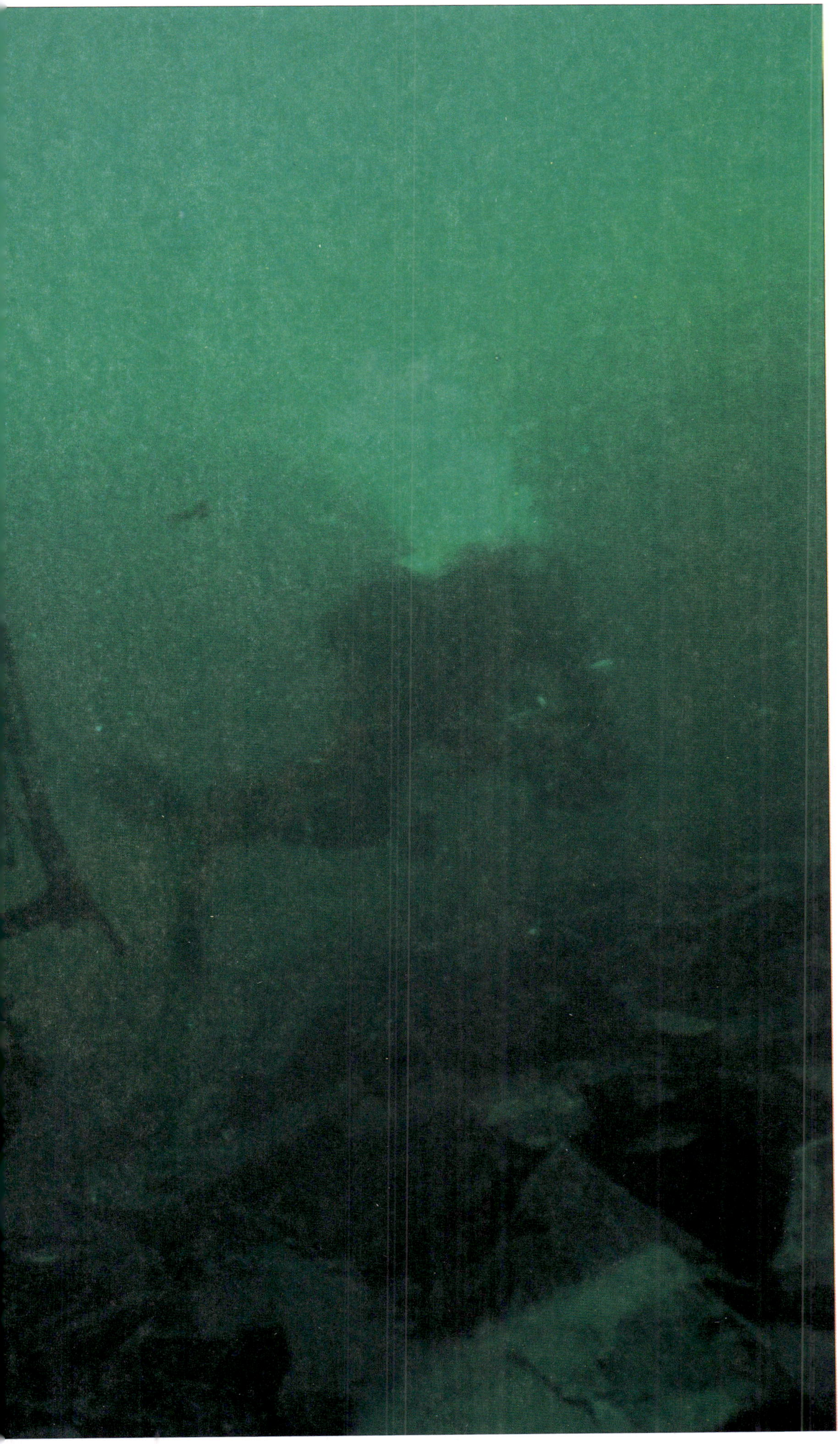

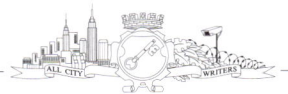

WWW.ALLCITYWRITERS.COM

CURATED BY:
Andrea Caputo

ART DIRECTION:
DFP Company — Milan

GRAPHIC DESIGN COORDINATORS:
Matteo Callegaro, Andrea Crestani,
Sara Pellegrini

CONTRIBUTING DESIGNER :
Greta Bizzotto, Domenico di Donna, Lorenzo
Antonioni, Noemi Caruso, Salvatore Lavieri,
Vera Marin

HEAD TITLE DESIGN:
Niels Shoe Meulman

LOGOTYPE DESIGN:
Tristan Vancini

TEXT EDITING COORDINATORS:
Fabio Falzone, Jada Parolini,
Elisa Sabatinelli

CONTRIBUTING TEXT EDITORS:
Laura Arrigoni, Francesca Cogni,
Elisa Mogavero, Lara Pollero, Matteo
Sacchetti, Serena Valietti

TRANSLATIONS:
Rosanna del Buono, Jada Parolini

PROOF READING:
Prue Keane

IMAGES POST PRODUCTION:
Zum Studio Milan

www.zumstudio.com

CONTRIBUTING PHOTO EDITORS:
Alessandra Tisato, Roberta Beltramini, Mattia
Campo, Stefano Incorvaia, Alessio Occhiodoro,
Stefano Macrino, Marica Moretti,
Luca Fontana, Federico Resega

FIRST PUBLISHED IN 2009 BY:

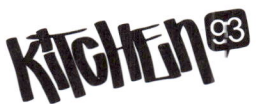

Kitchen93
Bagnolet, France
kitchen93@wanadoo.fr
www.kitchen93.fr

WORLDWIDE DISTRIBUTION:
Critiques Livres Distribution SAS
BP 93 – 24 rue Malmaison
93172 Bagnolet Cedex, France
33 (0)1 43 60 39 10
critiques.livres@wanadoo.fr

PRINTED IN HONG KONG BY:
C & C Joint Printing Co.
ISBN 9-782859-800161
EAN-13.978285980016

SUPPORTED BY:
Mariano Pichler
Istituto Europeo di Design, Milan

SPONSORED BY:
carhartt

Richard Ga liano

NEW YORK SUBWAY TIMELINE

Writing is a street culture that in the span of the last 40 years has been transmitted by collecting and interpreting direct observations of its protagonists. The various facets of the phenomenon however obstruct a view of the whole: a confused magma of voices in fact complicates any attempt at reconstructing and decoding this movement tied to the subway of New York in the 70's and 80's.

Though various researchers have ventured into the monumental effort starting from partial stories, it becomes almost impossible to encapsulate these variegated experiences into a single guiding direction. With that as a premise, summarising the genesis of Writing is a particularly complex and inevitably haphazard operation. Therefore, the timeline here will present the sum of personal testimonies and facts that have been analysed and accepted by the majority of the community as well as by various scholars.

Starting with the research – iconographic or textual – by Norman Mailer, Jack Steward, Henry Chalfant, Martha Cooper and Craig Castleman, we propose an integrated vision which attempts to render a partial view of that period of maximum splendour for the New York subway.

During the 70's and 80's the scope and the aesthetic shock of painted trains had such an impact that it became a real icon of the metropolis. The spontaneous character of the city on the subway shined with a new light, though the bad hygienic and security conditions of the public transportation infrastructures were conveying a critical and indefensible image. The progressive explosion of the phenomenon in the course of these two decades caused a crack down by the MTA, or Metropolitan Transit Authority, as well as the state of New York. The new measures took the concrete form of higher vigilance in the yards, more arrests, increased car buffing, up to the adoption of anti-graffiti carriages. On May 10th 1989, after having cleaned the last car, the MTA officially declared that the war against graffiti was over.

Elements and sources

MEDIA topic	**BOOK**		**RESEARCH**
	SA *Subway Art* Martha Cooper Henry Chalfant	**G** *Getting Up: Subway Graffiti in New York* Craig Castleman	**I** *International Dictionary of Aerosol art* Staffan Jacobson
1967 year	**SP** *Spraycan Art* Henry Chalfant James Prigoff	**M** *The Faith of Graffiti* Norman Mailer Jon Naar Mervin Kulansky	**J** *Graffiti Kings* Jack Stewart

FOCUS
GW *Graffiti in its own words* - New York Magazine

ARTICLES
number of newspaper articles published per year

S subwayoutlaws.com

MEDIA
book
newspaper article

movie
exhibition catalogue

tv program
music video

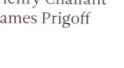 Kohl, Herbert. "Names, Graffiti and Culture". *Urban Review*, April issue.

• The New York City Transit Authority report on *subway good manners* includes "Don't write graffiti".

• **March.** The New York State Legislature creates the Metropolitan Transit Authority to oversee transportation operations in 12 counties. The MTA becomes New York City's parent transportation agency.

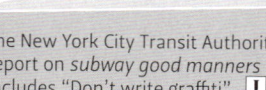
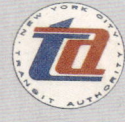
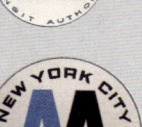

• The Transit Authority begins subjecting cars to highly caustic chemical washing called buffing. Cars are washed once a week on the inside and once every three weeks on the outside.

• Early tags by Cornbread in Philadelphia.

• Cornbread and Cool Earl: two Philly graffiti writers define the role of the modern day graffiti writer. (the major objective is fame). **S**

• Cool Earl uses the arrow as an element in his tags in Philadelphia. **J**

• Subculture is born in Philadelphia with a distinct style. **S**

• Early tag in NY by Julio 204.

• **May.** Riots at Columbia University turn graffiti political.

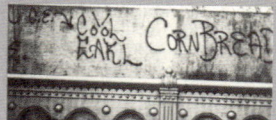

• Taki 183 starts writing in Washington Heights.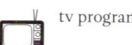

• Linear graffiti begins to cover NY, especially in Washington Heighst, Manhattan.

• **Late 1960's.** Buses and subway trains in Philadelphia are saturated with graffiti.

• Topcat moves from Philadelphia to NY bringing with him the first style: platform letters.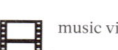

1967   **1968**   **1969**

EXHIBITIONS

- **December 2ⁿᵈ.** United Graffiti Art sts at City College, NY.
- Hugo Martinez with selected writers forms United Graffiti Artists.

MEDIA

 Padwe, Sandy. "The Aerosol Autographers – Why They Do It. *Philadelphia Inquirer Magazine*, May 2.

Charles, Don Hogan. "Taki183 Spawn Pen Pals". *New York Times*, July 21st.

Janson, Donald. "Spray Paint Adds to Graffiti Damage'. *New York Times*, July 25, 1971.

 total number 15

 Prial, Frank J. "Subway Graffiti Here Called Epidemic". *New York Times*, February 11.

 Golden Boy as Anthony Cool: a Photo Essay on Naming and Graffiti by Herbert Kohl.

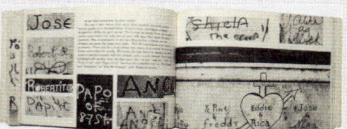

PREVENTION

- Graffiti becomes a political issue.
- Transit Police Chief Sanford D. Garelik declares war on graffiti.
- **M d September.** General Welfare Committee submits graffiti bill to city council stating the use of markers and spray cans to write graffiti has reached proportions requiring serious punishment for the perpetrators.
- **October 11ᵗʰ.** Full city council approves Graffiti Bill, it is illegal to carry aerosol cans into public facilities, Judges sentence writers "to remove graffiti under the supervision of an employee of the public works office, NYC Transit Authority or other officer or employee designated by the court".
- Most merchants n Washington Heights place the following sign on their shop windows: "For the benefit of our community and at the request of the Chamber of Commerce of Washington Heights, we are discontinuing the sale of spray paints and marking sticks to persons under 18 years of age"
- **October 27ᵗʰ.** Mayor Lindsay signs bill into law.
- **October 28ᵗʰ.** MTS Chairman Ronan instructs trans t policeto charge "such miscreants with malicious mischief".
- Private citizens get involved in the Graffiti War by helping to clean up the city

SUBWAY FACTS

- First tags appear on the outside of trains. **S**
- Joe 182, Taki 183 & Julio 204 begin bombing in NY. **GW**
- Eva 62, Barbara 62 and Michele 62 are the first female writers to gain prominence. **S**
- BabyFace 86 is the first to put a crown over his tag. **S**
- Barbara 62 & Eva 62 are the first writers to outline their name. **S**
- Cliff 159 and El Marko are the first writers to use outlines. **J**
- **Spring.** Writers start hitting lay-ups and yards. **J**
- **Summer.** The second generation begins hitting the subway system. **J**
- Cay 161 & Junior 161 paint a T-2-B wall at the 116th St. Station.
- «In 1971 I was in the Sheepshead Bay lay-up one night, that's the tunnel where trains rest in between rush hours, and we found the names of PAN 144, COCO 144 and ACE 137 on some of the cars. The paint was still wet. That opened our eyes to going all-city», Mico. **GW**
- Coco 144 creates the first stencil: Coco 144 with a crown on.
- "The first graffiti crew was started by SNAKE 1 and STITCH 1 and was named for the corner they hung out at: Writers Corner 188 or WC 188" **S**
- SuperKool 223 starts using a cloud like outline around his name.
- Most subway station walls in Manhattan, Bronx and Brooklyn are covered if not saturated with graffiti. **J**
- First masterpieces, writers attribute the invention to Super Kool 223. **J**
- **October.** Phase II starts hitting trains. **J**
- First "signature" pieces found on walls in Manhattan. **S**

- **Winter.** Every graffiti writer with ambition attemps to create graffiti on a large scale on the outsides of the subway cars. **J**
- "Brooklyn started the first real graffiti crew: The Ex-Vandals". **S**
- Arrows become popular in names. **J**
- Super Kool is the first to use polka dots in his name. **J**
- Honco 1 makes the application of dots and stars famous and introduces candy cane spirals. **S**
- 1st piece by Super Kool. **G**
- Cornbread stops writing. **S**
- **Fall.** City housing officials and other landlords start bemoaning the graffiti epidemic. **J**
- Charmin 65 gains fame by putting a big hit on the Statue of Liberty.
- Tracy 168 organizes the Wanted Club. **J**
- Super Kool starts using the fat cap. **G**
- Phase II unveils a rough version of bubble letters. **S**
- Use of stars, asterisks and circles. **J**
- **Winter.** Cay 161 and Junior 161 quit writing. **J**
- Each district has it's own style: Brooklyn, Bronx, Broadway, Queens. **M**

Mico starts tagging/writing in East Flatbush. **GW**

Tagging/ Hitting enters the inside of trains. **S**

EXHIBITIONS

- **September 4th**. UGA at Razor Gallery, Soho, NY.
- Twyla Tharps performance "Deuce Coupe" premiers with members of UGA painting a graffiti backdrop during the performance.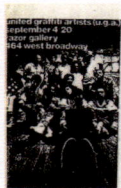

- Jack Pelsinger forms Nation of Graffiti Artists: NOGA.
- United Graffiti Artists at Chicago Museum of Science and Industry, Chicago.

- **September.** UGA at Artists Space, NY.
- United Graffiti Artists disbands and soon after Nation Of Graffiti Artists is formed.

MEDIA

total number
35

Ricklefs, Roger."Co-co 144's Underground Art School". *Wall Street Journal*.

Goldstein, Richard. "This Thing Has Gotten Completely Out of Hand", March 26th, (first published pro-graffiti forces support).

Urban Graffiti as Territorial Markers by David Ley and Roman Cybrivsky.

The Faith of Graffiti by Norman Mailer, Jon Naar and Mervin Kulansky. Alskog book / Published by Praeger Publisher, Inc.

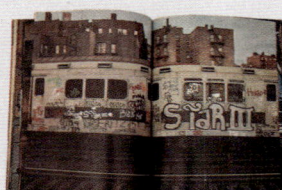

total number
22

Slattery, William. "Graffiti Champ Scrubbed." *New York Post*, February 9, 1974.

Grossberger, Lewis. "Frank Berry Takes It Personally and He Resents the Graffiti." *New York Post*, February 15, 1974.

Mazza, Frank. "Question Plan to Use Dogs to Fight Graffiti." *New York Daily News*, July 31, 1974.

United Graffiti Artists catalogue by Hugo Martinez.

Street Writers by Gusmano Cesaretti, Los Angeles.

total number
22

Opening credits of the TV series *Welcome Back, Kotter* shows a moving subway train with masterpieces by P-Nut, Jester I and Diablo. Years later the series was aired in London and became one of the most importan inputs for Mode II.

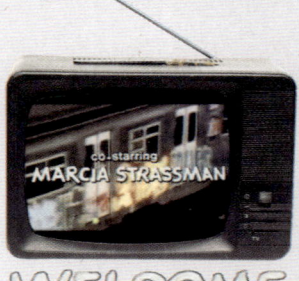

PREVENTION

- Steven Isenberg announces 1,562 youths have been arrested for defacing subways and public places. 426 sentenced in court to spend a day in the trains yards scrubbing graffiti.
- New York City Bureau of the Budget completes a detailed work plan for Mayor Lindsay's Graffiti Task Force.

- The Transit Police Graffiti Squad is constituted.
- All the Subway Trains are painted brand new.
- $7 million spent by the MTA to remove graffiti.

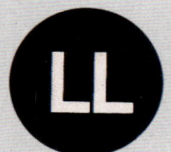   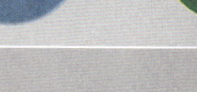

SUBWAY FACTS

- First whole car by Flint 707. [G]
- **Summer.** New letterform is born: marshmallow letters. [J]
- Priest 167 creates the 3D letter technique. [J]
- First 3D piece by Pistol1. [S]
- **August.** Flint 707 creates the most influential 3D piece. [J]
- Taki 183 quits. [J]
- Use of intentional drips. [J]
- IRT Redbirds are covered in graffiti, this triggers fights within the graffiti community. [S]

- Use of highlighted bubbles and homilies. [J]
- Blade inventes "tumble letters". [J]
- Tracy coins the word Wildstyle, soon the phrase became a generic term for a new lettering style. [J]
- **Mid.** Comic book iconography becomes prevalent. [J]
- First "Super Star" crews start gaining notoriety. [S]
- **September.** Sir/Dice 198 creates a crude version of the first top-to-bottom. [S]

- **Mid 70's.** Last important club is formed: The Fabulous Five. [J]
- Blade does a Halloween whole-car piece called "Booba" giving it an illusion of depth. [J]
- IN popularizes throw-ups and they become huge in Brooklyn. They are the favourite weapon of crews such as TOP, TC, SSB, TMB. [S]
- Whole-cars become common from '75. [J]

| 1973 | 1974 | 1975 |

OGA (Nation of Graffiti Artists) at Bank Street College, NY.

 total number
7

"Some Artful Dodgers Find a Different Line." *New York Times*, March 13, 1976.

Blumenthal, Ralph. "Subways Are Rated by Experts." *New York Times*, March 18, 1976.

Hectman, Michael. "New TA Paint: Graffiti Comes Off in the Wash." *New York Post*, May 11, 1976.

Mazza, Frank. "Future for City Graffiti Artists." *New York Daily News*, May 28, 1976.

"Graffiti Removal." *New York Times*, May 28, 1976.

Duddy, James. "Subway Graffiti Artists on Right Track in Exhibit." *New York Daily News*, July 9, 1976.

Burks, Edward C. "A Subway Elongatomus? Why, It's Preposterous." *New York Times*, November 18, 1976.

 total number
17

The Buff, NY Times, March 20.

Fischler, Stan, and Dave Rubenstein. "The Graffiti Gangs Are Painting the Town Red Again." *Soho Weekly News*, March 10, 1977.

"Subway Graffiti." New York Times, March 20, 1977.

"Paper Monsters Haunting Subways." *New York Times*, March 28, 1977.

Pienciak, Richard T. "MTA Thinks It Has a Way to Erase Tracy's $25 Subway Paintings." *New York Post*, April 5, 1977.

"Graffiti Is His Biz." *New York Daily News*, April 5, 1977.

"Art on the Lam." *Village Voice*, April 5, 1977.

Walsh, Edward R. "No Easy Mark." *New York Times*, September 18, 1977.

"San Francisco Students Who Cut Graffiti to Be Given Cash Awards." *New York Times*, October 2, 1977.

Dallas, Gus. "A Solution for Graffiti." *New York Daily News*, October 10, 1977.

Gooding, Richard. "The End of the Line for Graffiti." *New York Post*, October 14, 1977.

Sullivan, Patrick W. "Anti-Graffiti Chemical Called Health Hazard." *New York Post*, October 24, 1977.

"Fume Fear Halts Graffiti Work." *New York Times*, November 1, 1977.

Sullivan, Patrick W. "Graffiti Rx Washed Out for Tests." *New York Post*, November 1, 1977.

Malcolm, Andrew H. "Graffiti, 141 Giant Eyes along River Bank, Hint At Changing Japan." *New York Times*, November 10, 1977.

Dallas, Gus. "Critic-Cops Go Underground to Catch a Running Art Show." *New York Daily News*, November 20, 1977.

 Graffiti a New York by Andrea Nelli.

NOGA catalogue

 total number
5

 "Graffiti-Sprayer Shoots Super." *New York Post*, January 7, 1978.

Lochnowitz, George. "Save Thousands of Child-Hours Wasted on Ugly Daubings." *New York Post*, October 20, 1978.

Stivers, Cyndi. "Graffiti on Order." *New York Post*, October 17, 1978.

"Divine Graffiti." *New York Post*, November 29, 1978.

Moritz, Owen, and Richard Edmonds. "The New Subway Car: Fast, Quiet and Cool." *New York Daily News*, December 5, 1978.

April 12th. Car Maintenance Division – Cleaning Compounds.

May. John De Roos announces a practical solution to the problem: Polyurethane paint that is resistant to graffiti removing solvents (facilitates cleaning of graffiti without destroying base colour of trains).

• October. Train Wash Machine (The Buff) introduced using newly developed solvent.

• De Roos states $15 million spent to remove graffiti.

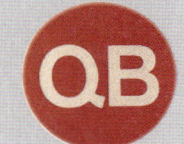 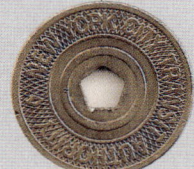 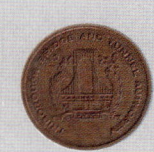 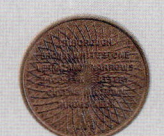 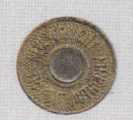 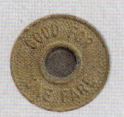 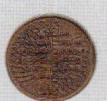

January 31st. Double whole-car masterpiece "Doomsday" by Lee. **J**

July 4th. First whole-train for the bicentennial (The Freedom Train): 11 cars by Cain I, Flame I, Mad 103. Unfortunately the train was separated and the cars did not leave the yard together. **J**

Whole-cars make resurgence with Cliff 159, Blade, Tracy 168 and Kindu. **S**

The Death Squad is formed by Kool 131, Mr. Jinx 174 and Chain 3 with Part as the first member. **S**

• December 10th. Fabulous Five ten car whole-train (The X-Mas Train) by Lee, Mono I, Slave I, Doc 109 and Slug I. **G**

• Due to looting during the July 13th–14th blackout, roll down gates are popular on shops and writers start painting them. **GW**

• Solid 1's death prompts one of the most important cars of the 70's, it reads "Solid, Bot, Don, Riff". **S**

• Wildstyle becomes the leading style. **I**

• Blade reaches a high point of letter design with an end-to-end done in what he calls his "Blockbuster" style. **J**

• "I wanted to make sure you could see a train from five blocks away and you could read it. COMET 1 and myself invented the blockbuster: very large, square words, but very legible", Blade. **GW**

EXHIBITIONS

• **December**. "The Fabulous Five/Purest Form of NewYork Art", curator Bruno Sakraischik, at La Meduza Gallery, Rome.

• "The Times Square Show" COLAB, at 41st St. NY.

• "Graffiti Art Success" Fashion Moda, Bronx, NY.

• Fashion Moda at the New Museum, NY.

• "New York / New Waves" PS 1, Long Island, NY.

• "Beyond Words Show" with Lee and Fab 5 Freddy at Mudd Club, NY.

MEDIA

The Warriors, Walter Hill, USA, 93'

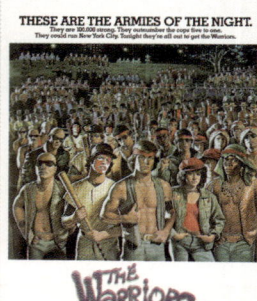

total number
5

Glazer, Nathan. "On Subway Graffiti in New York." *Public Interest*, Winter 1979

Toth, Robert C. "The Writing on the Wall: Public Is Tired of Graffiti." *Los Angeles Times*, August 6, 1979.

Allen, Henry. "Signs of the Cryptic Scrawler." *Washington Post*, March 28, 1979.

Wagner, Robert F. Jr. "Artists Spins Subway Scheme." *New York*, April 30, 1979.

Herman, Robin. "Vandals Take Psychological Toll." *New York Times*, May 21, 1979.

 total number
8

 Edmonds, Richard. "TA Dumping Toxic Wastes Into City Waters." *New York Daily News*, July 7, 1980.

"$5M Paint Plan Seeks to Halt Subway Graffitists in Their Tracks." *New York Daily News*, July 21, 1980.

"First Thing First." *New York Daily News*, July 22, 1980.

Stern, Carol, and Robert Stock. "Graffiti: The Plague Years." *New York Times Magazine*, October 19, 1980.

Whitcraft, Virginia. "You Get the Itch, You Gotta Paint." *New York Daily News*, October 24, 1980.

Wells, Jeff. "TA Cheers–Judge for Attacking Graffiti." *New York Post*, October 25, 1980.

Ravitch, Richard. "Graffiti By Any Name is Vandalism." *New York Daily News*, November 11, 1980.

Goldstein, Richard. "The Fire Down Below." *Village Voice*, December 24, 1980.

total number
5

Hager, Steven. "Graffiti: Is The Art World Ready For It?" *New York Daily News*, March 30, 1981.

Goldman, Ari L. "Dogs To Patrol Subway Yards." *New Yo[rk] Times*, September 15, 1981.

Wadler, Joyce. "Graffiti: Learn to Appreciate It." *Washington Post*, November 16, 1981.

"Who Can Do What About the Subways in New York?" *New York Times*, December 13, 1981.

Goldman, Ari L. "City to Use Pits of Barbed Wire in Graff[iti] War." *New York Times*, December 15, 1981.

PREVENTION

• MTA increases train washing activities in celebration of its Diamond Jubilee Year.

• All efforts failed far in vain of high costs.

• The Transit Police Graffiti Squad disbanded.

NYC subway lines map, 1975

• **May**. Kalkhof (transit authority general) provides $5.1 million for Graffiti Enhancement Program.

• *Daily News* and *New York Post* reveal toxic graffiti solvents being dumped daily by the authority into the city's waterways.

• New five man Transit Police Graffiti Squad constituted.

• **September**. Mayor Koch announces a $1.5 million program to provide fences and german sheppard watch dogs for the Corona train yard.

• All cars are painted white to test efficiency of the new progra[m].

• **December, 14th**. City contribution of $22.4 million to the MTA to install similar fences around other 18 train yards. Dogs to b[e] replaced by coils of razor wire.

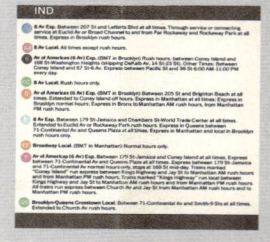

SUBWAY FACTS

• "Stop the Bomb" whole–car by Lee, theme: the Cold War. SA

• Mural by Lee (Handball court, lower East Side). G

• **December, 8th**. John Lennon tribute after his death, a masterpiece on two whole–cars. GW

• "Fuck the Buff" piece by Seen. SA

• Cap & Pjay take on a war against other writers by crossing over pieces. S

• Playground/ Handball court walls become the first alternative target to subway cars. SP

| 1979 | 1980 | 1981 |

n Gallery, NY.

rbara Gladstone Gallery, NY.

ash and Daze at Fashion Moda, Bronx, NY.

he South Bronx Show" at Fashion Moda, Bronx, NY.

One, Koor, Toxic at Fashion Moda, Bronx, NY.

- "Champions" at Tony Shafrazi Gallery, NY.
- **December.** "Post-Graffiti Art" at Sidney Janis Gallery, NY.
- "Lady Pink, Lady Heart" at Fashion Moda, Bronx, NY.
- **October 22th – December 4th.** "Graffiti" featured artists: Blade, Dondi, Seen, Futura 2000, Zephyr, Crash, Quik, Noc 167, Lee and Rammellzee at Booymans Van Beuningen Museum, Rotterdam, The Netherlands.

- **March – April.** "Arte di Frontiera" by Alinovi Francesca at Galleria Comunale D'Arte Moderna, Bologna, Italy.
- **April 5th – June 2th.** "Classical American Graffiti Writers and High Graffiti Artists" Gallerie Thomas, Munchen, Germany.
- Agent at Fashion Moda, Bronx, NY.
- "Urban Phenomena" at Fashion Moda, Bronx, NY.
- "3 Graffiti Artists" at Sidney Janis Gallery, NY.
- **September 8th – October 7th).** "New York Graffiti" at Louisiana Museum, Humlebaek, Denmark.
- **January 14th – February 26th.** "Graffiti" at Groninger Museum, Groningen, The Netherlands.
- "Classical American Graffiti Writers and High Graffiti Artists" at Thomas Gallery, Munich, Germany.

Getting Up: Subway Graffiti in New York by Craig Castleman.

Graffiti Talks by Joel S. Feiner and Stephen Marc Klein.

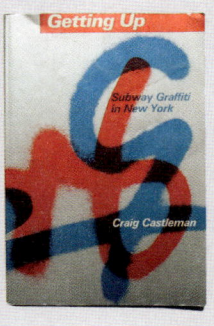

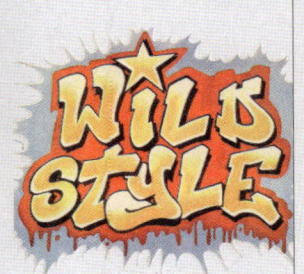

Wild Style by Charlie Ahearn.

Train as Book, Letter as Tank, Character as Dimension by Edith DeAk, Art Forum, May.

Buffalo Gals music video by Malcolm McLaren.

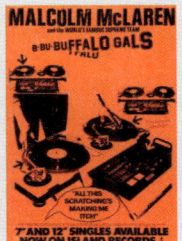

Style Wars by Tony Silver & Henry Chalfant.

Subway Art by Martha Cooper and Henry Chalfant.

Beat Street by Stan Lathans.

Hip Hop: the Illustrated History of Break Dancing, Rap Music and Graffiti by Steven Hager.

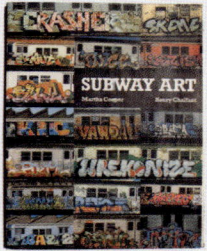

"Dump Koch" car by Spin: a response to mayor Koch's anti-graffiti campaign. **SA**

- **March.** International Graffiti Times – volume 2
  Broadsheet 17 x 22
  Duo Ink: black & red
  Accordion 12 way fold
  Interviews: Phase, Amrl, Coco, WG, TB, Stan, Vinnie, Livi, SaharaThe Empire Strikes Back, Video Reviews, Yanquijunkie.

- **Summer.** International Graffiti Times – volume 3
  Broadsheet 17 x 22
  Duo ink: black & green
  Accordion 12 fold
  SoledadM, Interviews: Chile/ El Salvador, June Trains 1984:
  Kenn, Cope, Spin, Swan, Mack, Rize, Sak, Flite, Alas, Thud.
  Danceteria, IGT Benefit: Hall of Fame.

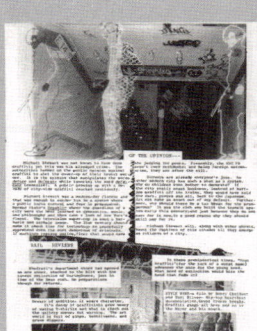

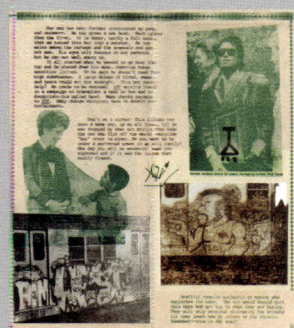

ew York City Rap Tour goes to London and Paris

utura 2000 tours with the Clash.

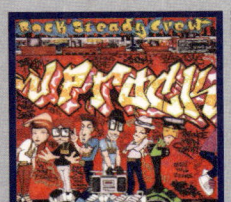

- Hip Hop goes to Europe: Rock Steady Crew is touring since the early 80's.

- **December.** International Graffiti Times – volume 1
  Broadsheet 17 x 22
  Black Ink
  Quarterly fold
  Bout & Graffiti, Yanqui Come Home, Rail Reviews, Micheal Stewart Vivid Interviews: Sak, Rize, Revolt, Quik

- **Election issue.** International Graffiti Times – volume 4
  Broadsheet 17 x 22
  Duo Ink: red & black
  California Freights, Cane2, Sharp in Lalaland, Foto One, Sidejackets, Gnosticism and the G Word, Zines, Berlin Wall.

EXHIBITIONS

- The Stedelijk Museum Helmond, Helmond, The Netherlands.
- **November 15th – Januar 6th.** Amerikanskt 80–tal. Liljevalchs Konsthall, Stockholm, Sweden.
- "Collaborations – Paintings" at Fashion Moda, Bronx, NY.
- "Off the Street" at Fashion Moda, Bronx, NY.
- "Quik, Seen & Blade" Sigmund Wenger Gallery, La Jolla, California, USA.
- "New York Graffiti" (with catalogue) at Museum Helmond, Helmond, The Netherlands.
- **February 10th – April 14th.** Gemeentemuseum Helmond, feauturing artists: Quik, Crash, Willy Bilast, Dondi, Futura 2000, Seen, Noc 167, Phasell, Rammellzee and Zephyr. Helmond, The Netherlands.

- **March 9th – May 4th.** "New York Graffiti" (with catalogue) Leopold–Hosch Museum, Duren, Germany.
- "Urban Aspects" Tweed Gallery, NY.
- "Fashion Mode" Denise René/Hans Mayer Gallery, Düsseldorf, Germany.
- The Stedelijk Museum Helmond, Helmond, The Netherlands.

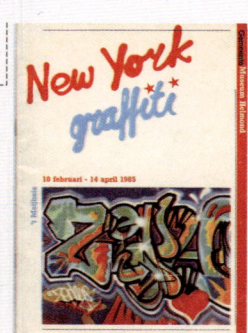

- September, 17th – October, 25th. "New York Graffiti" Scharp collection at Wilhelm Hack Museum, Ludwigshafen, German
- "Beyond Words" at Fashion Moda, Bronx, NY.

MEDIA

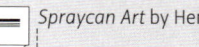 *Das Graffiti Lexikon* by Peter Kreuzer, Heyne.

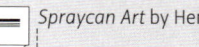 *Spraycan Art* by Henry Chalfant & James Prigoff.

 Graffiti – en kriminologisk undersøgelse by Anna Skyum Nielsen.

PREVENTION

SUBWAY FACTS

- **Spring/summer.** International Graffiti Times – volume 5
  Broadsheet 17 x 22
  Duo Ink: black & blue
  Accordian 12 way fold
  Get the Rich off our Backs, Bx Style Bob, Trains: Swan, Cem, Sak, Rize, Poke, Much, Psycho, Raz, T–Kid, Nel, Vulcan, Eleonor Bumpurs, Mayor Wisdom, Bama, TB.

- **Fall/winter.** International Graffiti Times – volume 6
  Broadsheet 17 x 22
  Trio Ink: black, yellow, red
  Accordian 12 way fold
  Freedom to Write, Koch gets Electrocuted, Trains: Apache, MadSeen, Demon, Raz, Psyco, Shame, Run, Jon, Sak, Cem, Ken, Interview: James Top, Sain Top.

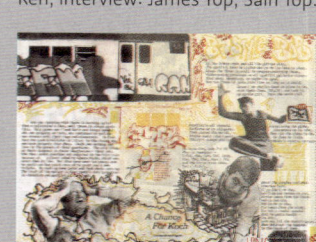

- The Subway Sun – volume 7
  Broadsheet 17 x 22
  Duo Ink: black & gold
  Quarterly fold
  Seeing is a Developed Sense, ATrain, E8thSt, Sharp, Phase II, Delta, Duster, Revolt, Zepher, Stash, PJay, The Cool 5, Jon, Klye, Bama, La/ Cholos, Part.

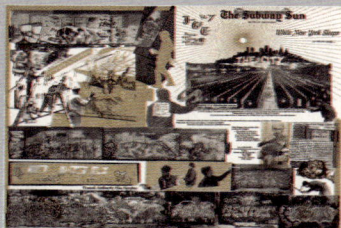

- The Subway Sun – volume 8
  Broadsheet 17 x 22
  Black ink
  Quarterly fold
  Misconceptions of an Art, Bear, A Look at the Myth, Poem, Sak, Klye, Mkay.

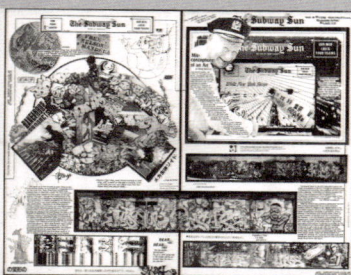

- Seen paints on the Hollywood Sign.

- The Subway Sun – volume 9
  Broadsheet 17 x 22
  Black ink
  Quarterly fold
  It's Serious Business, Sucker – Inner City Culture: Sharp, DC3 Shoroz, Centre fold interviews: Dero, Dome, Vulcan, Cries of the Ghetto, Skim/ Philly.

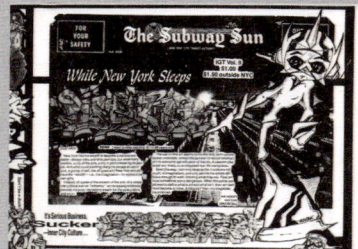

EXHIBITIONS

- **June 18th – August 27th**. "Graffiti New York– Paris" Musée des Beaux – Arts de Verviers (Neue Gallerie/Sammlung Ludwig Aachen, Verviers), Belgium.

- "Graffiti Between Anarchy and Gallery", curator Johannes Stahl (with catalogue).
  Travelling exhibition to: Helmond Museum, Helmond, The Netherlands; Heidelberger Kunstverein, Heidelberg, Germany; Nassauischer Kunstverein Wiesbaden, Wiesbaden, Germany.

- "New York Graffiti" at Stadtischen Gallery, Goppingen, Germany.

- The Art Foundation Academical Hospital Leiden, Leiden, The Netherlands.

- Nassauisher Kunstverein Weisbaden, Germany.

- Heidelberger Kunstverein, Heidelberg, Germany.

- The Stedelijk Museum Helmond, Helmond, The Netherlands.

 Subway Graffiti: an aesthetic study on the subway systems of New York City 1970–78 by Jack Stewart.

 The Hex and Slick battle, LA Downtown News, August 28.

MEDIA

Graffiti: zwischen Alltag und Ästhetik by Johannes Stahl, Scaneg, München.

- The last graffiti train is buffed. Train piecing in New York slowly died out. MTA, spending more then $10 million a year claims to have defeated it. Aggressive tagging on house fronts successively replaced it. In the rest of the USA and in Europe TTP shows no sign of lessening. ⬛

New York Times–May 10, 1989
>

Transit Agency Says: *New York Subways Are Free of Graffiti*

Constance L. Hays
>

On Friday, the New York City Transit Authority plans to celebrate the final journey of what it says is the last graffiti-covered train. That train, on the C line, will be taken out of service. Fifteen years after they began battling the initials, names and cryptic messages scrawled on subway cars, transit officials say the system is now graffiti-free. Almost the entire fleet -6,245 cars - has been replaced, rebuilt or scrubbed clean. When new markings do appear, they are promptly wiped away, officials said. About 250 of the 465 subway stations have been cleaned and are being similarly maintained. More than 10 years after Norman Mailer wrote "The Faith of Graffiti" and graffiti painters were celebrated in galleries as pioneers of an important form of self-expression, less-sympathetic forces appear to have prevailed. "When you're sitting in a graffiti-covered car, you don't feel safe", said the president of the Transit Authority, David L. Gunn. When the trains were covered with names, codes and epithets, "there was a sense that the system was out of control," he added. "Graffiti on the walls of trains or subway stations create bad karma," Mayor Edward I. Koch said last week. Although many critics of subway conditions say there are still major problems to be addressed, some of the critics add that cleaning up the trains was an important step. "I appreciate not having to get on a fun house of colors in the morning, and it makes me think somebody's in control," said Gene Russianoff, staff lawyer for the Straphangers Campaign, a consumer organization. He said the group had ceased rating the trains for graffiti this year, because "there's so little of it." State Senator Franz S. Leichter, Democrat of Manhattan, acknowledged that graffiti now constituted "less of a problem." "I wish that much effort had gone into more important issues such as safety, like the doors that drag people to their deaths," he said. "I wish they had improved on-time performance and dealt with trains' going out of service en route. I question how effectively they've dealt with the real nitty-gritty of running the system." Mr. Gunn insisted that maintenance had not been compromised as the cars were stripped of graffiti. 'We didn't defer maintenance," he said. "You have to be able to chew gum and walk at the same time. Part of maintenance is cleanliness." Safety From Crime and Defects Transit officials see additional signs of improvement, in statistics showing longer service between breakdowns. In April 1984, the trains averaged 9 031 miles before a failure; last month, they had improved to 22,744 miles, Mr. Gunn said. Safety from crime and mechanical defects is still an important concern to riders and transit workers. The safety director of Local 100 of the Transport Workers Union, George McDonald, said he did not think graffiti-free trains deserved much praise. "Big deal," he said, "if you can't get to work on time and you don't feel safe." "Nobody was ever raped by a graffito," Alfred A. DelliBovi, the Urban Mass Transit Administrator in Washington, said. "People need to see not only that the trains are clean, but that criminals are removed from the transit system." Taking Trains Out of Service Mr. Gunn said the overburdened courts hampered the transit system's quest for safety. "Ninety-five percent of the people we arrest for robbery don't serve any jail time," he said. Combating graffiti, however, was recognized as something the system could accomplish more or less on its own. Measures were devised to '

> CONTINUES ON PAGE 36

PREVENTION

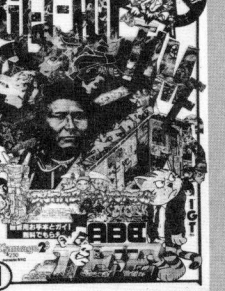

SUBWAY FACTS

FROM REDBIRDS TO

The unpredictable fate of New York's red cars. Their stop in the last deposit at the bottom of the Ocean, amidst the sea fauna

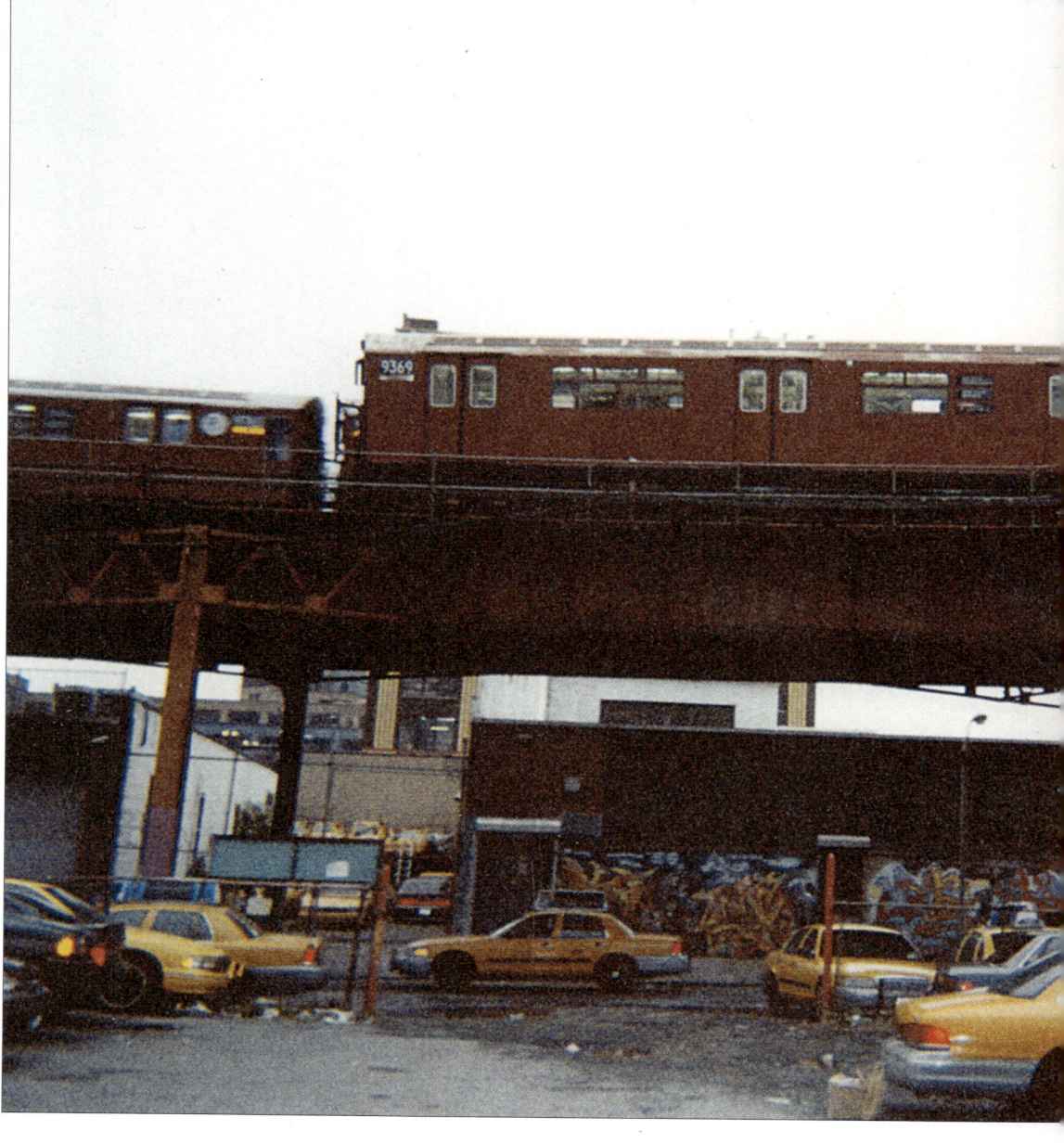

A dark red strip emerges along New York's skyline. It is not the fiery background of a sunset; a long, crimson arrow crosses through the rail tracks of the city, freeing the trail of a red phoenix flying towards its destiny, in the direction of the sea.

This is the story of a subway line and its Redbird trains, which brought new lifeblood to the Big Apple during the 70's and 80's. The uniform colour of the carriages, like pulsing arteries along the rail network, stimulated the imagination of commuters, becoming a real icon of NYC. Unexpectedly, what was supposed to be a simple means of transportation, a narrow red line connecting opposite poles of the city, became one of the most powerful images to be associated with the metropolitan scenario.

The story of these carriages begins with an evocative moniker, "Redbirds", and ends with another, "Silent Whales", thus re-baptised because they resembled whales resting in the train yards. Their trip begins in the 80's on the IRT Flushing line, a backbone through some of the most multiethnic areas of New York, ferrying thousands of inhabitants and tourists from Coney Island to Queens County.

Each day, about 1500 carriages traversed the city, exposed to the sight of passengers who gradually started noticing the shining new colours of the trains. The graffiti was modifying the subway liveries, its revolutionary hues indicating the rise of a movement that was gaining life in the urban surroundings.

For their ephemeral nature, the paintings were adding to the background noise of the city, an addicional distraction that could easily blend in with other large insignia, from advertising billboards to road signs. Though the first tags were mostly perceived as disturbing visual elements, the graffiti layer that took shape in coloured letters and large whole-cars soon began to baffle common citizens and inspire the few that lingered on the platforms to grasp their more interesting aspects.

The Redbirds circulated for forty years, until the last engine was switched off on November 2003 at the station of Willets Point/Shea Stadium, marking the end of an historic age for the New York subway and the beginning of a legend: the famous red cars were transported to the offing of the Atlantic Ocean on large naval platforms, and deposited on the seabed between the coasts of New Jersey, Delaware, Georgia, South Carolina and Virginia. They were part of an environmental project for the formation of artificial coral reefs to favour the development of aquatic fauna.

Far from the skyscrapers, the rail tracks, and under the curious eyes of jellyfish and turtles, the Silent Whales were launched on their last run, towards the sea, engulfed by the water in a matter of seconds, a dull thud on the sandy ocean floor, making them eternal.

> CONTINUES FROM THE COVER

and especially with the publication of the book *Subway Art*, the first sources of information regarding the dynamics of this yet unknown movement, reached Europe. Through these first productions, the Graffiti phenomenon was exported to Europe associated exclusively to the Hip Hop culture of the Bronx. The four founding pillars of the movement, Breaking, DJ-ing, Rapping and Writing, were considered as binding dogma.

The first musical tours, organised in London and Paris – such as the *New York City Rap Tour* in 1982 – were a showcase for the American protagonists which consolidated the idea of a movement as heterogeneous and comprehensive as it was inseparable. These concerts, in which graffiti represented a kind of scenic backdrop, constituted the prelude to a real exchange of direct experiences that would take form only a few years later, when the European contemporary Art market would start being interested in the phenomenon. Repeating a tendency that had already taken place years earlier in New York, various galleries in Holland, Germany, Scandinavia, France and Switzerland took notice of the potential business tied to the universe of Writing.

Between 1983 and 1988 such a high number of exhibitions on the theme were inaugurated as to generate contacts between writers from New York and writers from Europe, who were the unusual spectators of events aimed at a public of collectors.

The meeting between geographically opposite shores generated an intense exchange, which made it possible to rectify certain stereotyped visions which had been distorted by the media. It was a direct experience, until then inexistent, which gave European kids a new consciousness, and an opportunity to to perfect technique and styles, discuss the dynamics of painted trains and especially define with more precision the figure of the American writer and the reality of New York.

SILENT WHALES

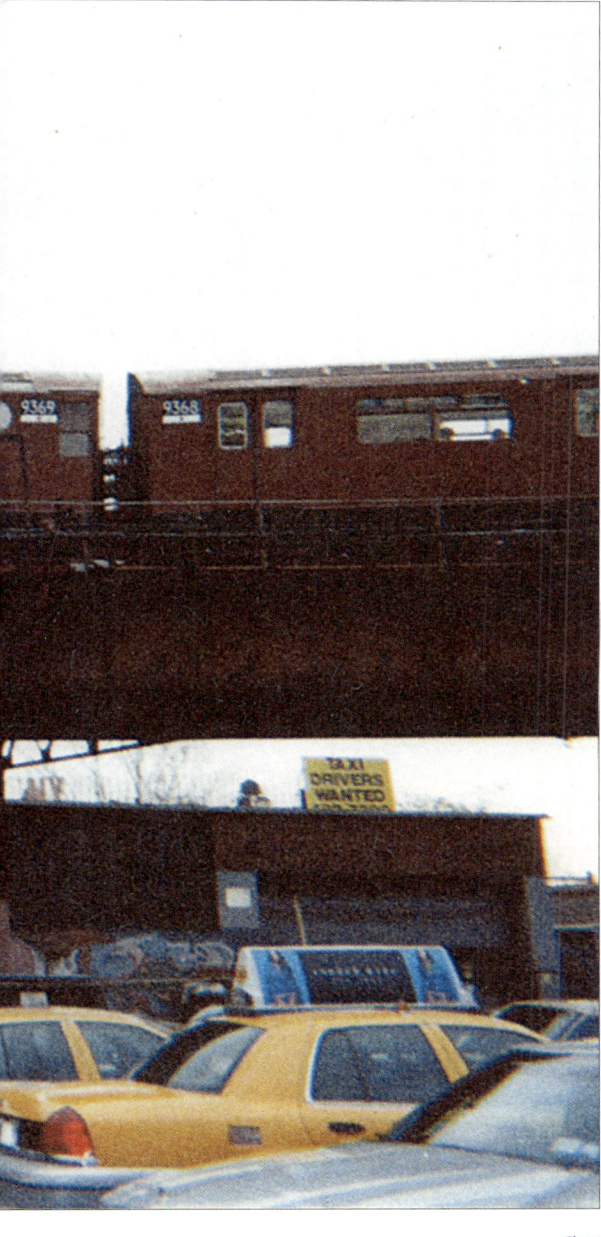

— Chero

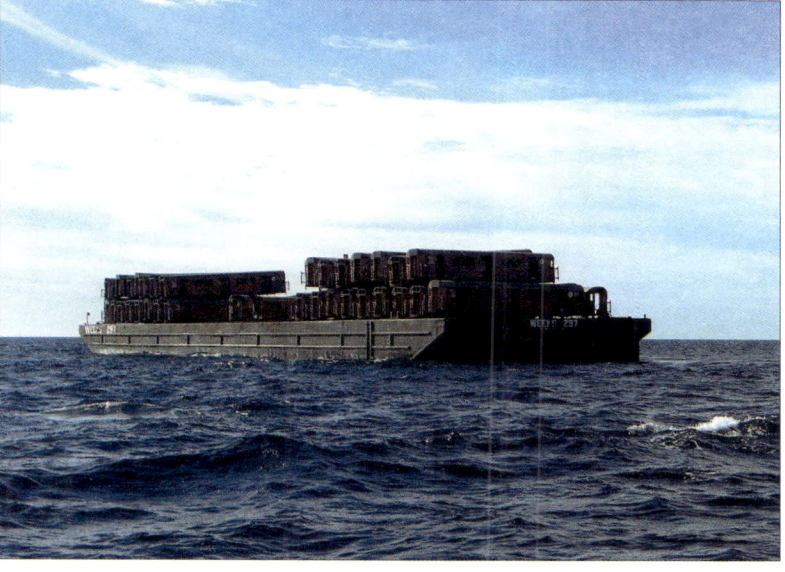

— Richard Galliano

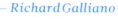

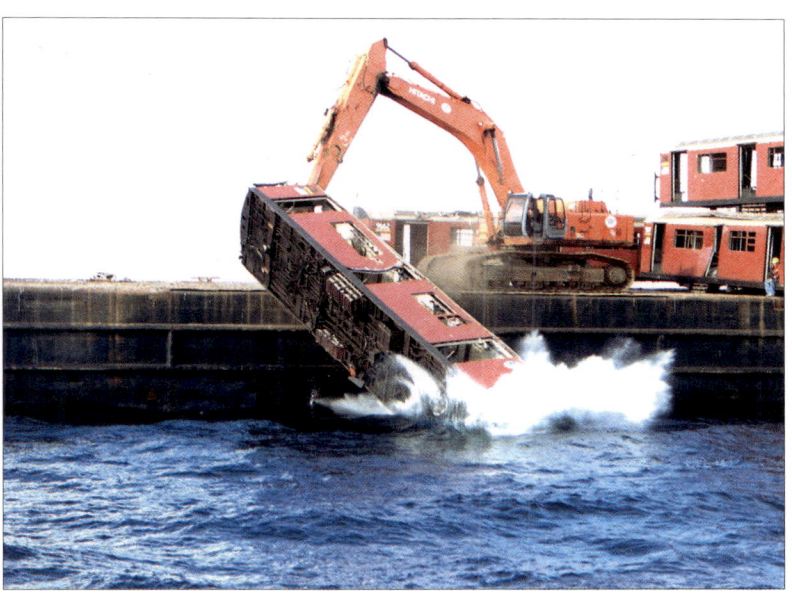

— Richard Galliano

INTO THE OCEAN

The long trip of the Red–bird carriages from the New York elevated line to the deep of the Atlantic Ocean

Metroglyphs

New York for some is the soaring skyline of the Chrysler and Empire State Buildings, the redounding canyons of overgrown towers. But for me, the city has always been the subway. Filthy, crowded, reverberating the hellish friction of the rails, all of my memories of New York as an overgrown biology experiment are there, underground. When I came back after a seven-year draft-dodging sabbatical-it was late 1975- something had radically changed. The skyline was the same-there were no new buildings thanks to the war and the Oil Embargo- but there was a new mood.
I found it down in the subways where brokers continued trying to read their Wall Street Journals without noticing. The cars had been decorated, some would say attacked.

Graffiti was everywhere, in full color, and layered. It was not the old sort of scribbles of obscenities and gripes-- no fuck you's or impeach Nixon's--but instead sublime frescoes of letters: ornate, arabesque, and seemingly nonsensical. The letters did not make words, or if they did, the words did not make sense.
All of a sudden that morose atmosphere of conformism and dread, captured so chillingly in George Tooker's *Subway* (1950), was shaken out of its lethargy with splatters of joy. Colossal droopy letters, stark shadows, bold contours, hatching, spots and polka dots, the variety of techniques were infinite and the combinations of forms unending. Graffiti was fit into the negative spaces of other graffiti, superimposed, blotted-out, fragmented. There was no control and little respect: subway art was never finished and never left unaltered; no one's work was better than someone else's.
What happened down in the New York subway had surpassed the dreams of modern abstract artists. Robert Rauschenberg, Jasper Johns, and Andy Warhol had met

their match. How unfair that the subway artists worked for nothing under threat of arrest while the gallery painters drank themselves silly while collecting their residuals! Many New Yorkers complained about the graffiti, arguing that it was an affront to public property and that it made people feel unsafe.
They never complained about all the advertising thrust upon them down in the subways however, that interminable assault of ads for chewing gum, hemorrhoid-shrinking pills, and pregnancy tests.
This spontaneous art form made people uneasy. It was anonymous and rebellious. When I first saw the graffiti they struck me as primordial, like Paleolithic cave-decorations. These metroglyphs were a type of sacrifice offered to the city in the only place where almost everyone went (saving the executives in their helicopters). In a world bereft of religious experience they begged for hosannas. In the thick of New York anomie they created a new cult of belonging. Subway graffiti restored the true purpose of art. — RICHARD INGERSOLL

AESTHETIC INVESTIGATORS
—

THE ELEVATED,

Following the few, sparse contributions of the first researchers, Writing was becoming the object of growing attention, witnessed by the numerous publications on the theme. The quantity of articles in the New York Times between the 70's and 80's attests to the topicality of the matter and the great interest it aroused in the media and public.

The decoding of tags, styles and dynamics belonging to the movement was however the prerogative of those few researchers who did their ethnographic studies in close contact with the writers of New York. Among these, Norman Mailer was the first, big author interested in this phenomenon that was all the rage among the teenagers of New York's streets in the 70's. Mailer investigated the private world of these youths, the mechanisms that tied them to their Name and in particular the choice of an alias that at the time was being prevalently traced on neighbourhood walls. When the book *Faith of Graffiti* saw the light in 1974, tags had already taken the form of real pieces, travelling on subway cars.

Journalism is chores. Journalism is bondage unless you can see yourself as a private eye enquiring into the mysteries of a new phenomenon. Then you may even become an Aesthetic Investigator ready to take up your role in the Twentieth Century mystery play. Aesthetic Investigator! Make the name A hyphen Roman numeral I, for this is about graffiti.

A–I is talking to CAY 161. That is the famous Cay from 161 Street, there at the beginning with TAKI 183 and JUNIOR 161, as famous in the world of wall and subway graffiti as Giotto may have been when his name first circulated though the circuits of those workshops which led from Masaccio though Piero della Francesca to Botticelli, Michelangelo, Leonardo and Raphael. Whew! In such company Cay loses all name, although he will not necessarily see in that way. He has the power of his own belief. If the modern mind has moved from the illumination of the first master of fresco, that sim-

ple subtle Giotto who could find beatitude in a beheading as well as the beginnings of perspective in the flight of an angel across the bowl of a golden sky, if we have mounted the high road of the Renaissance into Raphael's celebration of the True, the Good and the Beautiful in each human succulent three-dimensionalities of the gluteus maximus and bicep on out to our own vales and washes in Rothko and Ellsworth Kelly, why so, too, have we also moved from the celebration on the name, travelled from that mysterious, even frightening, notion that men and women in the sweetmeat of their bodies had wrested a degree of independence from Church and God down now to the twentieth-century certainty that life is an image.

From "The faith of graffiti"
Norman Mailer
Alskorg/Praeger
New York 1974

From *Faith of Graffiti* onwards, the number of publications steadily increased, focusing on various aspects of the phenomenon: the identity of the authors, an analysis of the dynamics, to more generic considerations on aesthetics and style. Renowned publications such as *Gettin' up: Subway Graffiti in New York* (MIT Press, 1982) by Craig Castleman, or *Subway Art* (Thames & Hudson, 1984) by Martha Cooper and Henry Chalfant were alternated by research and PhD theses of a certain importance, though unknown for years – above all, the dissertation by Jack Steward, *Subway Graffiti Kings 1970–1978*. We must mention Andrea Nelli, an italian photographer whose University thesis and discovery of the first Manhattan Heights writers is an essential contribution.

Nelli decided to dedicate an entire research project to them, following in the footsteps of Mailer's work, the only literary reference of the time. The thesis evolved into the publication of *Graffiti a New York*. Distributed in 1976 by a small Italian publishing house called Lerici Edizioni, the volume decoded the world of writers and for the first time drafted a reliable glossary.

In New York Nelli had met Coco 144 through Hugo Martinez and the U.G.A gallery. The friendship between the two youngsters, practically of the same age, created a trust-based relationship that allowed the photographer to get directly in touch with the protagonists and the places of a metropolis still to be revealed.

Andrea Nelli
>

One of the first images I remember from New York in 1972 is tied to the subway, which travelled with tags on the outer sides and the inside, almost a premise of what would happen briefly later. In the span of a year, when I returned, I immediately noticed an enormous fracture, reflected both on the surface of the cars and the looks on the faces of the common citizens. The trains were completely covered in drawings that, for their impact and formal completeness, provoked a real shock at the station. The letters had taken volume and from simple traces had become solid elements, to be filled and complicated with loops and evolutions on that theme. The contrast was evident: on one side the private property of the city was being compromised, on the other the result was remarkable and aesthetically devastating. The reaction of those taking the subway was embarrassment, almost Puritanism. There was tension among the platforms.

The lack of an immediate comprehension of the letters gave me the impression of a relation to ideograms; the ideogram contains elements that are much more than a written word: they involve sight, an eventual sound and a sign. These subway ideograms initially appeared mysterious and I considered them as a possible interpretation of the surrounding reality, other than the beginning of a new and marvellous adventure. They were like explicit road signs of New York in those years. The city was finally sending a mysterious signal: the problem that I think was common to many urban centres in the 70's is the lack of unconventional messages. Cities were too predictable and this additional layer of meaning on the surface

of subway cars finally caught me by surprise. In a short amount of time I finally got in touch with the authors of these signs. During my stay I had the opportunity to visit Hugo Martinez's workshop in Manhattan. United Graffiti Artists included some of the best writers of that time, putting together an almost explosive ensemble: the guys seemed enthusiastic of this shift from the streets to 'insides', canvases, maybe even dubious about the great leap they were about to take: from the ghetto to museums....who could imagine it?

Sure, what I had seen on the subway carriages of New York was not comparable to the works displayed in an atelier. A wild compositional instinct oozed out of every work – be it sculpture or painting – but the context was lost, the lion was caged and the risk of loosing oneself, high: those that managed to reinvent themselves and avoid a fall in style were the only ones safe. "Stylising equals killing" Lewis wrote. Attempting to reach the intensity of the painted subways seemed futile, though the commerce of these works would later become popular. The encounter with U.G.A. in any case revealed to be fundamental. Before I left, Hugo Martinez took a piece of paper and wrote two notes: the name of a Puerto Rican poet, Pedro Petri, and the number of a local writer, Coco 144, my future mentor.

In the tunnels and underground passages of New York, Coco 144 was my Virgilio, a unique guide due to a life spent around gang turfs, which in the early 70's dominated the city. With him I visited every street of Manhattan, from the tunnel of the subway to the interminable yards in the open. I remember secret deposits he would enter into easily, because in those years he had made copies of the keys. We were both twigs, easy preys for any gang, but nothing ever happened. Like every navigated writer, Coco knew how to move around and for two kids – I was 24, he was 21 – that was it. Coco nevertheless tried to calm me down; "I don't wanna hurt anybody, but if I have to....". I looked at him, not quite reassured by his slender physical presence...

On 188th street was the writer's corner and that's where Coco, Mico, T-rex and dozens of other adolescents would meet. Coco and Snake I were from Washington Heights while I was living around midtown, and spent my days painting canvases and snapping photos. I had bought a set of five oil colours and some art boards from Pearls Point, quite the Sunday painter. One time I decided to take a stab at depicting the skyline of the city: from the window of Mary Jane Ciccarello's, at about the height of Columbia University, I painted the view of Harlem. Lizard

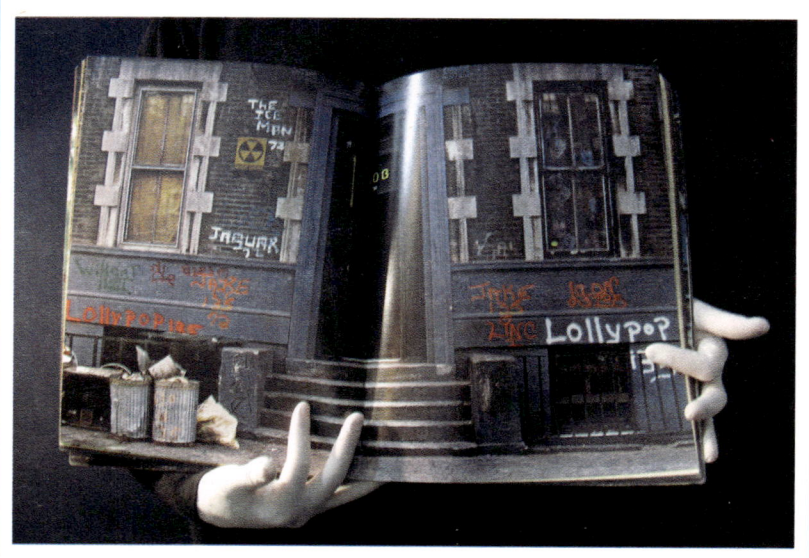
Laure Boudet

ANTICIPATIONS
MAILER AND NAAR
Faith of Graffiti – also known as Watching my name go by– is the first published volume on New York writers

A MOVING FEAST

green, yellow, red, blue, and ochre. When Coco saw it he picked up a fine brush, dipped it in white and, without even asking, filled the ground floor of my buildings with small tags: his, T-rex's, and Mico's. They were part of the urban landscape and reproductions that weren't faithful to the original were not admitted!

Coco continuously mentioned a great master, Cay 161, also cited by Norman Mailer in Faith of Graffiti. With no exaggeration, Cay was recognised by everyone as a key figure for the way he signed himself, his ability in choosing the best places in which to leave his tags. They were primordial, but all the writers I met already had very clear concepts in mind: the fame, the masters, the signatures and their respective collocation. Every tag, no matter how simple, complex, small or big, had to be written in strategic, special spots.

Only the masters, the Kings, had this gift, so connected to observation and an aesthetic of calligraphy. The spot was initially less connected to the idea of visibility, to the passage of an audience: this would occur only much later, when Writing would appear on the cars of the subway. In truth, the initial process tied to tagging was grasped as something much more intimate and secret; the clearest Writing belonged to gangs that literally marked their territory, but the writer tags, like in the fine arts or in music, followed a pure compositional discourse tied to context. A certain type of signature looked good on a determined surface, another on a corner, between a laterite wall and a cement one, another between two windows, on the second floor. They had this innate talent for compositions, absolutely urban and explosive. For the Masters it wasn't just a question of quantity or quality: it was their

way of being, acting and belonging to a group that made them stick out from other writers. The person had to coincide with the sign: if the person was not worthy, the sign wasn't sufficient to save him, even if it possessed an 'acrobatic' quality. Cay and Mico painted in a simple, intuitive manner, in the right places – and therefore the risky ones – with a pretty clear idea of what to compose on the surfaces they chose, if not the entire building, the typical American brownstones. And most of all, they knew how to deal with people, with kids. For this reason they were among the Kings of New York, at least the Kings of the first generation.

– "SOFTIES" AS A REFLECTION OF THE YOUTH

Conscious of the fact I was not really part of the writer universe I nonetheless tried to recognise the first styles, already identifiable on the sides of the subway by the mid 70's; I remember rusty, crowded cars running with the first 'masterpieces'. Next to these would be the first figurative designs, writers called them "animations", for the most part characters borrowed from the world of comic books. Since my first visit in 1972 the signatures had taken volume, the names could be read clearer and from afar. Among the calligraphies I saw, traced in 'bubble letters' or 'softies', I remember the names of SuperKool and then Phase II, painted in puffy, gum-like styles; they reminded me of the psychedelic graphics coming from the opposite coast, California and particularly San Francisco. There are numerous possible references, among which I wouldn't even exclude the album cover of Rubber Soul by The Beatles that I believe was one of the first to present such letters. The wild imagery of those years brought me to a make a connection....bubble letters and soft hair...from the 'wet' look to the 'dry' look, the greased-up hair a' la Elvis that had invaded Europe for me had become the puffy hair of the black kids. In that period the whole atmosphere of those streets in Manhattan was... gum-like;

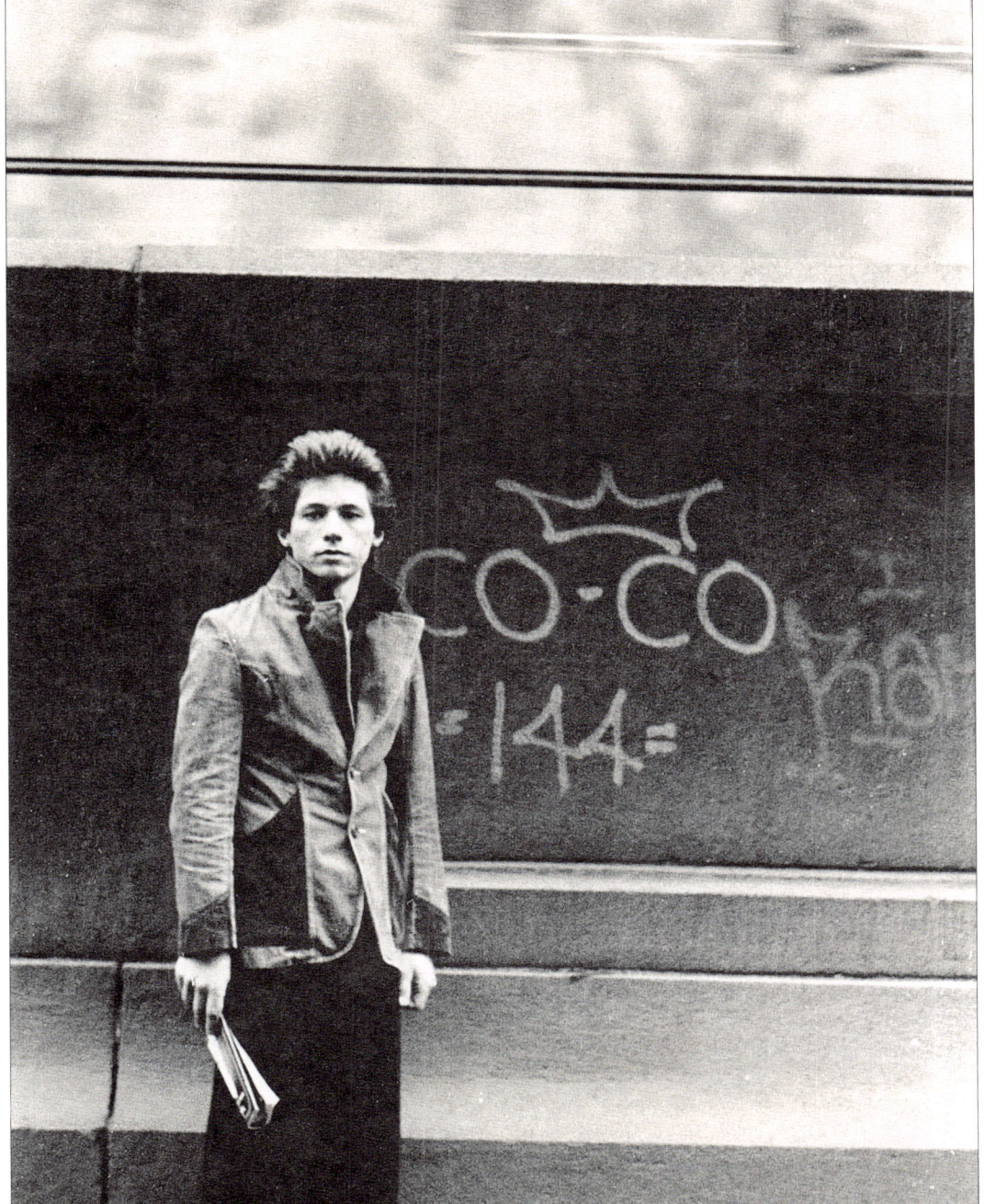

Portrait of Coco 144 by Andrea Nelli

– Andrea Nelli

> ## Since my first visit in 1972 the signatures had taken volume, the Names could be read clearer and from afar.

the parties in Washington Heights that Coco and Snake I brought me to catapulted me directly into the funk atmosphere of that period, not only musically but also in the same spirit of the people. I have a precise recollection of funk as the musical score of certain blocks in New York, present in the flat-top microphone-head of kids and in their rolling letters; coming from Europe it was initially difficult for me to get in direct contact with people... during parties they were taken aback, they called me and my girlfriend the 'Outs', though in a friendly way. My days would be spent in a very exotic mix of drinking, smoking and arguing in people's houses; this cohabitation with Puerto Ricans, Italians and Africans was something unique and new to me, light years away from the European University environment I was accustomed to. With respect to the immense collective happenings, big festivals such as Woodstock, in these houses you could breathe a different atmosphere. It was like a new kind of solidarity, different from those gatherings based on the hippy aesthetic and a communality of sentiments known to us all, perhaps because for the kids of Upper Manhattan or the Bronx, all imagery had yet to be invented. It was a work in progress, done on the spot, and even recognising one another was not to be taken for granted, as the dress code still had to appear. I remember only an infinite desire to escape the suffocating 50's, the asphyxiating mythology of the West-side story and Linetti brilliantine.

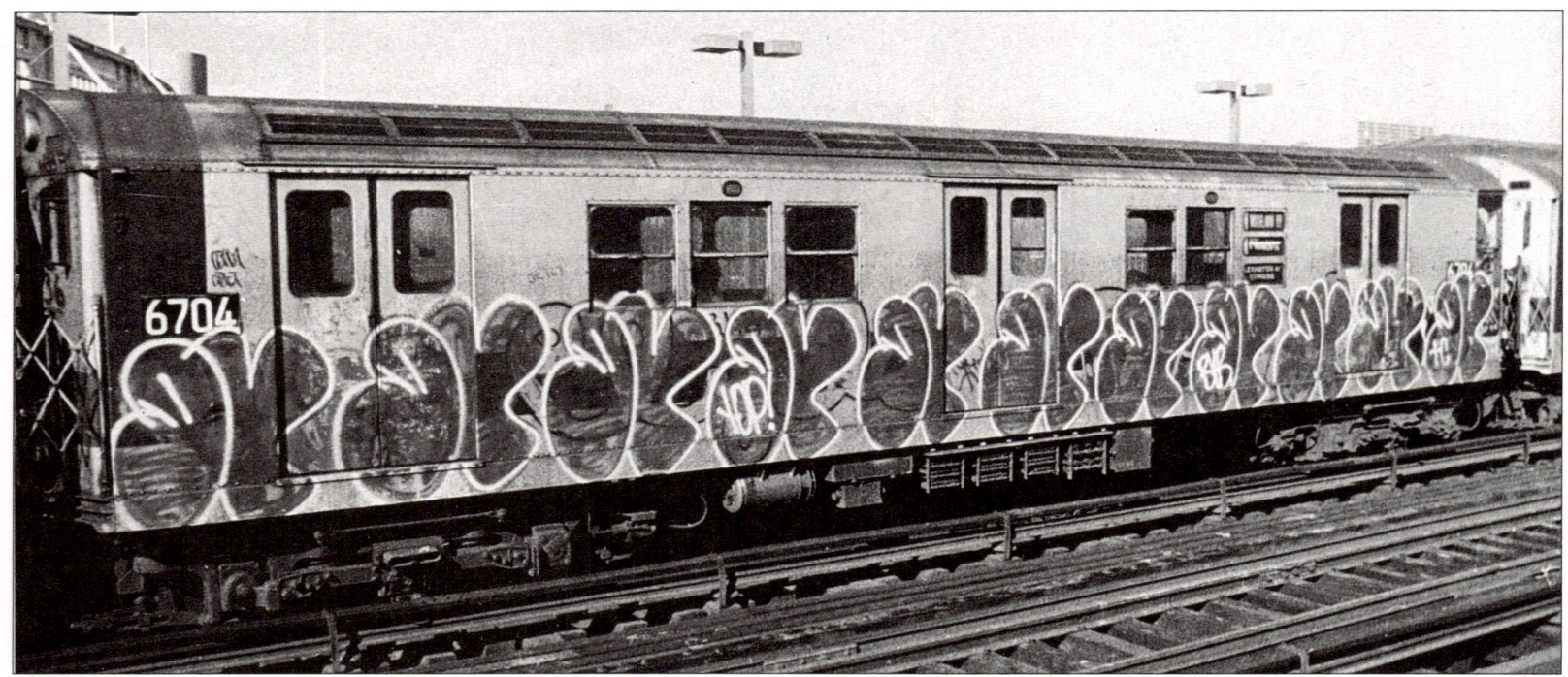

— Andrea Nelli

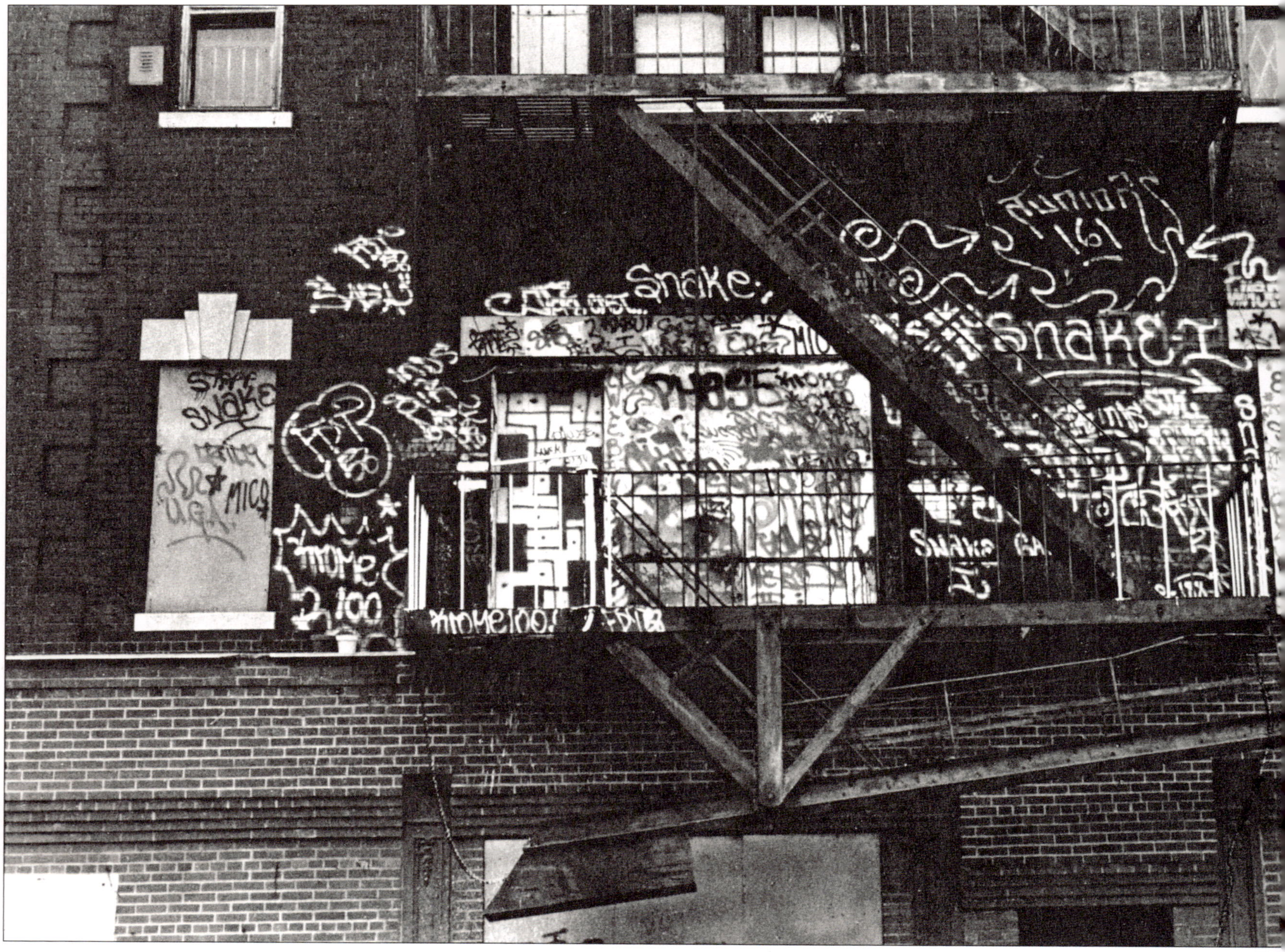

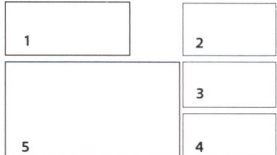

1 DY end-to-end
2 Cliff piece and character
3 5 Early writer tags in Manhattan
4 Comet and Blade whole-cars

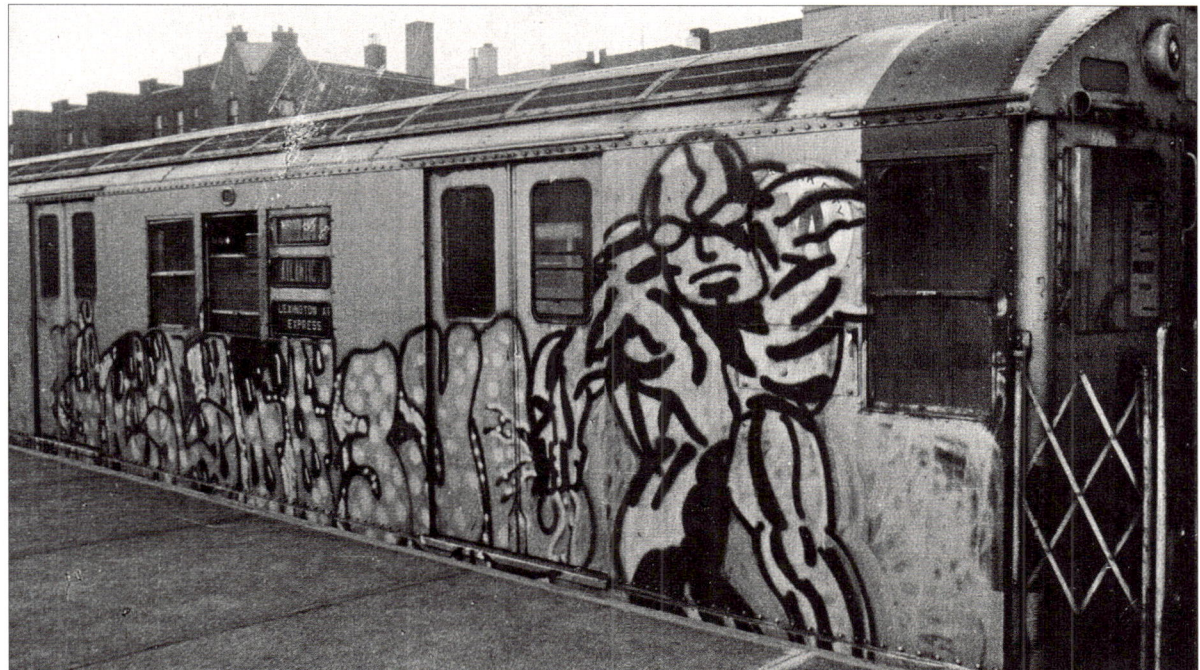

— Andrea Nelli

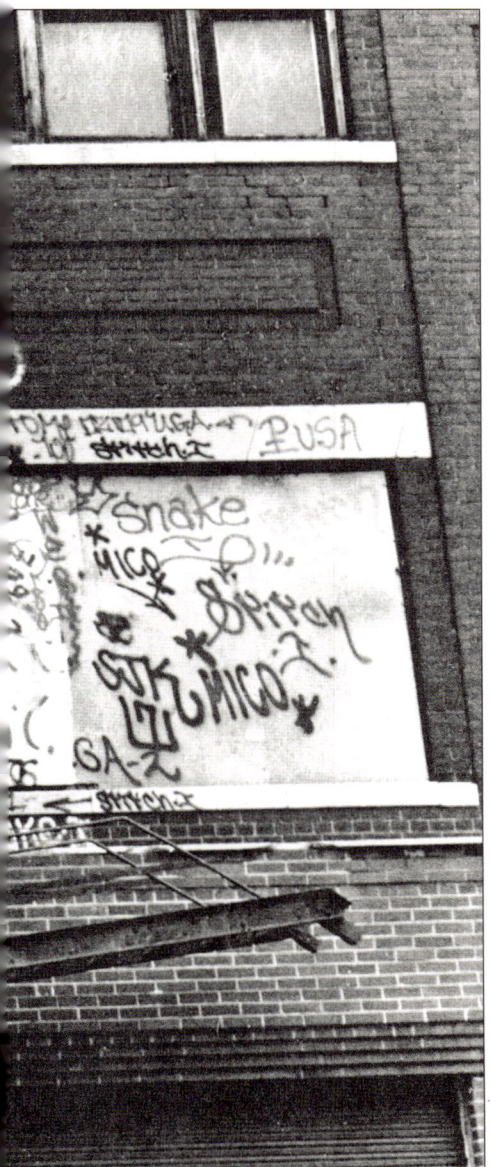

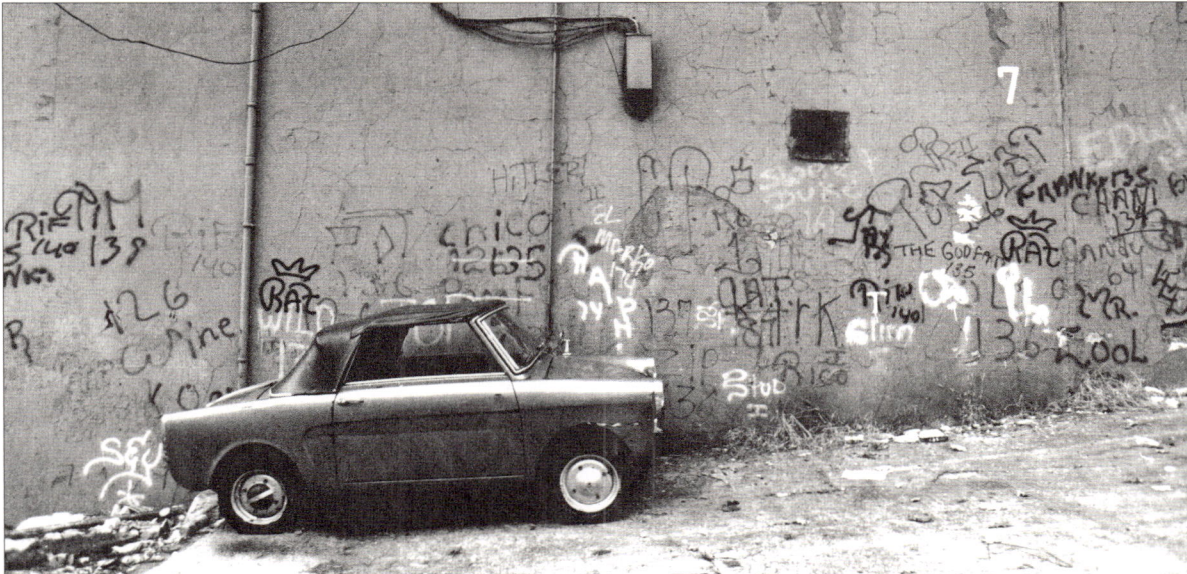

— Andrea Nelli

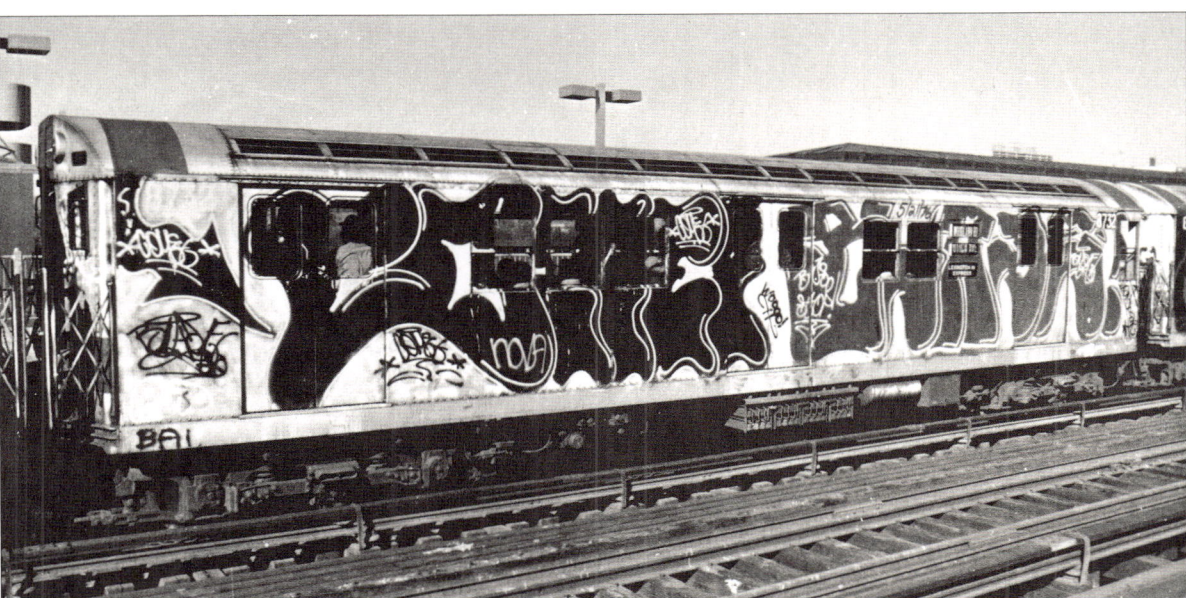

— Andrea Nelli

— Andrea Nelli

MEDIA

WILD STYLE BREAK

Wild Style, directed by Charlie Ahearn
and set in the New York City
of the 80's, becomes a classic
in Hip Hop filmography. An interview
with the author takes us behind
the scenes

What inspired you to make *Wild Style* and how did the project come to be?

It was a confluence of things that were happening around the late 70's up to the summer of 1980. I was finishing up a kung-fu movie that I had made in the lower East side, in the neighbourhood of Lee Quinones. In this neighbourhood there were giant wall murals, in the handball courts, with colourful images on them. While I was making the movie I met Lee briefly cause he came by while I was shooting a scene in front of one of his murals and I told him I would love to work with him on a film. He said it would be great and then he disappeared and I never saw him again for a long time. He was like this mysterious character and people didn't know where he was or how to get in touch with him. He was also probably the most famous subway graffiti writer at that time. So this was 1979, and it also happens that in 1979 Fred Brathwaite (Fab 5 Freddy), was working with Lee to try to organise a show in Italy. I think they did an art show in Milan to show their graffiti canvases. Fred had seen these posters up in the neighbourhood for the martial arts movie I was making that was called *The Deadly Art of Survival* and I was showing the movie in this art show called the Times Square Show which was right in Times Square, and one night Fred approached me there and said he would like to work with me on making a movie. He said he was working with Lee Quinones and I said "Oh I would love to work with him, if you could bring him here tomorrow morning we could start talking about how we can make this movie together". Fred had this idea of combining rap music with graffiti and bringing them together in a movie, and when Lee came the next morning I had him do a graffiti piece on the wall of this sort-of outlaw art show that we were doing in Times Square, and they wrote the words Fab 5 on the wall, and that was the beginning of making *Wild Style* in June of 1980.
The next thing we did that was really important was Fred and I went to this party that was sort of an outlaw rap party in a park in the North Bronx. It was a very large open space, it was dark and rappers were on the microphone with a little audience in front of them and I ended up speaking to this guy off to the side, who I later found out to be the chief rocker Busy Bee. I said to him that I was interested in making a movie about the Rap scene and I told him my name, and he brought me right out on stage and said "this is my movie producer, and we're making a movie about the Rap scene!" So it was right there that he introduced me as his film producer and right there in the audience were all these people from the Hip Hop scene, they were looking at us like "Wow, I wanna get involved in this". And it was funny because

at the time before I introduced myself, Busy Bee said he thought I was a policeman and he was really sweating bullets cause he was holding a big joint in his hand.

Why did you decide to give Quinones the name of Zorro in the movie, when he was already writing the name Lee?

Well Lee was his real name, it wasn't a nickname, he was writing with his real first name. When I made the movie I wanted to give him a kind of persona, in the sense that he represented all graffiti writers. I didn't want to make it as if the movie was about Lee Quinones, I wanted Lee Quinones to represent the whole movement in a sense. So I gave him an identity that was not really his. I had him write the name Zorro which is a Spanish name that means the fox, and the whole fictional Zorro character is someone who writes Z's. I had Lee living in the Bronx, like his character, and he got involved in the Hip Hop scene through Fred, it was a way to make a movie that would hold together, tell a story and introduce everybody that was there. So in a way people took on characters, like Fred took on a character and Lee did, they became characters that could then lead us through the scene, which was actually all real. It was as if we were going through a real world but with a kind of fictional context to it.

When you decided to combine the Rap scene with the Writing scene, which were part of the same movement in the Bronx, did you ever think of how the movie would be interpreted outside of NYC? In Europe for example the first generation thought that to be a part of Hip Hop you had to be a writer and a breaker and a DJ and an MC.

The funny thing with that is if you go into the reality of it, if you delve deeper, Lee Quinones was a break-dancer when he was younger. If you talk to someone like one of the great MC's in *Wild Style*, who is Grandmaster Caz, before being a rapper he was famous as a DJ. If you go back before that he was famous as a break-dancer, and if you go back before that he was famous as a graffiti writer. So in other words it's a deep story and it's a deep culture and it has many facets, but there is a lot of truth to the idea that these things were all interconnected. At the time I wasn't making a documentary, I wasn't trying to tell the whole history of this movement, I was trying to introduce the movement and project it towards the future, because to me it was new even though in reality it had been around for a decade. I was trying to introduce it as a new thing out into the world.

Did you imagine the movement would spread as quickly and as widely as it did outside of the US, to Europe and the rest of the world?

If you think about it I guess the answer is yes because when I struggled to make *Wild Style*, almost from the beginning, the first support I got for making the movie came from German television and the next support I got was from the UK, from the Fourth channel. In the summer of 1980 I had a friend that was involved in the independent film world, she was very up on things and she said there's people in England and in Germany that work in television and are interested in movies from America. So I sent them letters with images of the graffiti on trains, and that was it, that's all I sent. Just a few pictures of

pieces on subway trains and they agreed to make the movie. At that time I didn't even know for sure whether the film was going to be a documentary or a narrative movie. I guess I was always going back and forth between those two approaches and that's why the movie seems like it does. The first people that distributed it and really took to it were the Japanese though. When *Wild Style* premiered in Tokyo in 1983 it was a huge success in Japan, so you could tell it was going to be the big bang of Hip Hop. In Europe in a way it had already arrived through television, it had already played on ZDF and the first graffiti on the Berlin wall actually came from people who had seen *Wild Style*. I think it was on TV already in 1982 but I'm not 100% sure, and it was called *Graffiti* on television, they didn't call it *Wild Style*. After watching it the people had gone to the wall and started to paint things they saw in the movie. For example there was an image of the Zorro character and some of the other things in the movie and this was the beginning of graffiti on the Berlin wall.
It came in waves, it was shown on television and it had a lot of impact because people at that time were able to make copies of it and that whole thing was just starting. A lot of people saw the movie thanks to friends that had recorded it and made bootleg videotapes.
There was actually a celebration of the movie in Amsterdam in January 2009, and it was huge. One guy that showed up had a tattoo across his entire back, and he was

> **There was an image of the Zorro character and some of the other things in the movie and this was the beginning of graffiti on the Berlin Wall**

a very large guy, with the *Wild Style* logo. It was amazing. At the base of his neck he had an image of Grandmaster Flash and at the top *Wild Style*, done perfectly, just like the logo.

There's a specific part in *Wild Style* where you compare the legal aspects of writing with the illegal ones: Zorro painting the cars and Lady Pink painting the commissioned jobs. I wonder whether that was your way of showing two different sides of graffiti and suggesting something about the two. In Europe for example many writers interpreted it to mean that trains were the pure form of graffiti, as opposed to commissions.

That's a good way of looking at it, I would say that's true. In the larger sense though I liked the idea of this artist looking at the different options he has, what he does on the subway trains is one option, and he's looking ahead to his future and he's trying to understand what he's going to do. He's also got the mural painting with Pink, that's another option, then another is trying to become famous as a graffiti writer through this journalist. Yet another option is to make a painting for an art collector. There's the scene in the movie where he makes that little painting and it looks like it's not a success, it's just completely absurd, he's trying to make a painting and the canvas is way too small for what he does. The option I found the

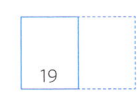
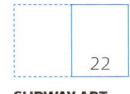
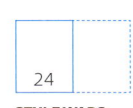
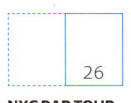
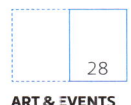
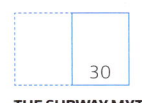
THROUGH

most interesting was him struggling to find his voice as a public artist to paint this amphitheatre, how he struggles with it at first and he fails at it. Then he finds a way to do it where he paints the star with the hands and everyone comes together in a way that is sort of an ideal image of Hip Hop at that time, where it becomes an integrated community with all these people coming together. I'm not saying any of those options is bad, and in fact they were all options that Lee Quinones as a real artist had done, whether it's paintings for a collector or murals. At the time I saw the mural he created as an expression of what I thought was some of his best work on the handball court. It was a kind of public art, it was the idea that a graffiti writer was a public artist, or a street artist, it was a kind of evolution from the trains onto something that could be integrated with the community, sort of revolutionary in a certain way.

Some people pointed out to me that the star could represent Hip Hop as a new nation, and in that sense Zorro was laying the foundation for the future by doing that. If you look at Lee as a representative of subway graffiti writers, up to that point he was still hitting trains, but after he finished the movie, that was it, he didn't go out into the subway system after that.

No matter how dedicated a graffiti artist is to hitting trains there's a point in which he stops and goes on with what he's gonna do.

While you were writing the movie and doing the research for it, were you working only with Fred and Lee or were you in contact with other people, for example Martha Cooper or Henry Chalfant, who were researching graffiti?

There were a lot of things happening around the same time. Fred and I were working on the movie together for a long time before I met or even heard of Marty and Henry. Then in September of 1980, and you have to understand I had already been working on the movie very graphically for some time, Henry Chalfant had a show of his photographs of subway car graffiti in an art gallery. It was there at that show that I met Lady Pink, and a lot of writers met each other at Henry Chalfant's show, because a lot of people weren't necessarily hanging out together just cause they were writing graffiti, so in a way it sort of brought people above ground. I think I might have met Marty around that same time, but it wasn't until much later that I saw her photographs. While I worked on *Wild Style* I had Marty come on and take some photos when I did my second shooting in the Spring of 1982, which was much, much later, like a year and a half later. She didn't actually work on the film when we did the original shoot, which was in the Fall of '81, she came on in the Spring of '82. But her photographs are amazing and of course the *Subway Art* book was a big influence on everybody, but that came much later, like 1984.

What really influenced me for the movie was seeing all the trains, cause it was so incredibly exciting, that Summer of 1980 there were blockbuster trains by Futura, by Blade, by Lee, by all these people that were busting out these amazing whole-car trains. In the movie I go to a specific spot, which was one of the best, because you could see trains from a distance there, you could see the trains coming, and that spot was in the Bronx. But you know just even being out and about in New York you're seeing the trains pull into the station and that had a big impact on me.

The impact of music videos

Hip Hop music videos of the 70's as the primary aesthetic and stylistic reference for the first European generation

CMP – CMPSPIN / Naestved
>

It was January '84, I was watching a German program on TV, and that was the first input as far as I remember. At that time television in Denmark was really poor; there were few channels: one national channel and a couple of German channels in my area. The language wasn't really a barrier because we studied German in school. I remember this small clip about electric-boogie from New York. There were these guys dancing on the street, and in the background there was graffiti. I was wondering what

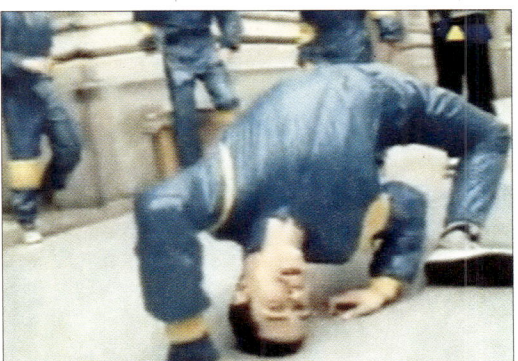
Crazy Legs dancing in a Rock Steady Crew video   — *Rock Steady Crew*

all this electric boogie, popping and locking and graffiti was about. This clip lasted 5 minutes or maybe even less. The truth is, that I went straight to my room and tried to copy those dance steps. I was 14 years old and I didn't even know what it was about, but at that age you see

At that age you see something and you are instantly influenced

something and you are instantly influenced and try to reproduce it. The same thing happened watching soccer on TV. I saw all these Brazilian players and the next day, I started to play. But when I saw the breakers, everything

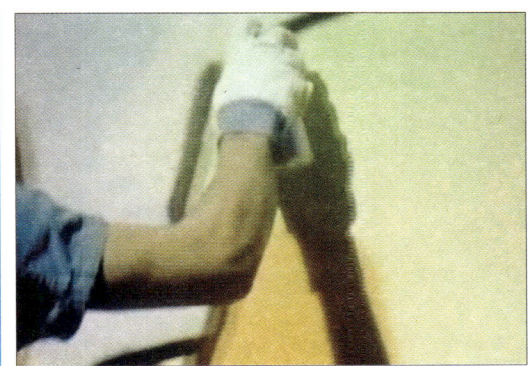
Dondi as he traces the outline of Buffalo Gals   — *Malcolm McLaren*

changed. Spino5, who is also from my hometown, was into dancing as well. We actually met in a B-boy battle at the time when B-boying was still new, but soon after there was no point in getting into battles, because most people had stopped dancing. So we joined forces.

A few weeks later there was another thing about the new movement on TV, but this time on Danish TV, and suddenly it was all over the media. Everything moved really fast, and then *Wild Style* was aired on Danish TV.

Honestly, at the beginning I was afraid of going out to paint illegally. One day this 15 year old loud guy, Inspe, said to me "I know you can draw, and if you don't get that sketch ready for tomorrow night, I will kick your ass." He really forced me to sketch and paint illegally. After some time, he suddenly vanished.

Funny how life sometimes works. Today, he is one of my best friends and the godfather of my daughter.

For the sake of efficiency, he organised the actions so we all had different tasks. One guy would sketch, one would bring the cans, another would watch out, and he would be the leader. That's how it was all organised the first months of my Writing career. Looking back 25 years later, I recognise it was a real good lesson for me.

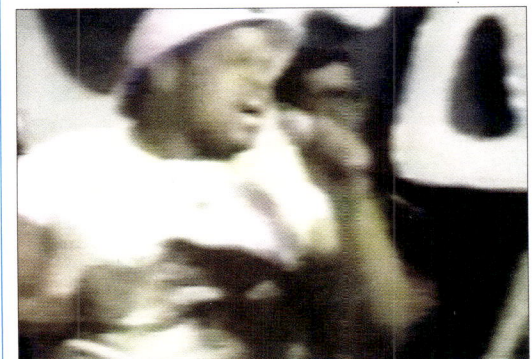
Rapper's delight music video   — *Sugarhill Gang*

The times of change: contaminations and the

Cemnoz – FBI / Munich
>

I started in spring 1983, I saw a picture of graffiti with some text next to it in a magazine. I was 16 years old and me and my friend were into the whole Punk attitude, but it wasn't enough for me, it was too destructive, there was "No Future" ... as their motto used to say! I wanted to do more and it was a kind of revolution for me; to express myself in that way. I started drawing and looking around, but there was nothing in the city, except anarchy signs. I was drawing all the time because my mother is an artist and took me to a lot of museums and galleries, she gave me the opportunity to paint so it was a natural development. I tried finding some more information on Writing but it was quite impossible until *Wild Style* was shown at the cinema. In that period, after school I'd go to another school so I could get my exams done faster, and the cinema where *Wild Style* played was really close. I went and watched it several times alone, trying to absorb every detail, I must have gone four, five, six times! I immediately understood this revolutionary idea of going out and saying something on the streets. After that I started noticing people were also doing it on the streets in Munich. The first guy was The Force, along with Flash and Loomit, and they did two pieces that were very long, with a concept behind them. It was done next to the subway tracks and it didn't get cleaned for a very long time, so I was going there with my bike pretty often. It really inspired me to go out myself because I was already drawing, but I didn't know how to translate it onto the walls. I did some drafts at home, my father gave me some paint and let me paint in a room in the house. I let my rebellious side run wild there. What he told me some time ago was "My 20% defiant streak turned out 100% with you". He was also the one who took pictures of the first train I did. Of course seeing *Wild Style* gave me the desire to hit a train in my city, and right after I did my first whole-car I went to his house and told him about it! I had no photos, so he offered to drive me and Loomit there and take some pictures of the painted train. Once there, my father said "You can do whatever you want, but I won't pay for it".

Alex Pistoja / Zurich
>

The first news about the world of Hip Hop was launched by TV in 1983, the year in which music videos like "Looking for the Perfect Beat" and "Planet Rock" by Afrika Bambataa came out, as well as Malcolm McLaren's Buffalo Gals.
But it was 1984, the year in which the German television channel ZDF aired the film *Graffiti*, which certainly marked the beginning of an important age for the Writing movement. The exact date of the broadcast is April 7th 1984. The strange thing is that a couple of months later the same movie was in theatres with its original name, *Wild Style*. ZDF (Zweites Deutsches Fersehen) had co-produced the Charlie Ahearn film and thus had the rights to

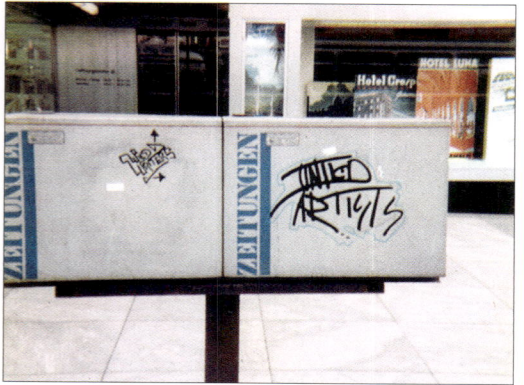

United Artists tags in Zurich's city centre   — *Alex Pistoja*

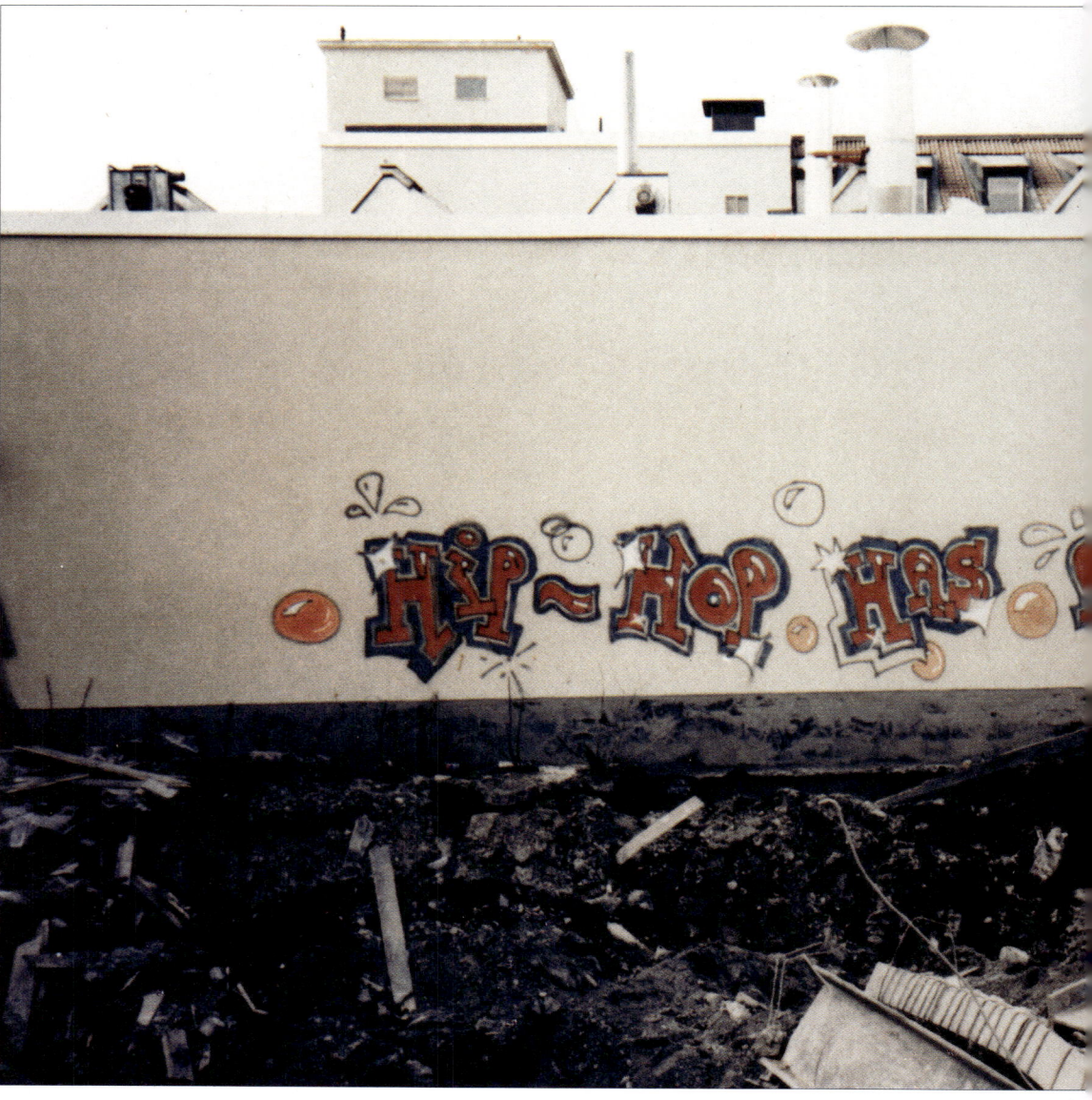

Hip Hop has arrived to Sweden. One of the first pieces painted by Puppet, 1984

air it before it hit the movie theatres. It was in that period that everything exploded inside me. Seeing such a thing on TV left me totally shocked. Later I realised that the same was true for many others: the movie had acted like a virus, contaminating kids with the desire to write. After having seen it I went to look for Rap records in the stores but nobody knew what I was talking about. Then when I went to watch it again at the theatre with Ivo, a friend of mine, we both decided that we would go tagging the next weekend. In those days I had already tried to use spray paint and knew I lacked certain skills, so I decided to limit myself to tagging with markers, thinking anybody would be capable of doing that. The next weekend we went to Banhofstrasse, the most expensive street in Switzerland, we walked up and down, it was winter, cold, and us two with our markers leaving tags upon tags! And we were not the first to do so: the Wild Writers had also been around. They already had a couple of tags even on trams. Then we started tagging next to them and another very innovative group that was called UA, United Artists. Wild Writers and United Artists had already been tagging close to each other, just as we had started doing. Nobody had the insight to think of putting the tags where they could be seen. We still used thin markers and all you had to do was leave a couple of signatures around to consider yourself a writer. Two weeks later we met Wild Writers and United Artists in person, and found out that the two groups didn't want to have anything to do with each other. It was only 1985, and everything was in turmoil.

Stone – SAK / Munich
>

The Munich scene really took off when *Wild Style* was shown. The world premiere was in Germany because it was done in cooperation with ZDF, it's a German state TV that financed it. The premiere was in a cinema in Berlin, but it had already been shown on TV before that, in '83. First it was in its original language with German subtitles and then it was translated. We actually preferred subtitles

> **After Wild Style was shown on TV the guy who really came first was Ray. He painted caricatures in incredible places**

because when the Hollywood production *Beat Street* came out, it was translated and shown on TV, but the result was so stupid. It was really artificial and it didn't have much to do with it, but it contained some information within it, some flavour, even though the real atmosphere was

outbreak of a culture

OUR SCRIPT
—

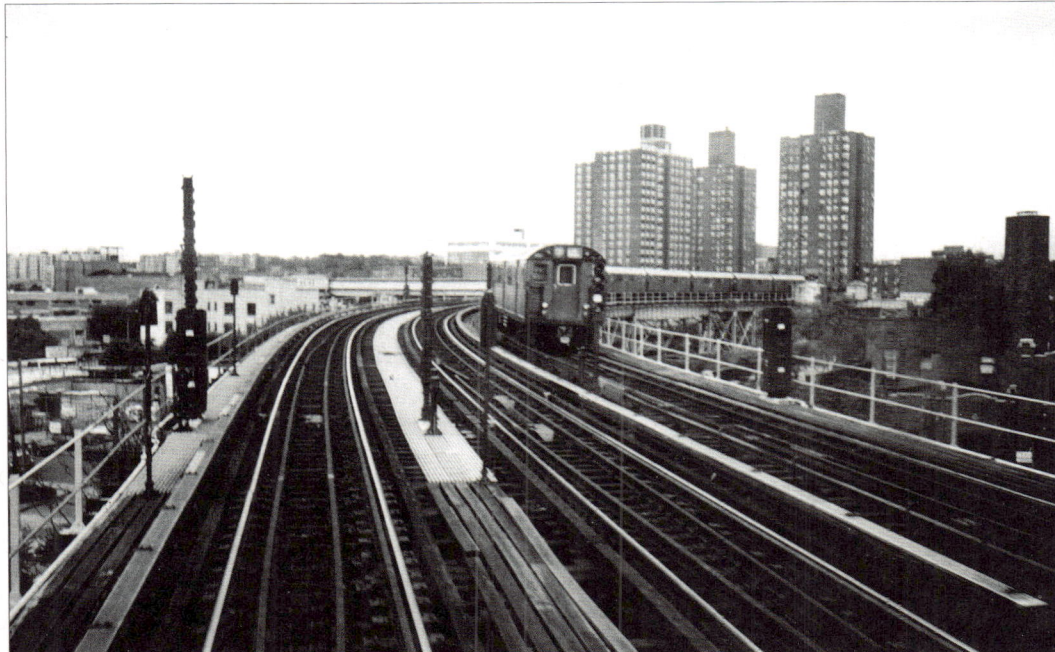

South Bronx elevated tracks   – Spino5

Chana – TWS / Dortmund
>

Once *Wild Style* the movie was featured on German public television, almost every kid from the first generation was influenced and amazed by the New York lifestyle, the Bronx surroundings and the atmosphere in general.
Besides that, there was a specific scene in which Lee (as train-writer Zorro) crit-icised the Union; a group of writers focused on graffiti commissions and jobs on legal walls, painted for customers in exchange for money.
When we saw this scene in Dortmund, around 1983/1984, the guys who started the whole scene took this sentence as a rule to abide to, as a manifesto. Chintz, Zodiac, Shark and me followed Lee's statement since the beginning, with no compromises. Back in the days graffiti jobs meant you were a 'sell-out' and what we saw in *Wild Style* immediately became a standard for the city.
Almost no one in Dortmund was compromising with graffiti jobs, the hardcore conditions became an intransigent factor for graffiti, fitting a city which in any case didn't offer commissions. Writing in Dortmund couldn't have another faith other than the one we built up years ago.

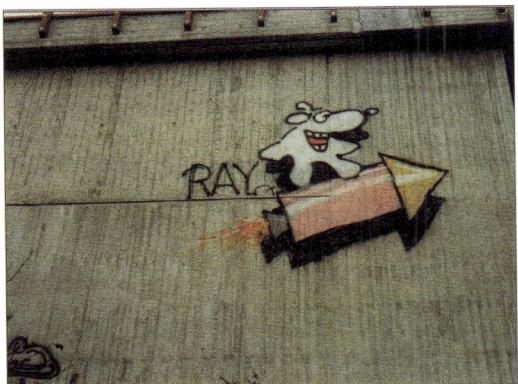

completely lost. There's a scene where they are painting in the tunnels and talking about the style of Phase II saying he was the first, well they translated it into "You have to stay in phase two". Of course we didn't understand what was happening, we thought they had started a secret language. They really hadn't understood the movie. *Wild Style* was subtitled because it was more of a documentary even if it was still a comedy. It was immediately shown all over Germany, not on local TV but on national TV. I think that's when it really started. You can't

really say it all started in Munich because it was pretty much everywhere in Germany at the same time, but with a different power. It took a while before everybody got connected. First everybody thought they were the only ones, even within the cities it was like this. Before *Wild Style* we didn't have writers in Munich, except one guy who was totally alone. We never found out who he was even though we had probably already met him. He was a German guy who had stayed in New York and painted trains there. After New York he came to Munich and did graffiti here. He knew everything we didn't know. He was shown on local TV once and someone interviewed him. Later on an article was published in the Munich city magazine with pictures of the pieces he had done on the subway in New York. He never got in touch with the scene in Munich because we were just toys and he already knew everything: when we reached a higher level, he wasn't painting anymore.
After *Wild Style* was shown on TV the guy who really came first was Ray. He was a little bit like Ray from the movie *Wild Style*. He didn't paint styles; he painted caricatures in incredible places. He was a climber so he went on bridges 35 metres high and made little characters there. He did a lot of actions like this and influenced many but he never got into style writing or tagging. In the end there was a bit of rivalry because we started going into style writing and into the culture while he stayed on the outside doing caricatures. He made fun of things, so the public could relate to his work much more easily than to our styles.

He was really influenced by *Wild Style* when it was shown on TV. I think one or two nights after he saw it he did his first piece and then some other pieces in very prime locations around the line. He also hit the first freight train which was standing in a very public spot, everybody saw it. That movie became the main reference for everyone; the ones who missed the opportunity to watch it on TV were simply cut out. I hadn't seen it so the first thing I imagined about Writing was "Ok, there are these guys from New York who paint graffiti, they surf on the trains, they make graffiti while they're riding and when they talk with each other they rap". Back then I was 13, I didn't have the chance to travel so what I did was I went into the libraries and checked out all the travel books from New York. After looking through dozens, I found one or two graffiti pieces so I cut them out and stole them. They were from the 70's; common pieces on the subway. They were really incredible, really precious. I kept them and showed them around the whole city. Everybody saw them. These pieces that I took from the library later made it into the *On the Run* magazine! Then I started to document the S-Bahn; the graffiti on the trains in Munich. In the beginning I was taking pictures of every tag; every time there was a train coming with a tag I would take a picture. Now when I look at the New York subway pictures from '71 I realise it was pretty much the same, style-wise. In the beginning a lot of people just copied what they saw from the U.S.! Many copies were made for example of the Zephyr and Revolts classic "Wild Style" piece.

– Puppet

Ray character in Munich, early 80's   – Stone

SUBWAY ART GOES

The techniques and dynamics of New York crews are revealed and contaminate the imagination of European writers who emulate these aesthetics and styles

Kapi –BTP / Barcelona
>

In Barcelona the Writing phenomenon broke out in 1984 with the first Breakdance movies: people started getting into Hip Hop through Breaking. Therefore they would write their names around, but without a real writer consciousness. So in 1985 all the groups of the city would meet up in Plaza Universidad and here they would sign the walls with markers. The names weren't as much individual as opposed to representing the group of breakers, the various pseudonyms they had given themselves. Koa. one of the first writers of the city, like many others had seen *Beat Street* and it came naturally to him to start writing his Name on the train cars of the subway. No tactics, no attention to what was going on around him. He just took the subway to come to my place and simply tagged the extremities of the train car with a marker when he got on and off it.

Things radically changed after I went on a trip to London with my dad. We went to visit some Argentinean friends that like him had run away from the oppression that was suffered by the intellectuals in Argentina during the 70's and 80's. The immigration of political refugees involved my family and other friends that were persecuted and found refuge in Spain, England and Western Europe. That time in London, around Christmas of 1985, an illustrator and friend of my dad's gave me *Subway Art*, which had just come out in the U.K., as a gift. He knew me and some friends had been Breakdancing, but he probably never grasped to what extent that present would influence the adolescence of an entire generation in Barcelona.

I got back with the book and finally all of us that gravitated around Plaza Universidad started understanding what it was we were doing: *Subway Art* made us conscious of the fact we were part of a bigger phenomenon that in the meantime had been embraced by many others in the city. Seeing other tags around had not led us to associate them to all this, simply because our decoding process had never begun. By January 1986 we had already started to observe somewhat more and realised that all the subway trains were running with an "L" painted on the front and back ends. We had already seen these L's times before, but nobody had put two and two together. The L's were by Lito, a kid of our age that was probably the first to paint the subway. Before *Subway Art* we had met Lito at Plaza Universidad and had even seen him in action; one day he waited for the train to arrive and while people were getting on and off, Lito would stand in front of the car, on the platform, writing with a spray can. The people around were impassive but we immediately asked ourselves whether it might be dangerous because of the subway guards. He said that they had already walked by and he had told them he was painting an advertisement. It really was another age.

Still in 1986 we started getting into Punk stencils, though punks usually didn't use the name or logo of their band. These were real artistic drawings and compositions, akin to the European Punk aesthetic of the 80's, but not tied to the musical band circuit. Among them I remember Frank from the group Trepax, he was a genius illustrator and artist: he also went from stencils to spray paint, however his graffiti, though technically admirable, lacked style and the principle groundwork of letters that constitutes Writing. The *flecheros* phenomenon of Madrid never existed here. The first couple of years there were no neighbourhood crews or writers tied to the halls of fame

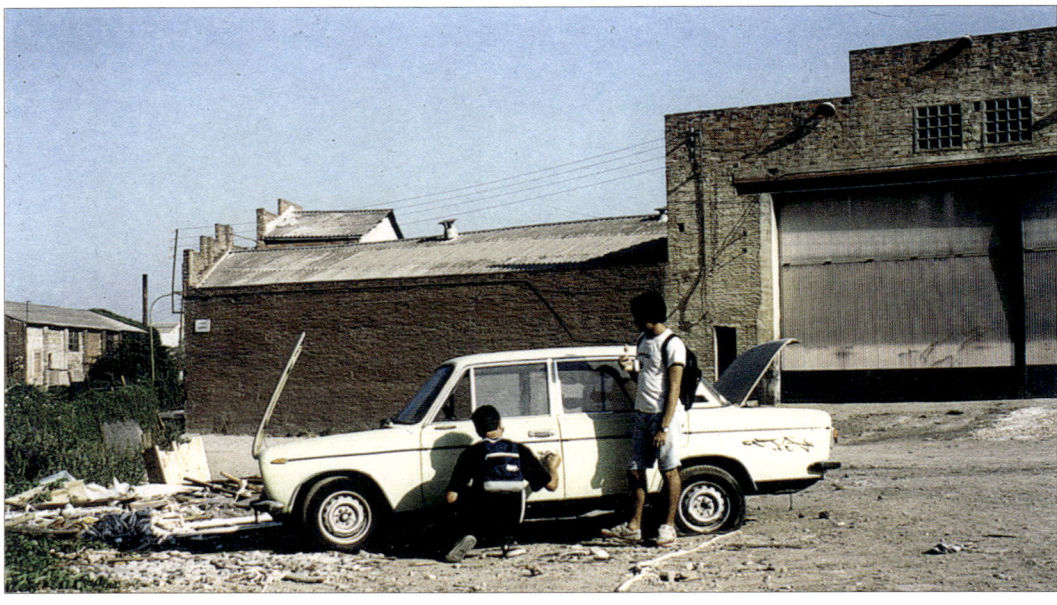
Kapi and Koas tagging the Barcelona streets. Mid 80s.   – Koas

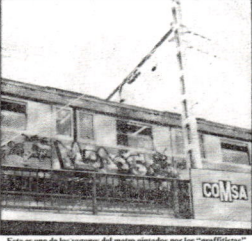

LUNES, 4 ABRIL 1988   Sociedad   LA VANGUARDIA 15

Los muralistas toman el área metropolitana de Barcelona y modifican su fisonomía bajo la atenta mirada de la Administración

Los nuevos pintores urbanos se esconden en la noche

El "graffiti" paulatinamente va ganando espacio en la ciudad. De las pequeñas inscripciones –los escritores– como se autodenominan los pintores de los "graffiti", han pasado a los grandes murales que pintan ilegalmente en las calles o en el metro. Son los nuevos amanuenses del fin de siglo que amenazan con pintar de colores toda la ciudad. Las autoridades, de momento, lo toleran.

Los "graffiti" llenan los muros de Barcelona con colores vivos

La policía actúa en la ciudad para localizar a estos grupos

JAUME V. AROCA

BARCELONA

KAPI

The subway remained a mirage during all the early years: already by the end of the 80's a sort of local Vandal Squad was created; the administration preferred to create delays and traffic jams rather than allowing even a single car to run painted

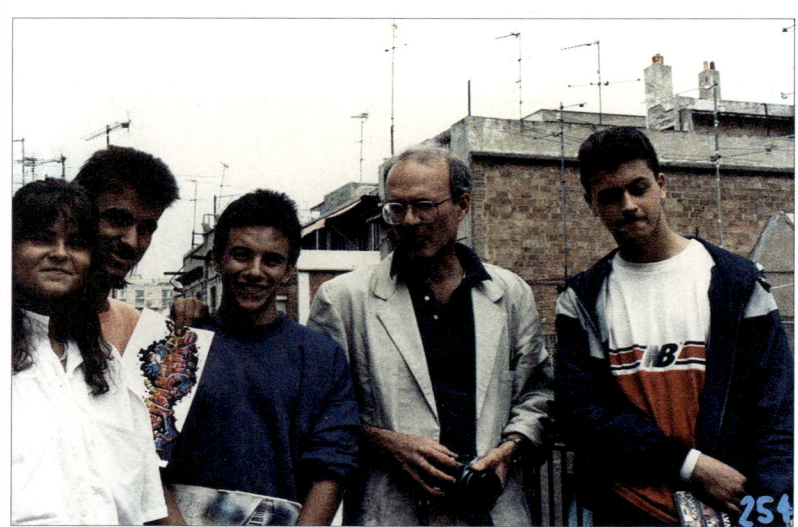
Henry Chalfant and Barcelona locals   – Kapi

OVERSEAS

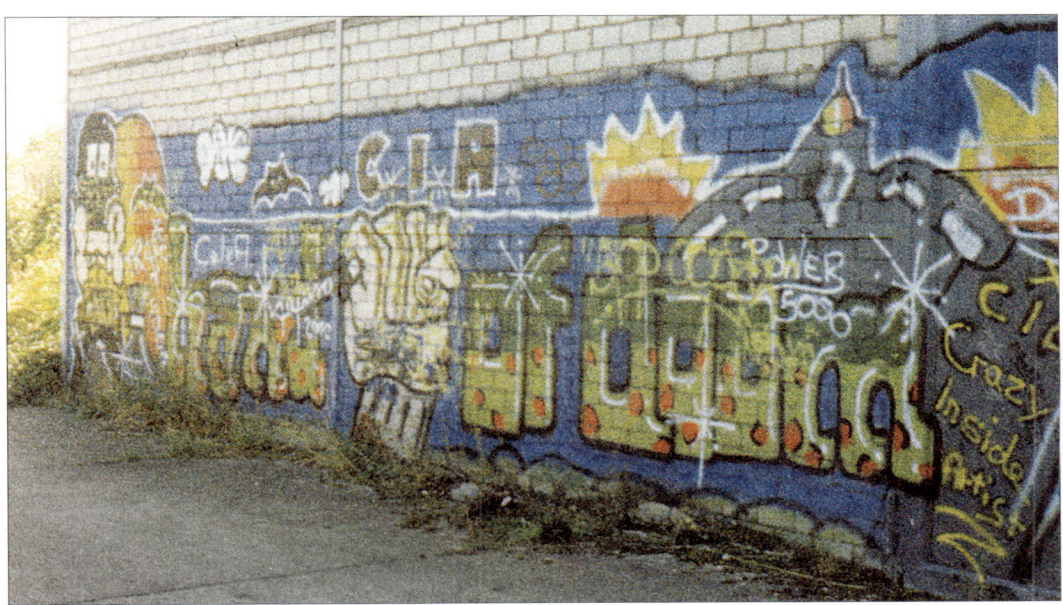

Dondi's Hand of doom piece replicated in Dusseldorf, 1985.   — *Mark Tedt*

in their vicinity because the only considered targets for writers were the trains of the subway. So crews mixed, at Universidad new friendships were born among people of different neighbourhoods, and the affinities gave way to the forming of groups who chose the subway as their reference point. So in 1987 we painted five subway cars and already then our tactic of entering, painting and getting out was extremely cautious: no leaving traces behind in the yard, we avoided forgetting empty cans around, same for caps. This strategy wasn't based on the English text of *Subway Art*, which we didn't understand, but by looking at the photos our conclusion had automatically been: painting cars is VERY illegal and risky (since *Subway Art* dedicated an entire section to the boys in blue), so we thought it was a good idea to be cautious. When, much later, we saw *Style Wars*, we relaxed: here writers were strolling in the yard and we saw the recreational and carefree dimension of graffiti. *Beat Street* and *Subway Art* on the other hand traumatised us, influencing our undercover way of painting in the first years.

The subway remained a mirage during all the early years: already by the end of the 80's a sort of local Vandal Squad was created; the administration preferred to create delays and traffic jams rather than allowing even a single car to run painted and this difficulty pushed the attention of writers to move towards the streets. Trains were momentarily forgotten. Even Renfe, the Spanish railway, though it had a capillary network, initially wasn't painted because it was considered a toy target, too easy to hit.

Stone –SAK / Munich
a.k.a. Don M. Zaza
>

Seeing all the trains in *Subway Art* was very impressive, it made our imaginations flow even though we were already close to those scenarios. My first piece was done on a train line so it was a natural spot to play with; it was just interesting and directly related to what we were doing with train painting. When I saw *Subway Art*, the general quality seemed so distant that I was like "I'm a toy and I'll never be as good as them", I thought it was impossible. We had a completely different life and environment: no shootings on the streets, no drug quarrels and no desperation. We thought that you needed this to do what they did on the trains. Initially for us it was

something that we could never reach, but once the book came out and we saw all those whole-cars, me, Loomit and Blash thought we had to paint a train. So we planned it for the 22nd of March 1985. It wasn't the first S-Bahn[1] train because Cheech had already done two trains before, one alone and one with a friend, but this time there were many of us: seven kids and a huge train that was even parked on my line. I knew the station because I'd been there with my parents before going on Sunday's

> [1] S-Bahn is a German Commuter Train. Other regional trains and freight trains were painted before, but the first S-Bahn piece had much more significance for the writers.

excursion: it's in the middle of a forest, surrounded by nature, and there's a really big yard. If you go through my hometown and you continue to the end of the line you'll reach the yard. So I took them there and we went inside knowing nothing. Nobody had noticed the first two trains Cheech had painted, but ours was done over the weekend and on Tuesday morning when my father opened his newspaper the train was published! It was such a shock, halfway between totally scary and cool! I went to the newsstand and kept all the pages of every newspaper that featured that train. In the tabloids it was over two pages, the whole-train with the story. It was the Deutsche Bundesbahn (German Train authority) that brought the story to the media, and they really regretted it because from there on the story went all over Germany. It was on the national news: two pages! They were wondering what was going on and of course they criticised it because they couldn't understand anything. They said "There's a character, a naked woman and thick colourful beans" - they didn't see the letters. Some made the connection with New York, it was considered scandalous but at the same time nice to show. This really did something because two months later it was being discussed in the German Parliament. They were talking about laws and a "graffiti problem". Somehow the government was really smart in predicting what was about to begin all over Germany in the late 80's.

Sabe –FYS,COD / Copenhagen
>

I started in '85 after seeing a documentary called *Hip Hop History* at school. Right after, just a few weeks later, *Subway Art* started to be distributed across Denmark and

I saw it for the first time. I was at a friend's house and there were six other guys sitting there drawing. When I saw them I just said: " Is this a drawing class or what? What the hell are you doing?" They all replied I had to see this publication from New York. I checked the book out and the first piece I saw was the Sab-Case full car. Still today I think it's one of the most beautifully styled and colourful whole-cars I've ever seen. Of course everybody was copying the *Subway Art* pieces! It was a whole new invasion. We'd never seen anything like it, they weren't commercials and they weren't meant to be, people were doing that because they wanted to and that's why it had so much power. I realised I really wanted to do that too, I'd always been drawing and I was kind of a strange child. I wanted to do something special. I was BMX biking and doing creative stunts at the time but I always broke my bones. Before that I played a lot of chess, I was a chess-head motherfucker! When I was 10 years old I was playing against guys that were 40 or 60... they'd been playing chess all their lives. So when I saw this graffiti thing I quit all these experiences and decided to focus on that. It was the only shit I could focus on. As I got more and more into it I bought a copy of *Subway Art* for myself. I read the book and started understanding the background of these kids. I figured out it was about having a name so I started writing down all sorts of names even if they just didn't have the right feeling. So one day I wrote down a long list of names, I put them up on my wall and decided. The connection between the letters was really important for me rather than the name itself and maybe I was unconsciously influenced by that Sab-Case whole car I saw. I started by copying all the pieces from *Subway Art* with poster markers I had stolen from the local shop. I'd been drawing for three weeks, every night! My mom thought I was going crazy but I wanted to get better and better. Then I came back to my friend's house, showing them all the drawings: they were laughing their asses off! My drawings were way too similar to the *Subway Art* pieces while they were already on another level. Pretty soon I understood the difference between being inspired by styles and copying them. I've learnt it the hard way through being ridiculed by my friends, but that's how kids tend to communicate: directly, maybe in a raw way, but definitely always honestly.

Bomber Johan / Tilburg
>

It was 1984 when Dutch national TV broadcasted *Style Wars*. I knew a bit about graffiti but this documentary came as a shock. It seemed like a parallel world compared to everyday life in the countryside of Holland. The colours...the ghetto.. the writers... Skeme and his mother, it was unbelievable that she knew what he was up to... the instant hate I felt for Cap. The doors to a new world were opened, and, once entered, I knew I could never leave. From there everything just snowballed. *Subway Art* was published in 1984, I bought it, read it and read it again and again, in bed, on the toilet, in the bathtub. One time I dropped it in the bath and had to buy another one so I could keep on reading it. I felt the urge to go out and paint myself. I started to rack paint in the small villages that surrounded mine. I had to bike for about 30 minutes to get to the nearest city but I felt that was the only right place to paint, so I had to go there. Possibilities were limited as I was a young boy, living with my parents and I really didn't have any business going out at night, let alone biking 15 km to a city where I didn't know anyone. I only painted walls and tunnels on the South side of the city as that was the nearest spot to reach. I had to do it very early as I wasn't allowed to stay out that long. Everything went well until I got caught red-handed painting under a bridge at 21.00 hrs in the early evening. The fine was huge, and the restrictions very harsh.

DECLARATION OF STYLE WARS

The American documentary from 1983 captures the actions of the first writers bombing the New York subway.
The chain reaction in European countries is immediate: train-bombing is imported

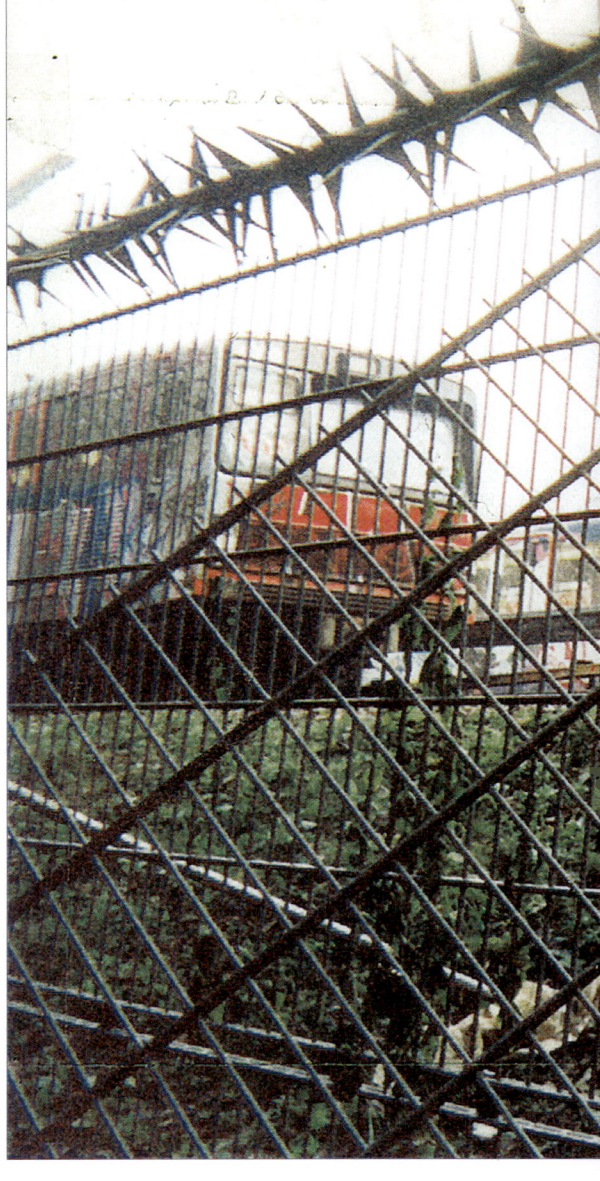

Ces53 –INC / Rotterdam
>

Ever since I was a kid I would draw cartoons on the street with my little markers, on poles, on street signs, everything. I was about 9-10 years old when I was doing that but it wasn't until '85, at age 12, that I actually did my first piece with spray paint. In Rotterdam there were already some punk guys doing graffiti, I remember tags from the early 80's

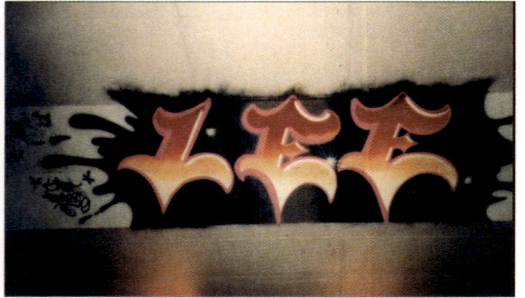

Close-up on the Lee rooftop painted in Rotterdam   — Wessels

done by older guys, mostly hooligans and punks, but nothing related to Hip Hop.
Then at one point I saw a documentary from New York: *Style Wars*. A teacher from school had the movie on videotape and showed it to my class because he wanted us

to make a graffiti drawing. Because I had already been drawing with markers, when I saw that movie I realised what it was that I really wanted to do. It completely changed my perspective: from the movie I understood I had to choose a nickname, while before on the poles I was just drawing small animals. I first chose Alias, as it fit perfectly with the meaning of using a second identity. That movie provoked an instant chain reaction: the following days we went directly behind the school to draw with our markers, totally inspired by the movie. We met other kids who were also interested in that stuff, everybody was just talking about tags and bombing. Little by little a first wave of young writers took form in my neighbourhood.
But it wasn't happening just in our area: other kids from several districts saw *Style Wars* and neighbourhood divisions started to take shape. Of course I used to walk around with the guys of my area. We joined other crews, and like a gang territory-game we kept to the centre of the city. The East was a little bit separate and then there was Hoogvliet, a southern area where kids were kind of on their own. This whole situation caused a lot of fighting between neighbourhoods around 1986-87.
One guy in particular was really bombing hardcore, his name was everywhere: Coke. Along with him guys like Call, T-Rex, Master and Save were really bombing throughout the city; some of them were already trying to be American by using letters with arrows.
I remember the first pieces started to be seen around '85 and already in March '86 there were thousands of graffiti kids on the streets, meeting in the city centre where the writers bench was. The police had to come with horses

and sticks, as if we were hooligans. But they couldn't do anything; we'd be 50-100 kids at a time going into shops and just taking whatever we wanted, each of us with a marker in his pocket! It was like *The Warriors* movie because guys from all the different neighbourhoods would come to the centre of the city to meet on Friday nights, and then start non-stop riots, sometimes there were 100 kids the cops had to battle. The writers bench was close to the central station and there was a piece by Lee from New York there; it was on a rooftop, in the middle of the centre, where all the shops were. Because of this Lee piece, the spot was kind of a Mecca. He had come for an exhibition in '83 and did this piece then.
In the beginning it was almost ignored by everyone, I guess because it just hadn't been decoded yet. But once *Style Wars* came out, everything changed, people started realising what it was and what it represented, and by '85-86 it was considered a Holy Grail of Writing in Rotterdam.

Rhyme –GVB / Amsterdam
>

Graffiti exploded here in '85, when the movie *Style Wars* aired on TV and really inspired our imaginations. Before this, the first book I saw was *Subway Art* the year before and of course it really blew me away as well. There was also this other book *Getting Up* that I really liked and still do. By then we were totally hooked and there were a few hundred writers in Amsterdam.
It was very competitive, only about bombing, bombing,

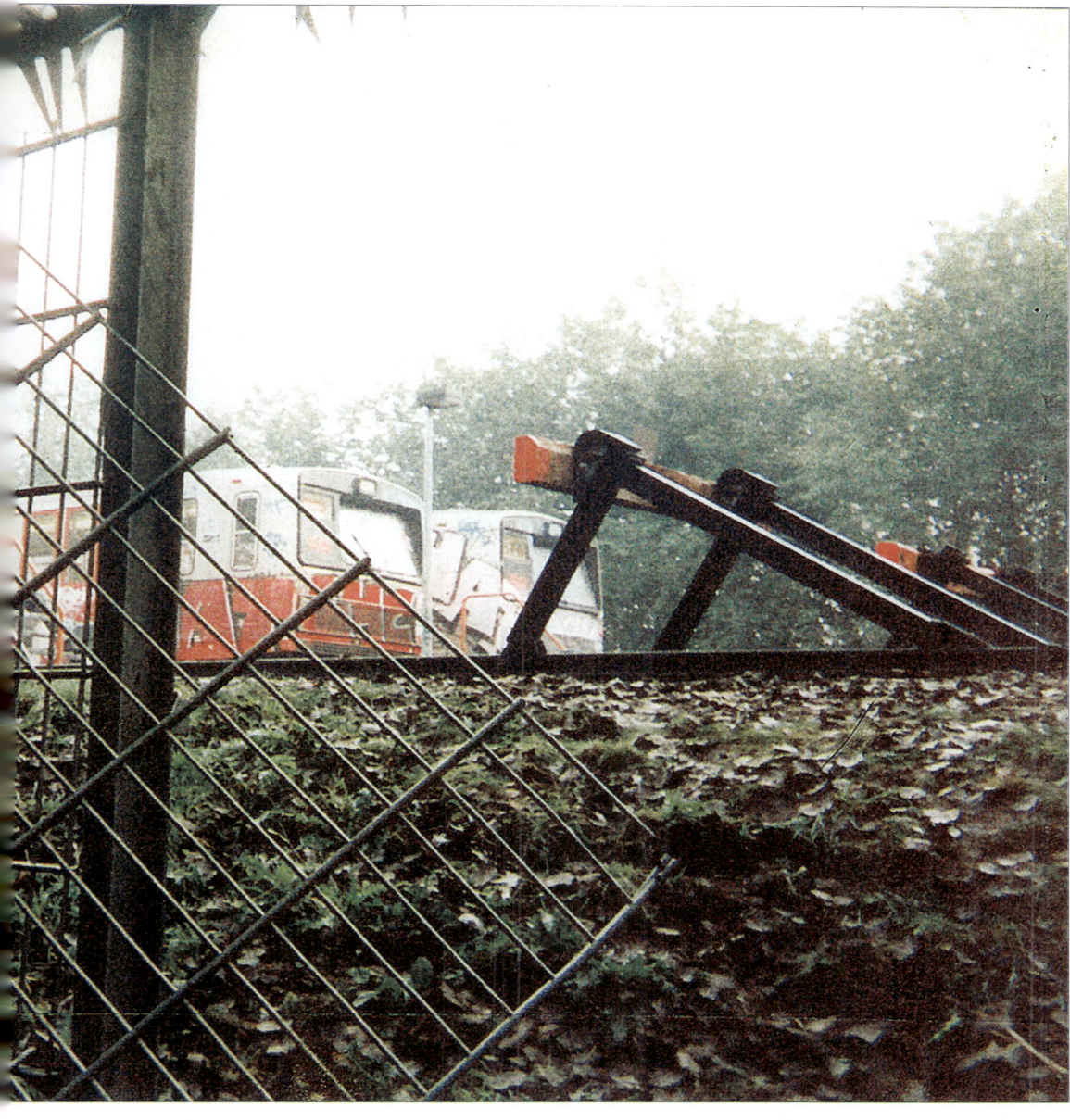

— Rhyme

SIMILITUDES

Amsterdam, mid 80's.
The destroyed fences
through which writers
entered the subway lay–up
are reminiscent of the New
York atmosphere

---

bombing. After they had played the movie on television the whole scene tripled! People came to Amsterdam from all over Holland. The movement was getting bigger and bigger, it was more destructive and graffiti gangs sprouted up like mushrooms all over the city.

A funny thing is that a week after *Style Wars* aired, the council for the city's public transit started making huge fences around the tram yards. They probably had been warned by the movie and in a rush they started to build this kind of barrier. They made some big fences, copying the ones from the New York subway yards. But the company was so stupid because underneath the high fences they didn't put any concrete or stones, just sand, and the sand under the fence was still fresh. So with Shoe, ZAP, Lino and some other guys we dug the sand out, passing under the brand new fence and trashed all the trams in the yard. That was our answer to this fence. And so you could say that the *Style Wars* movie really did come into effect.

Zedz –INC / Amsterdam
>

When *Style Wars* was aired on Netherlands' national television I didn't see it and I felt terrible, all the kids were talking about it but I had no idea what they were all going mad for. I was really trying to work it all out in my head, but I couldn't come up with the answers ... I had to see the movie! I really panicked until at last I found a guy who had recorded it. When I finally watched the movie, I think my

mouth remained open throughout the entire thing. My parents came into the room and said "Oh what a bunch of scumbags!" I remember my dad dropped in when Sach was talking about how to rack paint. He told us "Don't believe this, it's not normal", but by then I think we had already stolen some paint, so we were agreeing with him but at the same time trying to learn from what Sach was saying. Of course stealing paint, after seeing *Style Wars*, became the daily routine here as well, as we thought that was the attitude to keep if you wanted to paint a lot. We saw the movie in the daytime and that evening at 8 o'clock we were outside painting pieces, we were totally motivated! I remember when we saw my first ninja kung fu movie we beat each other up and it was the same with this. We watched it and were so inspired that we had to go out that same evening. The whole way trains were portrayed in the movie was a bit of a shock to us. I think it was unrealistic because in the movie all the trains were painted and the writers were speaking about painting over each other and all of that! I almost hadn't realised trains were running in my country, so painting them wasn't really an issue at that time, it wasn't like in New York where trains are everywhere. Our city's public transportation system is essentially based on buses, while in Amsterdam and Rotterdam it's trams. In our town there were buses passing by that you would occasionally take to go to the centre, however most of us were using bicycles, it's part of our culture. You'd see trains passing by sometimes but I didn't even realise people were inside. So we felt a bit unprepared and *Style Wars* was also overwhelming because our pieces were 1 metre by 2 metres at most. We were 14 years old, our arms were 50cm long and that was already big for us.

So to go on the train tracks was unrealistic at that time and if we painted on trains it definitely would have been window–down, because we couldn't even reach the windows! And as there was no train culture, it wasn't considered interesting in the beginning. However we started painting trains in '87, when we painted the first one I remember my legs were shaking and when the engine of the train suddenly started, it totally shocked me.

DORTMUND
—

Shark –TUF / Dortmund
>

The most remarkable memory of train–writing in Dortmund in the 90's is the sight of bombed trains. I guess *Subway Art* and especially *Style Wars*, the only images of graffiti we had in the very beginning, incited the passion for bombing trains. This means pieces but also tags and throw–ups. We were never satisfied with

just a piece on a car, we always kept paint for tags and throw–ups on the rest of the train. Putting tags between windows or on the front of a train was always nice and seeking the best spot on a car was great competition. Since the trains were running painted, hitting a car for the third or fourth time was just great. I love tags and throw–ups over a window–buffed whole–car. Painting a clean train just ain't the same.

IS EUROPE READY FOR HIP HOP?

The first Hip Hop tour arrives to Paris and London in 1982. Dondi, Phase II and Futura 2000 accompany the breakers and the MCs by painting on stage. The first live show of American writers

Bernard Zekri

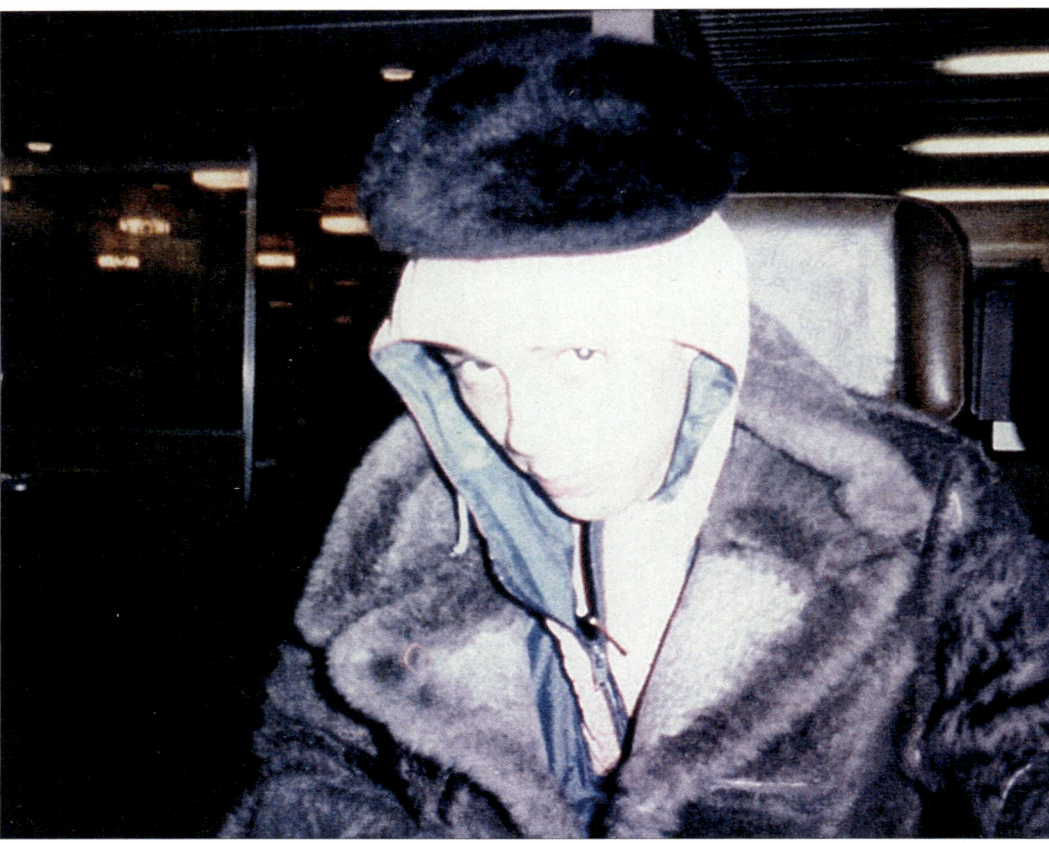

Futura 2000 travelling with the New York City Rap Tour   — *Phase II*

remember a dark staircase, mirrors on the walls and large black and white tiles that gave the dance floor a plastic tablecloth look. The Negril was a club on 2nd Avenue where Reggae was played, and there were never that many people, maybe two or three rastas, and a couple in the corner. That was it. I often passed by on my way home, and every time I would ask myself how the owners made ends meet.

And then Hip Hop arrived. A real tsunami (at the time neither of these words was known; neither tsunami nor Hip Hop). So Hip Hop swept everything away: the city, style, the walls, language, sound, and obviously the Negril! The Negril became a fashionable disco, smoky, overflowing with people, a mixture of fabulous creatures and blazing mixes. But very soon, the Reggae club was passé and the B-boys had relocated to the Roxy, a giant skating rink on 18th Avenue in which there was space for ten times the amount of people.

In that short span of time however, a couple of weeks, the dozen or so Hip Hop nights that took place at the Negril were touched by grace. The magic of a moment! Rap was a raw diamond. A bubble that bounced off of rhythms, scratches and break-dance moves. That unique moment, in which Manhattan the tireless was dazed by a joyous energy, a life blood flowing out of its ghettos. Period zapping, natural grandeur, there, that's what was going on at the Negril!

A new world was being invented and the bloodthirsty marketers had not yet pounced on these secret treasures coming from the street. It was there at the Negril that I came up with the idea of the *New York City Rap Tour*. There, while watching Crazy Legs, space juggler, human spinning top that made you dizzy with his breakdancing. The girl who organised the parties was called Blue, mysterious Blue, a 22 year-old from the U.K. Leather cap, violet blue eyes, she was managing the Rock Steady Crew. The first night I talked to her about going to Paris, Madonna was getting down to a breathtaking mix and DST, master-conjurer of the wheels of steel, was capturing us with an upbeat groove. Madonna sandwiched between two B-boys, that's what the Negril was!

In the beginning Blue was cautious, unforthcoming. She didn't believe much in this European venture. To convince her I brought her to Paris to do a tour of the sponsors, the radios and the nights at the Palace. Françis Bueb, guru of the FNAC, a chain store that distributes books and music, paid half the budget in advance. In turn, the tour had to stop in Belfort, Mulhouse, Metz and Strasbourg; Hip Hop was to invade France from the East. Europe 1,

a large, generic station threatened by the arrival of free radio and badly in need of a 'lifting', financed the other half, charging me with the delivery of five 12 inch records to AZ, a record label affiliated to the radio station.

As a journalist back in NYC, I was metamorphosed into tour promoter and record producer! Futura gave his ok on painting a canvas that would become the cover of our five singles. He had recorded a Rap song with The Clash and we agreed on including it in our compilation series. Consequently, Futura was the first to sign up for our expedition; he would paint during concerts and sing his song for the encore. Even better, he had promised to convince Mick Jones, the guitar player of The Clash, to come with us to the Bataclan, the first date in Paris. And Dondi, his painter friend, would join the party to add colour to our trip. A tour with two painters! Hip Hop didn't do things like everybody else, and I liked that!

Blue got her gang of dancers involved in the adventure, the 'Rock Steady Crew', who had not yet appeared in the movie Flashdance. In fact, they had never left New York, and it was the first time these kids from the Bronx were going to cross the Atlantic, with only one exception: Mister Freeze.

Let's stop a moment while I tell his story. Mister Freeze was the boogie-dancer among the breakers. You remember Michael Jackson's moon walk? Well the master of this move was him, Mister Freeze, a real character! Well, he was French this Mister Freeze, a Frenchman who had lived in the Bronx since he was five years old. He had almost forgotten his language and had a horrible

accent. Mister Freeze, who was a fan of the famous mime Marceau, was being imitated in all the streets of America; he would then in turn be copied by all those in Europe and France.

Conquer the world! Our happy-go-lucky gang of the Negril was bubbling with excitement at the idea! Who would take part in the journey? How long would it last? The time for negotiations had come.

We started talking money and the problems began. I was about to quit, call the whole thing off. I remember a meeting at my house, hours and hours of discussion. The final participants were to be DST and his MC, and Futura, Rammellzee, Bambaataa, Phase II and Fab Five Freddy, godson of Billy Cobham, a tough cookie when it came to business. Jean Michel Basquiat also wanted to follow us for a couple of dates without actively participating, at his own expense. Jean Michel was already a star. He had produced a 'cult' single for Rammellezee an out of space rapper, and was someone who took his interests much to heart. Freddy and I had a little financial dispute; he had recorded *Change the Beat*, a rap in French that I had written, the second record of our series, and he had complained that he hadn't been paid enough. So he had decided to be even more intransigent regarding the fee for the tour. I excelled in the role of the bad guy and greedy producer, and we tore each other apart dollar for dollar for the final total sum including expenses. I couldn't give in more than $150 a day and they wanted more. We had been arguing for hours when I blundered: "Freddy, yo boy". Yo Boy. The insult, the fatal error, I had stepped

The New York City Rap tour

over the invisible line, "boy" to a black artist! In the Hip Hop universe, you don't kid around with respect! And in that moment, in front of their appalled expressions, I understood I must have sounded like someone from the dark ages of the KKK. DST tried to pick up the pieces: he made fun of me and my English. And he was right. I had not understood that "boy" belittled a man!

DST's song, the third record of our series, had left a producer friend of mine called Bill Laswell enthusiastic, "It has the same rhythm as Tony William" Bill had said, nothing less! A legendary jazz drummer and legend is what DST wanted to achieve. It all happened even faster than I had thought. Rock It was a planetary hit! Seven million albums sold together with Bill and Herbie Hancock. Scratch aristocracy. DST the DJ! The scratch single Change the Beat was recorded right at the end of the tour. And "Fresh", the last word of Change the Beat became a

Futura gave his ok on painting a canvas that would become the cover of our five singles

cult, scratched by deejays throughout the world. Come on, admit it! Wahoo!! DST didn't drink a sip of alcohol. And in a millisecond he went from a brat's joke to bad boy violence. During the tour, in Lyon, I was afraid he would rip the head off of a fan who had argued with him. I had to physically intervene to make him stop. A ball of nerves! You died young in the housing project where he came from, and behind his impeccable look lurked the soul of a paranoid man. He had shown me a spotless case with an AK. Maniacal just like with his turntables. I have memories of funerals of brothers killed in their prime. I remember hours spent choosing a coffin, sky blue with stars. And inside the funeral parlour photos would be taken as if death were a game. DST looked good; an audacious elegance, he had a slight lisp and difficulty pronouncing the letter X. I liked the guy. His name, DST, came from Delancey Street. The youngest of our entourage were students, the Double Dutch girls! Malcolm McLaren had not yet made them famous. Bringing them along was like bringing a little piece of New York with us. Getting their parents' permission was not an easy task. Blue acted as guarantor. Finally, the last day before the plane trip, Bambaataa came to take stock of the situation in my Funk Room (That is what he had nicknamed my office, populated by mice and an old stereo, where he liked to sit on a rickety dentist chair I had recovered from the flea market). He had his little stock of White Castle mini hamburgers he was addicted to. "Is Europe ready for Hip Hop?" Bambaataa had asked me, worried. I had bragged something about it being a triumph, though the story is actually more complicated than this. I'll tell it in another article. It was nonetheless sufficient to reassure him. Bambaataa, the emblematic figure of a cool cat, already had two hits, *Planet Rock* and *Looking for the Perfect Beat*, "the ultimate Rap song" as the Village Voice had written. Thanks to Bambaataa's name, our tour would even stop in London and Los Angeles. When Bambaataa left the funk room he had the smile of an old lion as he roared "Peace". The *New York City Rap Tour* could begin…

– During the 80's you came to Europe with the New York City Rap Tour. Could you tell me about this tour? How was the show organized?

IT WAS A TOUR THAT WAS ORGANIZED BY EUROPE 1 AND IT CONSISTED OF THE SO-CALLED FOUR ELEMENTS OF HIP HOP. SOME OF US HAD RECORDED MUSIC BECAUSE WE WERE INTO HIP HOP ON THAT LEVEL, MAINLY DST AND THE INFINITY RAPPERS. I ALWAYS RAPPED AND FRED WAS A GOOD RAPPER TOO, EVEN IF HE AIN'T REALLY RAPPING TRUE TO HIP HOP AT ALL THOUGH. WE HAD THE ROCK STEADY CREW, FUTURA, DONDI, THE DOUBLE DUTCH GIRLS AND BAMBAATAA TO NAME A FEW OF THE MORE LEGITIMATE HEADS INVOLVED, ALONG WITH SOME DEVILS.

HOLDING IT DOWN, IT WAS THE FIRST TOUR AND CONGLOMERATE THAT HAD ALL THE SO-CALLED ELEMENTS OF HIP HOP UNDER ONE UMBRELLA AND WE TOURED DOING OUR SONGS, MCING AND DOING THE ART ON STAGE. IT DEFINITELY CAUGHT A BUZZ AND GOT PEOPLE ON IT BEFORE ALL THE HYPE AND MISREPRESENTATIONS.

WE DEFINITELY ATTRACTED THE ATTENTION OF A CERTAIN AMOUNT OF THE MASSES AND TURNED THEM ON TO HIP HOP AND URBAN CULTURE IN A WAY THAT THEY WERE NOT EXPOSED TO BEFORE. I HAVE BEEN TOLD THIS FROM HEADS OUT THERE AND THAT WAS BEFORE ALL THE MYTHICAL BOOKS AND MINSTREL SHOWS IN THE SHAPE OF FILMS AND DOCUMENTARIES CLOUDED THE MINDS AND BRAINWASHED THE PEOPLE. THEY WANT YOU TO BELIEVE THAT IF THEY HADN'T WRITTEN A SCRIPT OR A BOOK THEN NO ONE WOULD KNOW HIP HOP, AS IF IT GOING WORLDWIDE HAS ANYTHING TO DO WITH WHY WE DO IT IN THE USA, OR THAT NO ONE BUT THEM EVER DID ANYTHING THAT DIFFUSED IT FOR IT TO BE EXPOSED AND SPREAD AROUND THE WORLD.

THE 'FUNNY' THING IS THAT I START TO SEE CERTAIN THINGS DIFFERENT THAN I SAW THEM IN THE PAST… JUST LIKE FINDING A SNAKE IN YOUR GRASS WHEN YOU THOUGHT ALL THERE WAS WERE WORMS.

THERE ARE TIMES WHEN YOU DON'T SEE A PERSON'S HORNS AND HOOVES. BUT USUALLY THEY ARE THE ONES WHO HAVE THE STATUS AND PULL TO MAKE THINGS HAPPEN. SO GO FIGURE. IT WORKED IN OUR FAVOUR HAVING IT CONCEIVED THOUGH, BUT AS USUAL WE WERE DEALING WITH VULTURES. THE VULTURES WHO EXPLOIT THE CULTURE EXIST BECAUSE OF US; IT'S NOT THE OTHER WAY AROUND, EVEN IF THEY DID EXPOSE IT TO SOME DEGREE AFTER THE FACT.

WE DO IT BY NATURE AND BECAUSE OF THAT ONGOING REALITY THE SAGA CONTINUES: IT DIDN'T START WITH A BOOK OR A MOVIE. IF WE HADN'T DONE IT AND GENERATIONS HAD NOT CONTINUED IT, THE LEECHES AND VULTURES WHO CONTINUE TO WRITE, EXPLOITING NAMES LIKE MINE WITHOUT MY PERMISSION, WOULDN'T HAVE AN ARENA TO PLAY IN.

LIKE COLUMBUS DIDN'T DISCOVER AMERICA, NO ONE DISCOVERED US. HIP HOP IS THE NOISE AND HIP HOPPERS ARE THE ONES WHO BRING IT AND BROUGHT IT, FROM THE ORIGINATORS TO THE ELABORATORS TO THE CO-CONSPIRATORS AND MASSES.

– Coming from the Bronx, what impact did London and Paris, the people and the European culture in general have on you?

WE RAN THROUGH CITIES TO TOUR. HIP HOP WASN'T REALLY BUSTLING AT THE TIME SO THERE WAS REALLY NO REAL SCENE THEN BUT LONDON WAS LOVELY, ALL THE SHOWS WERE FUN AND THEY WERE REALLY RECEIVED WELL.

BUT, WHY IS IT THAT WE HAD ONE ALTERCATION THAT WAS STARTED BY A BUNCH OF FOOLS WHO THREW A BOTTLE ON THE STAGE THAT ONE ASSHOLE REPORTER FROM NEW YORK, (THE SAME ONE WHO WAS PATTING US ON THE BACK AND TELLING US HOW WE ROCKED) CHOSE TO FOCUS ON THAT AND HOW NEW YORKERS

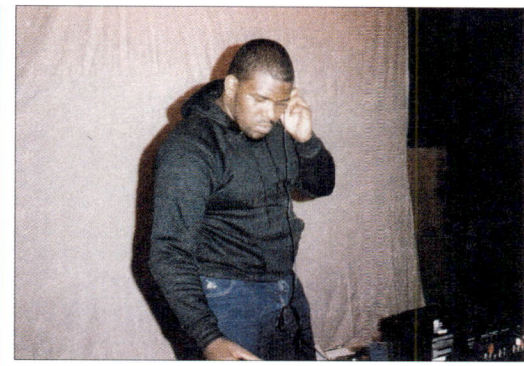
Afrika Bambaataa djing in Paris   *Phase II*

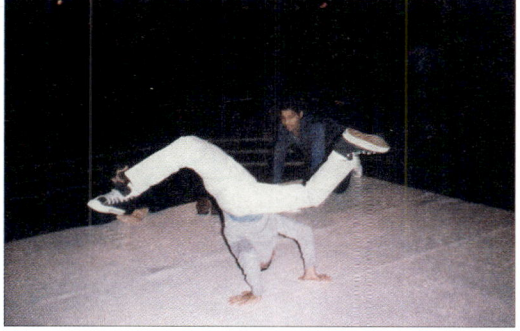
Ken Swift on stage in London, 1982   *– Phase II*

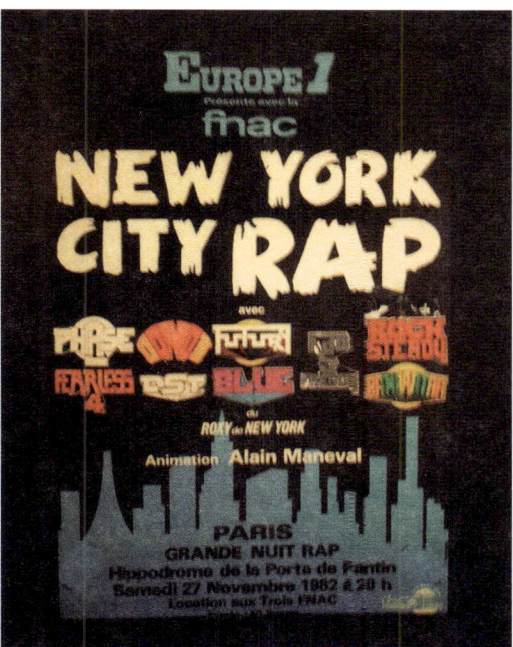
New York City Rap Tour poster   *ACW archive*

LIKE US WOULD PREFER MICKEY D'S TO FRENCH CUISINE, AS IF WE ARE SUPPOSED TO GIVE A RATS TAIL ABOUT CREPES AND SUCH.

THIS IS WHAT SOME OF THE SAME PEOPLE WHO INTERVIEW AND SMILE IN YOUR FACE REALLY THINK OF HIP HOP AND US.

YOU HAVE A LOT OF TIN SOLDIERS WITH COLOURFUL NAMES IN THE GAME FRONTING LIKE THEY ARE RAMBO WHEN BASICALLY THEY ARE GOFERS AND MICE THAT FOLLOW ALL THE CHEESY NONSENSE THAT DEVILS PUT BEFORE THEM AND THE PUBLIC.

THEY ARE NEVER GOING TO SAY WHAT I SAY AND TELL YOU HOW WHACK AND SUPERFICIAL AND UNREAL THINGS ARE IN THIS GAME MAINLY BECAUSE THEY FEED INTO IT AND LIVE BY IT, THEY ARE IT. –PHASE II

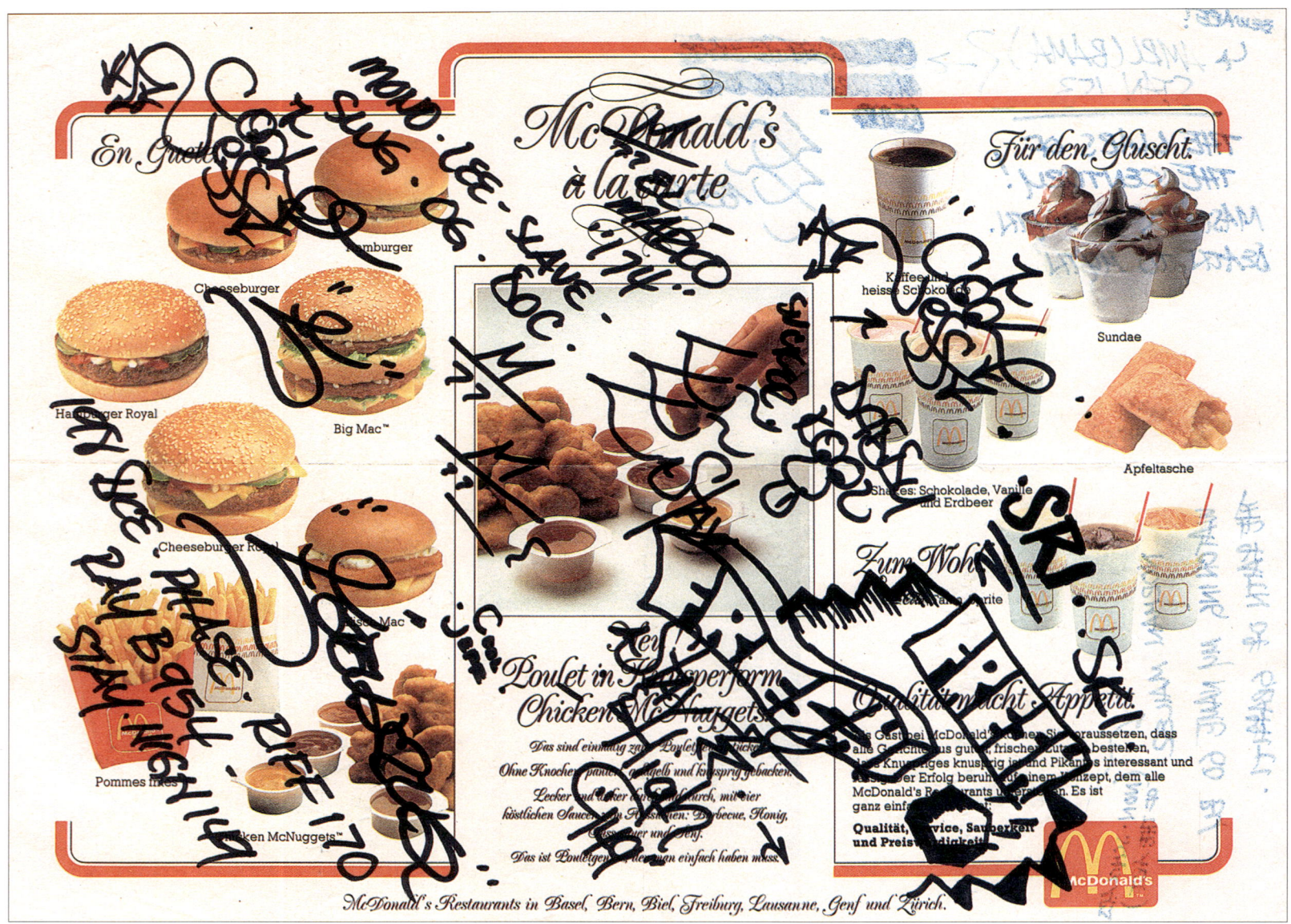

Phase2's different explanations on a McDonald's placemat –note his list of the "original" fabolous 5 with members: 198 Dice, Phase II, Riff 170, Ray B 954 and Stay High 149   – *Alex Pistoja*

ART & EVENTS

European galleries open the gates to American writers: direct contacts with the scene of New York

Gijs Van Hensbergen
>

The American Graffiti exhibition presently showing at the Boymans van Beuningen in Rotterdam is an important early attempt at making sense of the latest movement in New York painting. Organised in collaboration with the Groninger Museum, numerous private collectors, the Yaki Kornblitt Gallery, and the critic Edit Deak, much has been made in recognition of graffiti as a self-contained movement. The polemic surrounding the graffiti show concentrates on its transition from subway to museum; from train to canvas, hardly touching at all on any qualitative judgement. For some, the sampling of graffiti reverberates

> CONTINUES ON PAGE 36

Rhyme –GVB / Amsterdam
>

In 1983 the New Yorkers came to Holland through the Yaki Kornblit gallery, the owner really liked this new art form and brought the New York graffiti artists for an exhibition to his gallery, which was very close to Vondelpark. Seen, Blade Futura 2000 and Dondi were here in '83 while Bill Blast and Quik came in '84. Of course new signs started to appear across the city, there were all these crazy New York tags around! Amsterdam was already pretty bombed but that literally introduced the New York style to Holland. It was Shoe, Delta (than Lone) and maybe some other guys that hooked up with the New York artists and then the whole connection started, it brought an important change to the pieces. Before that Shoe was doing some crazy comics and block letter stuff, he had already done some pieces in his neighbourhood but then he started doing these New York style bubble letters. No one copied the New York styles but of course there was a big influence. It was stunning to spot Seen pieces around! One was in the park and they also did some walls in the South-East area, I still remember the pieces really well.

Quik was tagging and putting his beautiful throw-up everywhere, I've never forgotten seeing tags from Urban Blight, NOC 167, Zephyr etc. We traced the tags like we were Sherlock Holmes – it left a huge impression on us graffiti junkies...

Shoe –USA,CTK / Amsterdam
>

Around 1983 Dondi and Futura came to the Yaki Kornblit Art Gallery in Amsterdam for an exhibition of their work; this gallery was just a few blocks from my house so of course I couldn't avoid checking it out. It was around this same period that *Subway Art* came out, which influenced my style completely, and, along with the show, changed everything in Amsterdam. Until then the city had its own very distinguishable style in graffiti, coming straight from the Punk and Anarchic movement of the 70's. The kids belonging to that period had never seen a painted train or a tag, so they had a very different approach, just doing their own thing. When New York letters arrived, writers instantly forgot these 'roots' and adopted the new style that was evidently bigger and more interesting to develop: New York letters allowed colour experiments on shapes, which the original Dutch ones didn't since they were just black sticks, a sort of Punk typography. That is one of the reasons why I'm currently doing Calligraffiti, which is a mixture of various calligraphic styles, New York graffiti styles and protest lettering.

Yaki Kornblit was bringing different artists to the gallery every couple of months, and we would often enquire about the next exhibition in order to get in touch with more New Yorkers. Of course Delta, Gasp, me and a couple of other kids were all hanging out around the gallery to see the canvases but actually we were much more interested in street actions, cause the goal was to learn about techniques and styles that could be applied to walls, not canvases. Not everyone was that open, but for instance Dondi was, and he became a really important figure for all of us. Many of the Americans coming over were visiting Europe for the first time and seeing the graffiti here they must have thought we were amateurs. It took some time before we consolidated a real connection. Obviously one thing led to another and I would show them the city, the coffee shops, we'd go out tagging, a little piece here and there in the park. We really learned a lot from them because we were only 15, 16 years old while they were in their 20's.

Besides Dondi, also Zephyr, Daze, Blade, Crash and Rammellezee came through the gallery. I would hang out with Quik and Futura, even though he kind of kept to himself. It was mainly Dondi and Quik that were coming back to Holland quite often, especially Quik who was doing a lot of shows here. Following these inputs, the 70's style stuff in Amsterdam was practically dead, even if there were still a few guys tagging the old-fashioned way. Even Rhyme did, who used to write "Aids" with the three crosses on the "I", which was totally the Amsterdam style.

The whole New York concept of graffiti changed everything, and of course it had to do with the diffusion of the Hip Hop movement in Europe. Sure, the movement was strong in the Netherlands as well, but maybe in Amsterdam we were more writers than B-boys, as we were more concerned with graffiti than the actual Hip Hop movement. Via the gallery we got in touch directly with New York writers and were less influenced by the media. Meeting all these people allowed us to see the whole graffiti phenomenon through another perspective: we realised that it could be bigger than we had imagined and not have to be strictly about B-boys. Of course we were influenced by *Subway Art* and *Style Wars*, but thanks to the gallery we had met many writers from New York, each so different in lifestyle that it would be impossible to pinpoint a precise school of thought we followed. I mean, how similar are Seen, Futura and Quik? It's the broadest range of people you could imagine. They all have such different ideas and style. We didn't have a main reference to copy from but rather an ensemble of influences and teachers. In the beginning it was bouncing like a rubber ball from one side to the other, but very quickly all of us, like Delta and me, realised we needed to find our own direction. However, we did completely absorb the idea of 'crews'. Back in the days in Amsterdam, everybody used to go out bombing alone or maybe in twos at most. And on top of that you even had lots of people writing the same thing. In New York I don't think it was normal to have two or three people writing the same Name, while in Amsterdam it was really common.

The idea of being in a crew made more sense in New York, especially if you wanted to do a big whole-car; you needed to go with a couple of other people. It's a beautiful idea being together and sharing one, big surface.

In Amsterdam on the other hand we were primarily hitting streets; the idea of crews came directly from the American writers who told us about them in the 80's.

For them in New York it was often a matter of survival in the face of violence and danger.

For example, if someone confronted you and you didn't have the boys to back you up, you were basically helpless.

This was less of an issue in Amsterdam in the beginning: only when our subway system became a main target were the New York dynamics reproduced, and all of a sudden the necessity of being in a crew became implicit.

Stone –SAK / Munich
>

At one point there was an exhibition at Gallery Thomas, an important collector in Munich. When *Wild Style* came out in '83, the art gallery system picked up on graffiti, organising world tours for the original New York writers; first they were in Amsterdam and then they came to Munich and did an exhibition here too. I was not at the opening but I'm sure there were some New Yorkers. When I did go I was amazed by the canvases by Lady Pink, Daze, A1, Futura, Crash, I had never seen anything like it before. Of course through the art gallery some writers started to meet and recognise each other. I became friends with Cheech H and one day we decided to meet

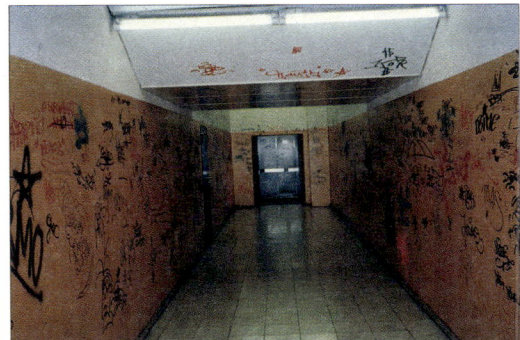

Pocchistrasse Munich, view of the bombed hang-out   — *Stone*

in the city; we skipped school that day and he took me to a subway station in Munich Poccistrasse. Behind it there was a very little stairway, which he took me through: it was completely covered with small pieces made with markers! Pieces from everyone in this small and hidden place, a sort of miniature hall of fame. All the writers in Munich went there using acrylic markers to make little pieces, it was incredible, like a sketch book painted on the wall. Besides the first meeting in the gallery, that was the first spot where we all got together. It was very special for every early writer of Munich.

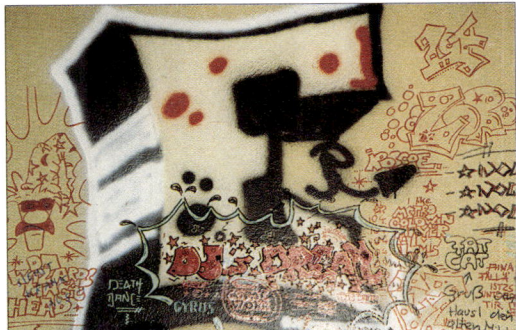

Pocchistrasse, walls details   — *Stone*

Alex Pistoja / Zurich
>

At the 1984 opening of Rammellezee's exhibition in the Ziegler gallery, three B-boys were present. Among them was Power of the Fantastic Rockers who came from my neighbourhood, and dressed in fat laces and straight-leg jeans ... they were very stylish. They had a record with them and asked Rammellzee to sign it, but he answered: "I don't do no tags, this is scribbles, scrabbles...get outta here!" So they never exchanged contacts and left almost traumatised. Not long later another exhibition was organised at the Ziegler, this time with Phase II. In that period I would always go around taking pictures of graffiti and especially of a particular hall of fame that I would visit once a week because there was always something new. One day, passing by there I saw something really beautiful, yellow and blue. I looked at it with care trying to read what was written: I deciphered "Phase II". I had already seen and recognised that same style in a book that is now

impossible to find. I immediately went home to call the others and warn them that maybe Phase II was in town. The next day we all met up in front of the wall to look at the piece. Close by there was a Burger King, a hang-out of ours at the time. Convinced that if Phase 2 was here he would pass by again, we sat for hours and hours at the Burger King and at the sight of any black person – there weren't that many at the time – we would ask them: "Are you Phase II?" Then he came for real. We were sure! He was with Steve, the leader of United Artists, who had met him a couple of hours earlier. Phase was real nice and stayed almost a month in Zurich, during which we spent a lot of time together. I was very interested in his story, how he had started in the Bronx, and he told me everything in detail. On a McDonald's menu placemat – I still have it – he wrote all the names of the original New Yorkers, and then showed me how he had started with letters. He made two lines and wrote F.R.E.S H, taking the

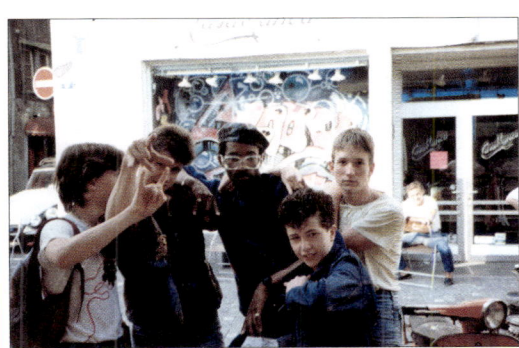

Wild Writers posing with Phase II at Hechtplatz. From left to right: Craze, Bost, Phase II, Star–T, Genius   — *Alex Pistoja*

necessary time to explain the structure to everyone. Kids from outside came, and we would go do pieces with him. It was a great period, and to hear the story in first person was unforgettable. When Phase II went to Milan he left a huge hole in all of us.

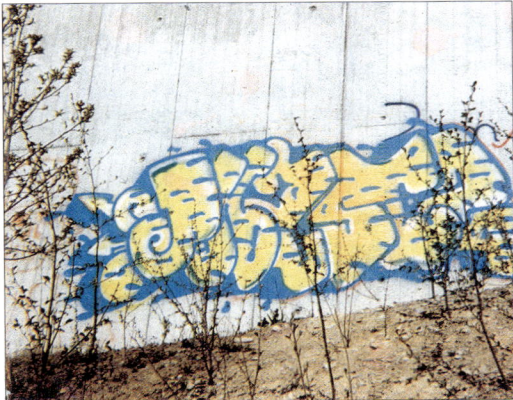

Phase II, first piece in Zurich   — *Alex Pistoja*

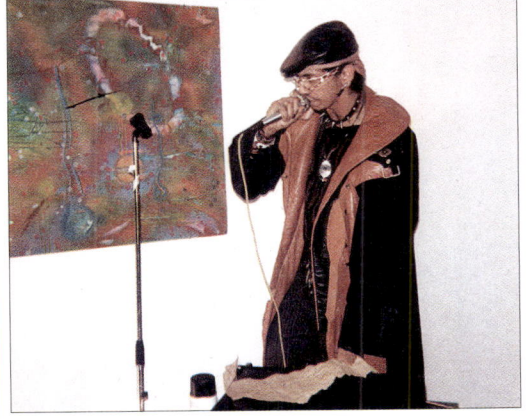

Rammellzee performing at Piranesi Gallery, Zurich 1984   — *Alex Pistoja*

A MYTH AFTERBIRD

WHAT THE NEW YORK

The myth of the New York subway, the desire to live the reality of the Bronx and to paint the cars where it all began

Following the shift from indirect experience – mediated by books or television – to direct experience – favoured by the galleries that displayed work by American writers – at the end of the 80's a new form of thematic tourism appeared, in which European writers directly catapulted themselves into the marginal areas of New York City. European crews felt the urge to experience the New York subway live and ventured into the South Bronx unconscious of the risks they were exposing themselves to. They pursued the myth of the subway and of the ghetto, where Hip Hop music was born and where you could see trains travelling between buildings. Painting in the United States was a tribute to the origins of the movement, a symbolic act that often represented a milestone in the 'career' of a writer.

Yet the delay with which the phenomenon got a foothold in Europe allowed only a few to experience the subway's moment of maximum potential, before the definitive cleansing of all cars in 1989. The majority of European kids in fact started visiting New York no sooner than 1990, and would meet a second generation of writers, the initiators of the so-called *Clean train movement*, representatives of a completely different way of experiencing trains, in which painting becomes an act in itself. Having to deal with a now efficient train buffing system, the only opportunity was to photograph the painted cars, freezing their slow but inexorable trip towards the buff in a snapshot; the photo thus becomes a relic and the tangible document of an instantaneous work destined to be short-lived.

Fume – MSN / Dusseldorf
>

When I went to New York I understood what Writing was all about. Before that I had the typical *Subway Art* conception, with fantasies about elevated trains and underground legends. Like many other kids, I had to find out about the main rules myself; nobody taught us how to do things so obviously we just kept on following ideas we had seen around, on photos or in spots.

Back then of course we were biting or taking some ideas as main references and somehow this lack of sources in the beginning provoked the evolution of a very defined style in Europe. For instance, many of the German styles became rigid, monolithic, and Dortmund took this even further, even more straight; if there was a big influence during the late 80's/early 90's, it was definitely coming from Dortmund. In my eyes the people from there didn't have a lot of creativity, but their blockbusters were impressively massive once you entered Central Station by train. Maybe this aesthetic was related to the working class mentality of this industrial city: locals who painted a lot were really straight in what they did and in how they made things happen. There wasn't an effort

to experiment with style, interacting with the fantasy-factor, but always one rule, a very well-known motto from the Ruhr area that sounds like "we are machines". Surrounded by this scenario I visited New York for one week. When I saw the locals' blackbooks I was expecting variety, but the styles were even more creative than I anticipated, even different from what they were showing in *Subway Art*. I realised that everybody there was trying to be unique and not follow just one direction. That's what I was seeing in Germany where almost everybody was trying to follow one style. So when I came back I started testing things and even if people might have thought I was doing ugly pieces I kept on trying and daring. I visited the New York subway in 1990, just one year after they had buffed the last train. Everything was over but when I first took the subway I was impressed: even though the trains were clean on the outside I could anyway understand in what context everything had started.

Underground everything was dirty, we didn't have this degree of filth in Western Europe back then. Every part of the infrastructure was dirty, slimy. When you walked in the subway and touched something you felt lousy and unsafe. Then I remember the noise. You went into the station where cars let off an iron scream! I was finally living a real metropolitan context and I only realised it at that moment. Back then local writers were in a transitory period, old and famous writers weren't painting anymore and new kids were hitting the streets with throw-ups or participating in the *Clean Train Movement*. Going out bombing with the newest generation was amazing as they had more energy and were really focused on insides. We took train rides at night just bombing insides and I could understand why people were doing it because the train rolled through the tunnel and you were just standing there with your marker, jumping from one car to the other. "Hey I've done five cars, but there are still five to do!" and there was nobody sitting in the train at night. I would go mad and destroy everything. It left a very strong impression, the subway and its system. From the point of view of a European kid you could really feel the power it had, you really wanted to do it.

From the first moment I set foot inside one of those cars I decided I had to paint at least one of the outsides, I realised I had to paint the New York subway. Once I had done this I felt my goal was accomplished.

Stone –SAK / Munich
>

In '86 Roscoe and I went to New York. I was 16 and through our link with Fashion Moda from the Bronx we met other writers. I really had to convince my parents to let me go, they kept saying "no way". They couldn't

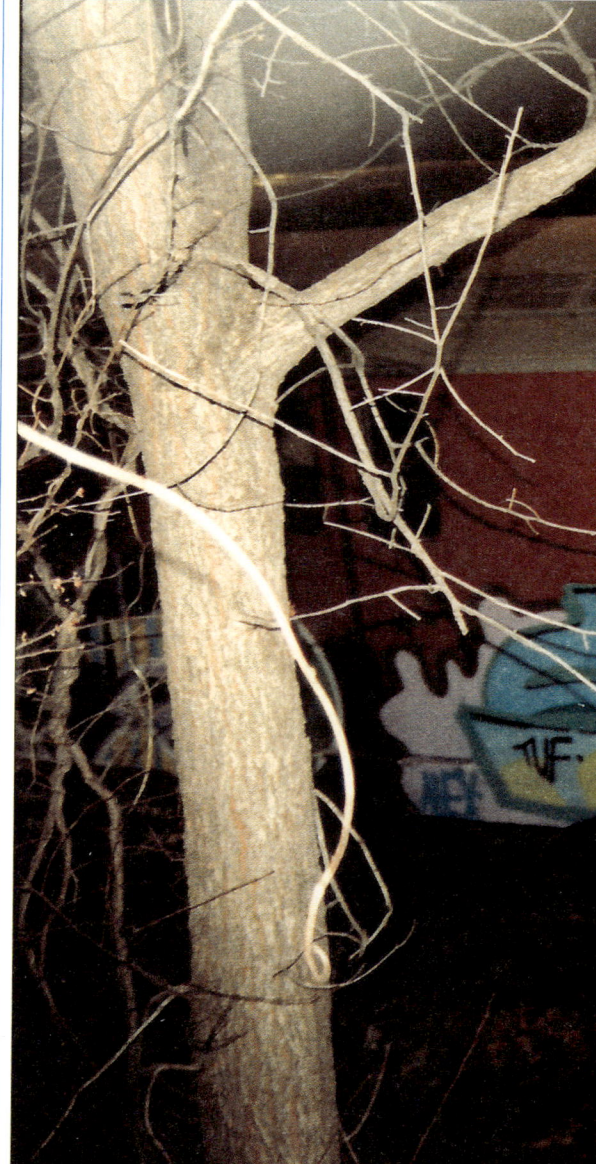

Shark from Dortmund to New York, 1993

understand what was going on but they accepted it in the end and I saw the trains running, it was a new beginning for my life. When I travelled though I had a pretty clear idea about what to expect of New York through the books and media, but after we arrived from Munich we crossed into town via the Brooklyn Bridge and stepped into the subway and it felt like we were on another planet or in a science fiction movie. So New York was more than I could imagine, totally shocking. The smells, the sounds...I was completely overwhelmed. We went to Fashion Moda in the Bronx, where we meet A-One and Koor and a couple of other writers. They really freaked out when we told them were we came from and showed them train

CHANA –TWS / DORTMUND
I can't forget the delusion when I visited New York for the first time. Absorbing Subway Art and Style Wars meant thinking about the

famous iron "giant-worms", and the size of trains connecting a million citizen metropolis. We were kids that had grown up in smaller cities, sometimes in towns where

even the idea of a subway was an abstraction as we had never seen one before. So once I arrived in New York, I dove anxiously through the subway gates, totally excited.

On the platform I discovered how small the cars were, how incredibly smaller compared to the German steel trains I used to take so frequently and unwillingly!

SUBWAY USED TO BE

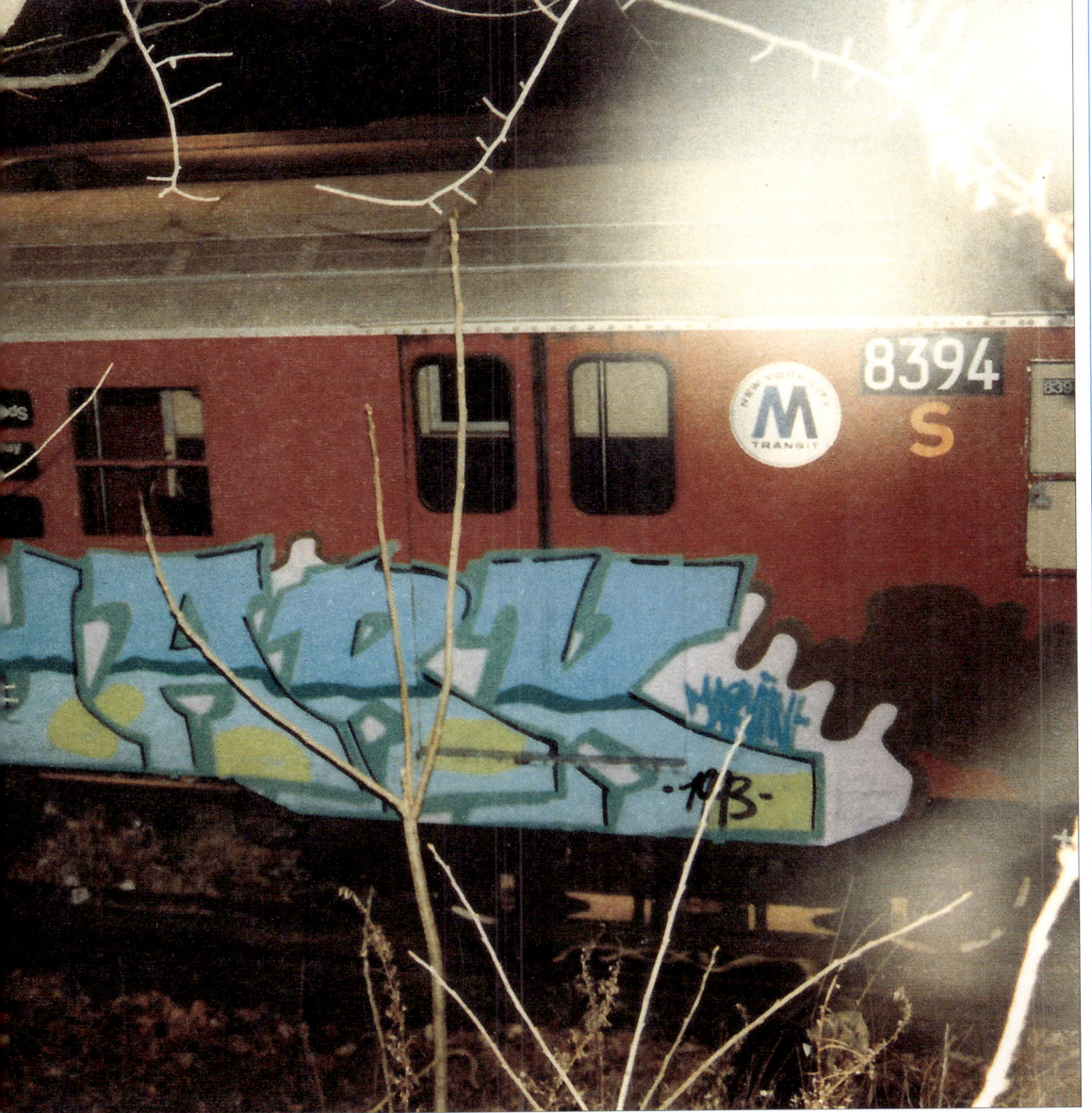

— Shark

were kids and had heard that as a writer in New York you can go everywhere!

Once when we were at Fashion Moda in the Bronx, we got lost and did end up in this really fucked up area. There were some guys with baseball bats coming out from every side, so we quickly moved out trying to find the next subway station.

Riding the bombed trains all day was great. One time we cruised to Brooklyn, and we started to talk to the driver of the subway. He was really cool, a Rastafarian, he liked graffiti and told us about a whole-train that he had seen recently. But he was very surprised by our presence there: he told us that the drivers called the last station "Whites off" because at this stop all the whites would get off and only the black people remained! We spent seventeen days taking pictures in the metro, we toured the rest of the city just once, a brief visit to the World Trade Centre and the Statue of Liberty, we spent one afternoon in Central Park, and the rest of the time it was in the subway. Who cared about the city when our greatest open-air museum was still open?

Bates –AIO / Copenhagen
>

If you were into Hip Hop during the 80's, you definitely wanted to go to New York to see where it was all coming from, to experience it and suck in all the information; above all, you wanted to try to understand where it was coming from and how it had started.

You can see the cultural movement in photos but it's not the same as actually being there, trying to paint and talking to some of the older guys.

Graffiti-wise, it was the same: when you paint you start planning actions, you want to achieve: painting an end-to-end, a whole-car, a good silver piece along the line and, above all, you wanna go to New York to paint THE subway. So I went there, it was my mission. I hooked up with Poem, the guy from *Flashback* and he took me out to paint. It was a crazy experience to go into a yard in the Bronx and see tags by Quik. Entering the yard became a big mission but once you were inside you were fine: of course the train didn't run, but as everyone back in the early 90's did, we took back-up photos at night, like a souvenir, like a postcard to take home.

Cat 22 –CTK / Amsterdam
>

I went to New York after seeing *Subway Art*. It was too much to believe... the "Hand of doom" car!

I worked in a holiday camp for poor black kids. They called me the "Glockenspiel" because of my language, and that was the only word they knew: "Frank Glockenspiel". I loved doing that. We were based in a town about 100km from New York. Every weekend the children went home, and we could go to New York, so I went every weekend. I stayed there for almost four months. New York in those days was nothing compared to how it is now. Now it's a phoney glamorous city which means

> CONTINUES ON PAGE 36

pieces from Munich. They just could not comprehend that. Through these guys we came to know about the 'Writer's Bench', even though it went pretty much unused as it was a real problem with the cops. We also met David Schmidlapp from the legendary IGT graff magazine. When we visited Henry Chalfant in his studio he showed us his huge photo portfolios. Seeing all these unknown trains was a blessing. He told us however that he had stopped taking pictures, mainly because all the kids had started to cross each other out on the trains. And this was true, at that time, much of the pieces were crossed, you had to chase after the brand new stuff. They also did a lot of marker tags on the trains so it was hard to see

❶ The writer's bench was a local hang-out where they used to meet to take pictures of painted trains. After a few years these hang-outs became off-limits as they were big hot spots for police raids.

nice, untouched pieces. We just checked out the lines, staying a lot on 125th Street[1] because the trains come out of the tunnels there. We didn't paint, but we tagged inside the trains. It was in the 80's and it was pretty dangerous. Once we were alone at a station in the Bronx we just sat there waiting for trains, imagine two pale boys looking like complete tourists with cameras in hand. Some cops came by and asked us what the fuck we were doing there, telling us to move out of the area as they didn't want to return to collect our bones. But we

The reckless attraction for infrastructures

Elevated infrastructures became an aesthetic reference, influencing the works of European writers that live outside of a metropolitan context. CMP narrates his experience

CMP – CMPSPIN / Naestved
>

When I was young, I really liked watching television. I used to watch Kojak and Tax, so I was already exposed to these American scenarios. Of course *Style Wars* is what really hit me, and that's why even today most of my stuff looks like it's from this specific period. Not the pieces, but the characters and the atmosphere. I've always wanted to catch that environment in my paintings, and it has become part of my private universe.

In '84 I teamed up with Spino5 because we were Breaking and battling together and, above all, living in the same city. He really inspired me to travel and understand the train systems. We painted together as a team and always represented our style together. The blockbuster style was what we wanted to do. It was important that it be legible. We wanted everyone to be able to read our Names. In our composition, my part was always related to the puppets and scenarios, while Spino5 used to sketch the letters; the outlines were traced by both of us. We really painted together as a team.

I guess we absorbed this method by looking at the guys from Sweden. During 1990 we visited Stockholm where we saw how Dutch and Terror operated as a team: one guy was doing the first lines, while the other was filling in. It was something similar to the way that Spino5 and I were working. It wasn't just about painting simultaneously, but producing something together.

Spino5 and I grew up in Naestved, a small city in Denmark. It made us hungry to experience and discover more, and forced us to travel because nothing came to you, and nothing happened if you didn't go after it. From 1991 to '93 our adventures were almost as important as the pieces themselves. I was hungry for more elevated tracks and tunnels, and every trip was about finding and discovering chaotic and congested scenes in Europe. Stockholm was just fantastic; we teamed up with VIM crew, and learned about the history of Stockholm. In Sweden there were trains parked in pitch black tunnels inside the mountains, 2km deep. If you're from a small city this is not something you grow up with. We don't have this sort of landscape. We'd followed these guys into the tunnels to find trains parked there and the only light was coming from really far away. This was a big part of my education. Spin always studied the train systems and he inspired me to do the same.

When I was 14, I never expected that one day I would write in the Bronx or Harlem, and it's amazing how all of this shaped my work. That's the reason why I still draw and paint the way I do, because of the feeling I got when I visited New York the first time. Of course, I was there because of the movement, but it was also about studying the whole cityscape. So New York has always been the most important influence on me because I've always been really interested in train system aesthetics. Even today when I paint I want to capture that special feeling. You know, it's like when you hear Lee talking about the old trains, that really motivated me through all these years, besides loving letters and studying the history. I started painting trains and images of trains before going to the Bronx, but the whole experience there really changed me. The impact was just massive! I love the whole system. This system plays a major role in my work, and wraps up 25 years of my experiences, adventures and tributes.

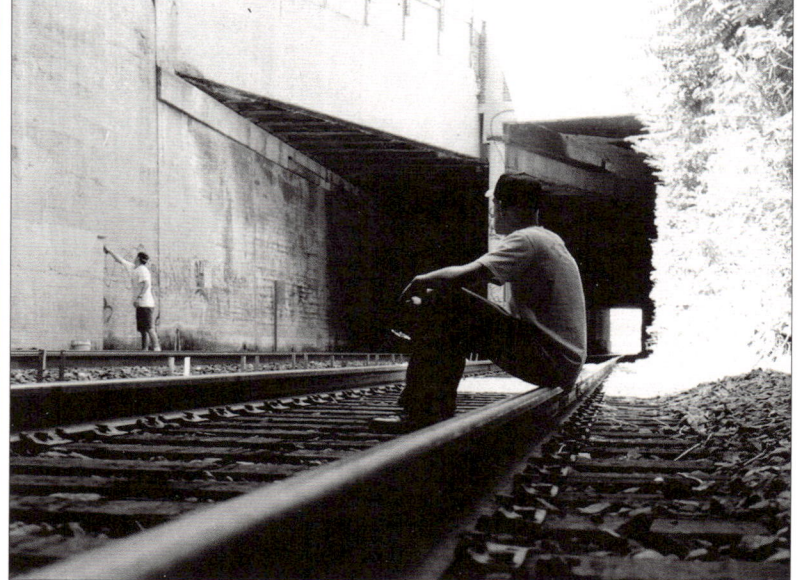

— *Spino5*

ADVENTURES

CMP
Swet, Spino5 and I painted this wall in New York in 1993 in the area of 72nd street. I remember this kid looking down from the street saying something like: "Hey mom, look!, homeless people!". Actually the homeless people and probably even the mole-people were watching us too.

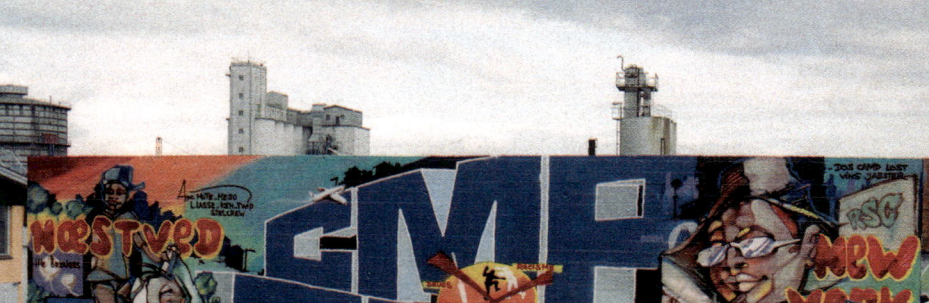

CMPSPIN, Naesved–New York

— *CMP*

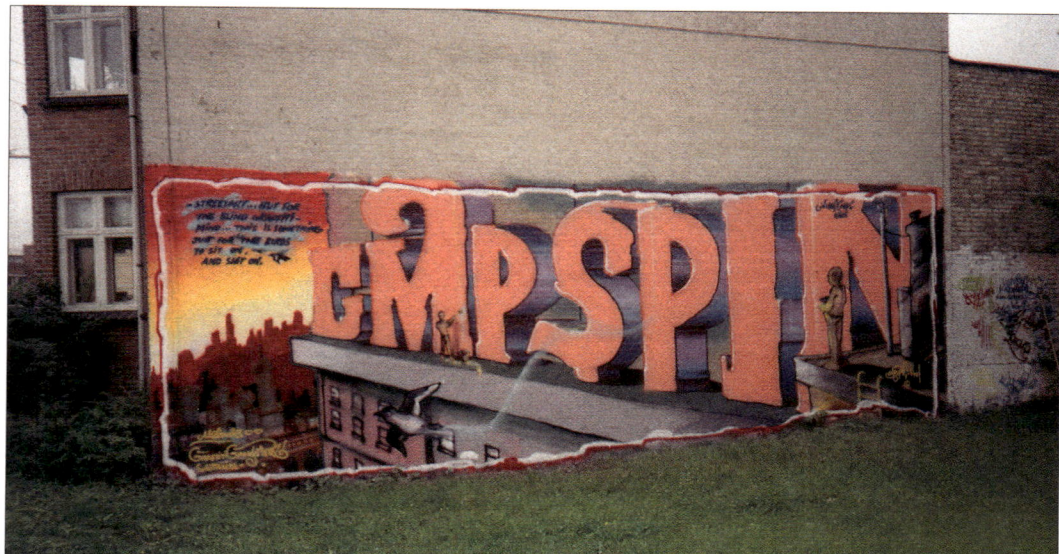

CMPSPIN on an imaginary rooftop

— *CMP*

Urban renewal

Along the Q Line, three European whole-cars cross through the city: the dream comes true

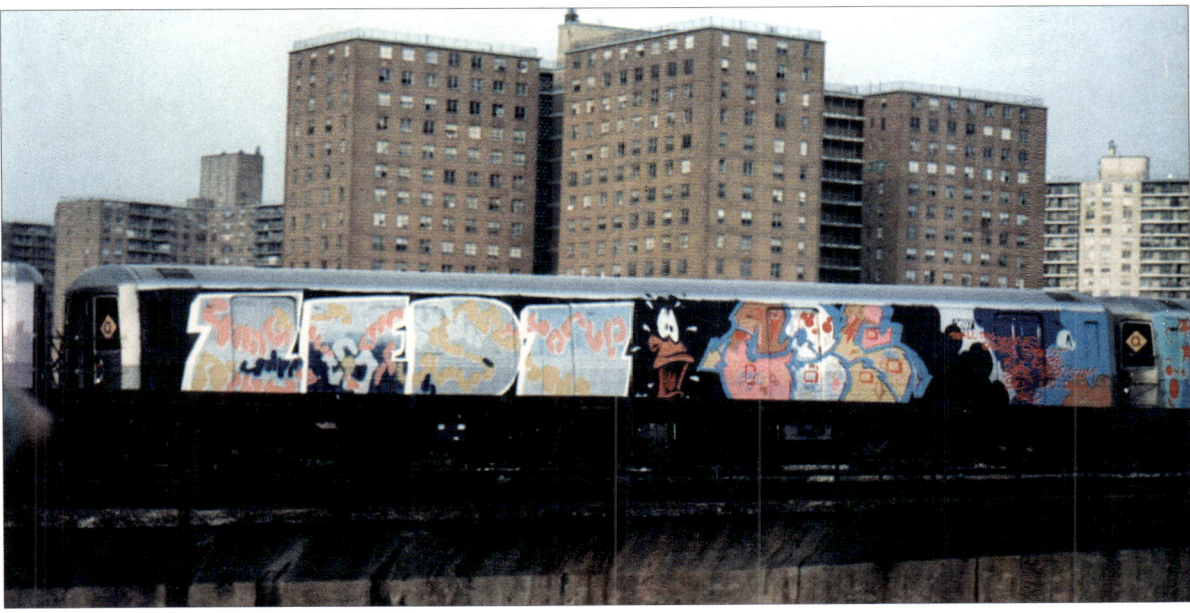

— Ces53

Ces 53 – INC, MSN / Rotterdam
>

In '92 I went to New York with Zedz. I knew the trains were already clean, for me the bombed ones were the real thing so I considered it kind of over already. I knew it wasn't like it had been in the 80's anymore. We ended up painting those clean trains anyway but it was just for the fact of doing a train in New York, to have been there, have seen what it was like and hopefully to see if we could find some old pieces or some scrap trains to look at.
I basically wanted to see the city and simply do a train there since that subway was mythological for every writer in Europe. In New York we were painting everyday, we did walls, a couple of trains and some other stuff. The first time we went to a yard we were by ourselves.
We also met up with Chintz for a few days and he took us where he had already done a whole-car. He had figured out how to go about things by himself, not with the help of the New York guys; this peculiar attitude to travel alone and spot yards was really typical of him, it was his style and indeed it worked in New York as well.
The next day we were all waiting for our cars to pull out and get amongst the traffic; watching 'em run and cross the New York skyline was a kind of sensation that you'll never forget, an emotion impossible to explain.

Zedz – INC / Leiden
>

The first night we arrived in New York we immediately explored the subway by taking the trains and looking out for where the yards were. If we found a yard we'd get off and check out the area. At first we planned on doing it alone but we accidentally bumped into some German guys who were also out there to paint. From that moment on we more or less put our eyes in our pockets and just depended on the information we got from them. We had already been making plans ourselves and had checked out some places, by the second day we had even bought wire cutters for cutting the fences. Though we had already planned how to enter the yards, this coincidental meeting meant we could also find out through someone else. But on our first appointment in Queens nobody showed up; we were just sitting under an elevated train track somewhere in the hood for an hour or so while gloomy people walked by, and cars passed by slowing down several times. We realised the area

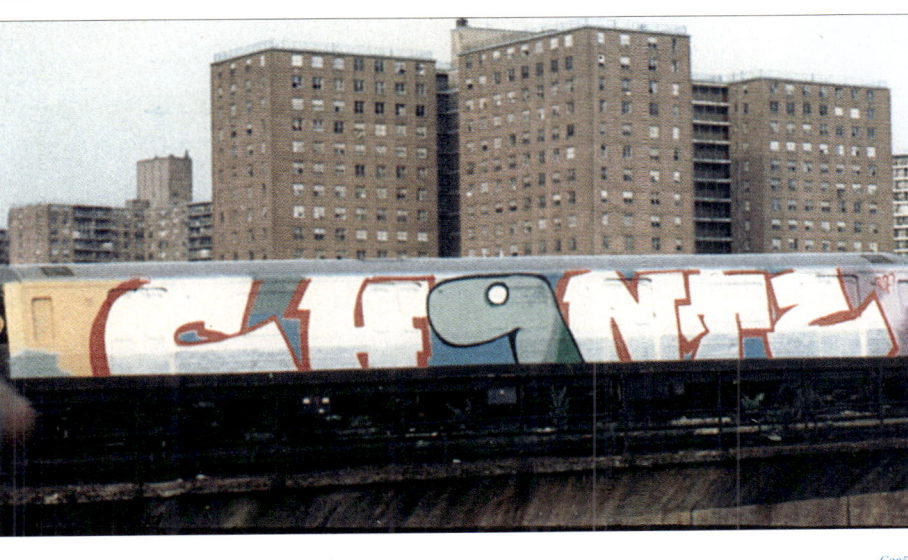

— Ces53

ACROSS NEW YORK

Triple whole-car painted by Euro writers in New York, on a lay-up of the Q line. Zedz-Ces, from Holland, Shore from Hamburg and Chintz from Dortmund. 1992

— Ces53

was fucked up and the guys weren't coming. So we went into the yard by ourselves and half an hour later, while painting, we heard "Yo guys" from the street and there was our connection. We thought they had just showed up so we told them they were really late, and they replied they had been painting in the same row

as us, just 200 metres away and had done top-to-bottoms! I remember while I was painting I had seen something moving but I hadn't gone to check it out, it could have been workers or cops! The reason why I give everything in detail is because I relive the moment; I see myself climbing up the yard, squeezing in between the space

under the tracks and putting my head through... my head sticks out and there are iron bars to my left and the right (the tracks). I'm basically coming out of the ground like a mole. This was the first time I entered a yard from under the rail tracks and I will never forget that image, the moment of entering the New York subway!

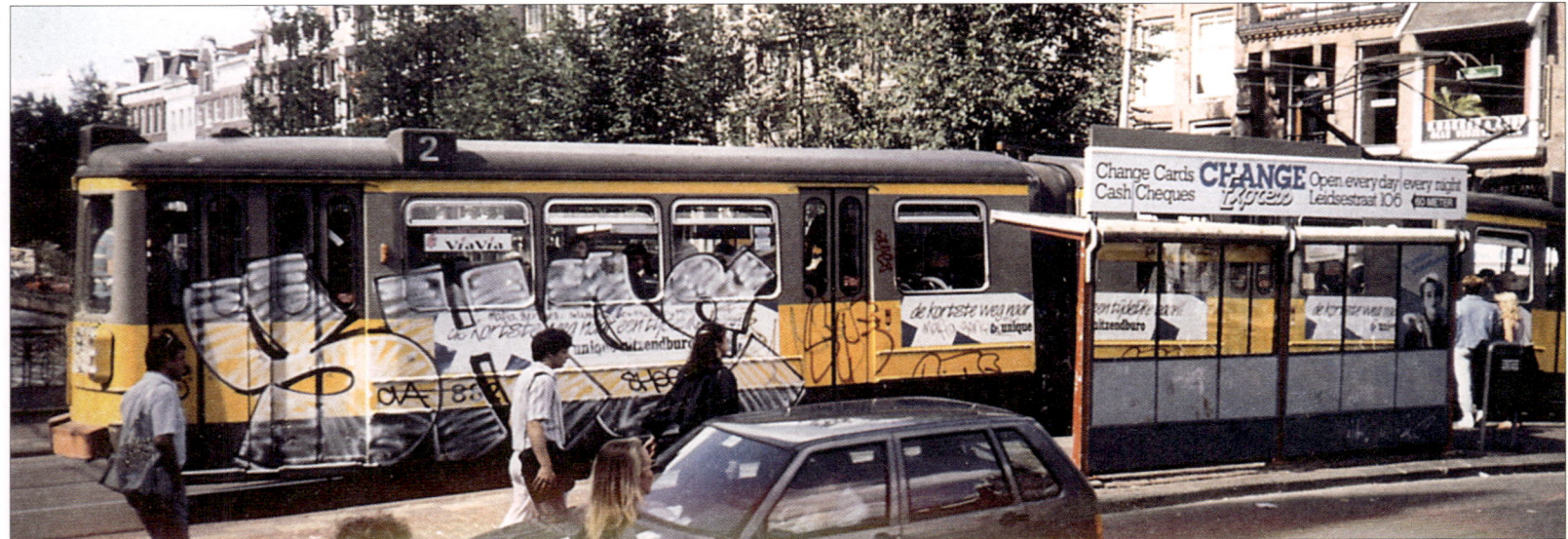

Shoe throw–up on Amsterdam tram, mid 80's   — Shoe

CITY TRAMS

The New York subway not only generated a flow towards the Graffiti Mecca.
Its dynamic character was translated to the transportation systems that were
available in Europe, from local trains to long distance ones, sometimes choosing
buses and trams as alternatives to a limited or nonexistent urban rail system

Rhyme –GVB / Amsterdam
>

In Amsterdam, just like in many other cities, there were specific targets we wanted to hit. There were a lot of worker's shacks where the construction guys working on the streets would have their coffee and lunch. I did a lot of these cars. I think I did most of them with High. That was our own little subway in my fantasy. These things moved all over town, and all over Holland, sometimes in the North, the South or near a highway. It was cool because they didn't get buffed immediately, sometimes your piece was there for a year or two. At the time the subway here was being buffed right away. We did some cars, I did quite a lot but it was only in the early 90's that the cars got totally killed. But since the very be-

> ## We were just cheering as the trams were pulling up "Yeaaah another one coming!" Everybody started running towards them

ginning in Amsterdam the tram system became our New York subway. They were the main form of transportation in Amsterdam so there was a lot of visibility. It was exciting to go to the yard or the end stop of the line to do throw–ups and tags.
In Leidseplein, in the middle of town, was the hang–out for all the graffiti writers. Everybody used to go on there on Saturday morning, it was Shoe who had started this thing. Every Saturday morning we were hanging out there and then the whole bunch of kids (between 12 and 18 years old), sometimes even 50 of us would hit the trams while

they were running, we killed them from back to front with passengers inside. We did insides–outsides, with markers, spray cans, shoe polish. Nobody was organising this, I guess it just happened spontaneously. First it was pure graffiti and then it started becoming vandalism. If you want to give it a name it was a mix of hooligan–like behaviour, not in the way of football but much more destructive. By this time more and more kids were getting attracted to the lifestyle of this bunch of loose canons, it just got crazier and crazier; robberies, lootings, people beating each other up, smashing windows for fun... it was just out of control. Most graffiti writers had already bailed out, the police didn't do anything, there were detectives around but they didn't know how to stop it. If you have something like that nowadays, there's media all over. If someone drives a bicycle into a car it's on the news right away. At that time it wasn't like that otherwise we would have been in the news every day.
It slowed down at some point, it was getting out of hand and the police started taking action by arresting more and more of the group.
One summer night I'll never forget was a Saturday while we were hanging out at Leidseplein, with probably about 25 guys and a few girls. This was also on a square where the 1–2–5 trams stopped. It was hot, full of people who were going out and we suddenly started bombing the trams. One, then another one, and another one. The police didn't show up. The whole square was looking! We were just cheering as the trams were pulling up "Yeaaah another one coming!" Everybody started running towards them; tags, throw–ups... filling up throw–ups. This was all on the main square with a lot of people watching, tourists maybe thought that it was part of the Amsterdam experience! It was total madness. That was one of the funniest graffiti things that the hang–out created.
With this guy Zap I went to a lot of tram–yards. He was a crazy guy. Suddenly one time he started driving the trams (probably bored of tagging) in the yard while I was doing a piece or tags. I said "what the fuck are you doing?" he was screaming out "yeaaahhh!". The pieces ran,

maybe just for one ride or a day, not longer. So that didn't make a lot of sense, there wasn't enough pleasure for all that effort we had to put in. So we took it to a different level and filled up everything with throw–ups and tags. Even insides. On the weekends we went to the yards non–stop. When his tag was on every tram in 1986, he retired. King ZAP.

Shoe –USA,CTK / Amsterdam
>

One of our main targets in the city were the trams. We had always wanted them to be really bombed, especially inside. They were our subway in a sense, since we only had a couple of subway lines in Amsterdam, whereas the trams were all city, so what could be better? Dondi once said Amsterdam is like one big train yard. That's because you have to watch out while you're walking in the streets, you may get run over. When the "tram–movement" took place, it coincided with the Writing boom of Amsterdam. In the beginning we were so few that I started thinking we needed to get more people involved in order to create a real movement. At that point Gasp and me decided to meet every Saturday at Leidseplein, like a regular hang–out, on a bench. Every writer I would bump into would be told we were meeting there every Saturday, and each week more people would come. After a couple of months there were about 100 writers meeting there every Saturday to go out bombing. That's when people really started talking, like "have you seen such and such picture, check out this arrow..". So when the trams became our target, we would bomb them at Leidseplein. Everybody would go on the tram or run after it. People would just watch us attack the cars! The mentality was "I don't care if people see, I'll just tag it anyway". I remember one old lady saw me while I was tagging and so she wiped her hand in my wet dripping tag and put it right in my face: I had ink everywhere! That was one tough old lady.

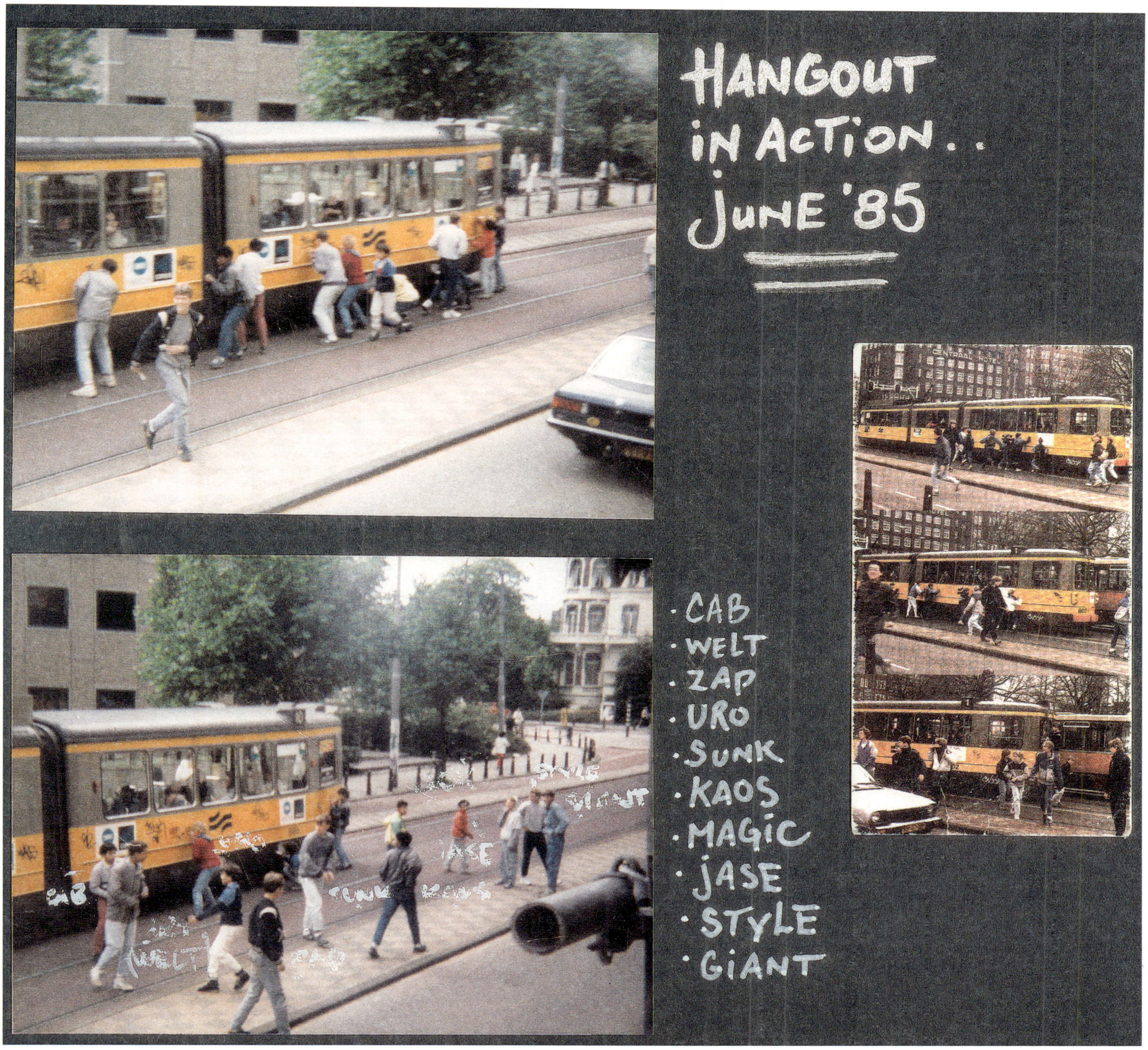

HANGOUT
iN AcTioN..
JuNE '85

- CAB
- WELT
- ZAP
- URO
- SUNK
- KAOS
- MAGIC
- JASE
- STYLE
- GIANT

Amsterdam kids attacking the trams at Leidsleplein hang–out

— Rhyme

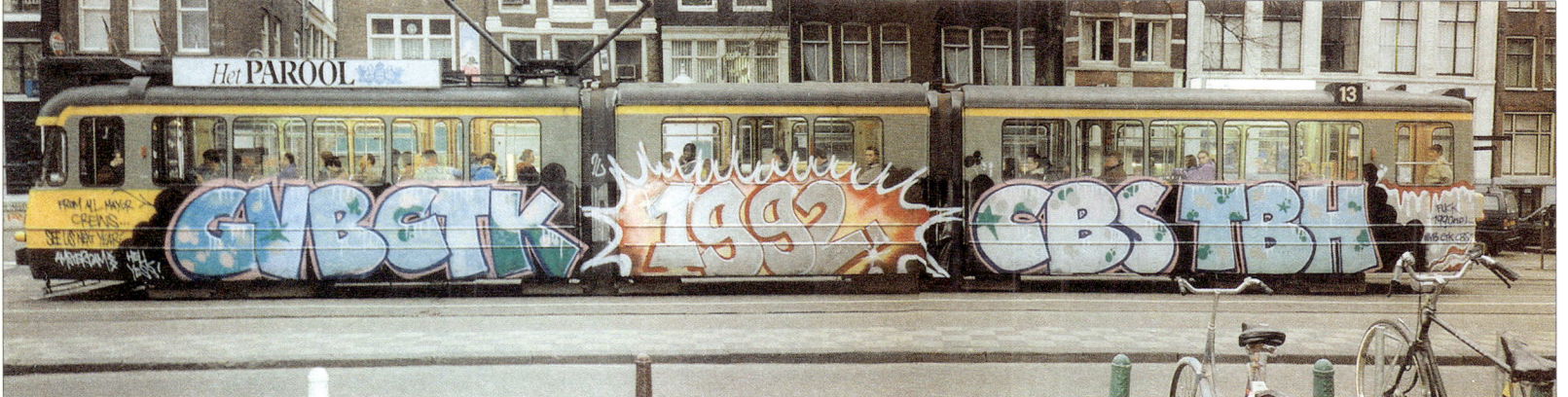

A GVB–CTK–CBS–TBH production, 1992

— Rhyme

Transit Agency Says: New York Subways Are Free of Graffiti

> COUNTINUES FROM PAGE 11

defeat graffiti's purpose - namely, the desire to see one's work on view. Transit officials ordered trains out of service within 24 hours after being marked. In the last five years, 10 trains were withdrawn in rush hours because they were marked up. The authority uses glycol ether-based cleansers, which workers swab over the graffiti and then rinse away, said the authority's director of environmental and occupational safety, Nancy Wittenberg. About 1,000 people were hired to clean the graffiti. ''Initially, it was labor-intensive,'' Mr. Gunn said. ''But once you get on top of it, it's not that big a deal to keep them clean.'' From White Paint to Crimson The cleaners are included in a $52 million annual budget for cleaning cars, which these days means scraping chewing gum from floors more than scrubbing away at graffiti. To thwart graffiti painters, the program, known as the Clean Car Program, assigned transit officers disguised as cleaners on the cars. Since the late 70's, a number of measures to clean and prevent graffiti have been tried and rejected. In 1983, workers covered car exteriors with a white paint that was intended to resist graffiti. ''It was like putting out a rolling canvas,'' said a Transit Authority spokesman, Jared S. Lebow. About 25 percent of the cars were painted white before officials decided to paint them crimson. The latest anti-graffiti project began in 1984 with the IRT Lexington Avenue Express and Flushing lines and gradually expanded. About two years ago, the number of clean cars began rising steadily, and the reported appearances of graffiti began falling. 'Hit' Every Three Months The graffiti problem has not entirely disappeared in the subway. Many stations are still decorated with something other than officially sanctioned paints and color schemes, and graffiti writers continue to carve legacies, using staples, nails and other pointed objects, in window panes and plastic panels in the subway cars. Each car gets ''hit,'' in Transit Authority parlance, an average of once every three months. ''It used to be every other week,'' Mr. Gunn said. Officials said graffiti had moved to other quarters. ''It's all over the highways now,'' said A. Richardson Goodlatte, the Transit Authority vice president for rapid transit, who until last month was in charge of the Clean Car Program. ''It's on bridge abutments, and there's been some increase on the sanitation trucks.'' It also turns up in parks. And it covers one wall of a building on the northwestern corner of Warren Street and Broadway, in view of Mr. Koch's office. Because of the wall, Mr. Koch said he was proposing a law to require landlords to remove graffiti from their property. ''Why should that be allowed?'' he asked. Are New Yorkers glad to see graffiti gone from the subways? Do they even notice? ''I believe that most of the people in New York were fed up with graffiti by the 1980's,'' Mr. Goodlatte said. ''Clearly it is a major achievement,'' Mr. Russianoff said. ''But do riders care more that service is unreliable on most lines? The answer is yes. I think the Transit Authority deserves a pat on the back and maybe a cigar, but I don't think they deserve canonization.'

—

Arts and events

> COUNTINUES FROM PAGE 22

with echoes of 'radical chic', comparable to Leonard Bernstein asking The Black Panthers to dinner. For others, there seems to be a perversity in taking graffiti, at least in the short term, from the public and making it private. The intervention of commercial concerns is opportunistic and distasteful. Painters should be like priests: the sanctimonious amongst us still plod on with the same arguments that it seemed Picasso had exhausted twenty years ago. If the strength of graffiti as a movement lies in part in its hermeticism, it is also the same quality that limits its impact. Hence, Edit Deak argues:

"The subway is not cross-Atlantic. True to what canvas has always performed in the history of art by being culture's means for transmitting visual information, these artists in their habitually swift dynamic manner, use this portability of painting for distances no train can travel."

What would be far more instructive is to see how graffiti has coped with the transition from a dynamic ephemeral art to a static contemplative one.

For the curators, the choice of whom to include in the show must have been easier due to graffiti's tendency towards meritocracy, (often based on quantity rather than quality). Titles abound...The King, The Prince, The President, The Duke, etc. Graffiti is old enough to have its history, folklore and myth, accompanied by a deep sense of nostalgia. The curators have fielded an all around team. So we have Rammelzee, the graffiti philosopher, Futura and Lee, whose aspirations are to become 'painters', and others like Zephyr who yearn for the return of those lost days of innocence, when you'd be on to tracks at 3 a.m. with spray cans in hand. Graffiti is steeped in a New World romanticism. This is, at times, one of its most infectious qualities. In an unabashed way it explicitly clarifies aspects of the creative process which others try to hide behind a wall of highbrow intellectuality and culture. In interviews the graffiti artists stress their desire for attention, for fame, for money. In short they want to 'make it'. When someone writes their name in eight foot letters the length of a train, we can assume he is in sympathy with Warhol's maxim about being famous for fifteen minutes. It is hardly surprising then that they should welcome absorption into the art world institution. They have come far since the semi-criminal days of 'bombing' trains. Outsiders and underdogs, underprivileged and uneducated, they create beauty from banality, or so the myth has it. If it is easy to dismiss graffiti as pubescent daubings, it is easier still to draw stylistic links between all that has gone on in New York painting since the 1940's. From the abstract expressionists they inherit the all-over action painting. From postpainterly abstraction, the branding impact of the large-scale single image. From 'Pop', the painters Dondi and Zephyr in particular inherit the comic strip, the advertising logo and the witty direct image. Unlike 'Pop', the images remain private and self-referential, they are not the media-based icons of an age. While the graffiti painters continue to contest their 'style wars', the intervention of the museum has forced the transition towards serious art. While for some graffiti is still the academy of the streets, for others it is now dead. If the best of its initiates, Futura 2000, has been likened to a "space-age Kandinsky", we may still hope for something positive and lasting from this dynamic phenomenon.

- Original title: "American Graffiti in Holland". Published on *Art Monthly*, December 1983

—

What the New York subway used to be

> COUNTINUES FROM PAGE 31

nothing. Back then the New Yorkers were proud of their city, their whole Hip Hop culture and the B-boys. The funny thing is that I'm a white man, as white as can be and I learned how to boogie from the kids there.

One time I was in the Bronx and there was a block party. It was illegal of course. They knew I could dance, so I showed them some moves and they wanted me on stage. Imagine, this older white guy in an all-black crowd. They were all wondering, "What is he going to show us?" So I started popping to the electro music and they gave me a huge applause! I'd never gotten enthusiasm from white people but there I got it from black people, and that's where it was all coming from. It meant a lot to me.

At night I used to dance on Broadway Avenue when people came out of the theatres. There were these popping guys wearing masks from Transformers. I don't know for sure if they were called Transformer crew, but they were the last crew to boogie on the street. I danced with them and they gave me money to pay my hotel bill of $6 a night. It was the lousiest hotel ever. You couldn't even call it a hotel!

During the day time I went to Jackson Ave. That's where line 2 and 5 come together. I found this out myself on the map. I saw that at Jackson Ave, just before the train entered the station, it curved. When the train pulled in you could see which car was painted. So I knew what spot I had to run to on the platform to take the picture. There

were whole window-downs and end-to-ends. I took so many photos of the 1-2-5 lines. In the end I started working on line 6, the whole-car line. I saw a couple of things but not so much, so I went near Coney Island. I knew there was a lot of Iz the Wiz stuff there. I started to check out the trains and they were really bombed. There were Quik throw-ups, Iz the Wiz pieces and I remembered them from *Subway Art* and *Style Wars*. That's why I took the photos. While in New York I got in touch with Mack from *The Nasty boys*. It was quite funny because I was taking photos of a car when suddenly the window opened and this black guy shouted "Yo man what do you write?" "I write Cat" "Cap? What the fuck!" and then he left. When the next train pulled in from the other side, the doors opened and Mack came towards me saying, "What the fuck do you want?" "I'm from Europe, I'm from Amsterdam, I'm just taking photos. I don't know what you're talking about" "Ah you're a European writer, they have writers there?" "Yeah in Amsterdam and in Paris" "Seriously? Let me see your blackbook." I had it with me so I showed it to him. He showed me his book and I thought "Ok that's how you make a blackbook" They were massive, huge! He was carrying it around and gave me two of his drawings. I went back to Amsterdam after all that time, and it took a while for the films to develop, maybe a week, and I was praying that the result would be good. Once, a whole film of whole-trains, 36 pieces in total, was gone into oblivion. I didn't have any money then and developing film was too expensive, so sometimes I would rack them. They would give you the prints and you had to walk to the cashier to pay them, so it was kind of easy. When the film was developed I showed the photos to certain people who were allowed to see them, I made a selection.

Of course these trips and the direct influence of the New Yorkers shown in the galleries somehow affected our process. I was talking with Gasp and he said that when I came back from New York the first piece I did was a "Julia" piece, which was totally New York. But a week later the whole influence was gone. I'm glad about that because at that point we already had an Amsterdam style. People were listening to what you had to say about your work, about your pieces, and people would give serious opinions. If you were doing a New York style piece they would say it was kind of strange. A week later I was back into the Amsterdam style, which is a typographical style with nice connections, not necessarily written like a block as they did in New York, in order to fit it below the windows, because we had walls. Rhyme in that period was doing the big swirl which was impossible on a train. You couldn't do it because you'd cover the wheels. Our style is different because of the way we started: on walls.

The reason why we developed this crazy style in Amsterdam was because we all came from cultural, artsy backgrounds. Shoe's mum was a judge and his dad a designer. Then you had Jazz, whose father was an actor. Perhaps that's what made the difference between us and other cities. Elsewhere it was more of a criminal thing, while here it was an artistic thing.

NETWORK REPORT

>

The European Writing scene expanded thanks to connections between writers from different cities and countries. Starting with individual travels, writers created relationships of reciprocal influence, considering themselves part of a single movement that began to become popular on an International scale in the mid 80's. The natural epicentres of these networks were European capitals, where the concentration of writers was fertile terrain for a widespread expansion into provinces and neighboring mid-sized cities. There were essentially four main elements that, in different ways, contributed to implementing the development of these networks: the forming of the first International crews; jams, which were occasions for collective encounters; the creation of fanzines; and the use of Inter-Rail. The first crews made up of members from different countries emerged in a spontaneous and somewhat casual manner in the early 80's, often following the trips of those who spent their vacations travelling around Europe. *Crime Time Kings* was the first international crew to include members of other groups: USA (*United Street Artists*) from Amsterdam, TCA (*The Chrome Angelz*) from London, and *Bomb Squad* from Paris.

> CONTINUES ON PAGE 39

> THE EUROPEAN **NETWORK**

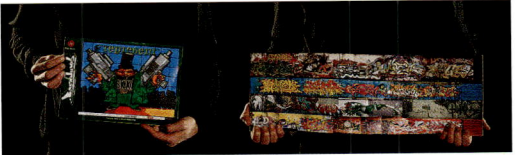

INTERNATIONAL CREWS

CRIME **T**IME **K**INGS

The story of the first International crew, formed by uniting the most representative groups of the London–Paris–Amsterdam triangle.

Shoe – USA, CTK / Amsterdam
>

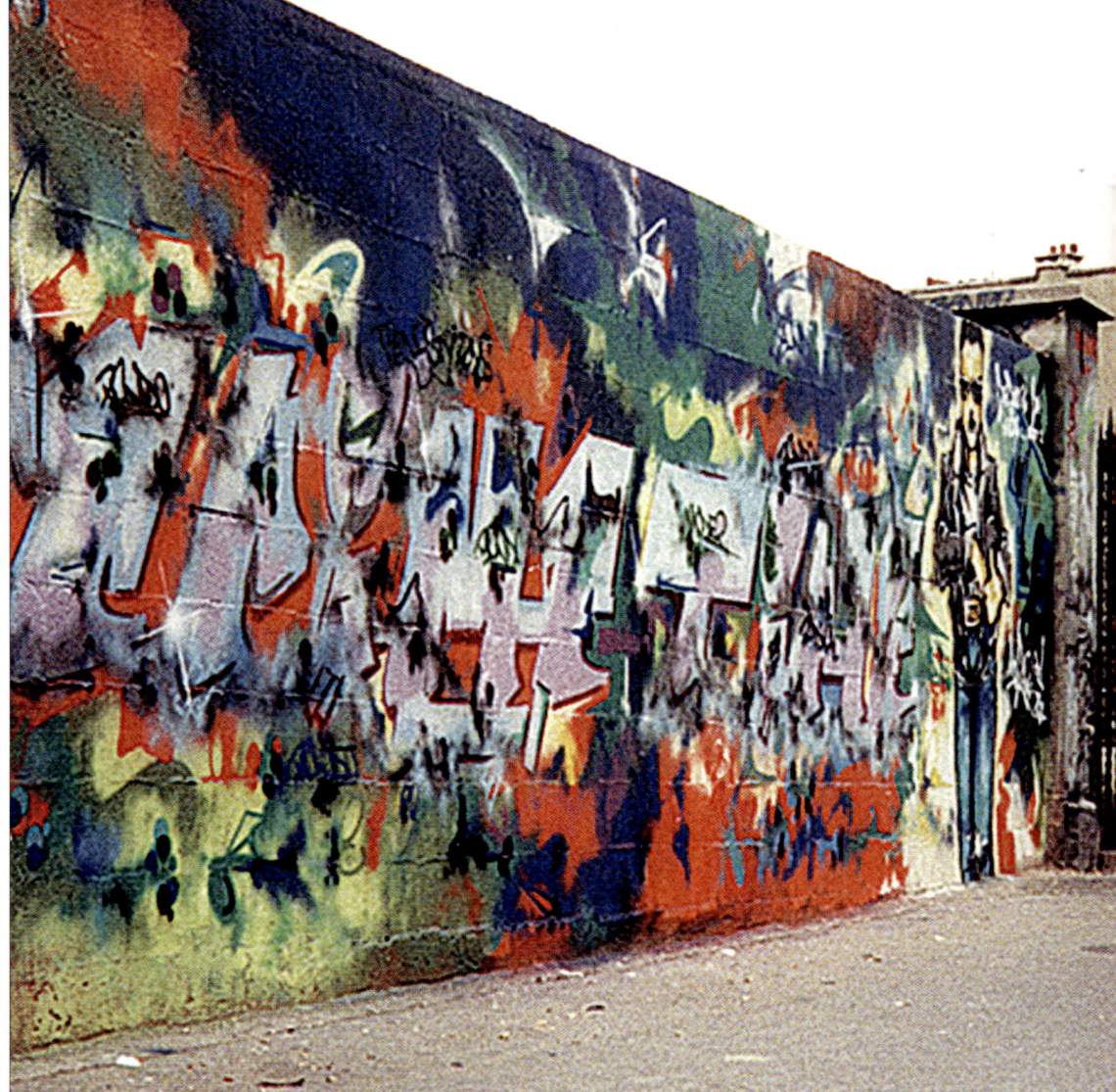

The infamous *Crime Time* piece outside Paris Stalingrad. April 1986

The main connection between Dutch and French writers started during the mid 80's when the guys that would later form CTK began travelling, mostly on individual trips without planning anything, as the Writing movement hadn't begun yet. I was painting in Amsterdam without even knowing that the same thing was taking root in other countries as well. There was no way of getting any information back then.

Around 1985 I went to Paris. It was just an Inter-Rail trip and graffiti wasn't a part of it at all. I did, however, spot the first, timid signs on the streets, like small tags here and there. Then, all of a sudden I saw a colourful wall along the banks of the river: I was totally amazed... Delta still has the postcard I sent him during that trip on which I wrote: "This is the incredible style on the banks of the Seine". I decided I, too, had to do something there, like a territorial message, thinking that it might somehow provoke interest and start a connection. So I did a *Shoe Jan Jaz* piece on the same river bank. The next day, as I was walking along it, I saw some dudes sitting in front of those pieces with Pumas and fat laces, and I thought to myself they must be some of the local writers, and that's how we met. Back then the dress code

was quite important. The French writers were with this crazy American black guy who was dressed like a Native American with feathers and stuff. His name was Rhett, and he was a funny guy. So we met this bunch of kids and Bando gave me his address. Bando and Mode2 were hanging out along the Seine and of course they saw what I did. I think they were also interested in building connections just like we were.

Since then a strong network between Paris and Amsterdam got started and continued for years; basically it was a friendship based on a shared interest. It was pretty clear that Bando was the most talented and charismatic of all of them. He formed the crew CTK, built first on the Paris-London axis and then including Amsterdam. Before CTK, every member had his own crew in his respective country: Mode was with The Chrome Angelz in London. Bando had The Bomb Squad in Paris, while I had formed United Street Artists in Amsterdam along with Delta, Joker and Jaz. USA was our first crew. It stemmed from the idea of using three initials like we had seen in many New York crew names. USA was kind of a weird name, but it was an abbreviation of United Street Artists. I remember painting it really big on a rooftop one time in super letters: USA. No tags or adding anything else, just

USA. Regular people thought it meant "America". They didn't get it. They would wonder why the USA was being promoted in the Netherlands. So let's say we already had a kind of identity, even style-wise, but Bando was really pushing his idea of merging every group into one big, ambitious crew.

We joined forces. At that time the whole idea of crews was just a bunch of letters and you weren't necessarily hanging out with all these guys but keeping the flag high anyway, writing CTK non-stop.

So the triangle was London, Paris and Amsterdam, even though we didn't go to London that much. I would go to Paris more than Bando would come here. London was always a bit isolated, even though things started moving there really early, and the UK-French connection really got strong once Mode moved to live in Paris. I guess those trips and visits became the main device CTK used to keep our crew together in a period during which getting connected was really difficult. But together we planned missions focused on hitting specific cities or specific train systems that no one else was doing in Europe at the time. Copenhagen and Munich were probably the most important actions ever, somehow even the most explosive, especially if we consider the whole mess we got ourselves

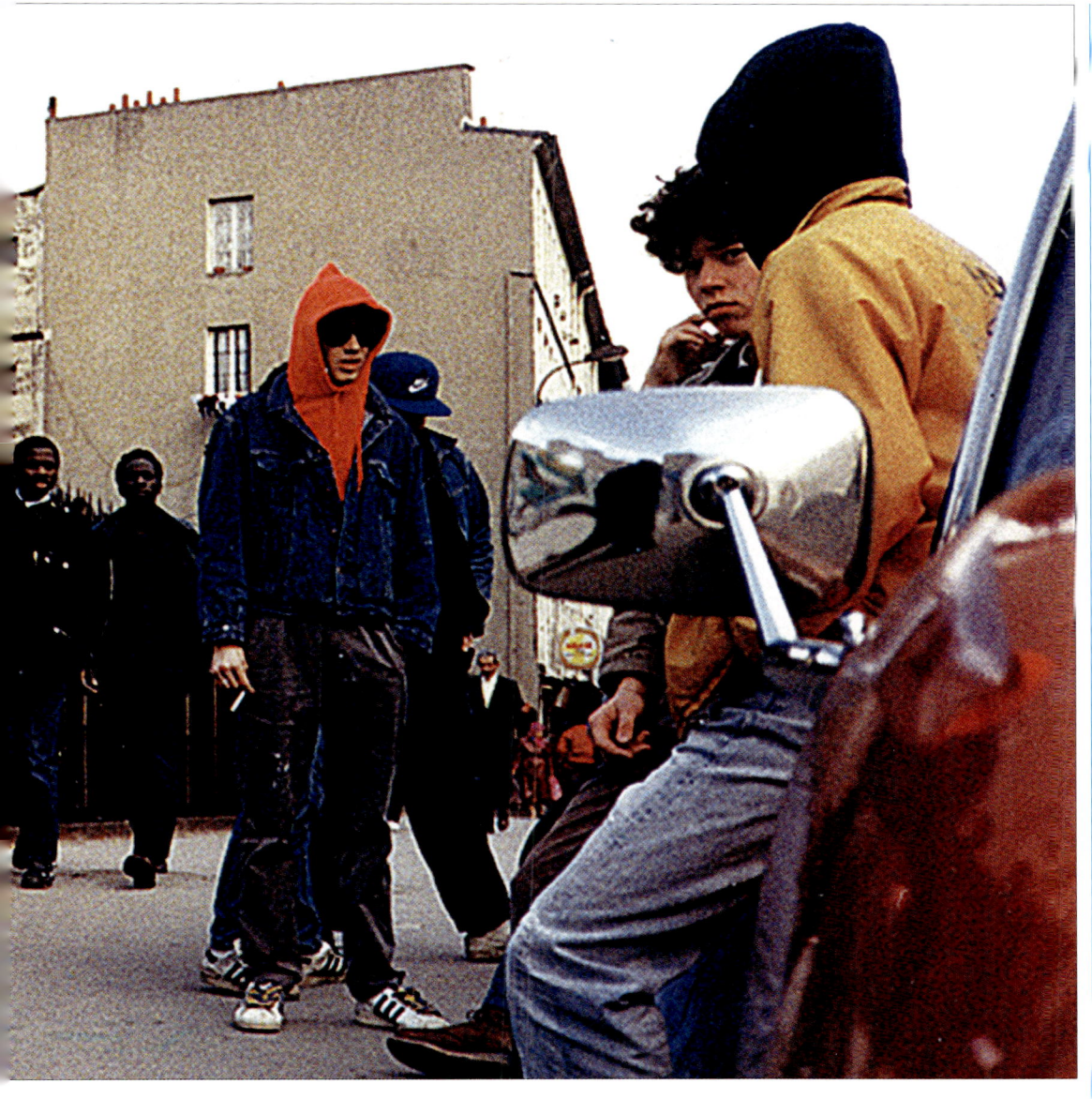

— Mode 2

NETWORK REPORT
—

> CONTINUES FROM PAGE 37

The Fantastic Partners was an important example of an intercontinental network, they were directly connected to Europe and acted as a bridge – from the 80's until today – between American writers and German, Dutch, and European contingents in general. RTA (*Real Transit Artists*) was one of the first crews in Europe to focus on targeting trains and travelling specifically in order to bomb German or other European railway systems. Another significant example was the Northern European network which, in the early 90's, was made up of the MSN crew - mainly Dutch – VIM from Stockholm, MOAS from Copenhagen, and ALL from Oslo. From single entities, in time these four crews united, forming a sort of alliance for promoting the Names of their respective crews. The strong bond between Scandinavian train-bombers created a sort of microcosm, a niche in the European panorama that was characterised by a strong sense of group, giving preference to their collective instead of their single crew Names, thus influencing future generations.

JAM– Events associated with Hip Hop music were also happenings of great popularity.

UK Fresh 86 in London, and some of the other first concerts organised in Europe, facilitated the meeting of writers from different countries. The natural evolution of these events coincided with the emergence of the first jams, a sort of reinterpretation of American block-parties. Already in the 80's, these conventions represented the only public opportunities to compare local scenes, which at the time were still fragmented.

FANZINES– A network of fanzines revolving around writers' works also contributed to cementing connections between writers. The birth of these independent and self-made projects managed to crystallise the habit of exchanging photos of pieces and open general horizons on the graffiti panorama, thus allowing scenes that were disconnected from the metropolitan network to emerge also.

INTERRAIL– Last but not least, the use of Inter-Rail travel in the 90's allowed writers to maintain international contacts and in particular identified the figure of train-bomber, defining the character of dozens of crews that travelled in search of new railway systems to bomb.

into in Germany. It was around 1987 that we went to Munich with Boxer's van. There was some graffiti there but definitely not a bombed system. It was Boxer, Cat 22, Bando, Sign and me hitting trains everyday, inside and out. I don't think the city ever looked the same after that. No less important were our trips to New York. The first time I went there was with my family in 1982, and when I saw all the painted trains I thought it was insane. The system was really bombed and when we took the train from JFK, I looked out the window without saying a word, just mesmerised by the trains, the rooftops. Once there, I met Dondi and he showed me the city as I had done with him in Amsterdam. In this case the Yaki Kornblit gallery had really been a strong bridge between us.

Just a couple of years later Bando and I decided to visit New York together. He was leaving from Paris whereas I was flying out from Amsterdam, and I left alone the day before we were supposed to meet there. I think I was 16 or 17 and my dad said "Ok son if I never see you again, you make it big!" He thought I was going to stay! Either way we had a great time in New York, not only because of graffiti. We met with Joni and went up to 175th street to do trains in the lay up there and that kind of stuff. I guess the friendship with Dondi and this exchange of

experiences in Holland and the US were really important for the development and evolution of CTK letters. Of course we were influenced by the New Yorkers and they were fundamental in developing and building our own stylistic path. Nowadays creating your own style is quite impossible; one of the reasons is the Internet.

I didn't invent my own style either, I think if I had to trace the evolution of these letters it would be through a series of references and influences. Along with that evolution however, I've always followed a linear path of solid and tangible shapes. If you see Futura 2000's style, it's so far out, and the same is true for Rammellzee's letters. I was always into flat 2Ds, very graphic stuff but never into colours or details. It was very much about the shape of the letters. At one point Bando and I decided not to bother with colours and fills but just do only silvers and outlines. Once the outlines became more visible and important I wanted to get them really perfect. Usually you'd trace one line and outline it but it was never perfect, so I'd add another one and it would get better. Maybe it's not how it should be done but in the end it's a better outline: a border made by adding layers and layers of several lines, to reach a thicker one. We'd do these fat outlines with just normal outline cans, and these types of tools were

also responsible for shaping styles, but we never cut the outlines with silver; nowadays it's something that a lot of people are doing but it makes it so sharp that it almost looks like a stencil. If you do a train it takes the speed out of the outline because you can really only do it a couple of times, especially nowadays. But besides the pragmatic reasons, if you then start cutting the outline on a train piece, again and again, it takes away the roughness, the dynamic peculiarity that brings to life a window-down. Probably the combination of all these aspects, defined letters, thick outlines, monochrome blocks, formed the CTK style.

This direction was taken even further by Bando who at one point started separating the letters, which immediately took up a very typographic identity. Bando was constantly adding something new. I had my direction, too, but of course sometimes you copy something without even realising it. It can be positive. I don't mind taking inspiration so much because if someone copies something, it's always a little bit different and it may be the birth of something new. It's an unconscious process of reinterpretation, you don't realise you're taking something and changing it. Then someone takes that and changes it further: after five times you have a very different style.

THE CHROME ANGELZ OF

Chrome Angelz crew
is born in London
and becomes a stylistic
reference point for the U.K
in the 80's

Zaki Dee – TCA, CTK / London
>

The Trailblazers (TB's) was my first crew, it was formed in 1983 and for the first months there was only one member, me. This one-man crew did quite a few track sides and tags in West London; Hammersmith, Chiswick, Brentford and Barnes (also fondly referred to as 'The Boogie Down'). I also had a hand painted jacket with "Blazers" along the top and a character (myself) holding a spray can with a B-girl embracing the character's legs. It was the 80's and at that age sexism wasn't an issue I'm afraid. This jacket was responsible for me meeting most of the writers I hooked up with in the early years.

Hammersmith roundabout in West London used to have a series of subway paths connecting the Underground stations. It was in one of these tiled subways that I was tapped on the shoulder and on turning around I saw two fellow early London writers who had noticed the back piece on my jacket. Their names were Eskimo and Zerox. Up until this point I wasn't aware that there were that many other writers around so I asked them to join the Trailblazers. Almost every Saturday we would meet up at Covent Garden along with many more of the Capital's ever-growing B-boy & B-girl fraternity. From this central London focal point, others would begin to break, rap and show their piece books and photos. It was on one of these visits to Covent that another writer spotted the "Blazers" jacket I was wearing. Whilst walking from Covent Garden tube station to the main meeting point I was stopped by this writer, the inimitable Mode 2. Mode had already painted the boards at Covent along with his partner Scribla. Pride was also coming down to Covent

Garden and he had a sketch book that was unbelievable! Colour felt-tip outlines & fill ins that were just head and shoulders above anyone elses's that I had ever seen in the UK, a bit like the man himself. His sketches and designs were amazing. It wasn't until the open air Hip Hop Jam at the South Bank in 1984 that we all painted together. Tim Westwood had organised a live event funded by the now defunct GLC. Mode and Scribla, Pride and 3D from the Wild Bunch in Bristol along with Eskimo, Zerox and myself were all invited to paint some boards while the jam was going on. Once we'd seen each other's work and realised our potential, we were driven to the natural conclusion of joining forces. 3D was a hugely respected artist and although he didn't join the crew we did form a Bristol / London alliance called the "Union" which we got up on the District line tube train a few months later. The

---

Mode and Scribla had met Bando at Covent when he was over from Paris to check out the London scene in 1985

Artful Dodger (of Weetabix advert fame) another Covent Garden stalwart with a super slick 'Old English' style tag was also asked to join the Trailblazers.

Around 1985 The Trailblazers were invited to paint the stage back drop for the Shaw Theatre jam in central London. The event featured DJ Red Alert amongst other high-profile US and UK hip hop acts. It was backstage that the Chrome Angelz (T.C.A.) where formed. The name was the brain child of Mode and this new outfit would trim the Trailblazers to create a new crew of the most artistically likeminded and creative writers left; Mode, Scribla, Pride and myself. Next to join TCA was Paris-based Bando and this was the start of an alliance between London and the other major European cities that had graffiti chapters.

Mode and Scribla had met Bando at Covent when he was over from Paris to check out the London scene in 1985. After seeing his style he was immediately invited to join the TCA. Around this time a lot of writers in London were beginning to realise that we couldn't keep on doing American stuff, we had to do our own thing. I think that we were among some of the first writers to try doing something a little different from the scene in New York, because everyone at this time was apeing what was happening there. At the beginning we were influenced by Hip Hop in a big way. You would see Hip Hop videos on TV, movies like *WildStyle*, *Style Wars* and read books like *Getting Up* or *Subway Art* and you would try to emulate. When Bando came along it was a big step for us to see a different way of painting.

His highly original approach to letters and colour schemes gave all of us a huge incentive to be different and create our own style individually and as a crew. I'm not saying we were the only ones in London doing that but we were certainly a major influence at that time.

It's also important to point out that even before Bando came along we were a collective group of artists who were interested not only in Graffiti but also in other elements of art and design.

We were influenced by painting, drawing, graphics and comic art and were looking at graffiti from every angle we could and from varied artistic perspectives. We all had an interest in an art medium, and rather than just going out bombing or tagging, we wanted a piece. Art was the most important thing to us, creating new letters or new colour schemes and at the same time each one of us had our own style. Even before Bando's entry added his innovative approach we were already doing something that was different. His presence in the crew was like putting the accelerator on a natural progression. Bando had an influence on the artists that were around him in Paris as well, and when TCA met the outstanding artist Shoe, on the banks of the Seine, the idea to form an extended European crew was born – the *Crime Time Kings*. CTK members were spread across Europe and when you see pictures of pieces by phenomenal writers such as Shoe and Delta you can see Graffiti was quickly turning into a Worldwide movement.

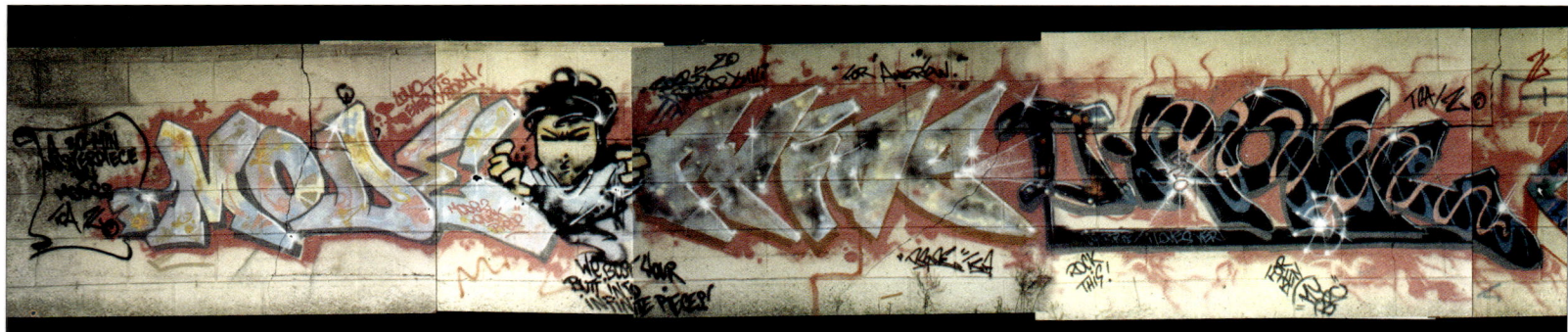

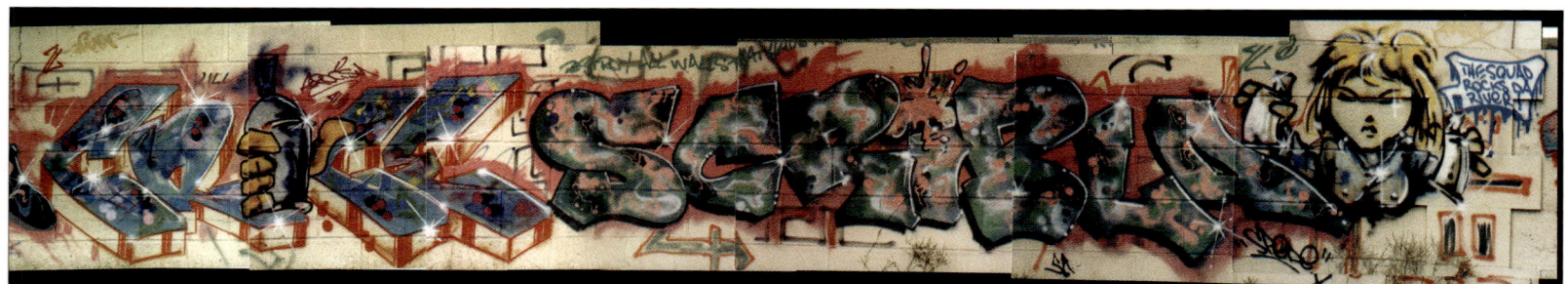

Mode 2, Pride, Zaki, Bando and Scribla along the Seine river, Paris. *The squad rocks da river.*

– Zaki Dee

LONDON

Mode 2 – TCA, CTK / London
>

Capital Radio's Venture Day, in Battersea Park, Summer '84, was where I first really hooked up with Scribla. There was a lot of Hip Hop and Electro being played on that hot day, with loads of people getting down in the park. There were also some fights and even a full-on stampede at one point. So he was telling me he was drawing and we found out that we lived in the same neighbourhood. That's how I got into it, kind of through him really; since I had been drawing on paper and with markers, but not painting with cans as yet. In our area of South East London there is no subway, just over-ground trains. I was this child that grew up in the Mauritius and before Hip Hop I was heavily into Dungeons & Dragons, Traveller, or painting lead figurines and so on. My brother and I had even won a national prize in '83, against guys who were like 60 years old, painting this Jabberwocky figurine from Ral Partha, with its own base and fake grass and stones and so on. We had a real painting interest, others would go to the park to play football but we were heavily into the stuff you could do at home or in the garden.

So I started painting and drawing together with Scribla, and later that Summer we saw Zaki Dee, with a back-piece on his denim jacket, walking up towards Covent Garden tube station, along with Eskimo and Zerox. They were called the Trail Blazers, and in August we got a chance to paint together. There was a thing that happened in London, where the London eye is, that big wheel. Jubilee Gardens, this little park there, hosted a jam on August 4th of '84. There was a stage with barriers, a big tent, speakers, and then there was a big square where the writers painted. On one side of the square was Scribla, me and Danny, who was a dancer, and we did a piece for Glide Master, of the New York City Breakers, who had died in a motorbike accident. On the opposite side to us was Zaki, Eskimo and Xerox.

Then there was Pride painting by himself to our right, and 3D from Bristol opposite him to our left. That was the first time we really met properly, it was the first time we really met 3D. It started to rain later that day, after we had just finished, and we all had to go inside the big tent where I remember them playing "It's Yours", by T La Rock and Jazzy Jay, as well as "Fresh, Wild, Fly & Bold" from the Cold Cut Brothers, amongst other great tunes of that time. Zaki put Scribla and I down with Trail Blazers, so that's where the "Devious TB's" piece in *Spraycan Art* is from, but Pride was still this big black guy from Wembley we just knew who continued to paint alone.

It wasn't until the RapAttack gig at the Shaw Theatre in April '85 that we finally became The Chrome Angelz, when Pride joined us. What we were really interested in was having this crew of guys who painted together. We did this "Urbanism" piece down at Labroke Grove, on the tracks, next to Brim, who did this "Nail" piece.

When Bando came over and joined forces with us, in May, him and I painted the piece on Powis Terrace, with Brim, Scam, and Drome painting underneath us, at street level. Our part only got painted out in Summer 2004, just before me and Bando were actually going to re-make it; using the same paint and same colours as then, Marabu Buntlack and Car Plan or Duplicolour, then me painting some of the real characters of the neighbourhood, who were all being pushed out as the area changed. That bullshit "Notting Hill" movie with Hugh Grant and Julia Roberts was partly to blame, and some people were very happy that the working class lot were making way for wealthier residents.

The only thing that really interested me, or most of our crew, was exchanging. We were influenced and inspired by each other, but we never copied, so everyone progressed really quickly. It was about how much personality you had and what you wished to interpret, not about making an inferior copy of somebody else's work.

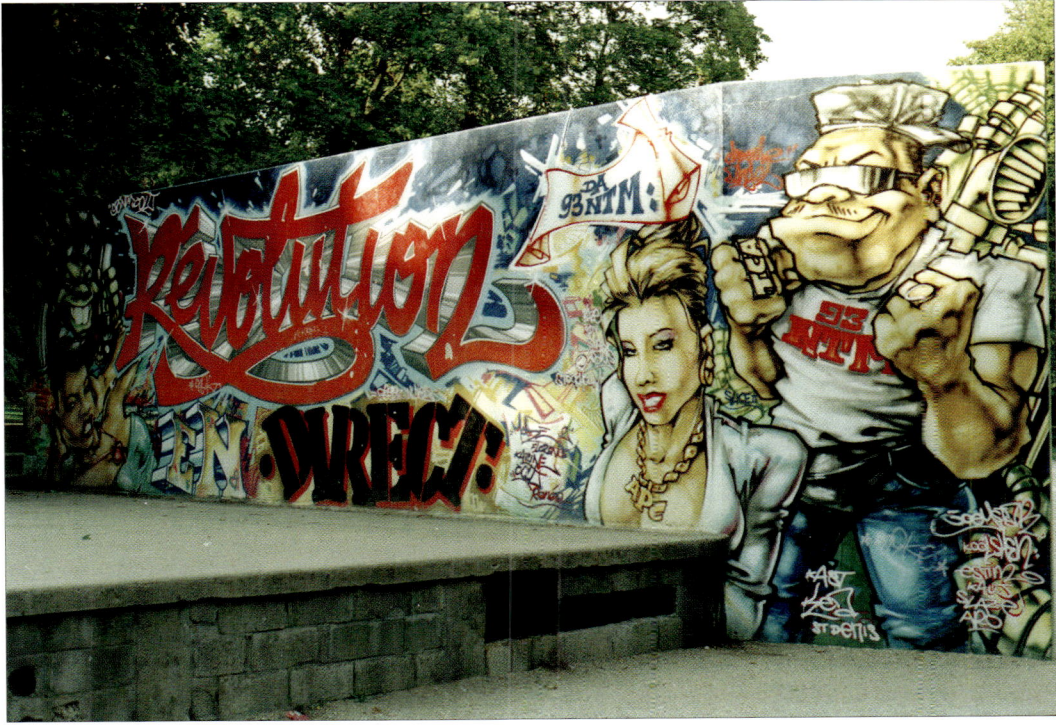

Revolution en direct by Mode 2 and Colt. Paris 1989   – *Le Truc*

At first we wanted to paint like the New Yorkers but then in '84-85 we thought "wait... I'm never going to get to that thing because I wasn't born there, I didn't grow up there". So we decided to do our own thing. We'd give our own interpretation of the vibe for London. So that was basically our driving thing with The Chrome Angelz. Many European writers get totally influenced by New Yorkers in the beginning, visiting writers like T-Kid were really inspiring Europe. I think New York is New York and the explosion of the culture that happened everywhere else in the world is something else. You can't put European writers in the context of a New York crew because it's a totally different thing. We didn't grow up in the original birthplace of this culture, watching it evolve around us.

In the mid 80's the scenes were really not comparable to that of New York because in London and in other European cities they were so few of us, so the dynamics involved in forming and expanding crews started crossing national boundaries. Bando came to London from Paris late in the summer of '84 but we didn't meet until early the next year. Him and his peoples had come because they knew the scene was vibrant in London and they just wanted to battle and burn the guys here. This was the mentality back then. When Bando returned to London in '85, Scribla and myself met him in Covent Garden. He looked like he was one of the Ramones, because of the black Ray-Bans and long hair. He had a really good back piece on his jacket so as Scribla and I spoke with him and when he looked through our book, and we looked through his, we forgot about the battling stuff and put each other down with our own groups; Bando into TCA, and TCA into Bomb Squad 2. So that was how the London-Paris connection started.

The first time I went to Paris was Sunday 26th of May, '85. The day before we did this thing called Swatch in Covent Garden. Swatch was doing the big launch of their first wristwatch, the clear "Jellyfish", so there were these big square canvases, our crew did two of them, working in teams of three for each. On Sunday I went to Paris to meet Bando and Steph, and I also remember there was another guy back in the day called Scam, from New Jersey. That was the first time I painted in Paris and saw Stalingrad, with the pieces from the Bad Boys Crew, like Jay, or Lokiss

from the Boucaneers.

Stalingrad was basically the spot where breakers and writers would hang out in Paris, it was closer to the outskirts of the city, on the side of the train tracks from Gare de L'Est and directly overlooked by Metro Line 2. It was quite a big piece of waste ground which stood where a building had been demolished. From that first trip the idea of CTK was formed, from a fusion of Bomb Squad 2, which was Bando's crew in Paris, with our crew The Chrome Angelz from London. Bando wanted to get rid of a couple of people from Bomb Squad so that's basically why he formed CTK. The driving mentality was just to bring good people in so we could all progress really quickly, not people who didn't fit in like Artful Dodger in TCA.

At the time London was somewhat lacking the inspiration we craved so it was good to go to Paris and see that there was a whole load of other people out there painting. So just one month later, from the 21st to the 24th of June 1985 I went back to Paris with Pride. On the back wall of Stalingrad we did "Aerosol Art" with a character in the middle, which got published on *Spray can Art*. By the Summer, about mid July, all the crew from London was out there painting.

Bando lived on a street that came off the river, 300-400 metres from his house, so we'd be painting on the river bank too. We saw some new pieces in July by people from out of town, and decided to stay about and just hang, waiting for them to come back, that kind of thing. And they did. We immediately recognised they were writers; even though there was no dress code, there actually was. I guess we were just different from other people. That's how we met Shoe from Amsterdam and his people, Jan and Jaz, on the river bank.

Shoe showed us some photos, Dondi had been one of his mentors at the start so when we saw his pictures we were stunned by the colours! We were really impressed and I think they were too by what they saw of our work. So as CTK was already on, and with the fact that it started with guys from London and Paris it already had the mentality that we could have included someone from somewhere else, Shoe therefore became 'president' in Amsterdam and ran the 'chapter' of CTK in that city

CREW ENDING
—

The Paris CTK connection started to come apart when Boxer was allowed to be a member, because he had a truck, which meant it was possible to go out of town to steal paint, as most of the spots in Paris had become too hot. He had absolutely no skills though, and also had his own private agenda when it came to friendship; he was just there for self really. Bando and Steph fell out over that, but we were all beginning to move on with our own things anyway. Initially the driving force that held us together was our common interests, the idea of a collective strength through crew, but when Pride and Scribla had to go seriously back to their studies to finish school, and I moved to Paris to work in computer graphics, TCA was really not meeting up so much anymore. I think that Amsterdam was the only place that really kept it tight. People grow up anyway, though. By the time I reached 26–27, people around me in Paris were having crises and some even had to get psychiatric treatment. A lot of people had lived on this Hip Hop fantasy for so many years and then reality was really hitting hard. We had not been educating ourselves because there were no parents around; we were just doing our own thing. A lot of people were not showing their insecurities, no one wanted to show weakness. So there are certain aspects of personal evolution that nobody went through, and when push comes to shove the lack of a certain set of tools in life becomes problematic. Echo, for instance, did his cinema stuff on the side. I think a lot of people just went and carried on doing their own thing. It's probably better to have a job somewhere and keep this thing for your own pleasure on the side rather than make your living out of it, because it's really hard when you have to do commercial work. The art form is

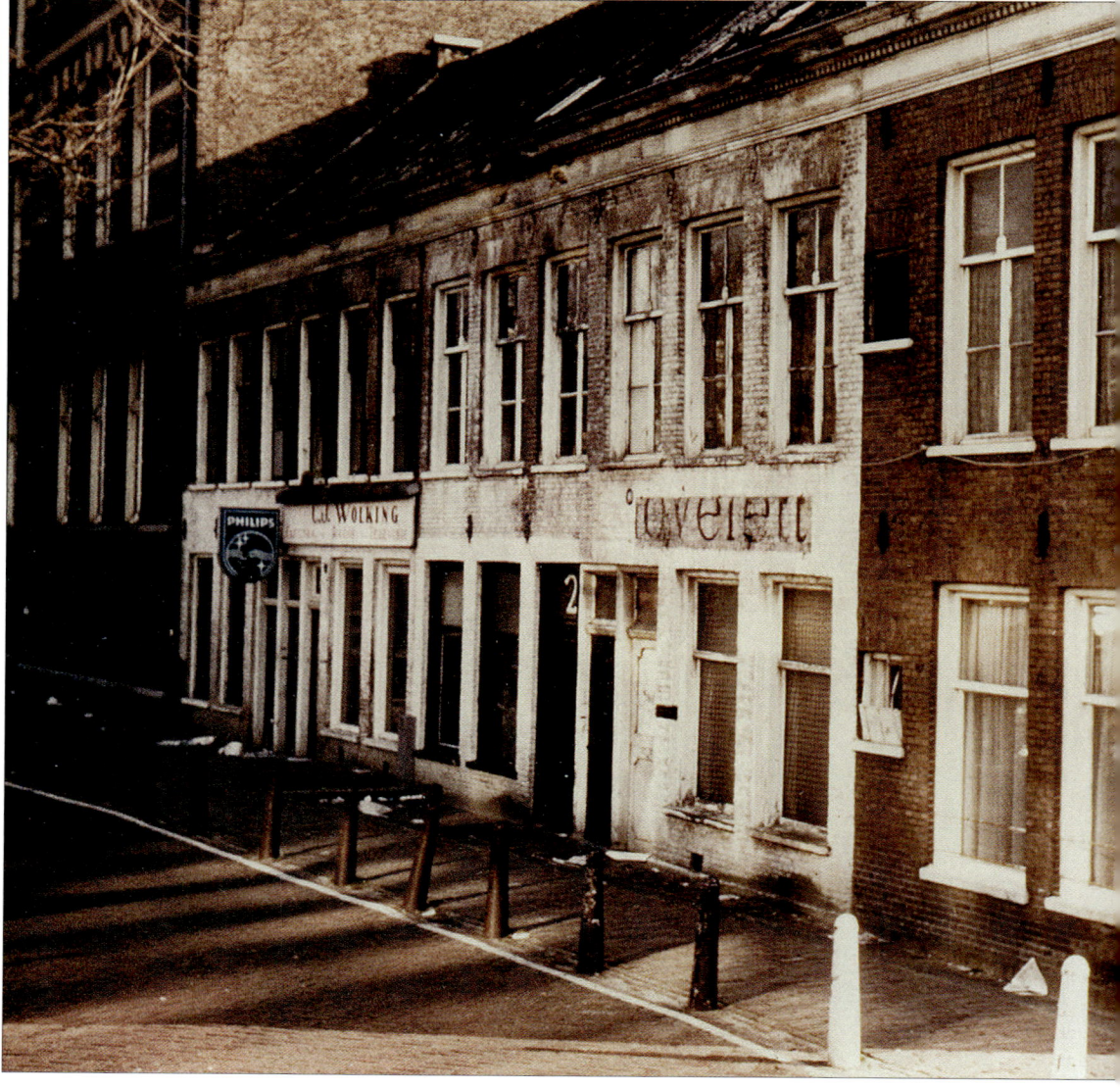

The art form is kind of independent by definition so how do you stay true if you're working under someone else?

kind of independent by definition so how do you stay true if you're working under someone else? What if the client is getting on your nerves and you're not feeling the work method? There are some things you can get done real quickly because you're into them while others you get done really slowly. I didn't get a graphic school education, I didn't do anything like that. I did record sleeve work and flyers and posters, the odd graffiti commission job, but nothing major. CTK was already over in the late 80's, even if the Dutch guys carried it on some more. Amsterdam is so small and those guys have known each other for such a massive part of their livese, seeing each other at least every other week. It didn't get broken up like it did in London or Paris. In Paris the crew was predominantly centred around the figure of Bando, but it also included talented writers such as Steph, who was later called Colt. He had so many names; he was also called Deen, Seme 2 and Sence. Apart from him there were also other members with other characteristics, such as Doc or Jonone, and perhaps these different personalities were the cause of the fragmentation of the Paris nucleus of the crew, which was the beginning of the end. Bando and Steph each went their own way and we never found the same cohesion we had once had. So it was already broken up from '87-'88. Chrome Angelz was something I kept with Zaki, Pride, and Scribla, but then Scribla moved away, and he now lives in the West of England, I think. His parents wouldn't pass on my messages though. I think they thought what he did then was no good and that I was a negative influence on him. I still have his phone number in my head. We haven't seen him in so long, but that's just how it is, people grow up and take different paths. I think I'll give it another try one day... —MODE 2

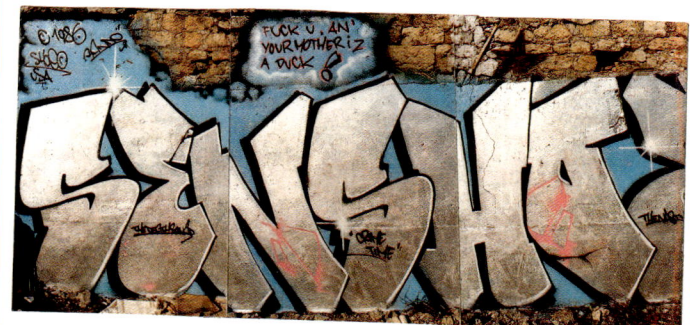

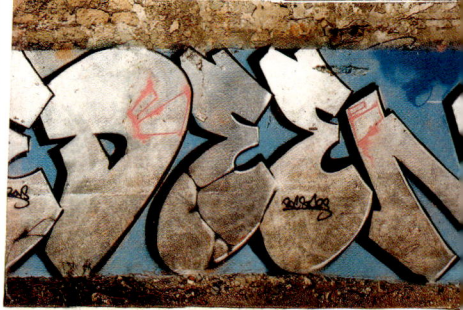

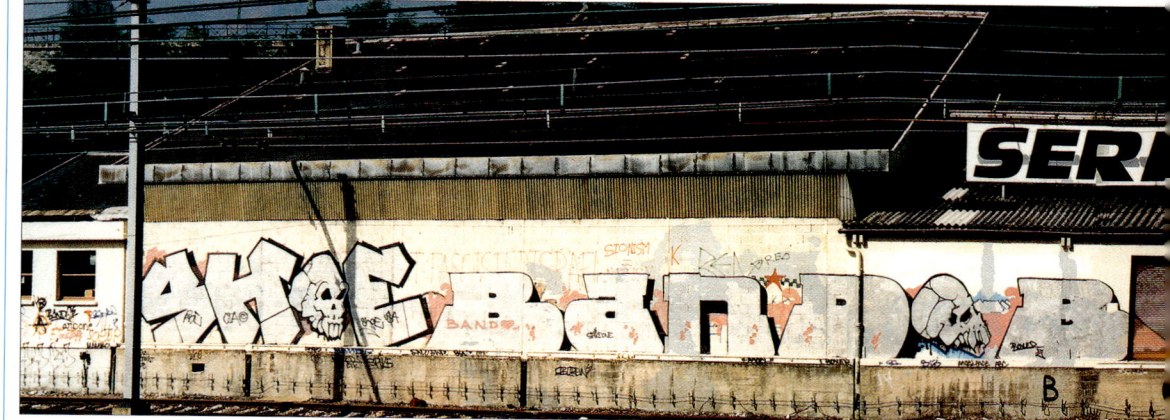

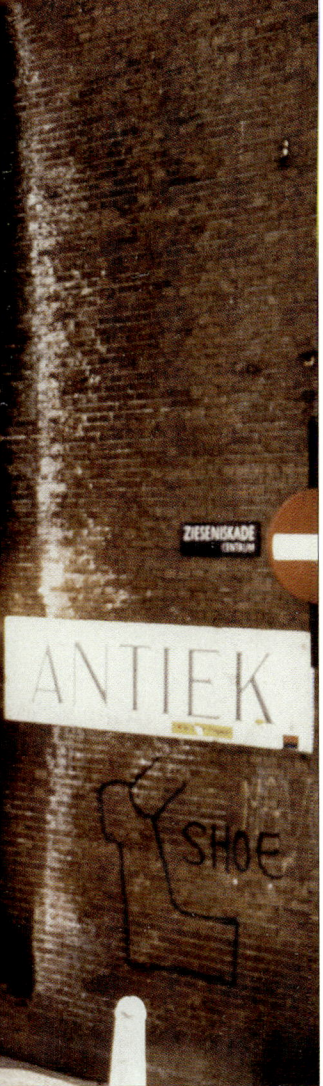

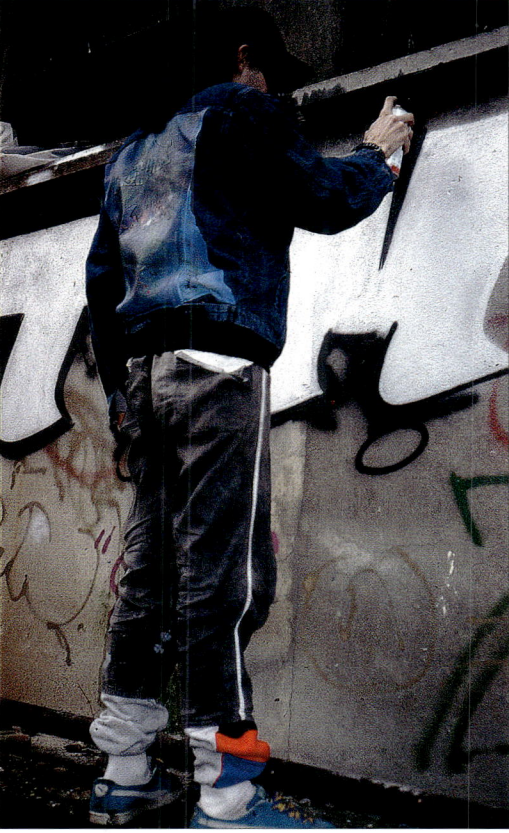

— *Cat 22*

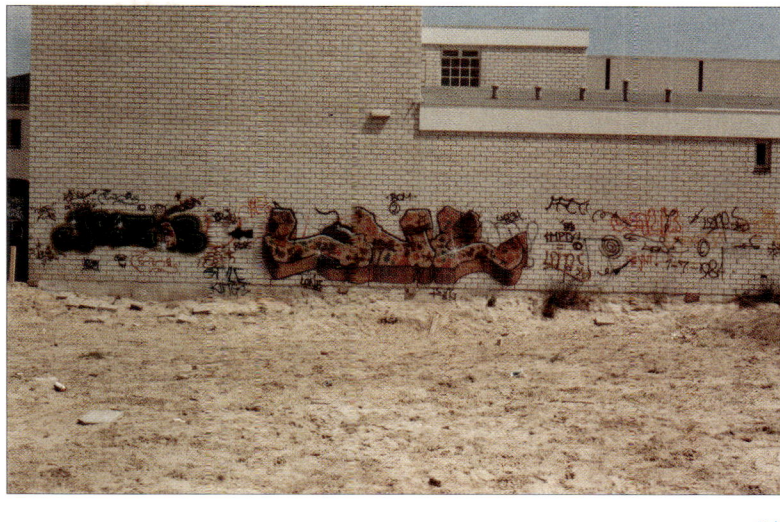

— *Delta*

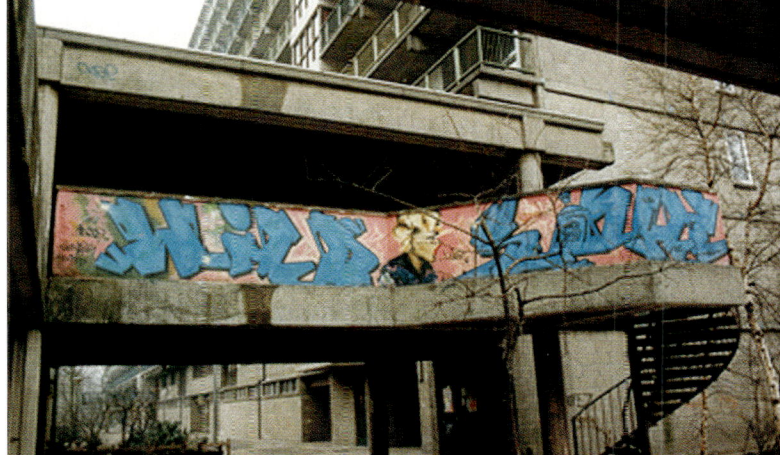

— *ACW archive*

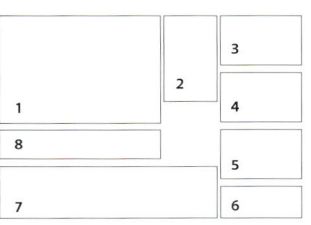

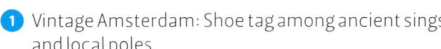

— *Shoe*

1 Vintage Amsterdam: Shoe tag among ancient sings and local poles

2 Bando painting in Paris, 1985

3 Jaz and Delta with his first "Lone" tag. Amsterdam 1984

4 Piece by Bando, Paris mid 80's

5 Delta at Waterlooplein, mid 80's

6 *Sho* by Shoe, Amsterdam

7 Silver blockbusters by Shoe, Bando, Boxer and Angel in Paris, 1986

8 Senshoedeen by Sens (Bando), Shoe and Deen (Colt) over the famous Aerosol Art piece published on *Spraycan Art*. The Mode 2 character was left intact

— *Shoe*

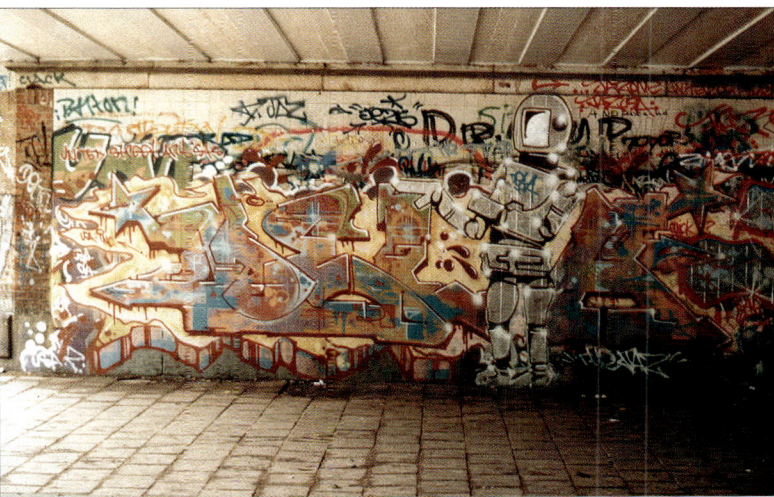

— *Delta*

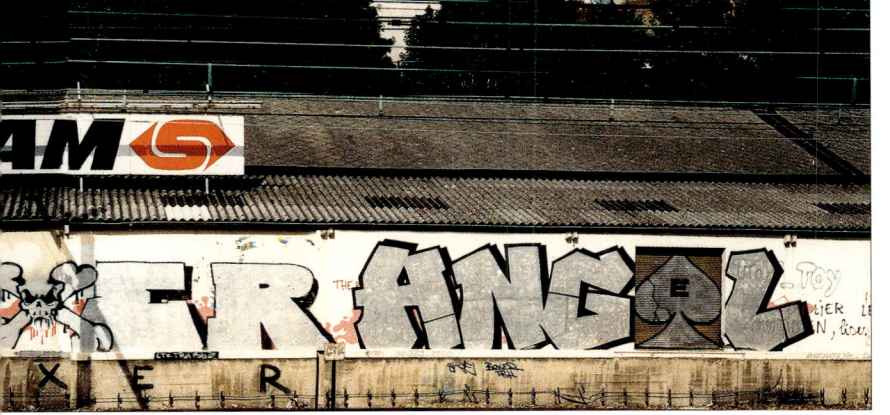

— *Shoe*

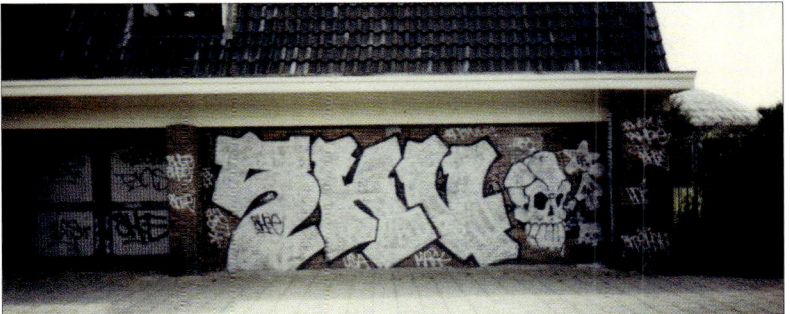

— *Gio at TOSHQ*

The headmaster's ritual: simple letters as a

Bando – CTK / Paris
>

One of the first flashes of graffiti I can remember is Futura
a long time ago, in 1980 or something; he was doing a
big backdrop for a Clash concert at the Palace in Paris. I
wasn't really into graffiti then but I thought it was cool,
even though I ignored what it was. I could say I saw graffiti for the first time in New York. My dad lives in New
York and my mom in Paris. Graffiti was everywhere there,
streets and trains, but mainly on the trains. Every single
train back then was completely covered either in tags or
paintings, and personally I liked tags more than pieces. I
immediately realised it was about writing a Name because
that's what was everywhere, everybody was writing their
Names all over the place. You would always see the same
Names, over and over, so I figured it out right away. After
a while I met Bear 167, it was 1982 and he explained what
it was to me, how you do outlines and how to draw and
all this stuff. So I started to think what Name to choose
and I found it at home: my mom had a painting in her
living room by a Japanese guy and it says "Bando" on it.
At the beginning I thought the Name was cool but actually after a couple of years I stopped liking it. I didn't like
drawing the letters, the Name was really hard to write, a
"B" and an "A" are two hard letters to write one after the
other, so sometimes I would write Sens and other aliases,
though mostly sticking to Bando. So I started painting
in New York and when I came back to Paris I was the first
one in the city to do this. It was 1983 and about four or five
months later BBC was also around, painting cool pieces. I
founded the first crew, Bomb Squad II with Scam, a B-boy
from New York; we went to England where we met Mode
and TCA and a friendship started. Then they came to Paris
one summer and stayed at my house and we decided to
form Crime Time Kings.

Even though we were all influenced by the New Yorkers, at least in the beginning, we all started to work on
our style, individually. Mode was more about characters
while me and Shoe were studying letter shapes. I think
that little by little you get better by practicing, and then
you start getting the technique to do whatever you want
to do. I just started drawing the way I did, there were no
particular references besides New York. I was seeing graffiti from many original writers but the guy I liked the most
was Seen, still today. I prefer simple styles as opposed to
really complicated stuff, because if you don't have a base
of real good simple letters there's no way you can start
doing the complicated stuff.

Too many people started wanting to go really crazy right
away without having a good base. So I always wanted to
keep it as simple as possible.

I think there are two ways of doing graffiti. One keeps the
whole group of letters together, with overlapping layers;
people do a lot of really good pieces like that, inventing
great ways of connecting letters. But another way is to
completely separate the letters. Each letter is detached so
each letter is its own piece, and since at the time nobody
was doing that, I started drawing that way. Also if you
have a really big wall, say it's 80 metres long, you can
fill up the whole wall with one word, you can separate
the letters and take the whole wall, and even though the
letters are separate the whole wall becomes one piece. If
the wall is along rail tracks you can easily read the name
and the shape even if the train is travelling at a high speed.
With graffiti the only thing that counts is the letters'
structure and the ultimate tool for me would just be a can
of black and nothing else, just the outline and shadows in
black. To reinforce this shape on the wall, the next best
thing is to use silver for the fill. So black outlines and silver: just two colours, because the only thing that comes
out with only two colours is the harmony of the letters.
There's nothing to mask, or camouflage or take away or
distract the eye from the style. I always thought silver was
the best colour for letters because it really makes them
stand out. So if your style is really good, then it's going to
be even better, but if your letters suck or if there's something wrong, right away everybody's gonna notice because there's no 3D or colours: the mistake is obvious. It's
like calligraphy, which is just black ink on white paper.

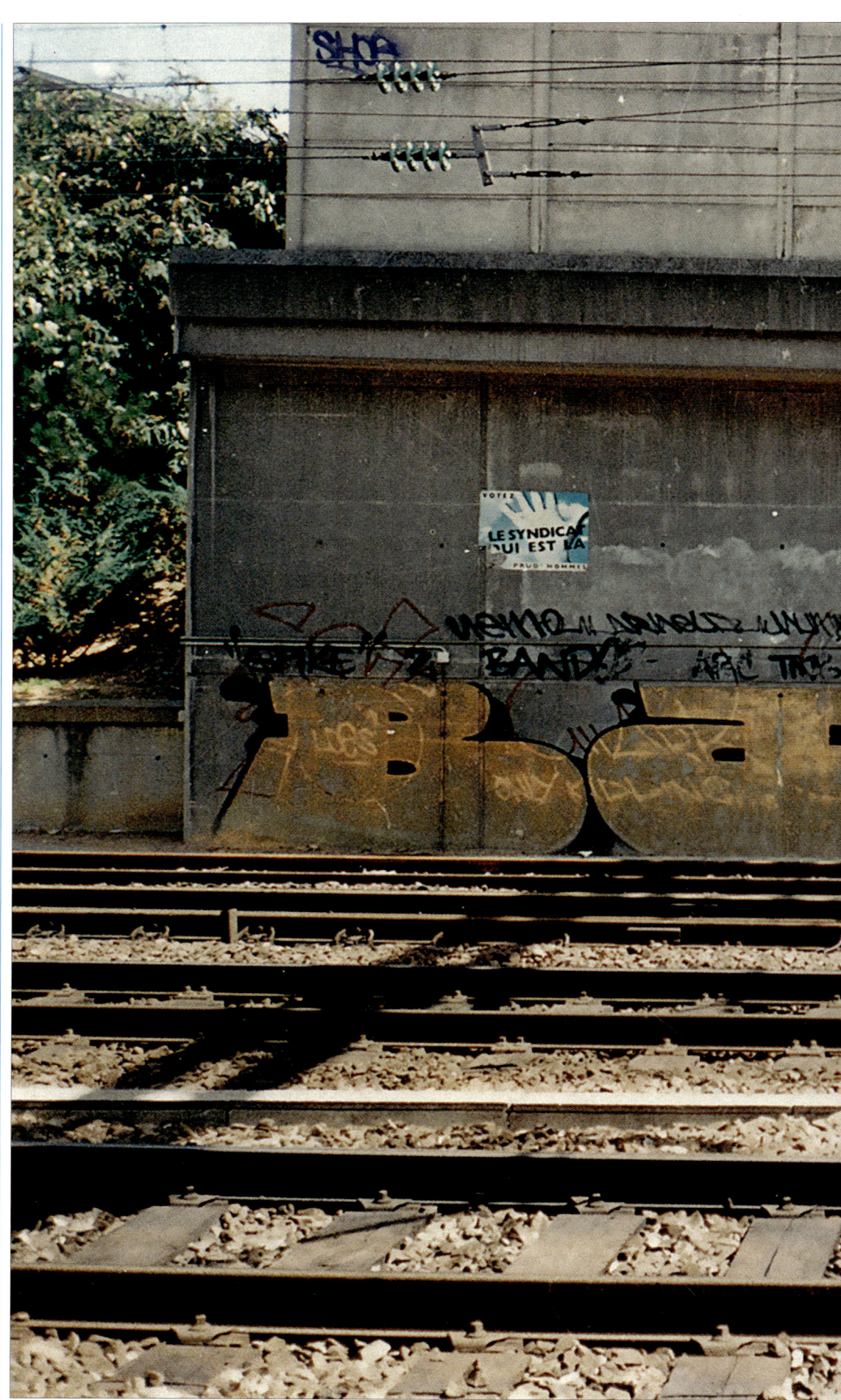

A classic Bando blockbuster, Paris

standard

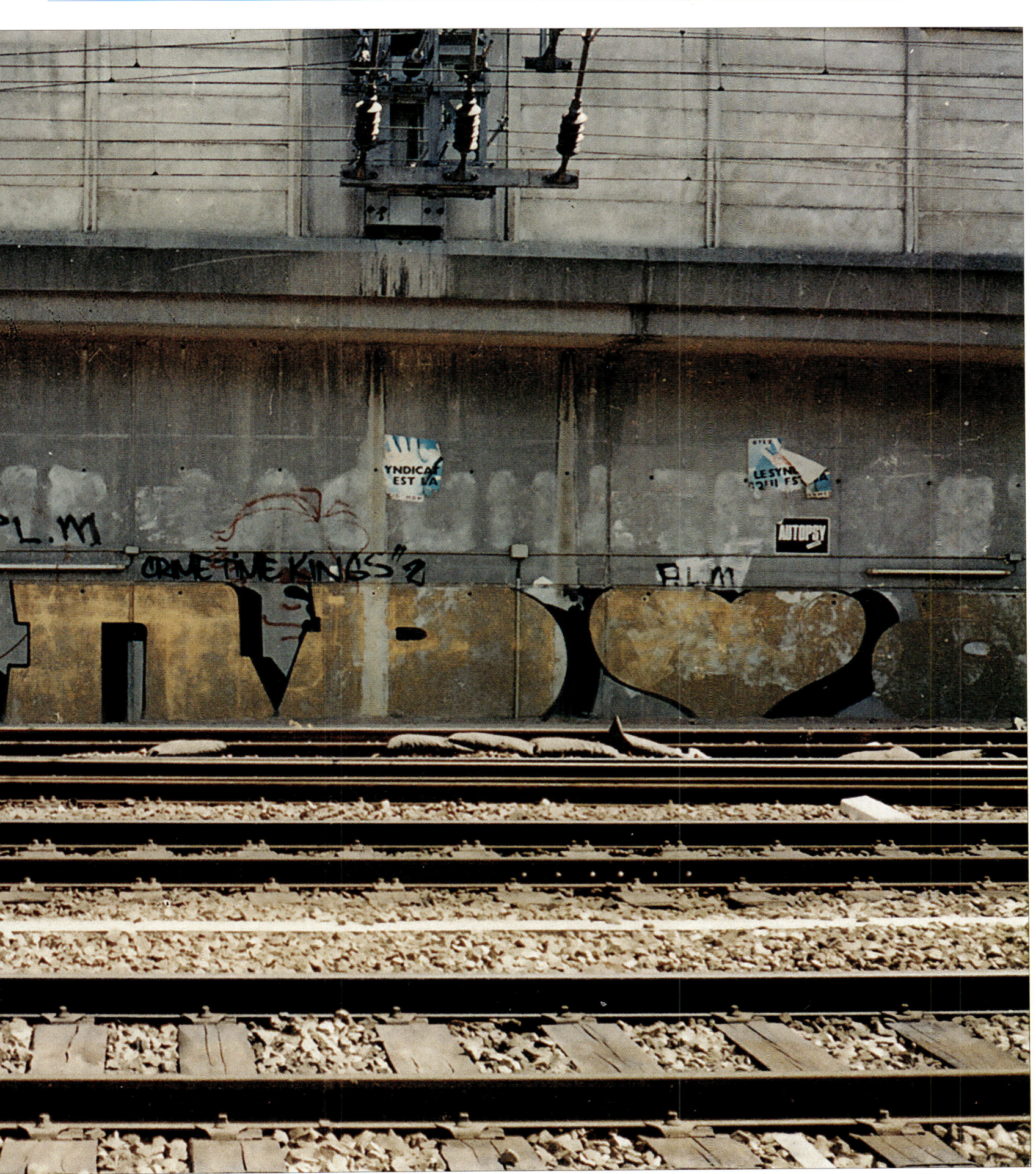

— Mark Todt

EXPORTING THE BOMBER

Cat22 – CTK / Amsterdam
>

CTK was the first International crew ever. Originally there were two presidents: Bando and one of his best friends, Steph. In 1982 Steph attended the New York City Rap Tour, the concert with Africa Bambaataa and other New York B-boys that first arrived in London and then Paris. Steph went backstage and as Bambaataa at the time was trying to expand the Zulu Nation to Europe, he wanted the Zulu Nation symbol to be everywhere. It was a "Z", the interrupted Crime Time Z; basically the Zulu Nation sign revisited.

Before Amsterdam, these two cities came into the picture, as there was a connection through Mode 2. In London he was painting with guys like Pride, Zaki, Scribla: TCA, The Chrome Angelz.

The president of the Chrome Angelz was Mode 2 and with Bando they formed a very active duo, painting innovative styles. In my opinion, nothing has been done better than the pieces in those days. All those walls along the Seine, all those amazing burners were top, they had new style with cool characters and beautiful colours. Those pieces looked really professional, they were all done with Altona paint, which of course helped but didn't create it. Rhyme and Delta came back from Paris and showed me some photos.

I remember a *Dawn* piece by Bando and a *Lucrezia* piece. It was a combination of Dondi's skills and the art form of Futura. It literally turned graffiti into art. At that point, for me at least, I finally thought a European direction had taken place in regards to Writing; the New York style was somehow forgotten. With all respect to New York, we had to do it and go on developing something peculiar and aesthetically independent.

Right after London the connection with Bando and Amsterdam came. This guy Lime said he had a photo shoot with some models down there and I decided to go with him. It was an opportunity for me to go check out some Bando stuff, so we drove to Paris and stayed in a youth hostel. I remember we arrived by car and driving around we saw the Louvre, where the crystal pyramid was just about to be built. On its wooden hoarding there was a silver Bando piece. I can still remember exactly how he'd made the B. There was even a Mode piece. If you like letters, it was beautiful. Anyway we went to the youth hostel, checked in and all of a sudden a guy, a courier came into the hostel, delivering a package. I looked at his scooter and I saw a silver Bando tag on the back. When we asked about Bando, he helped by giving us his address. We went straight to his house and his mum was there, she called him down. He welcomed us in, and

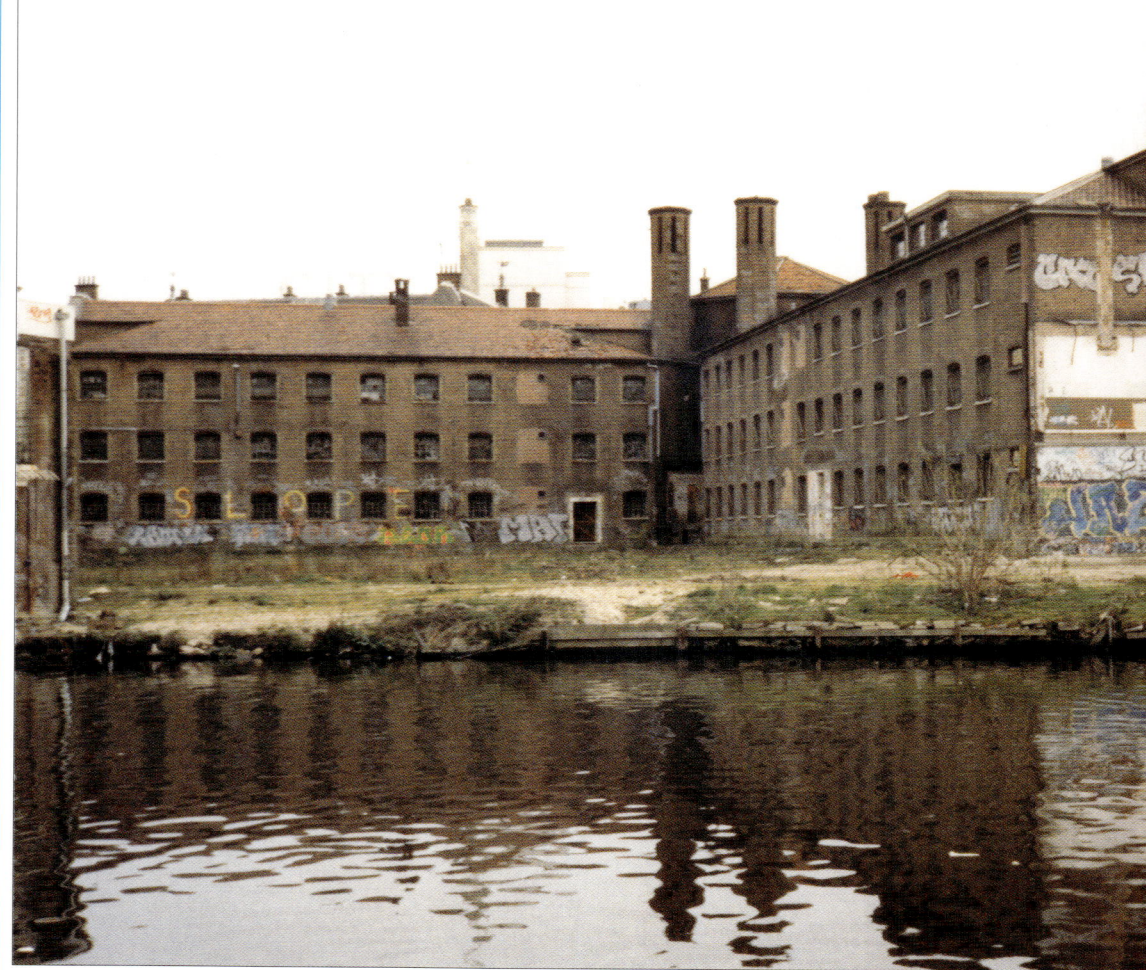

Mode was sitting there drawing. We had hit the jackpot! No photos of models were taken that weekend. We left our stuff in the hostel but never slept there because we ended up sleeping at Bando's. We got along immediately, Mode was a cool character and Bando was the nicest person in the world, but also a little strange. That same night we were out doing pieces, we went to the catacombs and got caught by the police. The other guys with them were Sign, Boxer and Steph. We went back to Amsterdam after that weekend, but the following week I was back in Paris again. All of a sudden Paris and Amsterdam started to be connected. When Shoe and Bando connected, USA stopped existing and became part of CTK. I need to say that Bando, Mode and the Amsterdam division of CTK were the most productive in those days.

When Bando, Shoe and I visited New York again, it was

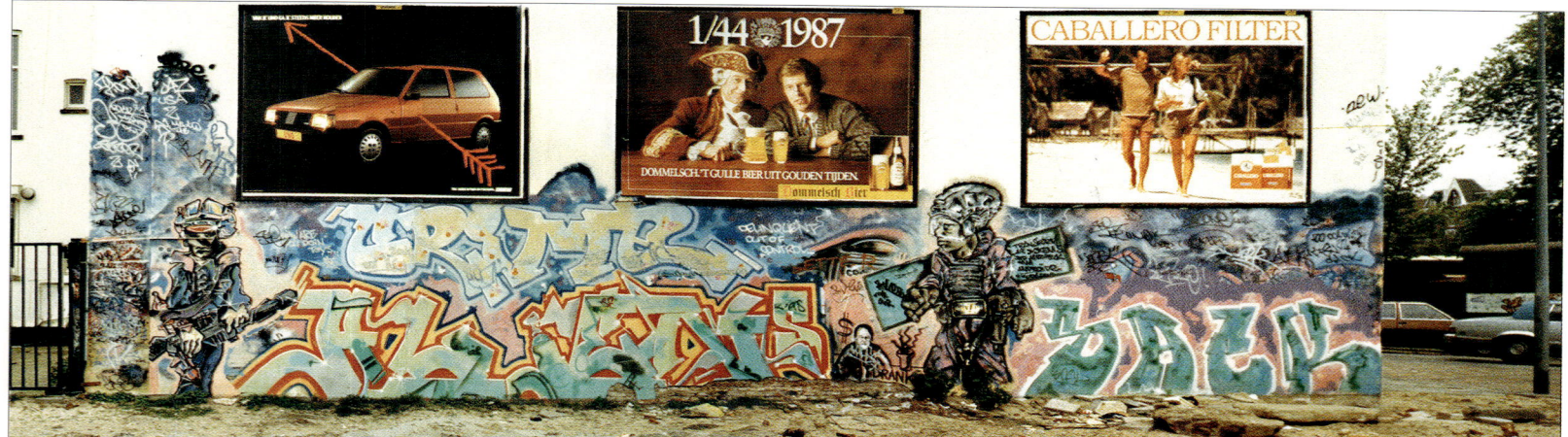

Alien, Saek, *Crime* by Cat22 and Jaz

— Mark Todt

ATTITUDE

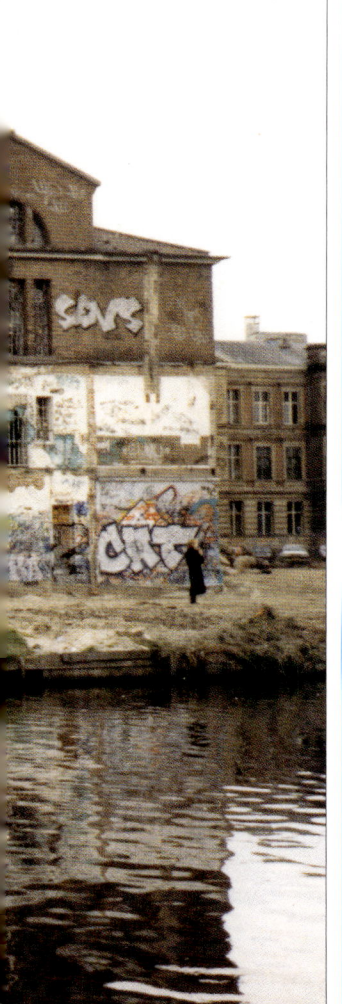

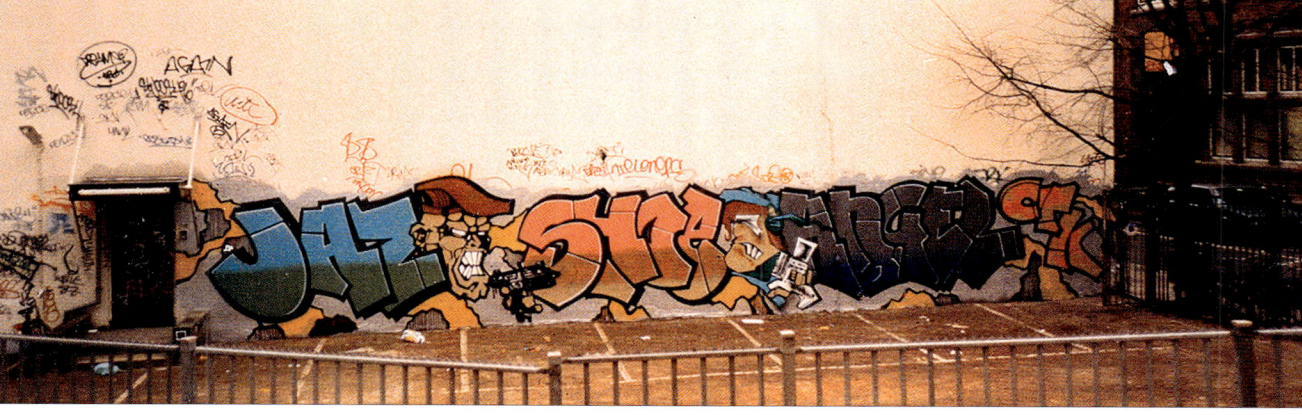

Jaz, Shoe and Angel of CTK crew

— *Shoe*

THE OLD JAIL

ZEDZ INC

Since graffiti was tolerated in Amsterdam, during the 80's a lot of places were being painted in the daytime. There was the old jail on Leidseplein that was totally painted: the rooftops, the insides, the courtyard. I think the police went easy on it; they were more concerned about other things like junkies robbing tourists. Of course many places were illegal, but this area didn't have a specific function for people anyway, and nobody would even walk down those streets.

— *Mark Todt*

then and there that we decided we had to go back to Europe to kill a city. So we thought of Munich. I had the number of this writer Loomit where we could stay. I had met Loomit and Don of the Stone Age Kids from Munich years before in Vondelpark, Amsterdam. I was doing a commercial job at the time, a really nice piece, so I met those guys and they showed me their books. I was impressed! I saw trains, window-downs, end-to-ends, top

-to-bottoms that even Chintz from Dortmund did. I was acting like a tough guy, "I'm CTK you know, this piece is cool but the style is totally wack", but it was cool to see trains painted in Germany. Anyway I got Loomit's phone number. So I called him up and he told us it was way too dangerous in Munich because of the cops, but I told him in a week we would be there anyway. First we went to Paris and did some shopping: racking everything until the car was full! We racked up strong, 300-400 cans or something, the car could hardly handle it.

We went to Munich and Loomit told us we could sleep at his place, even if we weren't there to sleep. He told us he couldn't come with us because it was a dangerous situation. The reason why he warned us was a few weeks earlier there had been a huge raid in Munich and had been arrested everybody. But once we arrived to the spots, the yards were beautiful! They were completely dark and in the middle of nowhere. Train after train after train I wondered what the big deal was. He'd told us that we could work from 00:00 until 06:00, 6 hours to do a train, I couldn't believe it! We thought we would do one piece and then destroy. We stayed there for one week and every night we did a different yard. Unfortunately halfway through the week Boxer's grandmother died so he had to leave, which ended up being a good thing as he didn't get caught. The last night we had no more paint but plenty of ink so we decided to only do insides, to kill and trash the place. They had trains that ran to Dachau, which to me was more than just an end-station, it made me think about the concentration camps. I deeply wanted to bomb those. I'm from Amsterdam, I have a strong hate for the Nazis and concentration camps. So I had no problem

destroying them, I was really attracted to that. I always had train keys with me and as the cars were like married couples, to get to one you had to go through the other. I remember I wanted to jump out of a train but I saw this big fat German man jump out from the bushes. We didn't have face masks in those days and he put the gun to my face. I jumped out the train with Cemnoz who was with us and we ran away. This is one of my top three most horrible escapes ever! I got away but it took hours of walking. In the end Cemnoz called his girlfriend who came to pick us up and took us to Loomit's house where I only had my blackbooks. I knew Bando had been arrested and Shoe too, it was only me and the German guy that escaped. So I took all their books, put them in a bag and decided I would take them with me back to Amsterdam. I was so tired because I hadn't slept the right before and I just fell asleep on the bed. The next thing I remember was someone pushing me and when I opened my eyes there were all these uniforms around. The first thing I did was look for the books and they weren't there so I looked at Loomit and understood he had hid them in his mum and dad's room. They arrested us and put us in jail for 2-3 weeks. The Vandal Squad in Germany was really organised. They had the right to even take family photo albums that dated back to the 1900s. If they did that to me my resentment would never die. South Germany for us free-thinkers from Amsterdam was a totally alien world! It was like a dictatorship. But anyway we killed the system down there, I was proud of that because they were not used to that in Germany. They weren't bombing at all; they were only making beautiful pieces so I think we changed the mentality over there .. somehow.

THE MUNICH MISSION

—

Stone – SAK / Munich
>

CTK visited Munich and went around on a bus painted with a beautiful *Crime Time* style and a character by Mode. Bando's *Crime Time* was so high that it was incredible even just going to see the bus. When they came to Munich everybody met at Loomit's place. It was Cat 22, Shoe.

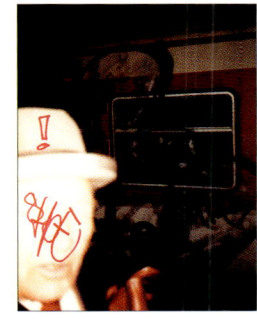

Bando, and Boxer. When they came we were already pretty much into trains, we knew what was going on but the yards were definitely not bombed, there were little pieces running here and there but the system hadn't been taken down. They thought they could do it in one week and they did. After the first night you saw trains running with Shoe throw-

ups and Bando throw-ups, it was beautiful stuff. So CTK continued the whole week like this, painting every night. The transit cops knew something was happening and made some efforts. There are different stories about what really happened. Some say that a guy may have talked and given information to the police about where they were staying, but that was just

part of the rumour. After all, we were just a few guys back then and with a little thinking the cops could have figured it out themselves. After one week of hard bombing the police showed up in a yard and arrested Shoe and Bando. Cat got away and slept at Loomit's place but got arrested the next day. They were put in prison because they were foreigners and had

done a lot of damage The action, the bombing session and the style they painted brought about a big change, it made us become more radical. What I mean by this is that if we'd go into a yard we wouldn't leave a single train untouched. We'd do a piece on one train but then tag the remaining and fill up everything with throw-ups. This was the idea they imported.

THE FANTASTIC PARTNERS

The global expansion of The Fantastic
Partners, historic New York crew
captained by Case 2.

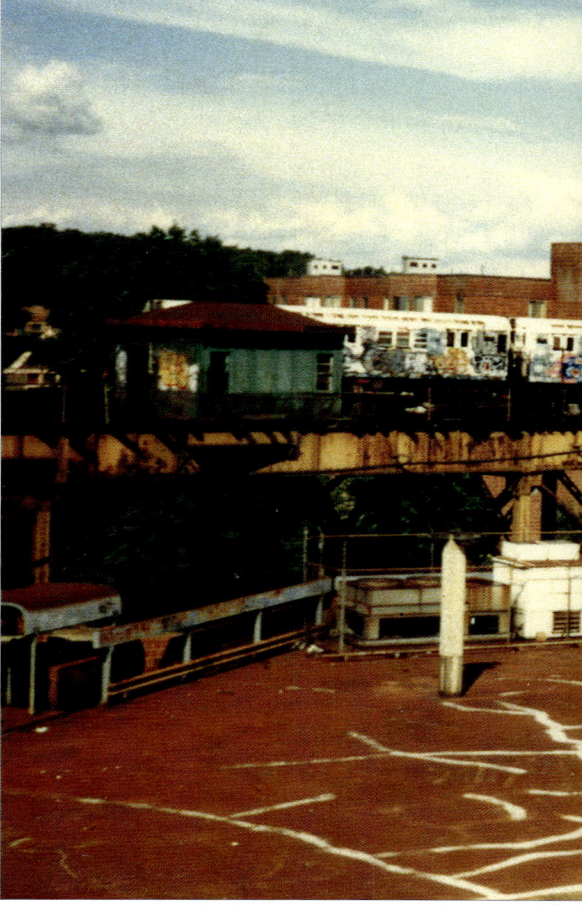

Sent whole-car pulling out of 180th St station in the Bronx

Milk –TFP / Munich
>

Case2 with his big arm. The photo everyone knows from the book *Subway Art*. I was 15 years old when I held that book in my hands for the first time. Intrigued by the concept of writing your name with a marker or spray can, having your name run on the side of a train. Little did I know that a few years later I would be standing side by side with the very same people from that book, painting my name on the walls and trains of New York City. But let's go back in time - a time before the World Wide Web, a time before mobile phones and global communication, back to the mid 80's. When your block was your world, your city your universe and you knew very few people outside that realm. You were surprised to find graffiti in places other than your hometown or New York. First there where rumours, then the first contacts where made and writers started to travel and look beyond the rim of the plate, first nationally then across borders to neighbouring European countries. But for that first generation of European writers, New York was still the ultimate destination. The Mecca one had to go to.

I had wanted to go to New York since I was 10 years old. Even more so since I had started writing Graffiti. The big moment came in 1987 when I spent a year in the US as an exchange student. I would cut school, hop on a Greyhound bus and make my way to the Big Apple.

It was then that the MTA was starting to win the war against graffiti. Line by line the painted cars started disappearing. Many of the older writers from New York where discouraged by this mass of clean trains and only a handful of writers, namely Sent, Ghost, Dero and Ven kept on going 'til the last one had been pulled out of service on May 10th 1989.

Once off the bus, I would spend from dusk 'til dawn riding the trains taking photos of pieces. Sometimes I would wait hours for a particular piece to make its long way back through Brooklyn and the Bronx so I could get a good shot of it. By spending countless hours in train stations, I eventually ran into other writers. They were curious to hear that there was a growing scene in Europe, that people were hitting trains on the other side of the Big Pond. No one that I met had ever been to Europe and most only had a vague idea of where I was from. Clark, a writer from the Bronx, took me painting and in early '88 I did a rather ugly Milk on a handball court in Crotona Park. But ugly or not - I was up in New York City! I wrote "Germany Style" next to it, which must have left the inhabitants of the Bronx who read it wondering what someone from Germany was doing there, painting their walls. In fact Sent told me years later that he had seen some of my pieces that all said "Germany" underneath and had wondered who the hell I was.

The fist contact had been made, but it was Neon, a writer and friend of mine from Munich, who really pushed the limit. He had come to NY in the summer of '88 and somehow had met Sent who took him to the trains and they succeeded in painting three trains on the J-Line. Sent was then vice president of the legendary writers crew TFP (*The Fantastic Partners*) and Neon was made its first international member. After coming back to Germany my only concern was how to go back to NYC. With the money we had made from an article on Graffiti in the German edition of Playboy, Neon and I set off across the Atlantic once again, to hit New York hard in the summer of '89. The plane ticket cost 1.300 DM (ap. 650 EUR), a big chunk of money for 17 year old kids at that time. We were house-sitting a building in Brooklyn, which ironically had been vacated by the owners for a summer trip to Europe. Well, we were never there at night. Out painting every night, climbing up burned out buildings, trees, trucks to get up to rooftops along the train lines. New York was still pretty bankrupt, the financial-crash of '87 had left little hope for the city, decay was everywhere, large parts of the Bronx were marked by burnt out buildings and even burned down subway stations. Tourists didn't dare to cross the bridges to Brooklyn or the Bronx and places like Williamsburg were famous for the Hisidic Jews and crack rather than art galleries. But on the other hand, you could still get away with a lot more things than today, especially Graffiti. We met up with Sent the first night and whenever he had time we would go painting together. One night we all went to visit Case2, who still lived in the same housing projects that everyone knows from the documentary *Style Wars*. I had come full circle. Here I was, four years after picking up *Subway Art* I was sitting in Case2's kitchen. Case2 was president of TFP at that time. The formation of *The Fantastic Partners* dates back to the early 70's and the original members had been such pioneers as Kindo, Fuzz, Bot707, Solid, Fred165, Og2. It was Case 2 and his partner Butch though that had a major impact on the scene in the early 80's by painting countless whole-cars on the 2 and 5 lines with incredible lettering leading to Case's title of "King of Style". But the driving force behind the crew at the end of the decade was Sent. He was the one who wook up the tradition of train productions that blew everybody away, sometimes staying in the train yard for ten or more hours.

He was also the one to maintain the name TFP on the now clean trains, by refusing to give in and continuously hitting trains like nothing had ever changed.

But it had. Once a painted train was spotted it was immediately pulled to the maintenance yard to be cleaned. Graffiti on trains had vanished from the face of New York. One day, we went to paint in a lay-up right under City Hall. A tight spot between two trains that were parked in an abandoned station. For my piece I used some German Sparvar paint that I had brought on the plane (yes, you could bring a bag of paint on the plane!). After chasing the train to catch photos we found it half cleaned in the Coney Island yard. All the American paint had been washed away, but my piece remained almost intact, because the German paint resisted the cleaning solvent.

What had so far been a one way street of visits to New York turned into a transatlantic exchange program when Sent came to visit Europe at the end of '89 and left quite a mark on Munich's trains. At the same time more and more connections between writers were formed within Europe and travelling for the purpose of painting elsewhere was slowly becoming popular. For me personally this was a revelation. I cut most of the ties that connected me to my old life of school and parents and embarked on a journey that over the following years would take me many places and result in close friendships that remain to this day. I had been made a member of The Fantastic Partners and took this name to many of the train yards of Europe, though also returning to New York almost every year. This later landed me a photo of a whole-car I had done in New York in the New York Times under the headline "Graffiti tourism". We had gone global and even the cops had figured it out. By the mid 90's travelling on our part had become quite extensive and it happened that one week Atome from Australia, Sent and I would paint in the Bronx, a few weeks later we would all meet again in Amsterdam, go to Germany for a Hip Hop jam, sneak away for a night to do whole-cars in Amsterdam again, then go to Munich and on to Italy from there. Atome from Sydney, being from the opposite side of the world, was the one who gave the thing a global dimension. Another very influential member of TFP was Pure from New York. He started writing in the early 80's and had been widely recognised for his perfect style. He had then been connected to the famous crew FBA, but in the late 80's had taken a break from Graffiti in favour of Rock music and partying. It was Sent who sparked the flame again and brought him back into the game in '91, which for Pure was rather painful, cause he broke his ankle right away while trying to climb into the 241st yard with Sent. You had to be a monkey and be able to fly up 15 metre high poles to go painting with TFP. I had first met him that same year while spending time in New York. Besides doing a number of pieces with him, he also introduced me

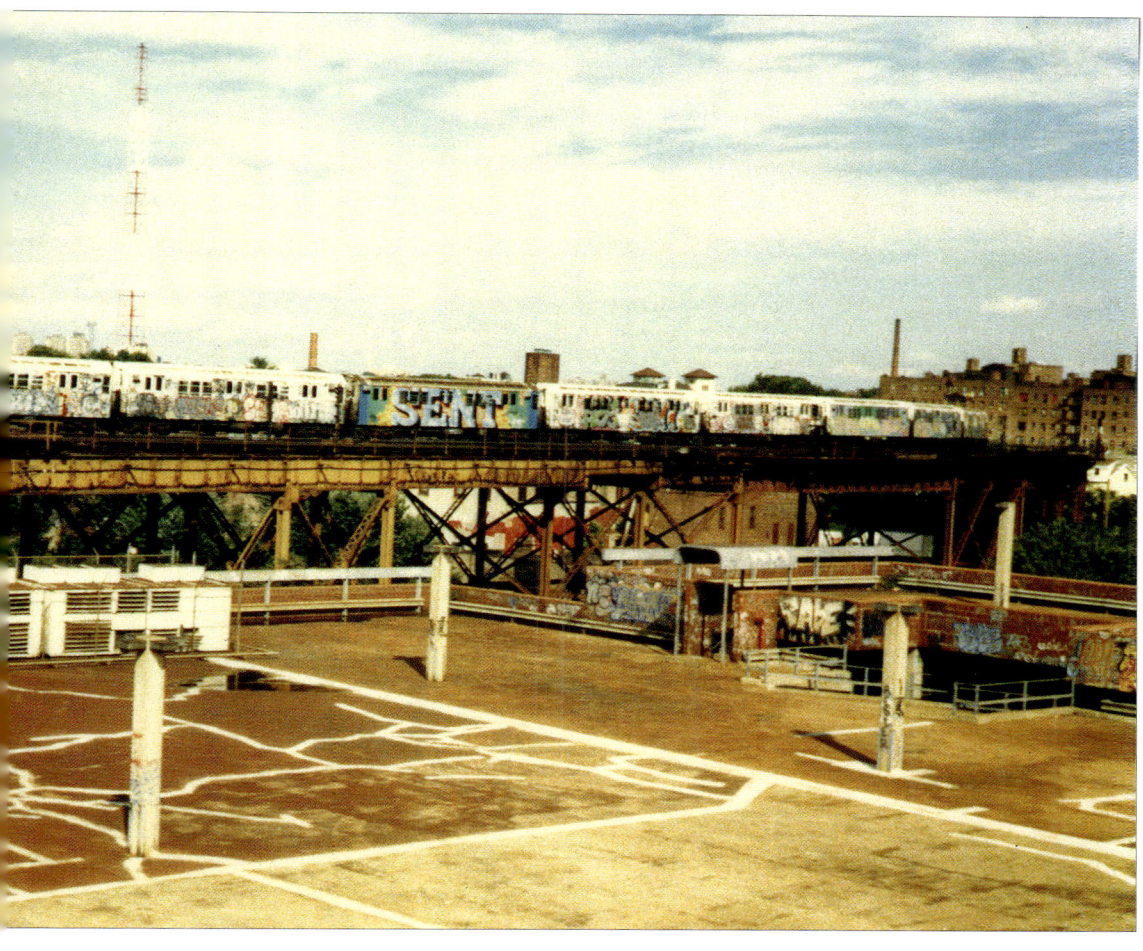

— Milk

NYC LINK
—

Pure –TFP / New York City
>

I met Milk via Sento, when he came to NYC in 1991, and we painted together while he was here, so when I decided to visit Germany in the Winter of 1992 I called him up, and while I was there I also met Cemnoz and painted with him. The Summer of that same year I decided to move to the Netherlands and that's where I hooked up with Ces 53, Gasp, Pone, Delta, Zedz, Reaze and Set and painted quite a bit with them as well. Somewhere in the Summer of 1995 I moved to Germany and since Milk lived in Munich I called him up and we started painting and hanging out together. Sent had visited me a couple times in Holland as well as Germany so we all got together to do productions and had a lot of fun, linking up with people like Fume and Ces and Shame as well as the Italian guys.

In 96' I went to a Jam in Bologna and painted together with Stand, Pane, Aser, and a bunch of the Rome Zoo. Sento had already been out to Italy to paint but this was my first time painting there, and we had a blast. I also made it out to Rome with Gasp and Set a few years later. We formed a pretty tight unit of people who were all really talented and just cool people to hang with. The TFP connection is probably the strongest around, with Milk first, followed by guys like Ces 53 and Stand who painted a lot with Sento directly. Then there is Spain… and that's Kami! He's the man, he lived with Sento in NYC and I flew out there to meet Noah who was painting at a Jam and we did many pieces…we painted every night it seems. Pocho and Nova were also rocking with us and we had a really good time with them in Madrid on that trip.

All in all I think that TFP is about people who are really pushing style and getting funky with it, that's what Butch 2, Case and Sento are all about

All in all I think that TFP is about people who are really pushing style and getting really funky with it, that's what Butch 2, Case and Sento were/are all about, but you have to be cool first, style comes second, because if you are not cool, but have style, who really wants to paint with you anyways?

That's my take on it, and having people who are better than you around will always push you to get better and make your impact that much more direct. My man Noah is a good example of that. I taught him a lot and Sento saw to it that he got his thing rock shockin' in the pocket! That's the way to go, and a lot of the European connection ran with it as well, people like Stand and Ces 53 seem to have picked up on the TFP vibe pretty hard, going for broke with their stuff and trying new things as they develop their art. Of all the crews I have run with I'd say TFP and AOK are the main two for me, no disrespect to anybody else I am down with, but the connection within the two crews is really tight, those are good peoples, they have mad styles and a lot of good stories to tell for years to come.

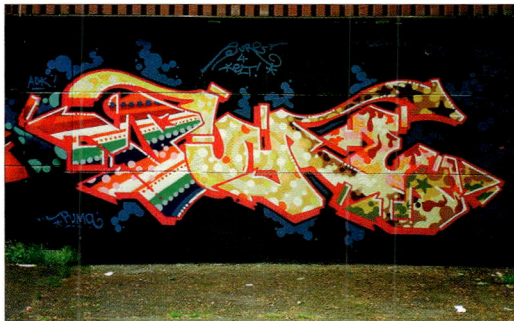

Pure –TFP in Hamburg   — Pure

---

to the music of Black Sabbath, Led Zeppelin and Rock in general. That was the sort of music New York's Graffiti movement was rooted to – not Hip Hop. Pure came to visit me in Munich in '92 and ended up staying in Europe for over ten years. His style influenced many writers on this side of the Atlantic. As the travelling expanded to even further locations throughout the 90's, new friendships formed and new members joined the group. There was also a constant flow of visitors to New York and at one point writers from Europe were responsible for larger part of the damage on the NY subway system. New entries to the crew were, to name a few, Delta from Amsterdam, Mason from Dortmund, Kami from Spain, Noah from New York, Mickey from Holland and Stand from Rome. They all added their own flavour to the group, stylistically and personally for they are all unique characters that stood out in this Graffiti game. There it was, a quarter of a century after its formation in New York, the letters TFP appeared on trains and walls all over the world. If you'd like to go way back in time, I recommend reading the book *A Bronx Childhood* by Fuzz, the founding father of the group. Looking back, it was an extraordinary experience. Something you can hardly recapture with words. The adrenalin, the moments of pure joy, excitement, the trust, the hospitality, the pain, the fear, all those countless stories that you could only tell to a chosen few and that only true writers can fully appreciate. No matter if I paint one or fifty trains a year, I remain a writer at heart and I am proud to have been a part of this phenomenon from an early day on. I have met some very special people over the years, who are my closest friends to this day. Between us, a bond built by the love of our lives "Graffiti" and three little letters: TFP

Atome –TFP / Sydney
>

The 90's were definitely a crazy time for us. (TFP International crew) My love for, fascination of, and addiction to, travelling and graffiti Writing was enabling me to see the world like few would or could. I fell into graffiti much the same way as most kids do, but through a series of

circumstances and the desire to see the world I started travelling in the early 90's. From that point, it was definitely on. New York was always going to be somewhere I would go to and when I finally got there in '91 it was everything I thought it would be and more. I met a few writers here and there, painted a little and then went to Europe for a few months. It was on my return trip to New York that I met Sent. We shared stories about Europe and being from Australia, we spoke a lot about 'the land down under'. There was a lot of goofing around before we actually even painted. In fact we hadn't even been introduced to each other by our 'names'. We shared a kindred spirit and that became the start of a very active and memorable chapter in our lives. We stayed in contact and in many ways we tried to travel the globe together. At this same time, the Hip Hop scene in Europe was exploding and with that, some of us were lucky to have friends in the right places. Suddenly all the talk of travelling together was very real, and once it started it became something we certainly looked forward to more and more as the years went on. We would sit around laughing and saying "let's go to Italy, let's drive to Prague, if we get to Belgium tonight we'll be back by……" I mean it was surreal in thought but very real in that it was all happening. It was an amazing lifestyle. We were all from different countries so travelling around Europe was something exciting for all of us on different levels. Sometimes we wouldn't even finish what we had started and sometimes we wouldn't even start… but each and every time we had a laugh. It wasn't until Milk and I were being interviewed by the NY Times in the mid 90's that I really thought that 'a lot' more people were taking notice of our trips than us and our friends. Keep in mind, we certainly weren't out there broadcasting our travels, but in saying that, a decade of travelling around Europe and New York was always going to attract attention, eventually. By the mid 90's, we were pretty tight. We would certainly go out of our way to meet up and go to places we hadn't been to or hop to a city to see some friends along the way, and this continued throughout the decade that was the 90's. As for the crew… TFP is still alive and although the travelling has certainly slowed down, the friendships and memories are as fresh as the paint we were throwing.

Holland and the U.S.: exchange writers

Mickey–TFP / Groningen
>

Until 1991 I mainly bombed in the Netherlands. My first meeting with an International TFP member was in 1991 when I met Milk at a jam in Munich. It was not such a good way to meet... he remembered my name because I had crossed a *Milk* piece in 1990 in Rotterdam thinking it said *Mick*. My International connection with the crew started during my first visit to NYC. In 1992 the Groninger Museum organised the exhibition "Coming From The Subway". Here I got to meet some legendary New York artists like Lady Pink, Blade, Quik, Dondi, Zephyr etc. Sar TMB mentioned me to Iz The Wiz, president of TMB, who wrote me a personal invitation to come visit New York.
In '93 I met Sach TMB in Groningen and he also invited me to come visit. So I did. Sach, Iz and Sar were true gentlemen, showing me the good life in the city back than... I remember NewLots yard on a hot Summer night and uncountable amounts of pizza slices, American accents and more spray paint than we could empty. We did a lot of beautiful work together. I cherish these times, and I'm grateful for getting this opportunity from artists I always looked up to.
KingKaseII put me down with TFP in '93/ early '94... I wrote TMB-TFP proudly. It was a definite honour to be put down in two of NYC's oldest existing crews ...even though TFP was not yet fully concrete to me, because I didn't know anyone from the crew. I returned many times to New York between '93 and '95 to represent my name and to enjoy Hip Hop and graffiti culture in a deep way. I was young and eager to get up and I met many other

writers, some of whom were also (or used to be) down with both TMB and TFP. But TFP became most real to me when I met mister Sento The Great. And through this connection I met most of the others that were down with the crew in NYC/Europe/ Australia. New York in the early 90's was

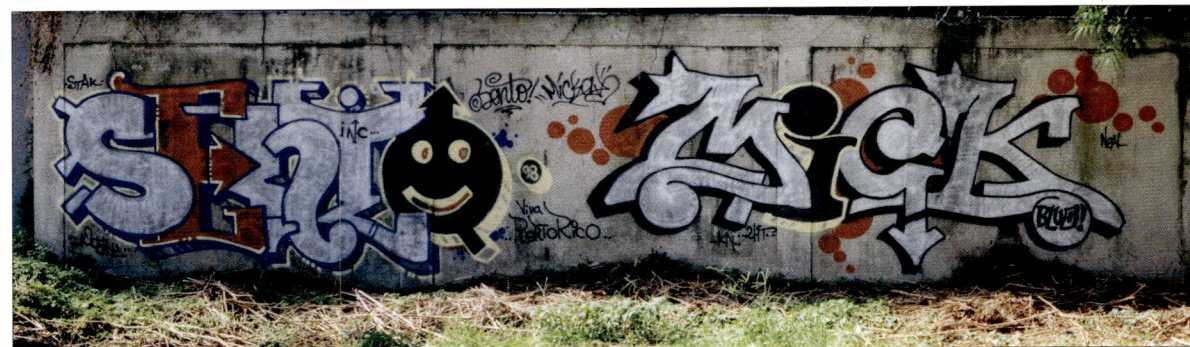
Sento and Mickey, *Viva Portorico*   — Mickey

very very very cool. It was in the days before the broken windows theory (and way before the war on terror). Denkins was the mayor and graffiti was not a big political or judicial issue like it is today. You could paint just about anything, even handball courts in the park were still painted. I went around the city and the boroughs, painting basically every day. But New York to me was so much more than graffiti. The city itself with it's buildings, traffic, subway system, different smells, the crazy heat in the Summer, the crazy cold in the Winter, its people and culture(s), Spanish food and pizza, the sneaker stores and nail salons. All kinda things we didn't have back home. I bought a zillion pairs

of Hip Hop earrings and Fila sneakers. In NYC Hip Hop was already part of daily life back than. It was the start of the commercialisation era of Hip Hop. I remember the FunkmasterFlex show on Friday night, Hot 97 pumping Hip Hop all day... I was taping radio shows like a madman. And there were The Rock Steady Crew Anniversary parties at Amsterdam Avenue where I was introduced to Afrika Baambataa, dj Kool Herc and got down with Zulu Nation. In Holland Hip Hop was still an underground subculture.

– TMB – TFP:
Two of NYC's oldest crews still existed in the 90's. TMB was the first I was officially inaugurated into. It made a difference in my graff career. Thanks to TMB (and Lady Pink) I was able to explore the city from the inside out, instead of being a tourist. Going into the late 90's-early 2000's, I lost contact with the leaders of the crew due to developments in life. With all due

respect to the early members, I have to admit I do not know that much about the early history of TFP crew going back to the 70's. It was a different time with different people in the game. When I started writing in the early-mid 80's TFP to me was one of the legendary crews I read about in books just like CIA, UA, TC5 etc. In the early 90's in my opinion European graffiti developed itself faster than it did in NYC. By putting some of Europe's best and most hardcore writers down with TFP, Sento brought a new vibe back to New York. As he also brought a certain style and class to Europe by uniting writers of that level in TFP. In the mid-late 90's being in New York became more and more a TFP-thing to me. Except for legendary all-time president Kase2, all members were from my graff generation, and we all had the love of definite lettering styles in common. We still have. All of them are writers on the highest level possible when it comes to style and actions.

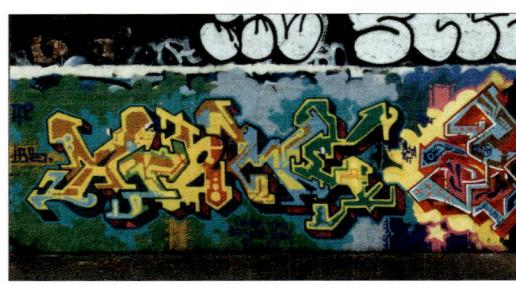
Atome from Sydney in New York   — Milk

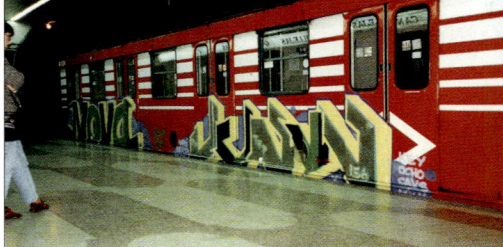
Nova and Kami – TFP, Madrid   — Milk

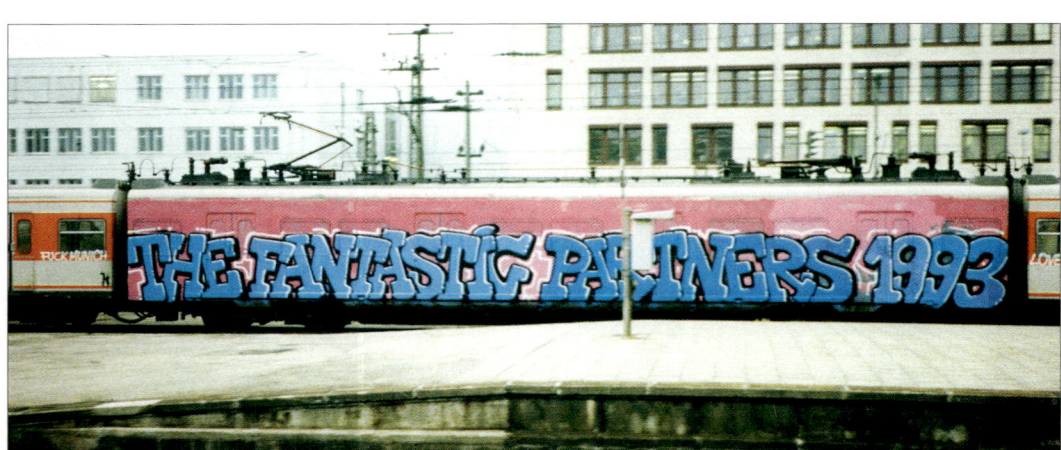
Whole-car painted in Munich by TFP's. One one side it says "Fuck Munich", on the other "Love New York"   — Milk

Sent production seen from the building on Cypress Av   — Milk

On a plane full of cans

Neon–TFP / Munich
>

I left for New York in 1988, I was 17 years old and had never set foot outside of Europe before. I went to the USA without having much of a clue. I was in search of contacts and information on Writing before even having any in Germany, at the time I wasn't really in that much contact with the guys in Dortmund or Frankfurt. I decided to go to NYC alone because I just couldn't wait anymore and I knew the only thing to do if I wanted to know more was live the experience live and direct; Don, Cemnoz and C from Dortmund had been there two years earlier and had come back to tell incredible adventures, and naturally this did nothing but increase my own desire. During that trip Gor had also painted a wall with Seen, at the time the subway had not yet become a target.

I got on the airplane with only one contact, of a writer in Brooklyn, and I brought with me all the German spray cans I had, you were still allowed to bring them on the plane then. The first weeks I was living in Queens, at an uncle's house, but as soon as he found out what I was here to do he kicked me out. I had called Clark, my contact, as soon as I had arrived, and we immediately organised to meet the next day in Brooklyn.

After having painted a wall together, he told me that in the Bronx on 238th street there was a hang-out under a bridge. You could paint even though it wasn't technically a hall of fame, those walls were illegal but generally tolerated because they were along the m-tracks, on the course of a river that nobody could see from the streets so it didn't bother anyone.

I met Sento in that spot a day later. There were many writers but I immediately started painting a wall without worrying about making friends right away; he came and introduced himself in a very mysterious way, though two days later I already knew who he was.

In a few days I got in touch with all the guys of that place. There was a lot of surprise amongst the NYC writers. They would ask what Europe was like, where it was, if there was graffiti. And when I answered that we painted and I had come to New York to learn about their styles, they couldn't believe it. I was 17, at the time I was pretty aggressive, I went directly to the Bronx to meet these people and this choice, together with my stubbornness about painting trains, seemed surreal and naïve to them. We surely each discovered new experiences, intersecting the lifestyle of two realities, that of the American ghetto and mine in Munich, light years away from one other. At the same time, my stereotypes on American writers slowly diminished.

In New York I discovered Writing was a very individual experience. Clearly the Hip Hop movement had swept over entire generations; if you think Afrika Bambaataa is true, and you feel it and it's good for you, of course you have to follow your instinct, your vocation. And Bambaataa of course influenced many people but not everyone. Graffiti was never part of Hip Hop from the beginning, maybe you hang out in the same barrio, one guy is a DJ and it's cool that he does what he does but I don't stick to it because I'm a non-stop writer and I like ACDC at the same time.

Years later in Europe we understood that all these early writers like Coco 144 weren't part of the Hip Hop movement. Hip Hop wasn't even born then, the term Hip Hop came later. I observed that the majority of writers in 1988 had nothing to do with this movement, some were rockers, Seen had rockabilly influences, Sento listened to heavy metal, Blade and many in his group were more tied to psychedelic stuff like The Doors, Uriah Hepp, many writers were involved in pacifist movements too, against Vietnam. In my opinion the hippy influence played a key role in certain styles like Blade's or Quick's, you could tell by how people painted that they came from another background. Reflecting on this I think these different inclinations could also be directly linked to the neighbourhood of origin.

Each of these styles and writers contributed to giving me

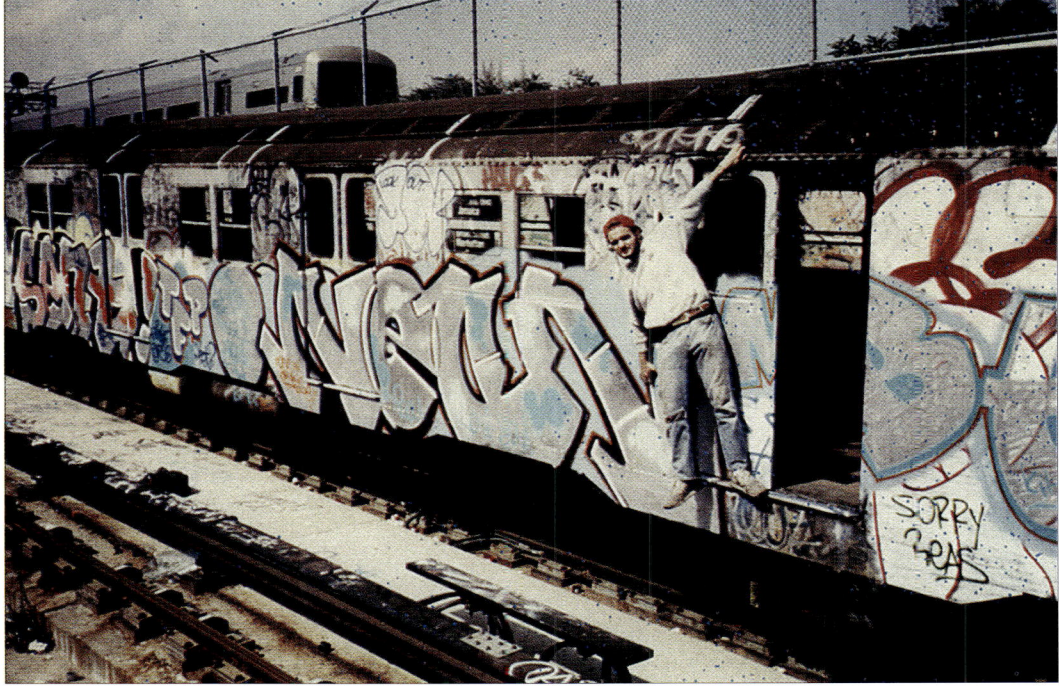

Neon along the New York tracks, 1988

— Neon

something and allowing me to understand the dynamics of the scene in New York a bit better. On my part I contributed information regarding the S-train of Munich and the first halls of fame like Flohmarkt.

But what left the locals really dumbstruck were my German spray cans. The first subway cars I painted were done with Sparvars, the incredible thing is that the paint thinners they used to buff trains worked on American paint but Sparvar resisted. So on end-to-ends the pieces on the sides would melt away and mine would stay, or else you would see my piece without the fill that was done with Krylons, only the outlines remained on the train, traced with the colours I had brought with me. Every single day was extraordinary and unforgettable. After spending a couple of nights in jail because I had been caught while doing a whole-car, I returned to Europe.

In Munich I started looking around with a totally new perspective, my point of view on Writing had drastically changed. I understood that many aspects had been overrated in Germany at the time, such as perfection and the obsession with painting technically impeccable pieces. German outlines and 3D's were rigorous, with perfectly geometric and clean lines. In New York on the other hand I discovered the flow, still a fundamental stylistic concept at twenty years' distance.

Sometimes these stylistic choices depend on the tools themselves, for example Sparvar allowed the possibility of painting with much more precision while in New York when you used a skinny on a Krylon it was the equivalent of a German semi-fat cap. The pressure of the colours was different and with Sparvar the degree of control you had was basically much higher. The tendency of being proud about being able to cut letters precisely started spreading, which is very German in mentality.

This misunderstanding tied to the Hip Hop package arrived to Germany with an autarchic name and at the beginning nobody questioned this lifestyle or even the B-boy dress code. It has to be taken into account that at 14 years of age you haven't yet developed a complete critical consciousness, we were 13, 14 years old, in full adolescence, and we sighed with admiration at the idea of skyscrapers and an elevated subway with whole-cars by Seen. Growing up you become more skeptical, you start doubting that everything you read in books or see in Hollywood movies is necessarily true, starting from *Beat*

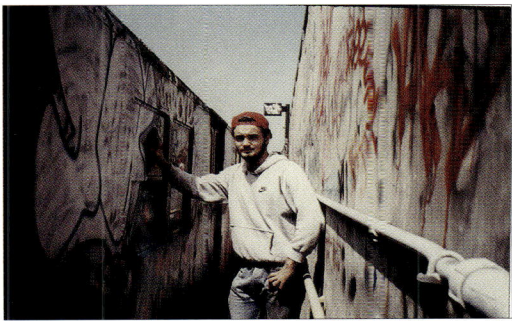

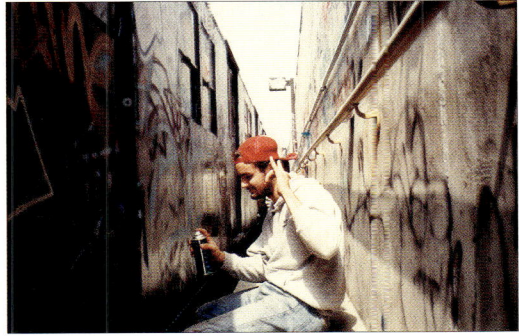

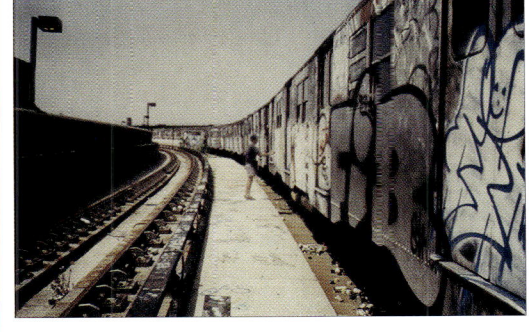

> CONTINUES ON PAGE 100

— Neon

REAL TRANSIT ARTISTS

The territorial expansion of RTA crew, first German formation to adopt strict strategies in the planning of missions on National and International railway systems

Sie –RTA / Germany
>

Real Transit Artist was a crew formed by a few writers coming from different cities of Germany during the late 80's. It was the first Intercity crew focused on the concept of travelling to paint different train systems all over the country, Europe and New York. Before RTA these kinds of missions had been achieved only by one International crew called CTK, who were the European pioneers in going over the boarders and hitting trains. But while CTK experimented this strategy a couple of times like in Munich or Copenhagen, RTA decided to do it in a systematic way, planning a sort of train bombing Risiko where they had to place their flag over every nation on the European map, organising specific missions.

This planning continued for years and it became the same goal of a few other independent writers like Mr C from Dortmund and Loomit. Everyone was travelling to discover new yards and new train systems. With them, during late the 80's, RTA bombed the whole Western part of Europe: London in '87, Stockholm in '88, Rotterdam in '88, Vienna and Switzerland in '89, Milan in '89, Belgium, France, Spain, Denmark and New York, along with almost every train system in Germany.

– ORGANISATION

RTA was organised like the navy seals, with various hierarchies amongst the writers. It was always a mission to experience. Few pioneer writers had all the information of what could happen, it was a very well-organised and precise team. The core was formed by a few writers who were the heads back then, they also tested and trained some new guys. They had to prove themselves before they could become official members. RTA was a small group, when you look at the names in the end you have like thirty of them, but it was like a maximum of six guys, maybe with a guest here and there. In the beginning every effort was spent for very detailed end-to-ends or whole-cars with a changing extension of the acronym RTA.

A Real Transit Artist end-to-end was more of a punch into the game than a series of names together, even because the sentence was often quite legible. In the end it was becoming more effective. And being more effective meant getting to a level where you could paint lines and be impressively fast, coming up with a new style wasn't the only goal. Sometimes the letters were simplified to be able to work with more blocks, more top-to-bottoms, or to be recognised next to the train lines. If you have a Wildstyle piece next to a train line it's not effective. It's better to have a piece with simple letters and do something with colours. That was the same concept followed in Dortmund where the guys used block letters to have a stunning impact while the train was leaving or arriving at the Central Station. Even the length of the names letters became somewhat fixed, it was a kind of short-name standard. Maybe there was a five-letter name in the beginning, like Prime, one of the guys who started RTA. Show had a four-letter name and She and Sid had three-letter names. For some reason the S letter became very popular at the RTA club! Of course the shorter the name, the faster you could finish it but sometimes there were combinations. Like in the beginning Ego-ism, whenever

Ego had time he would extend it. There were variations, like Rise sometimes wrote his name with a Z or with an S or other times he wrote Riser. Mens also wrote with S sometimes adding a Z-factor: Menzer.

– ORIGINS

RTA started as a circumscribed initiative during 1986, around the Hamburg area. The first impressive actions started along 1988, when a stable connection with some exponents of Munich took step. In Hamburg RTA hit the subways for the first time doing whole-cars. Through the first fanzines from Europe and NY this initiative spread all over the world and Germany was placed firmly on the map for graffiti and trains. The New York guys were like "What the fuck is going on in Europe?" when they saw all this kind of stuff. Those were probably the first images of whole-cars running across European cities and for the NY pioneers it was probably a shock to see their movement reach the trains of the old continent railway systems.

– STRATEGY

The objective was to bomb as many systems as possible. To hit them in the most effective way the Hamburg division of RTA was flexible in travelling, so they were going from one transit system to the other back and forth, and when they put it down too heavy on one they just moved onto another, waiting for the waters to cool down. But the whole yard planning was something really clean and organised, it wasn't just about going straight to the yards and destroying them. Normally the first night was spent checking the area and then the night after that was the good one. From the beginning they were using tools like timetables of train schedules, in order to know when the cleaners were coming, when the drivers were coming and at what time several trains would be running. It wasn't just about painting, it also had to do with every action

> ## A Real Transit Artist end-to-end was more of a punch into the game than a series of Names together

around them, which meant the first rule of thumb was to be safe and keep the place safe. All evidence of 'typical' vandalism was consciously avoided, as if RTA was a kind of ghost-presence that didn't leave traces besides the paintings. The few decisions relating to 'vandalism' were only done in the name of visibility: to let the pieces run. For example for some trains in Hamburg in the beginning of the 90's, RTA took out all the interior lights. So if the train ran in the early morning you could take a photo and not have the distraction of the light from inside. So those guys just took out the lights and used them in their private homes.

Then tagging started to be considered when the pieces

weren't running, so in some cases other train car windows were just filled with paint, and of course the railway company wouldn't put these cars in traffic. Indeed they were also thinking about the surroundings.

Once the job was done the session continued by taking photos of the trains. Considering that besides the subway system, RTA often bombed trains of unknown regions, where the possibilities of seeing the pieces running were very limited, this second game of 'capturing' became 50% of the whole process. Almost no one had considered train Writing before in these spots they were painting. In some cities there wasn't even a scene yet so try to imagine a group of people from all over Germany joined together reaching lost spots to paint a train. In this sense it was really ground-breaking stuff.

RTA was focalising on this, considering the whole area as a playground, but then more and more people showed up; so there was this situation where you had to deal with the government but also with local competitors. The yard situation got out of control once the scene started growing, from world wide you'd go back to local, preserving your yards and taking care of your area. Competition was the first rule to learn, comparable with the record label dynamics: first there were few labels and people were connected over a distance through a record label, then more and more labels showed up and the new ones concentrated first on their surroundings, then maybe only on their city and then maybe only on their block.

– TEAM WORK

RTA organised missions where one person did the sketching and the others finished the job. Usually there was one guy tracing letters and someone good for the background or for the characters. There were never ambitious people that aspired to be individually noted, to have their name up. It was more like a big goal to reach with the whole team, where everybody played a specific role.

Somehow militarism became the model, where the captain would say "You stay here and make sure nobody is coming from the back". If you're a soldier, you have to do it. This is how you can do something, if you only have crazy egos, then you're limited. Sometimes the experiences captains of RTA organised actions with new recruits in order to paint something bigger like thematic end-to-end's or coloured whole-cars. For example every person was given a specific task: tracing the outline, filling in, painting the background, surveying the yard and helping the others in the collective act.

The Stone Age Kids were another crew from Munich that treated the name of the team as something real important. This crew was more of an open group with changing guests, where everybody used the same name in different combinations. This example from Bavaria was really important, they showed that forgetting the ego was possible and that when train writers joined together they could achieve more, planning impressive whole-cars with backgrounds or details, like in a hall of fame.

– SYSTEMS

In the beginning the long-distance systems were not so interesting, it was mainly S-trains and subways. The Munich subway and the Frankfurt subway were not

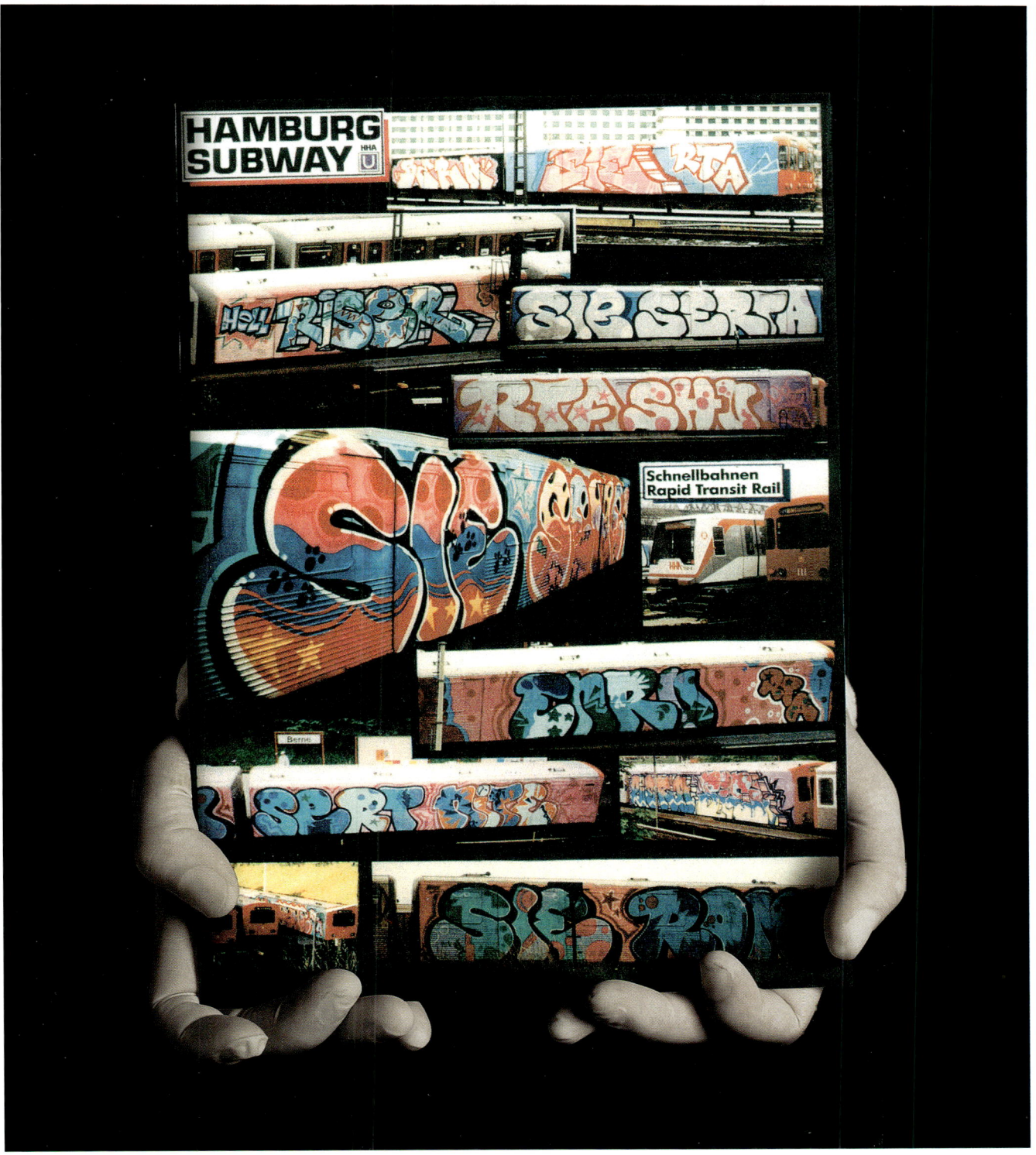

ON THE RUN HAMBURG SPECIAL

A focus on subway car productions by RTA crew in Hamburg. Photo from On the Run fanzine primary bulletin of information for German train-bombing in the early 90's

— On the Run

considered since they only ran in tunnels. But in Hamburg the subway runs above ground, sometimes on elevated tracks, so of course it was a great opportunity to see the pieces running. Over there the system was pretty efficient anyways, they were able to send every painted train directly to the buff. Sometimes you saw the best whole-cars just disappear and you never saw them again! So the local division of RTA started painting panel pieces while the trains were in service and running, it was the best way to have them run.

Of course everyone was studying the different dynamics of every system. In the beginning, besides some types of subway, the classic orange S-trains were the main target along with the Hamburg blue S-trains. But then they figured out almost every S-train or local transport system in Germany, discovering that for instance Stuttgart and Frankfurt shared the same scenario.

So it was a matter of understanding how the X system worked and then directly visiting that region and doing the job. Of course it also worked in other countries but

with difficult steps. Analysing the context and the surroundings is a bomber's prerogative and when it comes to train-bombing during the early years it was useful to understand why in some cities specific targets were being painted while others were being literally ignored. Sometimes it's even part of the local tradition to follow some systems instead of others, like the red S-trains in Copenhagen or the Berliner-U and S-Bahn.

The more RTA were into writing across Germany and foreign cities, the more they focused on hitting every kind of system, just because you didn't have this all-city situation you could reach in New York. It was impossible to imagine that all our trains could be painted, they were cleaned so fast, so instead of uselessly trying to demolish a specific one, the crew concentrated more on the idea of target collection and discovery.

Sometimes you had the situation where trains got bumped so much they ran painted for a while, for example when RTA discovered a local train which was a little bit more connected to the area they lived in. Why

leave your city to go 500km away when you have your own system? Even if it wasn't a closed system like the S-trains, these local line cars ended up running painted and looking a little bit like the New York subway. So a few years later a collective project began called Silver Storm where several key-people got connected and planned a massive attack in a short time frame. One week later almost every car of the Silver trains had a piece running, it naturally set a precedent as every writer then wanted to hit that target. These kinds of trains were used by the DB all over Germany, sometimes they were used for long distances but mainly they were saved for regional networks. They were utilised nationwide so DB used to exchange the cars to fill in a void in the system that could even be 300km away.

So in the beginning of the 90's some of those trains were imported from Dortmund, and Vola, Sak, Rio pieces were running in Mainz. But this came later, when the peak of the crew wasn't so high anymore and RTA began to take part in European graffiti history.

MSN
VIM
MOA
ALL

A pact between crews that aimed
at hitting every North European
railway system. A union of forces
that multiplies their firepower
in the 90's, creating a solid, ideal
and heterogenous group: MSN
and VIM – MOAS – ALL

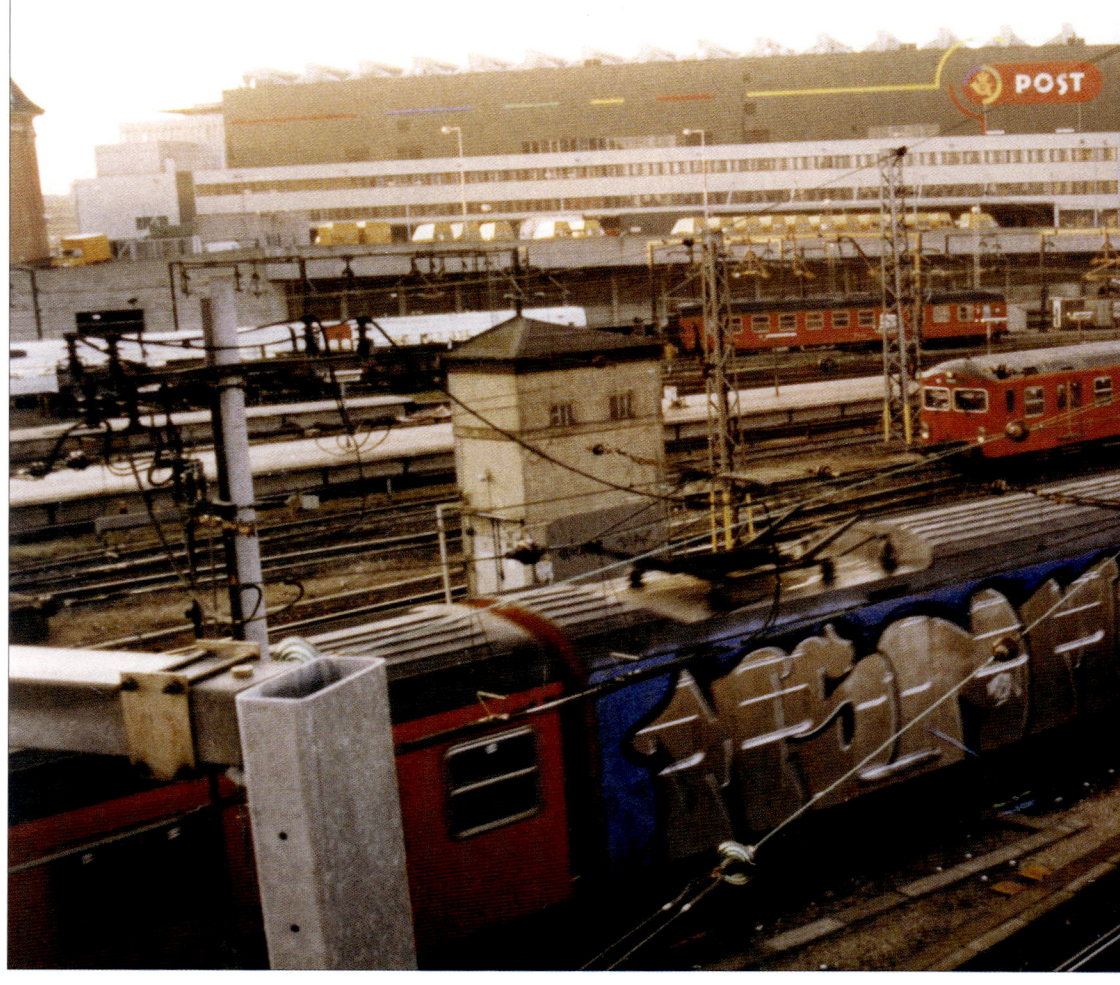

MSN and MOAS executed at Copenhagen Central Station, 1996

**Reaze –MSN / The Netherlands
with Mellie –MSN / The Netherlands
>**

I n 1990 a new crew called *Lazy Insane Lizards* was
erected in Utrecht. LIL consisted in five prolific writers from the city; Bisar, Eror, Mellie, Reaze and Sort.
Basically these guys were the people Mellie painted
with. Each person had his own characteristic humour
and style which was more or less inspired by guys like Ces
53, Shave, Pone and by New York writers with a similar,
cynical view on style like Reas, Sane and Ghost. LIL also
had a lot in common though: attitude, bombing, stealing
tendencies and having fun. In the beginning people really didn't get it, most of the pieces were so ugly; white,
organic, blubbery outlines instead of straight black ones,
but somehow it had an appeal because all of a sudden in
Europe people started biting it.
All of the LIL guys used to meet at the 'hang-out', meeting each other there or at school. Each of them had already been writing for a few years: Bisar was mostly
known for robbing toys and painting track sides; Sort
was a local and profound thief; Eror was a psychopathic
weirdo bus-bomber (because there were no trains in his
town) while Mellie was considered an 'old school' street
bomber. He was about the same age as the rest, but was
hanging out with the older guys like Shave, Camel, Tom
32, Rhythm 62 and Thrash 23.
Reaze on the other hand was a n***a with attitude, yet
he quickly understood that trains were the way to get up
quick in a quick, respectable manner. His style wasn't as
developed as Eror's or Mellie's, but he gave a lot of positive energy to the crew: "Every yard is cool" he would
say on a regular basis.
Within the first few months of the crew's existence, Sort
got kicked out because of not having painted enough
trains while the four remaining members, as LIL, bombed
cars non-stop from 1990 to 1993. The 'official' kick-off
was a whole-train in Belgium which for Eror was also his

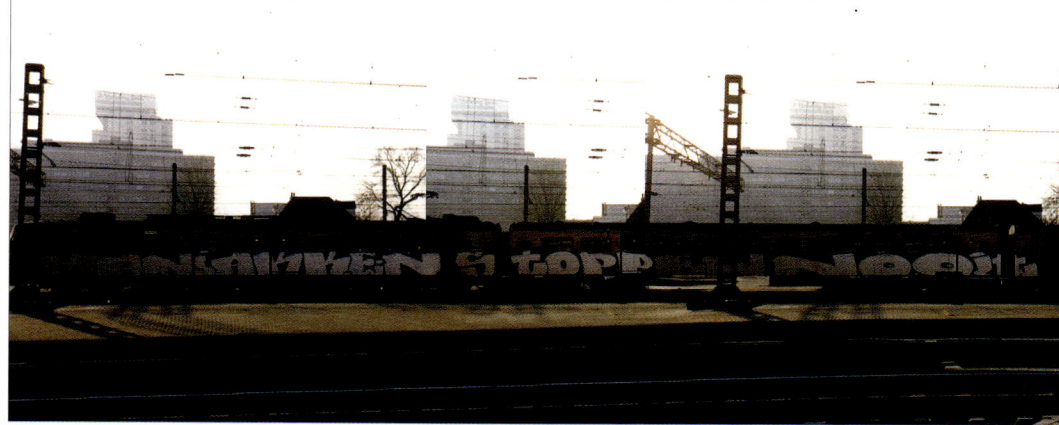

A double end-to-end done in the Utrecht yard, probably the 20th hit within the last four weeks —Reaze
                                                                                                  — Reaze

first train piece (a one-man whole-car). In 1991 these
four one-man whole-cars, painted with skinny-capped
Flexa's and Tintra's, looked pretty ugly. On that particular mission, the entire village's inhabitants chased
us after they saw us taking photos the next morning...
imagine running through a small village at 7 a.m.on a
Sunday morning! Luckily none of us got busted that time.
It's weird how such a traumatic experience ends up as a
couple of lines of text 18 years later.
Another remarkable night was bombing all of Amsterdam's subway stations with black, gold and chrome paint
along with Set and Beat 53 on Queen's Night 1993, the
Dutch festival held in honour of the Queen's birthday.
The hundreds of panels, whole-cars, tags and throw-
ups – a non stop hit on the 'Banana's – the Dutch national train system - was actually sponsored by the
authorities as the whole crew was riding for free with
their college student travel passes. The whole bunch of

us non-representative, drug-smoking youngsters, willing to paint 24-7, travelled the whole country to discover
train yards and steal paint, a true nightmare for some.
The heat was increasing. People were getting busted and
being harassed by the cops asking them about LIL. People
were already using dozens of aliases, and there was heat
on all of them. One day a writer wanted to test the vandal squad to see if they were really focused on busting
writers. So he phoned them saying he was going to the
yard that same night. When he arrived to the yard, he got
busted immediately. So definitely yes, the cops were focused and for some very unknown and weird reason they
thought they had busted Reaze. Besides the heat, we felt
like doing something 'new'. Eror came up with the phrase
Maniakken Stoppen Nooit - Maniacs Never Stop - and we
would write it beside our pieces and tags. Not necessarily to show that we were a crew, but to show our shared
mentality and state the fact that we were unstoppable. In

The German contingent

Fume – MSN / Düsseldorf
>

One of the first, tight nodes of connection between German and Dutch writers got sealed the year an event was organised in Bruhl, a small city close to Köln. Even if the happening had to be an important opportunity to spread the culture, we were all there for one goal only: racking paint. Once we met over there, Shame from Geldrop, Ces from Rotterdam, Rio and me started a strong partnership aimed at painting trains. A couple of years later Reaze from Utrecht joined us, he was already down with LIL's, a very active crew from the Netherlands. With him, the German commuter trains, Rotterdam subway and NL 'bananas' became the new designated targets. Once LIL reached the top of visibility, they strangely broke up and at that point Eror founded MSN. Even if at its origins

it began as Nooit Stopping Maniac, it soon became known as MSN... the same words just switched around. MSN formed by Eror, Mellie, Reaze, Bizar and a few others, started taking in the best bombers from North Germany and Holland.

Besides this strong connection, an affiliation slowly developed with some guys in Finland: during the early 90's, writers like Spy, Egs, Poe and Hick (RIP) were travelling a lot and hitting trains from Prague to Belgium and the UK. Egs later moved to London and together with Nema they started a strong series of burners on UK commuter trains: crazy letters and psychedelic colours. Nema knew of impressive outside yards in working places, where on Sundays from 12 until 3 it was possible to paint one man whole-cars in full colour, simply unbelievable with regards to style. Then, once Cake from MBC crew had moved

from Helsinki to Köln in the early 90's, the Finnish division of MSN finally had a stable spot in Germany where they could stay. His flat became a melting pot for Scandinavians and Germans, hosted by this crazy guy with one dreadlock in the front of his head – a great character. He was a fabulous partner in crime for many writers.

December, January and the whole Winter months spent in the frozen yards of Europe were dramatic, they were tangible proof of tenacity! Missions to close and virgin countries like Belgium started to be planned, where earlier writers like Ces had totally demolished the system of beautiful green commuter trains. Due to this network, full-colour pieces were running, intersected with burners by other strong crews and connections, like Nug and the Scandinavian Vandals In Motion. Vim crew was the first to be connected to the

Dortmund guys, like Shark and Zodiak. Together they did whole-cars during the Amsterdam boom, when Nug met Reaze. Once the Swedish writer got incorporated in MSN, the whole Northern European bomber scene closed circle: VIM crew from Sweden, MOAS from Denmark, the ALL's in Norway and MSN became part of the same network in which writers were usually writing crew names of others and vice versa. Some of those were literally non-stop bombers, but among the others *Monsters Of Art* were more than machines. No one could have ever gotten close to them neither in content or numbers. No one-man army like Chintz or Jon from Rome, because even as crew they continued year by year to recruit the most active bombers of the newest generations. The impact that MOAS had on the scene was like a bomb that smashed everything.

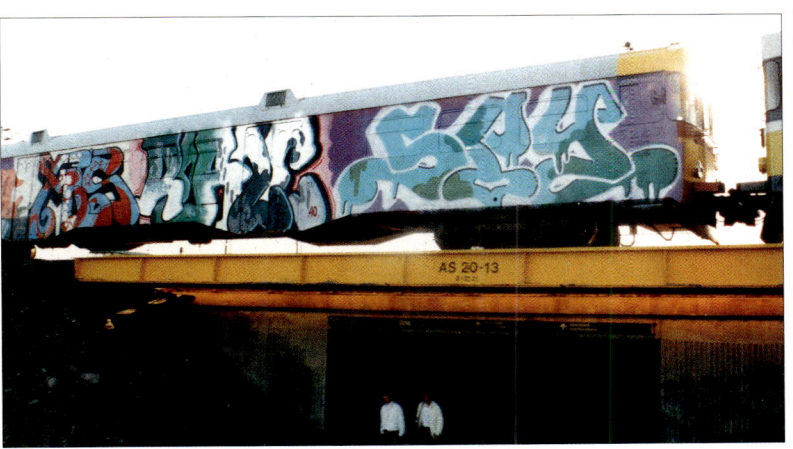

— *Reaze*

1992 Reaze went to Germany after talking to Ces 53, who had seriously thrashed some trains there, and met Fume, amongst others. Soon LIL was bombing with him almost every weekend. Fume had a car, which made bombing a lot more comfortable and successful. We would use our free train passes and go to Germany to visit him, or he would come over to Utrecht and we would bomb there. After a while we would meet at the border and go to Belgium. And back then, believe me, there was nothing, 'nada', 'geen' graffiti in Belgium – not from locals, not from foreigners. Just a few Germans, Dutch, and occasionally a few Parisian writers had been there. Belgium was heaven back then. Later, after an infamous raid on Milk and Fume, and another on some toys in the prior months, we decided not to go anymore: cops were hard on writers there, plus it became pretty obvious that the Dutch and Belgian Vandal Squads were communicating. It didn't make a difference anymore to write there or here in Holland, because the yards were equally hot.

As Fume couldn't become part of LIL, we asked him to write MSN. That guy was, and 20 years later still is, a hardcore bomber. Fume's participation was a reason to make MSN an 'official' crew.

Before all of that, and even before MSN and LIL crews were founded, Reaze and Mellie were doing some trains with other guys like Sorce, Colt, Deal, Vandel and Taser. Suddenly they were blown away from a very unsuspected angle. Within one Summer about thirty serious full-colour, Wildstyle end-to-ends with a never-before-seen style popped up by our friends Shave, Camel and Rhone – WOW crew. Reaze can remember getting a phone call by Mellie; "Yo, did you hear that? These guys did mad shit last night." Reaze went to the station and waited there for the train to pull in. Within half an hour it did. He almost died as it felt like all those panels he did –which looked shit anyway– were absolutely nothing compared to these. WOW were a crew specifically formed for trains by the same members that formed the *Bomb Steady*

> CONTINUES ON PAGE 56

FULLCOLOUR

REAZE

I remember Spy saying this was the first coloured whole-car in Finland. That night we got chased by a mcr.... we were just wasting time hanging around in front of the pieces when suddenly he showed up out of nowhere.

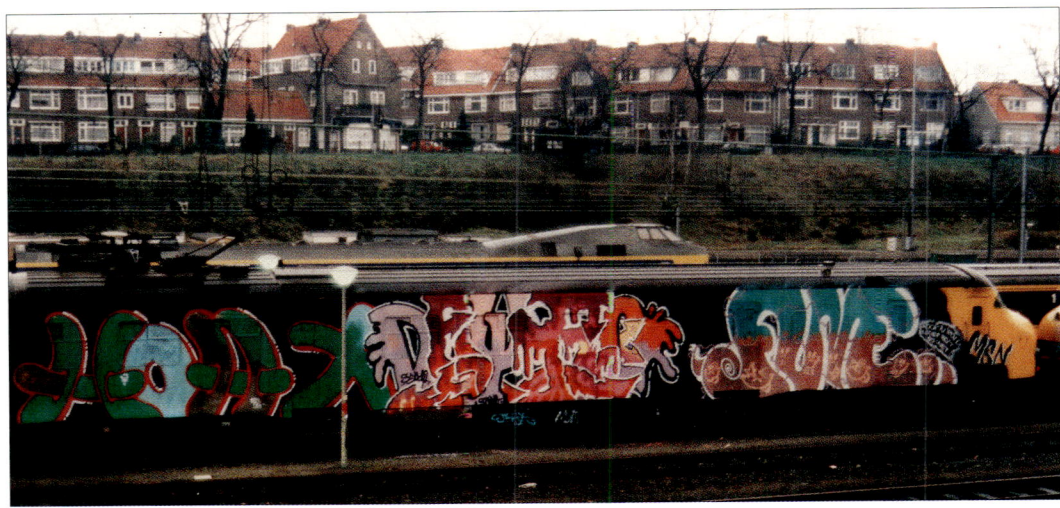

> CONTINUES FROM PAGE 55

Vandals (BSV), a crew founded by Shave. This sounded like a wake-up call. Mellie remembers: "I'd been sneaking in and out of that yard so many times, putting up tags with a shoe polisher or a marker, but I couldn't figure out how such a big group of guys could just go in with all these bags of paint and stay in there for hours, creating these full-colour Wildstyle double end-to-ends with B-boy characters on top. I mean the rumour was that they brought their own ghetto blaster and had an assistant to roll their joints. That shit just blew my mind, from that day on I was just focused on the fact that I would be either in or out, jumping over the fence and doing my thing, or stay a hall of fame toy doomed to rot in legal hell forever. We had to get organised." So when LIL started the only thing they could do was fucking work hard. They couldn't compete in terms of style, but they definitely could when it came to endurance and quantity, getting better with time, developing an identity. Some of the members of WOW won't like to hear it, but that first Summer in '91 was their best ever and this debut was so full of impact that it never reached that level again. Around one year later, Shave WOW and Reaze LIL started hitting trains together. Actually Reaze worked on an outline Shave had drawn. This was again some 'oil on the fire' as a new connection started and ended with Shave and Camel as part of MSN crew.

MSN was taking over the trains nationally, plus a big share of subways in Amsterdam and therefore dominated the whole Dutch scene. Combine this with some hardcore fuckers like Fume, Nug, Egs and Spy ... and soon the crew established itself in Europe.

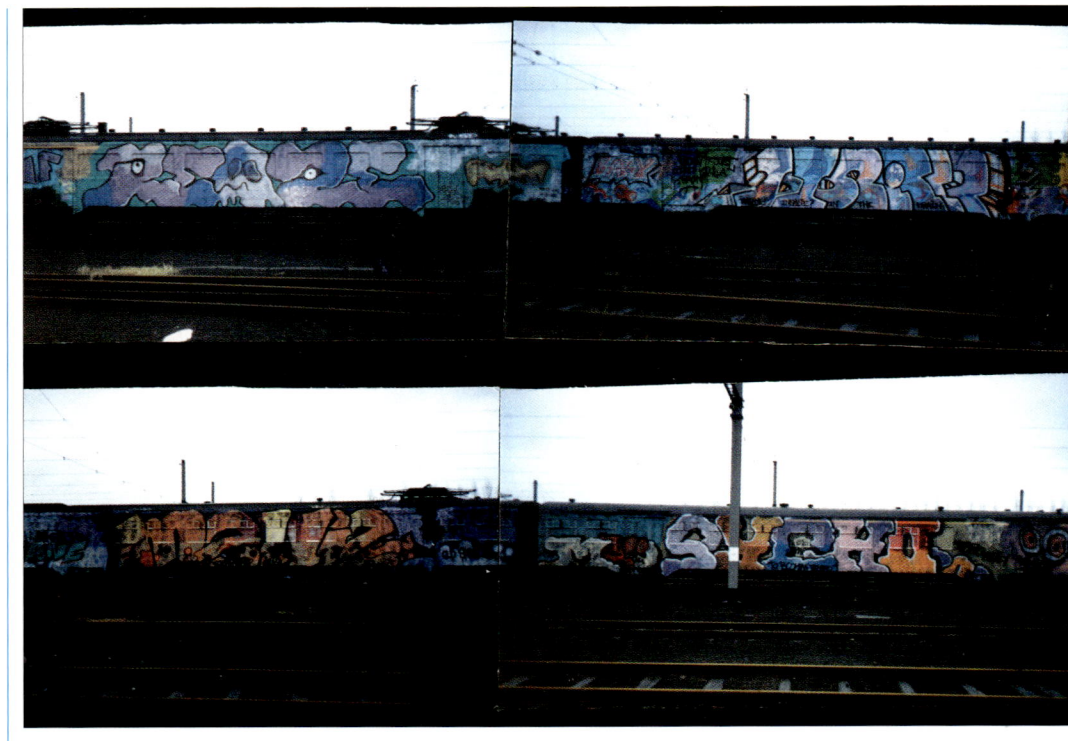

Whole-train in Belgio, 1991   — Reaze

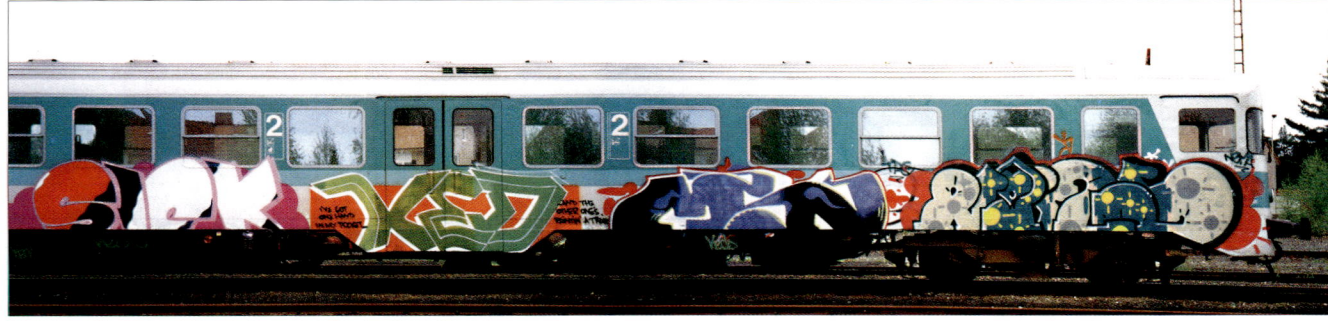

Sick, Ked, MSN, Nims. Germania   — Mark Todt

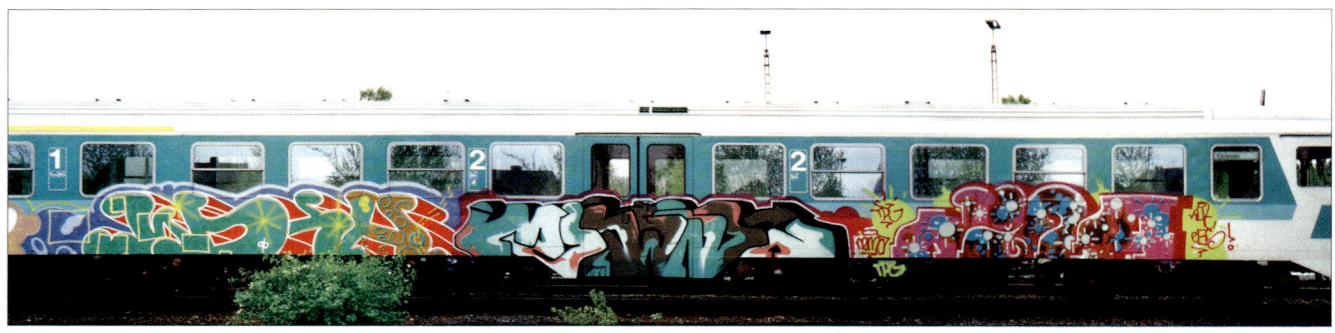

Wodka, Mellie, Nims. Germania   — Mark Todt

OFFICIAL PLAYERS

REAZE
When MSN was in full force the members were Eror, Mellie, Reaze, Shave, Camel, Serie, Line, Wodka, Sprite, Ces 53, Set, Gasp, Pone, Delta, Mir e Mickey from the Netherlands; Fume from Germany; Egs, Spy and Cake from Finland, Nug from Sweden

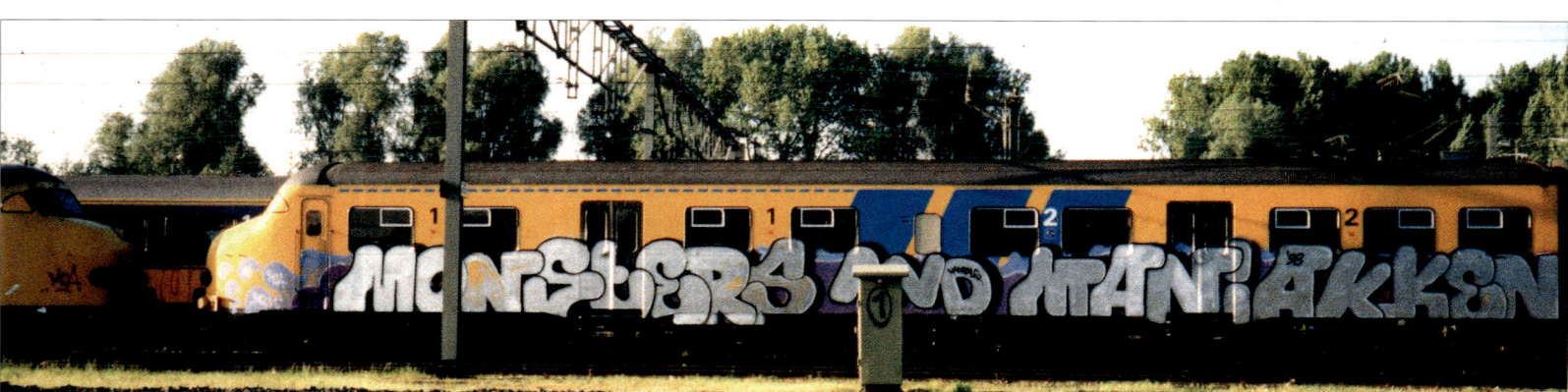

Making ourselves not very sympathetic to normal people by writing the first word of the MOA and MSN crews combined — Reaze   — Reaze

ALL CITY WRITERS   NETWORK
REPORT

INTERNATIONAL
CREWS

MSN &
THE VIMOALL

57

The Northern iron belt

**Reaze –MSN / The Netherlands
with Mellie –MSN / The Netherlands**
>

It must have been in '92 or '93 that Mellie went to Stock-holm and Oslo. Inspired by the stuff we'd seen in *Bomber Magazine*, the crew was keen to broaden our horizons and it seemed like Scandinavia was the next step. Vandals In Motion crew – VIM – was into trains too and the first connections took form by regular post and telephone. Mellie remembers: "After a few polite postcards I was in-vited to come over by Kaos from the VIM crew. When I arrived at Stockholm central station, a crew of ten soldiers including Kaos, Nug and this guy Hen from Madrid picked me up. First we went drinking and exchanging valuable information, and then we got to a spot, which was well-known for its raids by the police. Kaos told me not to wor-ry, *because we got the beer, man!* This night was the first of many; I went through a variety of burglaries, bar-fights and sleeping in subway tunnels for twelve days."
When Mellie came back, he had a pile of photos and was full of stories; "These guys are as fucked up as we are!"

> ## The year after Mellie visited Scandinavia, Nug came over here and together we went to Germany and Copenhagen; this whole International bombing network became a standard

That was another thing: we were very competitive with each other and with the rest of Holland's crews. This competitive attitude served us well. There were times when MSN would split up and meet again later during the night. For example me and Mellie were going to one yard, Serie and Line to another, and later the four of us would meet in a third yard. Sometimes we would paint (or at least try to paint), two or three times a day for a whole year. So the year after Mellie visited Scandinavia, Nug came over here and together we went to Germany and Copenhagen; this whole International bombing network became a standard and we actually did the European In-ter-Rail too. Serie and I met up with the infamous MOAS from Copenhagen, Mellie and Line went to Switzerland and Berlin... it was funny trying to explain to your par-ents or schoolmates how come you were down with all these foreign homies. Imagine meeting up with a bunch of Scandinavian writers at eight o'clock in the morning somewhere in Germany, having a Schulten Brau, talking about who did what and where that Summer. This travel-ling introduced us to other graffiti cultures and it was a good way to meet friends: Nug and Egs from Helsinki got into MSN in those years. Today they still bomb and are part of the crew.
Besides that, pretty soon we noticed we lacked caution when abroad. As soon as we crossed the border, whether it was Germany, Belgium, Copenhagen, Paris, London, New York, wherever, we just didn't care anymore. Of course we would listen carefully to the advice of our hosts, but deep down we didn't give a fuck. In Holland most of the yards aren't remote but rather in the middle of the city. In those other countries yards were in the middle of nowhere. We can remember being in Munich painting on trains that were laid up at least twelve min-utes from any civilization. Also there was this funny idea that being caught abroad would be no problem, 'cause they'd just kick you out of the country, which was a big difference to dealing with the Vandal Squad in The Neth-erlands. We never got into any serious trouble in Holland but as we understood, you could be interrogated and ha-rassed for weeks in jail.
We all reached the sublime moment once Mins (Mon-sters Of Art – MOAS) proposed the idea of combing the

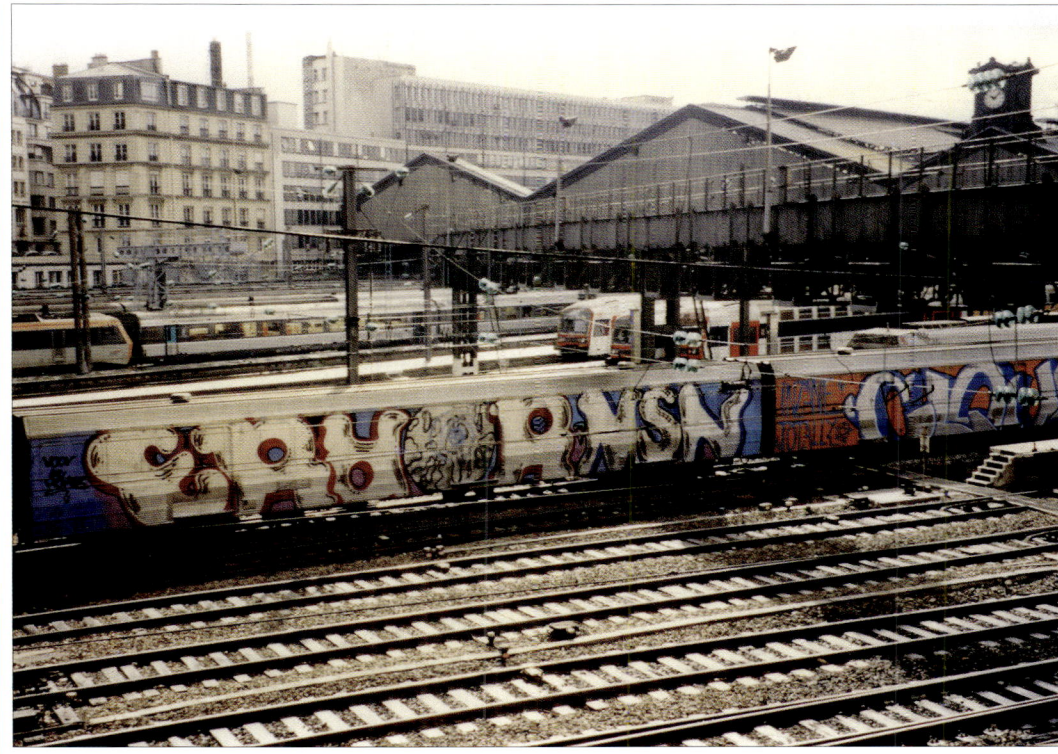

Error –MSN entering at Garde Du Nord, Paris 1997. Part of three whole–cars by MSN and SDK crews   *– Reaze*

energy, knowledge and spirit of the three most prolific train-bombing networks in Europe. VIM-MOA-MSN. The crews would remain separate in their content and form, but we would do pieces using other crew's names. MOAS would do VIM and MSN pieces, while VIM would do MSN and MOA and the same with MSN writing MOA and VIM. Seeing those three names pop up everywhere, people were stunned and we became undefeatable by anybody in the 90's: in style, in being hardcore and in quantity. We would go to Copenhagen on a regular basis for years and bomb there - whole-cars, panels, anything at night and in the day. Not that it was easy there but we just didn't care and of course we were in good hands

with Les and Mins (MOA). One night I was in Copenha-gen, chilling with Aman, Kaos, Nug of VIM crew, some ALL guys from Oslo and of course MOAS. Then suddenly somebody had the brilliant idea of doing a piece all to-gether, even if nobody had proper paint. It ended up with twelve guys walking into the yard, each one with just a couple of cans, managing to do a whole-car. Everybody was stoned and drunk as hell, just painting with a co-lour anywhere on the surface of that train. Only Aman took care of being legible. We never got a photo of this and perhaps it's a better memory than a piece itself. Of course there was only one guy we couldn't compete, and

> CONTINUES ON PAGE 100

A MATTER OF FRIENDSHIP
—

Egs –CDC, MSN / Helsinki
>

Pubblicato su Bombers mag-azine

I don't consider myself any-thing special for my personal achievements in terms of writing graffiti. I'm definitely not a king of style, a king of the line or a king of anything. The only true things I have developed through Writing on trains and walls are my friendships. When talking of Writing we immediately think of getting up, getting fame. Yes, it is the true and original motivation for Writing but at the end of the day what is fame. What does it give you? Isn't it just selfpromotional

masturbation with your ego? It's hard to imagine ourselves in a coffin with a dead self–absorbed smile; I got up, I was the king. Like other writers, I presume, I tend to live in my own fantasy world: a barbec wire wonderland. Some-times I forget that Writing, as when I started, is supposed to be fun, is supposed to be relief from our normal lives Don't get me wrong. I truly enjoy the thrills and happy moments of graffiti. My life without it would have been a tedious stay at Borings-ville. I had access to places and moments that I couldn't have experienced without being a writer. And I'm not talking about yards and tun-nels. When you live through

thrills and exhausting stress with your partner, you are testing the strength of your friendship. You are not only responsible for yourself; you also look after your friend. You never leave him behind and never drop a dime. Nev-er. Then again as time passes, we see people betray their friends. These were also the people who once swore not to drop a dime. What hap-pened? Did they get scared of their own future? Did they loose belief in their once so religious lifestyle or did they just 'grow up'? Could that happen to me? I hope not. Usually the people who say they will never stop writing give up the next year. Never say never. I'm happy to be

in MSN. For me it's not just three well–respected initials. It's proof of friendship. In my opinion I was not invited to the crew because of the quantity or the quality of my pieces. I'm not that good as a writer. I got in for my person-ality. Maniakken Stop Nooit to me represents the things in graffiti that I love: friend-ship, trust, thrills, dedication and fun. I know for a fact that one day our physical con-dition will prevent us from writing. These are friends. I would still love to spend my time with them regardless of their occupation. Graffiti gets buffed, new kings will come and go but true friendships need not end. They are never eroded: MSN.

VANDALS IN MOTION

Kaos traces back to the origin of VIM
and their memorable actions on the
local Scandinavean lines

Kaos –VIM / Stockholm
>

Vandals In Motion was founded in 1987-'88 by Akay, News and Dudge. At this time graffiti in Stockholm was focusing on hitting subway stations, mainly on the famous green line inner stations. Also bombing subway and commuter train insides was the thing to do.

At the time Akay was already a famous bomber and painter since 1985; News was the inventor of the name "Vandals In Motion" and also a famous bomber, while Dudge was a skilled train bomber with many panel pieces done. So when VIM was founded, we kept focusing on the inside of subway stations, and on heavy train bombing. On Christmas Eve 1988, Akay and Duck from Megatronic kings bombed the whole Vällingby subway yard with tags and throw-ups, covering all trains on both sides. The next day, that action was all over the news as the train company had to let the bombed trains circulate. It brought instant fame to VIM crew and now most people know who we are.

In '88-'89 I joined the crew after a short period of subway station bombing with my partner Ruskig; we had both recently moved to Stockholm from a smaller town outside the city, where we had started to paint walls and trains around 1985-'86. All of a sudden that town became too small for us and so we decided to move to the Capital. I had also started to explore lay-ups around the city and yards in order to write my name on the trains and stations. Now we were a group of four and just waiting to take the town by storm. In the beginning me and Akay hooked up and got along really well, mostly because we were neighbours and that made it easy to go painting together. In that moment we really started to paint on trains regularly: every week we went three-four times, mostly just us, but later with the whole crew. This period was maybe the greatest because it was just us and our target, the commuter trains. Those lines were not guarded so we just stayed around the yards for four-six hours, sometimes even the whole weekend, just painting.

We were isolated back them, without a clue of what was going on in the world of graffiti outside Stockholm. We didn't have any connections in Europe at all, so only what was happening in Stockholm had importance back then. Around 1989 Terror was the next to join the crew, he was already a partner of Dudge's since '86 so it was natural for us to have him join.

After some years of heavily bombing trains we planned on doing a whole-train, just to test the limit of our crew; we went racking for some weeks and then went and did it; eight colour whole-cars in four-five hours, the train ran once and then went straight to the buff. That was really something that we were all feeling proud of, that we'd

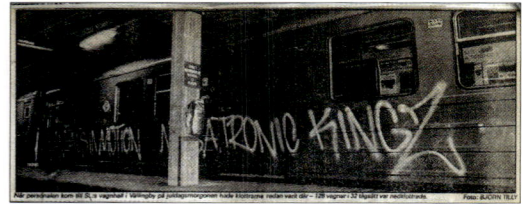

A famous action: VIM straight on the news   — Kaos

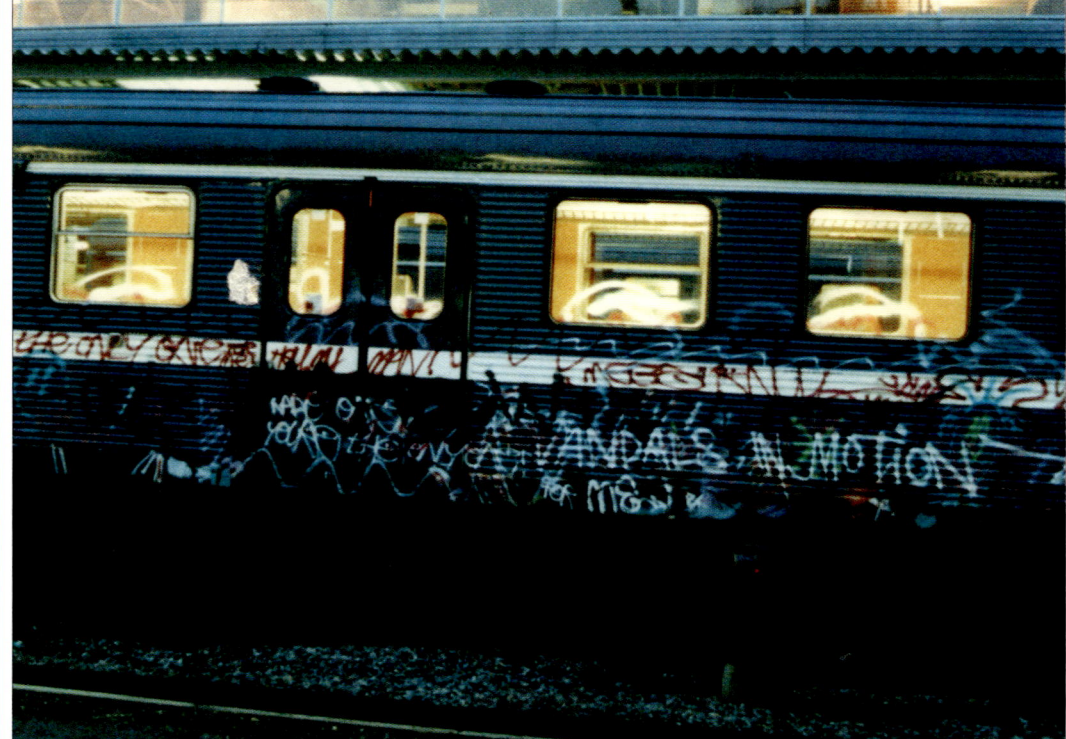

VIM–madness on the Stockholm commuter trains   — Kaos

pulled it off, us young kids. Then, during 1991 *On the run* magazine came out and it was really amazing to see that there were actually other dudes doing the same stuff as us: that was our first contact with Europe's graffiti scene. Later on we got in touch with Zebster from Germany who also took a trip up to Sweden. This was great for us but it was also a big collision of two worlds, his way of painting and preparing was something totally new to us.

He was used to guards and scoping yards, we didn't have guards up here at this time, so his sneaking style was really strange behaviour for us. Whilst we all thought he was a weird dude we also had a lot of respect for him as he was more experienced than we first thought. Also the paint he took with him was like something from another universe. We were used to shit Swedish paint that we thought was the best! And then we got a can of Buntlack Marabou in our hand... shit that brought a new world with totally new options.

Soon later we got in contact with other painters around Europe and started going on trips to visit them. The first country that was pretty close for us to visit was Denmark, so we started to go there to drink beer and take photographs of pieces from guys like Bates, Sabe, Rens, Sek, CMPSPIN and of course many others.

In 1992 there was a big International jam in Uppsala, North of Stockholm, where a lot of writers from all around Europe showed up. This was the place where we first met the Danish writer Mins from *Monsters Of Art* (MOAS). We thought that those dudes were totally

insane, but pretty soon we figured out we were sharing the same mentality and goals: after that meeting we went down to Copenhagen to drink beer and see how it was to paint over there, we were totally impressed by how much they were producing on the trains and how they did it. So after some heavy drinking sessions we decided to put our crews together and to see what would come out of it: and so VIMOAS was founded.

It wasn't really planned out from the beginning, it was more of a cool, crazy idea. This had never been done before and was a really strange thing to do in the eyes of other writers. But we did it and it turned out really cool. We got up in two countries at the same time, having the possibility of counting on two or several panels running at the same time in two cities. The year went on and we got to be really close friends so we'd visit each other's country more than we used to, it was like having a second home. Since then we have been doing this 24 seven. As the years passed, more friends with the same attitude joined, like MSN crew in the Netherlands and ALL crew in Norway. Later on it became even bigger with TPG, TKO, VTO and now even TAT from New York with How and Nosm.... we still don't know if they joined us or we joined them. The rest is history, up to now we are seeing each other again and again, sometimes to paint or just chill with some beers and our families. Without a doubt, the foundation for this successful project is based on friendship, on our attitude and devotion to train painting, year after year.

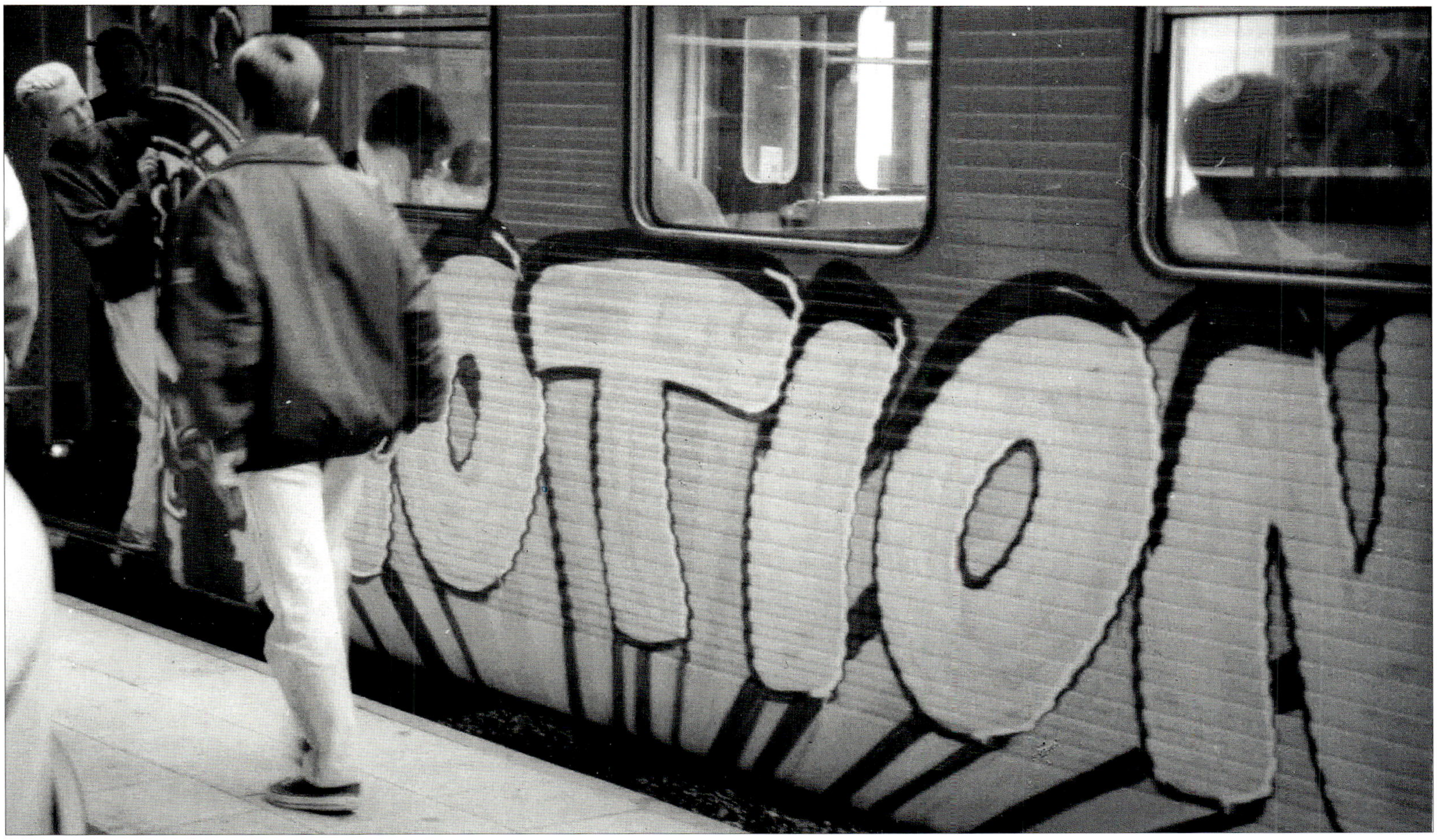

ALL CITY WRITERS   NETWORK
REPORT   INTERNATIONAL
CREWS   MSN &
THE VIMOALL   59

A classic *Motion* panel waiting at Stockholm central station

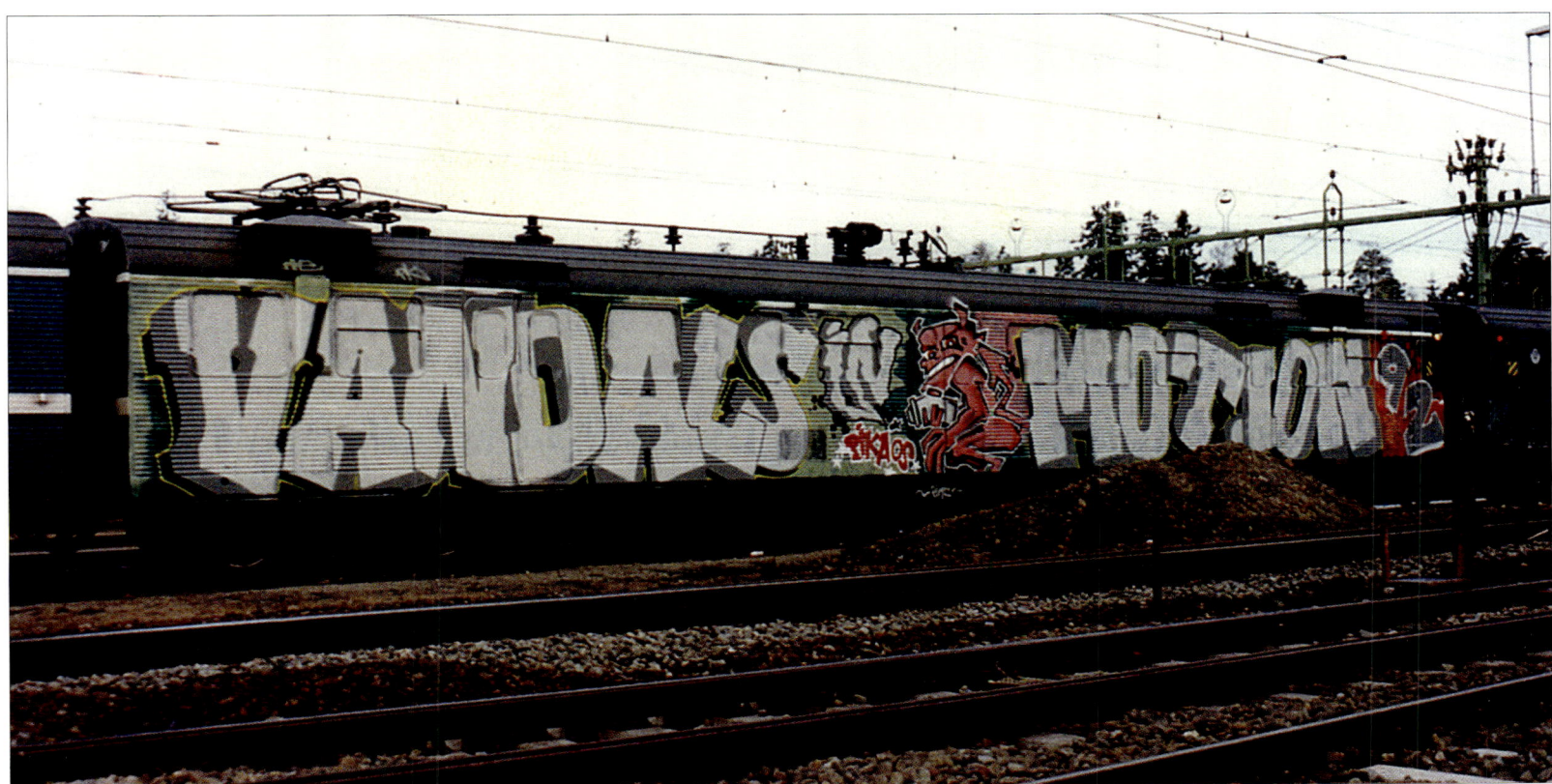

One of the infamous VIM whole–cars with Pike character, 1992

MOAS AND ALL

One of the primary European train bombers talks about his obsession with the Name, the actions and the honour of his crew.

Mins–MOAS / Copenhagen
>

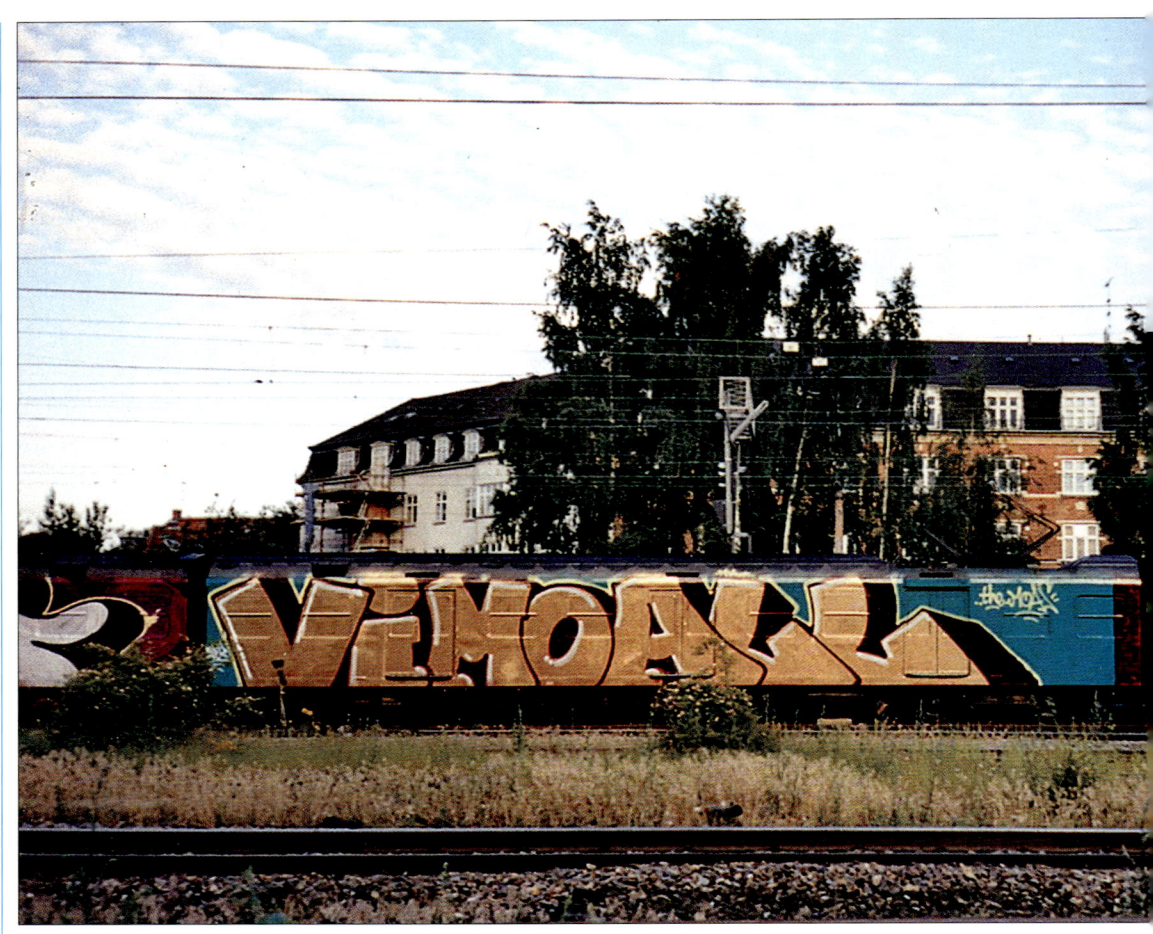

Hello, I'm Mr Mins. I started painting in 1985 as a little boy. In the beginning I only bombed the city that I lived in on the Westside of Copenhagen. One day some of the local writers took me under their wing and taught me all about graff, all about pieces. They still paint today, big up Toys crew! Later on in 1987 I met my mentor Rezen, he taught me everything I needed to know about trains. This one time when Toys crew and my crew were standing in a tunnel under our local station, Mode2, Bando and Shoe came and wanted to paint the tunnel as well. We couldn't believe our own eyes! We just stood there checking out their style. Fuuucccckkkk! That was the beginning of style in Denmark. It was like a dream spotting a Mode2 piece on a Danish train in 1987. After that I wanted to have the biggest train crew in Scandinavia. I started MOA crew in 1991 with a couple of friends, we went to Stockholm in 1992 to meet up with the biggest train crew in Sweden called VIM. We hit it off immediately and got along perfectly. We have always been like family since the very beginning. We were the first crews to unite our letters; VIM and MOA together made, VIMOA. We also decided to put a 'S' after VIMOA because there were more people in the crew. Our travels around the world continued, meeting other graff brothers and today we are in lots of countries. It's crews like MSN, TKO, TATS, that are our closest peoples and today we are one of Europe's legends, if we do say so ourselves. We all got older but we're still lively and we do this from our hearts, it's all about staying true and staying ablaze. Graffiti for me has evolved into something different from what it was in the 80´s, where everything was fresh. Now it's all about beef and that's fucked up for the graff culture, but where there are people there is beef. I hope graff will be around long after I'm gone and I hope MOAS played their part the last 20 years. All respect to the European writers of the 80's and one love to my crew.

ALL crew is based on painting steel and we have done a lot of it. It's what you could call a natural behaviour: bombing in the same, fucked up situations as always. Thats ALL.

Ridder, ALL crew Oslo

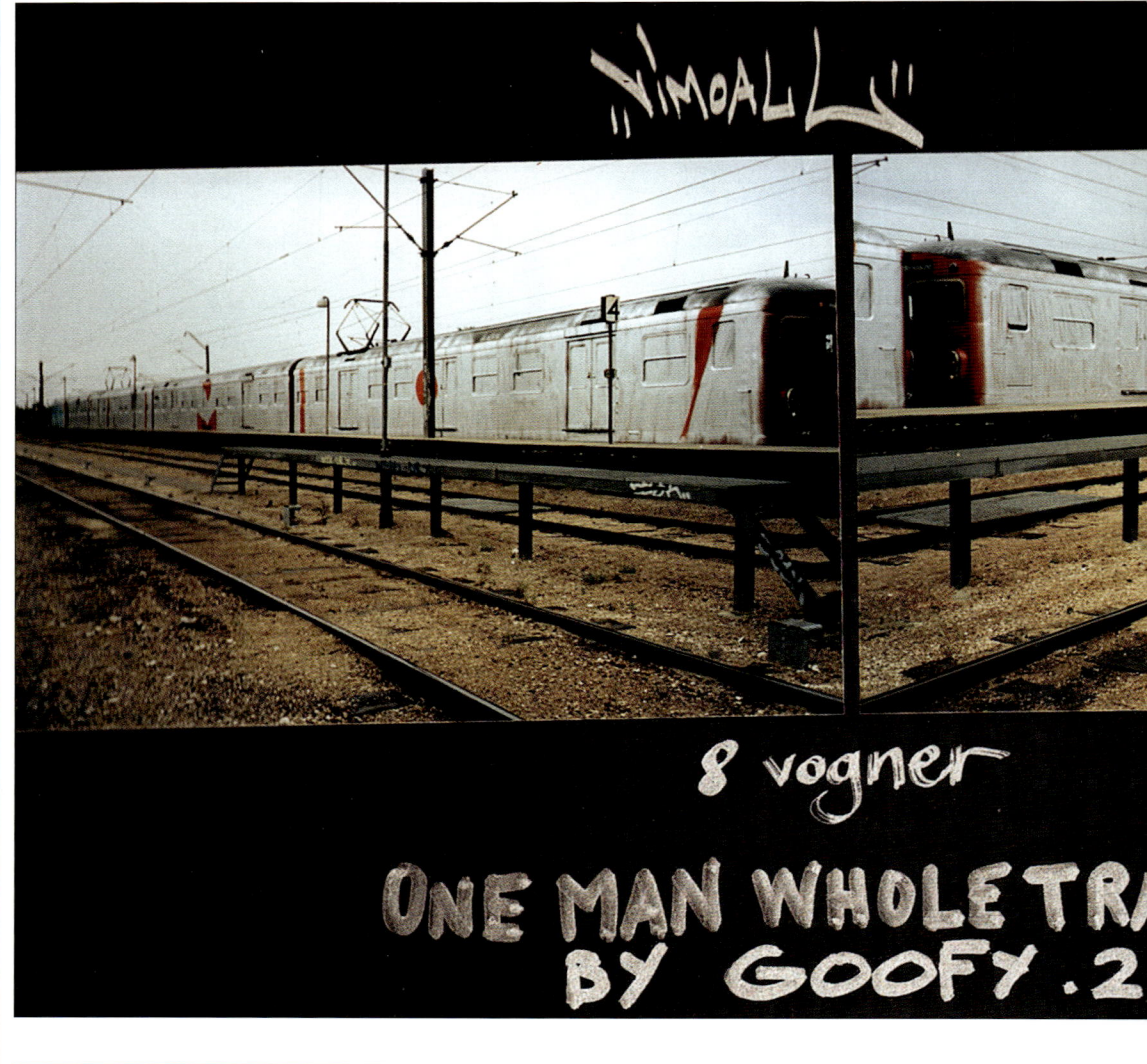

8 vogner
ONE MAN WHOLE TRA
BY GOOFY .2

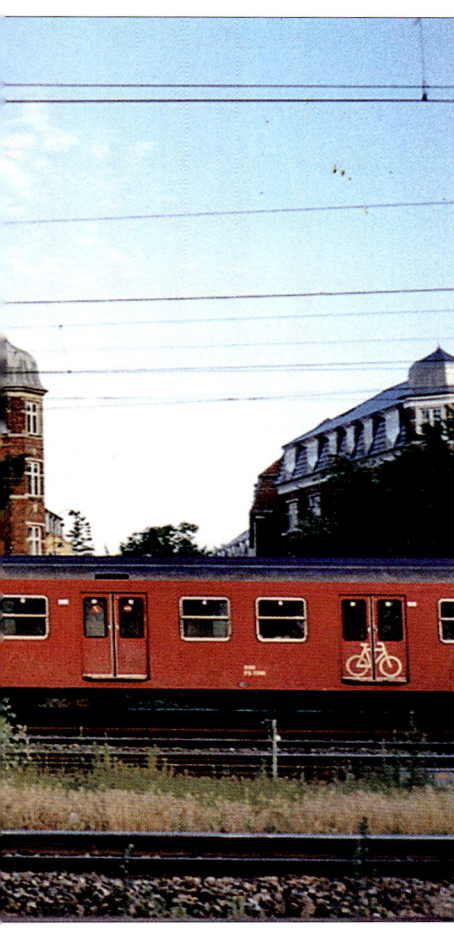

— *Fra 32*

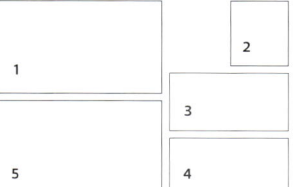

1 VIMOALL, Copenhagen

2 ALL crew, Oslo subway

3 MOAS and VIMS united

4 ALL crew in action

5 *VIMOALL* one-man whole-train. Eight
  cars by Goofy, 2001

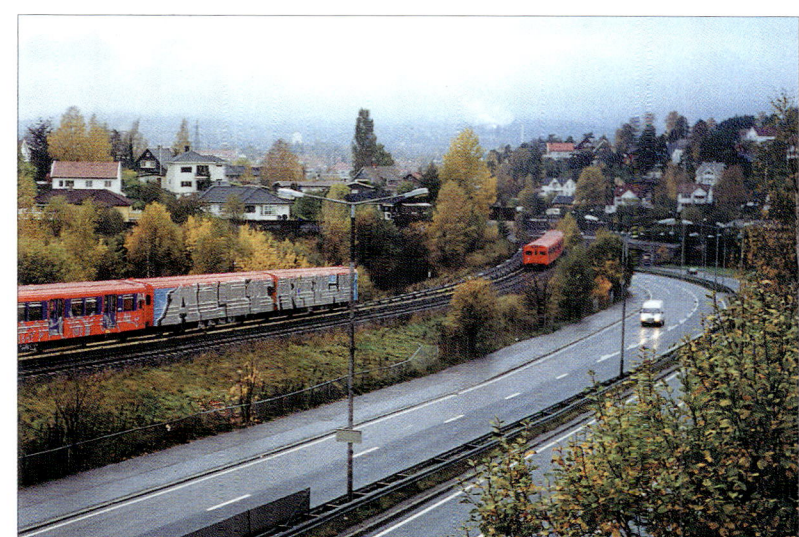

— *Ridder*

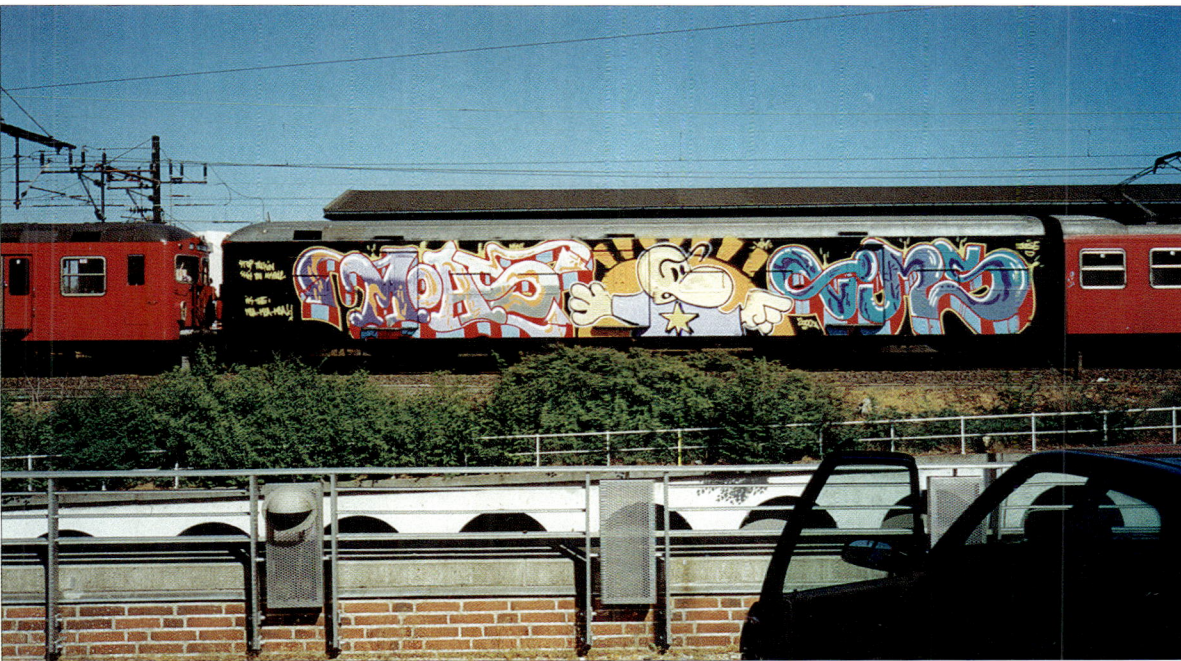

— *ACW archive*

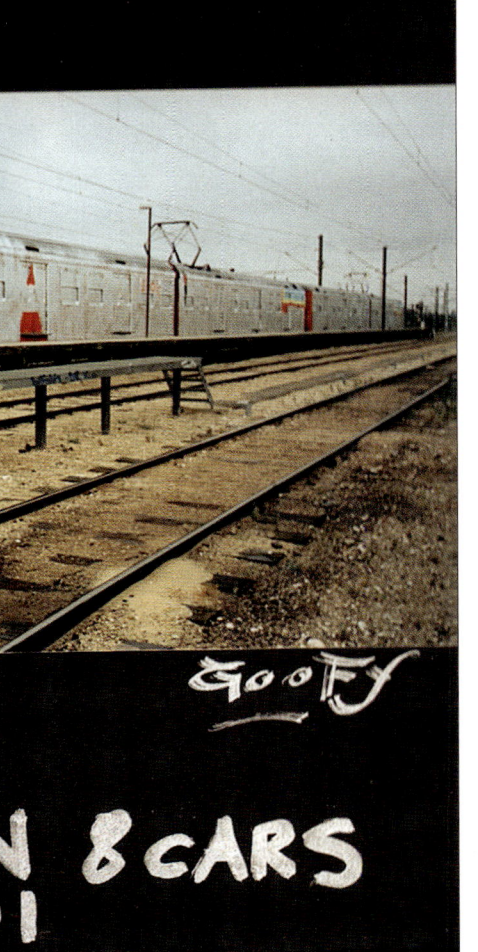

— *ALL*

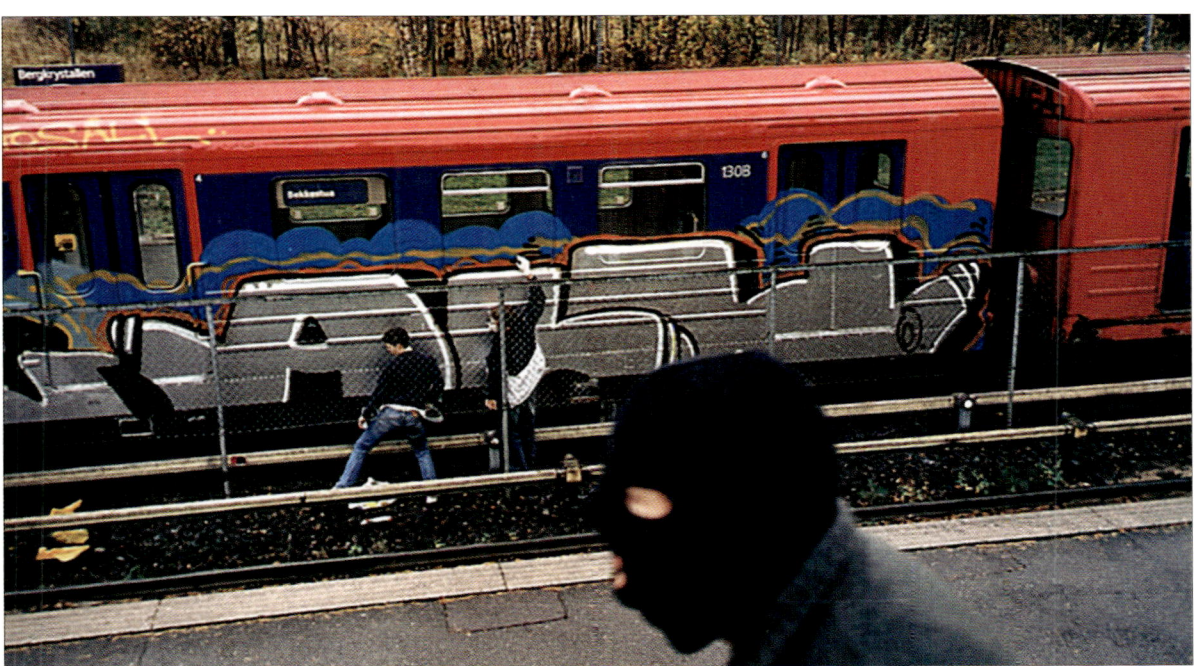

— *ALL*

WRITER'S MEETING: THE JAM

MZEE FRISCH

Zebster –COD / Germany
>

In Europe the first gatherings relating to Writing and Hip Hop culture were basically connected to the Break-dancing wave of 1983-'84. A sort of 'world championship' was organised in London, The UK Fresh. It was a mainstream event related to music, like a concert, not really a Hip Hop jam like the ones that came later. Of course a lot of people went there and made connections. I would say the B-boys were the first ones to really make connections. For example Swift met the Italian breakers, like Emilio from Genoa. This was before their own scene got organised. Starting from the mid 80's a series of underground Zulu parties started taking place in London. I went there with Gawky in 1988 and at the Limelight Club I met the UK writers, like Rex and some other B-boys. We were looking at each other trying to understand which country we were from. Zero-T from Florence also came and since then we kept the link; sending letters, sketches and photos.

Not much previously, in 1987, Dortmund's first underground jam had been organised, a very important event for every German B-boy of the first generation. It was organised in a youth centre and a lot of key people met for the first time, like Jace, JBK, Swift, writers from Hamburg and Kiehl. The majority of people were from Dortmund but at least 40-50% came from the rest of Germany because of this event. I remember Dortmund was three hours by train from our hometown, so we went there as a B-boy crew: Supreme Force, Crazy Rock, Thief, Can2, Vivid Legs and myself. During the whole trip we talked about what would happen there...we had no clue! When we arrived to the event it was really impressive. Me and the other guys from Mainz officially met the Dortmund guys for the first time, we met the Khissen B-boys like DJ Catfester, Skipthebeat and many more. This event was more like a Hip Hop jam. It was the first underground reunion and it had a huge impact.

It was through this event that I got inspired to organise something on an even larger scale. In February 1988 I put together a big jam in Mainz, in a youth centre, borrowing some of the formulas of previous events. Before that we had Rap concerts, Break-dance parties and a few happenings related to live Aerosol Art but they were never really put together on a larger scale. In Mainz we painted the background with spray cans, we invited the DJs and we had the B-boys on stage, not only on the ground. Breakers came from all over Germany, mostly people I had met during my earlier years of travelling. There were also the Munich writers whom I hadn't met previously, they came, left their stuff, took the bus to somewhere else, did their thing and came back early the next morning. I later found out they were Loomit, Neon, Cemnoz and Don. Then there were kids from Berlin, six or seven guys from Hamburg and a few from The Hague. The connection between Hamburg and The Hague was through Jase who had relatives in Holland and had put the Dutch kids in contact with the German ones.

So there were all these guys, let's say 25 people, hanging out in my parents' party cellar. We were all young, I was 18 and of course everyone was excited as it wasn't so common to go to these kinds of Hip Hop culture events. We used to meet in huge concerts, like the Run DMC one in Frankfurt where you'd go and meet hundreds of guys, but without the possibility of staying in touch or sharing something.

At the jam everybody was in a very cool Hip Hop state of mind - it's interesting how many connections were made in these events that still exist today. Everybody was into something, there were no spectators but only active kids dedicated to the so-called four elements of the movement: writers, breakers, DJs and MCs. There weren't many MC's because some were really young and the criterion was that you had to be able to rap in English. Maybe because they had the connection with the army base, where people rapped in their own language, or maybe because it was simply the language of the pioneers. For me it was always weak as I thought it was more original to rap in your original language.

The dresscode of course was really important as well. It was part of a whole scenario where the B-boys used to show off their proper outfit. Of course some writers had photos and blackbooks with them, at that time there wasn't much graffiti that you could look at on a visual basis or in magazines.

Few of them were already careful and advanced, for example the Munich guys who had started train bombing early; they had heavy problems with the police and were undercover while others were openly showing their blackbooks. Through these series of events the modern concept of jam was invented. Starting from this experience the organisation of a series of conventions took place in the South of Germany during the late 80's.

In 1990 I came up with the concept of doing the same line-up in two different cities. It made things easier because organising a jam was hard work. So we did one jam in Munich and then another one in Mainz.

The name invented for that organisation, MZEE, came from the M of Munich, the Z in Mainz and the double E stretched it up. The term Fresh, which was pretty in vogue that year, was re-invented: instead of *UK-Fresh* we chose a German version, *Frisch*, with a bit of competition in it, it became *MZEE Frischer*.

We even took it a step further developing the event into an International meeting: at that time connections had already been made in the U.S.; with New York. This Jam was particularly important because we connected the scenes of many European countries besides Germany: Sweden, Denmark, Norway, Finland, France, Switzerland and Holland.

The main idea underlining it was that we had our own culture and as people from France had already started seriously rapping in their own language we invited MCs from there, Lady Tail with DJ D-Nasty and the Flopstars from Denmark. Therefore at this time the crew I was managing was Advanced Chemistry, who were also rapping in German.

The most difficult goal to achieve was expansion because there wasn't a particular network of magazines or media focusing on Hip Hop culture. It was basically an underground rumour that reached all of Europe as far as Scandinavia, a combination of existing sources and a lot of mouth-to-mouth propaganda. Just as had happened for previous jams, people heard the event was taking place and like madmen took the train all the way over here to figure out if anything was happening.

The Scandinavian guys organised themselves to be able to come. CMP from Denmark was in charge of the Danish guys coming by train. It ended in a total mess, as at one point they got on the same train as the Swedish guys of VIM. They came to the location by bus but at one point the driver gave up because they were a bunch of crazy drunken Danish, Swedish and Finnish writers joined together.

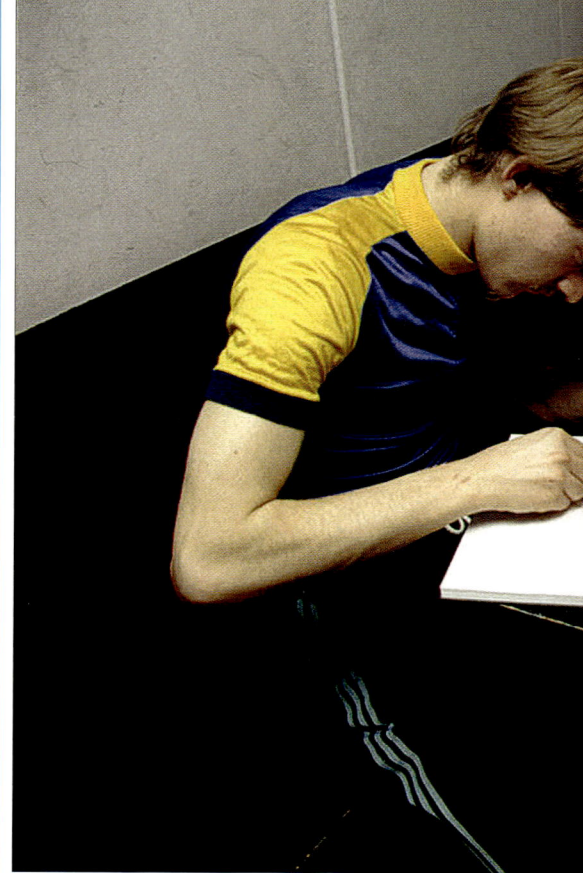

B–boys photographed by Le Truc at MZEE Jam

Beyond exhibitionism

Mode 2 – TCA, CTK / London
>

Personally, to me the Writing jams that took place in Europe during the 90's were more of a pain rather than fun times, maybe because I'm really more of a voyeur than an exhibitionist. When you're at a jam and you're part of the performance, you're totally exposed.

Often I improvised, in which case you risk taking too long. I would go there, facing that large wall and often just get carried away, sketching out too much. Before the jam starts, when people are not there yet, you have the time to think about what you want to do, how to fill the wall, the space, but then you sketch up too much and stay there like two days. Other people, they start, they finish, they go to the party, and you just stay there painting. You're actually giving a lot to the jam and the public, but don't get recognition for it. When you're improvising, sometimes for a couple of hours you may be going in the wrong direction and then have to go over everything you did and start again. People see that you make mistakes and stuff, which is not a drama but it's always a

Bates –AIO / Copenhagen

In '89 I went to England with Romance for a street art competition. People had come from America like Risk and Slick from Los Angeles and Vulcan from *New York. There was also Jonone 156 that has now moved to Paris and a lot of guys from England as well. Raide from Oslo was there because we were writing letters to this English organiser* *and he brought us to England for this competition. It was the first time I was part of something International, there were people from all over and this was the first jam I attended.*

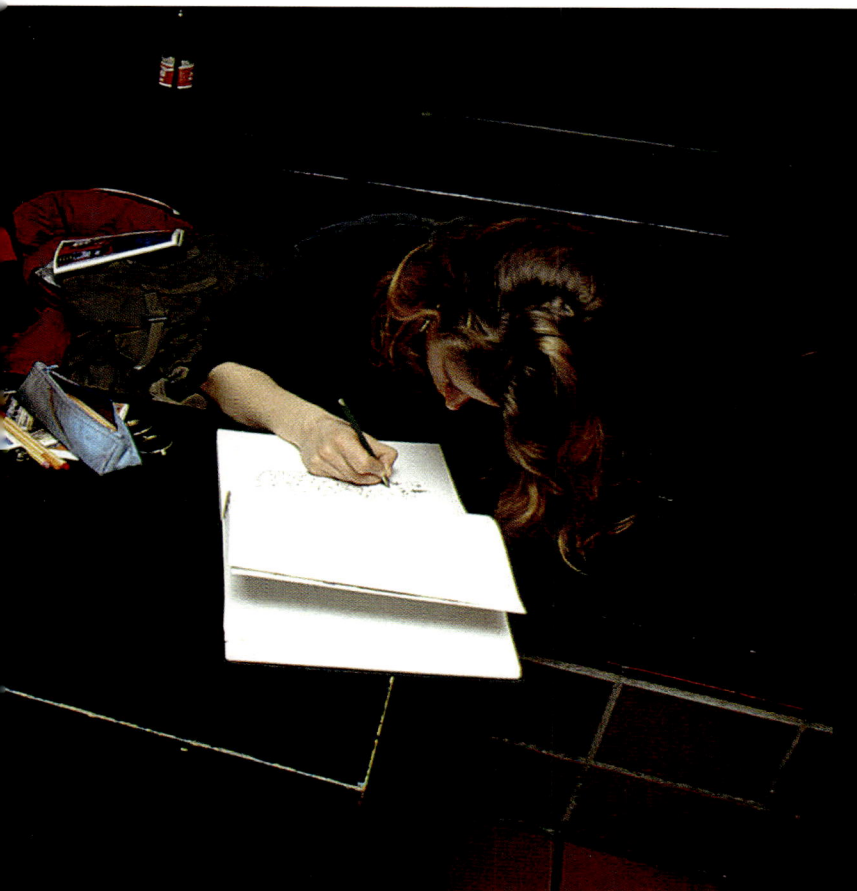
— Le Truc

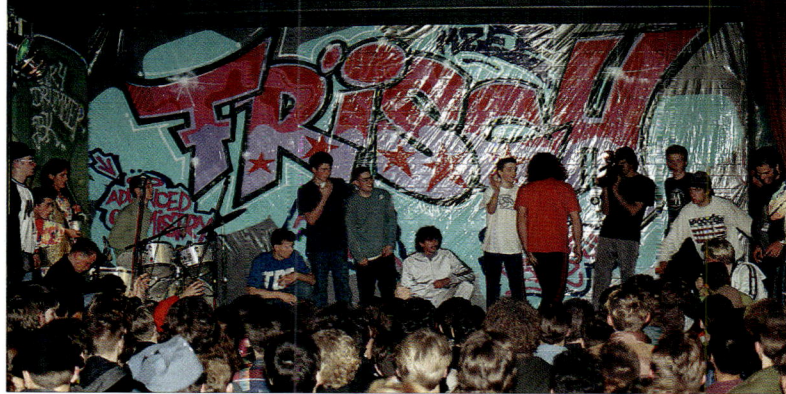
— Le Truc

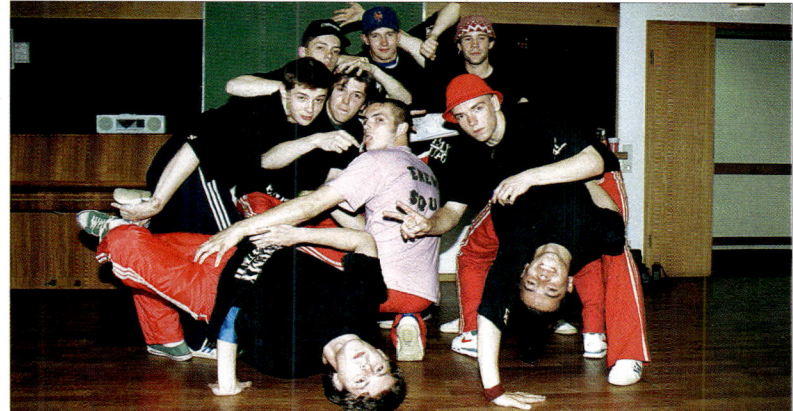
— Le Truc

matter of feeling overexposed.

I like it when people just come and sit down to stay for most of the day, eat something, go to the toilet and then come back and watch the pieces evolve. The problem with jams is that at one point people just turned into trophy hunters, trying to get photos and tags. They go from jam to jam, collecting. It's the kind of thing that puts me off because you see that the essence of the culture we are talking about becomes totally diluted and superficial.

It's the same if there is jam with 50 people on the roster. You should pick just a few of the best ambassadors of the culture, because when you put 50 guys on, it's like there is no hierarchy anymore. As far as the origin of the culture goes, the competition on who is up most, or who has the best style and who has many different skills, separated the good from the not so good. A lot of people who organised jams were doing it then and there, without really thinking what effect this would have 15-20 years down the line. Choose just a handful of really good guys, and use your budget to keep them in your town for a week, so that they can leave something of value behind. Many jams also had public funding, so when your local tax-payers walk by and see all these young people from all over the place painting away, it doesn't give us the best promotion for what we do. Better then just to have the local illegal scene that makes up its own rules.

Of course being invited to International jams was important because we got to meet Delta during the trip, or to travel with Sharp. There was a time when a handful of us would be invited to all those jams, year after year; so we would find ourselves again and again in different cities of Europe. We really just tried to get the best out of it for ourselves; the rest didn't matter as much. When you'd get Sharp travelling alone it would be different from when you're in a crowded jam with hundreds

of writers, or back in Paris, where everybody had their own thing going on. For a few days we could really have in-depth conversations that had to do with New York, how it was before and the kind of stress that he used to get, and where we were all going. You'd get to be with people when they're more open and focused on the discussion. It was a great excuse to meet long-term friends from others places and hang out; but the jams themselves right from the early 90's on just became a circus with no direction whatsoever.

The first meetings during the 80's were totally different, of course. Before, when you'd see someone else who looked like they were down with the scene, you'd talk to them. Exchange and talk. I remember one of the things that helped the scene in Europe was UK Fresh in 1986, a big one-day Hip Hop concert thing that started at mid day and went on until midnight. It was organised by Morgan Khan who used to do Streetsounds, Hip Hop compilations. So many guys who were out then came over from all over Europe. When there was a group playing that you didn't like, you could go to the back of the arena. There were people there from Scandinavia, Italy, France; so many people who heard that there would be this big event. I remember that at the back of the hall you were exchanging numbers with different guys, from Copenhagen for example; and that's how I ended up going to Denmark in August '86, and from there to Stockholm. Above all, UK Fresh was a chance to see so many rap groups, when it was still ok for rap to be called rap. Everybody was into every discipline back then, so it didn't matter if you were dancing or writing because compared with today, there was a lot of crossing over between disciplines and just doing one of those meant you were down; and most people were actually active in something then, not just hanging around...

FREAKS ON TOUR
—

CMP – CMPSPIN / Naestved
>

In 1990, Swet, Spino5 and I teamed up with a lot of people at the MZEE Fresher Jam in Munich. We organised the tickets for all the guys from Copenhagen and made sure everybody got on the train from Copenhagen to Naestved and on to the location. There were guys from all over Scandinavia mixed in the group. At that time it was really different, if somebody did something you would participate and back it up, just out of respect.

I can't really explain how funny this whole trip was. Imagine that the whole train was trashed, this time not outside with paintings, but inside by Swedish writers, crazy Finnish writers and of course the wild Danish writers. It was a crazy train ride... and a long ride, it took around 15 hours. Writers got connected and formed friendships that lasted for years.

On the way down there we were probably 50 people drinking, wondering around, drawing, listening to loud music and I remember writers walking up and down the train with a huge boom box! Honestly it was so much fun and at the same time both a nightmare and an endless ride too.

The jam took place in November 1990, it was really important because it connected people from all over Europe. You know, even Wane said that the most important trip to this day, was going to that Mzee Frisher jam.

At the jam, there were so many writers from all over Europe. I remember Central Station was packed with police, I've never seen that much police at a Hip Hop jam before

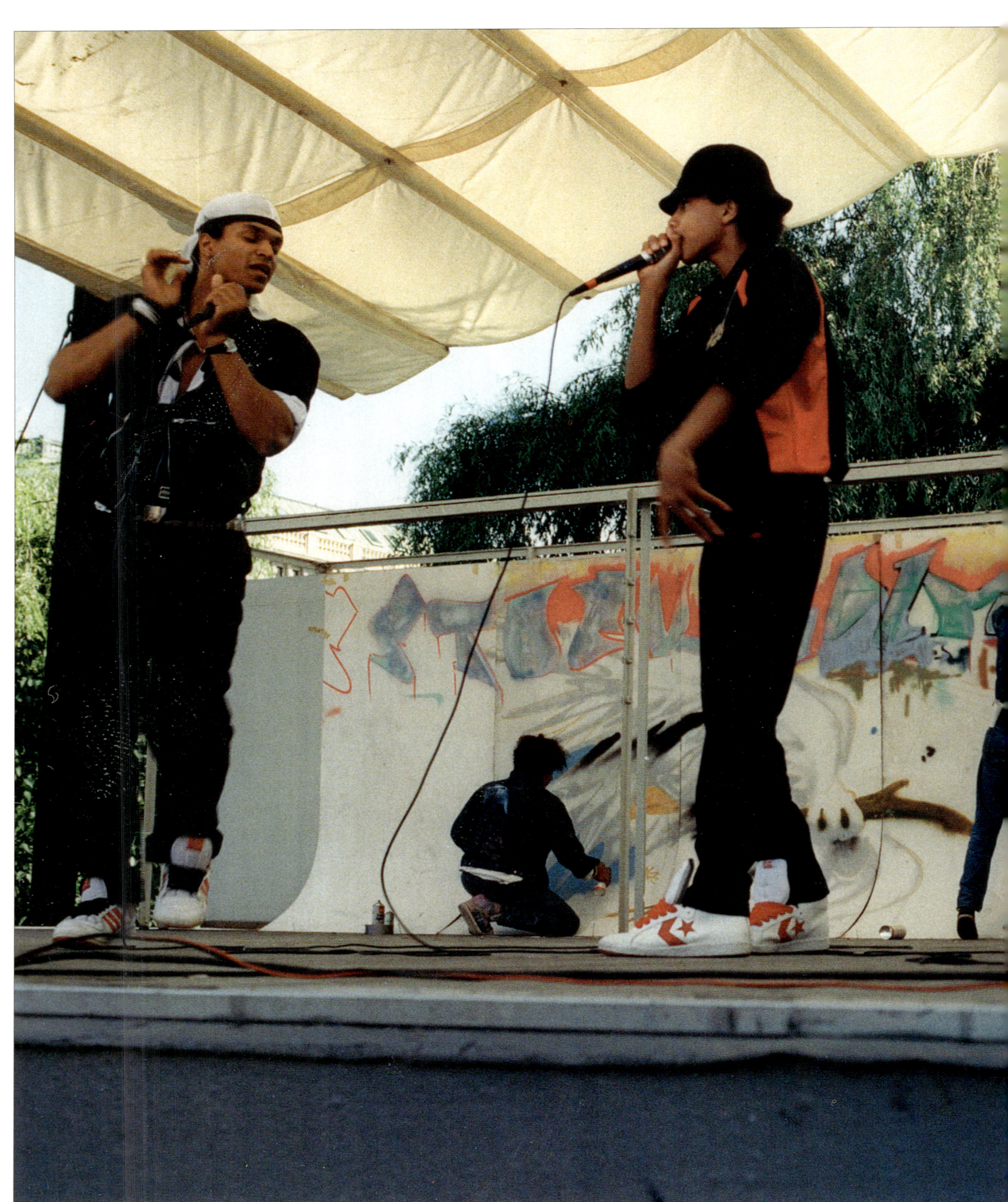

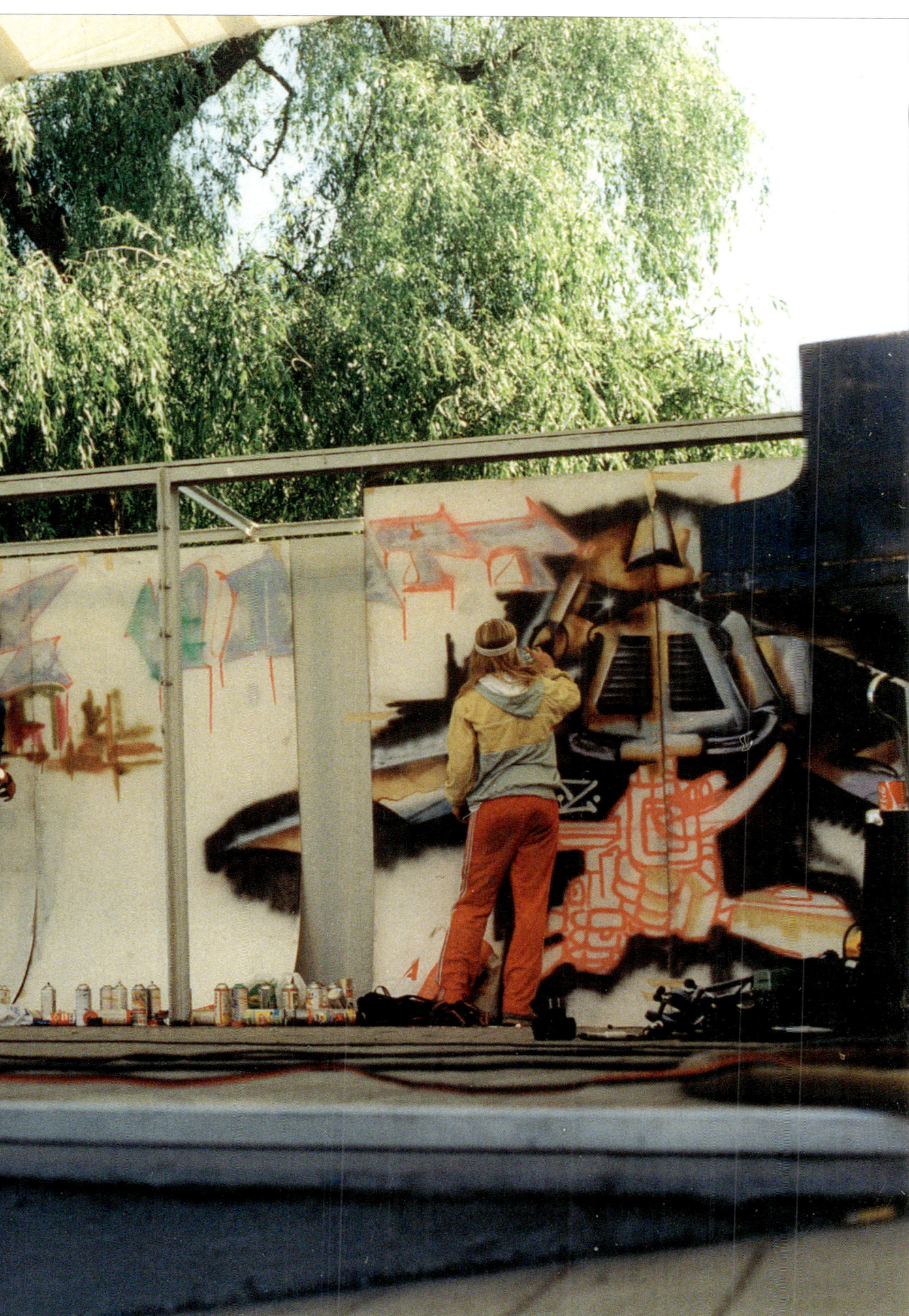

HIP HOP FORMULA

TOBIAS BARENTHIN LINDBLAD
This photo depicts Disey (middle) and Ziggy (right). The MC at the left is MC Too Fresh, or MC Carboo as he later called himself. It was a jam in Kungsträdgården in Stockholm for the movie Stockholmsnatt (Stockholm nights) which was released early '87 as a anti-violence film starring the elite of the Hip Hop scene at that time. The jam took place in late summer/early fall of 1986.

Nico Cley ndert

THE FANZINES CIRCUIT

HAND MADE NETWORK

From the exchange of photos and sketches to fanzines, the main circuit for stylistic comparisons

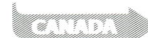

Montreal. Under Pressure
Vancouver. Xylene

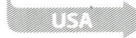

Miami. 12 Ounce Prophet
Kent. Can Control
New Jersey. Crazy Kings, Under Cover
New York. IGT/Tight, Flashbacks, Mass Appeal, On The Go, Stress
San Francisco. No Limits To Fame
Cincinnati. Scribble
Boston. Skills
Bethesda. While You Were Sleeping

AUSTRALIA

Sydney. Blitzkrieg Magazine, Full Effect
Brisbane. Hype Magazine

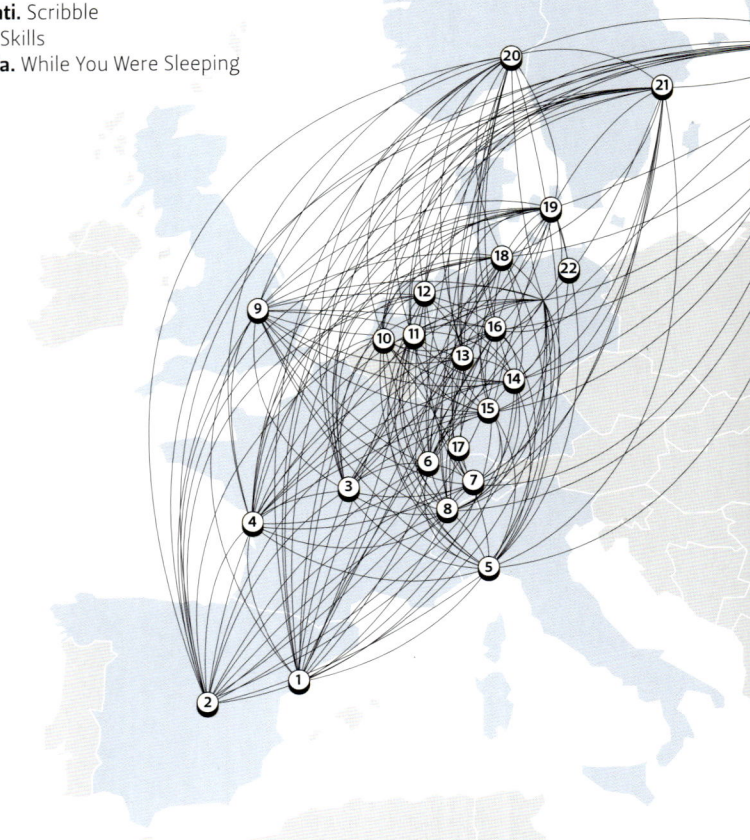

The following publications offer only a partial vision of the European network during the early 90's.

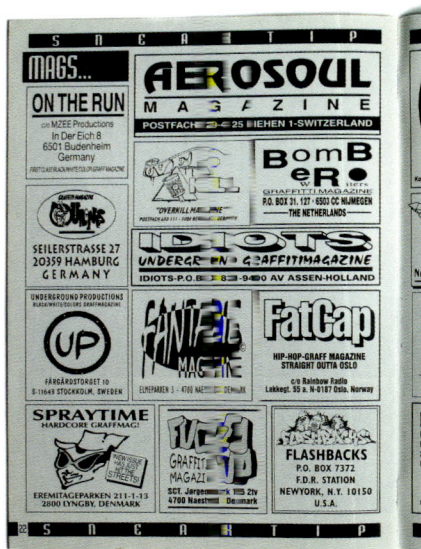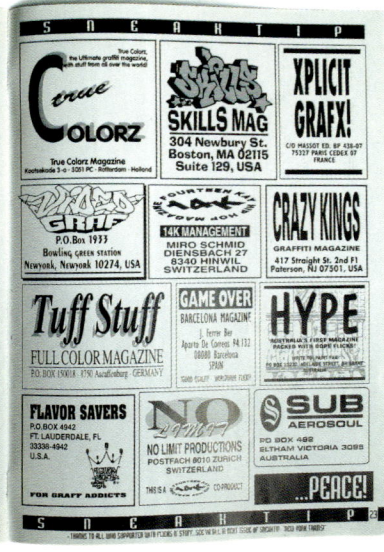

The first European fanzine network to be dedicated to Writing forms as the evolution of an already consolidated tradition tied to the barter of photos. The first collectors based their archives on images of painted walls and trains, often exchanged with those who had the possibility of travelling and getting in touch with foreign scenes. The photograph thus became the only resource with which to study different styles, follow the evolution of letters in other countries and consequently pursue a personal stylistic path. Eventually photos were assigned a specific value, quoted on the basis of their importance, organised into a precise hierarchy. For example, snapshots of the New York subway were considered precious documents because they were difficult to obtain. Writers became progressively more obsessed with protecting the material in their possession: particularly rare pictures had to be hidden from indiscreet eyes, shown only to members of one's group or to whoever had one of equal worth,

because they portrayed innovative styles.
With time, photographs became the primary divulging document: the information written on the backs of pictures revealed to be fundamental for knowing the author, the crew, the year, the country of origin, the target and the conditions in which the piece was realised; important details for images that often focalised on the design, to the detriment of any contextualisation of the work.
In a movement like Writing, based on risk factors, these details supplied a complete image of the author because they framed the conditions of a risky spot in which he might have had to operate. Certain expressions often present on the subway trains of New York – like "too fuckin dark in dem tunnelz", "sorry no more blue", "fucked up my hands were cold", "too late too tired" – in Europe were transcribed on the back of snapshots to justify or enrich the idea of what dynamics were adopted in the act of painting. With the development of fanzines, this information was synthesised into brief captions

placed under the images, furnishing generic information: author, crew, year, and country where the piece was done. In concurrence with the circulation of photographs, another protocol soon followed, as widespread as it was transitory: the exchange of sketches, easily reproducible through photocopies.

During this time we were either exchanging photos of the big names, the deal was like "You send me five photos from Rotterdam and I will send you five photos from Utrecht". These kinds of exchanges were going on and they were interesting because they built a sort of private, free magazine. Then some kids who were interested in putting pictures into a format came out with the fanzine concept. The first fanzines were simply collections of photos, just the best material they had and even some sketches. The magazines soon started focusing on extraordinary actions, like extremely well done trains or big murals by certain well-know writers. Before the fanzine boom, photocopies of sketches were exchanged as well. That

Next pages
>

30	81	82	83	84	85	86	87
14K MAGAZINE	GAME OVER	UP	BOMBERS	ON THE RUN	XPLICIT GRAFX	FANTAZIE	OVERKILL

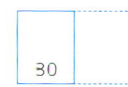
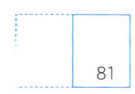
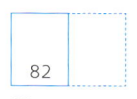
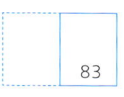
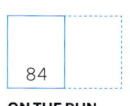
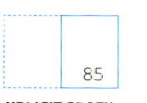
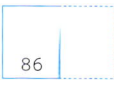
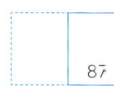

SPAIN

1 BARCELONA
Game Over
Sicopats

2 MADRID
Wanted

FRANCE

3 PARIS
Xplicit Grafx
1–Tox
400 Ml

4 BORDEAUX
33c Fresh

ITALY

5 GENOVA
Al Magazine

SWITZERLAND

6 BASEL
Aerosoul

7 ZURICH
14k
There's No Limit

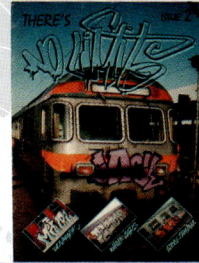

8 ALPNACH–DORF
Make It Better

UNITED KINGDOM

9 LONDON
Graphotism

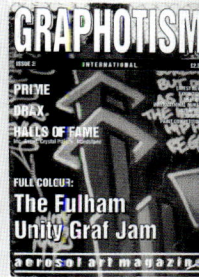

HOLLAND

10 AMSTERDAM
True Colors

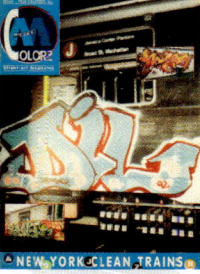

11 NIEUWEGEIN
Bombers

12 ASSEN
Idiots

GERMANY

13 ASCHAFFENBURG
Tuff Stuff

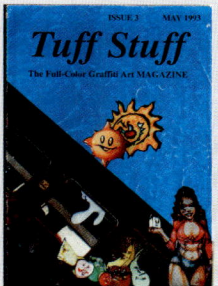

14 ERKRATH
Style Wars

15 FRANKFURT
Steel Is Real

16 KOLN
On The Run

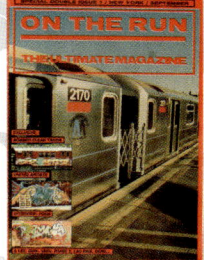

17 BERLIN
Backjumps
Overkill

18 HAMBURG
Backspin

DENMARK

19 COPENHAGEN
Fantazie
Sneaktip
Magic Moments

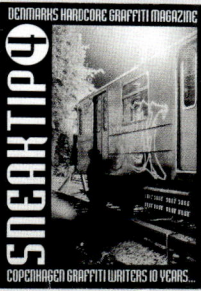

NORWAY

20 OSLO
Fat Cap
From Here To...

SWEDEN

21 STOCKHOLM
Underground
Productions

FINLAND

22 HELSINKI
Gas Mask

A complete overview can be consulted on the Art Crimes web site Art Crimes www.graffiti.org/faq/zines

– ACW archive

---

humoristic, funny graffiti. It was very innocent. After seeing the photos we started to concentrate on style and technique with the spray cans.

From an interview with Bates-AIO, for All City Writers, 2008

Moreover, the European circuit became the means of economic sustenance for every fanzine, which had an average foliation of 24 pages.

In each issue there was a page dedicated to the different Writing publications existing in Europe, a sort of informative window of the editorial landscape dedicated to the phenomenon.

The exchange of magazines between editors became inevitable, giving them the chance to become both representatives and distributors in their area of otherwise unobtainable International publications among foreign editors the exchange was equal and concerned a limited number of copies, usually a few dozen units.

As had occurred with the exchange of photographs, with time new qualitative criteria appeared in the sphere of zines as well, tied to the number of coloured pages and the importance of the writers published in them. On the base of these criteria, some periodicals were set in a position of superiority with respect to others, and the parametres for an exchange started varying on the base of their quality.

The distribution of other fanzines on a local scale represented an important source of income: the readers could ask the editor of their magazine to procure foreign ones. For many years, apart from the small business tied to unobtainable products such as markers or spray caps, this distributive channel became the only means of sustenance for these publications. At the time the advertising world was completely indifferent to graffiti and its target of reference.

The European fanzine circuit was fuelled both by what was coming out of the primary cities of the continent as by a more global network – active since the mid 80's – that comprised the American, Australian and Canadian publications. And yet, while fanzines from New York were created to document and re-evoke a phenomenon, like Writing in the subway, that was progressively disappearing, in Europe the production of the first fanzines was motivated by the need to foster and intensify a numerically meagre scene. At the end of the 80's the European reality was composed of numerous cases of isolated kids who had very few means of getting in touch: their scarce number and the very low concentration in a common territory – unlike the scene in New York – increased the attention towards fanzines, laying the foundation for the very first International network.

---

period expired fairly soon though, as the photo of graffiti replaced the sketch.

Also photocopying sketches was risky because it made it easy for people to bite, to start copying. A sketch reveals much more than a photo because when you have drawn letters you see their structure, the way the structure has been conceived and other important guidelines that painted pieces don't show. Also it isn't copyrighted like something that is done on the street, where everybody can take a photo. You can bite a sketch and then paint a public wall, claiming that you were the original inventor of those letters, and nobody can deny it!

From an interview with Zedz-INC, for All City Writers, 2008

Thus the experiences stemming from the exchange of pictures and sketches gave form to the first prototypes of photocopied fanzines that would gradually be perfected until becoming high quality publications.

In the first place, these papers contributed in defining the stylistic directions Writing was taking in every nation and in every single city between the 80's and the first half of the 90's. The fanzines from Berlin, Amsterdam, Paris or England show how each urban centre could recognise itself in the stylistic and aesthetic taste of the local writers, coming to define an easily identifiable standard.

In 1987 I went to Stockholm and that was one of my first trips out of the country. It opened my eyes, I realised graffiti was bigger than my local scene. Of course we knew some things about America but back in the days we didn't have much information. Someone had to go there to take photos and bring them back home, there were no magazines. I think Can Control and IGT were the first two magazines that we ever saw; this was in '87-'88. I knew some guys who went to Paris and Amsterdam with their families very early and took a lot of photos. Of course we looked at the photos and noticed that their graffiti was different from ours. We were doing graffiti that was looking like Subway Art and Style Wars, a

The original flix swap: what fanzines owe to

1 "Virus" Aug. 05
Vancouver
Canada

2 This is how we bomb
the subway in Paris!
Check out the
"Colorz" tags!
PEACE

3 The ilm ten.
Troubled children
da freeze mobbe
skore
by Ten & Skore
Brighton '94

4 Exit (secret tag).
I did this drawing
during the day,
by myself in a
yard in Melbourne.
I had never been
there before!
No one could
come + paint!!
I did more but it
left unfinished
–BROKE

5 Illegal Kasino
Spike Page
"ACR"

6 ID one UGG krew
on L–Line
in Brooklin 94.
Untouchable
Graffiti Giants

7 Wodka Holland

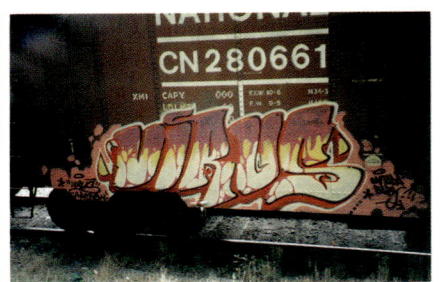

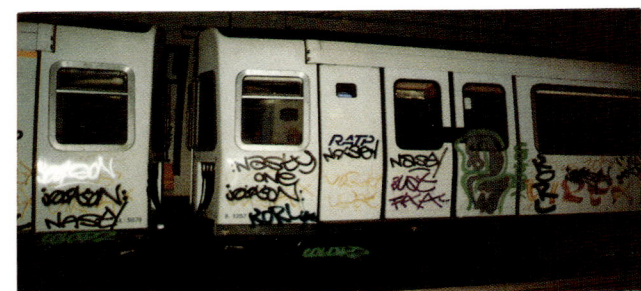

"VIRUS" AUG 05
VANCOUVER
CANADA...

This is how we bomb the
subway in Paris! Check out
the "Colorz" tags!

PEACE.

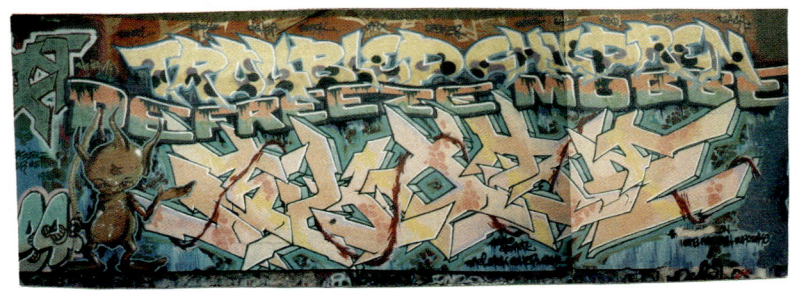

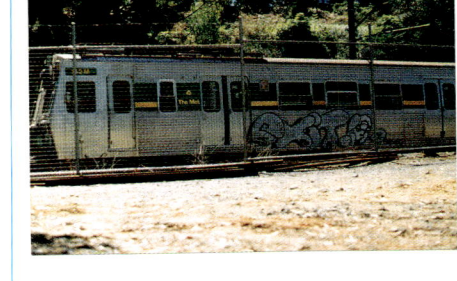

THE ILM — TROUBLED CHILDREN
TEN   DA FREEZE MOBBE
            SKORE.

BY TEN & SKORE
BRIGHTON '94.   LONDON

EXIT. (SECRET TAG).
I DID THIS DURING the day, by
myself in a yard in Melbourne.
I had never been there before!
No one would come + paint!!
I DID MORE but it left
unfinished _ BROKE.

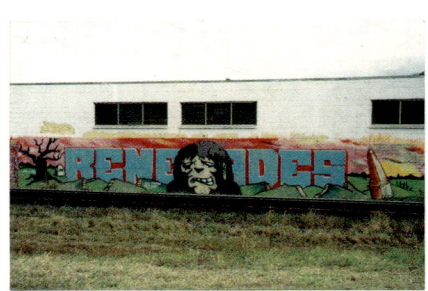

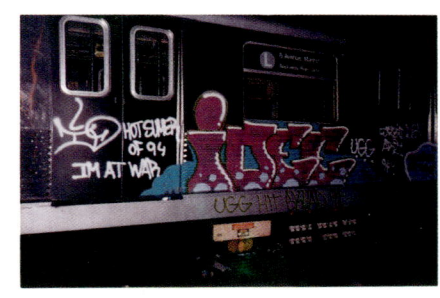

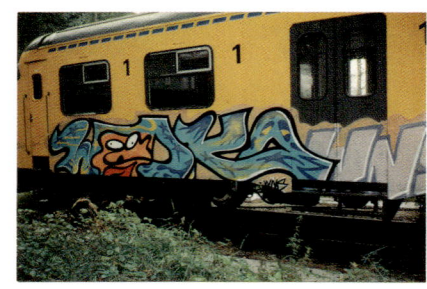

ILLEGAL

KASINO · SPIKE PAGE
"ACR"

ID one UGG krew on L-Line
in BROOKLYN 94

UNTOUCHABLE
GRAFFITI
GIANTS

WODKA
Holland

this habit

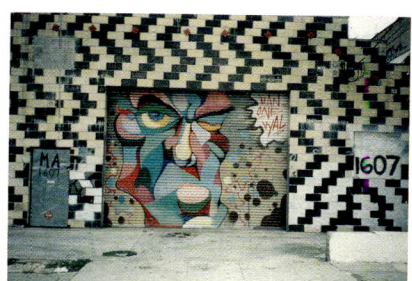

ManOne & Vyal
C.O.I.
1994. L.A.

(9)

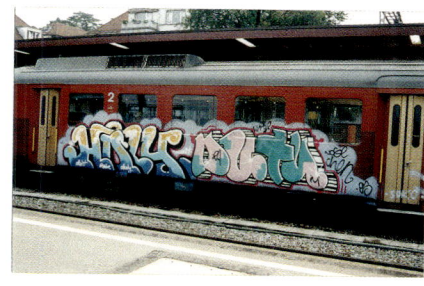

HOLY - DUTY

MIND
TERRORIST
ZH

I.R.A
CREW(D)

(10)

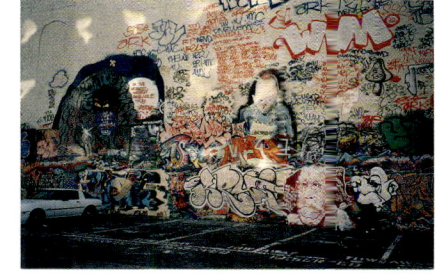

PSYKO CITY 1992
NOTICE THE SAN FRAN WRITER
ON BOTTOM CORNER

4
PAG 20

XANK MP-AVE-TKK

(11)

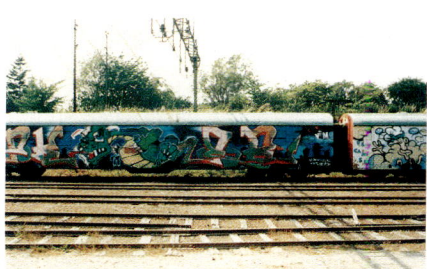

WHOLE-CAR   BY   PIKE

(12)

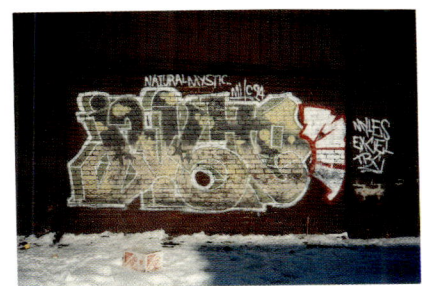

°30 BELOW ZERO
1993
BY ME

(13)

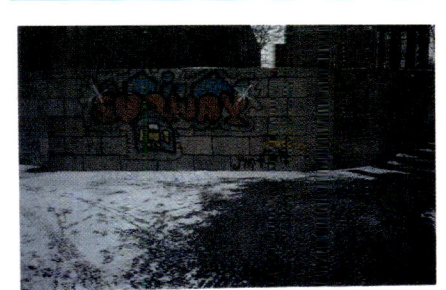

DUKE 1 ...
HANNOVER (D)
1983/84   "ZERO KIDS"
"BACK FROM THE
OLD TIMES" ...

(14)

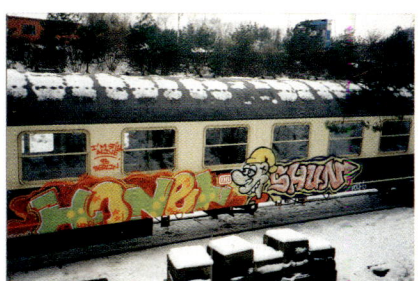

HONET SHUN
BERLIN 93

(15)

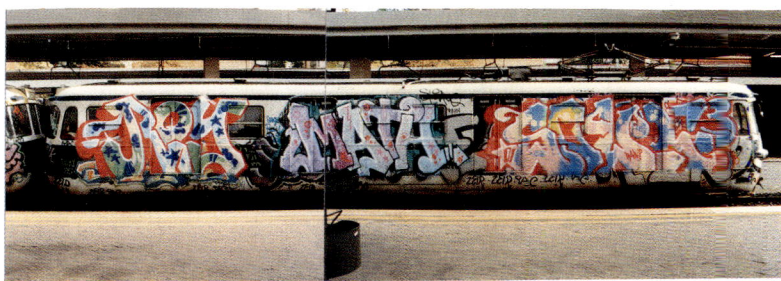

A proposito di pezzi crudi ...
Questo tentativo di Whole car di Roy Math (da
Amsterdam) e Soul '73... Abbiamo dipinto per tutta
la notte sotto la pioggia ; era completamente inutile
tentare di fare qualcose di dettagliato, cosi ci siamo
buttati sulla quantità — il Soul 73 è tutto fatto a FAT,
con marabou, come piace a te cara !!

(16)

TROPHY HUNTERS

In writer photo collections, other than snapshots portraying graffiti frontally or showing the author during an action, another type of thematic picture emerges, in which the writer is immortalised next to his or her newly-conquered 'trophy', almost as if to fix in time the image of them as train custodians.

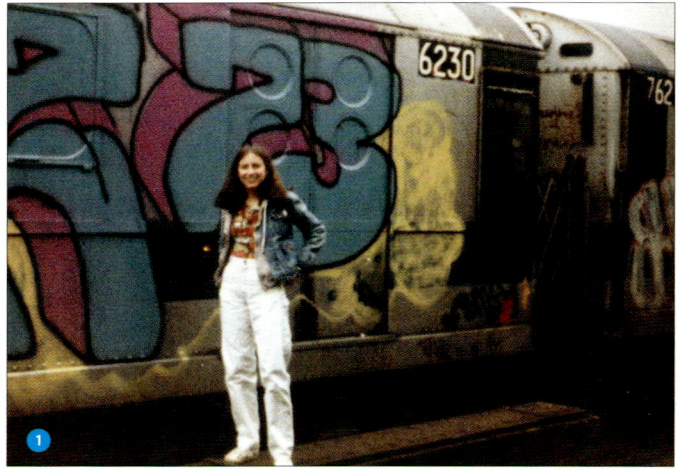

— Andrea Nelli

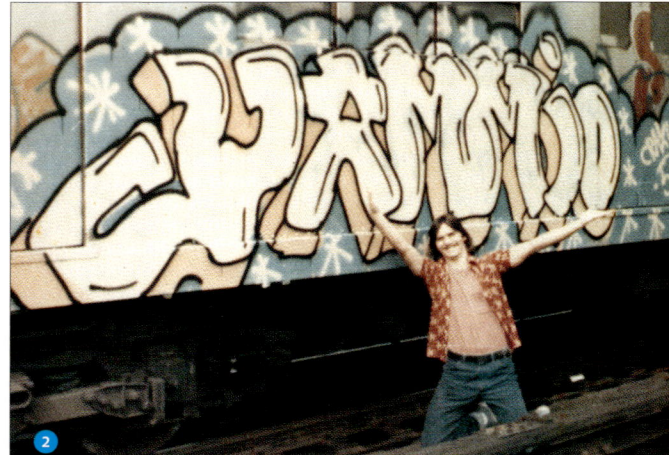

— Andrea Nelli

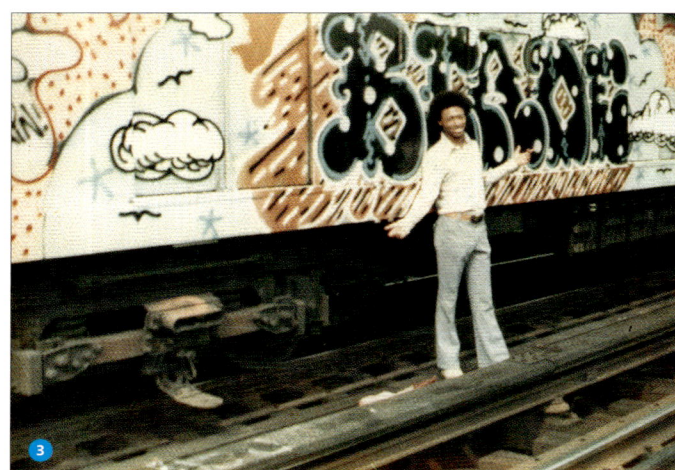

— Andrea Nelli

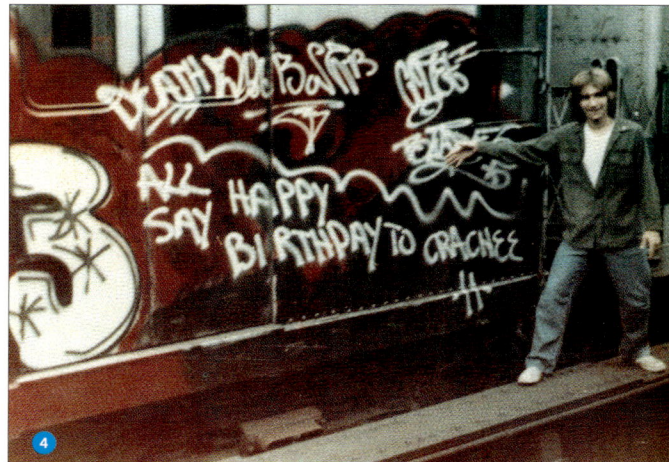

— Andrea Nelli

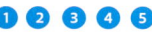

The souvenir photos of New York writers in 1973. Among these Blade, Vamm and The Crazy 5 crew

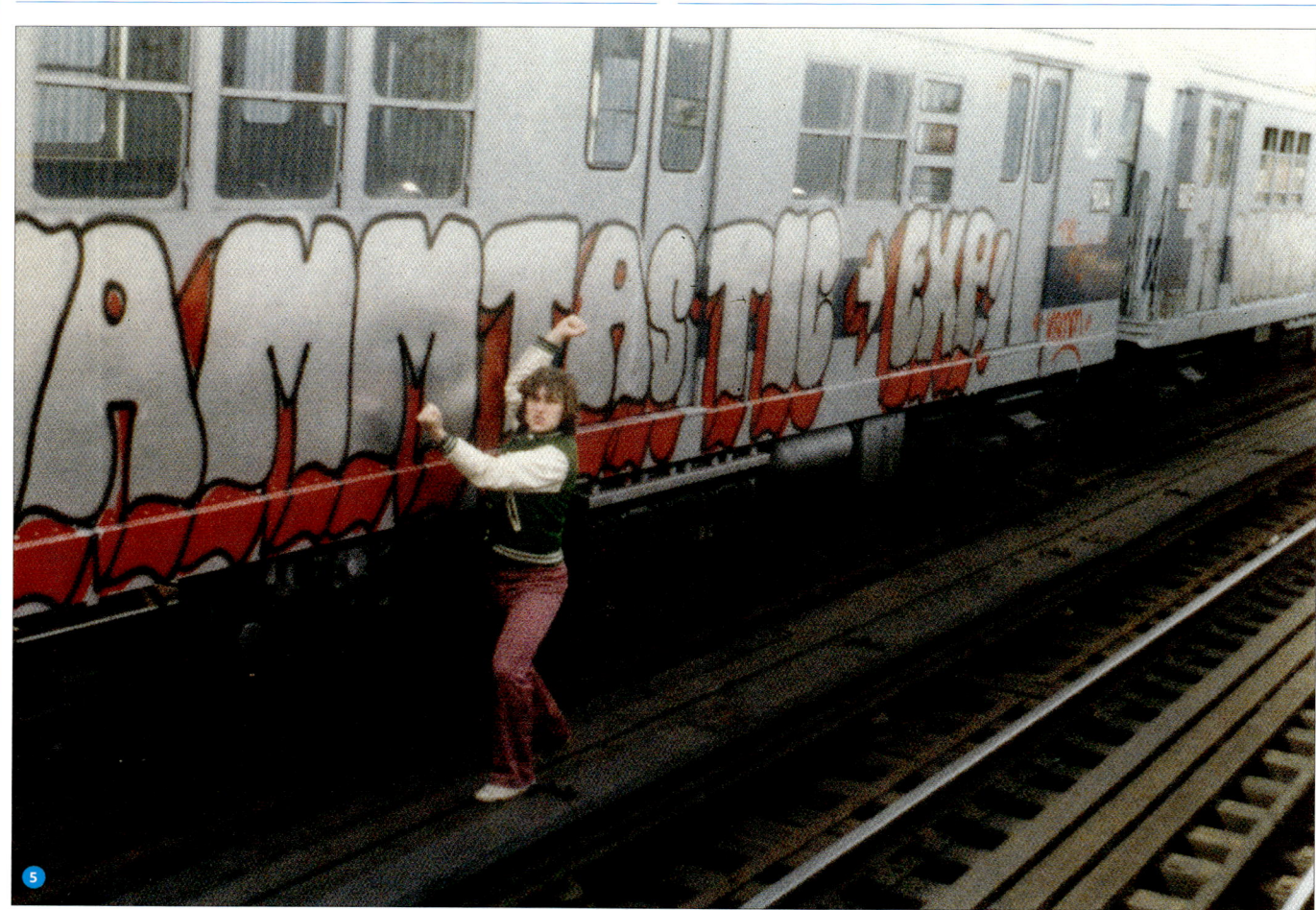

— Andrea Nelli

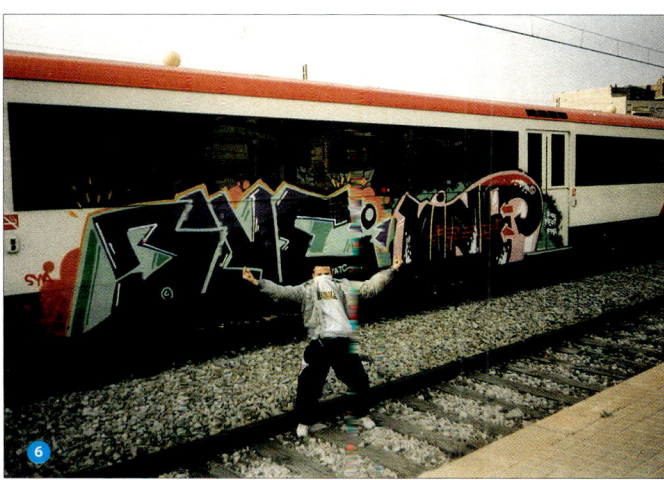

– Vino

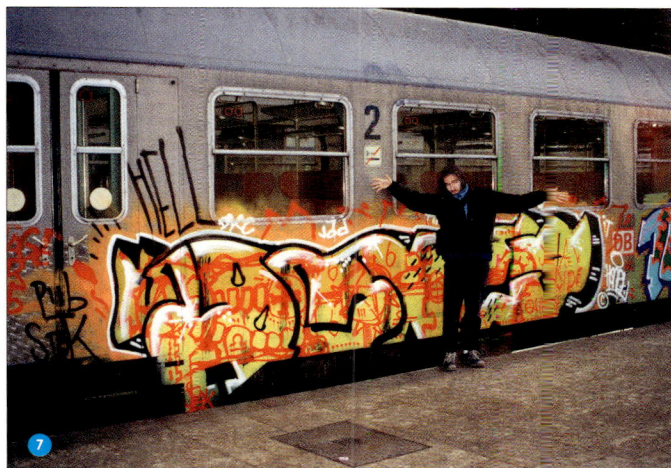

– Honet

6 Blue in front of his Cercanias. Barcelona 1997

7 Honet – SDK in Dusseldorf, 1996

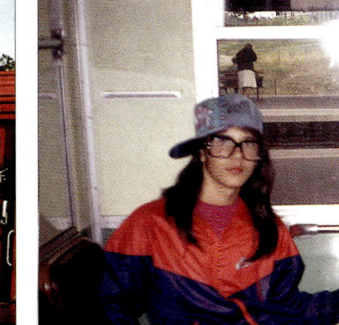

– ALL

– Puppet

8 All crew on Oslo subway, 2001

9 Puppet posing in front of his tag, Sweden 1986

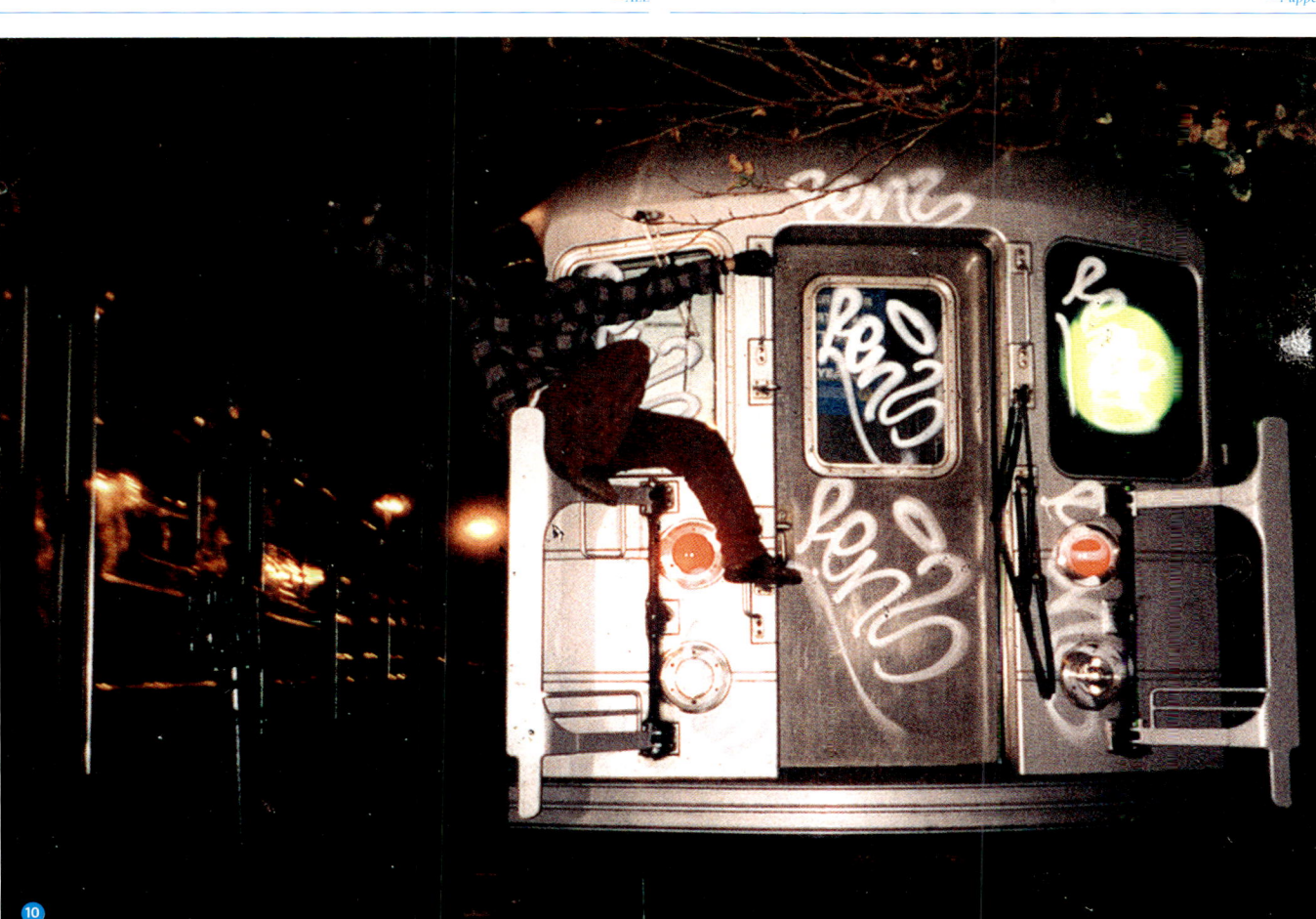

– Rens

10 Rens conquers New York. 1993

IGTIMES AND OTHER

The origin of Writing-related
publications narrated by the founder
of IGTimes

David Schmidtlapp / New York City
>

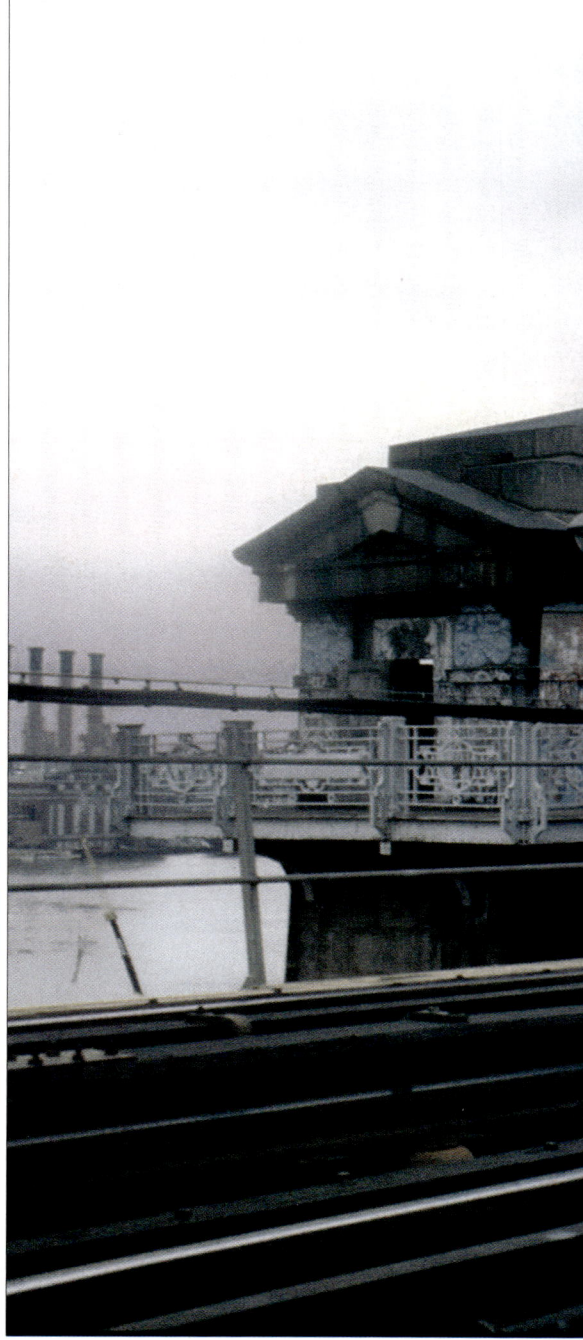

The idea of a publication whose focus would be this inner-city phenomenon of 'Aerosol culture' came some time in 1983, a good decade after Super Kool 223 painted the first masterpiece on a train. In the beginning the subway was the one and only medium for the art. That was its beauty, and its impetus: a travelling vision, a performance of an ethereal alphabet in a repressive environment. New York had lost its civic and corporate vision and was in total decline like all other urban areas in America. In New York, art was filling the vacuum. New York had the mystique of a 'crazy big city'. It was dangerous and dirty, and more importantly, a place in which to create. The city had become the art capital of the world since the last world war. Now an indigenous art form was emerging not from any art school but from the streets. Inner-city youth, mostly blacks and Latinos were expressing and developing a new visual language and a new understanding for the end of the 20th century. This illegal activity of spray-painting monikers on the side of subway cars would have an impact beyond these young 'writers', their generation, and their city.

I was a part of the population of artists in the early 70's who came to New York City from elsewhere to do our thing. I grew up in the counter-cultural scenes of the late 60's. I used to hawk (sell) the Black Panther and other underground newspapers on the streets of a radical, university, Mid-America town. One of my favourite underground rags was IT International Times, the notorious mid-60's London publication. I moved into downtown New York. It was offbeat, cheap and vibrant. By the mid 70's, when Soho was peaking as the centre of the downtown art world, I found my niche doing 'photopages', collages out of my own photography in a local cultural rag. The painted subways that ran throughout the city

> ## The next generation of International youth would soon emerge and Aerosol Art would explode. The culture would evolve into a worldwide phenomenon

(underground in Manhattan) were a part of the creative environment. Most artists downtown had an affinity for this new art but there was our pervasive cultural divide of class, race and age. By the end of the decade, this inner-city culture proved to be such a creative force that these barriers started to crack, allowing for cultural hybrids and cross-pollination. Group shows started to include 'writers', mirroring the collaboration of downtown musicians with the growing uptown Hip Hop phenomenon. Downtown street art became more creative and

abundant. By the early 80's the whole city was bombed and 'graffiti' was the craze. So too was the opening of 'graffiti' galleries. Downtown people were jumping up and down like they had discovered subway painting, Hip Hop and everything in between.

This is when the idea of an underground publication came to me. It would be a parody of this new hip scene. Major art magazines were claiming that the art was unique to New York and that it would soon disappear and now was the time to corner the market with your own stable of artists. The environment was ripe for satire. *Subway Art* and *Wild Style* were about to be released. A few, fellow downtown artists aided in getting interviews and photos. We were all anonymous, crediting only our nom de guerre. I first thought my audience would be the hip downtown crowd, but with Vol. 1, all the writers started to appear. The younger writers, who were continuing and evolving the traditions with their current subway hits, and were left out of the books and galleries. *IGT* was the place to publish their photos. The early writers from the 70's, the trailblazers and innovators, also had their story to tell. Vol. 2 featured an interview with these early writers. *IGT* became a forum for the artists and the voice of the emerging Aerosol culture – embracing its history, its current executions, and its undeniable future.

In 1984, worldwide youth had barely developed their Aerosol skills. I know, 'graffiti' has existed ever since someone put up a wall in Babylon and the Aerosol can had been the preferred tool in many, maybe most street hits since the 60's. In the mid 80's besides publishing *IGT*, I was travelling around Europe and the West Coast doing my slide/ lights shows, a skill I had developed earlier in downtown NYC clubs. Wherever I went, I would check out the streets. London, LA, Zurich, Amsterdam and later Barcelona and Paris. There were plenty of hits: art school scribbles, punk rock logos, political and personal screams. Among this barrage of street art, a couple of local up-starts had tried their hand at Aerosol techniques. A few NYC writers had also travelled and had gotten up. The International Aerosol assault of the Western alphabet had begun.

The next generation of International youth would soon emerge and Aerosol Art would explode. The culture would evolve into a worldwide phenomenon. New York carried a certain cache. Outside of New York, the art had more mass appeal. All kinds of people were amazed by it. It had a hidden marketing element in a larger cultural context. This art form pushed forth the name/logo game in a totally creative way on a large public scale at a time in the early 70's when corporate advertising was at an all-time low. It would take years for the ruling elites to figure out the formula and revalue the urban landscape. Labelling the art 'graffiti' was a good start. This "art import from the ghetto" became the cultural force of creativity and energy that people wanted to be around, to live off of. That is why photographers were photographing it, the youth was intimating it, and marketers were selling it. The culture would be exposed to the pitfalls of growing

consumerism. The negative aspects were resident, too. The obsessive nature of youth could always directly lead to vandalism. It seemed that the level of violence inside the culture among writers and crews grew with each generation. There was a built-in desperado quality to each new generation of writers in New York, as if they missed something, as if time was running out.

Someday the authorities would find the means and the capital to stop it.

How would this culture in the mid-80's speak to International youth? When the art was basically dead in the subways in New York in 1989, the worldwide 'Writing' phenomenon was in full swing and Aerosol publications started to appear. Aerosol proved again to be such a force of vision that it inspired youths to be adventurous and evolve the art form within their own repressive global

DECLINATIONS

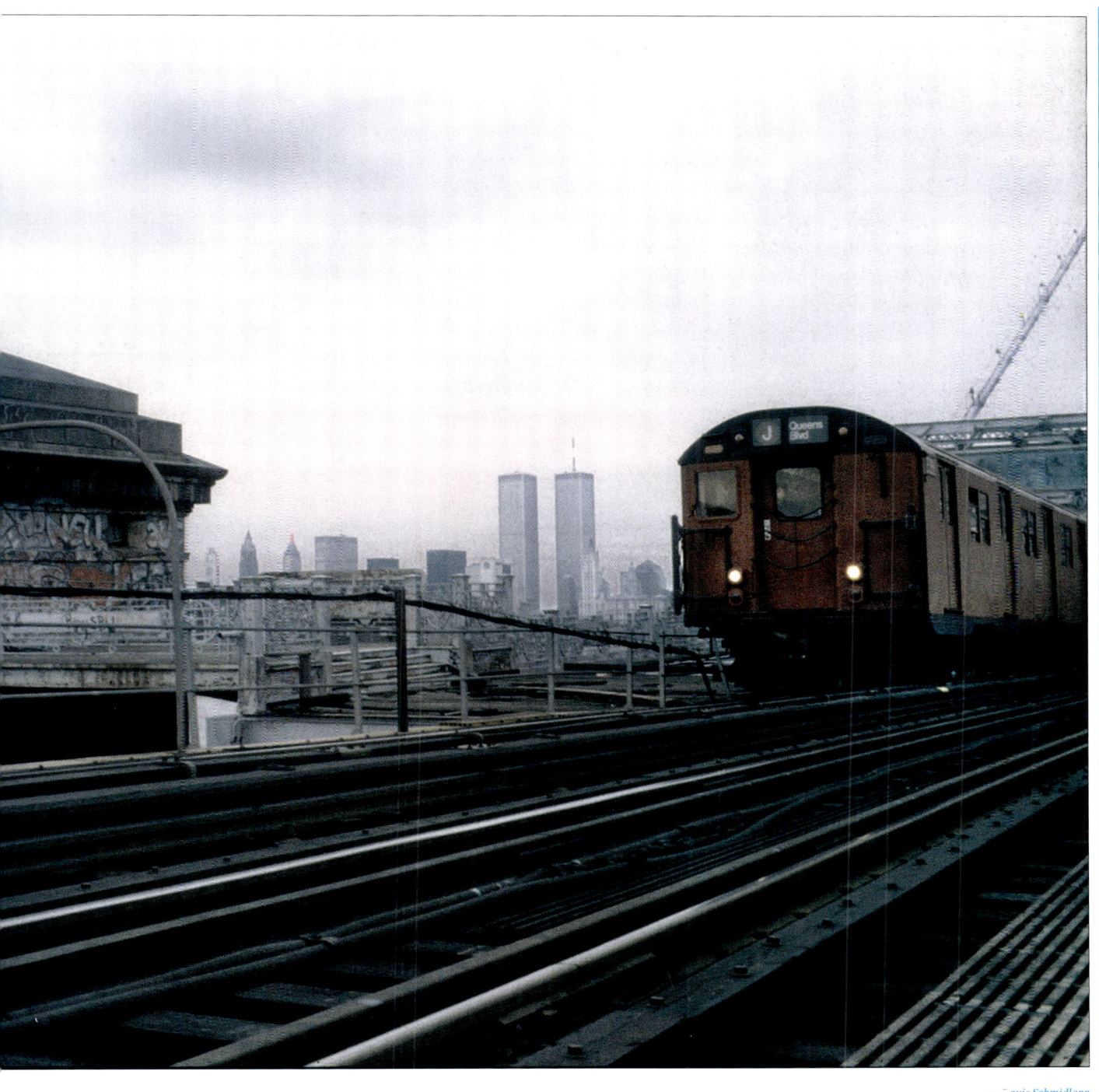

TWIN TOWERS

DAVID SCHMIDLAPP
New York 1988. "By the time the twin towers were finally full, only clean trains were running"
From Off Camera

— *David Schmidlapp*

environments. Western Europe was urban to the core, with vast mass transportation systems to embellish. Europe had strong traditions of working class solitary, International art, and street rebellions. Immigration in the 80's had also changed the face of Europe. Kids could paint in their local cities and the next day paint in another major city. A vision of a European community of *Aerosol* artists would become a reality before the corporate class had the means to capitalise on their own idea of an EU.

The energies and hopes of youth formed a culture of survival in an increasingly more consumer-orientated and global-capitalist world. *IGT* gained status as the precedent and reference point for all the Aerosol zines that would appear. It was the first and only zine for several years. There was a xeroxed zine, actually called *Aerosol*,

coming out of Belgium several years before *IGT*. It focused on all kinds of underground expressions, including 'graffiti': yet they made no distinction of style or the movement coming out of New York.

They were part of a mass underground of zines that were continuing the International counter-culture of the 70's into the 80's with mostly local and small circulations. *IGTimes* naturally became a part of this network for trades and listings. For distribution it was a 'word of mouth, travel by foot' operation. Hip Hop shops certainly didn't exist in these pre-digital era / Internet times.

Whenever I did my slide shows, I would search for any Aerosol attempts. *IGTimes* was my calling card at youth centres and school yards in immigrant and working class neighbourhoods, and all the funky art spaces. Copies were left at old head shops; comic, commie and anarchist

bookstores; hip fashion shops and galleries. Along with a couple of my associate slide-artists and a few travelling writers, the *GTimes* found itself in the first year of production in London, Zurich, LA, Paris, Rome, Amsterdam, Berlin, Australia, Hawaii, Barcelona and even Japan, Mexico, and Nicaragua.

By the time *Ghetto Art* in LA and *14K* in Zurich appeared in 1988, more than half of our 3000 plus circulation was outside New York City. There was direct communication with these early publications, plus others like *Graphotism* - London, *True Colorz* - Amsterdam, *Vapors* - Australia, *Game Over* - Barcelona, and *14K* - Zurich, comparing our growing distribution spots throughout the globe.

By 1986 with Vol. 8, the P.H.A.S.E. 2 collaboration had started, intensifying the standards and the direction

> CONTINUES ON PAGE 74

> CONTINUES FROM PAGE 73

of *IGT*. First, Phase was a pioneer who had an unquestionable influence in laying down the foundation and executing style in Aerosol writing. He was also a major influence in and on B-boy culture, a master and legendary 'collagist'. He visually promoted Hip Hop in the world with Hip Hop flyers, and was a formalist in terms of aesthetics. Culture to him was all about creation and evolution, like he has always said, " The art would have gone nowhere; if these elements hadn't existed." I, on the other hand, saw the culture as an extension, a jump-off for counter-culture, a post-modern culture with a sense of irony and critique. *IGT* became the third mind, it spoke for the strength of Aerosol culture and the unity of youth worldwide. It would scream at the perpetrators, the imitators, the marketers, and would satirise the globalisation of consumer culture, which now includes our beloved 'graffiti'. The 'g' word has always been a misappropriated label from the outside. The word 'Aerosol' was coined and was now in circulation.

Vulcan would soon add to the mix. This master stylist reported from the field in Vol 10. (1987) of his own trip with T-Kid to an 'alleged competition' in Brindligton, England. The promoter was scamming money from a local charity and council. A panel of two senior citizens and a teenage soap-opera star judged the competition. His cries in the *IGT* were for Aerosol activism, in effect. In the following year, Vulcan became this competition's new judge and jury.

Phase went Down Under with Daze on a Velore & Double - 0 tour and exposed Aerosol Australia and critiqued the local zine, *Vapors*. Again featured in Vol. 11 (1988). Travelling worldwide was nothing new for P.H.A.S.E.2, he'd been going back and forth to Europe since the first Hip Hop tour in 1982 with exhibitions and promotions. His presence and global executions have always been an inspiration to the M.A.S.A.I; Mighty Soldiers Armageddon International. A global call went out in 1988 for uniqueness, originality, expertise, and execution. It was the *IGT*'s Aerosol-Art Rock-a-ton. All the results from nearly a hundred entries were published in Vol. 11, 1989. There were ten winners. Beside those crazy cats from rocking Cali and the hard-core nuts from NYC, there were three European pieces: Intra Mural, Paris by Gor, Scale, Loomit; Capones Prohibition Rock and Fabulous Bomb Inability, Munich by Don, ZaZa and Cemnoz; and Public Enemy, Copenhagen by Jest, Dimer, Sketzh. Remember *IGT* was still only in the black and white offset mode with only some of the earlier issues in a funky duo color.

The 90's started as a slamming decade. Havoc reeked across America and in the 50th state of Hawaii, by the *IGT* Aerosol Armada, a slide/lecture extravaganza. The throw down came to Craigsfield Youth Centre in Scotland and The Whitecapel Gallery in London. I continued the Aerosol images in my slide shows in Paris and Barcelona and Phase parked a massive portion of the armada in Italy. More screams and shouts and photos of worldwide style – T.I.G.H.T. - Vol. 12, 13, 14, 15. And finally color! The *IG-Times* publishing project accumulated with Style: Writing from the Underground, another Aerosol first - the first book from the artists themselves. And in 1996, copies were printed and published in Italy in a duo language of English and Italian.

IGT set the standard of style worldwide, its cultural critiques and social satire illuminated the broader spectrum. And whilst it was a pioneer, it paid dearly for it. We were constantly locked out of distribution by the new mega stores and jealous punks. Too political, too judgmental, too visionary (they only wished), and 'Too Large for the Shelf!' As time went on, there were more and more twenty-year old 'know-it-alls'. The new millennium called for it. The digital era finally buried us. With the explosion of the Internet, bullshit became information, and self-delusion knowledge.

Had the culture become only consumerism and/or vandalism? Did fashion become the last refuge of art? Are the collectors cashing in and out with our Aerosol treasures? Will the retarded museums have the last say? IGTimes has now become a collector's item and New York a tourist town, yet the desire to create pushes on. Will youth once again take up the call in our brave, new and imploding world and evolve the art? As Jean Genet once said, "The creative act is always a criminal act." The human imagination cannot be conquered.

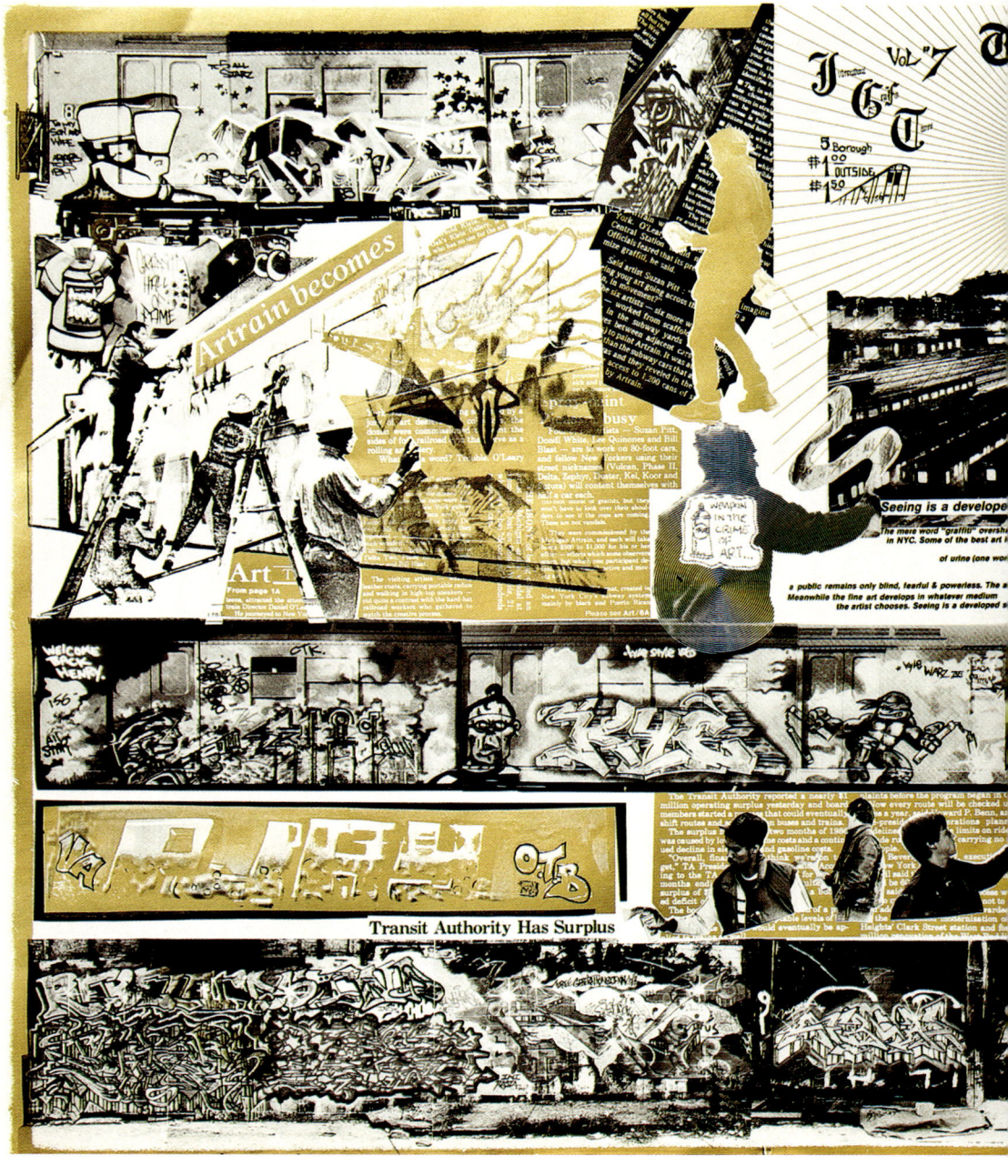

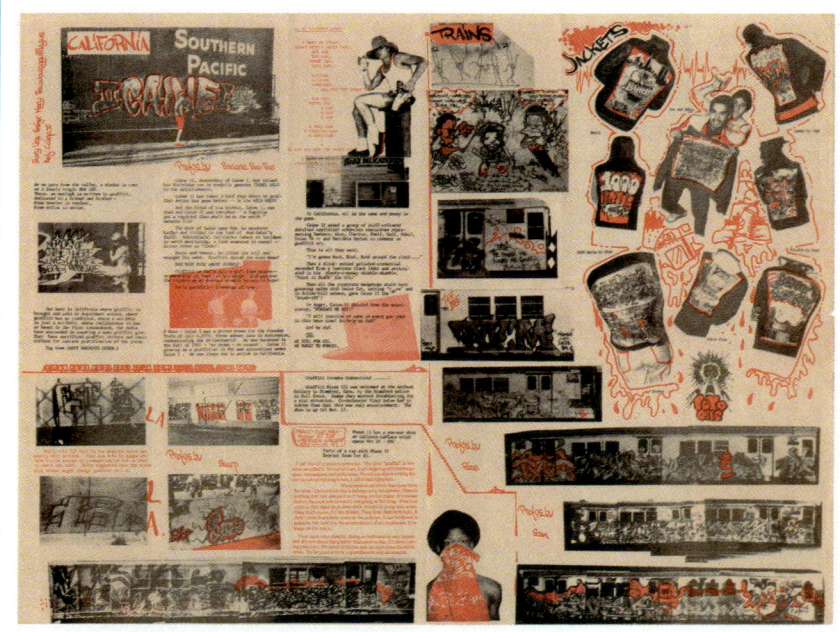

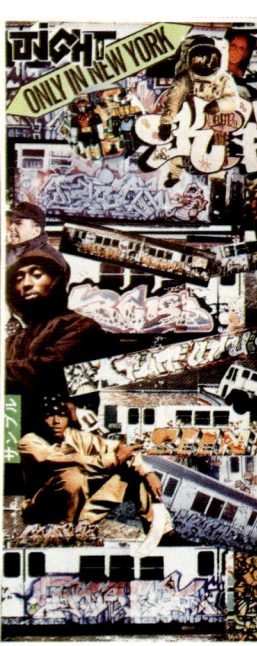

– IGT archive

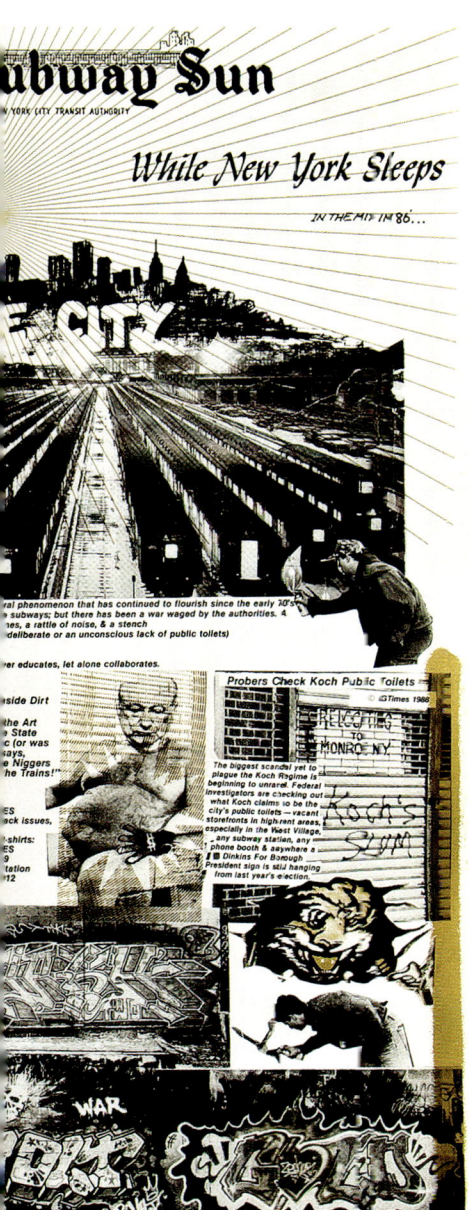

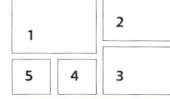

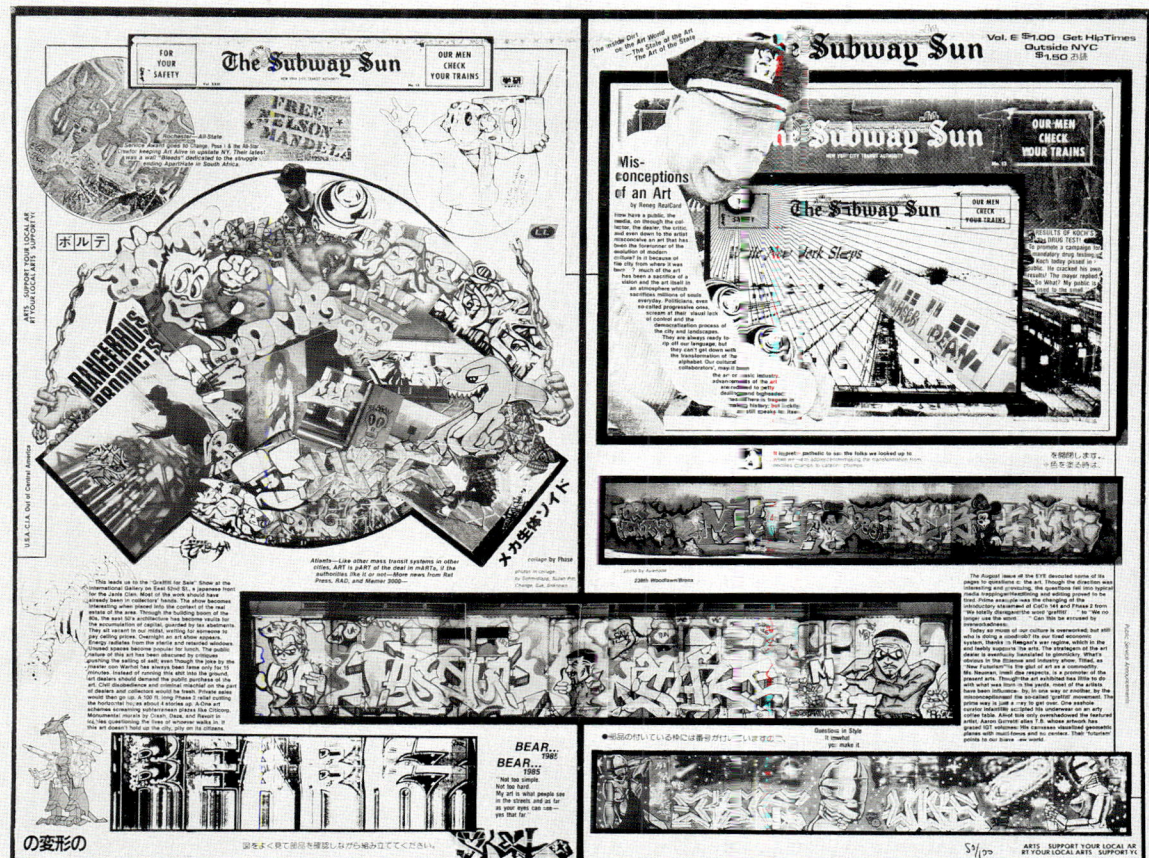

— IGT archive

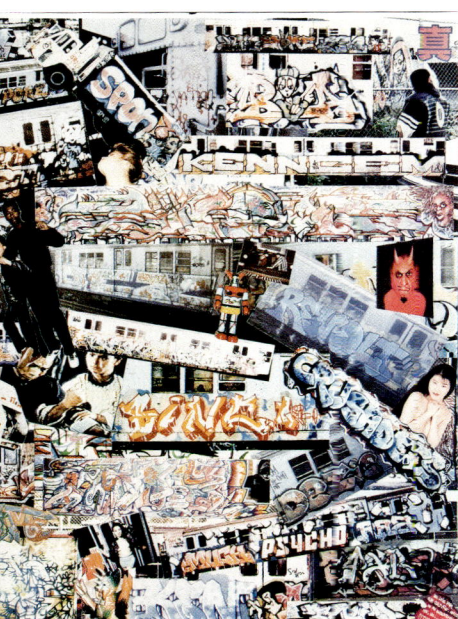

— IGT archive

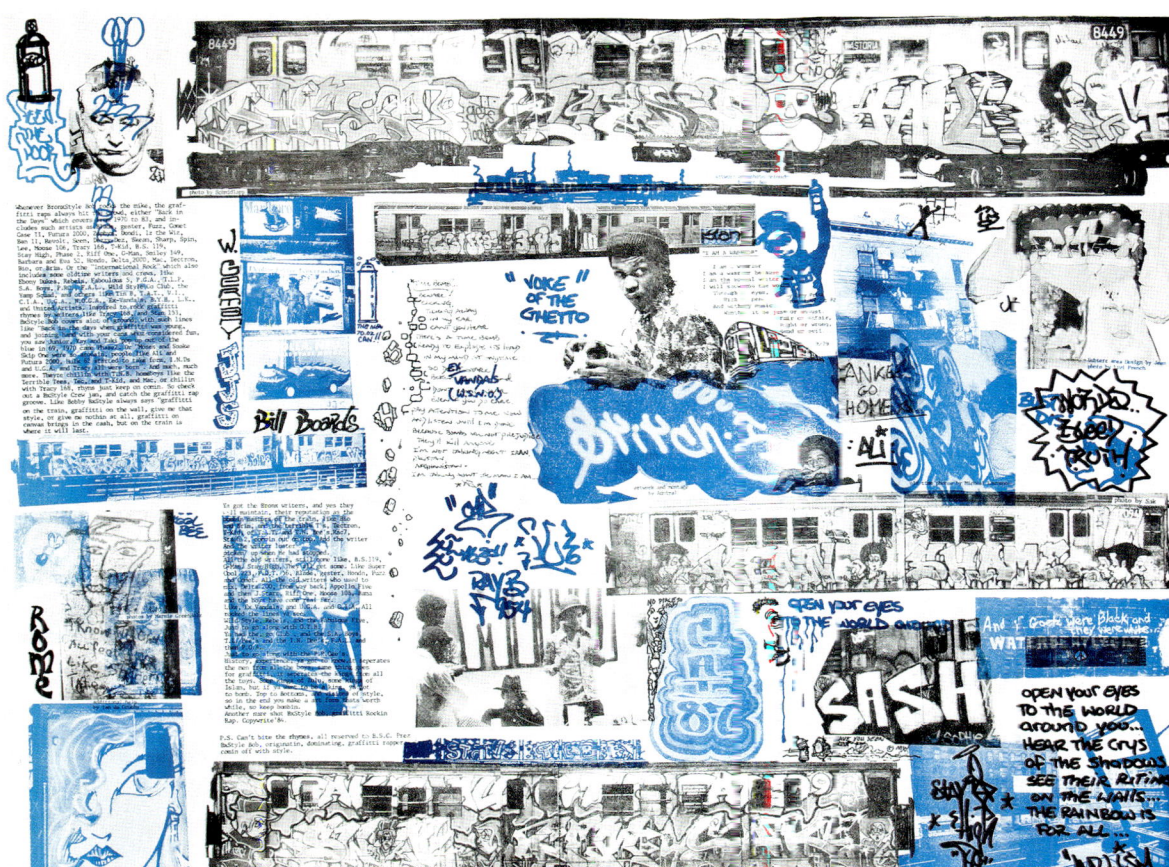

The man who saw it all

Buddy Esquire designed some of the most striking and vibrant flyers in the early days of Hip Hop in the Bronx. Here he talks about his work.

Interview by Johan Kugelberg
Courtesy of Soul Jazz Records

When did you start designing flyers?
It started around the time I was writing graffiti – that started roughly in 1972 and we didn't get onto the trains until 1973.

When did you do your first flyer?
I knew Tony Tone back when I was going to Stevenson High School. My graffiti start was after I quit school. I just kept going at it with the pen, you know, scratched it on paper, and I got better. And he was liking my style.

Do you remember what the very first flyer was?
Yes, I remember it very well. It was made in November of 1978 for IS 131. I don't

have a copy of that one right now; I wish I did. Actually, that is my second flyer. The first flyer I made for some outside jam back in '77.

When did it start getting really frantic in terms of workload and how many flyers were being made?
After I started getting into design – instead of designing backgrounds, I started using press type. The work got better and I was slowly getting more calls. So needless to say, I was spending a lot of time at home.

How many flyers would you be doing in a week?
Sometimes two or three a week, something like that.

And when did it switch so you started getting paid for it? Were Baron and Breakout already paying?
They were paying but they weren't paying. I was getting very little money - $5, $15, you know?

So a lot of times there would be a party that would have your flyer, but you didn't show up at the actual gig?
Sometimes, yeah. And then after a while, there was a time, like in '79 for a couple of months I just stayed home and made the flyers! And then, they were always talking about, "Oh, you gotta go, you gotta go". Because like I said, I wasn't really that

type. I just made the flyers, stayed home. And then finally I went to one, this was maybe around March of '79 and I noticed that it was different because they sounded different, more polished. Of course, I'm referring to the Funky Four. And after that I decided, okay, maybe I'd better go again, you know?

So when the first records came out and when Rapper's Delight got on the radio and all that, how did people in the inside community like yourself feel about that?
That's a good question. Me, I didn't really have too much of a feeling about it because I'd heard one or two things on the radio. Because mostly at the time, everything was just on tape, so we'd hear sometimes people on the bus with tapes. The first thing I can remember hearing on tape was "King Tim Personality Jock" by the Fatback Band. And then I heard Sugarhill, but when I heard Sugarhill, I'd heard Big Bank Hanks rhyme and I was like, yeah, he's biting off of Caz! Because in fact, I heard Caz do that rhyme back at the PAL back in '79. And then after that, I heard the Sugarhill record.

Tell me more about the period around '81, '82, '83. Did the community aspect of this start to drag a bit more, or what happened? Did the shows get bigger?
In '81 and '82, that was when they had the so-called "Downtown scene", which I wasn't a part of, that was more Phase.

So a lot of times what I did was just make flyers for parties out of state.

And then, go even later than that. We're starting to talk '82, '83. That's when it seems like a lot of the originators were kind of fading from the scene. Why do you think that was?
Why? I think certain people were maybe looking for something different. That's what I think it was.

And this was just like a phase of your lives that had passed?
Yeah, you had that and then you had other people coming up.
That was around the time '82, '83 – Run DMC starting coming out and then the Sucka MCs, that must have been about '83. And then after that began the decline of the old school.

I agree with that because I think once Run DMC came around, it was a different art form. It wasn't really the same. When did you do your last flyers?
My last one was, let me see, I was doing one for Rodney C back in '84.

How do you feel about the renewed interest in your artwork now, like people like me showing up?
I find that to be very strange because it's been 20 years, and to be honest with you, I never thought anybody would be interested.

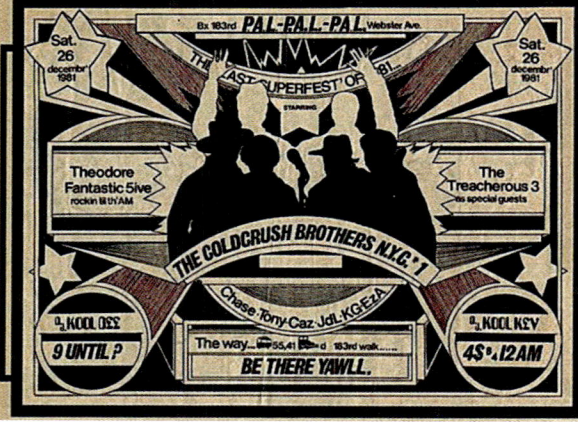

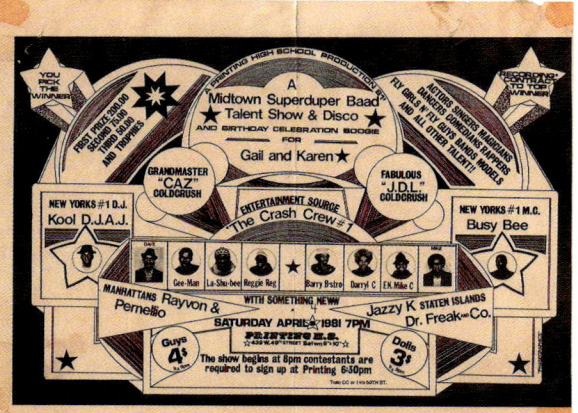

ICONS

Flyers for the block parties organised in the Bronx. Desgned by Phase II and Buddy Esquire

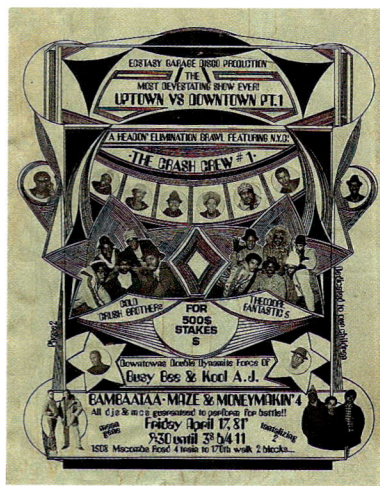

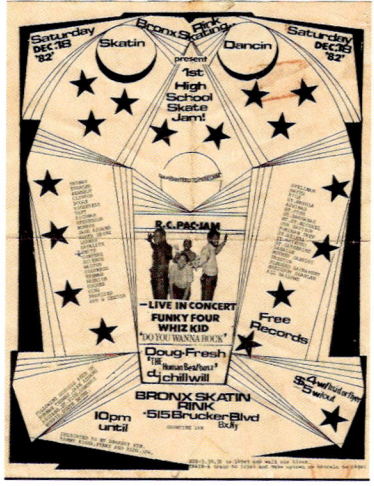

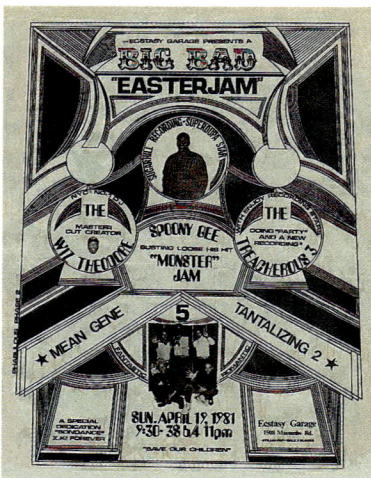

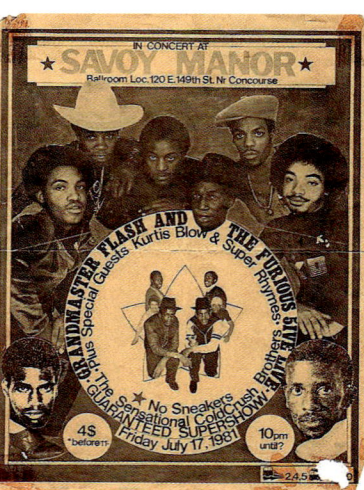

Wildstyle sommelier

The genesis of Phase II's Wildstyle collage and of an aesthetic originating from block party flyers. The style that contaminated IGT's layout and influenced an entire generation

Phase II / New York City
>

IGTIMES WAS CREATED BY YANQUI JUNKIE AND HIS COUNTER PART DAVE SCHMIDLAPP IN 1983/1984. DAVE BELIEVED IN THE CULTURE AND WANTED TO SHOW-CASE IT AMONGST ALL THE POLITICS AND REALITIES THAT IT WAS ENGULFED IN AND SURROUNDED WITH. I GOT WITH HIM AND WEEDED OUT WHO WAS JUST SUCKING THE CULTURES BLOOD, BASICALLY I GAVE IT MORE FLAVOUR AND SOME EXTRA INTENSITY. THAT SET IT OFF.

THE DIFFERENT LOOK CAUGHT MORE ATTENTION, EVERYONE FROM THE WEST COAST TO AUSTRALIA AND BEYOND RAN WITH OUR FORMAT. MY PARAM-ETER TO CHOOSE WRITER'S PICTURES WAS ABOUT A STANDARD, STYLE AND DEFINITELY SPIRITUALITY, EVEN IF I WASN'T THE ONLY ONE PICKING FLICKS. IN GENERAL, THE PROBLEM I HAVE WITH FANZINES IS THAT THERE'S NO STANDARD FOR WHAT THEY PUT IN THEM. SO BASICALLY A LOT OF FANZINES PREACH THAT BEING BASELESS TASTELESS WRECKLESS STYLE-LESS AND WHACK IS FINE. THEY JUST THROW ANY OLD SHIT IN THE FANZINE, THUS WRITERS DON'T EVER HAVE TO HAVE A STANDARD OR STEP THEIR GAME UP. SO THE WEAKEST STUFF IS ACCEPTABLE SIMPLY BE-CAUSE IT'S OUT THERE, NOT BECAUSE WHOEVER DID IT IS REALLY TRUE TO THE GAME AND DEDICATED OR EVEN A UNIQUE STYLIST.

IT'S LIKE ANYTHING IS ACCEPTABLE. WHEN ALL THIS BEGAN THE STANDARD WAS WHAT MADE CATS HUNGRY AND ACCEPTED. IF YOU DIDN'T RISE TO THE OCCASION...YOU COULDN'T HANG. IT'S LIKE WEAK BOXERS GET KNOCKED OUT. YOU COME WITH YOUR BEST. BUT THAT DOESN'T EXIST AND THIS IS WHERE UNDERSTANDING YOUR ESSENCE AND FOUNDATION ARE IMPORTANT. THE SPIRITUALITY AND SUBSTANCE GET LOST WHEN ANY ONE 'CAN' DO IT OR IS BEING DEEMED AS ABLE, WHEN REALLY THEY CAN'T ON THE ESSENTIAL AND TECHNICAL LEVELS.

IT'S JUST THAT THE STANDARD IS SO LOW THAT AN ARMLESS CAT CAN DO IT. AT ONE POINT, WRITERS WERE 'JUDGED' BY ONE OR A FEW THINGS: DEDICA-TION, TENACITY, GETTING UP, FLAVOR AND STYLE. BUT TODAY, AFTER THREE DECADES OF THE PIECE BE-ING IN THE GAME THE STAKES SHOULD BE HIGHER.

PEOPLE HAVE BOMBED BEFORE. TECHNICALLY IS THAT ANYTHING NEW? NOW IF YOU DO IT ON AN-OTHER LEVEL WITH FLAVOR THAT WOULD BE WAY MORE DYNAMIC AND A LOT MORE ACCEPTABLE FROM A VISUAL POINT OF VIEW. IF YOU'RE JUDGING STYLE WHAT IS WHACK IS JUST GOING TO BE WHACK, NO MATTER IF I DID IT OR WHOEVER DID IT. THERE WAS A TIME WHEN GUYS HAD TO INVENT WHAT TO DO IN ORDER TO ROCK, NOW WITH SO MUCH STUFF OUT THERE, THERE IS NO REASON TO BE WHACK. ANY-WAY AS I STATED BEFORE AS LONG AS THERE IS NO STANDARD THERE IS ALWAYS GOING TO BE ROOM AND A PLATFORM FOR THE BLANDEST STUFF TO BE 'AC-CEPTABLE', AND TO A BIG DEGREE THAT PART MAKES THE CULTURE SUCK.

TALKING STRICTLY ABOUT PIECING AND THEME WALLS, IF YOU LOOK AT THIS FROM A STYLE, LET-TERFORM AND WRITING PERSPECTIVE, CONCEPTS OUTSIDE OF ROCKING STYLE ARE NOT RELEVANT. NOT TO SAY IT DOESN'T TAKE TALENT. BUT IF YOU HAVE A WALL WHERE THE PIECES ARE MINIMAL AND THE STYLES ARE BLAND AND SIMPLE AND EVERYTHING ELSE IS OVERWHELMING, WHAT'S THE POINT IN EVEN DOING THE PIECES? GREAT ART IS DOPE BUT YOU CAN SEE THAT ALL OVER THE WORLD BY SO-CALLED ARTISTS.

IF YOU ARE A WRITER ROCK LETTERS. TAKE IT TO THE NEXT LEVEL. PAINTING A SCENE FROM THE PRE-HISTORIC AGE. THAT'S CUTE FOR THE PUBLIC BUT IT DOESN'T SAY MUCH FOR STYLE. A HALL OF FAME SHOULD HAVE A STANDARD BUT THAT DOESN'T EVEN EXIST IN NYC ANY LONGER. SUBSTANCE IS LOSING IT'S VOLUME. TODAY ANYONE CAN BE IN A HALL OF FAME PAINTING STUPID STUFF LIKE OCTOPUSES IN THERE WHERE THERE WAS ONCE A BIO OR A VULCAN, BUT THAT'S NOT EVEN CLOSE TO COMPARING. WHAT THEN IS THE POINT? BUMS ARE NOT INDUCTED INTO HALLOWED INSTITUTIONS. DO YOU SEE NOBODIES ON THE COVER OF TIME?

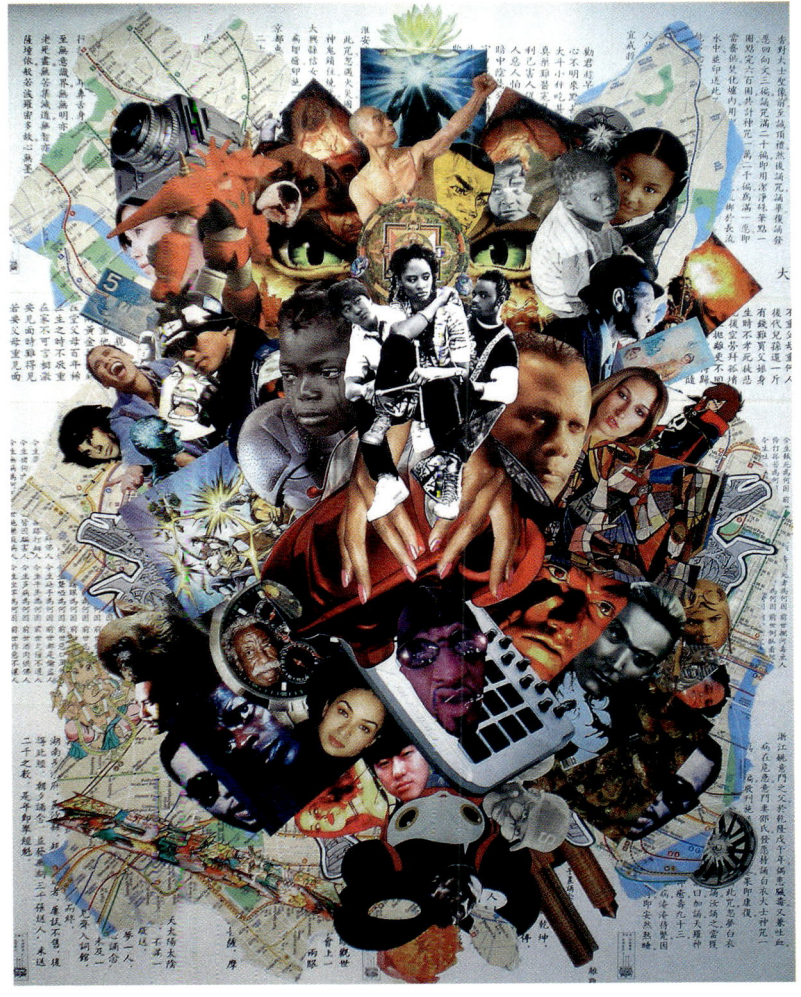

Wildstyle collage by Phase II   — Phase II

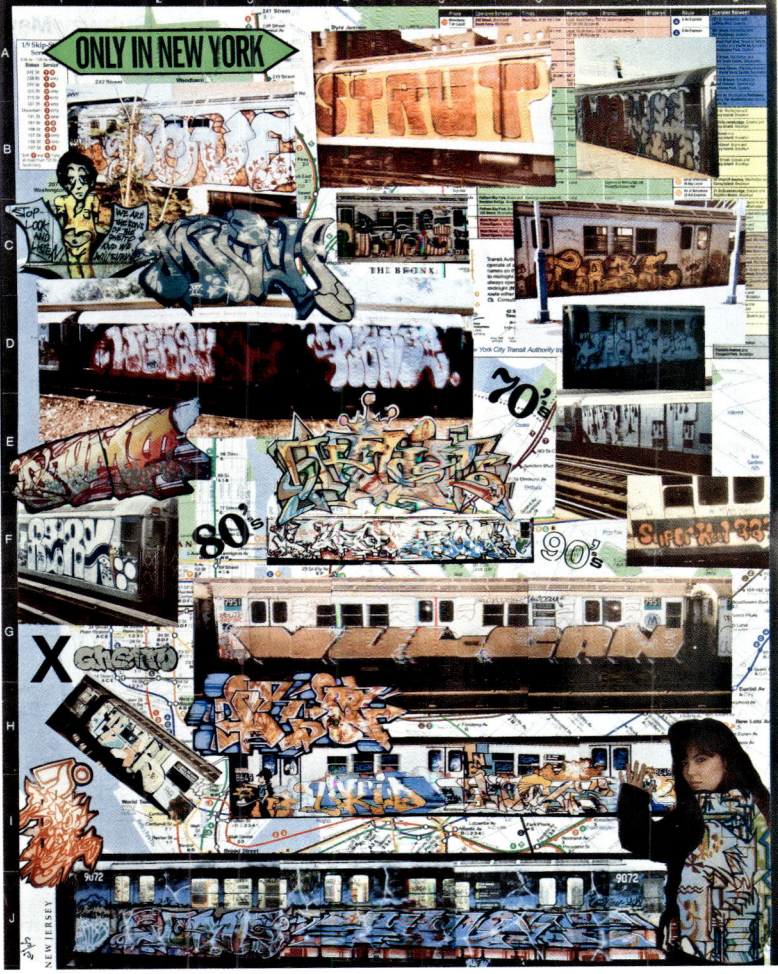

Twenty years of styles on the subway cars in New York assembled by Phase II   — IGT

Frames in time: formats compared

The first Writing fanzines conformed to a format that had already been adopted by other movements using self-production as their main communicative approach. DIY (Do-It-Yourself) became an essential condition in this field as well, fundamentally centred on photographs and brief text contributions.

In the early 90's the fanzine standard (vertical A4 format, photocopied and reproduced) appeared in a moment of total disinterest towards this phenomenon on the part of the European media. Self-production became the only possible means, in a time when the computer was not yet widespread and xerox machines were accessible to everyone.

The first numbers of *Fantazie* (Denmark), *Bomber* (Holland) and *14K* (Switzerland) gathered sketches and images and glued them on sheets of paper supplied with brief informative articles.

The presence of text is indicative of the need to inform and disseminate the rare input that was being whispered by voices in the background. Vice versa, sketches started divulging the first European styles, concentrating attention on the structure of the letters.

The black and white format of the first fanzines nevertheless ceased to exist fairly rapidly, seeing the demand for quality photographic material gradually increased, until becoming a prerequisite.

– THE COMING OF COLOUR

The first coloured pages were a personal bet of the editors, who undertook the risk of investing on an amateur project without any financial warrantee. This leap of faith flashed past all stages and allowed these zines to progressively increase the quality of their materials: the demand for colour on the part of writers became a fundamental point of comparison, thus generating a gap between the various publications. In general, the first pages to be offered in colour were the cover and the back, followed by the central page. This initial structure of the pilot format gave direction to all the fanzines present on the market, towards a strongly standardised disposition. The central page, as the second, the third, and the back, became a display for all the best burners, almost always coloured pieces painted in halls of fame or particularly well-executed trains. Colour transformed fanzines dedicated to Writing into volumes that can be compared to art catalogues, in which works were progressively listed in a dense, homogenous grid. Each piece was framed in an identical cell, presenting walls and trains painted with different styles on the same plane. The dense presence of pieces made up for the scarcity of publications dedicated to the Writing scene, allowing a limited number of pages to concentrate the vast landscape of International productions.

– HORIZONTAL FORMATS AND THE LIKE

Halfway through the 90's a new model of fanzine gained ground, still based on the A4 format, only used horizontally. The binding on the short end allowed

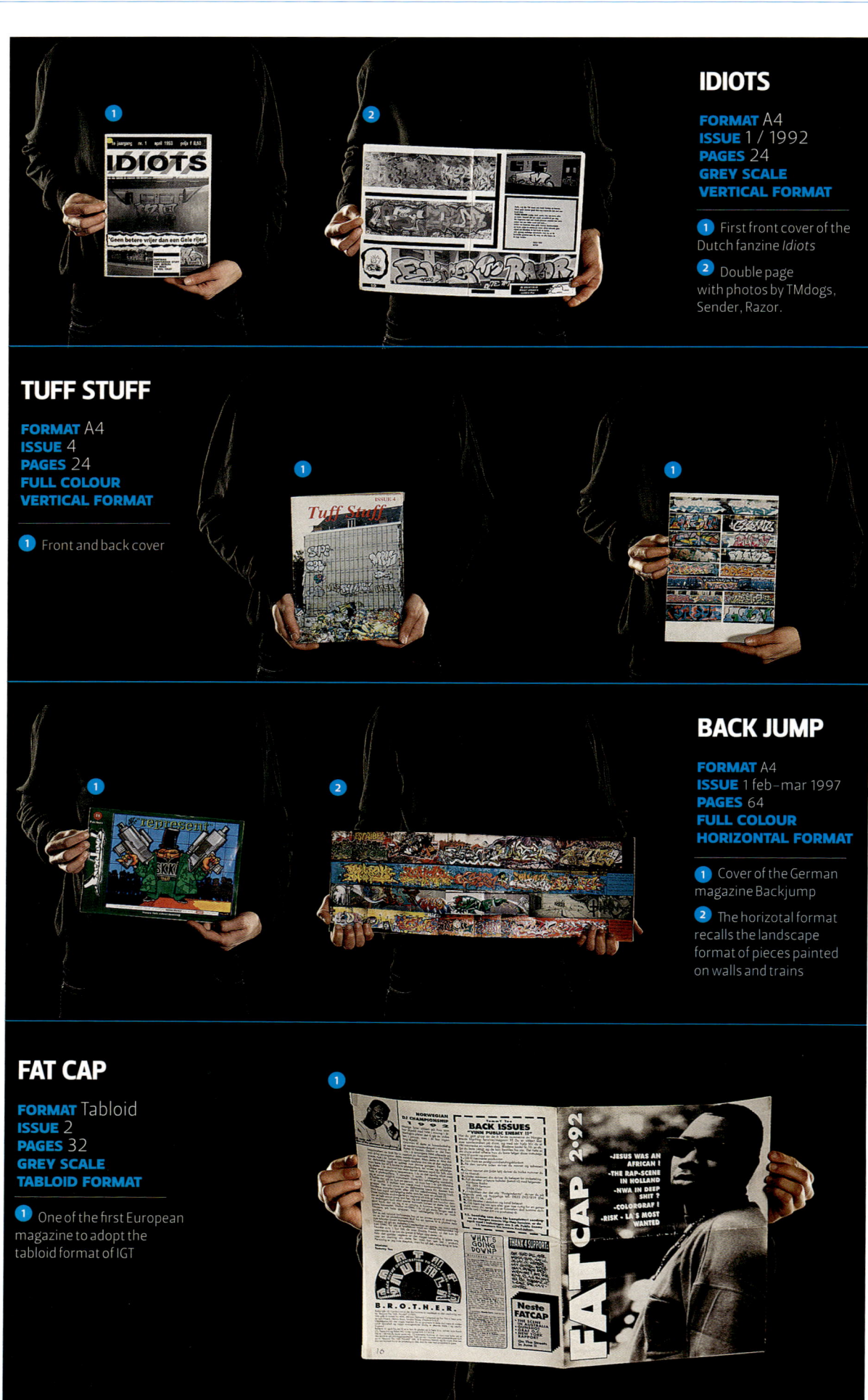

IDIOTS

FORMAT A4
ISSUE 1 / 1992
PAGES 24
GREY SCALE
VERTICAL FORMAT

① First front cover of the Dutch fanzine *Idiots*

② Double page with photos by TMdogs, Sender, Razor.

TUFF STUFF

FORMAT A4
ISSUE 4
PAGES 24
FULL COLOUR
VERTICAL FORMAT

① Front and back cover

BACK JUMP

FORMAT A4
ISSUE 1 feb–mar 1997
PAGES 64
FULL COLOUR
HORIZONTAL FORMAT

① Cover of the German magazine Backjump

② The horizotal format recalls the landscape format of pieces painted on walls and trains

FAT CAP

FORMAT Tabloid
ISSUE 2
PAGES 32
GREY SCALE
TABLOID FORMAT

① One of the first European magazine to adopt the tabloid format of IGT

the magazine to be leafed through like a photo album that well fits the panoramic format of many pictures. The double page, once opened, became a structure that facilitated the vision of long murals, whole-cars and end-to-ends.

The same view of a train recalls the orientation of these horizontal A4's, which became the standard for magazines such as *Backjumps* from Berlin.

Other than these variations on the theme, few attempts at reinterpreting the model took place, often coinciding at most with the use of a wider sheet of paper. *IGT* by David Schmidlapp and Phase II, as the Norwegian *Fat Cap* and the Swiss *14K*, were among the first fanzines to pursue a format that recalled the periodical and the tabloid.

Their pages embraced contents tied not only to Writing but to Hip Hop in general, with the urgency to publish abacuses of photos accompanied by a large quantity of textual information.

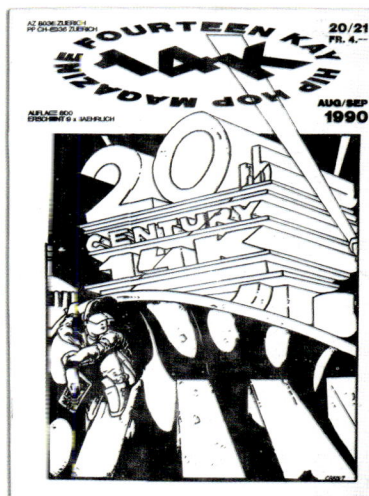

14K #20/21, 1990   — *14K archive*

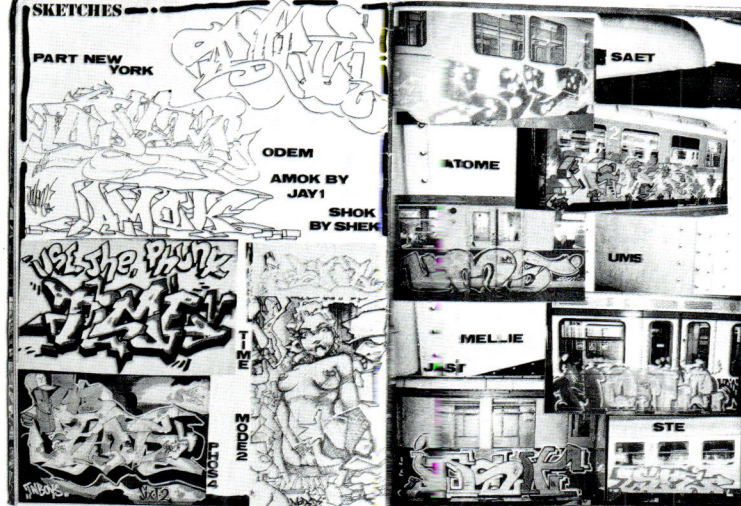

Overkill #7, September 94. Sketches and train pages   — *Overkill archive*

Opposition to style levelling

Mode 2, one of the most published writers in the 90's, explains the pros and cons of the fanzine network

Mode 2, TCA–CTK / London
>

Around '93–'94 there was a boom in the number of fanzines that came out, especially since the first *On The Run*. I also remember *Make it Better*, *AL*, *Fat Cap*, *Tuff Stuff*, or *Tuff Times*. *Bomber* was actually good, as was *Underground Productions*. Very few of the fanzines were really well done, while most were just like a catalogue of photos. It was really great from the consumer aspect because people were really hungry for information, and the more came out the more they wanted. You could observe this at jams, with everyone walking around with their blackbooks, ready to exchange photos and sketches. I still have a few, as people in jams would just give them to me; but I threw most of them out to paper recycling.

By showing the styles of every country the magazines killed this peculiarity, this individual research on style. People were connected already by travelling, and had been Inter-Railing before the fanzines came out. The train-writers were already moving and looking for other places to hit, those that were good at stealing knew they could get around Europe by winging it, trading in stolen goods like clothing or stationery to fund their travels. What happened when all these fanzines came out is that everyone ended up being influenced by the styles of the published pieces. Back in the days you couldn't bite from another crew in New York because if you got caught they would beat you up. You could get really hurt by the people whose style you were biting. This set some very hard parametres for evolution. You had to interpret, improvise, evolve, invent, innovate and all of that; and this all happened over the course of an intense 10–15 year period in a city in which so many people were doing graffiti at the same time. That's what made this particular art form evolve to what it was when we got lucky enough to receive it all on a silver platter.

Sure, publishing pieces was important because there was a real lack of information, but a whole bunch of pictures or a double page of a magazine gives no sense of the particular context of each, which can be totally different one from the other. The real scale of things cannot be properly represented. Only the person who did the piece knows how dangerous it was and what the police risks were but

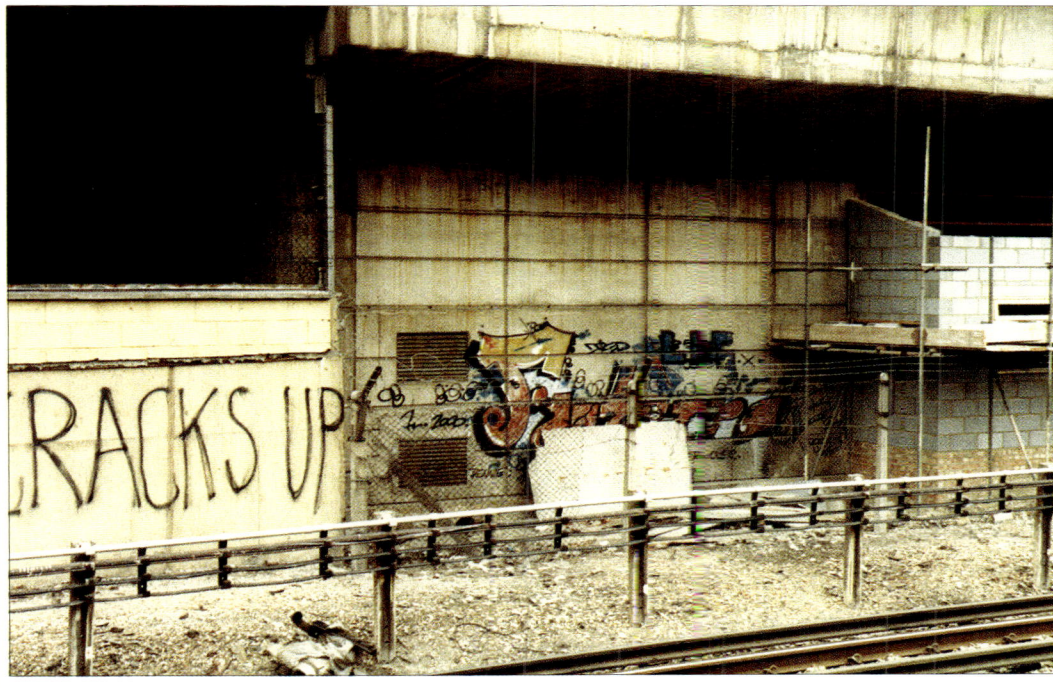

Futura2000 piece at Ladbroke Grove. London 1982   — *Zaki Dee*

none of this was conveyed. When we heard Futura had a piece somewhere down in Ladbroke Grove, in the summer of '85, a piece he had done in '82 from when he was hanging out with The Clash, we knew we just had to go and find this piece. So we set out, like five or six of us, and went hunting for it. We had to jump over fences, walk along the Hammersmith and City Line train tracks, until we finally we found it. When you're in front of it, looking at the scale, the colours you've never seen, checking out the technique up close, it's just totally different. All this cannot be communicated through a fanzine that only includes a photo and a one-line caption with author, city and year. People were sending their photos in the mail to the guys doing the magazines so there was communication going on but no one was writing any comments or taking the time to really describe the dynamics involved in painting. Magazines always contain a large number of photos but it only represented the aesthetics of style and not the process of Writing as a whole.

The same thing we're talking about can be seen in the evolution of the music when the record industry picked up on it and started to format. The fanzines kind of formatted habits in the scene, a lot of toys were doing pieces in any old place, taking photos and sending them in to be published. The road to fame is a lot quicker now. The whole fame thing had never been an issue for us though, even from the start because we were some of the first people to paint in London so we were automatically famous. You had nothing to aim for, it's not like you're starting and the big guys are on another level.

There was none of this with us. *Spraycan Art* just took that to another surreal level. With the fanzine circuits fame was just a matter of appearing. There was no hierarchy, no contextualisation, no analysis of quality and style, and they really did not take responsibility for the influence media can have in all aspects. Too many of them were there to steal from a glorious past they had never lived, push anything from their own period, but not take enough time to think about were it all would be in ten or fifteen years from then.

What brings the reiteration of contents in

The fanzine as a catalogue: repetition of a standard

The first generation of fanzines in Europe can be distinguished on the basis of their content into two categories: those that associated Writing to the Hip Hop movement and those that on the other hand concentrated on the stylistic evolution of pieces, considering Writing as an independent phenomenon.

Though the European scene was permeated by the figure of the B-boy, the progressive distance from Breaking showed to what extent writers had gradually identified themselves as an individual entity, without any association to external movements. Already in the early 90's certain fanzines were starting to pay exclusive attention to graffiti without considering the influence of specific music genres, with the intent of showing the phenomenon only from the point of view of the stylistic directions it had taken. The basic content of many magazines was the presence of two main photographic themes based on the target: walls and trains. Along with the pages centred around street-bombing, fanzines relied on two distinct interpretations of the act of painting, one tied to the idea of composition and evolution of style on legal walls, the other closer to the concept of risk, suggesting the image of a painted train as the only worthy heir of New York's Writing culture.

The first fanzines progressively set a standard marked by pages entirely dedicated to specific targets, in which series of images of walls and of trains rarely shared the same space. Bound to an inexpensive format such as the vertical A4 and to a limited number of coloured pages, the viewing pattern of the first fanzines tended to be homogenous. They would begin with a brief editorial introducing a series of photo pages. The space between

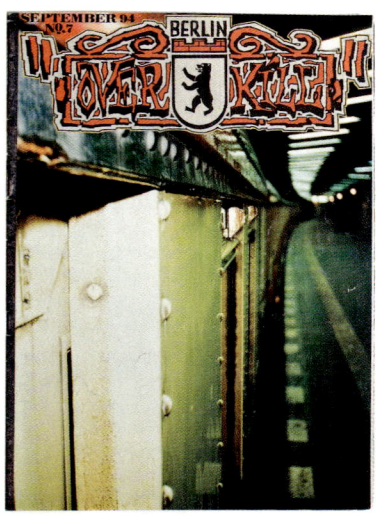

COVER
The front cover of *Overkill* #7, September 1994, depicting a view of the Berlin S–Bahn

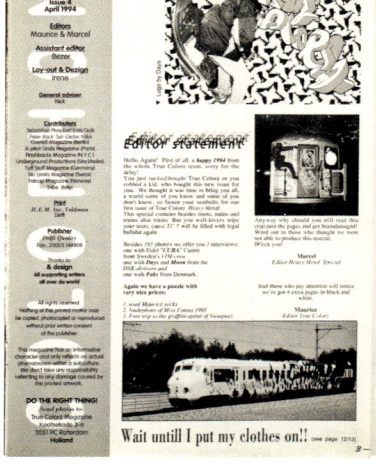

INTRO
Colophon of *True Colorz* magazine from Amsterdam. Logotype designed by Days. The logos of such publications are often commissioned to writers

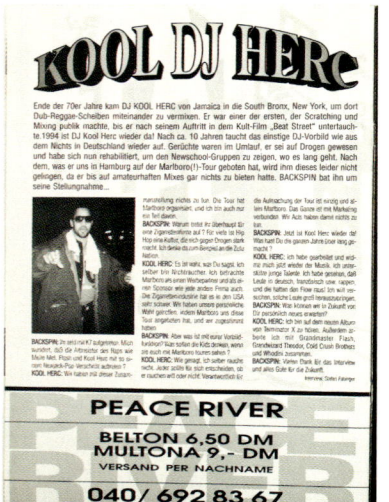

HIP HOP
An interview with New York's DJ Kool Herc published on issue 3 of *Backspin* magazine

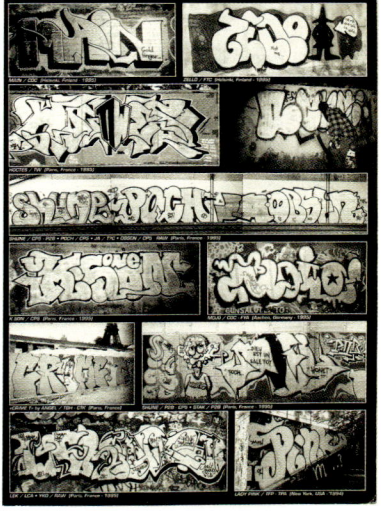

HANDSTYLES & THROW–UPS
The black and white pages were often dedicated to monochromatic flops, tags and blockbusters.

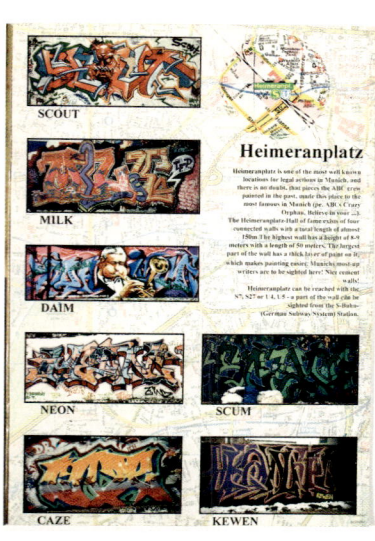

GUIDE
Special edition of *Style Wars* magazine centred around the city of Munich and the mapping of its primary halls of fame. The text adjacent to the styles explained how to reach the respective locations

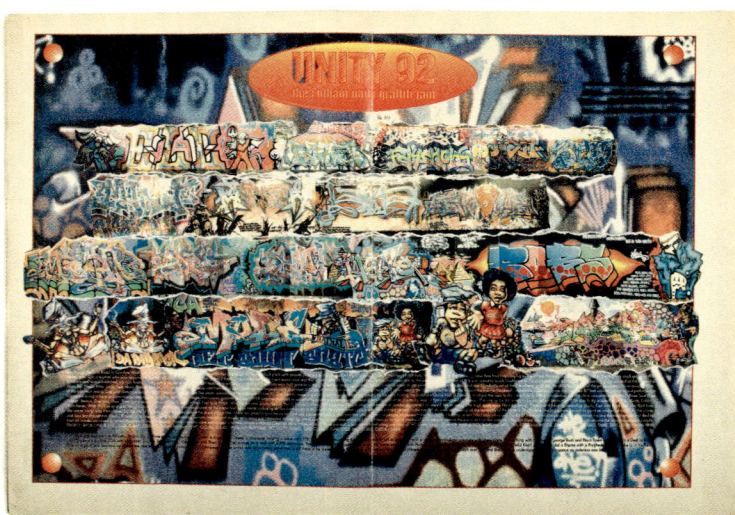

JAM FOCUS
Double central page of *Graphotism* dedicated to the "Unity 92" jam organised in London

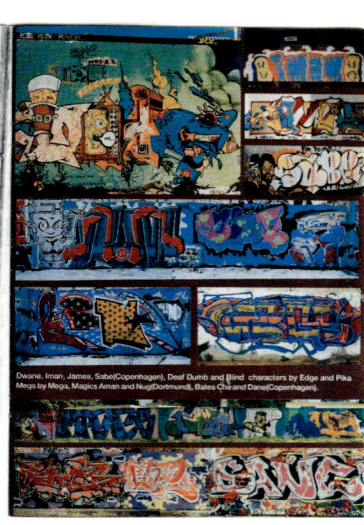

WALLS
A page of *Underground Production* focusing on the best wall styles in Scandinavia

fanzine layouts

clusters of photos coincided with the interview of the writer or crew, with a report on the scene of a specific city or on a particularly risky action during an Inter-Rail trip. The few extras were alternated with thematic pages, for example dedicated to hand-style; often tags and throw-ups were concentrated in the black and white pages at the extremities, whereas the few pages printed in colour were reserved for the more elaborate pieces.

The paradox of these publications was that within them coexisted an amateur product of high aesthetic value, almost an art catalogue, with contents and selling conditions that were practically illegal. Fanzines dedicated to Writing were editorial projects that were rarely registered and counted on informal distribution channels, presenting image content based on illegal actions. In the 90's the promotion of Writing on trains was opposed by the repression of police branches that, particularly in Northern Europe, aimed

at limiting the graffiti phenomenon and any form through which it might spread. Ironically it was the same fanzines that divulged names, crews, years and scenes of the crime on the captions of photos, available to anyone who wanted information on the authors. In the course of a decade the difficulties that arose because of this gave way to the publishing of contents that, though more explicit, were also less compromising: in the first period the most extreme enterprises were

documented through texts and anecdotes, subsequently information was limited to a simple photographic reproduction. The same picture captions, that in the fanzines of the early 90's specified every detail of the painted train, were progressively substituted by a blank conspiracy of silence, an omission that on one hand left writers the task of understanding the work's author, and on the other made the decoding even more complex for the calligraphers of the Vandal Squad.

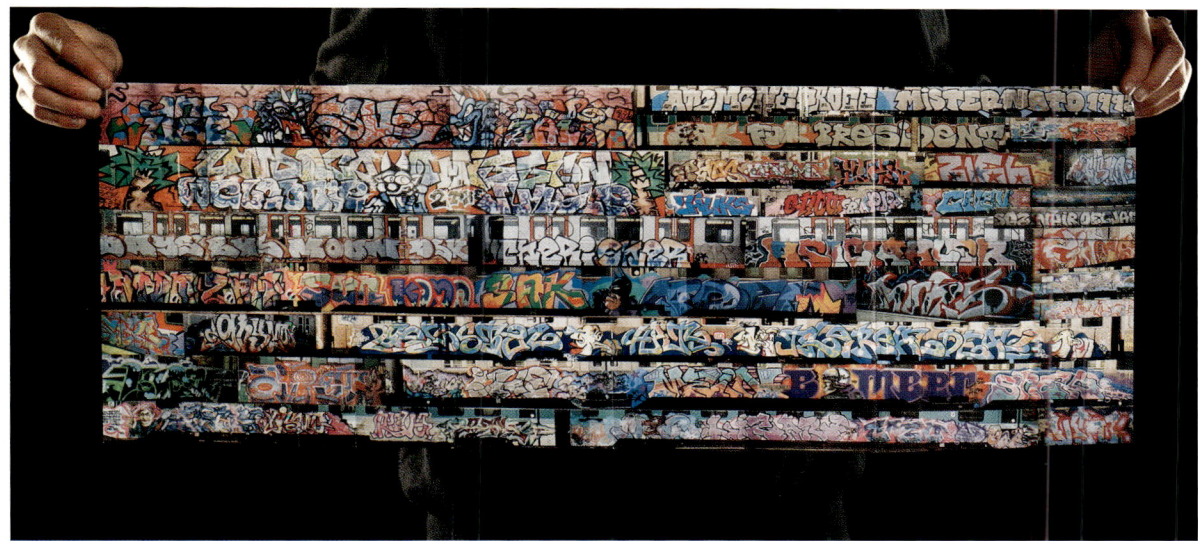

DOUBLE PAGES
Centerfold of *Tuff Stuff* magazine, entirely dedicated to Writing on trains

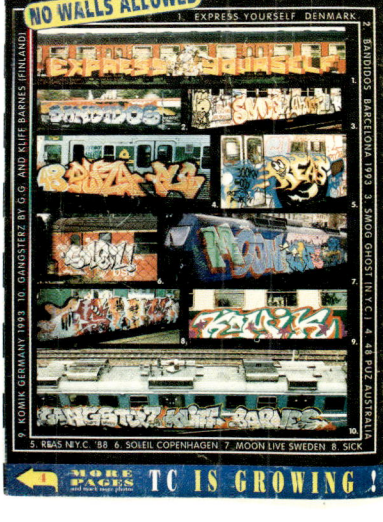

BACK COVER
True Co'orz magazine and many other publications often concentrated the photos of the best burners on their back cover.

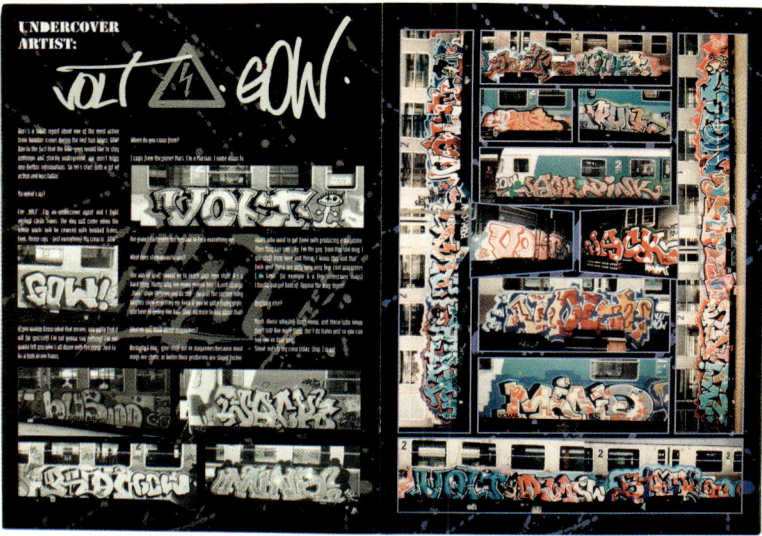

INTERVIEW
Interview with the Swiss writer Volt – GOW crew. The format was based on a very limited number of questions, often similar to those of other magazines, concentrating specifically on the activity of the interviewed artist

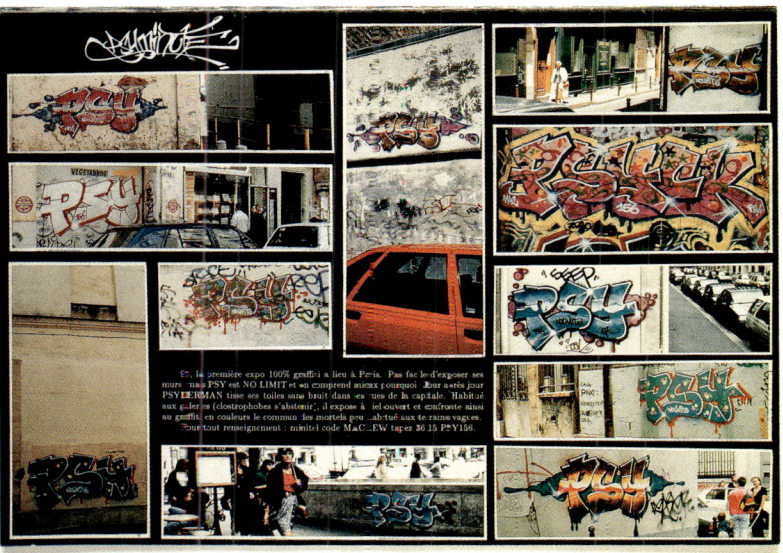

REPORTAGE
A special report on Psychoze, 156 crew from Paris, on *400ml* fanzine. Specials on a determined writer or crew presented a photographic abacus accompanied by a brief descriptive text

THE EDITOR'S VOICE : 14K

Alex Pistoja / Zurich
>

After his exhibition at the Ziegler Gallery in the mid 80's, Phase II left Zurich, and the rivalry between the only two crews of the city, Wild Writers and United Artists, was set ablaze once again. During his entire stay, the competition and dislike between the two groups had ceased, as if by spell, and the scene in Zurich had never been so cohesive. But as soon as Phase II left, the rumours and dissing increased excessively. It was then that, Charlie, Ivo, a fourth guy, Razzo, and I decided to publish a newsletter. We thought of taking all the rumours and putting them together down on paper, to understand which were true and which were false. We wanted to clarify what was going on in the Zurich scene, and give voice to whoever wanted to say something. These rumours concerned every aspect of the B-boys of the time; everybody - at least during the first years of the Writing movement - was involved in the controversy. The rivalries were tied to stylistic choices and reciprocal influences of every writer and crew. Therefore rumours were everyday occurrences; beef would ensue from nothing, like a letter too close to a certain stylistic current with respect to another. Our objective was to write all this up and publish the news that was circulating to give credit or not to whoever was putting them around.

At the time United Artists had the most style in their letters, they were more structured, and yet the book *Subway Art* had not even come out yet. Surely their references came from some other book or photo that Steve, their leader, must have had. What they painted were pieces copied from New York, without a shadow of a doubt. The Wild Writers on the other hand had letters that, to be honest, sucked, but the filling was unique, and considering the cans of the time they had done the utmost possible. There were beautiful letters on one side, and colour on the other. In 1985 I went with Bost of the Wild Writers to Paris by Inter-Rail and for the first time we saw pieces by Bando, United Street Artists, Shoe and Cat22, and we thought they were the bomb. It was something incredible, not only for style, but also for the beautiful fills we had never seen before. When we returned to Zurich, Bost, along with Gen, started copying the style of Paris and so United Artists beat them up, accusing them of biting, but at that time nobody had told them yet that they too owed quite a lot to New York!

So Zurich followed an anti-Paris stylistic current that was castrating. You couldn't copy, or brawls would ensue. I'm talking about '85 or '86. These years, previous to the birth of *14K*, became a key condition for the genesis of the magazine. When we put together the first photocopied attempt, we soon realised that it was a negative initiative, almost counter-productive, no longer creative because it caused conflict between the groups. So then we tried to get a slogan "Get Active!" as an incentive to be active, creative, better.

All this was concentrated in 4 pages of paper and 50 photocopied copies to hand out at the Burger King hang-out. The origin of the magazine's name came from a lyric of a rapper, Schooly D if I'm not mistaken, that said something like "14K B-boy Gold"; plus 14K was the name for gold in the States, and obviously we took New York as a reference. Even the fact we met up at a fast food joint had to do with this. It made us feel closer to the life of the original writers. When the first issues started circulating we thought people would get angry, because none of us four was really a writer: Charlie break-danced, Razzo had done a couple of pieces only, Ivo just had some tags, and ditto with me. None of us were really part of the Writing movement. On the contrary, the feedback was positive, and we would get asked for more copies. The second issue already had sixteen pages. In those days there were zines like *IGT* by Phase II in New York, and *Zulu Lettre* in

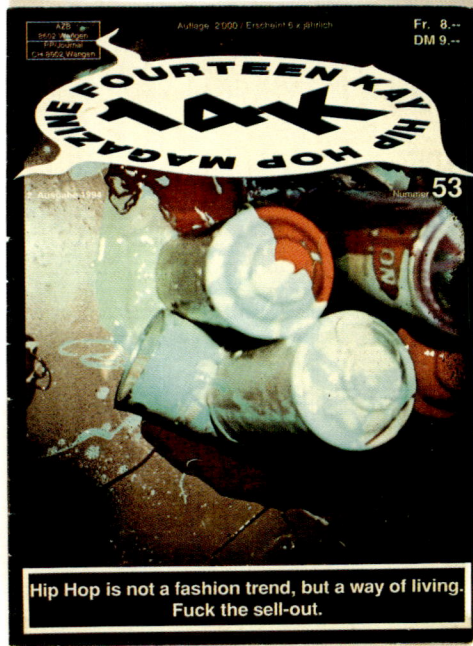
— *14K archive*

Hip Hop is not a fashion trend, but a way of living. Fuck the sell-out.

Paris, which was the first zine in Europe, and was produced by Candy, just a little before us. But talking with people around Europe, it's *14K* that is considered one of the first European magazines to really break the stereotypes of fanzines. In 1988 the zine *Bomber* came out, with stunning content. Many others followed, each in an independent manner and each with the desire to create something new. Our advantage was Germany, since in those days there were a lot of good parties in Biel, the number of German B-boys was very large and our zine was the only reference point of Southern Europe.

In Biel, parties were organised at La Coupole, that was the first relevant place where parties were held on a regular basis. People would come from Paris: Dee Nasty was more or less always there, and it was always packed with people. It was the place to be, and that's where I met Zebster. He showed me his blackbook of incredibly coloured whole-cars and I was astonished. From that moment on we stayed in contact and *14K* became the magazine par excellence, especially for the Germans for whom our zine was the only reference.

So to keep our readers faithful we came up with a subscription system. We would send the zine by mail. At the time there were no specialised stores so already by the second issue we had made fill-in forms to subscribe with. The response was so numerous that it seemed like people were really into reading this stuff and by the fourth issue we had subscriptions from Germany, also because it was in their same language. At the beginning it contained mostly texts because people were really starving for information; they wanted to know everything about what this new thing was. The dominant presence of text was also due to the fanzine format of black and white photocopies, and so pictures didn't come out well.

At that point our subscriptions were boosted by the stores that helped us sell, and therefore expand. We started with 50 copies and ended up with 7000. The magazine was everywhere: in Italy it was at the newsstand; the same in Spain. In Germany it was in stores, in the United States it could be found at Tower Records, who then sent it to Japan. In the end we were receiving pictures from all over the world, from Mexico, Australia, even though we didn't know how they could have found our mag in all these countries.

14K financially supported itself thanks to the subscribers

and foreign distribution, with hardly any ads. Nobody was interested apart from a brand of cigarettes during the last issues. That's one of the reasons why it cost so much. We wanted to keep it clean and unique, and trying to keep the price as low as possible was really difficult. In those years the production costs in Switzerland were very high, so the price of *14K* in Italy or Germany was sometimes unaffordable for the younger kids.

The evolution of *14K* from fanzine to magazine happened in parallel to the money we got from the first sales that gradually allowed us to go from photocopied fanzine to a full colour mag. Years later we totally changed format, going from a vertical A4 to an A3. The idea was to give more space to the photos, trying not to overlap the style of one writer with that of another. Even though *IGT* used the collage technique, we had found it visually disturbing when applied to *14K*, probably because we lacked the composition skills of Phase II and Dave Schmidlapp.

GASMASK
—

We started *Gas Mask* in 1990. Our main reference was *IGT* from New York, *Bomber* from Holland, *Fantazie* from Denmark and *14K* from Zurich. Me and Poe produced it ourselves, we collected photos or took our own photos and then photocopied everything. We didn't really have a set criteria for choosing what to publish, we just started putting in the guys we knew from Helsinki, the guys we knew were the most active, just basically the most 'happening' writers of the city, with the best styles, and also we tried to bring up some of the new ones. Then when we went to Stockholm we obviously took a lot of pictures, mainly of things that we saw on walls and sometimes we saw panels running, and from there it expanded to also include other guys from other countries like Norway and Denmark.

Then around 1993 some fanzines became really professional. Personally I would rather paint than concentrate on a magazine. If you wanted to make a high quality magazine you had to put much more work and energy into it. Basically I preferred to concentrate my efforts on painting. **— EGS**

German style focus   — *14K archive*

Barcelona Game Over

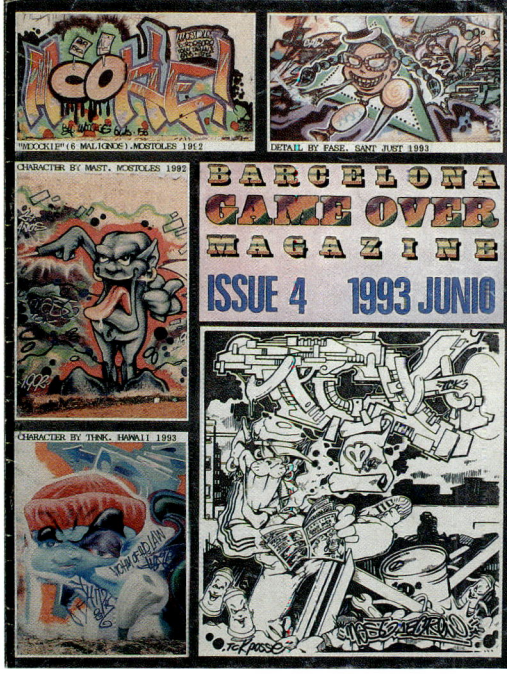

— Game Over archive

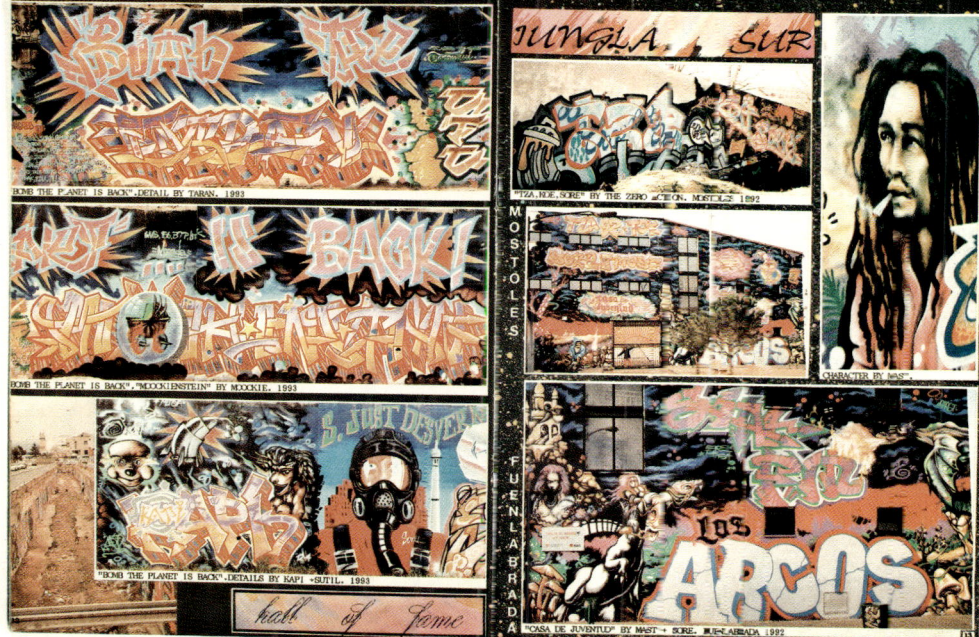

St. Just Hall of fame and Jungla Sur Madrid specials

— Game Over archive

Kapi / Barcelona
>

The origin of the magazine *Game Over* is directly connected to the collaboration between Kapi and Moockie and more in general to the period during which Catalonian Writing was exploding. Every writer was hungry for information and publishing a fanzine was just the first step in a series of important intuitions for the city of Barcelona. Moockie had already published a fanzine in black and white in the early 90's, and with time it was transformed into the principle point of reference for Iberian writing. The first contact with abroad was with Patrick from Zurich, who had been collaborating with *14K*, a well-established fanzine and one of the very first in Europe to focus on Hip Hop. *14K* became the reference for *Game Over*, which little by little was starting to build a network of foreign contacts: Zerok from Germany would send pictures of the German steel trains, Zeta and Chop contributed material from Madrid and Patrick from Switzerland. In 1993 I met Opak in Paris, who was getting ready to publish Xplicit Grafx, a new magazine which focused on the International train scene. But the most important intuition I gathered from travelling came from Four Star General in London and Ticaret in Paris. These two stores fully coincided my and Moockie's intentions: a shop for writers that at the same time would become the headquarters of

14K became the reference for Game Over, which little by little was starting to build a network of foreign contacts

Game Over. The real turning point came from an almost banal intuition: the European stores kept accessories for sale, records, fat laces, fanzines, everything.
That is, except for a key instrument: spray paint. So Moockie, who worked in a shop that sold products in rubber, convinced his boss to keep Feltons in the store, which at the time were one of the brands used by writers.

In this way we managed to buy them at factory prices to then sell them retail to writers. The difference was in a series of modifications that we came to suggest to Felton: fat caps, skinny caps, wider variety in colour palettes,

The most important intuition I gathered from travelling came from Four Star General in London and Ticaret in Paris.

and so on. Every request was regularly ignored until one day the new sales manager of the company, a certain Jordi, called us. The first thing he had seen on his desk was the pile of messages the secretary had written from all our phone calls. At the same time he had noticed that the rubber company in which Moockie was working was selling more spray paint than the hardware stores and so when Moockie explained the reason, the sole mention of the word "graffiti" lit him up, as Jordi was 25 at the time and snowboarded, so all of a sudden he was getting excited for the initiatives of the Catalonian writers. The first thing he did as manager was finance *Game Over*, which managed to become a colour magazine thanks to the advertisements by Felton.
Other than this, Jordi seemed like the perfect person to convince the president of Felton to finance the store the two writers had in mind. When Felton refused, Jordi lied to the guys and helped the store with his own money, saying that Felton was enthusiastic about the project. After a year, he decided to leave the company and went to speak with Kapi and Moockie. The roles were reversed, now it was Jordi asking for help, for information regarding which spray paint was the best for writers.
In April of 1994 the first batch of Montana spray paint was produced, a variation on the Felton product that had been improved in many aspects: pressure, paint density, colour range. The very first productions still had female caps but they were soon supplanted by the standard that was being used in New York and everywhere else. From the moment in which a company, for the first time in the

world, started producing spray paint especially for writers, the whole aesthetics of the game radically changed. At the beginning the productive process was very distant from the usual industrial dynamics, it was completely handmade: Jordi and his partner filled the cans themselves and would bring them directly to the store, which was the only Montana selling point.
The distribution broadened for the first time after Dafne, Sherif and Done came from Italy to visit Spain in April of '94, a week after production had started. When they returned home, the echoes of the enthusiasm of Italian writers arrived to Barcelona via Genoa, where the first writers started distributing the paint in an informal manner. At this point, the magazine was supported by a store that was working and this allowed *Game Over* to stay pure, with very few advertisement pages, a full-fledged magazine that was self-financed and self-produced.

OUT OF THE LOOP
—

Chana / Dortmund
>

I didn't like graffiti fanzines and I've never sent a single photo to the mags. Firstly, because in my opinion getting up is the essence of Writing and this kind of competition stands for single scenes, localised in one city
You can't compare writers from different cities as the context is not the same and the conditions change. So why do I have to be in a magazine when the battle is indoor and local? Graffiti fanzines were publishing good styles but avoiding information about the photos: for instance you often lost scale and size, as the shots were focused on the piece and every context was cut out. So you had incredible Wild styles being published like the Hildelberg style during the 90's, without realising that those pieces were really small. European Writing of that time was a 'live in the moment' movement, facing the real aspects of pieces and their proper context. Besides that, trains were still running painted for months on end and there wasn't a proper necessity to save masterpieces with photos.

Underground productions of Scandinavia

Jacob Kimvall / Stockholm

Underground Production was in the making for various years, but only in 1993 did the first issue leave the presses, and now, 16 years after the first edition, it continues to be regularly published. In the autumn of 1989, inspired by the Swiss magazine *14K*, we made a half-hearted attempt to publish a periodical. It became limited to a really ugly cover (created with the then entirely new technique of desktop publishing), but both its name and idea lived on, and in February of 1992 we printed 320 copies of the first issue. The print run was calculated based on our own circle of acquaintances (including International contacts), and a list of potential buyers in the Stockholm graffiti scene.

At this point, there were barely a dozen magazines with International distribution: *Hype* from Australia, *Can Control*, *Flashbacks* and *IGT* from the US (Los Angeles and New York, respectively), *Fat Cap* from Norway and *On the Run* from Germany (the first magazine to feature colour printing) – and about the same amount made their debut at the same time as *UP*. When I say 'International distribution', I use the term in its broadest sense. The magazines had very small print runs and were distributed through an informal network of writers and other graffiti enthusiasts, but were written in English and strove to reach beyond their home country's borders. In Sweden there were actually two magazines before *UP* – *Kilroy* and *Trains/Sniart* – but I would venture to say that *UP* was the first to court and receive international success. After just a few weeks, we had received responses from readers in several countries, and the same year, we printed 1,000 copies of a second issue. This was also the first Swedish graffiti magazine with a few pages in colour. International graffiti magazines brought intellectual insight and an increased feeling of being part of something bigger; they also put graffiti in the local and International limelight. This limelight was later further developed by the internet.

Among the early 90's graffiti magazine pioneers, four are still published with approximate regularity today: *Bomber Magazine* from Holland, *Graphotism* from England, *Xplicit Grafix* from France and then *UP*. Several hundred titles, probably thousands, have come and gone over the years, mostly with one or perhaps two issues. Because making a magazine is hard work, and in most cases this work meets with absolutely no financial reward. On the contrary, at first we paid to publish the magazine. Later, when it became more established, we paid with our work. But it is only in the last five or six years that anyone got paid actual cash for some of the work that goes into an issue. Fifteen years of mainly unpaid magazine work, the first ten of which were spent as part of the editorial team: that has yielded quite a few memories. Some good, others sad. There are memories of long editorial meetings in small, cramped cellar compartments in which the air would run out after twenty minutes (and with it, all patience and understanding of the opinions of others), doing layouts 24 hours a day a few days before the deadline, hunting colleagues whose copy and images had failed to come in on time (and to be honest, I myself have been the prey in some of these hunts).

Quite regardless of the fact that making a magazine is probably always a lot of work, publishing a graffiti periodical is associated with problems that few other publicists have to deal with. It entails facing attacks from people who think you have no right to exist at all. Resistance has probably been especially hard and well-organised in Stockholm. Over the years, local politicians, Transit Authority officers and the odd policeman have issued various decrees and promises that *UP* would be stopped. They never succeeded. On the other hand, they indubitably managed to create quite a few problems, and at least partly limit the magazine's distribution. And I will not hide the fact that it has been irksome, as an unpaid member of the editorial team (working double shifts, considering my principal job as an underpaid care worker for the disabled), to have to put in additional hours arguing with

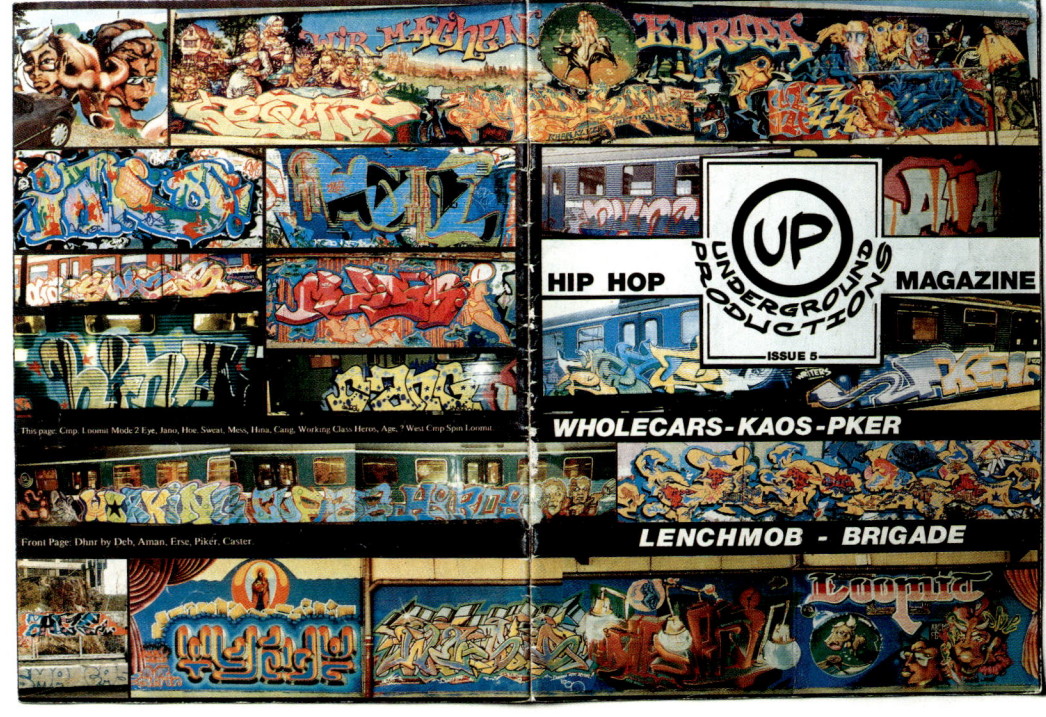

– UP archive

well-paid civil servants, well aware of the fact that you would lose regardless of the outcome. Lose, because you had spent yet another couple of hours on something that was at best a decent defence of your *right to exist*. There was nothing to win, as such, and these arguments stole time and energy from the project you really ought to prioritise: the magazine. It was not without some pride that you still attended the debates, and sometimes I still do. It was a feeling of doing something important, something that mattered. But the circumstances still brought about a feeling of insufficiency and a destructive, devouring sense of powerlessness against an invincible enemy who fought through envoys, field marshals and a constantly renewable supply of goons.

Worst of all was the climate of debate in Sweden in the last years of the 90's, and for a while we seriously feared that the police would hit the magazine with some far-fetched excuse to search the premises, then located in a small, 150 square foot cellar compartment at Thorildsplan in Stockholm. Editorial meetings were on Thursday evenings, and one Autumn afternoon during this period, I was alone in the premises, preparing for the meeting. Once the post had been collected, the agenda written, coffee bought and all other preparations taken care of, it was time to deal with the latest orders. After collecting the various magazines, I laid out a set of letter scales on our combined packing, conference and coffee table (which doubled as a desk), and laid down the orders, magazines and envelopes in stacks. Then I sat down and started my task of putting magazines in envelopes, adding names and addresses and affixing postage. It was time-consuming work that also required attention to detail, but at the same time it was quite relaxing.

Since the premises had no windows, it was always hard to tell what time it was, and you had to keep the door ajar so the air wouldn't run out. After working for a while, I heard the stair door slam. Aside from us, the building was also used by the owners of a number of similar compartments in the cellar corridor, and by some of the residents of the apartment complex as the laundry room was located right next to the bullpen (this is also where we did the dishes and got water for coffee and tea). In short, there was quite a bit of to-ing and fro-ing, and it was not surprising that someone showed up. But since our door was slightly open and it was soon time for our meeting,

I looked up, and glimpsed someone hurrying past in the corridor. I checked my watch, and saw I had been in the premises for about an hour, and it was time to go out into the yard to get some air.

After closing the latch so as to bar the gate, though leaving the door open in the hopes of getting some fresh air into the premises, I walked towards the yard door, in the corner of the corridor. The cold, humid raw Autumn air was liberating after the musty cellar oxygen.

I had been standing in the doorway for less than a minute when I heard the stair door slam again, and then a few steps approaching before it went quiet. The person had to be outside the editorial premises. Probably a colleague, coming in early and having forgotten the key, I thought. I turned back into the corridor, around the corner, only to find a complete stranger standing there, looking in

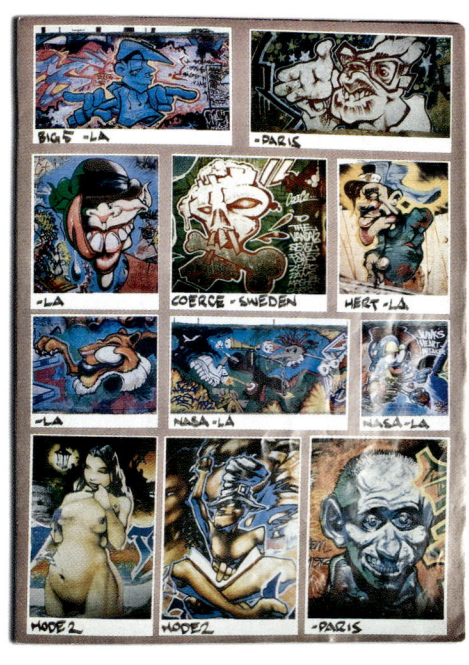

– UP archive

through our door. The man jerked, but quickly regained his composure and asked me in a confident voice if it was my compartment. Mine? Well, it belonged to the magazine's cooperative. but certainly I had access to it. Why? Could I help him somehow? Without answering, he took a quick step towards me, gripped my arm with one hand, as the other shoved his police ID into my face, and he asked me where my friend had gone. *Oh, so it's time now*, I thought, but not without confusion: what friends? Had they tried to arrest someone on their way to the meeting who had managed to get away? I had the keys to the premises in my hand, and he demanded that I open the gate. We exchanged some lines back and forth before I complied. Actually, I had nothing to hide, and everything to lose in starting a serious argument. Once inside, the man cast his gaze around, in a way I found, shall we say, curious – even though the whole situation was curious. With one hand still on my arm, he leaned around the room, looking horizontally at the bookshelves and above the books and files that stood there. On the table were two cardboard boxes, one with the latest issue of *UP*, and one with some caps that we were thinking of selling through mail order. They were both open, and he looked into them and examined their contents. He gave special consideration to the one with the caps, and dug with his fingers. "Where's the stuff?" he asked. My knees still felt quite weak, but I was slowly returning to my senses – I had begun to suspect the whole situation was a mistake, even though I couldn't exclude the possibility of a particularly devilish trap – and honestly told him I didn't know what he was talking about. He tried to ask me about my friend again, explaining that they'd been keeping an eye on him for a long time, and when I maintained that I didn't understand, he fell silent and stood deep in thought for some seconds. The grip on my arm started to weaken.

"What exactly do you do here?" he asked suddenly, and I told him we produced a magazine. Now it was his turn to look surprised. What magazine, he asked, seeming sceptical that any form of honest work might take place in premises like these. "A magazine about graffiti and Hip Hop," I answered, invigorated by his diminishing authority. "But what do you use that for?" he asked, pointing at the letter scales. After hearing me explain that we used it to add correct postage and seeing the rack of stamps on the table, he let go of my arm, and deflated a bit, as though the air was slowly but surely seeping out of him, and he looked at the bookshelf again. This time, he looked at the titles on the spines, rather than above the books. "A magazine about graffiti?..." he muttered something beneath his breath. "Yes, graffiti," I replied. "I thought that was what you were trying to nail us on."

He explained that he was on the drug squad of the county police while extracting a small walkie-talkie, into which he explained how it was all a mistake and the investigation must continue. I wouldn't say he apologised before leaving; rather, he seemed to think that I should have known better than to act suspiciously and detain him while he was hunting bad guys. It still wasn't illegal to publish magazines about graffiti, if you wanted to do something that incomprehensible, and what's more, graffiti was a stupid cork crime that only dork policemen dealt with, not real police like him – that was the spirit of his message, and after that he ended by asking me to keep my eyes open for anything suspicious.

I can't remember anything about the editorial meeting that followed, and don't think I got much done. But though the policeman's blunder was unpleasant for all of us, I felt relieved afterwards. He put things into perspective, and got me to understand that even policemen can be reasonable. What's more, I realised that the graffiti squad must be held in low esteem among policemen, which was probably the driving force in their endeavours to get graffiti to become regarded as more serious and problematic than it really was.

Today, *UP* is located in a well-lit, street-level premises, but otherwise everything is still much the same, and in some ways worse. Repression of active graffiti writers in Stockholm is probably harsher than ever before, and prospects seem bleak for graffiti writers' legal recourse. For the past year, Sweden has a minister for culture who, in her parliamentary career, has written propositions intended to further limit the possibilities to both practise and discuss graff. Graffiti magazines and the limelight they created are needed now more than ever.

Bombers magazine

Bomber Johan / Tilburg
>

— THE EARLY BOMBER DAYS

I think it was around '87 when the first Dutch graffiti-magazine appeared. It was called *Freestyle* and was in A5 format, about 16 pages thick and great fun! But along the way I felt I could do a better job so I started thinking about my own magazine. In 1987 *Bomber* was founded, but it took two years to get it really going and to publish my first, serious issue. That year 1989, I did 2 issues, 'o' and '1'. I was lucky to get to know a lot of helpful guys like Son 103, Eras and Dirk. We formed the first generation 'Bombteam'. Back then the content was based on photos from collectors, so in order to get some content I started to trade and collect myself. Pretty soon I was fortunate enough to have the support of big names such as Pike, Loomit, Cat22, Milk, Chintz and Ces53. Therefore the first focus was mainly Sweden, Germany and Holland. Son 103 focused on Paris, while Eras was close with Seen and PJay, and provided *Bomber* with nice NY exclusives. In the beginning Dirk illegally produced the issues during his nightshifts. The little money we made was invested in the reproduction and swapping of photos and the 'free' issues to those who donated photos.

— HIGHLIGHTS

With Issue 5 in 1990 I went to Paris to do an interview with Lokiss, that was exciting! I had been to Paris before but never hung out with a local writer. Lokiss took me to the secret spots he was painting at, they had to be secret in order not to get crossed out, hostility amongst writers was big in Paris at that time. NThe cover of issue 8 was actually a big A3 sized collage covering the back and front. It featured the 150m long piece with the phrase "The idea is to let you know that graffiti is rocking and it's on the go and there's a lot more to it if you check him to it, but the fallen is the fallen, they just can't do it." from Dortmund's legend! Zebster did that issue with me. Issue 10, a WOW special with a high WAUW character, issue 11 a special 'Stockholm Issue' again done with Zebster. Those who are into Scandinavian styles nowadays are 19 years behind schedule. Issue 12 introduced Dmon and issue 14 was 32 instead of 20 pages thick, it featured a Bando report, a scene report by Bates and an article on how an interrogation by the Vandal Squad works and tips on how to behave during the inquest. Issue 16 featured a brief history of the activities on the Amsterdam subway from 1985 to 1991. Bus and Dice, two writers who were up on the Amsterdam subway in 1991 were interviewed, so was CMP from Denmark. Issue 17 was the last issue of the photocopied era. In 1992 the *Bomber* series had a re-start with its first off-set printed issue. The issue had the notorious OMT report and interviews with Reaze, Delta and Erse. From that moment I had the support of the hardcore Utrecht posse that consisted of LIL, MSN and WOW crews. Their help played a big role in the success of *Bomber* Magazine, as they provided me with an over-whelming and mostly exclusive amount of real trains. In 1992 the LIL crew was 'up big time and Ces 53 and Zedz went to New York. Issue 4 had the first colour pages which, to be honest were totally fucked up, because the photos were scanned low resolution. In issue 7 we had a pretty controversial interview with the vandal squad who in the end withdrew their help and threatened us if we went to print. We published but nothing happened afterwards. The magazine kept on evolving and from issue 17 in 1998 *Bomber* was totally full colour. The printing market had slowly changed and due to new and less expensive printing techniques, full colour printing became affordable. This finally led to today's appearance, 108 pages full colour magazine madness.

— TODAY

The world has changed in the past 22 years. The Berlin wall has fallen down, bombings in Bali, the World Trade Centre, London and Madrid. Politicians and writers got killed, wars for oil, land and terrorism. Internet conquered the world and in the shadow of those events graffiti changed too. It became bigger, harder and bolder. The writers race for the hardest systems, most far out places and bravest actions go hand in hand with the struggle for exclusive, unpublished material and exotic video footage. We at *Bomber* headquarters always felt that the right time to do an issue is when you're sure you've got enough good content to give it a go. Sometimes this process takes longer because the other competitors in the magazine-game are fishing in the same pond, but most of these editors lack a 22 year old, solid reputation from which we can benefit.

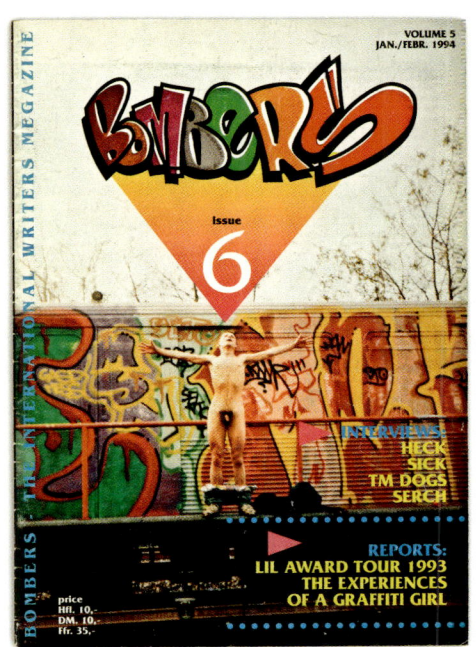

– Bombers archive

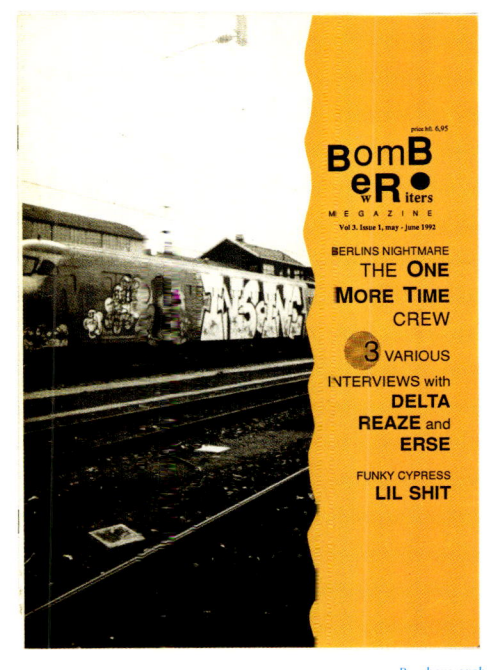

– Bombers archive

THE ULTIMATE MAGAZINE

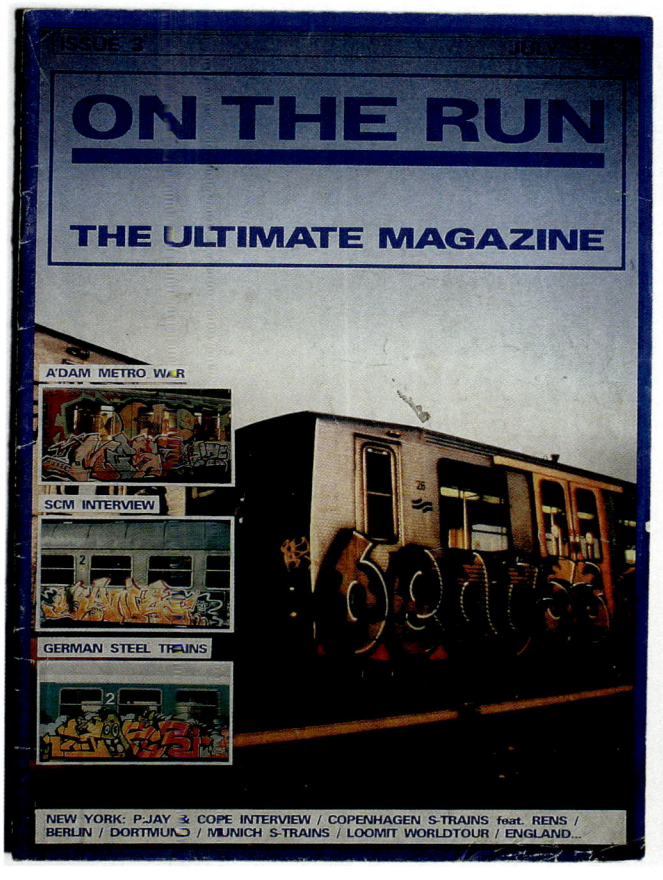

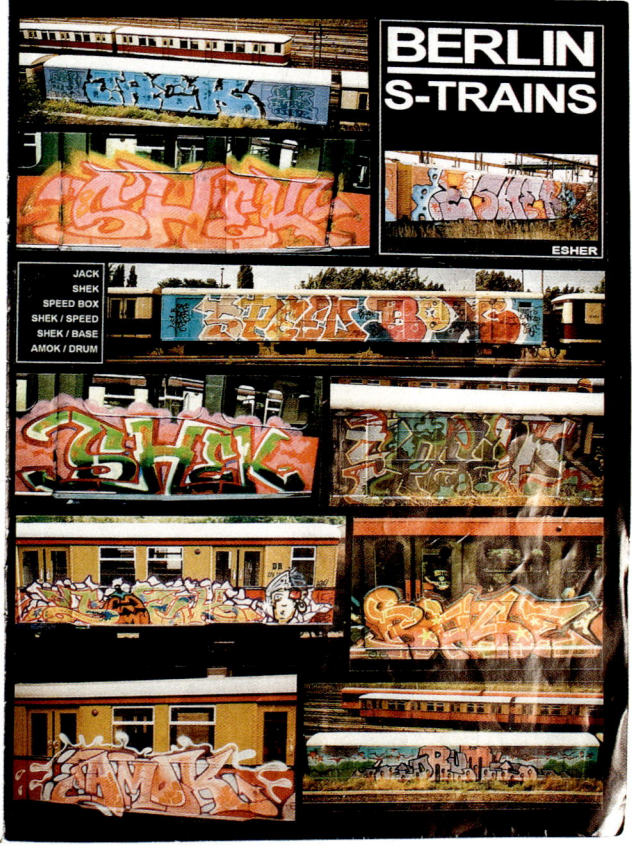

S-BAHN
SPECIAL

Back cover of a special
on Berlin's S-trains, one
of the primary targets
of the city after the fall
of the Wall.

Zebster – COD / Budenheim
>

Around 1988 just a couple of fanzines existed, and were sold via mail or in the few Hip Hop shops around. The first were Dutch: *Freestyle* and later *Bomber* magazine from Nijmegen. Then came *14K* from Zurich, which was more of a Hip Hop magazine and like *Bomber* mag, it lasted many years. When I found out there were magazines I decided to work with them. I did some work for *14K* and sent out materials. I worked with *Bomber* magazine making a complete issue, which was the Stockholm special. So there was already something going on when *On the Run* came out, and of course I had many good references like *Fantazie* from Naestved in Denmark. I just tried to reach a higher level with coloured pages, an effective layout and a better distribution. The magazine reached Europe because I was travelling a lot during the early 90's and I had friends who sold it on a commission basis, so it was well-extended, especially in the Netherlands. *Bomber's* Johan even helped me with the black and white pages, they were produced in Holland while the colour pages were printed in my home town. So there was this printing connection and we put them together. With the layout I tried to add something that belonged to the content. If you have pieces from London it's cool to know the subway

line or the tube line. Then I liked the idea of having these headlines like sensation newspapers, I transformed and translated this in the graffiti world with sentences like 'train yard destroyed' which was more fun than serious. The whole layout process was really home-made. I was cutting out stuff and putting it together, everything was cut, glued and done letter by letter, or it was typed down and photocopied to have different variations. So it was a little bit more complex and manual than today, but in any case it was a great learning process; we were always trying different

> ## I was cutting out stuff and putting it together, glued and done letter by letter

solutions for the layouts, working manually on the aesthetic and composition. We were young and hunting a little for fame, even with the magazines! In the beginning I put a lot of stuff in from our area or by us because we didn't have a lot of material. If you look through the issues you find you get less and less of us as we eventually got more materials from others.

AREOSOUL BASEL
—

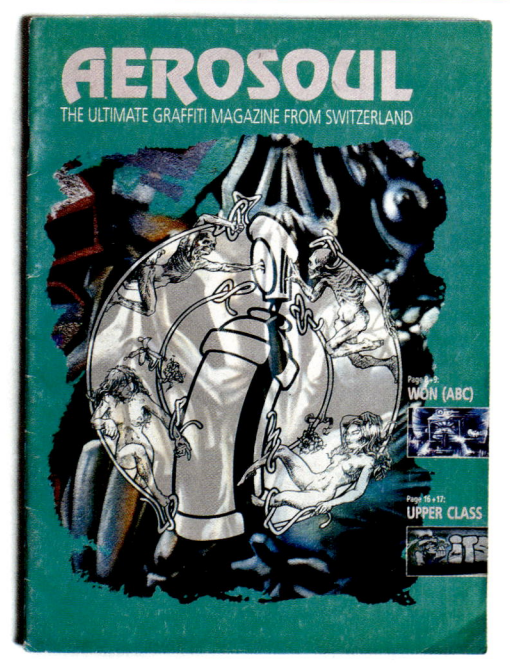

— Aerosoul archive

Aerosoul began as an idea around 1992 and as a fanzine in 1993, with the main goal of offering the best quality a magazine can strive for in terms of graphic layout, paper and printing. Every effort was pushed in that direction, for instance it didn't even consider black and white pages, as graffiti is a matter of colour. We decided to focus on the International scene because *Aerosoul* was distributed mainly in Switzerland and it was a good opportunity for locals to check out styles from all-over. That's why the pages were not mixed but thematic, so that each regarding specific cities. During the 90's it was still possible to recognise city styles and feature peculiar reports on Dortmund block letters, the Amsterdam subway flavour or Scandinavian crazy styles. **— DARE**

A matter of Xplicit grafx

Interview with the editor of Xplicit Grafx, a publication representing the French and International scenes

X–Man / Paris
>

How did the whole Xplicit Grafx project start?
There was no internet back in '92, so you only had two ways of getting info about graffiti or see pieces from other countries: go there yourself, or check out a local graffiti magazine. There were only a handful of them at the time: *IGT*, *On The Run*, *Bomber*, *UP* and a few others. Particularly, *On The Run* and *IGT* have been a major source of inspiration. I decided to launch an International one that would not only focus on Paris but on what was happening all over. One of the reasons was that I thought some cities like New York, Berlin, Stockholm or Helsinki were so far ahead in terms of styles & skills that I had to do something to show France what was going on in the rest of the world. The other goal was to release a proper documentation of the Paris train & graffiti scene, without necessarily getting trapped into those typical Paris styles I had to grow up with. That's how the first issue was born, on December 1992.

XG featured an International scene from the very 1st number, by including writers from the USA to the EU. Did you already have a network and if you did how did you build it up?
It was all about travelling and getting the right pictures from the right people, whether it'd be my own photos or other writer's personal flick collection. Travelling, painting and taking photos: that was the main part of the job.

With which magazine did you first start swapping issues?
Swapping magazines was one of the tricks that allowed this graffiti magazine sub-culture to spread so fast during the 90's. When I realised that, I started swapping *XG* with most of the other fanzines worldwide, so that any

small publication could end up being available anywhere in the world. It was a pretty effective system.

I've noticed a substantial difference between the very first issue and the following ones. It seems that after #1 you focused more attention on trains.
With the first issues I had to give props to those I considered some of the most talented Parisian writers, the few who made me love graffiti when I was a young toy. You couldn't be a Paris kid doing graffiti in the late 80's and avoid Mode 2, Bando, Lokiss, BBC or PCP crews. But I always had a preference for graffiti on steel – so after reviewing the classics, I quickly started to focus more on underground activities than just cool pieces in halls of fame: showing freshly painted styles on trains and letting people discover new talented writers and unknown territories became the main purpose of *Xplicit Grafx*.

You chose the vertical A4 format, as many mags did. Even the content layout was very similar to other magazines; do you think there was a kind of 'standard' in the layout of the magazines?
I don't think so, the fact is that in the late 80's and early 90's most of the magazines were doing collages, trying to follow *IGT's* style. Look at the old issues of *Tuff Stuff* or *Overkill*. The main reason was probably that computers were a luxury back then, in real life you still needed glue & scissors to cut & paste. I had the chance to have access to a Mac at my school, so I chose to do it the 'clean' and most effective way: simple layout, black background just like in *Subway Art*, and a maximum of photos. I'm not sure many graff magazines had already done that before. But it's true that after *XG*, dozens of fanzine editors followed the same path. I've always hated scrap-booking, so Quark Xpress and Photoshop it was.

In choosing new writers to interview, what were your criteria? Was it just a matter of style or did other ingredients come into play? (such as: Bravery – Personality – Tenacity).
If you were the most active bomber of your time but did shit styles, there was no way your pieces would end up in *XG*; or maybe with a big bribe! Quality was the rule, not quantity. But of course doing quality AND quantity should be a must. Unfortunately there have always been more toys than kings in the graff game, it's a fact that

brought us many jealous haters throughout the years. Fuck them. Still today, it's all about showing good styles and sticking to the good old steel canvas.

How did you get the best pictures? *XG* has always published original and unseen stuff, how did you keep this quality control?
Going to the source has always been more effective than just waiting for the postman to bring you a bunch of toy flicks. Graffiti writers are not rock stars, all you had to do was go and ask, most of them were cool guys like you and me who were happy to contribute.

How has *XG* changed with the Internet era?
Nothing really changed with the new edition that rose back from the grave in 2006, it's still all about showing the best photos of pieces that have never been seen before, and particularly not on the internet. The net is a good tool to see what's going on, but in a quantitative way. We choose the qualitative way. The only difference now is that we used to have 20 pages twice a year to express ourselves, now *XG* is 148 colour pages strong and released four times a year. We're finally able to show pictures in the size they deserve, and focus on the right people with a decent amount of pages to really showcase their work in the best conditions. It's always been frustrating to spend hours of work on a piece, which is then reduced to a photo printed the size of a stamp. Those days are over.

In 2000 the Paris vandal squad started this big war against the French graffiti train scene. Did these problems somehow change the way of making and publishing *XG*?
For the Vandal Squad *XG* became one of the main targets, because they thought it was responsible for the fact people were painting trains, which is obviously nonsense: Media usually report an existing phenomenon, they don't create it. Being *XG*'s publisher and an active writer as well, I became the perfect target. What's left today of these operations? I went to jail but won my case, and after a few years and a bit of reorganisation, *XG* was finally ready to be reborn. 17 years later, it's still here and our motivation remains intact: to show quality pieces from the real people who devote a part of their life – and sometimes their whole life – to playing this stupid game we call graffiti.

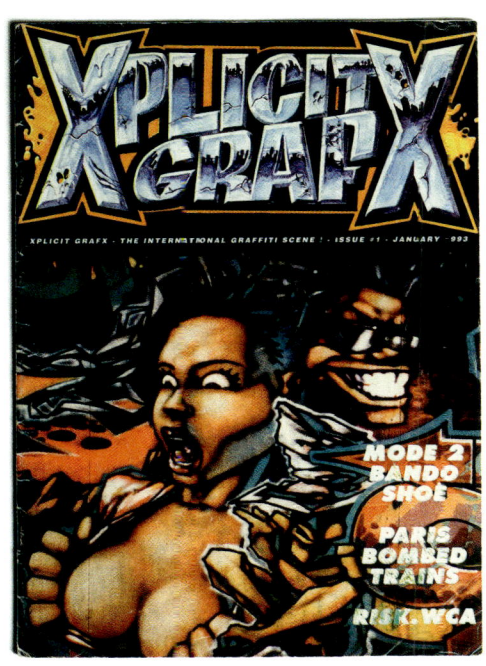

– Xplicit Grafx archive

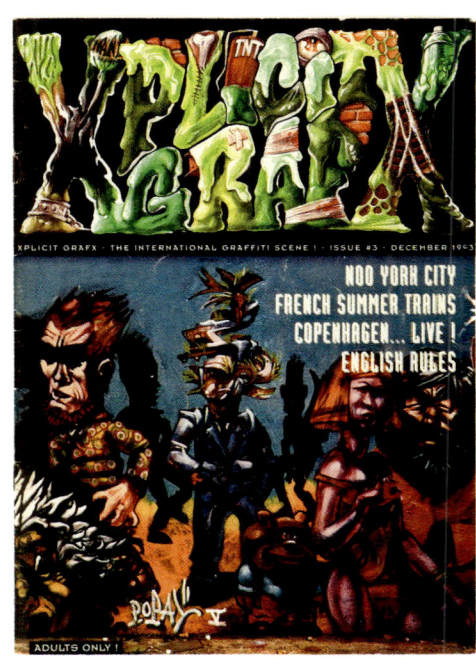

– Xplicit Grafx archive

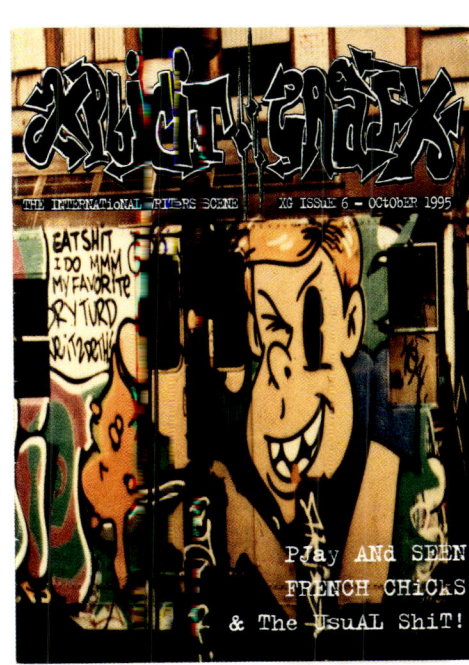

– Xplicit Grafx archive

DENMARK FANTAZIES

The story of the founder of one of the first European fanzines: a new way of promoting ideas and travelling non-stop

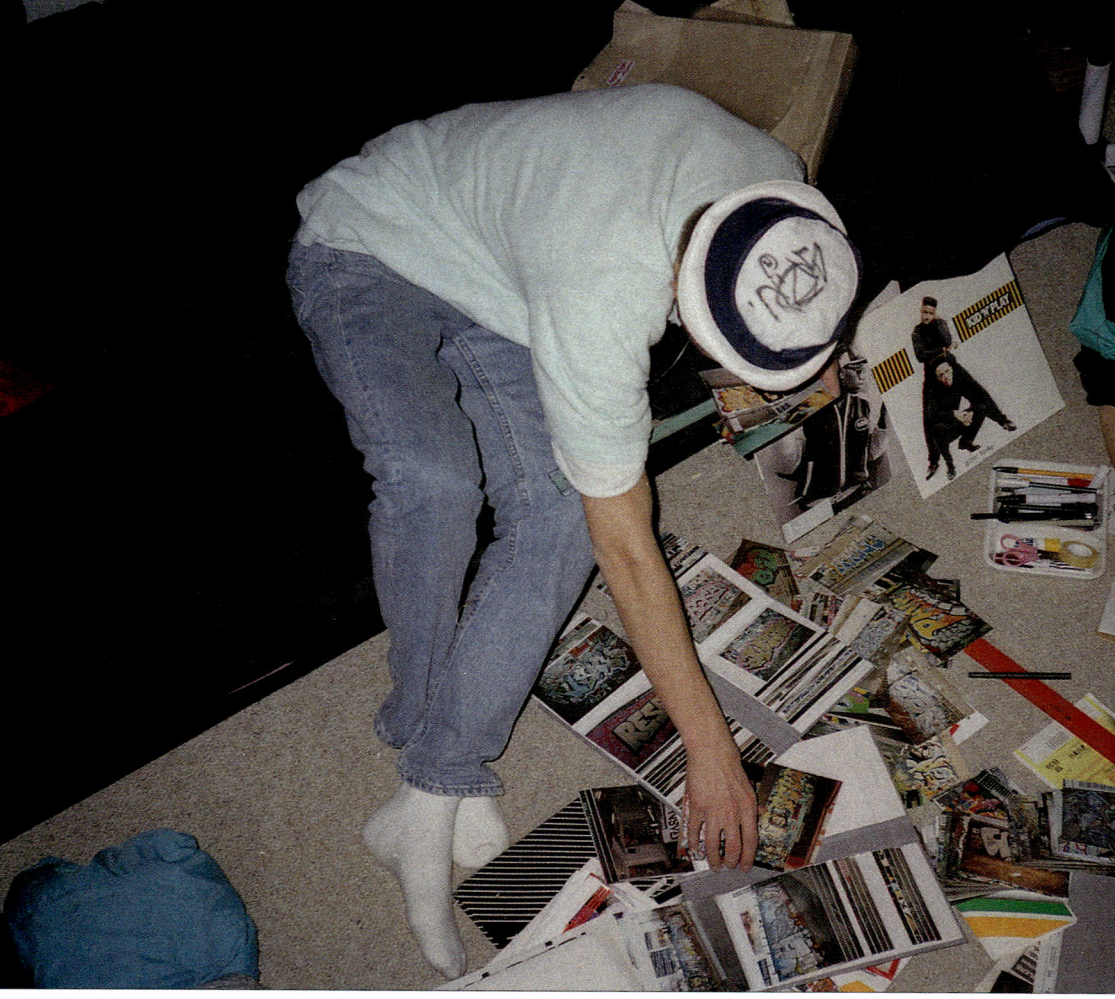

CMP – CMPSPIN / Naestved
>

Spino5 and I started travelling before most writers in Denmark. You see, we had to get moving. It was all really adventurous because we grew up in Naestved, a small city in Denmark. As Copenhagen wasn't enough for us, we created the magazine as a main motivation to travel and check out specific scenes in Scandinavia and Europe.

In February 1989 we named our magazine *Fantazie*. *Bomber* was already out since '88 and *On the Run* came out later in 1990. And the UK had a lot of magazines out as well. At that time Spino5 wanted to work with action photos, not just images of pieces, so we also took photos of people climbing under the trains and so on. We wanted to show the whole atmosphere. It was a bit different at the time, as everyone was more into publishing catalogues of walls and trains. Anyway our product was an easy-going magazine, handmade, cut and pasted, printed in black and white. After school, I had a cleaning job at the time, and at the office where I worked, there was a good photocopying machine, so we never paid for the copies.

In '89 we went to an LL Cool J concert, trying to promote it. So many writers were there, but even though we had been painting for 5 years, the scene was concentrated in Copenhagen, and of course nobody knew about us. We didn't really connect with anybody at the concert, we just talked to a few guys. Once the concert was over, we stood outside looking at peoples' shoes to recognise writers, and as we gave away the magazine for free, people started to come to us. This first issue had 25 pages. The guys were impressed because there were also photos of pieces done in Copenhagen. Sabe also got a copy and was stunned when he saw that one of his pieces was in it. But the guys there were skeptical and started confronting us asking "Why are you doing this? Are you working for the police?" It was so funny... they asked us so many silly questions. "This is Spino5 and I'm CMPONE. We are the CmpSpin. We've been writing for 5 years in Naestved, one hour from Copenhagen." Nobody knew except a few guys that had taken the train down there. We had this nice hall of fame close to the tracks which is still there. Then all of a sudden a bunch of UK writers joined the crowd, interested in the magazine. Months later – thanks to them – the magazine travelled and we started receiving up to fifty letters a week from the UK. It was crazy. Many letters came from Brighton, London and even Scotland. Things really started moving because of the price and the simple strategy; "Send us photos and you'll get a free copy". At the time, we were pretty focused on Scandinavian and UK stuff, which were the main ingredients of the magazine, and honestly, I have to say, that we didn't know too much about the scene in Amsterdam or Paris.

Suddenly we got to the point where it was too much. We were receiving thousands of photos. Among these letters one day, I got one from this German guy called Akim Walta. I don't know how he got hold of the magazine, maybe at one of the concerts we attended when travelling. We started writing back and forth and even if he had another style, he was really interested in the Danish scene. I remember he wrote something like: "It has another swing, it's a different style" and of course Spino5 and I were eager to know more about the culture in Hamburg, Munich and so on. Akim was a missionary guy and wanted to meet us.

On his way back to his hometown of Budenheim from a trip in Scandinavia, he heard the announcement "Next stop Naestved" so he just got off and called me. I was living at my parent's house, and my father answered the phone. I wasn't home. I was at a factory painting. Even though I had said nothing to my parents of where I was going, they knew. At this time it was pretty special when somebody from another country came to your house, so my father went to look for me at the factory in the middle of the city. He climbed over a fence, walked around a bit, and then came to the big building where I was painting. He shouted "Claus, there's a guy from England who wants to talk to you (he didn't know he was from Germany) what are you doing down there?" I was a bit shocked to see my father at this place, and quickly got my paint together. When I came out, Akim was standing right there... that's the first time we met, it was 1990.

He wanted to do a magazine so we went to my place and talked about other magazines. He said "We should do *Fantazie*, *Bomber* and *On the Run* together". Akim had a unique drive, and it was obvious that he had a plan when it came to connecting with people in Europe. We talked about Hip Hop culture, graffiti and how important it was to build these bridges from country to country.

We never got to the point of producing a magazine together, and Spino5 and I never got organised for that kind of business. *Fantazie* just represented our original idea of producing a simple magazine, that promoted the culture, and even helped us to get in contact with good people from all over the world.

– CMP

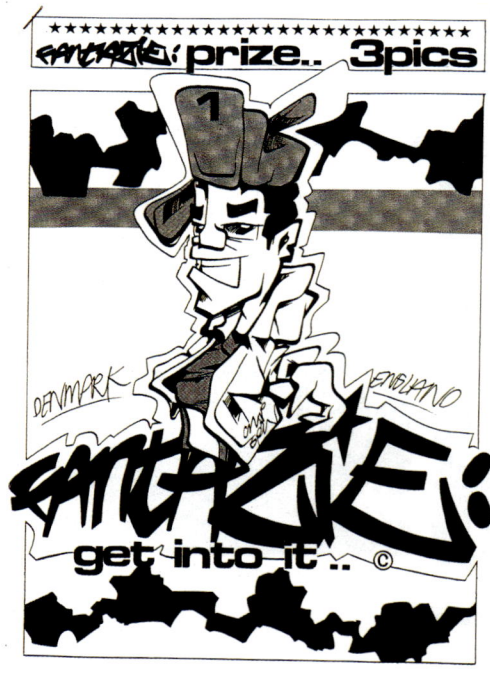

Berlin Overkill

Rew / Berlin
>

When I stared writing I just wanted to see more pieces, even if there was nothing around and no magazines. So I had only one option: to take the train and go see burners directly, then take a picture that I could look at at home and with which I could study the painted style. I got a camera and I took pictures of everything I saw, every throw-up, every piece, for years. The first time I travelled was in 1990 and of course I decided on going to Denmark and Sweden, rumour had it that the best styles were coming from up North. I took pictures of everything I saw, I remember I found an original Puppet piece in Stockholm! In Copenhagen I saw pieces by Rens, Sek, Bates, Sabe... pieces of kings. All of sudden, one day with Inka we saw for the first time *On the Run* and *Bomber* from Holland. So we noticed the same stuff we had seen in Denmark was being published, pieces by Rens and Bates and of course so many New York photos that were previously unseen. The fact we had these references and even a solid collection of Berlin pieces, at some point gave us to the idea of founding a new fanzine. After composing the pictures and gluing every sketch, text and design on, we took it to a copy shop to have it reproduced. That was the first issue of *Overkill*, totally done in black and white.

At the same time Hip Hop jams were taking place and everybody was participating, it became a ritual in Germany; some writer guests like Mode2 and B-boys like Storm were all over, in Hamburg, Frankfurt, Munich. It was a small scene in the beginning but really fundamental as jams were opportunities for making contacts and distributing fanzines: when we came out with the first issue in '92, we sold out at the parties and collected money for the next one. This time including a few colour pages.

Of course, since that issue the fanzine's format and content started to evolve; in the first issue we put pictures from everywhere, from all the trips; when we were in Copenhagen Rens gave me some New York photos so I put those inside too. It was all mixed. But then me and Inka met Mode2. At this time the Berlin style was really elevated and everybody was talking about the direction taken by the local writers.

Mode said, "You have so many writers in Berlin, so many individual good quality styles that it's better if you don't put pieces from other places in the world because it doesn't reflect you your magazine and your city". He was totally right, we had so much stuff we could have filled an entire magazine, and after a few issues *Overkill* started publishing Berlin styles only. This is how the idea was developed and why it is what it is today; only Berlin U-Bahn, S-bahn, city bombing and local halls of fame. We also made one issue called *All Overkill* and the concept was Berlin writers travelling outside the country, an issue mostly based on InterRail adventures.

The concept was to include productions that were done in the city within the whole spectrum of graffiti: sketches, throw-ups, bombings tags, trains, walls, sometimes canvases...it was all about the letters. Flavour and originality of styles were our criteria for selecting photos. The selection of the photos was only about the quality of the work. We followed some standards for specific pages, like focusing on silver pieces and placing the pictures one behind the other, like many mags were doing. It was an immediate device to let writers compare the selected styles, considering even 100 silver pieces and publishing the best ones only.

Generally it was me, Inka and Blake who were selecting the pictures, even if the team was always changing. For instance there was one issue in which I was not involved, one done by Inka and Adrian Nabi, another one by Force and Inka. We agreed spontaneously that changing the team would help a lot as in Writing it's important to have multiple opinions on the matter of style. It's very difficult to judge other people's pieces and select who has the skills and who is not ready to be in a magazine.

Sometimes envelopes would arrive with 100 whole-car pieces done just by one crew but they were all crap, so we would choose a burner panel piece instead. Quality has always been the concept of *Overkill*, it's not just about showing what's going on and who's who in a particular era. That's why sometimes we stopped producing the magazine for a long time, just because there was a lot of stuff around, but it wasn't that good. And even if I have tons of photos, I cannot go to print on an issue that could potentially lower our standard.

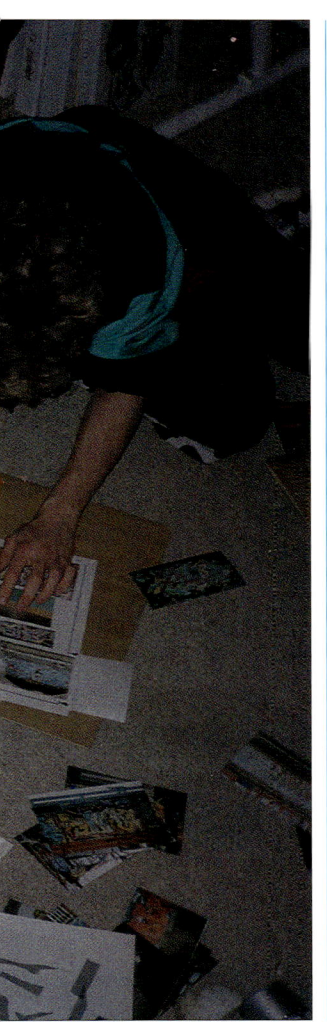

YOUNG EDITORS

CMP e Spino5 select the best styles to publish on Fantazie

— CMP

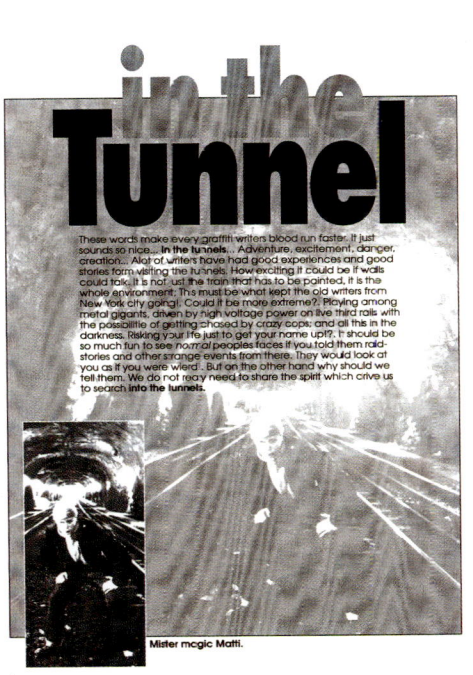

Mister magic Matti.

— CMP

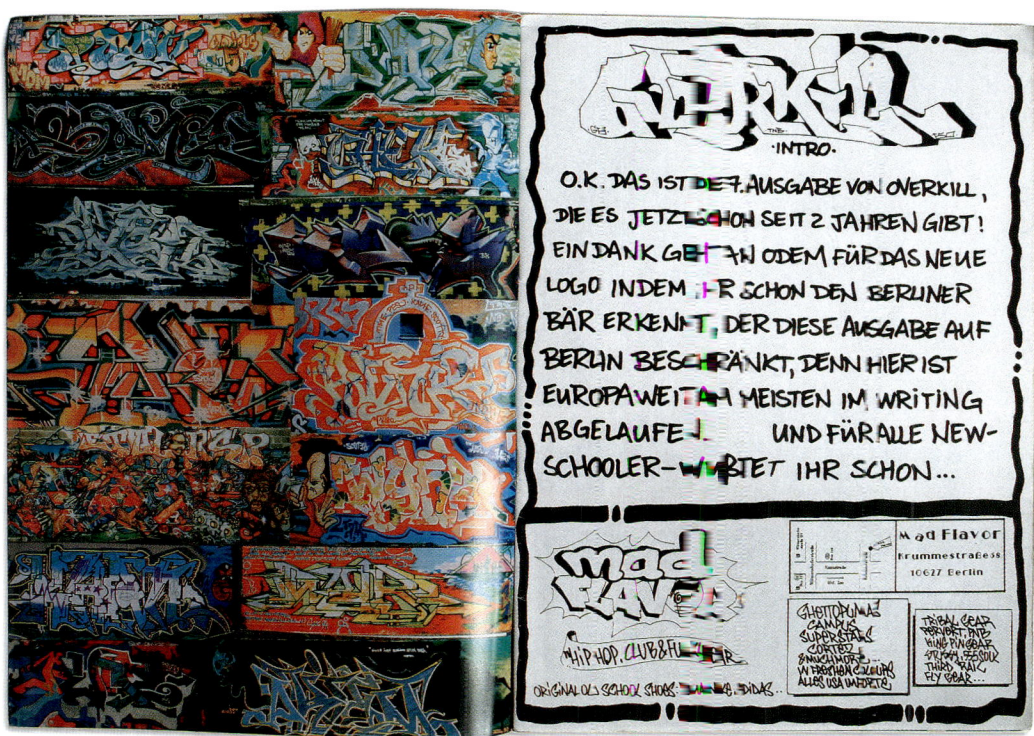

— Overkill archive

THE INTER-RAIL PASS

ON THE TRACK

An Inter-Rail ticket and a photo camera open the doors to the world of the railway and to the maps of European Writing, made of habitual spots and virgin territories

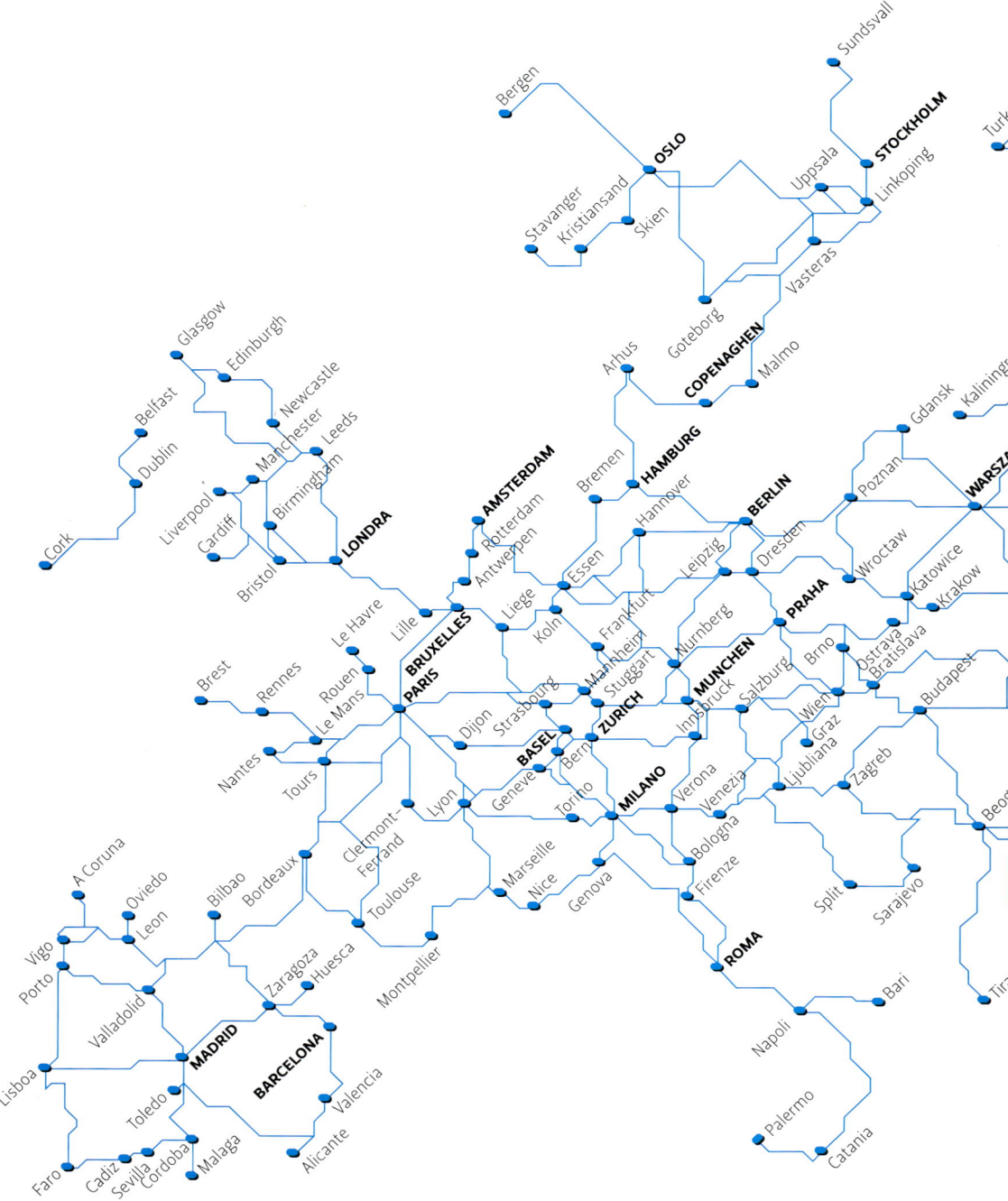

The European railway network, a means of transportation and at the same time a target for an entire generation

The Inter-Rail pass is a railway ticket that allows to travel throughout Europe for an unlimited distance in a predefined amount of time. The Inter-Rail program, born in 1972, had the aim of connecting young people in Western Europe, and its network was soon expanded to include every European state. As many other kids, writers too took advantage of the possibility to travel low-cost from one country to another, getting in touch with the crews that were forming in various urban centres. The experience of travelling by train – perceived as a real 'expedition' even before use of the Inter-Rail became widespread – was dictated by an impulse to communicate and the desire to discover other countries that could potentially have been contaminated by the Hip Hop movement. You would leave without any guaranty, fuelled by hearsay

or by the words of someone that had discerned signs of Writing on the railway lines of foreign cities.
The first contacts arose in a spontaneous manner: European B-boys recognised each other through specific clothing details such as fat-laces, name-belts or Kangol hats, and these initial approaches soon gave way to friendships that would form the first connections.
The Inter-Rail experience also appeased the desire to photographically document the styles of other countries in a time when fanzines still didn't exist and the circulation of information was rather scarce. In this case photography assumed the role of 'hunting' for tags or halls of fame, wild and episodic phenomena in a yet intact urban context. The searches thus corresponded to excursions in unconventional city spaces and visits to sites that were far removed from the habitual tourist destinations.

The map of attractions to visit coincided with the railway track lines, the respective city's hang-out and the various halls of fame, which could be located in the city centre – Waterlooplein in Amsterdam – though mainly they were found in the outskirts. The first actions to be executed in other countries were thus undertaken by looking for randomly acquired addresses, counting only on a home phone number: the trip was experienced as an exploration, a full-fledged adventure. The first Inter-Rail travellers had the common objective of painting trains and wanting to discover virgin railway systems. Their trips to almost immaculate countries and networks, such as Belgium, Spain and Italy, is indicative of the pioneering nature of these writers, who not only managed to establish contacts with the local scene - sometimes inexistent - but also to satisfy their collector's spirit by

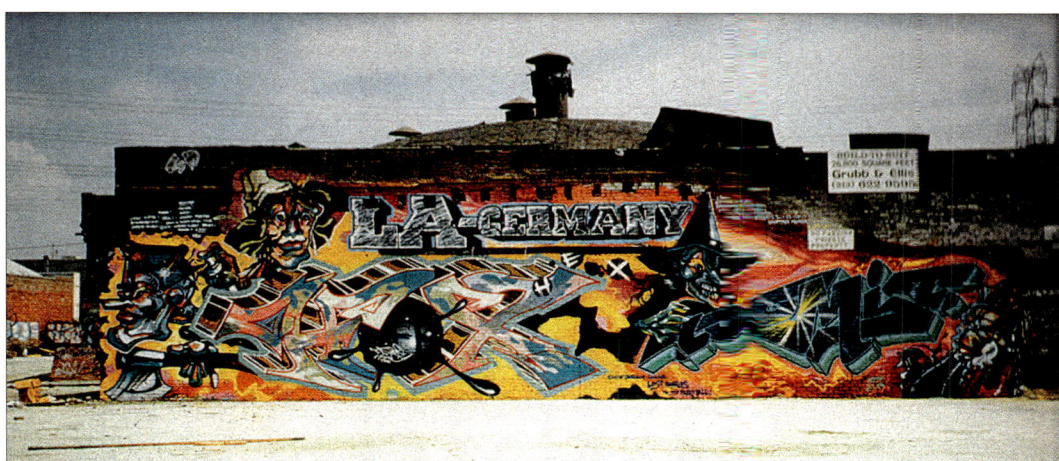

Loomit from Munich in L.A., guest in Hex's hall of fame. 1991   – *Loomit*

Beyond Europe

Loomit – FBI, UA / Munich
>

The absence of information regarding graffiti urged European writers of the first generation to travel, since only a couple of record cover sleeves and teen magazines were showing tiny little bits of what was coming out of New York City. There was definitely hunger for more. So around 1984/85 the scene in Munich shaped up with no more than 20-30 active writers, who met either around Break-dance performances, Hip Hop parties or through mouth-to-mouth propaganda. Every photo or sketch was gladly exchanged when you found someone that shared the same interest. An important figure of the time was Professor Peter Kreuzer, who worked for the Munich city archive and documented all the pieces that were done in this era. He gave lectures at the technical college and appeared in local newspapers with his motorbike, which he used for his research. In early 1986 he published the Graffiti-Lexikon, which was the first German publication on the subject, and though it did not include that many pieces it gave however a generalised view of Munich, the technical terms and a few phrases about what was going on around Europe. For the local writers reading their names printed in a book was a huge boost. But the publishing of this volume also incited something else: two writers from Dortmund, Chintz and Shark, who could not find anything about their hometown in it, though it was massively bombed for the standards of the time, came to Munich. This was the first encounter with writers of a different city, and with Dortmund boasting a pretty impressive Writing scene, they arrived with a style we had never seen before. They both painted at the Dachauer street Flohmarkt, which was the first legal hall of fame since April 1986. The insides were amazing and the style rather simple, but with a good swing. It wasn't over a week later that they left, and Don and me decided to pay them a visit in return. Since none of us had a car, the only option of transportation was the train, which was still a ten hour trip, but definitely the right choice. It was a night-train that arrived to Dortmund the next morning, so that we could see the impressive amount of tags along the tracks in the light of the rising sun. In the following days we were hardly ever separated from our cameras, in order to document as much as possible, particularly on the bus trip to Amsterdam. Over there graffiti was much more advanced in style and techniques and

meeting people like Shoe and Cat 22 was mind-blowing. On the way back we realised how much bigger the graffiti movement in Europe was, we had a huge appetite for more. So just weeks after our return, two writers from Mainz came along real true blue homeboys, who were going by the names of Can two and Zebster. Not that they really impressed us with their very clean line work, but they had already established contacts with a lot of writers and B-boys around Germany and even Paris. With more and more contacts it simply became a necessity to travel and since most of us were either under the age of 18 or anyway not in possession of a car, train travelling became very popular. Inter-Rail cards were standard on holidays and sleeping in waiting halls of all the big stations around Germany and Europe in sleeping bags was common.
At a certain point during the early 90's we realised the whole continent of Europe was involved in Writing; there

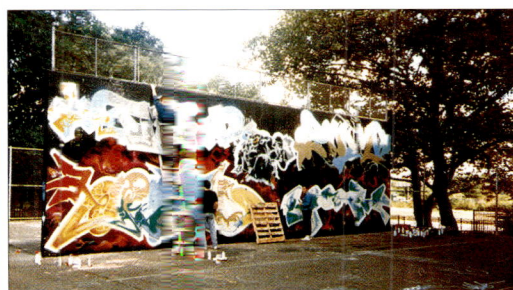

First wall in the Bronx – Darco and Loomit with Seen and Zoom 1987   – *Loomit*

were people from Finland down to Spain, from Greece to Ireland and they were all bringing their different flavours and ideas to it. Of course travelling played a role in the evolution, this is why it was so fascinating, so many people doing the same thing in totally different circumstances. There was a lot of travelling going on even in the late 80's; firstly to see what other people were doing and secondly cause once we had spotted cities where nothing was going on, of course we went for their trains. For instance when I decided to paint a full colour whole-car in Madrid I though the best moment would be on a Sunday afternoon during the siesta. I remember I went there thinking

> CONTINUES ON PAGE 92

– *ACW archives*

writing their name on a wide variety of European train models and liveries. During the early 90's the phenomenon spread primarily in Northern Europe, in countries like the Netherlands and Germany that already had the OV-Card, a very cheap student card with which you could travel on any train. The Inter-Rail did nothing but expand this model to an International scale; already by the mid 90's this network formed a wide web of travellers that, primarily in the summer time, spent as much as a month on trains. It's no coincidence that this new way of connecting gave way to the birth of many crews, joined by a passion for travelling. The lifestyle of these explorers was based on the freedom granted by a little coupon that gave access to the world of the railway, 24 hours a day, on board a means of transportation usually identified as the designated target.

> CONTINUES FROM PAGE 91
I would do the best I could but it was so hot; I had gloves on, and sweat was running out from under them, and just before I finished a guy came up. It was two and a half hours after I had started and he did not realise what I was doing, he saw that I was in the yard and he looked at me as I was leaving, but he had no idea of what I was doing there. To me it was crazy watching him stare without noticing my colourful train right behind me! The easier times have always been in systems that were not prepared for you and in which you could do whatever you wanted. In the beginning there was no way of just spontaneously going to a different city, it was always that a friend of a friend maybe knew someone there that did graffiti. You would then get this phone number and just randomly call people you'd never seen or met before and try to figure out whether they were who they were supposed to be. You couldn't outright talk about bombing on the phone, so you had to steer the conversation in a way that alowed you to understand if they were who you were looking for. The only way to do something and find out about something was travelling, you had to go with your camera, drive along the tracks, see if you could find people that looked like writers, with paint on their shoes, and approach them. You had to understand different systems in cities you'd never seen, there are always similarities between train systems, whether they're in China or South America, so you find this out, step by step. Even finding graffiti in foreign cities is something you get a feel for, you find the worst part of town in no time at all, you sense graffiti in the streets much faster than anybody else.

After you've seen a couple of tags you can then determine the standard of the town, whether they're backwards or they're into this or that scene, this is all stuff you find out by travelling. For me it was like the explorations of the seventeenth century sailors going to the new world. In the beginning we were more about just taking pictures of pieces that we found mainly along train lines or run-down parts of the city, but crafting and leaving your own pieces became addictive and the more we travelled the better we got at finding good places. From 1987 onwards, the focus for quite a few journeys was no longer cities with a vivid graffiti-scene, but rather the opposite. The local vandal squads were getting more and more successful in their work and so cities like Stuttgart and Hamburg became popular targets. We were lucky to have mom or dad's car for some of these endeavours, but in general we got there with the last train at night and returned with the first one in the morning, always highly paranoid about anything that could give us away. One final advantage of taking the train was that you caught up on all the lost sleep you had missed during the night, all while speeding closer and closer to home. The more we travelled, the more guests we had in return as well and after I moved into my first apartment, it became a kind low-star Hip Hop hostel. I had a lot of problems with my landlord, who had no understanding of late night jams with B-boys like Swift and Storm who stayed there, nor the regular house raids of the Munich vandal squad. In this same year Chintz, Darco and me hopped over to New York for the first time and started making the Intercontinental relations, where planes and visa applications became important. The prize was

about 36 roles of film, which cost a fortune to develop. The following years we spent most of our spare time going around Europe and trying to find lay-ups, rack spots and friends we could stay with. Of course we always returned their hospitality.
During 1988 the civil servant time arrived, it was supposed to be 20 months but after the Berlin wall came down the politicians cut this time down to 15 months; in any case the service itself allowed me to be really strategic, as I managed to be a receptionist at one of the local youth hostels in Munich, I made a lot of friends and collected their addresses all around the world.
Soon after that I left for Australia and New Zealand. I knew they had a scene in the 80's, basically a Maori scene; these guys were considered criminals and got locked away for it. I went there as a tourist, painting the first train after five years and they weren't prepared. When I returned a couple of years later with a friend from Dortmund there were only twelve lay-ups in the whole country and we did ten of them, basically rocking the whole nation! After this I went to Los Angeles, where I spent another two months doing intense research on graffiti. New York, Chicago, Toronto, Miami and New Orleans followed and it was Zebster who received most of the photos I shot that year. After coming back, I moved into an apartment that had no close neighbours and was located near the main station, knowing that in the times to come, I would have to host a lot of guests. Today I'm not sure I remember all the people who stayed at my house, but all the important ones left unforgettable pieces in Munich, like temporary traces fixed in my memory and in my pictures.

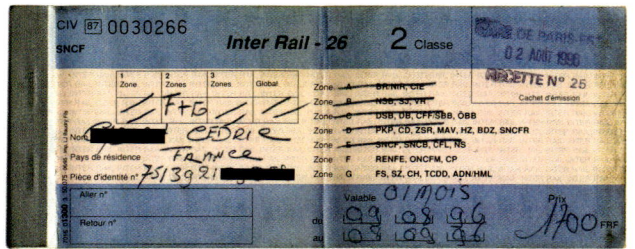

CARBON COPY ITINERARIES

The global pass gave maximum travelling flexibility, allowing access to any country in Europe. Unlike tickets valid only for 2-3-4 zones, which only included specific railway lines. To the side, Honet's Inter-Rail trip around Southern Europe in 1995

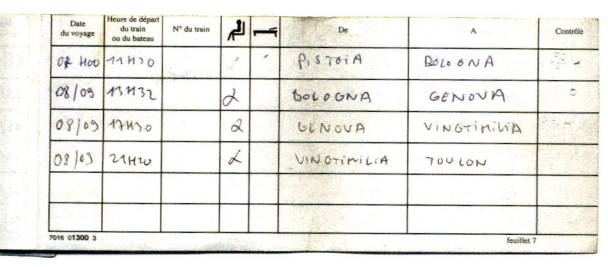

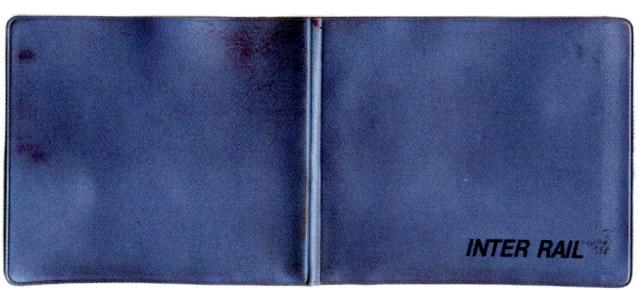

THE GREAT ESCAPE

Egs – CDC, MSN / Helsinki
>

think the first connections happened cause me and my friends used to go to Stockholm often. Sometimes even just for a day, not really to paint, but more on a holiday, and we'd take photos, since the scene there was more advanced than in Helsinki. So we'd take all these pictures, getting influenced by Disey, Ziggy, Baze, Buster, Erse, etc and that's how we ended up meeting writers that were also there taking pictures.

One of the first guys we got to know in Stockholm was Track. He is a really friendly and hospitable guy, so his house became a regular place to visit when in Stockholm. I still feel sorry for that fact that around ten Finnish writers were ringing his door bell every weekend. Track gave my number to Poze, a Finnish writer who had spent most of his life in Stockholm. He was writing with Nug, Aman, Kaos, Opera etc... so Poze came to Helsinki and through him we got to know people we started travelling with and who are still good friends today.

The first distant trip was in 1991 when we travelled by Inter-Rail. It was a big group of Finnish writers and Poze and Nug from Stockholm. We were actually travelling in groups to Switzerland, Germany, Belgium, Holland, France and Spain. We started Inter-Railing like every year or maybe twice a year after that trip.

Nowadays a lot of connections are made via the Internet. Back in the day it was a bigger task. We spent days riding trains to foreign cities looking for places that were painted and hoping to bump into some local writers. It was nice to get to know new writers, at that time we had one phone number for each city we visited and from each city we got some new numbers for the city up next on the itinerary. Of course travelling became an opportunity for new crews to form. MSN for instance was really based on those trips. Originally it was the Dutch crew from Utrecht and then it developed through the Inter-Rail. CTK was the first pan-European crew but MSN was the second generation and it became such a big crew thanks to all the Inter-Rail trips. It was nice to be in contact with like-minded people who loved painting trains, pushing new styles and partying.

It was a great way to travel, we met the coolest guys in every city we went to. It was never the usual tourist visit, it was crazy journeys in catacombs, yards, bars and coffee shops. One of the most exciting trips was when we went to Estonia in '94, we did some stuff there, it was totally up for exploration. We didn't have any local contacts, a friend of mine had been travelling through the country by train and he told me he had seen a yard in a small village maybe half an hour from Tallinn, the capital, and so I checked on a map in a bookstore in Helsinki. I looked up where that place was and me, Poe and Miro took a ferry to Estonia a few days later.

Tallinn was quite cheap and even though we didn't have much money -we were really young- we took a taxi from the harbour to that spot, only it was the wrong place. After a while we figured out that there were two places with the same name! Finally after another long taxi ride we found the yard. We were there during the day, painting. We just jumped over the fence and checked out the yard, there was a guard and a dog but they didn't really seem to noticed us at all. We did a nice colour end-to-end and some panels. We had tickets to travel back to Helsinki by ferry the same evening. A pretty stupid plan, and it wasn't that easy either. There were no trains or buses going back to Tallin, nor taxis.

We started hitch-hiking but no one offered us a lift until I started waving a note of 20 Finnish Marks. The next car stopped and gave us a lift to the ferry terminal via a Vodka store. The guy driving told us that he was DJ Raul Saarmets, the most famous Estonian techno DJ of the time. I don't know if that was true but he was cool anyway and didn't want any money.

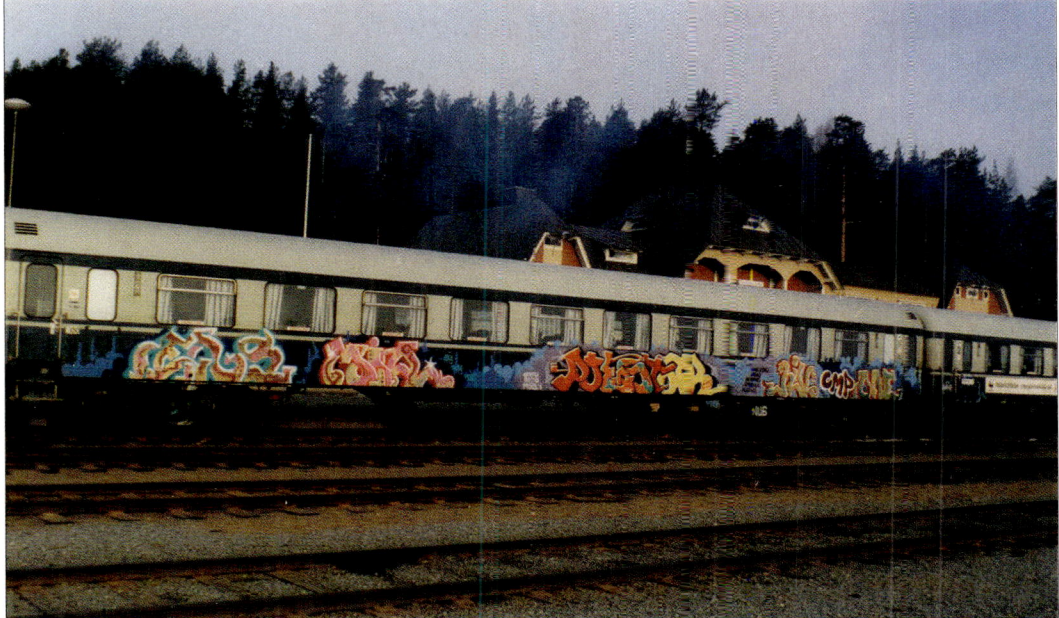
Egs, Mia, Poestar, Hiv, Cmp One   – Egs

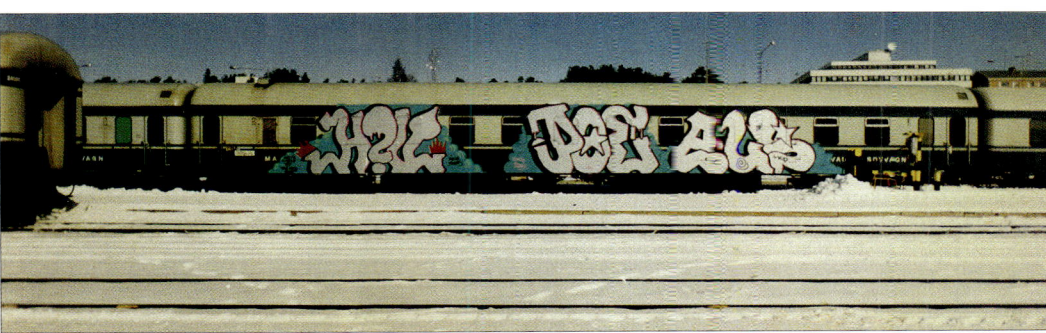
Hiv, Poe, Egs pieces painted on a long-distance train, Artic pole.   – Poe

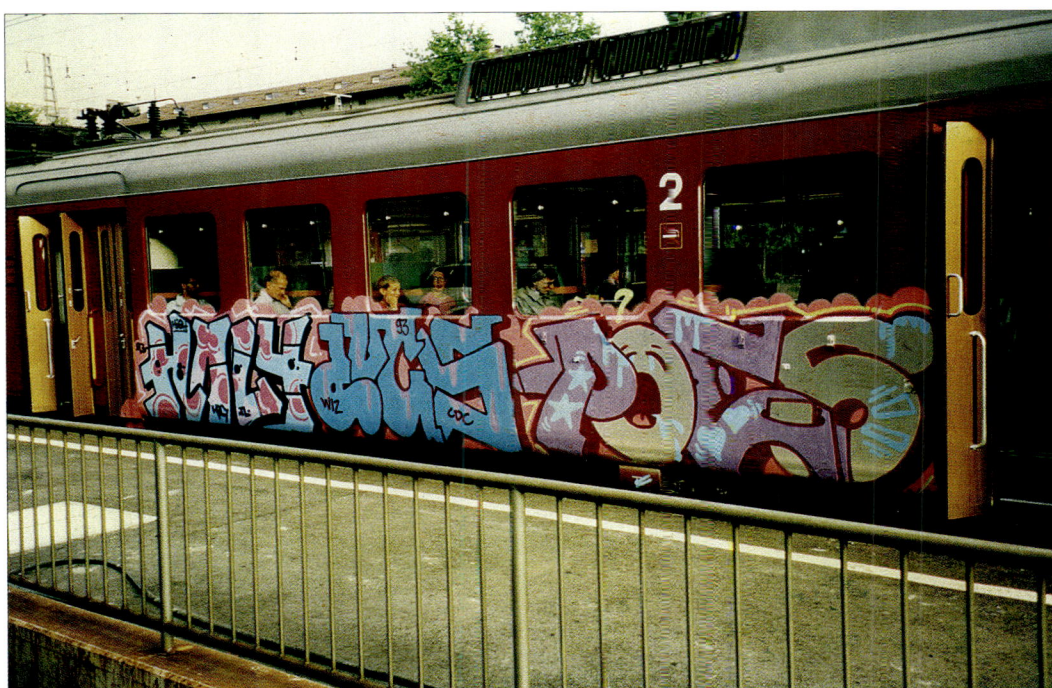
Holy introducing Finnish writers to the infamous Zurich "Red Beans".   – Poe

CES 53, ONE MORE TIME

Ces53's long trip across the German
railways and the deposits of East
Berlin after the fall of the Wall.

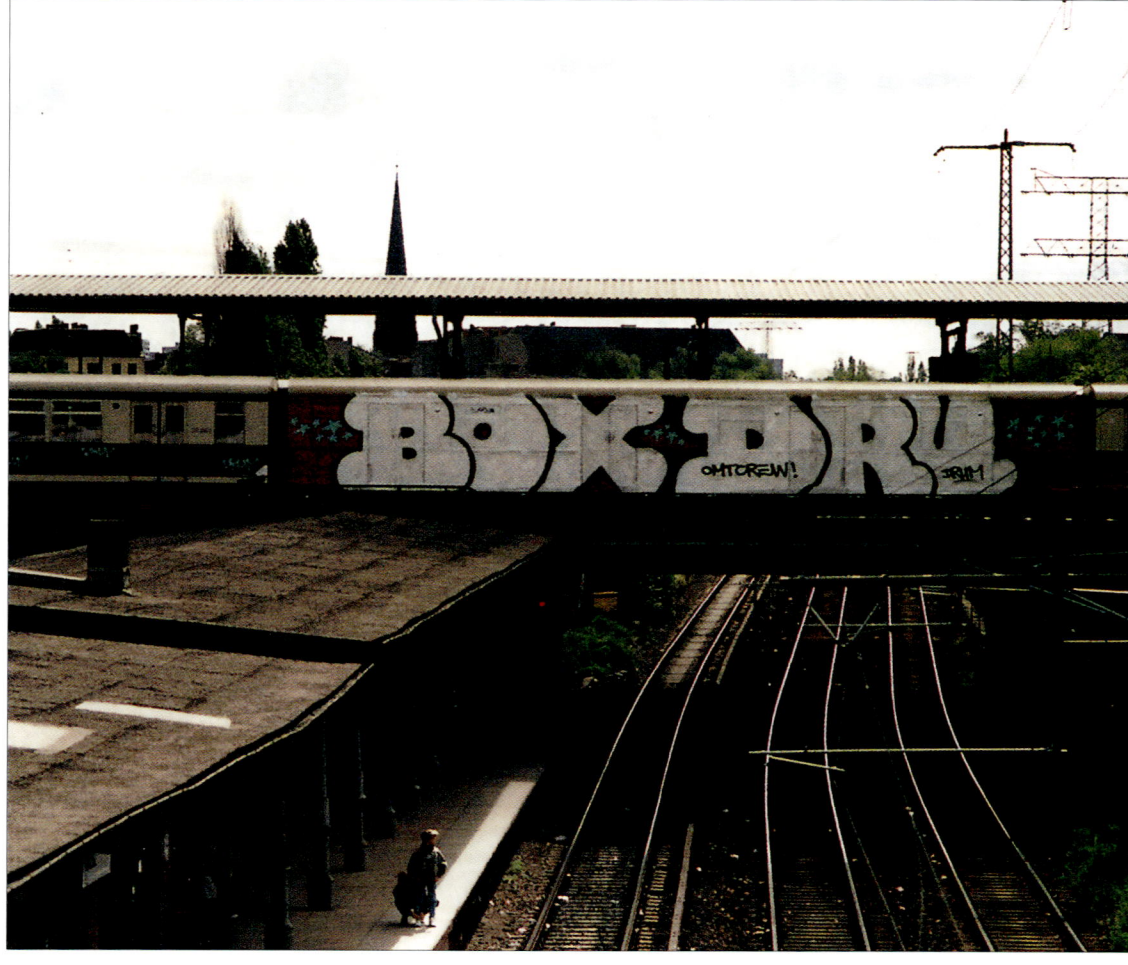

Ces 53 – INC, MSN / Rotterdam
>

Usually Inter-Rails last just a few weeks, but
when I left Rotterdam in September of 1990,
I embarked on a lengthy journey of several
months travelling across Germany. One of the
reasons I was away for so long was that I'd been
put in jail in Holland for painting trains that same year,
and so after that I decided to leave the country to get
the cop investigation off my back. I had tried changing
my name, and had started writing Dmon because they
caught me with the name Ces, but I was caught many
times, put in jail, and so I left. At the time it was possible
to travel really easily, to ride International trains with a
minimum amount of money and to survive by stealing
everything. I spent 1991 in Germany jacking whatever I
needed: food, clothes, and paint.
First I hooked up with Zebster in Munich, and that's the
first city I painted in, we did a whole-car right away (for
which I got caught live in the action). He had previously
come over to Rotterdam and met a guy I knew, so he was
one of the contacts I had in Germany, as well as Milk who
had also come to Rotterdam in '89. Painting trains in Germany was easier than in Holland. Here in Holland there
were always a lot of people around the trains, 24 hours a
day and so they'd never be left alone for the whole night.
You always had to be fast, you couldn't spend hours in the
yard. Plus, when I was younger, around '87, all this gang
shit started happening. There was a lot of fighting with
other guys because of the bombing and crossing. I was
kind of a rebel as well, I never bought paint. I would rack
everything, well... everybody used to rack everything. If
you bought paint you were a sucker so everybody was
stealing stuff. All of this was especially taking place in
crime areas, the fucked-up neighbourhoods where all
the kids were stealing and fighting. That's just the way
it was. In Germany I had the same lifestyle; I would steal
and write, that was the only thing I cared about, but in
Germany I stayed with friends and in squat house circumstances. I travelled by train, there used to be this
ticket in Germany that allowed you to travel all around
the country. It was very cheap, it cost €75 or €100 and
you could go all around the country for an entire month.
I used to buy one every month so if there was no place to
stay I could sleep on the train.

- BERLIN EAST

Whenever I'd go to a new place it was like a discovery
game for me. In Berlin for example I found the yards myself, I didn't have a connection with anyone from there.
I went with Milk and other guys but nobody was from
Berlin. I was checking out the yards and finding out the
times we could go, taking the time to investigate. Whenever I'd go to a new city the first thing I'd do was go to
the subway and note down all the lines and where the
yards were, every detail written on a little card. I've still
got some of those cards with stuff written on them. Then
I would check the yards and the timetables of the trains;
when they would come in and when they would leave. I
sometimes used to go check out a yard for a night or two
just by looking, this way I'd know what to expect. For

example in the bigger yards in Germany there were no
lights in the yards. These areas were totally dark and you
couldn't even see your own hands, let alone the colours
and shapes of letters painted on the cars. While in Holland the trains were parked in nice yards with lights and
houses next to them where there were guys working. It
was very different and for me it was more like New York
with all those trains in the darkness.
I remember I went to Berlin to scope it out in 1990, right
after the wall had fallen, and I thought to myself what a
great opportunity it was for hitting a new railway system
in a metropolitan city. So in the beginning of '91 I told
the Dutch guys we should go. Some Berlin writers were
already painting on the East side but the border had just

> ### I sometimes used to go
> ### check out a yard for a night
> ### or two just by looking, this
> ### way I'd know what to expect

opened and the bulk of the wall was still there. They were
still making holes in it, and the yards were enormous deposits in the open, without guards, fences or any control. There weren't even so many tags on the streets so
we used to bomb any building that was clean.
I remember there were some West Berlin guys going to
the East to paint, but I also remember some kids from the
East just starting so it was real fun. There were also toys

doing little pieces, I had never seen something like that.
It was interesting painting in the East part because the
West side already had graffiti, the situation was regularly
checked and controlled. They'd had graffiti for a couple
of years already in West Berlin, since '85 there had been
kids painting and from '86 they were also doing S-Bahns
and stuff, so I thought it would be better to hit a virgin
territory such as the East. We had already been trained
in Holland where they had a vandal squad, so this was
another reason why painting in East Berlin was easier, we
were already prepared for the hardest tasks.
I think I painted more than ten whole-cars in Berlin East,
but I nearly got caught three-four times. We nearly got
caught doing a whole-train, we had just finished it and
as we walked out of the yard the police came in. Then
another time I had just done the last line of the piece and
the train drove off! I didn't even have time to tag it and
there were still a few things to fix. I think I was doing the
highlights when it started moving in front of me.
It was anyway easy to catch pieces and take pictures of
them because they didn't know how to clean the cars in
the East, it was all so new! We did one train a couple of
days after another and they were totally shocked, they
didn't know how to react to it. We were four guys and
we did 22 whole cars in eight-nine weeks, it took a lot of
paint and there was a lot of organisation behind it cause
we had to check basically unknown places, sometimes
lost in the ghost part of the city. I remember the East Berlin police were really shocked and so were the writers.
It was me, Milk, this guy Shame (Deshamer) and Neon,
even though he only came one or two times. Neon was
originally from Munich so Milk knew him from there, he
was studying in Berlin so I was able to stay at his place. He

OVER THE BORDER

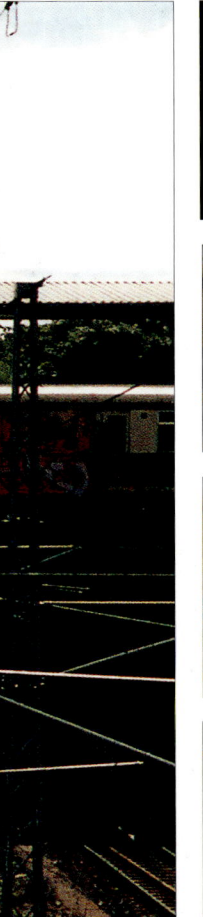

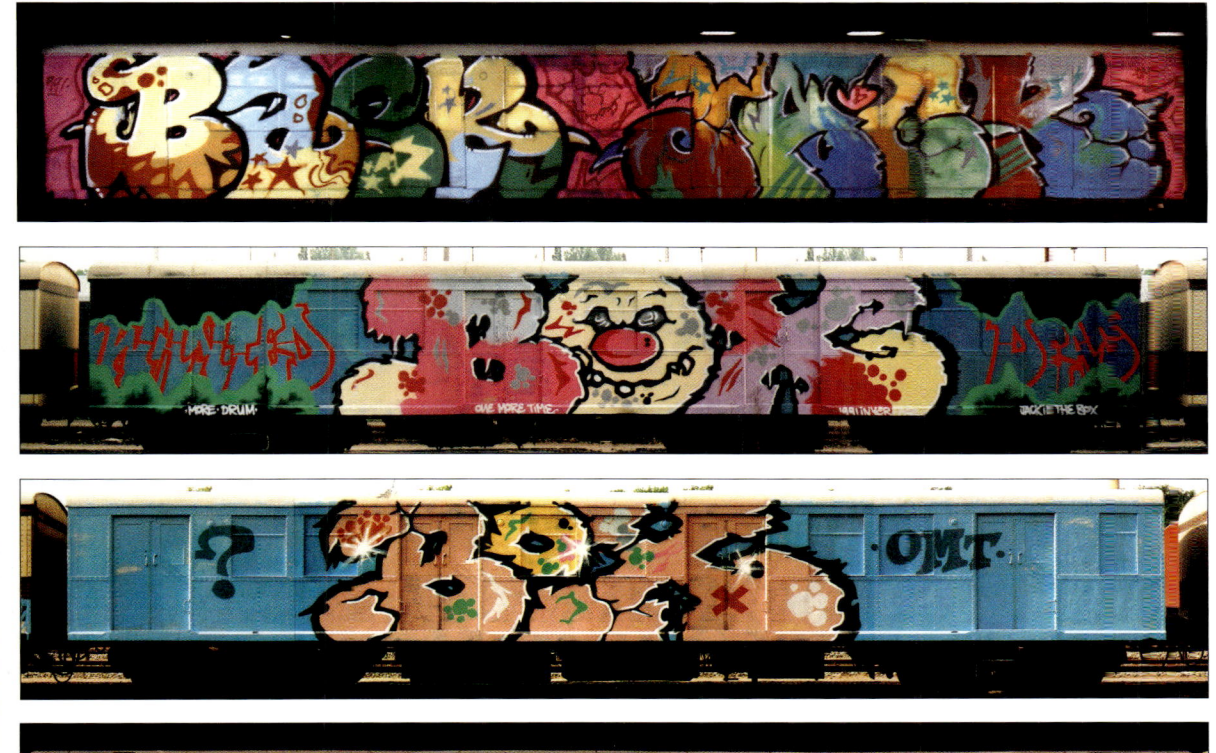

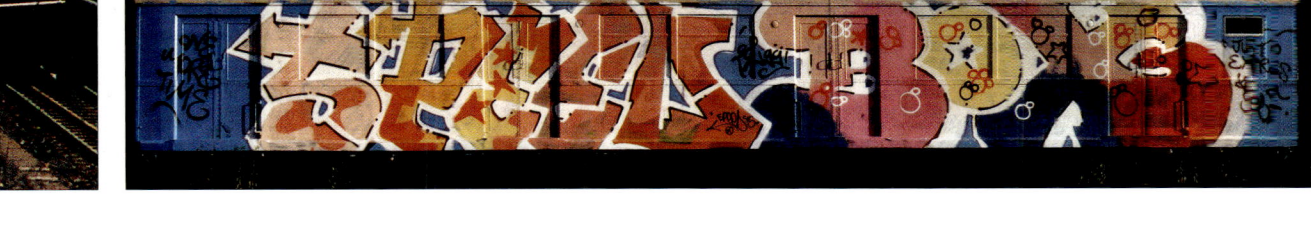

STYLE LESSONS

OMT

The full-coloured whole-cars painted by Ces53 and Drum left a clear mark on the scene. the "Drum", "Back" and "Jack in the box" series completed a non-stop year of bombing by ones of the most talented train writers of Europe.

was the main base, it was easy because he had an extra house and it only cost 20 marks per month to rent it. Well 20 marks was the price in East Berlin while in the West it was a couple hundred marks, it was mad cheap!
I stayed there for like three months with Milk and Shame, who's the other guy. Shame from Eindhoven was the guy who did the other whole-car pieces behind mine. He was also doing Desh pieces in Milan, in Berlin he changed his name to Drum. On the "Jack" full-colour whole-car he'd helped me do the background because I had helped him with a background on one of his pieces. It turned out to be an unforgettable action and I started to be published on every fanzine back then. It was in Berlin that I came up with OMT crew, One More Time. It was me, Milk and Shame, but I considered it more like a temporary project because I already knew that it would end when we left Berlin. I was always into project thinking rather than a crew that would last forever, even though I was in RTA with Zebster. I've always considered myself a solitary writer, not because I'm addicted to individual fame but just because it was and is my lifestyle. I stayed in Germany for about a year. I spent three months in Munich, three months in Berlin and six months in Frankfurt. It started like a sort of bombing mission and it ended up with whole-cars. I was painting a lot until '91, but after the mission in Berlin I slowed down because I was kind of getting crazy. I was carrying a gun on me to protect myself from the cops and crooks and when I realised how paranoid I had gotten I decided I just needed to stop. I had already been caught by the police 20 times since I was a little kid for stealing and all kinds of other things. I had a really big problem with them and this shit was getting too heavy; they were on my back, listening to my

phone calls and following me. It was just becoming too much and I was afraid the Germans were going to trace me down for doing this stuff. It was easy to buy a gun in Germany, they used to have the ones with bullets that leave scars but aren't real bullets. These guns were sold in regular stores so I started to get used to them. While I was in Germany I also painted with Chintz a couple of times. We used to spend the day talking about styles, techniques, train systems with Zebster, Chintz, Milk... all those guys were simply the best partners, they had the same skills. We knew each other quite well and shared the same background.
Chintz taught me how to steal cans with a shirt; normally I would put them down my pants, four or five of them sometimes. But he told me I had to do it differently: he told me to put my shirt in my pants, wear a coat over it and fill it up in the back. This way I could fit in 20 spray cans. It was kind of like a bag, with the coat on you couldn't notice anything. With two on top you could walk out with 20 spray cans. The secret was putting the shirt in your pants and pulling the belt so tight the cans wouldn't go down. Sometimes I took more than 20 in one go and then I'd walk out of the store looking like the Michelin guy. Around that time that I was painting whole-cars, so I would go out with 100-150 cans on any given day. Chintz and the guys in Dortmund were said to have a very undercover attitude, just mad sly about who they talked to and associated with, even among writers. but they were never like that with me because we immediately hit it off. Maybe because I was considered a style boy for German standards or maybe because Chintz considered me directly on the same level, during the early 90's we shared the same, wild playground.

LOCAL'S REVIEW
—

Rew / Berlin
>

The train system in the East was much easier compared to the one in the West. When the wall came down all the writers went to the East and found untouched virgin yards. There were many de-

posits, lay-ups, without security or workers. You could paint for hours and hours and it was the best time ever to be in Berlin. In the East there was the S-Bahn and a couple of subway lines. Ces 53 from Rotterdam came here to write when it was booming, around '91-'92.

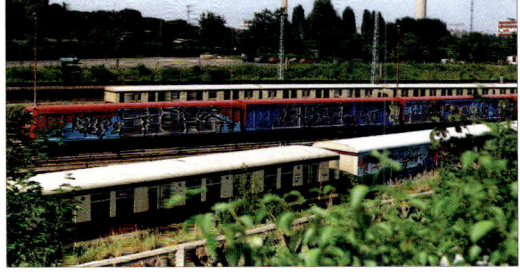

— Ces53

The Inter-Rail mania explodes: discovering

Vino – TSK / Barcelona
>

The first Inter-Rail I took was in 1996. Word was that you could find tickets that allowed you to travel throughout Europe and we decided to buy some together. Krash, Hove and I were the first Spanish writers to Inter-Rail. We went to Paris, where we had organised to meet Opak, which happened to coincide with a visit on the part of some Finnish writers – Mans, Sado, and Pablo – with whom we painted various panels. It was an incredible sensation: new trains of different colours, new yards... we had seen these trains published in fanzines...now they were in our collection! Cause the idea was this: to collect trains of railway systems different from our own. From there we travelled to Belgium, where we painted alone in an end station, it was really kid's play and in fact we did various panels for hours. From Belgium we continued towards Copenhagen, where we painted with some Parisians: Fizz, Vans and Vision. The Danish red trains seemed fantastic to us and we were impressed by the fenced-in yards...until then we had never cut the wires of a fence to get in. From Copenhagen we decided to go to France. During the trip, while we were sleeping on the train, they stole everything form us! We anyway spent some days in Paris, hitting subways and trains with Fizz; even though sometimes it got pretty bad, it rained, it was cold, we were sleeping in the street....but Inter-Railing was worth it; by travelling we formed strong

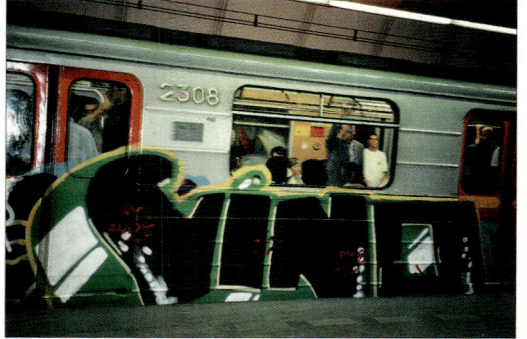

Vino, Prague, 1997   – Vino

bonds with local writers and from that year onwards every Summer would repeat: with different company and cities but with the same objective.

The following year Opak asked me to travel with him and we began our trip in Paris. The first stop was Zurich where we met VTO – Sexe, Zimtik – and painted various trains. It was the first time I saw anyone cleaning their fingerprints off of spray cans and it kind of shocked me, I wasn't used to that much precaution! After having passed through Berlin and Vienna, where we did some whole cars in the subway, we arrived in Prague. Opak had the contact info of some guys from DSK, even though he didn't know them personally. The first impression was rather negative, in some areas the city seemed abandoned and we even came to think our contacts would stick us up, because they kept asking what we had in our backpacks, if we had brought many spray cans, if we had money; the truth is they were ok, only they weren't used to seeing people from the Inter-Rail. We did some trains and they took us to paint a subway in the middle of the earth. We would call the guys guiding us "Ninjas". They weren't writers, simply guides... but the mission was incredible. We couldn't take any pictures of the pieces inside the tunnel but two months later a friend of mine from Barcelona managed to take some snapshots of my panels, still running on the local lines of the city.

After Prague we went to Warsaw. This stop marked a key moment, in a place that to us was absurd... strange people in the trains, destroyed cities and towns...when we arrived, we met Kobolt from Berlin who explained to us how things worked and advised us to be very careful. The first night we went to Zachodnia, a deposit of the city that hosted many trains. As we were going to the deposit we saw a load of shacks full of vagabonds, some were actually living in the trains. While we were hiding in the trees, we saw a group of people come towards us and we immediately thought of the worst....instead they were a group of Germans about 17-18 years old that were going to paint whole-cars! We did two panels each and the next night we returned with more cans to paint with. During the day you could see trains completely covered in pieces, and we bumped into Rew from Berlin taking a photo. One night we went with him to paint a whole-car together: everything went perfect. From there we returned again towards Berlin, passing through Hamburg – painting in both cities – to then end up in Stockholm: it was the city I had always wanted to go to. In

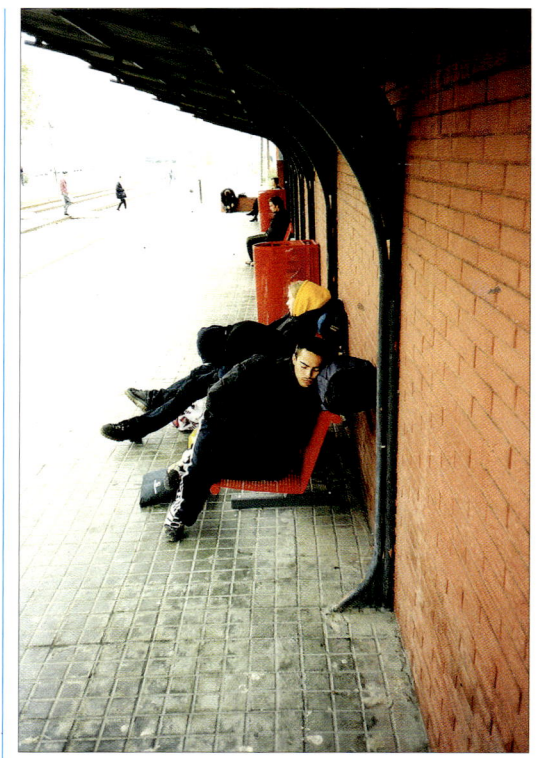

– Vino

Stockholm we hooked up with Ribe, Sear and Solo, and painted some trains and subways. We were coming from the paradise of graffiti – in Barcelona trains could be hit in all tranquility – but in Sweden everything was much more controlled: video cameras, sensors on the fences, trains buffed with blue paint. It was crazy....I ended up having to go straight back to Barcelona for family problems, 78 hours of train with an only stop, in Paris, where I did some subway cars with Fizz.

In 1998 I got back on the road with Kaze, Sioc and Fose: after having painted with Hulk in Paris and Brussels, we travelled towards London. It was my first time there and it was incredible, doing both subways and trains. We

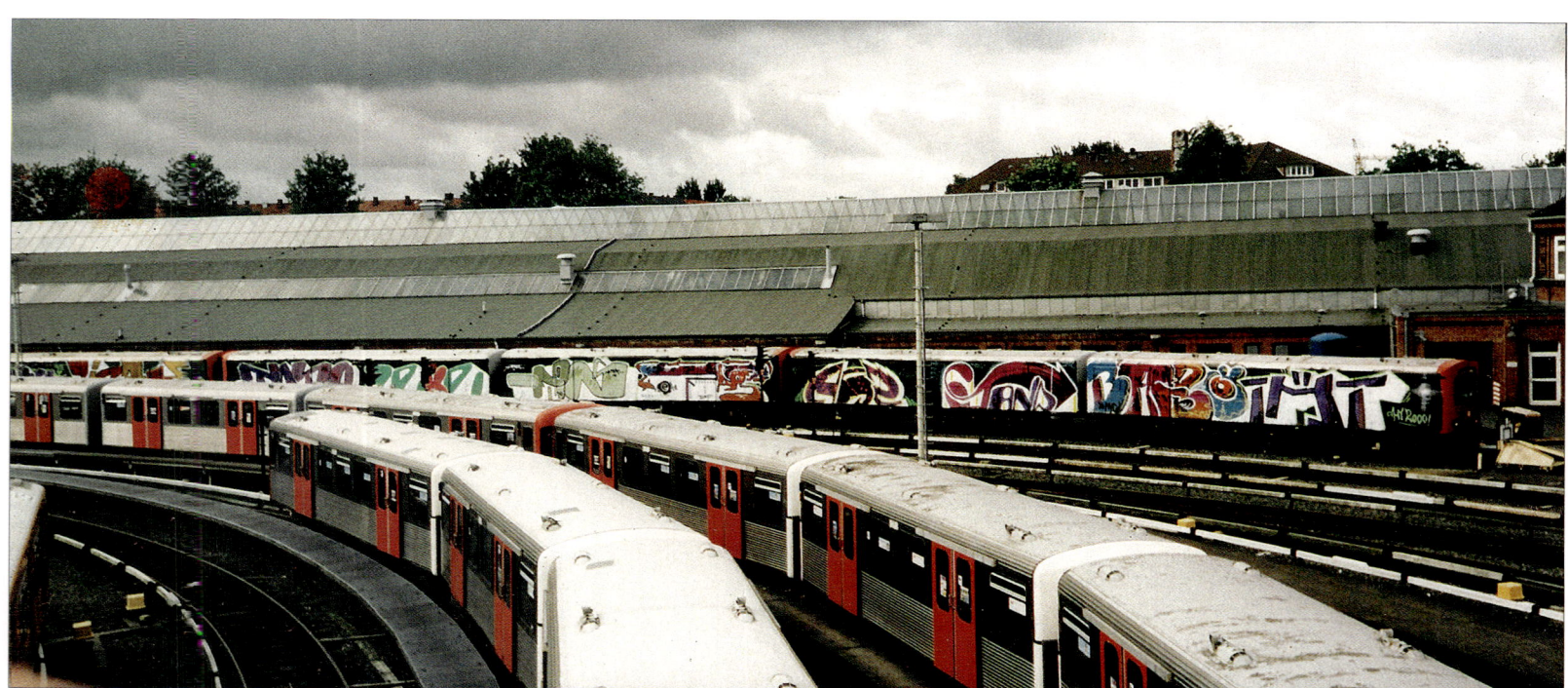

Whole-train in Hamburg, 2000   – Vino

East Europe

WARSZAWA ZACHODNIA
—

spent some days with Ano and Dodo, painting, drinking and just being stupid in the streets of London. When we returned home we still had some days of Inter-Rail, so Blue and I decided to go to Milan. We linked up with Shampoo and Dumbo there, with whom we hit the subways and the FN, but the thing that left me perplexed was seeing the city filled with tags and throw-ups.

In 1999 I then left with Fagor, with a more complicated objective: other than hit the trains we also wanted to target the subway of all the cities we passed through. Paris, Brussels, Amsterdam, and Rotterdam were the first cities we visited and it wasn't that hard to paint. Afterwards we spent a few days with Rocki, who was Inter-Railing in Copenhagen and Malmo, and we did some trains there. This is where it started getting problematic: painting the subway in Stockholm and Oslo. In Stockholm we could count on the help of Solo and Rilo with whom we did some back-jumps. I still remember when they told me we would have to paint in seven-eight minutes....I thought "what am I supposed to do in that little time"... in Barcelona we were used to painting for an hour! That was the acid test, and luckily everything went smoothly.

In Oslo on the other hand we didn't make it. We met with THT and painted some trains, but when we went to the subway a really strange thing happened. We got to the end station, checked out the people in the deposit and when we were about to start painting one of the guys of THT said he had seen someone with a pair of binoculars on a little hill close by and that it was a policeman, and that there were others on the platforms. So we got on the subway and left, thinking they were paranoid, only at the following station two cops in plain clothes got on and told us they knew who we were and what we had come to do and that sooner or later they would catch us. After this episode they spent the entire day following us around the city... we were incredulous.

On the way back home we did some S-Trains in Hamburg with Rage and DSF and until 2002 every summer went this way. We went back to Paris and Hamburg several times, where we did a whole-car with Rage and where again, I was struck by the way in which every movement in every deposit was controlled and by how much security there was. Incredible. And then Berlin, Brussels, Amsterdam, Stockholm, Rotterdam and London, where Blue, Sioc and I spent some kick-ass days with Ano and Dodo, this time indulging in both painted subways and litres of beer. In 2003, tired of painting the same cities, we decided to move progressively East. With Blue, Sioc, Thow and Rens from Madrid I took off for Vienna, where we did various subways and I had the sensation nothing had changed from the last time I had been there. Then we went to Prague, though this time we didn't manage to paint, to Berlin, where we did some panels in the subway, and then Warsaw. Here I realised the city had altered: it was more modern, full of young people, shopping malls everywhere, new buildings....we contacted some local guys and they told us it had become very difficult to paint trains at that moment. I ended up anyway going to the same place I had gone the last time and painted there three nights in a row, we even hit the subway. From there we moved towards the unknown: Budapest. We had imagined a very old and dirty city, but that was not the case at all. There were parties in the street, beautiful women and fantastic light blue-coloured subways. We met up with Rolex and painted various cars... it was hard to get into the tunnels, though once you arrived you could paint without worries. In contrast, things have changed a lot in Barcelona and it has become difficult to enter the deposits: if until then you could stay for over an hour, now you can't even paint more than fifteen minutes.

Back-jumps have become the daily routine in Spain as well. All these experiences I lived through have allowed me to evolve, helping me overcome the setbacks that ensued from the series of precautionary measures that the train system actuates year to year.

I have not been on the Inter-Rail since 2003. I no longer travel so much by train, I do so by car or plane thanks to the low cost flights, but the objective and the mentality have not changed at all.

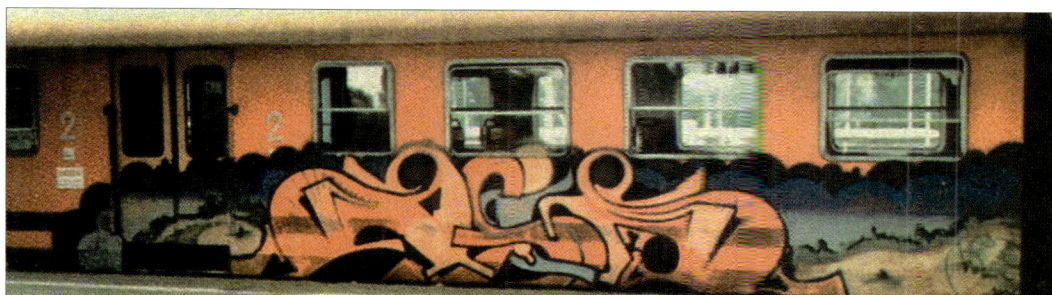
Asid–TT from Berlin in Warsaw.1996
— XG archive

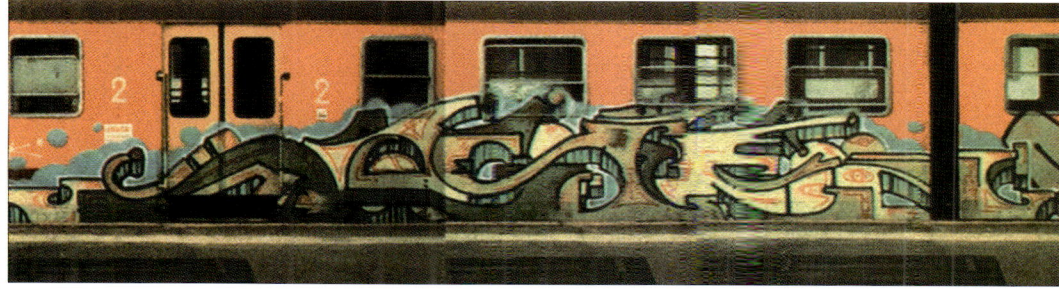
Dask–B3S, 1996
— XG archive

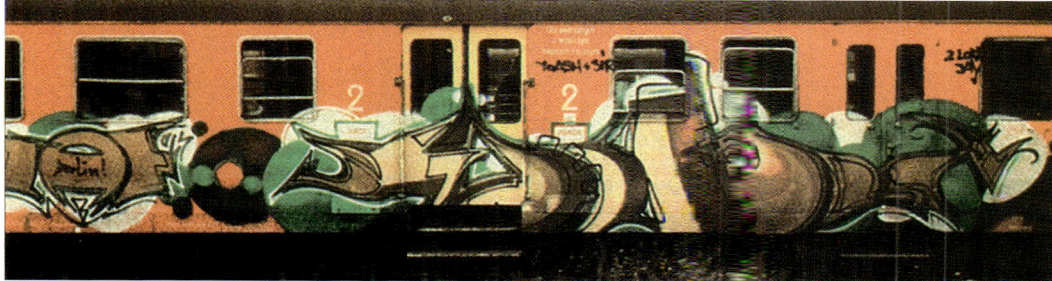
Kobolt–CAF from Berlin. 1996
— XG archive

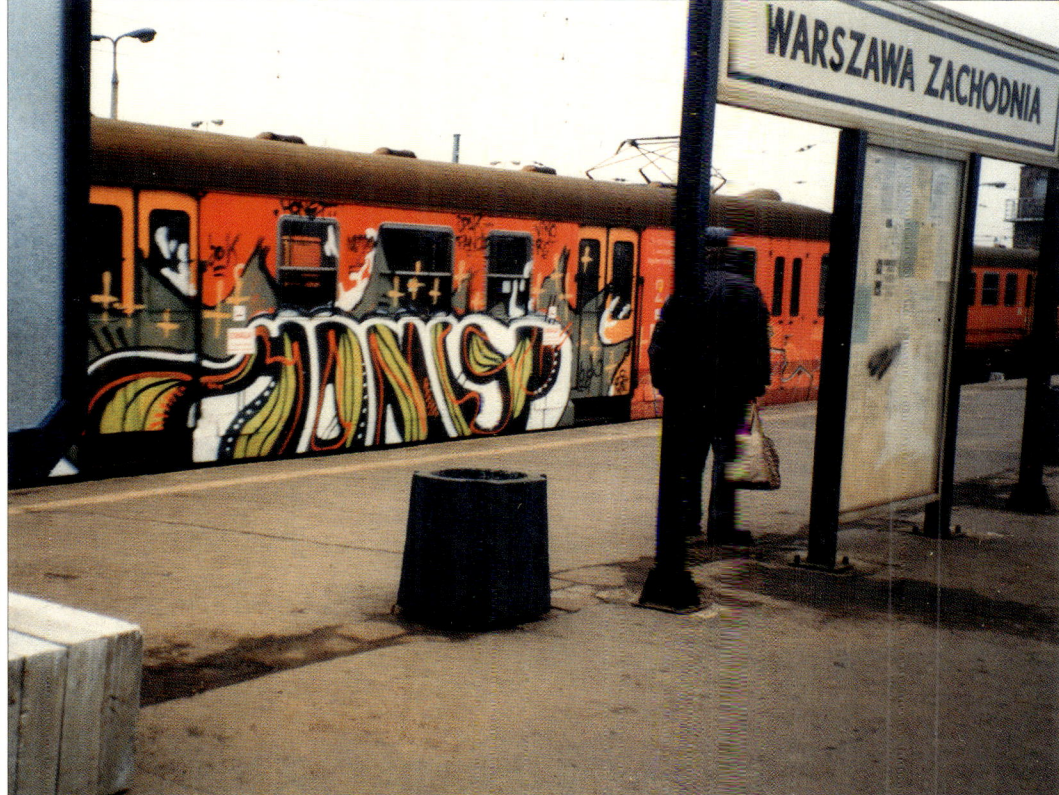
Honet at Warszawa Zachodnia
— Honet

Warnings of an exodus: the SDK experience

The journey to discover and collect photos of the widest variety of painted cars

Opak –SDK / Paris
>

I left Paris to go on my very first Inter-Rail tour in the Summer of 1993. I have always loved Scandinavian styles, not to mention Scandinavian girls, so it came naturally to me to go up North and check it out for myself. Nothing was really planned that much: the main mission was getting enough cash to actually buy the Inter-Rail ticket, once that was accomplished I just took off on this trip with a couple of phone numbers and a few sketches in my pocket. The itinerary started in Copenhagen, where I crashed at Ren's place, which is also where I met Chen from Munich. Chen and I quickly became friends and since he was also travelling by Inter-Rail we decided to hang out together for the rest of the trip. We started with the famous Copenhagen red S-trains and then we went to Stockholm to meet the Vandals In Motion, who happened to be the most talented, active and also the most friendly guys I have ever met: Kaos, Reson, Aman, Nuh and Pike just to name a few. Many of these guys were living in what was referred to as the famous "VIM House". During our permanence in Stockholm we would get drunk, rack stuff, paint trains and just have a lot of fun. Little by little we discovered the beautiful city of Stockholm in a very unique way. That's also when I did my first whole-car with top-to-bottom letters, together with Aman & Chen. It was an ugly piece, but it gave me the ultimate sensation! And so that was it: I became addicted to Inter-Rails.
In fact, travelling wasn't that new at all, but Inter-Railing was definitely not that common for most graffiti writers of the time, who rather preferred to paint in their own city or country rather than travel abroad. On the other hand I went almost everywhere you could possibly get to with an Inter-Rail ticket. Sometimes I was on my own, other times I would go with Honet or other guys from my crew, or whoever I had a good relationship with and was down for some action, there were many different travel companions throughout the various trips and years. It's not like you can put people who travel in one same category: the "Inter-Railers"; you get to meet all kinds of people when you're on tour, and graffiti was the thing that connected us. I guess some liked Hip Hop while some were into techno or heavy metal...but who cares? At the time of my Scandinavian tour, Stockholm was a real paradise compared to what it has become now, and it is one of the situations I miss most in Europe. In many of the other countries I visited things have remained more or less the same as they used to be, perhaps generally speaking there has been an improvement with regards to anti-graffiti security measures.
There is one exception however: Italy, which is now easier than it used to be! I'm not talking about specific private lines or the Rome subway system, which has always been a game of catch with the guards: I'm talking about the FS yards that have never been such an easy target as

> ## Nothing was really planned that much: the main mission was getting enough cash to buy the Inter-Rail ticket

they are today. Thank God we have at least one country in Europe where you can still feel the original flavour of painting a train without worrying about anything except completing a fresh piece. So what if you don't risk your

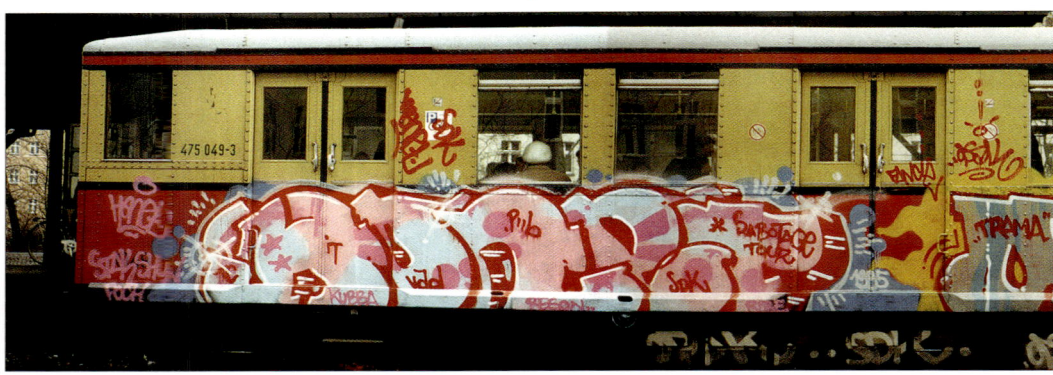

Duty, Opak, MR.Ira. Munich 1994

life doing it? What I enjoy is painting trains and watching them run, not fighting against Robocops and all kinds of electronic devices. I mean, if there's no other way, I'll do what needs to be done to reach my target but if I had to choose, I'd pick the chill painting session over the war zone any day.
Every city has had its share of golden years, and many times I've been lucky enough to be at the right place at the right time. I arrived a bit late to Amsterdam though: in 1993 there was still one subway line which was totally covered with paint, but they had already started increasing security measures in order to get rid of graffiti. There are, however, some places that were simply heaven on earth for the train-painting addict that I was... Warsaw was one of them. I guess it was around 1996, and very few people had been there despite a very talented local scene that couldn't paint as much as it would have wished to because of the lack of spray paint.
The main yard in Warsaw was a non-stop party, it wasn't rare for there to be more than 20 people in the yard at once, some would be painting while others were just chilling: locals, Inter-Railers, Berlin writers, and even people who had nothing to do with graffiti. The railway company hadn't realised what was going on yet – or at least no one had told them that graffiti was 'bad'. So you could just hang out there, say hello to the train drivers who sometimes seemed to appreciate the pieces, and keep on painting. What more can you ask for? I don't need to be on a mission to enjoy painting trains: all I want is a bag full of spray cans and those nice orange trains that allowed your pieces to run for years, and that was enough to entertain myself with!
The whole point of Inter-Railing was to discover places I had never been to before, so quite often we didn't know

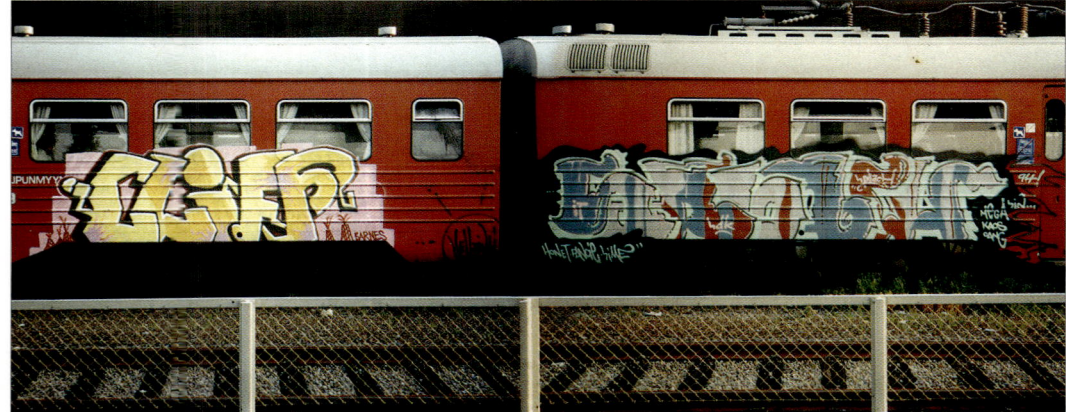

Honet, Berlin 1993   – Opak

Cliff and Splatch piece on Finnish commuter train, 1993   – Opak

> ## The main yard in Warsaw was a non-stop party, it wasn't rare for there to be more than 20 people in the yard at once

what to expect at first. Because it was quite early in the 90's, many places were quite virgin – or at least not under any sort of security control. I've done subways in cities that are now fucking mission impossible to paint: Athens, Stockholm, Rome, Naples, just to name a few. Nowadays it has become quite hard to paint in many European capitals, but as long as you're still motivated, you can always find tricks through which to beat the system: the most recent and unusual targets I have pursued were located in Hong Kong and China, and it worked out after

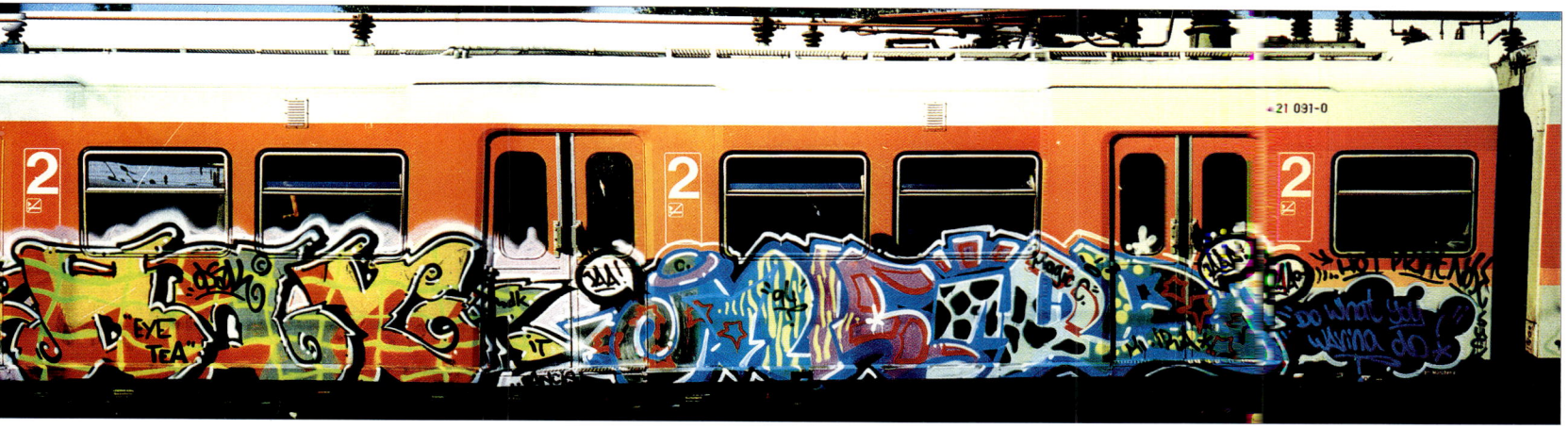

– Opak

all. I was less lucky in the Moscow subway, where the mission ended without success, but after what happened that time, I can tell you I was happy to be alive.

I've heard stories about people who got caught writing in a foreign country and are simply kicked out, but I've never really seen it with my own eyes. Like anyone else, shit has happened to me at times, and I even ended up in jail once waiting for them to decide what to do with me, whereas local writers might be set free right away. The reason is quite simple: locals have a home where the cops can find them whenever they need to, whereas foreigners who get caught will just run out of the country right after their release, instead of staying there and waiting for the trial. So quite often if you're a foreigner they'll hold you in a cell, it really depends on the policy of the country.

Personally, I've always had a preference for Italy, not only because of my family roots, but also because during the second half of the 90's Rome was the most exciting city to be in. When I first went there, there were hardly any foreign pieces except for a few burners by Delta, Sento, Zedz, Chintz or Milk. TRV crew was ruling the subway lines at first, that's the main thing I can remember. It was already hard to paint in Magliana, but the Lido line was a big joke and it was really all about having fun in the yard: like this lay–up they used to call Spaghetti, or Colombo, at the end of the Lido line.

I went there many times, but 1996 was perhaps the best year; I was with Pane who at that time was living in a sort of a ghetto area located near the seaside, at the end of the Lido line. The whole neighbourhood and all its buildings was just a giant squat. Inka and Fame45 from Berlin were there too. When we arrived the locals just gave us the key to an apartment there, which couldn't have been more perfect! One time I remember painting in the inner city yard, five minutes away from 'home'. The security guards saw us jumping the fence while going out of the yard and started following our car until we entered the neighbourhood, where they pulled back because guards and cops were not really welcome there... priceless.

I could go on forever: Rome's adventures have been some

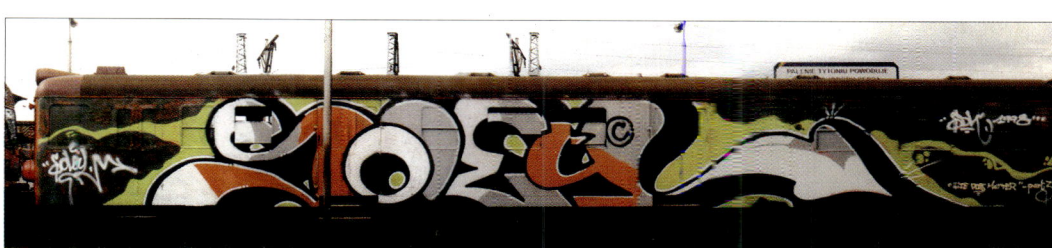

Soley – SDK, Warsaw 1998

– Opak

of the best ever. Milan was real fun too. At first, around '93/'94, the subway was not a target of choice because they used to buff it quickly – so no one was paying attention to it – while you could paint on the FN line and have your pieces run forever. What a blast to hang out

It's been 15 years since I started taking the ticket and I'm still travelling, just like in the 90's, not that much has changed

at the main station and see all the trains painted! And year after year, history repeats itself in Italy, since today some cities like Naples, Bologna or Perugia are still entirely painted. Over there it is still possible to enjoy a cool graffiti lifestyle, paint a lot of trains and not necessarily be paranoid and hide from society just because you like to put colour on steel. It's a luxury today, in this big brother world. During my first Inter–Rail trips I met many local writers, of course it was great painting with cool people

but there are also many places where it's much better or just more fun to plan actions by yourself rather than count on help from others. The best example is New York, where it was definitely safer to figure out everything by ourselves, rather than run the risk of being seen with local writers and end up at the VS office just because of a snitch, a tapped phone or whatever. When I went to New York I had never been to the USA before, so going to the big apple seemed like a perfect introduction to the country. Once you're there though, going around the yards and the city, you feel the weight of all these years of graffiti history, and it somehow adds spice to the game. And I'm definitely happy to have been able to paint some of those old subway models before they dumped them into the sea. It's been 15 years since I started taking the ticket and I'm still travelling, just like in the 90's, not that much has changed. The whole terrorism prevention thing is a big joke, because if a teenager with spray paint can sneak into a subway yard and paint a piece, what might a terrorist do in the same amount of time? Generally speaking, the 21st century seems to involve more & more CCTV surveillance and sadly we've got to get used to that. They already live with it in cities like London, and no matter how much energy they put into installing hi-tech cameras or brand new sensors: kids are still smart enough to get through and reach their goals. So let's see what they'll come up with next.

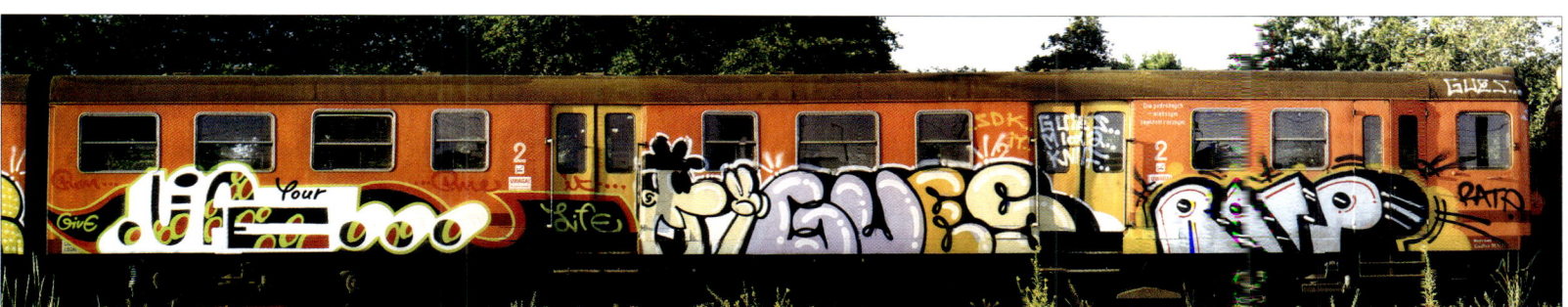

Life – PME, Guess – SDK and Ratp in Warsaw

– Opak

On a plane full of cans

> CONTINUES FROM PAGE 51

Street with it's invented characters or *Wild Style* which is almost fiction. From the moment you start searching for the reasons for something, you start asking yourself some questions, that s when you start maturing. But at the beginning how could we know Ramon wasn't a real writer? Munich was maybe an exception because Writing was absorbed as a phenomenon per se. When the Bavarian T.V channel BR aired *Wild Style*, for some reason the essence of the phenomenon that related to painting your tag all-city on walls and trains was fully captured. The other disciplines of Hip Hop were simply neglected at the beginning; the sole dogma that remained was tied to letters. Letters and styles were the only elements that guided everything, and it went beyond the specific personal passions of the kids practicing them. Nobody wanted to invent anything other than their own style, because, particularly in Munich, your stylistic level was considered a fundamental step and the only scale of judgment.

The trends, the various schools of thought, and Hip Hop in general were all part of a package that got to Munich only years later, as secondary aspects. In many other European cities a cliché of the B-boy was created and initially almost no one considered Writing and Breaking as independent phenomena. With time the initial influences were put into perspective and the arguments began, as well as a growing divergence of views with those that were B-boys and continued to convince themselves that the four elements were born together and should stick together.

The Northern iron belt

> CONTINUES FROM PAGE 57

we didn't want to compete, a guy from Germany whose name we can't mention, but people know who he is.

So MSN was growing and because of *Getting up*, we were meeting more people. Besides our personal influences, all of us were very impressed by the style and quality of many wall pieces that were being done by Amsterdam writers such as Delta, Gasp and Pone. Soon we got in contact with them, painting some walls - our pieces looked like shit compared to theirs - and some bombing on Amsterdam streets and subway trains, and since MSN wasn't just looking at the bravery of a writer but also their attitude and style, the former three guys were included in MSN too. I remember meeting Gasp for the first time in the daytime, at the subway yard of Amsterdam. Gasp was just walking around to see if anyone was painting and all of a sudden he spotted me doing my first subway panel. Gasp offered to watch out for me and I couldn't imagine that a legend like him would want to do that. After that the Amsterdam guys went with us several times to do bananas. All of a sudden the crew had a lot of members. This, combined with people all over Europe doing MSN pieces, made the crew a bit of an entity in itself, instead of a collective 'trust' thing. We saw MSN pieces done by people we didn't even know and as some original members quit writing or slowed down, the crew suffered a sort of self-proclaimed identity crisis. This didn't feel too good for the people who started it, so after more years, let's say by the end of the 90's, MSN had re-stabilised and that's how it still is today... writers who are in the know and feel that they are MSN. Right now, it's a handful of writers only. Since then, we've seen so many people come and go, there ain't so many soldiers left from the beginning, which is logical; people find other interests and responsibilities. Some feel like Mellie; "as much as I enjoyed those days, somewhere along the line I felt I lost the energy to really go out there and generate the bombing missions. Basically you could say the little voices in my head stopped talking, and the obsessive attitude just disappeared. So at a certain point I felt that I couldn't keep up my personal standards and stopped writing around 1997."

In the new millennium, we are still bombing without really caring about a crew or 'politics' or anything anyway, but after a while we realised that in the past year we had almost always painted solely together. Why not stay true to the meaning of a crew - the guys you trust, and like to bomb with - and keep pushing WOW a bit

more. Actually it wasn't a matter of bringing it back, it was more like 'let's be aware of the fact that we are a crew and put it up more conscientiously.' Yalt got into the crew. He had been bombing as long as all of us, but we just started hanging out more and more in the past years. We already met in 1995 in NYC where me, Camel, Mickey and Yalt, with locals like Sento, Sach and Smith did some serious damage. We could write a book solely about our adventures in New York.

What's up today? After 20 years of Writing, things have not changed that much for me and graffiti in general. Besides the fact that black outlines are the real shit. Many people quit saying stuff like "it's not profitable". I see it differently. I create my own rules. I don't care what you think, like or dislike. I do what I want to do and it feels good. I see so much graffiti, and I like its appearance and communication even if 99% of what I see looks soulless and feels irrelevant. Sometimes including my own stuff. For me, there's only one thing that lasts in graffiti: fun and endurance. Believe me, I'm going to keep doing it. Maniakken Stoppen Nooit!

STREETSCAPE

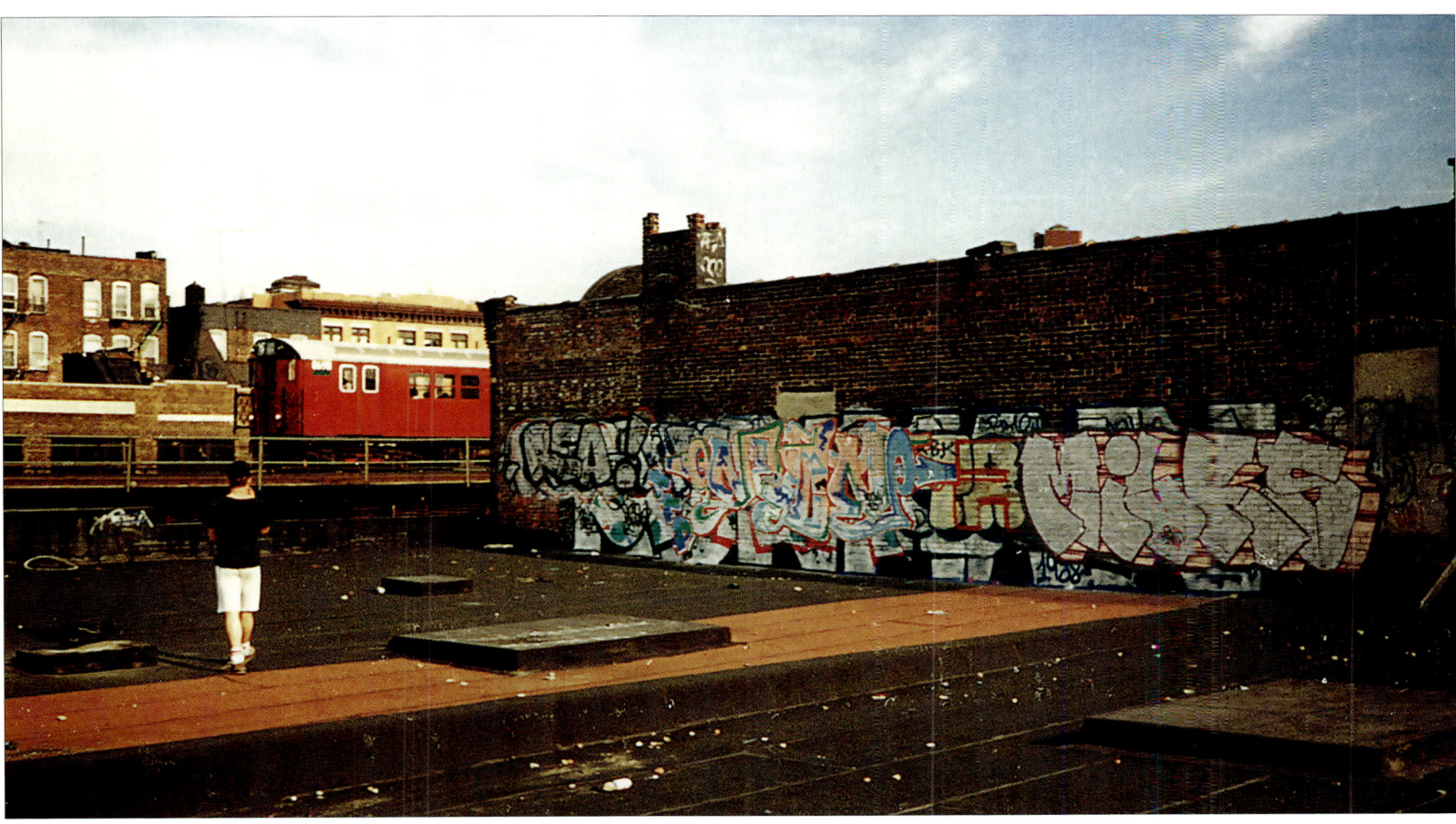

— Milk

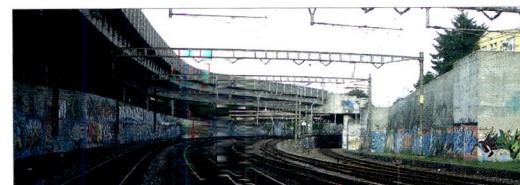
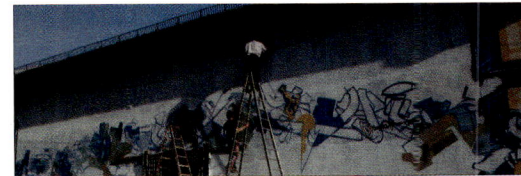
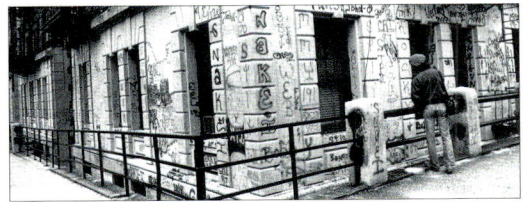

STREETS AHEAD: THE

With writers presiding over various urban territories, the groundwork for an inevitable development took form in Europe, beginning in individual metropolises and progressively invading suburban areas in a viral manner. The act of occupying specific spots can be traced back to the influence exerted by American writers in the late 80's, when they gradually shifted their aim from subway cars to city walls. Initially concentrating on the subway, writers in New York eventually contaminated every urban surface of the city, flooding the walls of railways and squash courts, penetrating the ground floor of buildings in decentralised areas and climbing all the way to rooftops. Graffiti had infiltrated every metropolitan interstice.

New York seems to be winning its war against graffiti in the subways, but many of the graffiti writers are using their spray cans and brushes on alternate targets: bridges, buildings, playgrounds and, particularly, the equipment of the Department of Sanitation. About one-third of the Department of Sanitation's 1,700 collection trucks are covered with graffiti, said Vito A. Turso, a spokesman for the department. It costs millions of dollars a year to remove. "Graffiti is no longer an underground problem," Mr. Turso said.
"It has surfaced in a very visible way on the side of our large garbage trucks, which, unfortunately, serve as an inviting canvas for someone who has a can of spray paint." Until recently, the Transit Authority was the prime victim of graffiti, according to Lieut. Kenneth Chiulli of the transit police. Graffiti writers - 75 percent of whom are boys 14 to 18 years old - were attracted to the subways by the fame, or infamy, that came from having their work circulate throughout the city, he said. But an aggressive anti-graffiti effort begun three years ago by the Transit Authority's president, David L. Gunn, has made the subways less desirable to vandals, Lieutenant Chiulli said. The "Clean Car Program" frustrates potential graffiti writers by virtually guaranteeing that fresh work will be removed within a day.
The trains in the program are inspected at the end of each run; cars that have been marked with graffiti are removed from service until they are cleaned. Improved security in storage areas and heightened vigilance by the transit police have also deterred vandals. In the last five years, Lieut.
Chiulli said, 5,000 graffiti writers have been arrested and charged with criminal mischief, a misdemeanor that carries a maximum penalty of one year in jail or a $1,000 fine. Few have served time in jail, he said. Among the graffiti writers

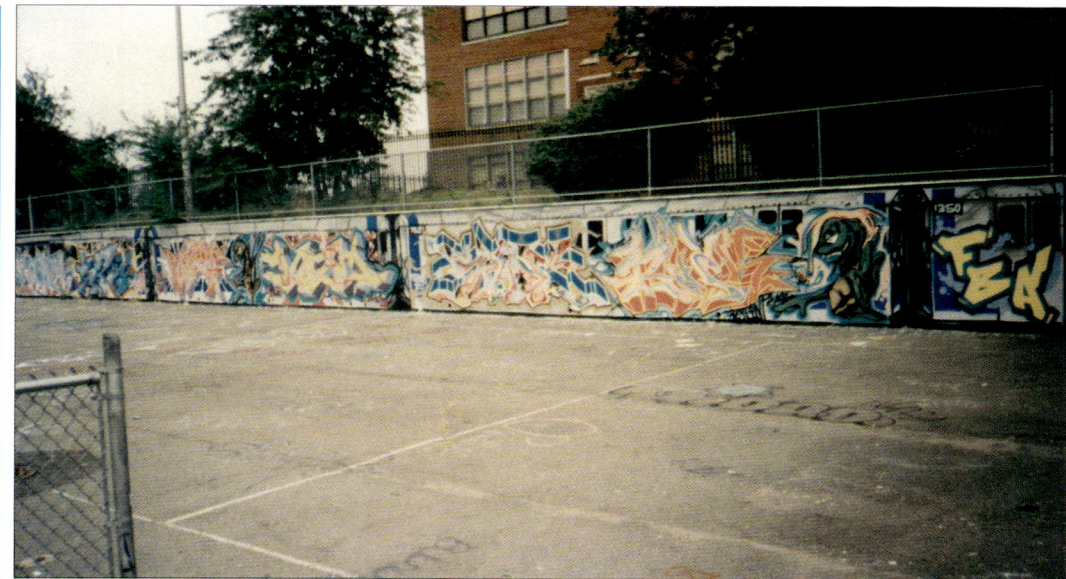

The memory of the painted subway, reproduced on the walls of a basketball court . New York 1996   *– ACW archive*

who have changed targets is Sean Perkins, a 16-year-old from the Bronx. "I haven't been hitting the trains because they are too hot right now - it's too easy to get caught," he said. Sean, who said he has written the letters "DKAY" on subway cars thousands of times in the last four years, has been arrested twice by the transit police. He recently began to paint handball courts, he said. Another graffiti writer, Louis Cancel, an 18-year-old from the Bronx who uses the tag "REA," said he recently switched from subways to rooftops. "People can see them from the trains, so you still get the fame," he said.

From the article "Battle line on Graffiti is shifting". New York Times, April 19th, 1987

–TERRITORIAL STRONGHOLDS

Until 1989, trains constituted an energy catalyst for the entire scene of New York; from that year on, severe preventive measures taken by the MTA forced local writers to abandon subway cars and venture towards vertical surfaces that were scattered throughout the urban fabric.

During this same period, the phenomenon exploded on the other side of the ocean. The repertoire of spaces already painted in New York doubly inspired European writers, who focused on both subway cars and walls from the very beginning. Thus, from trains to track lines, all the way to large hall of fame compositions, a vast scenario began to unfold.
Meeting spots directly connected to the world of Hip Hop – hence to music and dancing – constituted the first urban strongholds for writers: hang-outs were generally located in historic and tourist centres of the city, such as Covent Garden in London, Trocadero in Paris, Leidseplein in Amsterdam, the Nuevos Ministerios subway stop in Madrid, and Plaza Universidad in Barcelona. These spaces were characterised by a high concentration of tags traced with markers, where writers rarely had the chance to paint legal walls. In these spots, the legendary American city block was recreated, allowing the street life of New York to materialise through the presence of music, dancing, and graffiti.
At the same time, the need to find places in which to

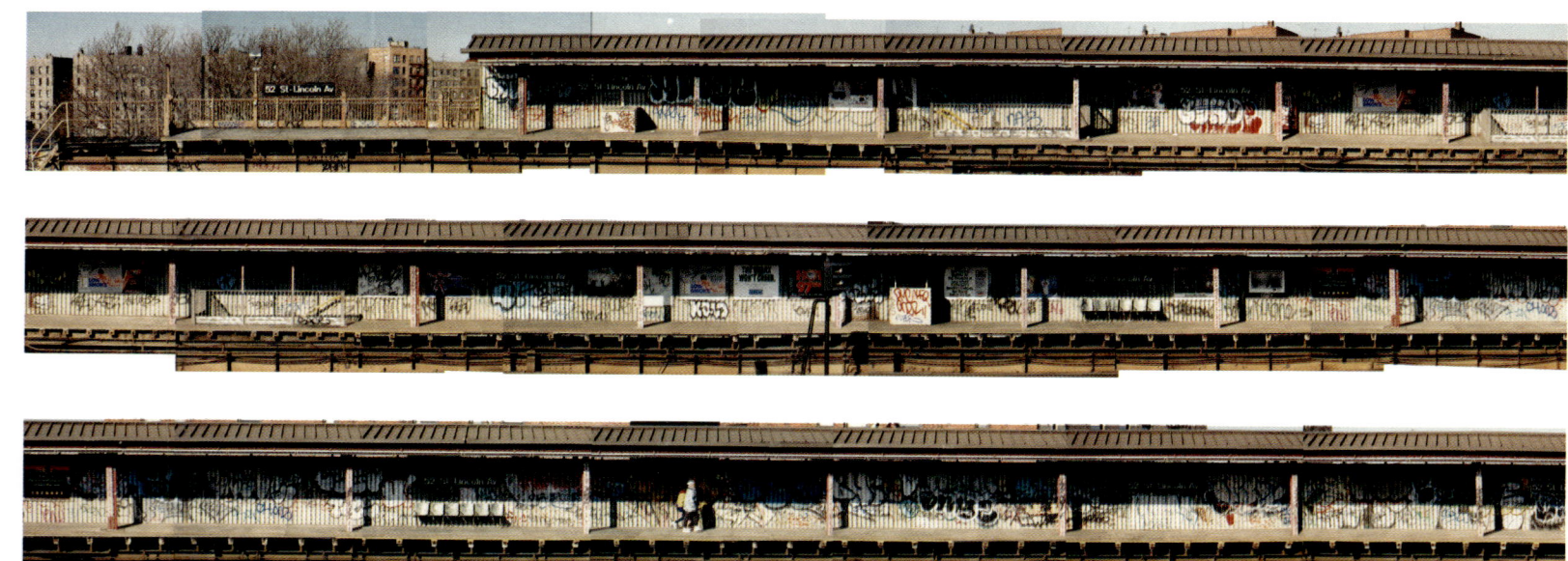

St. Lincoln Avenue station in New York, 1988

– Mark Todt

SUBWAY TRANSITION

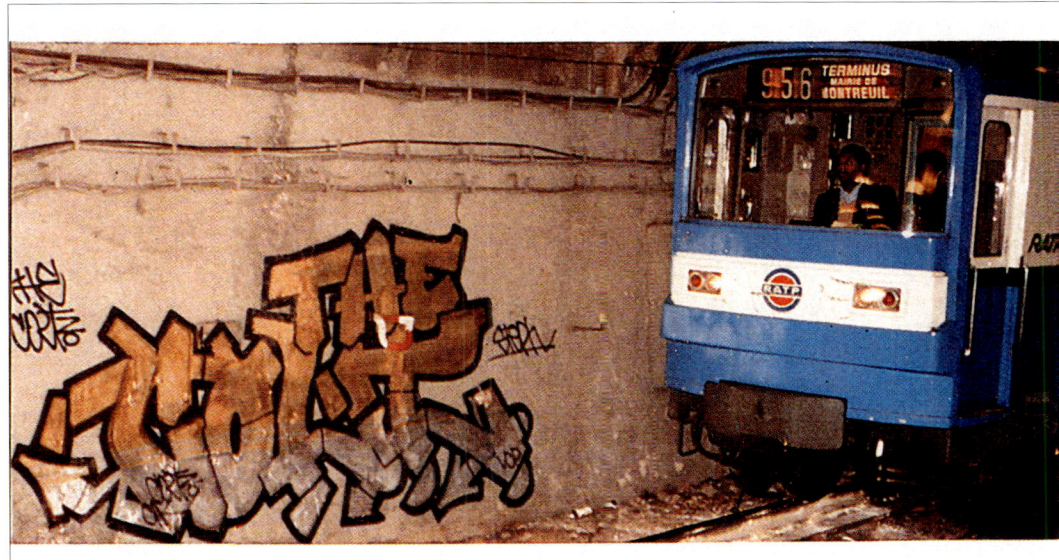

The Colt, by Colt. Burner painted along the Parisian subway tunnels.

— *Shoe*

paint legally began to emerge, leading to the European reinterpretation of the hall of fame concept, which in New York had been concentrated in the sport courts of outlying neighbourhoods. Unlike hang-outs, European halls of fame ignored the visibility offered by the city's historic centre and instead retreated to its unused spaces, often far from the busy areas.

Writers took refuge in marginal corners, amidst abandoned buildings – like Dachauer Flohmarkt in Munich – where it was possible to paint spaces forgotten by ordinary people, undisturbed.

Although there were some important examples of intermingling – such as Stalingrad in Paris, where the hall of fame coincided with the main hang-out for local B-boys – the difference between these two meeting places increased with time. While breaker hang-outs continued to be located in major pedestrian areas, the last 20 years of occupied halls of fame in Europe does not follow a precise logic, although it is possible to identify quite a few constant choices. The recurring elements go from infrastructure passageways (underpasses, viaducts, and tunnels), to empty urban spaces (construction sites, abandoned buildings, and industrial archaeology), and even parks and other locations characterising the city landscape, such as riverbanks. Also part of the same category are the ground floor walls of suburban areas, where painted surfaces took on an ornamental aspect, such as in the Mòstoles or Alcorcòn neighbourhoods of Madrid. These occupied spaces describe the urban development of Writing in European cities, which spread into interstitial areas that were reinterpreted through unexpected uses. The parasitical seizing of vertical surfaces for example rarely conflicted with any advertising slogans, under ining the visibility-invisibility paradox of the spots that had been chosen for painting. In fact, these spaces were part of a parallel circuit, with characteristics that were recognisable exclusively by writers and out of reach of those who were extraneous to the movement. European halls of fame, often forts designated to specific crews, became private space, guarded for their intimate value, where painting could constitute an act you do 'for yourself'.

– POPULAR TARGETS

The search for legal wall space, in which it would be possible to experiment with techniques and evolve styles, was accompanied by the necessity to be on display all over the city, to be visible, and to promote one's identity at any cost. Exposing an aspiring strength to one's Name: this was the umpteenth declension of the phenomenon. Any surface became useful, whether in central or outlying areas, but busier spots were preferred. Street bombing assaulted any typology o building, invading its every surface, victim of a sort of spatial bulimia: from ground floors to rooftops, all the way to store shutters, any target could bring visibility. Those who wanted to "get up" found an exemplary solution along the city's exposed nerves: the public transportation network, the flashiest metropolitan catwalk. In New York bombing had invaded subway stations just as much as tunnels and track line walls. In a similar way, writers in Europe occupied the barriers that skirted along railway lines, including station walls – like in Stockholm or Milan – or tunnel walls – like in Paris. Graffiti along the track line now constitutes the first sign of urbanisation for train travellers. Its presence announces the entrance into a city and progressively increases in proximity of stations. Hence, railway walls represented the target par excellence, and eventually became a constant in contemporary urban landscapes. Some cases were even more evident. In cities with heavily painted railway systems – like Dortmund, Amsterdam, and Rome, where painted trains were often allowed to circulate in the cars – the intensity of the phenomenon was perceived i an amplified manner in those places where painted train cars ran parallel to painted walls. Since the Writing phenomenon invaded every urban centre, involving metropolitan scenes and views of minor agglomerates, the city's image has undergone a transformation process, with a traumatic and irreversible aesthetic impact. Many writers were able to consciously reinterpret the city, classifying targets to hit, systematically distinguished according to various criteria such as visibility, risk, and prestige. Starting with subway cars, the New York phenomenon was reflected on an infinite catalogue of spaces and urban structures, which tended to repeat the same logic o occupation. Each urban centre became the object of a stratification of signs – above all the Names of writers – which progressively saturated disused areas, infrastructures, and in general any surface that offered visibility, transforming today's cities into temporary showcases.

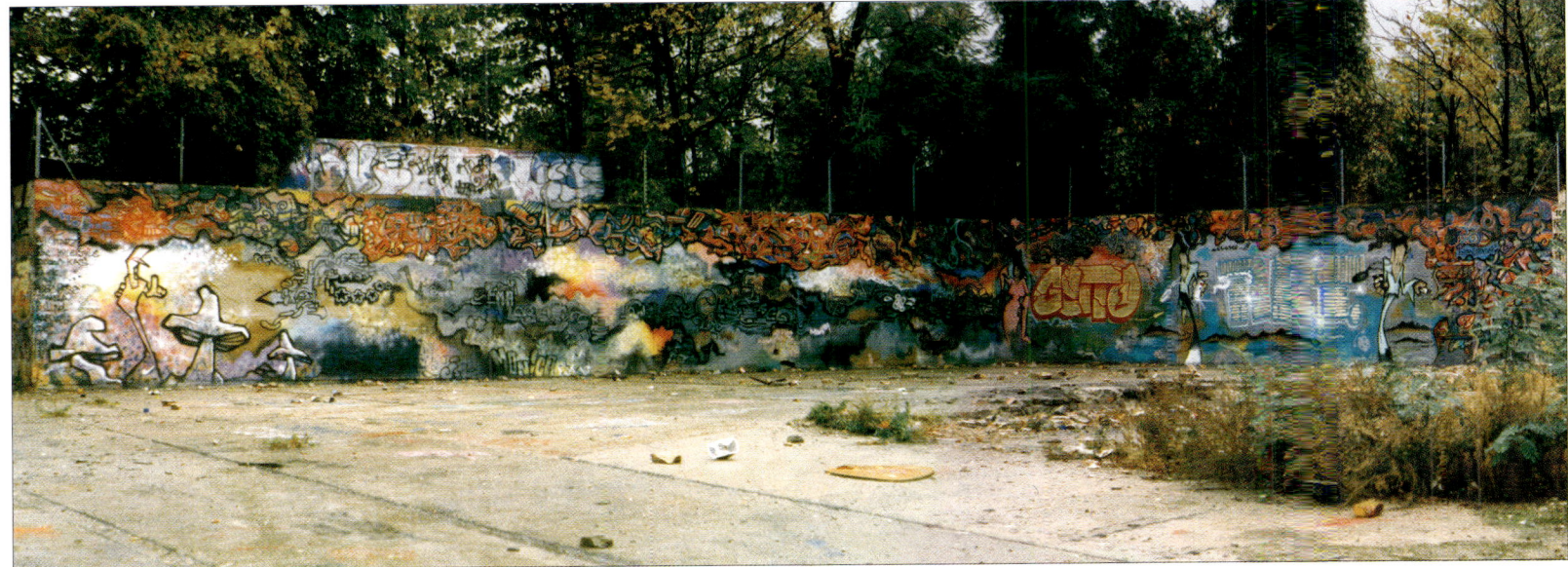

A Berliner hall of fame in 1988

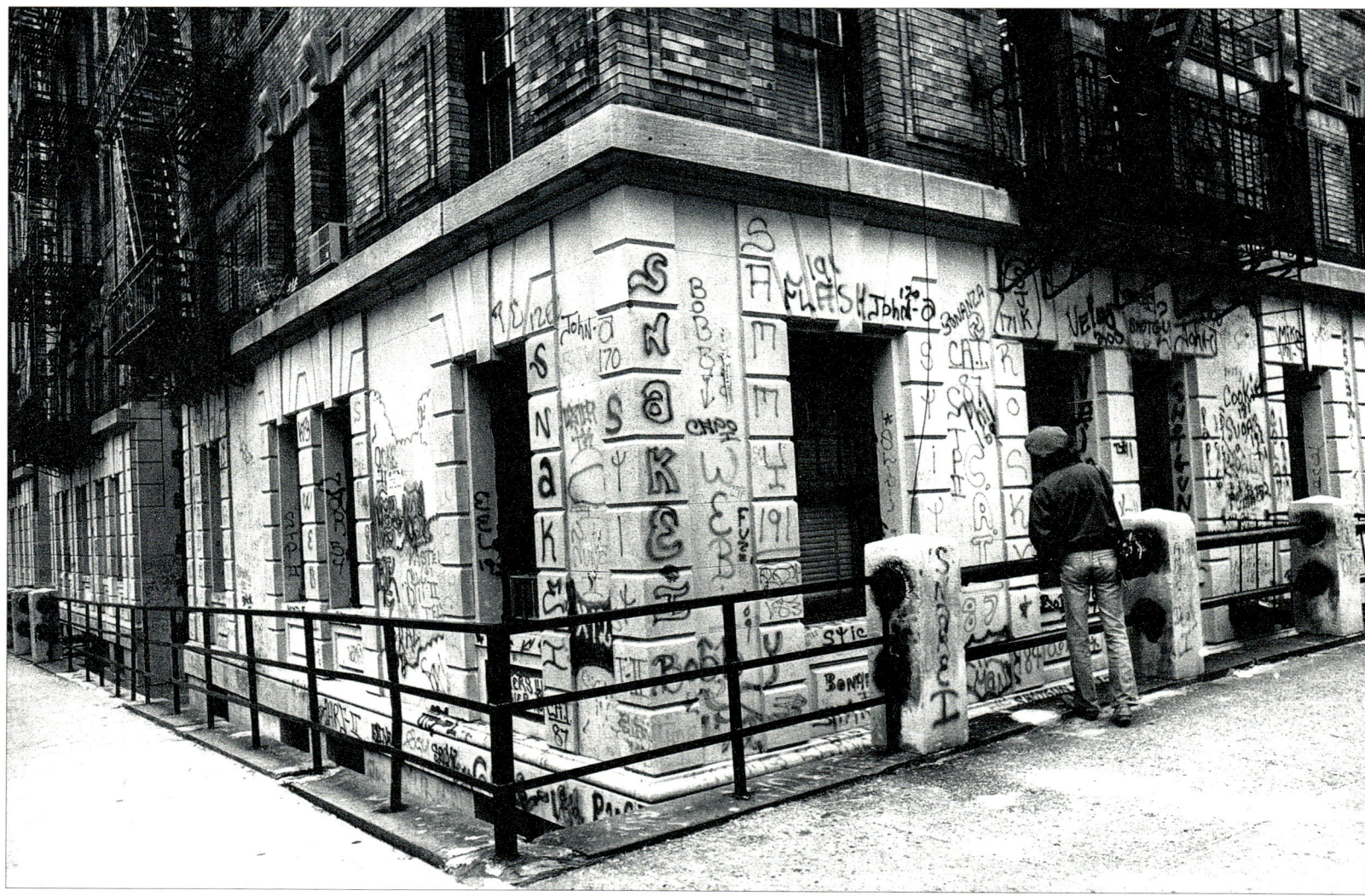

Writer's corner on 188th Street in Manhattan, one of the first hang-outs for writers in New York. 1973

— Andrea Nelli

COVENT GARDEN HANG-OUT

The European reinterpretation of New York hang-outs: the meeting spots of London, Paris and Munich as some of the first heterogenous forts

I moved to London when I was 8, from Mauritius, it was 1976. In the UK the first inputs regarding Writing arrived through the media, I saw Malcolm McLaren's Buffalo Gals on TV. The Dondi outline in Buffalo Gals was the first major thing. Then there was a sitcom titled *Welcome back, Kotter*. It was about a teacher of a school in the Bronx and in the intro they had a train go by, fully painted. At that time I thought they were hippy paintings because all you could see were the bright colours, and the train was seen from quite far away. But then on the Buffalo Gal's video you could clearly discern a defined shape of letters and the outline would magically appear around them. The power of that black outline traced by Dondi was a big hook and it opened the first door. One day, late in the summer of '83, my mother took my brother and I around central London, and we stopped by Covent Garden. There was a crew dancing and actually this was the crew Scribla was in, we just saw this white guy dancing with the others. They had these pastel yellow and blue Ellesse tracksuits. I literally got goosebumps, thinking back.

So the next summer, because I was finishing exams at school, I went back to Covent Garden and met some of the guys who were there, just hanging around, dancing, listening to music, sitting around chatting about who's the best and who sucks, or going off to the shops to steal, or else going off in small groups to go and dance somewhere for money. The music started being talked about in magazine articles, like the one that appeared in *Melody Maker*. Also, Tim Westwood would play it on the radio, on LWR Wednesday nights. There was a big overload in a few months: *Subway Art* came out early that summer of '84, then those movies *Breakdance* (*Breakin'*) and *Beat Street*, which confused us at first with the fake pieces done by cinema set-decorators. On Saturdays Tim Westwood was playing from 12 noon til 3pm at this club called Spats, on Oxford Street, so after 3 o'clock you saw all the people from there come back to Covent Garden, hang out, beat-

Chrome Angelz by Mode 2(left) and Scribla(right) at London's Covent Garden, June 1985

– Zaki Dee

box and dance. First it was on Saturdays, then when the school holidays started it was everyday, from 11 in the morning until the last train left; except for the 'blockers' who hung out all night too.

Covent Garden was an old fruit and flower market that had been shut down and converted into a pedestrian area, where the public could walk around, browse through the new shops that moved into the old spaces, or watch the

One day, late in the summer of '83, my mother took my brother and I around central London, and we stopped by Covent Garden

street entertainers who were allowed to perform there. The Royal Opera House was having an extension built, so there were these wooden hoardings around the building site. There was the old London Transport Museum there, as well as Jubilee Halls; where we had this jam called Freestyle '85, in December of that same year.

There was an office called Alternative Arts, who handled the licences for the street entertainers, and they got Scribla and me to paint some banners for their annual festival, and from there we also got permission to paint the hoardings, which were the first big pieces in Covent Garden. T-Kid painted in that same spot in 1986, when he had come over in the Springtime to paint an advert for TDK tapes.

Every Saturday we'd meet at Covent Garden because Pride lived on the other side of London, Scribla and me lived down South-East and Zaki South-West. Covent

Garden was the ideal middle ground and the subway by Charing Cross Station nearby was ideal for dancers to practice. We'd meet at McDonald's every Saturday, just hang out there, show each other sketch books, before going to where the others hung out. If during the week anything came up, you had time to talk about it. If you ever had a problem with someone, it was never left to linger and become bigger.

Compared to other hang-outs, like Stalingrad in Paris, Covent Garden was definitely different, from the writers to the dancers, the Mc's, or the DJ's who'd constantly be going on secret missions to find old beats. Stalingrad was a peripheral area, forgotten by citizens, whereas Covent Garden was a central public meeting point for people in general. The fact alone that they didn't understand English in Paris meant they weren't taking the rap stuff the same as it had been taken in London. People didn't understand the lyrics much, so they didn't import so much negative stuff that could be heard here and there, but it must be said that groups like Public Enemy did in fact export some of the political issues that they had in the U.S. as far as Paris. Anyone with an identity crisis could fall into the confusion of that, and a few did.

Still, the thing about Paris is that we were not affected by the Rave scene that was sweeping across the UK; so we really thrived off of what to me were the best years of Hip Hop, when those that had been teen fans of the Sugar Hill Gang or Grandmaster Flash, or Spoonie Gee, Cold Crush and so on, had reached maturity and were defining Hip Hop in their own way, before the record industry stepped in massively. The UK has a habit of eating up and spitting out all new trends and cultures as they come, and they did just that with Hip Hop too. Those who didn't have their game totally sorted out would soon fall out of favour as Rave culture swept everything in its path, and much of what existed in our time just disappeared.

Music and culture just evolved differently in Paris. as in England we had pirate radio stations like in the 60's

already pushing what the official broadcasters were not. In France it wasn't until Mitterand came to government in 1981 that they started getting radio stations that were not government-controlled. So culturally there were some very different things going on, influenced also by the racial mix ups from their different colonies. Because of the Jamaican culture we had a lot more DJ's and sound systems in London that would be playing Hip Hop on top of reggae or dub. In France these foreign influences were perhaps felt less, even though there were fundamental figures tied to Hip Hop such as Dee Nasty in Paris, who was one of the main people playing the music, and still active today. Amsterdam was also completely different, it's a much smaller city and had fewer writers but they were even more diverse, and with a good standard, maybe because Amsterdam was historically really rich in Arts and galleries. Naturally, venues and events also played an important role in the diffusion of the culture, such as the New York City Rap Tour which linked up local

Covent Garden was the ideal middle ground and the subway by Charing Cross Station nearby was ideal for dancers to practice

B-boys with ones coming from the States. The tour came to London and Paris as well, but was absorbed and reinterpreted differently depending on the local culture. In London, Pride and even Zaki went to see it. Then in Bristol jams were organised by The Wild Bunch. They

> CONTINUES ON PAGE 106

UK'S HIP HOP

> CONTINUES FROM PAGE 105

were a crew, a sound system, actually a lot of energies put together. At the time Bristol was very active. It was the first port where the trading ships would drop off the slaves, and was probably one of the most receptive cities with respect to external cultures. I remember seeing flyers from The Wild Bunch in summer '84, with 3D (Massive Attack) doing the impressive graphics.

Wild Bunch was one of the crews that took part in this contest at The Wag Club, back in January '85, hosted by Tim Westwood, to see who could win a record deal. Sipho (R.I.P.) & Darnel D had this kind of beat box rap thing, plus there was Duke who would later become Mc Duke. The Cookie Crew also came out and did their rap over an instrumental of Planet Rock, which seemed very marketable to the industry heads attending, as they were three girls, and they won the deal; but it was the Wild Bunch that had the roughest set there. So you were aware that something was going on not only around Covent Garden and London, but also in other cities like Bristol or even Birmingham and Wolverhampton, all adding their own local flavour to the culture.

Covent Garden, however, certainly represented an important epicentre for the movement in the UK. During the winter months, we'd also hang out at The Centre, a drop-in place for homeless youth, but we had practice rooms for the dancers upstairs, and the basement could

> ## Every Saturday we'd meet at Covent Garden because Pride lived on the other side of London, Scribla and me lived down South–East and Zaki South–West.

be used for parties or to prepare paintings in; like for Freestyle '85. The Africa Centre also held parties every once in a while, but by spring of '87 I had moved to Paris, and was less aware of what was going on in London.

As we grew older, and the Rare Groove scene switched to the Rave scene, heads just went their own ways, as some tried to follow their rap or dance careers, others as Djs. Many just fell off, disillusioned by what followed those great early days, some fell into drugs, or went to prison, and some just went back to regular life...

There were more opportunities for graffiti commissions, but these didn't last so long either. As opposed to other countries, you could say we were pretty big on advertising in the UK. Goldie and Artful Dodger, for example, both did campaigns for Weetabix, this breakfast cereal. Scribla and I had done the stage set for The Lenny Henry Show in May '85, and we all did paintings for the launch of Swatch watches; but after all of that there wasn't much else for a long while. To advertising companies graffiti writers were just good for things requiring graffiti-style graphics. They couldn't see us as graphic designers, capable of realising many different projects; maybe because we used another technique, the spray can. Ideally, what you were asked to paint should depend on the customer, it depends on the client's demands since experienced writers can do just about anything and everything, not just graffiti.

Similarly to Amsterdam, Paris on the other hand had a strong Art and Gallery scene, with fashion designers like Paco Rabanne and Agnes B who patronised and promoted dancing or art. The Paris transit system (RATP) even invited Futura and did this "Ticket Chic – Ticket Choc" with him. With the stuff he did when touring with The Clash, as well as projects with Agnes B, he was very quickly integrated into that Paris circuit. The French liked it because it was exotic, they were in love with it then, along with Keith Haring working with Grace Jones and so on, and it was great. Years later though, when the city started being devastated by tags, they quickly changed their minds and started complaining. Writing wasn't that interesting anymore; more of a threat to the order they were comfortable with.

Zaki Dee – TCA / London
>

Hip Hop had begun to hit the UK by the start of the 1980's. Although there was the odd clip on TV and article in the press, it was really through London's pirate radio stations and John Peel's groundbreaking radio show where he would play the odd Rap track in between Punk & New Wave, that I was mainly exposed to this new culture from New York. As I was already into my records, I had started to buy Rap from places like Our Price (they were no specialist record shops back then) on Kensington High Street and later Groove Records in Soho.

It must have been around the end of 1982 that I went to see Wild Style at the Brixton Fridge cinema. I can still distinctly remember sitting in the upper stalls and watching as these amazing painted trains passed across the screen. I was mesmerised by the graphics covering each carriage in a myriad of colours, letters and characters, appearing and disappearing too quickly for me to take it all in. Just as a bit of new art would blow me away, yet another even more spectacular moving mural would come into view and, just as fast, be gone again. Of course I loved the whole film but the part that really stuck in my mind when leaving the cinema and in the following days was the graffiti. I was already interested in art, so I knew from the moment I saw the graffiti that that's what I wanted to do. So I set out to get as much information as was available, which wasn't a lot at that time.

My mum was working in a bookshop and I asked her to find me any book about Graffiti. What she found for me couldn't have been any better. The book was called *Getting Up* (which was published before *Subway Art*). I read it from start to finish and inside out. When I reached the last page, I read it all the way through again. I was transfixed by every detail, every story, especially every photograph, as the all to quick images on *Wildstyle* had not been enough of a fix for this graffiti addicted kid. It gave me real insight into the history and the ethos behind my

new obsession. I was able to closely examine every aspect of graffiti, from it's beginnings to the latest writers of the time. The book also featured a writer called Lee 163 who particularly inspired me. I later used part of his name in my tag; "Zaki Dee 163".

This book and any reference to the New York scene was definitely a huge influence for me in that first year as when I started to tag and paint there wasn't any New York style graffiti in London. I know because I was desperate to find anything that was and looked out for it every time I travelled around London.

At the start of '83, after practising on my bedroom wall for some time, I had started to do a few trackside pieces along the train line near where I lived in West London. For the first two pieces the outlines were designed by my

> ## The Covent Garden hang–out was mostly based next to the temporary boards erected while the Opera House was getting done up. These boards were there the whole time that Covent was the place to meet.

brother, who is an amazing artist. The first "Crazy Dee" had a white to light blue fade in the letters with a drop shadow on the black outline and a broken rock background. Considering it was my fist piece, I found using a can and painting at night relatively easy. Perhaps this was because I'd done some spray can homework in my room already. The second piece, again designed by my

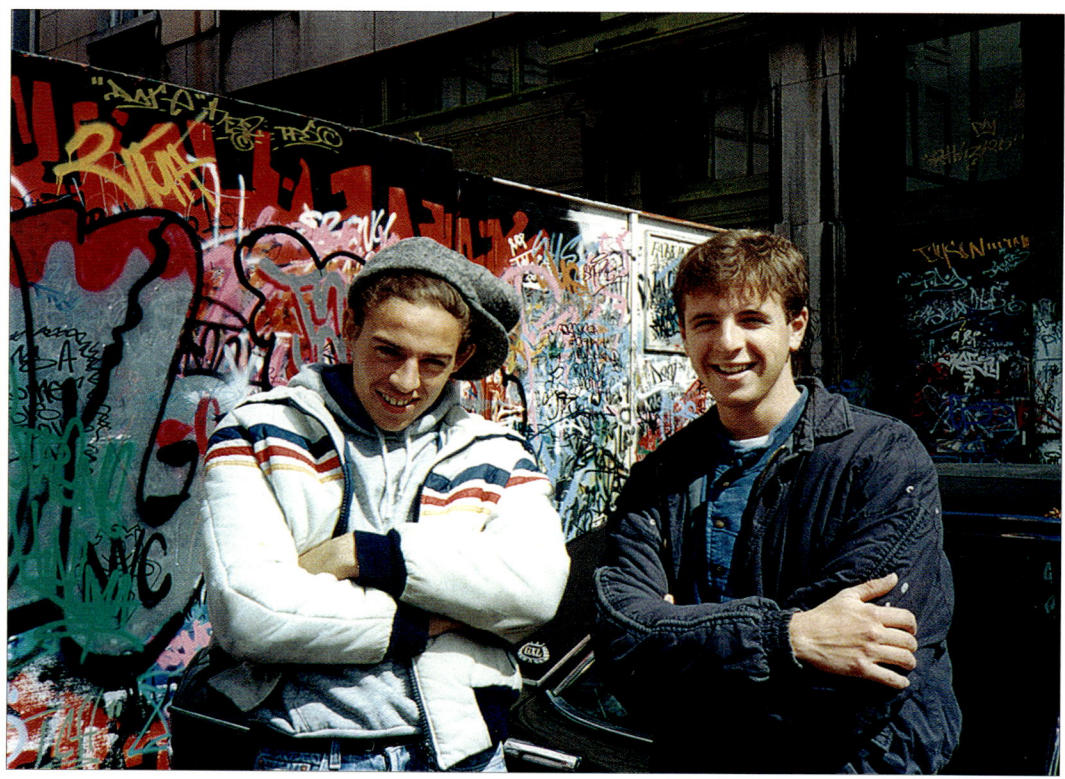

Zaki Dee and Scribla

SCENE

brother, was slightly more elaborate, it had "Hip Hop" in Japanese style letters with white to orange to two shades of blue fade in the letters, a red outline, and a Japanese sumo head character with a baseball cap on at one end and a dragon wearing sneakers at the other.

In the next few months I went on to do a few more track sides and also painted the outside walls of two platform waiting rooms. One featured a six foot high Father Christmas head with the words, "Whatever happened to Christmas?" under it.

It was around this time that I spotted two more bits of Graffiti. The first was on the outside of a tube train and took me totally by surprise! I was waiting on the platform at Turnham Green tube for a District Line train; it's one of those stations that have a fast non-stopping train running in between the stopping train tracks. As the fast Piccadilly line train passed by I caught a glimpse of the spray painted tag on the panel in between the doors. It read "Kosh". And there, a few carriages further along the same train, was another identical "Kosh" tag! I've never met the guy since but would love to because for me he was the first train writer in London. He also let me know that there were other writers in the city.

The second, I saw travelling from Shepherds Bush to Edgware Road on the Hammersmith and Metropolitan Line. On the train from Ladbroke Groove to Westbourne Park I saw a flash of letters under the Westway alongside the tracks. So a few days later, camera in hand, I jumped off at Westbourne Park and cut back on the opposite side to the Westway through some flats. I shimmied up the wall opposite and sat on top to see, to my amazement a "Futura" piece. I remembered reading about him in *Getting Up* as well as *Subway Art*. In fact he was one of my favourite writers from these books. I later found out that he had been on tour in the UK with the Clash and he must have painted it then. After that I started seeing some more pieces pop up in Ladbroke Grove by a guy called Skam, who, I found out a few years later, was also into graff around the same time as me.

COVENT GARDEN
CONTINUED
—

Zaki Dee –TCA / London
>

DJ Tim Westwood had an afternoon Hip Hop club at Spats on Oxford Street and every Saturday a hardcore nucleus of us used to go down there and straight afterwards it was down to Covent Garden. There was also another hang-out nearby which was Charing Cross Station, it had a network of subways connecting the Tube lines. This was where everybody used to meet with ghetto blasters and break, there was quite a few writers there also. So from Spats to Covent Garden to Charing Cross and maybe back to Covent, every weekend it was like that. At least this went on for quite a few years, from '83 to '86-87 I think. The Covent Garden hang-out was mostly based next to the temporary boards that had been erected while the Opera House was getting done up. These boards were there the whole time that Covent was the place to meet. TCA painted these boards many times over the years. If you come out of the tube station at Covent Garden and turn right there's a big square called Covent Garden Plaza. Over the years as the word spread more and more kids started coming down. Even from the outskirts of London and beyond: Bristol, Wolverhampton, and Manchester. Towards the end there were sometimes hundreds of B-boys here. The whole of the scene was there and surprisingly it was tolerated by the city. I don't remember the police breaking it up that many times.

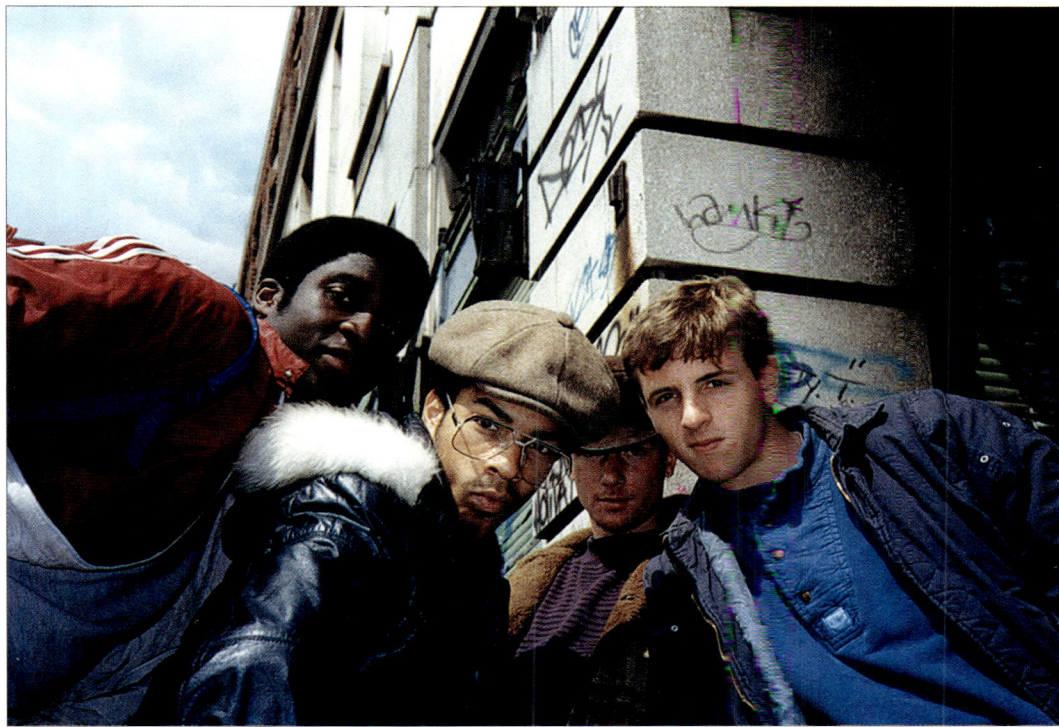

Pride, Danny, Eskimo and Scribla. 1985
— Mode 2

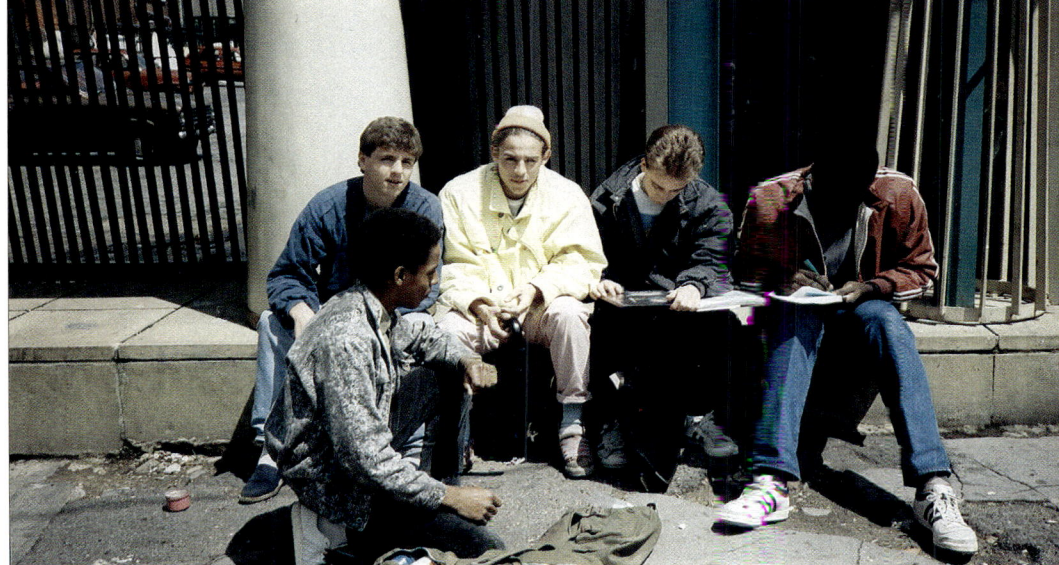

The Chrome Angelz
– Zaki Dee

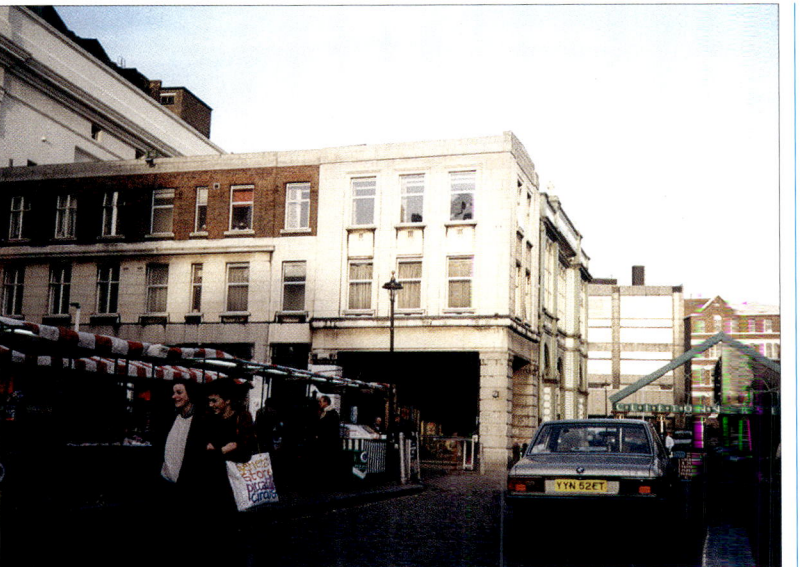

Coven Garden London in 1986
Mode 2

DRESS CODE

ZEBSTER

When I was in London in 1989 I met Second to None in Covent Garden thanks to the way they were dressed. I saw their fresh sneakers and thought "Those guys must be down!" So I ran after them and ten minutes later we were dancing in a subway station!

PARIS, STALINGRAD

The terrain vague of Stalingrad, pivotal
point of the Parisian Hip Hop scene
evoked by its founder

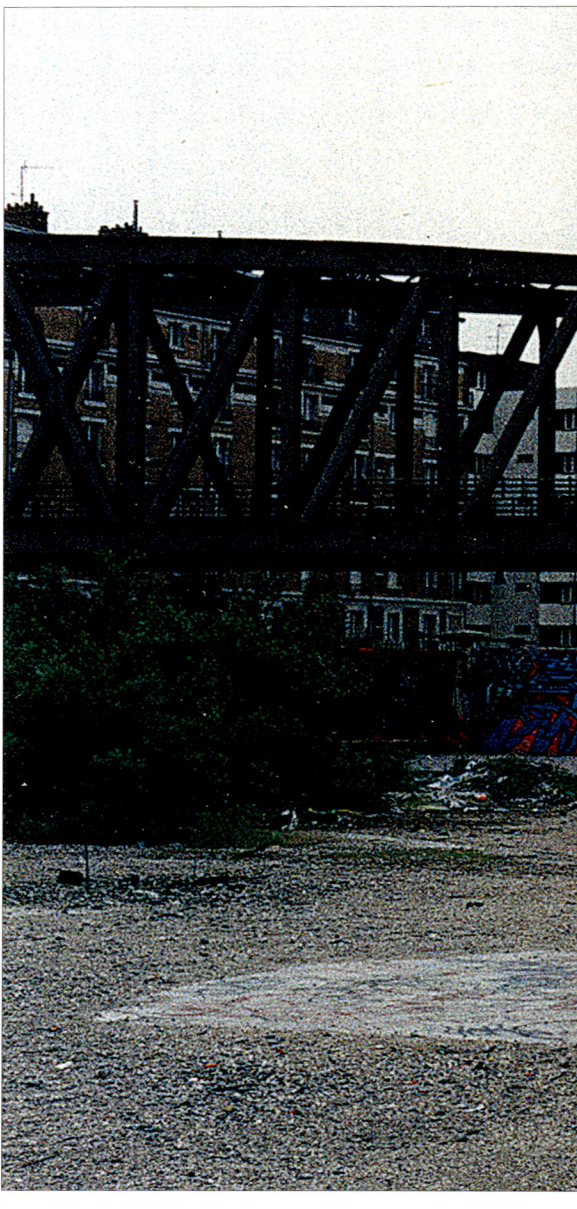

Overview of the Stalingrad area

Ash –BBC / Paris

>

The first graffiti writer in Paris was Bando, who started with one of his friends, a black guy called Scam, and probably one or two other temporary writers that were hanging out with them back then. After them came Blitz, Asphalt, Spririt, Lokiss, Jay1, Skki, Sciption, Irus and me; I also remember that Psychoze was doing some work in the catacombs. But above all of them, Bando was the most active in the Parisian graffiti scene. He was really good because he was completely obsessed by what he was doing and would work on it all the time, striving to develop his style.

I did my first piece in a tunnel near the Modern Art Museum of George Pompidou. Bando was already painting nearby on the metal hoarding placed on the side of the Museum. Before becoming a writer, I was more into Breakdance. In the beginning of my teenage years I used to hang out a lot at "Place du Trocadero" in Paris, right in front of the Eiffel Tower. In the early 80's, there were plenty of people that liked rollers, skateboards and all that kind of American youth culture that came to Trocadero. We loved listening to Funk on our big ghetto blasters and compete against each other with new-learned Breakdance tricks...it all began as a single thing, as I saw my first graffiti pieces on record covers and I guess that's probably why I became a writer.

I remember when I saw Stalingrad from the subway for the first time. The train was coming out the tunnel, running aboveground and out of the window there was the Barbes district and a big empty yard between Stalingrad

and La Chapelle subway stations. I immediately realised how overexposed that spot was. Perfect walls to be painted and to be seen from the subway. No one had ever painted there. I was the first one to discover these walls completely untouched by other writers. When I jumped into the so-called 'Stalingrad' hall of fame spot and started to paint that day, I'd never have thought that Stalingrad would become the Paris spot for writers, not only for French people, but also for the whole of Europe. Before discovering this place, me and other writers and people from the Hip Hop scene used to spend the whole week at a spot called the Paco Rabanne centre. The French fashion designer owned a building located at the subway station Colonel Fabien, in the North-East part of Paris, where young people could practice Breakdancing and meet to talk about styles.

At this same time there was the on-going construction site of the Louvre Museum. It was 1983 and a two metre-high wooden fence rounded the area of the Louvre, it was easy to access, and most writers started to paint on it. Even if the pieces were in a very central area of Paris, they were tolerated and the authorities didn't buff them. That's why that place became a spot where people like me, Bando and Blitz used to go painting. The Louvre was not a place where we could meet though, it was just the spot to see other people's work, the only ones I met there were Skki and Jay-1. At the time the Louvre garden was also one of the meeting points for gays at night, they always disappeared behind the bushes...we felt a bit

uncomfortable painting in that situation. Besides that, the other main reason that made doing graffiti there really bad was the fight with the students of the "Beaux arts", an art school nearby. These guys came to the spot and painted really ugly stuff over our pieces, so we crossed them, then they would cross us and we'd cross them again...you would make a piece and it wouldn't last. And I wanted to do something that would last as long as possible on walls, not on wooden boards.

The Louvre boarding aesthetic didn't fit my vision of where graffiti should be... I guess it didn't fit with the pictures I saw in books like *Subway Art* and my 'American dream' image of graffiti. That's why I loved Stalingrad. Long lasting works, no police to arrest you inside, and great exposure. It was just perfect. Nobody could see you painting except the people on the train. I did my first piece there on the biggest wall right in front of the subway, the most visible spot and I wrote Saho, that was my tag back then. Not long later the spot became so famous and crowded, Jay and Skki, Lokiss, Scipion and Irus all started to come there too. Little by little, writers covered every surface, both the inner and the outer walls, even those that couldn't be seen from the outside.

From 1984 onwards people started to connect with Rap music, Breakdance or graffiti, as well as starting to meet at the Stalingrad Wall of Fame. This all happened after a dark period for the French Hip Hop scene, during which only a few fans were involved in the movement. The fact is that Hip Hop's reputation was being turned into a 'ridiculous pop trend', mostly due to a very popular TV program presented by a guy called Sidney. It was a caricature of the 'black American ghetto culture' but presented à la French

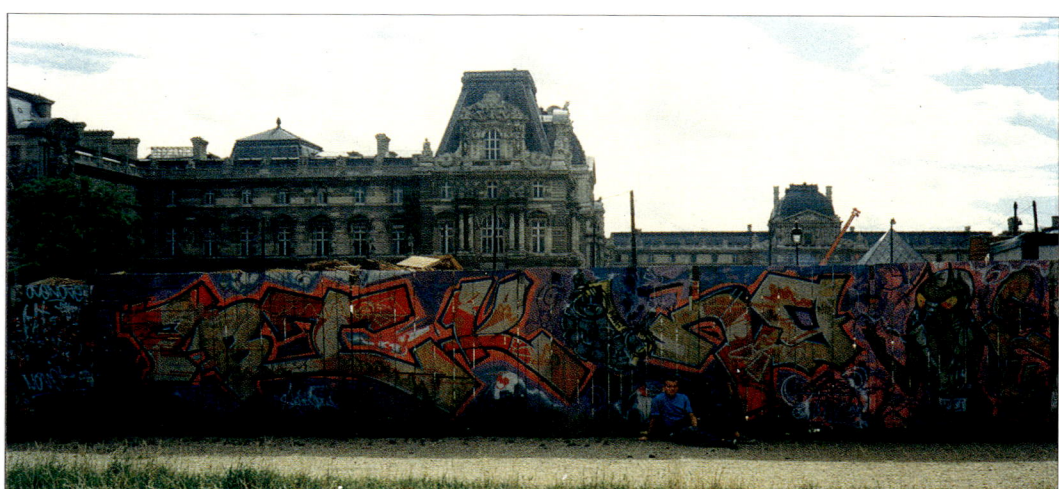

FBI king by FBI crew on the construction walls of the Louvre.

– Rendo

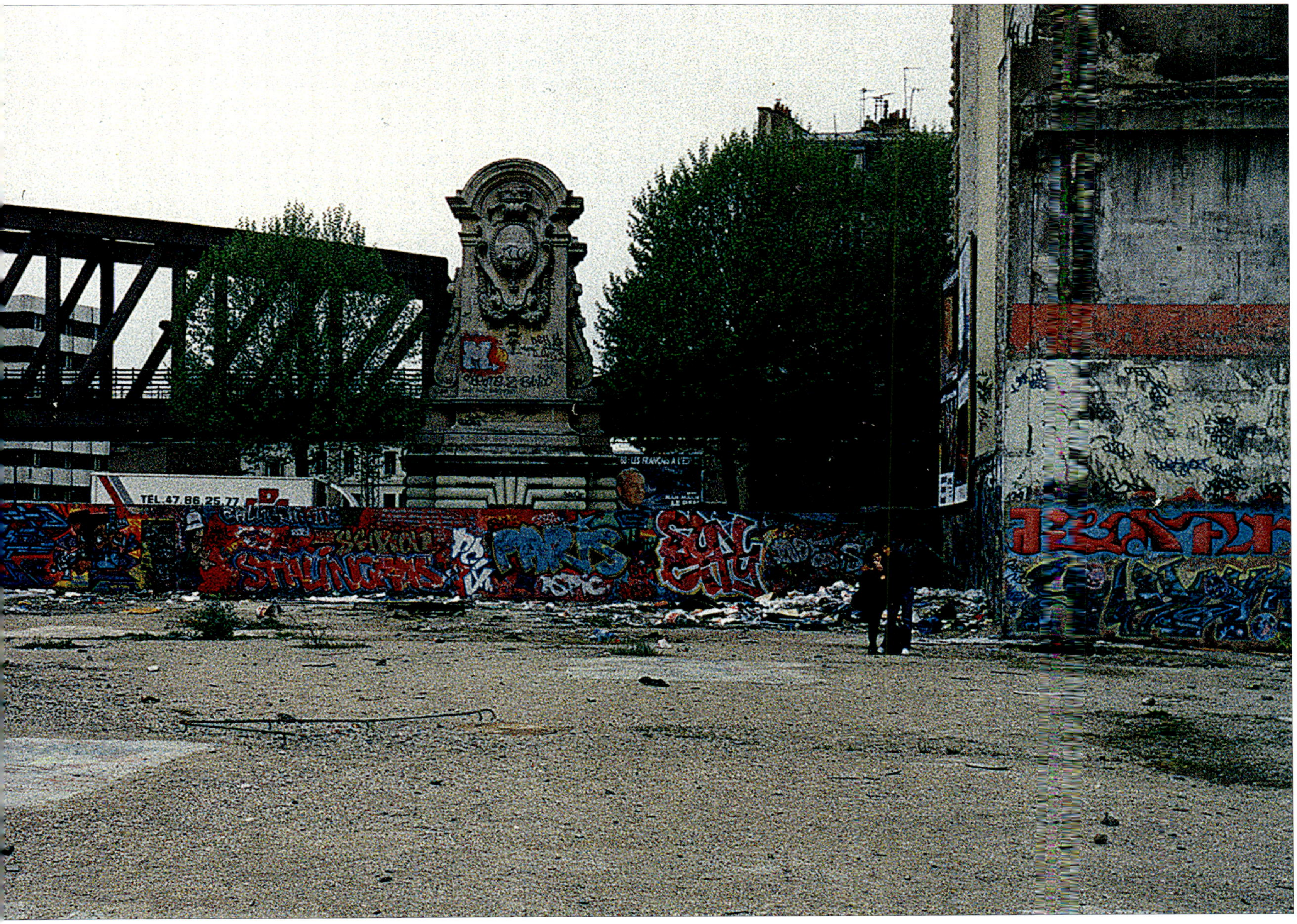

– Rendo

style, so Hip Hop started to be the subject of jokes for the majority of people. Even though Hip Hop was almost dead in France, a few people stayed true to the culture and didn't stop meeting each other at Stalingrad.

After a while Stalingrad was not only the spot for graffiti writers, but also for the whole Hip Hop scene. On Sundays for example there used to be jams with DJ Dee Nasty, he played music all day long and people would have loads of fun. In those days Stalingrad was the place of rebirth for French Hip Hop and in a matter of a few years, it became the best spot for everybody in Europe: there were guys

that travelled to Paris at the end of the 80's to check it out; from young writers to Henry Chalfant. In one of the early days of Stalingrad, Bando jumped the wall with a bunch of guys and a bucket of white paint to prepare it with, then he started doing his first piece there. There was plenty of space for everyone, and the more people came, the better it was from my point of view.

With time other writers came to Stalingrad, like Jay and Skki who painted the wall that couldn't be seen from the subway. But the spot was so popular at the time that the piece - even if invisible to people on the trains - was seen

by all the guys that came to the yard everyday. Jay, Skki and I would later become good friends and I started to integrate with BBC. BB crew came to Stalingrad to paint too: I think Darko and his friends were studying in Paris, but they were originally from Germany. Also from Munich in Germany came too: it, and JonOne from New York who painted the name his French girlfriend "Roxiz" in gigantic letters. From road Mode and Shoe also came, and one night they did huge green and blue piece with Bando on a wall facing the street. They were the first ones to paint on the outer s of a wall in the 'Stalingrad'.

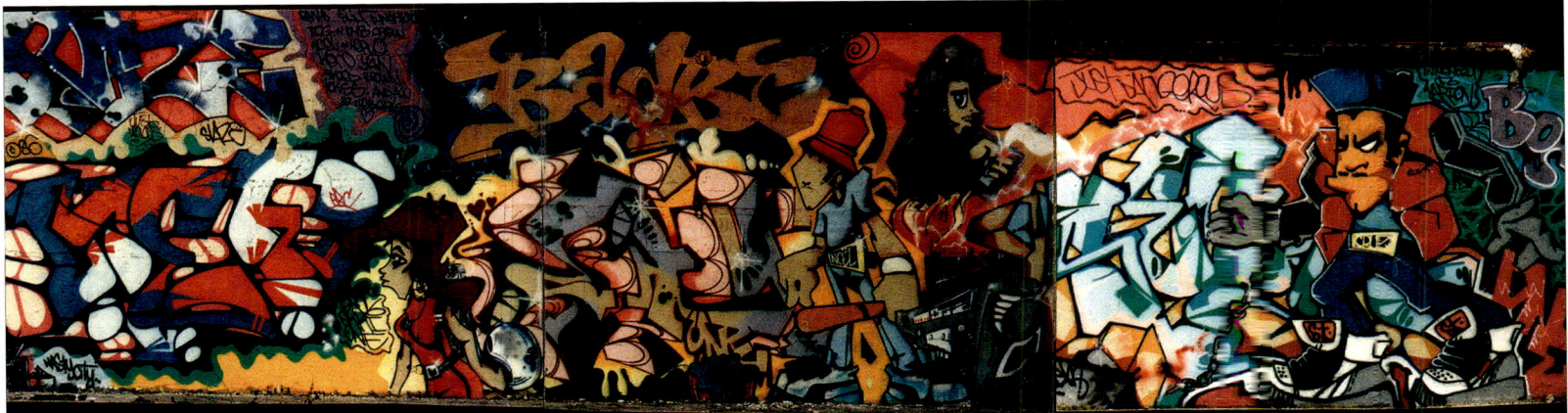

*Def*anc space Fly–girl by Skki©. *Jay* and B–boy with baseball bat by Jay 1. Ghetto blaster and puppet above by Skki©. *Seism* and mad B–boy by Ash. Stalingrad 19   *– Ash*

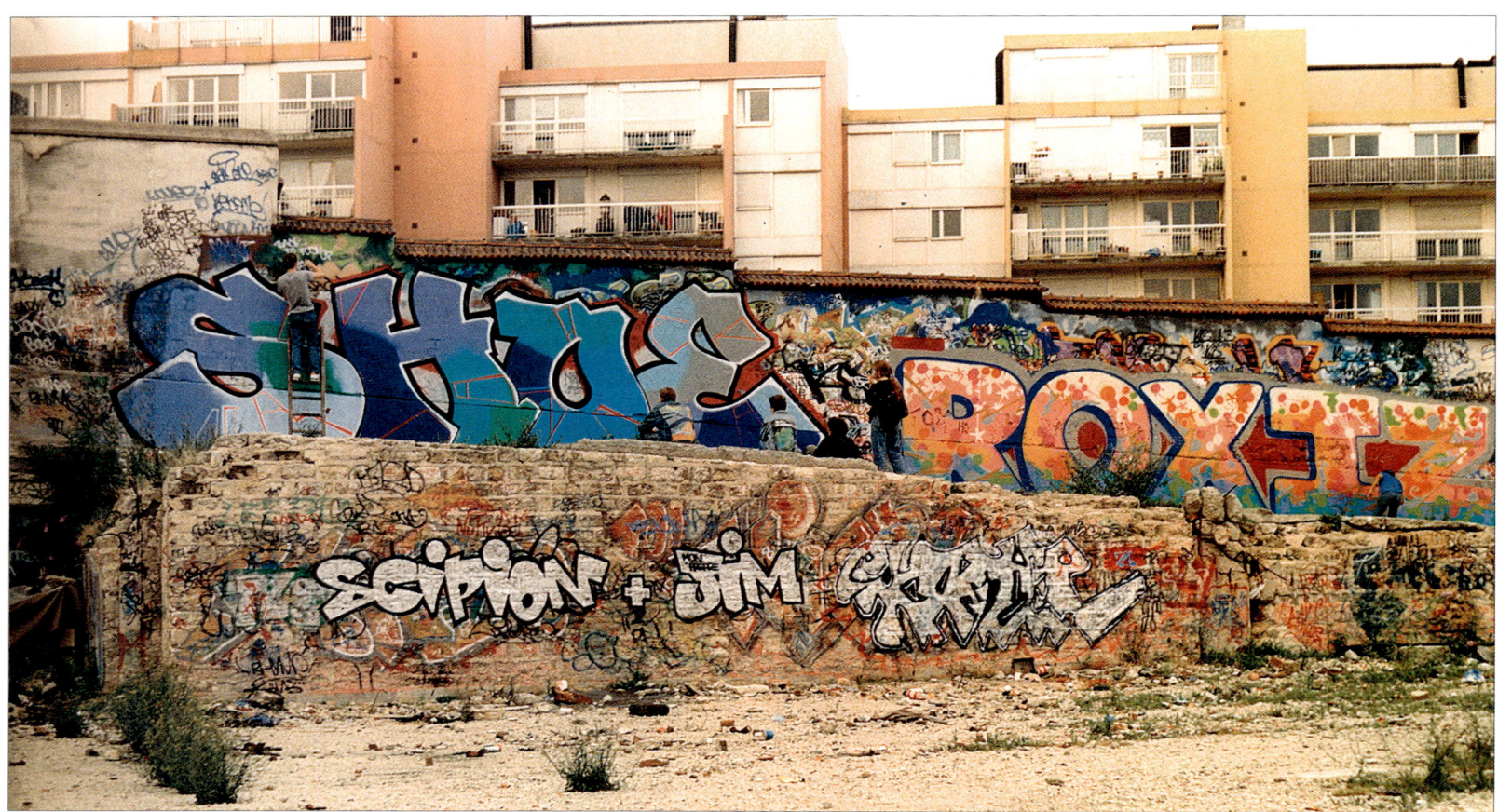

— Shoe

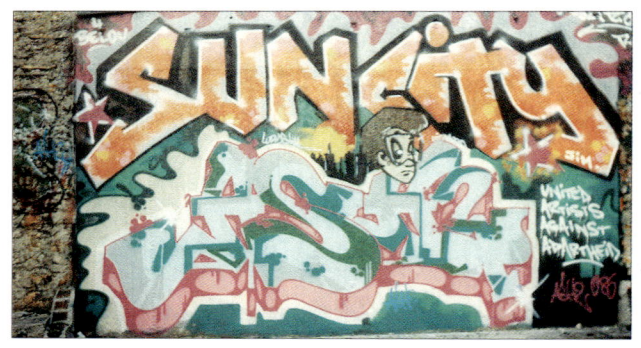

— Rendo

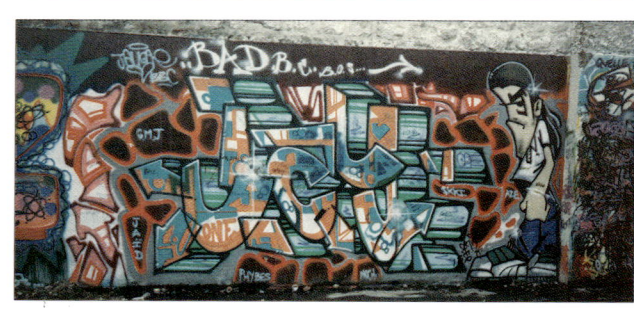

— Rendo

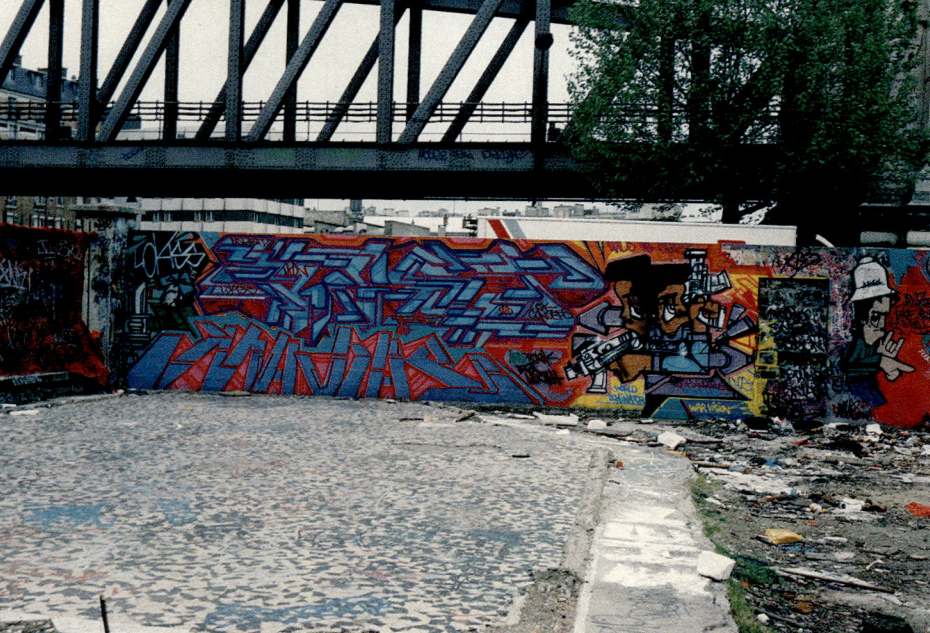

— Rendo

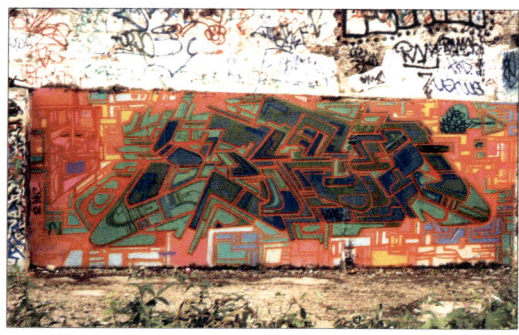

— Lokiss

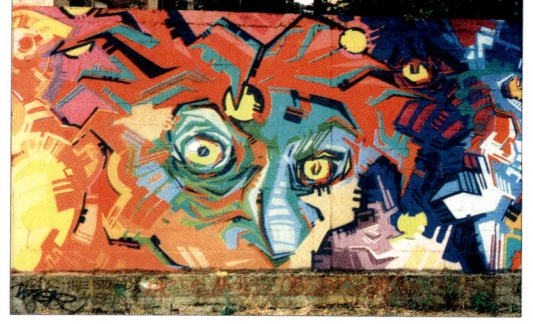

— Lokiss

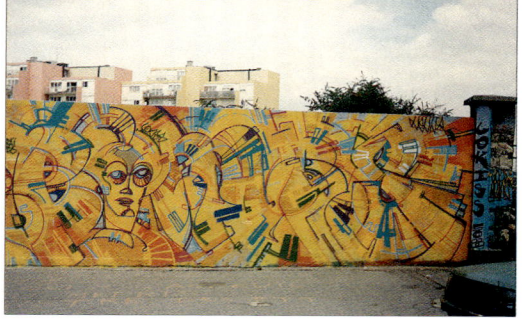

— Lokiss

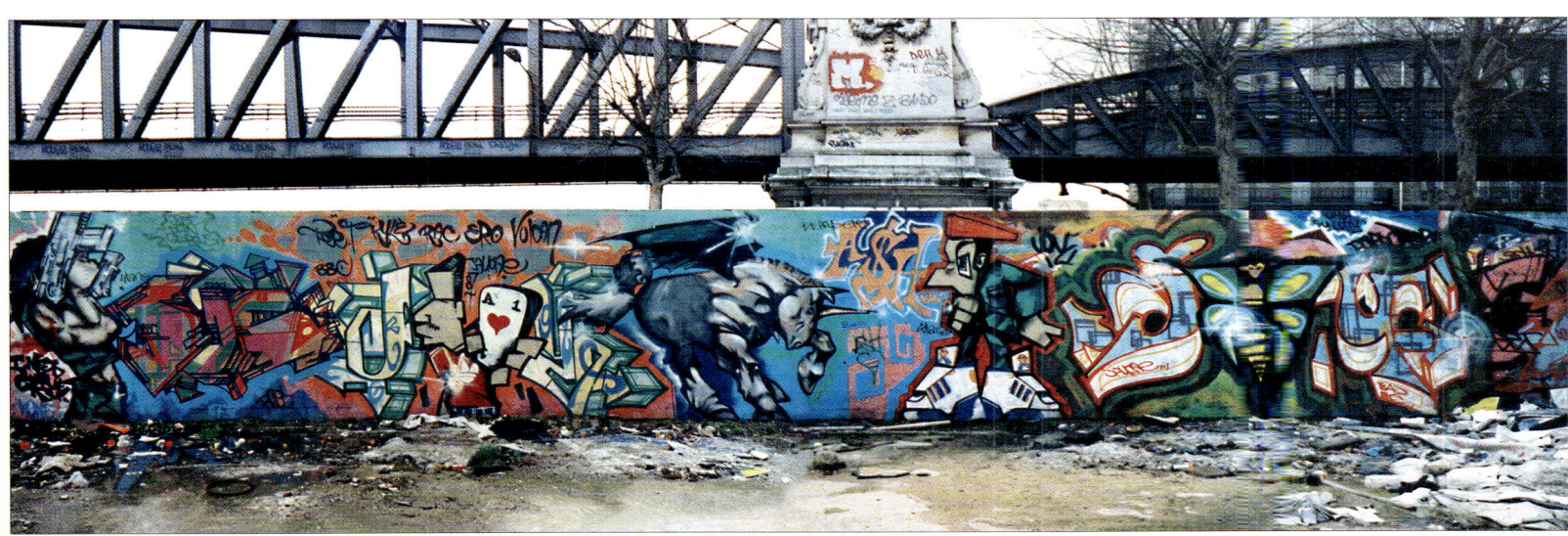

— Rendo

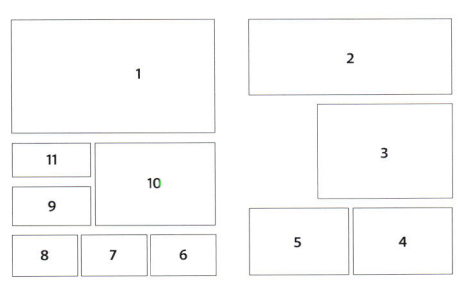

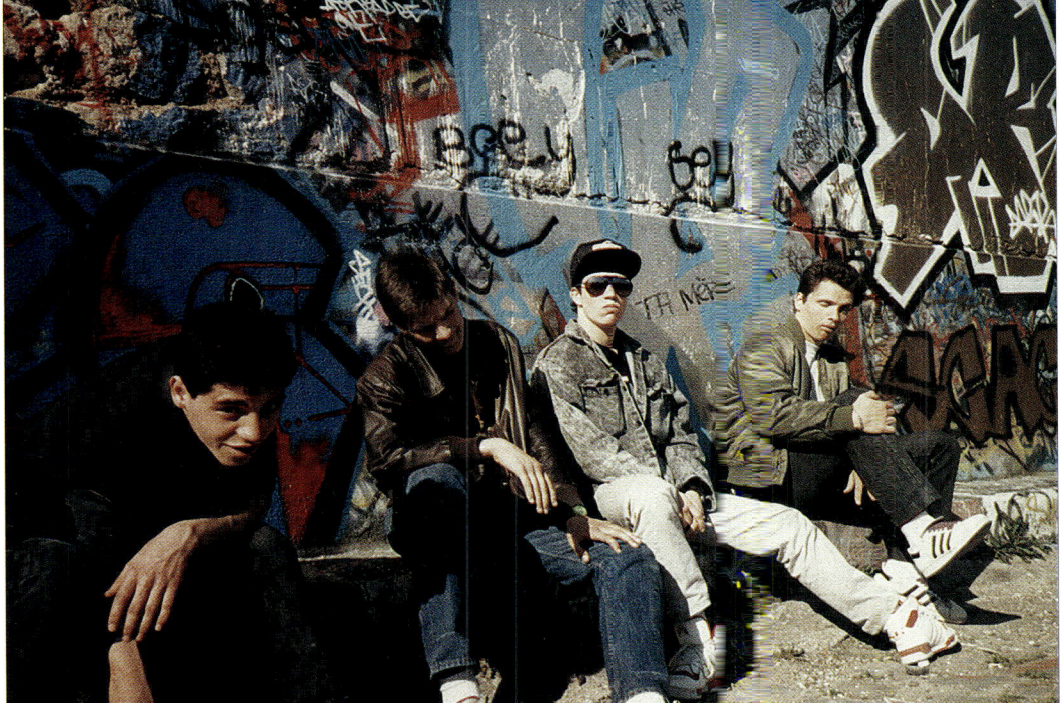

1. Shoe from Amsterdam and *Roxiz* by Jonone from New York

2. *Doe* and gun man by Skki©. *Jay* and game boy by Jay 1. Horse by Ash. B–boy camouflaged by Skki©. *Jay* by Jay 1, 1986

3. Ash, Sheek, Colt and Skki©. May 1987

4. Bando outside Stalingrad

5. *Escro* and B–boy power by Skki©. *Hero* by Jay 1. *Ash2* and crocodile by Ash, 1985

6. *Bomb* by Lokiss, 1988

7. *Diable* by Lokiss, 1987

8. *Jeez* by Lokiss, 1985

9. Jay One, Bad Boys crew

10. Lokiss burner

11. *Sun City* by Ash 2, 1986

— Mode 2

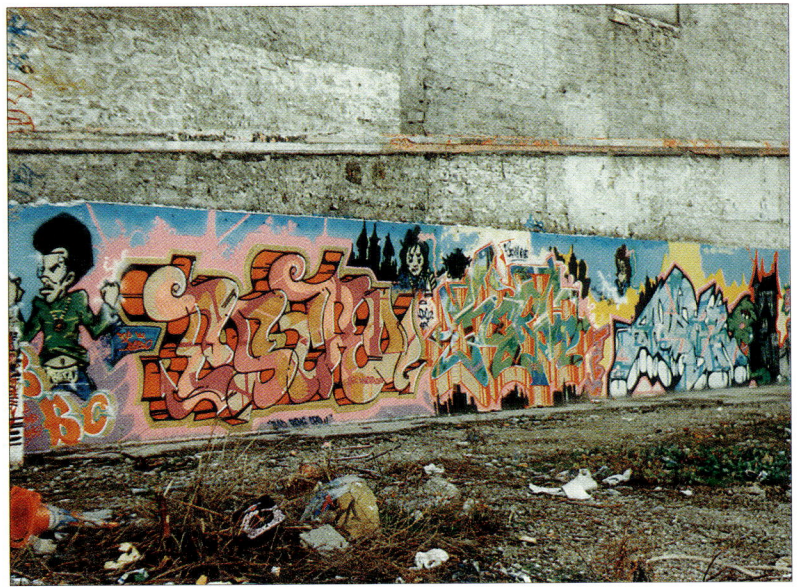

— Rendo

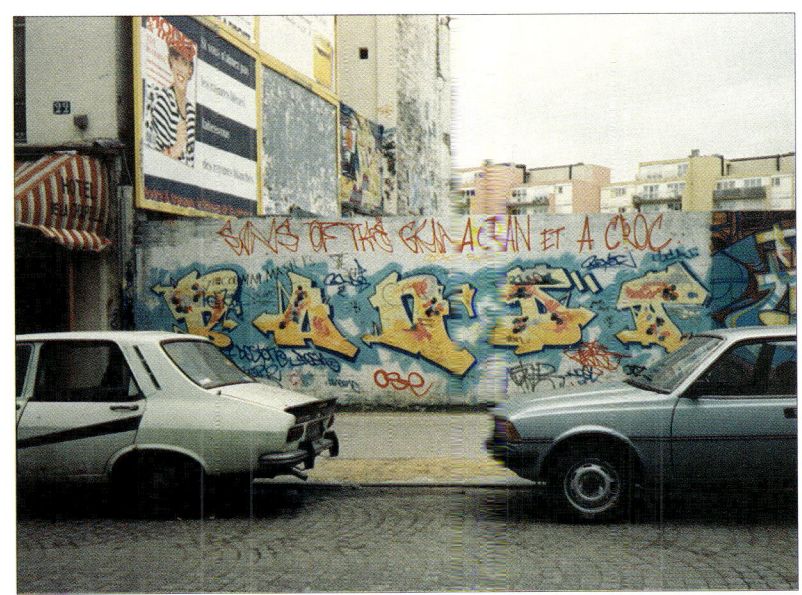

— Rendo

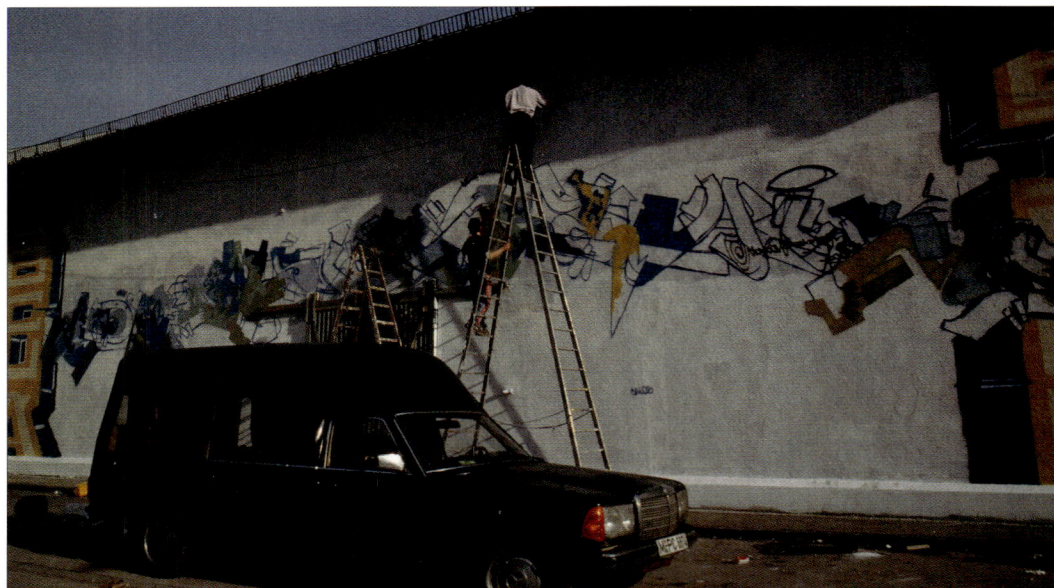
Loomit painting in front of his Mercedes Benz Station Wagon   — *Paolo Soglia*

DACHAUER FLOHMARKT

The striking thematic walls of Europe
originate along the surfaces of Munich's
flea market

Loomit –UA, FBI / Munich
>

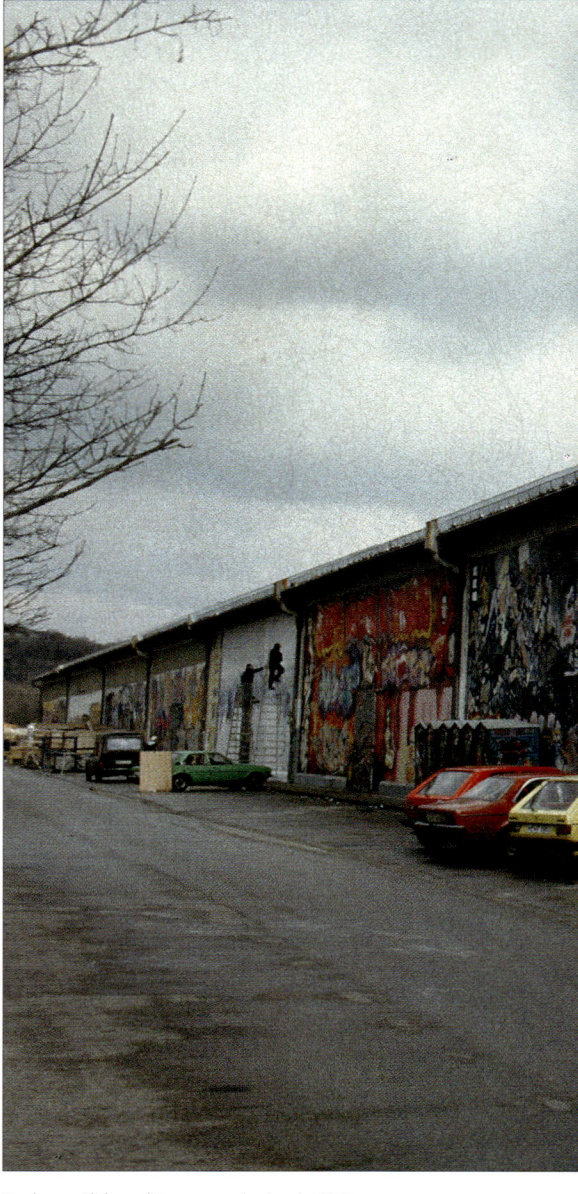
Dachauer Flohmarkt, panoramic view in 1988

Munich started with characters, pieces and backgrounds; the idea of tagging only came later, so the first things that appeared were really nicely done multi-coloured pieces and it just evolved into tags and throw-ups. We didn't see silver throw-ups with black outlines until '86, that was when we discovered that silver covered really well, but before that there was no idea. In '84 we had finally gotten some information, the book *Subway Art* came out so we knew much more about graffiti and we could look at the pieces for longer times, study the styles; having this book in your hands was such a big moment. Once we learned those aspects, the main Munich hall of fame was founded, the Flohmarkt. It was a military area used by the Americans to repair their tanks; after the American army moved out of the city, they rented this big open space and a couple of halls to flea markets, called Dachauer Flohmark as it was in Dachauer street. In the big halls there were also theatres, car repair places and antique furniture shops, so it was a pretty cool area. There was also a huge silo, I don't know what they used that for, it used to store grain and it was a pretty big structure, and even though it was far from the street it was anyway like the centre of the Flohmarkt.
It became a really cool place to hang out, we started painting the silo container but after a while we moved on to the walls of these halls where they had the tanks, and it got bigger and bigger because they were like seven metres in height and had no windows, one or two hundred metres long, and I was pretty ambitious by that time, So Won and Cowboy 69 came along, we shared the spots and I remember we were racking a lot of paint in those

days. There are some hilarious stories because I would take my mom's car and we would go out at night looking for paint buckets in construction sites, trying to steal ladders, from backyards, car repair places. We developed quite a criminal instinct trying to get all these materials we used for the big walls.
The first pieces were below the walls, but as soon as we discovered how well you could cover with normal rolling paint, that was it. The first set was cool but on the second we took the whole wall, there was no holding back. We got hold of the big ladders and got into contact with the company that was producing spray cans and got access to their leftover paint. All productions of paint take out a can every 20/30 to test it, so they can't sell it anymore, they put it to the side and it's basically scrap for them, so we got a deal buying lots of them quite cheap. By that time I had my first car, which was a Mercedes ambulance car I had painted black and looked like a Hearse, and it was a heavy car, it could hold a lot, but I recall the first time we went there it was packed. I think we had over a thousand cans, the whole car was hanging down real low, and we had 350 kilometres to go on the motorway to Munich, but we had fun, getting all that paint in the car, paying so little for it, and it was the first time we got a hold of fats caps.
Since we had the flea market every Saturday and Sunday we started painting always on the weekend so we could get clients, cause there were like 5000 people passing by every weekend, so there were always jobs coming up here and there, that's when I started thinking it could be a business. There was maybe a nightclub here or some student who wanted his room done, or some guy who

wanted his beetle painted.
That was my first encounter with the idea of making a living out of this. So it was interesting to have a hall of fame that wasn't lost in the middle of nothing but right there where the public was, and it was cool cause the market was just on the weekend so if you wanted to paint on a calm day you went during the week, and if you wanted to do just the last bits and pieces where people actually saw what you were doing and you attracted attention then you would go on a Saturday.
Of course at some point the area became totally painted. I was one of the first writers there though so I did a lot of stuff and occupied a lot of space. I recall there were fights between my crew and other crews, but I was just a peaceful guy with a lot of pieces, so my only problem was maybe when a guy from my crew would get into a fight with someone else, and I wouldn't know anything about it but would find my pieces crossed the next day and I had no idea what was going on. I didn't retaliate though, my idea of hitting back was simply of doing new pieces that took half as long and were twice as good.
With me it was never a question of blocking anyone else either, if you ask me I'm the first one to say sure let's do a wall together. One thing that I never allowed to get in my way was jealousy, if I saw people that did styles that were twice or three times better than mine I was appreciative of the fact I got to meet them and paint with them. All the other bullshit wasn't my style, I was about cooperation and having fun together, and it turned out to be the best approach, it's probably why I ended up organising places like the Dachauer Flohmarkt. Even after that was knocked down there were other Halls of Fame and I was

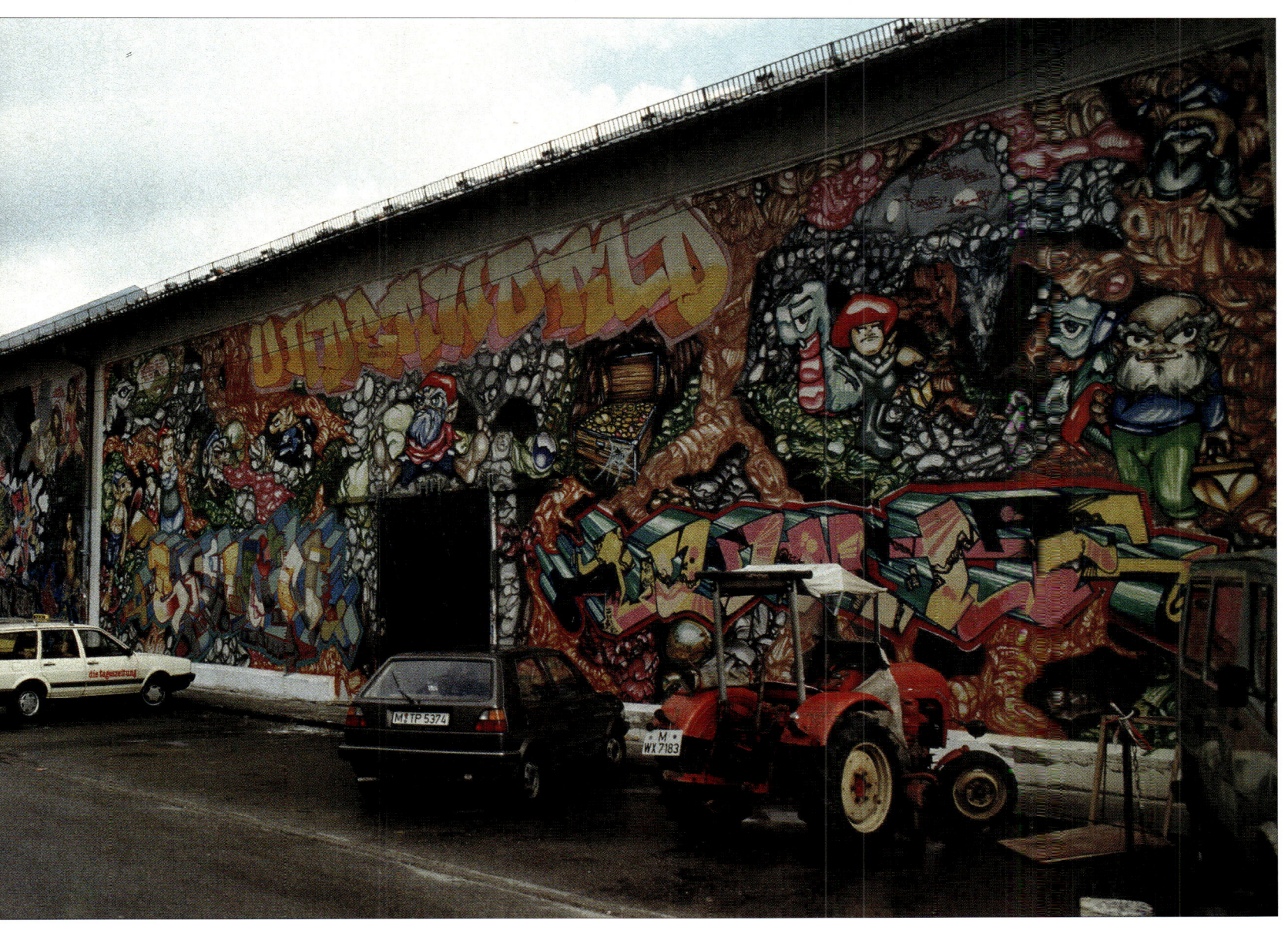

— Paolo Soglia

always the one that got hold of the private owners and managed to get permission to paint them and put everything together. If you do a lot of painting it's something that comes to you, you don't have to try that hard to look for Halls of Fame. I did so many pieces and big walls at the flea market that when it was knocked down I immediately got a job for a subculture concert hall that was going to be in an small ex-hospital from the II World War a little outside Munich. Basically I had to paint the walls of one of the barracks all around, and there was this one big building in disuse, it was the heating power station and I wasn't allowed to enter it but I asked the political community responsible for the whole place if I could paint it. They already knew me from the concert hall job so it only took a week for me to get permission, and again I had my own personal Hall of Fame.

When that was knocked down another coincidence happened, cause Munich moved its airport and the old one was still owned by the city but they rented it out for party occasions. During one of these we got hired to do long graffiti on wooden boards for the background, and while we were doing this a guy approached and asked me to do some interior designs for him at the airport in exchange for an art studio for free, and I had never had a studio, I worked sometimes in a youth centre where there was a studio for legal graffiti work but it had never occurred to me to have my own. It seemed quite handy to store my colours in, so I agreed, and while I was doing this interior work the city decided to rent out the whole airport to Mr. Noeth, who was a guy from the nightclub scene that owned a couple of clubs and he had the manpower and the knowledge to turn this airport into a huge concert

hall, and he hired me on the spot and gave me total freedom to paint it all. So we did a lot of pieces there and I had so many guests, we had CMP, Merda from Australia, Bates, Mode 2 and many others.

The big concept walls started to be the Munich standard, following the very first experimentations at the Flohmarkt. Huge compositions started over there by painting the bottom parts of big walls with pieces, then probably some problems arose, and the pieces were slashed, and this was the time when I started thinking of doing the whole wall in one go, not just a piece here and a piece there. So I invited some people to do pieces and characters and I was responsible for the background mainly, so I got the ladders and the paint and gave everyone their positions on the wall. I called people from other cities, I knew Zebster was willing to come to Munich, and Skena, so I tried to organise everything for a big wall, the ladder set, the colour set and I made sure there was no problem with the guys that had pieces there, that we would cover.

The background was a big part of it and had to be planned beforehand, because most of the colours if you see these walls are on the background, that's also why fat caps were so precious to me because I was always the guy that was filling the most and for the background I knew I needed twice as many colours as for pieces. So I had to think about the background more than the other guys as besides the pieces you have 80% of space left. I used to think about what to do with that entire space, and I had to plan ahead with the colours and structures. I had my piece on the wall but my main focus was always the background, how to bring everything together, and techniques to get the background done with the minimum

amount of colours in the minimum amount of time.
I did one wall with Erwin for example, it was like an underworld with a lot of rocks and dwarfs on it, and we basically white-wash did it and all these rocks and roots were done in very cheap paint that wasn't covering. Today you have transparent sprays but actually we've had them since way back cause these low-quality brands were basically transparent. I used them anyway though, you could do shades, like the grey wasn't covering much but after you go over one, two, three times, four times then it would become darker, so you could use the first hit as one light shade, the second hit as a slightly darker one, the third darker still and the fourth as an outline even. So I was trying various techniques to get as much done as possible with the least amount of colours, and this is how I trained two big surfaces, I was always the last guy to finish. It was fun for me cause I liked the pieces by the other guys and I was always convinced that they could do their parts better and I could focus on my part better, which was backgrounds and characters.
I was very ambitious but you also had people like Won, ABC, he was just the same, he was the guy doing huge massive backgrounds, Munich started with pieces and background and characters, so our understanding always included a whole surface, backgrounds, everything. When I met Chintz from Dortmund the first time that city was on a totally different trip, it was really bombed and tagged and we were really impressed by this because we had nothing like that, sure the styles were simple but they were really pervasive and numerous, we maybe had a third of the quantity but with colours and backgrounds

> CONTINUES ON PAGE 114

> CONTINUES FROM PAGE 113

and characters. This is something that Chintz noticed was typical of Munich, you don't see as much stuff but when you do it's always top quality.

At Flohmarkt we were experimenting, we were over this thing that everything had to look like New York and so we were trying new stuff, our own styles. I used whatever I thought would look good, or other times it was simply an economic question, if I only had certain colours I would have to think about what to do with these colours, for example a lot of cans of turquoise could become an underwater sea world, it was always just ideas of what you could do with the given tools, it just came along. It wasn't ever that we planned anything for much time, I might get inspired by something in a magazine, a T.V. show or a shop window, whatever, there were a lot of ideas around so we just tried to translate them to walls.

At the end of the 80's and early 90's, we noticed that New York walls followed pretty much the same scheme, and we were up for more. It might seem that we were breaking the rules, but what rules? Were there any graffiti codes written down in '72 in the Bronx act of train bombing? That's the whole point cause I started graffiti not to obey any rules, I was doing it cause I wanted to be free to do my thing at night. To me there never were any rules to break, I saw that people were doing this and that style and I really appreciated what they did but to me the only rule was not to copy and to take things and make them your own. You had to find your own style, that was the rule, and to do that you had to experiment, you had to find out what was possible and what wasn't.

The concept wall composition came out in a very simple way, we looked at each other's blackbooks, I saw them all, and I would say which pieces I liked the most and they would do the same with mine, that's how it came together. We each looked at the work of the other guy and then developed the idea, trying to accentuate each other's work, because it wasn't just about me, myself and I, just the opposite. It was always a game, there was a little competition, like maybe someone would do a sketch with a cool idea and then another person would take it and say he could improve it in various ways and things just evolved from there.

What you did really depended on the wall, if there was just a normal long wall then it would be pieces next to each other, in which case it wasn't a big deal what you did, cause there's not much you can do. There was a wall we did in Hamburg though, with Daim, Toast, Darco, Seak, Daddy Cool, Tasek, Stohead and Chintz for the birthday of the harbour, with Hamburg and it's partner cities, so we all got together, ten guys, in the studio of *Getting Up*, and they had all the books on the styles of Hamburg and the partner towns and we had a huge piece of paper and the first idea was to split 50% of the surface for Hamburg and the other 50% for the styles of the eight other partner cities.

I started to sketch a 3D style of Hamburg in the middle, with some arrows on the left and some movement on the right, and as soon as I finished the rough draft I gave the pencil to Mr. Toast, cause I knew he was the guy that could shape it up and make it look better and that's what he did, he re-sketched my style so he kept the ground structure but he did the letters much better than me, and then Daim came along and said he would do the scenery from this city, and everybody just pitched in and it was very much a game.

I recall we did something at the old airport with Bates from Copenhagen and Merda from Australia, and it came up that we do an A.I.D.S piece, and I discovered some gates in which I think the airport fire fighters kept their trucks, and it was four gates, for the four letters of A.I.D.S. Merda at that time in my opinion was way ahead, he had pieces back then that would be considered so modern even today, with techniques for doing really straight, precise lines. He had the tendency of making grids on the paper for his sketches, that way he made the architecture of his letters really perfect and it became a step by step process. Then there was Bates who was really good in swinging styles, so these guys matched each other perfectly, everybody was taking part in each other's strengths. The basic key for any wall to be a success is that everybody that participates has to work together, that's why having a sketch is so important, so nobody argues and everybody agrees on how things turn out.

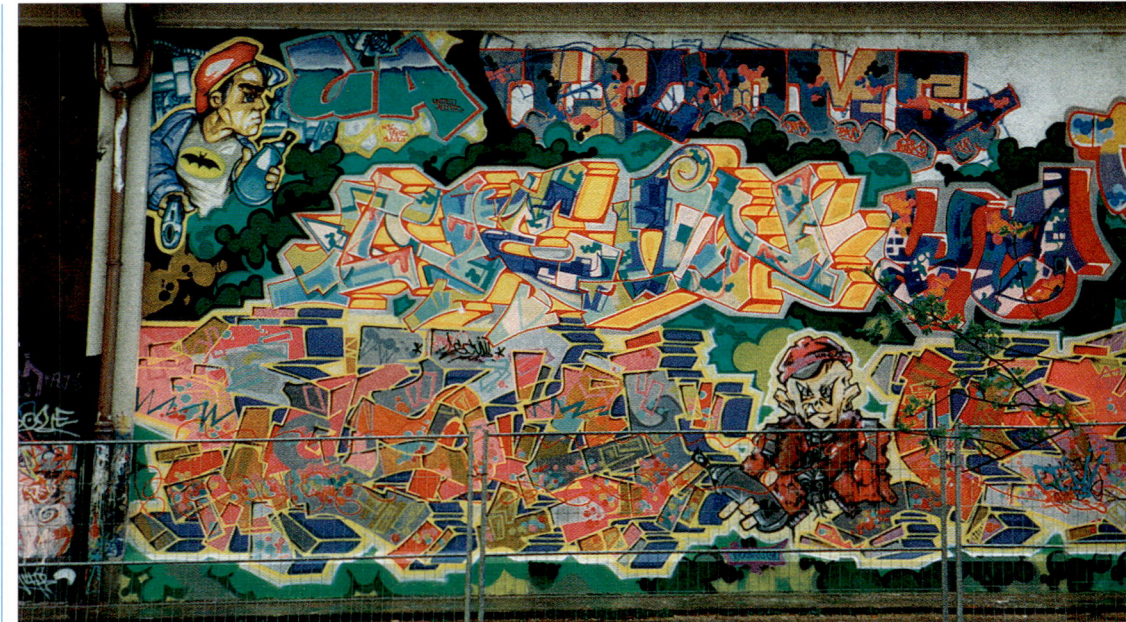

Neon, Scum, Zebster, Loomit, Skena. UA – TFP – FBI production

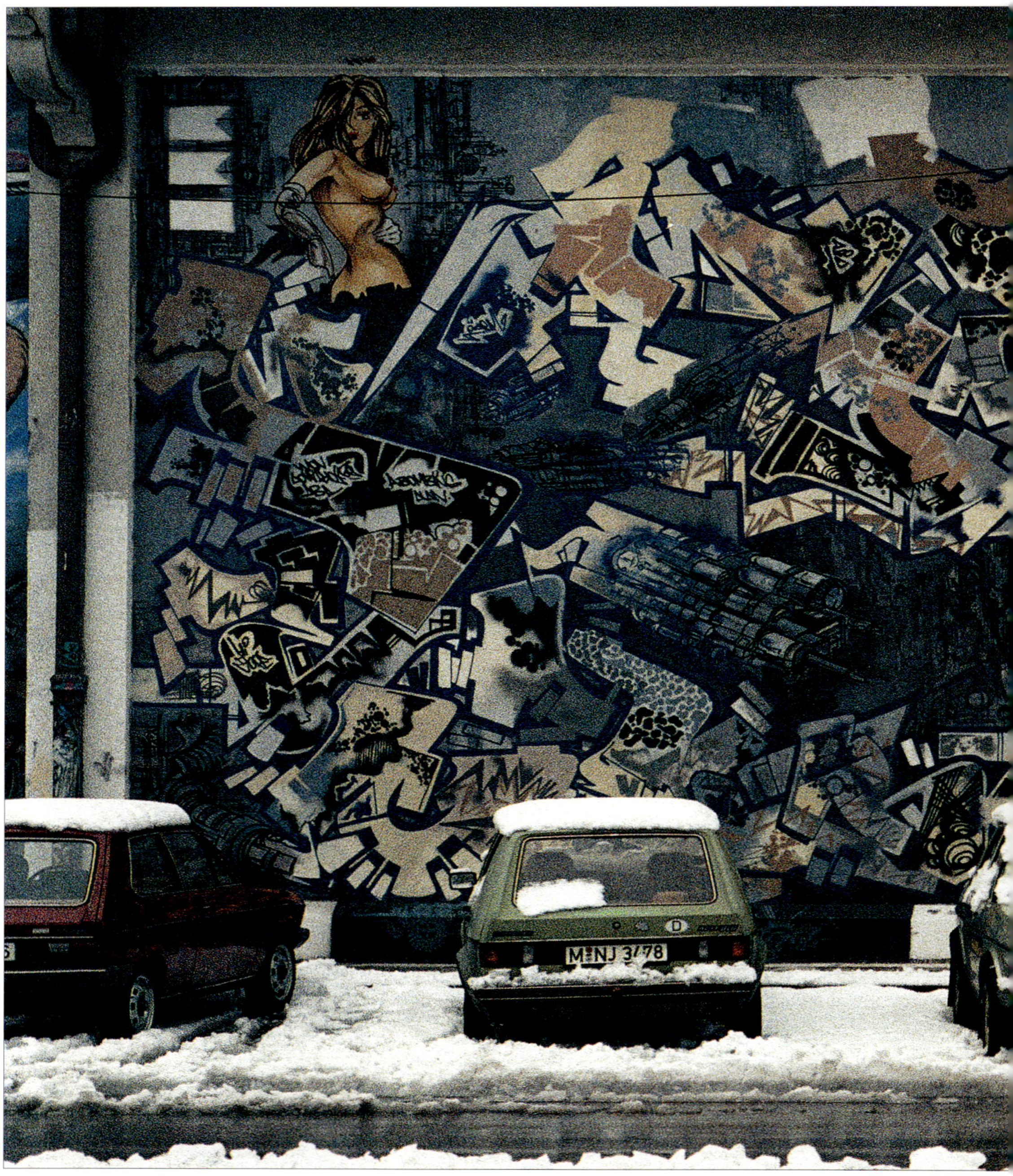

Megamachines by Won and Cowboy69, ABC crew, 1988

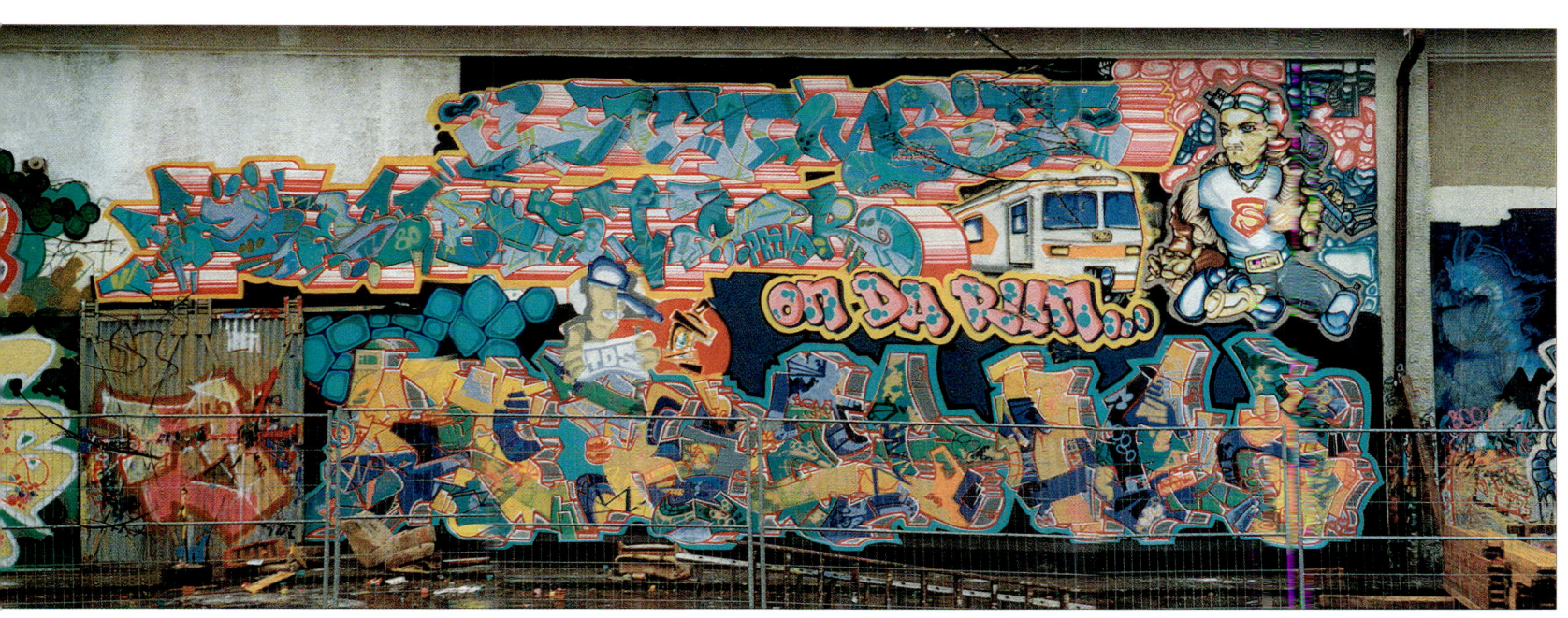

— Mark Todt

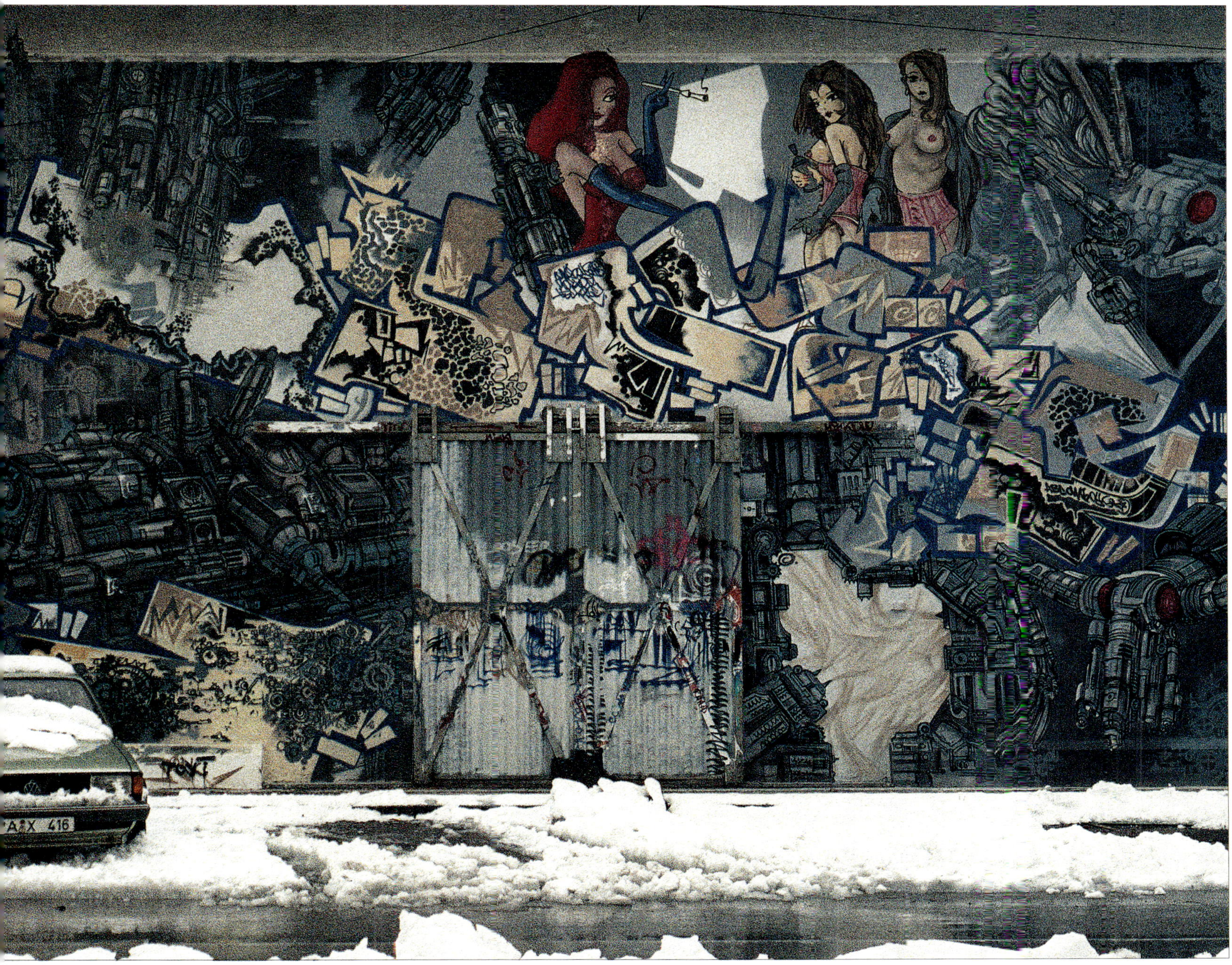

— Won

FROM NARRATIVE

The approach to a wall is often tied to the characteristics of the intended surface. In halls of fame for example, compositions were determined by the wall's characteristics, such as its texture, dimension and position: variables that would dictate the approach and aesthetic.

The stylistic evolution of Loomit and ABC crew would have probably taken different directions had the area at their disposal included a low, rectilinear perimeter wall. The possibility of painting the entire height of a large surface caused their compositions to be wide-ranging, where the background assumed a key role, that often determined the theme of the entire work. The large canvas that was offered by high walls recalled, though on a different scale, the proportions of the squash courts Lee had painted in New York.

Vice versa, halls of fame that had formed around the perimeter of basketball courts inspired other approaches and aesthetics. The low, longitudinal profile of these walls automatically triggered a series of Names often alternated with characters. In the 90's, this recurring theme became the source of inspiration for a sort of "Narrative walls" painted by Mode 2, where the pause between Names gave the opportunity to develop a storyboard distributed along the wall's surface, similar to a comic strip. "Narrative walls" became another occasion to give themes to compositions by multiple artists, like a sequence-shot on an urban scale that recalled the collective spirit of Writing, originally centred on group actions on long, rectilinear trains.

Mode2 –TCA / London
>

With respect to the monumental compositions of some writers, I tend to consider dimensions less important. I'd rather have a wall in which my piece can evolve along its length, so that children can walk along it and it almost seems to be narrating a story. I like to consider my pieces like comic strips on an urban scale. For many writers however making bigger pieces seemed like a natural thing to do, you take a given surface and proportionally increase the size of everything so as to cover it completely. The actual letters wouldn't change size but the figurative decorations accompanying them would be tailored to give harmony and balance to the final output. In this case the background that is painted assumes a lead role because it often sets the theme of the entire composition.

I've always preferred long and very rectangular walls however. I also have my blackbooks in landscape format so I was drawing in a horizontal way as well. The structure of horizontal painting is perhaps more traditional, most of the first halls of fame in New York on the sides of the basketball playgrounds were in this format. In a certain sense this structure also reproduces that of the subway cars, long and flat. What I intend as narrative painting is a wall in which the pieces set the rhythm and the spaces between them contain characters or drawings that set the theme and develop it in successive scenes. The same spaces above letters sometimes served this same purpose and part of our objective was to give the upper limit of our walls a uniformed aspect so that everything resulted in a continuous flow. You didn't need to tell a story all the time. The Sab-Kaze whole-car in *Subway Art* is just fat, like a good instrumental tune; just making you feel it, without having anything in particular to understand. The difficulty with painting in Paris was that these long walls were hard to find, especially in visible spots in the city, and when we did find them they were usually very bad surfaces. You couldn't spend too long in front of the really good ones, as they were just too 'hot' for big pieces. At the time my painting partner in Paris was Echo, we weren't in a crew together but we were hanging out a lot. He was working in cinema set decoration so he had Aerolux, this really top brand of paint, for painting movie sets; a really good quality acrylic. With that paint we had a reliable base for walls, which could fill up the holes and provide an impermeable surface for us to paint over. It was liquid but it really covered, and nobody had thought about this before; they'd just go paint the walls white and use up spraypaint to cover the entire thing. Instead of using a roller and obtaining an all-white surface, or buying a large quantity of coloured cans for a colourful background, we could use the various shades of Aerolux to create our base colour. We weren't good at stealing paint so we really needed to use the minimum amount to the maximum effect. We chose which walls to paint by walking down the street and checking their effective visibility in the city, the quality of the wall itself didn't matter because if it's tight bricks then you do bigger pieces. Echo told me about these brushes that were used for applying wallpaper paste, with long nylon bristles. They're very durable so you can use them again and again. When you've got one of those you can really get it into the brickwork, cover everything real good, working any crumbly bits into a kind of cement with the acrylic. Me and Echo would go out with all this painting material, scrapers, metal brushes, buckets, ladder, and we'd spend half an hour brushing the wall down and taking things off. Because of all the equipment we had, people thought what we were doing was official, legitimate, they never guessed we were actually acting illegally, because we wouldn't give that impression. Preparing the wall this way gave us a chance to check just how hot the place could get. Whenever they knocked down any buildings and an empty space was created, Echo mixed the Aerolux rests he had from work together in a bucket and filtered them through this sifter, like for tea, then we'd pour the paint through and this pure liquid would come out. When we did a wall with Futura in Montreuil in '95 we did the background black mixed with some ochre-coloured paint, and it really became the essence of the piece, especially since Futura painted abstract compositions without defined boundaries, each element he drew seemed to be fluctuating magically out of the background. Sometimes we encountered difficulties with other writers when we painted together, because their method was to start one piece right next to the previous, the way most halls of fame are done. People would always paint as though they were in the train yard, except we'd be on a street where time and space are enough to allow you to change the painting conditions. I need space to breathe, if we're painting together please count a couple of metres after my piece and then start, also because it is in those spaces that my narrative develops.

Things and times moved on though, as did the world around us; becoming more complex and moving faster. It was becoming harder and harder to deal with any given theme in the language we had developed, as many more factors came into play and started interweaving. We can only paint little anecdotes nowadays; the big themes would need a lot more space and maybe more text, more time, and so on...

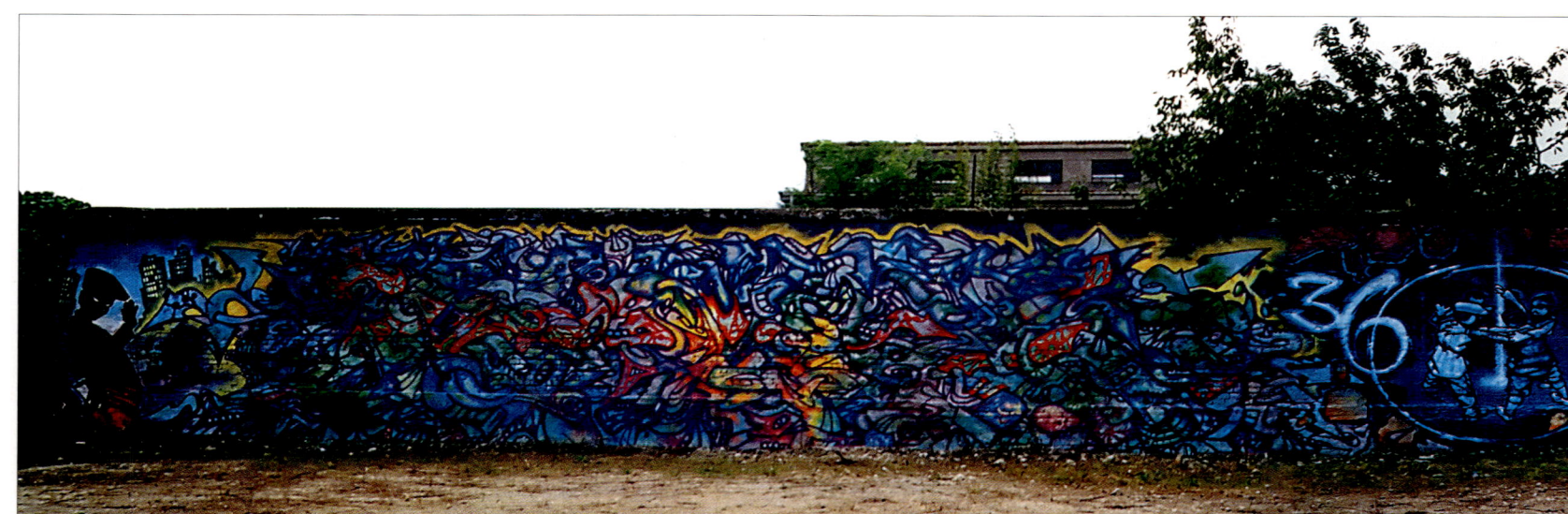

Phase II (New York City), Mode 2 (Paris), Sharp (New York City). Rimini 1995

TO CONCEPT WALLS

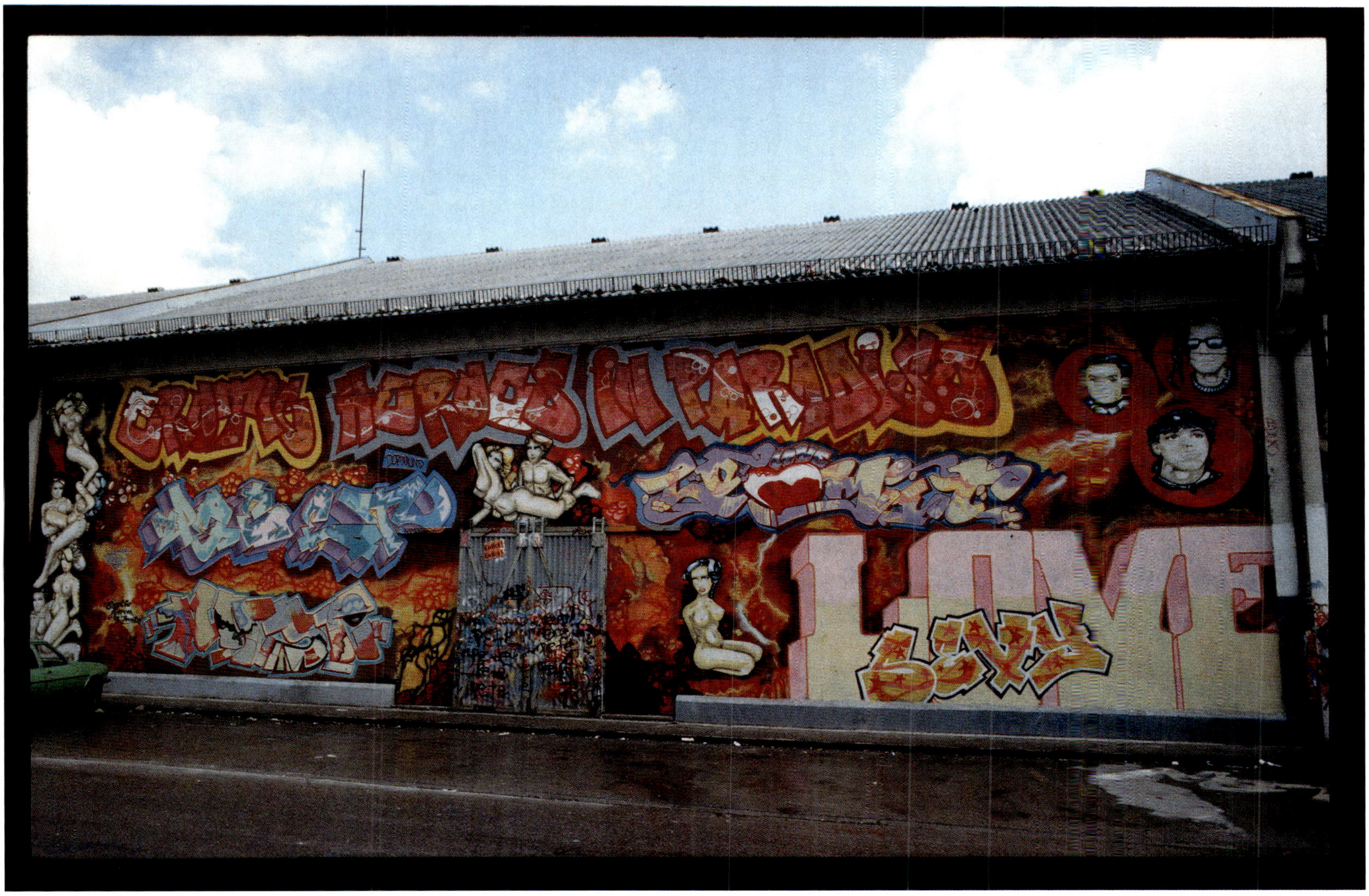

Erotic Heroes in Paradise. Theme wall on erotism painted by Loomit, Peeet, Nast

— Paola Soglia

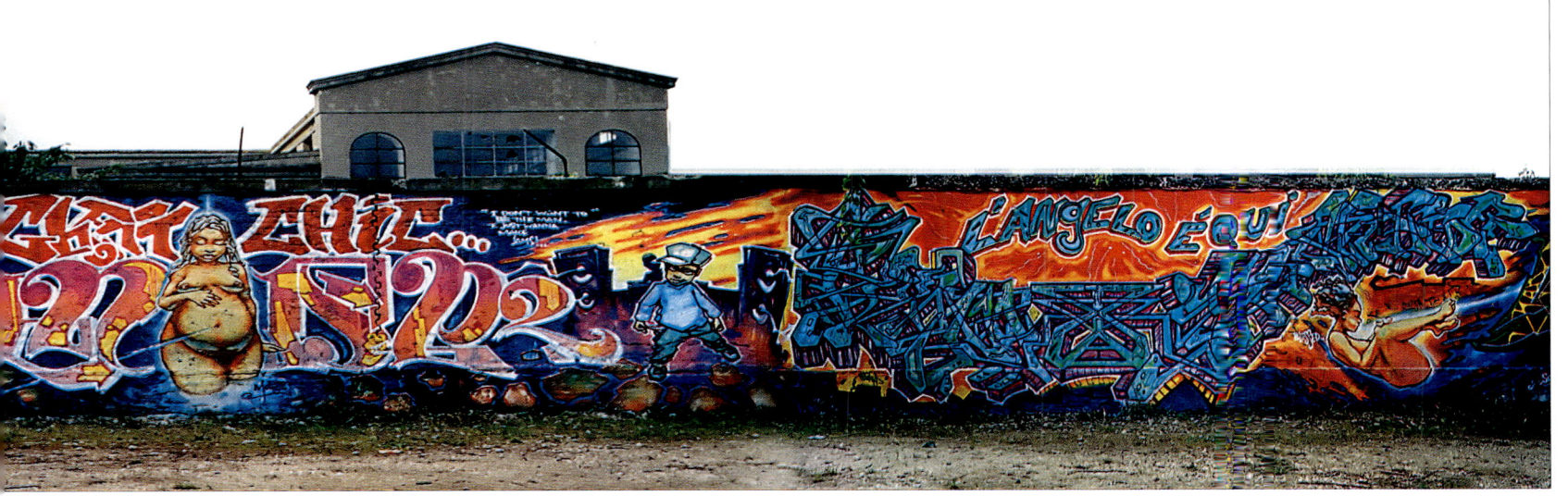

— Oida

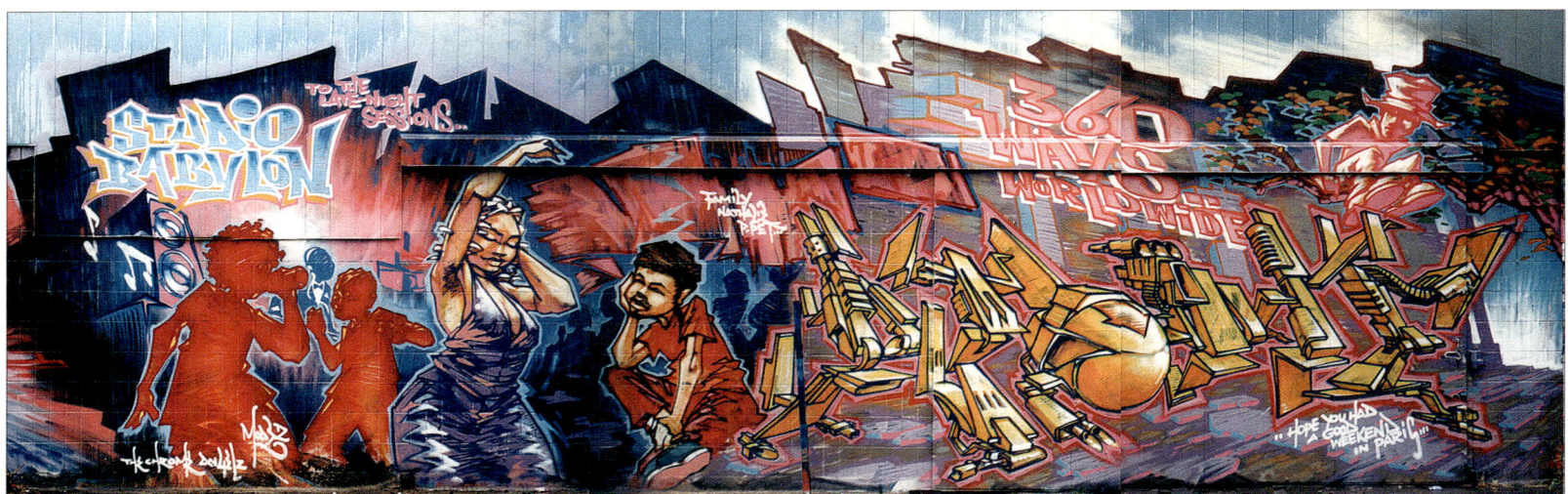

Atome by Mode 2, Wiesbaden 1997

– Mode 2

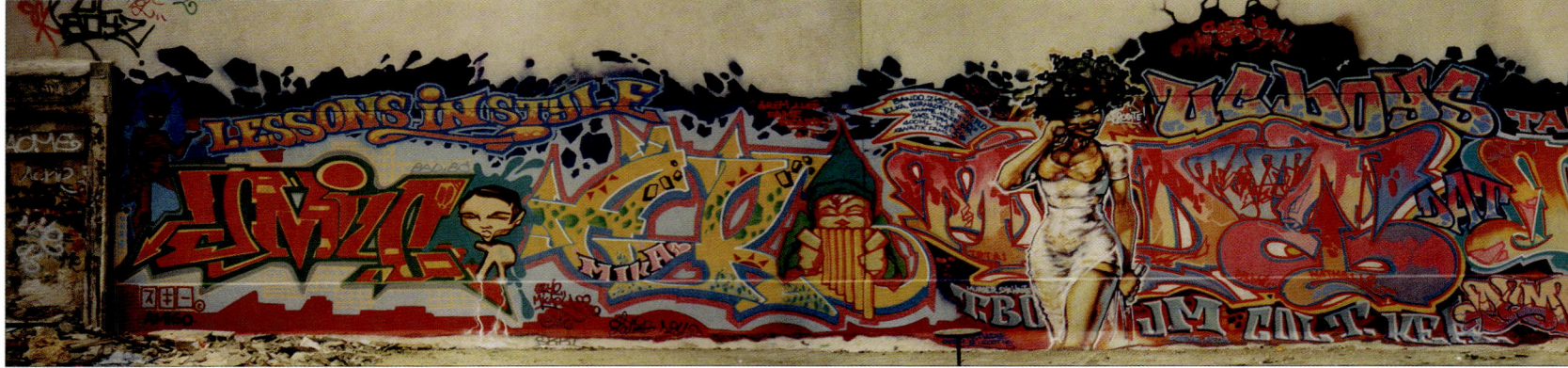

Skki, Echo, Mode 2 and Jay–1 at Paris Gambetta, 1993. First co-production between Skki, Jay–1 of BBC crew and Mode 2

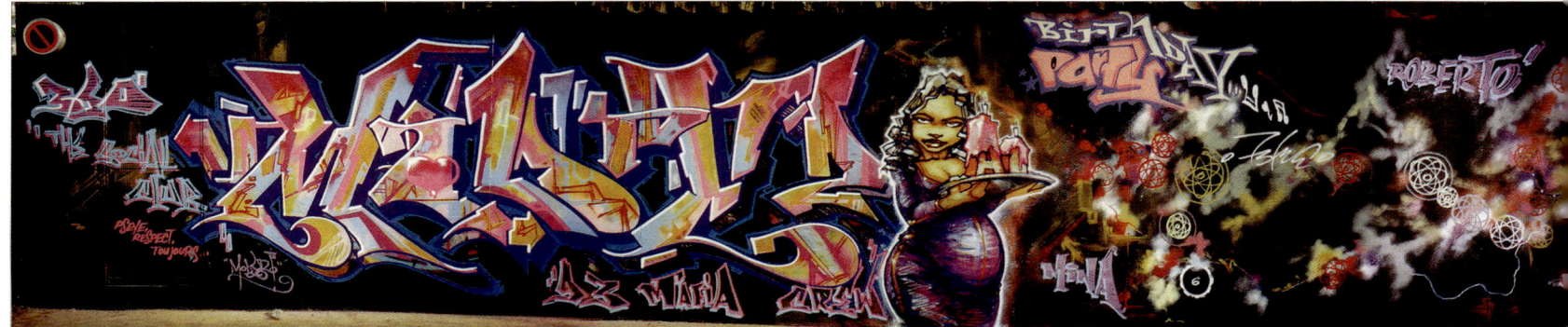

Mode 2, Futura 2000 from New York City, Echo and Jay 1

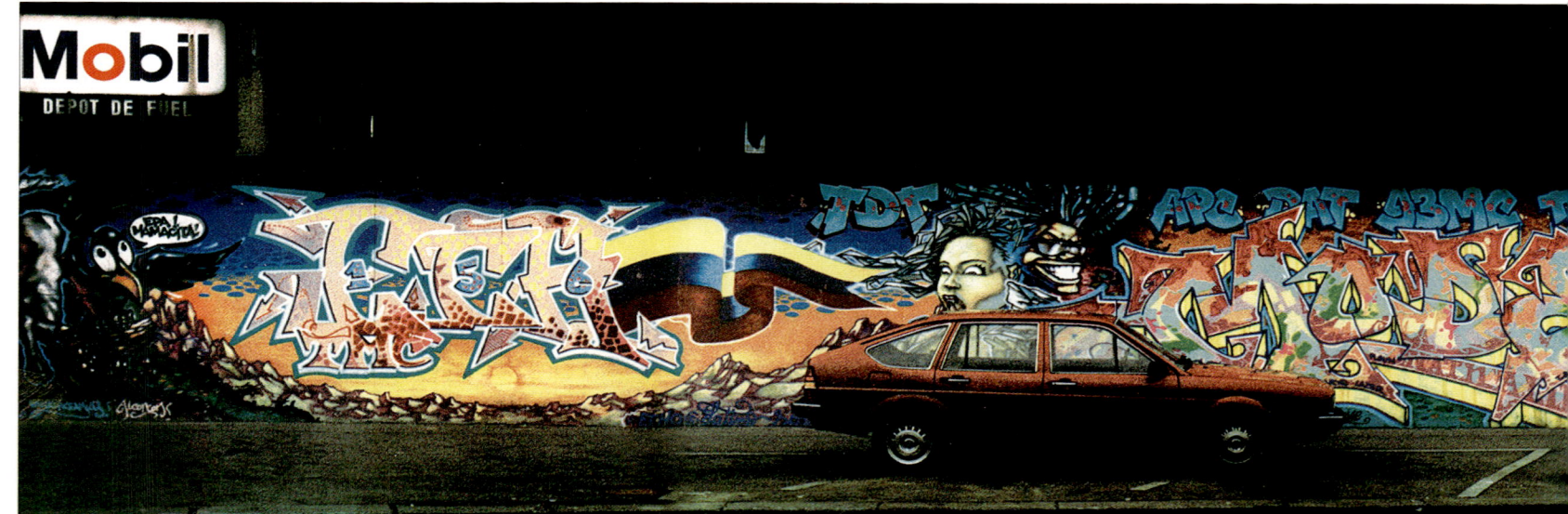

Echo, Mode 2, Zism, Rest. Montreuil Paris 1992

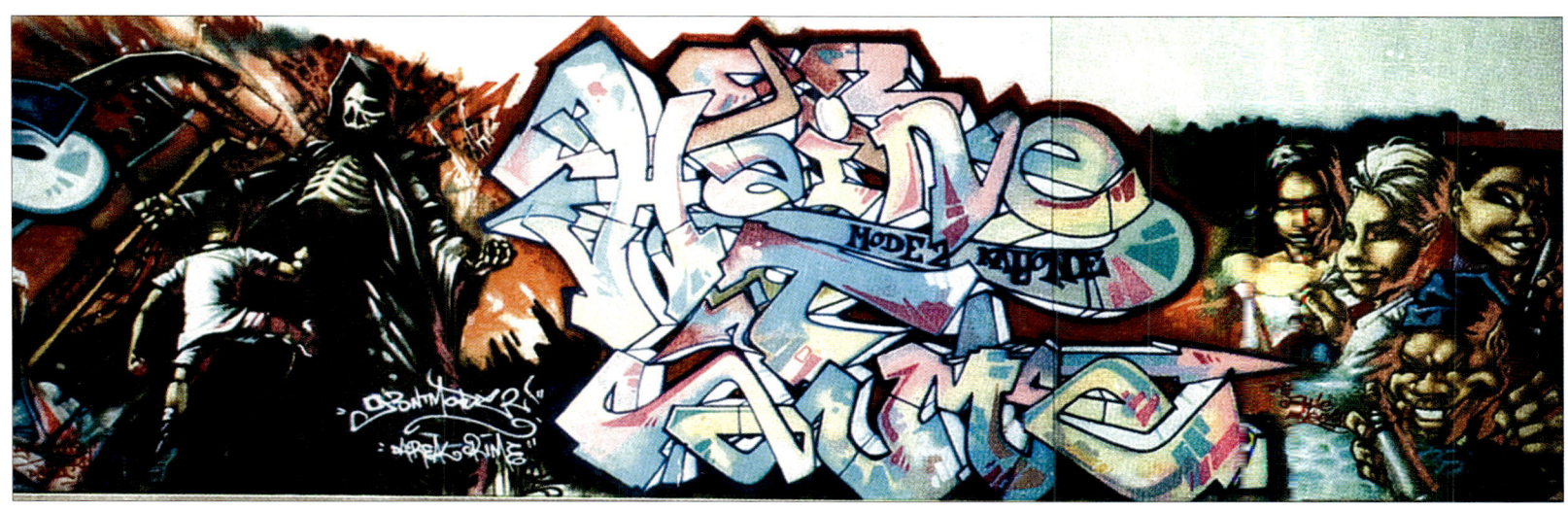

93 Haine t aime by Mode 2. Painted at Villiers Sur Marne, Paris 1990.   — *XG archive*

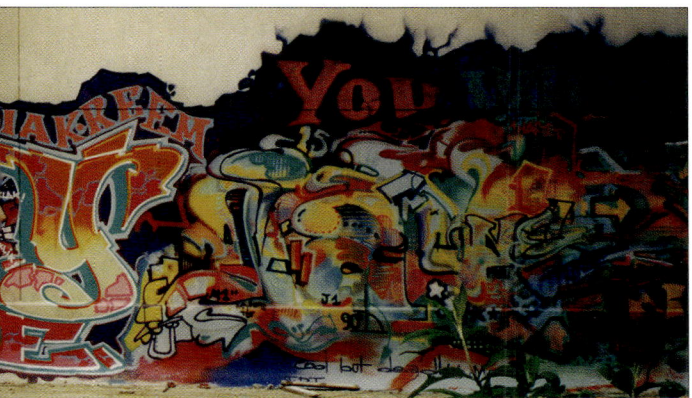

— *Echo*

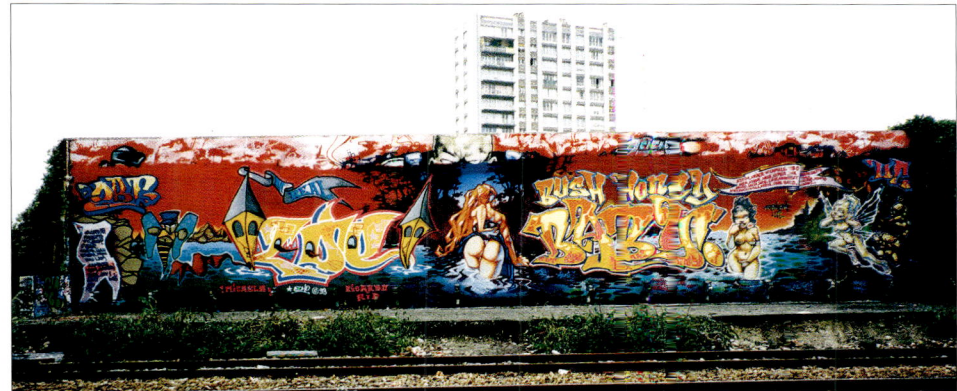

Koe by Echo, *bush honey baby* by Mode 2, St Ouen 1993   — *Echo*

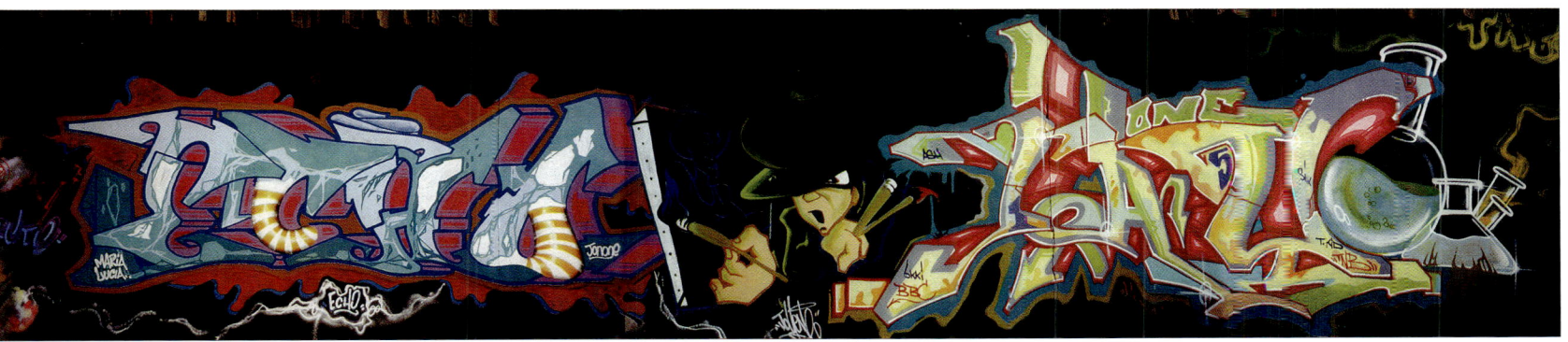

— *Mode 2*

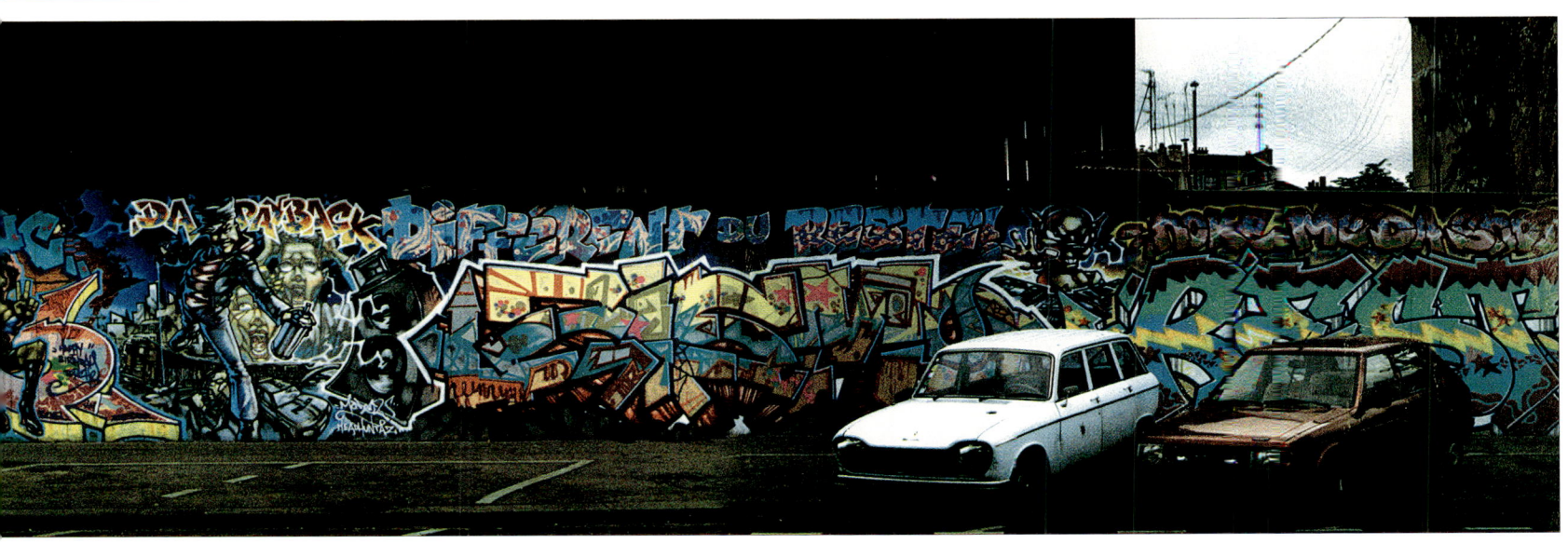

— *ACW archives*

Baseline

On the border between France, Germany and Switzerland, Basel accommodates three different national railway lines in its centre. Thanks to its location, the track line cuts through kilometres of city with a continuous wall distributed on distinct levels

Dare –TWS / Basel
>

I guess the reason why the Basel rail track line became so impressively painted is due to the location itself: as giant voids, the tracks continuously cut through the core of the city, forming long series of concrete open-air canals and deep tunnels. To connect the different parts of the city to the various directions going to Germany or France, the rail track had to be planned on multiple topographic levels. When Swet from Copenhagen came to paint the line walls he was totally amazed by all that complexity and dynamism, he was accustomed to the flatness of Denmark. As the three lines and stations connect different parts of the city to the corresponding countries, the track lines form a kind of Bermuda triangle where walking past every wall to check out the pieces takes hours and hours. Each direction has two lines going up and down, which form tunnels. On another level the highway also intersects these routes, increasing the visibility and complexity of this labyrinth. Arriving to Basel by train coincides with this infinite strip in which pieces today stand one immediately after the next or even juxtaposed; painting at +3 metres wasn't really necessary during the early 90's but today corners and interstices are seen as the last possibile spaces on which to show your stuff. As this illegal hall of fame became the main target, local writers started focusing on style and big productions, giving bombing a secondary role. In this case the urban conditions changed the behaviour of the scene, the rules and the target; Zurich's scene for instance went in the opposite direction, probably focusing on bombing and trains just because there wasn't such an important presence as our line. For the past 20 years writers have taken possession of this area as if it were their property. Though it was and still is illegal yet the city authorities tolerate it. In a city which lacks legal halls of fame such as those in Munich, and where the main spot doesn't really concern any private property, of course things go in this direction and are tolerated: the Basel line was convenient for writers and for the city as well. Today, considering that year by year every square metre of tunnels and concrete canals gets painted to saturation, writers and citizens have gradually lost the original greyscale memory of this infrastructure. The fact that 90% of pieces are condensed in this specific area has avoided conflicts with the city and it's citizens since no private property was damaged. The city's rail-track became the perfect spot for big productions; each one was well-planned and painted with roller coats as a background, complex letters, characters and combined colours when executed by two or more people. After I started this practice everyone adopted this way of painting as well: a standard that year by year identified Basel and its rail track line. It might sound contradictory: usually on rail track walls it's easier to find silver pieces and blockbusters, letters painted keeping in mind the speed of the train and their legibility. But in Basel large parts of those walls are inner city, where the speed of every train is slower and helpful. Moreover, as in NY, here too many writers paint for themselves and for the scene, not for the public: though an illegal spot, during the day the line was also the place where writers would meet, comment on new pieces, and take daytime pictures. So there is all the time to check every detailed character and appreciate the complexity of local Wildstyle.

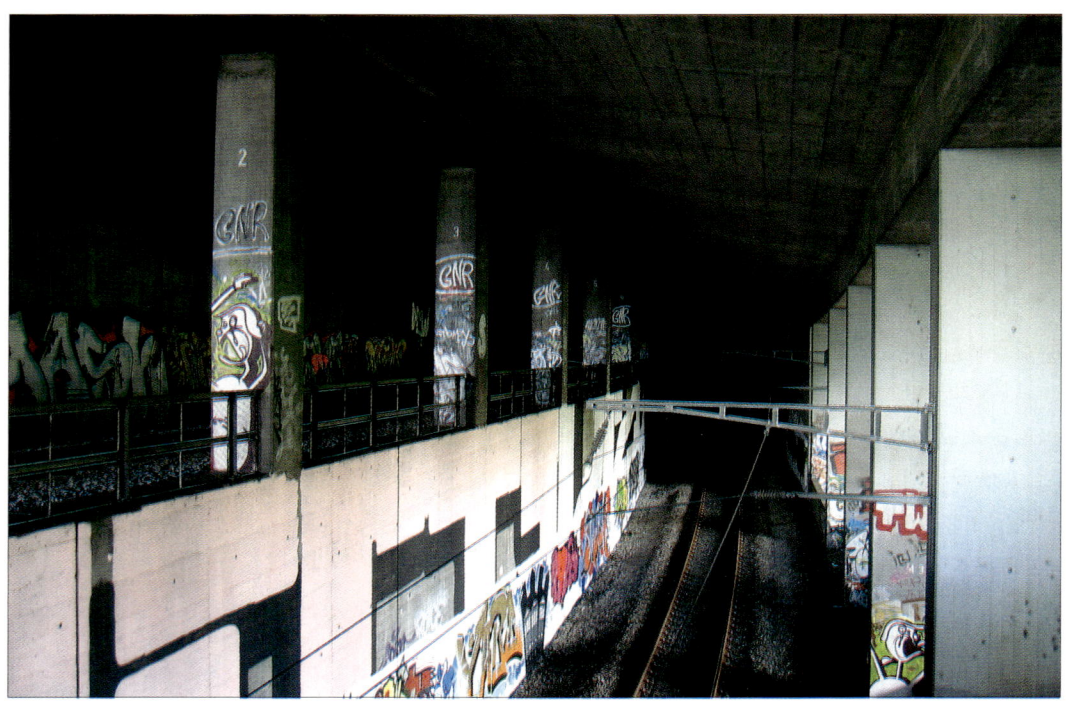

— Dare

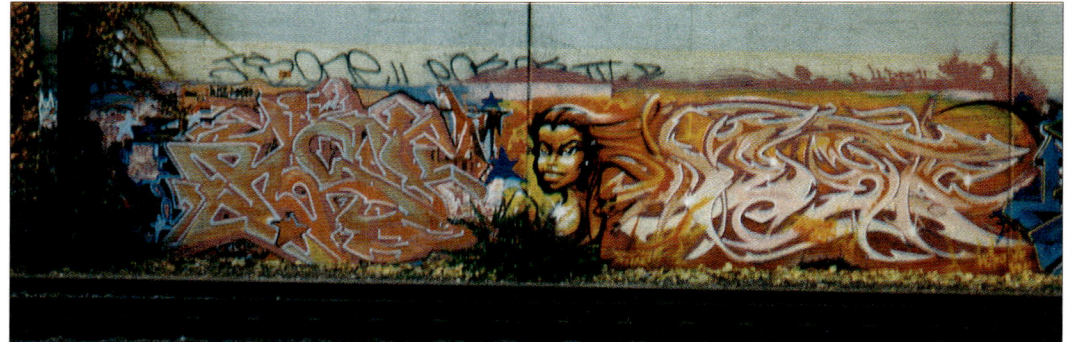

— Lay Up

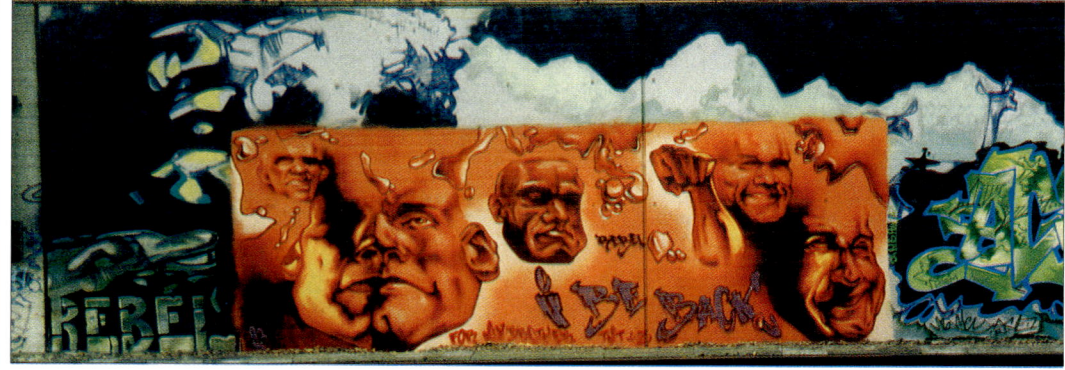

— Beka 70

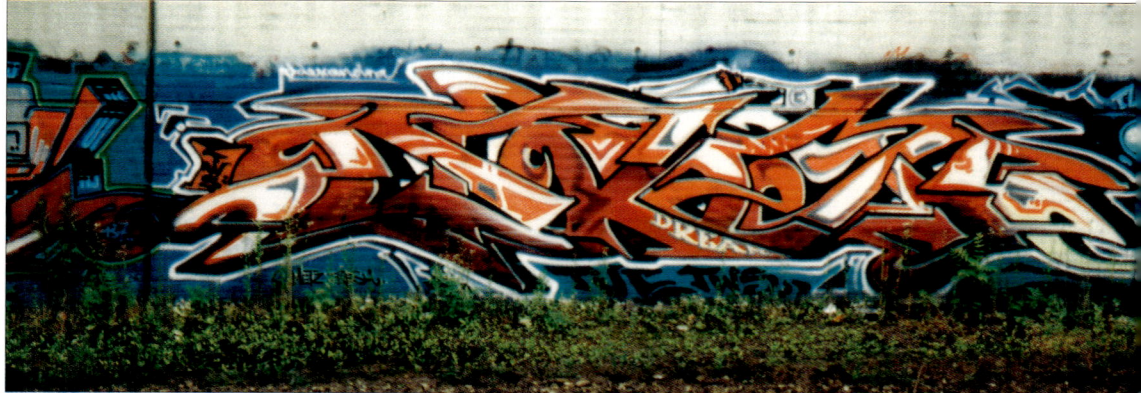

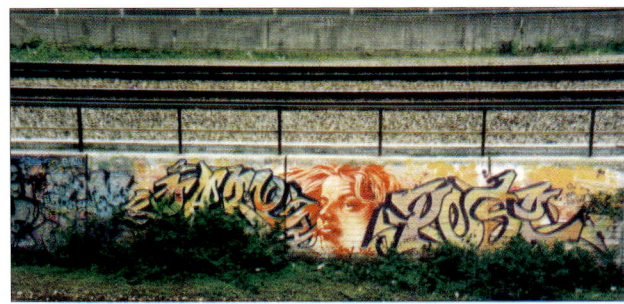

— Beka 70

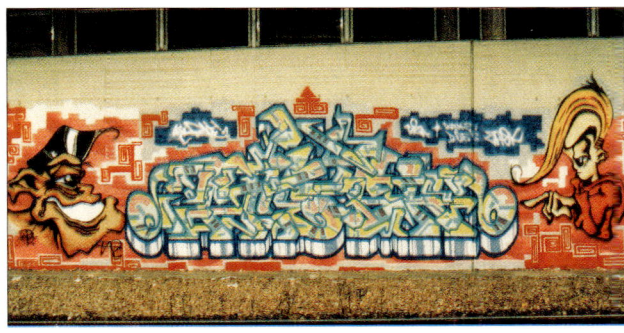

— Beka 70

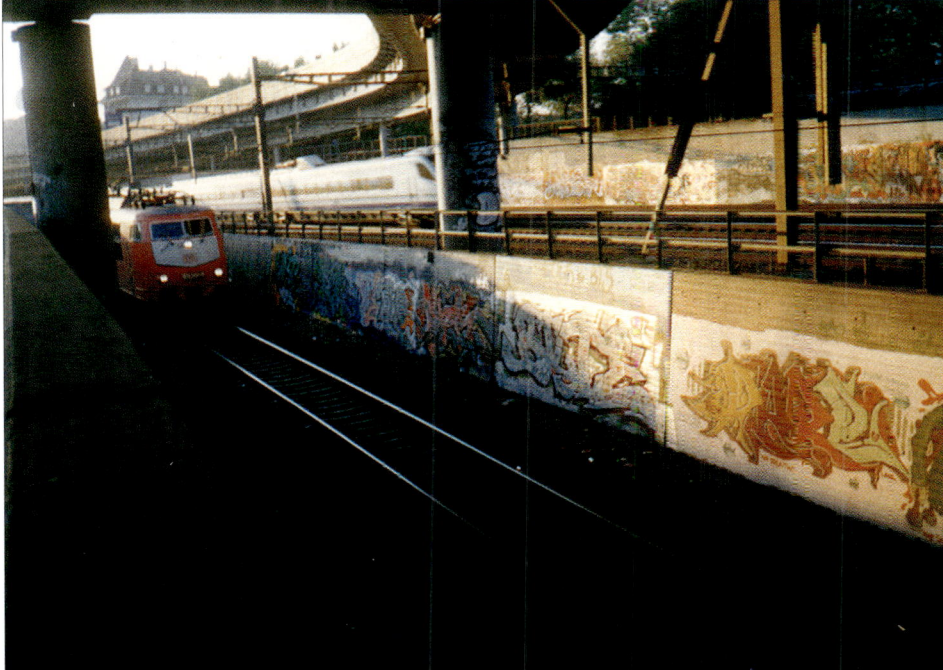

— Lay Up

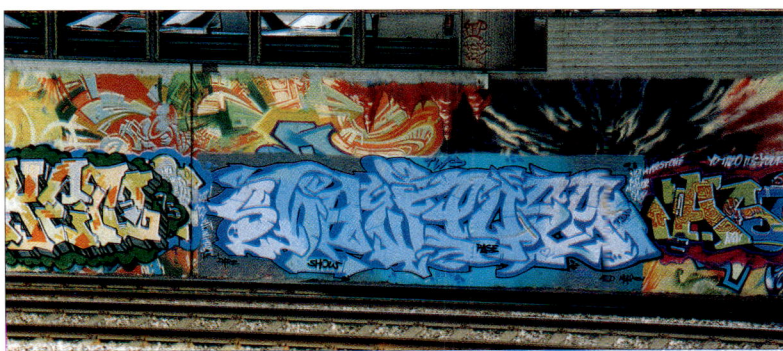

— Beka 70

	2	
1	3	4
10	5	
9	6	
8		7

1. Railroad headed to the German station of Basel DB
2. Dare TWS, Rebel TNT, Pose TWS
3. Skelt Zhock, Tiza –FTP crew, 1990
4. Multiple layers of the line
5. Show TWS and Pose TWS, March 1994
6. Dare TWS Character by Toast, March 1996
7. Primary stretch of the line, some hundred metres before entering the Swiss station of Basel
8. Dream and Dare –TWS, character by Sars April 1996
9. Rebel TNT, 1993
10. Pose and Desk

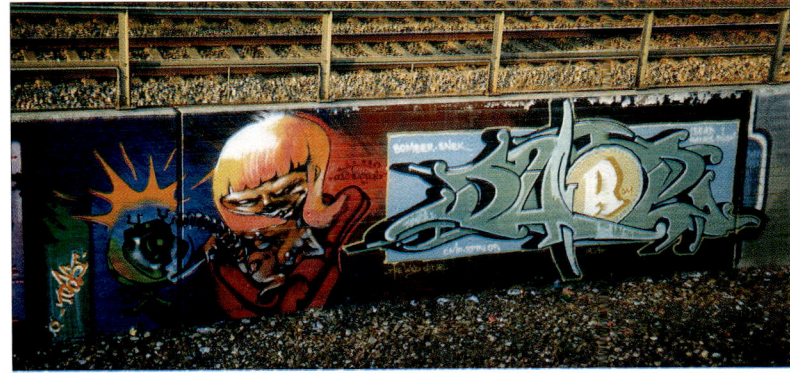

— Lay Up

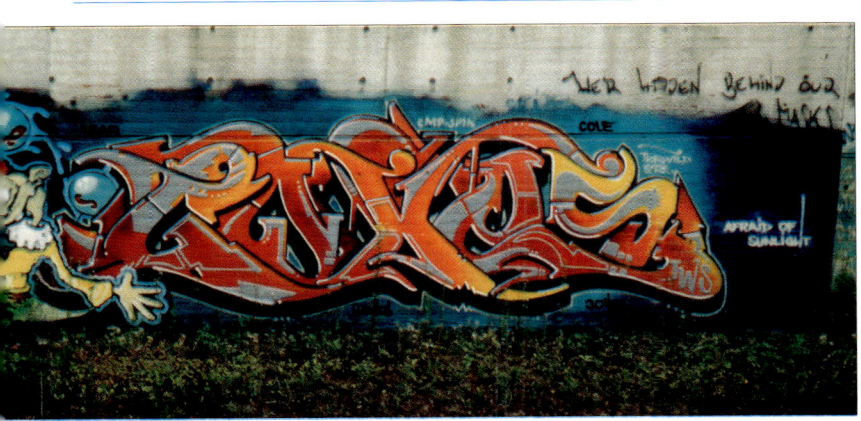

— Beka 70

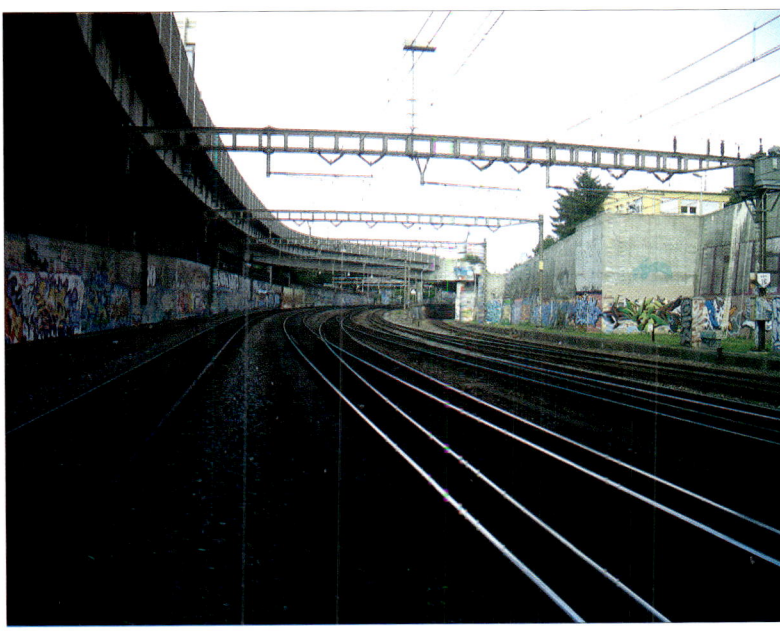

— Lay Up

THE BERLIN WALL

The local hall of fame tradition
and the Wall as historic catalysers
of Berlin streets energies

Rew –SKS / Berlin
›

While Germany had writers and a Hip Hop scene ever since the early 80's, in Berlin the movement didn't really get started until the end of that decade, probably because the city has always been detached from the rest of the country due to the war. It was only when the Wall came down that the scene started slowly growing. The first writers from Berlin to travel to other cities and get the connections started did so around '92–'93. Though Berliners from the West could travel freely, it was a hassle because at the time there was no internet and no mobile phones, only letters. If you wanted to see somebody's photo you had to go there in person or have them sent by post. But nobody did either; no Berliner went to another town and nobody came here, nobody sent photos, the local scene was really closed off.

This situation brought local writers to choose their own, private halls of fame, developing a very personal concept of style. Of course in the beginning the letters were closely influenced by Amsterdam, Paris and London, but Amok, Chic, Dane and Kaos didn't take that long to develop their own direction. These guys followed more of a New York flavour by looking at and developing the letter structures T-kid used. In my opinion what contributed to building the city's style in those years – the early 90's – was our isolated condition. These writers knew about the style of New York but there wasn't that much stuff to see. People were just forced to improvise, construct and deconstruct letters as they had no references. Once new magazines and books came out, the process became more complex. The next generation, with guys like Odem and Force, developed burners as well and you could say that the Berliner Wildstyle tradition didn't end there. At the hall of fame, they always painted and spoke about style and letters and how they had to be perfect. They weren't even talking about Wildstyle, it was more about pieces being perfect, through various elements, the connections, the proportions, the uniqueness. Original style was a way to judge and respect a writer. At this time there was a crew called SOS - Spirit of Style - which was founded in 1990 and was really starting to invent a unique style, as the crew name suggests. It was a group of guys: Odem, Force, Shek, Amok; this little group only focused on drawing the perfect sketch, no one was attending school or working. Automatically, they influenced some of the younger guys like Inka, me, Hulk and the rest, including the next generation that you have today like Akim, Sas, Nick, Cost or whoever. After 20 years, Berliners now have more than 50 writers with their own original style, dealing only with letters. At the base of this peculiarity, there were a few, perfect spots scattered in the city; these halls of fame were like small Stalingrads, just more spread out and not concentrated in a specific location. One spot was in Hallesches Tor, a small place with low walls two metres tall. Jay-1 lived in this area and he went down to paint everyday. It was a king hall of fame, if you went there in the 90's you'd only see burners. We used to go there everyday, taking pictures of new pieces painted by BBC crew with Skki and Ash. Before that, between 1986-89 there was another circumscribed place, a special hall of fame of Amok's with two walls, one left and one right, about four metres high; personally, the best pieces I have seen on photos are from this place, pieces painted by Amok, Chic and Dane. Until the early 90's there were about five places like this, which year by year

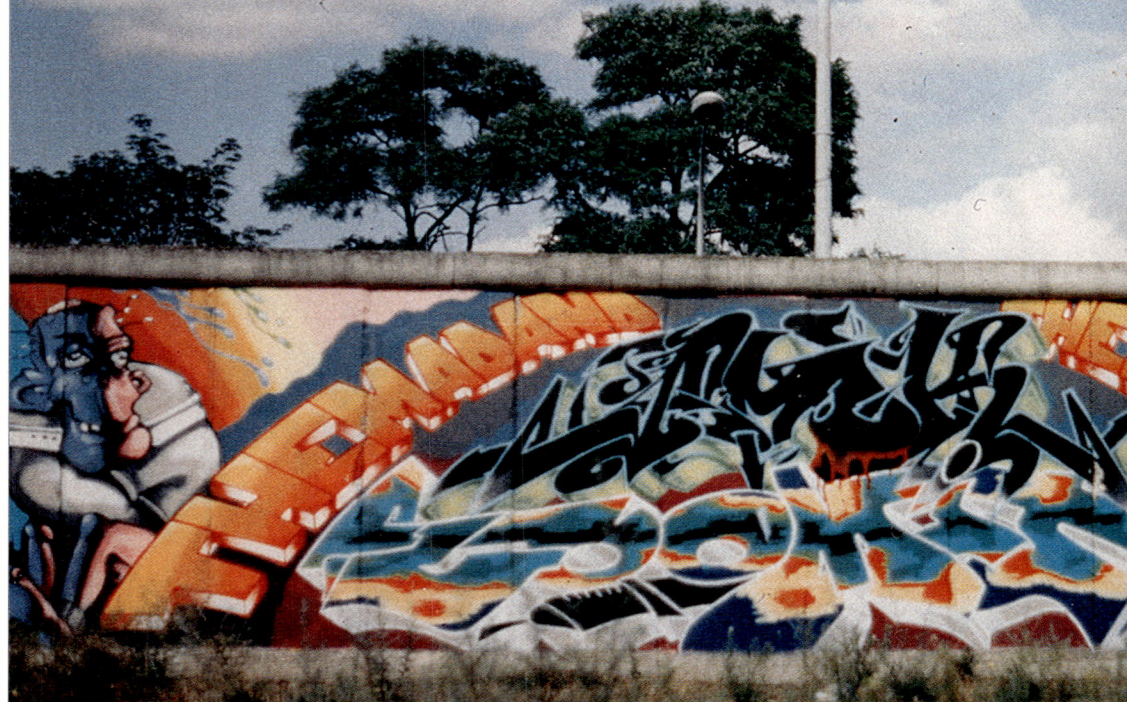

Amok and Loomit on the Berlin wall, 1992

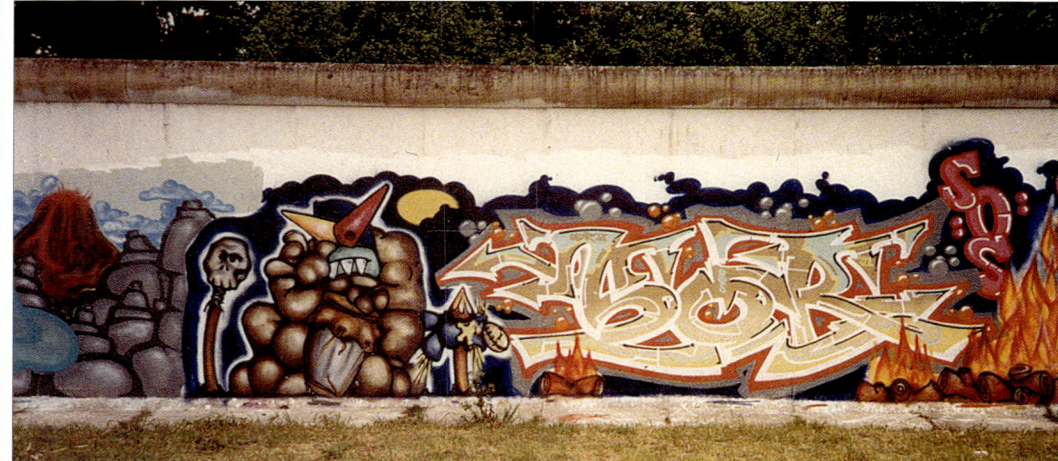

Sor by Odem – SOS crew on the Berlin wall   – *Mark Todt*

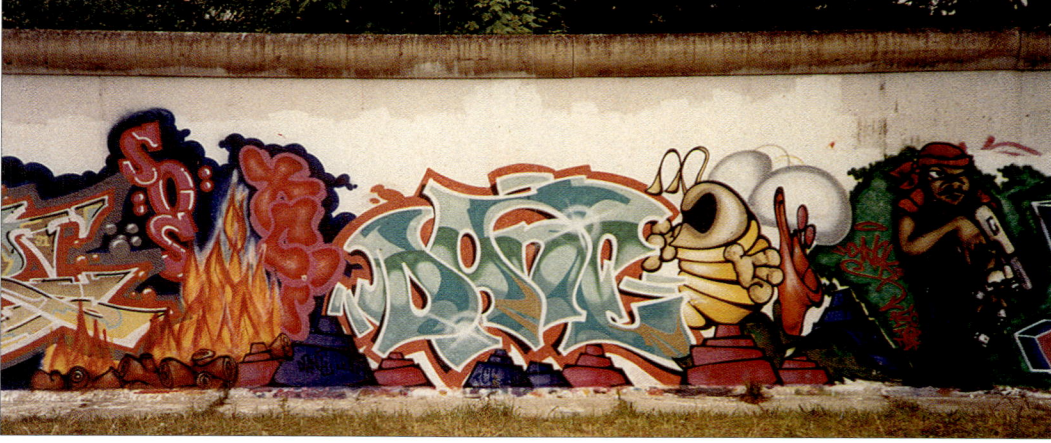

Dane   – *Mark Todt*

Salon de refusés

In the 80's the subway stations of Stockholm became the best showcase for writers in the city, becoming a valued alternative to trains during the rigid winter months. Two witnesses narrate the aesthetic developments

Jacob Kimvall / Stockholm
>

The "Exhibit of rejected works" – Salon de refusées – was a legendary art exhibition held in Paris in 1863. A great number of young artists of the time had had their artwork refused in the yearly exhibition. Some of the artists brought matters to a head and organised their own exhibition. Their intention was to let the public judge what they wanted to see. This exhibit came about as a reaction against mainstream taste belonging to the establishment. That's why they chose the name Salon de refusées.

The SL (Stockholm transit authority) consider themselves promoters of art and often declare that the Stockholm subway is the worlds longest art show. If that were really true I wonder why they spend millions of Swedish crowns every year on removing graffiti, of which some part, at least, can be regarded as art. This way of thinking depends on a principle that is more than twenty years old. In the mid 60's the subway station "Östermalmstorg" was built. A famous Swedish artist named Siri Derkert decorated the station's walls, portraying themes like feminism, peace, the environment and the joys of life. These themes were symbolised by children and dancing people. By the end of the 60's the walls opposite Derkert's work had been filled with drawings and messages written by anonymous travellers. In 1973 the SL decided to spend 60.000 Skr (300.000Skr today) to remove these 'scribbles'. Derkert and many others protested, they thought that these messages were a good complement to their art and that the money should be spent on restoring the original work by Derker instead, as it was not in the best of shape. The fact that Hip Hop-related graffiti was starting to appear in Stockholm at the beginning of the 80's was completely overlooked by the SL. Some people, mostly youngsters, had started to decorate the subway system on their own. Some of the pieces were thought to have an artistic value and were therefore left unharmed for some years. Around 1988-'89 though the methods changed. Masterpieces like Zappo's "Crush the War" or "Make Love, Not War" on the 23 line were buffed. It's funny to notice how at the same time the amount of pieces was increasing. SL often claims that their anti-graffiti stance is a form of care for travellers. They remove graffiti because the travellers want a clean and welcoming subway. Gunnar Schön, SL, in "Metro", November 9th 1995: "People don't like scribbled surroundings, that's a fact. One of the reasons for the campaign is just to create a secure atmosphere in the Subway." If you read SL's internal documents about "Operation Security" they'll leave you confused. In these documents it's hard to understand Gunnar Schön's point of view. The SL complains about the lack of support in their course of action. Their intention is to make people take a stand against graffiti. "There are some people, certain individuals in authority and creators of public opinion, that have an unconscious belief, a respect or even an admiration for what the scribblers do. They tolerate the scribbles, which in their eyes are only a sort of rascality that has been common among youngsters throughout time. Or they think it's a subculture that is not necessarily understandable but has to be respected for us to get respect from the youngsters. This naive and ignorant attitude shall disappear with the help of those that know better; us. That's a wish for the future".

It's not about whether a piece is ugly nor is it about caring for passengers. In that case SL should have chosen to save the most beautiful work. One can hardly understand why they spend hundreds of thousands of crowns on propaganda aimed at convincing travellers of the destruction graffiti is associated with. The same orderly art decorations that exist throughout the subway would never have survived had they been done illegally. Where would the advertisements have gone if all visual communication were not allowed?

Often the years of conflict between the SL and graffiti artists have been described as a war. This is an overstatement, it's not about a war – it's about power. Who has the power of judging and controlling what art should be displayed in public space? This power belongs to the following people in SL's management: Claes Åhnstrand, Elwe Nilsson, Jan Strömdahl, Birgitta Nådell, Majvi Andersson, Per- Erik Kull, Eie Herlietz, Barbro Noresson, Ulf du Rietz, Jan Olov Sundström, Ulf Uebel, Gunnar Thomén, Lars Randerz and Börje Flygel. Fourteen middle-aged people. It's their taste that decides and they instruct their subordinates on how to handle it. From a larger perspective it's all about the public authority's negative attitude towards the youth.

If the Stockholm Subway is "the worlds longest art-exhibition" I suppose U.P. is the exhibit of rejected works!

Originally published on UP #9 - 1996

PIECE ON EARTH
—

Tobias Barenthin Lindblad / Stockholm
>

Those pictures were all taken in October and November of 1988, in three different subway stations of Stockholm. In October writers realised that it was possible to enter the tunnels at night, especially on weekend nights, plus the pieces were not buffed. Within two months all stations were painted, mostly by writers from the following crews: VIM, COC (Controllers of Crime), STM (Stockholm's Tagmafia - Stockholm train mafia), DST (Da System Tyrantz) and MTK (Megatronic Kings). This period only lasted 'til winter of 1989, when pieces started to get buffed, though at a slow rate. The "Arcor" piece is by Archon, a member of DST who had one of the best tag-styles in town. Both he and his partner Trance invented a lot of new letter shapes and styles. This is a forerunner of what Swedish style would be like in the 90's: clear letters with a 'less-is-more' design. The Akay piece is strikingly modern when looked at now. Akay was definitely the king of stations, together with Code. This is one of the more minimalist productions, in a somewhat different style by him. Look at the first A: it looks as if it were made in Berlin today. It also has something of a New York-thing to it, with the connection from the K over to the first A. Amazing how good the technique is. This is when there were three good cap types and a handful of good colours. Triumph was one of Codes many names. For the station pieces he made up the name The Underground Kingz, Tu•z. This was one of several Triumph pieces, and one of the most elaborate. The late 80's were a time in which people focused on y on letters and fill-ins. A background was not necessary, and there's neither shadow nor 3D on this one. Great stuff from a very prolific writer. The tags at Sankt Eriksplan were done by several writers. Here it is possible to see a bit of the evolution during the fall. First out was Orgie (later Jason) and Triumph. The red tags at the right, Hades, Bored (Buzter), Trance, unknown and Yazi were also from an earlier weekend. News and Akay from VIM totally took over this space, crushing the competition, and giving a joking hint to the others: take up the battle! At the bottom Weird (Tarik) from Megatronick Kingz has added his tag too. A classic sight on one of the most painted stations during one of the greatest years: 1988!

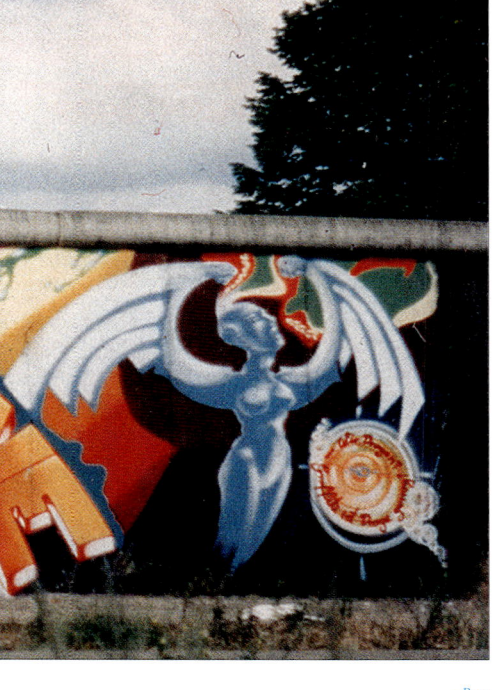

–Rew

always changed location due to the urban transformations of the city. The one in Hallesches Tor was demolished as well as Amok's, but now there are new places and the Berlin tradition of halls of fame continues. Somehow this tradition of painted walls is as as much a part of the city as the Berlin Wall, it was a tangible example of a painted surface for decades, at least along the Western part. The Wall has been considered an ideal surface by artists as well as writers, who definitely considered it as a target: a significant section of the S-Bahn line runs parallel to it, giving maximum visibility. You could see pieces painted by old school Berliners from the train. After 1989, when it was opened, the Wall passed through a transitory phase during which it was still paintable, as it had not been knocked down yet. There were still many parts of the Wall until 1992-94 just because the demolitions took quite a few years. It was easy as well, because there were two sides, the West side police didn't care much and wanting to have control of it was just pointless.

Besides writers, a lot of people were painting, from muralists to every kind of artist; there were so many parts of the Wall that the typical crossing behaviour of graffiti writers didn't occur, generating a sort of mutual respect. The writers took the North part where there were kilometres of wall with burners. The 'art' was in the centre of the city, more exposed to the ordinary public. This section definitely had more visibility and maybe the reason for this was that the artists had occupied it before the writers, but anyway it didn't affect their affair: writers often painted for themselves, staying in the shadows, while the muralists wanted to show their art (political) messages to the media and public, which were visiting the central parts of the Wall.

What this barrier really changed, was the local graffiti scene, which all of a sudden included writers from East Berlin. Before the boundaries were reopened, the East side wasn't painted because of the army. There were just a few writers using old cans from Hungary or Russia and painting with a brush. Obviously, once the West side writers went to the East to hit trains, yards and rail-track lines, a new generation of Berliners joined forces and the movement simply exploded all city.

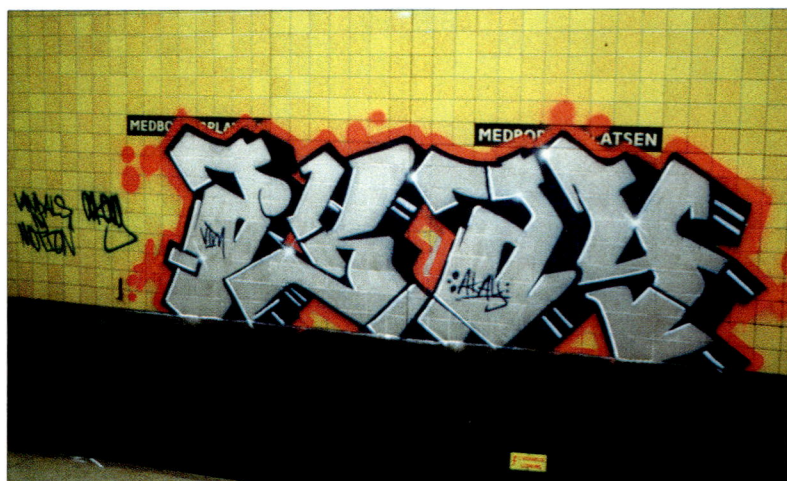

- Tobias Barenthin Lindblad, Dokument Press

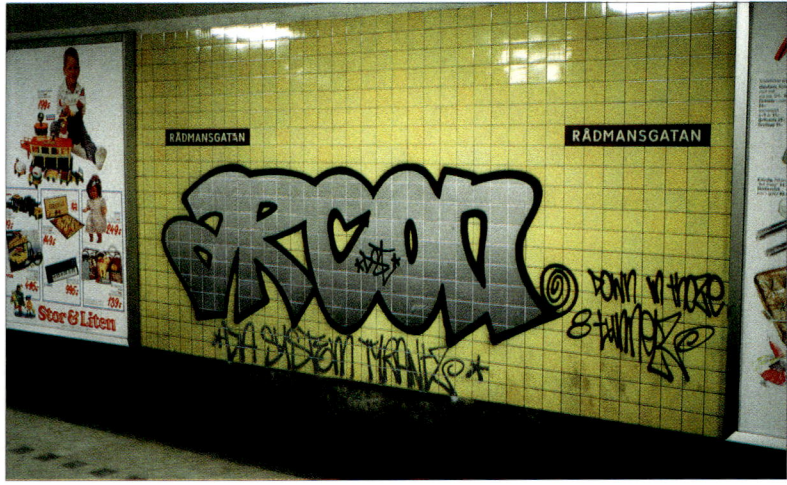

- Tobias Barenthin Lindblad, Dokument Press

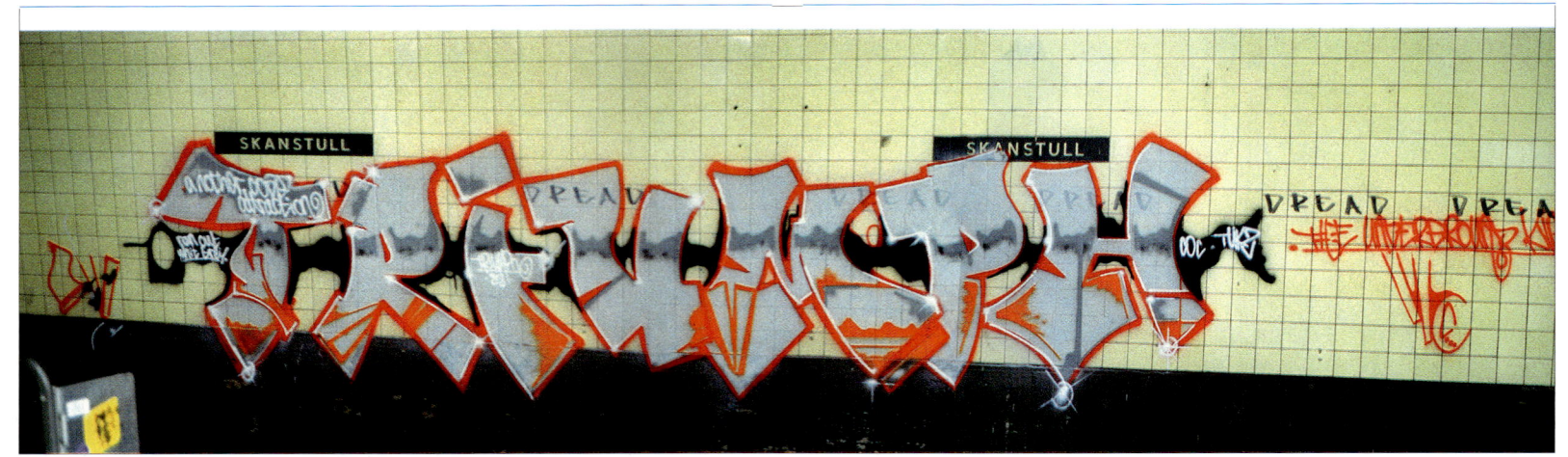

- Tobias Barenthin Lindblad, Dokument Press

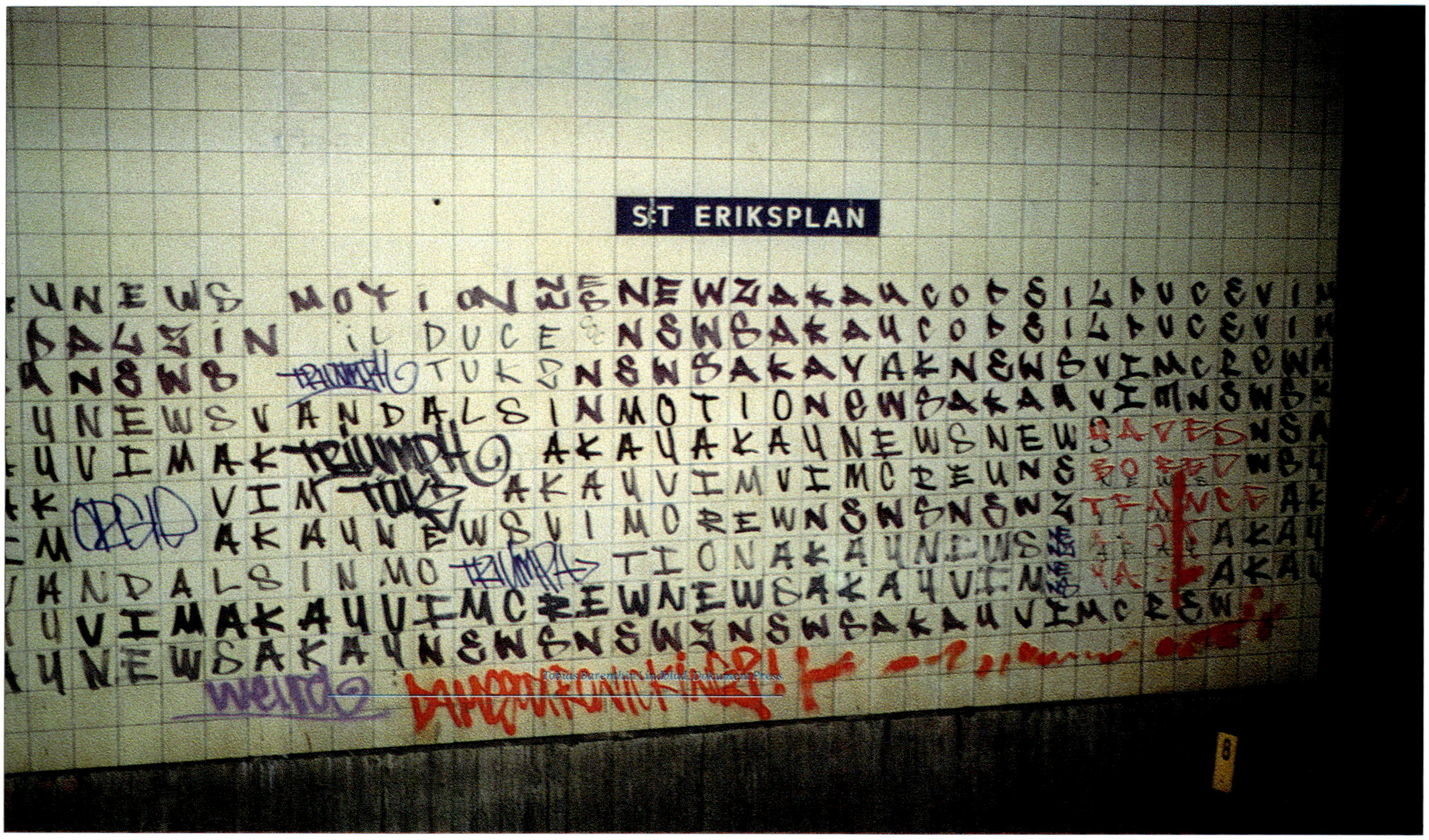

- Tobias Barenthin Lindblad, Dokument Press

All City Writers

LIFE STYLE

> Hip Hop transplanted from New York has noticeably influenced the first generation of European writers. Its interdisciplinary character, embracing music, dance and other performing arts, determined their lifestyle and generated a stereotype that often tied them to the figure of B-boys. Only in the 90's was there a gradual distancing from this cliché: the writer identity took various paths thanks to alternative reference points, portraying a kaleidoscopic image of the European scene, which included realities very distant from one another, sometimes tied to the Punk, Hardcore or skater world. Essentially diverse tastes and inclinations were juxtaposed: in England or in France for example many train bombers were an excrescence of other 90's movements, such as Rave culture. In truth, the cultural crossover that was taking place in those years was not new to the European scene. Writing one's name in the street had already been a prerogative of London punks in the 70's, while certain hints of 'autochthonous' Writing in Amsterdam and Madrid prove the direct involvement of various youth cultures active in that period. This multifaceted reality anticipated the real nature of an expressive phenomenon that was experienced individually and revisited even in terms of its tools, from blackbooks to caps, to markers.

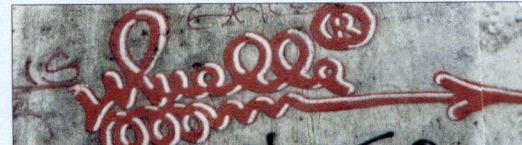

A STREET CULTURE

The unusual case of Amsterdam at the end of the 70's. The distribution of *Faith of Graffiti* influences the young punks of the city.

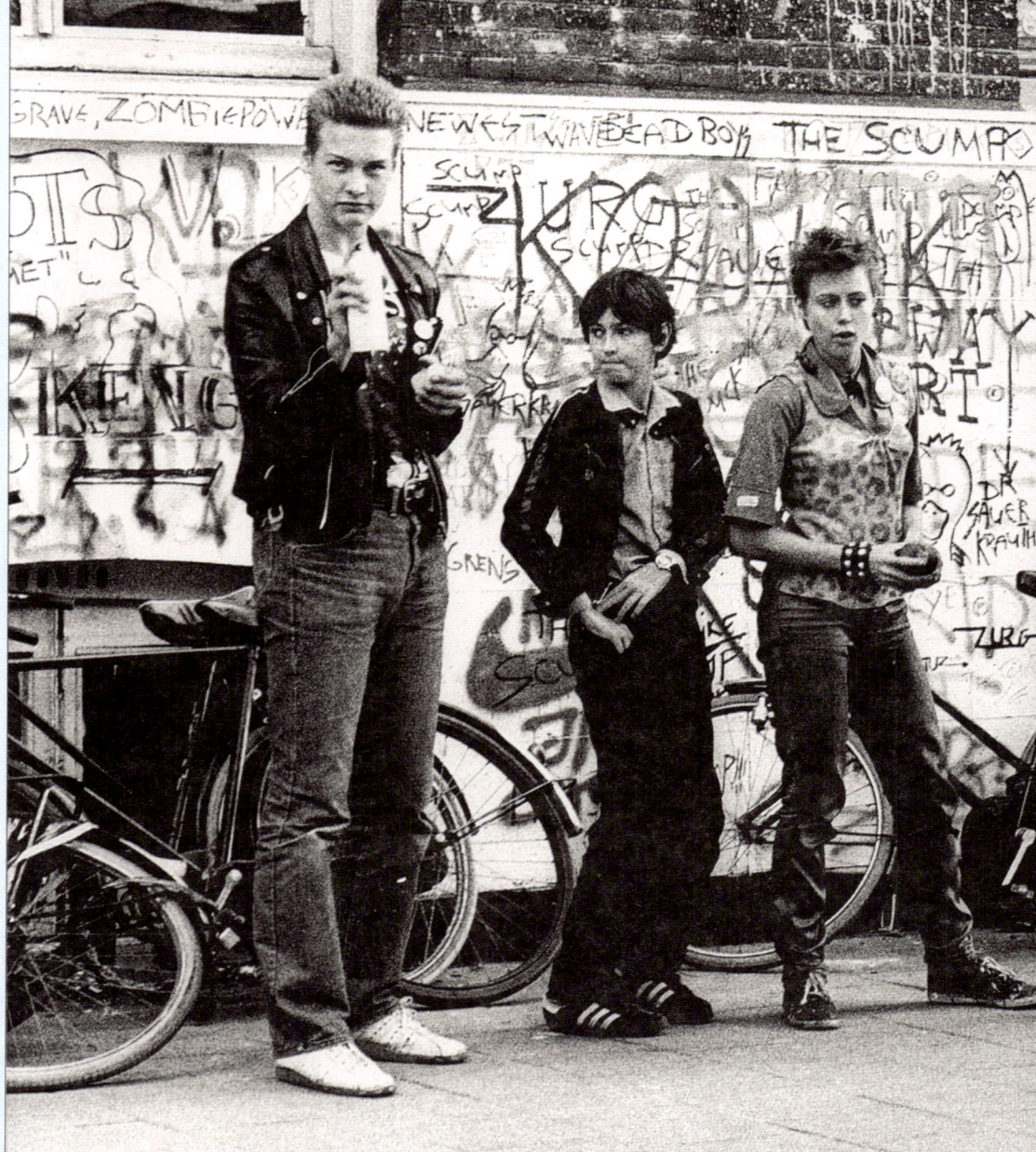

Interview with Cat22, formerly *The Dumb*

Could you describe the Amsterdam scene when the early Names started to be seen all over the city?
In 1977 there was a huge Punk movement in England and even here in Amsterdam. I loved that movement. I would go to concerts in these squat houses and everybody was tagging the walls with the names of the bands "Infection" "the Bugs" "Jesus and the gospel fuckers". Those are the names I remember. It was a very brief period, because within a couple of months people were writing their own names, which were not necessarily connected to the bands.

Was it a nickname?
Yes, it was mostly with "DR". Everybody was a Dr. Something, and with a marker they would put a character next to it which would stand for the person. One thing I can remember regarding bombing in 1977 was that in Amsterdam there was a police station with all their cars parked out front, and this guy, Anus Pelikanus, tagged every car door! So you saw all these cars driving around the city with the tags on the doors. Thousands of people must have seen that. It blows your mind!
A couple of days later I racked my first Eding 500 and I started tagging. But the very first Name I placed around with a spray can was Attack: I went to a local warehouse and stole my first can; it was a Ford Blue, metallic: 125ml

of lousy paint. I went to the post office and I put a huge Attack! on it. A couple of days later when I tagged around Amstelveen (a suburb of Amsterdam where I lived), I remember I hit a bus stop and a car stopped, the door swung open, and people dressed in plain clothes climbed out. I started running! They were after me.
That's my first chase: 1977. I got caught! I was 15 years old, I didn't even realise tagging was illegal; it didn't even cross my mind. I was sitting in the back of the car and the guy was asking me "Did you do that one?" and I'd reply "Yeah!".

The boys in blue...
Yes, they were undercover! I didn't even know what undercover meant. So I had to clean it, and the following

Thursday, the local paper came out, and on the front page there was a picture of the old "Attack" and then a shot of the clean spot; it said "Attack has been caught!" That article made me what I am today.

It was a kind of instant fame
Yes, I realised it immediately, and at that point I decided I had to change my Name.

You were probably the first European writer to change his Name for this reason.
Exactly, I got caught! Then I changed my Name to "Dumb", a dumb Name but I got out real strong with it. Gasp remembers that name from the period when I used to bomb his neighbourhood. At that point with Vendex,

CROSSOVER

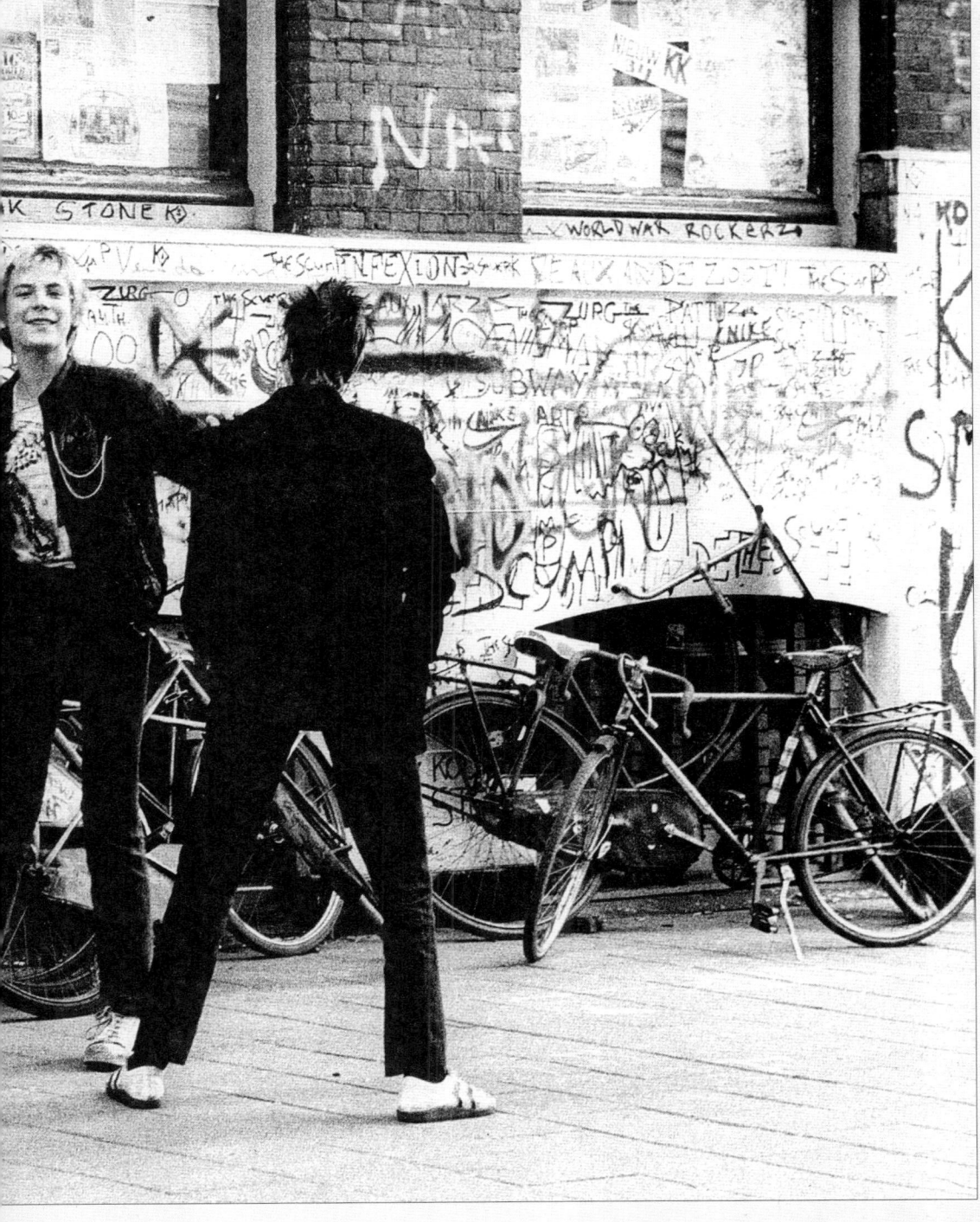

—*Steye Raviez*

NL PUNKS

PRIVATE ARCHIVE
Towards the end of the 70's
Steye Raviez portrayed
the first writers
of Amsterdam, coming
from the Punk scene.
In this photo: The Dumb,
De Kid, Cretchen, Vendex
and De Zoot

De Zoot, N-Power and Dr. Rat, we visited Weesperplein subway station which wasn't even finished yet, so we went and bombed it before it opened. We had walked a bit in the tunnels which were all fresh. It went well, it exploded! It was in the newspapers and it was huge! Then during 1977-'78 and late '79 it started to die off, because there was no progress. We had the article in *Parool*, we did so much more and you could have done so much more. But it comes to a point where the 'more' means nothing anymore.

Also because maybe you didn't develop a letter style.
Yes and besides that there was no competition. There was no battling. The state of mind changed too: at that point it became very political with the squatters. A lot

of writers left Writing like I did and got involved in Left-wing orientated political activism. That's what I did and I forgot about Writing. Some of the early writers were kind of intellectual. Vendex, for example, is a news reporter for the radio, De Zoot is married in Jerusalem with eight children, and N-Power became a very famous illustrator. Then after this first generation, around '82-'83 a lot of guys with ordinary backgrounds came up and started bombing: Zo, Ego, Mano. OK, Dr. Air, Trip, Walking Joint. They were all working class guys. They had a better approach: they were more into the New York way of bombing. Maybe they had the book *Watching My Name Go By* as a reference. The story goes that the three of them had a map of Amsterdam, they divided the city into parts, and each one would do a different part, taking

over Amsterdam with the all-city idea. Those guys understood what I hadn't.
I was too naïve so I quit and gave myself to political activism. I could see those guys becoming big Names, but I wasn't interested until one day in October 1984, I was on a bike with a friend of mine and I saw a green Shoe piece. I had never seen a piece before and it literally blew me off my bike. It's a very risky spot, always trafficked. I wondered how he had done it, but it was there and it was beautiful! That was the thing that turned me on! The next morning at 9 o'clock I got back in the game.

A complete switch in your life.
Exactly, I saw the light. So I started wrecking and I realised I needed paint. It was like a renaissance.

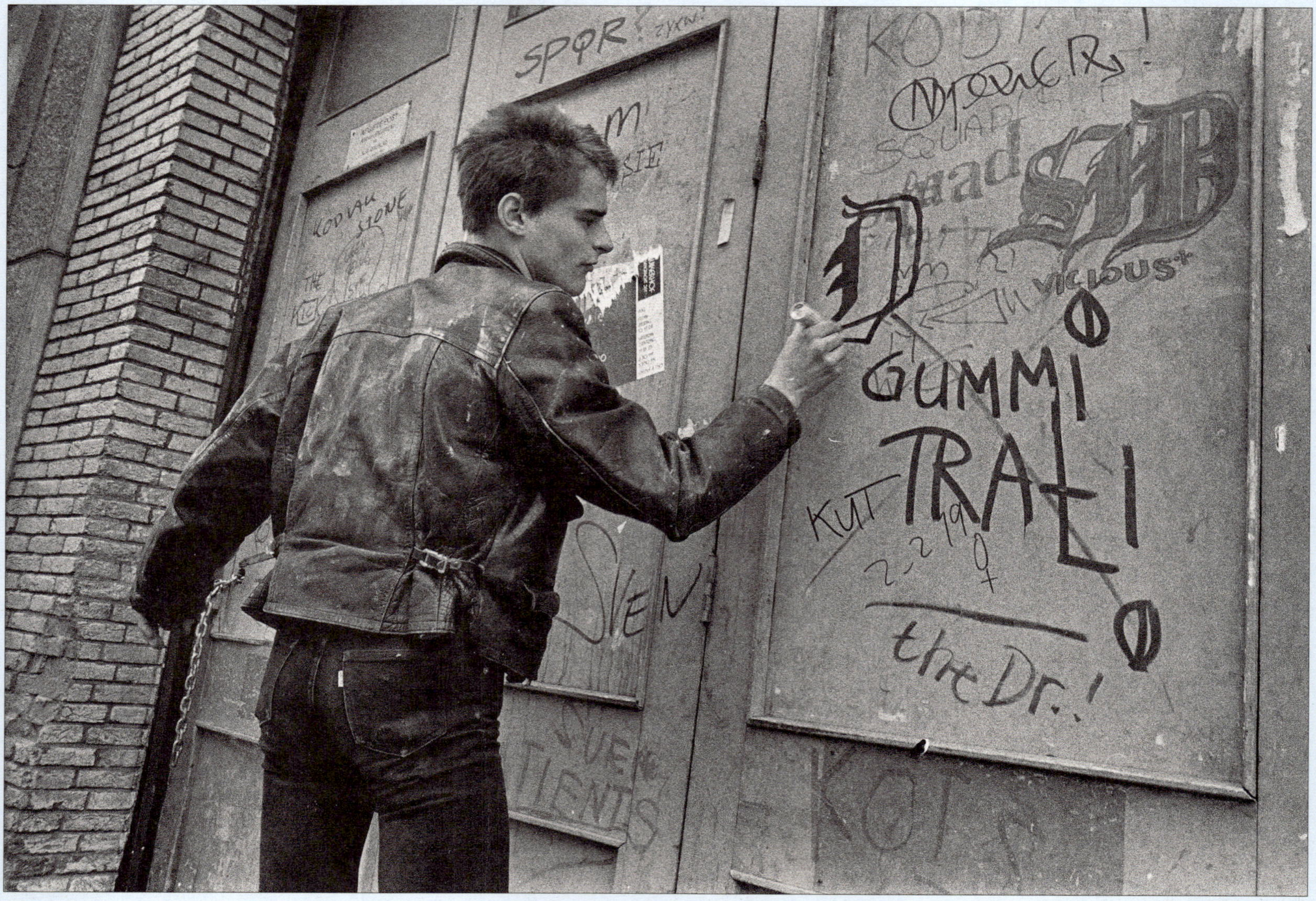

—Steye Raviez

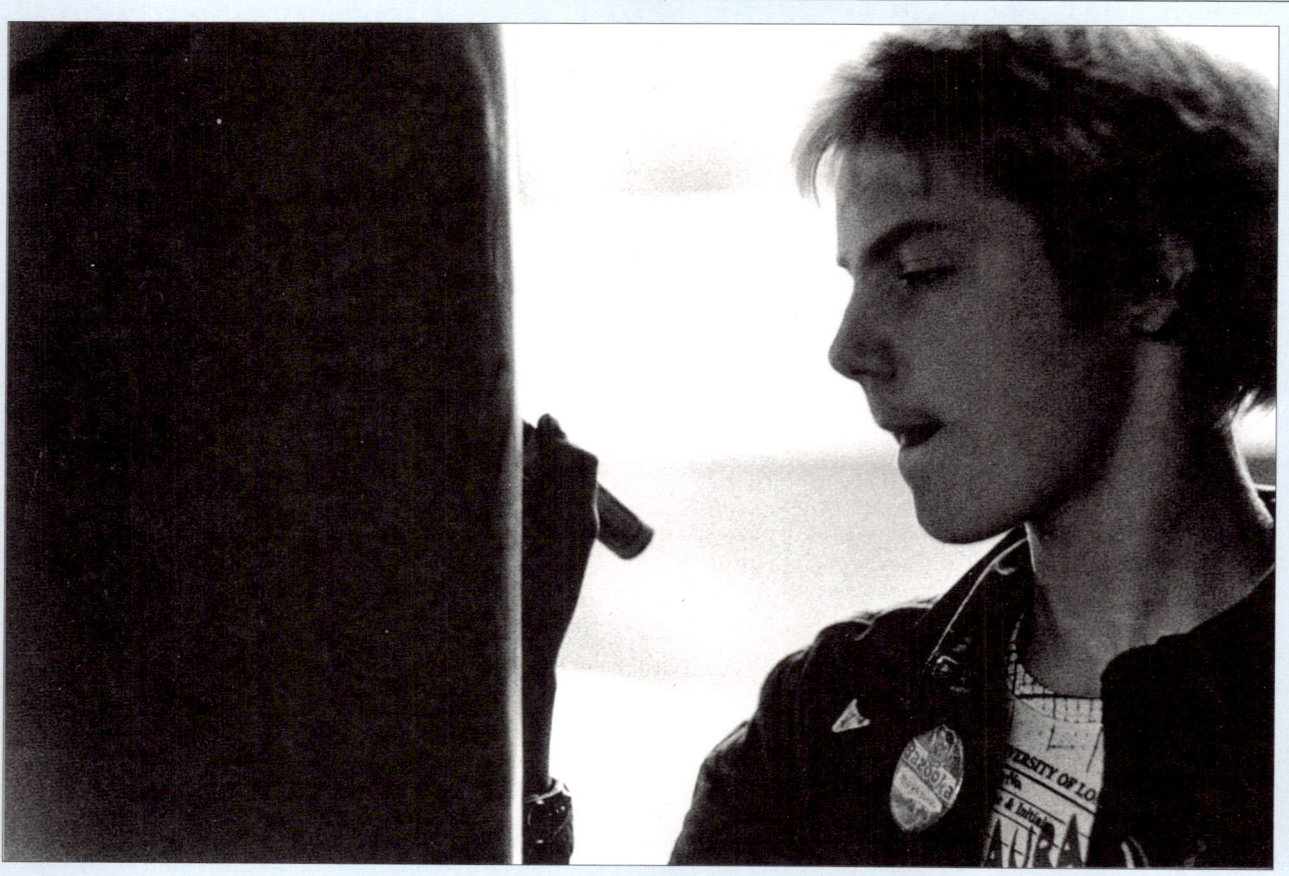

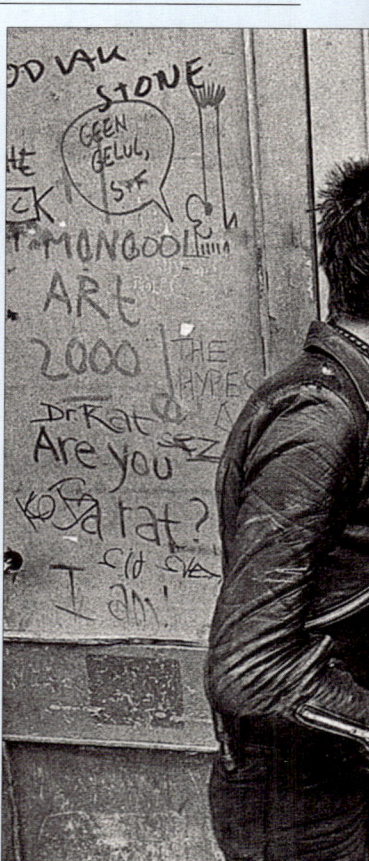

—Steye Raviez

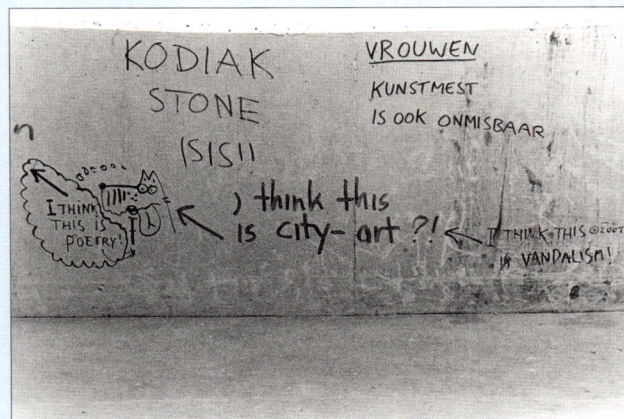

—*Steye Raviez*

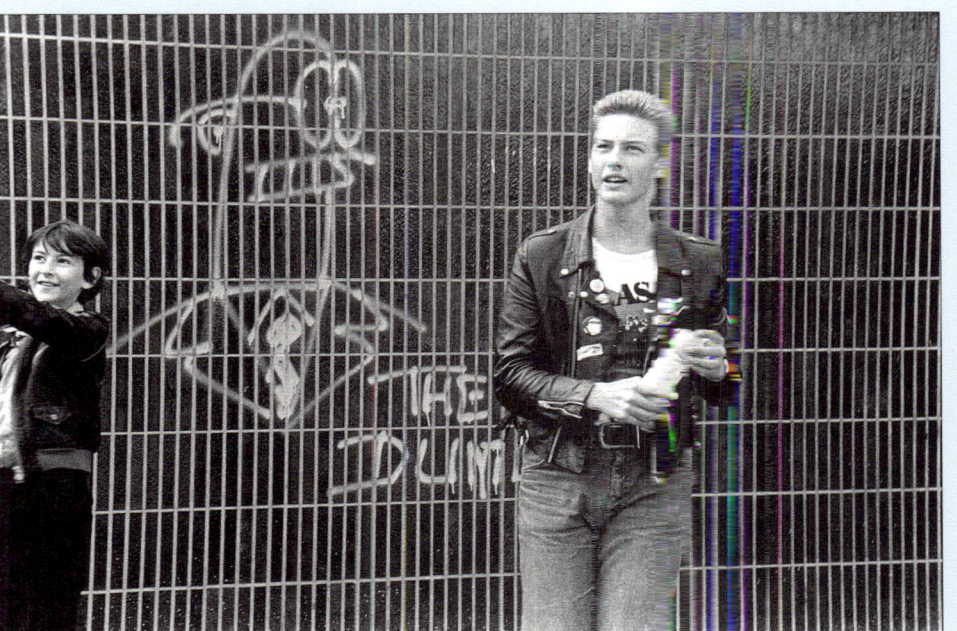

—*Steye Raviez*

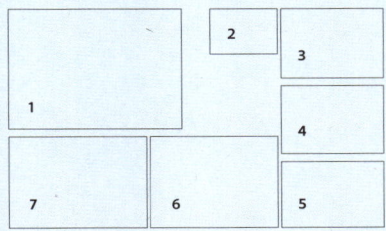

1 Dr Rat as he traces his gothic signature

2 De Zoot – Kodiak Stone

3 The Dumb

4 Vendex and The Dumb in action

5 Vendex

6 De Zoot and Dr Rat

7 Vendex

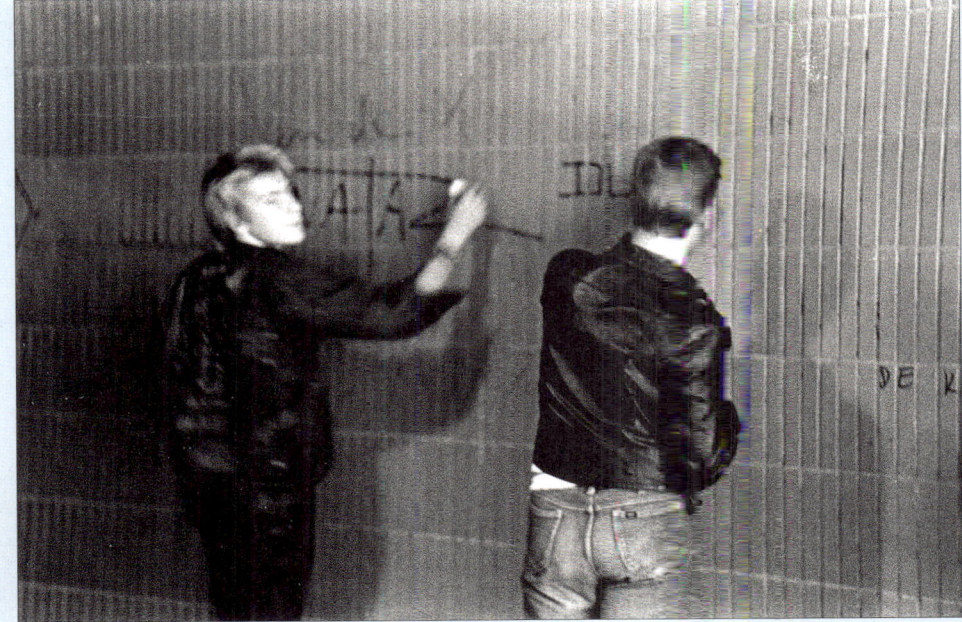

—*Steye Raviez*

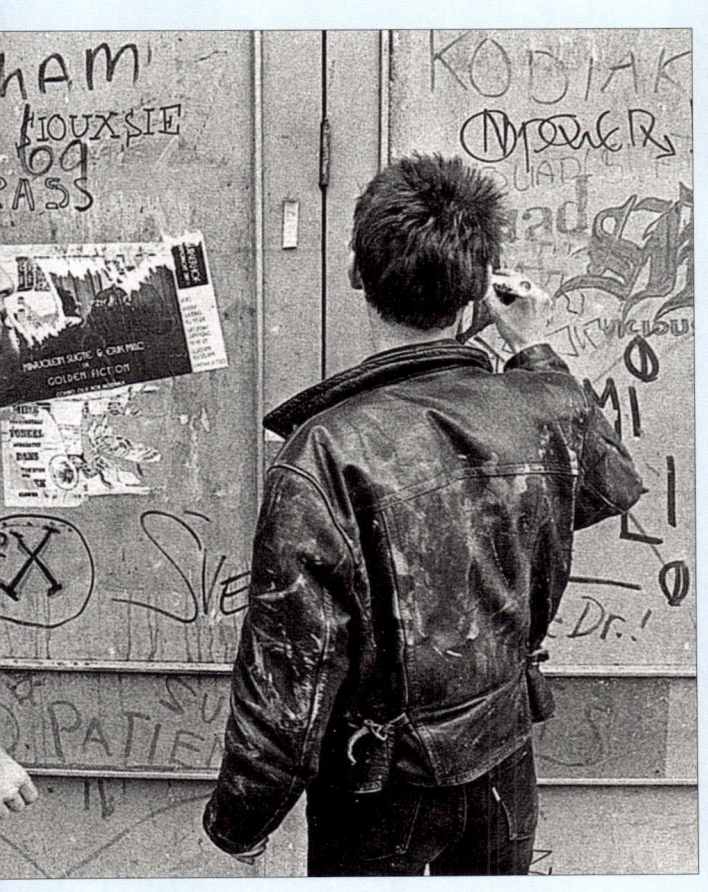

—*Steye Raviez*

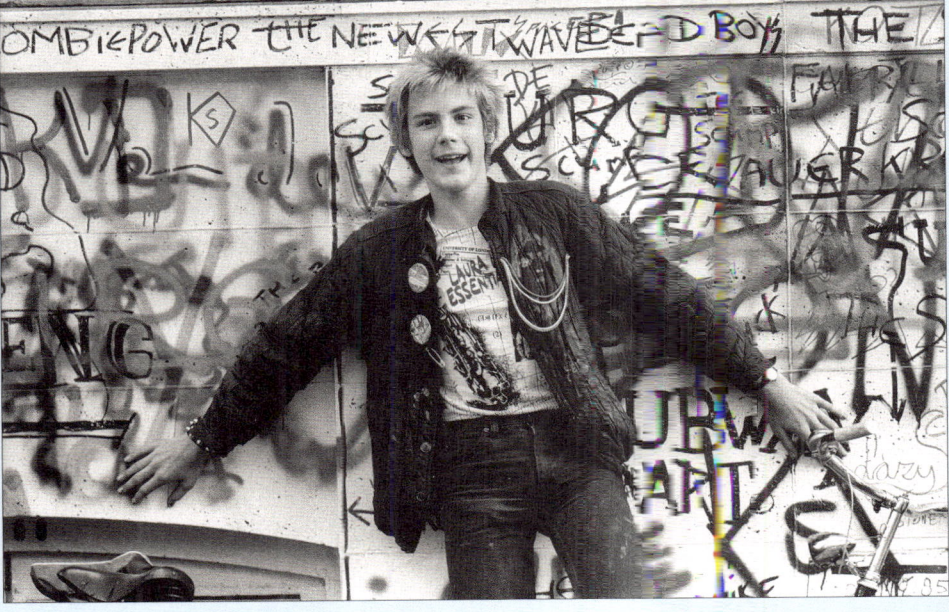

—*Steye Raviez*

Who said the province was dead?

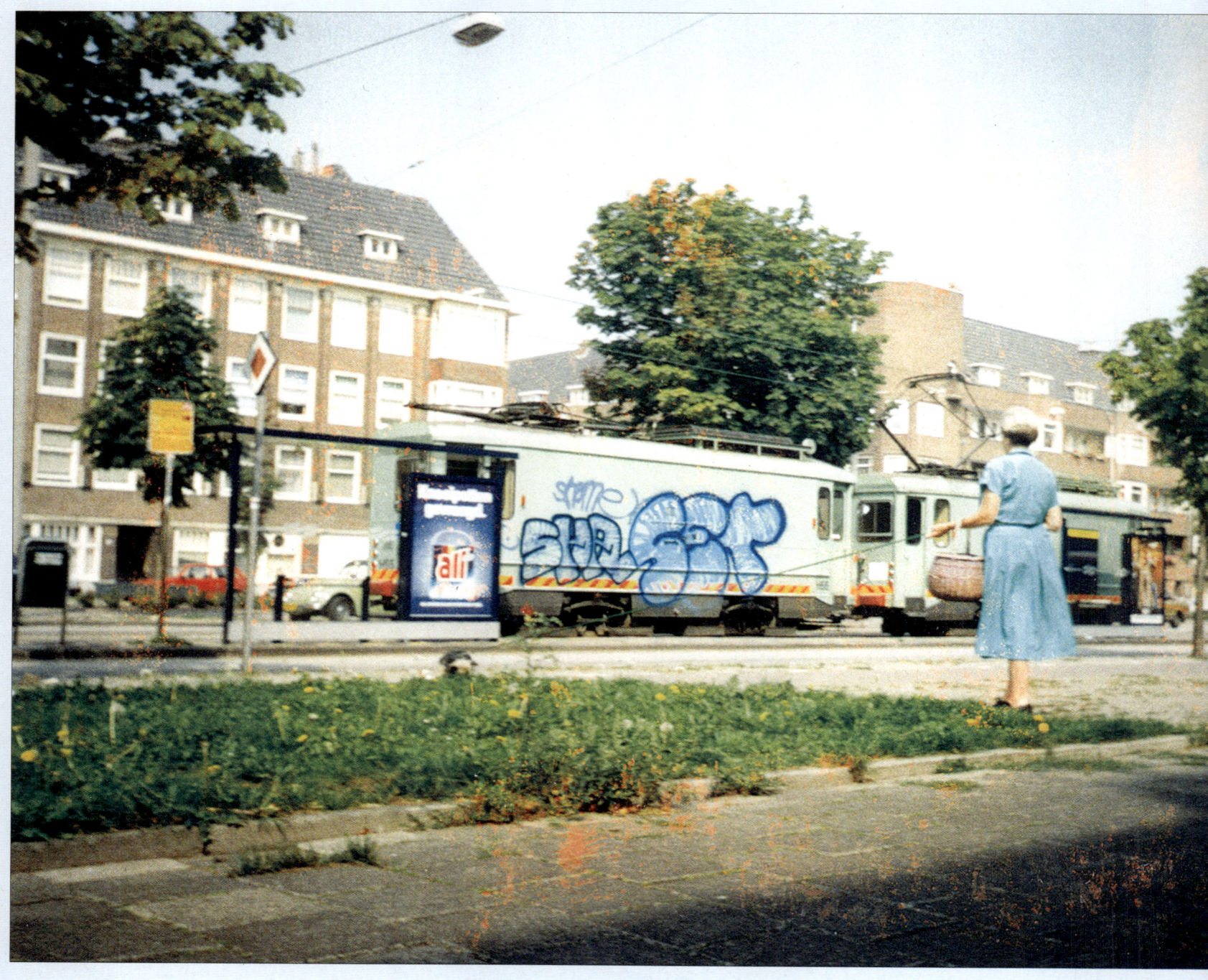

Zedz – INC / Amsterdam
>

grew up in Leiden, a small city close to The Hague and during the early 80's I used to see tags when I'd go out of the city by car with my parents. I remember those signs were more or less straight letter Names, mainly spotted in and around the cities of Leiden and The Hague. Names like Hunter, Leeds, Jackson, Xex... I was always looking out of the car window for the next one. If I knew there was a tag on a certain wall I would wait for it, imagining who the author could be. I figured out from the beginning that it was the Name of a guy or more likely a couple of guys. I thought it probably would have been a group of people and not a single guy because all of a sudden those signs started appearing all over the place. In this period my perception of time was really distorted, I couldn't imagine somebody being able to destroy the town in just a few weeks... back then everything was still

clean, the city was untouched, which of course made it easier to stand out. I immediately considered graffiti as a Name, not messages, and I got fascinated by this idea of having a hidden identity. So I was directly influenced by what I saw in the city, not by media like *Subway Art* or *Style Wars*. I just saw letters appearing across the city, not even complex tags but just straight-written letters, perhaps made by somebody who aspired to be legible, who wanted to get his Name out there. I remember big print capital letters, these people put a lot of effort into writing their Names clearly, adding only a few elements. There was someone who did a lightning bolt under the last letter; he used to write "Xex", and the letter X was just perfect for the lightning at the end.
Sometimes he drew clouds around the tag, implosion and explosion-type clouds. These were the few style elements. Then I clearly remember guys writing in my town later on, who used to tag their letters with big heads; a big top and a small bottom. In the beginning I did copy

the straight letter style, as indeed there was a straight, graphic identity to this Name Writing and it had a big impact on kids like me; to be legible seemed most important. Then one day this guy Zoré, hit up my neighbourhood and his style really impressed me, his style was funkier and harder to copy than others, there was flow and identity in this. Very soon, right around the time that the first Rock Steady Crew video clips were aired, I saw two proper graffiti pieces along a street in my town; by Zoré and his partner Yank. I was just a kid and my parents wouldn't allow me to go there and see them close-up, I could only glance at the wall while passing by car and then try to memorise the pieces. I couldn't wait to go downtown with my parents! I was looking forward to the next Saturday as this was the one and only opportunity to spot that small artwork. This piece was a step up even with respect to the first evolution of scribbles into outlined tags, no; these were proper pieces! Of course it pushed me to try and start drawing. There were two guys

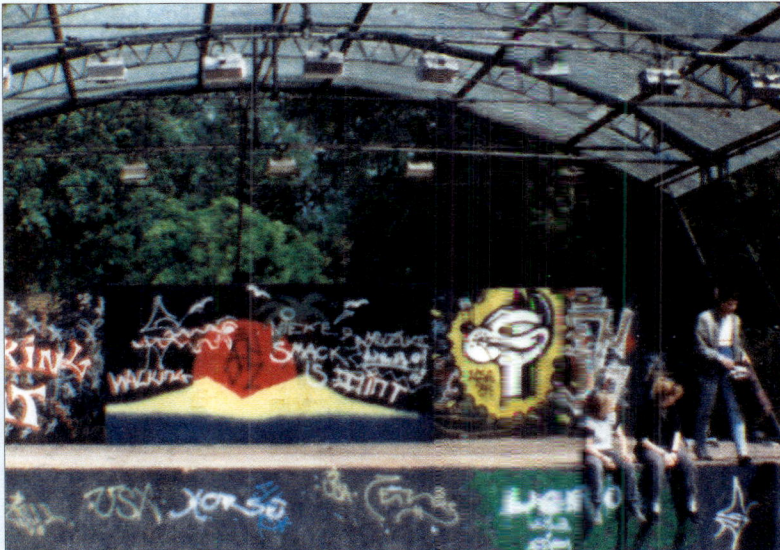

The Vondelpark stage, hang-out of punks and skinheads of Amsterdam in 1984 — Rhyme

living on my street who also shared this common passion; we would get markers and spray paint together. We started using them during the day and early in the evening as we weren't really old enough to go out at night. After school, around 4 o'clock, we would walk or take a bike to go across Leiden and try to do something but obviously our first tags were very straight bars, mainly capitals, legible lettering. I decided to write "Essex" as other people were finding tags based on the names of cities... we started looking in the index of an atlas and I found a name with an X, it was important to have an X at the end because this way I could do the lightning bolt which I fancied a lot. Right after using straight letters I moved to the new flow I had seen in the writings of Zoré. I started filling in, making the letters sharper, influenced only by the few inputs brought to me by the media. With *Subway Art* and the first pictures we exchanged, we finally had 'frozen' images, and the time to observe them. When you'd see the Rock Steady Crew videos on television you'd be waiting for those few moments to focus on the piece for one second. I couldn't grasp it but you could feel something; like the funky letters or the colours and from that you started filling in the gaps. Suddenly with printed books it all became clearer and more accessible. That was the only way to let us study the structure and composition of letters as there was still not that much graffiti on the streets and I was too young to totally style things by myself. Within two years I went from being a kid who wasn't allowed out in the evening to one that realised he had to sneak out at night. I would set my alarm clock for 3 am, and of course it was massively loud... you had to hit the button before your parents would wake up! The first time you'd shit your pants sneaking out

> **It was important to have an X at the end because this way I could do the lightning bolt which I fancied a lot**

because everything in the house made sounds. I think I figured out this night-factor when one morning I arrived at school and there was a huge graffiti piece... I understood it must have been done during the night and that was exactly the way to do it. Pieces started to pop up all over the city, quite randomly. Several Names appeared along the tracks, probably because some older guys were into travelling to Amsterdam, where so many pieces were concentrated along the lines. The rail track became the attractor everywhere and of course it brought us to visit Amsterdam, looking for new pieces to see. At one point, around 1985, we planned the first big mission! One day on TV they promoted a big graffiti job done in Amsterdam featuring the United Street Artists. My parents wouldn't allow me to go and nobody would take me either, so me and my friend decided we had to go there by ourselves. We simply couldn't wait anymore! On the way to Amsterdam we could see graffiti from the train and I think I had already seen some of those pieces on photos, we were literally glued to the train windows. We passed through central station and then went to Bijlmer because we knew the job was done there, asking people for directions all the time. Obviously we got off at the wrong station and the whole place was bombed! There were tags, throw-ups, even Quik pieces! I think we were nearly crying, our mouths were wide open. But to be honest, we were scared because we realised it was a shady looking area: you could get robbed and beaten up, and people looked like they could have been going around with guns or knives. Ok, well maybe it wasn't like that, but from our perspective as kids coming from a small town... indeed it was!

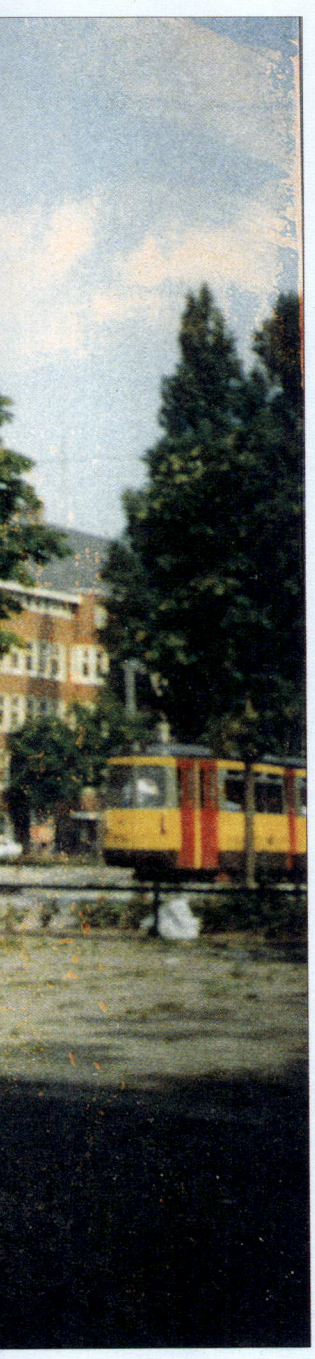

— ACW Archive

URBAN CONFLICT

The Netherlands in the mid 80's: the Writing aesthetic unsettles the equilibrium of historic European cities

Hitting the switch

Vondelpark, a convergence of all underground movements

Rhyme –GVB / Amsterdam
>

Vondelpark in the early 80's, especially in the summer time, was really full on, especially near the music stage. You had this big group of diverse youngsters just hanging out: skinheads, rastafarians, punks, squatters... just a whole melting pot of everything including guys and girls who were tagging or at least putting their Name up. The first big tags and pieces started to grow up here. Like the Walking Joint: three guys who drew a joint with arms and legs and there was smoke coming out from his head. They were all-city! They started doing really big outlines and made colourful drawings with nice backgrounds, and when they retired they gave me three bags full of left-over cans; the best present ever, for this by then 13-year old graffiti kid. Guys like Ego and Dragon also did their Names in really big letters. I'm talking about sometimes three metres high with shadows in different colours... just really big! Even DR.Rat was an inspirational multi-talent and his friends already did a lot from 1977, mostly with markers or paint brushes, this was graffiti on a different level... bigger and better! In Amsterdam at the time there wasn't a connection with Hip Hop, the whole concept didn't exist yet in Europe. That only started from 1983 and it was related to graffiti by 83-84, but it wasn't a must to be part of the movement as there were already all sorts of people doing graffiti and listening to all sorts of music. Of course when it really started booming it was Hip Hop influenced but as most of the graffiti writers were coming from all sorts of backgrounds, they we all really diverse. During those days, life in Amsterdam was very liberal, and there was also a lot

of anarchy. That started to fade out in the 90's, but during the 70's and early 80's there weren't a lot of jobs, or people just didn't want to work. They didn't give a shit, there were other things to be concerned about: a shortage of houses, the cold war between the U.S. and Russia, nuclear threats.

The young generation by then didn't feel like working, they would rather put their energy into anti-government movements and demonstrations. Obviously, along with this ruined scenario, graffiti was all over the city. Everything was bombed: from walls to public transportation, even the parks were bombed - regardless if it was a political message, a tag or just Names. That's what probably influenced me a lot: I started doing graffiti when I was 10. All these Names I was seeing around interested me, I couldn't avoid 'em so I just started doing what everybody was already doing. As before I was doodling in my school books, I simply transferred that diary habit onto the city.

Style-wise, Amsterdam played an important role in Europe. This city has a style of its own, it's very much art related and this is all part of the liberal mentality.

We could do for example a lot of pieces in the daylight and most people were like "good stuff you make the streets look better!" A lot of commissions came as well, of them a lot with Delta in '85-'86: shutters for shops, billboards for festivals; the art form became mainstream and fashionable. I don't know if somewhere else kids were open minded about telling their parents they had done a train the night before. I did tell my parents, I had a very open relationship with them and I told them about almost every action I did, or if they asked me I would be honest. I hope I can give my kids the same education. It's very important to have trust and have an open relationship. It's very much about confidence. If your kids have to do stuff in secret then you can't give them a goal or point them in the right direction.

MADRID FLECHEROS

The Flecheros phenomenon is born in Madrid at the hands of a single character: Muelle. The arrow he traces underneath his tag becomes a trademark of the Madrilenian streets

Fernando Figueroa
>

In the early 80's various signatures started appearing on the walls of Madrid. Their origin seemed very distant from the Writing of American matrix, though certain dynamics repeated themselves in a similar manner: the act of signing, the concept of getting up, the construction of an alter-ego and the accuracy of design and decorative finishes such as arrows, made these marks very similar to the tagging of New York in the 70's. In Madrid various counterculture environments were involved in this phenomenon, and where urban centres were concerned it often coincided with the common habit of youngsters to form groups. The principal divulger of this current was Muelle, a kid from the neighbourhood of Campamento – in the district of La Latina – who, with his trademark pictogram, achieved success far beyond the city's limits. His work and his example in a short amount of time managed to alter the urban landscape of a European capital that was opening up to the winds of change and democracy. Muelle's way of painting, his life philosophy and ethics, apart from a couple episodes that marked his life and his premature death, elevated him to legendary figure of Madrilinean autochthonous graffiti. He signed

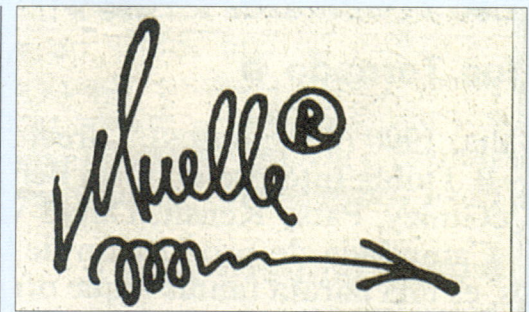
Muelle, original sketch   —*Felipe Galvez*

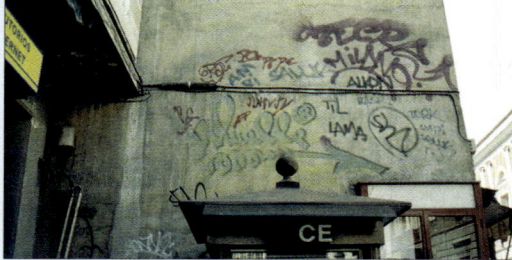
Muelle attracts other taggers   —*Felipe Galvez*

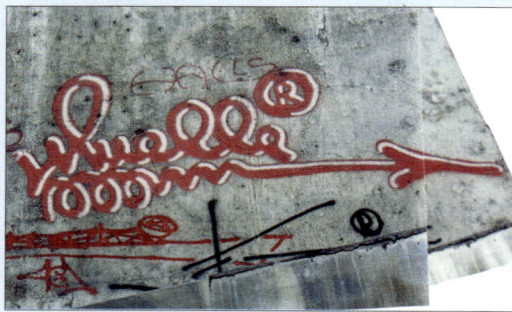
Muelle, tag with highlights   —*Felipe Galvez*

Bufon, Toro   —*Felipe Galvez*

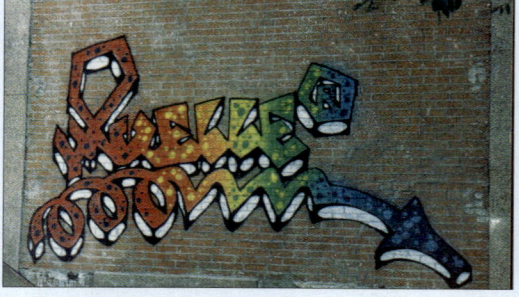
Muelle, tag as piece   —*Felipe Galvez*

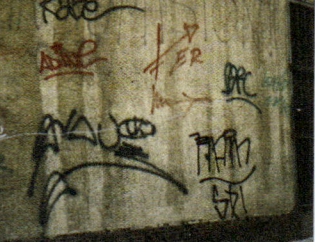
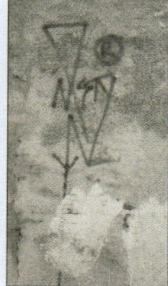
Fer, Msty and Flecheros tags in Madrid   —*Felipe Galvez*

> **Contrary to the New York tradition, those that signed with this style did not have the habit of grouping and forming crew Names**

spaces throughout the city and its infrastructures, becoming a promoter of road-tagging along the network of highways that connect Madrid to other regions.
With him a new movement took form in the Spanish capital that would be commonly defined *Flecheros*: those that belonged to it left visible signatures all over, in a way that was similar to that of the heavy metal, punk or new wave aesthetic. Contrary to the New York tradition, those that signed with this style did not have the habit of grouping and forming crew Names, apart from a couple of isolated cases in competition with each other. Generally speaking, the Autoctonos looked for spots where damage to private property was minimal or non-existent, and were interested in obtaining the maximum visibility and duration for their signatures. The primary hotbeds developed in the periphery of Madrid, with the district of La Latina as the most important epicentre, which included areas like Campamento and Aluche. Other neighbourhoods soon followed, such as Aganzuela, Vallecas and Moratalaz or, to the North, Fuencarral, Tetúan and Chamartín, which would then connect with and influence the areas between them. The outskirts of Madrid became school to the autochthonous taggers, concentrating the potential of these actions in these same peripheral neighbourhoods, especially in recreational areas tied to youth culture and laziness, other than the large roads or highways like the M-30. The connection between these epicentres allowed this phenomenon to spread from the outskirts

> CONTINUES ON PAGE 148

RIVALRY RISING
—

Zeta / Madrid
>

In New York Writing was something that evolved in the ghetto, and although it would not be correct to use this term in relation to the cities in Spain, many people were living in pretty scanty neighbourhoods.
Me and some other kids had grown up in Alcorcòn, a centre of the metropolitan crown around Madrid in which there was no money, and if it's true that in such conditions the necessity to feel like somebody easily emerges, in a barrio like Alcorcòn, this push was even stronger. We pursued our own career, in

the street, also because we were cut off from any other possibility, from university or an official profession. We had no opportunities.
Perhaps this is why Writing initially exploded in marginal areas. In a brief amount of time Alcorcòn and Mostoles were invaded by groups of writers, painting in the street, on the ground floor of residential buildings, in broad daylight and without asking for permission, and people were liking it; nobody ever said anything to us, it was almost as if the ground floor of every building in these cities had become a single extended hall of fame.
When the first crews tied to

the Writing style of New York started forming in Madrid, their presence was partially overshadowed by the media's attention towards the Flecheros. In that period Muelle was in his peak phase and had already filled the city with thousands of tags many years before us. Certainly he was an essential figure in Madrid, his work is incontestable, but it's important to recognise and distinguish every phenomenon: he was responsible for the birth of the Flecheros movement, a native phenomenon, while the diffusion of Writing was tied to us, as we definitely kept the style and parameters of New York in mind

when painting.
At the beginning these aesthetic differences generated much friction, Muelle often criticised us for the fact we were not autodidacts and followed dynamics that were directly imported, a thing he always tried to avoid, preferring a local source of inspiration. It's important to remember however that it was also thanks to this new American wave that Muelle became so popular. His art was erroneously confused and associated with the Writing movement by the media, that same movement that we were supporting in Madrid and that the Flechers were ignoring.

Perros callejeros

The obstacles writers in Barcelona have to confront at the onset of the phenomenon: the choice of abandoned industrial spaces and the division into factions

Kapi – BTP / Barcelona
>

In Barcelona kids started painting in the street only after the train buffing system had started systematically cancelling the pieces in the subway, which was the real sole objective of the first writers. A wave of discouragement swept through them and thus it was that almost by chance the first hall of fame was created at Alfonso X plaza. At the end of the 80's painting in the city centre was tolerated and the dangers you encountered were others; in Barcelona and all of Spain poverty was thriving and could be clearly seen in the streets, the transitional years after the death of Franco had turned them into a no-man's land: going out of the house was anyway dangerous for anybody that wasn't a junkie or a delinquent. For the writers it was worse, having to move at night to hit the most visible spots: in a brief amount of time we became the primary targets and the situation got tense. At night we would move armed with knives, sticks, and brass knuckles because the most common dangers of the street were the heroin addicts and the gypsies, or in the worst case heroin junkie gypsies that mugged you of everything: shoes, money, your coat, anything.

Then there were the organised groups: punks and skins. Today we see them shopping in the city centre but at the time you would hear the screams coming from the end of the road while you were painting, and then the first rocks would arrive, there wasn't much time to argue or understand what type of danger was about to occur: you just took to your heels and ran, and this was a constant, daily occurrence. So the diurnal halls of fame were the best solution because the streets were calmer during the afternoon and the police had more pressing issues to consider rather than treat Writing as something illegal. The first years, from 1984 to 1988, all writers were united and shared the spaces of an abandoned factory in Glories, where we'd steal electricity and whatever else we needed from the neighbouring buildings so as to organise

our first parties in pure Bel-Street style. With time things changed when the number of writers started increasing, each with his own ideas.

When we started assiduously painting the streets, writers were divided into two main or groups. On one side the locals of Gràcia and Sant Andreu, and on the other, people that came from Carmelo, Santa Coloma, Horta. These neighbourhoods bordered each other and sometimes kids from one group would be in the area of the other, but all in all their origin was not that different, you can't compare this reality with that of the American gangs and their respective turf.

The rivalry however was heated and the stylistic comparison often gave way to verbal and physical confrontations. A fundamental factor tied to this was the age of the writers: generally those that were over 18 or 20 years of age were free to go wherever they wanted, because the hordes of 15 year olds, though rivals, wouldn't say a word against them but rather picked on kids their own age. The Gràcia group started sweating the scenes of London and Paris; which consisted of tags and throw-ups everywhere, with bombing as the main objective. All of a sudden the French styles had become the main reference point and the general rule for this group of Catalonian writers. In an attempt to compensate the aesthetic delay of Spain, this crew, captained by Fase, started systematically crossing with tags and throw-ups any hall of fame that followed other styles. Needless to say that started an intense period of rivalry during which the pieces of the two groups would last only briefly, before being systematically destroyed by the rivals.

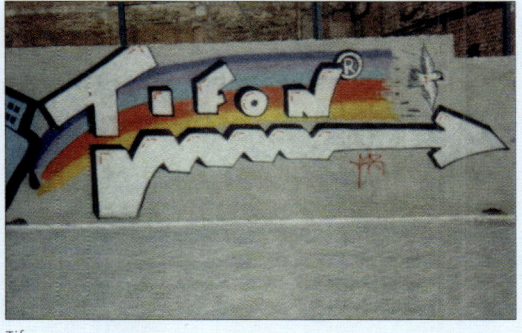
Tifon   —*Felipe Galvez*

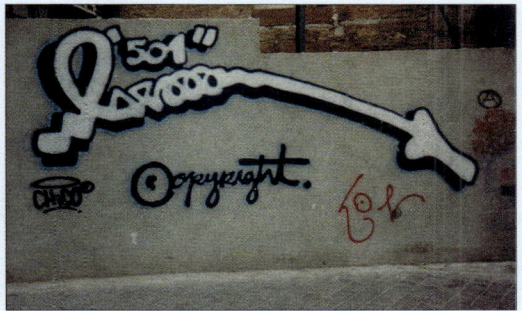
Max 501   —*Felipe Galvez*

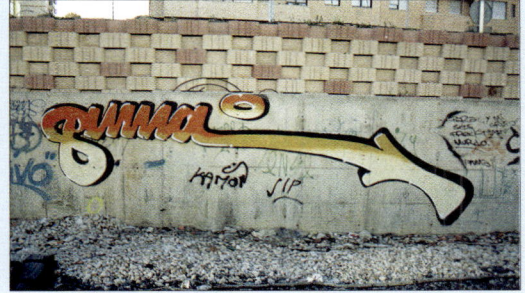
Puma   —*Felipe Galvez*

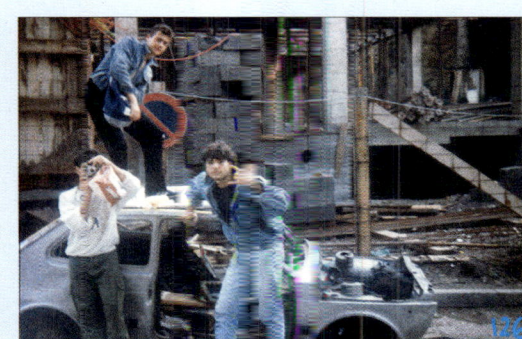
Koa, Taka and Sesac in 1987   —*Koa*

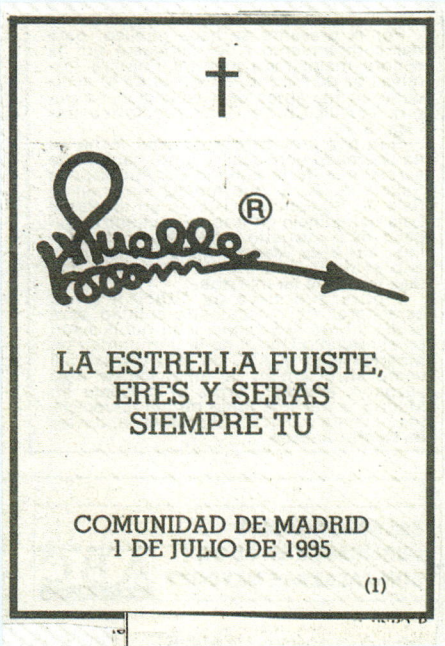
Muelle's obituary by the municipality   —*Felipe Galvez*

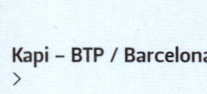

LA ESTRELLA FUISTE, ERES Y SERAS SIEMPRE TU

COMUNIDAD DE MADRID
1 DE JULIO DE 1995

(1)

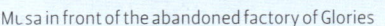
Musa in front of the abandoned factory of Glories   —*Kapi*

MODERN WRITERS

The European writer identity
and its progressive distancing
from the figure of the B–boy

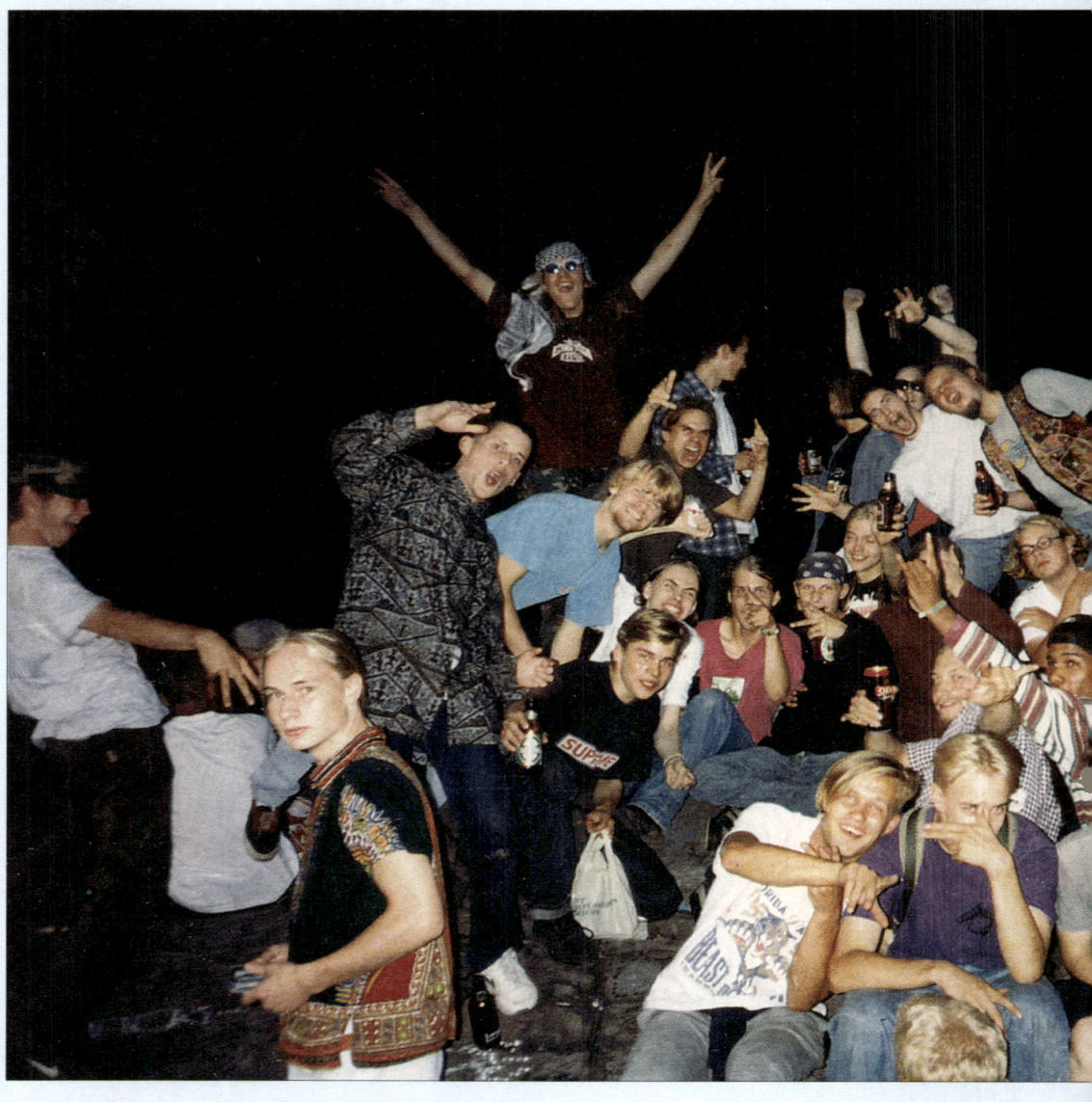
Crazy train bombers reunited in Scandinavia, early 90s

Zebster – COD / Budenheim
>

After the Breakdance wave of the early 80's, this discipline just faded out of mainstream channels. It wasn't in the public eye anymore, people just thought it was cool but 'out'. The only reason for this probably had to do with the fact that the next wave came through and the old one was forgotten. Only those that were really into the culture didn't give up. Breaking wasn't new anymore but in those early years, starting from 1983, it was a milestone for subculture in Europe.

A handful of people worked together to transport the New York formula and spread it everywhere; London and Paris were cities that Hip Hop had infected pretty early on. Through the New York City Rap Tour the scenes in Paris and London were able to hear the first voices of this new culture. This had a very strong impact, various scenes grew out of this context yet it didn't spread all over Europe that much. In Germany it started later because that New York tour didn't reach any city outside those in France and London, but once it began to spread it did so quickly throughout Germany as well. The development of German Hip Hop was radically different, probably because it wasn't centralised like that of France

or the UK, where almost everything was based in the capital. Our strength on the other hand was based on a network of many cities like Frankfurt, Köln, Hamburg, Munich, Dortmund and the Mainz area.

The same city of Berlin was initially playing a secondary role, since it was geographically isolated from the rest of the country during the whole of the 80's. So these capillary connections allowed a very positive competition in the scene to spread all over the nation.

A considerable opportunity during this building phase came from the German public transport authority, as there was a train-pass available for just 250 Marks. With 125€ we were able to use every train for one month without limitations. This gave us the chance to move around after school, to paint something or meet somebody and then come back home. Over the weekend we used to travel 1200kms! Of course a big issue every month was how to get enough money for that pass, after the first big jams in '87 - '88 people wanted to travel and meet others as much as they could. Rumour had it that in Dusseldorf there were some B-boys, in Heidelberg as well and even more in Dortmund. Swift, one of the most famous B-boy in Germany, lived in Kiehl, which is a rural place behind Hamburg. It was a long trip, 7 hours.

So people started to travel, there was a group of maybe ten people including JBK, Swift, Storm, Can 2, me and Jase who really did it monthly. We had no private life

back then, we were totally devoted to our culture! Then there were some writers like Mr C. from Dortmund or Loomit who were also travelling on an International basis to hit every type of train. Not necessarily as a crew, sometimes alone, sometimes in couples; there were combinations but it was kind of random. So we were in Sweden, Denmark and the Netherlands very early on. Personally, I became a workaholic, trying to bring people together from different countries. I simply started to look outside of Germany and understand how the Hip Hop culture was spreading around Europe. I realised that in France they had radio, and a magazine - at this time there was Hip Hop Connection, a professional Hip Hop magazine. It became clear we had to build the foundation. Step by step we kept the Hip Hop culture on a high level and a lot of people followed us. I would say there were a lot of strong heads that really pushed it hard, the German attitude to do things bigger helped a lot in this case.

There's also the market situation: Germany had 60 million inhabitants even before the Wall was knocked down, compared to other countries it therefore had more of an opportunity to conquer a slice of the market were we to come up with our own product. It's no coincidence that some of the most important businesses belonging to graffiti culture are based in Germany, like two of the biggest spray can companies. The fat caps and the skinny caps are produced in Germany as well.

RECALL

IN BETWEEN

Fume –MSN / Düsseldorf
>

Düsseldorf 1985. There were different youth groups: the punks, the mods, the skinheads, the poppers, new wave kids with nice clothes)… all sorts of different groups. Me and my friends didn't really feel comfortable within any of those, so when Hip Hop came it was newer and more radical than anything else. It was even trashier than the others.
There was the punk bar of the city where we used to go, The Clash were always on the air. Then all of a sudden you heard Grand Master Flash and we were really rocking the dance floor with our big chains, strange caps, baggy trousers and fat laces! We were doing all these moves and breakdancing while even the punks were looking dissed. They were looking at us like "What the fuck is wrong with these kids?"

Bates – AIO / Copenhagen
>

I was doing electric boogie in '84-'85. Then I started noticing the background behind the dancing, and there was some graffiti. I tried to find out what it was all about and discovered it was related to Hip Hop culture. So slowly I started to move into graffiti and left dancing behind. That's how I got into the culture.

Stone –SAK / Munich
>

In my opinion the whole concept of Hip Hop came out in a very artificial way. It was the media that actually connected Break-dance with graffiti and Rap music, there was no movement called Hip Hop, which had four elements, it was an invention of *Wild Style*, Martha Cooper and the media. Even many New York writers had nothing to do with Hip Hop, for example Seen was a rocker, he listened to hard rock. I think more than 50% had nothing to do with it, maybe they even hated it. Ces (FX Crew) came to Munich to a jam once and saw all these guys with name belts, fat laces and just said "What's wrong with these guys?" When this idea of Hip Hop arrived to Germany, it was taken seri-

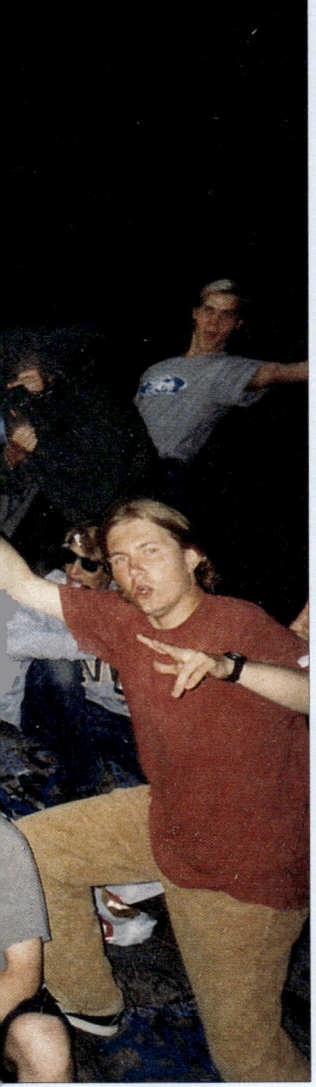
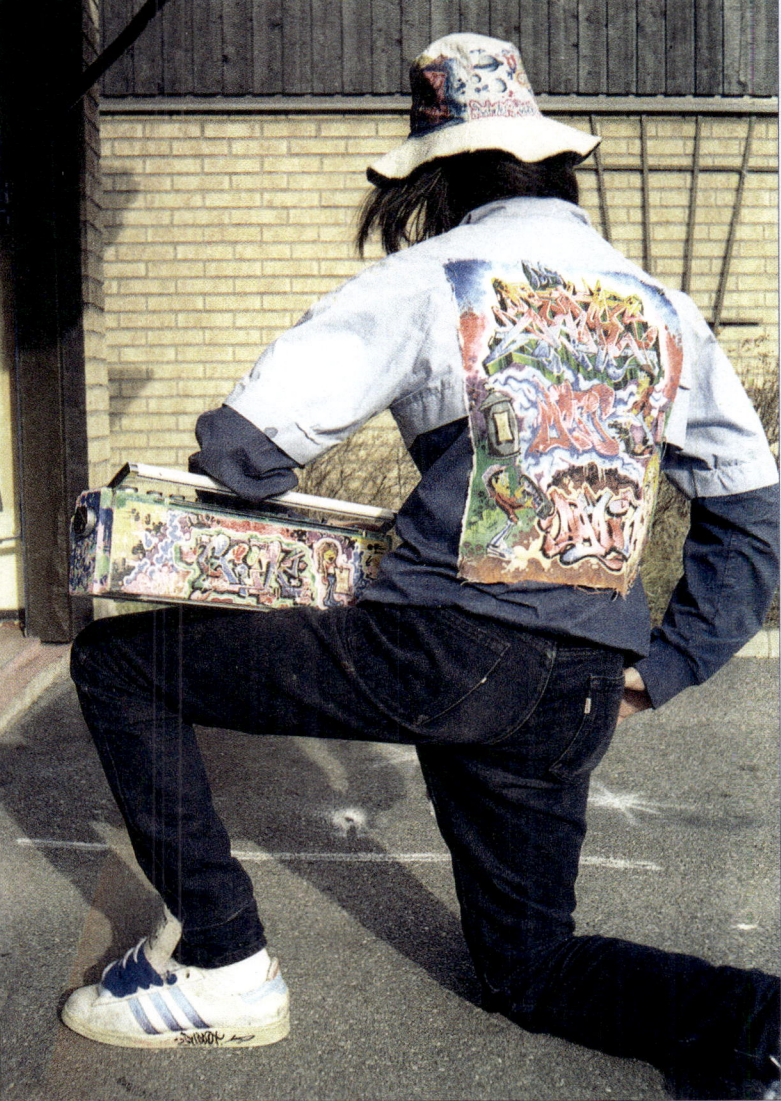

—Reaze   The Hip Hop wave inundates Europe: Backpiece and ghetto blaster customised by Puppet   —Puppet

– US ARMY AS LINK

For some cities like Frankfurt the early connections with Hip Hop culture were probably through the U.S. army bases. In Frankfurt an American soldier called Eddie Action formed a crew called *We Wear the Crowns* which was a major dancing group, they also had rap shows and produced music. This crew included Turbo-B who later became the rapper of Snap. There was another guy who was a DJ, Marcus Lipeld who became Max Spoon. Then Moses-P later became a major rapper and along with Three-P founded a successful German rap label.
They were all together in 1988, they hung out in this spot called the Funkadelic in Frankfurt and there was a piece outside. The first time we went to Frankfurt in the end of '84 we saw a "helicopter" live and some moves we were really impressed by, we'd never seen anything like that before. Then in Istbahn there was the roller-skating disco where a lot of army people went, we used to go to that place to battle them around '85-'86.
There was a kind of connection with the American soldiers, it wasn't a major impulse, but in terms of clothing of course they all had the coolest shoes, hats and Adidas tracksuits straight from the US. Back then you could really recognise people because of their shoes or clothes, whether it was a guy who had a connection with Hip Hop

culture or not. When I went to Copenhagen I just hung around during rush hour and it only took me 20 minutes to recognise three guys, one was a DJ and two were writ-ers. A similar situation occurred when Loomit, me and another guy from Dortmund went to Sweden to paint with a writer I had met before. For some strange reason he did not open the door, we had no place to stay so we thought "Should we go back?". We had already planned an action that night so we decided to stay. We hung out in Stockholm during rush hour when I randomly saw a couple of guys that were dressed perfectly. "They must be down" I thought. So that's how I connected with the first B-boys in Sweden. There were no shops back then, so during a trip to London you would maybe buy a Kangol, or steal it from a store.
Some people had Cazal glasses, which at the time you could only get in London. Dortmund writers came to a jam once, wearing this light vest that workers wear at night. It was a kind of creativity that mixed with clothes because a lot of things were hand made and customised. Of course the back pieces were customised. Sometimes people cut out their own letters to be stitched on jackets or t-shirts. B-boys used to buy leather sneakers, cut out the logo and put it on hats and clothes.
Hip Hop gradually became part of our day-to-day life, tracing a guideline that many of us followed as a way of life.

Personally I liked Hip Hop and I was listening to it but it wasn't my only thing. I never saw myself as a B-boy

ously. If you think of *Wild Style* it was meant to be taken as a comedy, not a serious commentary, but we took it very seri-ously, it was kitsch but in the end it was real life. We absorbed the whole Hip Hop attitude, it all the clothes and everything. So even if I say it was not real in the beginning, in the end it be-came a real culture.
Personally I liked Hip Hop and I was listening to it but it wasn't my only thing. I never saw myself as a B-boy; I saw myself as a graffiti writer or a style writer. I had a deep interest for style Writing and lettering which went much deeper than what I found in Hip Hop music. I was breaking before too, like robot dancing, but I was already doing that in the 70's when we were listening to Kraftwerk and that definitely wasn't related to any-thing coming from New York.
Kraftwerk started robot dancing, showing it in some concerts during '76-'77: they pretended to be robots on stage and we liked it so much that we started doing the robot dance at par-ties. When Breakdancing started it was completely related to Kraftwerk, even in New York they were a big success. When I was in New York I saw this big guy in the Bronx with a ghetto-blaster listening to Kraftwerk.

New tough line for crew behaviors

Analogies and differences
between crew and gang as told
by High and Pengo, CBS

What was your lifestyle in Amsterdam during the 70's?
HIGH– I started with small tags; in 1975-'76 I was already drawing on walls but I didn't know it was graffiti. I was just a little kid; I'd simply enter a store and steal a marker. I used to draw in tunnels, in my neighbourhood; in the West side of Amsterdam we used to play these sort of street games. Then in 1979 I found a book in the library, *Watching My Name Go by*. From there I just kept on writing letters, so a new phase began; I was 9 years old and I started writing everywhere. For years I didn't even know that was an American movement. Others probably knew, like Shoe and Delta.
They lived in the South of Amsterdam where all the galleries were, so they must have been influenced by New York writers. The only piece I had seen was in one of the worst areas of Amsterdam, "Bijlmer", by Seen. We didn't know who he was but we saw his Name at the subway stop. He contoured letters with a double line and we immediately defined it 'American style'. Only once *Subway Art* came out did everything start to develop really quickly. Before that we were pretty naïve regarding every aspect, and divided as well. I only met Pengo in '85 and Shoe a few years earlier; I did a piece in the centre of Amsterdam, on the Amsteel River. It had the American flag and Shoe put a tag next to my piece saying he wanted to meet me. So we communicated through Writing, "Next Saturday, Central Station, 1 o'clock".

It was an exchange of messages on the wall.

HIGH– Yes, but it didn't work. From our part of town a lot of people went to the meeting but he didn't show up, he was late. We all had this rule that if someone didn't show up within 15 minutes we'd leave. He arrived 20-25 minutes later so we missed each other. The next week we organised another appointment; in Leidseplein. We weren't the only ones who went cause there were 100 or 150 other writers. We didn't even know that they existed! By word of mouth everybody had heard about it and we all met there. You had this gang of little fuckers, 14/15/13/12 year olds that were inventing something new. Boom! The city changed completely, everybody was together and everybody wanted to write bigger, better and bolder. Competition was at a peak; it was a great revolutionary time.

Did you already have set targets? Like the tram...
HIGH– The tram was definitely a target. For me so was the subway because I lived in an area where the 9 tram had its last stop but I could also move to the subway lines. The various trams were divided, so one yard had lines 1 through 12 and the other lines 13 through 25. The trams I bombed weren't all city though, they only ran in a specific area.

When CBS was formed in '85, did it start at Leidseplein?
HIGH– It started in my area through me and some people from the same neighbourhood, twenty people maximum. We were in high school together and we were writing all the time. There were some graffiti groups in the earlier days but when we started we wanted to do something new; a real gang.
The other ones were only into Writing while we were pretty much into crime and fights as well. If you could fight and stand up for each other then that was it.
You know Amsterdam was a difficult city with difficult people. Sometimes it wasn't only about graffiti; if you had a problem then we all resolved it together. Violence was always just around the corner. Nowadays they talk about hooliganism if someone throws a rock; it's big on all the papers but the 80's were the real hooligan years.

Every week we were smashing trams, smashing each other for the Ajax home games. All the Ajax fans were together and there were big riots. I just grew up in these surroundings and I think it was normal enjoying gangs as it was just part of the daily scene.

Were you presiding over any part of the city? Rumour has it that Waterlooplein was controlled by CBS...
HIGH– It was Leidseplein in the beginning; that was the common hang-out but the police started checking it out so we changed places. We moved to Waterlooplein, just because we all lived on the line of tram 9 and it went straight to that spot. Waterlooplein was one of the first stops where a lot of writers came together and I did my first piece over there. Besides that, we did a lot of blockbusters next to the subway lines, it was the roughest period. Biba Straat, Waterloo station, Weisserplein... those were the famous graffiti stations.
We discovered those spots by walking under the subway. The first tunnel walks or runs we did were in '85-'86 and then we started bombing even at night. We'd ride from Waterloo to New Market and then we'd go up, wait for the train to pass, and then run again until the next station. It kicked ass! We started writing over there almost every week because someone stole the keys of the subway and we explored every tunnel and room, under and above the stations, where the workers would go. Some parts of those tunnels are labyrinths, as they were shelters in which people used to hide in during the war. I still have maps of Weisserplein, of all the areas, the levels, etc. Apart from the tunnels we also really liked bombing the streets ... rooftops in particular.

When did you start hitting roofs?
PENGO– In '86 I think. I did a lot of pieces on roofs; it came out in the newspaper. People on the radio stations were saying "Vandals like Pengo are writing on one of the most famous concert halls for classical music in Holland." That action went straight on a radio talk show, they were criticising the fact that I chose such an important monument to write on.

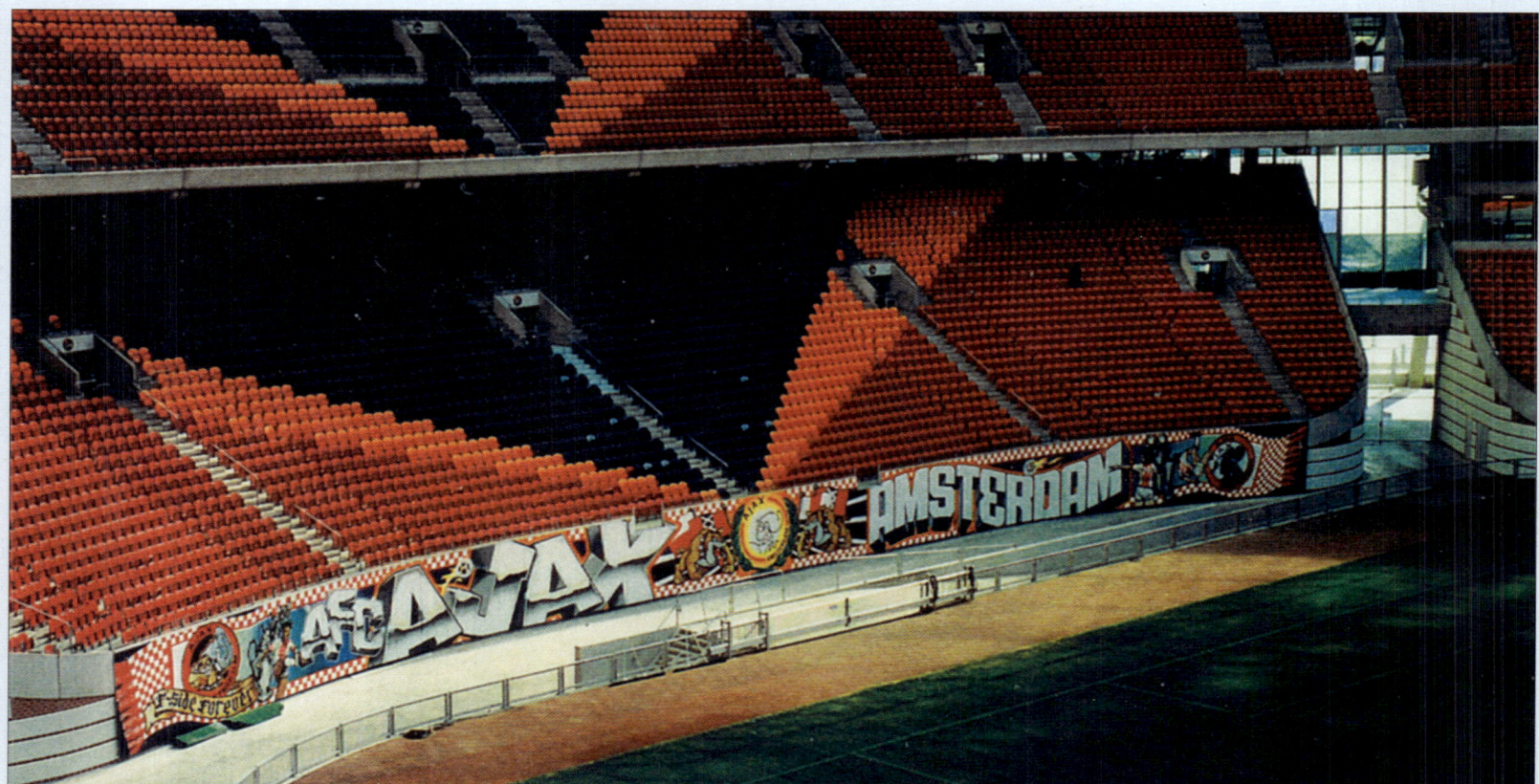

The Ajax Arena terrace painted by local writers

Breaking the mold

The emblematic case of a writer outside of the standards

RCF1 – P2B / Paris
>

So they recognised your name because it had simple letters?
PENGO- Yeah they could read it. It's simple. It was on the front page of the newspaper, and then again the next Saturday they were saying they were trying to clean it and the following Saturday they said it had been cleaned. Nobody dared to clean it initially because it was a difficult place to get to, so the person who did end up cleaning it was an ex graffiti guy. They had to tie him up with ropes.

So how did you do it?
PENGO- I just climbed up and stood on the rim. Crazy!

How did you choose the spots? Were you looking around the city and then choosing the most visible ones?
PENGO- If I was going to do something, everybody had to go crazy for it, no matter whether I had to walk, climb or crawl to do it. A piece on a wall where everybody can write was really not motivating.

It wouldn't bring fame...
PENGO- Yeah exactly, difficult places like Leidseplein, Dam Square on the monument, things like that were bringing fame, of course because those were just crazy spots to hit, in the middle of the city, where there are always people around. I did one in Dams Square. If you have the towers at your back on the right side there is a little tower and you can still see some paint...

When the big subway movement started in the 90's did you take part in it?
HIGH- When it started I was in jail for a year. I went to jail in '89 and I stayed there for a year when this came up... next to the prison you could see the tracks of the subway. From my room I could see other pieces go into the yard. When I came out I wanted to do the subway even though we kind of hated it because it had a coating that was easy to clean. It was always a matter of discovering other places, but unfortunately there were only a few lines to share amongst heaps of us, like 60 writers.

Did having such a small subway and being so many create a particular kind of competition among writers? Was crossing pieces a problem between the crews?
HIGH- I think that was only in the early days, but between Dutch crews we always respected each other. Besides that, we went to prison for fighting and violence and when we came out we had a fierce reputation. You didn't have to do much because you already had that to rely on, but you also couldn't become complacent, you had to be prepared in case something happened; your reputation could not last forever.

Where were the other gangs in Amsterdam?
HIGH- North side of Amsterdam. You had gangs on the West side, on the East side, up North and they were all fighting for territory. There were a lot of gangs but the ones that lasted the longest were from the North side, until the late 80's gangs were fighting against each other. The coffee shops solved the problem, at least one of the police chiefs said that in a newspaper many years ago.

So the coffee shops slowed this down...how?
HIGH- In the coffee shops everybody smoked and relaxed, so they started to mix. They were going to different areas and doing business with each other. Maybe police solved the gang problem but what they didn't see was that what came later was organised crime. The big criminals of nowadays come from the West part. The police didn't see that back then. There was a lot of money to make with the coffee shops; importing hashish. We were very small and we weren't into that but that's what we learnt. Territory gangs mostly died out but one big gang remained. And partially it was reunited under one single name: Ajax. With Ajax we are all together. You know each other because you're from different parts, you used to fight on the streets but then you get to know each other

> CONTINUES ON PAGE 148

During the mid 80's, I was involved in Paris' Mod scene, listening to 60's music, hanging out on my Vespa. I used to make scooter stencils, use drugs and even, write. I always had a marker with me; the first time I used a spray can to write something on the wall was because I had an urge to write, even if I didn't know what. I think I wrote something like "The Jam!" or other Mod band names.
In 1988 I went too heavy on the amphetamines; I had an accident and went to the hospital in the suburbs near my parents' place. When I left the hospital my mother and I took the train back home and I really saw tags for the first time. Initially I wasn't that interested in them, because I saw them as a rapper's thing. I remember the famous hall of fame in Paris: Stalingrad. I was on my Vespa and wanted to meet that crazy guy Mode 2. I already really loved his stuff even if I had never considered doing it myself, because it was coming from a totally different lifestyle. But that day I decided to quit drugs and I started to become more and more interested in Writing.
I got my name RCF1 from a Clash song, *Rudie Can't Fail*, and I started tagging by myself; I didn't know anyone from the scene. I would just go to the railway and see how they were doing it. All the drug energy went into this. Of course the first writers I met were into Hip Hop, so for a long time I was a kind of 'black sheep' in the Parisian scene. People from the Hip Hop scene had no idea what a Mod was, there were some prejudices as well; many of them believed that mods and skinheads were all fascists, without a clue about this street culture which was born in the UK. So I used to tell people I was a punk just to get over the subject quicker! I've never been a punk though. In any case, even if I never became a B-boy, to me being part of the Writing movement was a continuation of being a mod, going out dressing fine and listening to music. Of course the clothes were different, the music

even more, but I had the same approach. More than contradictions I see many connections. As a mod you always tend to have "style" even if surrounded by difficult circumstances; when I look at the 70's in New York, at those ghetto kids with no money, I see that same need and search for style. If you don't have the money then you have to create your style alone. The Mod scene was a creative movement with an upfront style and so was Hip Hop. The early mods wanted to be different from working class people; they came from the working class but wanted to be someone: they wanted to have the latest shoes, the latest scooter... all of it in order to create their own identity, to be different and have their own style. Besides the dress codes, this is something connected to Writing as well, as it concerns a style that refers to an aesthetic evolution. A study focused on being visible and unique. So even style-wise I tried to do something else, to avoid the New York influence in letters and characters. From the very beginning I didn't recognise myself in that. Doing drawings that were taken from Vaugh Bode comics wasn't my goal, as where it came from it just wasn't part of my upbringing. Obviously I had other references, such as classic European authors like Yves Chaland.
When I started doing graffiti, I had all of this in mind; even my letters came from 60's Garage-like letters. It took time; I didn't use it at first, not until a year after I started. The kids in my neighbourhood, the other writers, enjoyed it because it was different. Most of the others were saying it wasn't orthodox, it wasn't correct, it wasn't the way you're supposed to do graffiti but almost every P2B crew member would have a different approach to Writing, avoiding the Hip Hop formula and references. It was our intention; we tried to avoid stereotypes and follow other stylistic directions. Stak and Honet started experimenting with shapes and symbols while Shun was the first skinhead to paint trains and trams with chaotic letters. You had whole cars painted by a skinhead; he really was the first! During the early 90's, Honet, like so many other train writers was into raves and parties. A lot of hardcore people weren't into Hip Hop anymore; people like SDK crew were more into pills, spotting new yards, going to parties. Which is not better or worse than the attitude of some original New Yorkers, it's simply different.

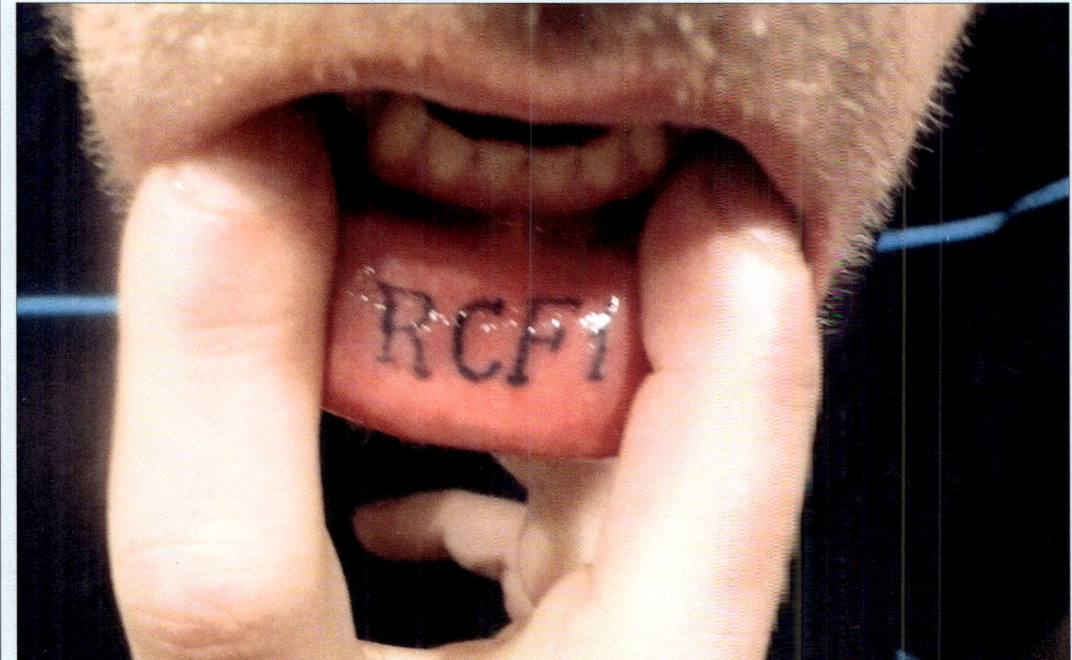

RCF1 bigmouth

—RCF1

REINVENTING IDENTITES

MY NAME IS

SKKI

I chose my 'artist' Name back in 1983, it was my nickname at school when I was 10 years old. Since my real family name is originally Slavic, it was difficult for the French kids to pronounce it correctly, they always shortened it and called me 'Ski'. So I later decided to use it and add the second 'K' (my real family name has two K's). In the beginning I called myself 'Lord Skki', using a title before Skki was directly influenced not only by Ragga and Dub culture from Jamaica, where musicians and singers used names like 'King tubby', but also by Hip Hop culture that had Names like 'Grandmaster Melle Mel'. In 1991 my Name was accepted at the International Copyright Organisation in France (ADAGP), any images of my work on the street were copyrighted. Media like magazines or television etc... were not allowed to use my work without my permission. So I decided to add this 'c' in a circle like 'Skki ©', and leave out the 'Lord' altogether.
I thought it was nice to have a circle in my Name, which without it would be all open letters. The circle at the end with the 'C' is closed and gives you the feeling of drawing a cloud or something round like the head of Mickey Mouse. It was also better than using the word 'One', which whilst having a circle for the 'o', was however too common ... everyone wanted to be 'the one and only' in the 80's. Somehow I didn't use my Name that much to do pieces, but instead I used the code name D.O.E (Directly.Operational.Element) and signed Skki© under or on the piece. D.O.E was made of two closed, rounded letters and an open one at the end.
To me the 'E' was like a dynamic element going right, with three straight, horizontal bars. I was then able to reconfigure it into an razor sharp calligraphic element that looked like a rocket or something with a weapon ready to shoot! Today, 26 years later, I use 'Skki©' and write the same way as I would with my real handwriting, slanting to the right, and knowing that 80% of other tags bend to the left!

MY NAME IS

CAT 22

At that time I was 22 and I used to occasionally take LSD sometimes. One time, when I was in the South of France, I climbed a mountain whilst on LSD. I started climbing at the beginning of the trip and eight hours later I was at the top. Once there, the trip was over. I felt like a cat. Even if going downhill was way more difficult. I had the feeling of a cat combined with my age.
Moreover Catch 22 is the definition of when you're in the army and you're not completely sane in the head. So it all fit together. It sounded good. I started writing that like crazy, every night. Soon I met other writers and I quit taking acid, I just dropped it on the spot. I didn't have time to space out for eight hours, the way my days were like before. Also, I had Norman Mailer's book *Watching my name go by* which contained a list of writer Names and it struck me that there were so many writers that added a number behind their Name. I thought that was cool, so I did too.

MY NAME IS

ZEBSTER

Ducky was my first writer Name. In the beginning it was Ducky-cool while Can-2 was Cool-candy. These were our first fantasy graffiti nicknames. Then from Cool-candy he went to Candy and then to Can-2. For me it was Ducky-cool, then Duck-ster and finally Zebster. It was kind of an imaginary combination of two writers I really liked and had got inspired by, their Names sounded cool: on one side Zephyr from New York and on the other Duster. Not the most well-known writers but they had some kind of cool image behind them. It was the combination of those two, and the -ster ending was powerful!

MY NAME IS

DARE

I chose Lord as my first tag. Looking at my real surname, which started with Von, it gave off a kind of 'noble' aura.
I thought it was a good reference until I discovered that there was already a 'Lord' in Zurich, which of course made me change to something radically different like Dare: besides the meaning itself, I think it really fits into the whole graffiti world, every letter and connection perfectly illustrating my idea of Wildstyle and its complexities.

MY NAME IS

BATES

I was using different Names from '84 to '86. In '86 I started brainstorming for letters that I liked, like the S, the E and the A.
One day I was watching TV and I saw some science fiction movie called Victory. One of the characters came to earth in a UFO and one of the leaders was called Bates. I thought he was a cool character so I wrote down the Name and started sketching with it. I had another Name at the time but Bates started to take over and I've used this Name ever since. It has been over 20 years and I took the challenge of keeping the Name. That's what I think it's about; it's about keeping your Name and trying to do the best you can with it. I tried having other Names but the feeling wasn't right. Every time I wrote Bates it felt good, so that's why I decided to push this Name as much as I could. I've always tried to write it in the most beautiful form. Me, Sabe and Rens have to be very careful because we have been around with our Names for 20 years. We do things at night and paint in the halls of fame during the day so we have to be careful, but I have never changed my style or Name to be unrecognisable for this reason. I've always changed my letters and style because I like to experiment, I'm renown for that. Whenever I do something, it has my fingerprint on it, no matter how I do it. Even if I'm trying to do something different it's going to have that iconic look that is recognisable to me. Sometimes it works out, sometimes it doesn't. I don't think all my pieces are good but I try out new things, if I don't experiment I can't come up with anything new. I could do the same outline in different colours but I wouldn't progress, if I hadn't progressed I don't think I would be here today. I can do anything I want because I'm still hungry, I still want to be better and I still want to experiment. I'm still pushing myself. I usually experiment first on paper, I draw a lot. It just depends what mood I'm in, what circus I'm in and the general surroundings. Whether you're on a train, in front of a wall in the daytime, at night, a silver piece... I sometimes try to fit the surrounding environment. I bring with me outlines that try to fit the situation. That's why it looks different, but it really depends on the mood I'm in whether I'm aggressive, sad or love hurt. I suppose this has an impact on the pieces.

MY NAME IS

LOOMIT

The first tag I ever had was Toy, I knew by the time I started painting what a toy was because of the stories. They were about these guys that were just beginners and weren't any good at it, and so they were known as "Toys". When I chose it I was basically the only writer around so there was no one else that knew about the meaning of the Name, and I thought that was cool. Unfortunately someone ratted on me; some kids got caught and gave up my Name, so I had to go to court for the first time and go on trial. Of course I couldn't use the name Toy anymore, and that's when I came up with the name Loomit. I used to see late night movies in black and white from the 60's, and there was one called "Niagara Falls" with Marilyn Monroe; the main character was called Mr. Loomis, with an "S" at the end. I thought that was a cool name, but also quite a difficult one too. No other writer would take those letters, an "L", two "O's", it was pretty hard to write. I managed to do the "L", the "O's" the "M" and the "I", but I fucked up on the "S" every time, so I switched to the next letter of the alphabet which was a "T". It worked really well so I started tagging with it.

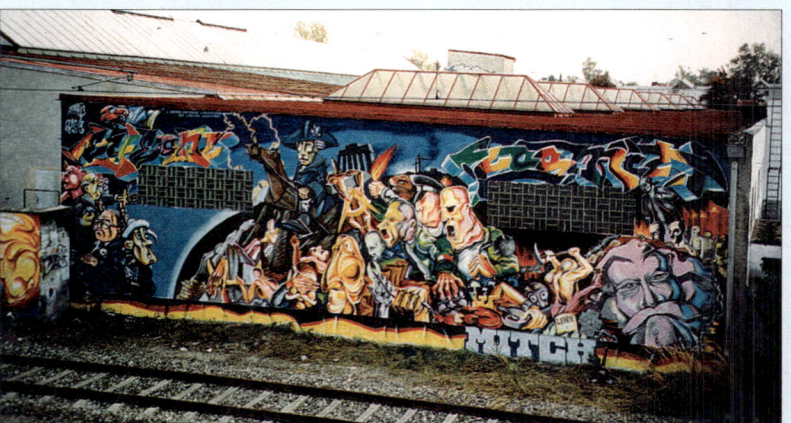

MY NAME IS

LORD

When I started using spray paint in 1983 I still didn't have a Name and would randomly write a bit here and there. A year later though I decided to form a crew, and we clearly needed a name. Since both our legal names started with the letter "P", my friend and I decided to call ourselves the "P-Lords". In the early days I was still signing with my real name! Then my partner baptised me "Ashes" and we founded a new crew: URP – Unrevocable Revolution of Paint. It was immediately clear that I would inherit the Name "Lord". Because to me Lord represents something bigger, a legendary figure, of which you can still feel the presence even if he doesn't have an identifiable face. Noble and mysterious. That's how my work should be. Clearly, being Swiss, my knowledge of the English language at 15 years of age was not that good yet: I realised much later for the first time that in more erudite English, the word Lord was also associated to that of God. I surely had no intention to make that analogy though. In spite of this, I had noticed that my Name, connected to my work, was starting to acquire a certain degree of respect both within and out of the scene, though there were

some days in which I damned it. Many writers will confirm that this combination of letters does not entail many advantages.
This does not mean to be a justification for the fact that I lacked a defined style for some time, but I envied Moniak a lot for his "M", Zombie and Zimok for their "Z" and Takit for the "A". But then again... if you have a Name, that's it in the end.
When in 1990 *UpperClass* reunited and became active, we abolished our previous individual Names, so that the members of UC wouldn't be known. So I abandoned my tag and only used pseudonyms (as many other writers do) on the surface of trains and walls. In any case, though we attempted to remain covert in the 90's, the scene was small enough and the news got around by word of mouth: in the end whoever wanted to know could find out that behind the pseudonym of Lord, was me. And so I thought about going back to my initial Name... or rather 'it' come back to me. It's right that it went this way because my Name has to correspond to that of the Family, to the Name of the Crew. Lord of Upperclass. It's right this way.

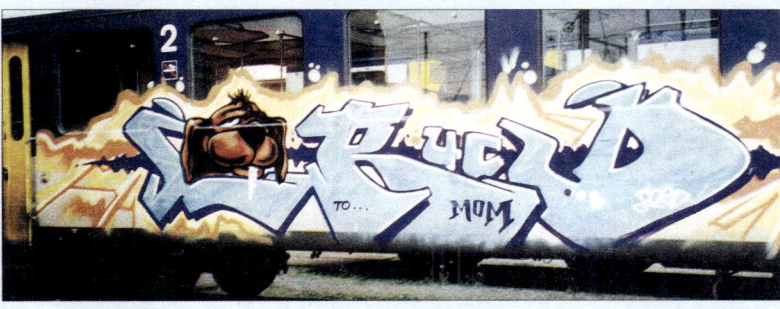

MY NAME IS

DRAX

Some time before I actually started Writing I chose my Name: Drax. I've had that name now for over 25 years. It was the name of a villain from the James Bond film Moonraker and I liked the way it sounded. Hugo Drax, the James Bond villain, was a megalomaniac bent on *World Domination*. That suited me. The name fit in with my aims, I felt it had dynamism and I loved the X. The only problem was that my attempts at writing it in a stylised manner, befitting the future King I aspired to be, were to say the least "shit". As a consequence of this the first Drax tag didn't appear until late 1985. So there you have it, I started writing in 1985. I've lost count of how many liars I've heard claiming they wrote in '84/'83 or even 1981. Very few people in England wrote in 1983 and some of those that claim they did would have been about 8 years old. In 1983 I was no more than a fan of graffiti, I watched from the shadows wondering how I could get involved. Then around 1984 the documentary *Style Wars* showed me that all I had to do was get myself a can or pen, walk out the door and write my name on something. After choosing my Name and gaining the courage to unleash my 'scribble' on the general public, sometime in mid 1985 I did just that. I've been a writer

ever since. The tag I have always written is Drax or variations of that name: Draks, DS or DX. I have at times done pieces that said different things but my Name has always been Drax. During the early 90's I had ongoing court cases. I was being prosecuted by the British Transport Police and London Underground Ltd for 'aledgedly' being the vandal known as 'Drax'. Consequently during this period and for sometime after I did train pieces under pseudonyms. These were nearly always a random word that I used just once, such as Daire, Brush, Bollocks, Thug, Insanity, Intercourse, Shinners, Combat, Lord, Bank, Why, Vision, Believe, Freaks, ABC and a bunch of other irrelevances. For a while I used the word "Germ" in a series of pieces: "The Germ", "Germ Warfare", "Germfest", "Infected by the Germs of life", "Germski One" etc but I never wrote tags relating to those names. My tag has always been Drax. From 1985 onwards I've done more pieces than I can remember, probably because most aren't worth remembering. But over the years I've done a few things that either made me proud or have stood the test of time and become, dare I say it, 'iconic' within the London graffiti scene. Here are a few such pieces.

MY NAME IS

CMP

My Name CMP came from my mother. All over Denmark during the 80's, everybody came up with nice names like Saba, Sketch, Faze, Bates or Cres which sounded good.
They sounded American and so fresh. In '84, one of my first names was Res 03, because I lived at number 3 on the street, but that Name wasn't really me; so I asked my mother to help me out. "What's a nice Name for me? A street Name, a nice nickname?' and she said "Call yourself Claus, that's your name."
"That's not really how it works, mum!"
So she replied "yes, but just use your initials: CMP." I had never heard of people using acronyms for a Name. Normally, of course, they are used for crew Names, but today I feel comfortable with one, even though, at that time I thought it sounded weird.
Besides that, soon I realised that these three letters were really interesting, offering very different structures, and the number ONE helped to balance the whole Name. It worked really well style-wise, especially for the blockbuster typography I used to do. Man, it was funny with these Names.
In '92, Swet, Spin and I met writers in New York

that believed CMP was a crew. And, like most people, they asked me where the rest of the crew was. And when Spin told them his Name, they said:
"Can't call yourself that bro, there's already a guy called Spin, he's an old cat, if he meets you, he's going to knock you down, people are crazy, this is New York." So Spin replied:
"But I'm not just Spin. I'm Spin05 and I got pieces from '85 to prove it."
After an embarrassing silence, everybody started laughing and said it was cool. They really liked our crew Name "CMPSPIN" and also our method of painting together, they even said it was unique.
The next year we did a piece on 37th street, I believe it's still standing, last time I saw it was in 2005. Anyway, in '93, Swet still wrote "West', but New York West didn't like that.
On the flight back, my friend changed his Name. He did a very smart thing: by switching his letters around he became Swet. It only took him a few months to establish this new Name. Man that's pretty impressive. Everybody knew he changed his Name, instantly recognising his style and letters.

MY NAME IS

WON

The Name Won ABC appeared out of pure coincidence. I started bombing around 1984/'85 in Munich Germany. Until 1986 I used various illegal Names but there was no use in thinking about a legal Name for that game.
This changed in 1986 when me and some other writers from Munich had to paint canvases together for a German film show called "Bambine". While I was painting I could hear one of my colleagues listening to one of my favourite rap groups, Public Enemy – the particular song was Public Enemy No 1, from the album Yo Bum Rush the Show, where the refain goes "Public Enemy one, one, one, one..." – I liked the idea of being a public enemy and I still do. After we finished painting, we had to look into a camera and introduce ourselves. I had heard that song more than a hundred times that day. There was still a writer from New York

named A-one (R.I.P.), so thinking on my feet I decided in front of the camera that my new Name should be won. Public Enemy no. Won, Won, Won, Won...
Towards the end of the 80's, Cowboy 69 and me founded ABC crew. Initially the Name referred to the 'Art Bombing Clan' but later it developed into 'A Bavarian Crew'. The first three years I went with the thing of combining letters with characters, but as Cowboy 69 became my friend and almost my twin as an artist, I found a way of expressing that my universe should be figurative. In each of my strokes of colour you can feel the rage and anguish that I openly and truthfully feel for this world. My images and thoughts are answers to that which surrounds me: hard, dirty, filthy and massive. This world doesn't deserve to be clean. That's why I'm smearing it to the max.

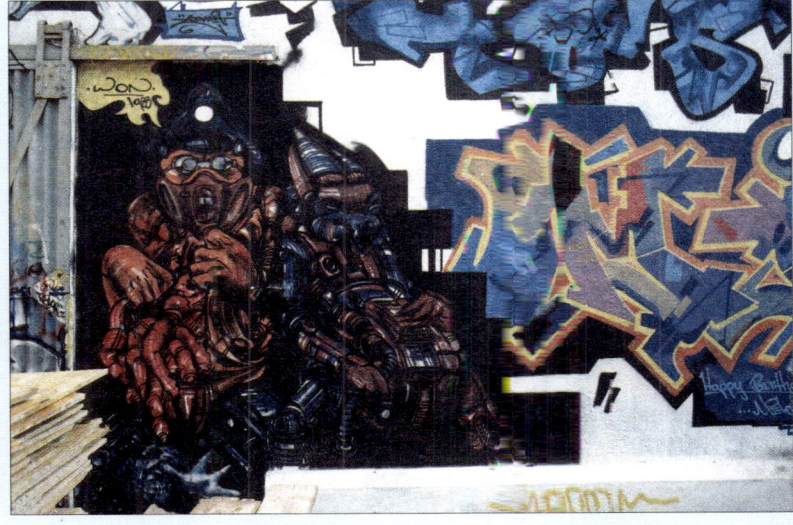

MY NAME IS

SKETZH

I started tagging and getting up in 1984. I was sixteen years old at the time and I remember wanting a Name and a tag starting with the letter 'S'. 'E' was also one of my favourite letters too, and as I was spending all my time doing Wildstyle sketches on paper, 'Sketzh' seemed to be the answer.

The Name 'Sketzh' defined what I was doing and at the same time it created the visual impact that I was looking for. My first tag was a combination of my primary school cursive handwriting, mixed with my influence and passion for the New York graffiti scene. Combining these two styles into one, made it distinct from other writers' tags at the time — it gave me instant street fame and put me firmly on the map of graffiti in Copenhagen. To me tagging is as essential as being able to do a masterpiece on a wall.

It's in a writer's DNA, a skilled craft and an art form in itself. It's the original way of getting up, and great late night entertainment.

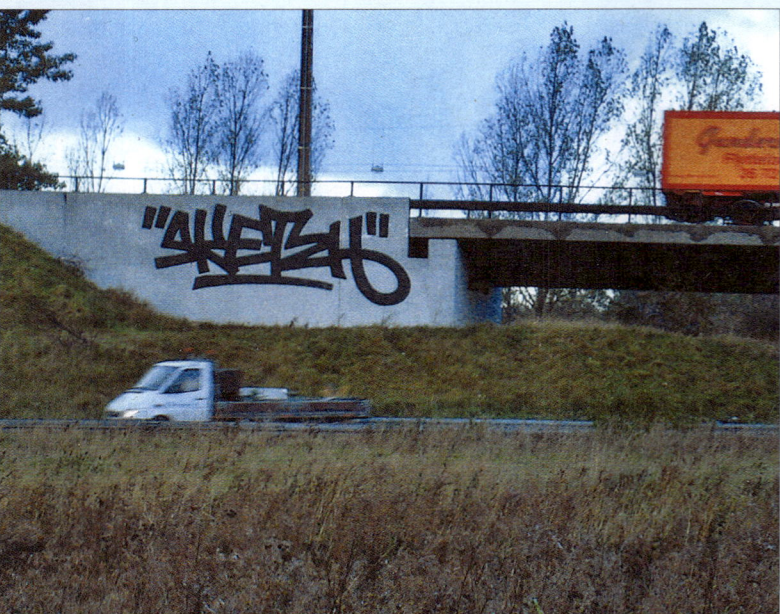

MY NAME IS

POSE

When I started spraying graffiti in 1989, I used different tags to keep people away from making connections between my pieces of work in case I got caught. Only later did I want to distinguish myself from other sprayers and so that's when I started looking for a unique tag.

It was very natural to choose an English Name, because me and my buddies were very much influenced by the New York graffiti scene. I wanted my tag to have both a great look and a catchy sound. After some initial thought and research into graffiti magazines I decided on the Name Pose. Nobody else had claimed it as far as I could tell, so it seemed just perfect.

Pose has something showy about it, and yet at the same time addresses this idea of self-display, which is after all what graffiti is mostly about. It's also got an 'O' and a 'S' in it, two letters I'm particularly fond of. I like merging my styles with characters that replace the 'O' in my tag and, in my opinion, the 'S' is simply the nicest letter to draw. It's good to have a short tag, too: when I tag special kinds of 'canvases' – glaciers, tanks or cows for instance – I need to get it done very quickly. Later I found out that there had been in fact a New York artist who sprayed under the pseudonym Pose That's when I changed my tag to Pose One, because abandoning my Name completely was not an option. Pirmin Breu had irrevocably turned into Pose. So far I haven't gotten to know another Pose One, although in San Diego I met a sprayer called Pose Two. He's a nice guy. The game is all in the Name!

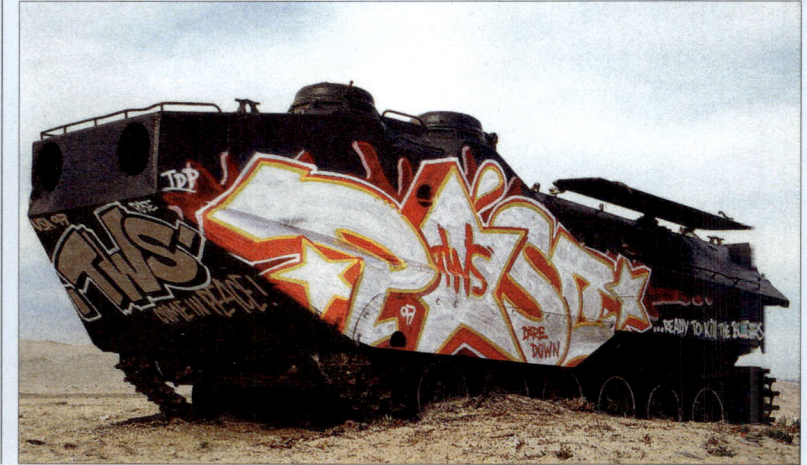

MY NAME IS

PUPPET

I started writing a shorter version of my real Name on buses, back in 1983: *Danne B.* It was provoked by a guy that was older then me, he had his Name on a heap of buses... I guess he was writing it to attract the attention of girls. He was the coolest guy in town! When I figured that out, I saw my chance and started to write my Name up there too, but a little bigger and with more detail.

I started getting my Name up on every bus and it wasn't long before I was getting all his girls too! During the early 80's I was a street dancer and my inspiration came from some videos. Some friends also found English music magazines where they where telling stories from New York, like about Breakdancing battles. It was so cool reading all these invented Names like Mr Wave, Crazy Legs, Grandmaster Caz, Double-Dee, Doze... so many cool Names and new expressions.

The words "cool" and "fresh" were pretty new to me then. Together with my popping-electro style of dancing I started to devise my graf name. It was Znake, but I wasn't truly satisfied. When I came to understand the whole Hip Hop culture better, I wanted a Name that was more complete, a whole identity that worked together.

One day as I was chilling and scribbling in the backyard with my homies, I had this idea that my dance style should also be my Name, if cool enough ... but I couldn't think of anything and was going to nowhere with it. I explained my style to my father, and he answered "the name you are looking for is Puppet!" I was a bit disappointed at first, it was really sucky letters for graf but as it was so cool for my dance style, I decided to keep it as breaker, without writing it. Years later, I even discovered that my dad got it directly from a song by Sandie Shaw '*Puppet On A String*'.

A few months after that I met some guys talking about graffiti, they were drawing sketches and testing out each other's skill. They said "so, you got this Name? Show us what you can do with it!" It was then that I thought ...Ok, let's consider Puppet again. Let's see what I can do with it!

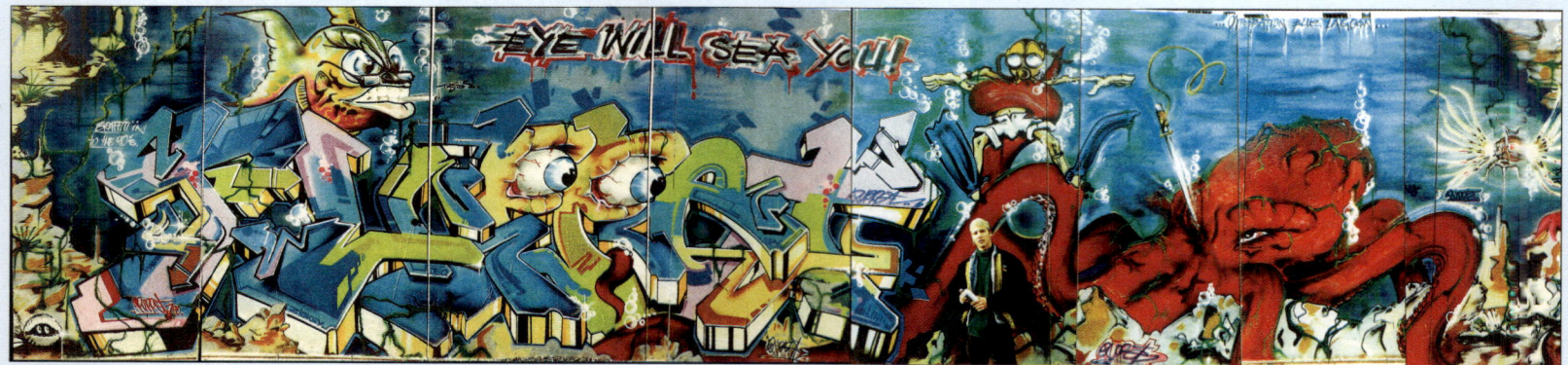

MY NAME IS

PIKE

I actually started drawing a lot of comics and even writing my Name behind characters. I would always write a little signature, which was JPD, the initials of my real Name. There was a little graffiti-style going on in my signature already during that period, but of course I couldn't use my real Name to write so I just had to make one up. I just took the "P" of my initials and it became Pike. Basically I came up with it by putting together letters I thought were cool, well not the "P" but the "I", the "K", and the "E". The graffiti scene in Malmö, which is where I come from, was really small and I just picked letters from other writers which had tag letters that I thought were cool and put them together. The evolution of my letters was totally focused on the combination of these four letters, drawn and composed following different connections and shapes. My Name on walls or trains used to come from sketches on paper, especially during the 90's. Then I stopped using them. I got a hang of it because it's stupid: you get locked into a way of thinking and what you imagine the sketch

will be is never how it actually turns out, so I prefer to go unprepared. Improvising is better because first of all you're always surprised by the result, and also it's easier to work with fat caps without a sketch because the style of your hand comes out in a much better way. I also encountered this problem... you could end up standing in between two people and that would be the space you had: between two completely different ends you would have to figure out how to make them meet, in which case it's better not to have chosen even an outline colour, but to just go with various cans and see what the background is, where and what the light source comes from. There are so many things that you have to think about, and this is what got me convinced to never make plans, the only plan you can make is to draw a lot of sketches beforehand, but just for your hand / head, maybe on a newspaper you then throw away. I really had a big problem trying to keep up with the sketch styles, so I just had to get rid of them, and I still think it's the best way, even if you are doing a hall of fame piece.

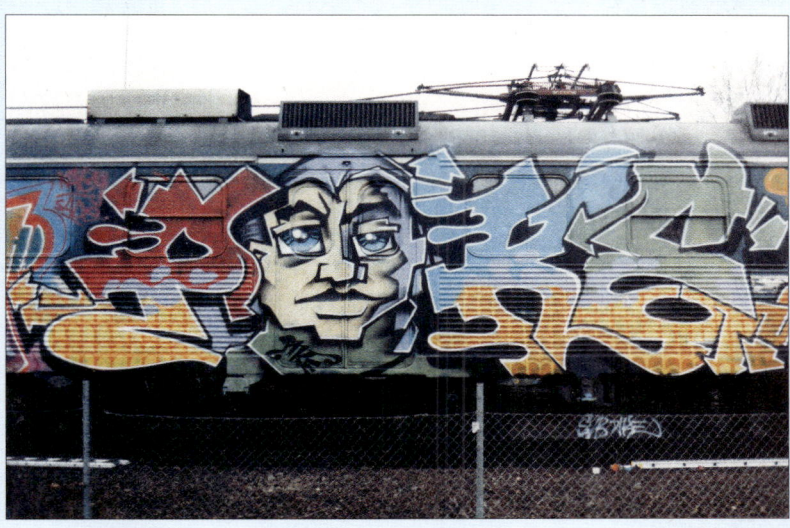

MY NAME IS

ZAKI-DEE

I've always been into vinyl ever since I bought my first 7" single in 1972 at the age of 8. By the time Punk / New wave came along in the late 70's I was spending all my money on records. As an avid listener of John Peels' seminal radio show I would hear him play the odd rap record amongst the Punk and New Wave ones. By 1980/'81 the Rap / Hip Hop scene was growing fast. As well as taping my favourite tunes from the radio, I was making weekly Saturday visits to Soho's mighty Groove Records on the corner of Bateman and Greek Streets. There I would buy one, or if I could afford it, two of the latest 12" US import Rap records. I was also listening to some pirate radio stations in London like Jazz FM and LWR, the latter of which was where Tim Westwood began his DJing career. This more soulful dubby sound coming out of the States appealed to me more than that of raw UK Punk. The Name Zaki was inspired by

a Name on one these record sleeves. Celluloid Records released a series of Rap records and on the back of each sleeve was part of a painting by Futura 2000. If you managed to get every record in the series you could join each sleeve together to form the whole painting (I never did manage to get them all). On the back sleeve of Grand Mixer D.S.T. And The Infinity Rappers – "The Grand Mixer Cuts It Up", there is a special thanks to Bernard Zekri. I liked the name Zekri but I wanted to change it a little so I turned it to Zakri. Over the months I dropped the "R" and it's been Zaki ever since.
I think I wrote Zaki 163 for a while, as well as Zaki Dee 163 which was inspired by the New York writer Lee 163 from the book *Getting Up*. I knew that the digits referred to the numerical Names of New York streets but it was the flow of the numbers after the name that appealed to me.

MY NAME IS

POE

Back in 1986 when the big graffiti craze hit Helsinki, everybody was coming up with Names that for some reason had four letters and started with a "G", like Gulp. I didn't want to be like everybody else so I chose Symbios as my first Name, but for obvious reasons that didn't last long. Then I changed to Rufus3, but I've forgotten why. Then in 1988 I began to consider graf a bit more seriously and spent a long time thinking of a new Name.
Names with P's and R's were popular around Scandinavia at the time probably because of Stockholm writers like Rode and Speed, who had also bombed in Helsinki in the summer of 1988. I had seen *Style Wars* and somehow Papo 184 stuck with me, and I chose to start writing Papoe. There was also a rap song by Papo, and I liked how the word sounded. It

wasn't too aggressive. I have always been keen on softer more sympathetic Names. I also liked the rhythm of P's and an "E" on the end. I wrote Papoe for some time and that was the Name I drew recognition and fame from.
In 1990 I shortened it to Poe and I've been writing it ever since. Sometimes I write Mugs or Gums when getting tired of the letters in Poe. I think my style somehow fits the word, Poe sounds round and smooth in the mouth and that's how I have wanted my pieces to be as well.
Once we painted a subway in Amsterdam with Mellie and Reze and I did a Poe piece and wrote "strong like whiskey!" next to it. Mellie thought there was some obvious contrast because my piece was small and neat and Poes means kitten in Dutch.

MY NAME IS

EGS

I was writing a couple of Names before I got stuck on Egs. I wanted a short three letter Name that would suit panels. At that time some of my favorite writers had three letter names: Poe, Sie, Due, Elk, Mer, Ket, Ven... I wrote Edge for a while and thought about shortening it to Edg, but then I thought it

sounded a bit stupid. So I did a couple of Egs panels and have been writing those three letters ever since. I don't think that it's a particularly cool or clever name but it has nice letters and people seem to remember it. My Name has nothing to do with Eggs, although I do like Eggs Florentine for breakfast!

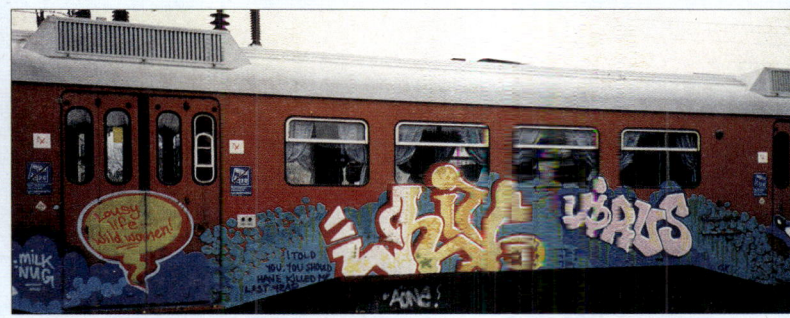

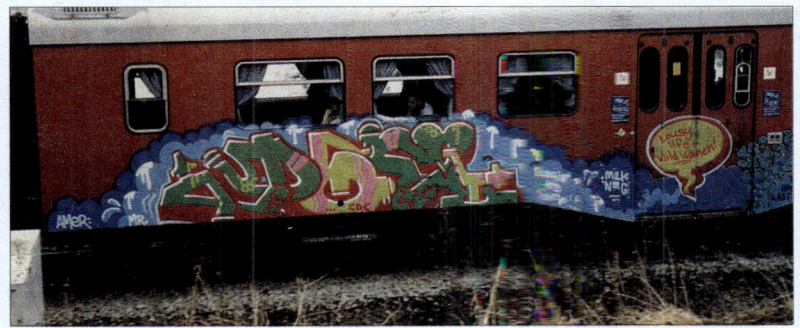

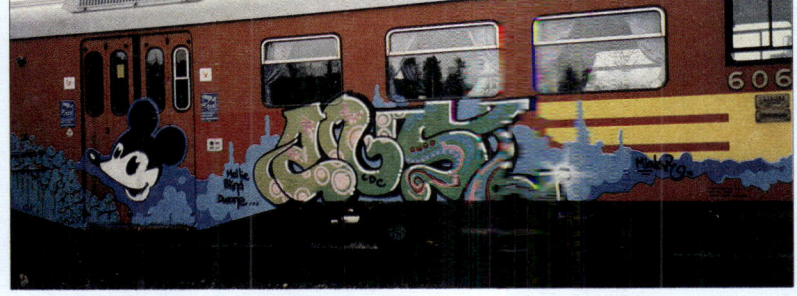

MARKER MARKET

Stefano Viola / Milan
>

From the onset, graffiti culture developed through the use of tools that had been created for completely different purposes with respect to those writers came up with. The chemical industry supplied a fundamental contribution: American companies like Marsh or Esterbrook Cushman & Denison – creators of the famous Flo-Master ink – have unconsciously contributed to the development of an anarchic, explosive and creative culture like that of graffiti.

Let's consider the example of the Flo-Master: an ink that responded to the need for a chemical compound capable of really being permanent, thus becoming the most contended object among writers between 1970 and 1980. Thanks to its opaque finish and its resistance to buffing, the Flo-Master imposed itself on the market, becoming extremely popular: once applied on a porous surface, such as the internal panels of New York subway cars, it was impossible to remove, especially when mixed with printing inks such as Garvey or with writing inks such as Pilot. The entire dawn of Writing culture is permeated by the use of non-conventional tools, in the States as much as in Europe. In France during the 90's use of a product called Corio spread, which much like the Italian Nero Inferno, had been created to fulfil totally different needs. Erroneously defined 'ink', both Corio (whose name derives from a deformation of the word Cuir – leather in French) and Nero Inferno, are nothing but hair dyes. Thanks to their extreme penetrative power and the absence of resins they have become fundamental compounds capable of resisting any attempt at removing them. These products could be distinguished from the competition because they left an indelible mark, which became their distinctive characteristic.

Necessity therefore forced writers to search within decidedly industrial markets for products that were right up their alley. When attention shifted towards markers, this practice was only further confirmed, indeed the most popular markers of the past were created with completely different goals in mind. The Mop, a tool for polishing shoes thanks to its dispensing sponge-like nib, becomes an extremely popular tool, thanks to the fluidity with which the ink flows out of the applicator. And even earlier the infamous Ultra Wide Marker as well as the precursor Magic Marker had been created for the world of advertising, which needed tools with which to write on wide surfaces, for ad posters or shop windows.

Already by the mid 40's in the United States it was possible to find rudimentary approaches to the modern felt-tip marker, but Magic Marker, invented by Sidney Rosenthal in 1953, was considered the first marker in history, so much so that its inventor embarked on a series of legal actions against certain imitators of the product, which he lost with clamour. The Magic Marker was a pad marker, with a felt tip, completely lacking a valve system, which was useful to control and dose the flow of ink. Which is where Ideal Stencil came in the following year, when it introduced the first marker in history to have a valve system, called Ideal-Mark. This is an important step in the industrial development of markers, because the use of a capillary system to control the jet of ink allows the industry, first American and immediately later Japanese, to develop products containing pigmented inks, rarely utilised until then. With respect to inks based on dyes, the pigment version creates a layer of ink that covers the surface on which it is used.

Coating enamels also started becoming popular in the world of graffiti in the 90's, when the first American and successively European laws ban the use of components that are harmful to health. The Flo-Master, deprived of the fundamental component for its long-lasting performance – lead – looses attractiveness, because it no longer satisfies its most primordial objective: leaving a mark. The same destiny is reserved, at the beginning of the new millennium, to other products in Europe like Nero Inferno, that deprived of aniline – an adjuvant in dying, with unparalleled fixing properties – looses its penetrative power. It is at this moment that writers search for alternative, equally effective products with which to leave their mark. Pigmented stencil inks by Marsh and other important companies become more appealing, together with valve system inks that supplant – or almost do so – the pad marker. 'Brands' of the rising sun like Pilot, Mitsubishi, Shachihata and Kuretake – inheriting a millenary tradition in the art of calligraphy – together with European brands like Edding, launch a series of products for artistic purposes, which soon become appealing to those generations of 'atypical' artists. Valve markers with wide tips such as those of Zig Biggie, Artline Poster, Uni Paint, Posca, and Pilot started becoming popular in Europe, thanks to the very large felt tip, the broad chromatic variety, and especially the ease with which they could be procured. In any case, despite the market offering an ever-growing quantity of products, writers continued to come up with new homemade tools. One of the fundamental characteristics necessary for the technical development of Writing has always been research. Thousands of 'recipes' with which to formulate homemade inks can be found on the Internet, which is indicative of the fact this culture has always proven to be essentially diffident with respect to the pre-packaged solutions available on the market.

Coming back to the comparison between pigmented inks and those based on dyes, it is therefore necessary to understand how the industry adapted to the new rules, to progress and to the competition of the world markets, conceiving multiple solutions the global scene could absorb. In the 90's Uni-Paint PX-30s could be found in the pockets of New York writers as much as in the backpacks of any of their European alter egos. The tools began to be universally accepted and recognised.

With the growth of the movement on a global scale, the last generations began to compete, other than on a stylistic level, also with regards to the tools to use. And this is when the turning point takes place: the market is approached, at times timidly at times not, by companies oriented towards satisfying the demands of that world that only a few years earlier had been starkly opposed. Montana in Spain is a shining example, as it is the first company created with the main purpose of serving its products exclusively to the world of graffiti. Halfway through the 90's an official Writing market is born and by consequence companies adapt to it. In that period, business is prevalently dedicated to the commercialisation of spray paint; markers, still in the background, will remain an exclusive of the historic leading companies of the sector for another decade. Paint companies like Peter Qwasny (Belton) or Motip-Dupli (Dupli-Color), together with the newborn Montana in Spain, compete for the sales of spray paint for artistic purposes in Europe.

This is a fundamental step to understanding how, in that period, there was still a gap in the graffiti market, filled by four-five marker producers.

It is in this moment that companies like On The Run approach the market. Founded by Tim Macke and Akim Walta, On The Run launches the first marker lines specifically tailored for writers. The now famous OTR 060 is none other than a tribute to the tradition of felt-tip markers used in the previous decade. All, or almost all, of what would be produced subsequently will be a series of cameo products already present years earlier: the black Grog is just an attempt at finding a worthy successor of the Nero Inferno, the Krink K-60 gives a nod to its Uni-Paint PX-30 big brother, while the Molotow Masterpiece is undoubtedly a tribute to that generation of Poster Markers – like Biggie 30 or 50 – so dear to the tradition of European Writing.

The appropriation of products for common use like markers and inks for other unintended aims has generated a new market for them, revisited for this parallel purpose. This movement has always availed itself of popular cultural references – like Bodé puppets or characters from Hanna & Barbera – just as its market, now prevalently managed by writers, applies the same principle of reinterpretation to products it comes up with, day by day.

Key points
>

1940
THe first rudimental marker models – sold empty

1950
Esterbrooks Cushman & Denison launch the brand Flo-Master, whose first product is the homonymous ink, famous for its opaque finish

1953
Sidney Rosenthal launches the Magic Marker, the first felt-tip marker to be sold in history – according to the documents and copyright and patent registrations.

1954
Ideal Stencil introduces the first valve marker in the market. Unlike its predecessor Magic Marker, the Ideal-Mark is composed – other than of a barrel and a felt-tip – of a valve system that permits the ink to soak the tip on the basis of the exerted pressure.

Mid 60's
Nero D'Inferno is born, an Italian product that imposes itself in the local and International shoe industry thanks to the formula that makes it extremely penetrating on leather.

1962
Yukio Horie founds the Tokyo Stationery Company, original name of the famous Japanese brand Sanford Berol, known today as Sanford. In 1962 he invents the first marker with a synthetic tip. Until then, marker tips were rough wicks of matted wool – hence the name, which would then remain to indicate the generic marker tip. Yukio Horie introduces nylon and polyester as the perfect synthetic materials from which to let ink flow, simulating the typical stroke of Japanese Indian ink and brush culture.

Early 70's
Writers discover that hardware stores in NYC sell bottles of printing ink (Garvey ink), stencil inks (Marsh, Flo-Master) and writing ink (Pilot ink). Now aware of where to steal them, writers start mixing the various inks in order to create an evermore indelible brew.

Early 70's
In parallel to the creation of the first highlighters, the Japanese introduce the first examples of poster markers: whose tips were about a centimetre wide, decidedly outside the ruling standards. The local market, strongly tied to the culture of calligraphy, demanded markers that were able to cover rather large surfaces, for artistic and advertising purposes.

Late 80's
In parallel to the creation of the first highlighters, the Japanese introduce the first examples of poster markers: whose tips were about a centimetre wide, decidedly outside the ruling standards. The local market, strongly tied to the culture of calligraphy, demanded markers that were able to cover rather large surfaces, for artistic and advertising purposes.

A do-it-yourself affair

Mode 2, TCA–CTK / London
>

All through the 80's finding caps was a real hassle. Today you go to spots where people paint and can find dead caps all over the place; everywhere. People just use them as if they were disposable. Back in the day you'd try to work out a way of recycling them, we'd use acetone, trichloroethylene, lighter fluid, or screen cleaner.

You'd be swapping advice and knowledge with people on how to clean the caps, because they were precious, like spray cans. England had Car Plan, Duplicolour and Marabu paint, if you were good at stealing that is, since Marabu Buntlack cost like £7 back then!

So if you wanted to improve on drawing characters at the time you had to manage with the limited colours available. The piece you made was related to the tools you had so it was very easy to recognise the London styles during the 80's, before Sparvar came into the market.

They were just different, you could spot the Car Plan and Duplicolour pieces in a second, in those simple car-painting colours: beige, blue, dull oranges and weak yellows; nothing too bright apart from Buntlack. I remember when we went to try to do some trains in 1985 with all kinds of car paint. There were six of us and it just wasn't working.

We had no fat caps, as we didn't even know about them; even though we did see them in *Subway Art*. Brim came over in April '85 to record the *Hip Hop history* documentary and was shocked by the fact we didn't have fat caps. We saw him use Buntlack with the regular caps, those little tank-shaped ones, and we were blown away by the technique and control he had; so clean, no drips.

Back in those days you really saw how long it took to get anywhere near good. Every country had their own brand, there was no universal standard.

In Paris they had Altona with lots of lead inside, 2.2%!

But they also had Krylon, which was pretty good for the time, in the mid 80's; original American cans with a French paper label over the top. We painted mostly with Altona because Krylon's pressure was really hard to control, you couldn't find many caps for that. In Copenhagen they had Quick, really limited; which was probably why they really innovated the mixing of paint from can to can. When the graffiti thing came out, the standard was to steal cans, it was a way of gaining street credibility, but it was very hard for people a certain age to learn how to steal. I think you learn from when you're young. If you practice enough, by the time you're 13 or 14 you're really good at it. So it was difficult for me cause I was definitely more art-driven than anything else, I didn't really know where to put the stuff I was trying to steal. I never really got into that, maybe the younger guys caught that bug more than people our age, as we were already 16 or so.

At one point when I lived in Paris, I stayed for 6 months at a friend's family's house. As an exchange, I did paintings for them and they'd buy canvases, but the Graphigro store only sold Krylon; so suddenly I had to try to work with those cans in a small format, trying to find a solution. Bando did all his outlines with Krylons but I felt they were a real nightmare because of all the pressure with which paint came out. Bando on the other hand could perfectly control outlines of big letters, painted in the street.

I always tried to keep the can control, the pressure of aerosol. With the original Krylon caps, when you're pressing down and you're listening, you can hear as soon as the air starts to come in, you can hear the paint bubbling down inside. When the hole gets large enough it comes up. It's not something you can do with a walkman on, or at a jam with music. I discovered you can really check this on a can of paint. I don't know whether it's like playing the trumpet or something, they must know how low they have to push the keys to make the right sound come out. With Krylons you really have to hold the cap constantly,

once you've pushed down far enough to let just the tiniest amount of paint out. It was something you really had to learn, there was no other way around.

Before paint was created especially for writers you had to improvise, so we learnt to control, and this direct consequence between tools and styles was evident not only in Europe. A lot of New York panel pieces looked so dynamic because they had to paint rapidly to avoid drips. The paint comes out quick, so you have to paint quicker. It's actually the best way to learn and also keep the art dynamic.

When the first Sparvars started to come over, the first default caps were the white ones, black-tipped inside, they saved me because less pressure was necessary to paint, so characters for example came better.

Bando had been bringing Erylons and Sparvar caps back to Amsterdam, and those were what helped him outline his pieces. I started with Altona before, then Krylon and then I switched to Sparvar in the beginning of '89; when Krylon discontinued so many good colours, and the paint was covering less than before.

Since then I've painted with a lot of different paint, but I've slowed down since summer '97, when I started to suffer the consequences of being exposed to paint for so long. I'm totally against the idea of people giving their Names to a colour of spray paint or a brand, as they never really did anything for us except damage our health. When Brussels decided that CFC should be removed from all types of spray, the paint brands adapted really quickly; but trying to get them to make safer paint is probably a lost cause to fight for, as too many people are too young to consider what effect prolonged contact with the paint and the fumes could do to them.

They've made so much money off of our health over the years, the least they could do is put some of this into research that could make non-toxic paint of good quality a reality one day...

TOOL DISCOVERIES
—

Zebster – COD / Budenheim
>

European writers didn't have good quality spray cans in the beginning, so we tried to figure out quite early on how to get better control of the spray. I was really into finding good solutions from the beginning, testing different caps. It was kind of logical, you had ten different spray cans at home and you wanted to test every possibility. For instance there was a very special brand for model airplanes, with special colours: when I tested one of the skinny caps on, it had a special effect, it would make a really sharp line and this pushed me to experiment a little bit more even if the same cap on the other cans was not really working.

When the value of a fat cap for the filling was discovered, what we were looking for was already on the market, it was used for cleaning ovens, like for foam spray. Through JBK I got the connection to find where the fat caps were produced, he gave me the tip. Then I figured out that another company made skinny caps, originally meant for Ellen Beatrix deodorants. So we called the skinny cap Ellen-Beatrix, the name of the deodorant became the name of the cap! We had L'Oreal as well, which was a hair spray, and L'Oreal was kind of a soft fat cap. I organised the whole thing, asking the company about all their different products

and then I simply made a test run.

In '89–'90 I tested all these different brands, writing a test report, like something a big company would do. When I finally found the skinny and fat cap standards, I turned it into a kind of business, through the cap sales we financed *On The Run* magazine because people were saying "Hey five dm is too expensive", even though a packet of cigarettes was the same price. There was this guy from NYC, Owen, he figured out where the Rusto fat caps were produced. So what we did was a kind of exchange "Get 8000 fat caps from me and I'll get 8000 fat caps from you". It was a primitive kind of business trade that was in the hands of the writers. Today it's in the industries' hands. Once this research on caps got started I tried to combine every single cap with every kind of spray can available on the market.

In Munich writers had Duplicolour which they used for commercials, the fat caps fit but as the can didn't have that much pressure there wasn't the usual blast of paint coming out. With skinny caps it was even worse, as they had a different means of connecting. Then in Hamburg there were Barbor spray cans which had thicker paint, the fat cap was working, but not as well as on other spray cans. When this process became clear it was really possible to manage the quality of pieces and the way you were painting. For example with the Marabu

and the fat cap you have a totally different effect compared to the Dupli kind. Dortmund guys had started wrecking cans very early on, they had like 60 Marabus while we only had one or two once in a while, and the difference became tangible, their pieces were shining on trains! They even had a spray called "Popolo", a very skinny spray with a very positive effect on the outlines.

Then, during a trip through Denmark I tried Quik cans, which was a spray can that was not compatible with the skinny caps. As a consequence Scandinavian writers had to learn how to work with regular caps, and since lines weren't 100% straight or sharp they had this effect you see on New York pieces, a kind of dirty outline but still with this kind of special flavour.

Another input that drove me into researching tools came surreally from a chewing-gum brand that started to add graffiti stickers to the candies. These weren't distributed all over Germany but when one guy found out the gums were produced in Scandinavia, me and Can-2 went there and bought everything; in '86 we had these 20–30 stickers which also gave us some kind of inspiration because some of the pieces were a mix of spray paint and air brush, so it wasn't 100% clear for us how it worked, we had no clue. They looked ok, they were sprayed but it was a bit strange for

us to understand how we could reach such an effect with the normal spray can.

Then all of a sudden in Europe we all started using Sparvar cans, they had a good colour range and were the best for outlines and details, even the fat caps were ok but it was impressive how much the quality changed: you could have a saffron yellow which during the filling faded into darker or lighter tones! But as Sparvar was first distributed in the North of Germany, in Mainz we started using Auto-K and Multona. The first time we painted with Sparvar was in '87 when we went to Hamburg. Then in Holland Henk was selling these spray cans at the flea market of Waterlooplain, in Amsterdam. So after many combinations I started selecting just some of the more unusual colours of different brands, so blue from Sparvar was perfect for outlines and some other colours would be chosen by other companies. Me and Loomit also talked about the idea of having our own spray cans, this was around 1992. We met and after this discussion we wrote down a list of colours that referred to writers, such as Chintz Blue, Zebster Red and many others; I wrote a letter to them but didn't get a response back. We knew exactly which colours we wanted to have and the shades we would need but in the end it was not successful, simply because it was premature.

Blackbooks compared: Delta's step by step

The double format of blackbooks:
from Delta's 'diaries', a collection
of sketches and images, to Rens'
photographic albums.
A direct comparison between
two masters of style

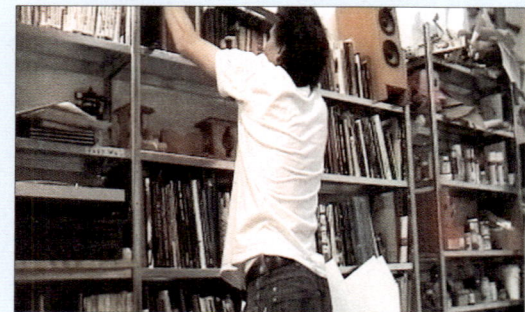

In the 70's writers in NYC used blackbooks differently from how we would use them in Europe. They had two books: one only for photos of the subway and the other for sketches, this was the original way.

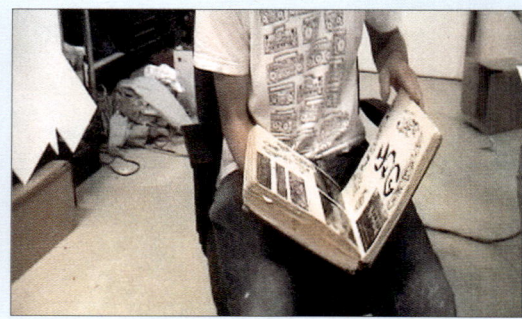

On the other hand we combined those two books into one, we turned it into a sort of diary with sketches and photos. We rein-terpreted their way and made our own.

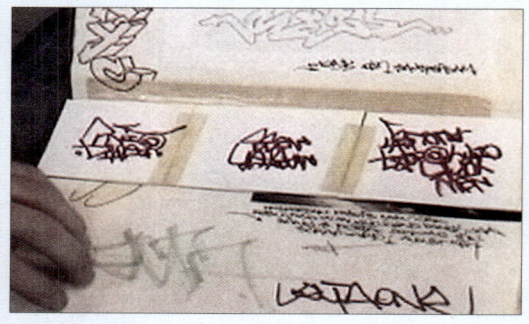

The first time I went to New York was in '84 and everything was still bombed. When I went back in '87 a lot of trains were clean yet a lot of lines were still bombed, especially inside. It was the best thing ever!

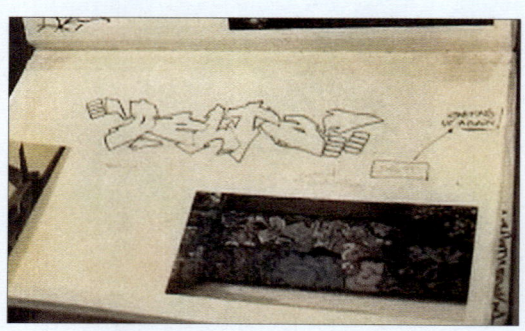

I did this piece in 1991. After that I stopped doing pieces for a year. In 1992 I started up again because of what was happen-ing to the subway lines in Amsterdam.

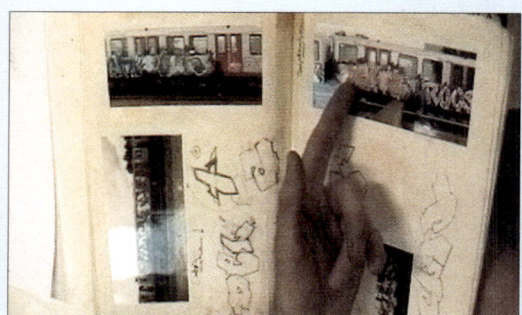

The trains weren't being cleaned anymore for environmen-tal reasons. They were building cement canals to collect the chemicals that would be used for buffing the trains.

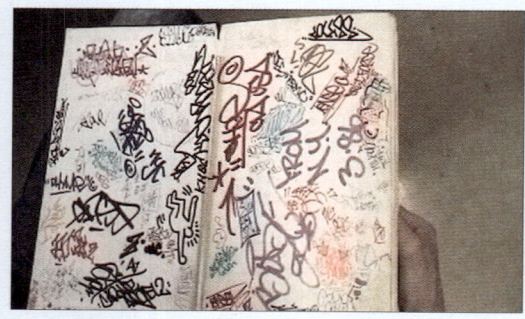

This is my guest page, a lot of foreign writers wrote their tag here. For example there is Rhyme, Zeb and Gasp. In 1986 Keith Haring and Blade came to Amsterdam, you can see their tags on this page as well.

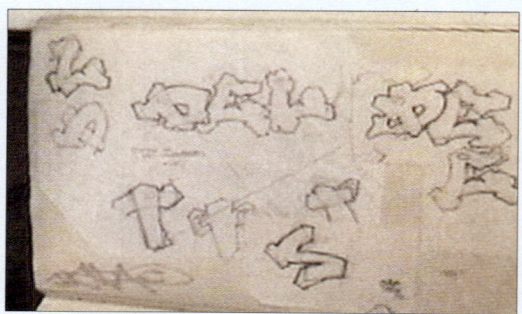

In the early 90's I was studying Industrial Design at the Univer-sity of Delft. On my way to Amsterdam I was always on the train for two-three hours with my sketchbooks, so I would keep drawing outlines.

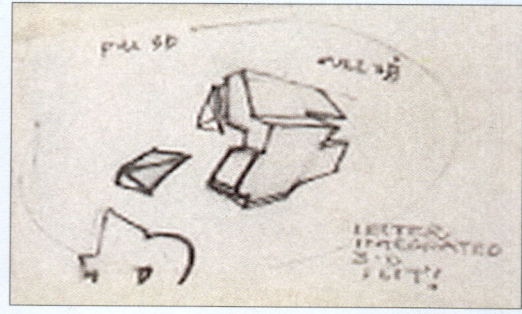

This is my first 3D realisation, it's an "E". If you look at it closely you'll see it's not actually an "E", but just a shape. I drew this ir-regular element and then I just sketched the XY lines. I realised this new shape was resembling an "E".

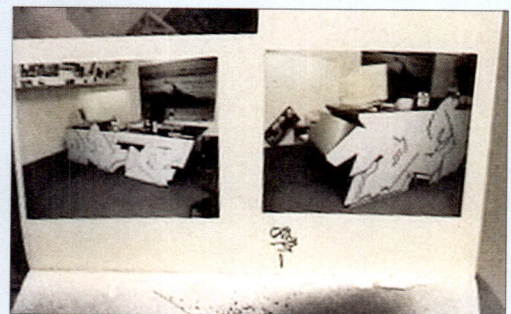

Even for architecture students it was common to draw 3D sketches or to make models rather than render them with a computer program used by professionals.

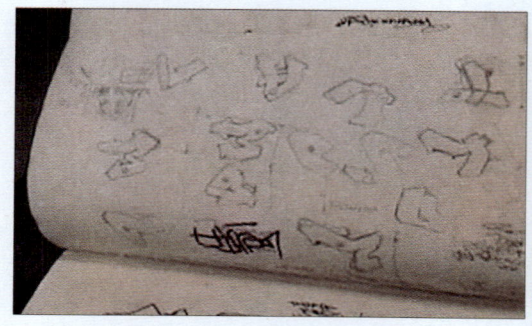

So I was trying to approach lettering as if it was something you could stick on the wall. I had the same approach with product design.

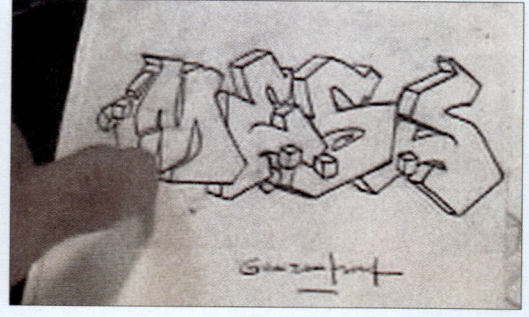

Then there was a turning point. I realised that maybe if I had an "M" I could make the length of the "M" go like this, even if this is not a real 3D, geometrically speaking it would be different, it would be bent.

guide to building 3D letters

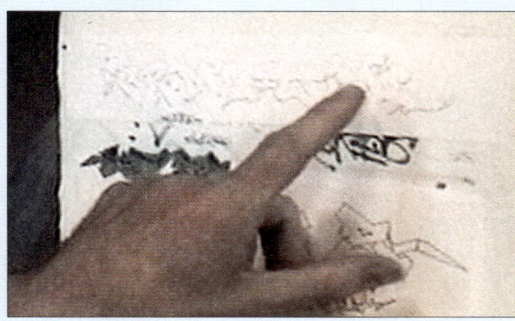

This was obviously my choice, as well as that of a lot of other writers from the first generation in the 80's. This sketch is from 1986 or so. It's the Bando influence. He was coming to Amsterdam a lot in the 80's because of his connection with Shoe.

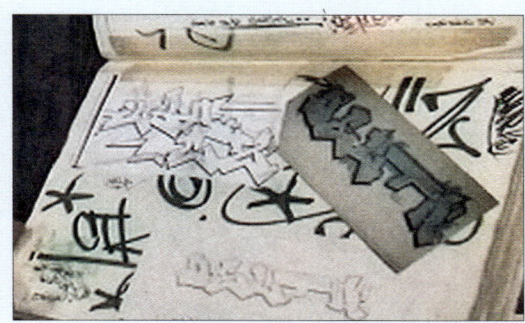

This piece was actually done in Rotterdam. I would go over to Rotterdam in 1986 to hang out with Eras and other guys from that city.

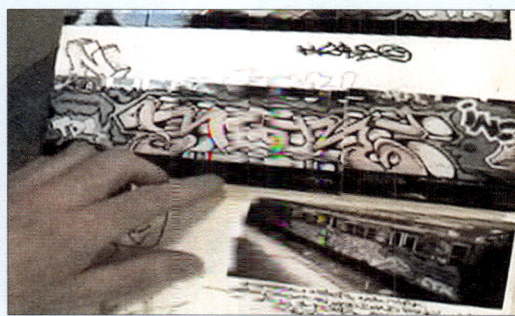

This piece was done in New York. I did the train with Sane, the guy who later died. I went over to Henry Chalfant's studio and asked if it was possible to do a trains, so we did a scrap train over in Brooklyn.

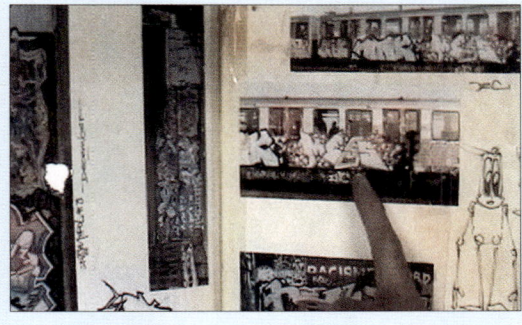

This situation brought a lot of foreign writers to Amsterdam. Everybody was going wild for our train lines, everything was bombed! This is why there were a lot of exchanges taking place between cities.

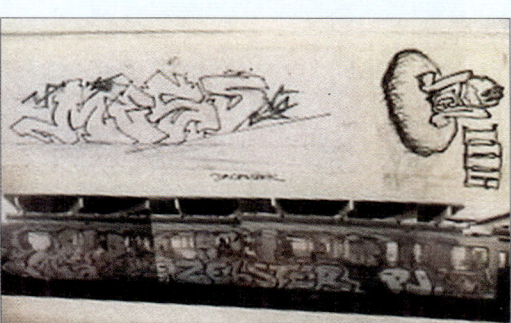

This is a piece I did with Zebster from Germany. He was the editor of On the Run magazine, always visiting different cities... during this time he published a special report on the Amsterdam subway.

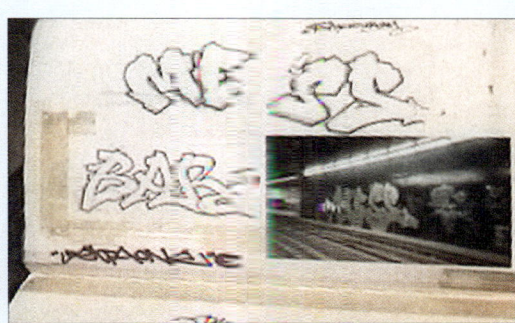

I was using two different names at the time, Mess and Delta. I liked Mess a lot because of the letters, you could do interesting things with them.

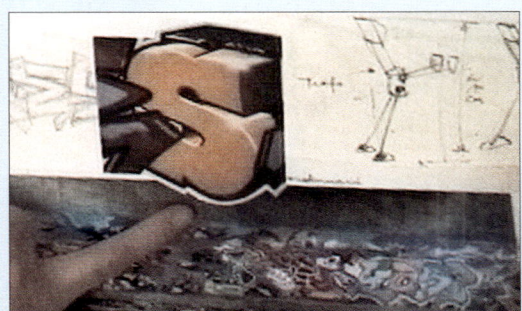

Honestly I didn't do anything with it for a long time, it came out randomly because I was always sketching 3Ds for a University course. I applied the same 3D study to certain letters which I then painted outside, like on this wall.

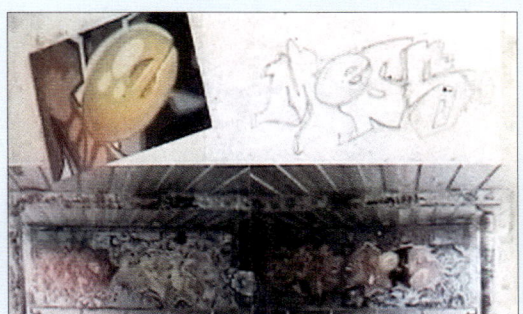

I was just experimenting by applying these rules to my letters. I was also playing a lot with perspectives, for example like the circle on this wall piece.

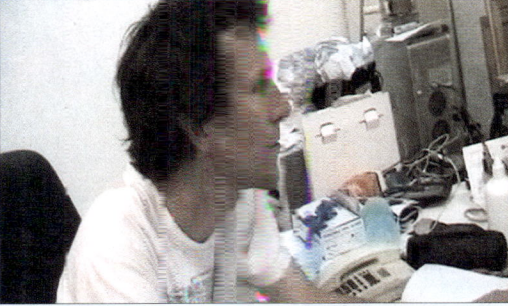

I was used to representing any object in perspective or by an axonometric design because in '92 3D computer programs were available but not that accessible. They were high-end graphic machinery which needed days to render one image.

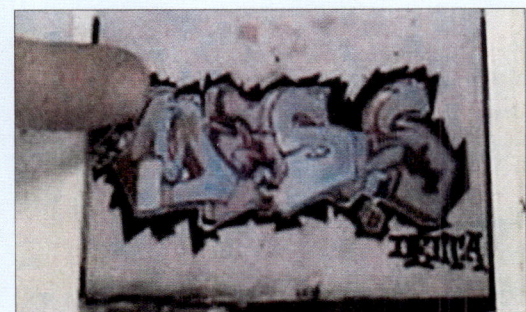

So I thought maybe there could be an arrow or anything else in the shape; at that point I realised that 3D could really have a form of its own. It was a completely different approach to building letters.

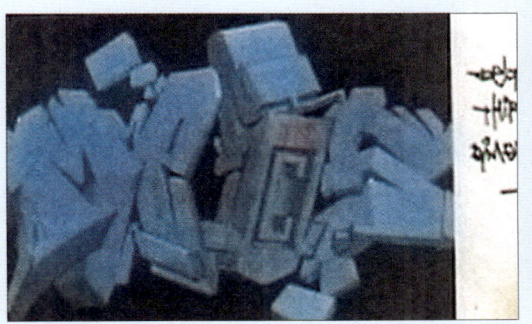

For instance this is a real 3D sketch. I spent a whole weekend studying these shapes and trying to draw them in a hyper-realistic way with lights and shadows as though it had been rendered by a machine.

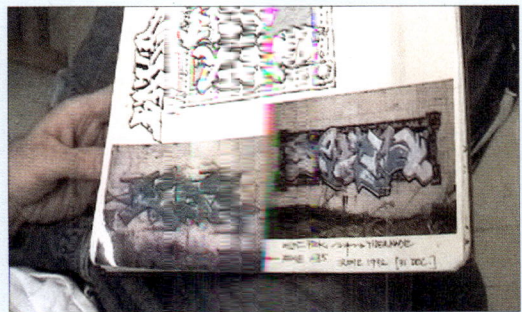

These were painted along the Roman Tevere river, you can compare my style from 1985 with that of 1992. I've painted the same spot again recently but it has been archived on my hard drive, which is a sort of contemporary blackbook.

A style profile: Rens' photo albums, reminiscing

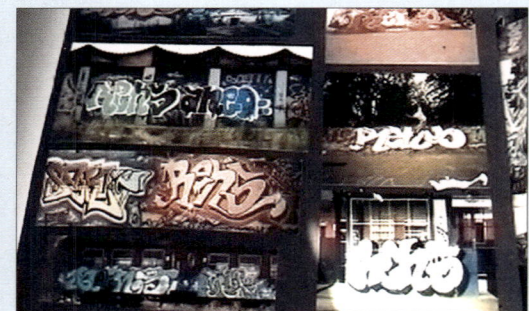

My blackbook is a ringed A2 black page album. It's done like the original New York blackbooks, a collection of photographs of the pieces I have done.

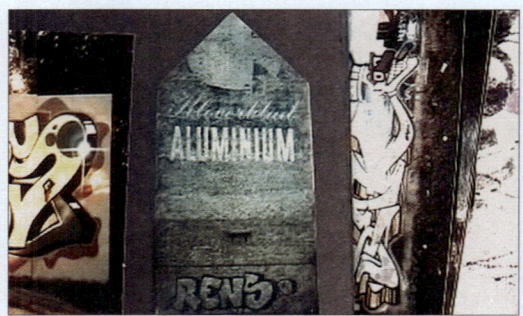

I've decided to keep all my sketches separate and only have photos in this book. It's a collection of memories with pages dedicated to my travels and the pieces I did abroad.

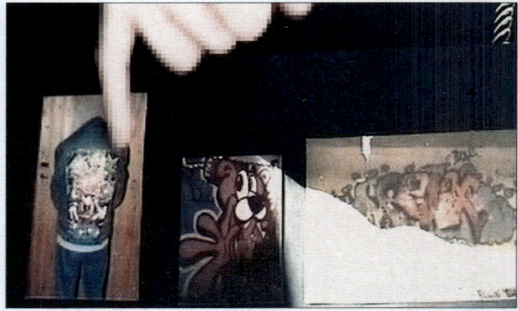

This was done in 1985, it is one of my first back pieces done on a jeans jacket. During the 70's in New York it was typical to paint the back part of your jacket so we did the same in Copenhagen.

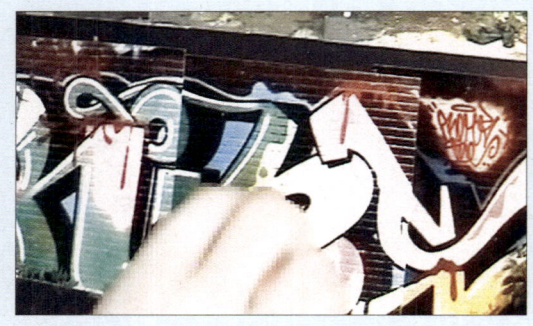

We learnt early on how to escape in such situations. In time we managed to paint the walls along the line and even though it was risky we used to paint fully coloured pieces. We have always preferred the hall of fame aesthetic with detailed backgrounds.

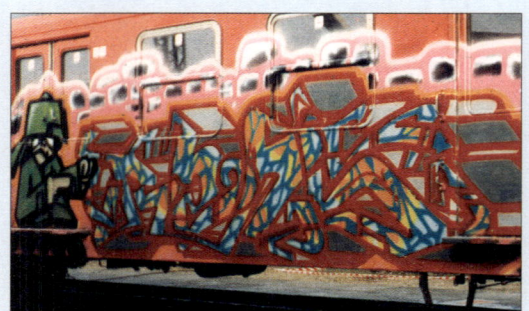

The spots on the line were chosen based on how visible they were from the train. The walls along the line became a very important target for every writer in Copenhagen aside from the famous red S-Trains.

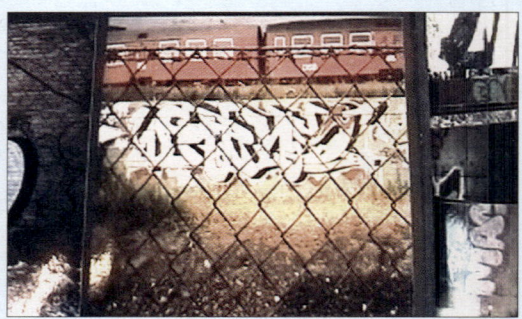

Even this is an illegal spot: as we don't have a continuous wall along the rail tracks like the ones in Basel, I had to go over my pieces so many times. I think I've painted this wall ten times!

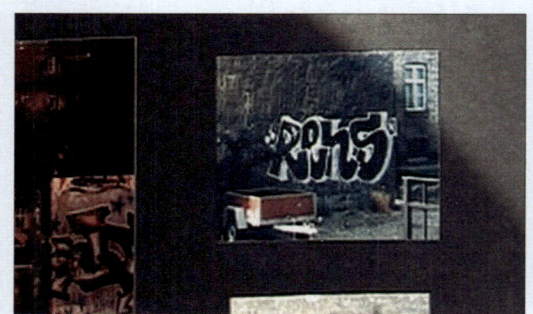

For my throw-ups I was keeping black as the filling and silver as the outline. I used to organise my street bombings by going out one night doing all the black fillings and then the next night tracing the silver outlines.

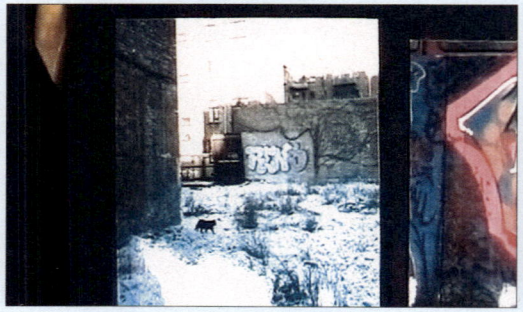

It was a good method to carry less spray cans and give no proof of what I had done. I had also made a guard uniform with a sign on the jacket, this way I could walk around yards without any problems.

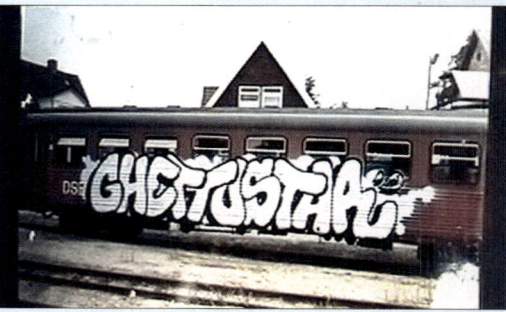

The S-Trains have always been the main target for all the writers in Copenhagen. It all started in the early 80's. They have always been considered an important point of confrontation for the scene.

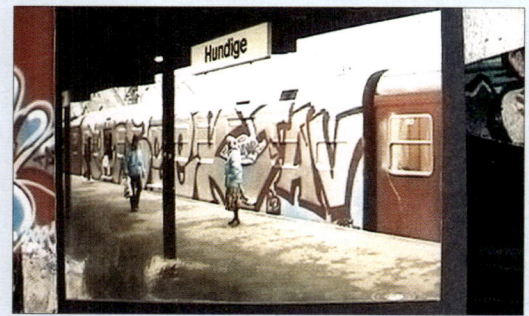

This piece was done with spray pumps. You'd put the paint in and then pump out the silver, it was really fast and exciting to fill a whole car with this method which was pretty innovative back then.

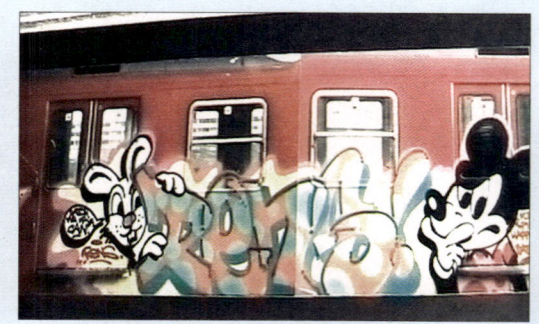

I used to bomb the A-Line because at that time I was living close to those yards. Most of the time we'd paint the trains during the day, hiding between two rows. TAV, my crew, got its name from this: The A-line Vandals.

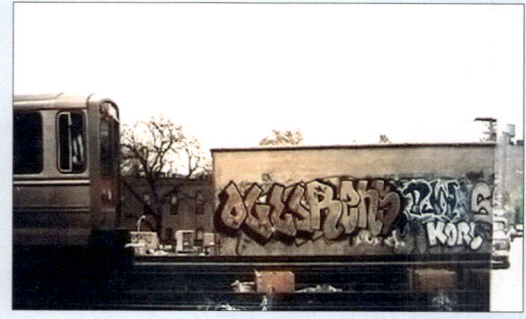

This is a photo of a piece I did in the States. I visited the U.S. a few times in the early 90's. I went to the major cities and hit their main targets such as subways and trucks. I was in Chicago for a while, it was pretty easy painting there even though they call it "Cop-Town" because the police is everywhere...

New York portfolios

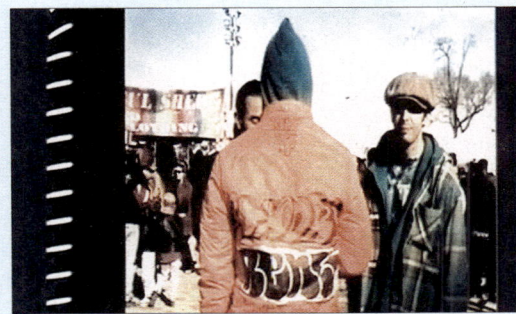

The dress code was important in the 80's, this way you could be recognised in the scene somehow. This back piece was just like the throw-ups I was doing back then all over Copenhagen.

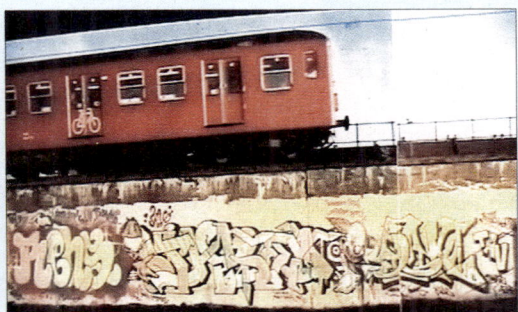

This piece was done with other famous Danish writers on the wall that follows the S-Train rail track.

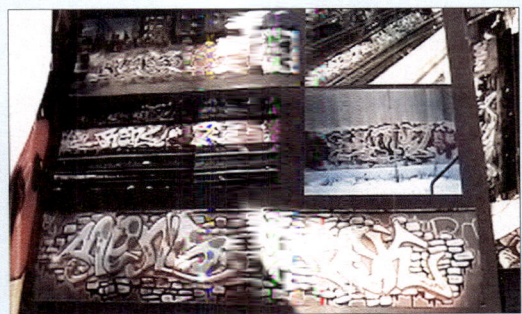

These walls in Copenhagen are illegal and I got chased on my first piece. Some cops rolled up screaming so we ran away. I don't think they had ever seen anything like it, they were wondering what was going on.

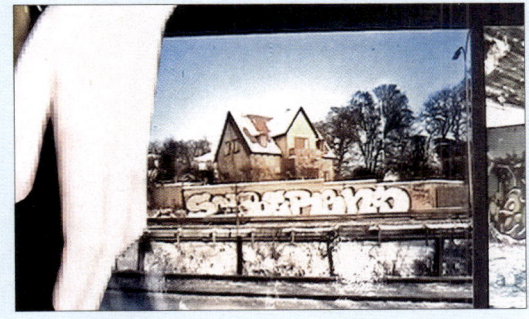

The scene in Copenhagen was pretty respectful. Me and Sek were always finding new spots so we never had to cross people out. Sabe was another great partner.

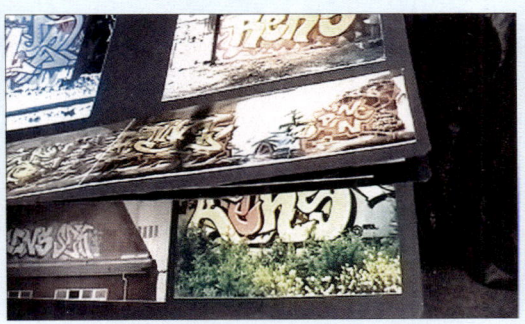

During the early 90's most of the colour pieces were done with Quik paint. There weren't many good colours available back then, you could only get green, grey, blue and a few others

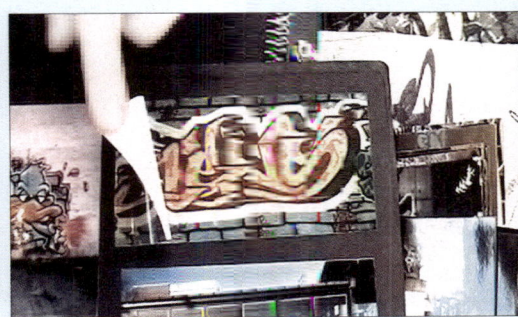

For that reason I started mixing paints. The result was fantastic and the whole scene was shocked by the variety of colours in my pieces. All sorts of colours came out like "his mother works in a paint factory!" or "he uses faulty colours!"

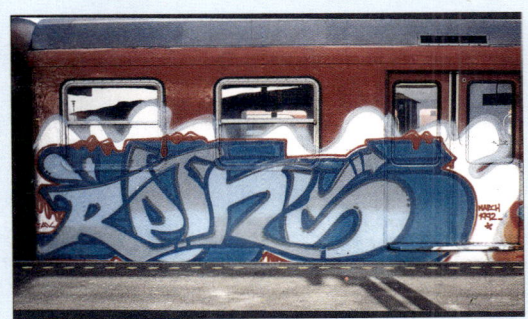

In the beginning the S-Train scene in Copenhagen was pretty friendly, my main partner was Sek. Every now and then there was beef but never a lot, it all started later.

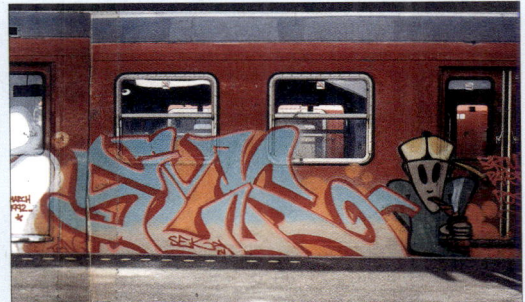

Besides Sek I was also painting with guys like Mins, Bates and Sabe. They were the best partners and I knew there was no problem if we got busted as they were very experienced guys.

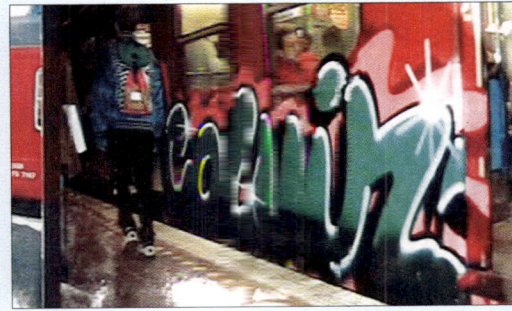

Calvin was my other name on trains. An alias proved to be useful in avoiding problems with the local Vandal Squad. Of course it was also a way to experiment with other letters, though keeping a recognisable style at least for writers.

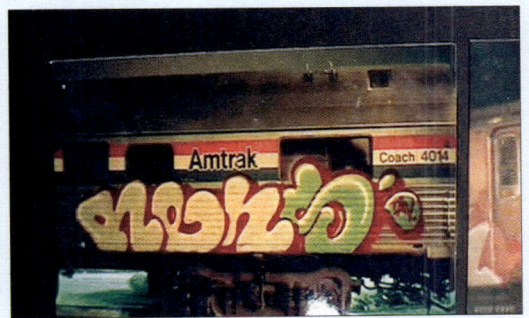

We painted the Amtrak trains in Chicago but not the subway. I was staying with Sek at Age's house, he kept telling us "we'll do it tomorrow, we'll do it tomorrow..." but time just passed!

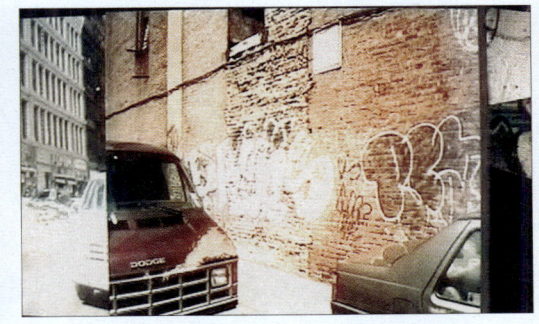

The first time we were in Chicago we stayed 14 days and the second time one month. In 14 days we finished 300 cars! We wrecked a lot there and then brought them to New York. Back then flying with cans was allowed. Once there we hit all sort of targets, besides the subway we did a lot of street bombing.

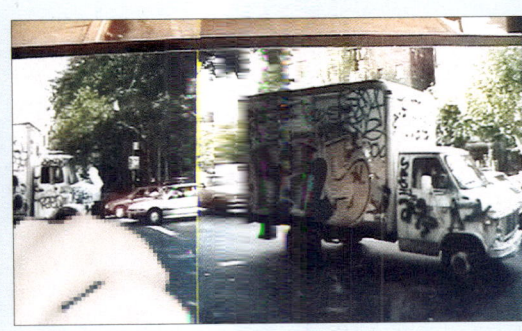

This is New York in '91, at the time the subway was already clean and we noticed that trucks were a sort of alternative target in the city. There was a truck yard where we would go paint, we did 50 pieces or something. I only have a few truck photos in my blackbook as a memory of that year.

Madrid flecheros

> CONTINUES FROM PAGE 132

of the metropolitan crown to areas in the centre. During this expansion and radication, as had occurred in New York during the 70's, a crucial role was played by the diffusion of the phenomenon through media (newspapers, radio and television), which concentrated on the same emblematic figure: Muelle, also thanks to these new communicative channels, became a popular character for the entire community of Madrid. The propagation of Writing tied to the Hip Hop movement, which only arrived to the Iberian capital in a successive period, produced an open conflict with Los Flecheros; a rivalry that was aimed at contending the spaces of the city as much as it was concerned with defending the various stylistic choices. Faced with the growing popularity of the American codes of Writing, the Autoctonos chose to increasingly emphasise the aesthetic and design of their signatures, even evolving the original tags into thicker, contoured letters, similarly to what had happened in New York. Their aesthetics however remained tied to a structural element such as the arrow, which, underneath the name, guided the style of the 'Autoctonos'. Gradually however, the passage from autochthonous to Hip Hop-oriented Writing became increasingly evident, until the total endorsement of the movement eradicated this peculiar local style around the middle of the 90's. A revival of the phenomenon took place around the end of the 90's due to some representatives of the early period, but in Madrid it would be the New York style of Writing that would conquer all the following generations.

—

New tough line for crew behaviors

> CONTINUES FROM PAGE 136

on Sundays, at the football match.

What was the link between CBS and Ajax?
HIGH– Not everyone from CBS moved across to Ajax, but when I got out of jail, the group was more important than the single individual. And since being in a group was more of a lifestyle for us, when I came out Ajax became a reference and everything was just part of the same big thing... graffiti, soccer and violence. I also organised fights. Since '85 we've been kickboxing so we are good fighters, Pengo is a world champion.

Mixing gangs and graffiti is kind of unique in Europe...
HIGH– Yes, but even if the rumours on CBS were always related to violence, I have to say there wasn't all that much beef between crews in Amsterdam. Sometimes we hate each other and so we cross each other but usually it's not done on purpose. For instance we had a good relationship with USA, of course there was competition and even also jealousy... they were artists, they weren't street guys. CBS only had two-three good writers, while the rest were just bombers.

In the 80's a lot of guys were visiting Amsterdam from London and Germany, were you interested in meeting others?
HIGH– A writer that has gained a lot of respect here is Chintz from Germany. He was the first to come here. He was standing at Leidseplein with us and all of a sudden said "Hey, look at my name on that tram!" so I looked and it was written over my piece! I put a knife to his neck and told him to give me some cans. It probably wasn't the best way to get in touch but only one year later one of our gang members got in touch with him when he went to Dortmund; so we kind of became friends. Things can happen like that but he shouldn't have written on my piece, even if it was just on the background. It was a good experience for him, now he's one of the best writers in the world. He is the ultimate writer. We even met some people from London in '87, who were Arsenal supporters. Among them was Drax. I was an Ajax supporter but we didn't bother about that. He later climbed up the Arsenal scene and I moved up the Ajax scene. The two teams are good friends though, so we don't fight each other.

I remember a huge "AJAX" piece painted inside the stadium, just behind the locals' terraces..
HIGH– Right, in '85 I made the first piece there. I wrote across the Ajax stadium the names of the F-Side leaders. They called me and said "Hey, can you come here and paint our logo?" They gave me 350 gilders and some cans, so I did the first piece for them. Later on it became my life beside graffiti and that wall got painted again, with Rayme and other Amsterdam writers.

CITY CHRONICLES

>

This section investigates the explosion of the Writing phenomenon in Italy. The national territory is mapped by focusing on the most prolific centres of the early 90's. Through the narratives of the direct protagonists, the characteristics of an apparently homogeneous scene are delineated and revealed as a eclectic reality, diffused throughout the country and often influenced by the peculiarities of the individual urban contexts. The primary common trait of this fragmentary universe, able to connect corners of reality quite distant from one another, is the national railway, analysed in the epilogue of this section. City Chronicles is thus a unique observatory, a case study that is introduced in the following pages through the testimonies of those who inspired specific local scenes. These heterogeniety of the contributors, chosen among protagonists whose experiences and contexts are completely removed from one another, is essential to faithfully render the complexity of such a landscape. Sean Martin, founding pillar of Milanese Breaking, here contributes his memories of the local Hip Hop scene; Monia Cappuccini, now a journalist, narrates the débuts of the Roman movement, lived through in first person, from a political perspective; and finally Zero-T and Deemo, trace back the first steps of CMC crew, remembering the beginning of the movement in Italy during the 80's.

BACK TO THE ROOTS

Sean Martin's firsts steps, a precursor of
the movement in Italy

The reciprocal exchange of experiences, information and contacts has always been at the
base of Hip Hop's growth. As a kid I too contributed to this exchange at the expense of the
poor woman that put me into this world: our
home was always infested with breakers – especially
French ones – and with a perpetual smell of tiger balm.
Laurent, Wilson, Michel, Nicolas, Didier, Aktuel Force,
Paris City Breakers...all names that have indelibly marked
the history of the movement in Italy and Europe. I was
about 12 years old, it was the 80's and Hip Hop would
never be as genuine in Italy as at that time. Many have
wondered who was the first person that set the example
here, obviously it's impossible to trace back to the very
first Italian B-boy and very probably it would be of no use
anyway. What matters in my opinion, is understanding
the artistic and cultural movement by analysing its genesis and development.
With regards to the Milanese scene, I was lucky to witness the beginning of this phenomenon and even be a
part of its development. It's inevitable to cite certain
names even though they might mean nothing to most
people, names that have never been mentioned on the
web because they left this world before internet was even
born. In Milan, the most significant, forgotten and isolated name is certainly that of Roberto Avellano (RIP). It was
the end of '82 and I was 11 years old, Avellano was five
years older than me and I met him through my brother
Paul, who was 14. A detail that may be important in understanding my story is the fact that my family had emi-
grated from South Africa to Milan in the early 70's. My
parents were musicians that had come to Italy in search
of the opportunities that South Africa didn't concede to
people that were not Caucasian. Nevertheless, in Italy we
also encountered difficulties due to the fact that we were
foreigners and had a different skin colour. Ever since I
was a child I understood that ignorance was a nasty beast
to be reckoned with, and whatever is different and unknown often arouses fear.
My brother and Robi hung out with the same company of
friends under Posterla, an arch between the two towers
in front of the church of S. Ambrogio and on Saturdays
they would mix with the first New romantic groups that
would meet up at the terrace of Linus, which would later
become Burger One, then Quick, Burghy, and finally Mc-
Donalds. In front of this place, cyclically managed by fast
food restaurants, was Muretto.
At night Robi and my brother would go to clubs like C.O.C
/ ZAM, the Odissea 2001 – later to become the Prego –
and most of all Il Punto Rosso. When, some years later,

the club collapsed due to an intense bout of snowfall, the
roof was removed and the dance floor became the courtyard of the renamed social centre of Garigliano. The resident DJ of Punto Rosso was a certain Maurizio Marsico,
so much time has passed that I hardly remember his face
but anyway it was thanks to him that Avellano and my
brother started moving the first steps, that they would
then study and perfect in the living room of my house.
They were absurd, Avellano resembled James Dean and
had bought himself a pair of white waiter gloves that he
would wear during these performances, he would put
the hood of his sweatshirt over his head and start moving
like a marionette, walking backwards and forwards in a
strange manner that made it seem like he was fluctuating
in my living room. My brother on the other hand looked
like one of the Jackson 5, and followed suite. James Dean
and Michael Jackson were floating in my living room!
I had already seen those types of movements in a music
video that was probably called Hanging out, by a group
whose name I unfortunately cannot remember, – a dose
of amnesia that has been pestering me for at least 20 years
– and there was a kid in it that danced as if he had no liga-
ments or joints. I found myself admiring those moves and
the next Christmas I bought a gigantic red sweatshirt,
with a zipper and hood, and a pair of white gloves that I
would colour co-ordinate with a white Kangol-like cap
an uncle had left me when he passed away. Avellano and
Paul were able to smuggle me into Punto Rosso in spite
of my young age, all I had to do was wear my gear and
move like a robotic puppet in front of the bouncer and a
second later I was in.
It was an afternoon early in '83 when Maurizio Marsico
started playing a selection of pieces that went from The
message by Grand Master Flash to Problems by the Fear-
less Four and also more commercial but yet banging stuff
like Ain't no body by Chaka Khan. I got goosebumps the
first time I entered that place and after a couple of minutes I had a circle of people around me staring in disbelief
as I danced. At the time I wasn't very good at it yet and
so I attribute all this attention to the fact that I was so
young; in any case, what was for sure is that in no other
Milanese club were there 12 year olds doing Electric boogie! Maurizio Marsico had started giving a more American imprint to the parties at Punto Rosso, someone at
the club had gotten their hands on some videos with the
very first Rock Steady Crew (1977/78) that were screened
during the arc of the night. These tapes showed a 14 year
old Crazy Legs Breakdancing on the streets of New York
and at some parties. At the beginning of the 80's Punto
Rosso had become the funkiest spot of the city without a

shadow of a doubt.
The first concert I went to, and participated in towards
the finale, was by Whodini. Oh Man! If I think back to
when one of their dancers came out wearing a silver
tracksuit, moving to the beat of Rap Machine, I still get
chills down my spine today. It was at that concert that I
saw a "hand glide" live for the first time (the turn-on-
the-hand as I had coined it), and the first "windmill" (for
us "eliccottero" or helicopter and later "webo", "we-
borg", "cupole", "cupola", "mulino"...) Not much later
there was a show by Broken Glass and, a few months after
that, finally a concert by Kurtis Blow at the Odissea 2001.
During the show some fucking punk threw a glass in Mister Blow's face, but, after consulting with the statuesqeu
breakers that had come with him, he recomposed himself and continued the show as if nothing had happened.
In that period, due to a dramatic family situation, I was
living a rather singular life for a kid my age, so much
so that by 12 I was regularly hanging out in Corso Vittorio Emanuele, the street where Muretto would be.
Armed with a radio, Avellano, my brother and I would
keep up with what was happening in the neighbourhoods of New York thanks to certain acquaintances, and
so started dancing in the street just like the B-boys in
that city were doing. It was '83 and we founded what
is still called *Muretto* to this day. There, at the time, the
rules in vigour were quite strict, definitely very distant
from the current situation in which whoever listens to
rap, wears baggy pants and follows the scene tends to
define himself a B-boy. At the time you could stand on
the side watching all you wanted, but you could not dare
wear a belt buckle with your name, or fat laces, (which
at the time we would make ourselves with scotch tape
and petticoats you could get from any tailor). Not even
nameplate necklaces, the medallions with your name on
them, or Kangols or a pair of Cazals were passable if you
didn't first prove your worth as a breaker or writer (the
figure of the rapper didn't exist yet in Italy). If you faked
it and weren't able to prove your worth, you were shit.
There was no such thing as the phony rapperism of today,
on the floor it was immediately obvious who you were.
Hip Hop, before it got commercialised, was a tight movement that was based on honour and codes of conduct
that made it a cultural form without objectives of eco-
nomical recognition. Moreover – and very importantly
– to be a part of this movement you couldn't ignore any
of its artistic expressions. With time this aspect got lost.
In the 90's the so-called four disciplines – Mc-ing, Djing, Writing and B-boying – were separated and Writing in particular took its own form, almost independent

by Sean Martin

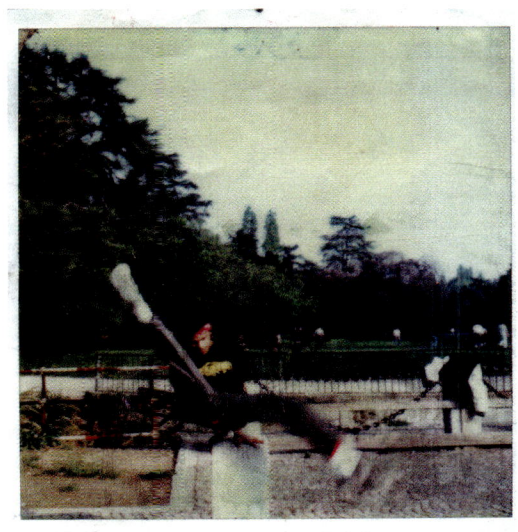

Sean at Parco Sempione, 1982   — *Sean Martin*

from the others. Many have taken advantage of the commercial rise of Hip Hop to promote their works and turn into writers. Today the world is full of crews with absurd acronyms, composed of people who enjoy a name and reputation in the Hip Hop circuit though they have no tie with the other three disciplines. Many of these are even good guys and good artists but they're spreading a movement whose spirit is very distant from what made Hip Hop such a pure phenomenon. Considering this aspect is decisive if you want to distinguish the movement of the early years from the current scene.

The first International artist I met that in my opinion contributed to de-contextualising Writing, was Keith Haring. He was painting the walls of Fiorucci, a world-renown store that is still today a few steps from Muretto, when one afternoon he told me he was setting up a personal exhibition. When I was invited to perform at the inauguration I met one of the most singular people and artists I ever encountered, A-one. He told me he was in Milan to promote his work and that in the meantime he was giving a hand to set up the show. Keith was a young artist who was rapidly gaining popularity and seemed to never deny those that associated him to Hip Hop, even though he had nothing to do with it. The media, at the time even more ignorant than today, even gave him

credit for spreading the movement.

A-one, who on the other hand had a very tight relation with Hip Hop, seemed not to mind this at all. Even though the whole thing left me quite perplexed, it was immediately evident that there were things in the Art business that I could not comprehend. I considered myself lucky to be there and would never have dared investigate further.

Then one evening of that fateful 1983, wandering around the station of Garibaldi, I saw a metal sheet fence that had been completely painted with incredible colours and strokes. The work carried the signatures of Toxic, A-one and Phase 2. A whole new world was opened to me. Until then I had only seen pieces in books like *Subway Art*, or on the cover of albums and movies that pertained to the scene in New York. Never would I have expected the privilege of seeing something of such incredible quality in the street, and even less did I expect to later actually paint with these great artists. It was pure magic, a dream, without even mentioning that I was just a kid in middle school. At night I was around painting until 2 in the morning and at 8:30 I was in school among classmates and teachers that couldn't even imagine what I was living.

My unusual family situation allowed all this, among the walls of my home, life advanced in a sad context and that's why it was important for me to spend my days practicing at Muretto, and painting at night with my friend Bogy Beat, also a breaker and among the first writers of Milan. Bogy was 16 years old and at night we'd go around with his motorcycle. Apart from us in Milan there was Graffio, his partner Fabietto and Tony a.k.a Seno, also a B-boy and among the most representative in Italy. There were other writers, newbies that made sketches on paper, jackets and t-shirts, but the walls of Milan were our privilege. Tritalo was another name you would hear of often but apart from never having seen a piece of his, I was sure he had no connection to the world of Hip Hop. Tritalo was a precocious example of street artist that is erroneously associated to Writing.

In any case shortly thereafter new solitary writers started sprouting everywhere – in Italy crews were a phenomenon of the 90's – and soon Writing became the passion of many night prowlers. In '85 I was denounced for a piece I had done on the Milanese aqueduct. My mother let all fury break loose also because I wasn't an Italian citizen and was thus risking much more than a simple reprimand and fine to pay. So, to allow things to settle, I had to suspend my activity as a writer.

That same year I ran away from home and went to London

to confront myself with the local breakers. London offered a scene that was impossible to compare to Italy's. Already at the time Hip Hop was obviously no fleeting phenomenon. In Covent Garden there were writers that spent their afternoons sitting on the sidewalk drawing in their notebooks, breakers practicing impressive human beat boxers and just a magical energy in the air. In that period they were even filming a movie about Hip Hop, called *Electro rock*, and at night there were jams everywhere in which memorable breaking battles would ensue, I felt more at home than ever. Another episode that left me speechless when I arrived to Covent Garden was the long fence of a construction site completely painted by the Chrome Angel, a name I had never heard before but that would change the history of writing. I was very impressed by the sleekness of the pieces, by the colouring techniques and the study of the letters. I had already seen something similar in some photos shown to me by some Parisian breakers. Among the many pieces those that stood out the most were by Bando, a name that would become legend, whose letters were destined to mark the identity of European Writing

Just as had happened in Milan, also in Turin, Bologna, Padua, Rome and other cities fabulous B-boys were sprouting everywhere, Writing was expanding and the Italian movement was acquiring a stronger identity. We would meet up regularly in different parts of the peninsula to battle and promote the name of the hometown crew. Deemo, Zero-T and Shangai (Sha-one) were the artists that most impressed me at the time.

In Milan skilled writers were appearing, a name that distinguished itself is without a doubt that of Kaos One, an inseparable friend and partner of mine. In the meantime I was given the opportunity to gain much experience in the field of breaking and especially Mc-ing, and soon rapping became a full-time profession.

Time seemed to pass faster and faster and Italy was slowly gaining a position in the European scene. Soon, thanks to names like Next One, we were recognised on a global scale.

Since then, everything has changed and during my artistic growth I encountered a multitude of contradictions in the message that many representative of this movement have been bringing forth for years. Peace, unity and having fun used to be the spirit but now racism, misogyny and homophobia transpire from the lyrics of many of the most regarded artists.

Hip Hop has indelibly marked my life but for various reasons – that may be subjective or not – it has lost the values that made it such a unique movement.

STARTING FROM

The dawn of the Roman scene, guided by
student protests and political opposition
in a time of social unrest

I magine a city with no tags, with no competition, with not even the slightest signs of graffiti. That's how Rome was in the 80's, a grey background in the life of a writer at point zero. Things were already starting to happen back then and in order for the culture to take root in the Eternal City, it utilised Hip Hop's energy. They arrived at the same time, arm in arm, to overturn the imagination and the existence of kids in those days. From the start we received muddled and blurred signs from that hotbed known as the Big Apple thanks to mainstream media: first and foremost, music - not just albums and covers, but also music videos played their part: an unforgettable Grand Master Flash in the middle of a run-down Bronx in "The Message" -; the first exhibits in galleries; some papers- mainly current events and fashion magazines-, and for the more daring, books like *Spraycan Art* and *Subway Art*; and films like *Beat Street* and *Wild Style*. 15-20 years olds at the time dove into this primordial soup and floated back to the surface revitalised. In the mid-80's, the first stone was cast along the Rome-Ostia line in the direction of the open sea. The perpetrator was Ice One with his 24/7, which means "24 hours a day, 7 days a week", just to give you an idea of how completely wrapped up this crew was in scratching, dancing, doing graffiti, and rapping. The endeavors of Ice One (100% original style, he was already a well-respected B-boy back then) and his crew became legendary, because on the one hand they revealed the presence (though still faint) of writers in Rome, and on the other they displayed a capacity that was anything but passive. Those first rudimentary maneuvers of style ended up stimulating other enthusiasts like, Crash Kid, Giaime (RIP), and Cromo at the Ostiense station a few years later.

The 1980's were a lame decade, a season of regression: façade of an internal void, a storm waiting for the right moment to burst.

Nowadays we're called "old school", it's rather amusing because if I think about how we were, I see a group of restless kids who, through Hip Hop, managed to find the energy to completely reinvent themselves. We were the children and/or the younger siblings of those who'd taken part in the protests of the 60's and 70's. From them we inherited a major defeat so we were forced to cope with the end of the class struggle, the tunnel of heroin, the upsurge of global Neoliberalism (for example: Margaret Thatcher and Ronald Reagan), and Italian-style yuppies (for example: Bettino Craxi and Silvio Berlusconi). Not even the no future philosophy of our punk brothers managed to console us deep down inside. Unconsciously, we wanted to break away from the past, rise from its ashes and imagine the present. Thus, every slight breeze that blew in from the Bronx became our own. We jealously protected any new discovery and as misfits, we only shared our aspirations with fellow misfits, whom

we would actively seek out, even though subdivisions (which now seem ridiculous) already existed within the Roman (micro)scene.

Some people, like Onda Rossa Posse, were direct line descendants of the protest movement of the 70's and used Hip Hop to manifest this affiliation; in a somewhat similar manner to the way in which signs coming from the U.S.A. during that period (it was the era of Public Enemy, KRS-One, NWA) openly referred to Hip Hop as a sort of emancipation. Onda Rossa Posse had a radio show on Radio Onda Rossa, the movement's free radio, which was founded in 1977 as a soapbox for the extra-parliamentary Left-wing movement of "Autonomia Operaia". The show was called Funk Theology: they played rap, read texts by Malcolm X, The Black Panthers, and Renato Curcio, they spewed out the first rhymes in Italian. Other people, like Ice One and Crash Kid, didn't subscribe to political alignments, to them Hip Hop was all about experimenting with style, there was no need to wave flags. They preferred hanging with the locals instead of associating with squats and social centres.

A variety of capabilities generated differences, each person laid claim to the authenticity of the language, but with the benefit of hindsight, I detect a pure and simple need to be the centre of attention. That unknown language contained unprecedented potential and nobody wanted to come in second. The daily routine was the same for everyone: constant experimentation, from rapping to Breaking, moving on to Writing and so on. Non-traditional and anti-fashion. Just take a look at the way we were dressed: baggy clothes, hats, big shoes and laces. Today's fashion would object. Yet 20 years ago, we looked like aliens from an unknown planet! Foreigners in our own nation. And by simply removing the cork, everything that was bottled up inside exploded.

In January 1990, students protesting the Ruberti reform, the first law that attempted to privatise institutions of higher learning, occupied all of Italy's Universities. Onda Rossa Posse was a large group made up of students, and they took part in the movement.

During the first days of occupation, Writing on walls was prohibited, you can only imagine how distant we felt from this form of protest even though the student movement was a well-respected political novelty.

During a circus-like protest march (with performances) on the University campus, the Posse performed on the stairs of the Geology building while 00199 painted "Temptation" on the wall below. Just to give you an idea of what the technical level was at the time, we drew the outline of the piece the night before... in chalk!!! Meanwhile, inside the Literature building, Onda Rossa Posse (whose members after the protests, went on to form the rap groups Assalti Frontali and Ak47, and the reggae sound system One Love Hi Pawa) was managing an

occupied hall, which was then renamed "Sakoa". It became a sort of pub, a meeting spot, there were dancehalls every night, DJs would get on the mic, and rhyming in Italian became an accepted and universal rule. The occupied Literature hall also hosted sociologist George Lapassade from the University of Saint-Denis (in the outskirts of Paris) along with a group of writers, breakers, MCs, and DJs for a series of lectures. Amongst them: Bangà and McSolar, who was still a nobody at the time. After that: a mural inside of the building and a jam on the stairs outside.

The movement proved to be a symptom-free carrier of an expressive renewal that hadn't been seen in ages, despite the fact that the approach to Hip Hop's elements was unconditional and undefined. Needless to say, the song "Batti il tuo tempo" by Onda Rossa Posse became the soundtrack for the Roman student movement, which was known as "La Pantera". After three months, the student movement disbanded and left the University, but the innovative force didn't lose momentum.

Social centres channeled this energy in the right direction- groups of young people occupied abandoned structures (for political activities, music, hanging out, drinking beers, organising solidarity events and parties), which was an absolute novelty.

For young people (and for the entire alternative culture) those places represented such a turning point that it's hard to imagine what would've happened if they hadn't existed.

From 1992, social centres started sprouting up like mushrooms, and each one had its own posse. We often went to them; our hangout was "Forte Prenestino" in Rome, an enormous military construction in the outlying neighbourhood of Centocelle, where, ever since 1986, the 'Non Labour Day' festival is held each May 1st.

We came from the movement and we were always considered the political wing of the scene. Contrary to the rules of Writing, we didn't worship our name as much as we should have, in fact we didn't care to write our name on pieces or systematically spread it around the city.

Instead, we considered graffiti as a new way of transmitting messages that broke away from the daily grind and incited emotions. In fact, by spray painting, we marked our differences. "Provocation" at the occupied university, "Menti Criminali", "Tocca a te", "Hasta Siempre" in San Lorenzo; "B. Sogno" at Brancaleone social centre, "Nessuna Dipendenza" at Forte Prenestino, "Sprigionarsi" at Askatasuna, "Conflitto" at Auro and Marco, "Non Credere nei Media" at Magliana.

We painted in lots of squats social centres, our art lent itself to direct communication; "If a wall is ugly, scribbling on it makes it even uglier", as Cheecky P always said. Seeing our pieces next to rhetorical slogans got on our nerves in a way we couldn't explain.

ZERO

by Monia Cappuccini

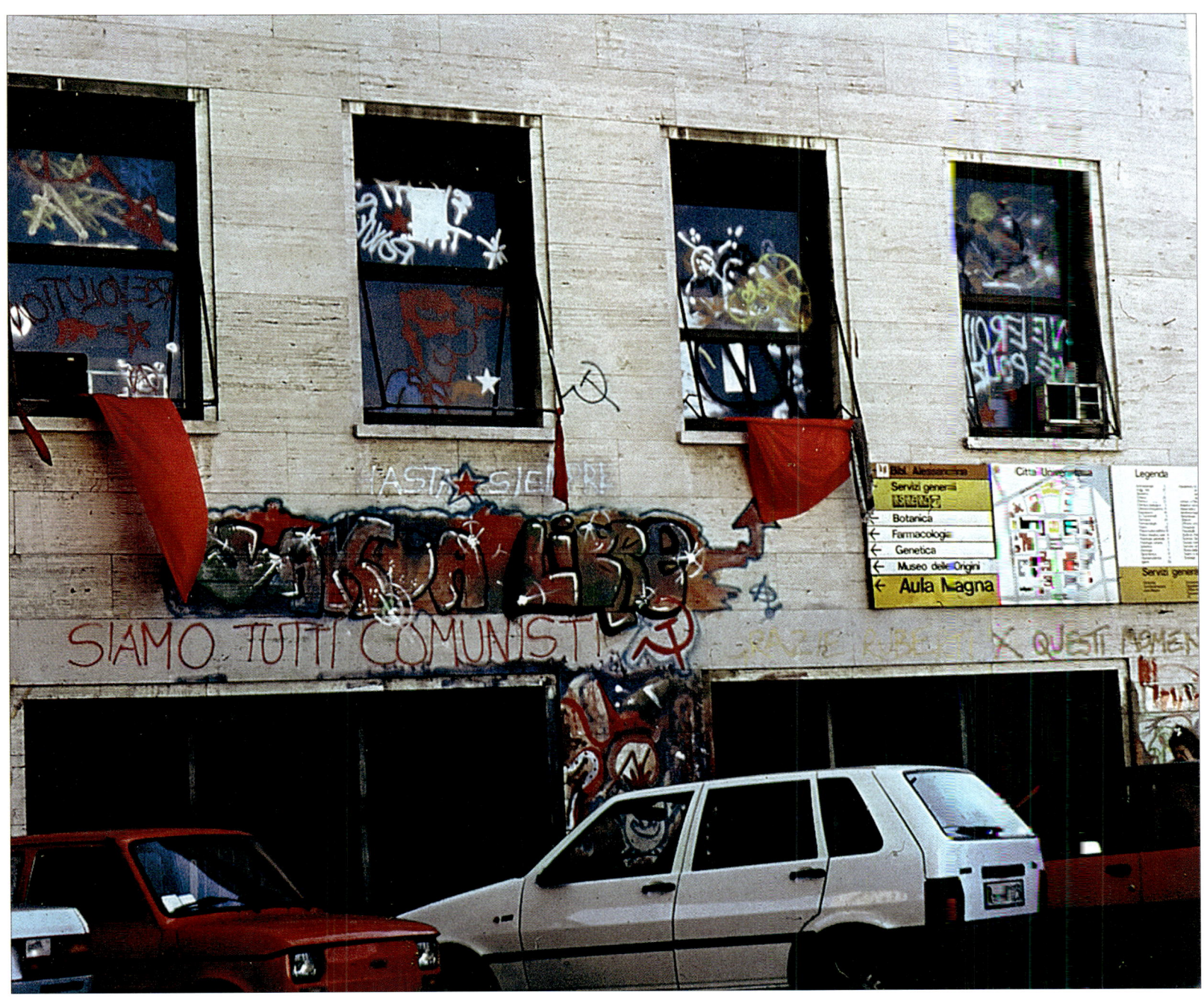

Sakoa libre written on the walls of the Literature Department of the University in Rome, 1990

— Monia Cappuccini

COLOUR MELODIES

During the first half of the 80's the encounter of two among the very first Italian writers determined a key passage for the diffusion of the movement in Northern Italy.

Zero-T

In a small and forgotten town of a couple hundred souls, close to Arezzo, lived Toxic, an American writer from TD Squad; what he was doing in the Italian province is something I never understood, but he certainly brought the first traces of spray paint to Tuscany. Apart from Toxic, the 80's in Italy, as well as in the rest of Europe I imagine, saw very few videos that could feed the imagination of the B-boys of the time: from Hip-hop Art Street History, tied to the New York lifestyle and distributed by Polygram video, to the feature films *Beat Street* and *Wild Style*, which struck Italy like a comet. In Florence they screened it at the Apollo, an old movie theatre that was falling apart. I remember the bill placed outside the theatre could hardly be seen, the owner had stuck a fluorescent green poster on top that said "Breakdance explodes!", which covered everything. Both *Beat Street* and *Wild Style* were dubbed in Italian, respecting our tradition country's of translating everything, from documentaries to comedies, and this caused the first trauma to our gen-

---

Terminology that was used by the kids in all of Europe like 'bombing' or 'footwork' reached us in the form of 'lo sbombo' and 'Buffalo'

---

eration: terminology that was universally used by the kids in all of Europe like 'bombing' or 'footwork' reached us in the form of 'lo sbombo' and 'Buffalo', but then again what did the translators know about this glossary? So Italian B-boys started calling things in other ways, even Maurizietto Next One would dance Buffalo the first years before learning the real term. Naturally the same inaccuracies weighed on our collective imagery for a long time, because while kids in New York could recognise the evident fiction of *Beat Street*, for us Italians it could well have been 100% true to reality. For example, with the knowledge we had in 1984 you couldn't tell and understand the difference between the invented character of Ramon and the concrete background of Lee.

Deemo-a.k.a. Dayaki, Deko 164, One Shot, Dumbo

How does your story begin?

My family moved to Bologna in September 1982. The city had a reputation as a counter-cultural epicentre, fuelled by a student population coming from every part of the country. Quite a shock for a sixteen-year-old kid who had spent the previous five years in a Catholic boarding school, in a vacuum. Coming from such a secluded environment, I had developed a strong distaste for authority in general, but at the same time I lacked real life experience and had a lot to catch up on. Hungry for life and mad at the world, I soon joined the ranks of the Hardcore Punk scene. That's where it all began for me.

How did you reconcile this association to the punk scene with that to the Italian Writing movement?

Writing came long after that, but I see it as everything's connected and one thing leads to another, you just need to be receptive. Hardcore had nothing to do with Writing per se, but it became instrumental in the process that led me to know about the art form and eventually express myself with it. First of all, it gave me a much-needed head start. The music and the lyrics reflected our mindset, but it wasn't even all about the bands. "Do It Yourself " was a primary driving force within the scene. Those of us who were more visually inclined contributed with artworks for flyers, record covers, stickers, murals, and banners. So you learned to design with a purpose, and your art would be seen and endorsed by a whole community.
There was definitely a strong aesthetic vocab and stencils had been widely adopted, to the point where they had become part of the style. People had been using spray paint forever, to write all types of messages. Stencils were even older, but much more interesting to me.
So right away I wanted to try it. That's how I started messing with spray cans and became fascinated with the tool. I did a lot of cutting and testing in my room, with different types of cardboard, different blades, and different paint. Black enamel, red nitro, white paint for leather, anything I could get my hands on, really.

Was that before Hip Hop came to Italy?

I'd say around the same time, 1983. It took a while for me to find out about it. Back then, the divide between different tribes ran deeper than today, especially if you didn't fit in with the mainstream crowd. I wasn't even interested in the trends happening outside the scene, but when Hip Hop took over the media, I just couldn't front. Other kids embraced it, while we admired it from a distance. You couldn't slam or stage dive to it, but..."Look at those acrobatics! Look at that guy in the back with the spray can...what's he doing?" We were all amazed. It was something from another planet.

Did you get to see the exhibition Arte di Frontiera?

That was totally unexpected. The catalogue says it happened in 1984, March through April, at the City Gallery of Modern Art, right here in Bologna. The late Francesca Alinovi had brought together an unprecedented all-star selection of artists hailing from the streets of New York City: Futura, Dondi, Daze, Lee, Crash, A-One, Toxic, Rammellzee, Zephyr and then Keith Haring, Basquiat, Jenny Holzer, Richard Hambleton, Justen Ladda, John Ahearn, you name it.
I think it goes down in history as one of the biggest events of its kind. You know what? Some of these guys actually came to Bologna and painted their canvases right at the gallery, on the roof. Daze did a couple of outlines in the heart of the city, plus he decorated the jackets of "i Puffi", two old school B-boys.
Me? I almost missed the whole thing: I got there on the very last day, at the very last hour. I tried to absorb as much as I could during that sixty-minute rush but, quite predictably, I left the gallery with too many unanswered questions.More than anything else, I was impressed by the canvases and pictures of Crash and Daze. They had that drawing element I could relate to. Letter styles and tags were out of reach; I didn't really know what to do with them at that stage. But I understood that spray paint could be controlled to paint my artworks like...huge, and that vision alone opened up new possibilities for me.
After "Arte di Frontiera", I started practicing a mix of stencils and freehand painting, adding more colours to my palette.

Considering the lack of reference points in Italy, where else did you learn about Writing?

Amsterdam, even before I got my hands on *Subway Art*. Despite our relatively young age and the lack of modern communication tools, the hardcore punk scene was

COMBO

by Zero-T & Deemo

well connected throughout Western Europe. 1984 was the year when bands started travelling from country to country, sometimes with a small contingent of close friends. Being linked with the squatter movement meant you always had a place to sleep and perform.

Plus we knew how to travel dirt-cheap to any destination abroad. You only had to buy an International railway ticket to any short route crossing the border (for example: Milan to the first city past the Swiss border, a mere 50 km, the equivalent of 6 Euros back then). This particular type of ticket was only available in selected travel agencies and had to be handwritten by the employee. Someone discovered that the carbon copy sheets could be chemically erased and then re-compiled as a roundtrip ticket to any European city of your choice: a little chlorine goes a long way! The secret to this all-Italian recipe was strictly kept among squatters and hardcore kids.

Can you describe the impact with Amsterdam and the Writing that could be seen in the city at the time?

On my way from the Station to the Dam, I realized that tags were all over the place. That was my first visit in August '84. I had never seen anything like it before. The next day in Vondel Park, I totally lost it. It was bombed on any available surface. I spent hours and hours staring at the pieces under the tunnel, checking out the different styles, the colours, trying to make sense of the names: Shoe...Delta... Zap... Arson... Jaz...Vampirella, one next to the other. This was even before CTK happened I think, the letters had a cartoonish feel to them that I still recognise as an Amsterdam thing, with a little Dondi here and there, I would say. That was the real deal, not a gallery show, not a picture in a magazine, but right in front of me.

On top of that, I started noticing some stencils that were a lot more detailed than the ones I was used to: samurai warriors, a Tutankhamen mask, zebras, monkeys, and police in riot gear. A friend told me they were made by an artist named Hugo Kaagman, who happened to live in a squat decorated with zebra patterns. This other guy, Walking Joint, had a signature logo that really stood out. Amsterdam offered a beautiful diversity in styles and techniques and I was totally overwhelmed.

I imagine this influenced you directly. Did you start writing when you got back to Bologna?

Not really. I went back to my drawings and the occasional stencil work. I would try my hand at random letters, but

since I had not taken pictures in Amsterdam I really had no reference.

I visited again in '85 and I found *Subway Art* at a bookstore there. The book answered a lot of my questions, but no matter how much I loved the art form, I wasn't really interested in that whole "getting up" game, the tags, the crews etc. I didn't see the point of it in my day-to-day life. In Bologna there was no one else but me, anyways. And if you take away those elements, what else is going to motivate you as a writer? It took me years to answer that, probably until 1987.

Whatever happened from '85 to '87, was very sporadic and far between. I used painting for some sort of visual performance during public protests and inside squats. From there on, people would acknowledge me as "the graffiti artist". I was asked to paint small murals, maybe a banner, stuff like that, here and there. I would enjoy doing it for what it was: just another visual outlet for me, alongside the flyers I was designing for live gigs and my first record covers.

My very first letter piece with character is also the first ever done in Bologna, and is still there where I painted it, after more than two decades. I went to the concrete garden called Giardini del Guasto and just did it. That was an early skate spot, so I wrote "Skate Tough" with a skater character on one side and my first tag "Dumbo", in all its primitive glory. It's been featured in books, even postcards I think.

Why did this adjustment occur only in 1987? What changed for you in that year?

Hardcore punk, I mean the music itself, had taken new directions that I wasn't feeling. Of course there was a strong bond with the scene I grew up in but the music itself didn't do it for me anymore. Slowly but surely I became one of the earliest adopters in my circle of the new Hip Hop sounds of Def Jam. Possibly as a consequence of that, I also started to spend more and more time practicing letter styles on paper, something I didn't bother to do until then. I changed my tag from Dumbo to One Shot, and started to tag around town, both with mini-cans and 0.6 inch silver markers. One Shot became quite visible, and without me knowing, some kids were taking notice. That was exactly my purpose, and my ultimate motivation. I wanted to inspire other people to go out and take over the walls. Bologna was as dead as can be.

I lived right along the railway tracks between the San Donato and Libia bridges, an area that offered many opportunities once I started to look at it with different eyes. For

the first time ever, I thought about doing a piece inside the railway territory, on the walls along the tracks, like the ones I had seen in Germany and the End. So I called a bunch of friends just to do all-ins. Five of us entered the premises and we wrote "Città Zombi" ("Zombie Town"). It's not like I couldn't do that small silver piece myself, but my idea was to teach them a thing or two about the technique, so they could start doing their own thing.

Did any of them start to write on their own after that?

Two of them actually did: Vined and Magma, who I knew from my days at the Liceo Artistico.

There was this abandoned area called Curtisa near the San Donato bridge, also alongside the tracks. It was enclosed by the bridge on one side, with a brick wall on the opposite side. Bricks were not the ideal surface, but I saw the opportunity for a very big piece that could be seen from bus number 19, which was always packed. So I did it. A huge "Egoism" piece with a character in the middle. I wanted it to be seen from a distance. Next thing you know, Vined and Magma both did their own piece there. Looked promising, there was potential for a Hall of Fame in Bologna.

I met Rusty right there, around the same time. He was this humble kid I had never seen before, carrying a big ass camera, taking pictures of those few pieces. I asked him if he was a professional photographer. He answered it was just a hobby. Or was it the other way around?

During your trips around Europe the previous years, had you met any other writers?

I had met Cowboy 69 in Munich a few months before. Munich itself was incredible. This girl I liked a lot had a place there, so I went to visit her by train. To my surprise, I saw mad pieces along the tracks. Tags everywhere. Munich wasn't featured in *Spraycan Art* so I wasn't expecting anything like that.

I met some Hip Hop kids in the subway and got directions to the local Hall of Fame, the legendary Flohmarkt. I couldn't even start to imagine that anything like those productions by FB and ABC existed. Walls like four meters high, perfectly executed, top-to-bottom. They were using so many different shades of colour.

How could they have so much paint at their disposal, it was beyond me.

Loomit had letters that reminded me of Arabic calligraphy in the way the connections stretched horizontally,

⊐ CONTINUES ON PAGE 156

> CONTINUES FROM PAGE 155
parallel to the ground. Cemnoz and Neon had crazy Wildstyles with thick, razor-sharp lines, and intricate arrows and loops. I asked Cowboy all sorts of questions, and he taught me some of the effects and techniques I was witnessing for the very first time. Like the halo obtained by spraying the paint sideways, parallel to the wall. Or getting a thin line by spraying with the can upside down. And of course the stone background. Those elements appeared in many of the pieces painted in Italy in the following years. Being the first Italian writer that made it to the Flohmarkt, I take full responsibility.
But there was one more thing I learned: these guys would actually bomb the trains and the subway stations with the same type of skills. I had never thought about it. I had yet to see a painted train. I thought it was something that belonged to the New York subway, and Europe was all about walls.

It wasn't easy to see painted trains in Europe during the early 80's, there were surely writers with this objective but the scene was probably in an early stage of development and the railway companies could still contain the phenomenon. Had you never seen a painted train before?

Well, I almost never took the subway in Amsterdam. Cowboy told me that they were buffing a lot in Munich in that particular time, so I didn't get the chance to see anything. But during my next visit I met plenty of writers and they showed me pictures. I also saw two perfect pieces at a subway station, both from Stone Age Kids. I was with Milano City Artist that time.

So you had finally met other Italian writers..

It was written I guess: one night I was in Milan for a hardcore gig that never took place. Amongst a crowd of ripped jeans and leather jackets, I spotted this guy wearing a Kangol. Turns out he's a writer too. I couldn't believe it: I wasn't alone any more. His name-belt spelled KAOS, first Italian writer I ever met. The same Kaos later became the hardest mc to ever touch a mic in Italy, someone I consider family. M.C.A. was his crew at the time. I told them about Munich but they all seemed skeptical, so we agreed to go there together for the first available event. When I finally took them to the Flohmarkt, their jaws dropped just like mine had on my first visit.
We stayed for a couple of days, four of us sleeping in the car. It was a major event, with writers from all over Germany and Switzerland. We spent an afternoon chilling at the Hall of Fame, watching FBI crew paint their outlines with the precision of a plotter. This was all new to us. Someone even tried to claim that "it's easier to paint like that big". I understood that in some Italian quarters, Writing had become a battle for the thinnest line. The smaller the piece, the better. I had my own share of ridiculous misconceptions too, so this time I won't mention names. But that's how backwards it was.

How did you meet ZeroT?

At that point I was on a mission and nothing could stop me. If anyone was painting anywhere in Italy, I had to meet him. I was missing some of that rock-solid networking of the hardcore scene.
One afternoon I'm watching this music video by the Steve Rogers band, an Italian pop band, when I notice that there are tags in the background. I call the TV station and ask for the number of the production house that did the promo. Then I call production and ask about the tags in the background. They tell me it's some kid hired by the art director. I ask for the number of the kid and they track it down for me. It's someone from near Florence. I call him, we introduce ourselves, I explain how I got hold of his number, we talk about styles and whatnot and agree to meet somewhere soon.
I was about to leave for Munich with the MCA guys. Last day in Munich we visit this other spot, an abandoned factory towards the end of the subway line. There we meet Zebster. He just got back from London, where apparently he met this very good Italian writer. I'm thinking: "there goes another one". Zebster hands me the contact that the writer gave him. As I get back home, I immediately call, without even looking at the digits. Turns out it was the same number I got from the TV station. ZeroT was the kid on the other side. We met a few weeks later.

Did you form CMC right away?

Pretty much. I invited him to visit Curtisa. He complimented me on my stuff, then opened his book: he had letters and the illest robotic characters. We both had drawing skills, but he is a natural, I had to work my ass off for years! I don't remember who started talking about a crew first, but we immediately agreed. He came up with the Color Melodies part.
I thought that Crew was too big for our two-headed monster, so I came up with Combo. Once again I changed my tag, this time to Dayaki. Our first piece together was another wall alongside the tracks, right behind Curtisa.

We wanted to write "Danger Zone" and split the job 50/50. It was done in two sessions: first time around I insisted that we could paint along the tracks in the afternoon and nobody would care. Of course we got stopped by police. A few days later we were already off to Rimini, where ZeroT had mad contacts for commissions in clubs. I had learned from Cowboy 69 how they handled commissioned works. ZeroT was a bit too enthusiastic: he just loved that free paint and would do anything to get it. "Yo D, they'll give us free paint!" I said: "Let's get the paint and the money". Right away I established a minimum fee with his clients, and received a fair amount of hate in return.
For a minute I was considered the Greedy Bastard. But who cares as long as we both got paid? Plus each major job ended with bags full of extra cans. That was another trick I had learned in Germany. We kept them in my basement, and we could use them anytime we needed to. Commissioned work was nothing hardcore, but we got the chance to work on some pretty big projects during our activity, like that time in Cervia where they asked us to do the whole facade of Rio Club. It was the closest thing to the huge productions in Munich and it took us a whole week to complete. It was all Duplis, not really that fast. We ordered an incredible amount of cans, directly from the distributor. When we got there to place the order, the employee almost cried for joy.
At that point we knew about MCA, Flycat, Grasshopper and a few more. They were our competition, if you will. But I still hoped to find others. Giorgio De Mitri was doing *Mente Locale* magazine, I had told him about Munich so he sent me there with a photographer. The result was an amazing spread with some great pictures of the Flohmarkt, and I asked to have my phone number published so people could contact me.
Now that I think about it, the first writer convention in Rimini would never have happened if it hadn't been for ZeroT's connections with the clubs. That was a historic event for the movement.

It was the first of its kind, right?

Absolutely. You had Zulu parties in the old school days, with deejays and B-boys. But this time it was specifically a roll call for writers. This art director asked me to invite writers and have a party at the club, with free drinks, free hotel, free paint.
I understood right away that this could be an opportunity to officially gather as many writers as possible from
> CONTINUES ON PAGE 158

by Zero-T & Deemo

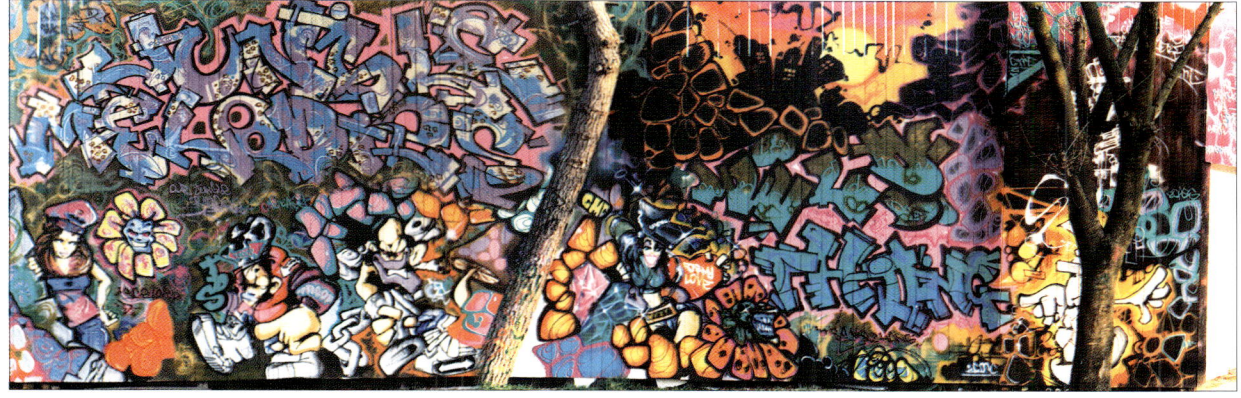

Walls of the Riò club in Cervia, painted by Zero-T and Dayaki at the end of the 80's   — *Roberto Verona*

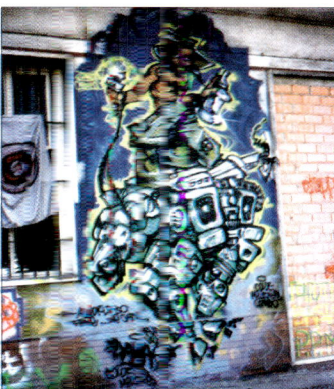

Dayaki's mechanical horse   — *Oida*

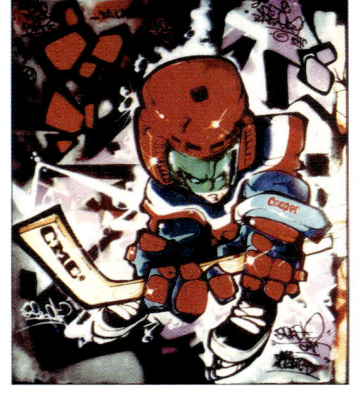

Zero-T Vans catalogue, late 80's   — *Zart*

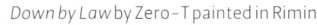

Down by Law by Zero-T painted in Rimini   — *Oida*

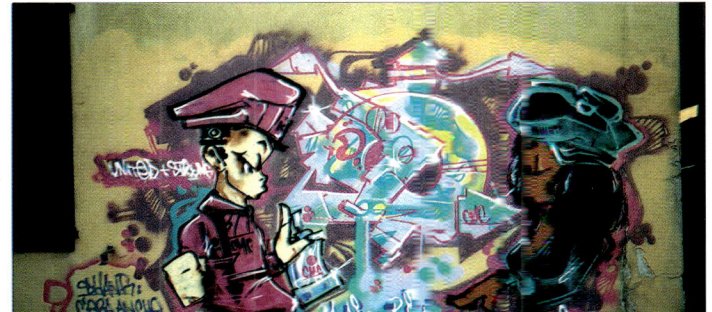

Dayaki in Rimini, 1989   — *Oida*

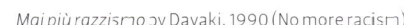

Mai più razzismo by Dayaki, 1990 (No more racism)   — *Oida*

> CONTINUES FROM PAGE 156

all over Italy, people that didn't even know about each other.

It was about time for us to start networking too. I called MCA in Milan, asking them for numbers. They called Flycat and gave me Grasshopper's number in Turin, who called some other guy, and so on, like a chain reaction. I don't remember how many people came to Rimini, but there were lots. They gave us a room for a meeting in the afternoon, we would paint our panels when the club opened, then party and bullshit. That day, new crews were formed and new careers started. That's where Flycat and Mace first met; Eron said it was some kind of rite of initiation for him, etc.

The movement also benefited from the increased sharing of information. I can retrace the introduction of soft caps and the demise of Duplis to a conversation me and Mace had after his visit to Paris in 1989. He told me that writers up there were stealing caps from a specific deodorant brand to get that sharp medium line. Next thing you know, we were raiding supermarkets for caps regularly. Those caps wouldn't fit a Dupli valve, so we switched to Talken and Marabus. Note: fat caps were still not that relevant to us at the time.

What type of link existed between CMC and Toxic, if any? He spent quite a few years near Florence.

ZeroT insisted that I should meet Toxic. Toxic was featured in Arte Di Frontiera, so I knew about him. At the time he lived in a medieval village near Arezzo and obviously had contacts with the Hip Hop scene in Tuscany. I think he realised that ZeroT was a natural talent, so he started building with him, engaging him in conversations about styles and developments in the art form. When me and ZeroT became crew, I was introduced to that too. I liked talking with him: he'd been expressing himself on canvas for quite a few years already, so his whole train of thought was coming from a deeper, artistic point of view. One minute we would ask him about his experience as a writer in New York, next thing we'd be there listening to intricate and fascinating theories on gothic futurism. That was probably way too advanced for little me, you know? He had all the basics already covered coming up as a writer in New York, while I was missing a lot of that step-by-step progression. If you try Wildstyle before straight letters, like some of us did, that's backwards. Even so, the Toxic sessions had quite an influence on my quest for a personal style. Best examples would be "Soul Side", the large mural me and ZeroT painted

in Modena for the "Spraycan Art vol.2" that never happened, or the Cellophane mural in Rimini. During that "Soul Side" production in September 1989, ZeroT nailed a shaded 3D piece, sans outline, which is quite remarkable in hindsight.

When did you realise that Bologna had a new generation of writers?

Rusty and Shan R (aka Deda of the rap group Sangue Misto) were the first new writers to take action after Mined and Magma, and the first incarnation of SPA. They started painting on the railway as TCT a few days after "Danger Zone".

Together we painted the first FS end-to-end car in Ravone in 1990. I painted with Shan R under the Suburbana bridges in Via Rimesse, and they both helped out with some of the early cars I painted in the Suburbana, notably the one we did to celebrate the liberation of Nelson Mandela. None of these cars ever made it out of the yard. A whole new breed of tags started to appear, and I was no longer alone. I stopped tagging because I always considered it boring, and somehow tags had done their job. Rusty went on to become a major player in the scene. Meanwhile, my people had occupied a venue right in the heart of the city, called Isola nel Kantiere. I started to organise Hip Hop jams there, and kept painting occasionally. Throughout the years I painted with most of the writers of the second generation. Eron always credited CMC as a major inspiration and I have immense respect for him as an artist and as a partner in the yard. Ciufs made us all proud and I enjoyed painting with him every time we did. Being recognised as one of the first Italian writers is indeed rewarding but I couldn't care less for my early pieces if they hadn't sparked that inspiration in other kids to get involved and take it to another level, the same way I got inspired by books and movies, but most of all by what I had seen with my own eyes.

MILAN

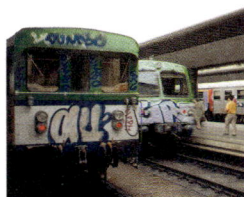

Page 184
>

The Northern line

A wild province

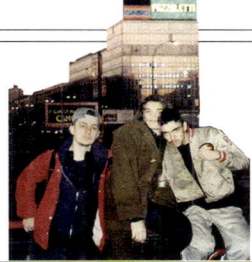

Page 166
>

East side story

Tales of the city

Muretto hang–out
>

❝

I remember a—at—pical Milan, with two faces a—ty ur der the control of fcg. wit— the attitude of a metropolis w—ilein the mere route from ce—tre—to periphery, a few hundred—met—es, it became provincial —A—EN

THE LAND LORDS
—

Robin
>

Exclusive groups fc—me— the city's first crews, especially the —more f—ous—ones. All young writers obviously dre—med of belonging to them, but that was nearly impossible. The crews were sp—ea—ch—ughout the city, but were predomir—ant—y on the East side, where it all began. Each crew—ed its own distinctive features and was—tied—to its neighbourhood of origin. Most of them had lrg ish acronyms like: PWD (*Pals Wi—Dr—am.*); TDK (*The Damage Kids*); TkA (*T—o Kr—s A—ne*); and they all

> CONTINUES ON PAGE 164

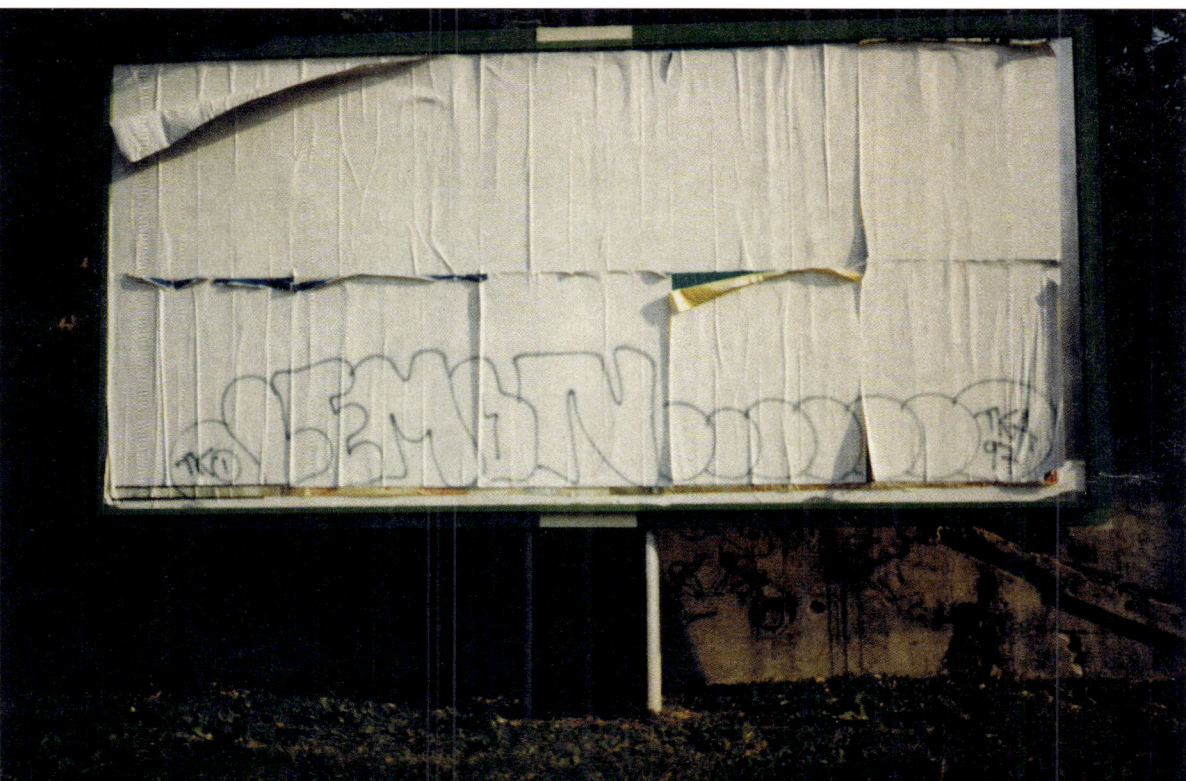

— Moe

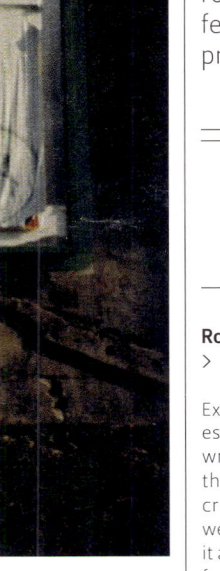

Names as pictures

The Writing years in Milan and the consequent seizing of the city

---

The evolution of the Writing movement in Milan can be summarised by delineating three fundamental historic phases, each with its own well-defined styles, influences and relationship with the surrounding urban space.

The first phase coincides with the 80's, during which two different meeting spots for writers established the two opposite directions of Milanese Writing: one tied to Hip Hop and the other close to the Anarcho-punk movement. The writers following the first direction would hang out in Corso Vittorio Emanuele, a central street of the city with a high concentration of stores, offices and tourists. The *Muretto*, a wide arcade facing the Corso, in those years represented a world apart, where B-boys would meet to dance and

battle. In that same period other groups of writers were approaching the first Milanese social centres, real incubators for counterculture. This reality, tied to the Anarcho-punk movement, would gather prevalently around the Libreria Calusca and occupied spaces such as Virus. They combined assertive political activism with a strong cultural consciousness, a union that was perfectly represented by one of the leading intellectual animators of that environment, Primo Moroni.

Sensitive to social movements, and led by characters such as Atomo and Schwarz, this small group however had only a brief existence, quickly giving way to the Hip Hop-oriented scene influenced by New York. Painting, for these two groups of writers, had radically different meanings: on one side – that close to Hip Hop – aesthetics and the American way of life were exalted; on the other – the Anarcho-punk – writers sought to spread a message to the masses rather than write their own name or image. During the early 90's a

change in perspective takes place. Having abandoned the two primary points of aggregation, writers started scattering throughout the city, transforming their neighbourhoods of origin into matrices of precise territorial identity.

It was the followers of the Hip Hop movement that formed the first crews from neighbourhood to neighbourhood, distinguishing themselves on the base of the specific area of their belonging.

The creation of these groups entailed a real seizing of territory throughout the city of Milan. From the moment it was no longer necessary to gather the few practitioners of this passion in an only hang-out, kids started occupying the walls of the parks near their homes. Within the city it became important to locate which walls were 'tolerated', so as to experiment with spray techniques, still at a primeval stage. Halls of fame became the preferred target for writers because they could be painted during the day, and each writer could experiment his own uniqueness

until reaching, with—time, a more or less identifiable stylistic connotation. Halls of fame witnessed—he particular obsession for letters and style—that was shared by the entire first generation of writers in Milan, influenced by New York masters such as – above all – Phas—II.

This phenomenon was initially concentrated in the Eastern part of Milan, in that area that includes Fantano, the Amphitheatre of Marte—an—Piazzale Loreto all the way to the neighbourhood of Lambrate. These places combined, represented the new version of *Muretto*, diluted in many different spots where writers could meet not only to paint but also to hang out and exchange information.

Gradually the adjacent areas of the city also got involved, with more writers and the consequent occupation of surfaces: crews formed in the Southern area of Milan, until reaching the district of Giambellino. Of fundamental importance to these groups was the neighbourhood

> CONTINUES ON PAGE 182

ACW INTERNATIONAL / MILAN

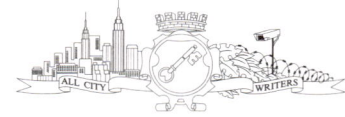

Main contributors:
Airone, Alberto WAG, Aken, Amok, Atomo,
Bang, Bean, Cano, Chief, Craze, Daze, Dosey,
Dra, Dumbo, Dust, Flycat, Gees, Graffio, Lark,
Kid, Mace, Mastro K, Mind, Moe, Phase II,
Phobia, Play, Raptus, Rax-E, Rendo, Riso,
Robin, Sand, Shad, Shampo, Shot, Sky 4, Stying,
Tawa, Teatro, Zaki Dee, Zeta

In collaboration with:
16K, CYB, CKC, DCN, IVA, MCA, MNP, PWD,
TDK, THP, TKA, UAN, VDS, VMD70s, ZONA 13

Cover photo:
Lemon -TKA, 1997

Illustrations at pages 172, 174, 178, 180, 186 by:
Davide Rapp / büro / www.buro.it

Blacksheep
>

Coming from the Punk movement

Marco Teatro
>

I started in 1986, Milan was plastered with political graffiti and colourful stencils, punk culture was at its apex. When I started using spray paint I was a punk, I lived in squats, I was politically active, I had very few friends in Hip Hop and no interest in it. During a trip to Northern Europe I was struck by the presence of tags in many cities and it confused me: I was accustomed to the fact that in Italy spray paint was exclusively used to write political messages on walls, I didn't understand why this medium was being used to spread a Name that was personal, individual and illegible to most.

Despite all this, I found this practice extremely fascinating and appealing, perhaps because of its elegance, the style, the diligent calligraphy, and the effort made by the writer to give the best of himself. Usually with Italian political graffiti, this aspect (the style and art) was entirely absent: the collective message was usually crude and aseptic, or else it was simply bad and disturbing. Up North I discovered true graffiti situated in no-man's lands: places hidden beneath overpasses or along the railway lines, places where no human being would ever consider going. Spaces that were usually immensely empty and forgotten by everyone, but present and familiar to all urban infrastructures. Grimy and abandoned places which, thanks to graffiti, were subjected to a live, human colonisation with boundless impetus and power.

In Amsterdam I bought some lively coloured spray paint at a market because it was cheap, they had hues and coverage that couldn't be found in Italy. Once back in Milan, I did my first 'real' piece on the walls of a squat I hung out in called Virus. Obviously my first pieces were influenced by my world, totally detached from Hip Hop, which was only just beginning to reach Italy. During that same period, we finally saw an elegant and decisive tag appear, it was the only one in the entire city that resembled the ones I'd "discovered" in other countries and it belonged to

Spyder 7. I had no idea who he was but at the same time I already understood what it was about. I'd watch people walk by quickly without even noticing the presence of that "blotch", which in their eyes was incomprehensible but premonitory of what was soon to come. That same year, the first figure of Milan's underground scene stepped forward and had the courage to tag with his nickname: A.T.M. The periods between the letters were so big they looked like little O's so many people started to call him "Atomo". The first piece I saw executed live was his, on the shutters of Calusca bookshop, which was on Corso di Porta Ticinese back then. Meanwhile, the tag "Hip Hop", executed by a different mystery hand, could be found all over the city, it was the first rough draft of tried and true graffiti.

Only in 1988 did Writing forcefully push its way to the fore front: during the night increasing amounts of tags would appear, and at first the media assumed it was Arabic writing done by new immigrants. Aerosol Art began to spread exponentially throughout the city, and at first it was only done by a handful of unknown hands. Atomo had been active long before I came into the scene, the centre of Milan was full of his pieces while everyone else was practically exiled to invisible spots in the outskirts.

During this time, squats and social centres were genuine stimuli for people, even for kids in the Hip Hop scene, simply because they were places where you could do as you pleased. It may seem unbelievable, but back then the Police persecuted us much more than they do today; often, anyone found with a spray can in their pocket was suspected of belonging to some political extremist group. In 1990 the Hip Hop phenomenon exploded, focusing on Writing and music: dozens of kids created a budding Italian scene, the phenomenon expanded and practically became mainstream. Squats and social centres definitively claimed the role of main hub for this scene.

On the one hand, the more underground side of the phenomenon came to the surface, but on the other hand, a historic chapter came to an end with the demise of collectively managed squats and social centres in which part of the Italian Hip Hop movement had its roots.

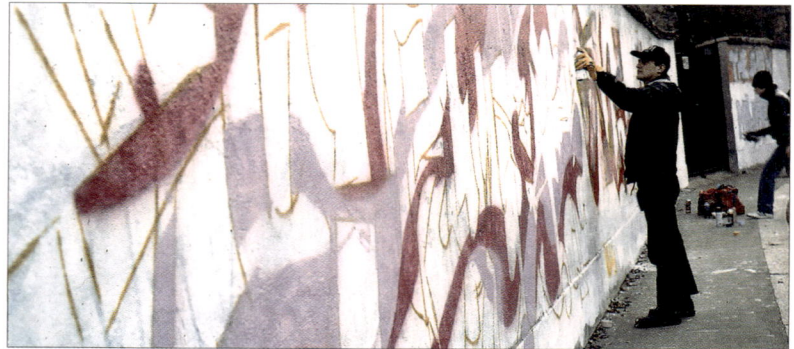

Teatro painting at San Eustorgio wall, 1988   — Teatro

Greyscale decorum

Atomo
>

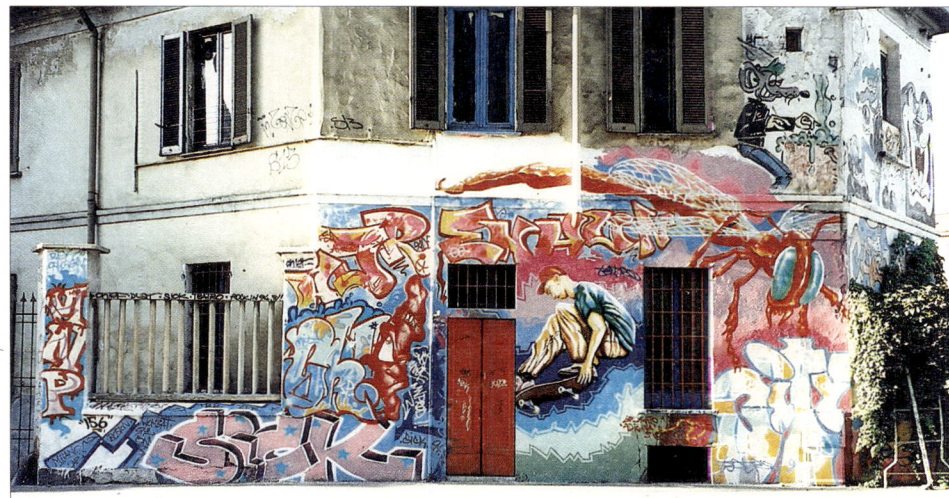

The insect, the skater puppet, and *Andrenalin* by Jet 4, '94. Chief and Sick from Boston. Above: Atomo's rats, '84   — Teatro

At the age of 17, I already lived on my own and had been working for a few years. I hung out in the most infamous spots of the Milanese outskirts and what struck me most was the amazing shades of grey on the buildings, which matched nicely with the colour of the city's sky: a perfectly elegant combination between business suits and pigeons' cloaks, perfectly representing the personality of the city's inhabitants. At 6:30 in the morning, while still dopey, I would face the foggy Lambrate station and squeeze through a gap in the enormous wall which led to the subway. Around me, hundreds of frozen faces with collars raised as protection against the cold, all walking toward the same destination at the same Milanese marathon-like pace. No time for emotions (how could there be, since everything's so horribly grey?), greetings, or chitchat, the objective was reaching the subway to get to work.

I wanted to have an impact on those people and distract them for just a moment from their daily life revolving solely around work; for a moment I wanted them to feel something other than grey, I wanted them to feel an emotion. Relying on the complicity of the night, I decided that the endless, run-down wall (unchanging backdrop in the routine of everyday life) should represent something different. Armed with spray paint, I unleashed my passion for drawing by spraying lines, curves, colours, and rebellion.

Mission accomplished: the next morning the fast-paced herd of raised collars slowed down for a few seconds to look at what I had done on the wall. Even the eternal presence of fog seemed to clear and that place suddenly seemed warmer and more human to me. That's why I started doing graffiti, to liven up non-places where architecture was so absorbed in functionality, rationality and speculation that it forgot humans were supposed to inhabit these spaces.

Thus began the war between colours and street cleaners, chasing after graffiti with paintbrushes so as to restore that grey-toned decorum to the city, painting over any symptom of transgression. Those were rough times because none of my efforts lasted more than two days before the Grey Squad (that's what we called them) unfailingly came around to restore that elegant Milanese greyness with square or rectangle patches.

Schwarz and I decided to make scissor stencils out of cardboard and spray them on the edge of these patches then adding dotted lines around the outline.

The wall of an enormous military compound that flanked an abandoned garden full of shrubs and trash, near my house, became the main grounds for our battle with the Grey Squad.

One night, we painted it with stylistically thought-out geometric patterns and wrote: "Transgress"; the next night it had already returned to its grey state. The newsvendor nearby, who woke up before us and appreciated a bit of colour in his daily existence, told us what time the Grey Squad would show up with their Milanese decorum kit. One night we waited for them to have a talk, we immediately understood each other when we spoke of work hours, obligations, and greyness. With beers in hand at the snack stand of Piazza Gobetti, they admitted they liked our work but explained that the list of streets they were assigned to re-paint grey were provided by the DIGOS (Italian FBI).

They told us that the Lambrate neighbourhood was scheduled for Monday, so if we painted on Tuesday, our graffiti would last a whole week. Bingo! Then as the years went by, there was an outbreak. All the neighbourhoods on the outskirts were coloured and the Grey Squad had so much work to do, they couldn't keep track of it. One night, a vigilante who was probably resentful and unsatisfied with his life, cursed us out and called the cops, who unfailingly caught us... when the vigilante left, pleased with his doings, the cops looked at the duckling we had just started on the wall and told us their kids liked to draw and would certainly appreciate it.

They succumbed to sincerity and said these words, which seemed magical to us: "Hurry up and finish before that asshole comes back, bye".

Flycat
>

OUTSIDERS

In those days, I was opposed to the fusion between squats, social centres and Hip Hop; I wanted nothing to do with it.

These people wanted to tell us what Hip Hop was, while we had a completely different and distant view from theirs. In any case, there was some common

I wanted to have an impact on those people and distract them for just a moment from their daily life revolving solely on work

ground: the student movements followed the deeds of Oakland's Black Panthers and we listened to Public Enemy, who promoted the same logos and ideals... these were constructive and important sparks. And shortly later I became acquainted with Shake publishing house. Shake was associated with Cox18 social centre in Via Conchetta.

The presence of some figures like Gomma and Primo Moroni helped shape us in some ways: the scene was unlike most social centres because there was a more direct approach, they were more open-minded, and certainly interested in our first steps as writers.

We were sick of posse social centres that had completely fucked up what we considered Hip Hop, and in some way Gomma and crew understood us, they all had a punk background and perhaps considered us the antechamber of an underground phenomenon similar to theirs in some way.

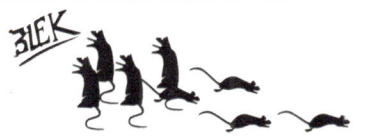

RATS
—

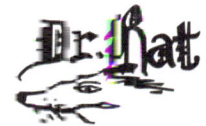

In the early 70's the rat became an emblematic figure of counterculture aesthetics. This rodent, it is parasite of society, was evoked by various independent artists. Some of which include Paris's Black Le Rat who was the first to paint it throughout a city using stencils, and Dr. Rat in Amsterdam, who drew a stylised version of it next to his gothic signature, almost to indicate a complete identification with his borderline condition.

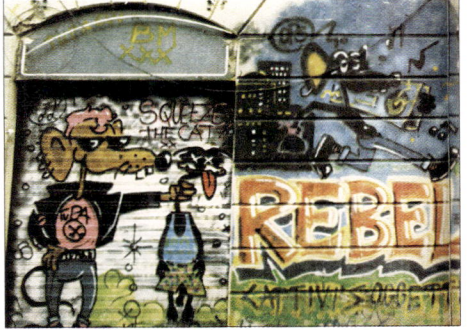

Cox18 in 1988. Rat by Atomo, Rebel by Teatro   — Teatro

Shad
>

When I think of the first pieces in Milan, I remember the little house in Via V gevano where Atomo and Schwarz hit – they did this sort of punk-mouse stirring a bowl of soup on the first floor. Their contribution towards the middle of the 80's was important because the few writers of the time mostly moved alone, and would manage at most a throw-up or tag as opposed to these big coloured murals. These guys on the other hand came from the context of the social centres and would move in "masses", sometimes protected by a procession of protestors during a demonstration. The fact they were often sheltered by groups of people allowed them to paint with a little more ease. In Via Laghetto there was another occupied building, Cox 18, with a huge wall completely painted by the kids of that social centre. Atomo and Schwarz would spell the word "animals": these would be typical squat pieces but certainly very well executed. Me and my people were initially on a middle ground between the two schools of thought: writers versus social centres. We had painted the Leoncavallo with Zero Fapilli when it was occupied in 1990. We would hit those places just like any other spot in Milan, bombing in pure, wild, PWD style.

Landmark
>

Muretto skill code

Rendo
>

The *Muretto* is located in a small square surrounded by a colonnade near Corso Vittorio Emanuele, also called Corsia dei Servi, in the centre of Milan. My first encounter with that place happened thanks to Play. It was Spring of 1984 and one morning while we were going to school he said: "Hold on... let me show you something I learned" and out of the blue he started doing some Break moves standing up. I was astonished; I'd never seen anything like that before.
A few months earlier, Play had discovered these guys who would perform strange moves called Breakdancing near Piazza San Babila. Without telling anyone, he started hanging out at the *Muretto* and, fascinated by this innovation, he started learning the basic moves. Only once he was sure he'd reached an acceptable level (hence had a competitive advantage over us, as he himself admitted), did he decide to show us the basic steps, convinced that we would've followed hot on his heels. Essentially, he wanted to be the best right off the bat, in fact when he saw how enthralled I was by it he said: "Even if you practice every day, you'll still be a step behind me because in the meantime I'll have learned new moves". In that moment I thought he was a dirtbag for having kept this passion a secret, but in the end, we were 15 years old, we were just kids. At the *Muretto*, Breaking was the discipline that won the most respect and everyone attempted to learn it, especially floor work, which was hard to perform

because it required substantial athletic abilities. Most people did uprock; it was customary to perform choreographies with two dancers, a choice that greatly enhanced the impact of the moves.
I recall every weekend we had to face the problem of buying batteries for our ghetto-blaster in oder to have music. Since batteries were expensive, someone came up with the idea of stealing electricity from a billboard near Burger One, one of the first fast-food joints in Italy. Naturally, at first the manager pretended not to notice because our frequent improvised Breaking performances attracted new clients for the place. But then he cut us off so we had to go back to using batteries.
We spent most of our time practicing moves and comparing sketches during the week. Doing graffiti was considered a heroic, almost mystical activity. Preparing sketches on paper, choosing the colours, going out at night with spray cans in a backpack, telling friends about the adventure the next day, still today this

At the Muretto, Breaking was the discipline that won the most respect and everyone attempted to learn it

wields irresistible allure for the new generations, imagine back then when it was all brand new.
Contemporaneously to the development of Writing and Breaking, people started rapping in English and beat-boxing.

Actually, the first lyrics were based more on punchlines rather than the desire to say something in particular... so long as it sounded good. Nowadays this might sound funny but we must keep in mind that back then, everything was just starting. Our young age played its part, and because we had nobody to learn from, we often proceeded by clumsy trials and errors. In the early 90's a few people started rhyming in Italian, but up until then everyone thought English was the only language suitable for rap. The appearance of the first deejays occurred when those of us who worked managed to acquire the funds to buy Technics turntables and reliable Stanton needles.
Despite everything, our crew continued to grow following a purely meritocratic logic. Nobody cared about who was from *Muretto*, all that mattered was personal ability.The spray paint we used was from craft shops, the colours didn't cover well and the nozzles were hard to manage. The caps sprayed in a way that didn't allow you to create thin lines. Not to mention we only had a dozen or so colours to choose from. That's why we were forced to improvise with the most disparate solutions. Full spray cans were only used to fill-in colours, while nearly empty ones were used for details. For the caps, we would extract the nozzle for nebulising and substitute it with the inner tube of a Bic pen.
This was cut to the length of 2 cm, melted using a lighter and sealed at one end. Once it cooled off, we'd pierce the plastic tube with a needle. At that point we were able to create relatively thin lines, but it wasn't a uniform stroke and the cap clogged up quickly.
Thinking back on it now, we must have seemed insane for our stubbornness in

trying to overcome these obstacles, but we were so overwhelmed by this passion for Aerosol Art that nothing could stop us. Obtaining photographs of graffiti from New York was nearly impossible because Milan, unlike Paris, London, or Amsterdam, was disconnected from any sort of informational exchange; we only got our hands on info by chance. Apart from some images from the movie *Beat Street* or images from the album covers of *Wild Style* or the Rock Steady Crew, it was rare to find material to study. Only upon looking at *Subway Art* did we realise the true substance of the NY scene, and subsequently, with the release of *Spraycan Art* in 1987, the existence of European scenes, especially the one in Paris that demonstrated to everyone the possibility of creating an entirely autochthonous style. Both books served as real turning points.
I vividly recall that Saturday afternoon at *Muretto* when I managed to leaf through *Spraycan Art* together with Fly Cat. We were spellbound, in fact while we were going home on the bus, we swore that from that day on we would start painting seriously, otherwise continuing made no sense.

Cano
>

In the mid-90's, during the North Railway upsurge, me and 16K went back to our old meeting spot, San Babila, with the breakers (Twice and Paolino's WRC crew). Black also hung with them, he slept in a garage under the *Muretto* since the 80's and was somewhat of a symbol of that

HIP HOP TO A DEGREE IS OR WAS ALL THINGS DOPE
—

THE FIRST PEOPLE I MET WERE BOGGY BEAT, MICHELE THE BOOGIE BOY, SEAN WHO REALLY WAS A PHENOMENAL B-BOY WHO COULD HAVE TAKEN ON ANYONE IN NEW YORK CITY BACK THEN, TONY AND OTHER HIP HOP HEADS. I THINK THAT WAS THE FIRST TIME I WAS AT *MURETTO*, AND IT'S A BEAUTY THAT THAT PLACE IS STILL WHERE B-BOYS GET DOWN.
GOT TO SHOUT OUT OMEGA ZULUS AND DJ/BBOY 2WICE, A TRUE PERSON AND A TRUE HIP HOP HEAD FOR KEEPING THE SPIRIT. SHAMA ROCK TOO, HONESTLY BECAUSE SHE WAS ONE OF THE MOST IMPRESSIVE PEOPLE THAT I NOTICED UPON RETURNING, WHO HAD CRAZY FREESTYLE FLAVOUR ON THE DANCE TIP.

IT WAS A BEAUTIFUL THING TO SEE AND THERE WERE MANY HEADS FROM DIFFERENT CULTURES DOWN THERE. WHEN I CAME BACK IN THE EARLY 90'S, MUCH HAD CHANGED.
RACIST COPS CALLING US NIGGERS. ANYWAY I FEEL THAT HIP HOP WAS CRAZY FLY THEN. WRITERS WERE ROCKING MAYBE A BIT TOO HARD BUT THEY WERE REALLY DOWN.
THEN IT SEEMED TO CHANGE BY THE MID 90'S, BUT IN THE BEGINNING SOMEONE WAS ONTO SOMETHING: WHEN EVERYONE HATED RENDO FOR HIS PROFESSION I WAS AMAZED THAT HE WAS USING THE WORST PAINT TO ROCK REALLY TIGHT PIECES WITH. SKAH IS STILL ONE OF MY FAVOURITES AND HIS BLACKBOOK IS PROBABLY

ONE OF THE SICKEST, MOST INTRICATE AND TECHNICAL THAT I HAVE EVER SEEN. DROP AND RAE AND SKY 4 WERE DOING IT AT ONE TIME AND FLYCAT WAS ON TO SOMETHING EVEN IF HE JUST STOPPED.
CANO AND TAWA SEEMED TO BE INNOVATING. AND AS FAR AS ADVOCATING THE CULTURE (THOUGH HE COULD PAINT TOO), SHAD WAS A REALLY TRUE SOULDIER.
BREAD 'N BAZOOKA ROCK THE HOUSE! OUTSIDE MILAN, THERE WERE A FEW WRITERS THAT I LIKED LIKE JOYS AND THOSE CATS FROM BRINDISI WHO I THOUGHT WERE BRINGING THE CULTURE. DADO AND DRAW FROM BOLOGNA TOO. I WAS IMPRESSED WITH THE WHOLE-CARS OF DAFNE AND SHERIF

AND I WOULDN'T KNOW WHO WAS PAINTING WHAT IN WHICH CITY BUT BLEF AND SIR WERE ANOTHER TWO I LOVED BECAUSE THEY WERE ROCKING BURNERS AND WERE UP.
MY CRITIQUE IS BASED ON A TOTAL OVER-STANDING OF WHAT STYLISTS DO AND I DON'T NEED AN ART CRITIC TO MAKE ME REALISE THAT.
THE MAIN THING IS THAT IF PEOPLE ARE JUST GOING TO "ADAPT" THE MOTIONS AND NOT THE CREED, IT'S NOTHING. IT'S LIKE TASTELESS SPAGHETTI. THERE ARE RECIPES THAT MAKE FOR WHAT GIVES THINGS THEIR MEANING AND FLAVOUR AND THERE ARE LEVELS OF IT THAT DEFINE IT. YOU DON'T JUST DABBLE IN THIS.
THERE ARE THOSE OF US WHO DO IT

JUST LIKE WE WAKE UP IN THE MORNING BECAUSE IT IS REALLY JUST AN EXTENSION OF OUR HERITAGE. MUSIC, ART, DANCE.
PEOPLE WANT TO IMITATE BUT NOT RESPECT THE FOUNDATION AND THE INFRASTRUCTURE THAT MADE THIS WHAT IT IS, AND THE REASONS WHY IT EXISTS TODAY. I WAS NEVER ONE TO DWELL ON OR LIVE IN THE PAST BUT IT HAS ITS SIGNIFICANCE AND IT DEFINITELY IS A GATEWAY TO THE FUTURE'S HOW, WHY AND WILL BE.
PEOPLE SAY THEY LOVE HIP HOP BUT HATE JAMES BROWN, THE STONES AND THE BEATLES WHEN ALL THAT IS HIP HOP. OUR GUMBO. HIP HOP TO A DEGREE IS OR WAS ALL THINGS DOPE..
— PHASE II

The 90's
>

Generation turnover

place, which was deserted back then but still a historical spot for Hip Hop in Milan. It all started under those porticos, a meeting spot for B-boys like Sean, Spit, Tony, Seno, Elektro; or MC's like Flaco, Loso, Fluido, Articolo 31, Kaos, and Space One; and writers like Rendo, Flycat... Tawa, Memè, and Vincenzo had already been hanging out there along with the skaters. Back then, people like Afrika Bambaataa or The Rock Steady Crew used to stop by, it was cool.

By the time we got there it wasn't as cool, there weren't as many of us and it was full of chavs, but eventually word got out and people started coming back: DJ Elektro with his radio, Mad Bob, and occasional visitors like Flaco, Rusty, and Nelson (who died shortly after). Lots of new kids like Dura showed up wanting to learn how to dance from Twice... plus a few posers from the Duomo area, we couldn't tell if they were into this Hip Hop stuff or not.

Soon enough, there was a substantial group, people like Noce, Vacca, Vincenzo and his brothers came back, Memè, Ste, and Angi, then Roger came back and the chaos spread, even criminals started hanging out there... Teo, Toya, Sam, not to mention drunks from the centre and nutty poets like Walter, Brambilla, the General or Black2, then Romeo with his Buffalo boots and pocketknife, Fausto and Aldo, Tony with his Durango boots in hand like a bludgeon who'd cry every time he talked about his son, and Donato who was always ready for a fight and would stretch his leg on the wall while talking to you, what a character! Or the nutcases like Inox who would show up dressed like a 15-year-old girl with dyed blond hair, even though he was a 35-year-old bearded man who had fried his brain on every possible drug. Poor guy, he was convinced that if he dressed like a girl, he'd get laid. Or Johnny, the Albanian who'd go around with a leather raincoat and hat even in the summer because he was obsessed with American R&B. By day he'd be shouting strange Albanianised American words in our ears, and by night he'd steal bikes. He was last seen singing on a stage in the streets of Manhattan, I guess his dream came true.

I remember the brawls with the Albanians, Iraqi-style carnivals, the shouting-matches with Debby, Cri, Lucia, and Elena, the wannabes who came from outside, the Chinese, the birthdays, Sunday afternoons at the Indian joint where fights always broke out, drunken Christmases with everyone, rows of bottles, brawls, Romeo trying to knife us over an offside call, barefooted soccer games with the Arabs till 5:00 am, radio always blasting, stolen McDonald's menus, Rap, Enzainer with his stories about Somalia, Romania, and butter... Aldo, Codino, Tony the mason...

I remember we used to hassle security guards, cops, and people who lived upstairs from McDonald's 'til dawn... Phase II and Vulcan would come by, Non Phixion, NextOne, Genius, Killa Priest... basically, everybody and their mothers.

Rendo
>

Around the 80's at *Muretto*, just a few metres away, a trend was born that would characterise that era, and, first in Milan and later in the rest of Italy, would influence the collective image of thousands of youths for a couple of the following years: the *paninari*. To be a *paninaro* meant following a simple set of rules on how to dress and act, nothing more and nothing less. And that is exactly why the *paninari* style was so quickly embraced by an entire generation. But then every social phenomenon that aspires to becoming a fashion has to be "easy". Easy to understand, easy to handle, and not that demanding. In those years all you had to do was go into a store, buy the right clothes, assume the relative behavioural codes and there you had it. It was an easily accessible trend. A disposable fad. On the other hand, the first thing you were asked if you wanted to be part of

"

To be a part of our group, especially at the beginning, you had to be able to dance or paint, and you had to do it well. .

Muretto was: "What can you do? Are you a breaker? Do you paint? Do you toprock, do you downrock? How many steps do you know and how well can you do them? How many hours do you practice every day? Do you dance with a group or alone? You feel like battling?". These questions, posed to kids between 12 and 15 years of age in rapid succession, I think clarify the philosophy at the base of our getting together: to do. To be a part of our group, especially at the beginning, you had to be able to dance or paint, and you had to do it well. Naturally that required commitment and discouraged most. Today, when a teenager decides to be a writer, even if he never enters a crew, he knows he can count on a solid web of solidarity, composed of kids the same age that understand him and with whom he can share his experiences. He knows his choice is identifiable by many and he no longer runs the risk of being considered a weird and eccentric kid. On the other hand we were alone, too few to be a recognised community. Nonetheless when I think of those years I believe the initial isolation was a stroke of luck for our movement, because it didn't stem from a trend, it managed to evolve thanks to a few motivated people that grew artistically for the pleasure of developing common interests, in a healthy way that didn't compromise with the inconsistent dictations of fashion, here today and gone tomorrow.

When we went to *Muretto* for the first time we ran into 16K and WRC, who were the city's only Breaking crew. 16K and WRC represented the real spirit of that place; the previous generation had passed it to them, almost as if they had "inherited" it. Obviously, you weren't automatically considered a friend just by showing up there. In order to be accepted at *Muretto*, it took months.

I particularly remember Twice, the best breaker. He was fascinating. He was quiet and bashful, he didn't talk much, but when he did everyone listened.

He had such an intense stare that if he looked at you, you'd inevitably look away. Not because he was scary but because he was intense. One night there was a fight between us and the chavs, who hung out at the *Muretto* in the afternoon.

The leader of their group, which was more numerous than ours, was encouraging his friends to fight, so in order to shut him up, Twice personally faced him and beat him senseless. That was the end of it; they left with their tails between their legs and none of them ever dared to bust our balls again. — ROBIN

I remember an atypical Milan, with two faces, hidden by the yellow lights of the street lamps at night a city under the control of fog, with the attitude of a metropolis while in the mere route from centre to periphery, a few hundred metres, it became provincial. The city in that period was reminiscent of a commercial version of *The Warriors*: you could see numerous groups aggregating in gangs, but only sustained by the trend of the moment. It was the *Milano da bere*[1] of groups of adolescents that reflected the ad posters placed along the primary streets of the city.

I remember the Saturday afternoons spent in the city centre when Corso Vittorio Emanuele was still open to traffic and the *paninari* fronted like they were the gang masters of the city, while instead our reality was quite distant, relegated to the margins. This rich and glossy city was counterpoint to the outskirts that watched it intensely, with a mixture of contempt and envy: hordes of kids that

spent their weeks in the squalor of popular neighbourhoods anticipated the weekend, when they could reverse themselves on the store windows of the centre, as if to fill an unbridgeable gap. I was starving like everybody else, and perhaps that is just what pushed me to the *Muretto* of San Babila, where I had the luck of meeting the first B-boys of Milan. There was a crew called *Dynamite Force* and others like Michael, Sean, Kaos, Argelino, Electro, Nelson, Spit, Fabio and the Pizzuto Brothers who were from my same block of project houses. I started dancing with my brother Memè and at the same time got interested in the high-sounding names of the first writers like Tony, Seno, Flycat, Rendo, Space One. All engrossed in their outlines and in the study of colours; they seemed to have come straight out of a cartoon. I remember they were so jealous of their sketches and photos, so reluctant to show them to strangers. Sometimes I asked myself what was so precious about those pieces of paper that they wouldn't show them to me. The street had already taught me to take what others had, but this time, not understanding what goods were at stake, I was even more curious; then one day I saw one of those guys tracing unreadable and complex letters with a spray can, that however I was able to grasp immediately, so much had I fantasised about them. The execution of that simple throw- up opened the doors a parallel world and reconnected me to a new way of communicating, distant from the ad posters, similar to political graffiti and yet different; tags were something I didn't understand but that however attracted me. All I saw while returning home was that way of painting, but I started understanding its dynamics only by assiduously hanging out in *Muretto* and conquering the trust of the others. That place was a type of non-school where I received primary lessons from non-teachers, empirically learning from what others did. — ENZO

❶ Literally "Milan to drink" from a famous ad slogan of the 80's, during which Milan was the epicentre of Italian wealth and fashion and was characterised by a lifestyle based on consumption and self-gratification

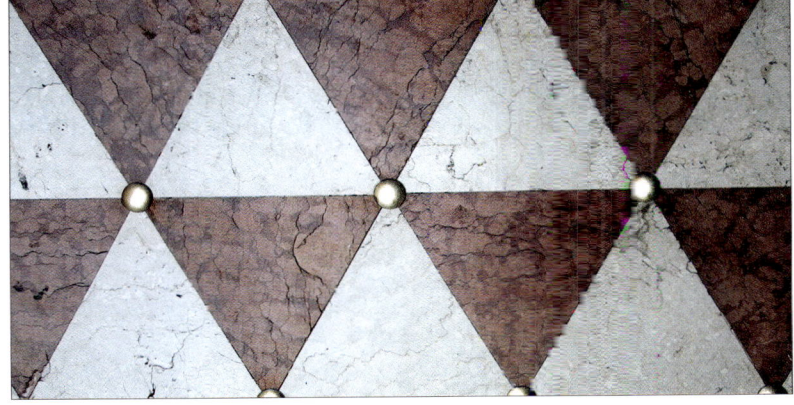

The floor of *Muretto* with studs to prevent breakers from dancing   — *ACW archive*

Mentors
>

Flying on a Spyder

Flycat
>

In the early 80's, the few Breaking videos that actually made it to Italy were our only source of information about American urban culture: more than anything, the surroundings, the background, and the settings we saw struck us and inspired us to daydream... Behind the breakers we saw lots of painted walls, we knew nothing about it, all we knew was they were done with spray paint. We assigned the same hierarchy we observed in these videos to aspects of street culture: in the foreground, the B-boys who were the protagonists; and in the background, the pieces. Therefore, we figured that dancing came first and all the rest was secondary- Writing included. That's how it was up until '86, we had nothing more than some Writing on our jackets. We basically gathered together to dance and listen to music.
Sher and I formed the first duo, TFS (*The Fabulous Sprayers*), but we didn't paint. He lived in Piazzale Repubblica and I lived in the Loreto neighbourhood, so our tour began by traversing Corso Buenos Aires to San Babila, where everyone met up at *Muretto*, which had already been a hang-out spot since '82. The few tags we did were along this route, unaware of the future consequences for the city. We were also unaware of the risks, we went

out tagging in the day, before and after school, on trams, while people walked by and saw us. We caught word of other writers in Milan. The guys from *Muretto* (who usually kept their distance from us due to our young age) told us one day that some American writers had painted in the Garibaldi neighbourhood. Seeing pieces by A-one, Toxic, Koor, and Phase II was truly mind-blowing. They painted on metal sheets in construction sites: for us those were the all-time greatest works of art, fundamental for our initiation.
Back then we always went around in groups, as if on a mission; even if it was just to go look at new tags or watch new videotapes. I still remember when Sher and me were invited by Sean (who danced with the super famous *Dynamic Force* back then) to go see *Electro Rock*: it was a true upheaval in our B-boy existence. The new tags we saw in the beginning stimulated us to try our hand at it and sparked our curiosity to find out who these artists were.

– IN MEMORY OF SPYDER 7
What changed everything was a tag we saw everywhere, perhaps the first person to gain visibility: Nasty. He started in Loreto and made his way to the city centre... this went on for an entire year. It was the most stylish name you could see back then, and it was done with a silver felt-tip marker to boot, extra-swanky. But Nasty suddenly and mysteriously disappeared from the scene. Then, a few months later, a new name appeared, even more stylish than the first: Spyder. It was a shock

for everyone at *Muretto*: some tags were done with spray paint, some were made with enormous felt markers, something we'd never seen before, and we were speechless. We couldn't understand how he had done it. Month after month, our astonishment increased. Spyder decided to take over the city and did something that had never been done before: he became omnipresent. Kids came to *Muretto* from the Navigli saying they'd seen his tag there too, I told them I'd even seen his tag

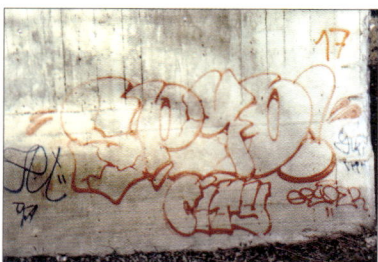
Spyd City by Spyder 7   – Rax-E

in Loreto, others had seen it in the centre, and others saw it on the North side of the city. Not only did Spyder choose the area, he also chose the spot: at eye-level, above shutters, on the corner of two buildings, up high in driveways.
Only Nelson (RIP), a B-boy who hung out at *Muretto* caught sight of him one night as he quickly tagged up an area... Nelson told us he wore Adidas Superstars with fat laces, a tracksuit unlike anything we'd ever seen before, and a Kangol hat. The legend expanded and we were all

convinced he was American. I decided to search for him until I finally found him one night. Nelson's description was accurate; he was even carrying a plastic bag that was dripping with red paint. I followed him for quite a while until he realised it and turned around saying: "What do you want???"
Thus, I managed to reveal another mystery: Spyder WAS Nasty, he had just changed his name because he realised there was another Nasty in New York. He instinctively added the number 2 to his name but then decided to definitively drop it. Back then, the search for an original and one-of-a-kind name was essential, you'd change your name if you discovered another writer from a different city had the same one. Spyder and I became friends. I found out he was 5 years older than me and had already been to NY. He had not meet writers while in the U.S., but he had been heavily influenced by the city and its scene: 1980's streets full of tags somehow coincided with his passion for heavy metal music, which consequently led him to graphics... Iron Maiden and other crazy album covers that inspired his mania for calligraphy.
One day he showed me a studded jacket he had hand-painted on the back with incredible lettering. Through heavy metal he grew to appreciate Hip Hop and it all melted together: Gothic Writing, new letters, urban settings full of tags, and a city, Milan, where things were just starting. As the years went by, it was just me and him drawing, and everything I learned was thanks to Spyder.

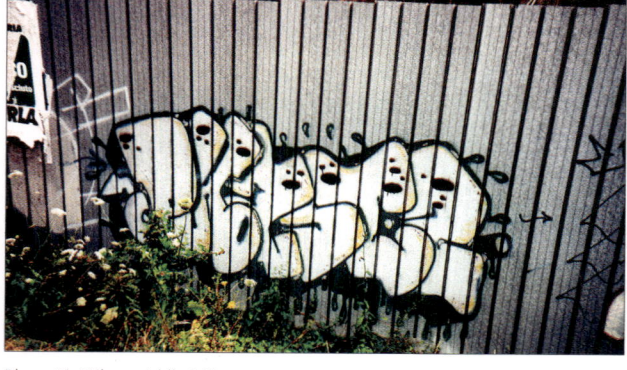
Phase II in Milan, middle 80's   – Mace

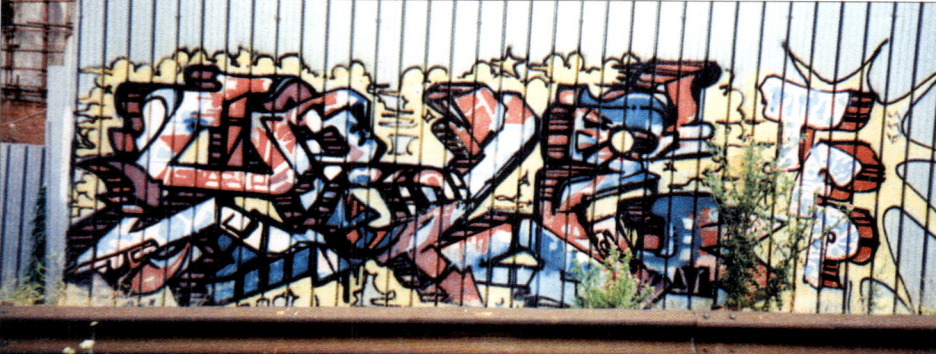
A-one, 1982   – Mace

> CONTINUES FROM PAGE 159
tried to stand out from the others. Competition was the stimulus that stirred everything up. In Milan in the early 90's, the most famous crews were PWD, CKC, TDK, TKA, MNP; also 16K, TGF, and even ZONA 13. CKC and PWD were from the East side; founded by Flycat, they had the best bombers and a style similar to the American writers. It was Wildstyle, the most complex and original style from New York. They hung out at Piazza Aspromonte and on Via Bazzini, and for years they were the "kings", meaning the city's best

writers. TKA, another historic crew that hung out in Piazza Aspromonte, were equally good.
They often painted with CKC and were one of the most respected groups. For a period of time they even published a cyclostyled fanzine called *Trap*. It was in black and white, but was nevertheless one of the best during those years.
Other crews from the East side, the Lambrate neighbourhood, were TGF and Zona 13, who were especially good at coloured murals. A bit further North, in the Martesana neigh-

bourhood, was TDK, a crew that was considered the best for murals in Italy. Their illustrations and compositions were exceptional, captivating generations of young writers. Many young kids started writing after seeing their pieces: the effort, the technique, the dimension of their work was without equal and remained unrivaled. If you wanted to see how unskilled you were, you'd go to their hall of fame to admire their pieces.
On the South side, in the Giambellino neighbourhood, was MNP crew,

famous for their more European style: they had been drawn to the style of famous writers from Paris like Bando and therefore did pieces with a style that was new to Milan. That's why there had been debates with the Wildstyle fans, because even though that style was new and original, it was not considered fresh by other crews.
A writer from the MNP, Kayone, then formed a new crew called THP. This crew, apart from their contribution to graffiti, also created a self-published magazine called "*Tribe*"

which was about graffiti in Milan and was the city's most important source of information for many years.
In the Barona neighbourhood, not far from where THP crew was based, was another group composed of kids with great talent: 16K. Their strong point was their unique, almost pictorial style. Their pieces contained letters that were avant-guard and original. The originality of their method and the freshness of their style made them perhaps the most innovative writers. – ROBIN

European influences
>

Milano City Artists

Rendo
>

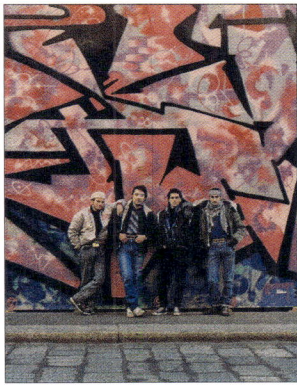

Kaos, Rendo, Play, Graffio   — *Rendo*

Wild Style, MCA by Kaos, Rendo, Play and Graffio. Milano City Artists, Bologna Biennale, 1988   — *Rendo*

MCA (*Milano City Artists*) was born on April of 1987 at *Muretto*, thanks to the encounter of Graffio and Yassassin with Rendo and Play. Kaos joined some months later, slightly before Yassassin left the crew. Our union was favoured by a series of stylistic affinities that in those years made our group unique: with respect to many other writers that painted in Milan we were attending art schools and had a passion for comics and illustrations.
More importantly, we were tied to the European stylistic current, a fundamental base to develop a personal style over time that was distant from everything that was arriving from New York. Our stylistic journey and growth as writers were marked by two determining factors: keeping contacts abroad and getting paid commissions.
In 1988 we were invited to participate at the Biennial of Young European Artists in Bologna. In that occasion we created a sixteen metre long by six metre high piece, but the most important thing is that we managed to convince our sponsor to give us ten times the necessary amount of spray cans. When we returned to Milan we started painting constantly, getting better with each and every hit.
Kaos visited London and Rendo Paris, but the trip that most had an impact on our growth as a crew was when we went to Munich in 1988. We spent our days taking photos and studying the pieces in a hall of fame of monumental proportions: the Writing was inserted into scenery that completed its meaning. In particular we finally observed expert writers in action and learned new techniques.
In those same years, thanks to a series of commissions for public and private institutions, we could afford a large quantity of spray paint this allowed us to notably improve the technical aspects of our work, but even more importantly, to experiment with new styles and modes of expression, faithful to the murals seen in Munich's Flohmarkt.

ANGEL
—

Rendo
>

This was painted by Zaki Dee in the summer of 1988, over a piece Grafio had done a year earlier. Zaki was in Milan to be with his girlfriend who modelled, so he came to *Muretto* and met us. We brought him to Parco Martesana and before going back to London he painted this piece without saying anything to us!
According to Graffio, Zaki did us the discourtesy of covering our piece, in this case his. In our opinion, he painted over it without malice. Consider that at the time no one in Milan went over anybody else's stuff, it was considered an offense to be washed in blood.
However, perhaps in London it wasn't considered disrespectful and so Zaki just did the piece, period. We'll never know. In any case that event allowed us to observe and study a TCA work live and up close!

Zaki Dee
>

The Angel piece came about in 1987. My girlfriend at the time was working in Milan and I stayed with her for a few months. Whilst walking around the centre of the city near the Duomo, I spotted some breakers. I later found out this was also where all the local B-boys would hang out, in an area called *Muretto*. There were some graffiti artists there, maybe four or five, I can't remember their names. They didn't speak much English and I didn't speak much Italian but we soon worked out that we were all writers. After that first meeting I went back to see them a few more times and they told me about a big wall where some

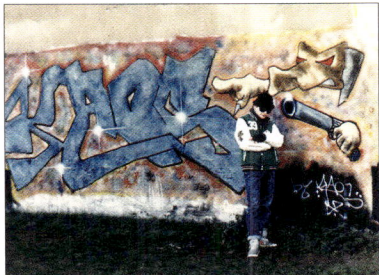

Kaos, 1988   — *Rendo*

writers had already painted. They gave me directions to get there by train, because it was quite a way out from the centre of Milan. There were already a few pieces there so I was a bit worried that if I went over them the local kids would go over me. It was a tall and wide wall and I tried to paint as much as I could, I think I finished it in a day. I had to stand on crates or anything that would get me as high as I could reach because didn't have a ladder.
The letters were around seven or eight feet high with the background maybe reaching about 10ft high and around 30ft long. At one end was a dedication to the Chrome Angelz; Pride, Mode, Scribla, Rendo and Colter.
I remember the paint selection was quite good over there, so I was able to do a colourful piece. At the time the Milan graffiti scene was in its infancy compared to some of the other European countries so I thought maybe the local kids would find the piece and get inspired. A few weeks later I moved back to London. The 1987 Milan "Angel" piece along with several trackside pieces and dubs in and around Brentford Chiswick and Gunnersbury tube stations later that year, were probably the last illegal things had. I then drifted out of the graffiti scene and got into DJing and record producing. "Angel" was probably the biggest piece I ever did. Thanks to those early Italian writers, Milan is an important part of my graff years and I hope it influenced some of the kids in that area to start up writing.

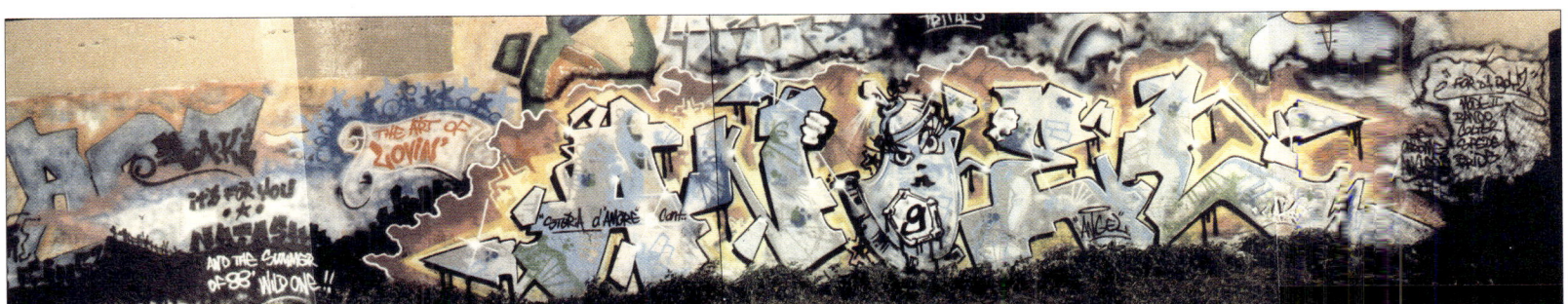

Angel by Zaki Dee - TCA from London. Summer 1988   — *Zaki Dee*

East side story

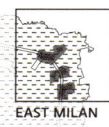

EAST MILAN

In the 90's the area of East Milan became the focal point of the first Writing scene to spill out of the experience of Muretto. Rendo and Flycat started searching for new talents amongst the kids of the neighbourhood, and the latter in particular animated an entire generation of writers gravitating between Piazzale Loreto and the Oratory of Casoretto. They later formed CKC, a group that would guide the original Milanese Writing movement. The reason why the Writing scene of that period was concentrated in that area can be identified by the presence of the railway line, which penetrated the urban texture from the East, deviating towards the North, to then weave its way in the direction of Central Station. This linear infrastructure running on a lengthy, elevated rail bed certainly influenced the activity of many crews that formed along the lines of its route. Originally demarcating the limit between the urban centre and the first industrial areas of the city, in those years the double wall of this structure represented a sort of no-man's land, an anonymous and completely unutilised space that appeared simply ideal to the local writers.

From the pieces along Via Ortica, to those in Zona 13, or those by TFG in Lambrate, many are the halls of fame that configured themselves along this embankment or the intersections radiating out of the city; such as Pantano and Argonne, two halls of fame composed on the sides of the tunnels along these walls.

These initiatives were never excessively impeded, nor were they perceived as invasive, for no private space was being violated and the occupied surfaces were not deemed strategically fit for propagandistic ends.

The decision to paint here, other than guaranteeing a certain degree of tranquillity while doing so, with time revealed to be an extraordinary intuition: after over twenty years, all the halls of fame that had formed along the rail bed of Eastern Milan are still in their place. The pieces have faded, perhaps enriched by the coating of time, yet they resist, unlike other marginal areas of the city that have progressively transformed. This kilometric wall, now integrated into the new urban centre, has never been claimed by anyone, not even by the advertisement that upholsters almost any useful or over-exposed surface in Milan.

Even if I hadn't grown up in Via Bazzini, I might have become a writer anyway, but surely not with this attitude. I probably would have followed the European style, maybe concentrating on puppets or block letters. But I would not have used Wildstyle, which took root in Italy and automatically spread through Lambrate in East Milan. We adhered to it because our idea of Writing was a faithful evolution of the unwritten rules of New York, of the Wildstyles that Phase II had passed down to us years before.
— BANG

Current CSOA Leoncavallo

Martesana

Pontano

Lambrate

Former CSOA Leoncavallo

Casoretto Oratory

Piazzale Loreto

Piazza Aspromonte

Politecnico

Ortica

Muretto of San Babila
Galleria dei Servi
The main hang-out for writers and breakers in Milan during the 80's and mid 90's.

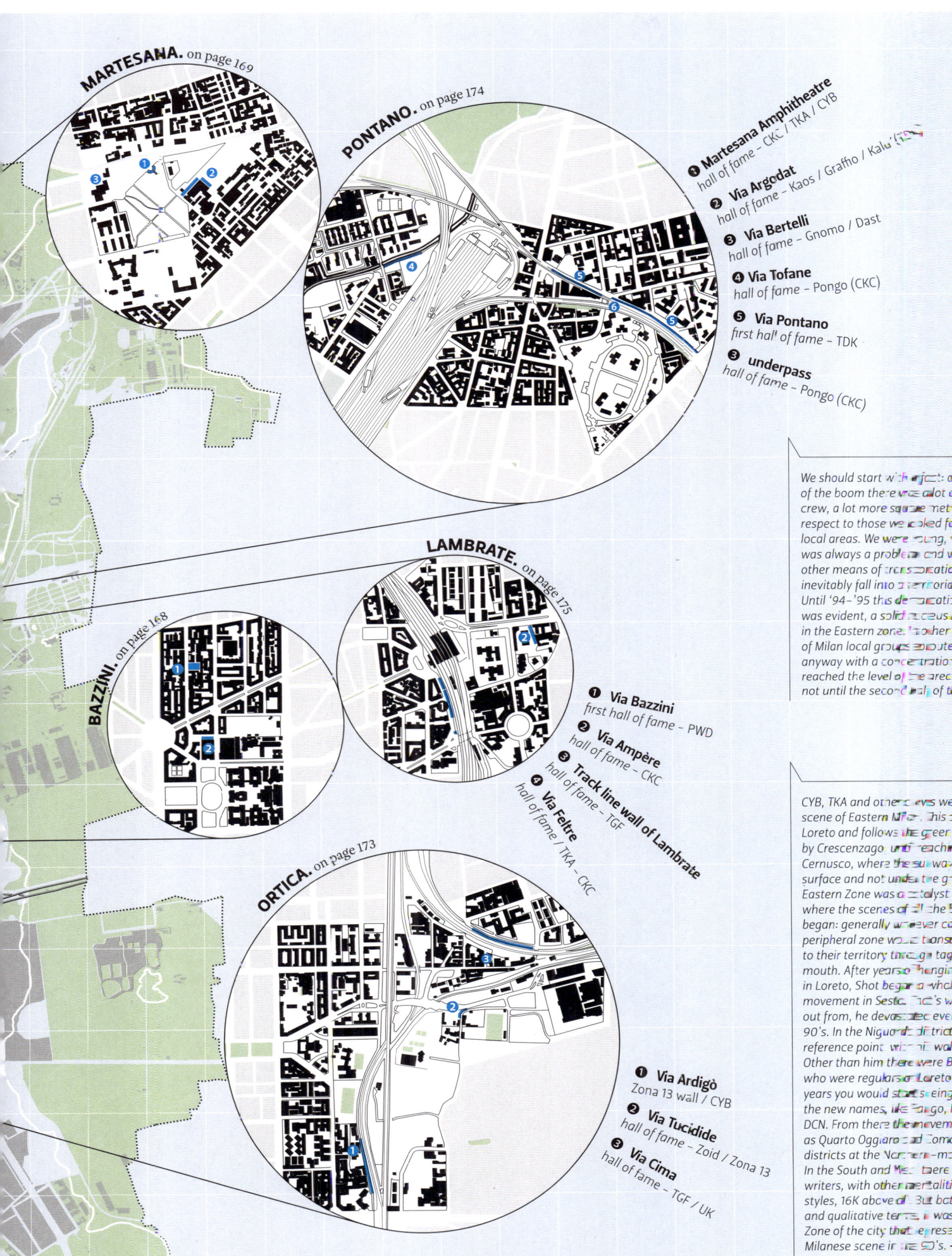

MARTESANA. on page 169

PONTANO. on page 174

❶ **Martesana Amphitheatre**
hall of fame – CKC / TKA / CYB

❷ **Via Argodat**
hall of fame – Kaos / Graffio / Kalu (?)

❸ **Via Bertelli**
hall of fame – Gnomo / Dast

❹ **Via Tofane**
hall of fame – Pongo (CKC)

❺ **Via Pontano**
first hall of fame – TDK

❻ **underpass**
hall of fame – Pongo (CKC)

LAMBRATE. on page 175

BAZZINI. on page 168

❶ **Via Bazzini**
first hall of fame – PWD

❷ **Via Ampère**
hall of fame – CKC

❸ **Track line wall of Lambrate**
hall of fame – TGF

❹ **Via Feltre**
hall of fame – TKA – CKC

ORTICA. on page 173

❶ **Via Ardigò**
Zona 13 wall / CYB

❷ **Via Tucidide**
hall of fame – Zoid / Zona 13

❸ **Via Cima**
hall of fame – TGF / Uk

We should start with reject: at the beginning of the boom there was a lot of space for each crew, a lot more square metres of walls with respect to those we looked for inside our local areas. We were young, moving around was always a problem and without a car or other means of transportation we would inevitably fall into a territorial mentality. Until '94-'95 this demarcation of districts was evident, a solid that caused had taken root in the Eastern zone. In other neighbourhoods of Milan local groups sprouted only later and anyway with a concentration that never reached the level of the area around Loreto, not until the second half of the 90's. — **SKY 4**

CYB, TKA and others crews were part of the scene of Eastern Milan. This area begins in Loreto and follows the green line as it passes by Crescenzago until reaching Cologno and Cernusco, where the subway travels on the surface and not under the ground. The Eastern Zone was a catalyst because it's where the scenes of all the bordering areas began: generally whoever came from a peripheral zone would transport Writing back to their territory through tags and word of mouth. After years hanging out with CKC in Loreto, Shot began a whole new movement in Sesto. That's where Dra came out from, he devastated everything in the 90's. In the Niguarda district, Flaco was a reference point with his walls and spaces. Other than him there were Bread and Drop, who were regulars in Loreto. After a couple years you would start seeing the pieces of the new names, like Fango, Haok, and all DCN. From there the movement spread as far as Quarto Oggiaro and Comasina, the districts at the Northern-most tip of the city. In the South and West there were other writers, with other mentalities and different styles, 16K above all. But both in quantitative and qualitative terms, it was the Eastern Zone of the city that represented the Milanese scene in the 90's. — **SHAD**

The garrison of neighbourhoods
>

From Muretto to the city

Flycat
>

After a few years, the *Muretto* was no longer the main meeting point for writers. Around 1987, Sher and I began looking for a spot in our own neighbourhood- Loreto. Near Via Bazzini I found a semi-abandoned urban garden full of shrubs. When we got there, we saw a huge wall that wasn't visible from the street because of all the shrubbery, so we could paint without being seen. Since we constantly pushed through the bushes to reach the wall, the shrubs started to thin out, and the garden was reborn thanks to our pieces. Kids from the neighbourhood began meeting up there: Fox (who then became Bangsta), Ask, Kray, and others who had grown up in the streets as kids. The Bazzini hall

of fame attracted everyone, at the end of the 80's it was a true magnet and in time it even became a regular stopping point for writers in Northern Italy.

The new generation of local writers was very young and couldn't move freely around the city, they were tied to the Casoretto oratory, so they painted in that area. I gave them names and their first tag styles, so they considered me their reference point and often rang my doorbell looking for me. Our connection became evident through their first felt marker tags around the neighbourhood... This coincided with the early 90's. Loreto remained a reference point even for the later generation of writers like Mad Bob (who then became 2Mad) and Sky4, until we began to isolate ourselves in our own microcosms, with an attitude that could be considered snobby, but was in line with what would happen years later throughout the city: in Giambellino MNP crew protected their

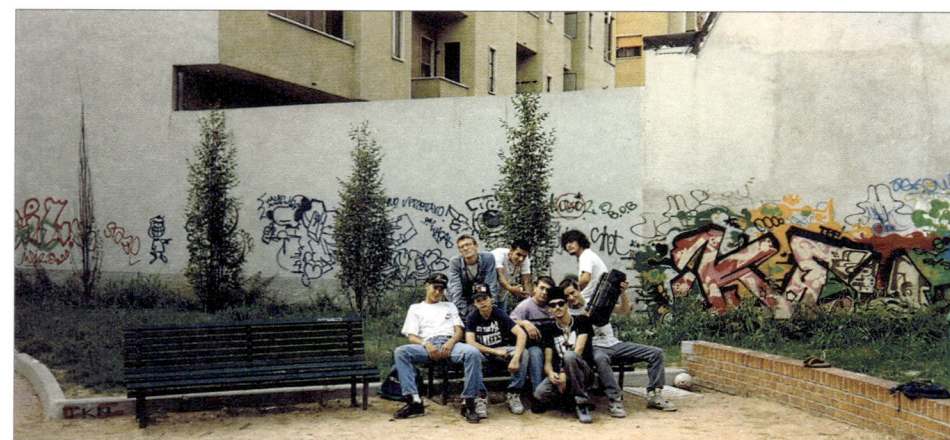
PWD chilling in Bazzini gardens, early 90's   — Mace

wall, in Lambrate TGF crew protected theirs, 16K in Barona did the same, as did TDK crew in Via Pontano and Zona 13 with the infinitely long wall that bordered their area. Crews would meet up at night; we'd go to Plastic Club when Skizo played, otherwise we'd guard our territory. There

was enough space for everyone, but often the coexistence of several crews in the same neighbourhood led to some harsh conflicts over wall space. For example, in Loreto PWD crew was at Bazzini, then came CKC, and lastly TGF crew: in the 90's, the relationship between them

wasn't exactly idyllic. TGF crew often hung out at Leonkavallo, they all lived in the Lambrate neighbourhood. Initially there was serious tension between them and CKC because even if they shared the same New York-inspired style, they didn't want to share the same territory.

A secret garden
>

Bazzini's

Mace
>

My first approach to Milan was through Flycat, but I already knew about the Via Bazzini hall of fame because the son of my neighbours (an elderly Venetian couple I always called grandma Elsa and grandpa Marco) from Treviso lived there. My mother was actually born in Milan, on Via MacMahon in the Bovisa neighbourhood: it was quite the working-class neighbourhood before the University and Bovisa Triennale came along. I had some relatives who lived there, all working-class people who were more or less Communists and Unionists: my maternal grandfather died with his union- he traveled throughout Italy but then fell ill. My relatives have now moved to Legnano, which is outside of Milan, and from what I know they've become supporters of the North

League secessionist party (Lega Nord). Bazzini's hall of fame was near the Piola station, at the Politecnico: in one of those little parks, squished between two buildings (actually, it was more like a flower bed) with nice walls that enclosed it. At the far end was an especially nice reinforced concrete wall that was three-four metres tall. Fly, Fox (Bang), Sher, and Shad would occasionally paint there. This was around '87-'88, and there wasn't that much stuff in Milan. When I think about it now, it's strange how much of an emotional impact the first tags stirred up. Now they're just part of the urban landscape, you barely notice them anymore, but I'll never forget the first tags I saw. It was exciting; you'd look at the same pieces over and over. I could describe every single piece on those walls back then. There was even a dragon, a sort of gremlin that I think had been done by Sher: not that many people know him, but back then he was Flycat's partner, they had founded TFS crew together. After bonding with Fly, I began visiting him regularly in Milan and this led to the formation of the PWD crew: Spyder 7, Flycat, Sky 4, Mad Bob, and me. We would drink Matheus, this crappy wine in a round bottle,

and our mission was to paint the city. One time, Fly, Mad Bob, and me went to get drinks at the seedy Mexican place called La Piedra del Sol before painting a subway station. Then, at the last moment, we decided to go to a nearby amusement park. While on the roller coaster, Mad pulled out a spraycan and started tagging the railing before the drop; he practically risked his life to leave his tag on the roller coaster car! We were bombers, obsessed with the need to see our works around because at the time the city was clean and we wanted to prove that you could paint trains and stations: we were the first in Italy to bomb full-force with CKC, TAS, and TKA crews. We wanted to be real writers, we didn't give a shit about painting well with skinny caps... actually, to be honest, we were pretty raw back then, we were vandals who idolised New York. For us, a panel piece was worth more than a detailed whole-wall piece, and this is what allowed Writing to spread throughout Italy: an amazing wall piece might intimidate you to never attempt picking up a can of spraypaint whereas a station bombed with tags and throw-ups makes you feel you like you can do it too... without this, Writing would have never evolved. What we

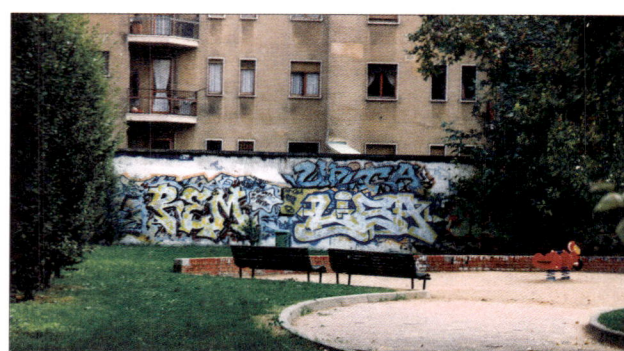
Bazzini gardens, early 90's   — Mace

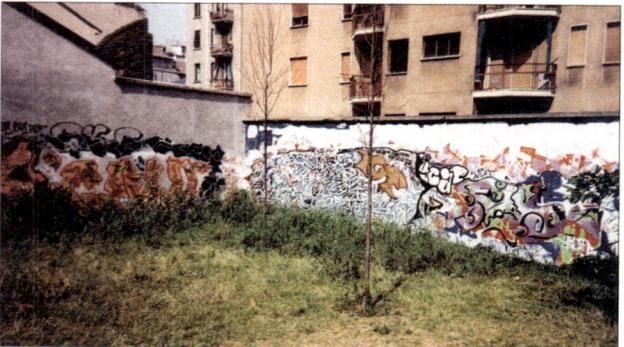
PWD crew   — Rusty

did wasn't enough, so we had to draft new recruits from the next generation. As the months passed it became increasingly

evident: new people began painting and the phenomenon spread like wildfire. Shortly later, it became something serious.

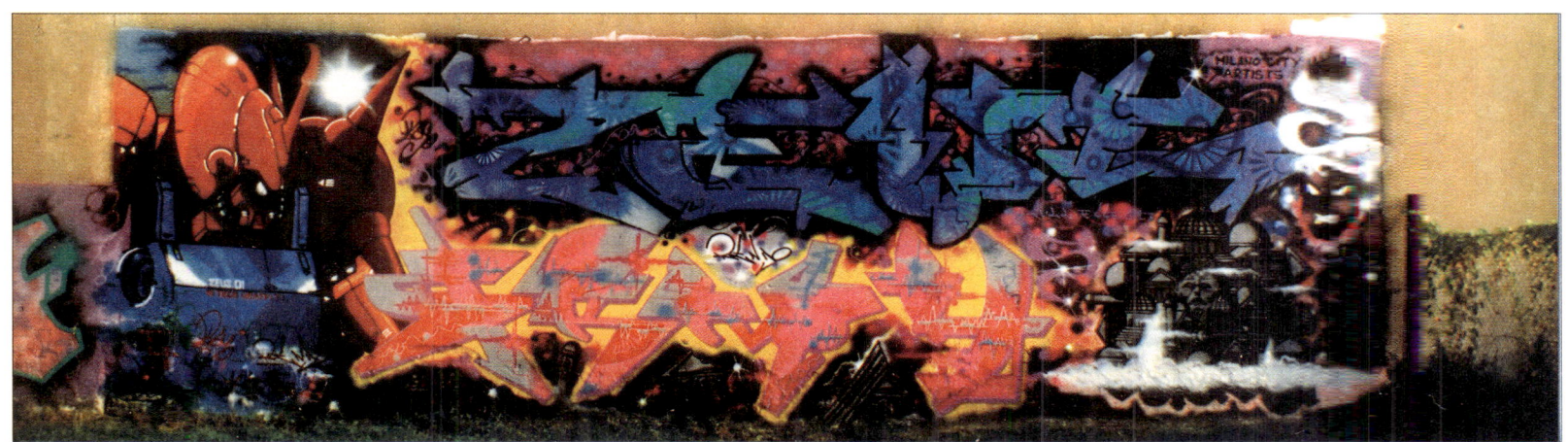

Zeus Army by Rendo and MCA, Martesana hall of fame

— Rendo

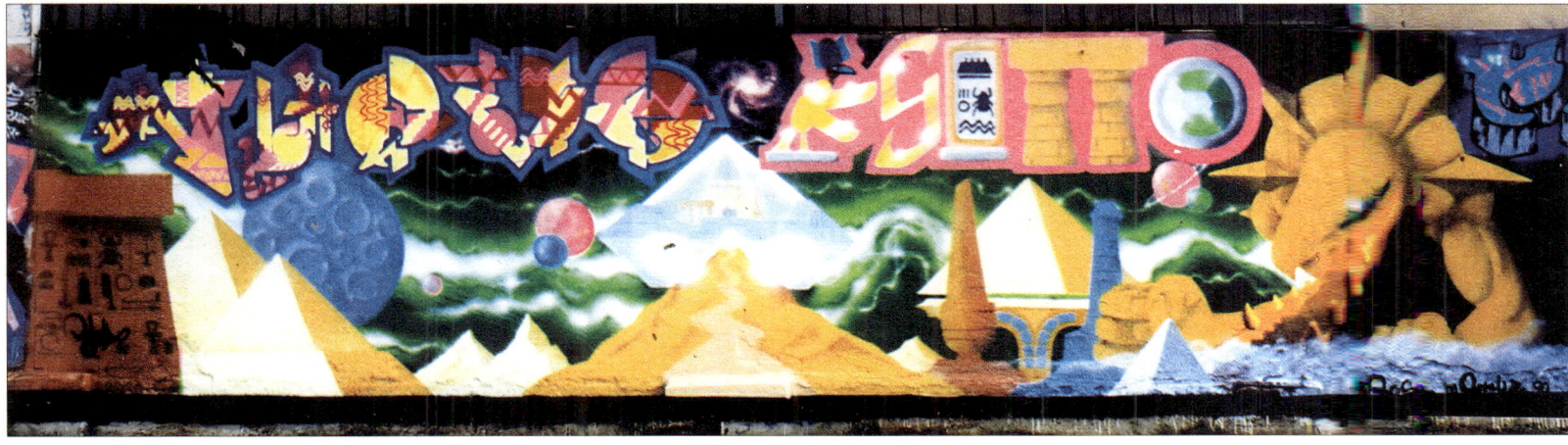

Antico Egitto (Ancient Egypt) by Rendo and MCA

— Rendo

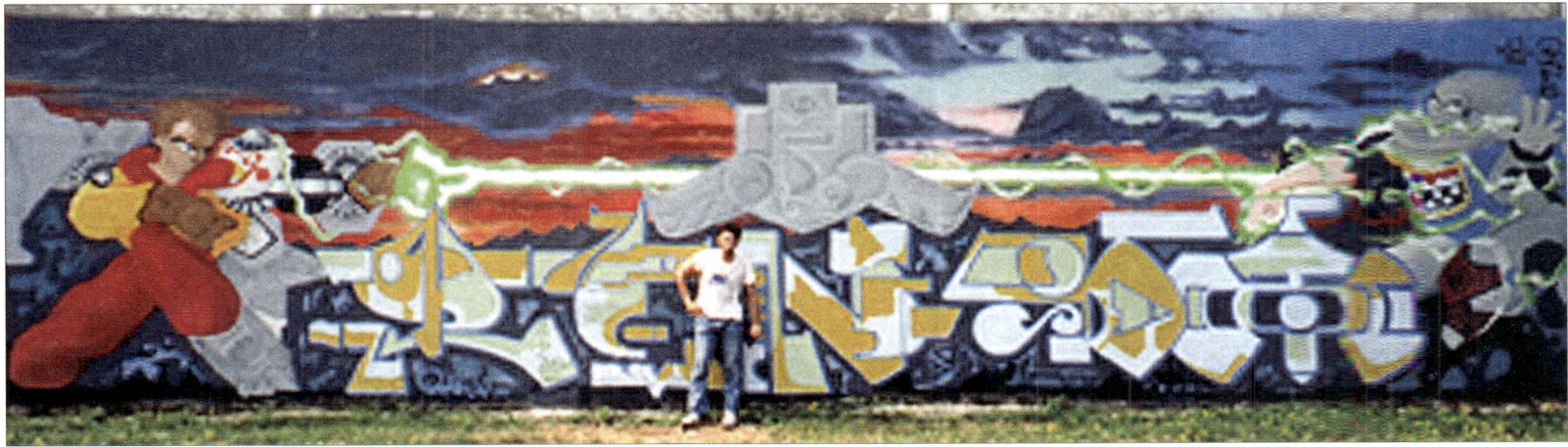

Rendo-TDK

— Rendo

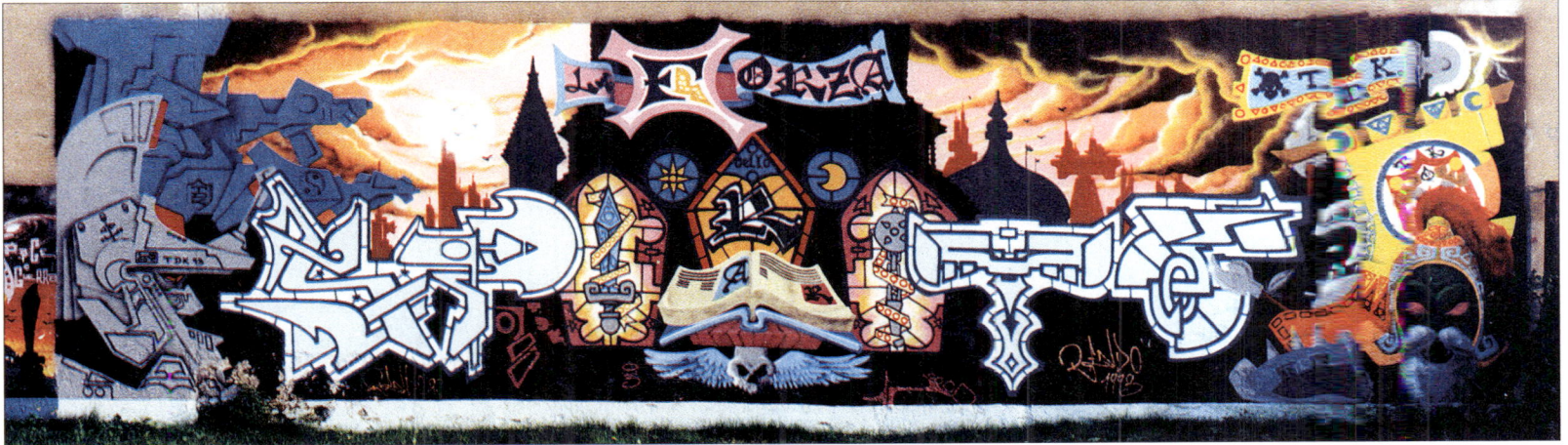

Forza dello Spirito (Strength of spirit) by Rendo and TDK crew

— Ens

Direct influences
>

PWD: New York Wildstyle

Mace
>

**Writing since childhood, legendary feats
and the first painted roof in Italy**

PWD crew belonged to a generation that grew up in the streets, unlike the generations that were to follow. From the age of 5, you'd go out after lunch and go back home at night to do your homework. When talking about crews, it's easy to get confused because in those days in Milan, everybody hung out on the streets, first at the oratory, then at Via Bazzini, then Loreto, and lastly at Aspromonte... a typical park that kids played in for years before painting in it. We weren't looking for halls of fame, we were just painting the walls in our territory, our playground... the same thing happened in Treviso.
In many ways, I think Writing is an extension of those things we used to do as kids, like building go-karts from shopping carts, guarding our football field, or lifting girls' skirts up; that was the initial spirit, then people grew up and took Writing to another level, but that's where it all started. In Italy, there were no gangs, just kids: if a new kid moved to the neighbourhood, he was immediately put to the test. Writing had the same dynamics, you would appropriate the place you often played in. Who else had the right to appropriate it apart from you, who had lived in that place forever?
Our targets in Milan were stations, some trains, white roller-pieces on the subway walls. As soon as Line 3 was constructed for the 1990 World Cup, Fly, Shad, Sky, Starch, and me bombed it. Unfortunately, we weren't able to finish our pieces, I had almost finished the outline but hadn't done the background or 3D effects...
Mad Bob and me were also the first to go into the tunnel of line 1, no one ever had

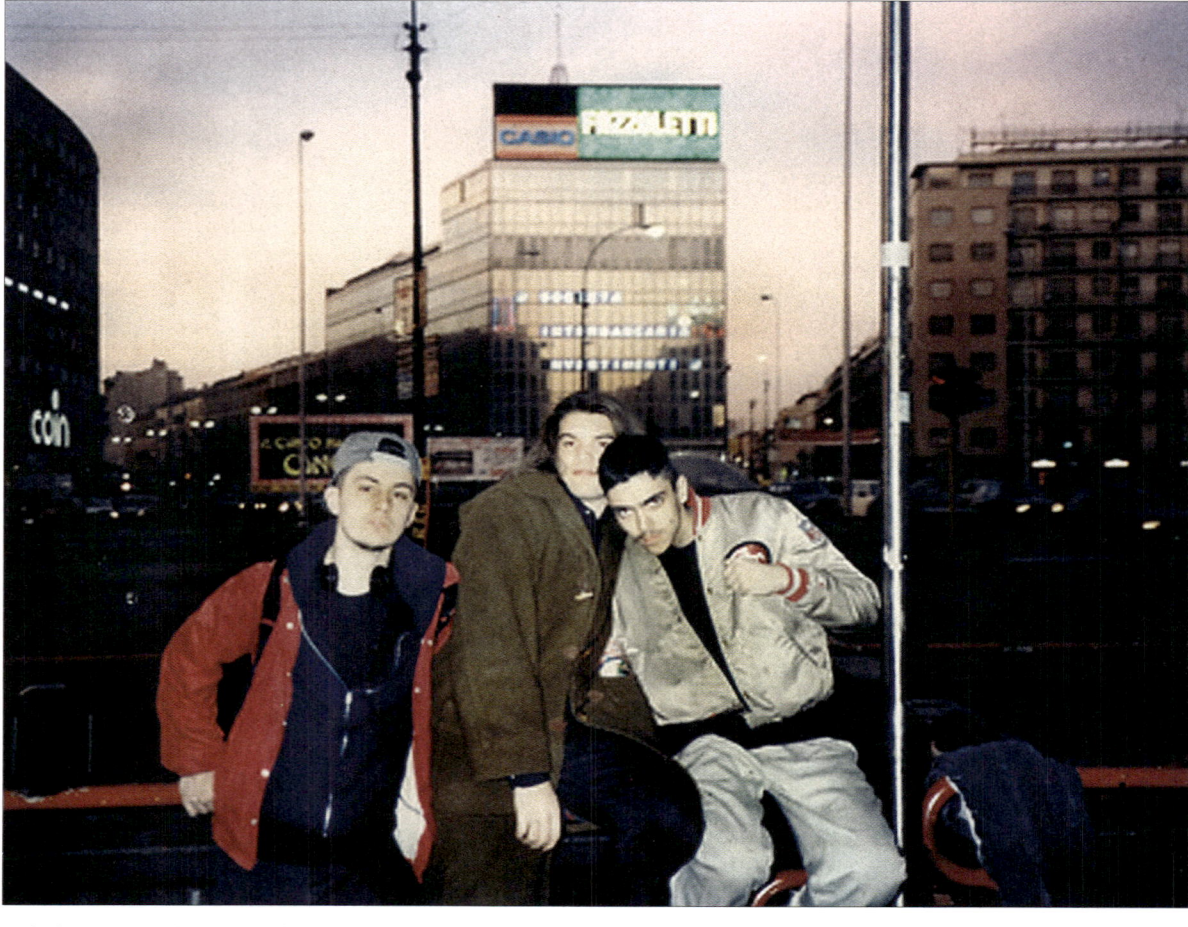

Mad Bob, Max Cortez, Flycat in Piazzale Loreto on the opposite side of the XI *blocco* hang-out, 1991   — *Flycat*

the guts to do it out of fear of the third rail. One night, Mad Bob and me snuck in to tag up the platforms and then we started jumping around all over the place. If I'm not mistaken, we walked from Loreto all the way to Lima, tagging along the way and even leaving a few throw-ups. Since we came out of the tunnel safe and sound, everyone else started doing it too.
Mad Bob was a key figure for bombing in Milan, few met him but he was a

fresh guy... we'd listen to The Geto Boys, he was crazy about Scarface, Bushwick Bill, and company; we'd drive around the streets of Milan in his compact car all night, if he decided he wanted to paint, nothing would stop him, he'd even go alone. He was the protagonist of ventures that were legendary for us: one night he stole a bike from a subway security guard and bombed five or six stations all in one night, riding through the tunnels on the

bike. He stopped at each station, bombed it, and then pedalled off. He was the first person to paint roofs in Italy, for example, the one next to the COIN sign in Piazzale Loreto, where there was traffic 24-7. Not to mention subway roofs: one of them is still intact and every time I go to Milan, I stop to look at it: arriving from Brescia on the left, shortly before reaching the central Station, near Via Padova, it's all covered in ivy, but still there!

GATHERINGS AT LORETO
—

Flycat
>

It was the early 90's. The idea was to have a gathering of all the crews in a single spot, to have a sort-of assembly, as if we were the protagonists of the city.
Movies like *The Warriors*, with a gathering of all the city's gangs, had sparked our imaginations, but we were unaware of the radical differences between the Milan of those years and New York City two decades earlier. Thanks to an idea Bang had, CKC crew had given all

its members bomber jackets of the Portland Blazers, an NBA basketball team.
On more than one occasion we gathered underground at the Loreto subway stop together with other city crews: it was all about making an appearance. In those days, CKC crew had established the first real writer's bench at the Loreto subway stop, and so writers met up at the exit of that subway, on the corner of Via Padova and Viale Monza. People flocked there from all over Milan and even from Cernusco, like Kid, who would pedal kilometres on his bike so as to reach Loreto.

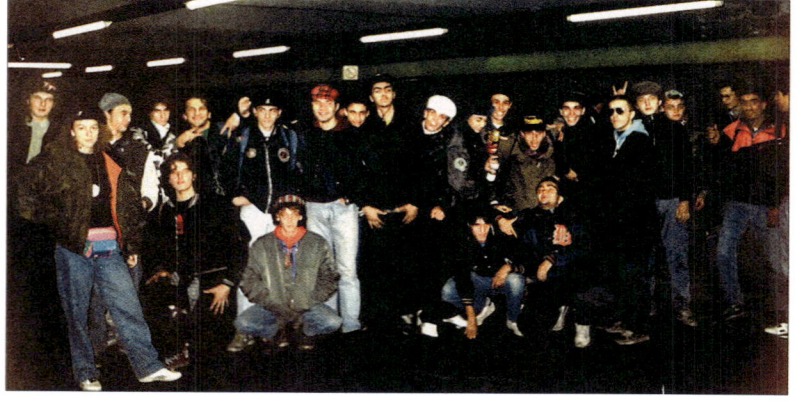

The first crews of Milan meet up at the station of Loreto   — *Sid*

as liturgy

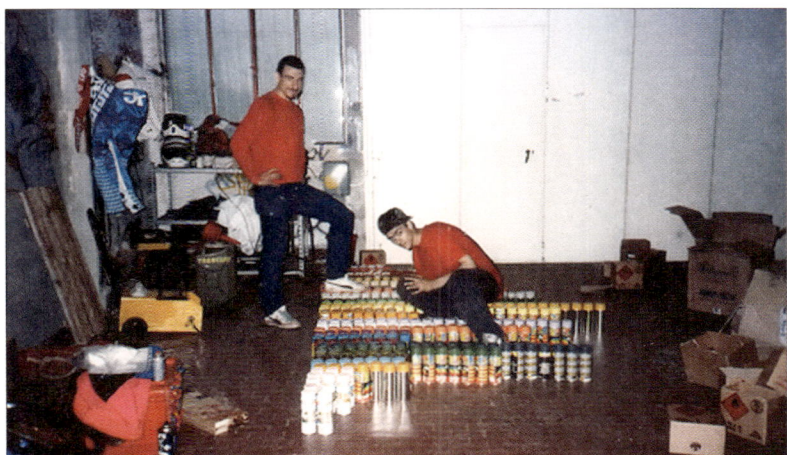

Spyder 7 and Flycat   — *Flycat*

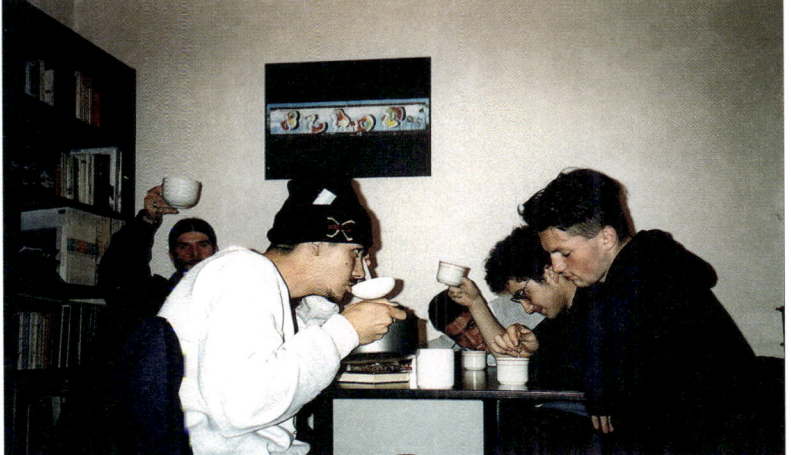

PWD crew under the Blade sign   — *Mace*

Pressure increases on self-production

With the early 90's came a change of attitude, less poser-like and more active. There was tension in the air since Falcone and Borsellino had just been killed, Italy was on the verge of exploding, turmoil was everywhere: in occupied Universities, high schools and squats.

There was a worldwide crisis in effect, like the '92 Los Angeles riots. In this state of ferment, people started connecting with other scenes, people who were part of Italian and European counterculture movements. We writers though were rather dense, we were so autistic that we didn't care to understand and interact with others. I'm referring to people like Primo Moroni, intellectuals belonging to the movement, people who were protagonists of the 1970's worker strikes but had no problem relating to us kids, or even Tommaso Tozzi in Florence, and above all, Gomma.

We met them because we painted in squats and social centres but we knew nothing about the history these people had behind them. Gomma started hanging out with us to film and take pictures, he realised something important was happening. At the time he was publishing a fanzine that would later became legendary: *Decoder*; of which he was the special correspondent, an observer of this new underground scene: concerts, small pamphlets, raves, the budding Hip Hop culture, cyberpunks, and the possibilities offered by new media like the Internet. These guys were the first people to approach the concept of "community", of antagonist networks.

Many scenes rose from the ashes of the punk movement, and in part from the Hip Hop movement, such as some members of my group, like Shad. The parties that took place at Isola nel Kantiere squat in Bologna were organised by people who had seen it all, people that had experience with independent radio stations and the first indy record labels of the country.

Italy has always been pretty indifferent to underground cultures, perhaps because it has lots of history and a sense of culture that is rather orthodox and academic. This prevented people from immersing themselves in underground phenomena like Writing, which instead was looked at from afar, like a passing fad. People like Gomma showed us what they were doing, their distribution and self-production, making us realise we could be part of a movement without a political banner or a specific ideological dogma, it was all about militancy as a way of life.

Most likely these people considered Hip Hop as a way out of certain ideological patterns, once they met us "kids", they sensed the dawning of a new attitude in us. But most importantly, they listened to us. They respected us, and back then there were very few people who did so.

Tommaso Tozzi was also an important figure; I remember he produced the first interactive CD-ROM in Italy and a beautiful book about the 80's. He had been in New York during the years of Fashion Moda gallery, he was familiar with the scenes of the Lower East Side and the East Village; he gave us tons of material because he knew it was pointless to keep this stuff locked away in a drawer.

With time, we understood the choices made by these individuals who had based their existence upon a lifestyle: for me and for others, this meant living off our passions that evolved throughout the years or simply changed, though the desire to share them remained intact. — **MACE**

Attitude
>

Faraway from Europe

From the day of our first debut, all of Eastern Milan's crews were hooked on the New York style. We didn't care about what happened in Europe, Paris, or Amsterdam. This was one of the reasons why we started bumping heads with other Milanese crews who were into European styles like Bando or the Dutch stuff.

Spyder and PWD crew were into the evolution of New York's "armamental" letters with arrows and loops, Bars & Arrows, Wildstyle, wild throw-ups, tags with drips, and original caps, avoiding cutting and re-cutting pieces. Milan based itself on this style, which was exported to Treviso and the entire Veneto area.

TDK crew was the exception in Eastern Milan because they were into other styles, they always maintained clean lines. On the other hand, for us it was all about pure instinct: we worked at night in the most visible spots and in the least amount of time, we never spent too much time on one piece, even a large wall in the hall of fame would be done in two hours, or else it seemed like a waste of energy to us. At the end of the 80's and in the early 90's, I recall lots of kids went to Paris or Munich in search of halls of fame by local writers, whereas we were purposely chosing to remain isolated.

For us, the network was composed of one vector, a direct line between Milan and New York, Spyder "exposed" us to it first, then A-one and Phase II told us about it. Phase first came to Italy in the early 80's and then often returned. He stayed at my house in Via Padova for quite some time and inevitably influenced an entire generation with his letters, his Bronx tales, and stories about life in New York.
— **FLYCAT**

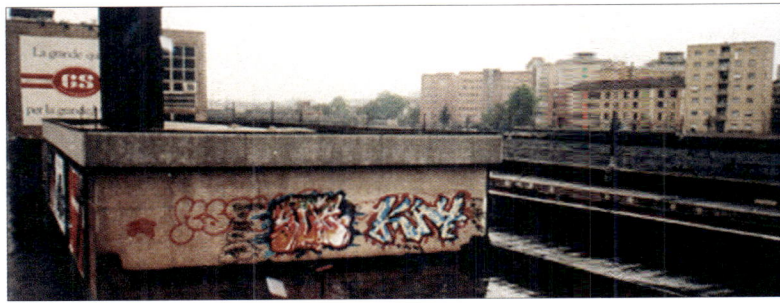

Soe by Spyder 7, *Kay* by Flycat on top of the FS station of Porta Garibaldi 1990   — *Mace*

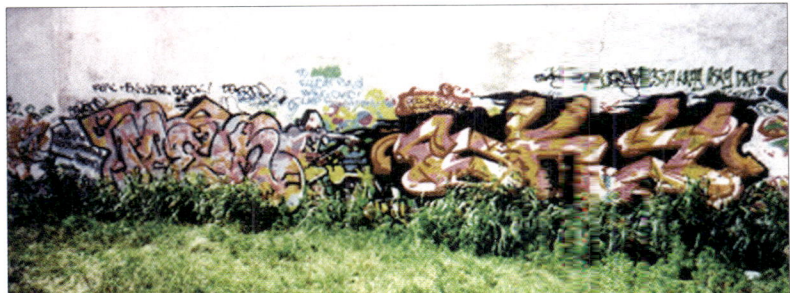

Men by Mad Bob. *Sky* by Sky 4   — *Rusty*

Concentration
>

East end

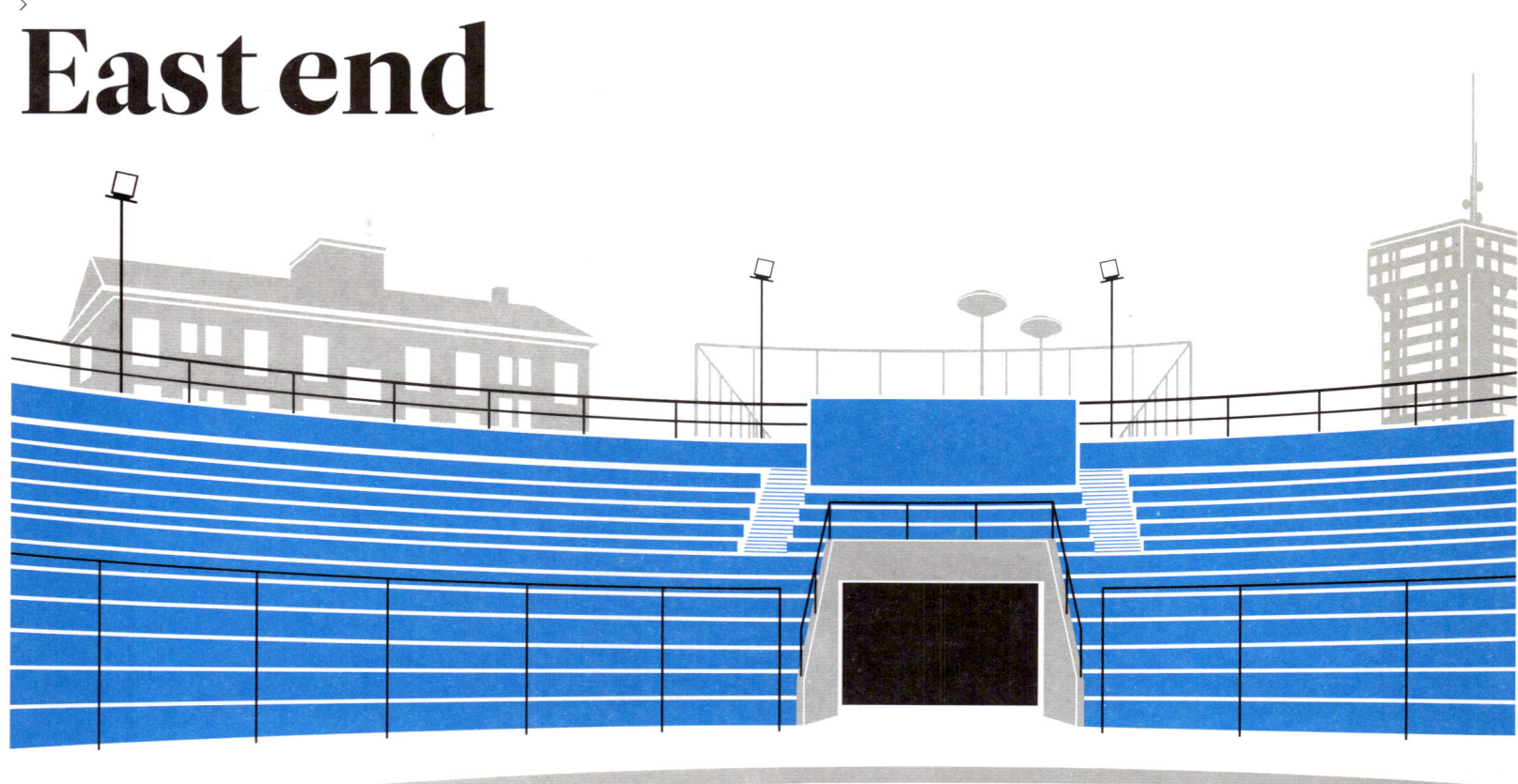

Bang – CKC
>

We were side by side with the greats: PWD, kings of the city and our main reference point. We of CKC were friends from the oratory, the one in Casoretto, Lambrate. Flycat had baptised all of us; me, Kray, Spik, Staze and Ask1. Then Sky 4 joined, he was an old-time friend from the days at Leonkavallo squat. From there, from a little room in that social centre, the whole Writing movement of East Milan began: additional kids would later enter CKC came from Cernusco and Vimodrone like Sly and Kid. Others just came to meet us and smoke, so much so that after a while they kicked us out because we were the only ones in Leonkavallo that weren't politically active. At first they looked at us as a sort of operative arm: they thought we might be useful during demonstrations, to spray the slogans they were screaming in the streets on the walls of the city.

Since this was not the case we had to part ways. From there, we moved to Piazza Aspromonte in 1990. In those days we were already at a crossroads: some of us got lost in synthetic drugs and clubs, while other kids gravitating around the Piazza joined as new arrivals. All our nocturnal expeditions to the various urban spots stemmed from that Piazza and the subway platforms were the main target. Sometimes we would meet so as to discuss who to let in of the new names, it always happened in an informal manner, just us talking. Each of us would speak the name of the writers that had most style and were the most active, and obviously closest to our mentality.
When we "adopted" Starch and Clout from Treviso it signaled a pivotal point, because it sanctioned the historical twinning between two cities that were already close thanks to Mace. Clout couldn't believe it, we were all reunited in via Bazzini and it looked like it was the most beautiful day of his life. The same with Kid, who came from Cernusco. Kid tagged like a madman so that we would take notice; you could say he joined CKC because it was owed to him.

He was crazy, he'd come to Lambrate by bike from Cernusco sul Naviglio, pedalling down the whole Martesana canal at night in the cold, tagging everywhere. That's how it came about that Sky, without even asking the others said "Guys, Kid is with us, him and Code". There was a period during which Kid was everywhere, the platforms, the Nord trains, in the street.

Sky 4
>

CKC

CKC was created by a narrow circle of friends, diffident of large groups and of the public in general: no commissions, many chillooms and a lot of time in the Piazza. With time however this attitude of exclusivity gave way to a different idea of crew, maybe even innovative for the majority of Italian groups.
CKC started recruiting new members: a chosen few, selected among the most active writers of Milan, picked on the basis of friendship and stylistic affinities. So the

original core formed by Flycat with Bang, Kray and Ask1, was expanded to include Staze, Spik, Bread, Drop, Shot, me and others. This extension coincided with the second half of the 90's and brought us to spread out of the neighbourhood limits: while the first CKC's were formed almost exclusively by kids from Lambrate, eventually lone writers from nearby areas were included. So Shot from Precotto brought Dra from Sesto, and then Bread and Drop from Niguarda.
My debut is linked to Bang who was the first to show me a piece. I wasn't too fascinated, interested maybe, but not that much. It was more of a gradual process, made of quick glances. Mad Bob was maybe the first real instigator, he was crazy and had an unstoppable bombing tenacity that got me involved in a way that would change my life. In East Milan we pursued a stylistic evolution based on the foundations of New York Writing, the Wildstyle of Phase II and Vulcan.
For this reason the variations regarded elements that often recurred in pieces by CKC, like loops between letters, arrows, complex colour fillings or even how we made the 3D effect.

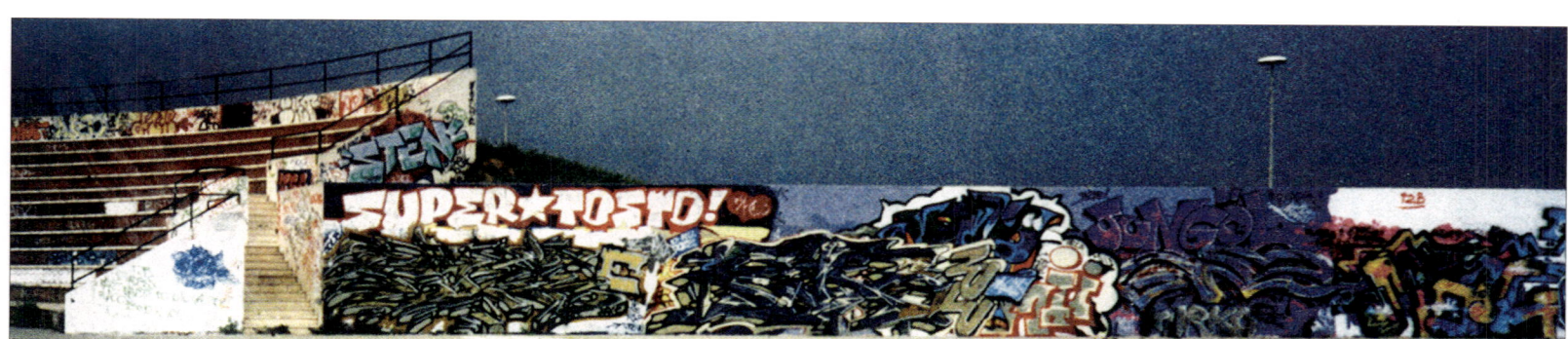

View of the amphitheatre of Martesana. *SUPER TOSTO* by Type, Rae, Sky 4, Guz, Shad. CKC– TKA crew united

—Ens

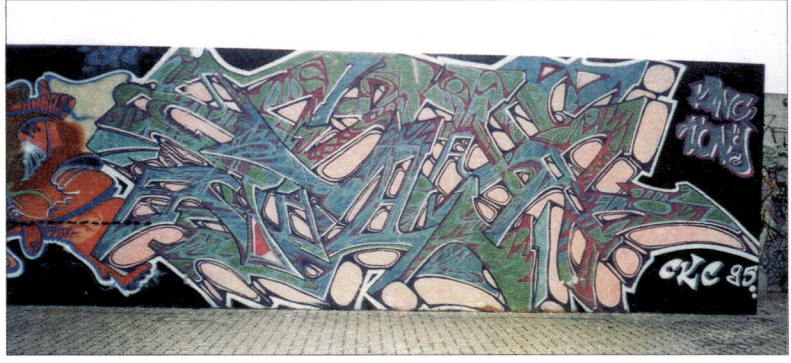

Sky 4 Wildstyle at amphi theatre hall of fame, 1995   — Lay Up

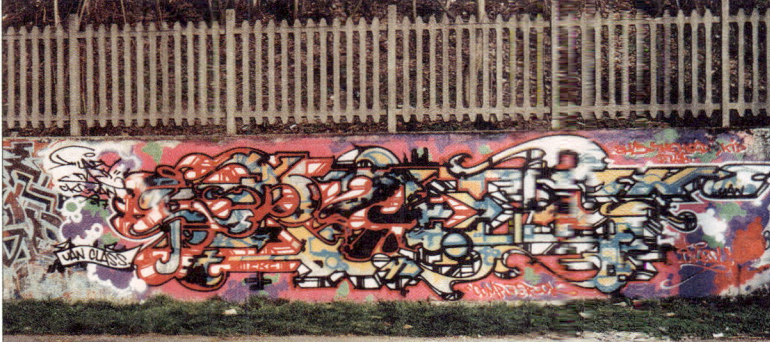

Rax–E at Ortica hall of fame, 1997   — Rax–E

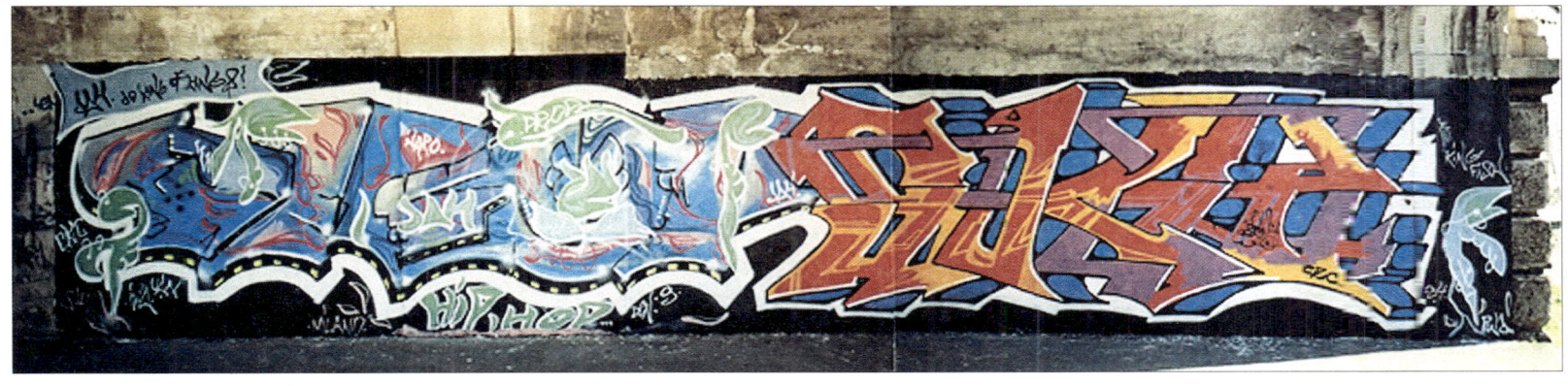

Drop C and Sky 4, Argonne, 1994   — Rusty

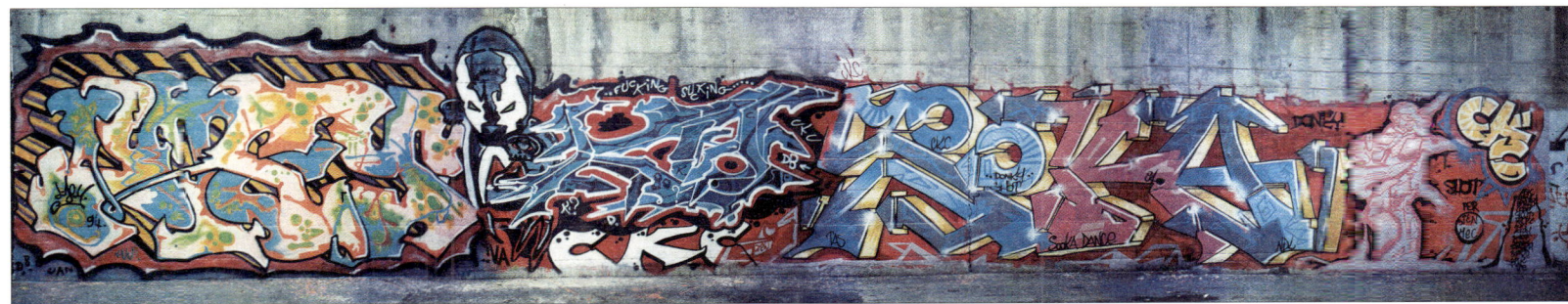

Dosey–UAN, Kid–CKC and *Sooka* by Shot–CKC painted in the hall of fame of Pontano, 1994   — Dosey

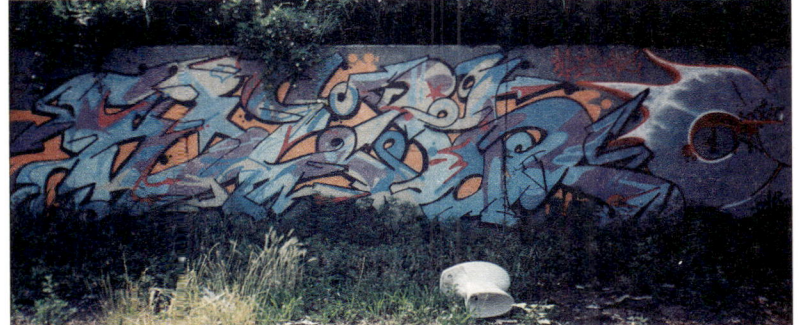

Flash–CYB, area of East Milan, 1992–1993   — Moe

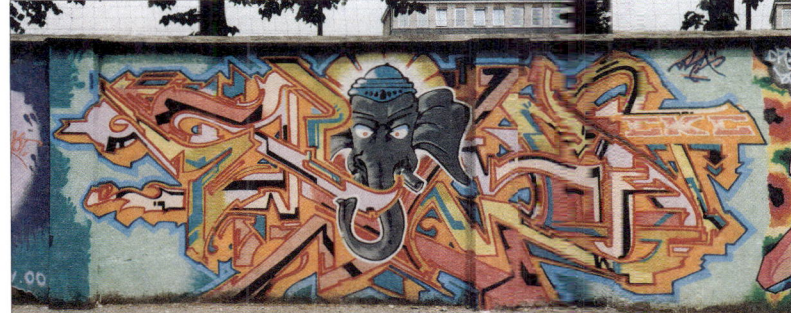

Dra–CKC   — Dra

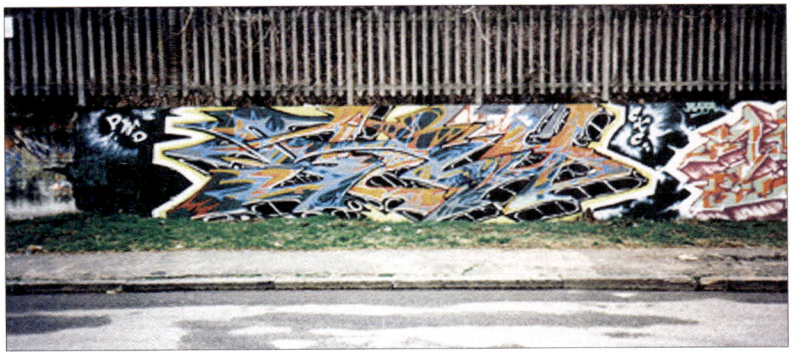

Sky 4, Ortica hall of fame   — Rusty

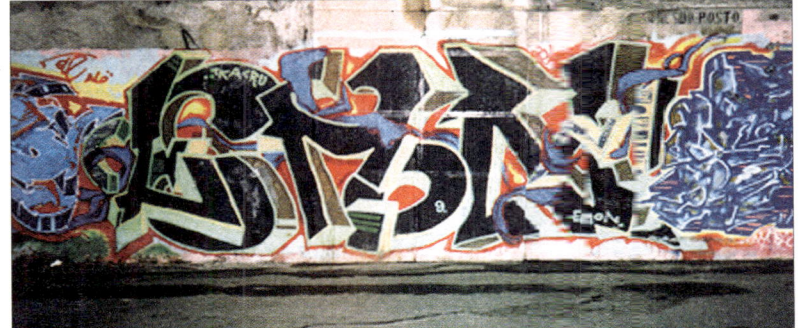

Lemon–TKA, Argonne   — Rusty

Looking for urban landscapes

The hall of fame of Pontano was born in a unique and unusual place of the city, where the elevated line of the railway branches out towards Central Station on one side and on the other goes to the towns of the Milanese outskirts in the North. In this urban stretch trains run more than five metres above ground, following the double rails that intersect the driveway underneath until forming an unusual and irregular Piazza, an urban corner as unexpected as it is evocative. The charm of Pontano can be attributed to its strongly metropolitan atmosphere, which made Italian writers feel closer to the crews overseas, as it evoked imagery tied to the elevated subway of New York City.

Rendo
>

In 1990 *Muretto* was no longer considered the exclusivist spot it had been until then, since the various crews started meeting prevalently in their respective halls of fame. Our hang-out in those years had become the hall of fame in Via Pontano, which was mostly painted by Sten and Mec. For weeks we had been trying to come up with an acronym for our crew that would be easy to pronounce and that would 'sound good', but every idea lasted less than a day.

We were in a rut and among the many initials we concocted, the letters T. D. K. casually came up. Naturally everyone started laughing, especially Sten and Mec, who felt the letters were too well known and strongly associated to the brand of recordable media called TDK.

Thus TDK crew was founded in spring of 1990 by Rendo, Raptus, Mec, Sten, Skah, Onis and Dext One; we wanted to create an extended group in which even the most marked stylistic differences could become a strength for the crew, as well as a stimulus for the artistic growth of each of its components.

Approaching Aerosol Art and the world of design in general with commitment has always been a fixation of mine ever since I was a child and shared a passion for drawing with Play. The problem is that my ideas almost always sparked conflicts with those of the other writers.

In those years there was a non-written code of conduct, whose rules determined the spirit with which you would paint. Many considered the act itself more important than the result, in the sense that doing graffiti had to be principally an experience in adherence with that of the writers of New York.

Early on however I realised I had to start painting with a new mentality. I understood that trying to act like a New York writer, though perhaps charging the action with an almost heroic nuance that could be narrated with pride to friends, would often leave you with a mediocre piece of work once the memory of the action had faded after only a couple of days. That's why Play and I started planning every piece in the smallest detail. To realise a sketch could take us as much as two or three days.

To better understand the final effect of the piece we would paint it with an aerograph on paper, and to trace the outline of the letters on wall exactly as planned could take us an entire day, and the same is true for fillings and borders. But the most maniacal job was that of eliminating all the drips of paint, because the piece had to be perfect.

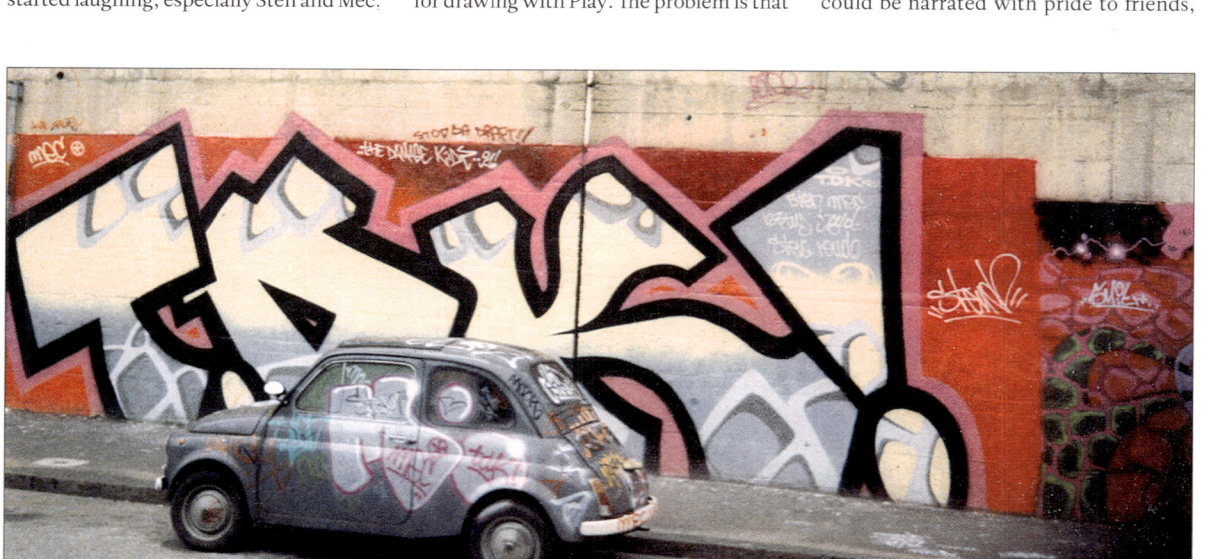

TDK by Sten and Mec, 1991, Pontano hall of fame

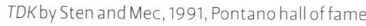
— AL archive

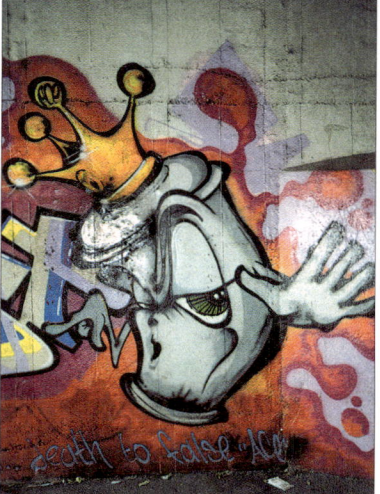

Death to False "Ace"
—Oida

Back Street Edge

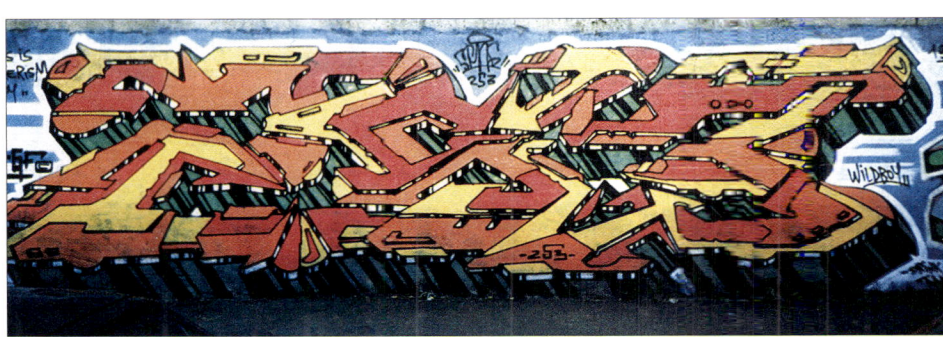

253 by Styng – TGF, Lambrate   *— Styng*

Lambrate's hall of fame came about by chance in the summer of 1995. Styng 253 and Tha Good Fellas had already been around for several years, we were born and raised in Lambrate. Despite the fact that this neighbourhood was on the city limits, it was still possible to pursue your interests without too much hassle: if you were wise enough to follow certain rules, during those years there was still enough space to be able to express your own energy and talent.

During the day we guarded our neighbourhood and forged ties with the piazzas' and the kids who hung out in them (in order to defend ourselves and gain their support in handling our business). During the night we marked our presence anywhere and everywhere with tags and throw-ups. Making sure we were visible and respected by day allowed us to paint in peace at night. More than once, these precious 'contacts' of ours saved our hides.

In the summer of 1995, on a day like any other, I was out with my brother Kez. The railway wall had been around for ages, at least since our neighbourhood had been built in Eastern Milan. We had passed by that amazing wall many times, it was like Newton's apple for us: we had always been too close to see it and focus on it clearly.

On that scorching afternoon Milan was like a sauna in the summer, we were going home after having painted a wall in Ortica (another historic TGF hall of fame), and happened to stop in front of that wall and look at it in a simple and ravenous way. We were left speechless. It was covered with tags, crappy throw-ups, and political slogans straight from the 70's when Lambrate was the headquarters of Italy's militant extreme Left wing. "Tonight we'll bomb it" Kez said. "Why not now? Do we rule Lambrate or not?" I said without even thinking. Thus the most 'looked at' hall of fame in

Eastern Milan came to life. It was 1995, the last years during which we could paint without having to watch our backs much. There were lots of brawls, but they were never harsh or violent enough to keep us from painting. We fought tooth and nail for that wall, with any means we had, we guarded it day and night, nonstop.

In the early 90's, you either chose a political affiliation, went dancing and dropped pills from morning 'til night, or nullified yourself by chasing after a University degree to make mom and dad happy.

Being a writer was an original and sincere alternative for us: it allowed us to develop our own

identity with conviction and self-sacrifice, trusting ourselves and only a handful of friends with whom we shared everything: not only a passion for Writing, but also values. In painting and 'defending' our colours, we attempted to take a different path, out of the ordinary, living in symbiosis with our neighbourhood during a time of immense political turmoil that was felt even at the lowest levels.

That hall of fame gave us the opportunity to try to improve ourselves without compromises, as well as give our neighbourhood some luster.

Upon that wall, I definitively consecrated 'my' letters, examining them constantly and

developing them day after day. Throughout the years, upon that wall I developed a purer Wildstyle, learned Computer-Rock, and professed Iconoclastic Panzerism and Armamental letters. With my loops, I could have gone anywhere, that wall made me feel even more invincible. At the end of the 90's, when the best writers from Los Angeles and New York (the masters I had learned from ten years earlier) came to Lambrate, they were blown away: that was one of my greatest victories.

Still today painting there means 'living in rainy winters and bright springs, with rage and commitment, with heart and without fear. — STYNG 253

From 13 on

Zona 13 crew got its name from a neighbourhood on the East side of Milan, a neighbourhood which no longer exists (at least on maps) after the number of official districts in the city was reduced to nine for administrative reasons. A mix of various urban elements added together throughout the years (strong presence of factories and workers, immigration of Southern Italians, mass use of public housing, arrival of foreign immigrants) gave rise to a potent concentration of problems typical of outskirt neighbourhoods.

A wall alongside a barely-paved road enclosed the area, and nearby freight trains traveled towards Central Station without interruption. This massive cement jungle was designated as hall of fame by the guys who created the crew, who resided in that neighbourhood and in nearby neighbourhoods. The state of marginality caused that area to become partly dumping ground for all sorts of trash (fridges, washing machines, stolen cars); and partly a place where you could spend an entire day painting undisturbed or swapping advice on how to modify a Vespa scooter.

Amok was one of the founders of the crew: "Until it was demolished in 2005, our wall wasn't just a spot for painting but a full-blown garrison where we had

developed genuine friendships with the local inhabitants (gypsies and Moroccans) with whom we spent our free time. It was rather common for us to have improv dinners and lunches near the wall, not to mention entire afternoons spent smoking with the locals.

Come to think of it, the nature of the characters that lived in the nearby trailers and shacks undoubtedly discouraged any possible invaders from coming in and buffing our pieces. Though nobody ever really considered doing so: we never had problems with crew rivalry, we always followed the 'Live and let live' code. More than anything, we shared the hardships of debuts with other crews- Amok explains - when the world of Writing was still uncharted territory.

Between 1989 and 1990, the emerging skateboard scene in Milan also generated the first signs of the existence of an urban culture (street culture, as we'd say today), which was impossible to identify until that moment. Perhaps this is what started it all, at least for us.

The first fanzines and pictures from the U.S. came with the skaters. We'd had a few glimpses from the extremely rare videos of the first Hip Hop groups and from some movies filmed in New York, but the boundary between skating and Writing was still unclear to us, or at least those two worlds didn't seem to be independent of each other.

It all became clear in time by meeting and spending time with the few existing writers in Milan. Through their stories, we managed to gather some additional

information about what had been done in Milan before and what was happening in other Italian cities. Eighteen years ago, the relationship between writers was more intimate, there were so few of us that we all knew each other. We each had our own style, fundamentally ascribable to the two schools that were present in Milan: one followed and preached European style, the other New York style.

Perhaps simply due to the first input we received, our crew was always more 'European'. In '92-'93, some of us began taking our first trips to Paris, returning home with fanzines and pictures of pieces, which back then were like science fiction to us, in fact they definitely opened our minds to a new way of painting that had yet to be seen in Italy.

We began to conduct our own research by personalising this style, just like other crews, such as Craze (MNP) and some members of TKA had also been doing.

For years, we painted on the same wall (without having permission) until we had transformed that cement jungle, a symbol of urban decay, into an element of vitality for the neighbourhood.

Our hall of fame, during its golden years, boasted 1,000 square metres of uninterrupted pieces, and continuous visits by friends and writers, thus creating a citadel within the city. Maybe this is why we liked it. It was our place.

Later, public opinion began manifesting its increasing intolerance toward this phenomenon of Writing causing the Police to intervene, and forcing us to leave that place definitively.

Today, the group spirit and the spirit of the kids who founded crews lives on in the friendships that still unite us, in the work we share and our lifestyle, which has barely changed, reinforcing memories of a part of the city and a time that belonged to us". — ZONA 13

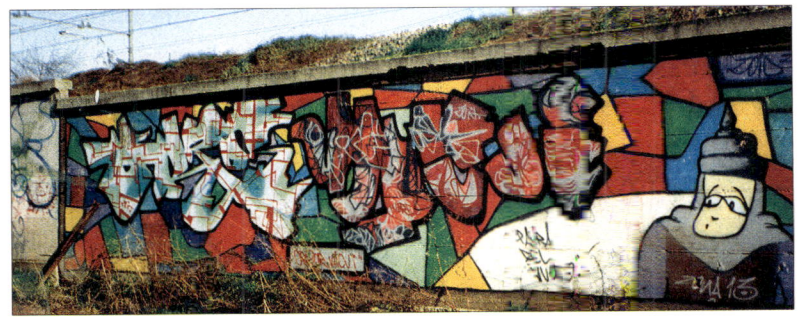

Colouri Vivi (Vivid Colours), by Zoid and Zona 13   *— ACW archive*

IN THE CITY

After finding the right place we would set the pace with a couple flops: we painted them at night and would then keep an eye on the wall in the following days.
If the flops lasted long enough we

would then paint the wall white and do a mural. If the mural lasted then the wall became a sort-of new hall of fame.
SHAD

❶ Spyder 7, Argelati hall of fame
❷ *Dope* by Mad Bob, *Biz* by Spyder 7
❸ *Kelo* by Flycat

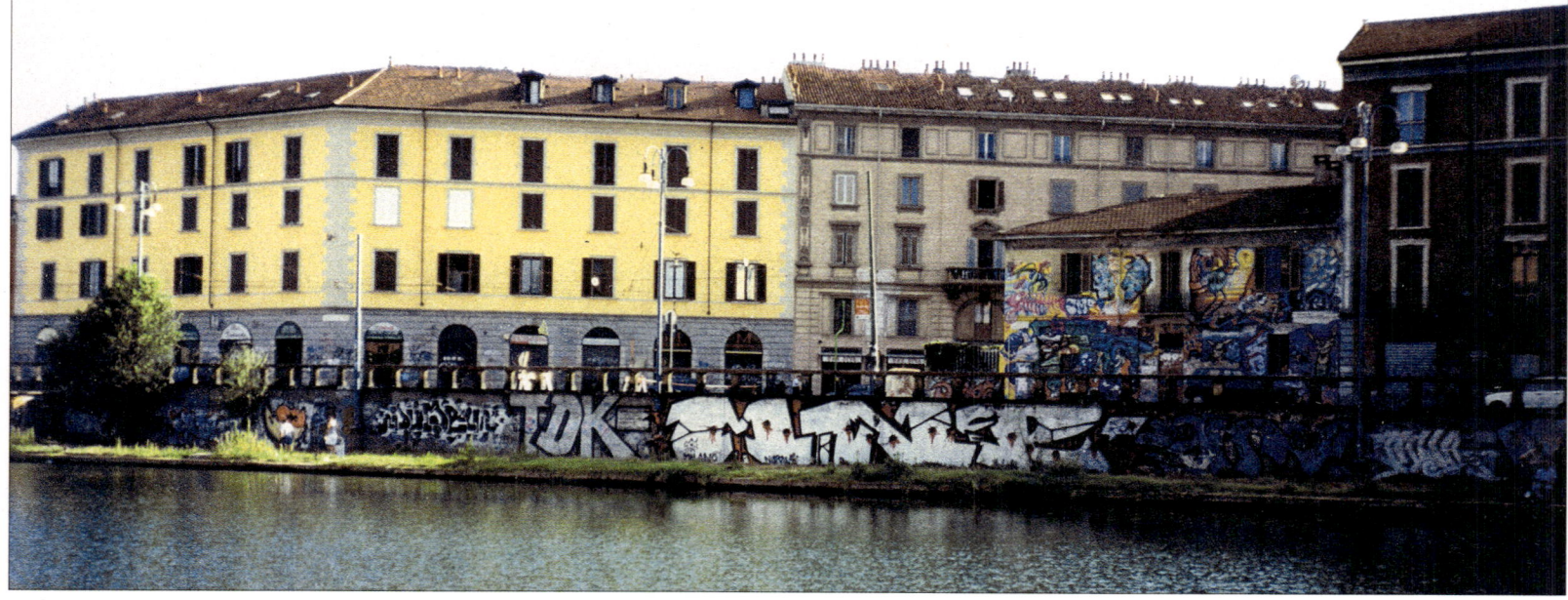

Writing long the Darsena, in the Navigli area, one of the most visible spots of the city

— *Siso*

Unlike the Eastern part of Milan, which was densely populated by halls of fame, up to the early 90's, the tolerated spaces in the rest of the city were spread out in multiple spots in both highly visible areas of the centre, like Darsena, as well as peripheral neighbourhoods like Barona. Also in these same places, Writing had arrived thanks to the activity of a limited number of kids who started painting the abandoned spaces and forgotten infrastructures of their neighbourhoods. The demarcation of the walls, generally tolerated by the residents, took place by associating a crew with a specific spot. In East Milan groups had appropriated very defined urban spaces such as Via Bazzini, or the amphitheatre of Martesana. The same process was repeated in the Southern area of Milan, where the most important and heavily painted spot became the overpass that connects the district of Giambellino to that of Barona, occupied on one side by THP and on the other side by 16K, who designated it as their territory. Years earlier, just a few

metres from the overpass, MNP had already occupied the surfaces adjacent to the weekly market of Via Carriera: a wall that was perfect for a hall of fame, as it faced a large open space that allowed pieces to be photographed frontally. On the other hand, the meeting spot of this crew was situated right in the city's historic centre: WAG, the first Milanese Hip Hop store, in a few years became a crucial node for Writing and was also active on the scene producing and distributing the magazine *Tribe*, which monitored the stylistic evolution of the city.

Shad
>

Ortica, Via Dottesio and Spina Park are just some of TKA's halls of fame, a couple walls were shared with the crews residing in the neighbourhood and others

were exclusively ours. Even though our headquarters was Eastern Milan, TKA had halls of fame spread throughout the city. We even had one at the vegetable market on the last stop of the 23 tram, in the area of Piazzale Cuoco. Moving upwards from there you got to Via Bazzini where Fly and Spyder had already been painting for years. Among the many, I remember the one in Argelati which I hit with Kaos. It was a wall bordering a park. Fly and Spyder had painted just a couple of throw-ups, which at the time was the main tactical approach: we would wander around the city until we found the right spot, preferably in our own neighbourhood since we were teenagers with no real means of transportation. After finding the right place we would set the pace with a couple flops: we painted them at night and would then keep an eye on the wall in the following days. If the flops lasted long enough we would then paint the wall white and do a mural. If the mural lasted then the wall became a sort-of new hall of fame: the owners of the wall or the inhabitants of the neighbourhood took it

for granted and allowed us to never need permits or signed papers, everything went down spontaneously as in many other cases of urban parasitism. After PWD had hit the wall with their throw-ups, me and Kaos went to white it and paint a piece: he did a characters, and I did letters. We had a good connection because Kaos was devoted to puppets and not really a fanatic of the New York style like the other writers of the Eastern Zone. Even his letters followed the wave coming from Paris, which worked well with me, since after seeing Amsterdam (USA crew in particular) halfway through the 80's those had become my stylistic references.

DARSENA

The Naviglio Grande and the Naviglio Pavese meet next to Porta Ticinese, on the Darsena. Built in 1603, it was meant to facilitate the transportation of goods to Milan from Lago Maggiore, Switzerland and the Adda river.

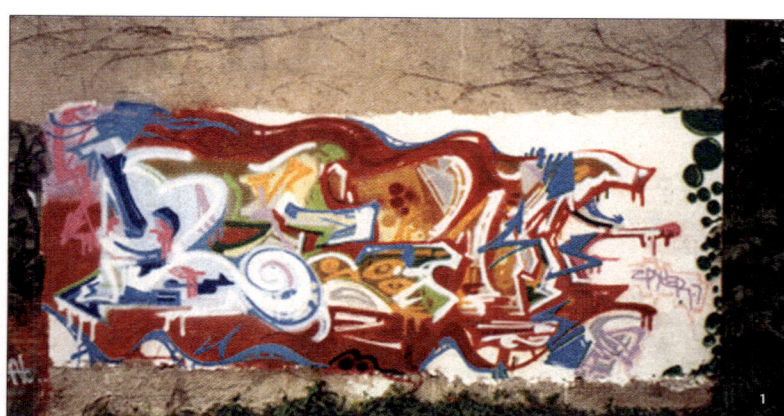

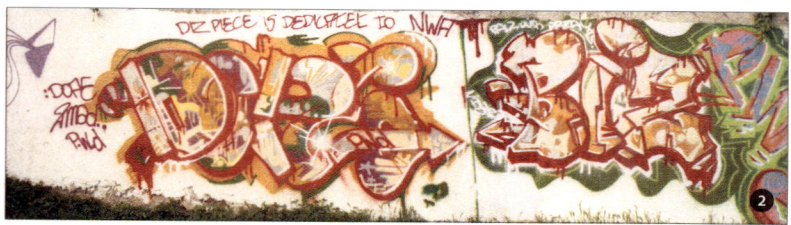

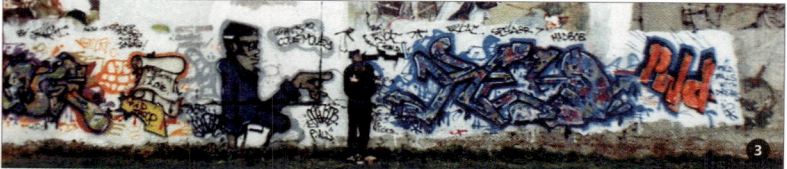

— *Mace*

Via Carrera

Airone
>

Growing up in the "South" isn't easy anywhere in Italy, not even Milan. In my case the South was called Giambellino. At the end of the 80's this was an area of scualor and junkies on the outskirts of the city, like many others. It bordered Barona on one side and Baggio on the other, a vast territory inhabited by a minimal number of writers, five or six at most. I'm not able to explain how the 'contagion' occurs in such cases: really the visual inputs were so few, perhaps what came into play was a sort of predisposition to feeling like outsiders in a society normally based on rigid social structures. It was love at first sight, and neither I nor Rush (TKA), my ex-classmate from middle school, could oppose any resistance. Given the initially limited number of us, we inevitably seemed something 'incomprehensible' to the majority of writers that lived in the area of East Milan and we ended up configuring ourselves through our own pretty evident local peculiarities. For starters, here a case of real cultural 'schooling' like that of PWD, from which CKC was born, never occurred. With this I don't mean to say that we didn't also gravitate around the kings that were particularly gifted and influential, like Kayone and Craze but their characters were different, often very reserved, with a more free and independent attitude. Nevertheless for a brief period of about two years

> On one side it became the THP wall, and on the other 16K

around 1990/1991, following the birth of MNP, South Milan was perceived as a compact entity that was counterpoint in style and culture to the writers of East Milan. It was this competition that emphasised a series of differences we had: flexible artistic references (Paris, London, Amsterdam and not just New York), greater attention to technique, a better relationship with certain local institutions, and less ties with social centres. The names I remember most from that period are Kayone, Craze, Yazo, Rush, Price, Chief, Choze, Tebò, Robot, Das 8. Tawa, Krema, Dust, Zen and our female friends Guelfa, Isa and Elfo. Almost all of us gravitated around the historic hall of fame in Via Rosalbia Carriera, born in 1989 and removed after twenty years due to a decision of the district council. At the time the wall was hidden behind an old and precarious factory populated by junkies and bums. Between the wall and the factory there was a parking lot in which the carcasses of stolen cars would be abandoned, on the other side of

this was one of those small neighbourhood market places that once sold food goods at regulated prices. In such a situation of urban decay the people in the neighbourhood loved us: the constant presence of dozens of kids allowed the elderly to feel safe taking the dog out for a walk or crossing the parking lot to shop at the market. The meeting spot at night in those years was the FS yard just a few metres away from our wall: San Cristoforo. In Summer we would spend entire nights there, bringing both male and female friends: it was as calm as painting a hall of fame. Very few photos remain of those trains, at the time few of us had cameras or thought that in the future it would be nice to have something with which to remember the pieces we had done: we lived day by day (or night by night), more for the experience itself than for what we painted, there was no reasoned or finalised artistic intent. Towards the end of 1992 the situation in Milan was evolving, the 'friction' between East and South seemed forgotten and some of us – Craze, Chief, Monè, Zen, Dust and I – in order to bridge the gap we felt still divided us from the rest of Europe, decided to undertake a trip to Paris in '93 to meet some of the big names of the time and see their works live. This was a significant experience that was probably the beginning of a more mature consciousness for all of us. In that same period, together with Kay (who had in the meantime left MNP), I had already published two or three copies of *Tribe*, one of the first Italian Writing magazines. This project had been conceived in 1991 when we had formed the production group *Tribe Hip Hop Posse* (THP) with Alberto – owner of the historic Hip Hop store WAG. At that point, in a completely natural manner the partnership turned into a real crew, absorbing a series of talents that were chilling in our hall of fame in Giambellino: Yazo, already well-known at the time, Done, Zeta, Clock, Mastro K from Saronno and finally Teatro, an Italian writer from the oldest generation.

In concurrence with this process, not too far away from us, 16BC was formed, later to become 16K: Tawa, Monè, Phobia, Krema. Since the space of Via Rosalbia had been consumed, in 1993 we moved just a few steps away to Via Brunelleschi which hosted a large overpass. On one side it became the historic THP wall, and on the other 16K. It was the beginning of a long saga that in future years would see us no longer clashing with the rest of Milan but rather with those in our same neighbourhood. The stuff we produced in those years was memorable, many historic names painted these walls as well, like Phase II, Darco, Smith, Jame, Spon and Sharp, fuelling a continuous flow of young writers from the hinterlands and North Italy, caming to take photos of it. Many started hanging out in our area: South Milan finally had a writer population. The new names, RNS, TAK, GR, and BN were those that gave place to a real generational turnover that with time moved from South Milan to Piazza Vetra.

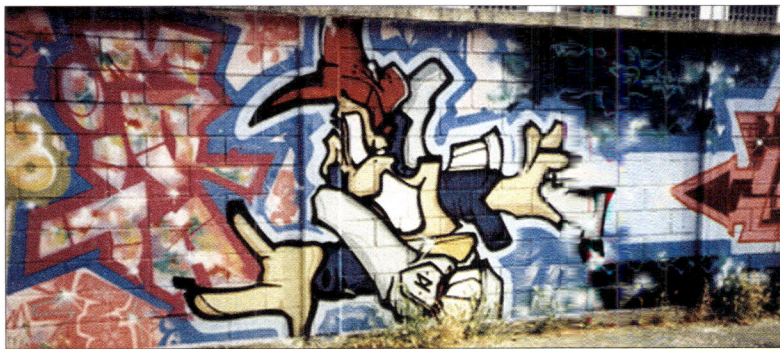

Character by Kay 1 – MNP, early 90's   – Chief

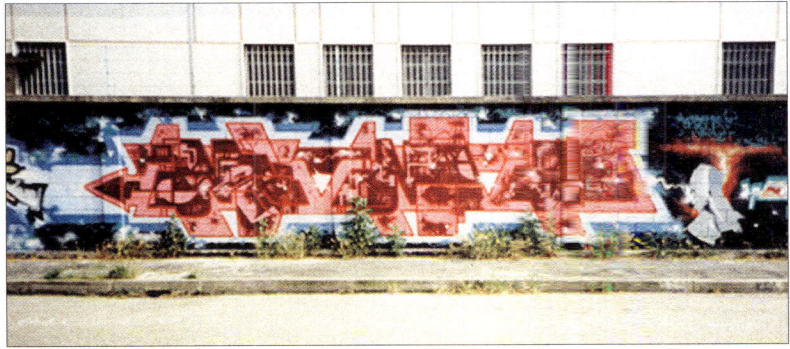

MNP by Kay 1   – Chief

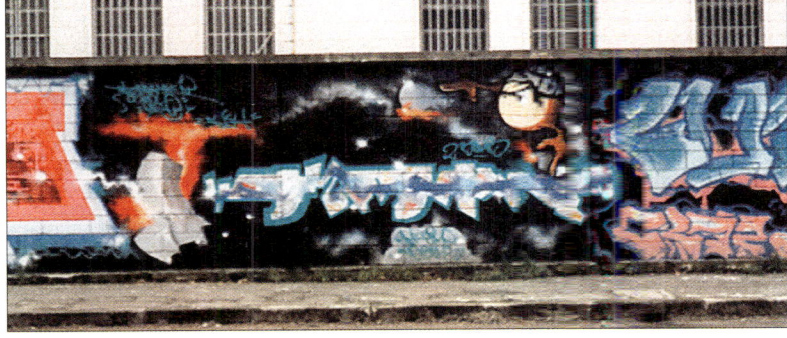

MNP crew   – Zeta

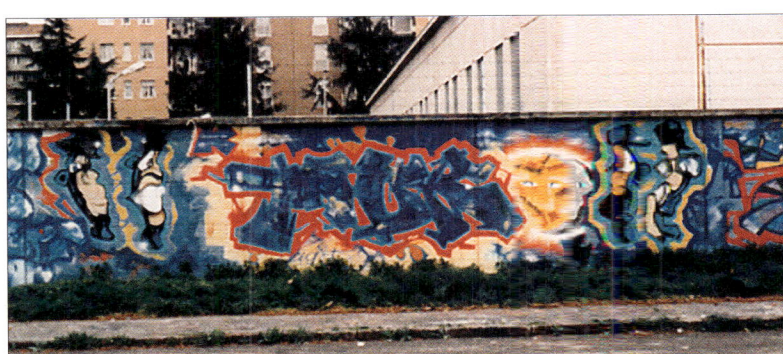

Characters by Kay 1   – Zeta

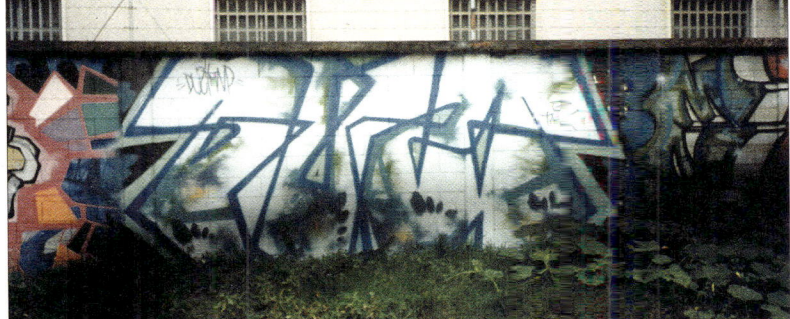

Dust – MNP   – Moe

Barona neighbouhood
>

Giambellino side by side

Cano
>

The crew was born in 1993 AD in Milan and was composed of: Tawa, Debby, Krema, Phobia, Monè, and Cano. Later additions were: Aken, Orma, John Dura, and Roger. The name 16k comes from the old divisions of the city: in the early 90's, the Barona neighbourhood was branded with the number 16.

In this neighbourhood, under a bridge that crossed the train tracks and one of the city's two Navigli canals, was our wall–16K's hall of fame.

This wall represented both a painting spot and a symbol for 16K, at least until we found San Babila. "K" stood for "kru", an Italianised version of the word "crew". From the very get-go, our scope was to create something new and different (though inspired by the New York masters), at least within our 'kru'. Near the wall on the other side of the river was the FS (state train) yard, it was about 1 km away and we'd walk there at night from the bridge. We often went to Porta Genova too, at the opposite end of the train tracks. It was riskier, but the yard had various types of trains, we could paint on the platform, and it was well-lit. It was cool to have everything we needed in one neighbourhood; it was like having our own little world, we didn't care about the rest.

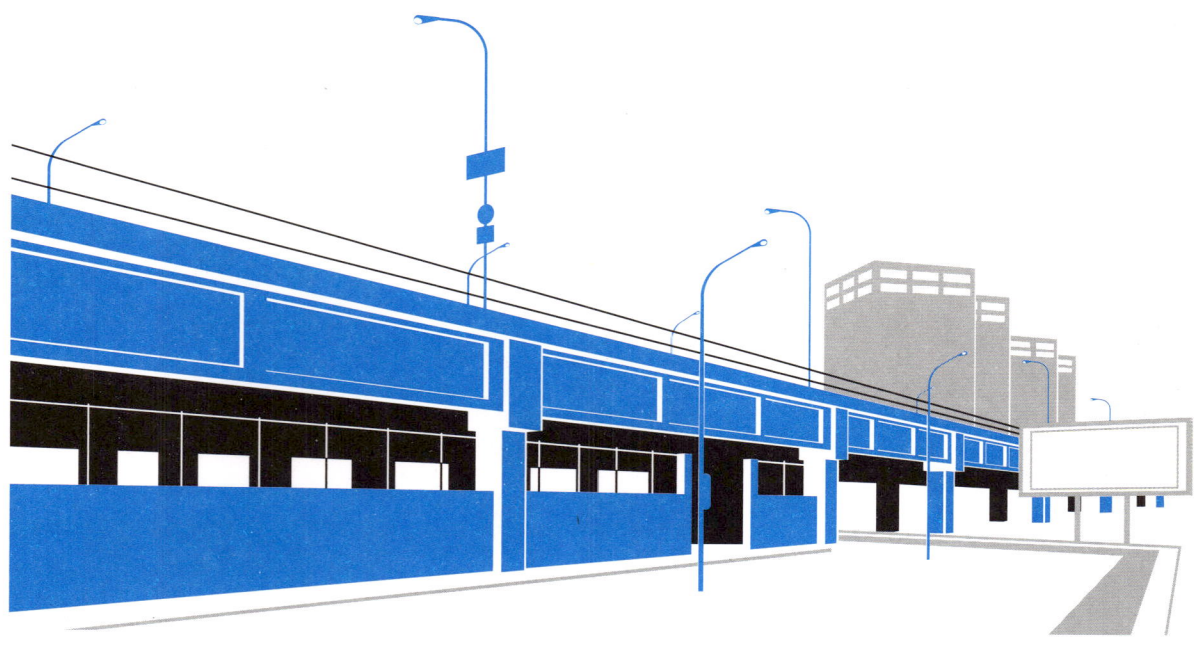

Tawa
>

Following various individual experiences in 1992 we founded 16K. The name came from the place where I was living and where our hall of fame was, in Barona, an area in which the air you breathe is proletarian and in which "trams proceed no further". I was 7 years old in 1980 when me and my mum moved here to these luxurious buildings...still today I would like to meet the architect! You couldn't even leave your umbrella outside your door because it would get stolen. Therefore before learning how to read and write you had to know the unwritten rules of the neighbourhood. Between drugs and jail I don't even know how many friends I lost and perhaps what saved me was my passion for Hip Hop and especially for Writing. It was in Barona that I did the first stuff, throw-ups and wall pieces, in which I would evolve and refine my

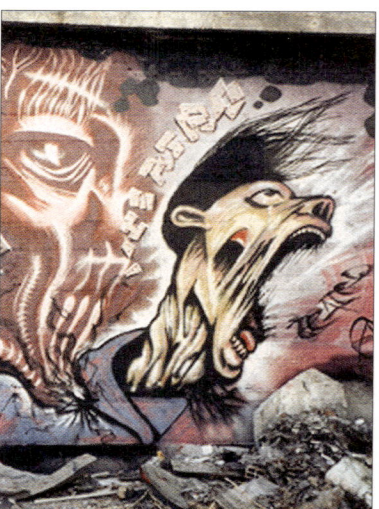

Character by Teatro, 1995   — Teatro

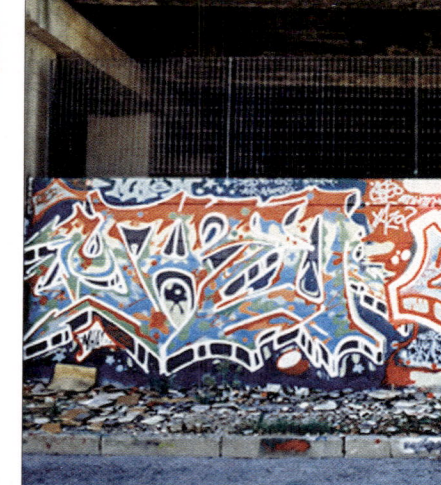

Yazo pieces by Yazo – THP   — ACW archive

technique. There were already various writers around that were killing it but the desire to emerge and distinguish myself brought me to pursue a unique and innovative direction, which I call "Anatomic style". The idea was to give life to my letters, inspired by animal and human anatomy. I gave a bone structure to every letter and integrated it with other organic parts like tissue. Instead of the typical arrows used in Wildstyle I painted tentacles and crab claws. The final result was a strongly symmetrical piece, characteristic that allowed me to immediately

distinguish myself from the styles of other crews in the city.

Craze
>

The wall of Giambellino borders the area of the neighbourhood market place; the first to have painted this stretch was Kayone at the end of the 80's. This was soon followed

by me, I outlined an enormous MNP piece with litres of white plaster paint in the continuation of the wall, right next to the overpass. In this part, perhaps attracted by the hue of the MNP blockbusters that could be used as background, Air and Yazo of THP would take over years later. The area of Giambellino, with the market wall and the nearby overpass was big enough to become the hall of fame of more than one crew. So though it was MNP that baptised it; the first part of the overpass, was taken by Air and Yazo of THP, while the other side became 16K territory.

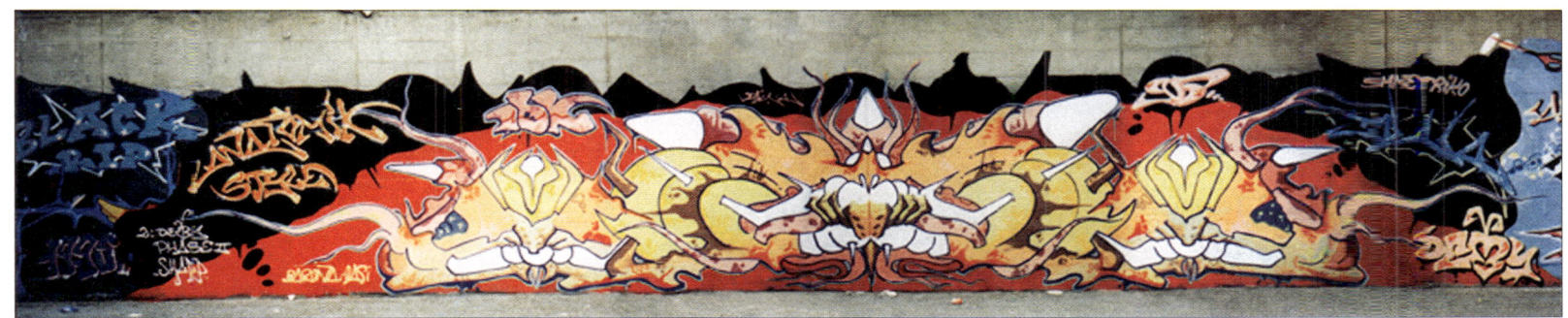

Tawa – 16K
— Tawa

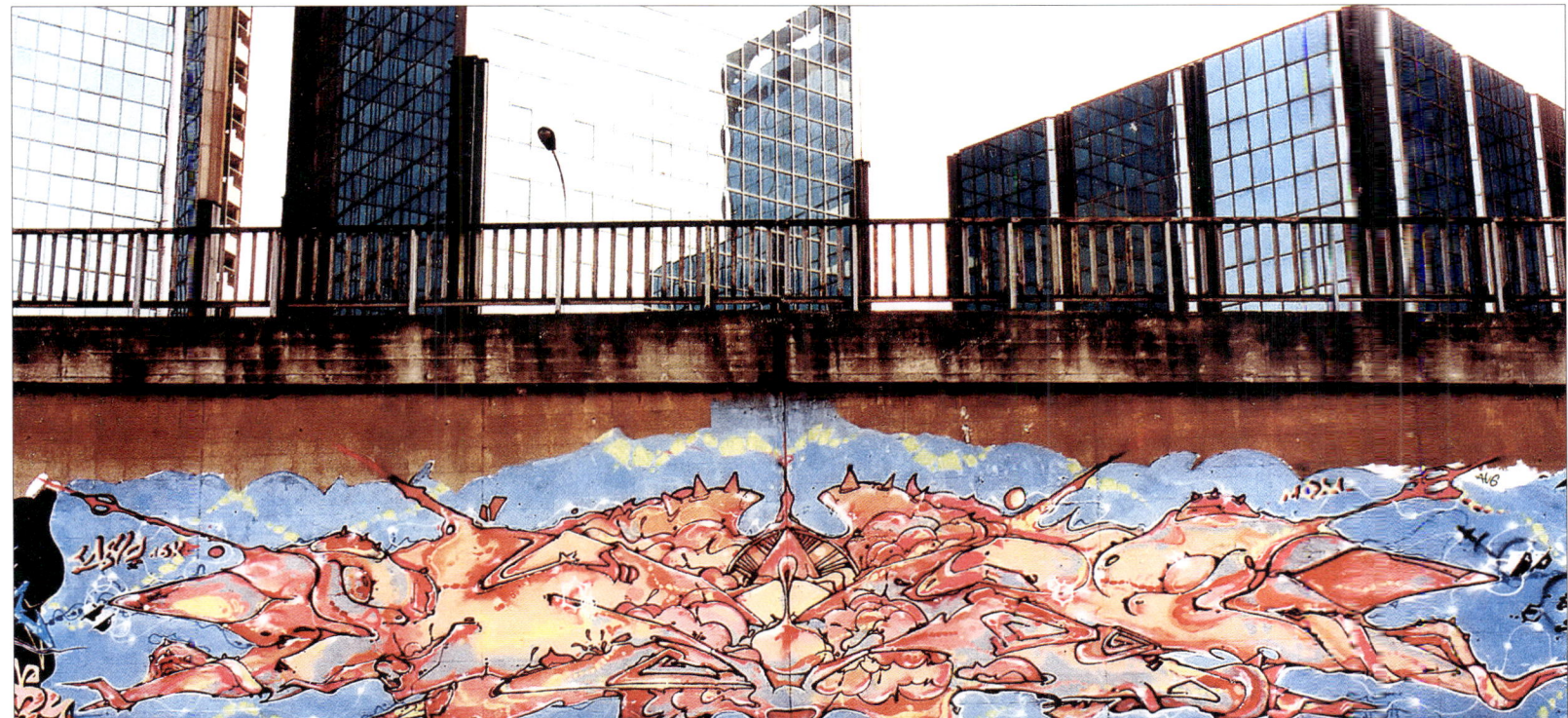

Cano – 16K
— Cano

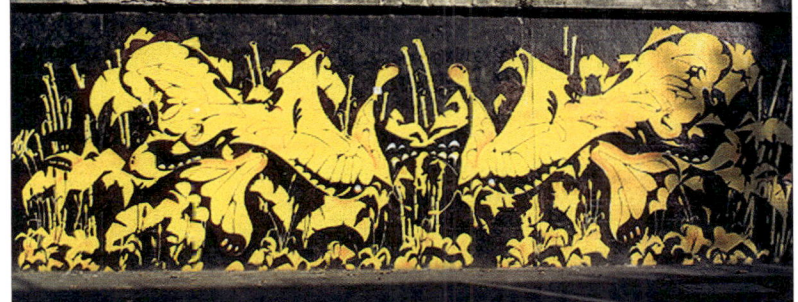

Phobia – 16K
— Phobia

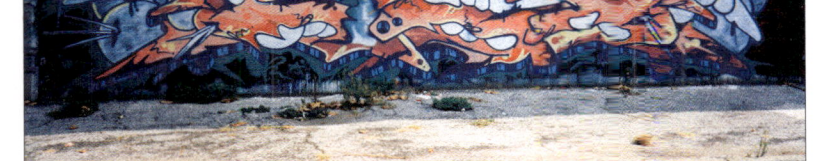

Tawa – 16K
— Tawa

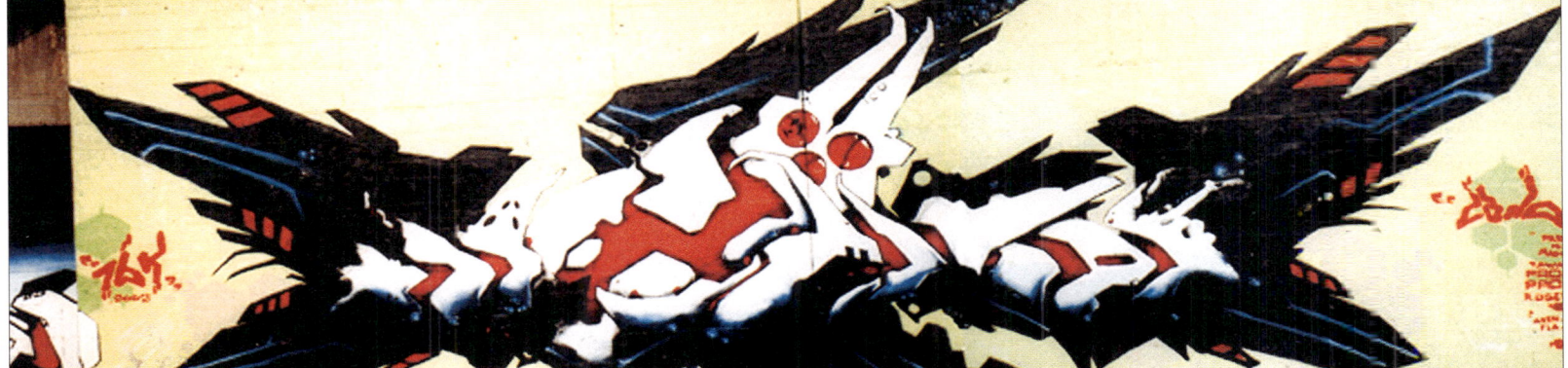

Cano – 16K
— Cano

GENERATION VETRA

A new approach to Writing
>

When words collide

Robin
>

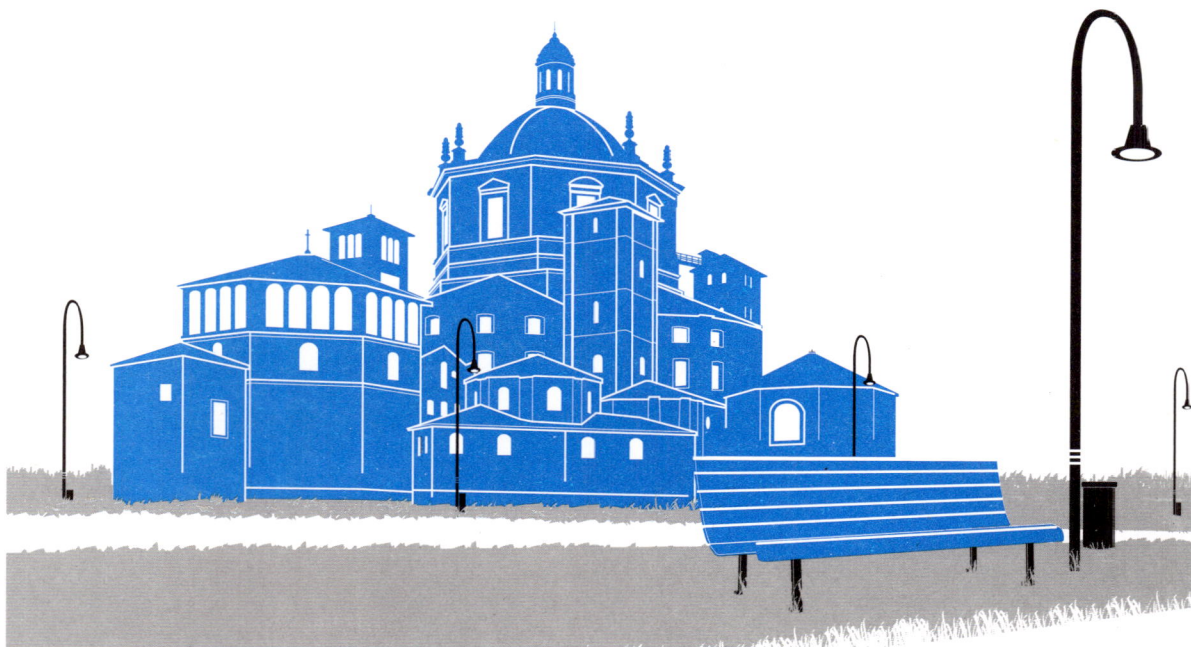

In Milan during the 80's and 90's there were two parks that were infamous for drug pushing: Parco Sempione and Parco Vetra. Parco Sempione is Milan's main park in the city centre, and unlike Parco Vetra back then it was fenced in, closed, and guarded at night. Parco Vetra on the other hand is located in the Navigli area to the South, it's smaller, always open and quite well-lit.

Parco Vetra wasn't the best of places, it wasn't kept in good shape, the grass was ruined and it was generally neglected, but that area was full of nightclubs and pubs. Back then if you wanted to have a beer or smoke a joint in peace, you would go to Vetra and hang out with your friends. Then, as often happens when a place becomes popular, people would flock there so it became a meeting spot for hundreds of different people. There were chavs with their techno music blaring, Moroccan drug-pushers who were actually pretty cool guys and rich kids who hung out at a pub called Cocktail. Then, amidst the homeless people, hawkers and potheads, there we were: the writers.

Between the end of '95 and the beginning of '96, we began hanging out in Piazza Vetra, which was also the meeting spot for TAK-GR crew, with whom we became good friends. GR crew was made up of various kids from Milan, and the Piazza was a great neutral ground for all of them. The crew consisted of Spice, Duplo, Rain, Mind, Bean, Cleph and others. In those years, we of RNS crew had already been bombing the Northern railway for quite some time, while GR crew mainly bombed the FS.

In 1998, when the crews decided to unite and form The Lords of Vetra, in honour of the piazza, our exposure and power increased exponentially. Our meeting spot was a park near the street where Cocktail was located. It was a great place with benches, a pub nearby, and a good view of the rest of the area. At times to get there we had to park our car on the other side of the park and cross through the crowd of people that had gathered; to reach our corner we had to walk past all the drug-pushers. With each step you took they'd offer you hash, marijuana, pills and whatever else. It was like a theatrical piece, in which drug pushers with all their goods would appear: in some ways it actually had a folkloristic feel.

Apart from this, in reality the park was a mellow place, where there was room for everyone and everybody respected each other. Plus, a couple of times a week, we got to witness a real-life scene like the ones on "Cops". Police raids were fun: patrol cars would screech to a halt and there would be mass panic, people running in all directions while the cops chased after some poor souls who usually got away; the park had various exits so people could run and hide in the city's streets. Then, after ten minutes, the same people would make their way back and it started all over again. We sympathised with the Moroccans because, apart from the drug-pushing and the racket, they were just guys like us.

Once I found three or four "marugasch", as we called them, who were cutting lines of coke on the hood of my car. "Excuse me, but that's my car..." "Oh sorry, just give us a second and we'll leave". They finished up quickly and even offered me a line. Since I declined, one of the guys grabbed a cigarette, licked it and wiped up the remaining coke residue with it. "Here, smoke this". They left, and instead of throwing it away, I went back to my friends and said: "Who wants a cigarette with coke?" Suddenly I heard of chorus of "Me, me, me..." everyone rushed to be the first. "Zio" Cake beat everyone, but since he was a good friend he split it with the others. To be honest, it didn't have much of an effect on them, they acted stupid as always.

– NO MORE UNITY
Early in 1995 during election time, there was tension in the air of Milan. For weeks the newspapers had talked about nothing but graffiti and graffiti writers. Albertini, who then became the city's mayor, had proposed the idea of putting a bounty on the heads of writers. Atomo, an ex-writer who got involved in politics, managed to organise a gathering at the Leonkavallo social centre to discuss the situation. It was amazing to see the various crews from Milan come together, many of them had never met before. The gathering of all these crews of young kids resembled the opening scene from *The Warriors*.

Atomo suggested he act as our spokesperson and prepared a statement for the newspapers in which we, as a community, pledged not to cover monuments and to paint less in the city centre. The purpose of this statement was to placate the hostility of the public and the local politicians against writers by demonstrating our good intentions. Nevertheless, this proposal, due to its scarce credibility, wasn't well received and a heated debate ensued, which led to the abandonment of the idea of releasing the statement.

Atomo wasn't exactly a writer in the average sense of the word, he'd always been very political and wasn't respected by everyone. Furthermore, the Milanese Writing scene was not a cohesive community. In the 80's, there were very few writers, and they were all part of a group that was localised in the colonnade near a spot called *Muretto*. In the mid 90's, there were over 100 writers, and it was nearly impossible for them to all get along. By then the scene was variegated and complex. Due to the competition, writers didn't get along and fights and envy were part of the daily agenda. Each writer wanted to be the best and wanted his style to rule, there were

AFFILIATIONS
—

Airone
>

Around 1995, when the attention of local writers was prevalently focused on trains, all South Milan ended up meeting in Vetra. Even though it was called "Piazza", in reality Vetra was a park in the historic centre of the city, in which the crews of the old and new generations had started hanging out for some time. This gathering marked a substantial difference with respect to the rest of Milanese writers: our older generation had not entered in conflict with the powerful wave of fierce younger writers, but peacefully co-existed and actually even made some new ties. So in Vetra you could find young writers like Cleph and Robin but also guys that had been present on the scene for years like Dust and Craze, Clock and Zeta Tawa and Monè, Esa and Polare and many others. Friendships were mixing, and not too many years later some kids were even sharing an apartment, like Phast that lived with Dumbo of VDS. That was probably one of the happiest and most productive moments, we felt we were a force of nature, impossible to contain! In "piazza" Vetra, as in other previous "piazzas" of Milan, a good deal of history was written, and it wouldn't be unjust to say that the popularity of Corso Ticinese, despite the big brands that give it recognition today, is also due to the many writers that characterised it in the 90's.

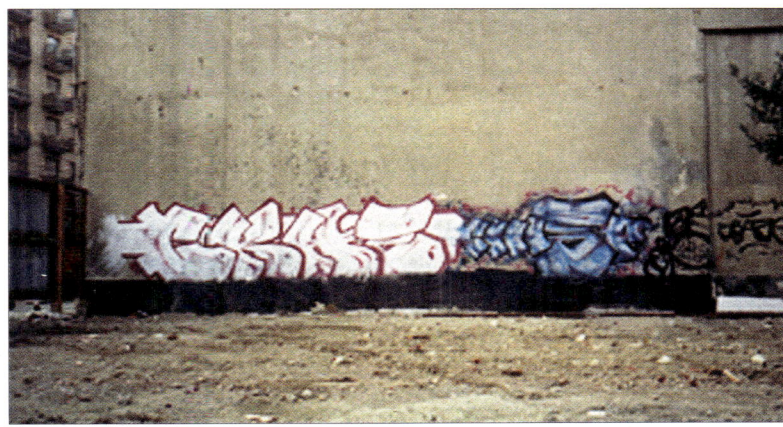

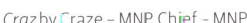

Craz by Craze – MNP, Chief – MNP   — Craze

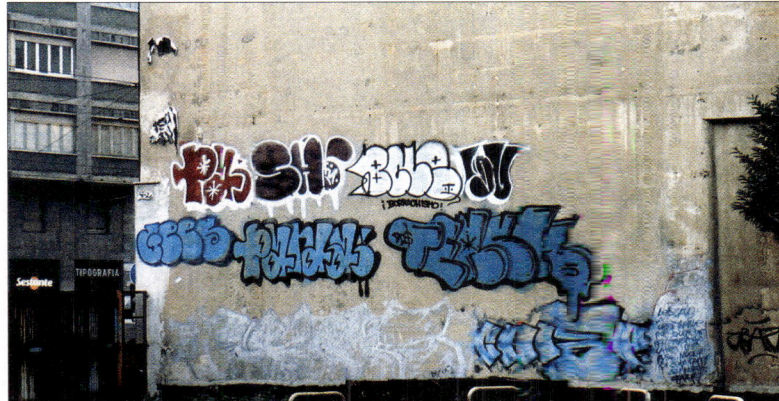

Throw-ups by Gees, Panda, Shampo, Buni (Madrid), Teach (London). Ten year later   — Gees

lots of ideas on how to dominate over others. Some guys only painted trains, some only legal walls, some filled the city with tags, some were pissed off at those who tagged the city, and some were just adrenaline junkies.

This divergence of views created lots of tension but at the same time was the sustenance of Milan's scene.

The clashes that arose were very productive for the development of individual style and character. That night proved that Milan had changed, the feeling of a united group disappeared from that moment on; upon seeing new tags in the city, writers no longer cared to meet who was behind them.

– GENERATION VETRA

After a while we started understanding the dynamics of the city, of the FS (the National trains), and of the FN (the Northern railways). During the mid 90's, which was the FN period, we'd meet up in the Piazza of Trezzano before going out to paint. It was a small satellite centre outside of Milan, connected to the city by the Naviglio canal. The locals had re-baptised the place Trezzangeles; it was a small green patch of land with a crowd of potheads who serenely smoked joints while the law enforcers let them slide. 7SN, a crew from this Piazza, then joined our group. One of the more noteworthy members of that crew was Dumbo, whose main weapon from the get-go were tags. I don't think it was something he planned, it was instinct, and that's what Dumbo was like even when he tagged as Waeze. He had to write everywhere, he couldn't help himself. Painting a wall or a train wasn't enough for him, he wanted to be omnipresent. I'll never forget the first time I went to Dumbo's house.

As soon as I stepped inside I came face to face with his clone: Fency, his brother, who was unbelievably identical to him. In the old family photos hanging around the house the two of them looked like a matryoshka doll. Their parents were truly wonderful people: both were Sardinian and incredibly generous and hospitable, always available and smiling.

It seemed like a family from another era, from the 70's, with a Formica table and loudly coloured tiles. His father, with his moustache and round Puerto Rican-like face, looked a lot like Seen, so we already liked him for that.

What really changed everything was the meeting with Hekto and Panda from Rome. The first time I saw them was at the 1995 Jam Juice in Ancona. Back then, I

had already seen some of their pieces published in AL and I knew they were part of the Roman scene. I was immediately impressed when I saw them.

They never stopped moving: they tagged everywhere- with felt markers, then with spraypaint, any spot was good for writing. One would stand on the other's shoulders to reach higher up spots, which is something I never saw in Milan, and they even signed each other's tags. Even in Milan there were writers who tagged

everywhere, like End and Kal. But Panda and Hekto did it unscrupulously.

I believe the encounter with them radically changed the concept of writing for our crew and for all of Milan. They weren't very concerned about the style of their pieces, they tended toward a more essential writing style made up of big block capital letters that were very legible.

The most important aspect to them was visibility. Upon seeing them, Dumbo and Onaman flipped out, as if someone had

taken their blinders off. It was a crucial moment. Having imported this attitude to Milan, we found ourselves in the middle of endless arguments, with most of the crews against us.

Feral pieces and bombing without style were not understood in Milan. But in no time, the Lords came and painted the entire city, infrastructures included.

Maybe this is part of the reason why few recognized the explosive value of Dumbo, Panda, and Hekto.

DIVERGENCES
—

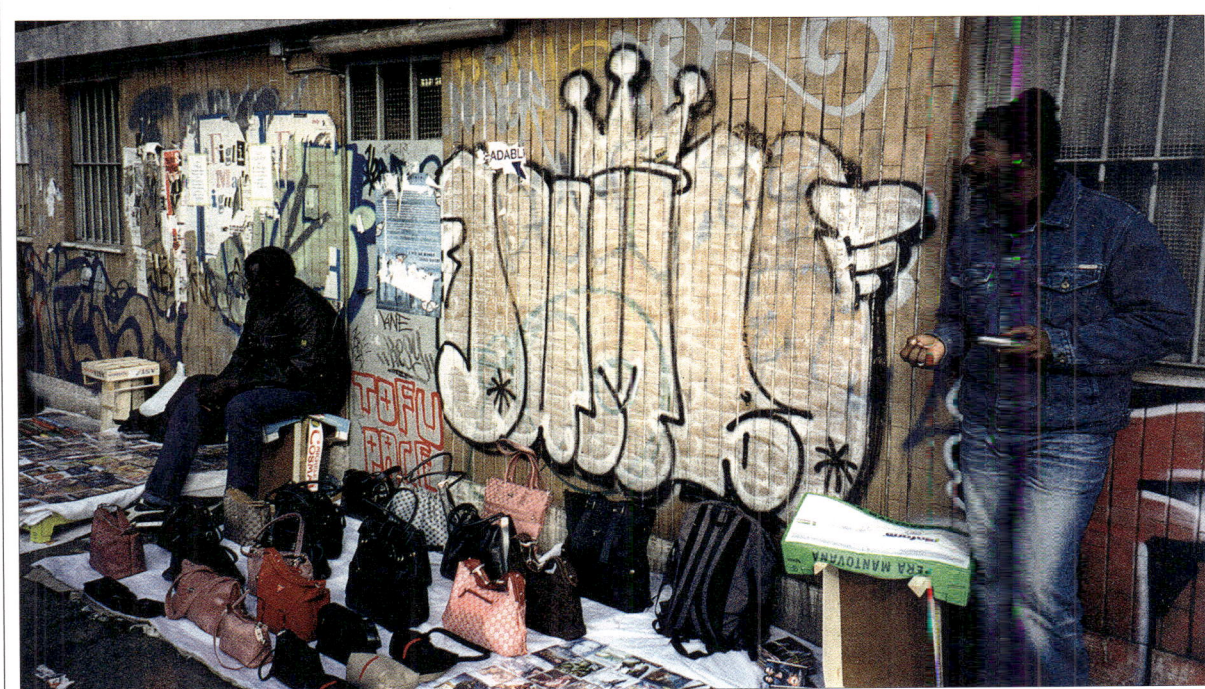

Dumbo, Darsena area   — Siso

Sky 4
>

It's a commonly shared opinion that the first generation of writers in Milan was closed and unaccessible to the new wave, that they were a bit haughty. From my perspective, it wasn't so: we lived in the piazza and kids from all groups would come visit us in Aspromonte.

Yes, there was tension and the competition was at a maximum level, but one thing is for sure: we were fighting one against the other with style. With letters. It was a race, just like in scenes outside Milan or outside Italy, aimed at acquiring the ability to paint the best, possibly inventing the best styles or anyway of improving one's background knowledge. The gap with the following generations is due to this point: they were not interested in this aspect of Writ-

ing. It was just about getting up for them. Not that the old guard wasn't active in the streets or on trains, but for the younger guys that's all it was about. What counted was leaving a mark, whether beautiful or ugly.

When we realised this, I think most of us chose to simply ignore them, perhaps through a form of snobbery, but there were no arguments of comparison, not even when it came to bombing, which is the ABC of Writing.

BATTLEGROUND

> CONTINUES FROM PAGE 159

of origin, which defined geographic and stylistic boundaries. One's belonging to one or another was often even asserted by the crew name: such as 16K from Barona (a district that at the time was indicated as Zone16 on city maps) or Zona13. Essentially tied to the territory, style became an identifying, almost ideological criterion, distinguishing crews that were open to the innovation of the very first European styles of French and Dutch matrix, to those – primarily concentrated in Eastern Milan – that loyally followed the aesthetics of New York City's style without half measures.

The third Milanese period begins in the second half of the 90's, and coincides with the progressive diffusion of Writing in every area of the Lombard capital and its outskirts. The concept of getting up, that is being present on any urban surface with tags and throw-ups, was already present in the very first generation of writers (PWD and TKA), but it's in this third phase that the idea of being all city becomes an indispensable condition for the new writers. Thus attention rapidly shifts from halls of fame and individual areas of the city to a new target, trains, and Writing assumes a more destructive, vandal character. A return to 'neutral' meeting spots takes place and the new *Muretto* is located in the Parco delle Basiliche and in Piazza Vetra, in the Navigli[1] area, where writers would meet and plan their actions to 'kill' the trains of the Ferrovie Nord, of the Ferrovie dello Stato, as well as the subway. This obsession with tagging radically distinguished the attitude of the new writers with respect to their predecessors, which had made style their flagship. The concept of quality soon gave way to the idea of quantity, to a constant presence in the city landscape at the loss of a purely aesthetic effort. It was a new mentality for the writers of Milan, directly imported from the Roman writers Hekto and Panda that had influenced Dumbo and VDS with this new way of interpreting Writing: occupying every area of the city, every centimetre of available space in the urban scenery, in the name of visibility. With the experiences of Vetra, suddenly the complex and studied letters of CKC and of the first Writing scene were joined by the easy-to-read, block letter characters of the new school, generating a conflict between the two generations with regards to both styles and attitudes. At the end of the 90's the Milanese scene was modelled by the sum of these three phases that progressively changed the aesthetics of the city in the arc of a decade, cyclically concentrating on different targets, real parametres with which to evaluate the Writing phenomenon in Milan as a whole.

❶ The canals in the South of Milan

Bang
>

FLOP MANIA

We would often go to Kray's crib and smoke hash instead of going to school. We were teenagers and all those chilooms were getting to our heads and hands with sick loops, transforming our first, primeval letters into Wildstyle throw-ups.
Each of us was aiming at having our own throw-up, our own individual loop, even though we were in the same crew. Me and Kray came up with a similar one, which later most of Milan would adopt on a stylistic level. Like in all softies, it would start with a number of circles that got more and more complex and interwoven: where the circles crossed is where the loops came out. As the intersections

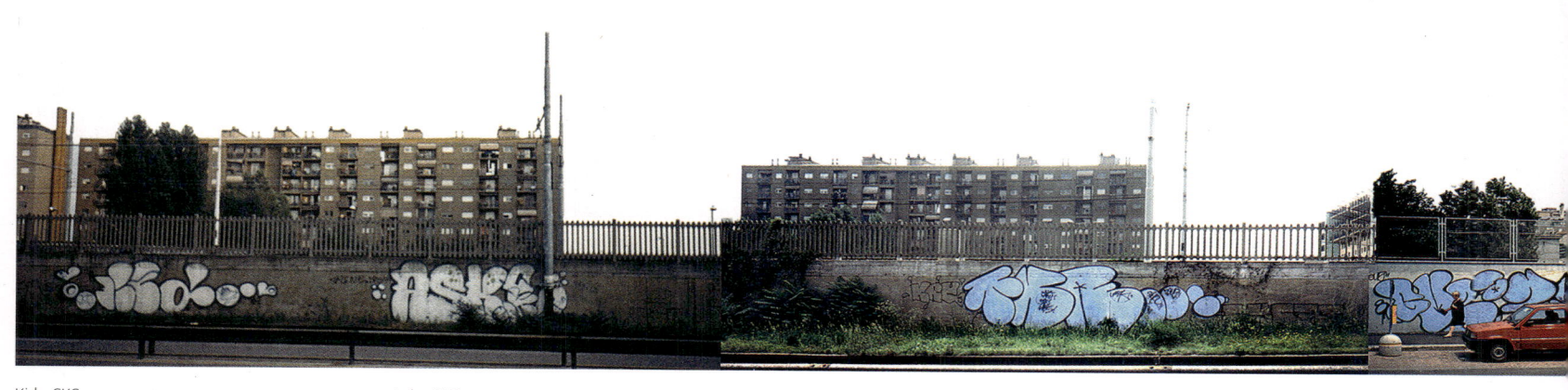

Kid – CKC   Ask – CKC   *TKA* by Bzk   Guz, Bzk, TKA, *Sh* by Lemon and Snad

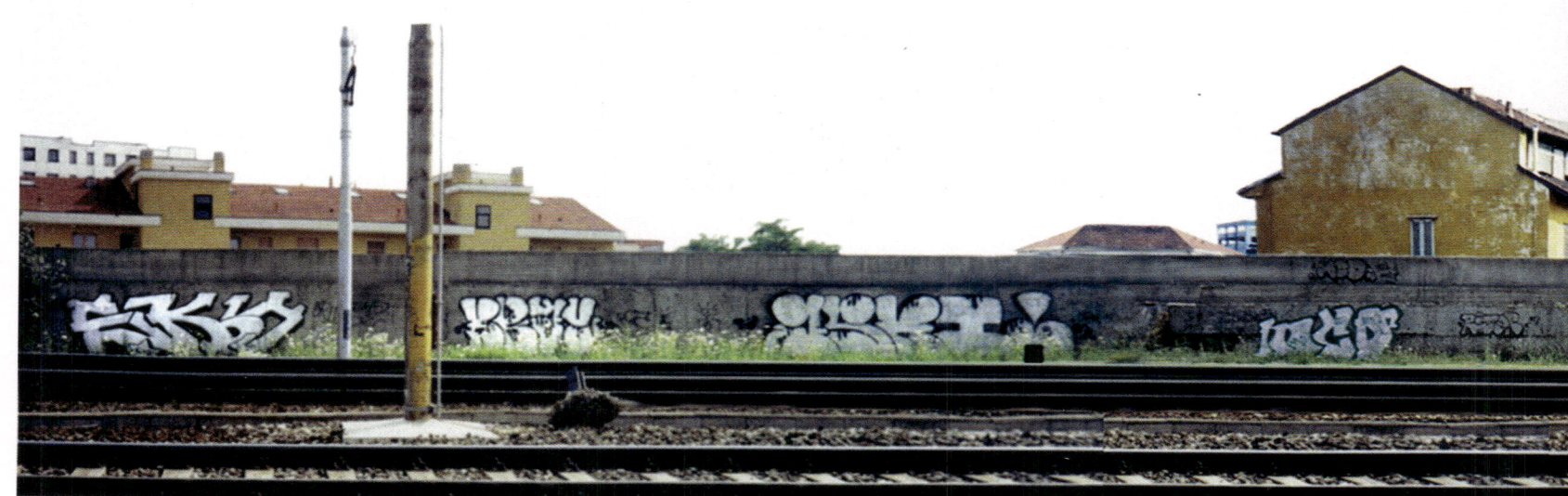

Sky 4 – CKC, PWD   Kray – CKC   Ask 1 – CKC   *MCD* by Unknown

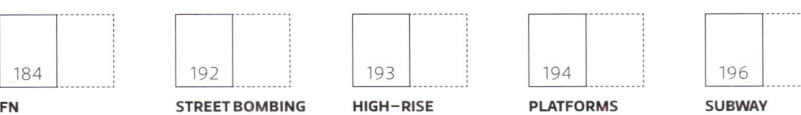

and loops got more complicated it would become Wildstyle. Drops and shadows would then complete the rest: the drops were placed in the highest and lowest points, with the criteria of balancing the composition when some letters weighed more than others.

At a distance of twenty years, even if you stop painting, throw-ups and tags remain in a writer's DNA, and sketching a loop becomes almost automatic, as if it were an instinctive motion.

Shad
>

TKA AND BAZOOKA

We would meet up primarily in Via Bazzini, and also at the subway stops of Piola and most of all Loreto. Loreto was a focal point because many kids studied at the arts highschool in the nearby Piazza Durante, plus others would come from Niguarda, Cernusco, from Viale Padova, the oratory of Casoretto, Sesto and Lambrate. In a couple of years the Aerosol movement exploded in Eastern Milan as well as in all the adjacent areas.

CKC presided the neighbourhood for years. At first they had their own space in the Leonkavallo social centre: a room identifying them as a real club. From there they moved to Piazza Aspromonte. Another crew also chilled in that area, called CYB, with kids that came from Viale Padova and Cernusco.

Then there was TKA, a crew from Vimodrone, composed of only three individuals who initially hung around Via Pontano, an area whose Piazza and hall of fame were mono-crew: TDK.

In the beginning TKA were hitting that area for mostly geographic reasons, seeing it was halfway between Vimodrone and the centre of Milan. After I joined them however we expanded our horizons and became an All-City group; in 1993 we started bombing the entire city. It coincided with a very creative period, we were all in it with the right spirit.

We had tanks upon tanks of white plaster paint - water paint - in the car, and rolls for making huge throw-ups. Bazooka would go all out and sketch the outlines of enormous bubble letters and then everybody would fill them in, independently of the traffic around us.

Sometimes we would go out at night with a very precise idea of what spot we wanted to hit, other times we'd wander until we found the most visible wall.

That year we bombed most of the Circonvallazione, the Navigli, Via De Amicis behind Wag clothes store, Viale Palmanova, Romolo, the Darsena.

The choice of white plaster paint raised a lot of criticism because of the resistance towards mixed techniques: they considered us outsiders with respect to the others, maybe because we weren't following the trend tied to the Hip Hop phenomenon. In that period I remember Rusty would always come paint with us and we got him involved in roller bombing, which was quick and cheap.

Bazooka was experimenting various mixes of micro and plaster with different types of rollers. We jacked five-six buckets of quartz plaster from the University so as to exchange it with litres upon litres of coloured water paint.

The fact that our group was composed of kids from outside Milan and that our idea of getting up comprised rollers and simple outlines differentiated us from the other crews - we didn't have our 'own' neighbourhood and thus the entire city became a generic target to hit in the name of visibility.

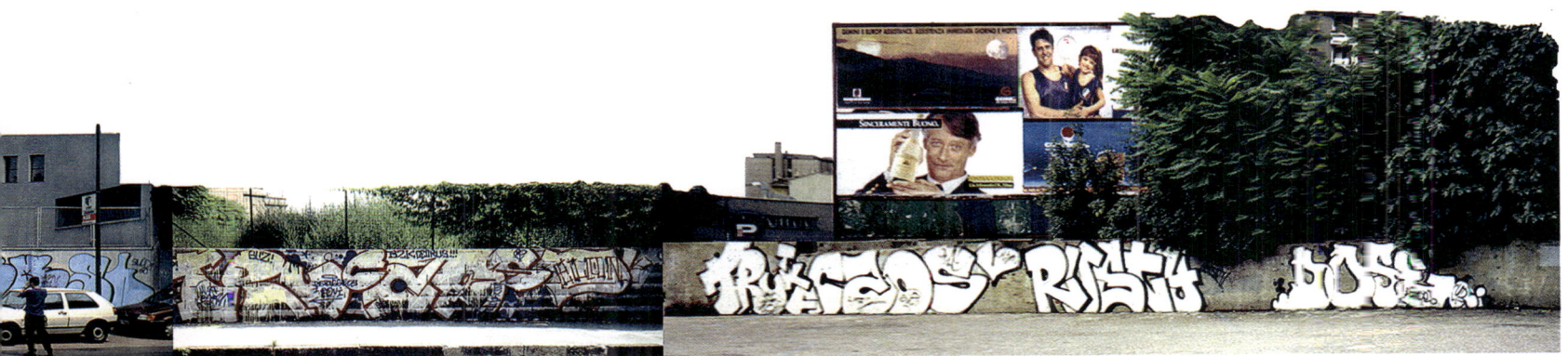

Tru Caos   TRU TKA CAOS by Bzk   Rusty – SPA (Bologna)   Dose – JAK

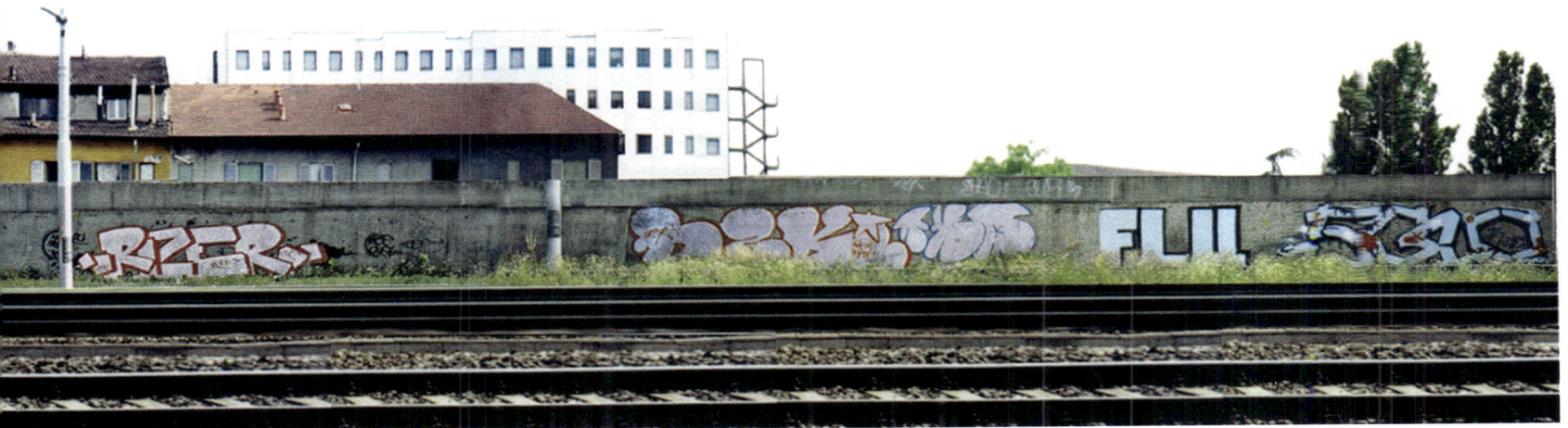

Riser by Unknown   Bzk TKA   Flu   Soldy Mace

NORTHERN LINES

Hinterlands

>

The wild province

Mastro K

>

Wanting to compete: a writer from the province falls for the charm of Milan and begins pursuing his Far West on the line of the Ferrovie Nord

I n the early 90's, in the triangle between Milan, Varese and Como, a singular situation was taking form with regards to the world of Writing. The context was that of the Milanese fringes, an area in which the density of buildings surrounding the city centres was slowly making the distinction between one province and another indistinguishable, almost transforming the territory to the North of Milan into its own city.

In this area, the thick web of rail tracks belonging to the Ferrovie Nord spread, and are still active, from the centre of Milan (Cadorna station), branching out to Varese and Como, crossing through the urban centres that compose the Northern Milanese outskirts (Quarto Oggiaro, Novate, Serenella, etc, up to the small towns immersed between countryside and industries).

Here is where my story begins, in these desolate areas we might call wild provinces. In fact, from the early 90's 'til maybe 2004 the Ferrovie Nord became the stage on which numerous crews coming from much of Northern Italy as well as farther away, met and confronted. While Writing spread in Italian cities halfway through the 80's, in the rest of the provinces the phenomenon started to manifest itself only around 1988-'89. The first pieces I saw on the Nord were by Shad, Airone, Cyrus and Bread around 1991.

In those days I spent about two hours a day coming and going to school by train, and I knew most of the line real well. In '91, Skrim Def Dee, Crisis, Phast and I formed a small crew called FKP in Saronno (crucial node of the Ferrovie Nord) that, along with some writers from the hinterlands of Varese, later became the better known SIC: Phast, Intru, Zoc, Krana, Nega, Bach, Ranx, Aster and Mastro K.

In the beginning we would invent crazy meanings for the acronym SIC so as to fill the whole-car and do the first top-to-bottom ever realised on that line. I would usually paint an illustration on the engine and the others would compose the letters, sometimes filling with nail polish instead of spray paint. The crews in Milan were pretty well acquainted with the Writing

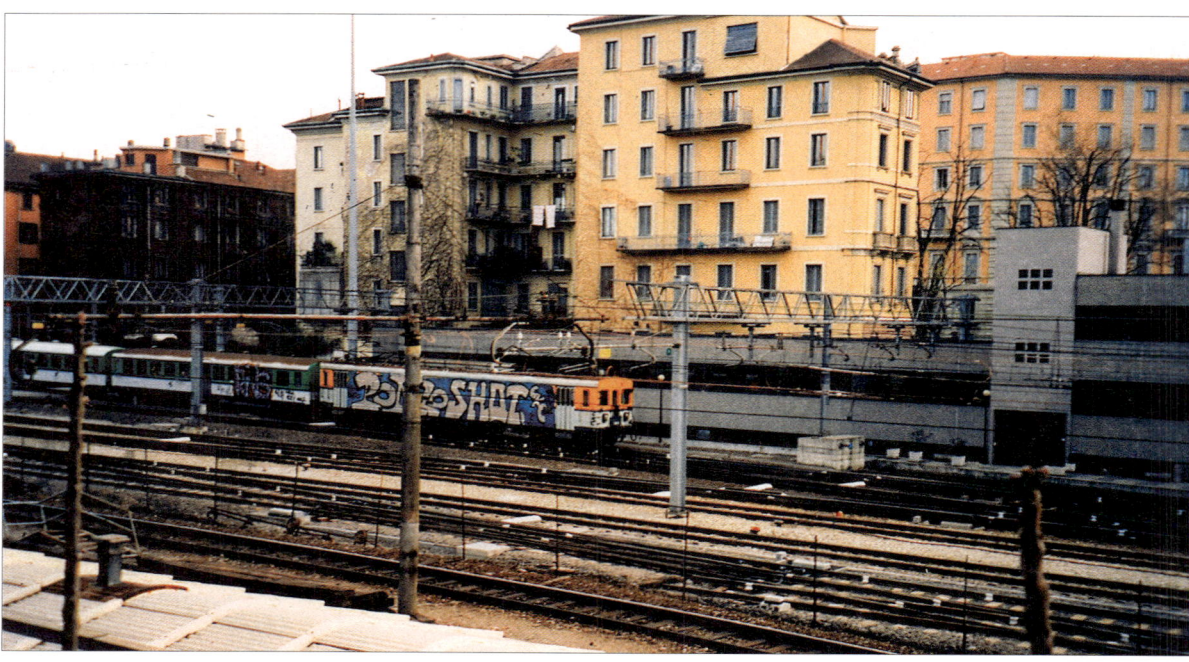

Pongo and Shot's whole–car entering Cadorna Station

— Shot

of New York, from the study of the letters to the styles, they had learnt a lot through contact with artists of the caliber of Phase II, Sharp and Jon One. We were initially behind from that point of view, we had to rely on research, on having fun and on our familiarity with the yard. I was particularly fascinated with this thing of strolling in the middle of the tracks and sometimes I would cover entire kilometres walking on the rails just for the fun of it.

Many of us lived close to the track lines and knew very well when and where the trains would stop at night. Once the evening was ripe, it was time to go paint and we would leave on expeditions to Saronno, Tradate, Asso, Varese, Como. The same thing was going on with some of the Milanese crews, CKC in particular initially organised real convoys captained by Bread. Until then it was mostly the platforms in Milan that got bombed, and this situation offered a new and open ground for confrontation. Everyday we would scamper around from one town to another, from the house of one friend to another, fooling around and checking out deposits. Phast and I would spend our time looking for photographic material, fanzines and books. I still remember our expedition on a NSR fifty motorbike in the middle of the COX 18 social centre in Milan, to attend a meeting with Phase II.

At one point we ordered the first numbers of *1Tox* fanzine from Paris: it was a revelation. In that moment the French

style captured us entirely and I went nuts for the illustrations of N°6 from the Parisian *PCP*. All us outsider writers felt the pull and fascination of Milan, but also a certain desire to compete. There exist numerous territorial reasons for which Writing developed in some areas as opposed to others, and Milan presents all the characteristics attributable to big cities. To enter this game and impose yourself can be difficult if you come from outside.

The North line system was our Far West, a no-man's land in which we had our chance to conquer four metres of notoriety. The deposits, at night were oases lacking any effective control. Nobody would have expected such an escalation. We would enter ten at a time, with trekking backpacks full of spray cans. There were kids battling each other with fire extinguishers, other kids tearing metal tubes from the trains with which to make the coping on a skate ramp and others painting with an unnatural and forgotten calmness. Some would come just to watch; others, wasted, would wait asleep in the car. One time me and my friend Lego spent the entire night painting, pushing our colours in a baby carriage we had found abandoned on the tracks. Wane-COD from NYC told me he had never had that much fun.

This situation was surreal and very distant from the pressure that the Writing of New York, Paris, Berlin, London and the first very tense missions in the Milanese subways suffered. Nonetheless those trains,

just like the ones in New York, Paris, Berlin and London, by moving from the province to the city would take our names through the stations, and we took advantage of it without moderation.

With time the crews present on that line grew exponentially, and with them the security measures. SIC progressively fell apart and contemporarily I joined THP in Milan, with whom I started painting trains even more intensely.

On the North lines the pieces could be counted by the hundreds, the wagons were literally devastated, covered over dozens of times. Writers from all of Italy and other countries would come to paint on that line. The unusual thing, as opposed to other lines around the world, is that the pieces would last for a long amount of time, even for years. Among writers an unusual rule was in force, whereby not to cover anybody else's piece, and it stayed that way for quite some time. You could see your piece running for a whole year. As the number of writers started increasing emphatically this rule was progressively abandoned, returning the situation to a normal regime. The crews in command alternated, contending the title week by week, month by month, a bit like what happens on the lines in the rest of the world.

This is the competition of Writing: monologues and dialogues, proclamations and beef, in which the only words at your disposal are those of your Names.

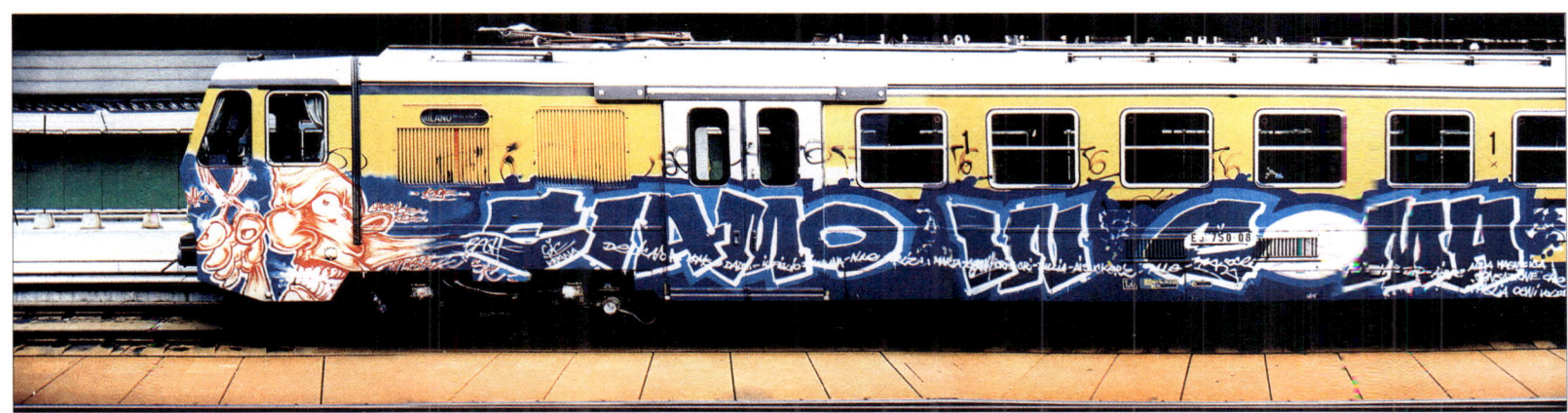

Siamo in coma (We're comatose) by SIC crew, Saronno, 1995. Character by Mastro K   – *ACW archive*

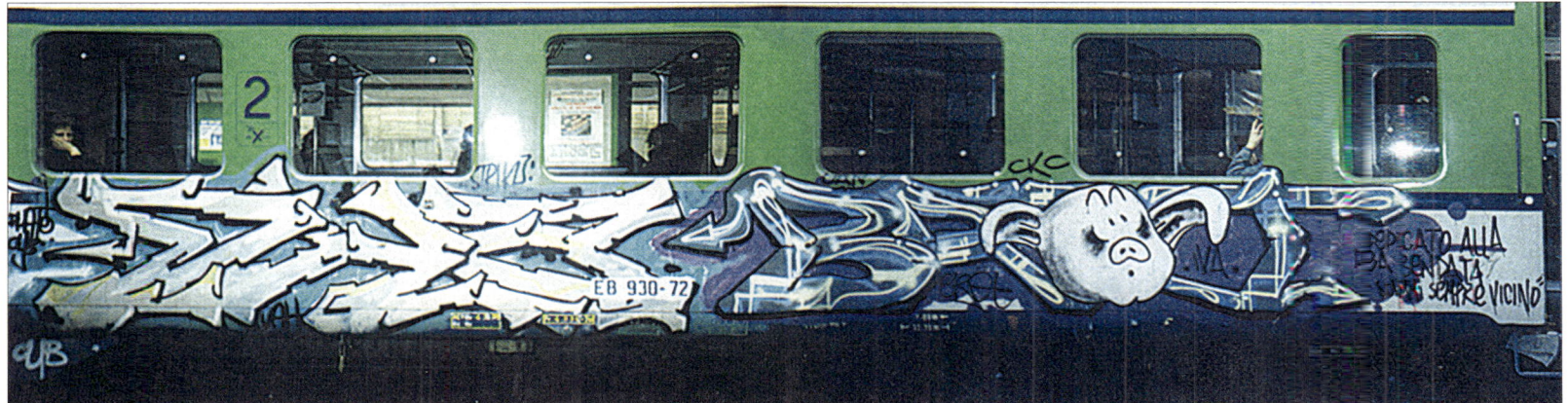

Pha by Phato – CYB, UAN, *Brot* by Bread – CKC, *Dedicato alla dea bendata, stammi sempre vicino* (Dedicated to the goddess of luck, stay close to me)   – *10000 Maniacs archive*

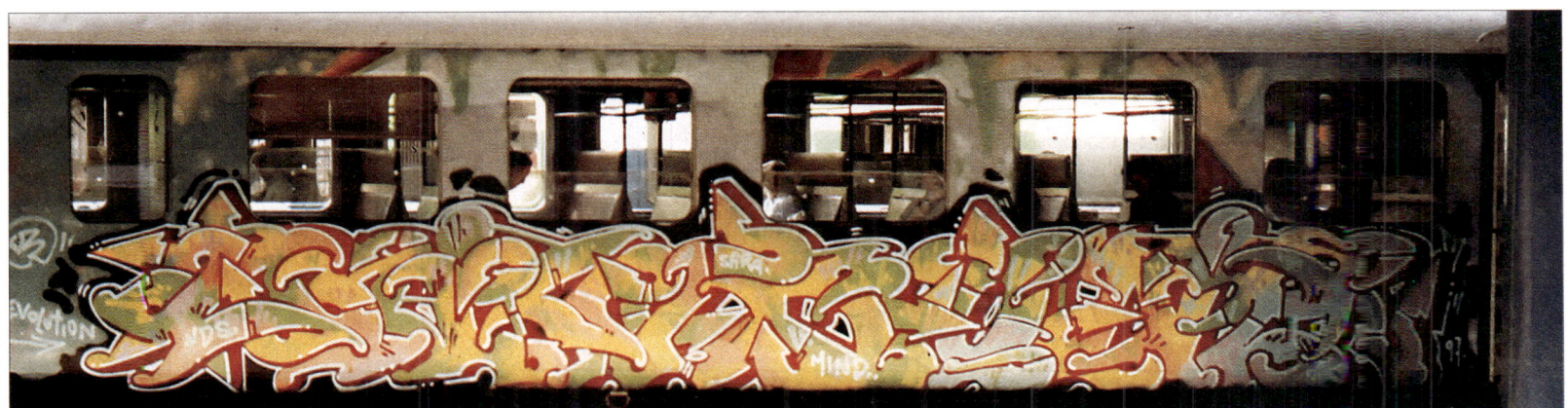

Window–down Wildstyle by Mind – VDS, GR, TAK, 1997   – *Mind*

Writing in Brianza
>

North Line System

Air One
>

When in Milan we finally took notice of the Ferrovie Nord and of trains in general – around 1992/1993 –, writers had already been painting the city for years. Not that trains had never been taken into consideration, it was simply that until then the writers of Milan had given their all on walls: an anomalous path that saw the birth of some of the most famous halls of fame in Italy.

Rome on the other hand, during those same years of the early 90's, had given start to a train-Writing movement that was envied throughout the world for over a decade, and it was through the subway that its myths were created.

Thus the difference was substantial: when the Milanese scene suddenly threw itself onto the trains of the Nord, it had already developed very specific traits and included considerable writers for both quantity and quality, therefore it was a mature and

prepared movement. The difficulty and harshness of a scene so aggressive and competitive could only spotlight extraordinary artists: style matters! That's how we could summarise the philosophy of that era.

Not quantity – though that was surely present – but quality, originality with styles, independence from the most common European trends, direct ties with the first masters from New York City (Phase II, Vulcan, Sharp), as opposed to those from Europe.

> CONTINUES ON PAGE 190

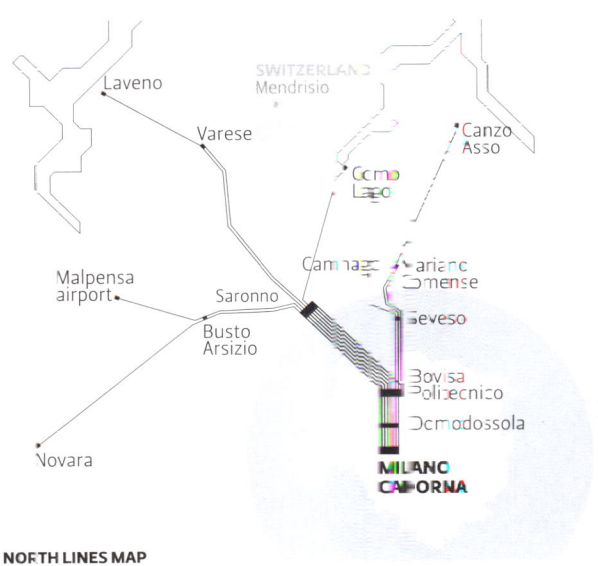

NORTH LINES MAP

Cadorna station as a meeting spot
>

Epicentre

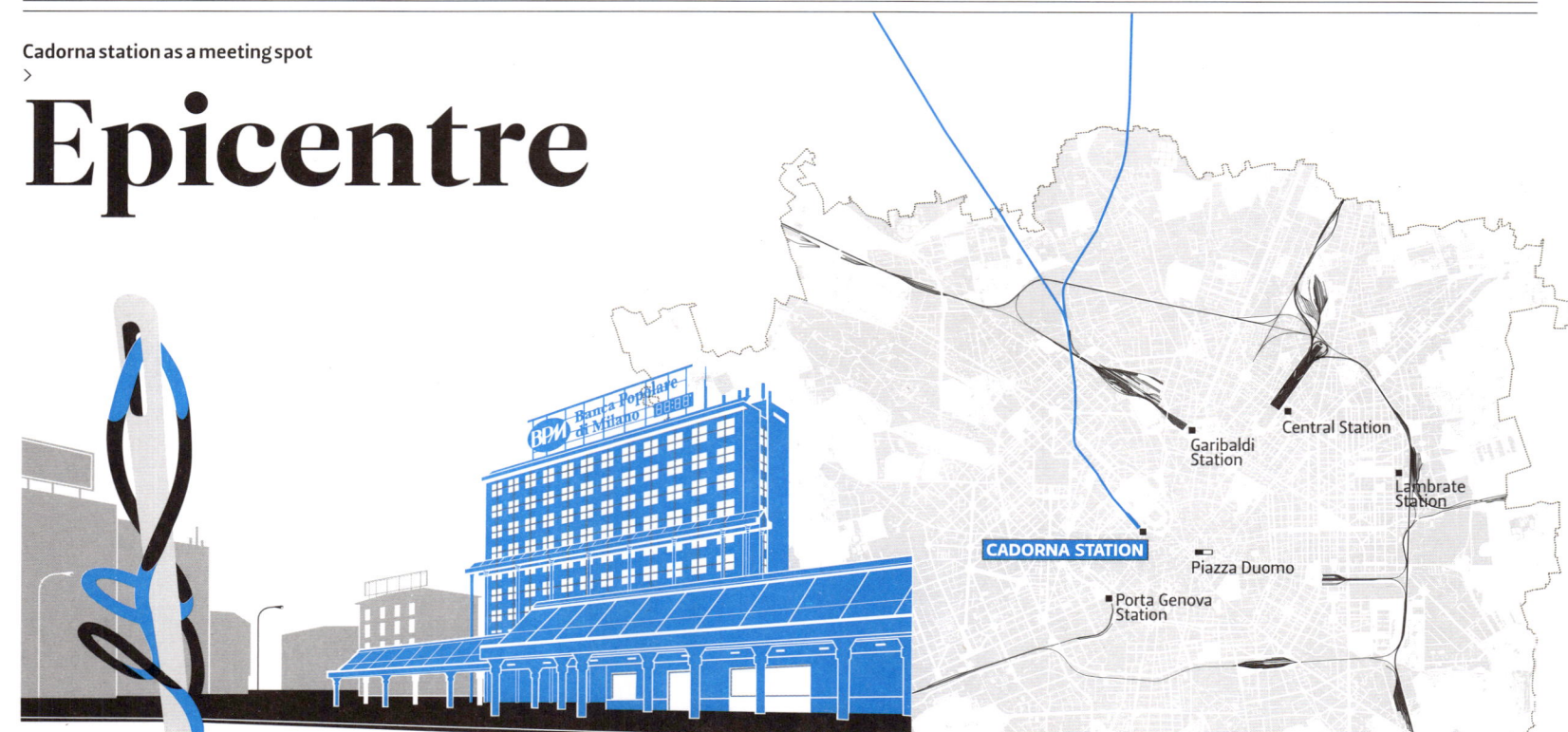

About halfway through the 90's, when the target of writers switched from the historic neighbourhood halls of fame to the Ferrovie Nord, suddenly the pulsing heart of the Milanese scene became Cadorna Station. The Ferrovie Nord were preferred to the Ferrovie dello Stato for various reasons: first of all, the presence of numerous local lines circulating frequently gave writers the possibility of seeing the panel they had painted various times in the arc of a day. Secondly, the deposits of the Nord trains were positioned outside of the city, surrounded by nature and without much surveillance, therefore being particularly easy to hit. In addition, during that period the Ferrovie Nord were facing a deep economic crisis, which didn't allow them to sustain the costs of buffing their carriages. Regardless of these reasons, the choice also revealed purely aesthetic preferences: though disposing of railway lines that

This railway was perfect because it was less extensive than the state line

were limited with respect to those travelling on a national scale, the Nord possessed an extraordinary variety of models and colours. The first post-war cars in military green and brown were followed by carriages in the style of the Italian littorine, bright green and yellow; and when the number of commuters rose drastically during the 90's, additional double-deck convoys were imported from France. Thus Cadorna Station, like a funnel, channelled all the energies of those painting in the city outskirts right into the centre of Milan. It became an attraction, a place where the Milanese writers could meet and stylistically challenge themselves with those spread throughout the various towns of Brianza on a daily basis.

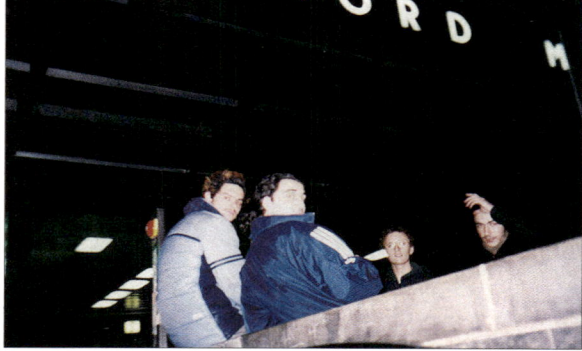
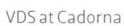
VDS at Cadorna   —Robin

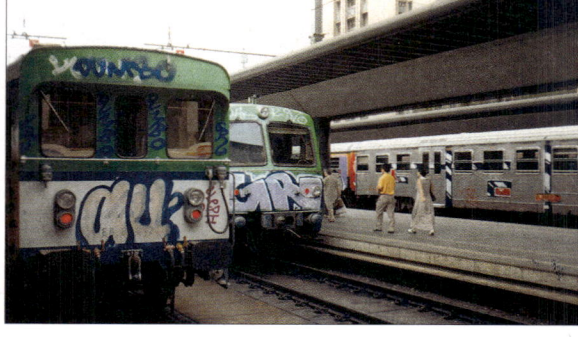
Bombing in Cadorna station halfway through the 90's   —Siso

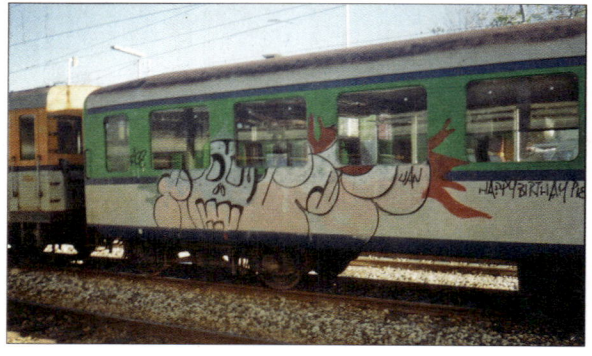
Face – UAN   —Lay Up

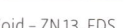
Zoid – ZN 13, FDS   —ACW archive

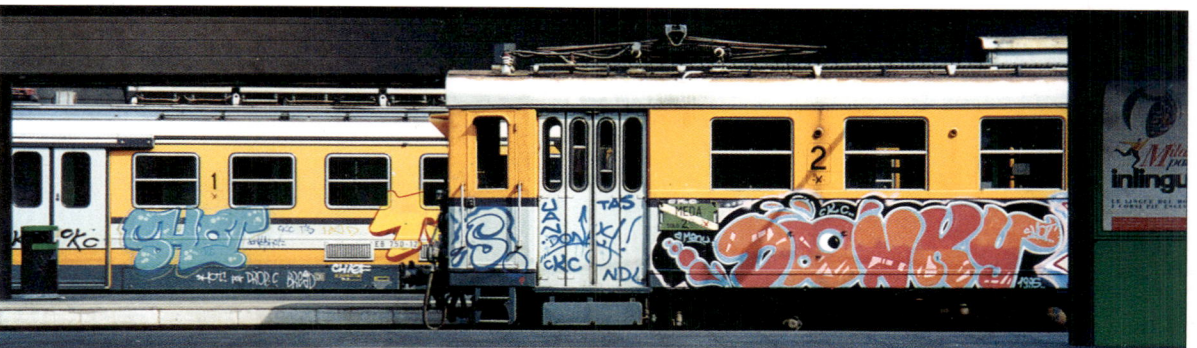
Shot and *Donky* by Shot – CKC, 1996   —Shot

Revealing the myth of CKC crew

In the spring of '94, the period of the Northern Railways, or Ferrovie Nord, began. During those years, the state trains weren't painted that often. First, because they got buffed quickly; and second, because they traveled the entire country so you might not see them again. When you painted the state trains you'd spend the whole day at Central station, or in the yards in order to find a bombed train. It was frustrating because the trains would disappear and you'd never know why: either they got buffed or traveled to some other place. All you'd have left were the photos you'd taken at night. So when we heard, in September of '94, that the Northern Railway trains never got buffed, we went to Cadorna to see. We were all curious. We discovered that the Northern Railways had been struggling financially for years, so they couldn't afford to buff their trains. We didn't think twice about it! Furthermore, this railway was perfect because it was less extensive than the state line, so you had the possibility of easily seeing your pieces and other people's pieces circulate. The Northern Railway covered a limited section of Lombardy, so if you stood at the station for half a day, you would see most of the trains pass by. For the first few months, the only pieces you'd see on the Nord belonged to CKC, even if there were many trains painted by SIC, a crew from Saronno who painted the Northern Railway because they were the only trains to pass through their area.

In no time, the novelty caught on and the FN became a real battleground, a place where you evaluated yourself and challenged each other with strokes of style and strength, reflected in how present you were on the trains. When I went to see this line for the first time in September '94, it was already bombed; the quantity and the quality of the pieces was rather remarkable. From then on, for years we had the habit of going to Cadorna to hook up with crews who went to see their pieces and others people's pieces. I was particularly curious to see those by CKC,

the best crew in Milan and probably in Italy. At Indelebile in Rimini, I saw Sky and Shot but I didn't recognise the other guys. I wanted to see people like Drop, Rax-e, who did fantastic pieces, Bread, Bang, Dose, and all the others. In those years, they were a true reference point, what we aspired to be. I recall I was dumbstruck the first time I saw them. In the beginning, especially when we used to go to Cadorna, we didn't want to attract attention, cops were on patrol looking for writers taking photos and could arrest them. One Sunday I was at Cadorna alone,

the station was nearly deserted. All of a sudden, a group of writers I'd never seen before started heading towards a freshly painted train to photograph it. Without a concern in the world, they stood photographing the train for ten minutes, then left as casually as they had arrived. It was CKC crew! They were so brash, they didn't seem to worry about being noticed. They really seemed like a gang. Moreover, one of them actually stayed there. It was Dose. He was a legend in Milan. Everyone knew his story: he'd lost a leg in a motorcycle accident but despite this he painted

subway platforms and trains. So he was respected and admired for this. That day in the station, he couldn't photograph his piece because the train doors were open. He stood there waiting for them to close. He waited a good 30 minutes and then finally managed to get the shot.

I was a few meters away and stood there the whole time watching in admiration and fear that the police would show up. It was very obvious he was the creator of the graffiti, but he didn't seem to worry, he just stood there waiting until he got what he wanted. - ROEN

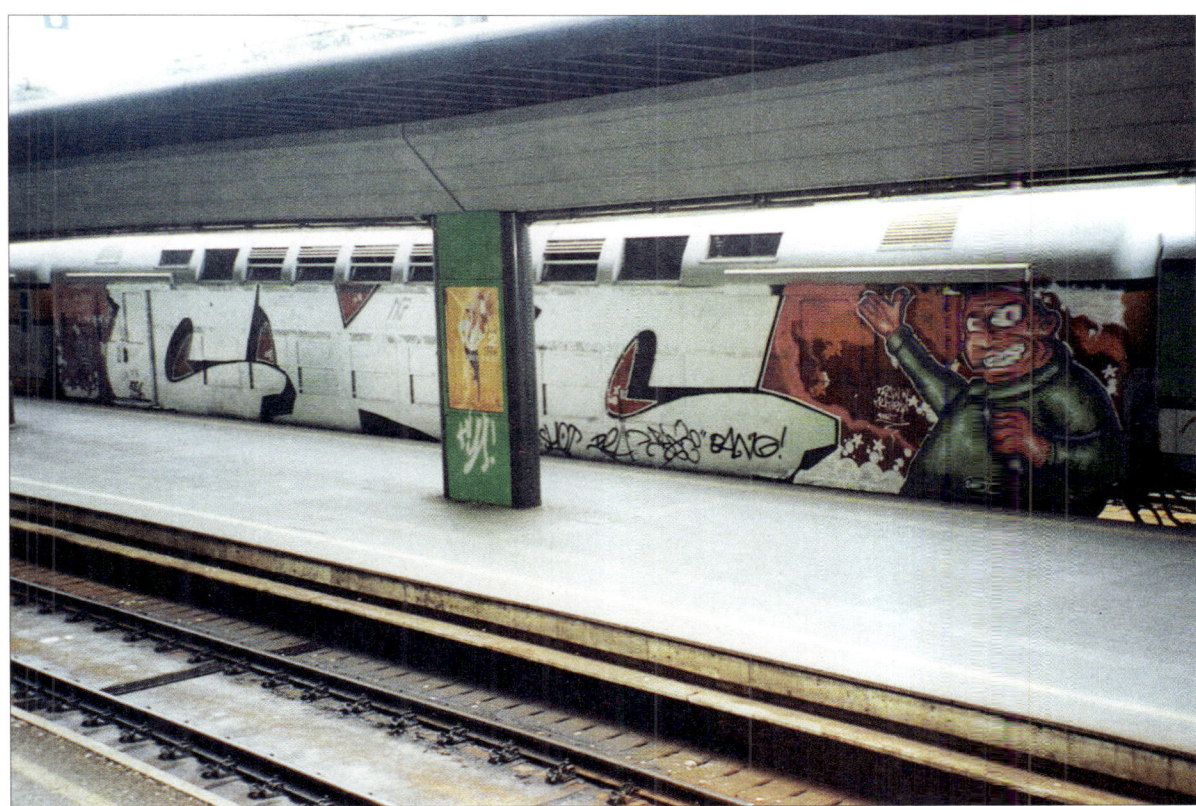

CKC whole-car by Dra, Bang, Rae. Character by Shot. Cadorna station, 1996   – Dra

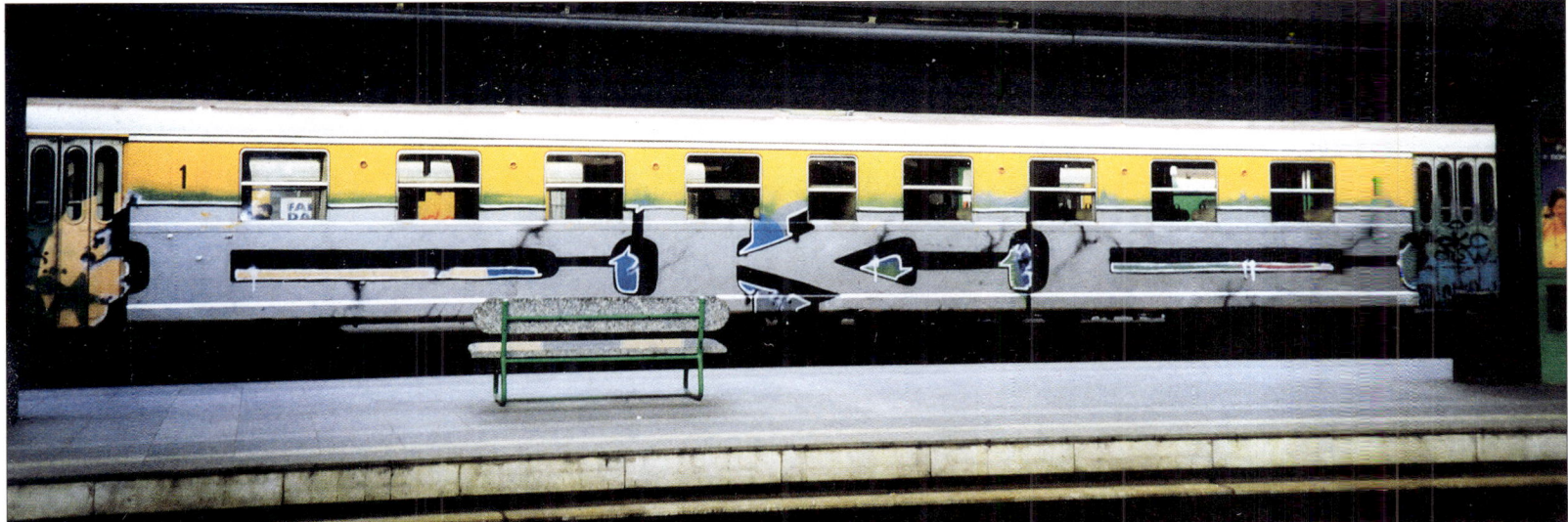

CKC crew: end-to-end blockbuster   – Siso

LOVE & PAIN
—

Rae
>

The period during which we were heavily hitting the Ferrovie Nord coincided with my love affair. This might seem surprising, after all, today it isn't trendy to wear your heart on your sleeve in these contexts. And yet it was a turbulent and overpowering relationship that has survived and blossomed throughout a thousand obstacles. Perhaps it was these same averse conditions, implicating precariousness, envy and betrayal, that allowed it to bloom. A love affair with a new world that found lifeblood in the determination of a child.

A love so encompassing that it would push him to evolve the letters of his name without pause, improvising on trains after months of practice on paper, preparing the paint, the caps, the gloves, finding and scheming on spots, arriving, entering in silence, with the cold that makes your hands freeze; checking that no one is coming, no dogs are barking, no window lights are on, that cars pass by without stopping, trace, fill, close the outline and concentrate, in a deposit embedded in a city that seems not to belong to it.

We never had enough of it, we looked for yards so that we could be where no others were, to then distance ourselves from the train and behold a piece as it comes out, is born, sometimes as large as an entire carriage itself, or long five windows but so elaborate that it would resemble a spaceship with letters that only writers can read. Others are excluded. And while at 8 in the morning they're going to work you're still there looking for your train so you can see it shining underneath the sun and take a picture, knowing you'll be painting thousands more because you just can't stop. And then you return home or perhaps you don't go back at all, who cares? To me all this was Writing on trains, living life with that inexplicable drive, a personal creative mission that you can't fully comprehend until you try it yourself, and explaining it is perhaps just a waste of time.

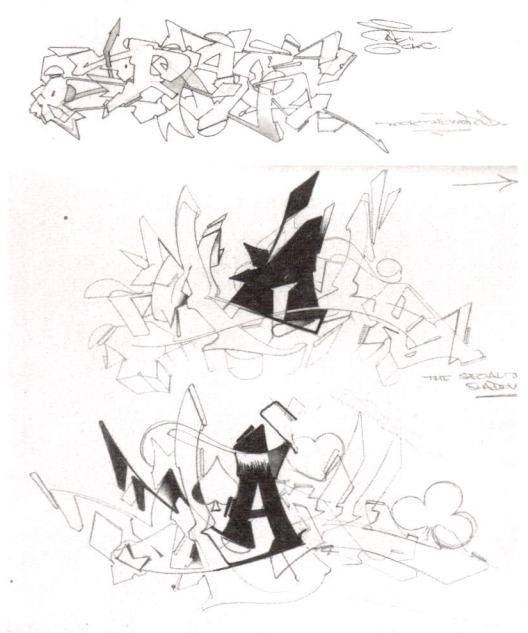

Sketches by Rae   — Rax-E

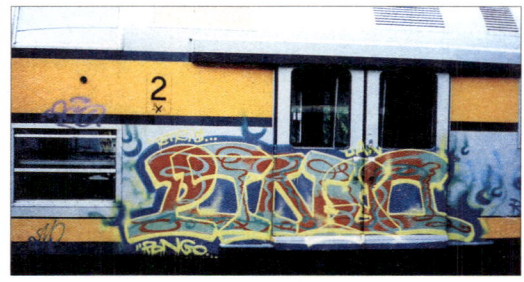

Pongo – UAN, CKC   — Siso

Writing is not a democracy. Writing is a monarchy where Kings reign on the forced silence of toys. — RAE

The city was something to be used, we wanted to rule it and for some time we did, in a contradictory way. There was a period in which we spent so much time in stations and yards that it felt like we worked there! It was as if we did shifts, as soon as the transit workers left, we started. — ROBIN

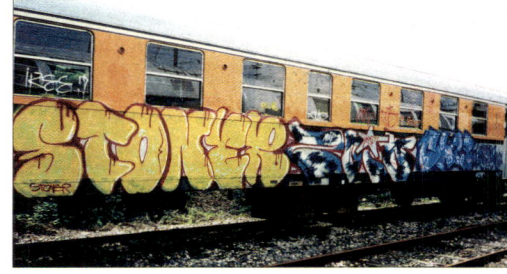

Stoner, Zoid, Craze   — Craze

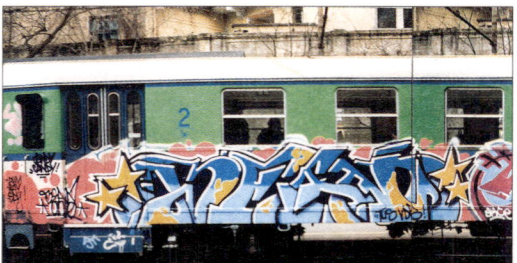

Bean VDS   — Bean

Mastro K – SIC, THP   — Robin

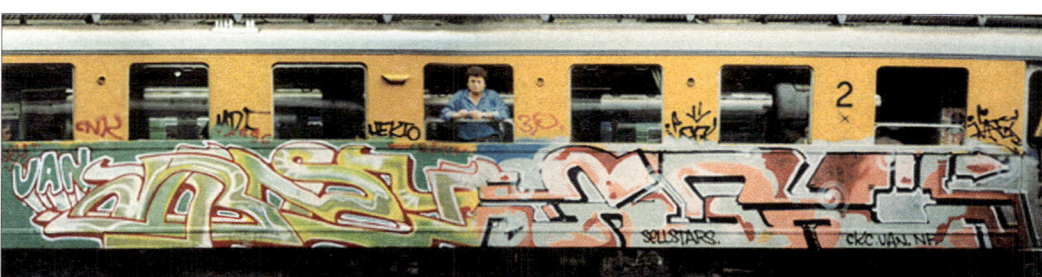

Dosey – UAN and *Sel* by Pongo – UAN, CKC   — Siso

We all knew each other in person. Being part of the first wave that had personally discovered every possible yard, I considered the whole line as if it was my home.
— AIRONE

Rae – CKC, 1999   — Rax-E

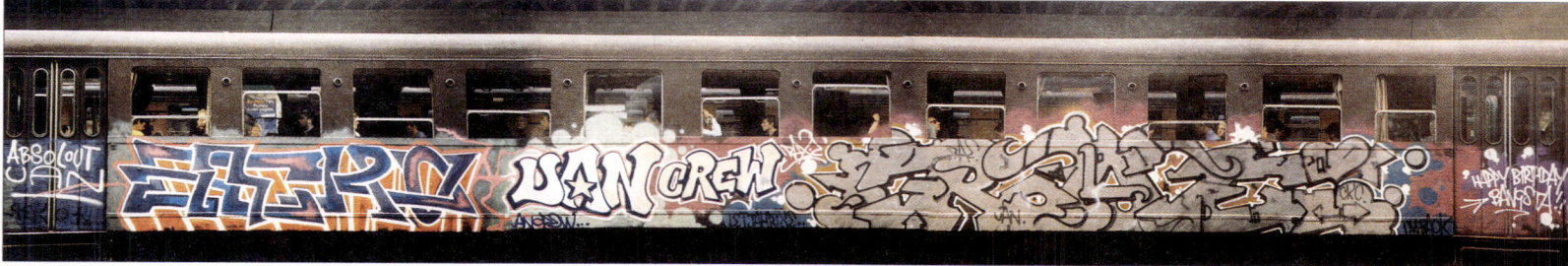

Geko – UAN, Rae – CKC. 1996   — Dosey

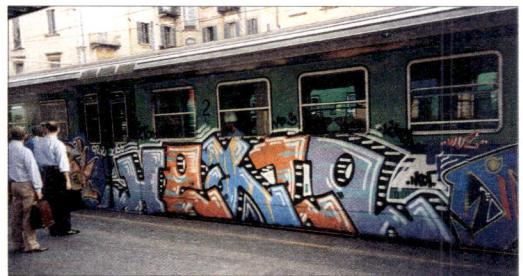

Hekto – MDF from Rome   — Siso

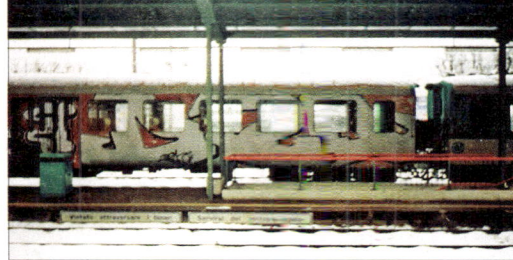

Sand – VDS, 1998   — Sand

Dra – CKC   — Dra

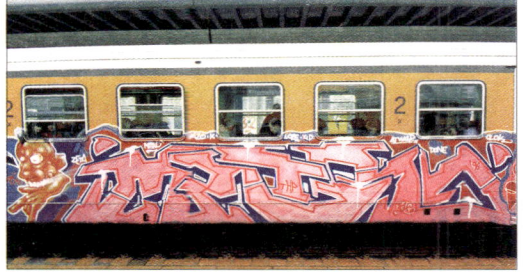

Character by Mastro K and *Metro* by Airone – THP   — Airone

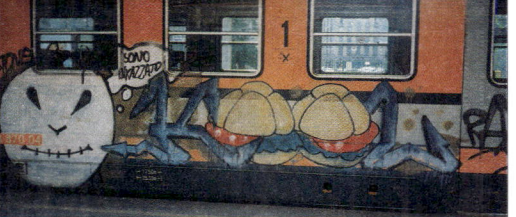

Kool by Bread, CKC   — Lay UP

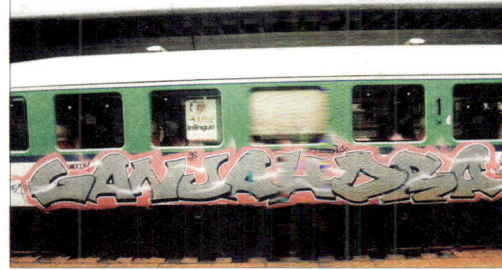

Ganjahdra by Dra CKC   — Dra

> Once our fixation for FS (state) trains faded, we moved on to the North Railway, or the regional line which was shorter. The competition with other crews was more direct, trains circulated more often, and above all, there were more yards. That was even cooler. — CANO

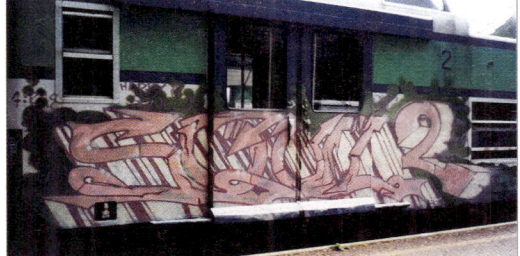

Soul 2   — Siso

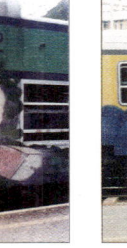

Stych UAN by Pongo, JAN 1996   — Lay Up

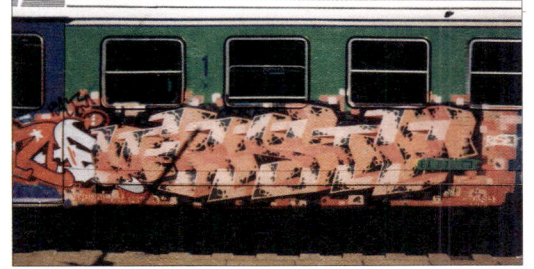

Riso – PDB from Vercell   — Lay Up

> Asso, Canso, Castellanza, Laveno and the territory to the North of Milan became our new playground: writers preferred covering great distances by car as opposed to bombing Cadorna Station, as it had become much too dangerous. — SHAD

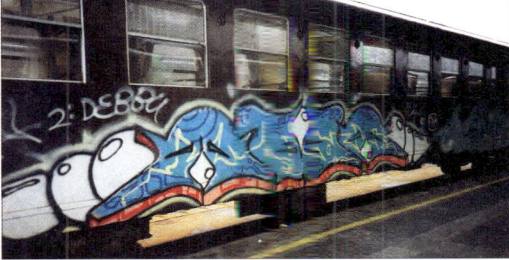

Tawa – 16K   — Siso

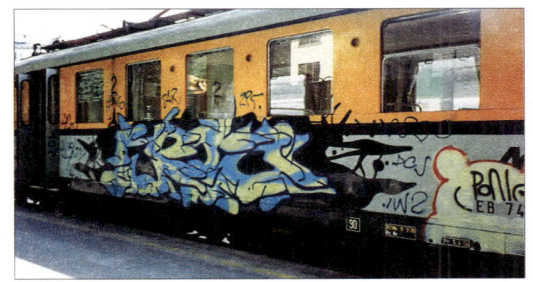

Furto – DCN   — Siso

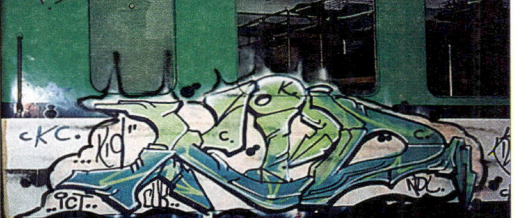

Kid – CKC   — Shot

> The North line system was our Far-West, a no man's land in which we had our chance to conquer 4 metres of nobriey. — MASTRO K

> Spyder kept insisting on painting the FN: he couldn't resist the appeal of New York City, be it stylistic, attitudinal, or urban. He kept urging me to consider the areas North of Milan as part of the city. A painted subway car that goes from Queens to Coney Island travels as far as the Milan–Saronno line. Once writers realised this, they all attacked Cadorna station. — FLY

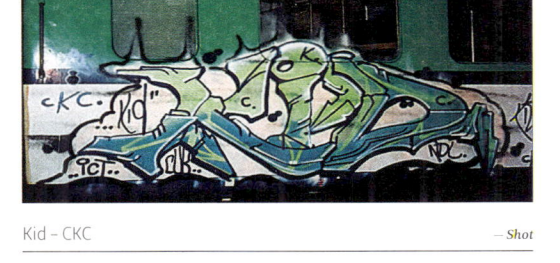

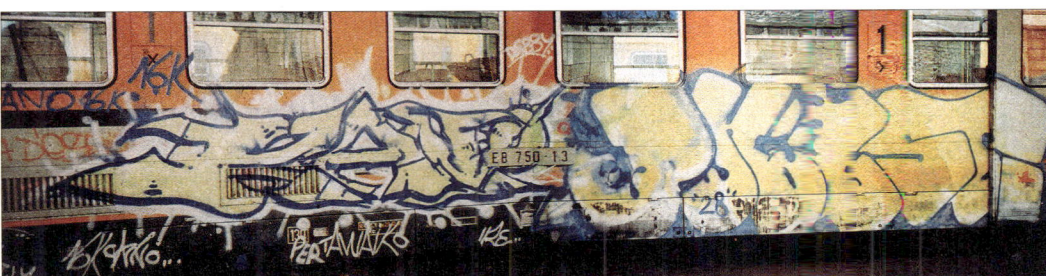

Cano – 16K and Phase II from NY   — Cano

> CONTINUES FROM PAGE 185
We of THP, formed at the end of 1991 and still active today, were no exception. On the tracks of the Nord I lived four very intense years, from which I learned a lot. Together with Clock, Done, Yazo, Mastro K and Phast, I formed a compact nucleus in which, however, each had his own personal style. Many thought there were more of us in the crew because we used other pseudonyms. Done wrote Sea, Luana or H2O, Yazo wrote Pepor, I would often use Aria, Metro, Chart, Opium, while Phast wrote Moma. Add to this the pieces painted by Teatro and KayOne and it'll be easy to understand why I found it absolutely normal to meet my friends in Cadorna Station and spend entire days there. In those same years Kay gave birth to *Tribe*, the most famous publication of the time in the area of Milan; we had International contacts few others possessed and so it was difficult for a month to pass without us bringing some foreign guest to the Nord. I remember Sharp, Smith, Opak, Honet, Bates, Loze, Kid, Jame, Vons, and many others. With some of these I've stayed in touch, though the paths we may have undertaken are completely different. The Ferrovie Nord were really their own microcosm. We all knew each other in person. Being part of the first wave that had personally discovered every possible yard,

The Ferrovie Nord were really their own microcosm.

I considered the whole line as if it was my home. Well, perhaps this is a significant point; we're not talking about a subway line, but a regional line, with much longer routes and more trains, something that could really be compared to New York City in the 70's. Italian subway systems in fact, are limited to a few, shorter lines: on the Nord you had to know yards that were distant, like an hour's drive from Milan to be sure you'd find your train the next day and could photograph it in Cadorna, for not all of them reached the station. So it was pretty easy for us "explorers" of the time to bump into each other in these places. Or even for crews to mix in order to optimise the use of cars (for at that age not everyone had one). Many were the times in which I went painting with Shot, Drop, Dra (CKC), or Krana, Ranx, Intru, Zoc (SIC), or also with Furto and Guen (DCN). There were some periods in which certain yards would become over-crowded, with situations on the limit between comedy and paradox. And how to forget Asso? In the beginning we went there with beers in our backpacks, painting whole-cars on the platform for entire nights and taking the same trains we had painted to return to Milan the next day! For over three years we hit without almost ever having to cover anybody else's work. When the new generations started crossing our old pieces, for many it was a real shock, the end of an age. Some retired, others adjusted to the new rules of the game. In truth it wasn't but the beginning of another era, under many aspects as important as the previous: those that could not accept it were soon surpassed by the train of history. – AIRONE

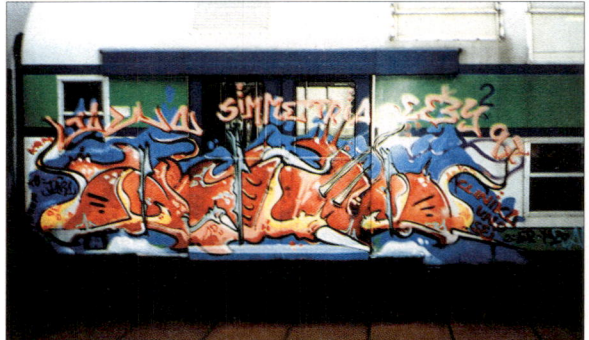
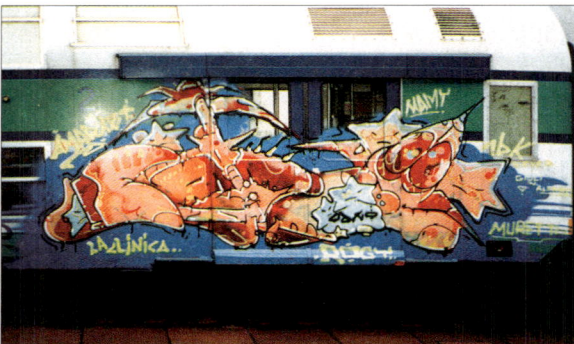

Tawa and Cano – 16 K   — *ACW archive*

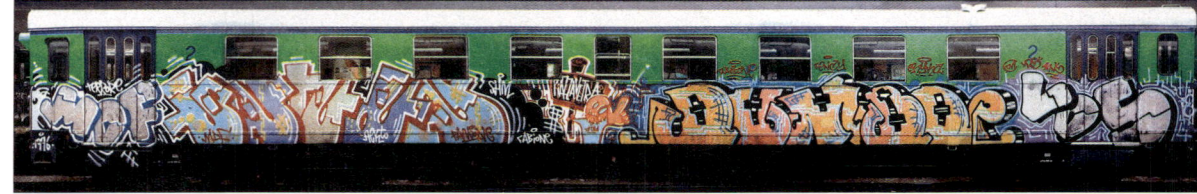

Panda – MDF from Rome, Dumbo – VDS   — *Siso*

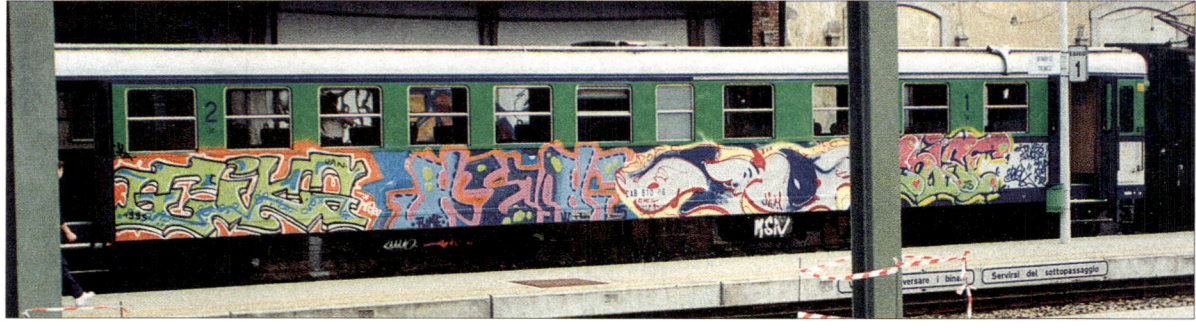

Geiko by Dosey – UAN, Fume – MSN from Dusseldorf, Drop – C – CKC, Chief – MNP   — *ACW archive*

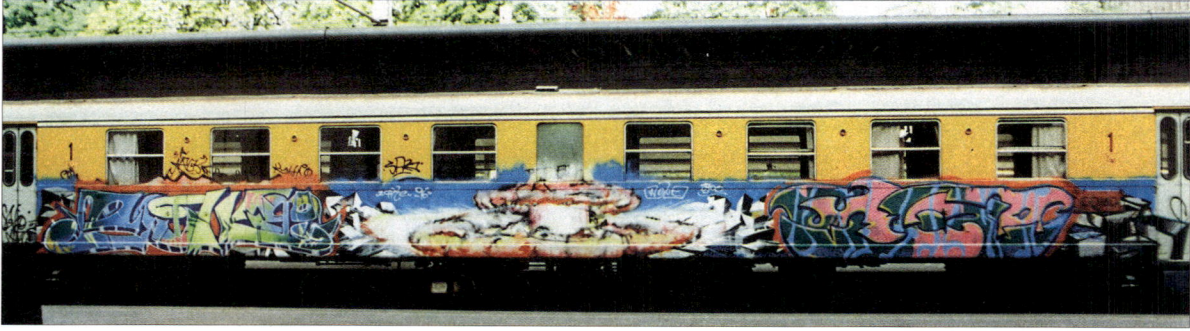

2 Cake – VDS and Woze , 1996   — *Sand*

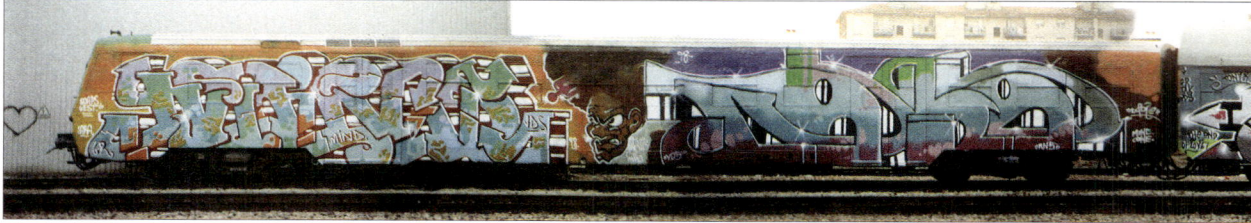

Whole–train by Lords of Vetra: Mind, Cake, Kill, Spyce, *Lords of Vetra*, Dumbo, Dance, Robin, Rain. (continues below)

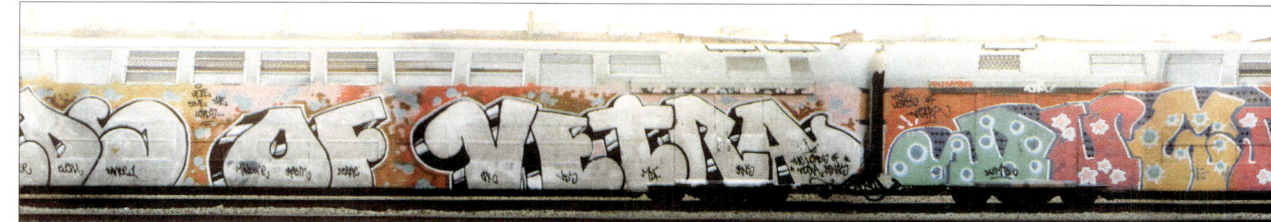

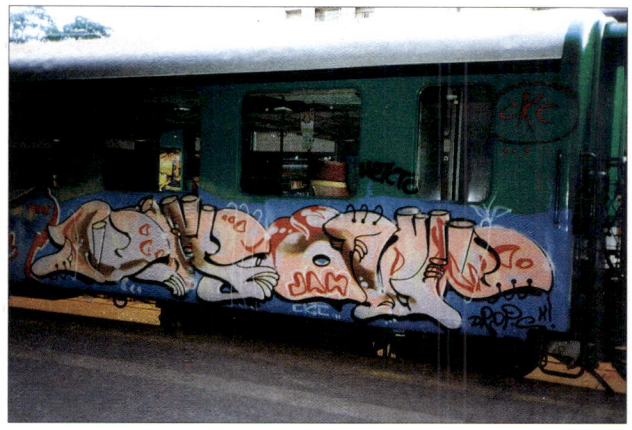

Drop C – CKC

— Siso

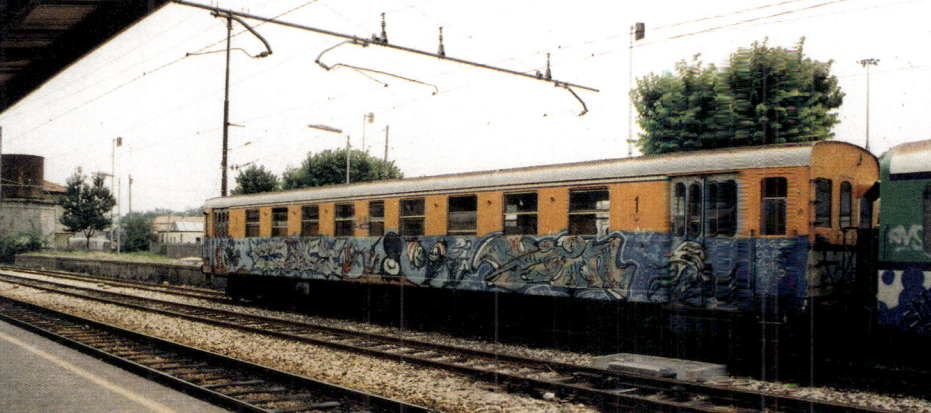

Guen and Crisy – DCN

— Lay Up

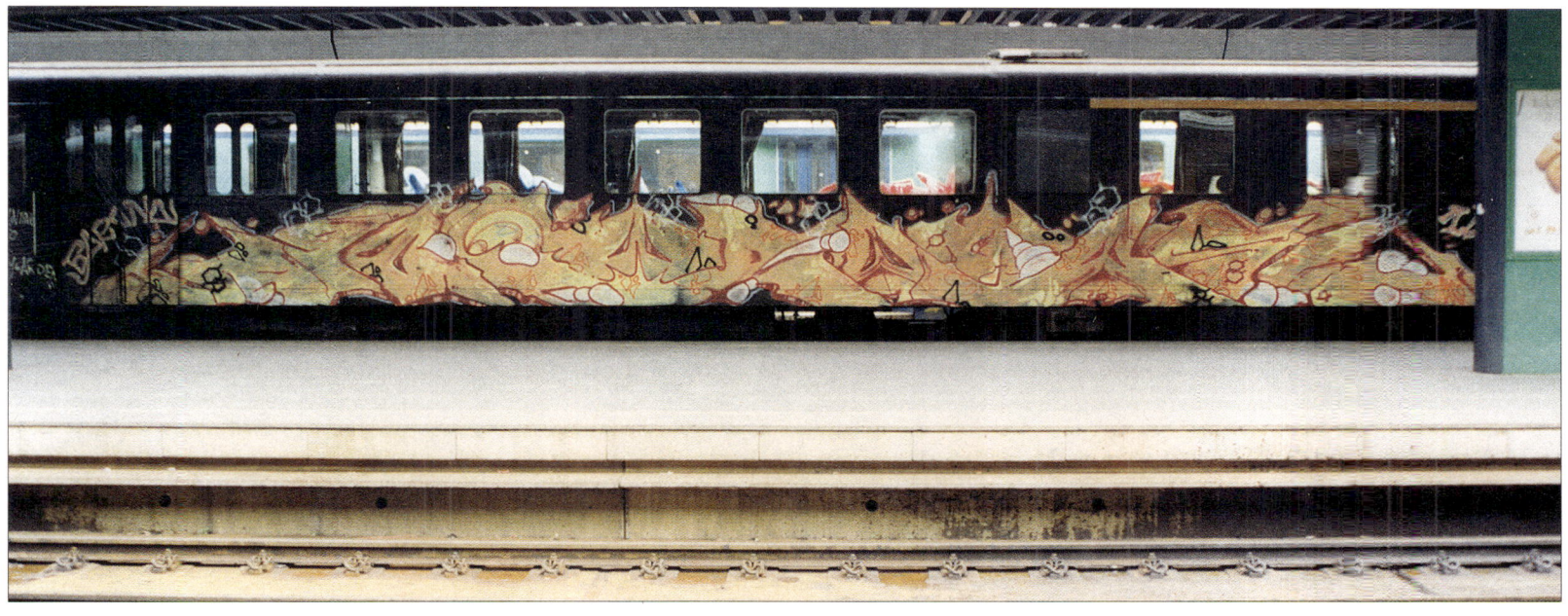

Cano – 16 K

— Mark Todt

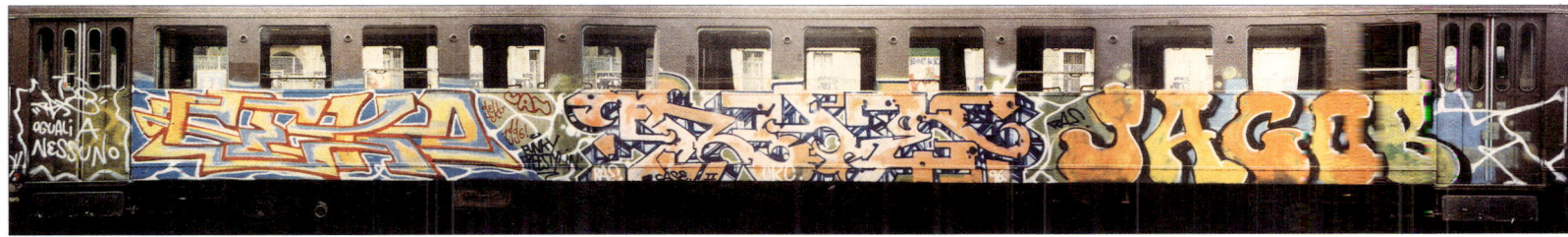

Geko – UAN, Rae – CKC and *Jacob* by Shad – UAN *Uguali A Nessuno* (Equal to none)

— Lay Up

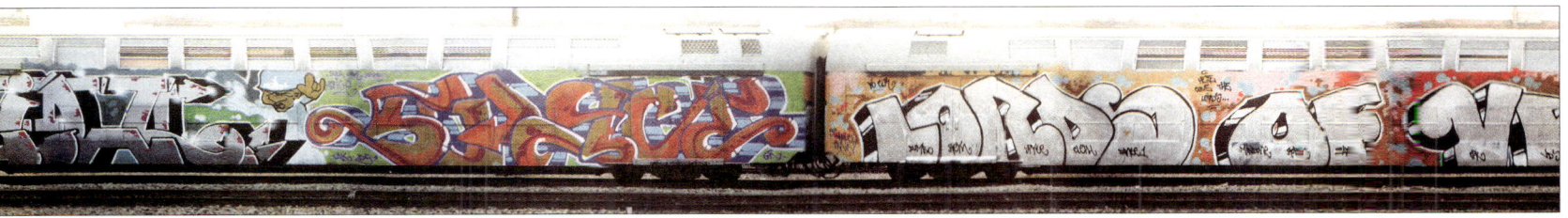

— Robin

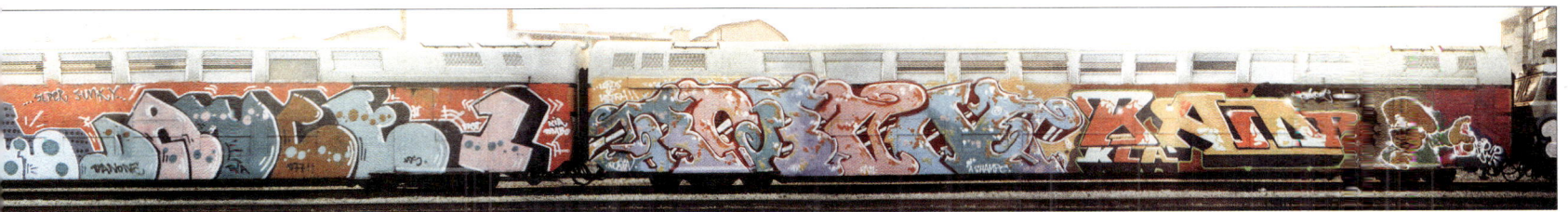

— Robin

COLOURFUL BOMBING

Craze
>

"The whole conviction of my life now rests upon the belief that loneliness, far from being a rare and curious phenomenon, is the central and inevitable fact of human existence."

Thomas Wolfe "God's Lonely Man"

This condition, which has always been a part of my way of living, is a state that truly stimulates the real act of a writer: bombing. Soon enough, this became the only sincere mode of interpreting Writing and will always be my method of approach.

At first, bombing adhered to my "urban lifestyle" and I painted the places I often hung out in. Something I could see any time I wanted to by wandering around Milan. Bombing, as an evolution to reach the result of whole-city hall of fame, conceived and shared with friends from various posses and crews: the city itself, in its entirety, was seen as our own personal illegal hall, covered with bombing and pieces with backgrounds and colours...

No longer banished to a wall or a specific area, but rather spread out to any visible vertical surface. Since subway pieces weren't very visible (Milan only has three subway lines which are mainly underground and on which fewer people ride compared to cities like New York or Paris), it was necessary to go into the light and colonise the city aboveground: bombing became a strategic choice, essential for achieving our goal.

In the beginning, when I started painting the subway, the act of bombing was saturated with energy and meaning... but as soon as I realised that the end result was visible for a limited amount of time and to a limited number of people, I started considering going above ground

and 'invading' the part of the city that was used by the majority of Milanese people. Then there was the Northern Railway "outbreak": these lines established contact between Milan and the dense structural territory of the Northern parts of the city, all the way to Switzerland. The walls of the city spoke and challenged everyone; and thanks to the Northern Railway, our presence could reach all those satellite towns that were part of the area that extended from Milan to Canton Ticino. Bombers are interested in visibility! The strategies I employed since 1988 while illegally Writing all over my city, alone or in company, can be summed up by years that correspond, more or less, to a progressive

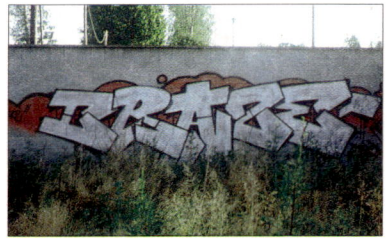

Craze   – Craze

appropriation of the territory and the achievement of increasing visibility.

1988-1989: weekly tag-tours take place, hitting, above all, the city's centre; passageways, stops, and exits of the subway lines I used.

These were daily and nightly tags done with homemade markers. For example, the 5.4 cm one, made with snowboard wax and the handy liquid shoeshine dispenser- emptied and filled with Flo-Master ink, closed with a Bic pen cap, and sealed with duct tape. Then there were daily and nightly tags done with fats from the original caps: the mercedes fat was made with a Duplicolour cap and a cutter, making three incisions; the Uni-Wide cap had a horizontal incision; and then you could experiment other types of used caps tracing giant tags with silver Talkens, after which you threw away the

cans and burned your jacket.

At first, the tag-tour only passed through my neighbourhood and neighbourhoods of other posse members. Then it spread to all the neighbourhoods we hung out in day and night. And lastly, only in neighbourhoods that weren't ours. Throw-ups? Yes, but not enough time.

1989-1990: the first bombings in the centre. In the beginning on the *Muretto* near Corso Vittorio Emanuele, the first meeting spot for writers, deejays, breakers, and thieves of Milan; who would later meet at the sides of the Duomo.

1989-1990: the first subway trains. We started at a time during which it was likely for bombed trains to circulate for a long time. At the same time, the first subway platforms were being hit – to be honest I only did a limited number of them because they didn't really appeal to me.

1990-1991: hitting the Railway lines. Central station (silver pieces along the lines), Garibaldi station (piece along the line), Porta Genova, Piazza Tirana (trains). The outbreak of Milan's Northern Railway (similar to Paris' RER) with repeated double roller pieces in white and black on the line's brick walls – which were mad absorbent –. The first trains to be done directly on the platforms of the Cadorna yard. Later, along the Bovisa lines (colour, silver, and tags). Lambrate was in the hands of other writers.

1992-1993: hitting the majority of main

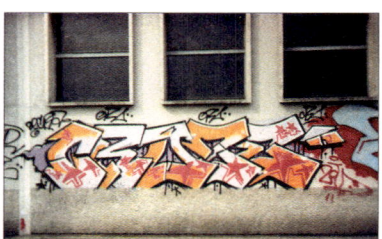

Craze   – Craze

roads to the city (Milan-Laghi, Milan-Turin, Milan-Novara, Milan-Bologna, Milan's Linate airport), subsequently the

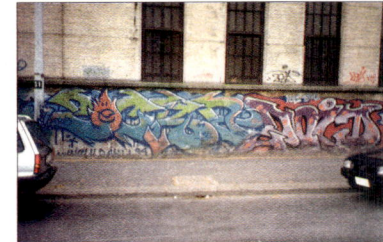

Zecra by Craze, Zoid   – Craze

bridges and walls on the beltway (external highway connecting Milan's various areas and the outskirts), Navigli roads – which guaranteed us visibility with the 'entertainment crowd' – and Darsena as the city's first illegal hall of fame. The idea was to hit all of the beltways outside of the city and then make our way to the inner highways, the ring roads, typical of Milan's urban structure. During this time Zoid and I started toying with the idea of bombing, doing quickly executed pieces, with a background, two internal colours, one colour for the details – bubbles or stars – one colour for the outline, and always finished off with shading and drops. We did all this without getting arrested, since we'd already faced a storm of trials, we did what we could to avoid facing more!

1993-1994: the emergence of the idea of whole-city halls of fame with pieces throughout the city, favouring more visible locations, 'hotspots', places in which I would stop to smoke and eat something after a night out, before returning home to bed.

1993-1994: no more sketches. All of my work becomes freestyle. I stand before a wall and the letters come flying out... and my hand swings.

IN BOMBING YOU FIND AN IMMEDIATE STYLE THAT COMES FROM THE DEPTHS OF THE UNCONSCIOUS AND BECOMES CONSCIOUS THROUGH MOTION... WITHOUT THINKING OR LINGERING ON HOW THE MASSES AESTHETICALLY DEFINE STYLE. THIS MENTALITY WILL ACCOMPANY ME THROUGHOUT MY LIFE...

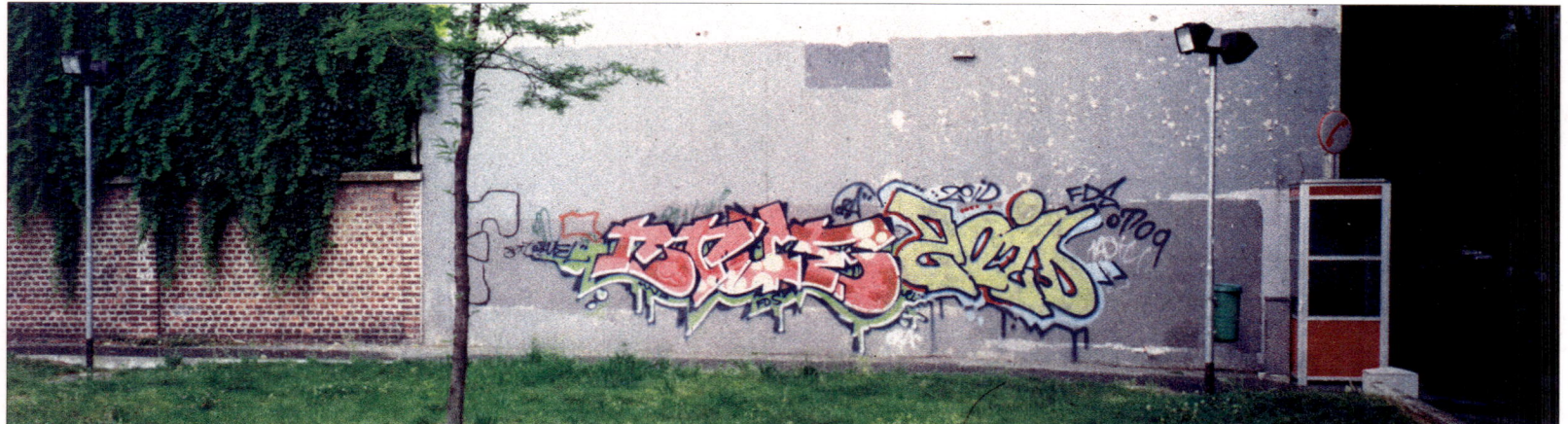

Crue by Craze, Zoid

                                        – Craze

HIGH–RISE WRITING

Robin
>

In 1996, Noce was only 14 years old, though he looked much older. One night he told me in secret that he was planning on climbing onto a roof of Piazza Duomo to paint there.

Apparently Dreca, a writer who was part of QVS crew, had challenged him by climbing up to the tenth floor of a building, so he planned on outdoing him. When he saw Dreca's roof piece he was taken aback, it was very high up, but despite everything, it was still feasible.

Noce's endeavor though seemed truly absurd, even just the idea. Aside from the actual difficulty of climbing to the top of a building near the Duomo, there was also the risk of getting caught by the cops: there was always a police van patrolling the Piazza. Out of respect, I didn't object, but I honestly thought he'd never pull it off. Since he was so convinced, I was curious to see what would happen.

The day after D-day, I went to Piazza Duomo and looked around... until I saw it. I was dumbstruck, he had pulled it off! In defiance of the cops, he managed to paint a spot that was practically unreachable. Thanks to that stunt, Noce ended up on a fantastic newspaper article in the Corriere della Sera in which he was depicted as a superhero, a Spiderman of graffiti who, dismissive of the danger and the laws of gravity, had climbed to the most un-

> ❝ One night he told me in secret that he was planning on climbing onto a roof of Piazza Duomo to paint there.

thinkable places, stirring the imagination of all the city's residents. We were thrilled to read about it. Noce and his roofs taught us that anything was possible, if you wanted it enough. From that point on we were convinced that the city was ours and that we could do anything.

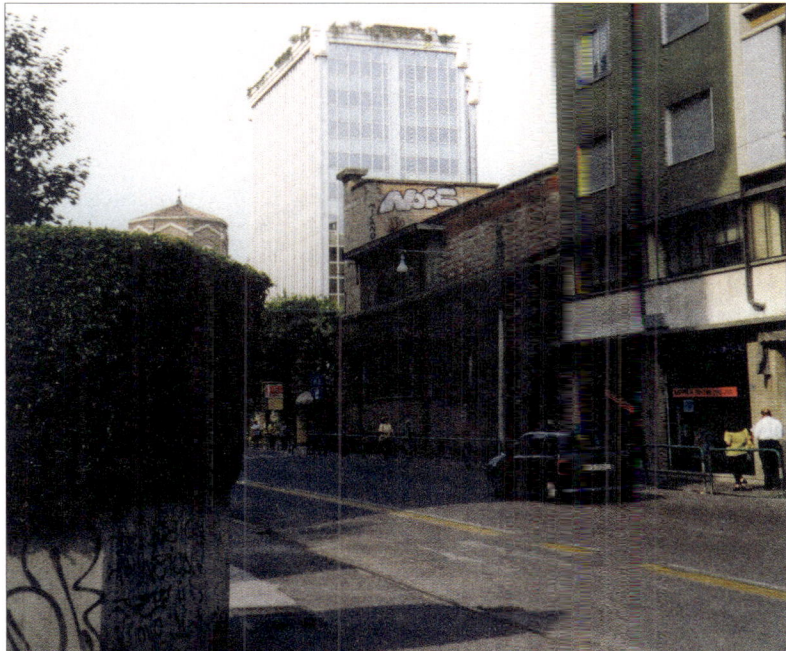

Flying Noce on Milan's city centre rooftop　　　　　— Siso

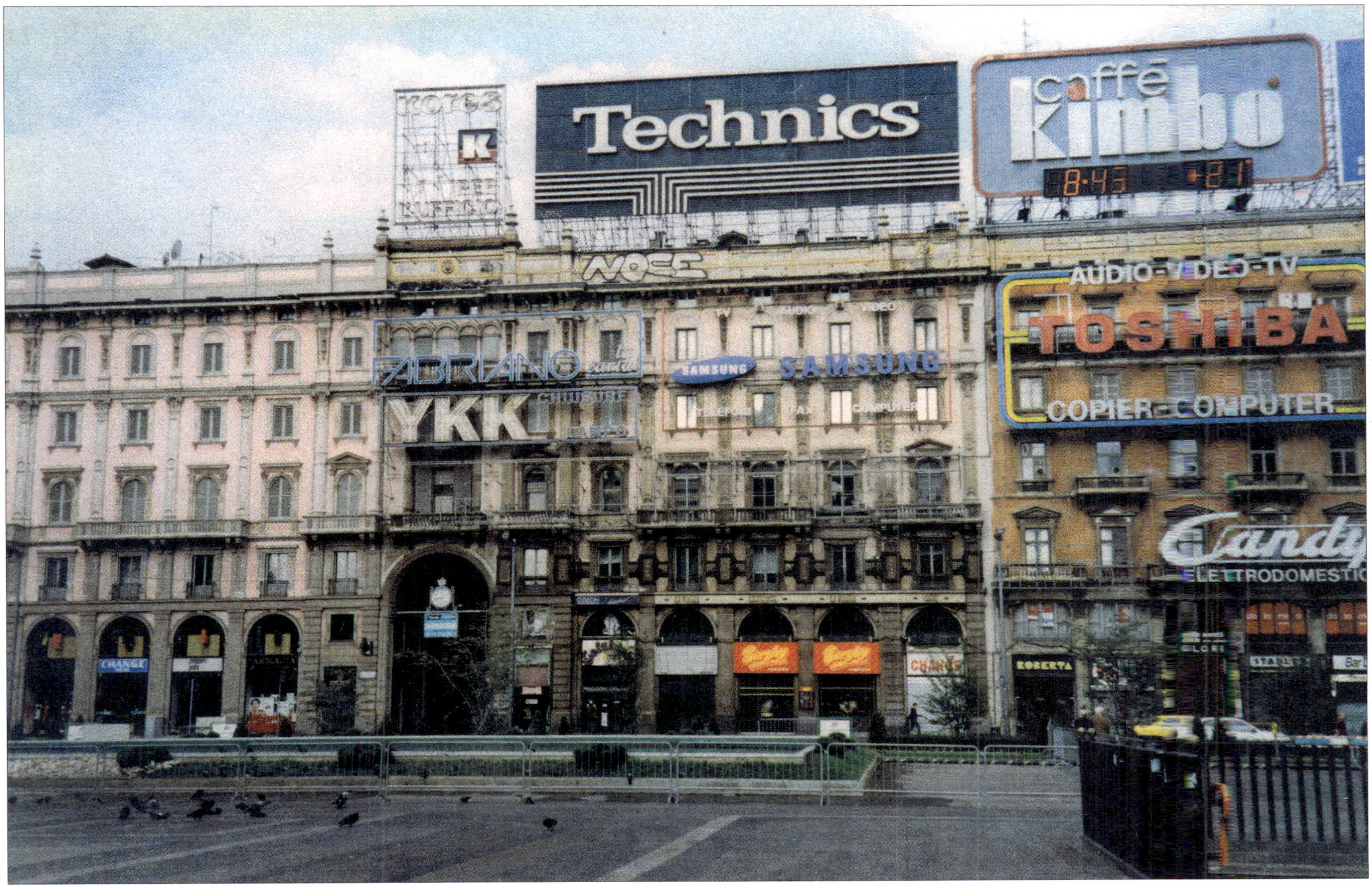

Noce against advertising in Piazza Duomo, mid 90's　　　　　— Siso

SUBWAY STATIONS

Into the darkness

Robin
>

In Milan during the early 90's we painted the walls of the subway. It was the riskiest thing to do. More than trains, stations represented the biggest challenge, a battleground for the most hardcore writers. They were a great way to showcase your pieces to passersby and other crews, due to their location in busy areas and also because the pieces weren't buffed immediately, actually they usually lasted weeks or even months. It was a daring move because you were in full sight of the cameras, knowing someone was about to come get you. So it was essential to be quick and know when you could get in. How to enter and how much time you had were big secrets.

Naturally, nobody would take you along to show you the ropes. So if you wanted to paint, you either figured it out for yourself or stood by, watching enviously. You had to know which entrance to use and where the cameras and the trapdoors were. Obviously the situation was different in each station. During those years, almost all of the inexperienced crews who attempted it got caught. In the beginning of 1994, lots of writers did subways, but one of the kings was Kid from CKC, a real mole. He always managed to get in without being caught. If you took the green line you could almost always see his platforms, stylish and effective.

But I think the greatest expert on tunnels and platforms was Electro. Electro was a truly curious character. He would wander in the tunnels just for the fun of it. He was obsessed with ninjas and always dressed in black. He had tons of Chinese stars, numchucks, plus other ninja weapons and moves. He was the biggest mole out of us all and he knew all the subway's tunnels, entrances and hiding spots like the back of his hand. He possessed every key and had lots of info on the surveillance setups.

Electro didn't draw, but he did an awesome electro boogie (the robot dance his name is based on), collected Hip Hop albums, and hung out at *Muretto* from the very beginning. He told us that when he went into the tunnels he'd bring a black curtain with him. If there happened to be security guards or workers in the tunnels and he had no way out, he'd stand flush against the wall and camouflage himself with the curtain. He was a good and kind person, but he definitely had a dark side. Once he showed up with some little white

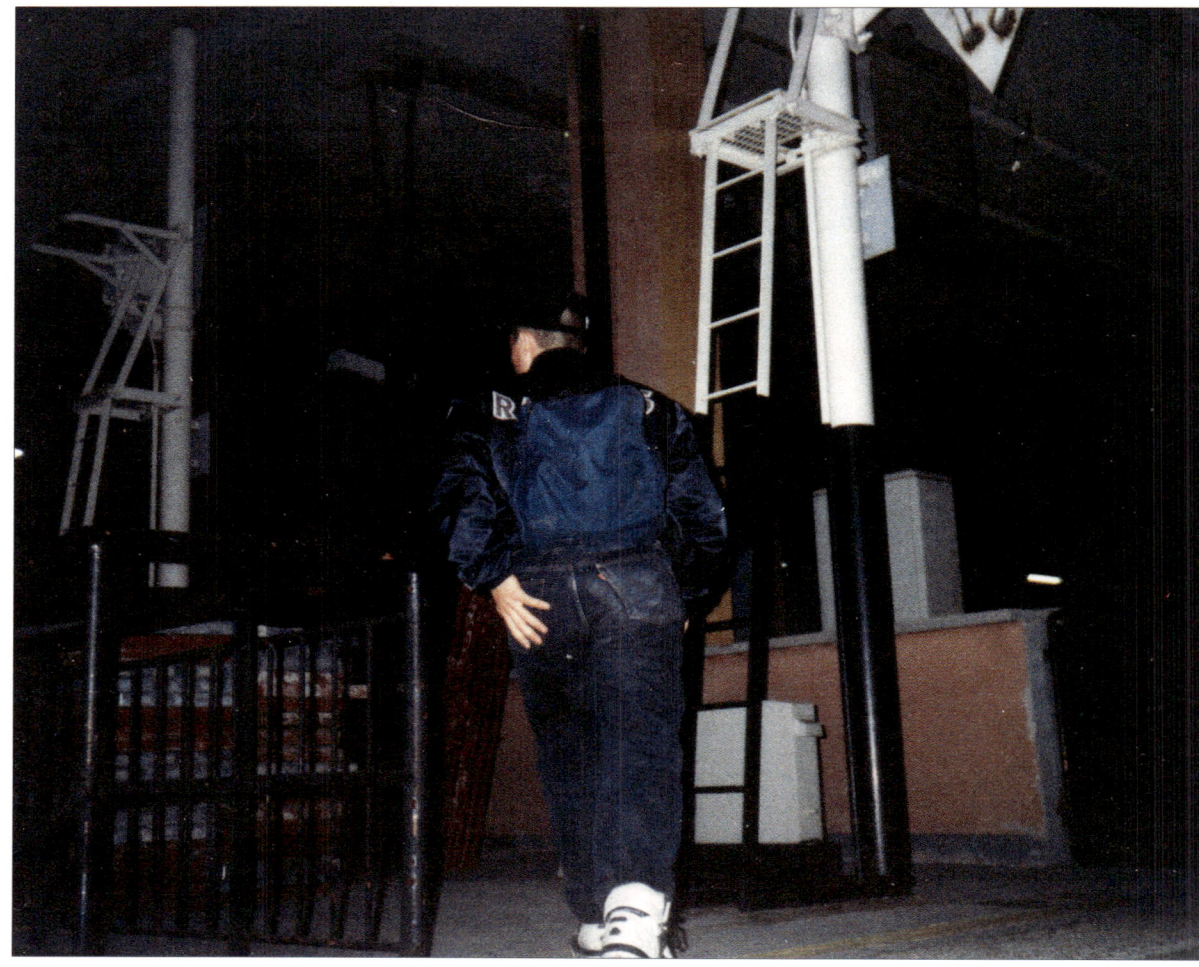

Mad Bob sneaking in the subway tunnels, 1988   — *Mace*

balls saying that if we threw them on the ground a cloud of smoke would appear and he would disappear. It was fun to listen to his stories, but partly due to all the joints he smoked and partly due to his craziness, it was hard to distinguish between reality and fantasy, perhaps he doesn't even know! In any case, he was a maestro and taught many things to the kids of the city.

Raptus
>

Toward the end of the 80's, the Writing scene was quite different from what it would become 20 years later: the main focus was painting, there was no competition to conquer a spot in the

Writing-business. We painted out of passion, for the thrill of the risk, in order to outdo other crews, and to demonstrate our own abilities. Back then there were only a few of us, rivals yet friends, who all knew and respected each other. We'd run into each other at night in the subway tunnels where we'd all hide out of fear of encountering on-duty subway police, but once we heard the sound and smell of spraypaint, we knew it was just a 'friend'. At night we'd meet up at pubs to organise a sort of bombing contest between crews: we'd go down to the subway and would each do our tag, then race back to the starting spot; the last ones back would have to buy drinks for everyone else. At times we'd steal the subway keys, break through the shutters, explore every tunnel in order to have an escape route. In the subway, our companion was the sound of the ventilation system, a noise which was imperceptible by day but

deafening at night, constantly churning; and the dense fog was our friend.

This was also the era of halls of fame that we'd conquer on our own without asking the city, without permits, funding, sponsorship; galleries and the media didn't give a shit about us, the city's walls were preserved through talent and sweat. We painted, period!

Bang
>

The walls of the subway were the ultimate destination for every bomber of Milan during the early 90's. Every once in a while we'd do some sporadic throw-ups on the sides of the train, but the surfaces of the stations were the primary target.

Painting them resulted in a concentrated dose of adrenaline you'd unleash outside, before even gettin' in. In Porta Venezia there was a roller shutter at the entrance of the escalator: from outside we would wedge a hand in the weave of metal and then 'play' with the lock, using rudimentary keys such as the skeleton key of the subway engineers. My first attempt at bombing was in the Porta Venezia station. We'd stay down for five minutes and then run out of the entrance. In the case of anything unexpected, we would hide in the tunnels or in the nooks of the stairs, waiting for everything to calm down. The manholes, for example those of the stops on the red line (Pasteur, Turro, Gorla), were a good alternative to get in/out: there was a grate that led down the middle of the tunnel passing through the fan room. Some kids even liked painting on the black surfaces of the tunnel, or on the last metres of wall that are visible thanks to the light coming from the platforms, but with respect to other cities such as Paris, the Milanese writers didn't consider these spaces of the subway much. Most of all, Lambrate was maybe one of the most targeted spots because that's where all the commuters getting off the regional trains would arrive, as well as students of the Politecnico Institue .. all potential spectators of our nocturnal actions.

Flycat
>

The platforms of central subway stops were the most sought-after painting locations because they corresponded to the busiest spots of the city, so they were great showcases for our pieces. When Mad Bob painted the wall of the Porta Venezia platform it was a turning point for us all. Since then everyone had their eyes on Lima and Loreto, the other two subway stops running beneath Corso Buenos Aires, perhaps the longest commercial street in Milan. Spyder was the absolute first to paint platforms back in 1987; the following year he and I painted one at Vimodrone, on the extreme outskirts of the city, and slowly made our way towards the centre. Electro was with us one day, and while we were painting he managed to break into the subway conductor's booth and find the keys that opened the subway's doors and turnstiles. That was a stroke of luck for us! He closed the door and from then on we were able to go in, paint, and leave without a trace of entry.

Authors
>

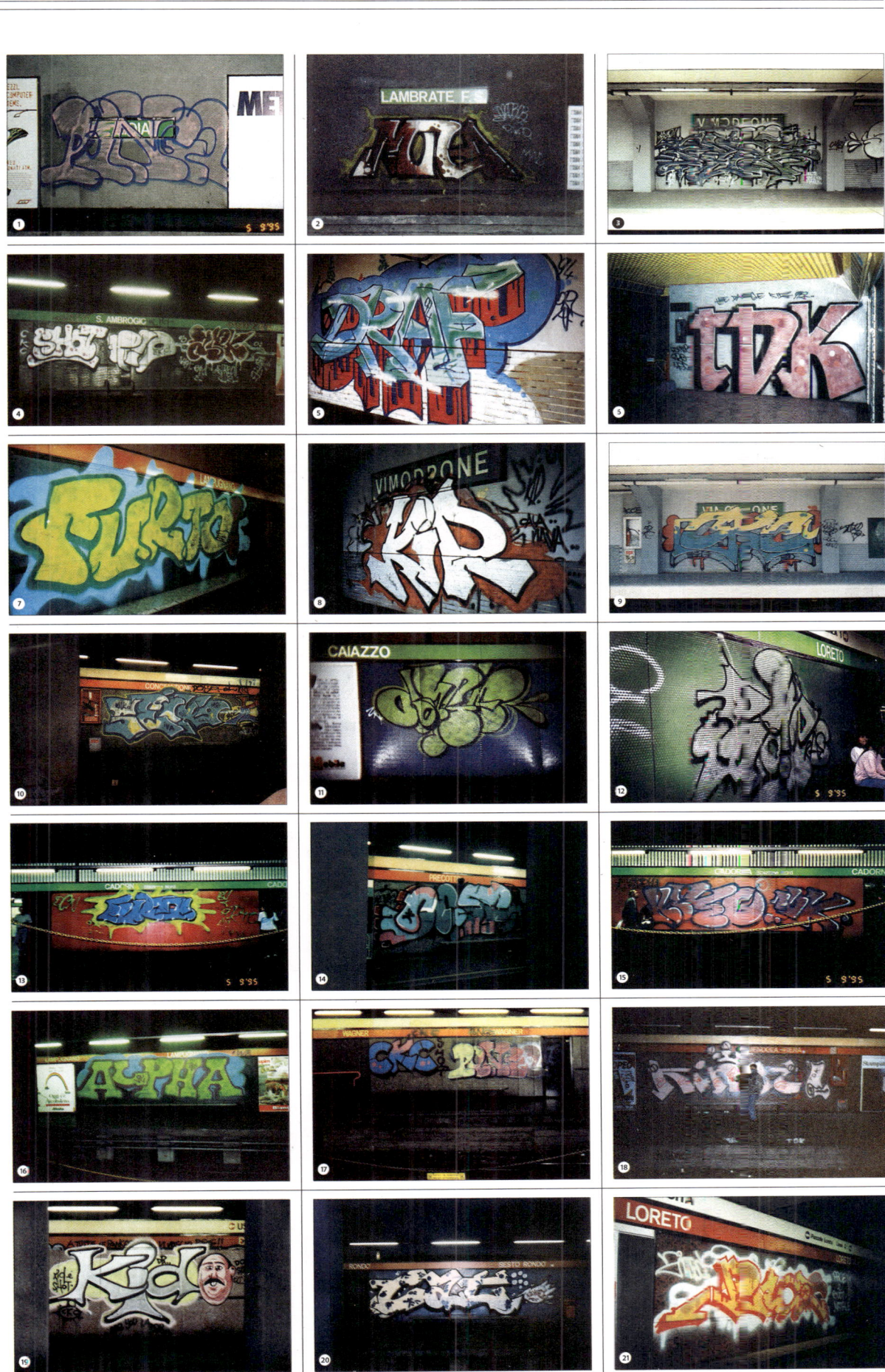

GOING UNDERGROUND

Dismantling the system
>

Hijacking: tales and tools

Robin
>

1st MAY 1995

It was the first of May 1995, the only day in which public transportation in Milan wasn't in service. The idea of taking advantage of this circumstance to paint the subway had been considered for quite some time. We had already been to dozens of railway deposits, but inside a subway, never, so it was a special day. The round-up was us, RNS, TAK and SAD. It was a strange convergence because before then we had never really hung out together. The fact itself that there were so many of us and that there were writers from other crews with whom we had never painted really made the day exceptional.

Together we had decided to attack the deposit of the green line, the 3, which was the newest. We always saw it from the tangenziale ring road when we went to Cologno to buy paint, and every time a train passed our eyes would be glued to it. As soon as we arrived we saw the guards finish their rounds, so we knew we had about 15 minutes to act undisturbed.

To get in you had to pass through a pair of automatic roll-up doors in hard rubber, like those that are used to unload goods from a lorry to a warehouse. As soon as we entered we found ourselves in an environment straight out of a science fiction novel. The deposit was new and illuminated. Everything was immobile, even the air. All sounds were muffled. The trains emitted a continuous buzz, it was like being in another dimension. The yellows and brilliant whites conferred an even more space base-like atmosphere. It was really a surreal spot and seeing all those trains together was moving. In a moment, without thinking twice, we threw ourselves on them with a sole objective. The excitement could be felt in the air, it was tangible: elation mixed with mad adrenaline.

This adventure united us a lot and many of us ended up forming lasting friendships from this shared experience. I was particularly impressed that day by a young beanpole that wrote Shampo. Though he was only 16 years old, when me and Dumbo went for our rounds of inspection he came with us and after an initial hesitation he jumped in to look. He did what I call "the mental leap" in front of my eyes. It's a particular moment for a writer. The first time you overcome your fears and take a leap of faith. I liked what I saw in his eyes because I understood that like us, he had the same madness in his brain.

Robin
>

NEW KIDS

In '97/'98 as a crew we had become an important reference point for the many kids that were getting into graffiti in Milan. We called them "ciampolini", I think Oneman came up with the term. It sounded good because it gave the idea of these small, timid kids. Since we had also been through it before we tried to be friendly when they came to the Piazza, some of them really inspired tenderness. We would give them the first pointers. The majority of them limited themselves to just hanging out with us, looking at what we did, others that were particularly into it, like Dance or Risk, with time became active members of Lords. Some even became quite daring and courageous.

OAS for example, were sick! It was with them that I went to the tunnel to do my first coloured whole-car in the subway. They were maybe 14 years old at most, but they were so into painting in the tunnel that they managed to find a brand new spot and figure out how to get in all by themselves. On their first attempt they actually did a whole-train, the maximum you could aim for. With much patience they had spent days monitoring the situation and figuring out how the surveillance worked and how to deactivate the alarms. They would lift the external grates to make the alarms go off, and then, hidden in the vicinity, would check how long it took the guards to arrive. Mirko in particular, had started experimenting many different systems to disconnect the alarm and even figured out how to bypass the electrical circuits. Going down into a tunnel is no easy task. Apart from the problem of the alarms, the grating you had to lift to get in was real heavy and it was impossible to open from underneath. Many a writer was arrested in the tunnel and I remember at least a couple of heart-thumping escapes.

Daze
>

ROMOLO

August '98 in Milan was a summer month like any other: crazy heat and nothing to do. In that period subway actions were sporadic, we had only gone to the shed on Labour Day when public transportation wasn't in service, but at night nobody dared paint in the hangar. When the first nocturnal raids started occurring they sparked a pretty inflamed period with a situation that had never been seen: the green line was trashed, one every two trains had panels, end-to-ends, even some top-to-bottoms. I remember one of the first T2Bs I saw was by Hell, Mirko and Humus from OAS. That train kept running, it was absolutely incredible and unthinkable only a couple months earlier. Everybody that painted in that period would meet up in Cimiano and that's where we passed our days, smoking joints, eating junk food, taking mad photos. It was an idyllic situation, no beef, you'd just go to Cimiano whenever you could and always find at least ten other kids waiting for their panel on the benches of the platform. Usually we'd paint in Gorgonzola and Cologno, getting in at night by sneaking under the tent of the shed, there were almost always ten or more of us, so even when we got caught we'd walk instead of run away, there were only two guards so they couldn't do anything but send us out: in some cases they even had a heavy set of rocks thrown at them in response. The only limit to painting in the shed was that there were no platforms on top of which to reach the whole-car, so when the first T2Bs by OAS started circulating it aroused a fair amount of surprise in all of us. Those kids were on point, we thought they must have surely found a spot in a tunnel since in Milan they're 'platformed' the whole length through. And so it was. A few weeks later we organised a whole-train together which should have been the first whole-train in the history of the Milanese subway. The line-up was composed of Mirko, Humus and Hell who were to realise an OAS triple whole-car, Robin who did a single whole-car, me and Neuro doing a whole-car together and then

Dumbo. We agreed to meet at the subway stop of Romolo at 6:30 on a Sunday morning, close to the staircase that accessed the mezzanine of the station. The air was a mixture of tension and excitement, like that of a big event that keeps you holding your breath until you're out of the manhole. A whole-train on the green line was not an everyday occurrence. We waited for Dumbo for a while but there was no sign of him and we could wait no longer, it was getting late and so we walked towards the park next to the station where the manhole was.

That was my first time in a tunnel and I was mad nervous. We got closer to the grating, one step after another in the grass, between needles, until arriving on top of it with our feet; a gust of air coming from the ventilation fans warmed us and we started smelling the typical tunnel smut that fills your nostrils. Robin checked the alarm and, as expected, it was deactivated. Mirko had blocked it the day before. Until '99 in fact ATM alarms functioned only at night and so you could easily go in the day, open the grating, deactivate the alarm and go back later without anybody having checked on it. Even though it was day it was anyway a wise precaution to shut it off before going down, and so that had been done in this occasion as well. All good, we shook our cans and with our backpacks on our shoulders started descending the ladder that brought us to the tunnel.

Once down we were in a small room with a yellow door that separated us from our target. The subway was already in service and the parked train was about fifty metres away and positioned on the opposite side to us, so we waited until the trains coming from both directions had crossed this stretch, so we could be sure they wouldn't surprise us as we're running to

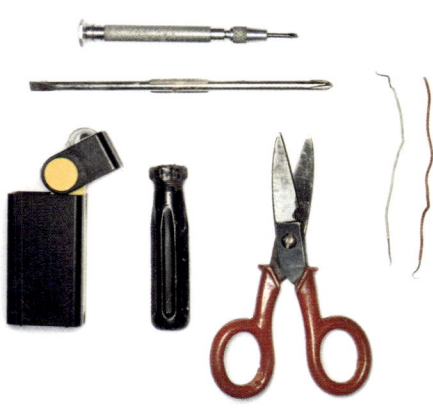

Alarm bypass kit.   – Daze

the lay-up on the other side. You could hear a train coming when it was still far away by putting your hand on the door and feeling the first vibrations of what in a couple dozen seconds would become a deafening roar echoing inside the pit. Once both trains had passed we opened the door and ran towards the parked train, crossing the tracks with ease since the green line is not electrified, and climbed onto the platform of the third rail that opens towards the right side of the tunnel (the lay-up is on the right side and in that point the tunnel becomes wider, forming a nook). There was also an emergency exit there, but we didn't know this yet. We passed the yellow door and got closer to the train, positioning ourselves in front of our respective carriages.

We started painting, making sure not to cover the glass windows even though we were doing whole-cars. There were headlights every ten metres behind us so the spot was pretty well-illuminated, the passing trains might have noticed the coloured windows. After a couple of minutes two trains almost surprised us and we all crouched to the ground so as to not be seen, after they'd passed we started filling the windows to then finish the outlines seeing we had to be done and ready to get out by the time the next trains came through. And that's exactly what happened, everything went smoothly and with the tunnel behind us we climbed out of the manhole and closed it. Even though the whole-train wasn't complete it was anyway the biggest composition the subway had ever seen and we were all pretty hyped. Big hugs were given out all around. We agreed to meet the next day in Cimiano to take photos and then each went his own way. That train was a real jab in the teeth, of those that leave a permanent mark. And the icing on the cake was that it ran for months.

A couple of weeks later OAS were organising another whole-train and to be sure the yard stayed calm until that day they thought it would be a good idea to put a huge chain on the manhole, the type that weighs like ten kilos with a lock that was impossible to cut. It was a big mistake. We didn't take it very well and so the night before the date they had fixed for their whole-train we went there and filled the lock with glue, so that the grating remained shut for both them and everybody else. Nobody ever went down that manhole again. but luckily there were other access ways: one very close to the station that was used only for nocturnal hits (cause it was too near the entrance of the station), and another unusual one in the middle of a forgotten parking lot. That yard rested for about a year after our attempt at a whole-train and only later was used for some night actions. The guards were on duty knowing that various people were painting there, which is why that area was later equipped with an alarm, perhaps the first magnetic alarm I remember ever having seen, and there was little to do against it. Or at least that's what it seemed to us at first. After a while Rute and I went to work trying to find a way of painting in Romolo like in the old days, early on Sunday mornings. We pondered on it a while before finding a solution: in the park from which we had descended the preceding year other than the grating there was also an emergency exit with a very narrow cement staircase that disappeared under the level of the ground, closed however at the other end by an alarmed door. If we had managed to open that door from the inside then we would have been able to enter with total ease from the park, which was definitely less visible than the station. To reach that door from the inside only one operable manhole remained, positioned smack in the middle of a parking lot where junkies and gays hung out, between the park and the station. It was different from all the others we were accustomed to using, indeed on top of the base in cement that rose from the ground there was a cage almost three metres high that covered the entire perimetre and was closed on top as well. On one side was a door, obviously closed, equipped with an anti-panic handle that could only be opened by slipping your hand in underneath it, basically you had to already be in the cage to do that. We walked around it for quite some time without actually achieving anything useful, but then we tried to get smart and look for helpful tools in a nearby construction site. We found a two-metre long rod and took it back with us. The situation was not of the best, with cars continuously passing, ATM buses full of people getting on and off, junkies taking their doses behind the bushes. We waited for a calm moment and slipped the rod between the bars of the cage, trying to hook it onto the handle of the door, which was certainly no simple task and took various attempts. In the end we forced it open and the door made a noisy "clank". We were now on the grate and what still had to be opened was the manhole, so we stuck in a pair of hooks and managed to lift it pretty easily, though doing everything in the light of day certainly complicated things. We risked being spotted by the drivers of the buses that could warn the ATM vigilance. After the manhole had been opened only one of us went inside, until reaching a nook in the tunnel. Once the trains had transited on each side he could cross the tunnel and briskly walk on the platform until reaching the opposite side of the train. Here is where the emergency exit we knew nothing of a year earlier was. Once the alarms were deactivated with the usual shoestring technique that door could be opened, after which was the long spiral staircase that led to the middle of the park. It was done. This door, once it had been opened from the inside, became the entrance for the rest of the group; we waited for about half an hour just to be sure everything had gone the right way, and then descended to the tunnel. Once down, the train of the green line would be five metres away from the exit, a small concentrate of magic. Unfortunately, just like in Bisceglie, this yard never saw a panel actually circulate, because only three months later they stopped parking trains in this lay-up and so an era was over: a train of the green line has never been seen parked along the rail line since, a real shame, because it really was one of the most adrenaline-filled moves ever, as well as the best way of starting a Sunday.

Robin
>

GREEN LINE

VMD and the younger OAS and CRZ found their dimension in the scene of Milan by painting the subway. The green line was running painted! It was the first time. In the beginning we were hitting the deposits three or four times a week, maybe with seven-eight people at once, sometimes even fifteen. Each of us would paint a different train so that the ATM (Transit Company of Milan) wouldn't have the time to buff every single piece and was forced to let at least a couple of painted cars out. In addition, the attacks would continue during the day inside the trains.

Armed with markers loaded with Nero Inferno (an ink called Hell Black) we would sign everywhere. The ATM were unprepared to deal with this explosion and the rest of the Writing scene of Milan was impressed. People that had ignored me for years were now looking for me, wanting to come paint with us. In the Milan of 1998 there was talk of nothing else. Some friends came from Basel to paint, and with them other foreigners. Milanese Writing became famous in all of Europe and also an attraction for many writers abroad.

Daze
>

EURO TOUR 1999

It was July of 1999 when we left for our tour of Europe. That trip ended up being more than we imagined as it would affect all our actions in the following years. The Inter-Rail was fairly recent and few people in Italy were going abroad to paint. There was no sign of the low cost flights that abound today: you either took the train or moved by car. It was me, Toni and Sway and the first stop was Barcelona. We had stocked up on what were supposed to be enough Montanas to last the whole journey, not including the ones we would jack along the way of course. We didn't have a set plan, you just leave and see how it goes. I remember the first person I heard by phone was Opak.

Luckily he gave me the contact info of Vino, a really great guy who immediately set up to meet us at Bunker Store, the historical shop of Barcelona. Not much later we were already hitting various spots to paint trains. The graffiti mentality in Milan, especially when it came to bombing subway trains, was still pretty unripe at the time and apart from a couple of hot spots, the general situation was chill. I realised the enormous difference that separated Italy from the rest of Europe when I saw kids like Sear of TD, a Swedish writer, brilliantly close a panel in 15 minutes when our average was still going around three quarters of an hour.

Sear explained to us that the situation in Sweden was real tense and you had to adapt this way. Perhaps that's one of the reasons Sweden became home to some very simple styles of incredible visual impact. Abroad I learnt to move in a completely different manner from that in which my crew and I had been used to. Day by day we experimented new techniques: first the palanca[1] in Barcelona, then in Paris, where we did a backjump with Kesie of GAP in broad daylight while people were getting on the train.

Today this is the norm in many European cities, but ten years ago it was experimental, at least in Milan we had never tried it yet. In our yards we had an "indefinite" amount of time, it was useless to risk more adventurous spots for a ten minute panel. But for that extra something that made the difference , adrenaline, it was worth daring.

After Barcelona the next stop was Rotterdam, then Cologne, until arriving in Switzerland, where Dent of TS brandished his theory of "No risk no fun". That was his motto: if it was too easy he wasn't feeling it. "Everybody can do it, I'm not interested" he would repeat before every action. His fixation was the *Red-bean*, a completely red train that no longer circulates now. It was substituted by the hummingbird-coloured ones, a difficult switch to swallow for any writer who grew up with a determined model of train. Time passed and we continued to practice on panels and whole-cars. We were nearing the end of our tour, just a few dozen kms from Milan.

Everything was about to go back to normal, the usual yards, the usual 2 hour panels in FS. The daily routine, nothing more. But something was stirring in our minds: the idea that what we had done so far was just a waste of time. All of a sudden we realised we had never taken advantage of a series of possibilities that, after our trip, were now within our reach. The legends surrounding the subway finally gave way to a new view, and we would go home with the hammering thought of killing the subway. And that's exactly what happened.

❶ Method for painting the subway invented by the Spanish: wait for the train to surface above ground, out of the tunnel, then pull the emergency lever, at that point all writers exit the doors and bomb the car in the few minutes it's blocked

Daze
>

SEPTEMBER 1999

My average day was that of your typical lazy-ass student, wake-up at 11 tops, and days spent smoking thousands of joints in the University plaza. Every once in a while I would slip a class in, but mostly I spent my time drawing.

It's at University that I met Truffa (Rute), who became my regular partner in all actions, one of those people you know you can count on 100%. At the time you couldn't trust any information regarding the subway, simply because there was none. Today you can say "I'm going to check out the situation in Molino". Ten years ago nobody could have imagined there were even trains down there, and even a simple logic like ours was really quite abstract.

We studied the map of the lines and came to the conclusion that in the morning almost surely the atemmini[2] could not have been using only the trains parked in the yard at night, since it was too far away. The line we wanted to hit was the red, practically immaculate at the time (the green had already lived through a wave of heavy bombing in '98), and on this premise the result was automatic: on the Bisceglie branch there were no yards. There had to be trains in the tunnel, it was mathematics. And indeed we were not mistaken.

❷ ATM workers, the Milanese transit company. Literally Azienda Trasporti Milanesi

> CONTINUES ON PAGE 198

> CONTINUES FROM PAGE 197

Robin
>

BOMBING THE TUNNEL

To paint subway trains in the tunnel we would get in at 9:00 in the evening, just like any normal subway rider, and we'd stop on the platform right under the surveillance camera. We'd wait about 15 minutes to see if the ATM worker sitting at the monitors was paying attention or not, and if all went well, as soon as the trains had passed in both directions, we'd slip into the tunnel and run to the train sitting in the middle of the two main tracks. Once we got there we'd hide inside of it. The doors of the carriages weren't blocked from outside, you just had to be careful not to close them behind you. Then, once inside, we would shake our cans and wait until the subway that passed in front of the side we intended to paint had transited. As soon as it passed we'd get out in a rush and start painting. At that hour trains would come through about every ten minutes so we had to stop every seven-eight minutes to get back into the convoy and wait for the passage of the successive train, to then start again. In the span of two or three rounds we usually managed to finish a piece. Obviously the more you stayed the higher the risks were. Sometimes the driver of a passing train would notice the pieces, or even worse, see us creeping inside the still train and give the alarm. The 1 line also had high tension in the third rail so you had to be careful about where you put your feet.

Daze
>

BISCEGLIE

What we were now missing to get the operation started was finding the right grating through which to descend into the tunnel. To the battle cry of Take-me-to-la-grada, two of us set off on Truffa's scooter in the direction of Bisceglie. It ended up not being so difficult finding the grate. It was between a parking lot and the primary street that passes in front of the station, in a little depression of the ground that slightly hid it, a few dozen metres after the end of the platform, but on the same level as the street. A 100kg cast-iron giant. Opening it was child's play, there was a cylinder with a square slot under which a small metal plate had been welded to block the opening of the manhole; all you had to do was stick a metal rod in and turn it 90 degrees and you were good to go. You could even close the grating again when you left, kind of like you would with your own home. In our eyes it was unbelievable. I still remember Sway's expression when a couple of days later we were organising a whole-car without even having the certainty there were actually trains down there. We had not actually gone down the ladder of the tunnel and were simply planning based on hypotheses and considerations. But everything went as programmed: Sway descended towards the tunnel and came back up super fast all hyped, rejoicing "it's there, it's there... right in front of the door, I don't believe it!"

The reply was immediate: "okay, let's do a married-couple, we should have enough paint". And the next morning on the platform of Loreto we saw the first whole-car in the history of the red 1 line flash past, a silver 70's outlined in black. That would mark the beginning of a new era of massive bombing in the subway tunnel. In concurrence with the first actions in Bisceglie, the friendship that had already tied us to VMD for two years was consolidated, bringing to the fusion that gave birth to VMD70's. In a matter of four months the yard was literally trashed with over thirty whole-cars in different compositions, of which two whole-trains, a triple whole-car and I don't even remember how many married-couples, silver and coloured, all stuff that had never been seen on the red before. The ATM staff, as dim as they may be, were anyway among the most reactive and as expected the party didn't last forever. One night we had organised a really crazy move: since it was practically impossible in those days for a painted train to get more than a run, we decided to change technique. We planned four whole-cars on four different trains, one of them had to run the whole morning, they couldn't just cancel all four at once. And so we went down that ladder we now knew by heart, divided in the middle by a landing, and then down again towards that door that to us was the entrance to paradise and for the atiemmini was the door to the toilet (the room under the grating contained the bathrooms of the subway drivers); we positioned ourselves and some were already tracing the first letters. I was looking around a bit more than usual, I was quite far from the exit, and when you're in a tunnel this becomes a disadvantage in the case of an escape; I tried to convince myself that everything was calm, but this time around things were not going to go as usual. At first nothing seemed out of place: the trains, the silence, the smell of paint that was starting to saturate the little air that circulated in the tunnel, but when I raised my head upwards I saw a brand new video camera right above me. At that point I called for a getaway, filling my lungs with all the air I could. We didn't run out from the manhole we usually used but from the emergency exit (much more agile when you're in a hurry). Our car however was parked right in front of the grating that had been left open since it was too heavy to close above our heads. So we had to go back there. To be honest nobody was to be seen and so once we were outside we weren't too worried. Too bad they had been observing us from the station that was only a couple dozen metres away. And so as we approached the grating a security vehicle screeched to a halt in front of us. From that moment on everything happened real fast, we raced to the car and put it into reverse gear. We left the parking lot and threw ourselves into a small street on the right, the security car was following us pedal to the metal but we managed to keep them at a distance of about twenty metres, and after having taken a couple of one-way streets in the wrong direction and another couple of small alleys we finally lost them. After that night we never painted that yard again, we tried a couple of times but without that much effort. If I have to compare it to other places we hit, all in all it was the easiest spot; we had mad fun that winter and that chapter was closed in this way, somewhat haphazardly, with a car getaway and no regrets.

Daze
>

INGANNI

I had known Mirko (aka Fube) for about two years and he was someone who knew a thing or two about subways. His crew, OAS, was a pretty young group and they had all become known in those years after doing an OAS triple whole-car on the green line in Romolo in '98 that ran for various months. While we had Bisceglie ablaze they were painting the shed of Molino Dorino, but that's not all they were up to. OAS also painted in the 'platformed' lay-up that was a couple of stops after Inganni, where trains were parked the whole night. We knew this because in the morning, while we were waiting for our trains to pass so we could photograph them, we'd see some of their stuff coming from that direction and vice versa - they were seeing ours coming from Bisceglie. So Mirko started looking for the manhole we were using and ended up finding it and they did a triple whole-car there. And so a few evenings later when we saw each other he said: "Hey basley, no getting away this time, I got your hole". I played vague until he started flaunting some details that could leave no doubt on the matter and so we decided to go there together in the following days. We organised the whole deal and that night I also met Ank (aka Erotik), who would later become my favourite partner in extreme actions. We got to the manhole but once we reached the door we found nothing but a naked tunnel without a single train. We climbed back up pretty disappointed about the whole situation. So Mirko, to alleviate the shitty mood, proposed we go to Inganni, seeing it was only a couple of metres away. We ran to the car and drove the distance that separated us from the manhole of Inganni. What was down there resembled a maze, there were various emergency exits, rooms hosting the polling booths that electrically fed the whole line, corridors and other rooms, in total there must have been at least ten doors, but for the moment the route we had to take to get to the lay-up was rather simple compared to what we would end up doing in the following years. The manhole we used was one of the earlier ones from the 60's, they were already rare at the time, I think they no longer exist today. It was made of two very light gratings that opened like a pair of windowpanes, except on the floor. If you weren't careful you risked setting off the alarm that was positioned under one of the gratings. You could easily see it from the outside: a box with a little arm that was pressed by the weight of the manhole cover, once you raised it the alarm would signal the breach to central control and the ATM security guards would arrive in a matter of moments. Basically it was a shitty alarm that could at most have kept children away. All you needed was a shoestring with which to tie the arm to the box and that was it: you opened it, went down and served yourself. The only catch was that you had to do this trick from the inside cause you couldn't just open and then block the alarm, you would have been back to square one. Time was in our favour and the rust did the rest. The left grating was a little loose and blocked by the right one that kept the alarm pressed. But if one

person put their weight on the left and another pulled forcefully on the right 'sklank!', the grating without the alarm would open. Because it was very narrow, the first to go down would block the alarm so that the whole thing could be opened completely to facilitate both the entry and exit of the others. Then down. Ladder, landing, ladder. You're then in the tunnel, under your feet a putrid marsh that collects the water discharges of the station, filled with a greenish foam they use to clean the railways with. To the left is a door and in front another double door, but the time for those entrances had not yet come. We first had to go around the water, then go back the other side and slip into a hole in the wall that seemed intended for a non-existent door; from there you had to pull yourself up and climb the ladder that took you up to the tunnel. In that stretch there was a boardwalk of a couple metres and then a staircase that step by step ended up on the cement platform in the middle of the tunnel. Already from the stairs you could savour the view of the red and white muzzle of what was waiting for you a couple of metres away. In the meantime however, you couldn't forget what you had behind you: at least three minutes separated us from the exit of that yard (without calculating the pauses along the way to check the situation), but when you run, jump, climb and descend ladders and tunnels, those three minutes can seem like an eternity. The situation was still calm in that period and everything went smoothly, as in various previous occasions. It was one of the most fun and most dangerous yards. Following a number of close escapes at night we took the habit of going there when the station was open (that is with the subway in service) to avoid the night rounds of the guards, and that added even more adrenaline. Hidden in the nooks of the boardwalk above the tunnel we would wait for the trains to pass in both directions, usually they would transit a couple of minutes apart, and then we'd go down to the platform. The trains would pass about every seven minutes and because we were in the middle of the tunnel we couldn't just stay there cause the drivers would have seen us. So we'd hide in the train we were painting, forcing the doors open and laying on the ground so as to not be visible. Once the trains passed we'd go back out and continue what we had started, but we had to get a move on, because only seven minutes remained to finish everything and be out. Too much paint in the tunnel wasn't good, because if trains passed they'd push the air towards the station and the risk was for the smell to reach the platforms. The last time we tried this move on that manhole was a Sunday afternoon during the summer. The grating was in the middle of the sidewalk, thirty centimetres from the road, in full view. Basically we slipped out of the tunnel onto that sidewalk with dozens of cars and people passing by and then we quickly ran off in front of the astonished bystanders. In that occasion I was the first to climb out and behind me on the ladder were Mirko and Toni. Before lifting the grate we always checked outside, to avoid finding anyone in the immediate vicinity of the manhole. That day there was an asshole with a bicycle standing right on top of the grating with his gaze towards the tunnel, scanning underneath. Toni, who couldn't see him, asked "Hey Daze, is everything ok? Can we go out?", and I answered "Yes" without a hint of hesitation. I hit the grate and got out as if it were nothing, behind me Toni and Mirko did the same. Once outside we flung ourselves into a park nearby, we threw all our spray cans and continued running. We hid ourselves for a while and after 20 minutes returned in that area to pick up our car but all hell had broken loose: a number of automobiles, belonging to police and ATM vigilance, were all around the manhole and our friend on a bike was animatedly gesticulating in the middle of all those cops. If we had been hesitant about exiting it would have been much worse, a hazardous decision can in some occasions save your behind. Something similar happened again in Inganni a few years later. The situation had greatly changed, on the platform a surveillance camera had been installed that monitored the train, so we had to paint on the rail tracks, plus the manhole had been changed with a much heavier one made of cast iron, with a magnetic induction alarm. Other doors in there had also been protected with alarms, so getting in became a labyrinthine experience that forced you to go through seven different rooms and open a total of nine doors before actually getting to the train. That time we had been painting about 15 minutes when some loudspeakers started diffusing a number of confused messages like "graffiti bastards", "you ain't 'getting away this time!", and "we closed you in", but without anybody actually appearing in the tunnel. So we thought, well, if they were really here they wouldn't be calling us from the speakers they would just come

to Vimodrone, where Fuck had left his car because he had gotten to Milan with mine. I thought that if I couldn't find his whip in Vimodrone it would have meant they were safe and had returned home.
But when I got to the piazza my blood turned cold, Fuck's car was still there. I thought they must have been caught, there was no other explanation. I didn't move for a couple minutes, as if trying to convince myself of the opposite, but there was nothing I could do and all that was left for me was to return home. After ten minutes I received a phone call, it was Erotik, who asked me "Where the hell are you? I've been waiting outside your house to go to work, did something happen?" I couldn't understand, (the normal procedure when you got busted was not to call anyone), and besides that the question was absurd because I didn't work with him, so after a brief pause, I turned the question around: "I'm fine, what about you?" An explosion of yells filled my ears from the other line. It was a vortex of curses at the ATM! We all met up in the piazza of Vimodrone and celebrated with mad joints while we recounted how we had gotten away.
The way the whole thing went down was actually pretty weird when we put everything together, those bastards knew we were down there and were stupidly hoping that by talking out of the loudspeakers we would run out so they could catch us in the square outside.
They only waited for 15 minutes, after which, not seeing us, they probably thought we had used another route to get

and the situation of the subway in Milan was already pretty heated. The previous bombing waves at Inganni and Bisceglie had awoken the passion for Writing in mad people and that's why you could notice many panels by other crews apart from the usual names. The competition started rising and the hunt for spots was open to everyone. Among the available yards, Molino was missing in the roll call, it was one of the last to be discovered seeing everyone prevalently painted in the end stations of the tunnels. That there were trains parked in Molino was something everyone had guessed, they could be glimpsed at in the evening if you scrutinised the tunnel from the platform, but from there to actually finding the right move to get to them was a long way. In that period there were many of us scheming on it, trying to figure out how to get there, apart from us VMD70's there was OAS as always, plus another crew, NBW. Though we had more experience than them when it came to tunnel incursions it was NBW that stole the record as the first to hit in Molino Dorino and they immediately came out with two or three diurnal whole-cars. They anticipated us by only a few days, just a couple of nights earlier Rute and I had gone scouting the area without finding the manhole hidden by the high grass in the field. OAS on the other hand had already found the manhole but had not yet organised a nocturnal action, so we decided to do so together briefly later. We organised the first night incursion in Molino early in October, five of us with five personal whole-cars. It was me, Mirko,

not do so? We spent the following months doing whole-cars upon whole-cars, even five or six at a time a real pandemonium for the ATM that fell into its knees before this fire power. It the year of the turning point for the green line was '98 – when it started running painted – for the red it was 2000. We had no restraints: the norm on the green had been panels and end-to-ends, on the red it was whole-cars. In November I remember some days in which you could see as many as 15 whole-cars running contemporaneously, some of which had been circulating for over a month; in little over a year we had gone from a situation in which the legends of infallibility of the red subway seemed to preclude any possibility of success on that line to having dozens of whole-cars moving every day. Having so much stuff circulating gave us a strong sense of penetration of the city as if, finally, after all the years of myths surrounding it, we had managed to contaminate it in a profound manner. If you live in Milan you cannot avoid the subway and entering a carriage covered by a whole-car is like entering in someone's home as a guest, the moment you step over the threshold you implicitly accept its rules. This idyllic situation lasted almost a year, in the meantime they put a new alarm on the manhole, forgetting however to notch or the second shutter of the grating over the first. This complicated the access seeing there were some moments in which you would remain clasping onto the manhole without much else to hold on to, your legs hanging over empty space, until you could hook your foot onto the first step of the ladder. The real problems started later on however, following a summer in which week after week we had had various InterRailers coming from every part of the world, the situation was really at the limit of sustainability for the ATM. It was one particularly unlucky evening that Neuro and Rute got busted, while they were with Dent and Beam from Zurich. They were doing four whole-cars when various guards, practically when they had finished everything, arrived from the station. With the emergency exit at hand they all flung themselves towards it, sure of an easy escape, but security had them in a trap; once the last door had been opened, the one that let out into the open, they found two guards holding their guns at them and threatening them to stop right there. They immediately turned back the other way to try and escape from where they had entered but by then the tunnel was full of vigilantes, one of which actually shot straight at Rute, who in the meantime had reached the head of the train closest to the manhole from which they had entered. Luckily he didn't get hit but the glass of the train window behind him shattered to pieces. They all hid, some on the roof of a convoy, some on the floor of another, others under the platforms. The last to be found was Rute, at 6:00 in the morning. When they brought him out, passing through the mezzanine in handcuffs, there was a crowd of people waiting for their train that started insulting him: the line had been blocked to complete the hunt for the man on the dead track, where he had stayed hidden under the platform only a few centimetres away from the electrified rail. He was only found after they turned on the tension of the line to move all the parked trains away. Two hours later, after

> CONTINUES ON PAGE 200

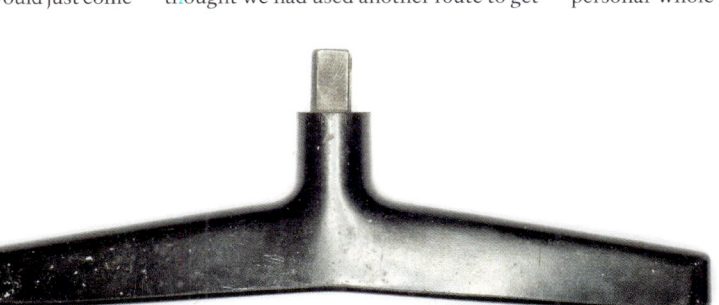

The key to the subway doors   – Daze

and get us, so after initially distancing ourselves a couple dozen metres from the trains we went back, finished our panels and took an abundance of photos in no hurry. In reality the vigilantes actually were there. We were busy taking pictures when two arrived from the station. We ran in the opposite direction towards the exit and started the rigmarole of doors and rooms, one, two, three, but at the fourth I found two guards about three metres to my right, that started shouting "Stop, stop!" as soon as they saw me. I turned to the left and threw myself towards the next door, the others backed up and ran the other way, so we were separated. I got out of the emergency exit into the middle of the square (that would shortly be invaded by police and ATM security), and flung myself over the perimetre wall of a villa. Once in the garden I climbed over a wire fence that bordered a construction site and there I decided to hide until morning. In the following minutes I heard those bastards yelling from a distance and in my head I pictured the worst for my partners. I only left at 6 in the morning, after almost three hours. I went to my car and rushed

away, which was not the case of course. So when they entered the tunnel they left all the exits open and we managed to escape in that labyrinth because the paradox was that we knew how to get around better than they did. Again it was a hazardous decision that actually saved us. We said our goodbyes and all went home, not however, before I gave Fuck the keys of his car that he had left on the dashboard of my Fiat before going down the tunnel.

Daze
>

MOLINO DORINO

Molino Dorino was more than a simple yard, the quantity of stuff that came out of that spot cannot be compared to any other deposit of the Milanese subway. Under that field of wheat rested three trains of the red line, apart from those inside the shed nearby and another one parked in the station: a real luxury. It was the year 2000, more precisely it was September

Rute, Fuck and Sway, and after opening the grate we hurried down the little ladder, one by one with our bags overflowing with spray cans held by our mouths so as to have our hands free and be able to hold on to the rungs. We got to the nook of the tunnel and leaned our heads towards the station for a couple of seconds, checking there were no workers on the platforms; from there we then ran towards the end of the dead track, jumping over the shaky blocks of bricks that were found every ten metres on the platforms to the sides of the tunnel. Once at the other end, close to the emergency exit, we would arrange ourselves so as to paint more than one train, this way we kept everything in check from various angles and made sure we didn't have any undesired visitors. We didn't take hours, in that period 30 minutes were sufficient to finish a coloured whole-car, with a couple of tricks we would close it really quickly. Speed was everything, reducing the time it took meant drastically reducing the risks and every effort in this sense was welcome; filling a piece with a single hand was just stupid if you were doing a whole-car and could use two, so why

> CONTINUES FROM PAGE 199

the crime scene investigators had finished collecting all their evidence regarding the shots fired in the tunnel, the line went back to work and the guard that had fired his gun was taken to the police station. For a while Molino slumbered in the calmness that followed, nobody wanted to go there for some time, until Neuro, Fuck and Due inaugurated the second season of bombing with a completely new approach; they no longer painted at the end of the dead rail with the risk of getting closed in, but at the opposite head of the train, the one in proximity to the grating and station. In addition, to obtain the maximum security possible, they put a lookout on the manhole, in a position from which the parking lot was clearly visible, so that in case security arrived their cars could be seen pulling into it. Another lookout was placed under the manhole to check in the direction of the station, and would call out to those painting were there to be problems from there. With this new technique we painted dozens and dozens of times in the following months without ever being seen. It was a reliable method, we always managed to exit before the vigilantes even reached the platforms of the station. It went on this way until too many people started knowing about Molino, by then it was so crowded that various times I met other writers in the tunnel or found freshly painted panels; it was time to change setting, or invent something new. We wanted to paint at unexpected times and moments so as to avoid the routine rounds. By doing so we could always be the first to paint on any given evening, without the risk of someone preceding us. Plus the ATM probably would never have dreamt of instituting extra rounds, they weren't used to incursions outside the normal time frame. Normally at night they would leave three trains in Molino, the first two were parked shortly after dinnertime, staying there until about midnight, when they would park the third. This meant there were about three hours of useful time during which to work and co-ordinate a plan. The other side of the medal was represented by the regular situation during ATM service hours, painting the red line meant you had to keep in mind that the third rail was electrified. When you cross tracks through which you know 700 volts of tension are passing, your priorities radically change; speed and hurry take a backseat, your gaze is fixed

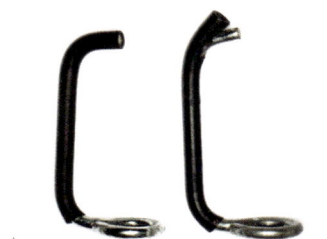

Hooks for lifting manholes   — Daze

underneath you to avoid taking a wrong step. We would organise ourselves once we arrived at the manhole in the middle of the wheat field, but not before having checked that the ventilation system of the tunnel was on, so as to avoid the smell of paint reaching the station. Once we descended we would lie and wait for a while, trying to sharpen our sight and sound so we could catch the best moment to fling ourselves over to the lay-up. All this was done in plain view of the station, which was perfectly aligned to the dead track where our target train was. The standard procedure was to wait for the train at the platform to leave for Sesto, so as to completely empty the place of people. From that moment we had 2-3 minutes to reach the parked train before another would reach the platform with its driver facing exactly towards the lay-up. Once we got to the central platform we would hide behind the ladder that was used to reach the lay-up at the centre of the tunnel without having to cross the tracks, which we avoided so as to make less noise. We would stay there, with our eyes fixed towards the station until the train would position itself at the stop and remain immobile. The passengers would exit and enter in a rush and not much later the headlights would turn from white to red: it meant the driver had inverted the direction of the train and was about to exit one end to get into the other and leave after about ten minutes. That was the moment! Index finger pressing on the fat pink, then silver fill, black outline, whole-car "VMD". That night it was me, Siero and Erotik: everything went smoothly, without a hitch, the typical well-executed plan. It all lasted about twenty minutes with a pause in the middle to avoid being spotted by the second train that was pulling into the station. When we concluded the whole-car we quickly gathered our stuff and swiftly made our

way towards the exit. The thing I preferred about this plan of action was the lapsing of minutes that made everything even more adrenaline-full, you couldn't mess up, the passing of time was highlighted by the trains arriving at the platform, everything was over in a matter of 20 minutes and when we got out it was only 11 in the evening. Too bad it lasted so briefly, very soon it became impossible to enter from that manhole. They welded it as usual with a slab that prevented you from opening the second shutter without opening the first with the alarm, which made it in fact impossible to go through there without setting off the alarm; well perhaps not really impossible, but it was anyway sufficient to make things a lot calmer in that yard for a while. Various people in that period were talking about Molino like it was played out: the more people think that, the easier it is for others to paint there once things have settled down. All you need is a minimum level of ingenuity to devise a new move, especially when you're dealing with the alarm systems that the ATM uses. When everyone hits the same spot only because they've heard about it you really risk loosing control of the situation, you're on the very limit and they can bust you in any moment: when a yard gets played out like that nobody goes there for mad long, until someone else finds a new way of getting in and others find out about it. Luckily we never lacked in imagination, it took us a couple of weeks but in the end we managed to get back in. We had in front of us two manholes: one with a ladder but also an alarm and one with neither. Initially we thought of building a ladder ourselves with ropes so we could descend the one without alarm, but in case of a getaway it would have been a lethal trap. And if we used the ropes to climb down then somebody would have had to stay outside to hold on to them. There was nothing left to do but find a way of opening the manhole with the alarm; which was pretty complicated seeing the old piston ones had by now been replaced and were only a distant memory. Seeing I had spent an entire summer installing electrical gates I started studying the new ATM alarms, mostly they were electromagnetic induction systems on which the old shoestring technique didn't work. The alarms were composed of two elements, an inductor and a magnet; the magnet was normally inserted in the block that was welded to the grate shutter, the inductor instead was fixed on the framework of the manhole

itself. As long as the two elements were touching, when the grate was closed, the magnet exerted a magnetic field on the inductor, maintaining the circuit of the alarm in a normal state. Once it was opened however, the variation of the magnetic field signalled the breach of the manhole directly to the central headquarters of ATM vigilance. It was definitely not an impeccable system and so I tooled up so as to have a 'kit', that is everything necessary to bypass the sensors. What was needed was a medium-sized Torx screwdriver, another smaller flat one to work on the clamps of the system, a couple of pieces of electric cable skinned at the extremities, a pair of scissors, a flashlight and an ATM ticket. Starting from the sensor you had to locate the different boxes of the system and understand if it was sufficient to work on those in proximity of the alarm or whether you had to work on the others as well; then you proceeded to bypass them with the necessary care. The first thing however, was actually being inside the tunnel and to do so without setting the alarm off. The most painless solution seemed to be that of lowering myself down with ropes from the other manhole without the alarm. We got hold of a rope of about ten metres and knotted it in such a way as to form a sort of noose in which to slip a single leg. My partners held on to the other end with the necessary force and I made a little jump into the void until the rope was tight and there I was, with my ass dangling about six metres above ground. They slowly lowered me down and once on the ground I freed myself from the rope and climbed up the ladder of the manhole with the alarm, after having played around with the junction box underneath. Once right under the manhole I completed the operation by opening the box of the alarm. Between wires and clamps, I managed to bypass the system and close everything up, leaving a small piece of ATM ticket sticking out of an opening between the box and the cover, as a safety measure. Then go, everyone in! Seeing that manhole open from underneath and all my peoples invading the tunnel for the umpteenth time was a unique experience, it was like taking back a precious space they had withheld from us for a while. Molino was the yard par excellence. There is no spot in the subway that has been as known, controlled, schemed and studied as Molino. As much as we may have literally destroyed it, we felt that yard was like a second home.

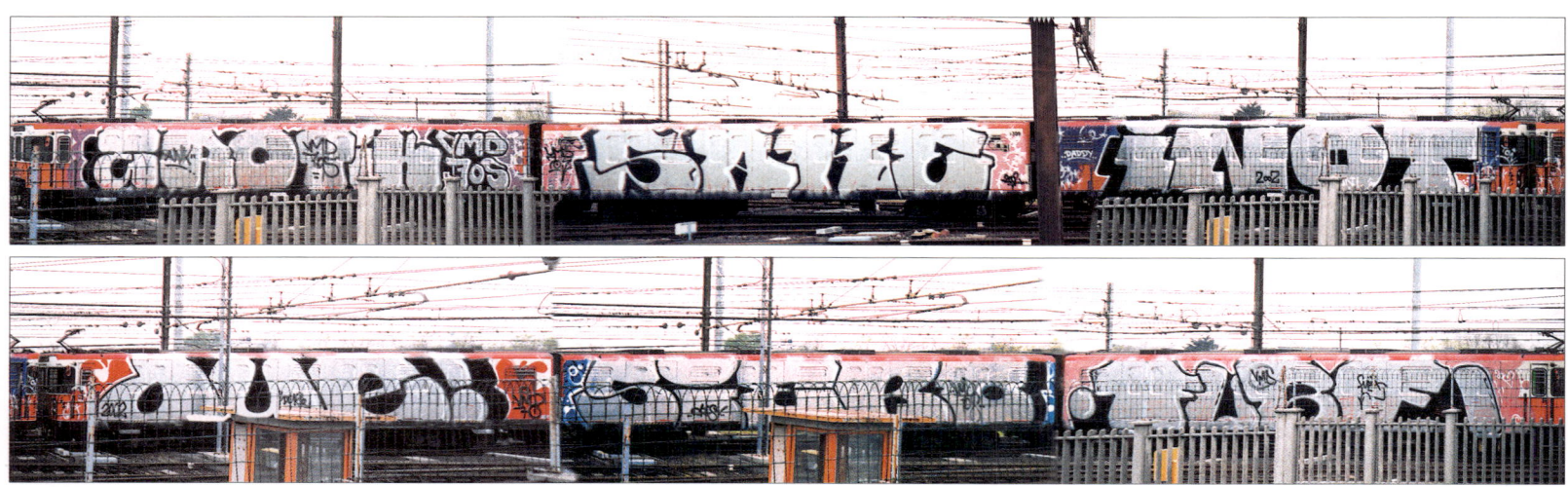

Whole-train on the red line by Erotik, Sake, Inot, Due, Siero, Fube : VMD '70   — Daze

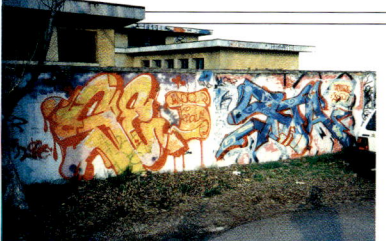

Page 206
>
Occupied Terrain vague
Treviso meat district

RAILWAY
ABACUS
—

The connections in Veneto during the 90's
>
Behind the scenes

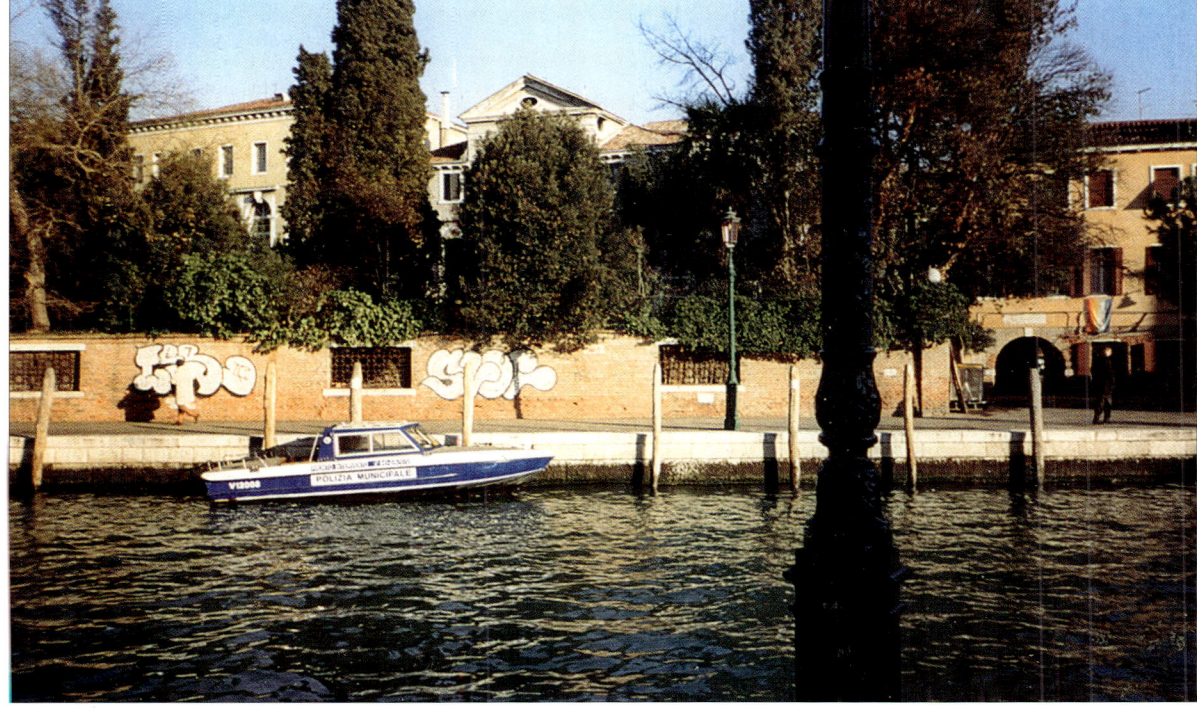

– Slog

During the 90's an intense network of encounters and exchange of experiences was taking place among the writers of the North-East, a circuit already strong in itself, that was further enhanced by the intensity and capillarity of the local railway system. Other than the principle State lines that branch out from the North-East to Milan, Bologna and the rest of Italy, the region can also count on an elevated number of private and semi-private lines that, however circumscribed and brief, compose in their entirety a particularly intense infrastructural weft of an almost metropolitan character. The first scene of the 90's came to instinctively associate the names of certain writers or of entire crews to a precise model of train. The *littorine*, the local orange trains, the whole National system of Interregionals, Regionals, and Intercitys, allowed the formation of groups of writers that were active on determined railway lines, almost as if in control of a specific portion of territory. The guys from Treviso and Bassano were associated to the typical *littorine* of their area, F2D from Venice to the *Prercioni* trains on which they concentrated all their productions, while the writers from Padua were identified by the red or maroon livery of regional and intercity trains that travelled on a national scale after leaving the local deposit of Campo di Marte, a yard of immense proportions.
The numerous types of carriages constituted the train playground of North-Eastern Italy and the different Names that were painted on them became testimonies of a scene that was numerically intense, stylistically heterogeneous, and difficult to contain.

The Writing scene in the North-East of Italy – particularly in Vicenza, Treviso, Padua and Venice-Mestre – grew with network logic, creating tight connections with other Italian cities.
Since the early 90's a triangle was formed between Bologna, Milan and the towns in the region of Veneto, stimulating reciprocal influences and collaborations. The contact of Mace from Treviso with Flycat from Milan for example gave birth to PWD, probably one of the first Italian groups to grasp the importance of street bombing and Writing on trains. This union was followed by a second, just as important, between CKC and writers Clout and Starch from Treviso. Vicenza also established a privileged relationship with Milan, thanks to the friendship that tied Skah, Onis and other local writers to Rendo: the common conception of Writing as the design of great murals, essentially connected to the obsessive study of aesthetics and theme compositions, led to the formation of a crew – TDK – that at the end of the 80's became a reference point for writers throughout Lombardy and Veneto. In Venice, Natas, one of the first writers of the Laguna[1], got in touch with TKA from Milan, with whom he shared

a real bomber spirit. Padua on the other hand became a set destination for certain writers of Bologna. One name above all is that of Rusty, who spent his military duty there, and together with Boogie formed FCE crew. A few years later, local writers EAD would establish a brotherly affiliation with DSP from Pesaro.

> [1] Or Lagoon, the figure of speech used for Venice as it is surrounded by water

Along with the connections to Milan and Bologna, writers in the North-East also developed a thick internal web of collaborations and exchanges between neighbouring cities: the kids from Vicenza, Treviso, Padua and Venice-Mestre shared their first experiences, mutually visiting each other in their respective cities during the weekend. The primary destination of these trips were halls of fame and hangouts, meeting spots loaded with meaning for writers but to which the rest of the population was indifferent; corners of the city, sometimes right in the historic centre, sometimes scattered in the industrial outskirts. In Vicenza for example, writers would congregate at the *Poste*, an apparently anonymous gallery in the centre, but an ideal place for breakers to dance in due

to the marble flooring. Additional activity in the city was concentrated in Skah's private hall of fame, which attracted writers from all over Veneto in search of TDK pieces to photograph. The hunt for these murals was so intense that it pushed Skah to white his walls right after he had painted and photographed them, so as to preserve the styles. In Treviso on the other hand, writers would gather on the benches of *Macello*, an empty urban space soon transformed into a hall of fame, through that typical process that occupies what is abandoned. In Padua the meeting spot coincided with the *Banche*, a garden at the back of a building complex which bordered the city. This was not only a gathering place for local writers but also for skaters, breakers and for an entire group that would subsequently take on the name of EAD. The fact that the spot was adjacent to a wide wall EAD had painted turned the *Banche* into a popular destination for writers from all over the region. And finally in Venice, given the particular conformation of the city, the place of reference for the Writing movement was the industrial zone, transferring the idea of halls of fame to the abandoned spaces of ex factories and particularly of deposits, which were

among the first places to be occupied. These locations allowed writers to paint undisturbed, experimenting in full freedom, almost unconsciously giving character to those small and intimate environments, visible only to those who knew them and thus characterised by a strong sense of belonging. Within the territory of the Lagoon the search for these abandoned spaces became a recurring practice throughout the years, urging the local writers to progressively paint the internal walls of the buildings with care in respecting the industrial architectural context. Keeping in harmony with the edifice, without subverting its pre-existent identity, neutralised the aggressive and wild approach of tags and throw-ups. It is for this reason that places like Forto Marghera hosted a form of Writing that was only slightly invasive, in which the aspect of content was joined by an emerging attention to the composition as a consequence of the specific characteristics of the spot the pieces were destined for. In addition in Veneto the possibility for the different local crews to meet and join was also favoured by the activity of the Palladium, a historic club in Vicenza and forefather of

> CONTINUED ON PAGE 202

ACW INTERNATIONAL / NORTH-EAST

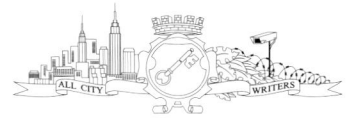

Main contributors:
Boogie, Capo, Cento, Fakso, Iave, Joys, Kato,
Mace, Natas, Pako, Siso, Sat, Sika, Slog, Skah,
Vons, Zuek

In collaboration with:
©>>, 668, B52, EAD, F2D, GCT, LDR, MKS, MOD,
NYS, PWD, SI, TC, TDK

Cover photo:
Lab and Slog in Venice, 1999

LE POSTE IN VICENZA
—

Iave
>

I remember 1986, when I lived on the outskirts of Vicenza, a small town in the productive North-East. To evade the neighbourhood we would go to a games room right outside the city centre: 50 lire games guaranteed an excellent afternoon of fun and escapism. The place was called Markus and was full of skinheads, we would go in the back and play Pacman and Supermario. The upper-class centre of the city was only at three kilometres distance, but at the same time light years away. Tags and graffiti popped up on every corner, witnessing the existence of a hidden world, violent and fascinating. I would read and decipher everything, trying to find my own interpretation of this unique language. Rebel, 352, ESK, Jeffrey, KDS, DextOne, Lazer and Tronik filled my fantasies, I imagined them as warriors fighting against society, moving at night to leave their marks on the walls of the city. Jay-one was my first tag, dating back to '88, of which the only remaining traces are on my school notebooks, to which followed Javo, obtained by joining bits of my name and surname, which would then be transformed to Iavo and finally Iave.

Every once in a while on Saturdays I would go as far as the city centre, wandering down Corso Palladio and Via Gorizia, which were full of pieces, until arriving in Piazza del Duomo. At the *Poste*, under the fascist-period arches, was a group of thirty-fourty people, all closed in a circle, big kids, all dressed in a similar manner and with no smiles to spare for those that didn't belong to the group. Those were the years in which skins, punks and metal-heads would meet up and form gangs at war with one another, and each group was very protective of its affiliates. Other than them, at the *Poste* you could also find the breakers: on the walls was their writing, on the ground a giant battery-powered stereo full of laser rays drawn in acrylic markers. It was these guys that had filled the city with elaborate stickers of colourful outlines on spray-painted backgrounds, with tags and messages in English. Their headquarters was in Via Gorizia and if you wanted to talk to them and let them know you existed you had to hit that street. One day I decided to make the first move and leave a message on a big sticker. I don't remember what I wrote but it had a striped background with a colour-coordinated Zulu Nation "Z" on top, and a sort-of poem written in an improbable English. Some days later next to it was another sticker, less elaborate than the one I had created, which in a friendly manner said something like "Show yourself, who are you?". The following Saturday I went to the *Poste* claiming the gesture as mine, but my 13 years of age aroused the usual dirty looks and the typical perplexities that are always reserved to rookies: that sticker and the few tags I had left around the city weren't enough to be accepted by Nex, Skah and Onis, the only female breaker and writer, inacces-

sible dream of every adolescent.
At the *Poste* the most experienced guys usually scorned or mistreated us, as kids we had to obey them if we wanted to hang around, some newbies wouldn't even get close for fear of their judgment. At the time there were only two crews, 352 created by Esk from Bassano and Rebel, and the *Supreme Vandals* with DextOne and Skah, and shortly later came SIA with Nex and Onis, which were then joined by the tags of Xeba, Kean, Xencs and Dottor Sax.
One day Nex told me I sucked and that my pieces had to become much more fly, I had to improve a lot before I could even think of chilling with them, Esk defended me but they were all pretty strict, for them style was of the utmost importance and if it even remotely resembled that of someone else it was a sign of little originality and therefore of wackness. Everyone had to have his recognisable style and to me this represented the brand seal of Vicenza writers: originality at any cost and a unique personality, two characteristics that years later would take the explosive concrete form of little Mich and his works. With time I got tight with Esk, who was extremely energetic, rebellious and reserved, not as tall or imposing as Skah, nor as aggressive as Nex. I started hanging out with him and Rebel, who was very outlandish, always on his Alfetta: he had done most of the pieces in the centre of Vicenza and in my eyes he was unreachable.
At 16, after a long ceremonial, I was authorised to write 352 next to my tag: Iavo 352, the dream became reality. As a skateboarder in Vicenza I would spend most of my time at the church of San Pio X; I started painting illegal pieces characterised by a quick and gestural style, the fill wasn't necessarily flat, but often striped to evoke a sense of movement. After meeting Boogie and the guys from Padua I discovered a new reality, far from the severity of writers in Vicenza: EAD was an enormous crew of breakers and writers that drank alcohol and smoked joints, which in Vicenza never happened. I started to distance myself from the clean and rigorous style of 352 and with Boogie and Crez from Mestre went on to form HIV, a group dedicated to painting energetically, without too many refinements. Our crew just didn't give a fuck and Skah got mad over the name we had chosen, because lately some old-time punk friend of his had died. But I was tired of feeling like I was always under exam and so I ended up taking my own direction, made of skateboarding, hardcore music and graffiti. With time I developed a more personal style, abstract, with colours that would often escape the outline of the letters: it was experimental stuff, not always successful but stimulating and aggressive. My inspiration came from the artists that followed the Futurist current, above all Balla, Pellizza from Volpedo and Hundertwasser, together with writers I had always been impressed by; Vulcan, Futura 2000, Jay One, Phase II and Rammellzee, from his theories I determined the conversion of my ending "o" in a sigma, that is an "e".

> CONTINUES FROM PAGE 201

many Italian black music venues that in the 80's started promoting a musical program imprinted on the new sounds tied to American Hip Hop and Funk.
Indeed among its primary clients were numerous American soldiers from the Nato base of Camp Ederle, who influenced

the musical tendency and became a cultural bridge between Veneto and the United States. In a brief amount of time, right when Hip Hop was inspiring the Writing movement, the Palladium encompassed all the energy and the potential of an effective ground for meeting and exchanging experiences.

The obsessions of an aesthete
>

A private universe

Skah
>

One of the first times I found myself to be drawing puffy or billboard-like letters was as a kid when I was making scenery for the car race-track I had built. The inspiration came from the writing on the background of the advertisement photo's of different models in the fashionable magazines and papers my sister read, like Lei, that in the early 80's was already posting essays and special reports on the trends of the ghetto. I kept the articles on Crazy Legs and the writers of New York for years.

Then I remember a TV series with an extremely young John Travolta, in a class of ethnic minorities: during the opening credits they showed a van with a silver throw-up with black outline, I think it was from Brook-

> Those were really years of study for us

lyn. All these inputs established the groundwork for everything I would study in the following years, a kind of writer conscience that only later, in 1984, would emerge, initially through other disciplines of Hip Hop, Breaking above all.
Thanks to B-boying I dug deeper, discovering the details of Aerosol Art, to come back full circle to what I had absorbed as a kid from TV and magazines. A new period began of which I still conserve pages and pages of letters, tags and Writing. Entire days and nights spent perfecting every mark and tracing lines upon lines in the search of a style. Those were really years of study for us. The little information that reached us was charged with an infinity of re-interpretations, touching everything from tools to styles to clothes. People in the street would point at you for a baseball cap and I would go around with a japanese doo-rag on my head, fuchsia feather earring, torn wife-beater and chains on my linen shoes. Still today, in the province, when I enter the sports store of my town, the owner stops me to inquire what year it was that I started asking

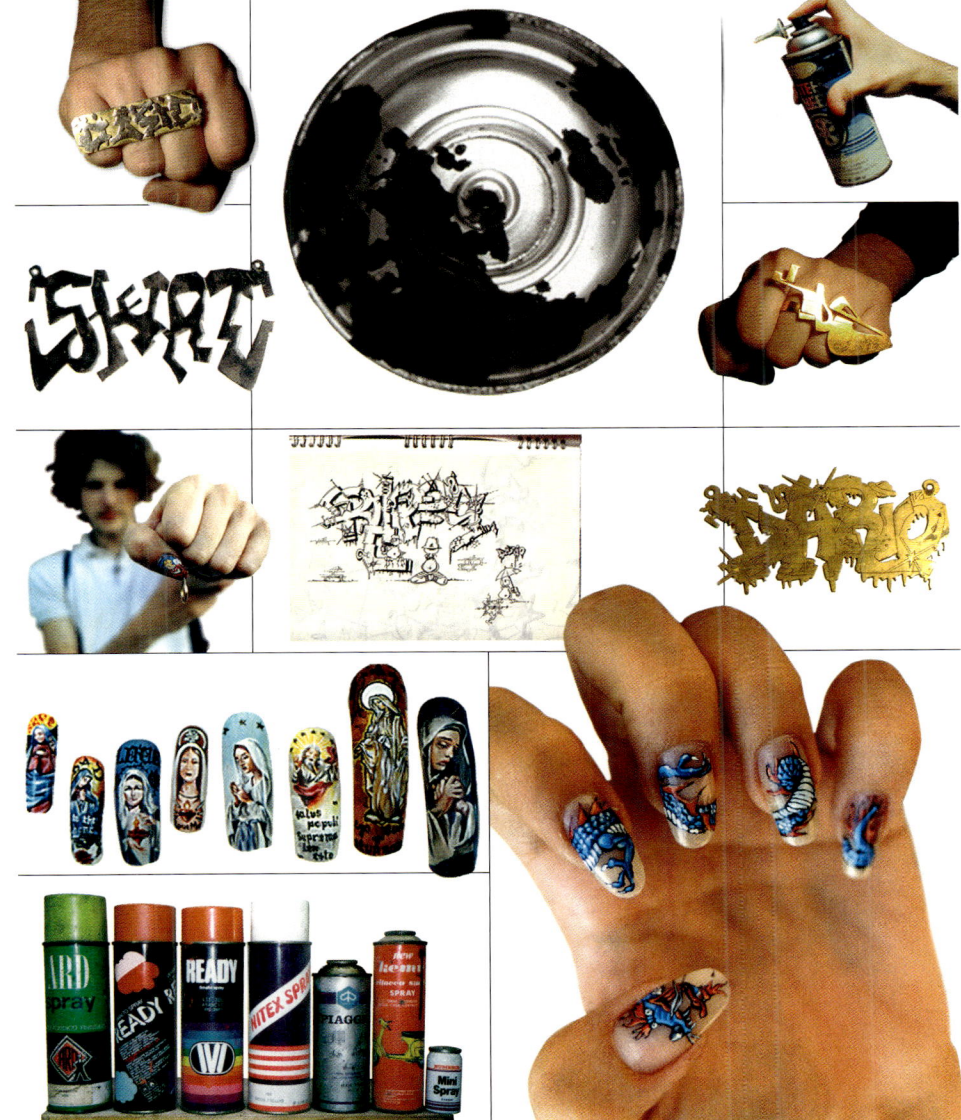

Collect on of customised objects by Skah   — Skah

for suede Pumas, to then shake his head when I remind him it was the spring of 1985.
During those years the search for information or objects connected to Writing and Hip Hop became a real incentive to travel. In 1988 I went to Paris with Dext one, it was a real reference point for many kids in the North-East. The first B-boys from Mantova had handed us a sort-of alphabet of French origin that they called Parisienne, from which all letter variations, experiments and elaborations stemmed, it was a kind of underground Rosetta Stone. In those years on the walls of Paris and London you could see a "Z", the same sign was re-interpreted in Vicenza and this plagiarism can still be seen on the walls of the city today. On our visit to Paris we met

Boxer, one of the legends of the city. We were at a flea market and approached a group of teenagers we had recognised were B-boys like us, because of how they were dressed. Paris has always been one of the capitals of style, both in Breaking and Writing, as well as clothing. We talked with them a bit, then Boxer asked to borrow some money, a small sum, 20.000 lira, or ten euros today, with which he wanted to buy a Kangol bucket hat: the point isn't the hat per se, (he could have stolen it in the street, along with its price-tag). At the time many kids were wearing their price-tags on their clothes, it was the sign they had bought them instead of stealing them. In exchange, Boxer proposed he give us a tour of the most private and hidden halls of fame

in the city. We trusted him and arranged to meet the next day, ignoring the possibility he might ditch us. Boxer acted loyally, he came back with his new electric blue Kangol, price-tag around his ear and big smiles of gratitude as he said: "Guys, today you will see some fabulous stuff...". We started walking but after a few metres three cops in plain clothes approached and stopped Boxer. They searched his pockets and extracted XL markers and some paint, then started squaring us two. At that point Boxer intervened, saying we were just tourists that had gotten lost around the city. The cops believed him, it was kind-of true in a sense, but they took Boxer away. Before getting in their car he turned and raised his arms, as if to say "...my bad". We never met him again.

Skah
>

I think the story of Bac caps is in the memory of all the first European writers, at least the italian ones. In stores writers would pretend to smell the deodorants so as to detach its cap with their teeth, it was the best spray nozzle for certain colours. After a couple of months the company producing them changed the nozzle mechanism because the deodorants on the shelves kept getting guillotined.
Apart from Bac, each of us would invent the most improbable system to improve tools and techniques: for example we would melt two caps together, connecting them with plastic straws and adhesive paste so as to mix the many colours together, while to make skinny caps we would use syringe needles. My alternative was a metallic structure on which hung a cardboard with a hole at ten centimetres from the cap. Then there were those that would use tubes of woodworm treatment and "duck bust" caps with a 15x0.2 centimetre jet. For a while I would use a pair of cans tied together with tape, a system that allowed both

> I used a pair of cans tied together with tape, a system that allowed both caps to be pressed at the same time, to make tags that were parallel doubles. Gothic stuff.

caps to be pressed at the same time, to make tags that were parallel doubles. Gothic stuff.
I quickly abandoned these experiments. You have to realise that if you want an airbrush effect, you have to use an airbrush. Every art has its tools, you can use a spray can to create the effect of a brush stroke. For writing, I began with a spray can to have a spray effect, even though before all this I have to admit I built a cap on which I attached the metallic part of a paintbrush, the one that holds the bristles. By applying light pressure the nozzle would spray the colour and the bristles would get soaked with paint.

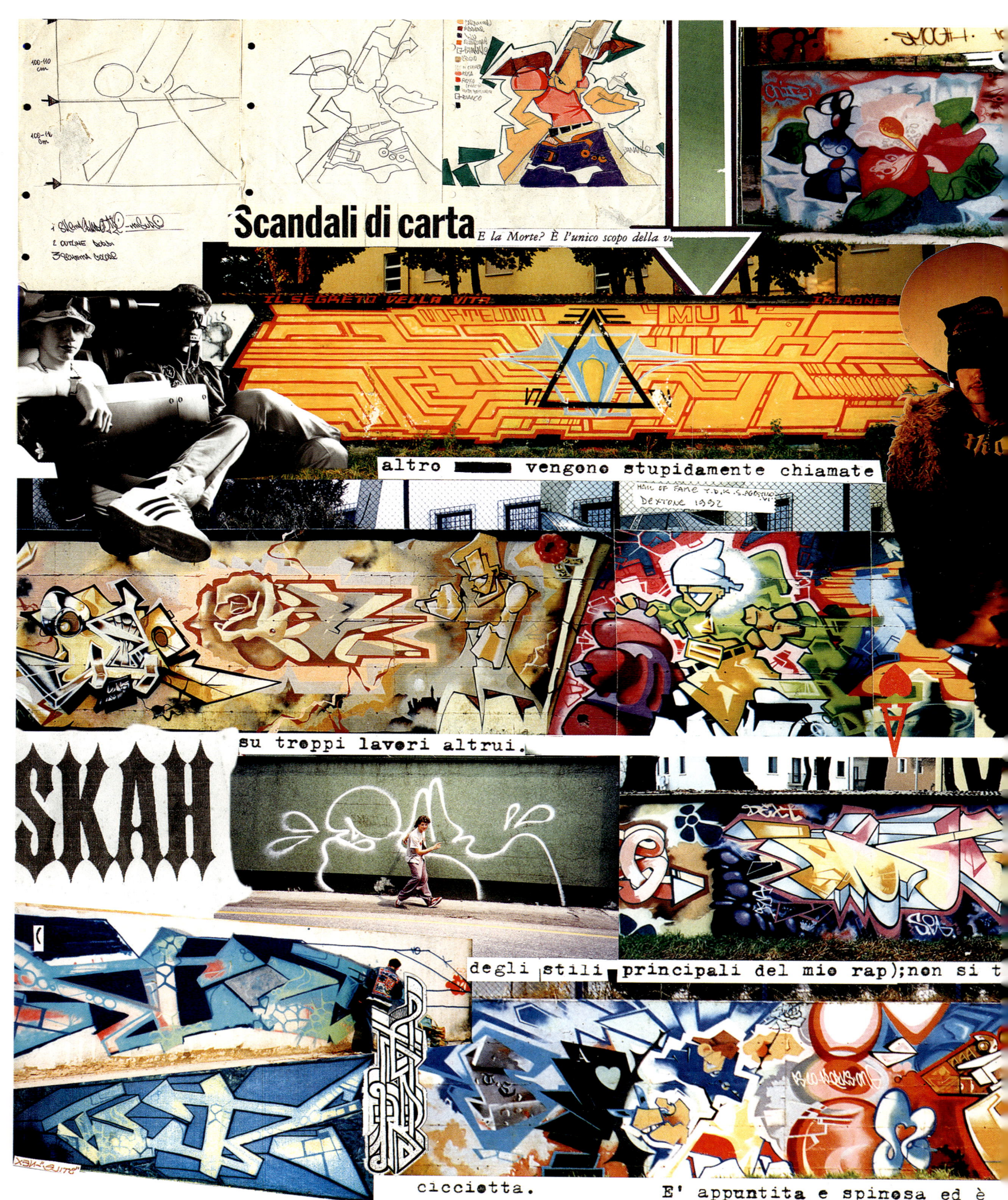

Collage by Skah, Dext One and Onis during the 80's and early 90's

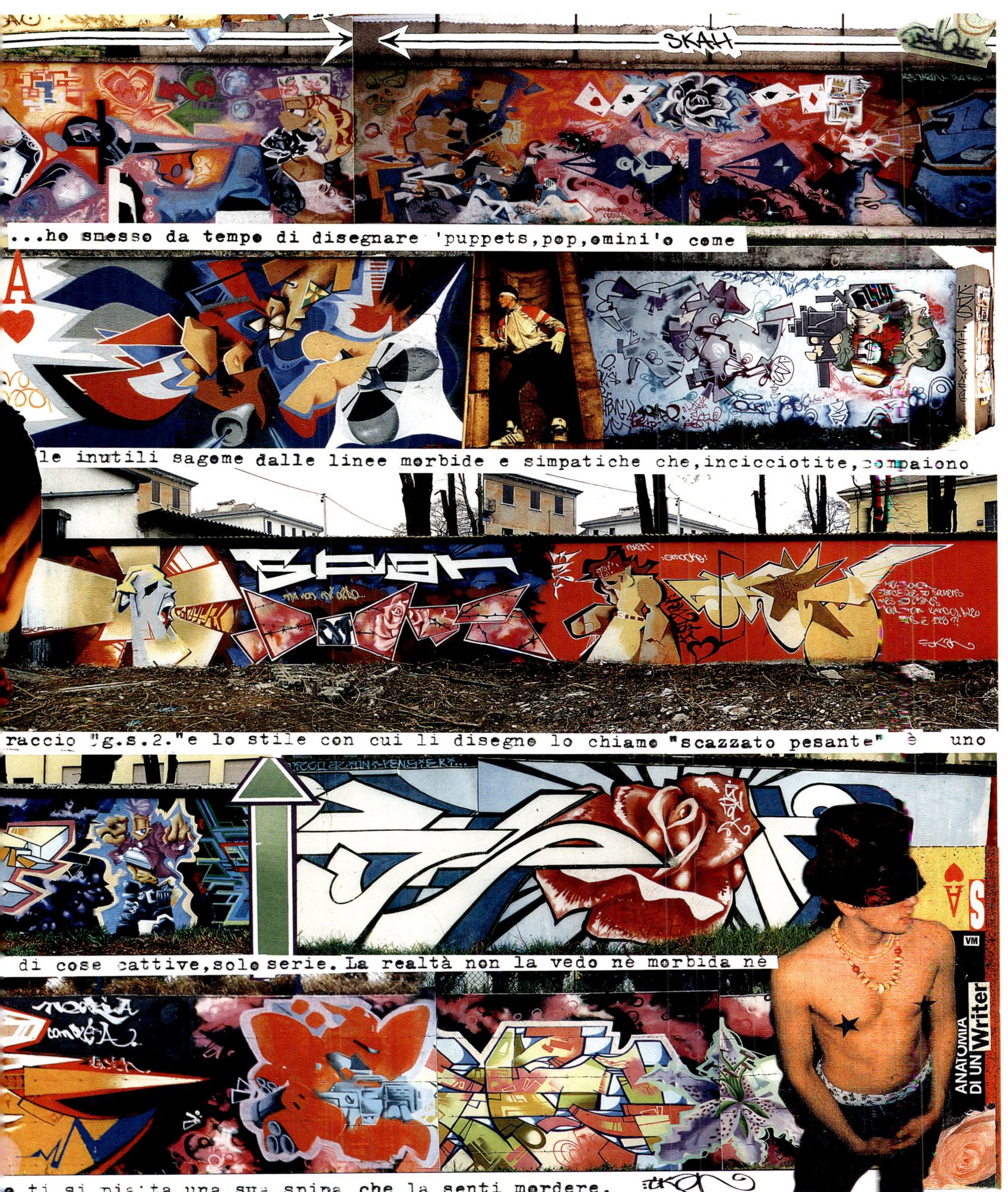

...ho smesso da tempo di disegnare 'puppets,pop,omini'e come

le inutili sagome dalle linee morbide e simpatiche che,incicciotite,compaiono

raccio "g.s.2."e lo stile con cui li disegno lo chiamo "scazzato pesante" è uno

di cose cattive,solo serie. La realtà non la vedo nè morbida nè

o ti si pianta una sua spina che la senti mordere.

Treviso meat district

Mace
>

From 1988 to 1992, Milan and Treviso walked side by side, thanks to various crews that evolved together. CKC crew also included Starch and Clout, I was in PWD crew and we often painted with people from other Milanese crews. Fly often came to Treviso, so did Sky 4, Rae, Tawa, Debby, and Shot, each time they'd leave a piece in the hall of fame. We shared the evolution of New York styles and letters; at the hall of fame in Treviso Sky did his first pixel... imagine the local kids when they saw a Wildstyle piece full of pixels.

We had a great spot in Treviso: the Macello, an enormous ex-slaughterhouse next to a freight yard that served as a cattle market in the 50's. There, each morning, cattle were bought and sold and transferred to the slaughterhouse nearby. There were three long reinforced concrete platforms that rested upon long rows of pillars which, since the 1970's, had been the home of musical events, concerts, Communist unity parties, and one of the most feared companies in the city from 1970-1980. A real integration took place between what was left of the neighborhood's crew and this group of nutcases who only cared about painting. Starch had grown up on that soccer field, when they demolished it to build a parking lot they erased a piece of this shitty city's history. At night we'd go paint trains in the adjacent yard or go tag up the city centre... the same old story, years of life spent on benches waiting to paint. In some ways, Treviso was more difficult because people couldn't begin to understand why we would paint walls and they tried to repress us immensely.

When the first rewards for catching writers began, it started here. And even though this phenomenon caught on quickly with other cities, it caught on the fastest here in Treviso.

The city was bombed before other Italian urban centres because we had a "trade off" with Milan, so we started off on the right foot.

Unlike in other cities, attitudes here immediately became more radical, also in regards to the military aspect of bombing: planning the action, dividing the tasks, trusting fellow crew members, sharing illegal experiences that still bind us indissolubly today. Some people listened to Hip Hop music like me, some liked hardcore or straight edge like Clout.

He was a skater who got hooked on bombing; he bombed roofs, but mainly trains, and some streets. He did throw-ups and some cool blockbusters with spray paint from Standa department store.

I have no idea what those spraycans contained, some coloured chemical plutonium solution... we inhaled way too much shit, but some pieces we did in 1990 are still perfectly intact!

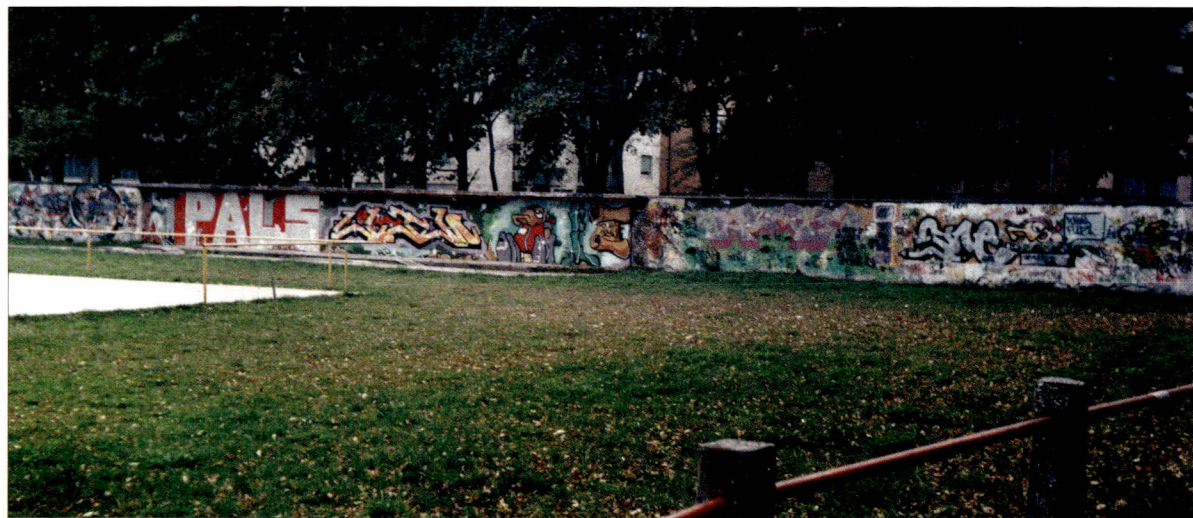

Panoramic view of the ex-Macello, Treviso   *— Mace*

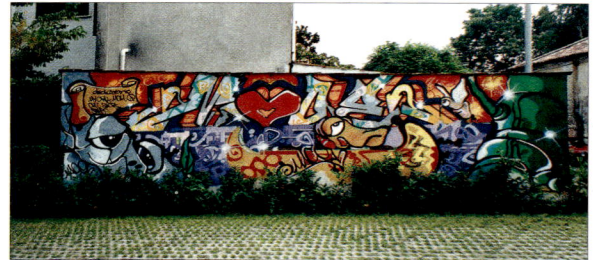

Mace – Pwd, 1998   *— Mace*

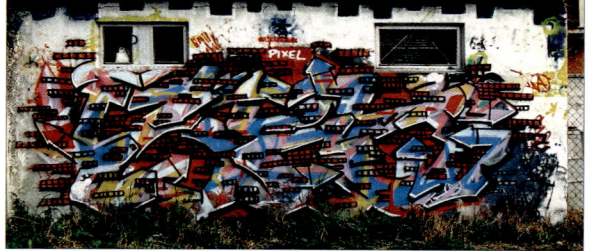

Se by Mace, Starch – CKC   *— Mace*

Pixel Piece by Sky 4 – CKC Milano   *— Mace*

Mace – PWD, piece against heroin, 1990   *— Mace*

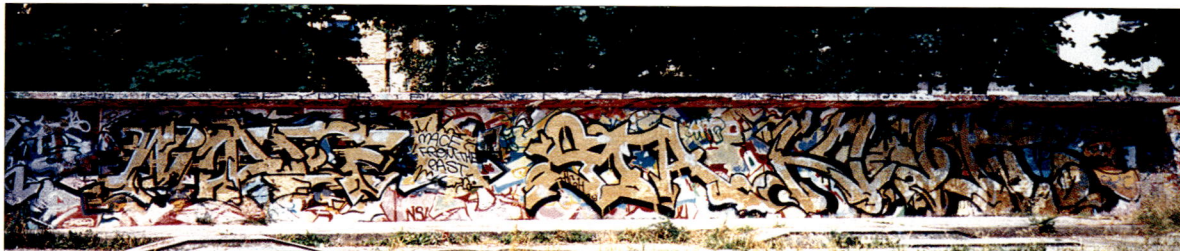

Mace, *Sta* by Starch, *Klout* by Clout, 1998   *— Mace*

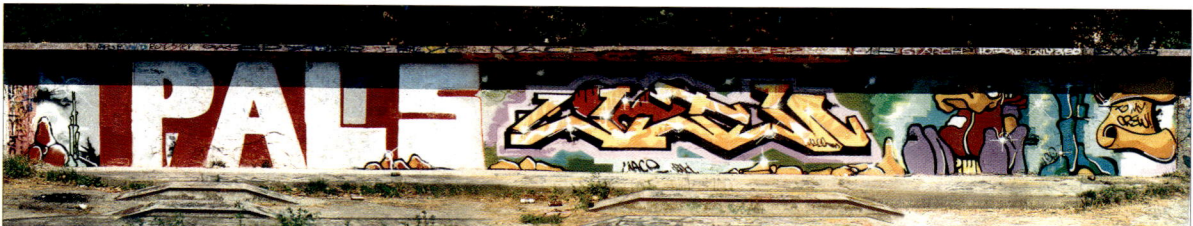

Pals With Dreams by Mace   *— Mace*

An anomalous place
>

Behind the business

Joys
>

In Padua everything began towards 1984: it was then that the first tags and pieces started appearing.
The very first generation of writers was composed of Streeken, Udy, Mila and Crazy, there was no real consciousness about what they were doing but just the desire to have fun.
Towards 1987 a new wave of people emerged, first Boogie and Ozone, then years later Mirror, Jeff, Spatter, Zagor, Trace and 3Art, up until 1992.
In those years the hang-out par excellence, not only for writers but also breakers and skaters, was the *Banche*: a compound of buildings with marble floors, low walls and porticos; here a generation of writers was raised, every Saturday there were kids reunited from all of Veneto and beyond, that went there just to chill, compare experiences, or make projects and plans for their next hit.
In 1992, given the close relations that had developed, some writers and breakers decide to form a group that was created not only because of their common interests but especially due to the strong friendships that tied them: the crew would take on the name of EAD and would later include a relevant part of the Writing and Breaking scene of Padua.
In that same year Joys, Riot, Retz, Themo and Riff start moving their first steps, the city is in ferment and the competition in quantity of tags and pieces starts becoming noticeable. From 1993 to 1999 the

growth slows down to a near halt, just a couple of writers a year: Made, Peeta, Yama, Cupo, Hase, Mote and the guys of SPC, Axe and Curdo. A mass initiation never existed, the scene was always small but lively, everybody knew each other and the beef was quite limited.
The reactions of the city have always been positive, both when it came to public opinion and local administration, I think the reason for this is that the city was never excessively tagged. In Padua everyone has always tried to do as much as they could without causing too much annoyance, it's a bit of a strategic move: to fill a provincial city like Padua with tags, one week of nocturnal actions is sufficient, it wouldn't take long to become the king of the moment.
We've always painted a bit everywhere without asking for many permits and apart from some sporadic cases there has been much tolerance towards graffiti. The Writing scene of Padua grew in close contact with the cities of Treviso, Vicenza and Venice, each of these realities developed their own style and taste without influencing each other too much.
At the end of the 80's, Rusty, who was serving his military duty in Padua, met Boogie, that together with Mace from Treviso and Skah from Vincenza created the groundwork of the Writing scene in Veneto. The very first magazines that circulated were mostly French (*1tox*, *Paris Tonkar*) and Swiss (*14k*), therefore it was from there that the first influences arrived for the local scene; during the 90's the quantity of material regarding Writing was constantly growing and this factor, together with the possibility of travelling, brought an ulterior influence and boost for everyone.

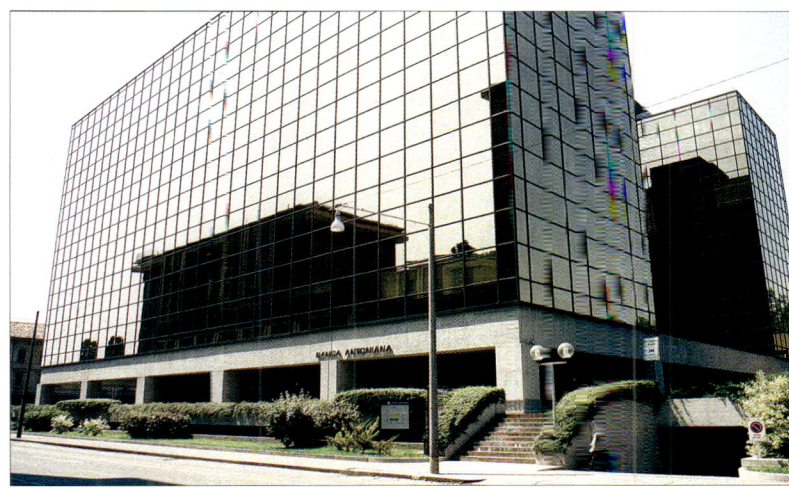
Le Banche, EAD main spot, external view — *Joys*

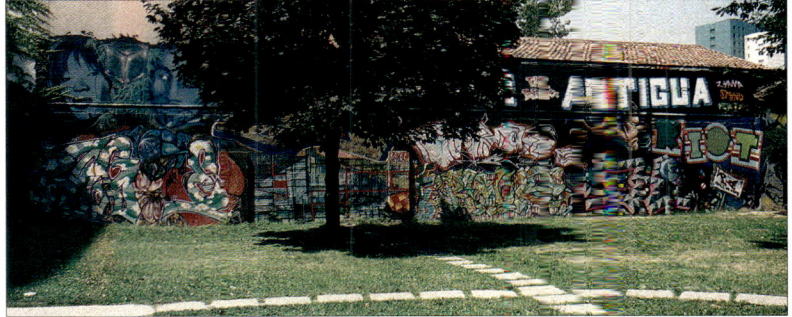
EAD hall of fame, the bank buildings seen from inside the garden — *Joys*

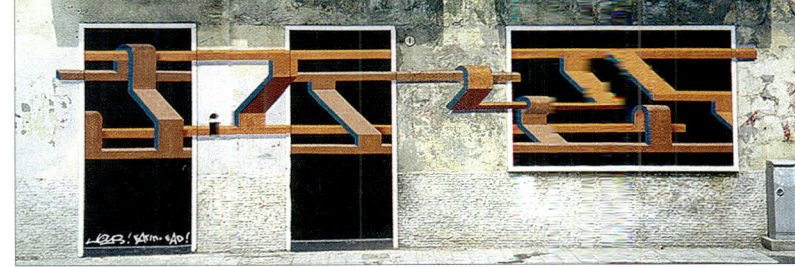
Joys – EAD, 1998 — *Joys*

BOOGIE DOWN PRODUCTIONS
—

Boogie
>

To me bombing is a phase that every writer should experience in order to acquire style, speed and technique. When I started in '89, I wanted to be free to express myself with the same impact of an advertising poster. I studied

to evolve my letters, prepared sketches, observed the highest and riskiest spots that were most visible, to attack at the right moment. My preference was for trains and the roofs of the city, in solitude or in the company of friends. There were few of us in Padua but with time we got in touch with kids from other Italian cities. In Bologna I met Rusty, with him and

Mace I found some passenger trains parked in the yard of Campo di Marte one night and we painted the one that was least exposed, while keeping a check on everything around us in case someone arrived. It was the first time I weote on metal, the smell of the paint made me giddy, I couldn't understand whether it was fear or adrenaline that made my heart

pump. Only once the piece was finished did I grasp the accomplishment, my first windowdown. I liked the risk.
When the police caught me and put me in their files, I went through hell. My counter-move was organising a bombing with my crew EAD that said "Fuck the police" on the roof in front of the train station of Padua. And so I got even.

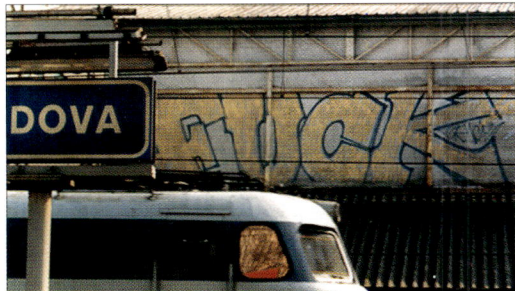
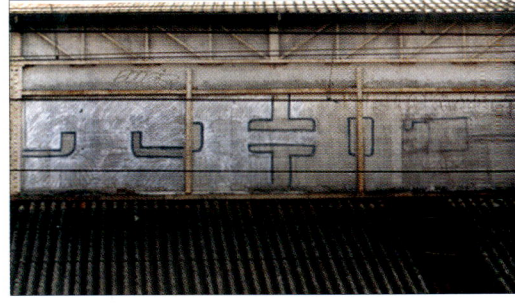
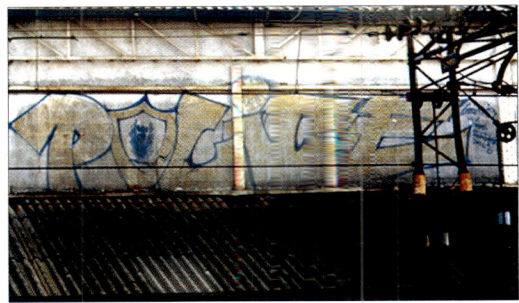

Fuck the police by Boogie – EAD, rooftop painted along the railway station of Padua — *Joys*

Double fantasy

Capo

\>

MESTRE

Word is that the first writer to leave a mark on Mestre was a certain Dozo, who is said to have painted the wall of a school in 1985. During that same period Stone and Side signed their first pieces in an underpass close to the city centre as well as in other spots, while Eugene and Skyone had also started making their first moves in the city outskirts. The first masterpieces of Mestre date back to the early 80's, they were colourful, with thin outlines, and simple, hard letters that were made even more beautiful by the many light and shade effects. East and Mesh with their crew, DWA were the initiators of the Mestre school, and were then joined by Sook, Hype, Sly and Bill. DWA was very active, tagging and bombing the walls along the FS line and in parks such as the Piraghetto next to the station or Parco della Bissuola. Their base however, was the *Deposito*, a large building in construction with various floors, and that was very soon entirely covered with graffiti. It would represent a real school for the next generation. With time the Deposit would become a real pole of attraction, not only for writers from Veneto like EAD from Padua, but for those from the entire North of Italy; Cento from Treviso, Polo from Naples and Rusty and Solow from Bologna. All of whom were the authors of many a black and white piece along the track line. In '94 DWA broke up and crews started forming with writers from different cities of Veneto, from HIV+ to OFC, LDR and MDF – the crew that represented the first real union between Mestre and Venice. Then in 1995 F2D and CF were created, and TWP followed shortly after, a crew whose writers followed very different styles: Hate was specialised in puppets as well as letters, primarily animals. Braco was the most eclectic of all and would sign pieces full of shadings and unsettling characters, while Slog, Sat and I were fans of interwoven letters and Wildstyle. Then, after having painted together for four years we each went our separate way.

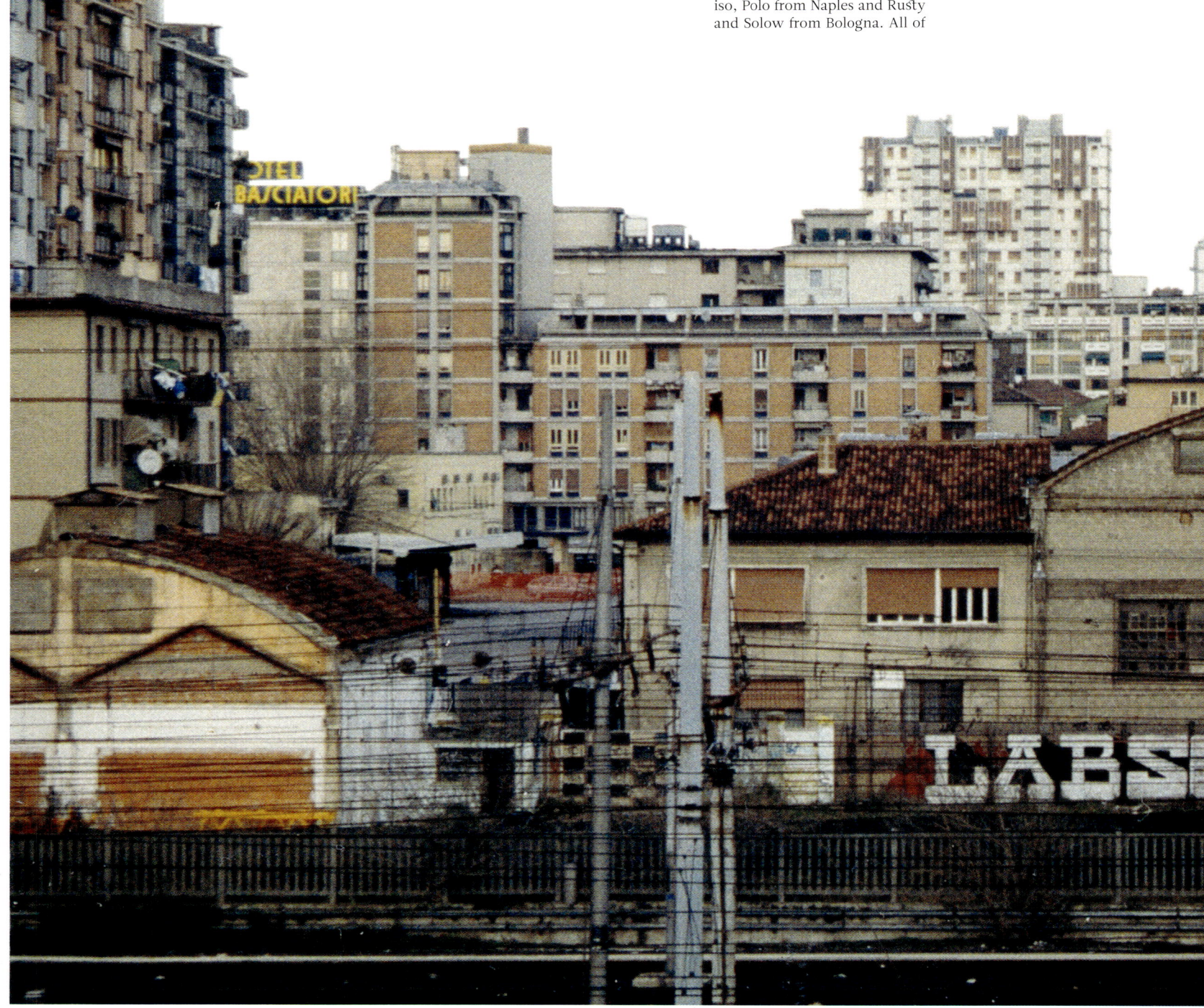

The track line that connects Mestre to Venice: blockbuster by Lab, Slog, Zor

Slog
>

Sat and I joined LDR, a group from Mestre, almost immediately after an initial period of distrust from them, as we were just kids at the time. The scene of Mestre in 1992 had a different mission as opposed to the writers of the earlier days, perhaps tied more to the action itself rather than to the style. On a stylistic level, Mestre looked towards the writers from Padua, particularly Boogie, who was really ahead of his time when it came to letters and bombing.

After the boom of posses took place in 1992 (which did more damage than anything else), giving birth to a massive series of toys, the scene in Mestre began its decline, so much so that by 1994 almost all the real writers had either stopped painting or did very little of it. I on the other hand continued, and actually that was perhaps the period in which I bombed the most, sometimes with Sat, but essentially on solitary missions, seeing that for a number of reasons I had the possibility of staying at home alone for large amounts of time. In the meantime I was changing stylistic orientation: from the "European" big letters I was doing in the first years, I became fascinated by both the pieces by Natas from Venice, who was hanging out in Milan, and those coming from the scene in Treviso, of which Mace, Clout and Starch were a part of: I therefore switched to the more complex New York-inspired Wildstyle, which from that moment on would represent my main reference. The Lagoon was our action territory, characterised by the contrast between Mestre and Venice, two completely different entities, separated by water and connected by a bridge: Mestre is an ordinary town, rich in grey suburbs, industrial areas, and devoid of any artistic attraction. Naturally this context brought us to paint with an attitude that was the opposite with respect to Venice, where once you crossed the bridge you entered another dimension in which the dynamics of bombing radically changed.

Sat
>

In 1992 when I started out in graffiti, I used to put together very simple letters with few colours. Then I moved on to a crazy style with thousands of colours and three million arrows. Looking at my pieces I thought "Yeah, guys I'm doing Wildstyle!" but the reality was that I was actually just doodling on the wall without any minimal skill or knowledge of what Wildstyle meant.

Things changed when I had the chance to see some real Wildstyle pieces by three writers: Starch, Clout and Mace had painted the hall of fame they had in the area of the *Macello*, in Treviso. After a while I met the first two in person and when I showed them my sketches they gave me a lot of useful tips and feedback.

These guys were part of PWD and CKC, two Milan-based crews, famous for the development of their own style, which was created by taking inspiration from New York kings like Phase II and many others. I felt captured by their style, by the shape of the letters, coloured and looped together so well. So what I've basically been trying to do since 1994 is study the New York lesson learned along the walls of *Macello* and apply it to my pieces, together with my crew, fellas from LDR, NYS and TC.

Capo
>

VENICE

Mestre was already at its second generation of writers when the scene in Venice started forming, even though in '91 Natas and his various aliases had already hit the all areas with pieces and throw-ups. Other than him, the Lagoon city had been targeted by Zoero from Bordeaux, Sten and Mek from Milan, Polo from Naples and the three legendary Parisians Bando, Mode2 and Odace, who as well as tagging everything also bombed a wall adjacent to the Canal Grande with one of his block styles. Their traces were not left unnoticed so much so that in a matter of few months the museum-city started filling with tags like Verter, Charlie, Succo, Andy, Schizzo and Jahllo.

After an initial reciprocal indifference the two realities of Venice and Mestre started interacting and growing (thanks to DWA) into one scene.

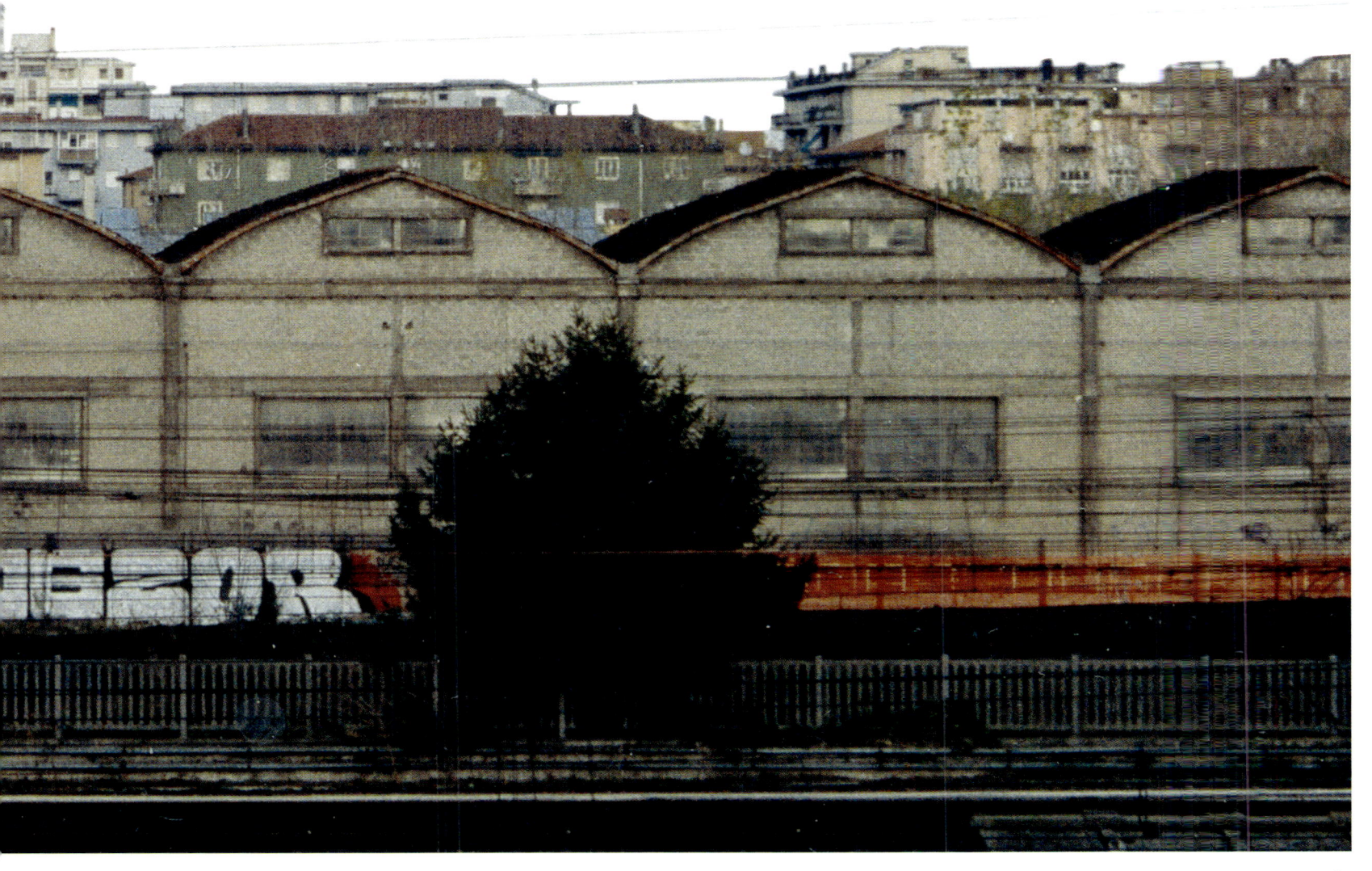

Venice bombing strategies

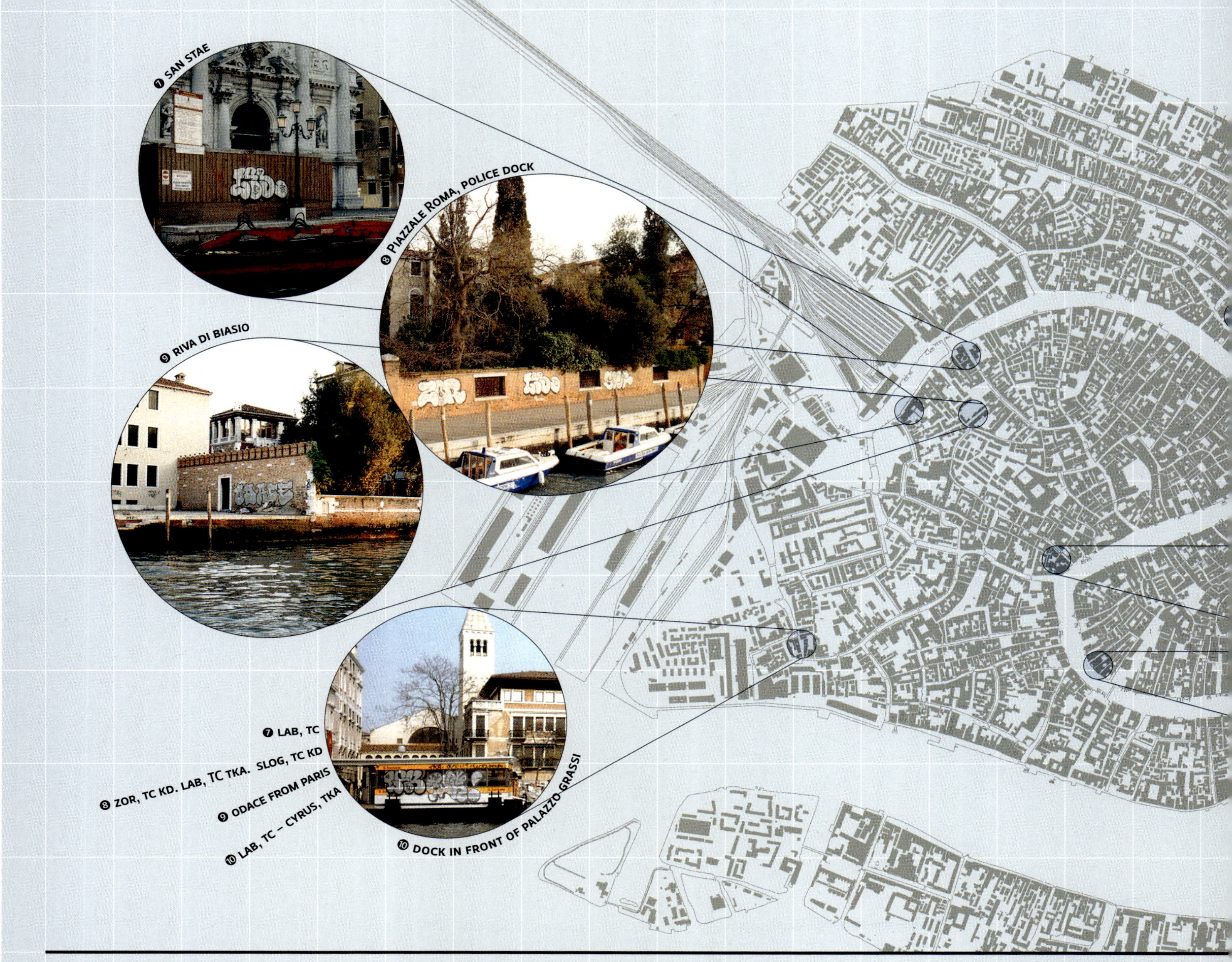

❼ SAN STAE

❽ PIAZZALE ROMA, POLICE DOCK

❾ RIVA DI BIASIO

❼ LAB, TC
❽ ZOR, TC KD. LAB, TC TKA. SLOG, TC KD
❾ ODACE FROM PARIS
❿ LAB, TC – CYRUS, TKA
❿ DOCK IN FRONT OF PALAZZO GRASSI

Natas
>

In Venice the best conditions in which to bomb the street are when you're alone, with nobody else. Bringing foreigners is out of the question because whoever doesn't know the city inevitably falls in the hands of the police. Painting in the tortuous calli streets of Venice means immersing yourself in an infinite maze in which even the people living

just a few kilometres from the Lagoon sometimes loose their bearings. With respect to normal urban conditions, there are mad more hazards tied to this context, for example the cops can arrive by sea, on a boat. In this case you almost always have enough time to run in an alley because the interval it takes them to haul in the boat wins you a few crucial minutes to escape. The situation becomes more tense in the calli, which can play as much in your favour as against you: on one hand they're good to hide in and loose the cops, but on the other hand the circumstances

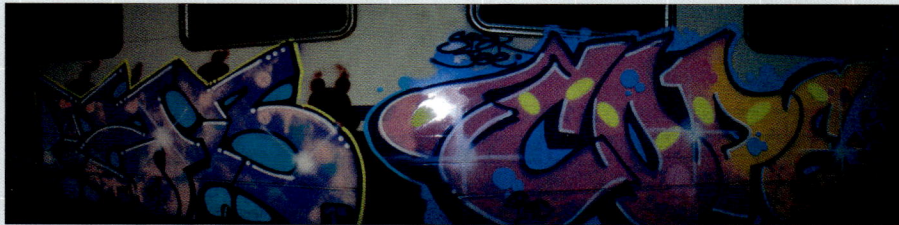

Lab and Cope from New York

— Natas

in which you're painting are loaded with unexpected events and presences that one impossible to anticipate. Sometimes throw-ups were sketched and filled one night while the

outline wouldn't be closed 'til the day after. Every spot in Venice falls within a precise hierarchy of risk and danger: in general the walls on the fringes of the city, that look towards

the lagoon, are calm because there's nothing in front of them except an immense extension of water; you'd immediately realise whether you were alone or not, if anybody

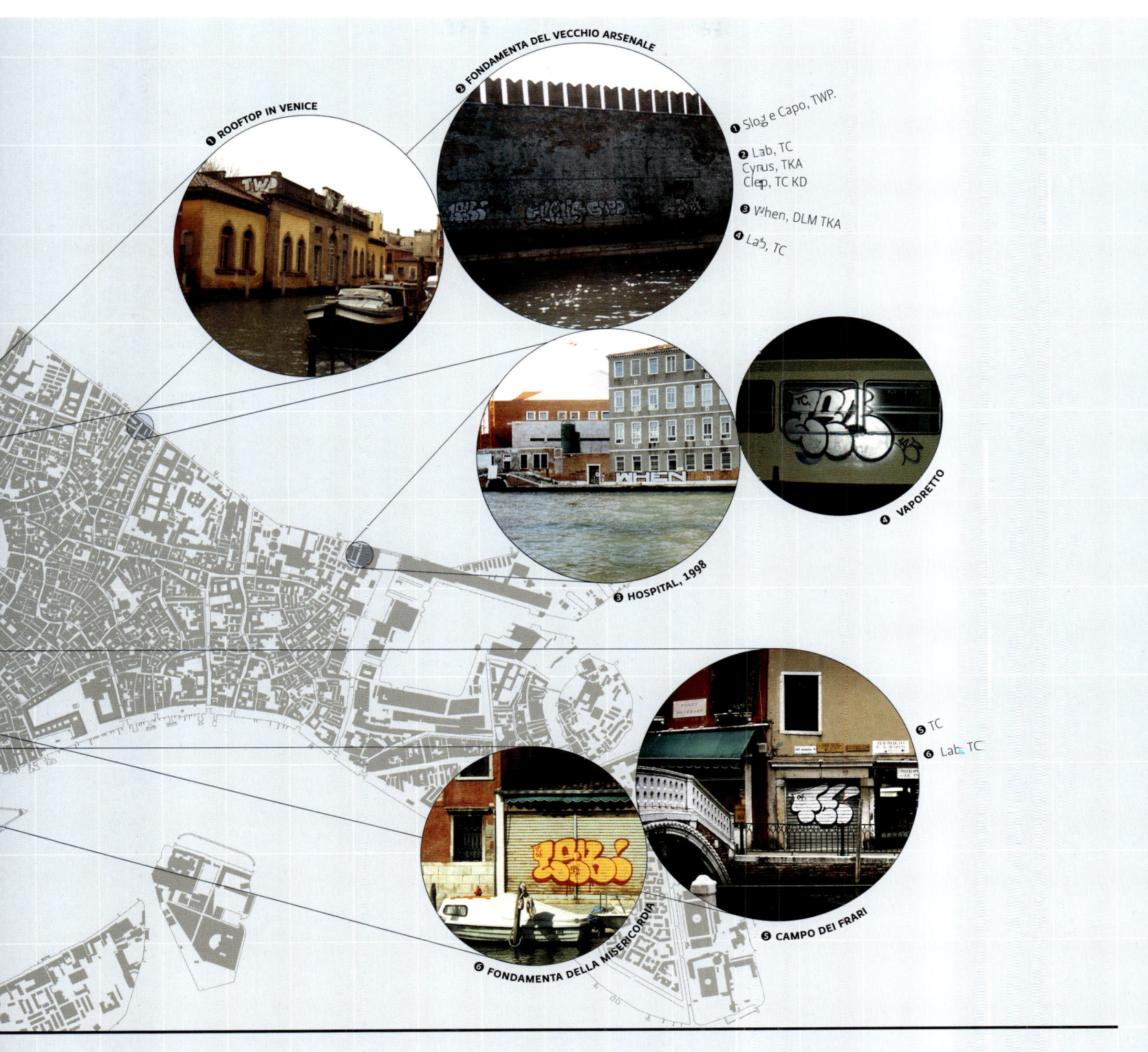

❶ ROOFTOP IN VENICE

❷ FONDAMENTA DEL VECCHIO ARSENALE

❶ Slog e Capo, TWP.

❷ Lab, TC
Cyrus, TKA
Clep, TC KD

❸ When, DLM TKA

❹ Lab, TC

❹ VAPORETTO

❸ HOSPITAL, 1998

❺ TC
❻ Lab, TC

❻ FONDAMENTA DELLA MISERICORDIA

❺ CAMPO DEI FRARI

arrived by boat you'd notice it in advance, while anyone on land would have to take the same street you'd be painting on, which is a long rectilinear parallel to the water: so in this case as well you'd notice any stranger from a distance. The risk increases when your target is a road that runs along any of the primary canals inside Venice. Canal Grande for example is one of the most difficult spots, one minute tops to bomb it. In this case the pilot boat of the police can arrive from at least four different angles because of the intersection of the various watercourses, and that's not even counting anyone coming from the streets. Then there are specific spots, like the Arsenale, which is pretty calm since it belongs to an area of the city in which tourists and locals do not transit that much. At the same time it's a very scenic place, where a photo of a flop taken from afar becomes incredibly suggestive. One of the issues that often touches Italian writers is vandalism in the historic centres, in a context that is always of historic and artistic value. Venice is itself a continuous monument, even the most recent buildings become part of what is generally considered an artistic heritage. This condition inevitably influences the way you paint and the choice of places to hit; writers would target only certain elements of the city centre, like shutters, walls of plaster and cement: they're anyways rebuilt every two years because though the edifices in Venice may have hundreds of years, the coatings suffer from the saltiness of the air and need continuous work. These surfaces are generally considered with less esteem than marble or other durable materials. Naturally there's always some kid that doesn't even consider this distinction, but they're pretty isolated cases. These are the ones though that the press and local authorities like to use in their generalisations and in their 'talk' of a social plague. One of the most prestigious spots is alongside the bridge that connects Piazzale Roma, the Piazza of the station, with the city: it's a sure stop for every tourist and citizen. There's always people around and it's dangerous, but whatever mark you leave near the bridge will be seen by thousands every day. Personally speaking, the district I hit the most has always been San Polo, the heart of the city.

First of all, because I grew up there so I knew the calli better than anyone else, and then because it is in a strategic position of the city: it's a middle ground between the area of Rialto, one of the main tourist attractions, and the bridge of the station. Considering that the aim of bombing is mostly to gain visibility, this choice was inevitable: painting means, to see myself every day to compete with the other writers of the city and most of all for the tourists, who come to Venice and remain surprised at seeing these traces.

Siso's photograph collection
>

Track life

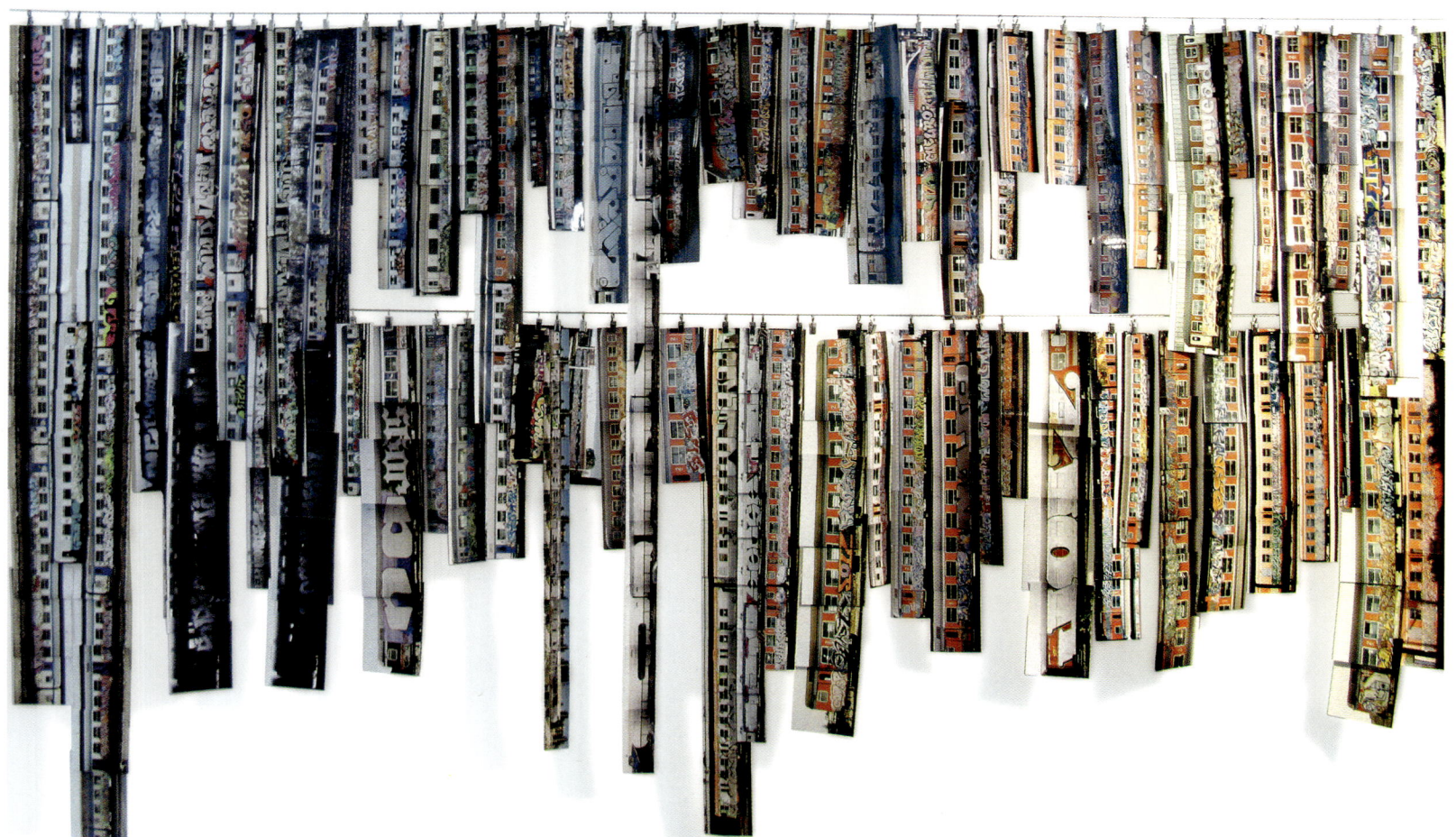

— Laure Boudet

Siso
>

I dedicated most of my youth to hanging around the various platforms of many stations of Northern Italy, trying to photograph trains that had been painted by writers. It was halfway through the 90's, a golden era for graffiti on trains, much before the year 2000 and the appearance of the protective film coatings. The first generation of bombers in Treviso (whose main representatives formed one of the first train Writing scenes of Italy), was personified by Mace, Starch and then Clout, but I didn't see my first panel until much later, in 1995. The first to paint the *Littorine* were these guys, and between 1989 and 1990 various Milanese writers such as Sky4 also came through to Treviso. The next generation included Cento, Med, Clyde, Grace and others that together with Starch and Clout formed TAS (*Tasso Alcolico Superiore*, or *Superior Alcoholic Blood Level*). Another old school writer was Shadow, who also painted trains and was part of NBA, of which other writers such as

Lazy were a part of too. Cento was also in B52 with Shadow and Cash.
Getting back to me, the first panel I saw on a passenger train in the region of Veneto was in the city of Treviso, I'm talking back in 1995. It was a *Littorina* model 668, with pieces by SI crew from Bassano, MKS, and Konso, a kid from Vicenza that had painted a pumpkin along with his letters. Fakso, Zuek, Chea, and Resoan were part of SI, which stood for *Super Idiots*. When I saw that train I had already been taking pictures of graffiti for a while, I had been to the *Macello* in Treviso, a place full of pieces by local writers. I had also been to the station of Cadorna in Milan, where the trains of the Ferrovie Nord had been devastated by the writers of the city. The idea of seeing in person a train painted in Veneto excited me and spurned the desire to immortalise this emotion, not just the pieces, but the whole experience per se, that is, seeing the name of writers on a carriage, while travelling. In the hope of catching the pieces again I returned to Treviso the next day, on the same track, same time, with a photo camera. I was unprepared. The train that arrived was yes a *Littorina* 668, but without a single piece. I felt lost, "Damn they already cleaned it" I thought to myself. A couple of weeks later, it was January 1996, I took

the train from Treviso to Milan to photograph a bit of graffiti. It was early in the morning and on track one there was a *Littorina* with some pieces. They were by SI and MKS, and I particularly remember a square, orange-filled piece by Fakso, that said "MorteUomo" (Death Man). From that day onwards I would often see panels when going to the station of Treviso. In '96 you could see stuff by LNF, with Rego, Siko, Kacio and also Slay. SMA also painted on the *Littorine* and before that also a lot of freight trains, that sounds weird now but at the time they were customary targets in Treviso, seeing that passengers were very rare.
Then one day in 1996, while strolling through the station, I again caught sight of the painted train I had first seen in Treviso, with the Halloween pumpkin piece by Konso, and I started to understand that trains were not immediately buffed as I had thought but actually had rather complicated routes, which is why there were periods during which you wouldn't see them. This was finally confirmed when I began seeing the same *Littorine* time and time again and in addition I noticed an increase in the quantity of pieces circulating, the number of painted *Littorine* was constantly rising. In Treviso the *Stronzi* were also running painted, these were

really old, completely brown trains with a rounded shape that were used for local distances like Treviso-Vicenza. I remember one that ran for a real long time, with different pieces: the first was "Love" by Kacio and next to it a silver by Rego, then another with "Deepone" and "Rush", two skaters that had done a couple of panels. The *Littorine* on the other hand travelled much farther: through Bassano, Castelfranco, Venice, Treviso and many other cities. I noticed LNF and SI often painted together. Only later did I start seeing other train models, for example the classic *Regionals* writers called 3-5-3, a name that derived from the distribution of the windows: the panels to the left and right included three windows and the central part had five, divided by the doors. Not much later I saw the first married-couple: it was a silver "Kso" by Fakso on an orange background, with the words "Il trionfo della giustizia"[1], and then there were also pieces by Zuek and Iave, a writer from Vicenza that painted with SI and also with LNF. Even though this train had clean windows it was running quite a lot and could often be seen. Then I saw a *Littorina* with two coloured top-to-bottoms by SI, these still had their windows intact! It was quite exciting. Obviously I was taking pictures of all the pieces I was seeing and I

North eastern liveries
>

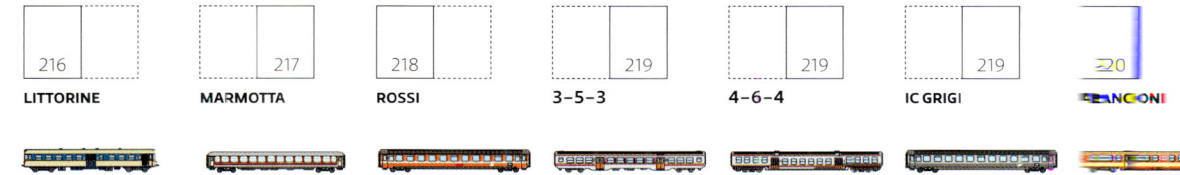

216	217	218	219	219	219	220
LITTORINE	MARMOTTA	ROSSI	3-5-3	4-6-4	IC GRIGI	FRANCONI

---

ended up with quite an impressive collection. In '96 you could also catch stuff by Manjar of NSB crew, a kid from Rome who studied in Venice and did a lot of really banging *Littorine*, some friends from Rome like Washe even visited him there, as well as the French Legs and also Tekne. The pieces by Manjar were really high quality for the time. He often wrote "Pastaman Flava" next to his pieces and when I met him he told me it was a phrase that identified a certain way of living things, which belonged to him and his friends. Again in '96 I saw another whole-car by Fakso, it was a "Fakkso" with two mirror K's. Him and his crew loved doing whole-cars! I saw others by them later on, they often used Nitro paint, you could see the marks left by the roller. It was a pretty "impetuous" way of painting. I think it was done in an attempt to fill surfaces more rapidly (let's not forget that we're talking about the 90's, the super fat caps of today didn't exist yet) and anyway it was a way of saving a bit of money: instead of buying a lot of spray cans all you needed was a bucket of paint. The number of panels steadily increased with time, I would often go to the station to take pictures of the pieces and every once in a while I would bump into Siko on the platform, waiting for the 18 o'clock *Littorina* to see the panels. He was cool and I gladly stopped to talk to him, he would tell me about when he had gone painting the last time in the central station of Treviso, a big deposit full of *Littorine* (at whose door a lot of people went a' knocking during the years, including CKC from Milan and DSP from Pesaro years later).

With time the variety of names appearing on the trains also started increasing. I started seeing new tags, such as Kato from Vicenza. Then I started seeing Clove paint *Littorine* and 353's. CRA crew was also present, I remember they had some beef with LNF. Not long later Clove, Verò and Sewor also started appearing with a certain frequency. The massive presence of Cento's name started being noticeable, he painted with Blace and Ricie 407, and together they planned actions with Kom and Sewor, to achieve some very detailed pieces. There was also Shadow in that period, from the old guard of Treviso, who was delighting the railways with what in my opinion were really beautiful pieces on some 353s and 668s. There was one on which he had written "Lisa" that was always running. You could also see stuff by Hope and Crow of MS with Bablo. I also remember a crew called 668, who were killing the 353s and 668s (from which they got their name): names like Fankool or Naso, who could be read for many years to follow. Then there were others like Pauno or In, you could see their stuff running, especially on the engine convoy. In those years I often started going to Venice to take photos of trains, some friends of mine had told me they had seen pieces there and wanted to go check out whether they were coming from other lines, to understand if many painted trains were arriving from other cities or whether those circulating in the North-East were prevalently from the writer circuit of Treviso-Bassano. Among the first things I saw in Venice I remember was an *Intercity* restaurant carriage by Mich, Iave, Elics and I think Iktron from Vicenza; then

I remember seeing a train by some Swiss guys again on an *Intercity* and from that day a saga of photos began that would last for years. I went through a pretty reckless period, if you can call it that: I had left school and spent a period going to Venice early in the morning and staying maybe 8 hours, going through three or four rolls of film every time I went. I practically always travelled hidden in the restrooms of the train. I didn't have much money and used it all on film, usually I used 400 iso which worked well at night but during the day 100 iso which cost less, was sufficient and so I could buy an extra roll. Many a time I didn't even leave enough cash to eat a slice of pizza and so I would return home in the evening starving but satisfied to have been able to photograph all that stuff. What was even more satisfying was finding panels I had seen previously but didn't have any pictures of because I had already finished all my rolls: I'd swear I would catch them again and spend days thinking about certain 353's by this crew or a certain *Littorina* by another that I might have seen running but hadn't been able to photograph for whatever reason. I was really determined, I could remember which pieces I "had" and which were missing in my archive. Catching one I had not photographed the first time gratified me, because it added another item to my mission as a reporter and naturally I got hyped when I found new stuff that had never been seen before. I cannot forget a top-to-bottom by Res on the central part of a 353, it was off the hook and I had found it with the windows still to be cleaned! In Venice I also witnessed the pervasive presence of panels by EAD crew from Padua (*Escuela Antigua Disciples*), an old-school crew with members of the calibre of Boogie, who also wrote Orange, a respected pioneer writer of the scene in Padua. EAD, with Boogie, Trace, Zagor or Roule, Made, Riot, Joys (and others like Omaex and Noem from Pesaro and Vire from Milan) painted many *Inter-regionali rossi* as well as *Marmotte* and Intercities. The most active two were Joys and Zagor, though in many end-to-ends various other members of the crew appeared. EAD from Padua would later connect with many writers in the Veneto circuit, like Cento. Fakso and Zuek from Bassano also often went to visit Joys. Ditto for Boost from Udine. Iave from Vicenza, Iktron and Elics.

I did my first panel in Padua in '97 with Joys, Zagor, Made, Boogie, Cento and my partner in crew Newe. I remember a Moroccan kid was sleeping in the train car, when he heard us arrive he got off and started chatting with us. He was 16 years old, like me, and just like me he was in this place at this same time that night. I often ask myself how his life was from that night onwards. In Padua we painted in a huge yard called Campo di Marte, a place where there were various types of train cars: Intercity, *Inter-regionali*, 353, *Marmotta*. They weren't entire trains but a composition of assorted carriages:

surrounding these was an entire community of Maghrebis, both in the yard and in the train cars, sleeping. We got into absurd situations with them, I remember one night Joys was supposed to do a one-man whole-car, and as soon as he got into the yard he found a Magrebi guy threatening him with a knife because he thought Joys was an undercover cop. Then another guy intervened and explained everything to him in his language and the man with the knife started laughing and said to Joys: "Oh, you're here to paint, sure, go ahead!" That same night I remember another Maghrebi crawled out of the window of a car behind Joys and asked if he could be more quiet cause he couldn't sleep with all the noise of the spray cans. Sometimes many of us would go in at once, ten or twelve people even. A lot of guys were organising real excursions to Campo di Marte in that period, some even including foreign names like Sharp, who had many panels run around these parts in '98 painted with Cento; or with the German from Berlin like Biboe and Mr.X. Other than what was going on in Bassano, Padua and Treviso, about halfway through '97 the presence of F2D (*Forze del Disordine*[2]) started becoming noticeable in Venice, and included Snow and Senor who hung with Hazk. The first panels they painted were on 664s, I remember a panel by Snow that had the words "Io amo la Natura"[3], with the fill done with leaves and a little river. Then you could no-

tice the private *Littorine* of the Adra Mestre line with pieces by Heez and Rage of CF. Rage was also a member of OFC (*Only Fat Cap*), a crew from Mestre that was behind many tags and bombings in the city. These *Littorine* were also painted by other writers like Slog, Sat and Capo from TWP crew of Mestre, which also included Hate and Colera. This crew that later changed its name to VBF, primarily painted the *Inter-regionali rossi* in Venice. In the meantime the presence of F2D had really become pervasive. 664s, double-decks and also the rounded

Arancioni were running with their names on them. I think Senor was one of the most persistent bombers of the time, all the *double-decks* had a lot of his tags on them, all the *Arancioni* carried at least one panel by him and also the 664s were trashed. He always went around painted up with Snow. They didn't paint in the traditional way, rather, you could say Senor in particular painted in a very "gestural" manner. Subsequently Senor and Snow formed GCT (*Gestualità Cultura Tradizione*[4]) with Rage and Elics.

The gestural stylistic current had origin in Vicenza with characters such as Iktron,

➤ CONTINUES ON PAGE 214

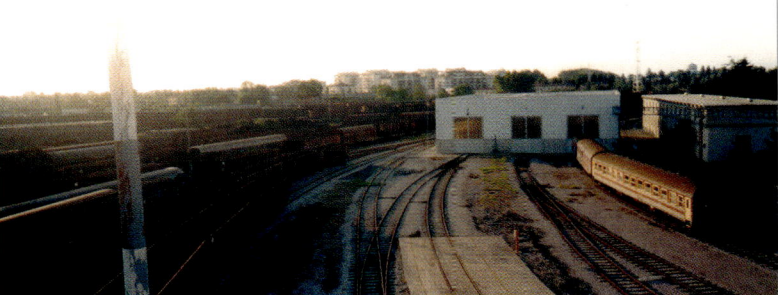

View from above of the yard of Campo di Marte, Padua   – *Capo*

Whole-car in Campo di Marte by Joys – EAD, Capo – ©>>   – *Capo*

> CONTINUES FROM PAGE 213

lave, Elics, Mich. When speaking about the scene in Vicenza it is necessary to remember the influences of Skah, Onis, Dext1, Konso and Solo24. These experimentations gradually influenced other writers in Veneto as well, among whom Senor of the Venetian F2D and Rego, who at one point changed his tag to Molok. With this name he started painting more abstract pieces, sometimes even without letters but just coloured compositions. Now I don't know if he did it as a provocation or as a joke, or maybe because somebody had gotten them confused, but I remember a *Littorina* by Molok where he had written "Sono Molok non Senor!"[5]. I also saw some double-decks and other *Regionali* by a certain Divieto that was from PV crew, I think from Trieste. This Divieto painted a lot of stuff together with Asone as well as DC crew, who up until '98 were doing very colourful pieces with simple letters on *Regionali* trains, 3-5-3s and the *Rossi*, a whole lot of stuff. The legend says that Klaun from DC always defecated in the yard every time he went there to paint. Apart from DC, Klaun was also part of *La Cremeria*, a crew dedicated to wall murals but that also included a couple of train bombers: every once in a while you could see a *Marmotta* by Spazio, Smile, and Zap. It has to be remembered that theirs was the first whole-car to be done in Udine, a Bteam on a *Marmotta*. Boost from Udine also painted in those years and did some really killer panels with characters, especially on the *Interregionali R ossi* and the *Marmotta*. Rame and Creo (TIA) also painted with him. Then there was also Safe, Base, the Cowboys and Penso. Rame subsequently became a member of MOD (*Masters of Disaster*), a sick crew that was born between '98 and '99 and that produced mad pieces on 668's, 3-5-3s and *Inter-regionali*. Originally it included Naso, Zuek, Res, and Sika. Then Cento joined and later on Rame (in the following years, after 2000 so did Bask and finally Neo).

You could say that like Padua, Udine was also a meeting point for many people and dozens and dozens of train cars came out of there, among which the *Sleeperette*, which were like the *Rossi* except with different colours: they were blue and white and had reclining seats inside, I remember a beautiful one by Boost and Sembro. From Udine you also got stuff by Waste, Darma, HC and Spano who painted many trains with an alien character and phrases regarding the existence of aliens. Then towards the end of '98 the first panels by Sexer appeared.

I also remember a crew from Verona, TSM with Shen, True and Dean who all painted a lot of 4-6-4s and 3-5-3s.

In 1998 in Treviso many of what we called *Verdigrigi* (greengreys, due to their colour) started circulating, a kind of newer version of the *Stronzi*. The route they covered was mostly always the same, the local Treviso-Vicenza. These trains had been sent from the region of Lazio and were filled with stuff by the Roman writers. I was psyched to be able to photograph different styles from the ones of my area. I remember some names: Trota, Gel, Blues, SIP crew. Obviously writers from Veneto also painted those trains, but not that much. I only remember a couple of very nice pieces that ran for months, a

---

"Love" by Clove and a piece by Sewor. Next to the panel by Clove was written: "Per Elisa, un sogno perduto"[6]. Between '97 and '98 the number of trains in the regional department grew tremendously, I continued taking pictures and cataloguing the styles that evolved out of the North-East in the 90's.

❻ For Elisa, a lost dream

Apart from the experimental stuff by F2D from Venice I remember work by Fank, sort of a set of explosions he drew between the windows, as if going in and out of them, plus stuff from the current of Vicenza, always very unique style-wise, such as the letters by Elics. By the end of the 90's the network was so thick and intense that almost every crew was formed by writers from different cities of the North-East.

In '99 Capo broke away from TWP and started hanging out prevalently with Joys and also Snow (who had become Wons in the meantime). MOD started getting bigger and in 2000 the first whole-train was done without it being a 668 (in which case a whole-train merely meant two whole-cars). This whole-train was on an *Inter-regionale, a Rosso*", and was a seven-car job done by four guys: Cento, Zuek, Naso and Copper (Rame). Nobody had ever seen anything like it in the history of North-Eastern train Writing. Four people had produced an enormous silver and black snake that had slithered with intact windows throughout the region, until reaching Venice! I don't even dare imagine what the buffers and tourists thought at the station of Venice when they saw it arrive: doing big, unprecedented things is definitely a characteristic of kings.

– COVERING THE TRAINS

In 2000 the protective film coating that allows pieces to 'melt' by spreading a specific acid and then washing away with water slowly but surely took the upper hand. In 2001 there were no longer variously coloured trains but a homogeneous white, green and blue on *Intercitys, Inter-regionali, Marmotta*, or any other type of train indistinctly. These were the colours

---

of the film coating. The match between writers and FS was now 1-1.

But I cannot forget the many periods spent with my eyes fixed between platforms, the emotion that filled my heart, the writers that said they had not taken a photo but weren't sweating it because they knew they could count on me. Sometimes I'd meet Fakso and Zuek about to board a train in Venice, or I'd bump into Senor taking pictures, I've lived many pleasant days and remember that at times I would imagine how everything would look were it to be clean one day, if they would ever manage it. Graffiti on trains gave me mad enthusiasm and inner gratification, a passion I have dedicated myself to for most of my life. From 2000 onwards the situation radically changed, it is no longer possible to spend entire days in the station trying to recognise the styles of the city. It has to be said however that even though now there are these damn film layers, stuff is running anyway. In these years some have stopped, others have started, others still simply continue, like MOD and ONE, "
>> crew " and other crews of Treviso, like 407, or people that actually skinned the film layer from the train before painting, like Naso, Rene, Kese. The story of Writing in North-Eastern Italy is not over, it has simply changed with the passing of time and I have only narrated one chapter of it.

---

lave
>

VENETO

During the early years nobody painted trains in Veneto except those nutcases from Treviso, everyone else focused on walls...word was that Mace had gotten a fine of 24 million Lira! Year after year the respective scenes started getting to know each other more, also for reasons that had nothing to do with Writing. Many kids were skaters before getting into graffiti, and this facilitated contacts because most of them knew each other

---

already. I skated with Naok and for this reason I often took the train to Padua or the Roxy Ring of Verona, to Bassano, where we met Fakso, Smek and Martino Orso, skaters that did graffiti just like us. We immediately became friends, Fakso had understood it was possible to paint trains and he was the first to guide me in the deposit. Writers would mostly hit the yards of their own city but many times we visited the neighbouring ones, in Venice I would paint in the train yard of Santa Marta, whose atmosphere was unique: on both sides it was bordered by the water of the lagoon. It was the most romantic and surreal deposit I have ever seen.

Natas
>

VENICE

The yard of Santa Marta is a surreal place, where painting trains becomes something cinematographic and unique. The primary entrance is obviously from a bridge that

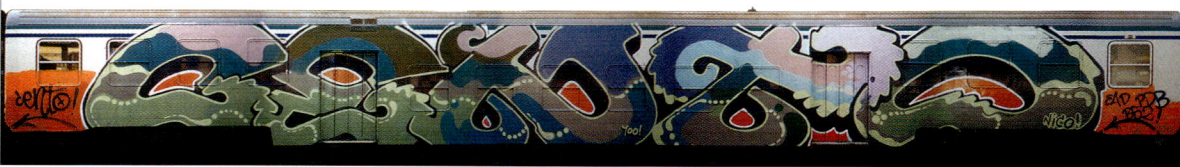

Whole-car by Cento – MOD, EAD, PDB, B52 crew, 4-6-4 train   – Cento

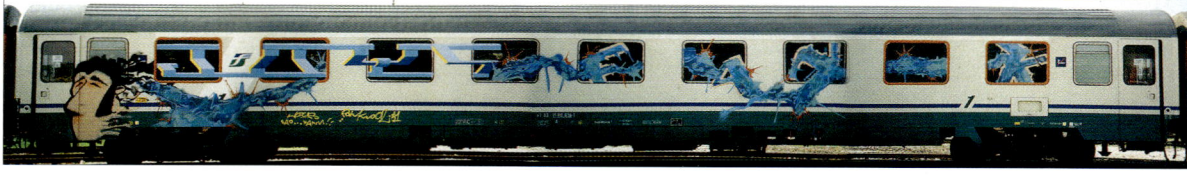

"Fank" by Fakso – SI, MOD, Joys – EAD, Intercity train   – Fakso

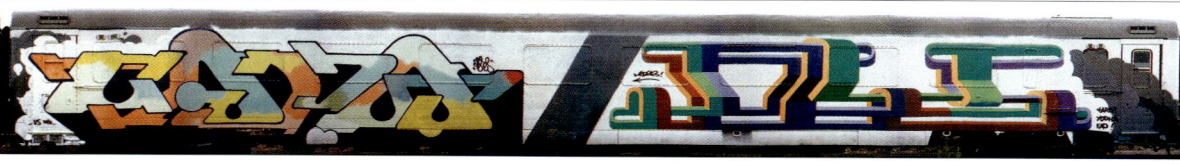

Whole-car by Capo – ©>>, Joys – EAD, Intercity train   – Capo

connects it to the rest of the city, after which however, there is a police checkpoint. Therefore to get in you had to pass through a series of alleys that eventually took you to an overpass, then a bridge to cross, at the end of which you were in the yard area, which was anyway a big blind alley since there's nothing but water around you. It's a pretty central area so there were a lot of tourists passing by on the vaporetto boats that would see the painted trains, parked in Santa Marta.

Joys
>

PADUA

The first trains in Padua were done at the end of '89 by Boogie and Mila, as well as by writers from Treviso like Mace, Starch and Clout. There was no systematic bombing, but rather sporadic episodes, you would paint whatever you found, from freight trains to postal ones. This continued for years, we'd go, do a panel, take pictures and then everybody went back home: the trains never ran. Then in 1996 the turning point, when bombing was taken up massively, trains started circulating painted and the yards were under regular assault: that was the golden era, when painting was chill and everything, I mean everything, was running. Padua is in a strategic position from which trains would move on both a regional and national scale: towards the South on the Bologna-Ancona line, towards the West the Milan-Turin and to the East the Venice-Trieste line.

Capo
>

MESTRE

The stations of Mestre and Venice have always been the end destination of the lines between Udine and Trieste, Treviso

Mestre that nobody had ever really taken advantage of since they were considered unfeasible in those years, due to the limited knowledge and interest of the old writers. They then started entirely covering the line of the *Arancioni*, the regional trains of the area, with violent end-to-ends and top-to-bottoms; they wrote things against the system, indeed it was no coincidence the initials of their crew stood for *Forze Del Disordine* (Forces of Disorder), they were against any form of legality and compromise with the institutions, you couldn't go to the station without noticing their trains. It had gotten to the point that actual police investigations were opened and bounties were put on their heads.

Zuek
>

BASSANO DEL GRAPPA

Writing down these memories while I'm riding in a train car of the same line we hit

on hitting the train deposits. In those days it was me, Fakso and Ceo, under the name *Super Idioti* (SI – Super Idiots), chosen by Fakso when he was trying to give some sense to the initials "SIS", which stood for a local cleaning company that was responsible for collecting trash, and whose trucks had been brutally bombarded some months earlier.

For all intents and purposes we were train writers, I don't remember ever having spent more than two hours in front of a wall. Plus I had problems planning pieces that didn't have the "shape" of the train panel. That's why I only painted certain models. For example we avoided the *Arancioni* trains of Venice because the bottom end of the cars curved, kind of rounding towards the wheel trolley so that they didn't cut the piece: it was like painting without the main characteristic of trains, without a set limit between the space that was useful and that which wasn't.

When we figured out that painting freight trains was for toys, we started hitting passengers: we realised a painted convoy had been running for over a month and from that moment on our attention was

that train and that other than us three, included also Iles, Eka and Pa1. Contemporaneous to us, on the same line which travelled the whole North-East of Italy, the *Littorine* were being painted by two other groups: NSA-TV (Rome) which included Washe Tears and Manjar, who studied in Venice at the time and painted the yard in the lagoon, and also LNF, who were in fact continuing the Treviso tradition of Wildsty started by Mace, Starch, and Clout. If it been groups were extremely distant from our way of conceiving graffiti and only after a couple of years did I start understanding and appreciating their take on style and lettering.

In the early 90s there was no connection between the kos in Venice and those in Treviso and so when the *Littorine* would arrive in Bassano with styles that were totally different from ours everybody was wondering who these guys were. At the time we tended to create mental manifestos that were difficult to change, then with time we started acquiring more consciousness and becoming more flexible with respect to Writing. Up until then the scene in our small city was circumscribed and provincial and pieces by other crews, especially the Lema group, were a sort of jab in the teeth for someone like me that was getting inspiration from the Letraset font catalogue and could not conceive that the shaft of an "R" could stem from the belly of an adjacent letter. Our vision of Writing and lettering was markedly defined by the school of Vicenza, by Esk, Skah, Iktrones, Ones Solo 24 and Iave. At the time Vicenza was partly tied to the Milanese scene but it actually developed a very personal and singular vision of letters that I would go as far as defining experimental. At the time many train productions were dictated by the desire to realise something new at any cost, which would include a strong conceptual component. This factor pushed us to realise pieces that were very removed from the traditional schemes, maybe even questionable and often unappreciated. It's a fact however that this way of conceiving Writing, whose origin can be traced to the primeval piece of Iktronex, soon expanded to include a wider circle of local writers, and then ended up characterising all the productions on the *Arancioni* in Mestre, painted by the insurrectional group F2D, with Sicov and Senor. As for 668 crew, with time it halved it's initial number and became the current MOD, first including Falso, Res and me. The crew reflected the maturity that we were acquiring with time as well as the desire to broaden our horizons, visiting yards outside of the city and all over Italy.

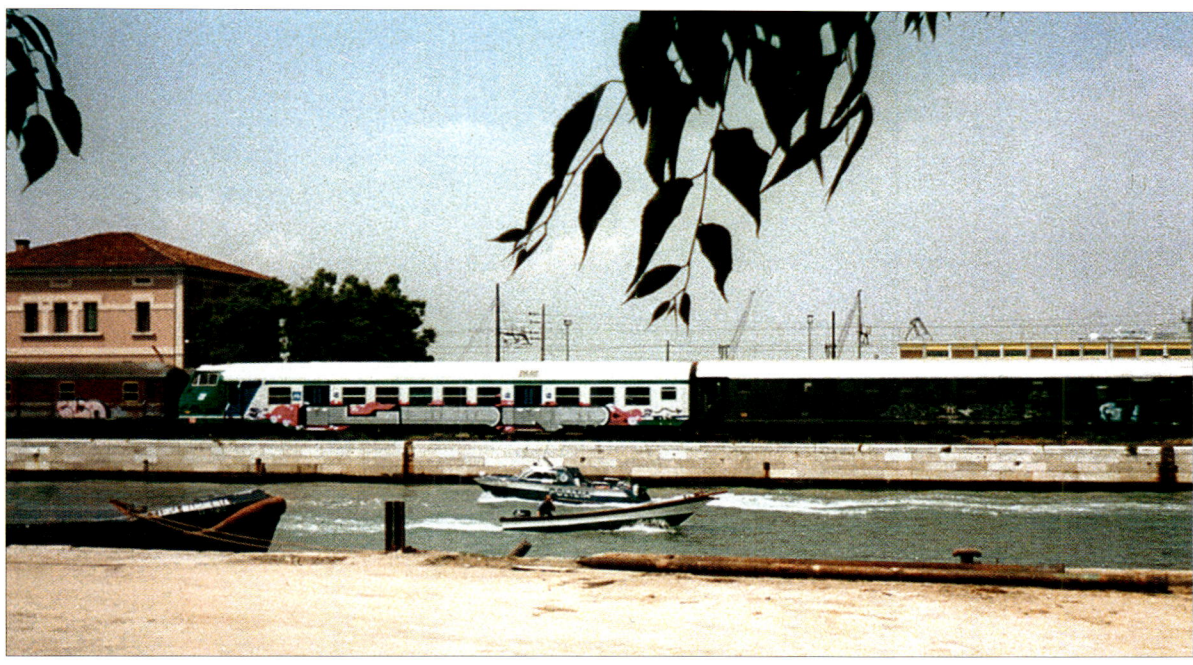

LDR end-to-end, painted in the yard of Venice and monitored by the police　　– *Slog*

and Belluno, and the Milan-Venice. Many trains would arrive from the South, from Bologna and Rome, or from the North, such as Switzerland and Eastern Europe.

The fact that the cities of Veneto are so close to each other enabled the train scene to explode between 1995 and '99. There were a lot of us painting assiduously and everything was running. We would see works by friends arrive in the station, the movement was very cohesive and we all respected each other, each of us was taking this thing pretty seriously. There was practically no buffing and going to the station always filled us with joy.

The first trains to be done in Mestre were by DWA and guys from outside, like Clout. The boom occurred in '95 when, together with Sat and Slog, Braco, Hate, and others, I started seriously hitting the FS trains, first the postals and then the passengers, beginning at Mestre and then in Venice. Quite soon later Senor, Wons and Hask started painting in the deposits of

for over a decade, until it was fully saturated, makes me smile. At the time we weren't even 18. It was a period in which we preferred freight trains to passengers, in spite of the fact they were adjacent to each other in the deposit.

It was more gratifying to sit on a bench in front of the station and observe the top-to-bottom of a freight train last for months as opposed to seeing pieces cancelled on the passengers after 48 hours. Fakso and I would enter the deposit in the day, with a ladder each. We'd get to the yard by scooter on Sunday afternoons, in August, when the sun still illuminated the cars at 7. Before me there had been others from my city that had been fascinated by what in Italy can be considered "a parcel shipped from overseas", in which you found Writing, Break-dance and rap, neatly tied up under the name of "Hip Hop culture". I would anyway prefer to trace back the history of Writing in my city to the period in which writers concentrated

focused almost exclusively on a sole train type, the littorina. The AL 668 was in fact the train model that all three of us, me, Fakso and Ceo, took every morning to go to school. These trains travelled the whole North-East, from Cortina to Venice, from the sea to the mountains. We developed an almost maniacal attention towards these convoys that pushed us to make a real census. Every painted train was coupled with its piece and transcribed on a sort of register, probably on what at the time was my school notebook. The entry would be something like: "KSO, silver piece outline blue AL 668 n.1220". In this way we had control of the cars and knew when pieces were cleaned or covered, though this didn't happen for various years, which is why it was the golden age of the Italian railway, before they applied the film coating to the trains that is.

Our attachment to the *Littorina* was a pretext to create 668, a new group whose name was inspired by the number of

Immediate and also unusual was the union with Cento with whom we had had a sort of stylistic rivalry and antipathy that however became the pretext to establish a long-lived friendship and an inevitable exchange of shapes. The presence of Cento allowed our group to get closer to Ble first, with whom he had formed a sort of "newer pack" of Italian Writing, and later Rune, with whom we had an experimental stylistic affinity even before this union.

And finally MOD was joined by Neo, a young writer from our city, at a time during which trains were already covered by the film coating.

To continue having them run painted, we started carving the film off, an extreme remedy to an extreme measure.

LITTORINE

YEAR OF CONSTRUCTION	1954–1981
MAX SPEED	110/130 km/h
CAPACITY	68 seats
DIMENSIONS	22 x 23,5 x 2,8 metres
QUANTITY PRODUCED	787 units in 12 series (diesel)

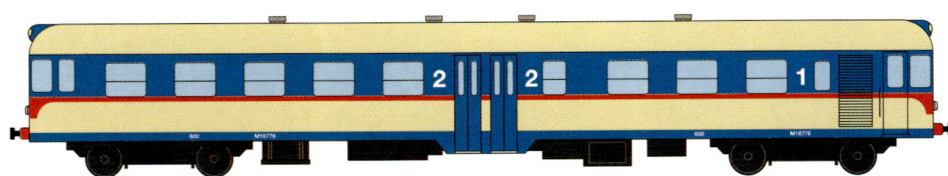

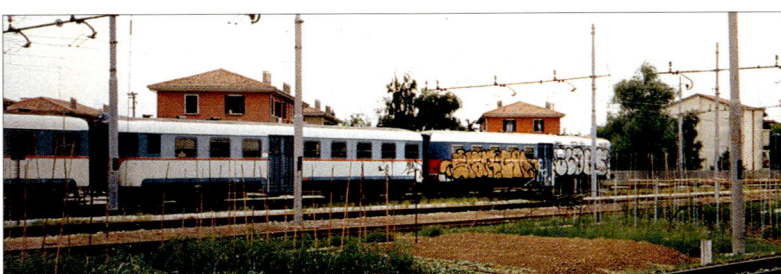

Top to bottom by Starch – CKC, Littorina train, Treviso, 1990   — *Mace*

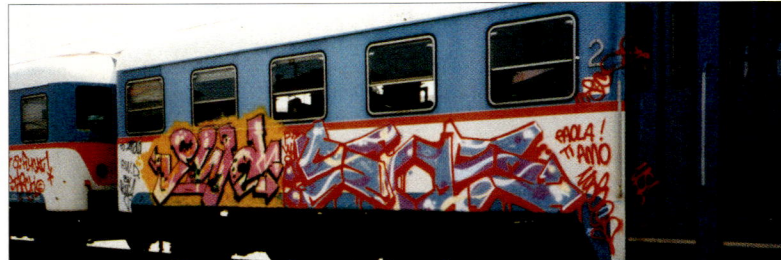

PWD by Sky 4 from Milan, "Sos" by Mace – PWD, Littorina train, Treviso, 1988   — *Mace*

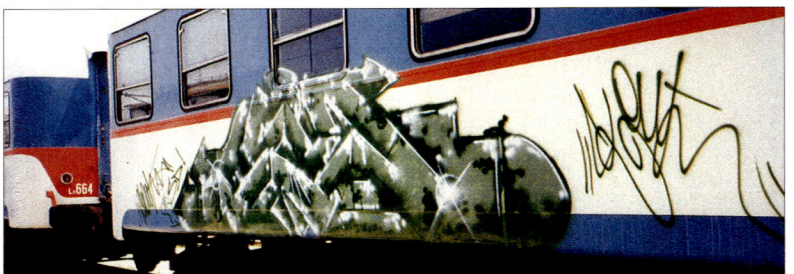

Clout – CKC, 1989   — *Rusty*

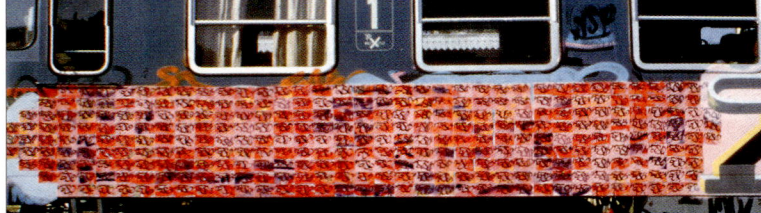

Sticker piece by Fakso – SI, MOD, 1996   — *Fakso*

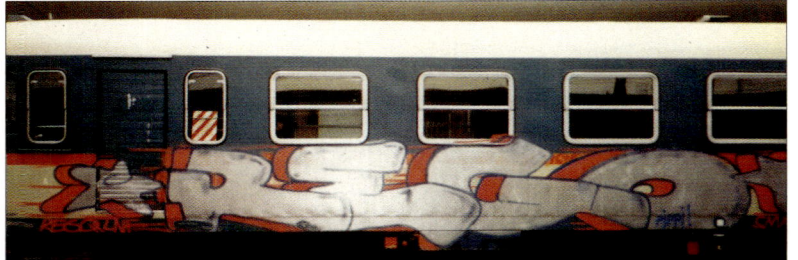

Rego, Littorina train, mid 90's   — *Siso*

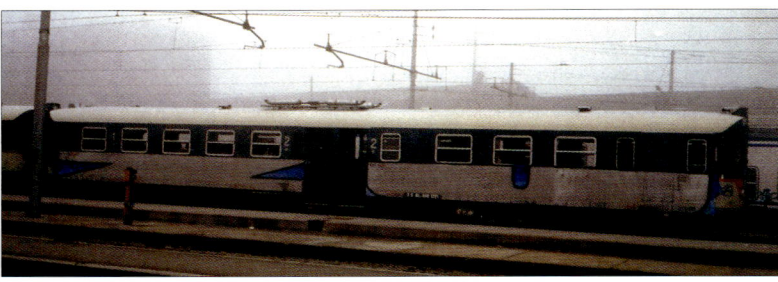

"Zu" end-to-end by Zuek – SI, MOD, Bassano del Grappa station, 1996   — *Siso*

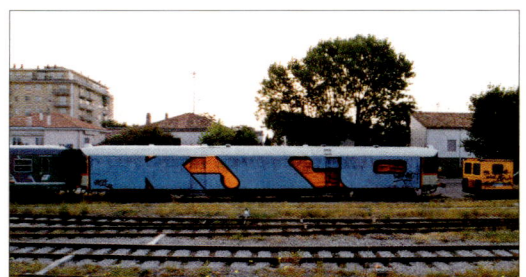

"Kso" by Fakso – SI, MOD, whole-car on Littorina train   — *Fakso*

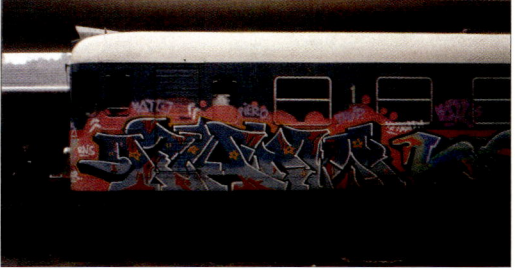

Kato – TM, RNS crew from Schio, 1996   — *Siso*

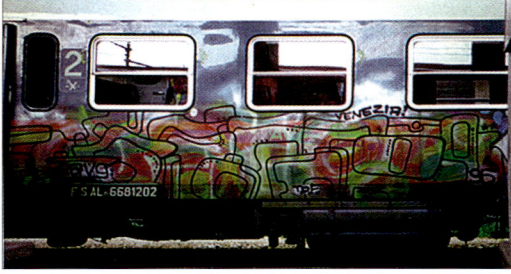

Iave from Vicenza on Littorina train, 1997   — *Siso*

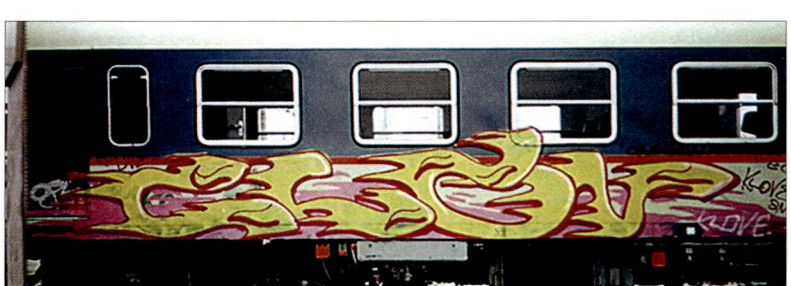

"Cbv" by Klove, Treviso   — *Siso*

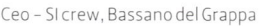

Ceo – SI crew, Bassano del Grappa   — *Siso*

CARRIAGE UIX-C " MARMOTTA " OR "BORDEAUX"

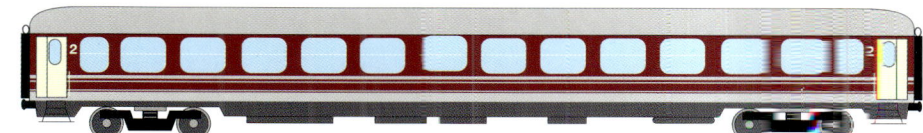

YEAR OF CONSTRUCTION	1964-1985
MAX SPEED	160/200 km/h
CAPACITY	60 seats (1 class) - 72 (2 class)
DIMENSIONS	26,4 x 2,8 x 4 metres
QUANTITY PRODUCED	4300 units in 6 series

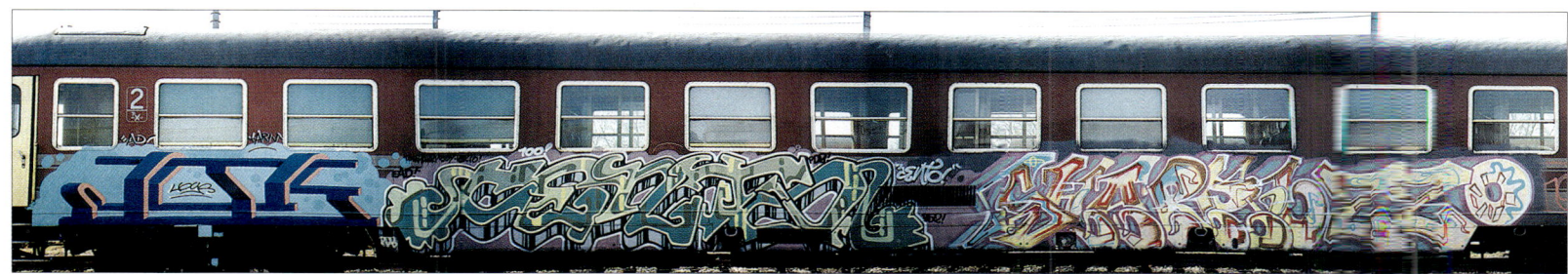

Joys – EAD, Cento – EAD, "Sharpuzzo" by Sharp from New York City, 1999   – D90 Maniacs archive

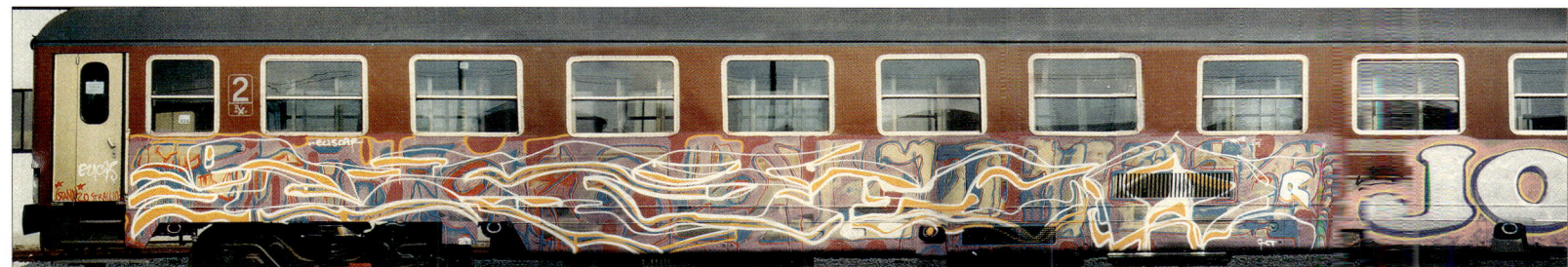

Elics piece in the yard of Campo di Marte, Padua   – Siso

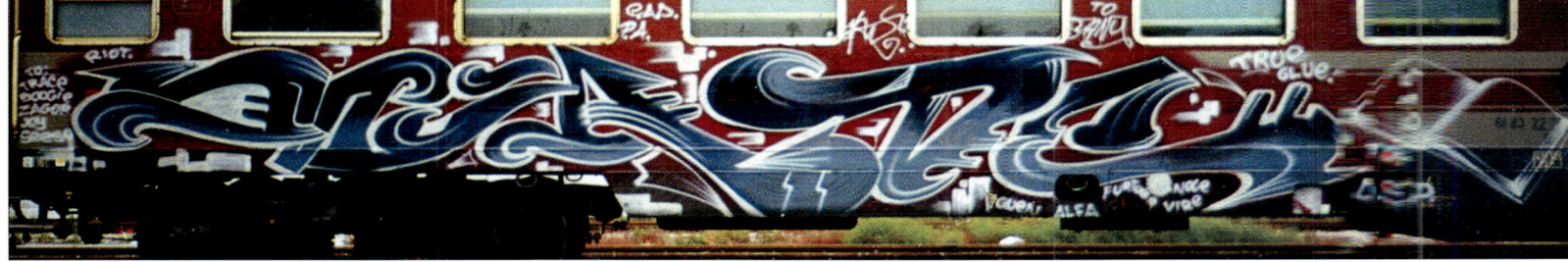

Made – EAD crew, Padua   – Siso

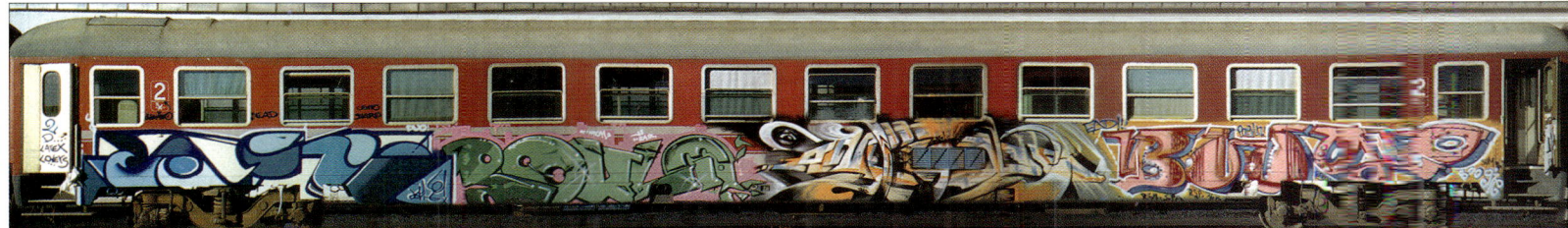

End-to-end by Dafne – 2D, Roule – EAD, Made – EAD, Boogie – EAD, 1998   – D90 Maniacs archive

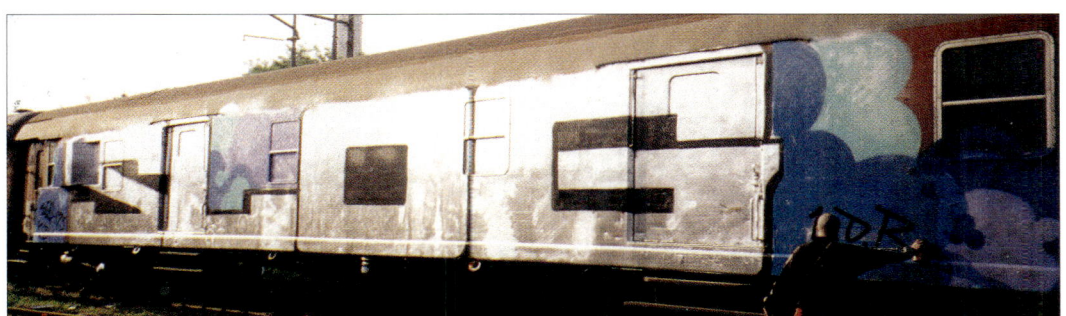

Top-to-bottom blockbuster by Slog – LDR crew   – Slog

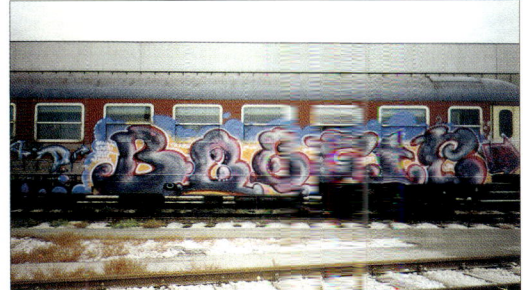

Boogie – EAD crew from Padua   – Siso

CARRIAGE MDVE "ROSSI"

YEAR OF CONSTRUCTION	1982–1985
MAX SPEED	160 km/h
CAPACITY	64 seats (1 class) – 84 (2 class)
DIMENSIONS	26,4 x 2,8 x 3,9 metres
QUANTITY PRODUCED	981 units

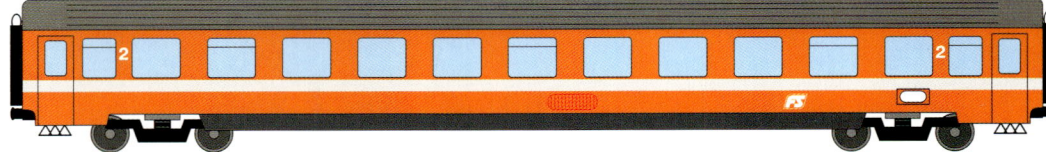

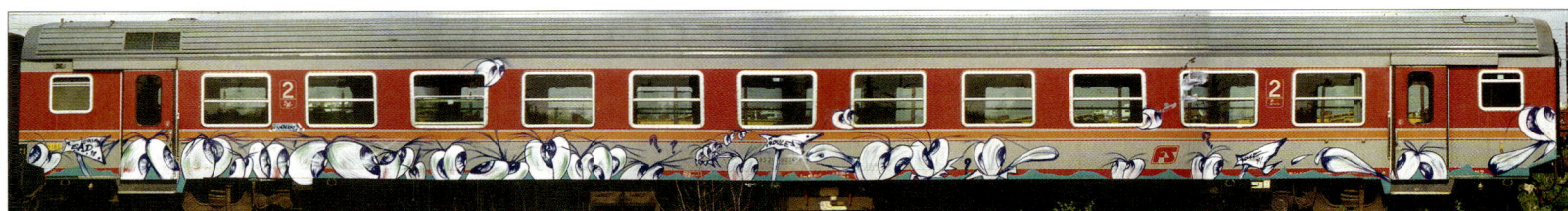

Eyes end-to-end by Roule – EAD crew, 1998   — *10000 Maniacs archive*

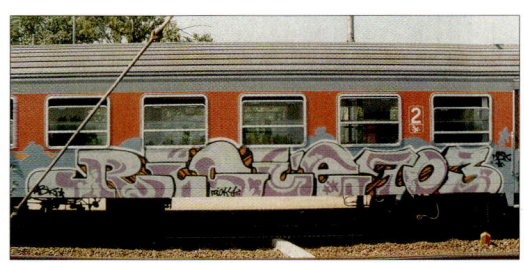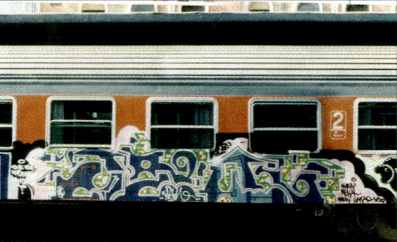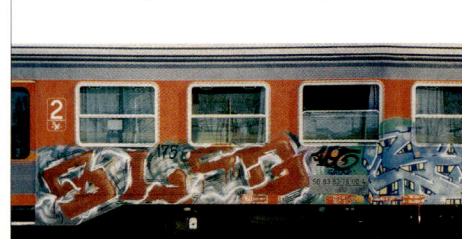

" Ricie 703" by Ricky – MBK   — *Siso*   Klaun – DC crew, late 90's   — *Siso*   Slog175 and Sat – LDR crew, 1995   — *Siso*

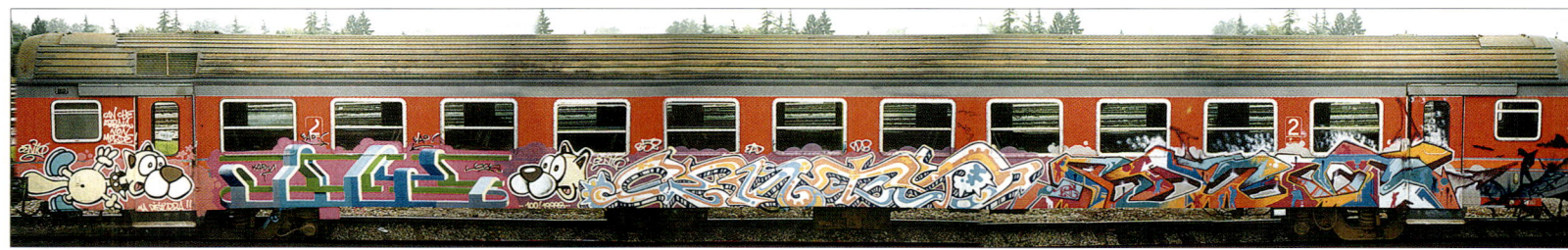

Loys – EAD, Cento – B52, MOD, B52, PDB, Boost – LAC, 1998. "Can che abbaia non morde! Ma disturba!!" (Dog that barks doesn't bite! But disturbs!!), dog puppets from Cento   — *10000 Maniacs archive*

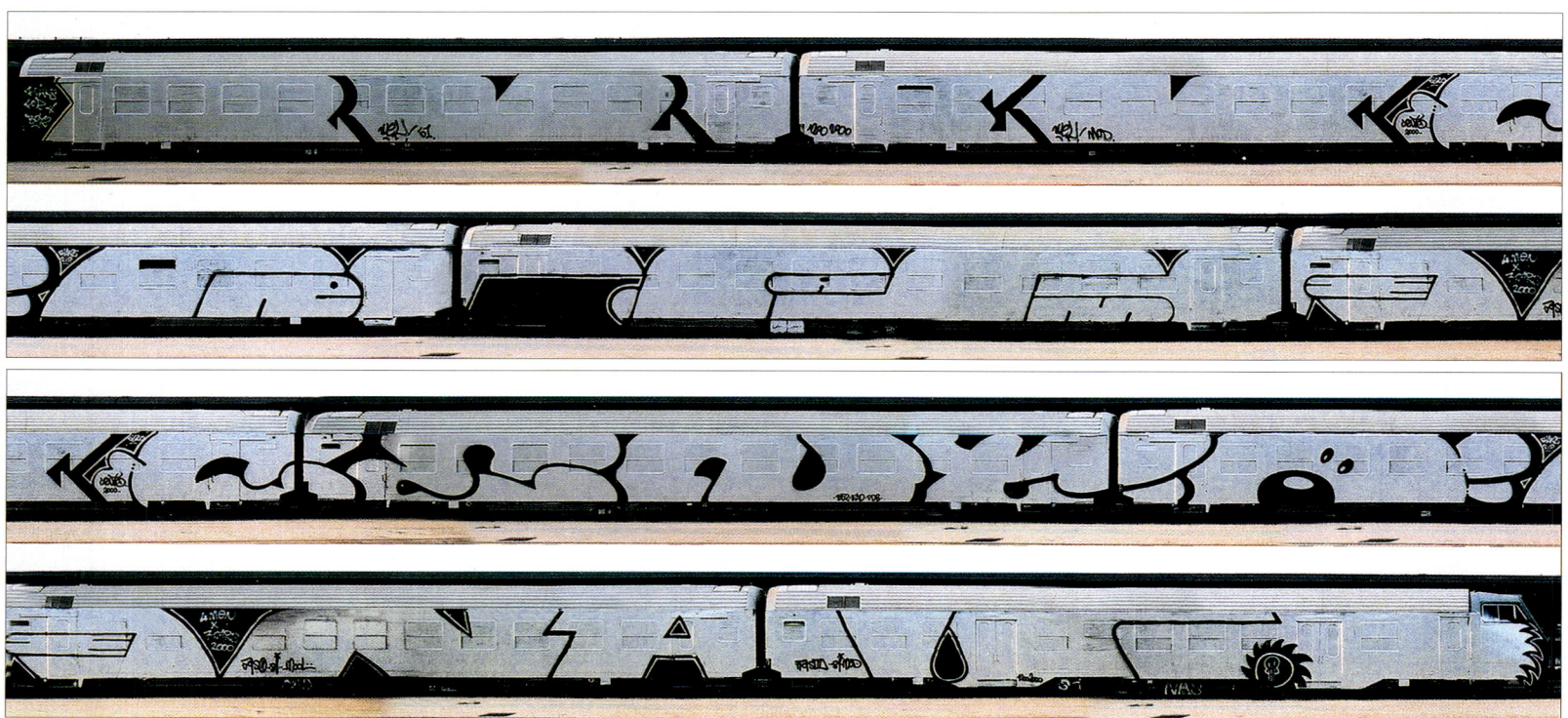

Silver whole-train by Zuek – SI, MOD, Cento – B52, EAD, PDB, Rame – MOD, Fakso – SI, MOD on local *Rossi*, 2000. First seven-car whole-train painted by four writers in Veneto   — *10000 Maniacs archive*

CARRIAGE MDVC "3-5-3"

YEAR OF CONSTRUCTION	1979–1989
MAX SPEED	160 km/h
CAPACITY	82 seats (2cl) – 28 (1cl) + 44 (2cl)
DIMENSIONS	26,4 x 2,8 x 3,9 metres
QUANTITY PRODUCED	1.313 units

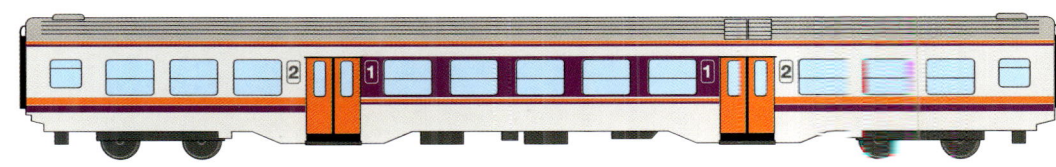

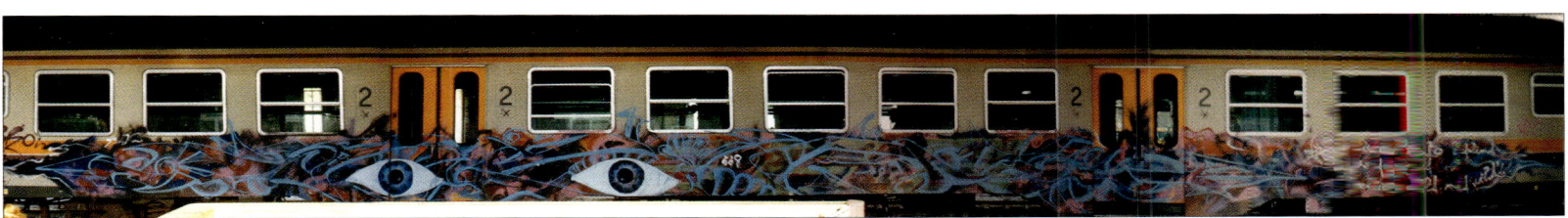

Sika – MKS, SI, 663 crew, 3-5-3 train. "Ho incontrato l'anima che avanzava sul sentiero della mia vita" (I met the soul that adavanced on the path of my life)   – Siso

CARRIAGE NAVETTA "4-6-4"

YEAR OF CONSTRUCTION	1965–1982
MAX SPEED	140 km/h
CAPACITY	100+70 (2class) – 76+50 (2class)
DIMENSIONS	26,4 x 2,8 x 3,7 metres
QUANTITY PRODUCED	1.076 units

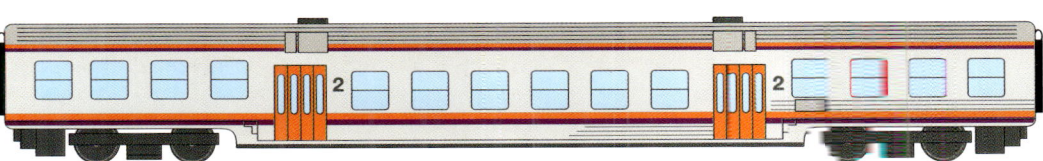

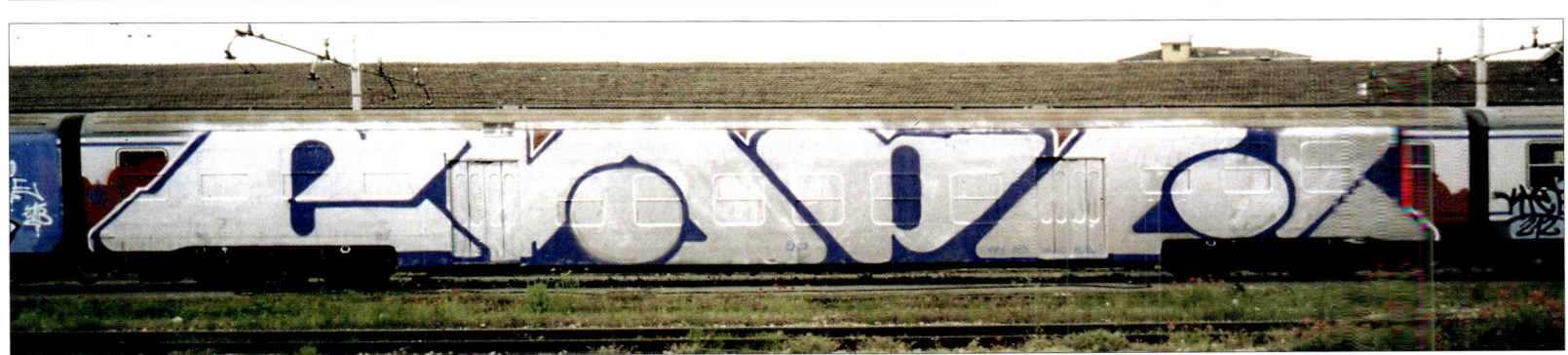

Silver one-man whole-car by Capo – ☺>>, painted in 2002 on a train with protective film coating   – Siso

CARRIAGE UIC– Z1 " GRIGI "

YEAR OF CONSTRUCTION	1985–1993
MAX SPEED	200 km/h
CAPACITY	54 seats (1class) – 66 (2class)
DIMENSIONS	26,5 x 2,8 x 4 metres
QUANTITY PRODUCED	830 units

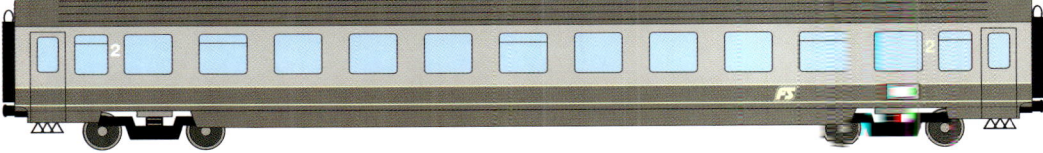

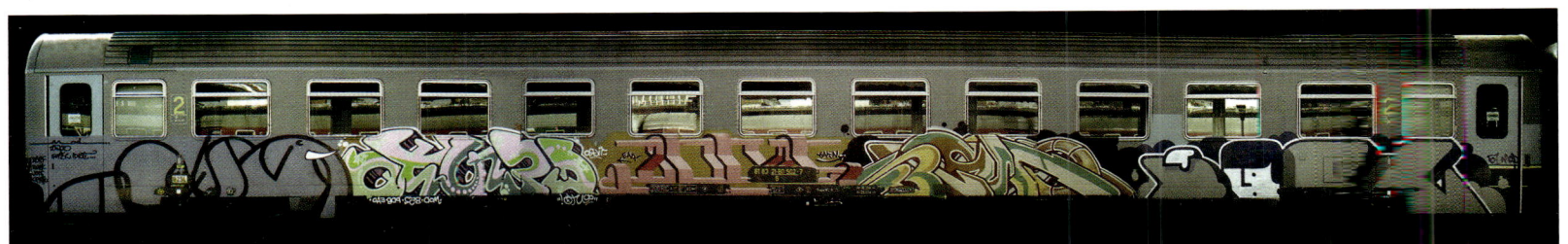

Naso – SI, MOD, "Otnec" by Cento – B52, EAD, PDB, MOD, Joys – EAD crew, Blef – B52, PDB, MOD, Zuek – SI, MOD, end-to-end on Intercity *Grigi* train   1000 Maniacs archive

CARRIAGE UIC–X "ARANCIONI"

YEAR OF CONSTRUCTION	1960–1985
MAX SPEED	110 km/h
CAPACITY	68 seats
DIMENSIONS	26,4 x 2,8 x 3,9 metres
QUANTITY PRODUCED	800 units

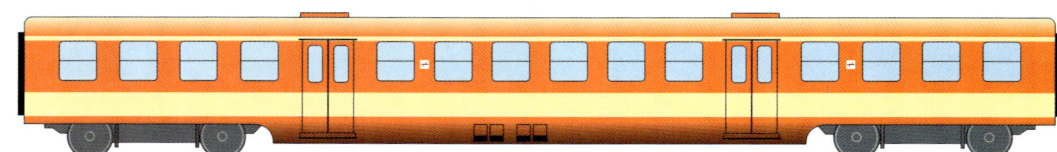

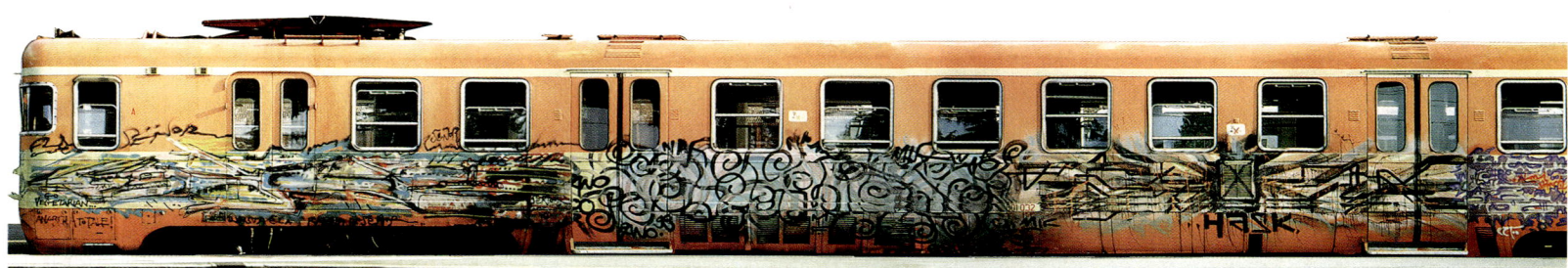

Senor – F2D, GCT "Questa è la rabbia di Senor" (This is the rage of Senor), Bano – MIF, Hask – F2D, GCT , Wons – F2D, GCT, 1998   *– Siso*

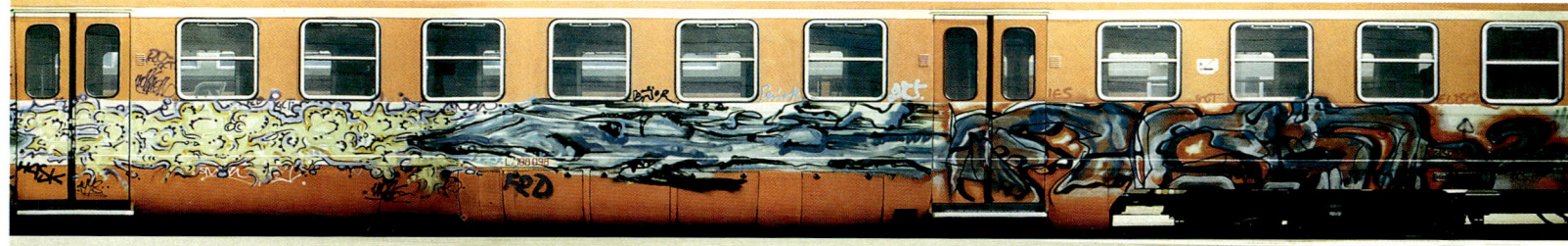

Hask – F2D, GCT, Senor – F2D, GCT, Elics – GCT, 1998   F2D – "Forze del disordine" (Forces of disorder)   *– Siso*

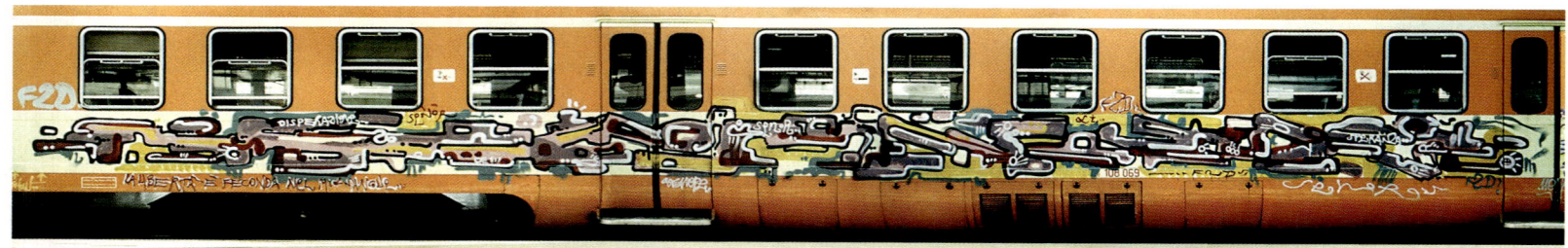

Senor – F2D, GCT " La libertà è feconda nel mio sangue" (Freedom is ingrained in my blood), 1998   GCT – "Gestualità Cultura Tradizione " (Gesture Culture Tradition)   *– Siso*

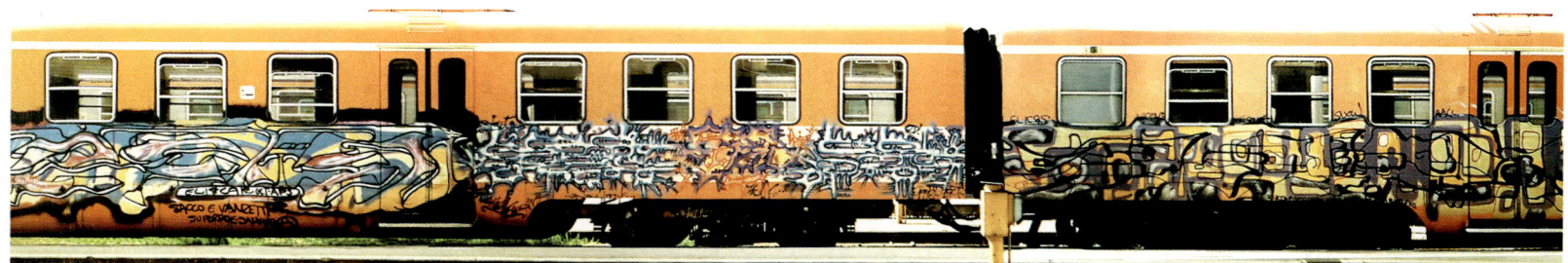

Elics – GCT "Sacco e Vanzetti su ferro e sangue"(Sacco and Vanzetti on steel and blood), Wons – F2D, GCT, 1998 (continues below)   *– Siso*

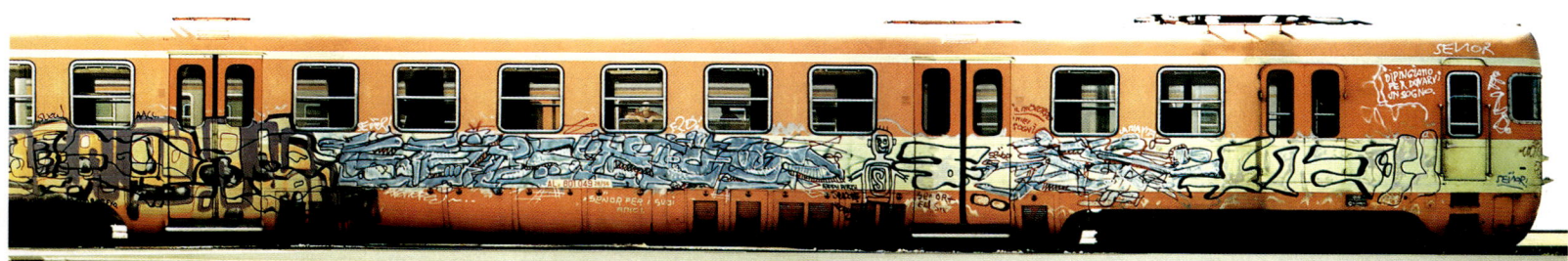

Senor – F2D, GCT, Senor + Elics" Il mio corpo…I miei sogni…La mia vita"(My body…My dreams..My life), 1998. "Dipingiamo per donarvi un sogno" (We paint to give you a dream)   *– Siso*

Page 225

>

Railway arena
City overview

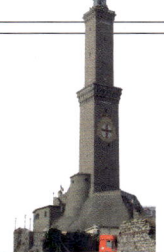

Page 232

>

Mythology today
Video-Sexy-Trama

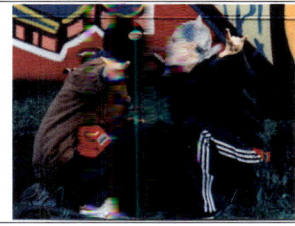

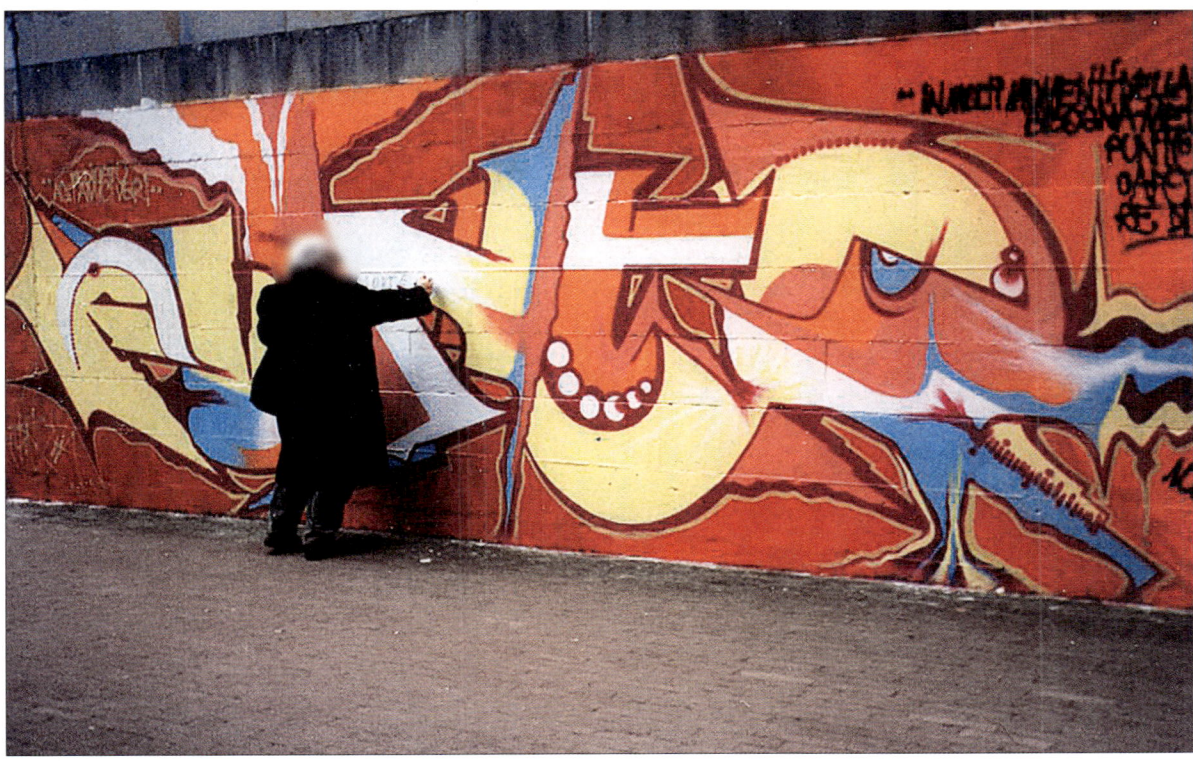

— Simone Poggiali

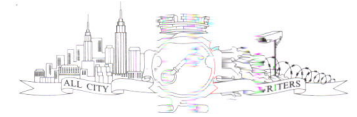

ACW INTERNATIONAL /
GENOA

Main contributors:
Blef, Dafne, Emis, Easo,
Mer, Pam, Rais, Sherif,
Siti, Tabo

In collaboration with:
ACD, DIAS, FL, G3, FDB,
RAL, SA

curated by
Cesare Bignotti

Cover photo:
The M crossing a Sed piece

M and the secrets of the city

In a city that offers few spaces to paint in, every tag or piece was systematically crossed by a mysterious "M"

The case of M is unique in the world, both in consistency and duration, an enigma which has generated urban myths and legends: twenty years of destruction involving the walls in the streets of Genoa. With the appearance of the first tag, writers became engaged in a conflict with an anonymous enemy, provoking a counter phenomenon, a negation of graffiti with constant crossing of pieces and Names, a gesture that occurs in the city of Genoa and extends to include the whole territory, from East to West. Every tag, piece, sticker or poster is daily targeted and destroyed.

The wiping out of graffiti in Genoa is neither an episodic nor a casual phenomenon but is part of an almost symbolic process that is now a trademark of this city. It would not be possible to speak of Writing in Genoa without reconstructing the history and origin of a "scene" in conflict with this invisible enemy. But who is

behind it? Where is it coming from? Why in Genoa? These are unresolved questions dozens of teenagers who have had to deal with this systematic repressive system, more constant than any anti-graffiti team, more tenacious than any vigilante, have asked themselves.

Inevitably, the determination of this M, the "vecchia", as she was referred to throughout Liguria, pushed the graffiti of the alleys and historic centre of Genoa out to the forgotten areas of the city.

In this city many chose to do not give visibility to their work, unintentionally baiting an exactly contrary reaction resulting in a relentless acceleration of the local scene's fragmentation. Pushed by the urge to be invisible and immune to M's deadly attack, attention has been moved toward hidden almost inaccessible spaces for outsiders.

On the other hand, the few writers exclusively devoted to trains, have not been trapped by this dynamic destruction of notoriety. With one or two exceptions, they were the only writers to enjoy immunity, and it is still not known why, given the audacity of this *all city* plague contaminator to wipe out every trace of the writer. It is as if the ephemeral works

painted on the sides of train cars remained invisible to the eyes of a big "urban" brother.

Like many other social and urban phenomena in Genoa, there is also an aura of mystery surrounding writing. It was here where one of the first seed of the Italian graffiti movement was planted, and also the network between Italian activists.

Alleanza Latina, an early magazine which began with modest resources and went on to be more and more organized, represented a pole that attracted a large number of different fans. AL was one of the few which showed what was happening in Europe making it possible for Italian readers to compare themselves with others and giving them a voice. It also became a means to distribute other European and American publications imported into Italy in some cases for the first time. The arrival of this press was responsible almost exclusively for the tendency of some local writers to become passionately involved with trains. Chintz, Mellie, Rens, Pike, are only a few of the names the locals considered as role models. They didn't necessarily want to imitate their styles, but were fascinated by the atmosphere their work communicated, almost in a subliminal way. NYC was

present but somehow it seemed worthy of an archaeological study. In 1996 "Coloriamo" an event sponsored by the municipality and organized by AL took place. It went almost unnoticed, but in addition to many locals, Phase 2 was present. Today it makes us smile to think of a young bunch of rookies, stuffed with graffiti, meeting this key role figure. The scene was cut in half: on one side a group of locals intended to show their skills and on the other an exotic writer remaining virtually isolated in his wild lettering. Our smile is bitter sweet, because the two worlds never ever really met.

Towards the end of the 90's Genoa had become one of the most active train writing cities. All the stations and part of the two coasts of the neighbouring regions were massively bombed.

Gradually the result has been a territory in which traces of writers are rare compared to other cities. This must not to be interpreted in a simplistic way but rather analyzed taking into account the manifold obstacles that the city writers had to confront for a long time. The circumstances had a strong impact which hardened some and revealed the weakness of others.

– SHERIF, ACD.

The role of 'M' in the collective imagery of writers

>

A lonesome legend

Cesare Bignotti

>

A BRIEF PORTRAIT

At the beginning of the 90's, seeing the absurd dynamics with relation to the destruction of tags, the scene in Liguria had started posing continuous questions that led to a series of outlandish urban legends. At first we had guessed the cause had to be attributed to an ex-writer, or anyway an individual "close" to the street scene, perhaps envious of the stylistic progress of others. This theory became even more credible after some pieces on trains got trashed. The anti-graffiti phenomenon was represented by a key word, "Merda", (shit), covering tags and pieces in Genoa, and later reduced to the single letter M. With the passing of time this sign became a logo of the city, repeated an infinite amount of times. While you walk along the alleys of the historic centre, or through the tourist harbour, you can distinguish it because of a specific stroke that can be synthesised in four essential movements; the majority of Ms were in fact executed tracing from the bottom right corner, with the left side of the letter tending to stretch downwards.

Though this mark was repeated in the serial manner typical of tags, with time different alternative theories were gaining ground with regards to the author. One of these referred to a Right-wing group of people who didn't appreciate the urban disfigurement of graffiti. Indeed, some of the letters done by political propaganda groups were completely lacking any calligraphy, just coarse, ignorant, letters very similar to those present in the word "Merda" such as the "E", the "R" or the "A". The only anomaly was the size of the letters and the tool used, since the Right-wing groups didn't use Pilot markers to write their messages. But why cross tags with an "M" when they could do it directly with a Celtic cross?

Another curious theory is the one that evokes a person deeply rooted to the city, who never goes beyond its limits, as if M never went on holiday. It's a fact that in Genoa during the summer the phenomenon stops or anyway decreases notably, as if the author had difficulty getting out of the house. On the contrary during spring and other seasons it's possible to see tags covered in freshly applied quicklime in the middle of the day. It is also said that in the 80's, with wide advance with respect to the arrival of Writing in Genoa, the same author had been repeatedly writing accusatory phrases against the world throughout the city. Strolling through the streets it was possible to find yourself before an interminable series of lectures written on the urban canvas of the city, phrases that directly accused the regional political class, with as much as names and surnames. These words, contorted and often making no sense at all, were multiplying all over the city. The practice underwent

a change towards the end of the 80's, when another urban phenomenon, just as 'enigmatic' and unusual, started appearing: tags and Writing, that shared a common environment and illegality with the messages of M, yet were perceived as competition, a battle of one against all, between her and the multitude of kids that were starting to get into graffiti. M evidently felt usurped of the public space she used to express herself and reacted with a counter-attack made of contorted, often illegible elements. This conflict with Writing induced her to radically renovate the way she manifested her discontent: it was no longer necessary to write ranting speeches, the message was transformed into a challenge, a battle on the field of the street that continuously reduced her personal expression into a quick, gestural action that aimed at completely destroying any other sign.

Tabo

>

CONTENDING THE CITY

From the end of the 80's to the present time, whoever is concealed behind the sign "M" has used different increasingly evasive techniques, to guarantee the success of his/her action, for instance, the switch from whitewash for the tags to black mortar for the pieces, or the stickers period. Also by using markers, "M" has followed the evolution of the early writers from Genoa. Comments and insults, written with indelible markers. often concerning people involved in local and national politics, appeared on buildings and crash cans for years. Like many other people in the city and before I was involved in writing, I personally saw an elderly woman several times writing slogans on a trash can. This phenomenon slowed down with the appearance of the first tags and their consequent coverage with the "merda" scribble which is why "M" was identified immediately as an old lady. At the same time she became invisible. Taking advantage of this mad woman's notoriety in the city, Sid One succeeded in finding out the name and last name of her, oddly they had both the "M " as initial letters. Together with Zek, Crim, May, Feibol and later with the VIA crew, we started to put up stickers with our tags on. Just as she had done with the tags done with markers, she started to use the stickers too. It started as a stickers battle that lasted for a long time: stickers over stickers, everywhere, until large format stickers were used. Then her trademark was replaced by long rambling messages, sometimes with the use of tricky or odd words. I remember a few of them: " Skateppista " (a word generated by the mix of skate and mugger) or " Skamerduso " (a word generated by the mix of Skate and shitty). This step into the skate world could be due to a rumoured violent attack this women suffered by some local skater, somehow

connected with graffiti. Some references were impossible to decipher; others were of a dreadful precision. This was the case of some very violent stickers like the one which predicted that we would be found dead in a trash can with our ass broken, which at the time we only answered with stickers tags. During the the same period we found stickers with names, surnames and other personal details. There were a lot of these, and the scale of this phase was really *All City*. One of these names was unknown but the others, enriched with many threats were a neighbor of SidOne and the other, "Billo", a friend of ours, guilty of having a Crim tag on the side of his scooter. Using the plate number she found his identity and address. In a short time, his neighbourhood was full of "merda" scribbles, not over tags, but placed with arrows, placed at intervals across my house garden and pointing directly at his house door.

At that point we started to go over her mad stickers with big adhesive sheets setting a place and a date for a meeting. The place designated was the "Depurator Park" in the Quinto district, famous for Flycat and SidOne pieces, and one of our daily playgrounds. It was chosen for being a place particularly easy to control, especially the entrance, where you could remain hidden inside. We wanted there to be many of us at that rendez-vous, but instead there were only Crim and I. It was 8 o'clock in the evening, a dark and cold winter day. We sat on a bench and waited. We saw some cars parking in front of the park. About 15 people came out of the cars and immediately gathered around the park iron handrail. A couple of men about 30-35 years came out of the group toward the entrance. We were 16 years old and were afraid that the old lady had a group of supporters, or that perhaps they were people whose property had been damaged by tags. We left our few defensive "weapons" hidden in the potted plants . Then we came out too, swallowing saliva. As we passed by them, they sized us up intensely without a word, as did the crowd outside. The air was really heavy. This incident didn't help us to find out who was behind the "M " identity. Instead it increased the mystery. On the way back, we decided to give up covering the "M" stickers. Continuing to do so was useless at that point. The result was a phaseout and finally the writing of specific names disappeared. Accordingly we also concluded and it was taken for granted among us that if you were piecing or tagging in the streets, it might last an hour, and it might last a month, but eventually they would all be smashed.

Emis

>

WRITERS AGAINST

When I started, M had already been around a while and kids were starting to get an idea of what was going on.

Everybody was talking about an old lady, sure, but how many fucking years was this lady old? Had she been an old lady even as a kid? Full of curiosity, and pretty pissed off, we started looking for her.

I had my doubts regarding the age of this ghost because I just couldn't associate everything M had done with an aging woman. She went as far as crossing Sherif's tags with white squirts of quicklime, and they were really unreachable due to his height. It's also true that if you have a decorator's brush you might manage to reach up that high, but if you're an old lady you can't make it, in some points buckets had even been used to cover two, three pieces, and I just couldn't envision an aging woman walking around armed with buckets of quicklime. Had it only occurred around the area where she lived I could have understood, but underneath the bridges of the rivers of Staglieno, in the cemetery, in the sewers, in places you could only reach by climbing, walking between brambles and weeds, there was no way you could be sure it was an old woman. Looking at it from the perspective of "getting up" - key concept for writers, she had left her signature everywhere, more than anyone and all over: walls, buses, trains, stations, trucks, toilets. If she really was an old lady, shit, props to her. We came up with theories and myths: one told of a woman, mother of a dead skater, that had gone mad and hated pieces and tags because they reminded her of the environment and memory of her dead skater son. It was said she was the same person that was writing political slogans on garbage cans. Her name was M and we went searching for her. She had a shaved head, and was already old, like 65-70. When we started looking for the person responsible we had hoped it was a group of people rather than an aging woman, because in that case we could have taken it out on them. Most ordinary people associated this phenomenon to a battle between gangs of writers, they thought that groups of writers were clashing in competition for the territory, and that the method they used to mark it was writing "Merda" over the work of the rival crew.

Blef

>

DIRECT CONTACT

From what I know the story of M dates back to the end of the 80's, it emerged in contrast with the first underground inputs of Genoa. I remember a spot where skaters would meet up, among them were those who were scribbling the first tags, the first attempts at Writing, nothing serious, but all expressions that in their way would increase the interest and the thirst for knowledge regarding the movement. In that period clear messages of dissent against the first tags had been emerging: vegetables had been thrown directly on pieces, onions, crosses and insults were appearing on top of any gesture that recalled the street message. You could say that M has always existed and was born with us, I limited myself to doing what I did, and what I did was mostly panels on trains, which she would normally not reach. In the city there were some walls that I used as training for the study of fonts, hidden spots in the centre and outskirts where I still go today and which I won't reveal to avoid the risk of getting crossed. In the early period the general curiosity was evident, one day we were resolute, we decided we had to understand who she was; to find the person we wrote messages on stickers and left them around the city, next to the crossed tags and pieces, in which we clearly expressed our disappointment with regard to what was happening. With time the first replies started appearing, and we were unprepared, the words sounded like threats, stuff like: *may a bulldog attack your throat.* I remember Tabo once found some arrows that indicated directly towards his house with sentences like: "Hit one to educate a hundred". Among the most absurd things I remember is that around 1998, M even appeared on train panels; I've always asked myself how she managed it, and I came to the conclusion that she reached the trains from the platforms and the dead end rail tracks of the regional trains. One time I saw a crossed piece on the wall of the track line, which was under a pedestrian overpass, a strange thing since the pedestrian bridge had pretty tall security grids; it would have taken a lot of strength to climb over them and throw the bucket of quicklime straight onto the piece, but she went to that extent. That's how it's always been here, unfortunately this has become part of the tradition of Genoa.

Mer
>

MULTIPLE IDENTITIES

When it comes to M I've always been in favour of the theory that considered an organised group of people, not a single individual. Perhaps the first few years everything started just as the legend claims, with the famous "old lady of quicklime", but even if initially it could have been a single person, in my opinion in the course of time other characters joined the club, let's say in "emulation" or maybe to protest against graffiti. I've never personally seen someone write over a tag, but more than once I've found my tags crossed only a couple of hours after I had done them. In twelve years I have heard them all, from those claiming to know the home address of the "old lady", to those that say they have seen her at work along with her daughter. The most "romantic" and imaginative story I prefer to remember interprets the gesture of the woman as a sort of revenge for the death of her husband, a blue-collar worker in a company that produced spray paint.

Pam
>

OVERTURN

M was up before I even started, ever since I was a little girl and didn't know anything about Writing, I grew up with it. When M inevitably got to my pieces, I tried not to give it weight and concentrated instead on the evolution of the letters in hidden halls of fame which she couldn't reach; or else I painted pieces on the panels of trains destined to travel outside Genoa, so the problem didn't subsist. I tagged a lot in the street, especially with Pilot markers, but any name would get crossed, or quicklimed as we called it, by M.
I didn't take it badly, actually if she didn't cover a tag or piece of mine I would be surprised, like: "What's goin' on? She didn't like it? How come she didn't go over this one?"
I have heard all kinds of stories regarding this thing with M and the quicklime, the legend which is most well known by everybody is that of an old woman that wanders around the city with a bucket full of plaster and a decorator's brush that she uses to squirt the lime on tags and pieces… this is one old lady that knows how to hustle!

Kaso
>

ALWAYS WITH US

Already in 1994, when I started painting, M was present wherever there were tags and pieces, but the whole thing had started earlier and still today tags in Genoa are all messed up. We knew of an old lady but ignored what she looked like, whether tall, short, fat, thin, so we stared at every aging woman that came our way; we thought we had found M when we noticed an elderly lady with a walky-talky in hand, wearing a red trench coat with a hood, a cap and sneakers. We thought it was her because we'd always see her around everywhere, then it turned out she was just reporting license plates to the traffic police, a real nutcase.
When I started painting and saw the tags crossed with quicklime I thought there was some kind of organisation behind it, like people united against the diffusion of Writing. But the phenomenon was so frequent, so widespread throughout the territory that there was no way of making sense of it. I hung out around the Govi area, in Corso Italia, that was one of the spots in which you chilled and got to know other writers, some kids were breakers or MC's, others skated, among us word was that this woman went around the city drawing M's on top of every tag. I was told that in the beginning the tags were covered with spray paint, generally black or dark brown (there are still a couple around), chaotic strokes in order to eliminate the name. Sometimes "Merda" ("Shit") would appear on top instead, again executed with spray paint.
At first I imagined this whole M thing as a group of kids, a crew united in the destruction of Aerosol Art. As a teenager I often hung around a piazza with a lot of others the same age, these guys were obsessed with scribbling the initials PPDN everywhere, which stood for *Piazza Paolo Da Novi* (the name of the piazza and the gang); and it was them that told me other kids were covering their stuff. But the members of PPDN were outside of the Hip Hop culture, they had nothing to do with it, they were just guys that went to the stadium and had the cult of the piazza, of the area and of the territory and perhaps it really was a rival gang that was crossing them. At the time a friend of mine had tagged underneath a bench in Nervi, and he had been covered by M, which seemed quite bizarre to me and I began thinking there might be some envious writer anonymously doing this.
I also noticed that the ink M used lasted longer than that of the writers, absurd rumors were circulating, surely urban myths, that told of the old lady ordering paint from Switzerland, a different type of ink that was more resistant to the atmospheric agents.
Sid told me of this one time he had gone with some other guys to do some shit in Quinto, in the station, and on the way back at night they saw in the distance an old woman with a bucket inside the perimeter of the rail tracks, they tried following her but she disappeared around the bend. At the time I skipped school to go around looking for halls of fame by Sid and others, they were always hidden in forgotten places. 1996 was the period of the "Coloriamo" project, an experiment that included the redevelopment of an urban neighborhood by delegating the embellishment of the walls of Piazza Faralli to writers. I had my photo camera with me because at that time I photographed anything that was pertinent to street culture. By pure coincidence one morning I caught an old woman with a shaved head writing the word "Merda" over a piece by Sid, I tried talking to her but she started flipping, shouting and drawing the attention of some security guards, I was just a kid and so I took off; I hid with the idea of following her, but without results. Then I met her again along with Dema in Piazza Piccapietra, and the crazy thing was she recognised me right off the bat, as if she knew who I was; in that occasion she murmured something and then hid in a bar. Again with Dema we met her another time on a bus, and he plunged towards her and rudely started asking why she messed with tags and pieces. In that occasion again she started tripping, going off about how she was against these symbols, that is tags, because the school where she taught was chock full of them, but she seemed real vexed and paranoid, quite aggressive. I don't remember the exact words, also because it was like a flow of consciousness so rapid and violent that the only thing that remained impressed was that she taught at Liceo Doria in Marassi. Then she started screaming that we wanted to rob and rape her, and since I was a kid I decided to get off the bus, because people were starting to give us these bad looks.
The most unusual thing that happened to me occurred one winter afternoon in 1994: I was at the Marco Polo Liceo, the hospitality-industry high school, with Dema, Geno and Emo under a kind-of overpass. We had met up to look at the piece we had done not much earlier, and found fresh plaster on top of it; so we divided up and started looking around, asking everybody if they had seen a lady with bags, maybe plastic bags. The guy at the news stand told us that an old woman had just passed by, fact is we never found her then either. It was crazy how she just managed to disappear all the time, she was invisible. The next day around the parts of Geno's house, in Via Burlanci, in the Piazza Manin area, where never ever had anything been quicklimed, we found everything covered and Geno even found a little note under his tags, with something around the likes of a message.
The next day I found all the tags I had done around the area where I lived busted. I was speechless, that gesture had me completely dazed, maybe due to my young age, or maybe it was the power of suggestion, but everyone was under the impression that the crazy old woman was following us.

Tabo
>

STAKE-OUTS

To catch M red-handed we started organising real stakeouts: among the many I remember the one when I changed address in Genoa. I relocated to an area that M would often hit, a favourable logistic place. I was there with my mother, she knew about my obsession with Writing and even about this M thing. I told her everything, just to avoid any family fights.
When we finished moving I installed a video camera outside the window of the kitchen that looked onto the street and decided to stay home until I caught M.
I was on serious surveillance four, five consecutive days, people would be calling me to go out and do stuff but I would be like "no I'm busy!".
Whenever I couldn't be on guard I would set the camera to start recording. Incredibly, after all this organisation and so much effort, she got away right under my nose: one Sunday morning I woke up, disconnected the camera to rewind the tape and went to the bathroom. Later while I was having breakfast I took a look out of the window – there was my tag, busted. She had done it while I was getting dressed, in less than twenty minutes. So I ran down and got my scooter, going up and down the streets to see if I could catch her, but nothing. Thus ended the cognitive approach with respect to the character of M and we started taking for granted that if you do tags or pieces around then they would get slashed. The first appearance of quicklime was in the form of almost insignificant squirts, just smears, that then turned into big blotches, evidently she had noticed the space she was covering was too small and non-intrusive.
So she started thinking of different approaches, throwing substantial "blocks" of plaster on tags and pieces. Then she started writing messages directly. Some of the phrases were explicitly referring to writers: "Skateppista merda", or "merda merda merda merda" arrow – "merda merda", for about a kilometre. Those words would follow one another all the way to the home of the writer crossed. Whereas the phrase "Skateppista merda" referred to another legend that told of an old lady that had been insulted by a bunch of skaters. It was the skaters themselves that told us of this, there was after all a shred of truth. Perhaps the rage M unleashed on tags was due to an association between Writing and the skating scene, indeed at the time everything was a bit mixed without too many distinctions: punks, skaters, B-boys, we were all contributing something that fed the street scene.

❶ *Play on the words "skater" and "teppista", or hooligan.*

Destructive methodologies:

❶ SPRAY PAINT

M's first attempts at covering pieces occurred with the same tools used by the writers that had been painting them; spray paint. The battle between M and the writers of Genoa thus initially started at even weapons. This type of crossing, executed in a systematic way, was used only for a brief period of time, during which pieces were slashed with crude, vertical lines.

❷ PILOT MARKER

M also utilised another tool typical of Writing, the fine-tip, permanent ink marker, which was used to write insults and entire dissertations, like a stream of consciousness sometimes without any sense, filling the city with confused words and her indelible mark. With time, and in the attempt to get even closer to the characteristics of a writer, M moved from fine-tip markers to the fatter Pilot ones. The original political statements were substituted with the word "Merda", that little by little was reduced to the single "M". This letter – that would become legendary – was executed from right to left over tags and pieces that M wanted to cross. Executed with quick, nervous strokes, the letter "M" witnessed the urgency of eliminating as many tags as possible, by allowing a greater number of destructive actions.

❸ THE "M" WORD

The word "Merda" would be written along the whole length of the tag to be covered, juxtaposing itself with the pre-existent name. The result aimed at making the signature unreadable.
The most curious aspect of this practice was in those cases when M had fun playing with the tags, using them as schemes for a crossword or boards for an ideal urban Scrabble, in which the term "Merda" stemmed from the same letters that composed the words the writers had traced. The evident impertinence with which M poked fun at the painted names, does not however subtract anything from her capacity to decode the lettering of writers. With time and the increasing presence of tags in the city, M had to adapt to the speed with which they were being executed, and ended up synthesising the entire word into the simple initial "M" thus repeating – for irony of fate – an action typical of certain street artists that obtain a more immediate symbol from a name, almost a more decipherable icon.

❹ BLACKWASH

Crossing with black plaster is something M expressly did on those pieces that went from the big silvers to the light-coloured murals, in such a way as to emphasise her

passage and her undeniable presence on the territory even more.
Initially it was thought that the liquid substance M threw over tags was ink, but given its density and dark colour, it was soon believed to be more like tar.
In any case the black mix she used appeared in the form and consistency of a thick and covering muck that ruined the tag, at times obscuring it completely.
On a visual level, the black plaster slashes produced an even more traumatic impact than the ones with white plaster.
Among writers the feeling something anomalous was disturbing their tags, obscuring them in such a wild and cruel way, was growing. To the eyes of the citizens on the other hand, the effect of the black quicklime was that of a fastidious dirty spot that added to the already disturbing tag.

❺ SPRINKLER

Towards the end of the 90's, M turned to the quicklime sprinkler for help in destroying pieces or tags with a squirt that was as wide as their entire length.
These were actions that were aimed and executed in a single shot, with what had to be perfect precision so as to extend over the entire tag and cover it enough to make it unreadable. Sometimes instead of a horizontal line M traced a cross: this symbol of death, 'the end' and negation was read as an almost dictatorial stance on her part.

❻ WHITEWASH

M adopted the use of a decorator's paintbrush in the early 90's, so as to splatter the tags and pieces of writers with globs of white plaster. M used a flat brush dipped into a plastic bottle filled with liquid quicklime. The effect it produced on pieces was similar to that of a white blob that, given the material consistency of the substance, assumed thickness and managed to cover any trace of spray paint. These plaster blotches, whether similar to large drops or enormous stripes, disturbed the view of the piece as a whole, hitting it in its entirety.

❼ PAINT BOMBS

The quicklime bombing technique wasn't used frequently because M only reserved it for pieces that were executed on higher floors of buildings or anyway in hard-to-reach places. Throw-ups would be bombarded with balloons full of liquid plaster that created an invasive blotch righ

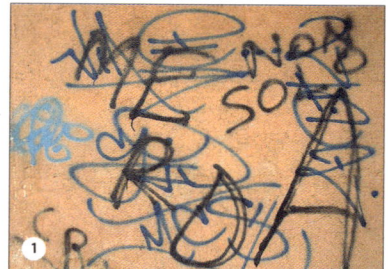

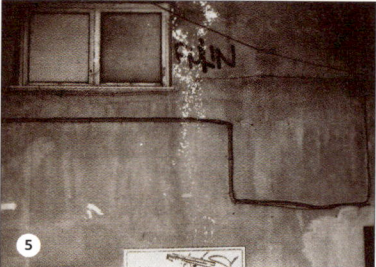

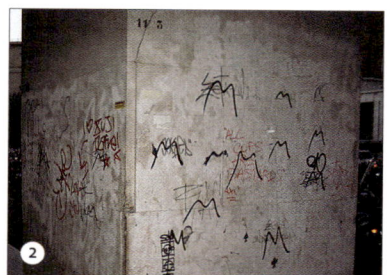

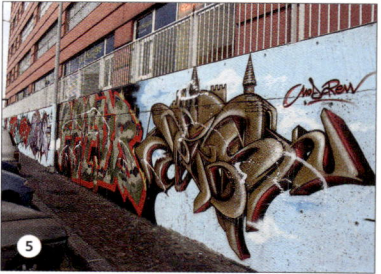

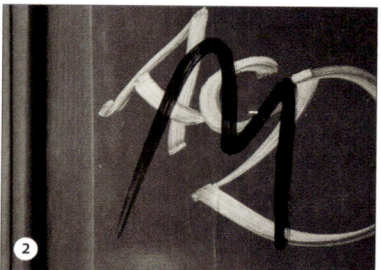

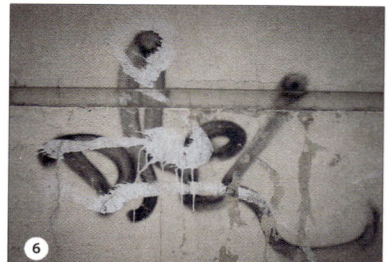

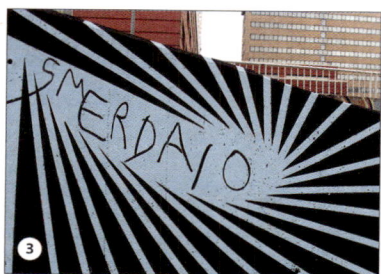

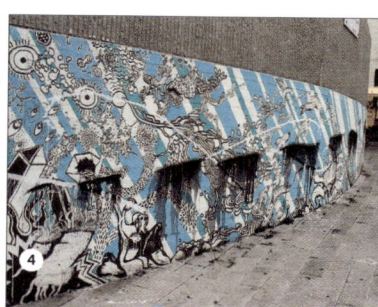

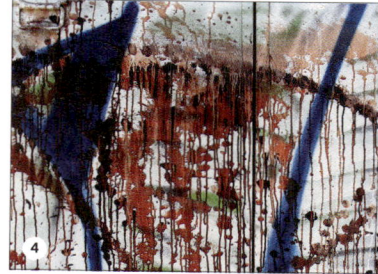

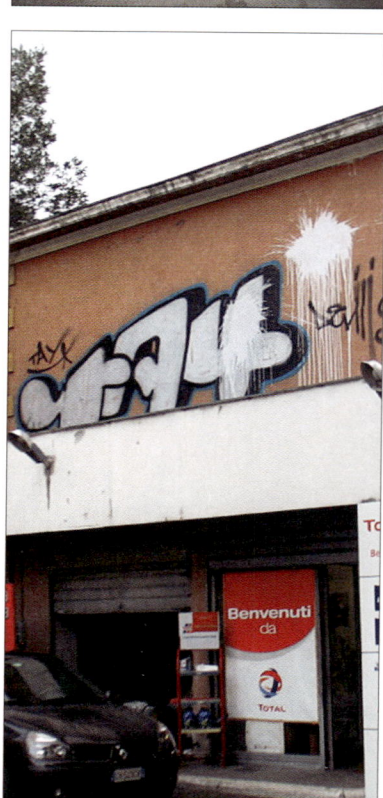

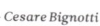

- Cesare Bignotti

the 'M' case enquiry

Rois
>

As far as I'm concerned, this old lady was never really a problem. I always did my thing as if I were living in any other city where this plague didn't exist. It is true that at the outset, the fact that anything I painted was destroyed by this person disturbed me a lot. But later, I learned to cohabit with her and put up with her ruthlessness.

My attitude was a form of resistance to her ongoing hostility. I never let myself give into the temptation to explode because I was against the idea of confronting her directly. In any case, I never did bend to her presence, and adapted my practice to her invasive activity. I always considered that it didn't matter what I did; in the end, the battle would be won by her.

Finally, we are forced to recognize that She was and still is the most prolific bomber of the city: she is everywhere and strikes everyone. As to her identity or the possibility that there were several individuals, one dropping whitewash, another one staking out the pieces, and yet another to tag with an M drawn with a marker, I would say that there are many theories in Genoa. All are possible, but no one knows for sure.

Personally I am more fascinated by the method than the quest to know who the individual or the organized group is behind this anti graffiti crusade.

We are talking about a sort of continuous censure, a mark adopted by someone or by something which thereby reacts to the daily signs left by the writers and is ready to go after new ones the next day.

It may sound like a paranoid vision, but considering that it is a truly obsessive phenomenon, this is the most credible interpretation I can find.

As far as scribbles on the walls are concerned, Genoa has maintained a predominant position for decades. It is still possible to find some very old signs around like those from the post war period or from the "red brigade" years. To write on the walls in this city seems more important than anywhere else.

Political scribbles, personal rambles and fragments of lived life are all traces that want to tell something to a public audience, contrary to the cryptic signs made by writers whose message is for insiders only. This whole flow of anonymous confessions makes its mark and solicits attention from others. Attention to what you think and who you are rather than to the sign itself. So, writing is covered with whitewash to contradict and to remember what was marked before and maybe to photograph. It would not be that strange then that someone actually records every type of writing and stuffs files with documents that are catalogued and archived and maybe preserved for future reference. It is true that nobody can swear to having seen this old lady in action, bombing with whitewash, and no one has actually seen someone take pictures of the writing. I should mention that immediately after the G8 meeting the individual who took pictures seems to have been hanging around for some time. Later, and contrary to everything else, all those writings disappeared in just a day.

Only the train pieces were saved, perhaps because the trains have serial numbers and so they consider censure unnecessary.

Basically the mystery has been persisting for years. An alternative to this theory and one which I also hold as possible is a territorial one. In Genoa the sense of defending space has always been stronger than in other cities. There have always been beefs between writers, and sometimes they have degenerated into violent conflicts focused on territorial domination. Perhaps the "Old Lady" has played her role in this story, recognizing at the very outset that writers were invading a space which until then had belonged exclusively to her. This theory could be substantiated by the fact that first witnesses saw an "old lady" write delirious sentences on trash cans and electric meters. This is would be a sort of intersection point between the writers and the old lady, based on the threat of invading a space cut out for work, especially in a city like Genoa. This theory interests me because it reveals the psychological and social aspects of the first wave of writers who considered territoriality as something sacred to protect at all cost, an attitude that with time has lost its meaning.

Apparently it seems that the old lady has lived for a long time in total impunity, perpetrating a proactive action, even more so than writing. Whitewash has been thrown systematically on every kind of surface in the city including those which could be defined as sensitive targets. It is not possible let this action go unnoticed for so long and that it continue for so many years without the old lady being denounced for degradation or damage as so many local writers have been.

In this city as elsewhere, this kind of event could not happen without it being known. Paradoxical in certain cases, the collateral damage caused by the whitewash cases is worse than the tags.

Finally, it is necessary to mention the fact that some really cowardly writers, especially in recent times, have taken advantage of this easy "M" trademark in order to hit other writers in total anonymity.

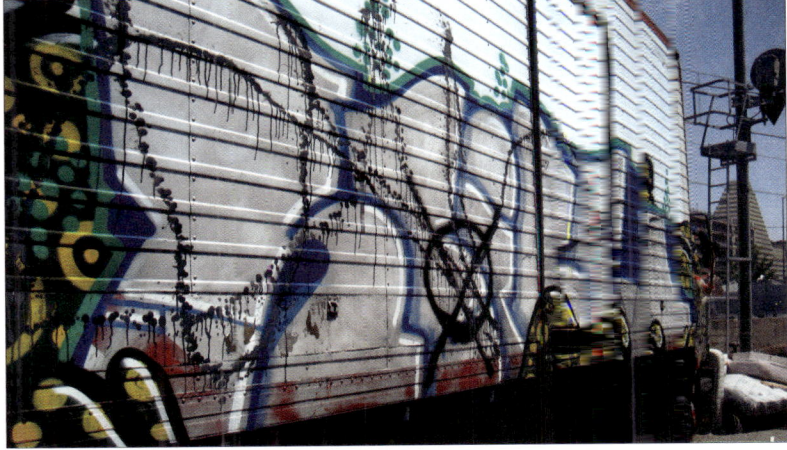

Rois crossed by the M   — Sherif

RAILWAY ARENA
—

As in every other Italian city, in Genoa the onset of train-bombing was influenced by the books on the Writing scene of New York, and by the direct comparison of national and international experiences. With respect to other cities however, the singular situation of the Ligurian capital – afflicted by an anomalous destructive phenomenon like that of M – had forced certain writers to paint the national trains out of necessity. Tabo, Sherif, Blef, Dafne and Emis were some of the protagonists of the original group that for various years targeted thousands of carriages throughout the region of Liguria. What fuelled this phenomenon was the same topography of the city, in which the urban settlements climb up the coast of the Gulf of Genoa towards the Apennine hills, dominated by the ancient fortifications and the *Mura Nuove*[1]. The texture of residential buildings, made of levelled terraces overlooking the train station, favours the possibility of having multiple angles from which to look at the convoys. Similar to the steps of a theatre in which the stage is exposed to observation from numerous perspectives, these terraces offer a striking view on a scenario of great impact, drawn by the railway lines that cross through the city. From an elevated position writers had the possibility of photographing trains from much wider angles, with often very scenic results. The Writing experience in Genoa was quite unique: for many years trains represented the only concrete opportunity writers had – if not an actual obligated choice – for showing their pieces, defending them from M's attacks, who only rarely went as far as the track limits to cross painted train cars.

❸ *The most recent wall built around the city between 1626 and 1639*

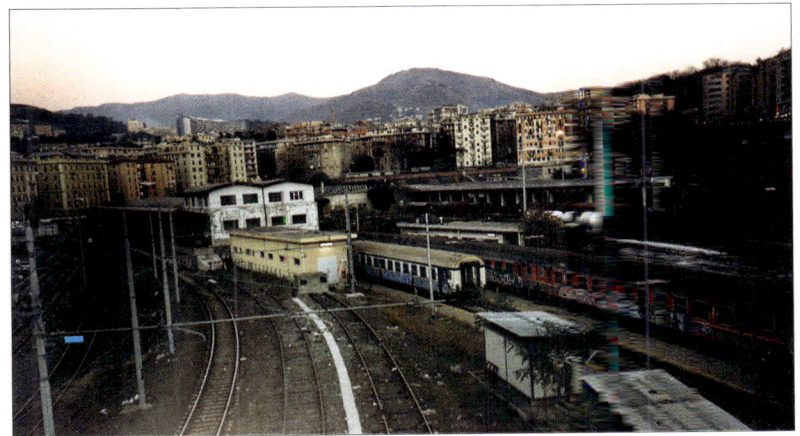

Overview of the city's yard   — Tabo

Genoa from scratch

Tabo
>

The first tags I noticed were those of Sid One MCS, when I was 13 years old. Later on, some movies on tv and few books such as *Arte di Frontiera*, *Subway Art* and *Spraycan Art* revealed the meaning of signs to me.

In 1991 when I confessed to a close friend (a writer later known as Crim) that I was writing, he invited me to his house where a big painting reproduced the Suicidal Tendencies album cover: Feel Like Shit / Deja Vu in his room.

We started to buy the spray cans and write large at first and for a long time in a quarry and then, when we felt ready, in a few roads like corso Europa, via Sapeto, via Vernazza and via delle Casette, behind Perasso and Marco Polo schools, in some city stations as Quinto and Sturla or in Nervi and Quarto alta.

Crim was a skater for a while and in that period the Contati brothers with their "Totally" distribution were pushing the street scene. In their warehouse you could find *Trasher* magazine or *Propaganda*. From those people from whom Punk/OI! or hooligans fanzines arrived, it was a jump into the future.

I remember a cool "D" from Dado from Bologne on their home wall and some tags

The writers of that period took a lot of care to protect the uniqueness of their routes and to protect every kind of information about the "discipline" from potential wannabees

around it. On Saturday's we would catch a train to Milan to see the hall of fame of the MNP and to spend some time outside the WAG shop, trying to gather anything that came up.

The writers of that period took a lot of care to protect the uniqueness of their territory and to protect every kind of information about the "discipline" from potential wannabees. As outsiders, It was really hard to get in touch with them.

The skaters' meeting point in Genoa was the Gilberto Govi Park, that it is still frequented because there is a ramp with a R.I.P. dedicated to a skater.

Here in 1991 the first chrome bombing of the city by SidOne was painted. It was a big "Genova " piece with a character of a sailor man that indicated the route, with this dedication: "To the historic center and the harbour that is going under, stop talking, We have to react !".

The Park was also visited by the B-Boys because it was used by Marcella and

Emilio from the *Battle Squad*, as an alternative training spot to the "Longines", located in piazza Piccapietra. Our turning point came when a friend gave us the first and second issues of *Alleanza Latina*, the magazine created by Sid One.

The phone number was on it so we got in touch and later with him we formed the VIA, the first intercity crew of the area. Sid One was really close to the Hip Hop culture in its original form. His style was already mature at that time, almost too cultivated for the young guys.

I owe to him the introspective approach that I have persued all these years: the search for equilibrium through knowldge, the respect for history and that of others, before any kind of ego-trip. I consider my

The Our turning point came when a friend gave us the first and second issues of Alleanza Latina

train bomber activity as a complementary experience to this type of research.

The VIA period was a pioneer journey into Hip Hop: from a closed-circle cult to a big business. It was a unique opportunity to have seen closeup a phase of the ascent of the magazine that became for a short time the number one music publication in terms of sales.

Through it I met people like Rendo, Shad, Flycat, Lemon, Won, Phase2, Neon and other absolute masters. And again, thanks to it I saw many of the historic events such as "Indelebile" in Rimini, "Hip Hop Village" in Turin and others in foreign countries like the 1994 jam at the Rote Fabrik in Zurich.

Here the few italian writers saw a preview of how the European railway lines would soon reproduce the NYC subway reference, on a large scale.

In 1996 the exibiton " Paroles Urbaines " at the Laiterie in Strasbourg made clear to me the necessity to distinguish nation by nation between the crowd of disciplined players and the hundreds of artists who thought they were developing their ways. Genoa during the 90's saw the creation of a small scene thanks to the arrival of some crews like the FNP of Maze and Boz, who refreshed our view of graffiti, and others who had different energy and potential.

It was necessary for us to know about how to evolve a style in an urban context beyond the Writing that was created overseas in the past. So after having learned the basics, it was our time to give it the correct interpretation.

Since 1995, my Writing has been mainly on trains. From the very outset, this is what I tended to do, and it is also why I never write legally.

For a long time, we were in the yards more than the train workers, and sometimes we went there for the sheer pleasure of going there.

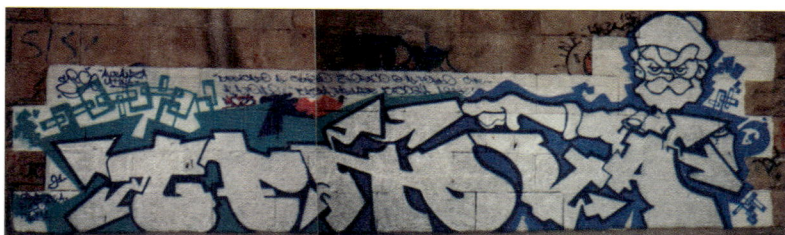
The *Genova* piece, painted by by Sid   — *Sid*

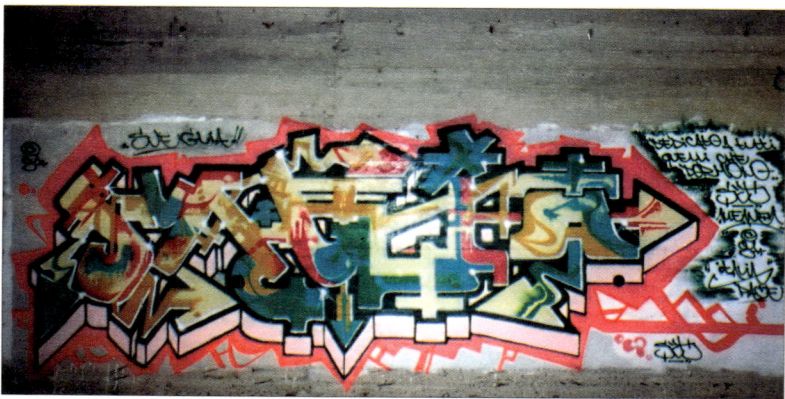
Sveglia by Sid, 1991   — *Sid*

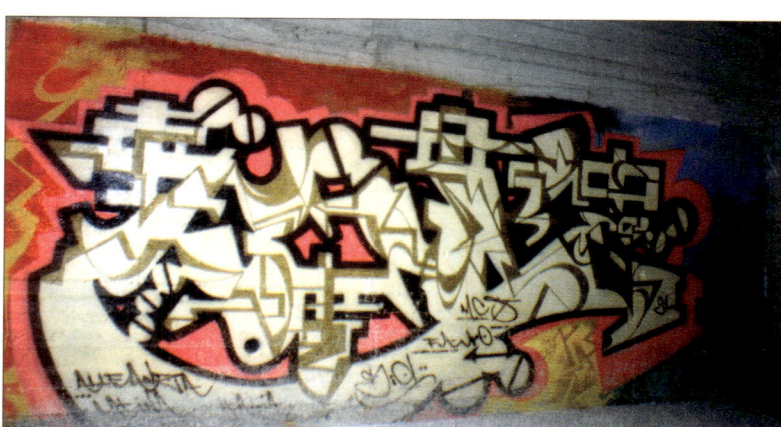
Sid 1991   — *Sid*

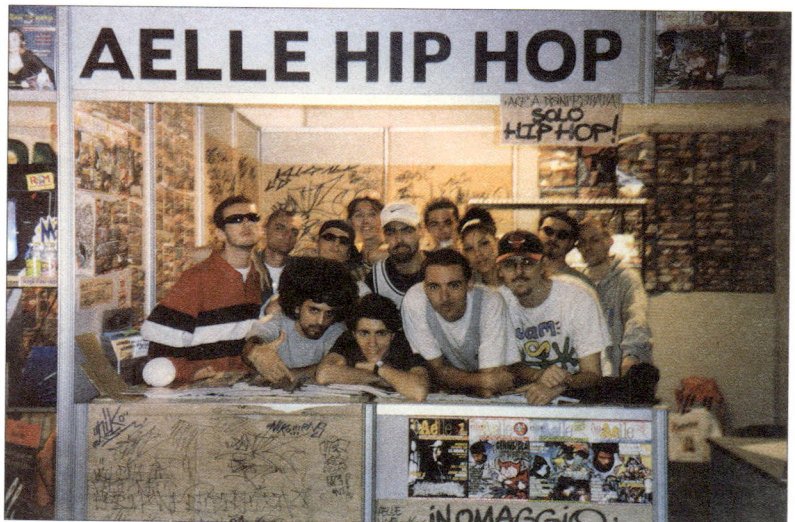
AL crew and friends, 1996   — *Sid*

Our microcosm

Emis
>

Emis describes his philosophy as a train-bomber, based on a bizarre paradox: not to leave any traces

When Blef left for his military service I started hanging out more with Sherif, with whom I got along real well. We had similar characters and together we killed it wherever we went. The strongest personal memories I have of that period were the time spent in the yard, such as when the spray cans were "frozen" and paint would drip on the stones under the rail tracks. When that happened we just turned the stones over; then once the piece was finished and the pictures were taken, we would look for the solvent with which to erase the paint that covered the serial number of the train. If we found a sheet of paper attached to a train car with the words "car out of service" we would remove it before painting, and once we were finished and had taken our photos, we would put it back on, over the piece, as if the piece had already been there when the train arrived at the yard. We were basically invisible; nobody was supposed to know we existed.

In a yard outside the city we concentrated on trains which were immobilized on the benches for washing. That way we could paint over the windows without running the risk of seeing them clean the next day. This is how it worked: we knew the timetable of the trains, and we also knew which were washed before the others. We would paint them as soon as the cleaners moved on to another side of the yard, to be sure that we were the last to see the pieces. The next day the train would run as we had left it. In some yards we moved real well and knew where everything was inside the carriages and in the sheds.

We might steal small things, like something to drink, but there was an unwritten code not to go beyond certain limits and to respect the place and the people who worked there.

We knew these things because we would go there many nights and days, learning the movements, studying the place and the possible escape routes. It was such familiar territory that after a few years we no longer went at night but in the morning or afternoon. We tried to hide our traces as much as possible.

There were spots we would hit two or three times a week for five, six consecutive years, and there were a lot of us, sometimes six at a time. All this lasted until the new writers came, and then the fun was over. In my eyes the scene got played out. A lot of kids started coming out who weren't interested in keeping the place a secret and leaving it clean.

Their goal was to paint a piece and show everyone they had been there. It was in that period that the first problems started because these guys did tags and pieces all over the place.

I remember there was one spot in which the railway workers had put up a gate, and Sherif and I broke the lock, substituting it with another, so that when we went there we could open the lock, get in, paint, and in case of a swift escape just close the lock behind us, so that whoever was chasing behind could go no further than the gate.

One time, to get away, Sherif threw himself from the bridge near the "keys layup ", which is 5 metres high, and broke his ankle. That area was fucked up, full of sheds, police patrols, and transit guards passing by every 10 minutes.

The trains parked there were always unknown and you could find a bit of everything. Many times back from failed action in other stations, we went to paint the 4-6-4 (the grey or beige trains of Liguria: 4 high windows, 6 low ones and another 4 highs) or the *Rossi* (the red trains with 13 door to door windows). We passed there as a last resort and happened to see some unpainted wagons. The piece you did was based on what train you found: sometimes you planned to execute a certain sketch and then couldn't find the car you were looking for, so you'd have to paint by heart, off the cuff.

The fact we studied our spots helped us avoid improvisation, because we knew everything beforehand, and it was good for many reasons as the case of the restaurant car, since those carriages had high windows with an 80-90 cm panel, much bigger than the others, and so much cooler to paint. Since we had gotten our hands on duplicates of the keys, we also

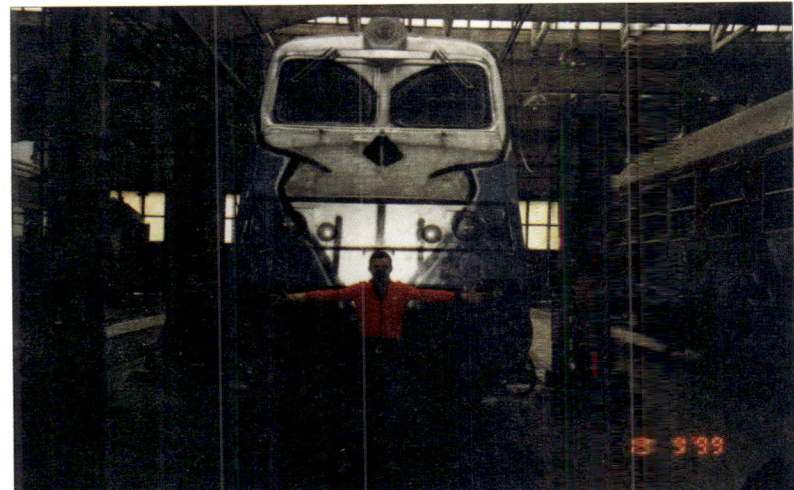

Emis in front of the train head he painted in a deposit of Genoa   — Emis

tried getting into the restaurant carriages to eat, but most of the time we only found fruit juice.

Sometimes Sherif and I would arrive too late to paint the right train, and we would have to wait 4/5 hours in the winter cold before the rush, so we started bringing whisky or limoncello, so we wouldn't freeze. After hours of waiting, we entered the yard. One guy began painting the train and the other stayed on the lookout rotating roles every 5 minutes. Once I was on the lookout under a train and the engine car suddenly arrived with 5 workers ready to hook it up the carriages. They got off right in front of us and we were petrified, silent, waiting for the right moment to make a run for it. It was no tea party, but still we had our spots, and since we kept

them tidy and clean, without bothering anyone, nobody knew we went there, or else they knew and pretended not to since we weren't causing any damage. It wasn't even a real workplace: there were pieces of rail tracks that had been modelled with a grinding machine and welded together to form sculptures, a of random junk, and a couple of bikes. The workers there were pretty informal.

There was a sort of silent "respect", because it didn't take a genius to figure out that three or four people had painted a train, going as far as wiping off the paint on the serial numbers. Seeing the huge drawings covering windows, it was impossible not to understand, but obviously it was in everyone's interest not to say anything.

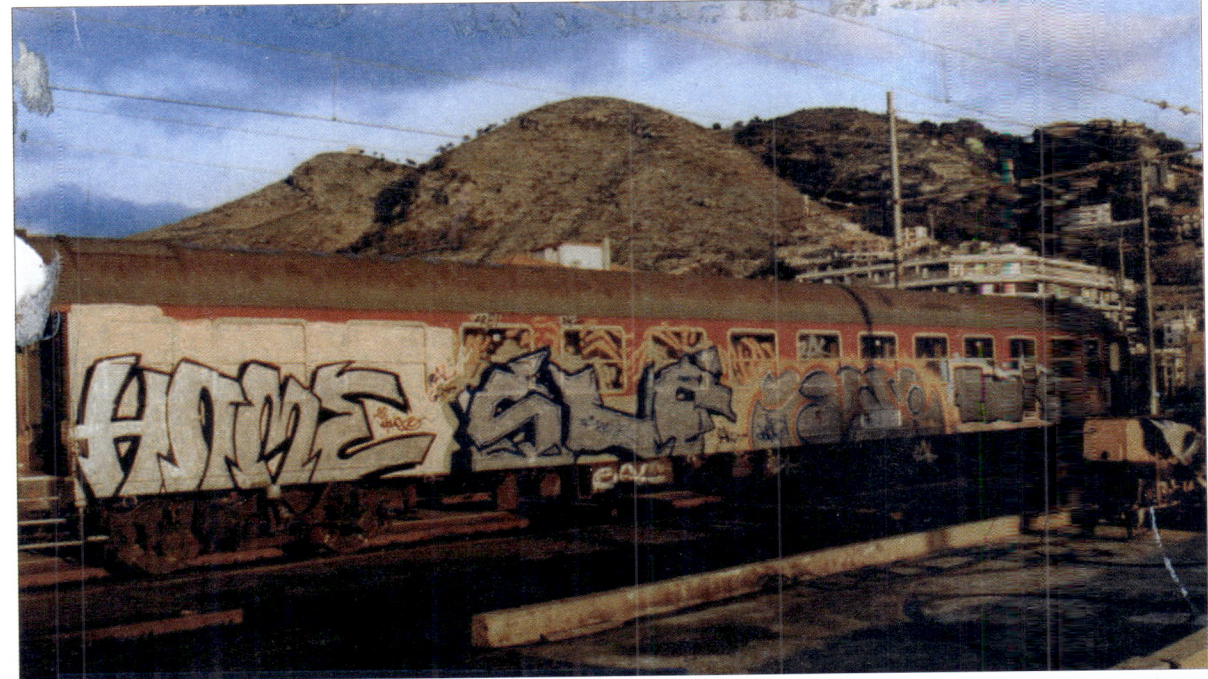

Home *She* by Sherif, Dafne ed Emis. End-to-end on *Marmotta* trains   — Emis

Back on track

Sherif

>

Sherif and his experiences as a writer; his fixation with train cars and the world of the railway

I started drawing simple, block letters, like the ones you see on school backpacks, then others were zig-zagging with thousands of arrows. It was 1986, I would write the names of my classmates on my school books, and when I took up spray paint, my first two pieces were "City" and "Break". The fact is I didn't have a Name and to be honest I didn't even know I needed one, so I would just write whatever I came up with, influenced by the title of a song or by the cover of the Rap albums I had.

In those first years I didn't know that much about graffiti; for a kid from the province like me, there was no way of obtaining any real information.

This "absence" had a strong effect on the way I experienced Writing. I think this frantic search pushed me to always move forward and just deeply believe in it for so long... it's not a question of how many fanzines you read, the books, the caps or the brand of paint, in the end all that counts is the desire to understand what is behind things. Today there are a lot of good starting points through which to understand Writing and so decide what route to undertake, trying to create a personal visual identity amongst the millions of stylistic references; if you have the skills and put your heart into it, sooner or later the results will come. In its totality a piece should give a glimpse of its author: like an extension of your character.

When a piece impresses me it's because it communicates something to me and I immediately think of who realised it, trying to imagine the executer, asking myself who he really is. This same curiosity pushed me to travel: meet other writers and enter their worlds for a while, disappointing or fascinating encounters as they may be. It's by traveling that I found my dimension in graffiti: metal. My first train was a German DB, that had stopped in the station for the night due to an engine failure. A train full of tourists, I think. Until then it was as if I had never been writing, it was 1992, six years later...then, for a year nothing more, until I went to live in Genoa.

This city, though fundamental for the Italian graffiti movement due to the editorial office of *AL* magazine, was never in the forefront when it came to Writing, never had a defined scene of its own.

This is partly due to the fact that writers and their crews obstructed in every possible way the development of the new generations. In 1993 the number of Italian writers painting trains was very limited, and even less were the ones doing

so with a train-writer mentality. Me and my friend Boz had hit some *Marmottas* or *Bordeauxes*, as we called them. The interesting slang that evolved in that period, like *4-6-4, 3-5-3, Aragosta* and *Rossi* came from us, at least around these parts.

1993 was a fundamental year because I met Dafne, a girl who immediately started painting trains with us and revealed to be a really kick-ass writer. She was ahead

under the title "If the kids are united" in *Report* fanzine. Many of the kids that participated would later become active writers on the national scene, pioneers of bombing on the FS line. The following years, at least up to 2000, were unique for all of Italy: a remarkable period where painting meant competing and seeing the concrete results on the rail tracks day by day. The continuous passing of pieces

that could be painted by six-seven kids at once. It was a way to get known in Lombardy and Tuscany. Trains from the Bologna-Ancona line would also arrive, with other names and other styles. The trains that were present in the yard would rotate, more than now, also because there were more trains.

Unlike other cities, here we were never that interested in painting clubs and

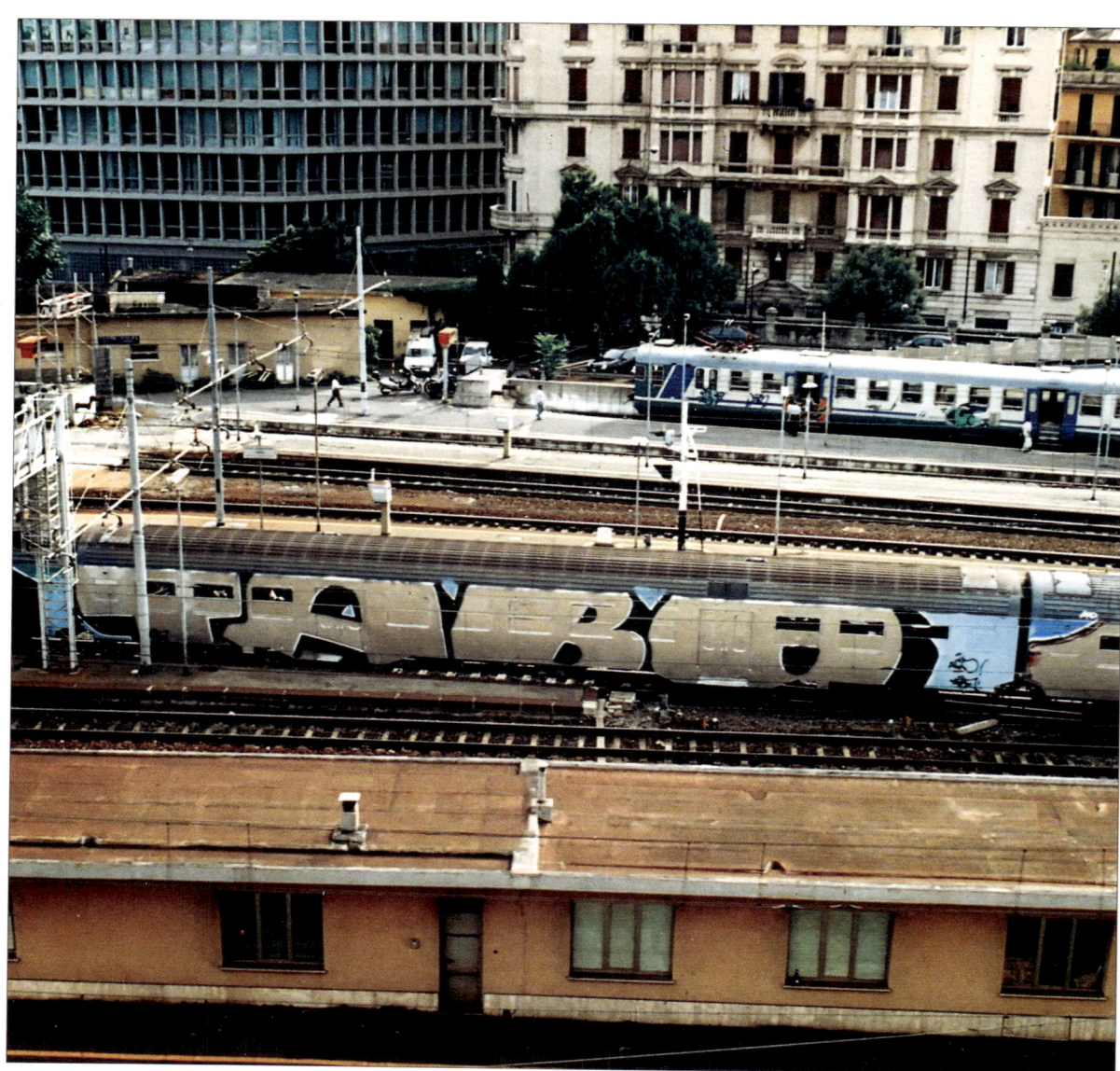

Tabo and *Sher* by Sherif–ACD, entering in Genoa station

when it came to technique, with a style that had already taken form but mostly she had a very deep and personal vision of Writing that fascinated me.

With her we formed RAL crew and began a real bombing campaign: end-to-ends, whole-cars and trips to hit the yards of more or less far regions, and we realised that train-writing had exploded in many cities in Italy. An event that in my opinion marked the beginning of everything was the whole-train window-down that we organised in Turin, which was published

had us spending hours in the station, who knows how much time we lost there... cars and cars of graffiti, circulating up and down all of Italy.

An afternoon at the station was enough to realise what was going on all over the country, there was no need for fanzines. In many cases the only way to no longer see a panel was to go over it, and in a single day it was easy to see a couple of your own pieces on every train that passed.

In my area writers were concentrating primarily on the *Interegionali*, the *Rossi*,

perhaps this aspect also affected the development of the local scene: we wanted our pieces to run far, on the Intercity, travel kilometers of distance, to Rome, to France, and of the various yards we particularly bombed two: the "yard grossa", a medium sized deposit deflowered in a spree of whole-cars, and the "yard delle chiavi" (the keys yard) a spot in which Emis had broken the lock of the entry gate, substituting it with one of our own, hence the name. Not that they were indispensable to get in the yard, quite the opposite, but having those keys in our pockets was cool... we were just playing! Among the many things I remember of that period is the massive quantity of work produced by Blast, the end-to-ends of FTR, the style of Enist, which you would have to check out on the subway lines of his city to fully grasp, and then I remember the panel pieces that would arrive from Rome on the blue TENs (Transit Euro Night), or other long-distance trains, way ahead of their time if you ask me, though they were dissed by many then.

Due to a series of misunderstandings with Dafne, together with an exasperation of the idea I had of train-bombing, I started hanging out with other writers and from there ACD was born. End-to-ends attracted me particularly, and even in the

with a background and everything else. Personally I liked big pieces that covered windows and doors.

You could say my ideal hit is a classical silver bomb that can be read even from a distance on a speeding train: in my opinion visual impact counts a lot in graffiti. Then there were panel pieces that, though having the same dimensions, had completely opposite end results, because of the elaborate letters and colours. The time factor was not a big problem in that period. With Dafne I had learnt the importance of experimenting and that pushed me to come up with a couple of filling styles, like the fishbone one, called "the funky piss" with five-six different colours in contrast or in similar tones, sprayed at a parallel angle to the panel. Dafne had an ill fill, the "video

me was more than a simple piece of metal, but a surface that can add something to a piece, as if this could be extracted from the same shapes of the train.

Unfortunately at a certain point they applied a film layer on every convoy, that together with the generation turnover rapidly downsized everything. MOD had started tearing the film off, an aggressive act of the moment, and indeed I thought the time had come for a change: to hit trains you had to step it up a notch, just like what had already been happening in other countries.

The age of Panettone and wine bottles left in the deposit for the workers during Christmas, an attempt at an impossible friendship that never took place, had ended. If you wanted your pieces to

in the station at 6 in the morning. From that moment my third and final phase would begin which was lived through alone. I think writing is mostly a private experience, max exception for those crews that promote themselves through the charisma and unity of their collective name. Personally, I don't see others as a necessary presence to calm my nerves, but at most a pleasant company with whom to spend a couple hours. Being in a crew should be an intense experience, to me the guys are most of all friends, with whom to share something that goes beyond the passion for graffiti. What had joined me, Kyro and Argo was writing, thanks to which a strong friendship ensued, that lasted even after we had stopped painting together.

For me a crew is also a small army, that's why I've always liked to think of Writing as a sort of war-game, in which you study the best tactics for hitting the designated target. When the others stopped painting I continued alone. In CC4 I started all over again, except with more experience and mastery. I think it was the most intense period of my activity, in which I felt a passion permeate me until I would get lost in it, for better or worse.

This phase was defined by an almost maniacal attention towards control: "if I get busted there's nothing I can do about it...", you know the risks you try to avoid the worst, and then you let go for it. In the end that's the beauty of painting alone. In that period I came out with a lot of pieces that I think are at the very limit,

"
In its totality a piece should give a glimpse of its author like an extension of your character

creatively speaking and at the same time I lost a lot of other things that should not be neglected. This is the difference between trains and the rest of graffiti, trains are a drug, a real addictive thing. But to me it's not about the adrenaline rush cause you're doing something illegal, and it's not about the compulsive level of satisfying an otherwise uncontrollable part of yourself. What counts most for me is the fact you're creating something in an unusual context, through revenue, you unleash your creativity in the only way you feel is true. It's a creative urgency more than an egoistic one. Of course if I then analyse the results in detail, I myself would save 1 out of 50 of my early pieces

The sensations a solitary, well-positioned and running piece gives me are still strong today, but even more intense are the emotions you feel just being in the yard. To me the context is a very important component, is what gives a special touch to an "Action". The fact is, after many adventures what has remained most impressed in my memory, other than the final results have been the backdrops, the areas of the deposit, the sounds, the strategies to get in and stay the right amount of time

It's in one of these places where the basement of a London building meets an underground subway line, that I read a slogan, I think by DLS, which perfectly fits some writers, and I still 'TRAINS... TRAINS... TRAINS'

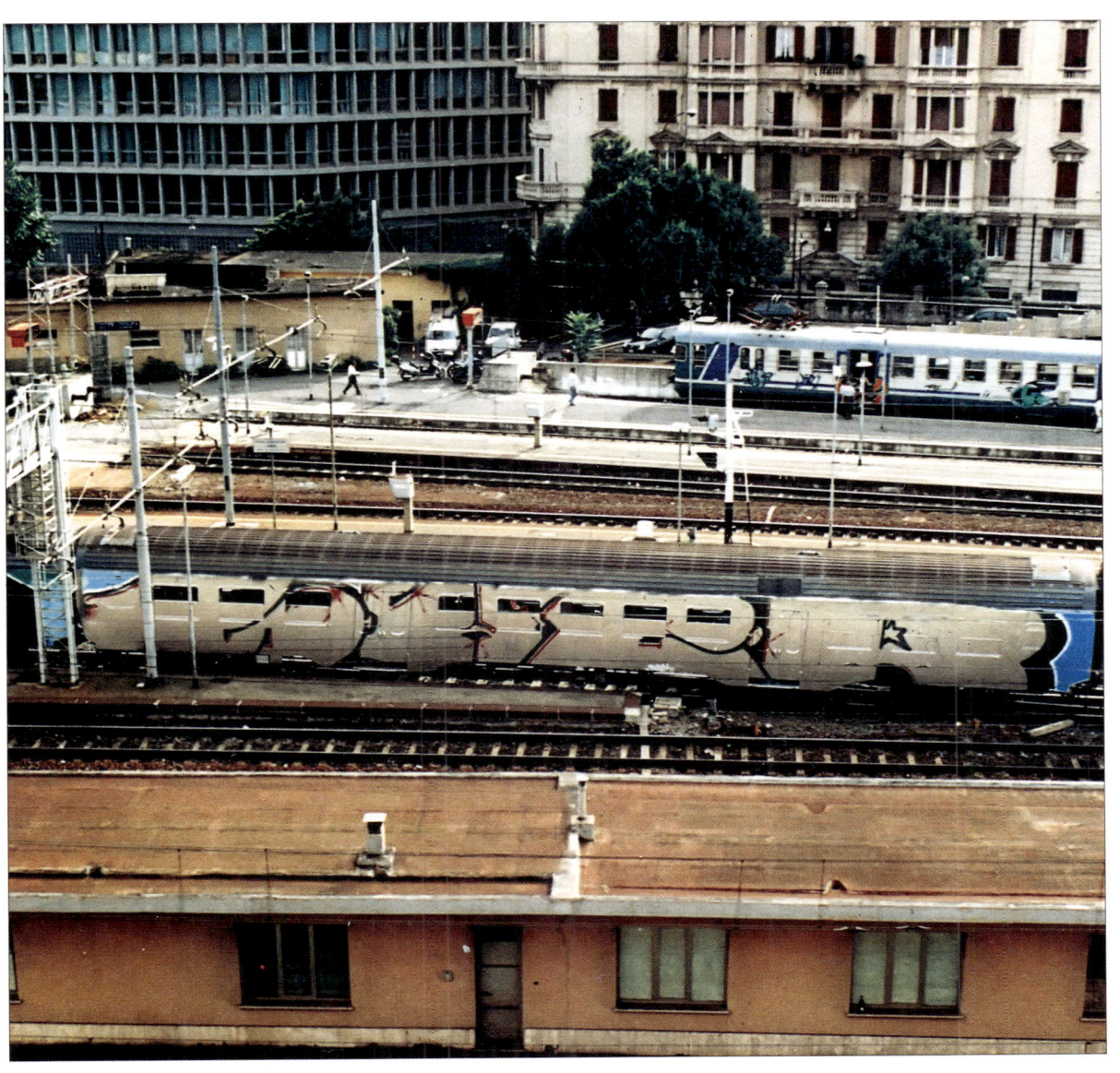

— Tabo

situations when it was just two of us we would tend to paint panels six windows long so as to close the whole-train car. It was the anti-buff philosophy, block letters, facilitated by the freer styles some of us were exploring, known as "swedish" and appreciated by very few at the time. The most successful pieces were those painted with Kyro, because he was a writer that was completely in tune with my way of seeing things, in the yard and out. Those painted with Blef and Tabo were also good, usually three well-balanced panels

sexy trama", I think it was called, a kind of grid with various colours, that gave a nice wild effect, especially since it bent the standard rules of execution.

In those years Writing was focused on the act itself, on the preparation of the piece to be realised in the best possible way, and not that much on the intangible part like tactics and strategies to avoid getting caught.

This "relative" tranquillity in action helped me mature stylistically, experimenting with lettering and its support, which to

travel now, which is something that has always been fundamental for me, you had to identify the right train, the right yard, kill the other cars with tags so as to slow down the buffing, and in general make other writers desist from working the same spots: you had to react if you wanted to paint as consistently as before.

In that period many writers around me started quitting, it took too much energy, both in and out of the yard; it took hours just to catch a glimpse of your panel circulating, otherwise you had to look for it

Daytime evolutions

>

Genesis of a Name

Blef

>

Freight trains witnessed the beginning of the career of one of the most prolific Italian writers ever

I started I started doing freight trains to understand the approach, seeing I wasn't quite clear on what exactly I was supposed to be doing. I practiced on freight trains before taking the big step and doing passenger trains. In Genoa I started doing my first stuff with Emis, Loez, Fiore, then one day I went to hit my first passenger train in Biella with Crim and Tabo.

In Genoa the places in which you could paint panels were primarily Trasta and Bolzaneto, a yard and a lay-up in which trains were left for hours. On the other hand, in the summer, trains would stop in a random station, among others, Arenano, Voltri, Nervi; they were all 10 minute quickies.

Thinking back to the early years, one of the most important moments was the Sangue Misto show at the Albatros towards 1994. I remember at the concert a girl asked me about FNP, the crew that included the first bombers in Liguria – Sherif and Boz – guys who already knew how to move and anticipate everyone else. They knew how to write also because some of them studied in Milan and therefore had more references. I found out the girl from the concert was Dafne. That show was the most important in Genoa because all of us were there. The whole scene of Liguria which was in some way connected to Hip Hop had gathered for this event.

Years later Dafne, initially active on trains with Sherif, invited me to go paint together. I liked painting with her because she was organised. She knew everything: the places, the timetables, the risks, whereas I was much more haphazard. Thanks to her I found out about new spots, and a desire to create a healthy competition was aroused.

In that period I started understanding

When you're alone you live it 100%, you feel it on you, and every undertone becomes fascinating and involving

what it was about Writing that interested me and thus began obstinately pursuing the path to becoming a bomber & styler at the same time, an obsession that increased year after year, until I would hit the yard 4, 5 days a week. The bomber regularity was accompanied by the intention to paint hall of fame type pieces on trains, with complex fillings and wild-style letters.

At that time the central station of Genoa, as in other big Italian cities, was the only place in which you could compare pieces by various writers, read into the styles, understand who was active and who wasn't.

If you went to the train station you weren't able to see interesting styles yet. The majority of works were pretty low standard, but when you saw the *Bordeaux* Intercity trains arrive from Rome, those painted by NSB, it was impossible not to be moved!

Genoa became a focal point for train-writing in the North-West of Italy, and during trips new friendships were installed with those that had initiated the Writing movement in other areas of Italy. In Turin, during a jam, I painted my first whole-train window-down with Emis, Sherif, Dafne, Done, Eron, Rok, Real, Sir, Ciuffo, and others. It was the first in Italy, it was the beginning of 1995 and everything was just starting to happen.

With 2D, the group I founded with Dafne, we spent a period travelling along the railway routes that were near and far: we were constantly moving, Tuscany, Liguria, Piedmont, we went everywhere. We saw each other with the sole objective of painting, often on the weekend. Dafne wasn't as panel-hungry as me. I never had enough. It was my drive.

2D remained active until 1999, but we never actually dissolved the crew. The positive thing about painting with Dafne is that we could pretend we were a couple just getting it on in case we were found out. Along with PDB crew, we started to paint the FS during the day. My pieces were getting better partly due to this aspect: the day light helps the paint not to drip and also allows you to work better on the graphic aspect of the piece. During my trips around I remember feeling quite surprised at how much freer Genoa was when it came to doing certain things. I understood this in Veneto when I heard talk of putting out a reward for catching

writers, and in 2001 it was again there that I saw the first anti-graffiti film coating on train cars. You could feel repression in the air. Anyway, the wildest experience remains in Naples: I hit the ETR, FS and subway in two days, it was total anarchy. You could paint anywhere, with such incredible ease.

1999 to 2002 was a period of major activity for me, during which I painted the most. Together with Sherif and Tabo I managed to get 3 carriages whole-car out of central station for the first time ever. In those years the best part was recognising the author of a piece, even from a distance. Everyone was following a personal study, with their own style and trait. At the time, if you didn't find your space, you didn't paint. I had my own measure of evaluation: I would cross any Genoese writer lacking style or whom I didn't respect. Then I covered the faded silvers that had been circulating for too many months and also the pieces by foreigners.

8 years abroad

>

1	**HOME** – 1996		
2	**BLEF** – 1996	**14**	**BLEF** – 2001
3	**BLEF** – 1997	**15**	**BLEF** – 2001
4	**BLEF** – 1998	**16**	**BLEF** – 2002
5	**BLEF** – 1998	**17**	**BLEF** – 2002
6	**BLEF** – 1998	**18**	**BLEF** – 2002
7	**BLEF** – 1999	**19**	**BESK** – 2002
8	**BLEF** – 1999	**20**	**BESK** – 2003
9	**BLEF** – 1999	**21**	**BESK** – 2003
10	**BLEF** – 2000	**22**	**BESK** – 2004
11	**BLEF** – 2000	**23**	**BESK** – 2004
12	**BLEF** – 2000	**24**	**BESK** – 2004
13	**BLEF** – 2000	**25**	**BESK** – 2004

Killer 1990

Dafne

>

As I leaf through the TV guide I see the title of a film: Wild Style – the TV premiere– I glance at the picture and see guys doing freezes in sporty uniforms and sweatshirts with Gothic-lettering, the tags in the background bring to mind Francesca Alinovi's words. The movie starts with an urban version of the Grease title sequence, then come the scenes of writers painting with their backs to the camera, in the dark, silhouetted, the shake of a can and an owl's hoot to warn others that someone is coming... I discover New York isn't that distant from the place I live in, I discover it's possible to repeat the same gestures with different results, with different extensions... those movements immediately become a physical necessity... the following night my search for trains begins, Marika Rock drives me to the yard, I follow my instinct, I know nothing about technique, the only practice I ever had was on the wall of my mother's garage, the spray paint is shoddy, it's like trying to make water stick to a wall. I have a plastic crate to help me reach the height of the panel, with no platform underneath, I stand on the tips of my toes to start painting and realise that the idea of doing a whole-car is pure utopia... once I'm done with my piece, the only thing I can think about is that tomorrow my work will be circulating, autonomous and out of control... KILLER?... just like any other thing...

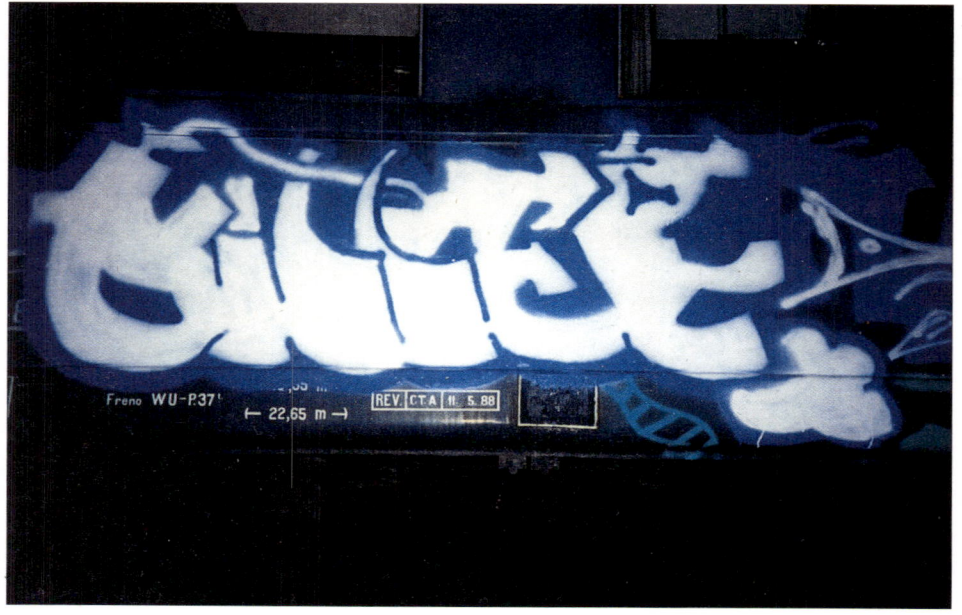

Killer, Dafne's first piece

— *Dafne*

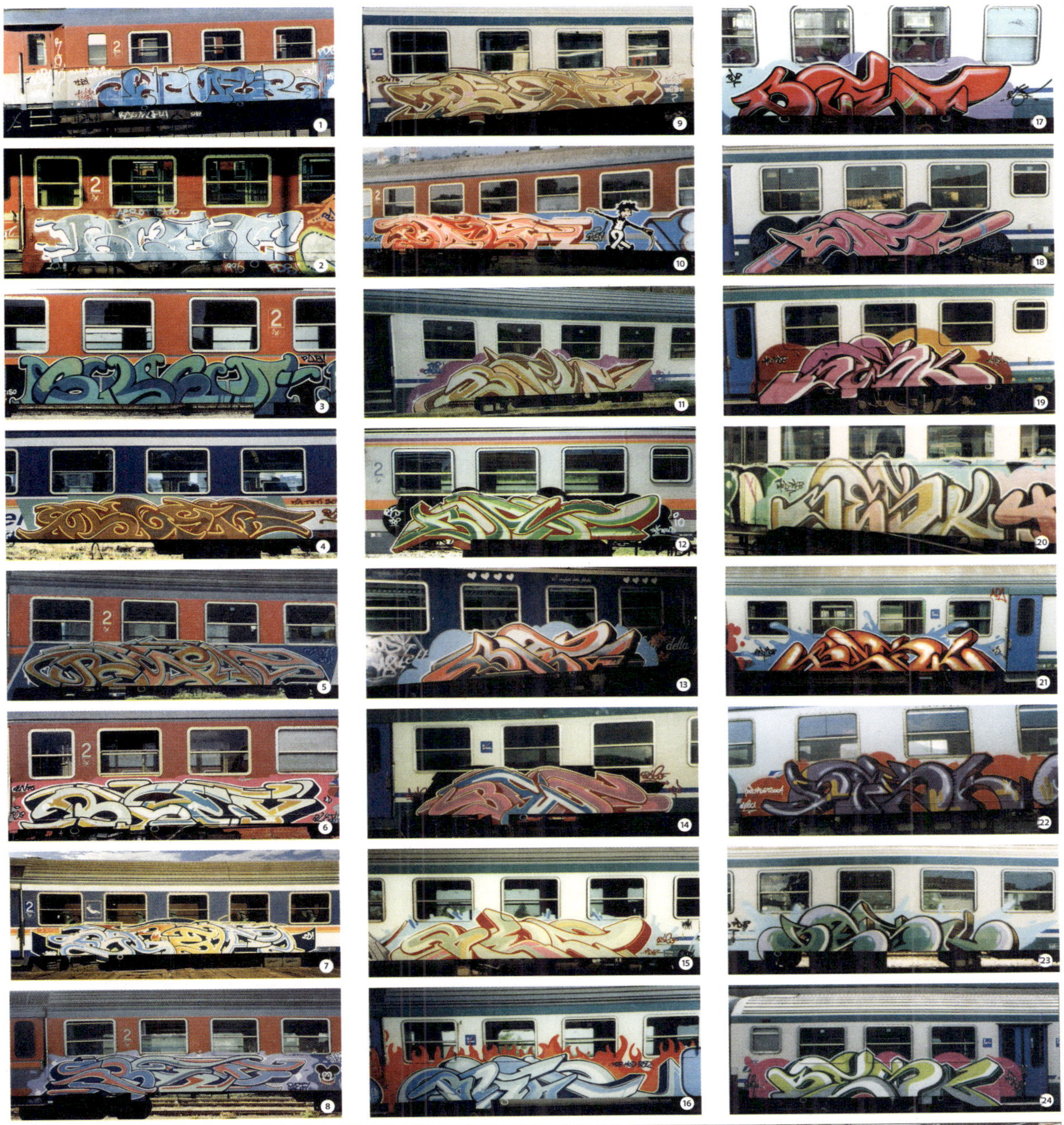

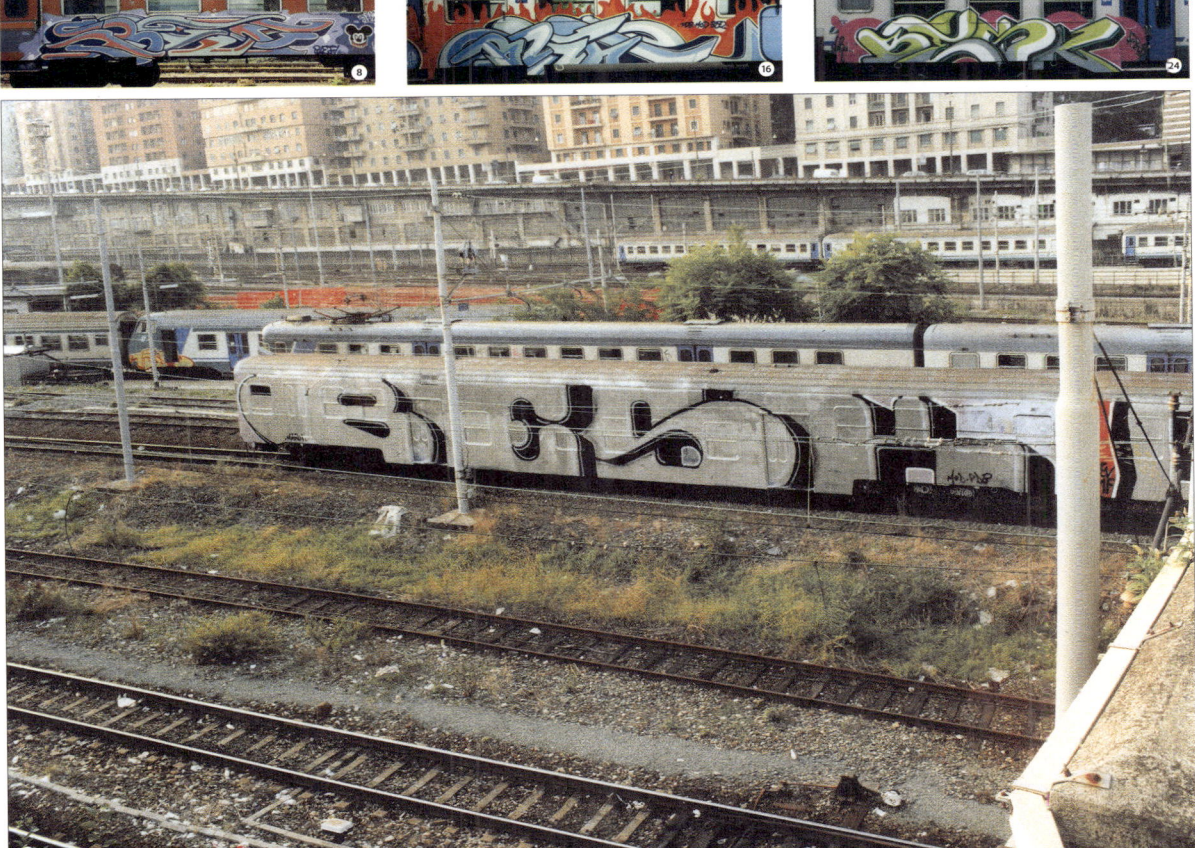

GENOA AND SURROUNDINGS
—

Dafne
>

During the first half of the 90's we'd paint in the principle yards of Genoa and in various lay-ups or small deposits spread throughout the territories of Liguria, Tuscany, and Piedmont. Naturally, with respect to the reality of Genoa, painting outside the city meant following other dynamics and using other tactics, especially when it came to "hunting down" our painted panels.

In Genoa you often found them in the central stations of Brignole and Principe but outside you could go crazy: we were obsessed with diurnal photos of the painted train and had studied a method to understand which stations it would stop in.

By mapping the territory and calculating the timetables we would anticipate trains in the stop that followed the yard and therefore photograph them without problems. A kind of New York subway strategy except diluted in a wider area, because the scale here was terri-

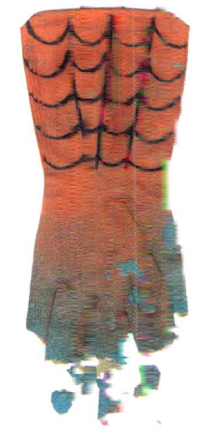

— *Dafne*

torial and not urban.

In the beginning it was me and Sherif, then after some time Blef joined towards '94–'95. We would organise real regional tours, painting many spots for the first time: the locals, if there were any, had never bombed those yards. All the months, years spent along the rail tracks reduced us to zombies, physically exhausted and socially isolated. Aside from trains, we had no other life.

We would sleep in the day and live at night, chasing after our pieces at sunrise, along the classic Sanremo–Genoa line I don't even know how many times. We went to Novara da Riso, to Vercelli, to Turin and if I'm not mistaken also to Pisa and Livorno. To then return to the lines in the region of Piedmont.

The last years are those with 2D (*Dynamic Duo*) crew that was created with Blef. Initially we observed one another with a bit of skepticism, him being such a latin lover, me more a latex lover; but with time we found a meeting ground that signified maximum trust in each other when in dangerous situations, and maximum esteem for the style of the other. The many nights in the mountains, spent freezing our arses off in flimsy sleeping bags before entering the yard, are still fresh in my memory.

The first female train-bomber of Italy
>

Mythology today

Dafne
>

Music, dancing, street-Writing, dress codes in a time before the Internet. How to buy a pair of Superstars in Zurich, leaving from San Remo without a precise address just because a friend heard there was a store downtown that had some pairs on display in the store window...

I painted from 1990 to 2000, I was in search of something to fulfill my quest to define who or what I was and why... I wasn't looking for a way to belong, I was curious to discover the chemical connection between things, to sketch a map of influences, and develop a personal language. In the 90's, the evolution of Writing from America to Europe could be witnessed on the pages of independent publications like *1Tox* from Paris, *400ml* from Zurich, *On The Run* from Munich, *Trap* from Milan, and *AL* from Genoa, or by leafing through a rare monographic book about a European city: *Paris Tonkar* (1987-1991)... the first time I brought it to Milan's WAG store, everyone was blown away. It was all underground, any information was precious and hard to find just like Bac deodorant caps that could only be bought in German supermarkets...I remember going to Stuttgart and Frankfurt with Skah and Onis 135 from Vicenza, going to to see B-boy battles, as well as the Zulu parties at the subway stop of Loreto. I found my Name in a book about classical mythology, the phonetics and the shape of the letters were exactly what I was looking for, 2+1+2. As I read the story about the main character, I thought it might bring me good luck and maybe I'd even be transformed into a bay shrub if I was being chased for painting... that's more or less what happened one night in Rome while I was painting trains with friends, we heard some shots and saw security guards running towards us, the fence was so slippery we weren't able to climb it, as I attempted to I fell into a bamboo thicket that hid me so I could observe the movements of our pursuers... I mainly painted trains at night, in an exquisitely inverted parallel dimension where fatigue was enough of a drug to alter the following day's clear-headedness. We'd arrive by car all tense, and during our activity we felt responsible for the safety of others. I always wore a plastic dish glove on my right hand. Layers and layers of toxic paint pretty much destroyed that glove...

The first RAL rail tour was in '93-'94. After looking over the train schedule, we figured out where the most isolated yards were and which trains would leave first the next morning and where they would go, so we could take pictures of our pieces at that station without looking suspicious... More than once we'd be on the road driving side by side with the train we'd painted... people looked on in amazement as the train passed through the countryside, trains hailing from tiny towns... the tour lasted a week, by day we slept in Marica Rock's car. New renaissance – this is why Francesca Alinovi's articles in the magazine *Flash Art* during the 80's were so important, they were my own private window on New York, stirring up images in my mind that then became a reality right in my own backyard, much to my surprise. In July 1984 in Quattordio, Delta Two, Ero, Phase II, and Rammellezee arrived from the Bronx and Queens to paint a building and shock the small village with their "army of letters" and their "Armamental" style.

-VIDEO-SEXY-TRAMA

VIDEO because the final result of chromatic fragmentation is similar to what happens to light in a cathode-ray tube; SEXY because it's an exasperation of "Aerotism" (Latex Lover/ Blef) hence, it automatically becomes sexy when executed; TRAMA (Texture) because it's a dense composition in which the colour stratification order gets lost.

It's the only type of colouring I used on trains, apart from the flat and uniform background. I wasn't interested in traditional 3D effects with the lettering; to me, using them was like triggering a mechanic repetition that negated the level of effectiveness of the letter, rendering it standard, integrated into the language of Writing, harmless, and almost sedated. I searched for something that was more edgy, something never seen before neither in Writing nor elsewhere, something that when in motion would give the idea of an "ultra colour", inexistent, the result of a fusion of all the tonalities used to make the piece. But at the same time I was very doubtful that I'd be able to control the lines while in a yard, in the dark, working quickly due to the tension of the moment; it was very likely the VST piece would be left incomplete. The first time I decided to use it was on the last day of the year, to "inaugurate" a new yard (1994). I was painting on a platform and ended up

having to change my "rhythm", I roughly finished and then went back to the outline after having "minimally" filled each letter in separately.

Time seemed endless, and my progress was at a standstill, after I finished painting the last series of lines, I realised I hadn't even started the hardest part yet. It was nearly impossible to find my outline since it was buried under the paint, the end result was disastrous; there were too many doubts between the lines. With practice, it all became easier, I got results by mixing fat lines and other marks with skinny lines, and the entire thing was contained by a winding outline, which enveloped the rigidity of the texture. In those days, I was listening to Surf music, especially The Ups! from Livorno, cascading guitar, drums, and bass... with Skah_bulous and The Capriss Girls '69, we often went to their concerts, it was natural to combine the idea of wave-shaped letters with that kind of music. A "wave" that was meant to unwind on the side of a van, with crests and crashing... SURF.

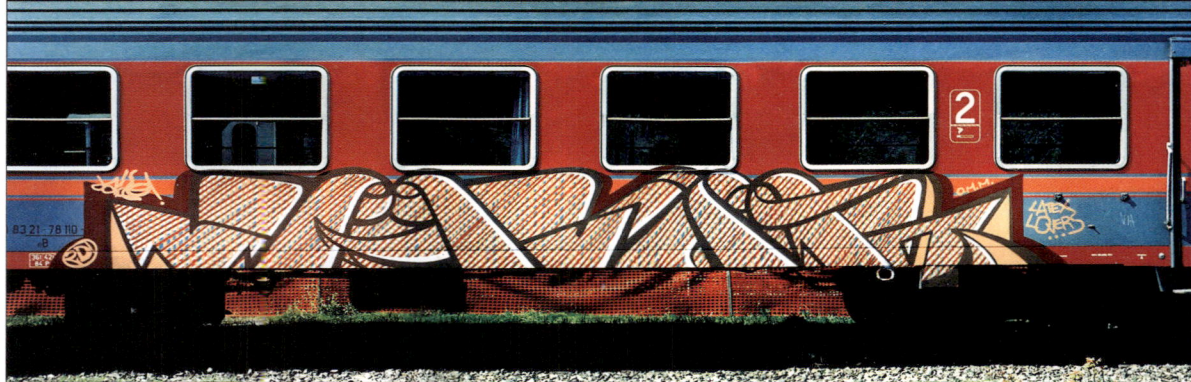

Dafne piece with video-sexy-trama filling

— Dafne

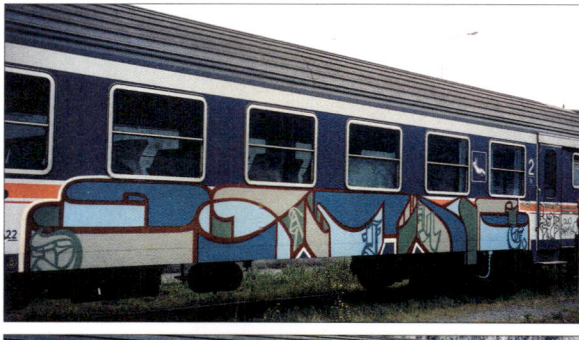
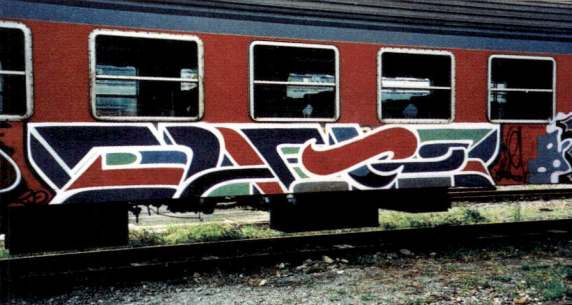
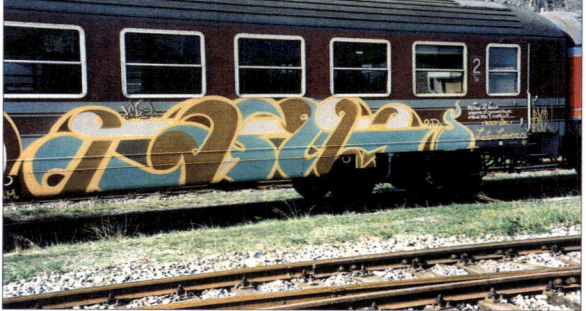

Panels Dafne painted in Liguria during the first half of the 90's

— Dafne

Page 248
>

Ravone by night
The city's main yard

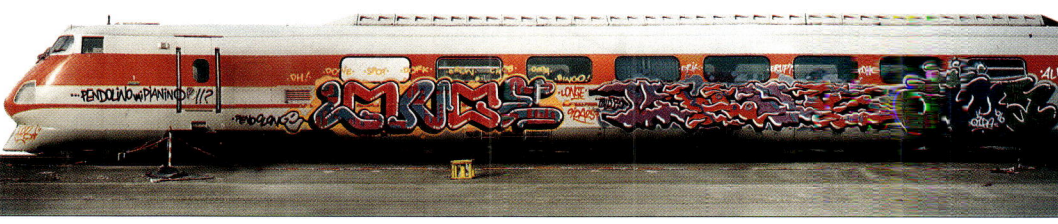

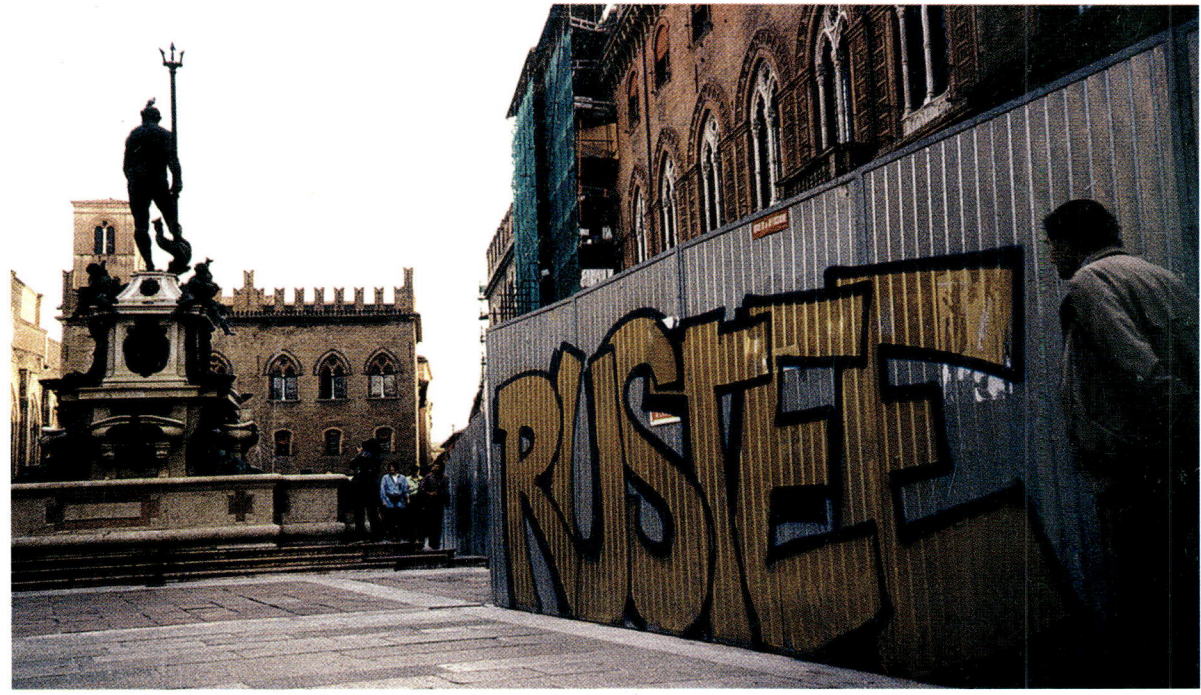

— *Rusty*

Forefathers of Bologna's Writing
>

Love of indifference

Fabiola Naldi
>

A t the end of the 70's, when political unrest in Italy was giving way to expressive outlets like politically charged writings and drawings on walls, writers in the U.S. were defining their territory by invading spaces with a communicative system in which they themselves represented the only viable ideology. All of this can only happen and grow through a love/hate relationship with the very spaces that contain writers and their deeds: the city must allow itself to be penetrated, and only when this happens can we truly speak of a cultural metropolis. The framework is almost always the same: a structure that reflects social, economic, and cultural forces in the relative organisation and planning of the city. It's the ideal perimetre within which the indicators of personal and collective identity are visualised in a democratic space. If this does not happen, then cultural penetration cannot occur, hence

halting the development of an urban space that, slowly but surely, will deteriorate. Bologna runs this risk during the late 70's to the early 80's, but the expressive momentum (also due to the presence of incipient creative groups within Universities, especially at the 'infamous' DAMS University) prompts the city to suddenly wake up to the sound of new thoughts, signs, and harmonies.
In Italy the term "Metropolitan Indians" was adopted by one of the many youth protest movements of the late 70's. The protest, led by these bizarre and irreverent young people with bright clothing and fresh yet scowling faces, is directed at the bourgeois and reactionary values and ideologies of the current society. This new 'creed' is infused with linguistic codes drawn from the cultural rifts of historic
avant-gardes movements (especially Futurism and Dadaism), which through irony and verbal violence, aimed at overturning the communication systems of their era.

● E.DI NALLO, *Indiani in città*, Bologna, Cappelli Publishing, 1977, p.9

The "Metropolitan Indians", who were active around 1977, faced "a desert of squalor, of missed opportunities, of

improbable alternatives, of wasted values".[1] In reality, the creative structure that houses the various forms of expression in the late 70's had been built upon the foundations of the second half of the 60's. Underground art stems from the encounter of multiple needs associated with the totalitarian behavior of the 'counterculture' which is drawn directly from Futurist-Dadaist experiments, where the cultural act identifies a new provocative reality in the act of playing a game.
Thus a new way of creating is born, a new way of working, of being politically active, of operating in the cultural and artistic realms in order to freely express all the taboos that had been imposed up until that moment.
Let there be a game to be played, and so be it. The game of protests, political actions, attacks on the Establishment, carried out on a daily basis and in such a programmed manner as to end up being anything but programmed because it becomes a vital component of everyday life.[2]
This affirmation by Mario Maffi refers to

● M.MAFFI, *La Cultura Underground*, Rome-Bari, Laterza, 1973, p.202.

> CONTINUES ON PAGE 252

ACW INTERNATIONAL / BOLOGNA

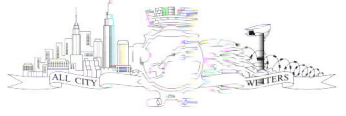

Main contributors:
Stefania Cavicchi i Choo, Ciufs,
Dado, Deemo, Draw, Fish,
Longe, Fabiola Naldi Cida,
Repo, Eox, Rusty, Shorty

In collaboration with:
BBS, BSA, OMC, DH, RB, SPA

Cover photo
Rusty, Piazza Maggiore 1991

Railtrack magnets

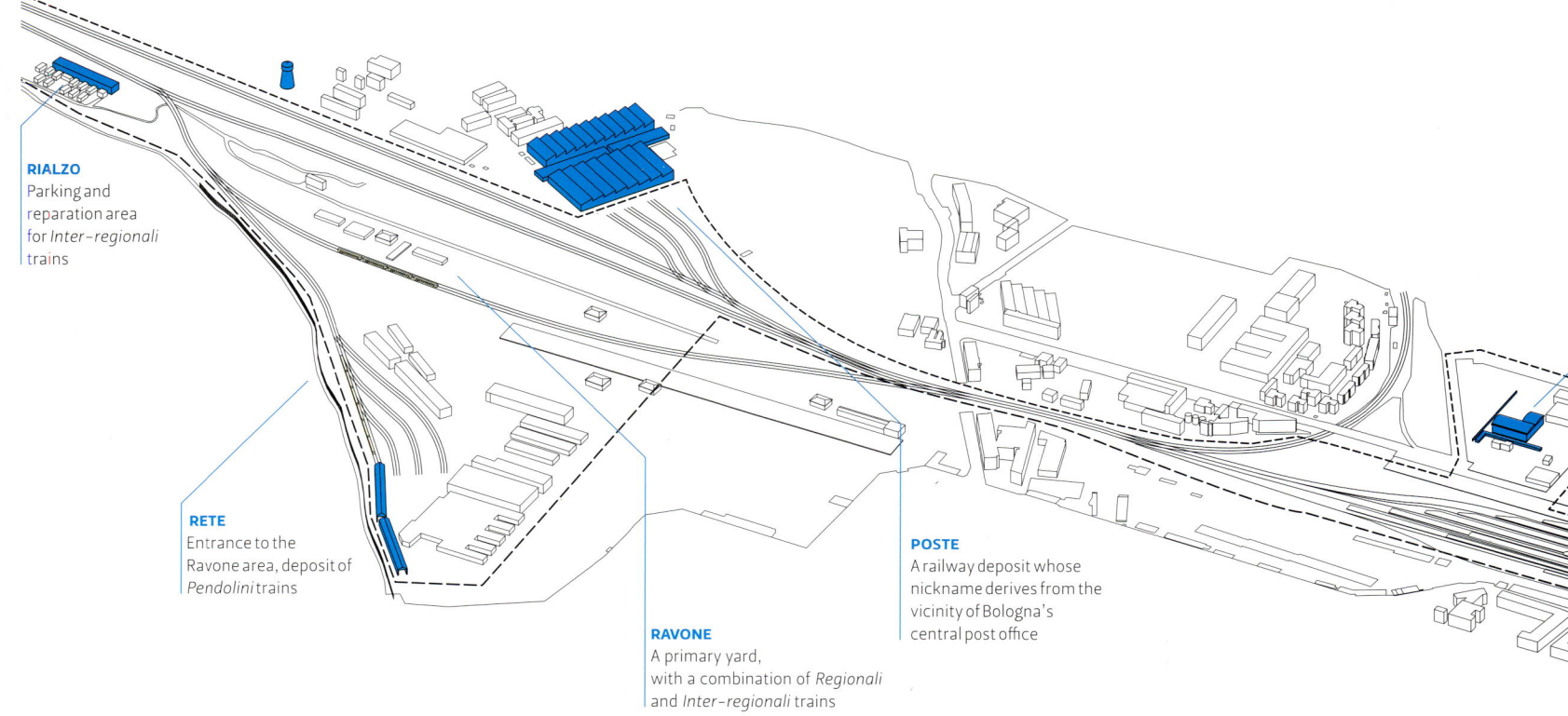

RIALZO
Parking and
reparation area
for *Inter-regionali*
trains

RETE
Entrance to the
Ravone area, deposit of
Pendolini trains

RAVONE
A primary yard,
with a combination of *Regionali*
and *Inter-regionali* trains

POSTE
A railway deposit whose
nickname derives from the
vicinity of Bologna's
central post office

Unlike other railway stations, like Stazione Centrale in Milan or Santa Maria Novella in Florence, the trains that arrive to Bologna pass right next to the city's historic centre. The railway line runs alongside the perimetre of Bologna's ancient walls and along its trajectory of industrial sites that have been progressively abandoned. In the urban spaces scattered along this route, around the end of the 80's, a first generation of writers was formed, whose aesthetic adapted to the type of surface they intended to hit, the speed of the trains travelling next to it, and thus the visibility of the piece.

In the part farthest from the station, the style of pieces was often simple, with the predominance of monochromatic blockbusters by SPA, painted on the laterite walls along the tracks: in this stretch, trains run at a standard velocity and for it to be discernable Writing has to be clear and legible. Advancing towards the point in which regional and inter-regional trains stop to give intercitys priority, the walls were systematically painted with a different objective, more related to the hall of fame aesthetic. In proximity to each bridge, the walls were first whitewashed and then completely painted,

giving life to chromatic flashes which resist time and unfavourable atmospheric conditions, thanks to the guaranteed protection of the bridge itself.
The first pieces to be painted on the walls adjacent the station itself were primarily spaces on one of the laterite facades, sectioned by a series of columns at regular intervals. The columns delimited the portions of wall: each writer occupied one, identifying himself with it and respecting its boundaries. The spatial restrictions resulted in a sequence of square pieces often coinciding with the initials of the crew the author belonged to.
The railway area behind the station then became the preferred spot for writers in Bologna.
The track line, passing underneath the bridge in Via Stalingrado, follows the urban stretch of ex-industrial buildings that border the historic centre. In this zone was the Livello 57 squat, whose yellow walls hosted SPA pieces for years.
The same portion of track line attracted many; on one side was Livello 57, where one could paint freely, on the other the cement walls that surrounded the perimetre of DLF, one of the primary yards of the city. At the end of the 80's, perhaps for the first time, the ducks of a local

artist called Pea Brain appeared on these walls. Even though she stayed outside of the writer circuit, she left traces of her presence in the city.
Following the tracks you then find the houses of the railroad workers and the cabins and junction boxes of the railway: micro-surfaces that allow the dissemination of tags and throw-ups, pieces of more limited dimensions with respect to the big designs that could find no adequate physical support in this area. A few hundred metres further is where the biggest railway deposit of the city can be found, Ravone, in which tracks branch out towards the primary directions of Milan (to the North), Ferrara and Padua (to the East), and Florence, (to the West). Along each of these routes, towards the end of the 90's, writers came to occupy the surfaces of the industrial buildings spread out between the railway and the highway, and the walls of the abandoned areas that border the tracks at a lower level of the ground. Over the years the railway line of Bologna became part of the urban texture of the city, and the construction of residential and tertiary buildings in place of the industrial complexes upset the aesthetic of the track line landscape: from

the detailed, coloured pieces of SPA, who generally pursued compositional criteria, to an uncontrolled appropriation of space on the part of an increasing number of writers and crews.
The cement surfaces built in substitution of the laterite walls favoured the diffusion of blockbusters and throw-ups, where beforehand had been hall of fame pieces.
The durability of these designs was notably lower, partly due to the large number of writers competing for available space, as well as for the same ephemeral quality of throw-ups. In certain railway tracks it became almost automatic to cover the recent writing of other crews and yet leave older pieces intact, pieces that had survived the passing of time and though faded and undefined were still respected by the new generations. The railway line of Bologna represents an interesting observation point from which to understand the alternation of crews that have been protagonists in the city's scene. The first pieces were painted by Deemo at the end of the 80's and right after him came Rusty and Shan-R. The formation of SPA – with its historic nucleus Rusty, Deemo, Dado, Ciuffo, Benja and then

Rusty
\>

THE TRACK LINE

The primary target of the first years was the wall along the track line, simply because it allowed for maximum visibility. We had transported the hall of fame aesthetics to the walls under a couple of bridges, instead of the usual blockbusters or silver throw-ups. Once the walls had been painted white, the surface would be smooth and protected by the structure of the bridge, so that the pieces would last and the colours wouldn't fade from the rain. The bridges were colourful pauses between the various stretches of the line, which were prevalently painted silver and without a background. Only initially was it possible to do coloured pieces with a background, as the walls along that track line have now been substituted by solid reinforced concrete. Before this though, the border between railway and city was delimited by a brick wall and interrupted only by a couple of columns, again in bricks, every three-four meters. Under some aspects it resembled the track line of

\> CONTINUES ON PAGE 236

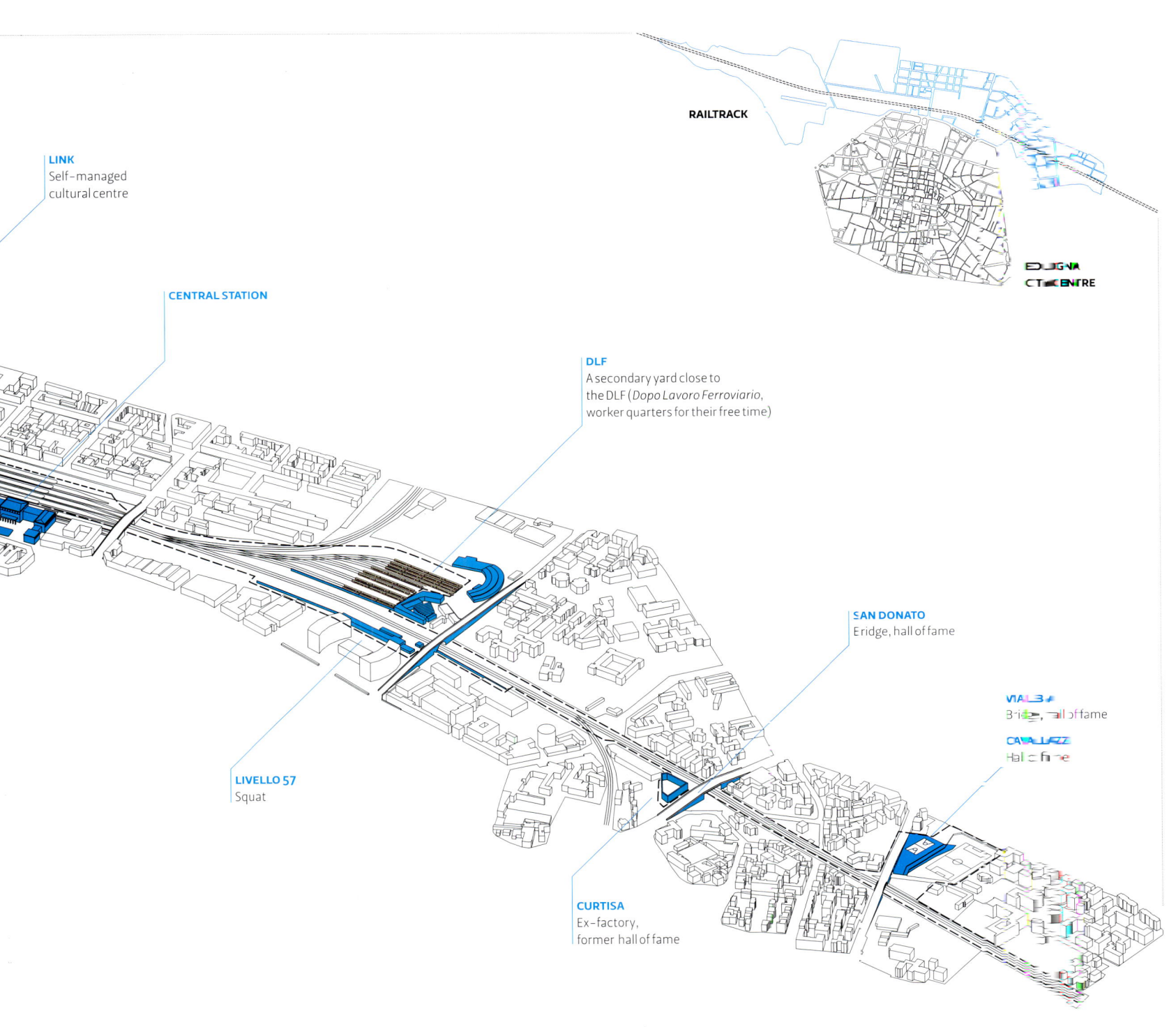

RAILTRACK

LINK
Self-managed
cultural centre

BOLOGNA
CITY CENTRE

CENTRAL STATION

DLF
A secondary yard close to
the DLF (*Dopo Lavoro Ferroviario*,
worker quarters for their free time)

SAN DONATO
Bridge, hall of fame

VIALE
Bridge, hall of fame

CAVALLAZZI
Hall of fame

LIVELLO 57
Squat

CURTISA
Ex-factory,
former hall of fame

Rimini, the way these pauses often defined the limits of a piece. The columns were perceived as vertical frames and the first pieces all respected these standards: "FCE", "TRAP" and "DFA", Dayaki and Zero-T's "CMC", and even "Città Zombi" (Zombie City), the first piece in history to be painted on this urban filament. It was a relatively simple work but anyway advanced for the time: black outline traced by Dayaki and a monochromatic fill done by Magma and Mined. About ten years later that piece

would be celebrated through a second "Città Zombi", this time in full colour, under the bridge of Via Libia. "Città Zombi II" is next to a drawing of the typical housewife from Emilia, rolling pin included, done by Dayaki, a good rendition of the sleepy life of the province. The letters this time were mine and, along with other pieces using this alphabet, greatly affected the style of Bologna at the time: stiff lines that became broad curves at the end, often used to connect one letter to another. This style, not

too wild, almost made of block letters, greatly influenced other writers of the region who were inevitably impressed by the coloured walls that could be seen – and photographed – while riding the train.
I would often paint the track line with Mined, and it's with him that some time later I did "Show me your shoes", jokingly dedicated to the writers of Rimini, long-time friends but also distant from our reality: they were too obsessed with their Hip Hop aesthetics. We would

go to Rimini in the Summer and as soon as you got there the local kids would look you up and down from head to toe, especially if you weren't sporting baggy jeans and fat laces....like us. We traced that piece along with the members of Cammelli crew, and I remember that while we were painting that night, at a certain point two people approached, with flashlights in their hands. They said they were cops but were foreign and didn't even have a badge, the truth is they were wandering around the

rail tracks looking for something they wouldn't like us. The track line was a sort of continuous hall of fame, a bit of a territory where you could easily encounter all sorts of shady people. Though it was in the proximity of the city centre and at spitting distance of the houses on its side, it was considered a free zone by the writers who took possession of it. There was no police and when there was they turned a blind eye, at least on the track of San Donato, far from the station, where trains picked up speed.

RETROSPECTIVE OF THE LAST 15 YEARS

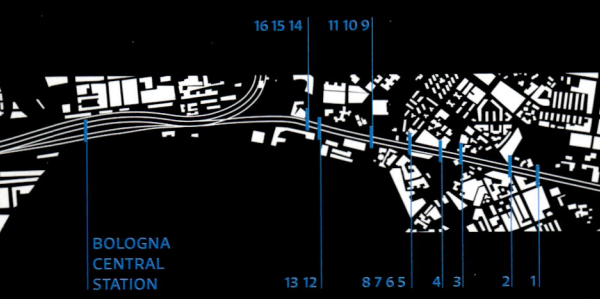

16 15 14   11 10 9

BOLOGNA
CENTRAL
STATION

13 12   8 7 6 5   4 3   2 1

> CONTINUES FROM PAGE 234

the large wall work under the bridge of via Libia. The crews that formed in the second half of the 90's, like BBS, occupied the spaces along the track line in their own distinct manner, almost always preferring throw-ups and silver bombings to big murals.

Observing these works from the windows of a running train leaves a particular impression of this track, that seems dominated by the ground noise created by the silver and black of contemporary bombings, at times interrupted by the silence of walls that have been weathered with time, real flashbacks to the past of Bolognese Writing. Rusty-mined for example, one of the first pieces to be painted, dated 1990, is still visible, in spite of the light colours of the letters, eaten away by the laterite bricks.

– ATTRACTORS

The railway in Bologna immediately presented itself as an excellent target for writers, who could count on considerable visibility for their pieces and such a variety of supports as to ensure a variegated body of productions. Other than this, along the same urban stretch was a concentration of other important elements of attraction: the Curtisa and the Cavallazzi, historic halls of fame that directly bordered the rail tracks, as well as social centres like Link and Livello 57. The line thus represented a magnet and a catalyser for all the Writing-related energy of the city, starting with Central Station, which

1992

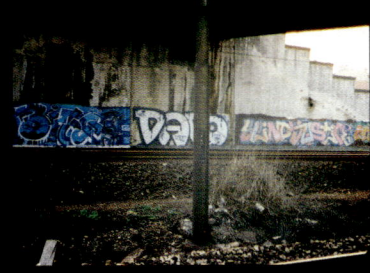

1 BRIDGE OF VIA LIBIA

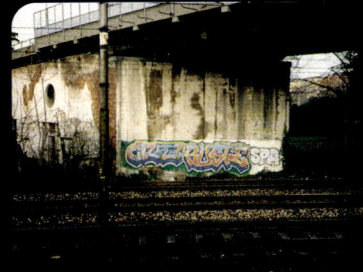

2 SAN DONATO BRIDGE

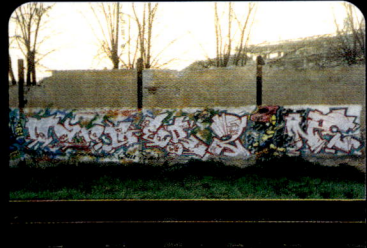

3 WALL OF THE EX–FACTORY OF CURTISA

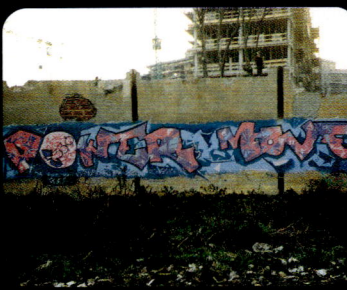

4

2007

1 BRIDGE OF VIA LIBIA

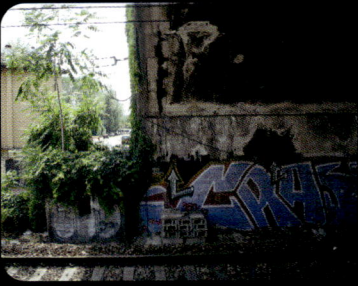

2 SAN DONATO BRIDGE

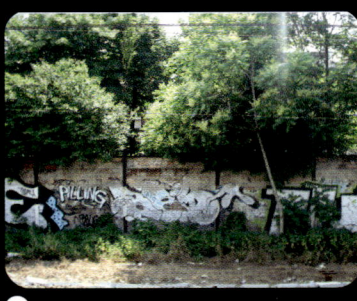

3 WALL OF THE EX–FACTORY OF CURTISA

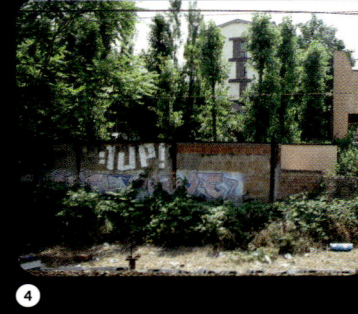

4

1992

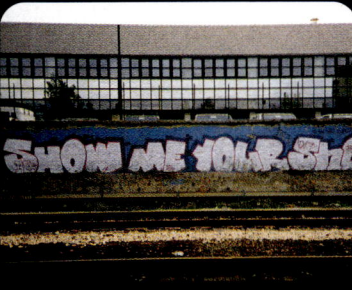

9 WALL OF ACOSER CAR–DEALERS

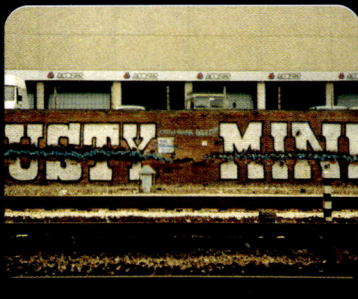

10

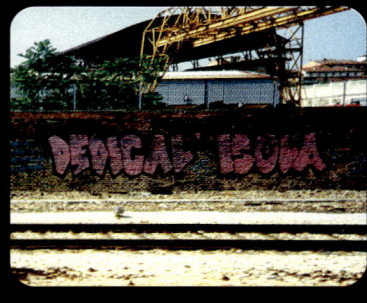

11

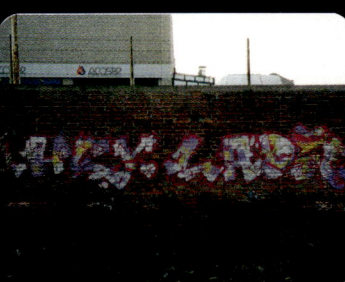

12

2007

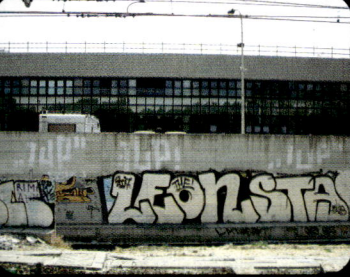

9 HEADQUATERS OF HERA (LOCAL CLEANING ADMINISTRATION)

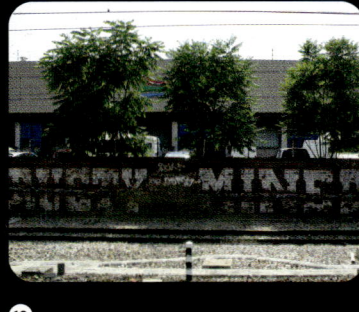

10

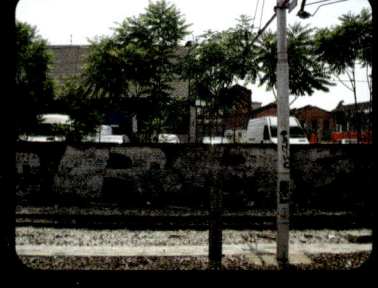

11

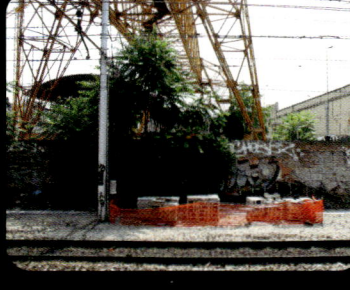

12

with the explosion of the train-bombing phenomenon became the ideal place to photograph painted cars. Of great importance also were railway deposits like Ravone and DLF: the first for example, forms such a wide expanse in the railway area inside the city that it creates an imaginary neighbourhood, in which writers lived as much as the people working there. Soon enough, the Ravone yard experienced a dual routine: the diurnal one involving railwaymen and workers, and the nocturnal

activities of the writers and the immigrants living in the trains at the yard. In Bologna, the railway line has established itself in the course of time as an excellent over-exposed target, with multiple possible uses. Similarly, the cars who passed through it were the only medium through which different generations of writers were able to confront each other, causing this railway track to be the perfect key to interpreting the temporal evolution of the Writing phenomenon in Bologna.

Oida
>

The story of Writing in Bologna is prevalently tied to the walls of the railway line that crosses through the city, where the pieces that would influence a whole generation took form: right next to the station you could read "Alta Tensione" and

the blockbusters by Rusty and Mined, and still in place, on the initial stretch in bricks that faces the South, there was also "CMC" (1989) by Dayaki and Zero-T from Florence, and also, "Power Move" (1989), by Rusty and Shan-R.
The 'graffiti' of those years was often a message that could be easily read from above a moving train: I remember slogans like "Love for Indifference", "Show me your shoes", "Dedical'isola", "Cani Sciolti" by Ciuffo, "Golpe" by Dado, when there was still

much to say and less evolution to represent.
The fact remains that these pieces gave colour to boredom, and represented the social unrest and desire to change things.
Many, I'm sure, jumped over the barriers of the track line to personally see and document this art. Just as I'm sure that all those that passed through here left their heart and eyes in front of "Danger Zone", by Dayaki and Zero-T, the perfect piece: writing and puppet both extremely precise, everything in place.

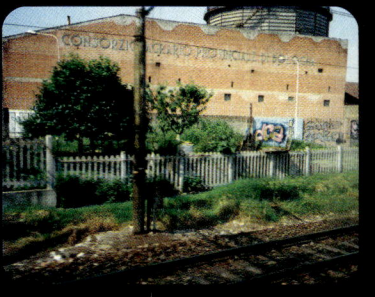 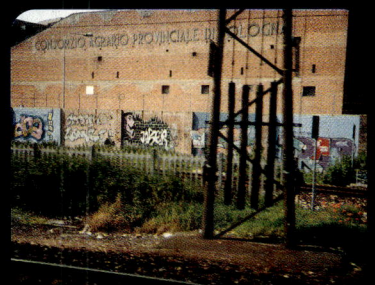 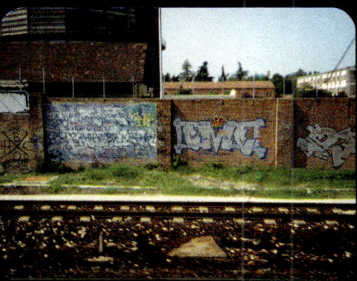 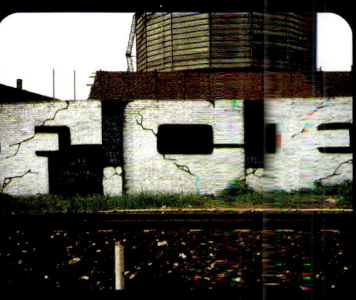

5 **THE AGRICULTURAL CONSORTIUM OF BOLOGNA** 6 7 8

1992

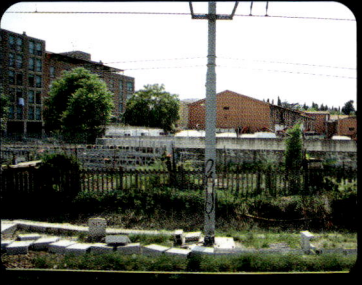 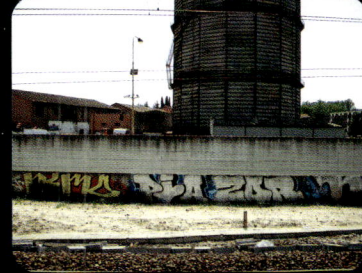 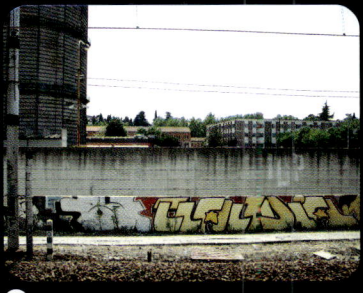 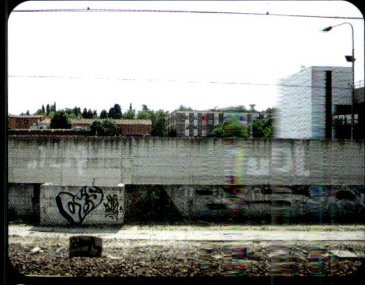

5 **EX–AGRICULTURAL CONSORTIUM OF BOLOGNA** 6 7 8

2007

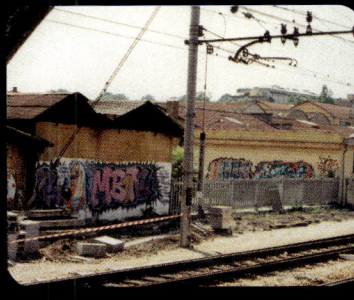 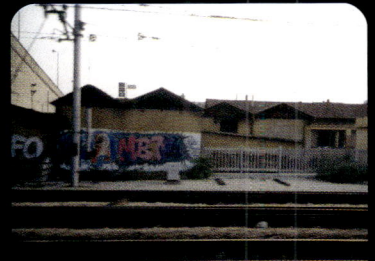 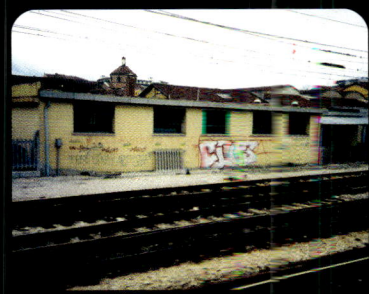

13 **BRIDGE OF VIA STALINGRADO** 14 **BUILDINGS OF LIVELLO 57** 15 16

1992

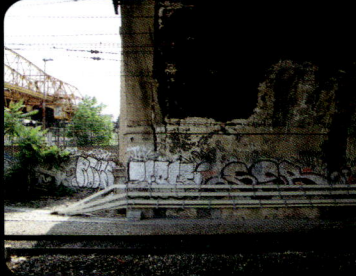 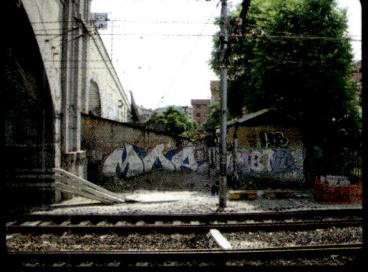 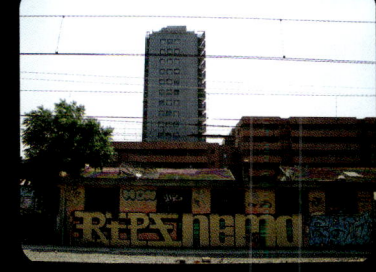 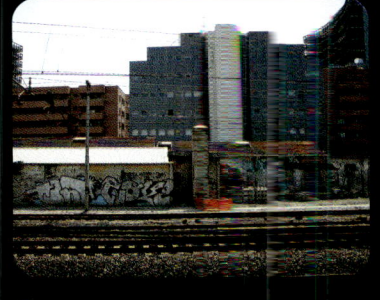

13 **BRIDGE OF VIA STALINGRADO** 14 **BUILDINGS OF FORMER LIVELLO 57** 15 16

2007

WALLS TYPOLOGIES

Mutations

❶	LINE Ancona/Bologna	SPEED ●●●●●	FUNCTION barriers	SIDE right	H/LENGTH 2,2 m/500m	MATERIAL bricks
	STATUS crossed	RISK FACTOR ●○○○○	BACKGROUND —	CREW–90's SPA	FIRST PIECE Rusty	PIECE TYPE blockbuster

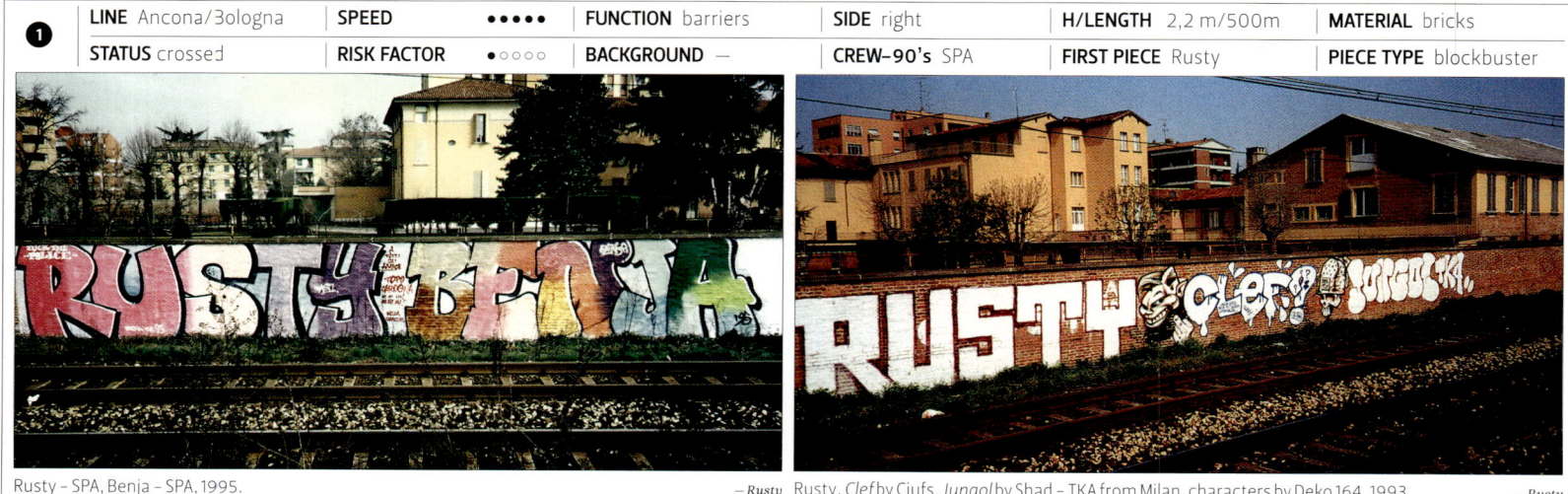

Rusty – SPA, Benja – SPA, 1995.   — *Rusty*   Rusty, *Clef* by Ciufs, *Jungol* by Shad – TKA from Milan, characters by Deko 164, 1993   — *Rusty*

❹	LINE Ancona/Bologna	STATUS crossed	SPEED ●●●●○	RISK FACTOR ●●○○○	FUNCTION bridge walls	SIDE left

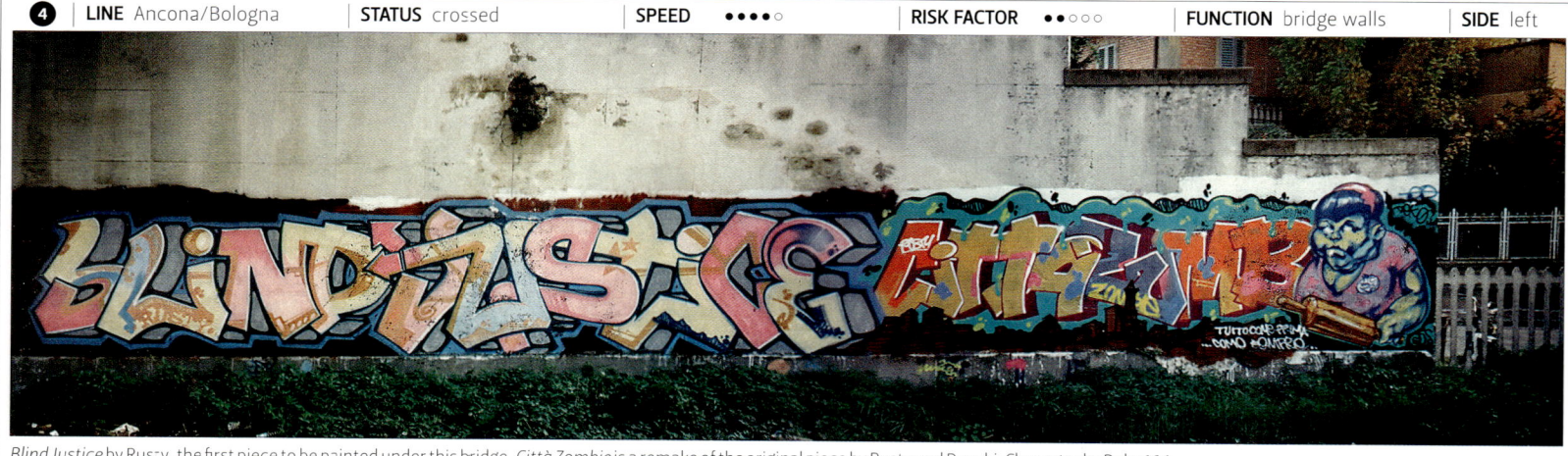

Blind Justice by Rusty, the first piece to be painted under this bridge. *Città Zombie* is a remake of the original piece by Rusty and Dayaki. Character by Deko 164   — *Rusty*

❺	LINE Ancona/Bologna	STATUS demolished	SPEED ●●●○○	RISK FACTOR ●●●●○	FUNCTION barriers	SIDE left

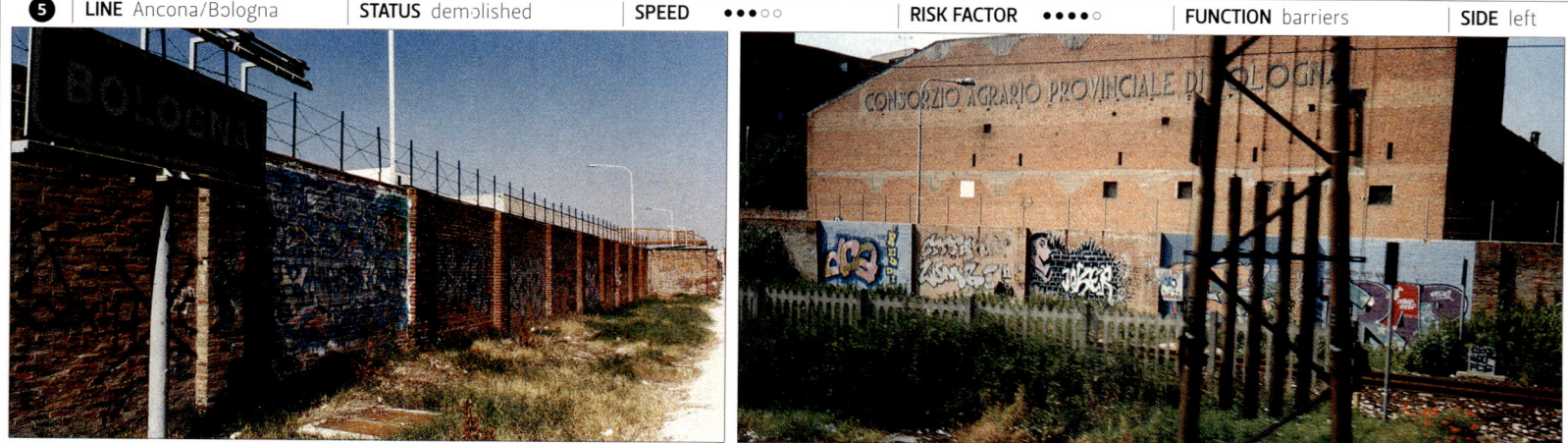

Alta tensione (High tension) by Dayaki, Mined and Magma, painted in September 1987   — *Rusty*   *DFA* by Rusty, view of the old line with the first piece to be painted on it: " Città Zombie", 1987   — *ACW archive*

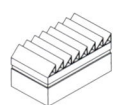 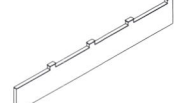 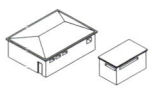 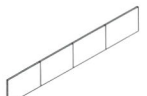 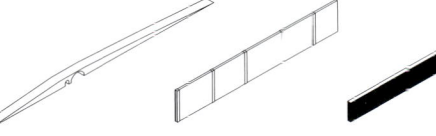 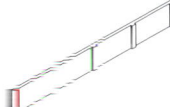

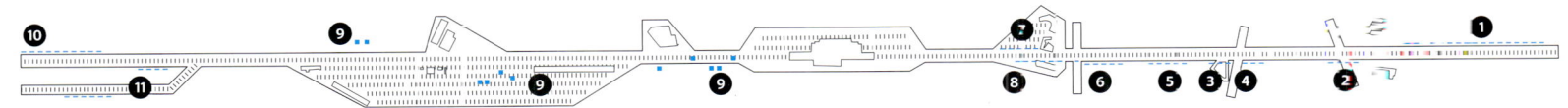

②	LINE Ancona/Bologna	SPEED ●●●●●	FUNCTION bridge wall
	STATUS crossed	RISK FACTOR ●○○○○	BACKGROUND none

③	LINE Ancona/Bologna	SPEED ●●●●○	FUNCTION factory
	STATUS existing	RISK FACTOR ●●○○○	BACKGROUND plaster

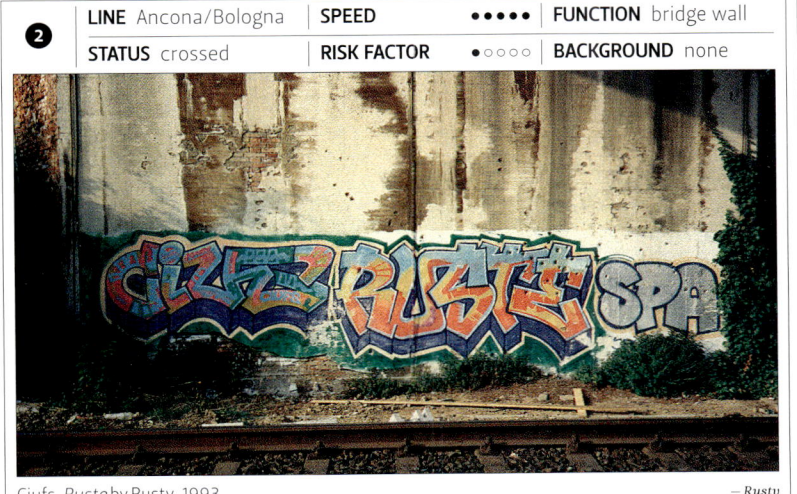

Ciufs, *Ruste* by Rusty, 1993.   — *Rusty*

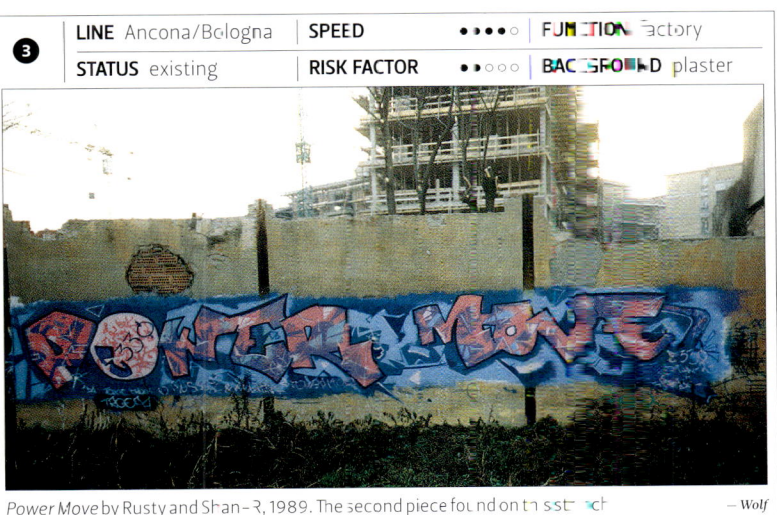

Power Move by Rusty and Shan-R, 1989. The second piece found on that track.   — *Wolf*

BACKGROUND grey plaster	H/LENGTH 6,5 m / 15 m	MATERIAL concrete	FIRST PIECE Blind Justice	CREW-90's SPA	PIECE TYPE colorful

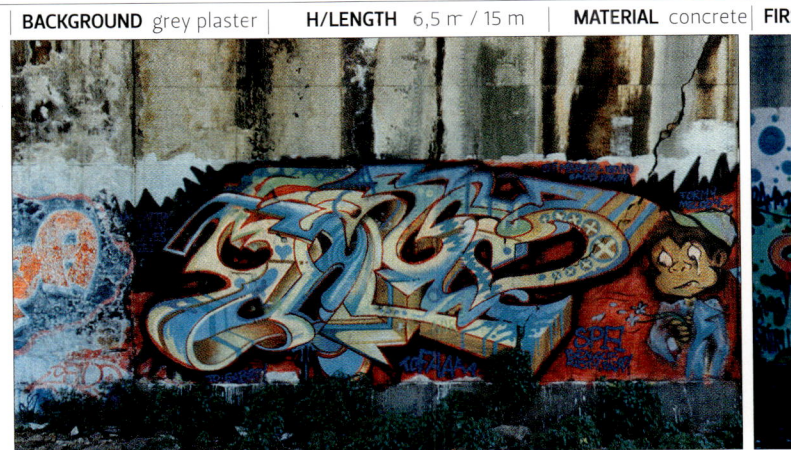

Dado – SPA, 1994   — *Oida*

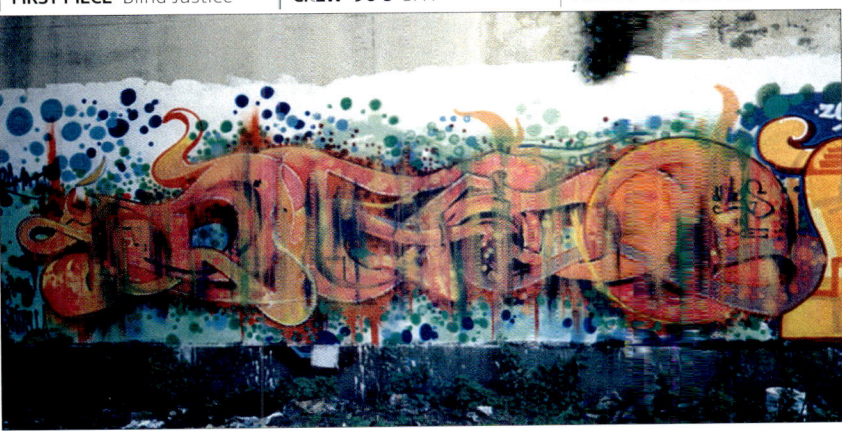

Dado – SPA, 1995   — *Dado*

BACKGROUND —	H/LENGTH 2,5 m /500 m	MATERIAL bricks	FIRST PIECE Città Zombi	CREW-90s CMC-SPA	PIECE TYPE blockbuster

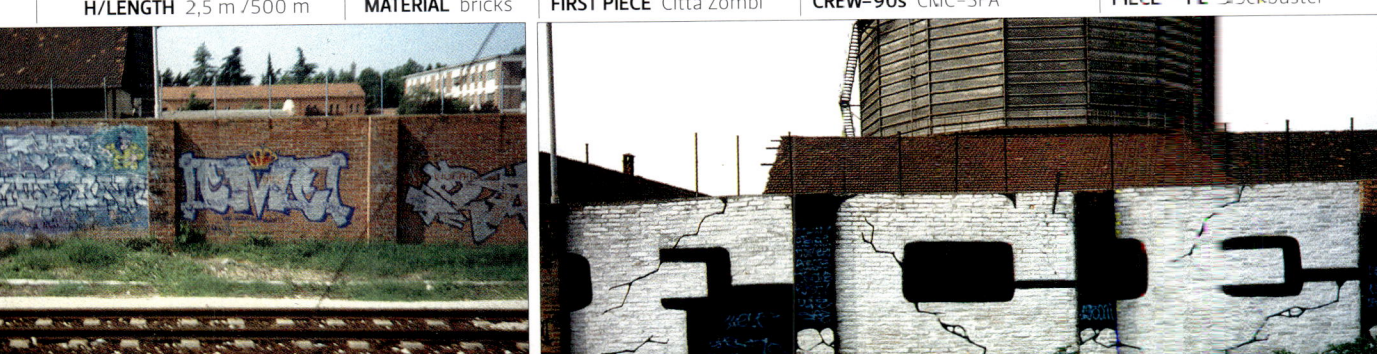

CMC by Dayaki and Zero-T from Florence, 1989   — *ACW archive*   *FCE* blockbuster by Wolf and Shorty   — *Oida*

| 6 | LINE Ancona/Bologna | STATUS demolished | SPEED ●●○○○ | RISK FACTOR ●●●●○ | FUNCTION barriers | SIDE left |

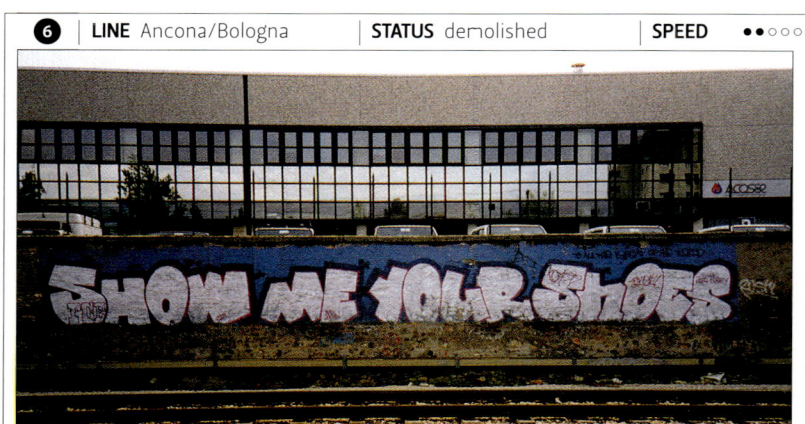 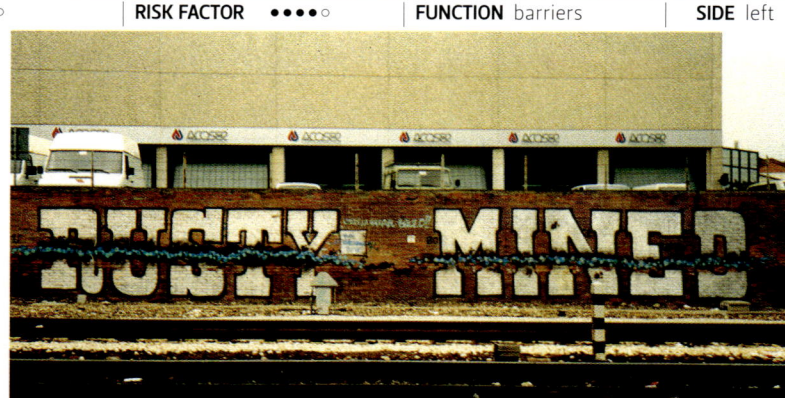

Show me your shoes, ironically dedicated to B–boys by Rusty. Shan–R, 1991   — *Wolf*   Rusty and Mined, 1991   — *Rusty*

| 7 | LINE Bologna/Milan | STATUS crossed | SPEED ●○○○○ | RISK FACTOR ●●●● | FUNCTION barriers | SIDE right |

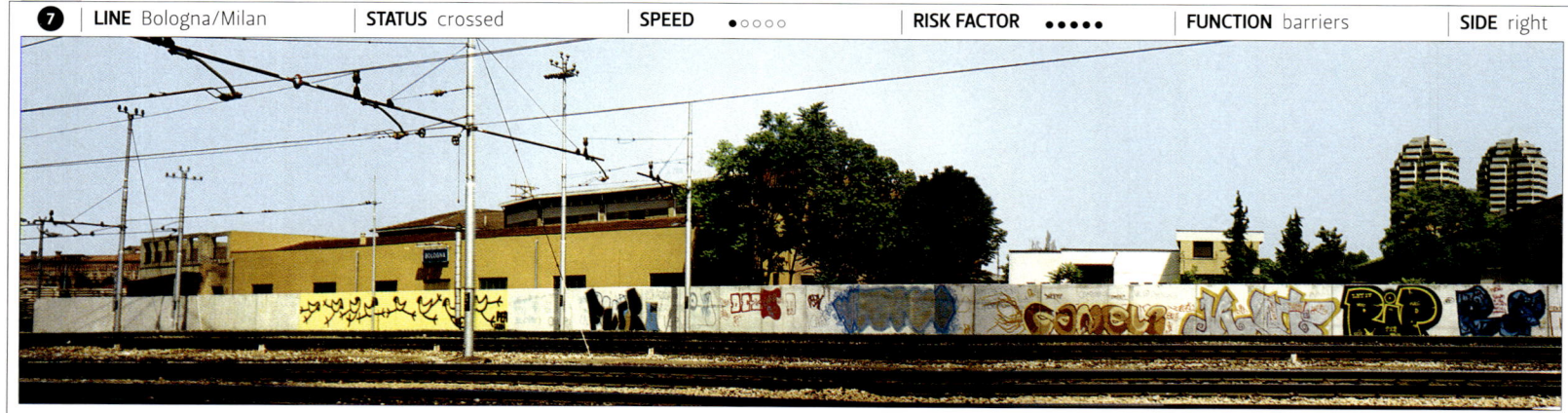

To the left ducks painted on a yellow background by Pea Brain, first piece on this wall of the track line, 1991. Among the various designs is *RIP* by Rusty dedicated to Isola nel Kantiere when it was cleared   — *Oida*

| 8 | LINE Ancona/Bologna | SPEED ●●○○○ | FUNCTION ex squat walls | SIDE right | H/LENGTH 2,5m / 7m | MATERIAL concrete |
| | STATUS crossed | RISK FACTOR ●●●●● | BACKGROUND none | CREW–90's SPA | FIRST PIECE Bombin' | PIECE TYPE colorfull |

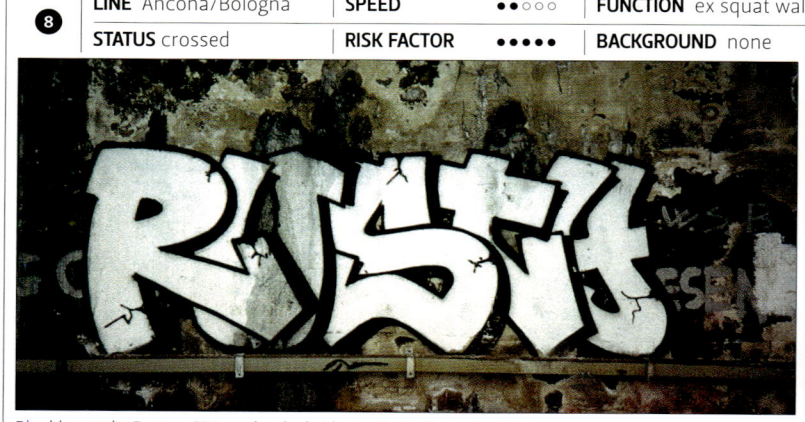 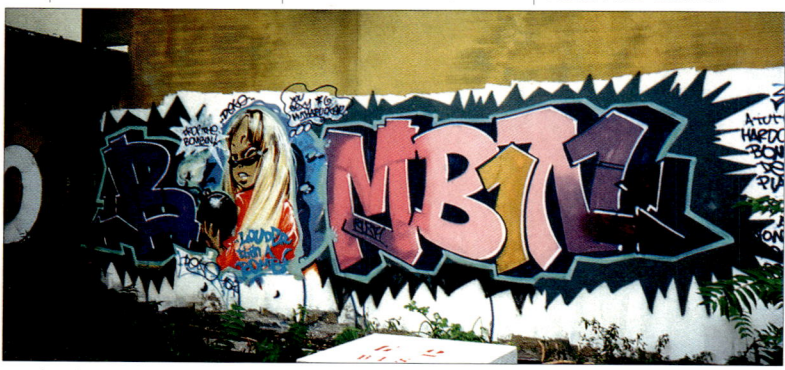

Blockbuster by Rusty – SPA, under the bridge in Via Stalingrado, 1993   — *Oida*   *Bombing* by Rusty and puppet by Deko 164, 1994   — *Oida*

| 10 | LINE Bologna /Padova | SPEED ●●●●○ | FUNCTION factory wall | SIDE right | H/LENGTH 9 mt /50 mt | MATERIAL concrete |
| | STATUS crossed | RISK FACTOR ●●●●○ | BACKGROUND yellow plaster | CREW–90's SPA | FIRST PIECE Rusty | PIECE TYPE colorfull |

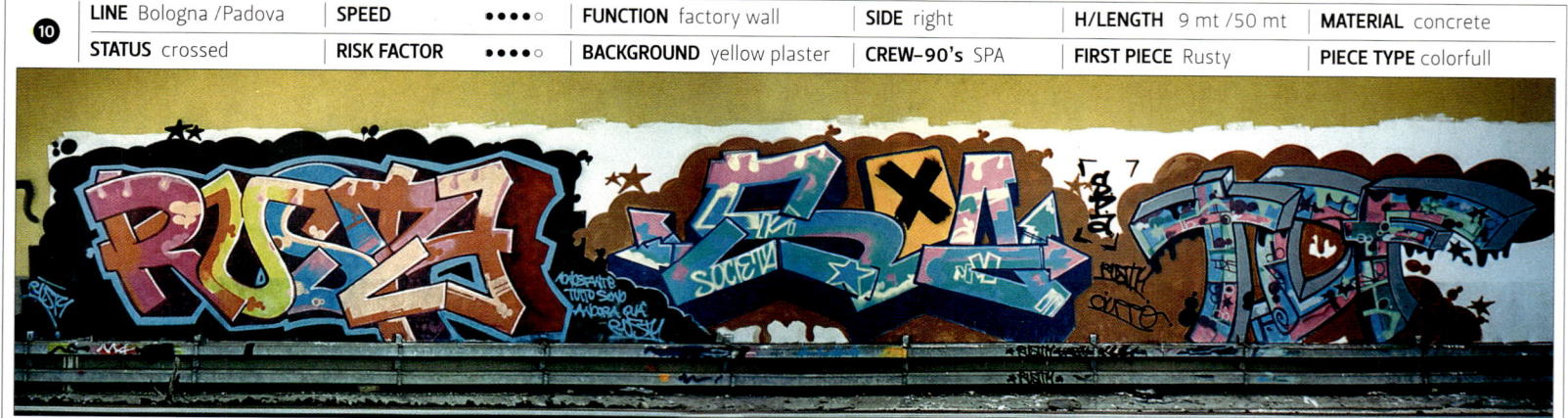

Rusty, *SPA* by Rusty and Ciufs, *TDF* by Ciufs, 1991   — *Rusty*

| BACKGROUND — | H/LENGTH 2,2 m /150 m | MATERIAL bricks | FIRST PIECE Rusty/Mined | CREW-90's CMC-SPA | PIECE TYPE blockbuster |

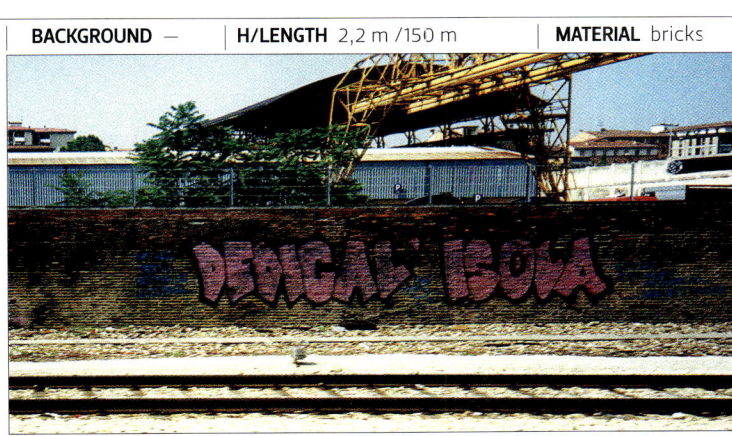 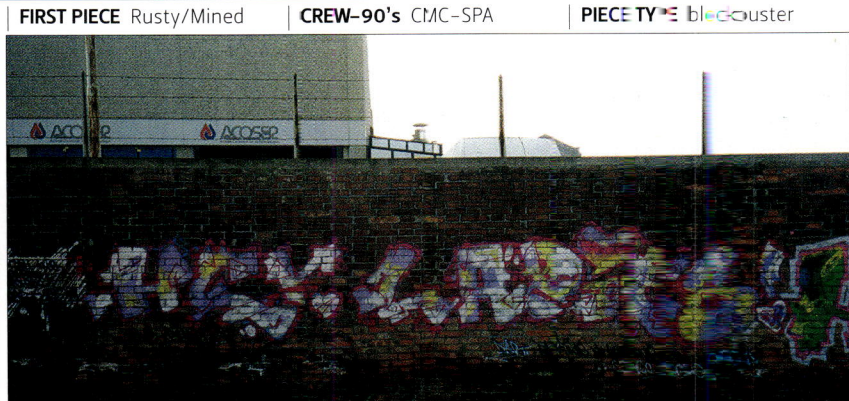

Dedical' Isola Josha , Kelso and Ciufs, 1992   — *ACW archive*   *Hey Ladies, Da king is looking for a queen!* Painted by Dayaki, 1988   — *Wolf*

| BACKGROUND — | H/LENGTH 2,6 m / 250 m | MATERIAL concrete | FIRST PIECE Pae Brain ducks | CREW-90's FCE – SPA | PIECE TYPE colorfull |

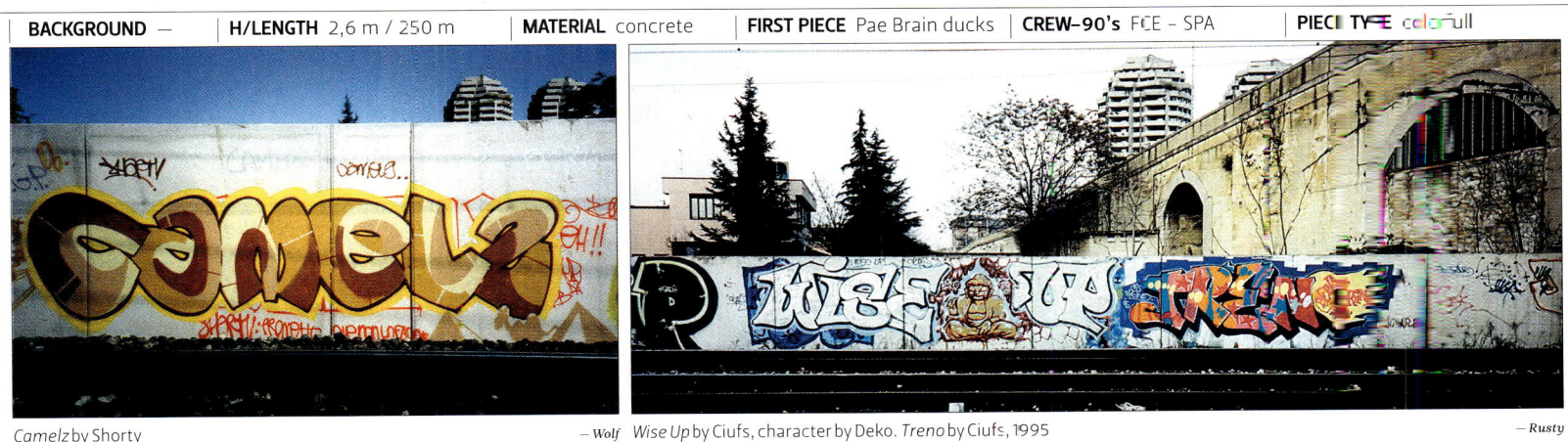

Camelz by Shorty   — *Wolf*   *Wise Up* by Ciufs, character by Deko. *Treno* by Ciufs, 1995   — *Rusty*

| ❾ | LINE Bologna/Milano | SPEED ●○○○○ | FUNCTION various | SIDE left/right | H/LENGTH various | MATERIAL various |
| | STATUS existing | RISK FACTOR ●●●●● | BACKGROUND various | WRITER BBS/PMC | FIRST PIECE Panik | PIECE TYPE throw-ups |

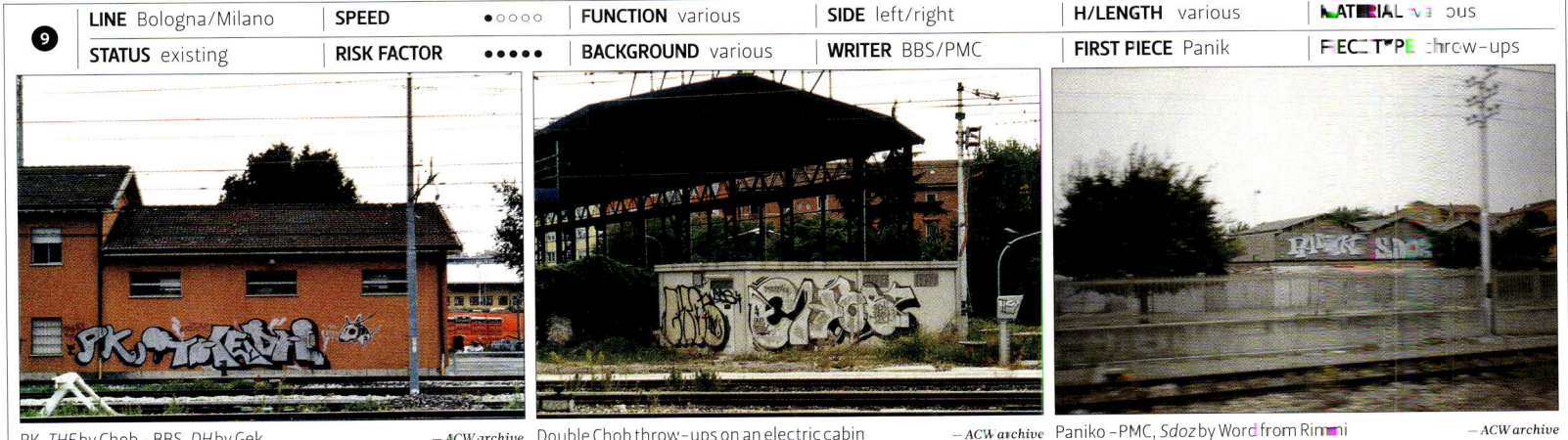

PK, *THE* by Chob – BBS, *DH* by Gek   — *ACW archive*   Double Chob throw-ups on an electric cabin   — *ACW archive*   Paniko –PMC, *Sdoz* by Word from Rimini   — *ACW archive*

| ⓫ | LINE Bologna/Milano | SPEED ●●●○○ | FUNCTION industrial border | SIDE right | H/LENGTH 3,2 m /240 m | MATERIAL bricks |
| | STATUS existing | RISK FACTOR ●●●○○ | BACKGROUND — | CREW-90's SPA | FIRST PIECE Rusty | PIECE TYPE colorfull |

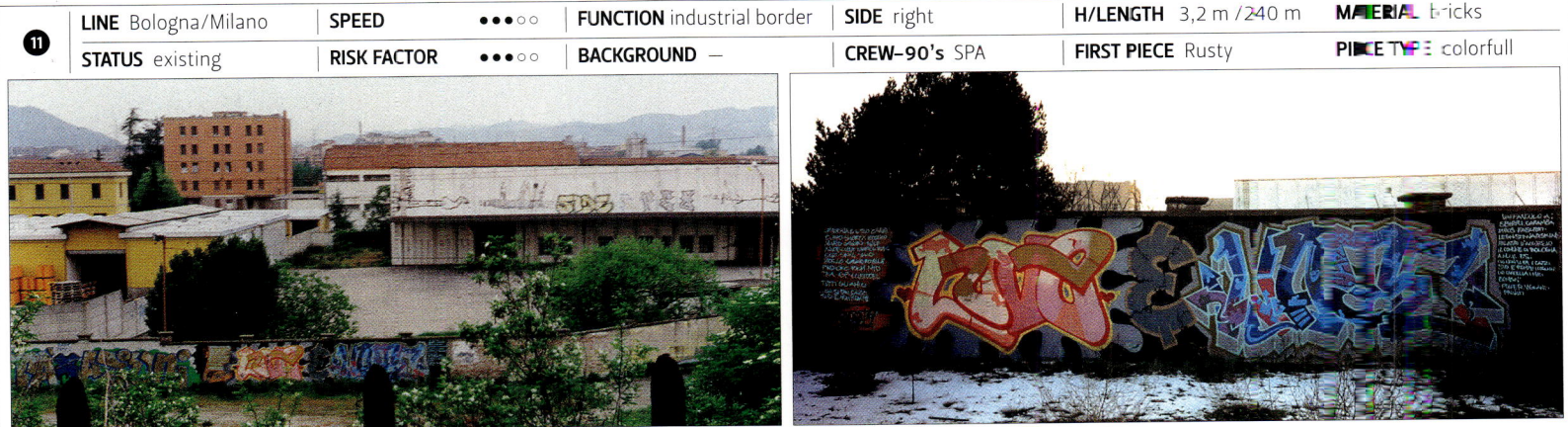

Along this stretch of the Bologna–Milan, the first SPA hall of fame was born. On the roof to the back pieces by Pea Brain and Side are discernible. A close-up of *Love and Hate* by Rusty, 1992   — *Oida*

HALL OF FAME

Free zones
\>

Enclosed halls of fame

CHOB

In the beginning between SPA and BBS there was that typical rivalry that exists between rookies and the more experienced writers that look down on them. One of my first pieces was at the Cavallazzi, the city's hall of fame. It was bursting with pieces and I decided to cross over a work by Andrè that I couldn't decipher, an absurd composition, too pictorial even for us. Due to this episode I would often find guys waiting for me outside of school, Ciuffo's cohorts, as at the time he was somewhat considered gang leader of the young writers of Bologna.

The début in Curtisa halfway through the 80's and the official switch to Cavallazzi

The first two halls of fame to rise in Bologna, though occupied in different periods, were just a few hundred metres away from one another, united by the vector of the railway line. Curiously, both were located on the bridge structures crossing over the same line, becoming meeting places for local Writing. Curtisa was the first spot of the city to be occupied towards the end of the 80's, by Dayaki who lived nearby. It was at the site of a key factory which had been demolished, leaving a large open space in its centre, surrounded by a wall. Writers thus had the possibility of painting both the inside and outside, with a double exposure of pieces within sight of the public: on one side the external walls faced the railway line, and were therefore visible to passengers onboard the trains, on the other the internal walls could be seen from the buses that transited over the bridge.

From the moment in which the city authorities decided to classify this portion of land as suitable for development, the hall of fame stopped existing. Deprived of their meeting point, writers started to notice a new opportunity in the Cavallazzi sports centre, which became the Bologna's official hall of fame a few years later, and would remain so for approximately two decades.

One side of the Cavallazzi is enclosed by the bridge of Via Libia, whose structure presents a series of consecutive blind arches, each circumscribing a specific space, a sort of frame on which to paint. The wall that delineates the remaining sides of the sports centre includes the gardens and the sports fields, suggesting other available surfaces.

Given its characteristics, the Cavallazzi can be interpreted as the transposition to the Italian province of the famous neighbourhood halls of fame in New York, which appeared on the walls of the city's game courts. In N.Y.C these spaces dedicated to sports were created in plots of land that were perfectly calibrated for the size of the court, constituting a well-defined wall perimetre: almost a box in which every square metre becomes a precious surface for the writers of the city, who painted directly within the game area. In addition to Cavallazzi, innumerable other Italian halls of fame also arose in places dedicated to sports activities and kid's recreation areas, transposing the congested spaces of the American cement playgrounds into vast metres of public gardens.

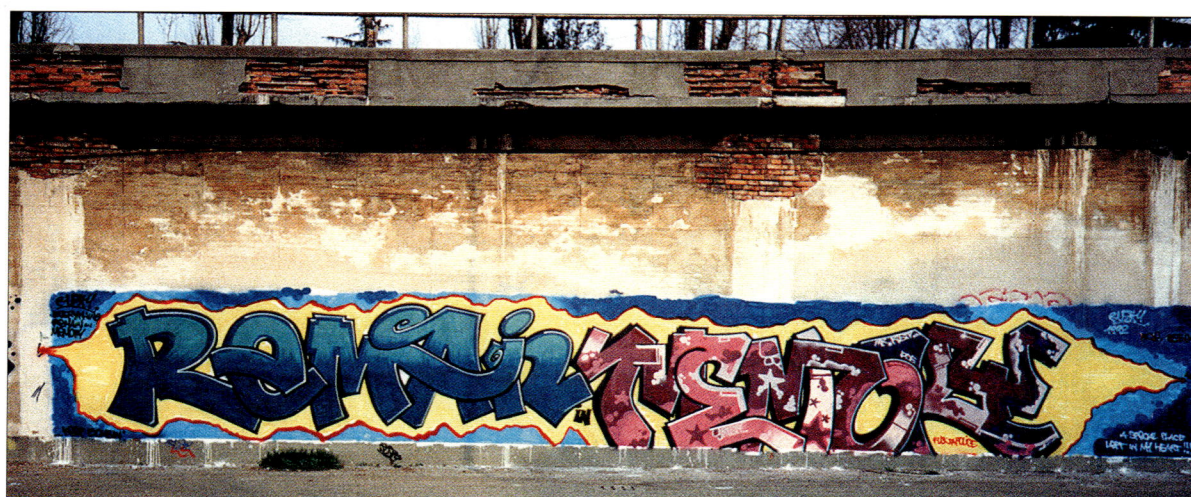
"Remain in Memory" first piece to be painted on the hall of fame walls of Cavallazzi by Rusty – SPA, 1992   *– Oida*

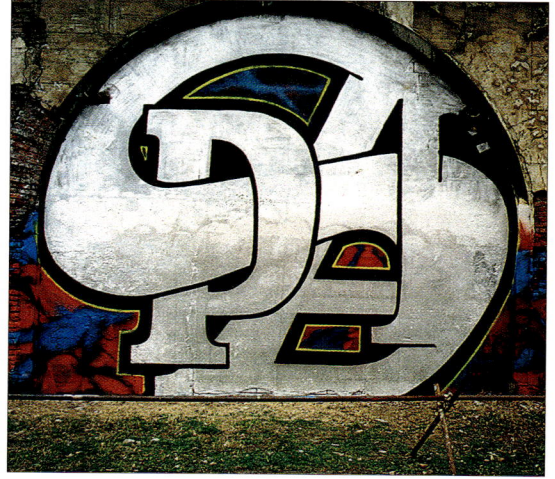
"SPA" logo painted by Rusty and Ciufs on the structural arches   *– Rusty*

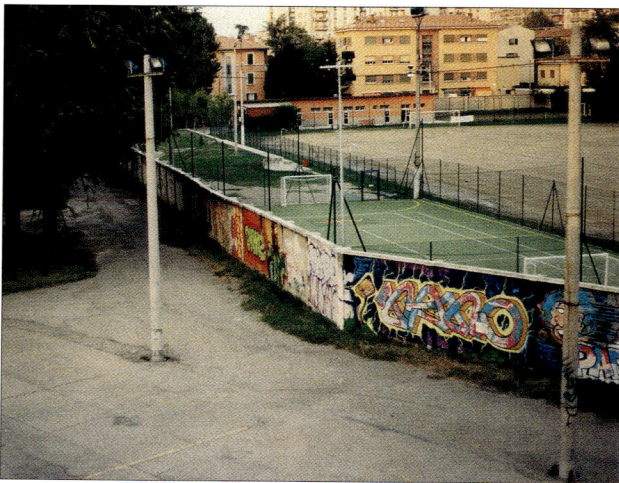
Dado on the perimetre walls of the sports fields, 1993   *– Ciufs*

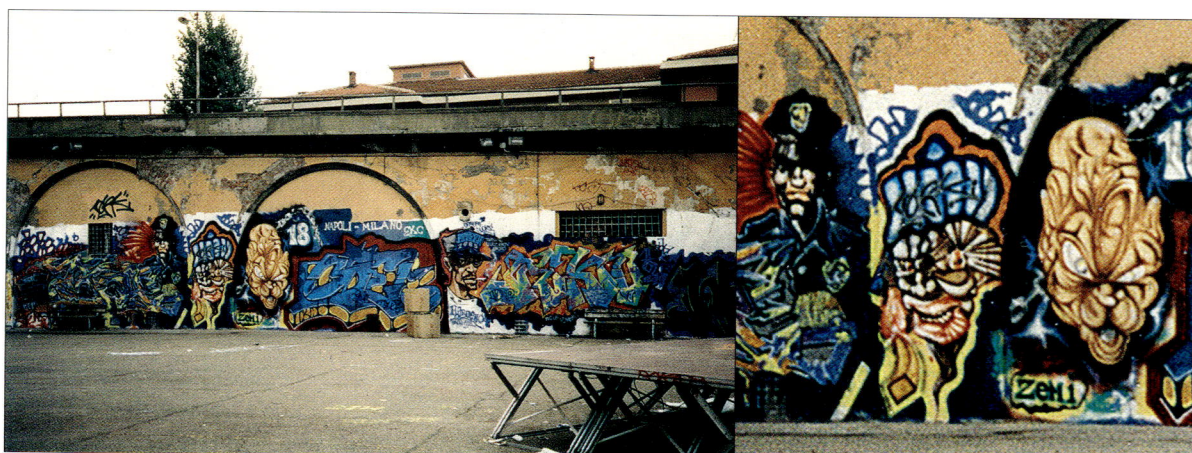
Wall by Mace – PWD Treviso, Tork, Zemi – KTM Naples, *Ciel* by Sky 4 – CKC Milan, Deko 164 and Waz – MT2 Rome, painted to commemorate the first jam to be organised in Bologna in the spring of 1993   *– ACW archive*

RUSTY
The first piece to be done outside the Cavallazzi was "Remain in Memory", which, after being covered a first time by the authorities, was repainted again:

so the local administration decided to forget it. That´s how it was the first years, if you wanted a wall you had to take it, and to make it last and become a hall of fame the only rule was stubbornness.

Once the games were set, all of Bologna went to hit that wall, until Cavallazzi became a public hall of fame that has been lasting over twenty years.

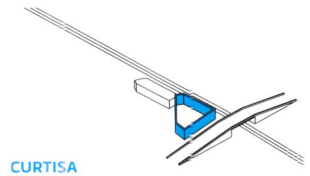

CURTISA

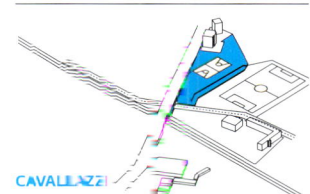

CAVALLAZZI

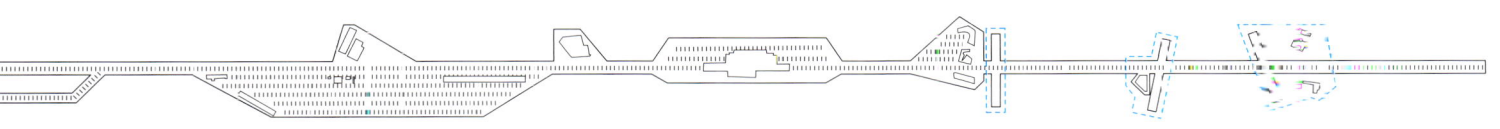

Rusty
>

BOLOGNA SPA

The first contact with Dayaki and with Writing in the city

In 1988 Bologna hosted the Biennale exhibition and invited MCA crew from Milan: they painted an enormous panel, maybe the biggest I ever saw in that period. Other than that, I also started noticing stuff by Dayaki around the city, especially in his area, San Donato. There was a bridge over the railway next to Curtisa, a former key factory that had been destroyed at the end of the 80's. This is where Dayaki would paint with Magma. The lot of land around the factory bordered the railway, and its walls, that had survived the demolition, became the best surface to hit for the first writers of the city: I would see them paint almost every week but, perhaps held back by shyness, only later did I decide to go down the stairs of the San Donato bridge. They

were painting right next to the bridge, and I was looking at them from above, but when Dayaki raised his eyes, I ran away. Ten minutes later I went back to the spot and finally decided to go down: unexpectedly Dayaki immediately started explaining the tricks of the trade, leaving me the address of the tool shop where he bought his colours. An hour later, in Via San Lorenzo, I bought my first spray cans, some Dupingos mixed with Duplicolor. It was the 24th of December 1988 and two days later I did "Illusione", written under a bridge in the mountains. That winter changed everything: I started tagging behind Dayaki, who would hang out in ATAC, headquarters of an independent label of Bologna that produced Punk groups like Disciplinatha and CCCP. I would always walk past there and ask after Dumbo (Dayaki's first tag), until one day I met Deda, who at the time was the singer of Rabbid Duck, a local hardcore group. It was the first time I saw him, and he told me he had also done a couple of sketches but hadn't painted yet, so we decided to go together. By instinct, we chose the railway line as our first target, and wrote "Power Move", next to "Danger Zone", by Deemo and Zero-T. Both were on the

walls of Curtisa facing the track lines. Me and Deda formed our first crew, TCT, the initials of *TreCentoTrenta*, (OneHundredThirty), which indicated the formula of some food colouring, one of the most toxic. Me, Deda, and many other kids that hung around Isola Nel Kantiere in those years were involved in battles supporting self-production and LAV[1], we lived day by day, between writing, skating, and hardcore music, which was a reference point, musically speaking.

1 Lega Anti Vivisezione, an activist group against animal testing and vivisection

Me and Deda would bomb the city sometimes with the members of Cam-mel i, a Hip Hop group that was active in the street through Galante and Duke-T. Most of my actions however were done alone, which was the condition I preferred. I was alone when I bombed Piazza Maggiore, the Vai Via Ugo Bassi and the most visible streets of the city.

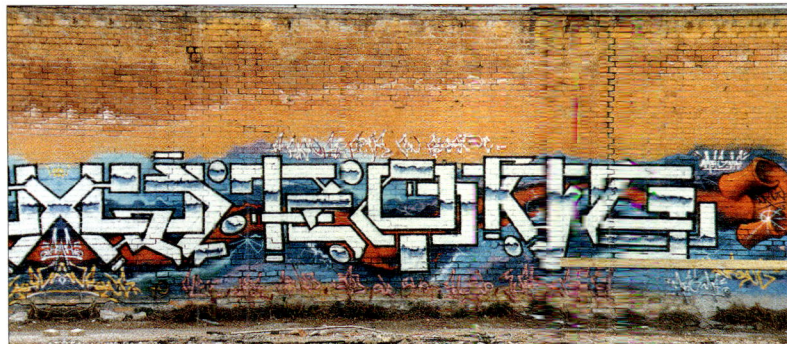

Wrong by Magma, painted on the internal walls of Curtisa's hall of fame in the late 80's   — Rusty

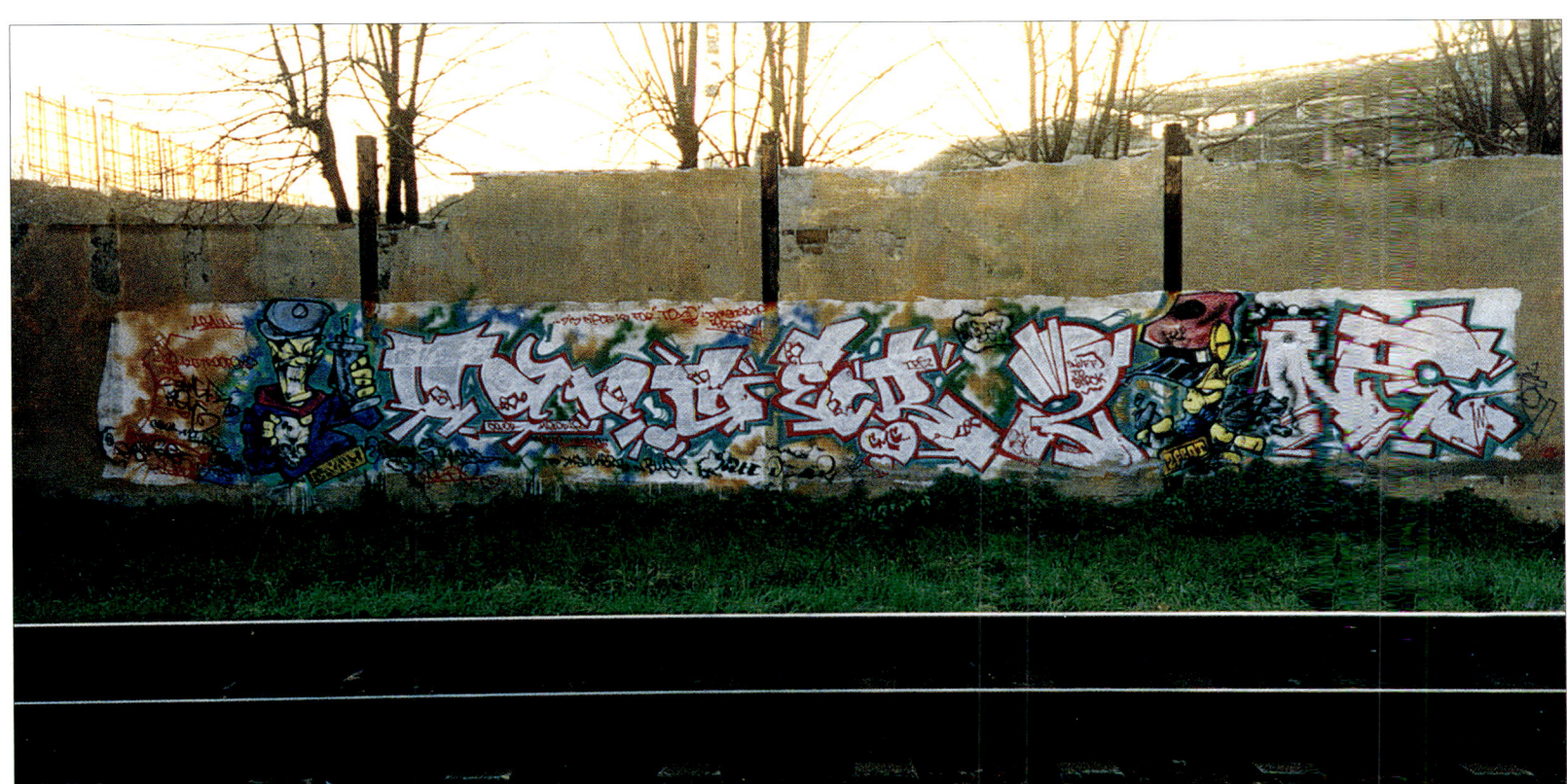

Danger Zone is one of my favourite pieces done with Dayaki. We painted it with Marabu, a spray paint used in the fine arts, that a professor of my graphic design school had recommended, it was very expensive, but after a series of commissions we managed to paint this piece with the best colours, and Bad caps, stolen from deodorants, a tip that came from Zebster.   — Wolf

SQUATS

Local writer hook–ups

The squat circuit

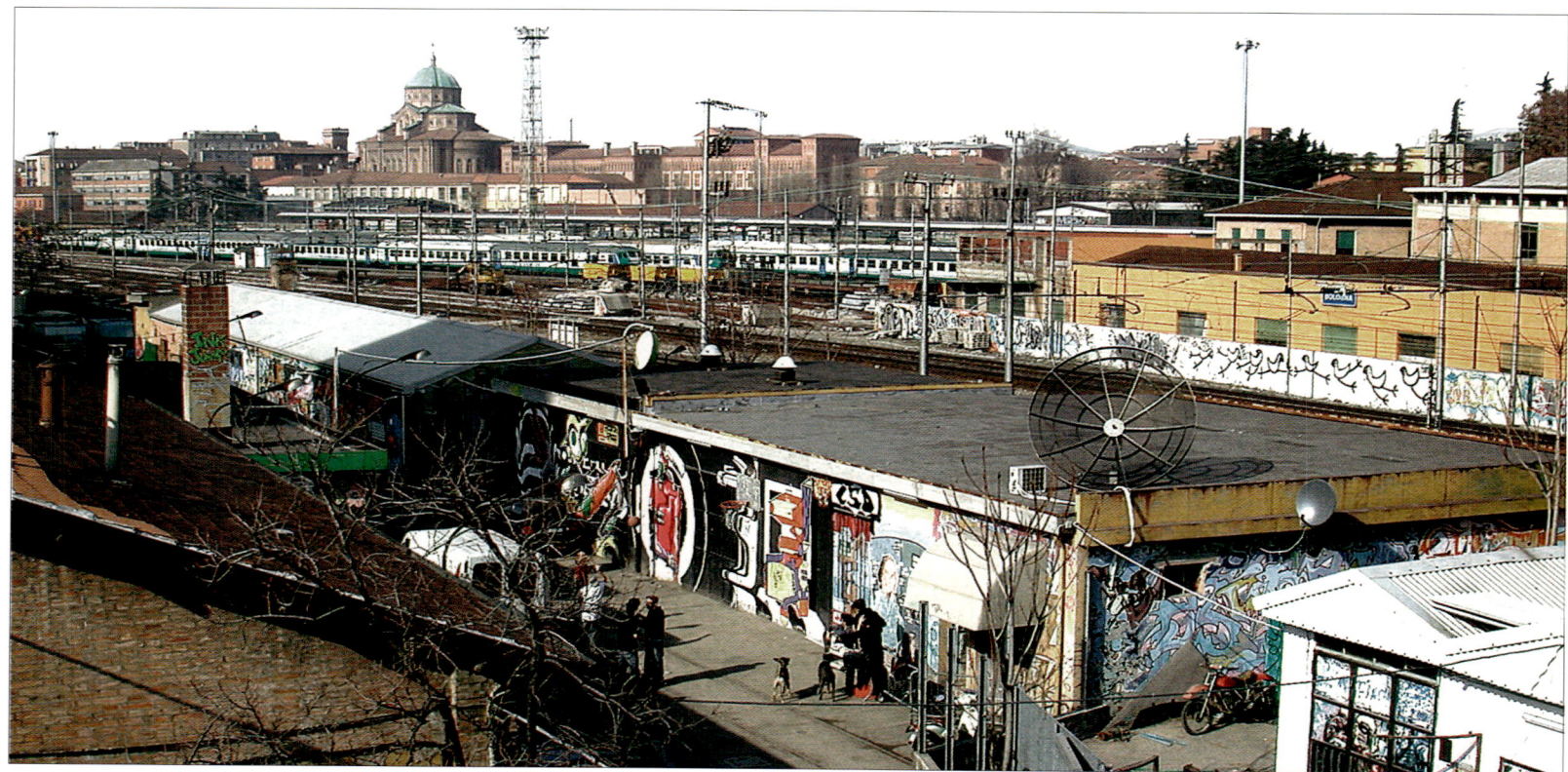

Livello 57, in the background the yard of *DLF* (Dopo Lavoro Ferroviario)

— *Renato Montecristi*

Rusty
>

LIVELLO 57

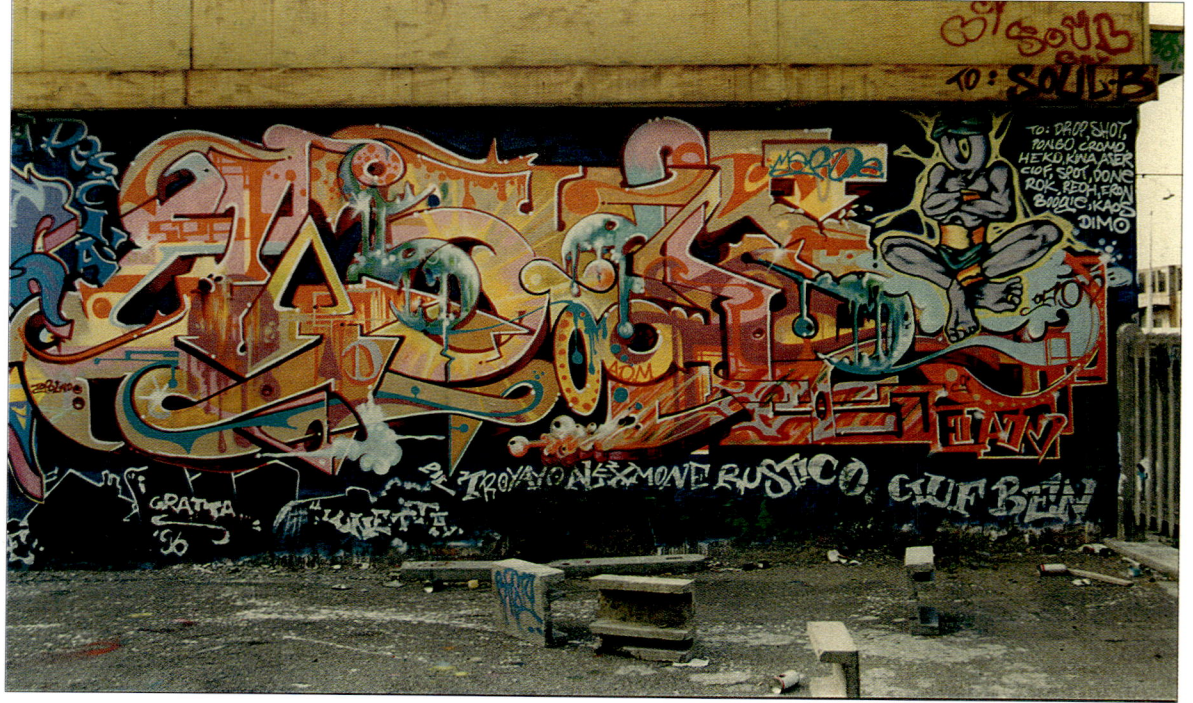

After Isola Nel Kantiere came Pellerossa, in Via Verdi, then Bestialmarket and finally Livello 57 and Stalingrado. Link was also created in those years, around '93-'94. Every squat and social centre, as in the rest of Italy, was a hang-out for writers. Many squats were the setting of some of the first big conventions, such as In Linea, that was organised at Livello 57, right next to the railway. During the day everybody would paint the legal walls of the centre but at night you would inevitably see people jumping over the fence to throw themselves on the trains of DLF, Ciuffo's yard. Pongo and Shot from Milan decided to hit the walls outside of Livello, those in front of the rail tracks... and naturally ended up running away with the railway guards behind them! When it comes to Writing, Livello was a border territory: on one side of the fence hundreds of legal square metres to hit, and on the other, the walls of the railway along with dozens of train cars, what better reasons for it to be an epicentre for writers.

Dado & Draw – SPA, 1996

— *Dado*

CIUFS

Zona Dopa was the sorting centre for all the crazy writers that wanted to hit trains at any cost.

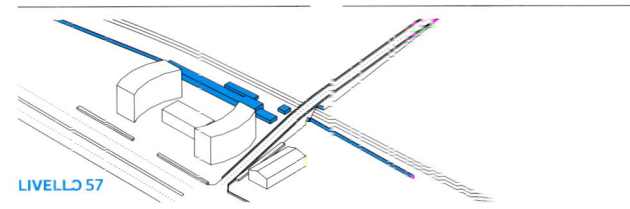

LIVELLO 57

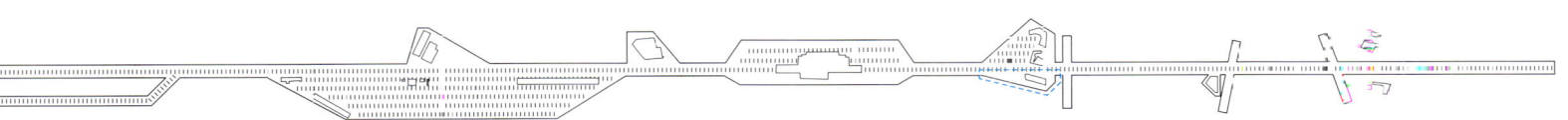

Mace

>

ISOLA NEL KANTIERE

Though Dayaki didn't bomb that much, he played an important role in Bologna's history; he was an activist involved in hundreds of projects. Unlike the breakers he came from the Punk movement and had a Hardcore background, he was part of the squat scene of Bologna, which was perhaps the most vital in Italy back then; there was a historic record label where everyone hung out, but above all there was Isola Nel Kantiere squat, which was smack in the middle of the city, on Via Indipendenza. Isola was

painted back to back, we had no idea how they could've done that. Dayaki hit that neighbourhood, the streets, often alone or at times with Zero-T, their crew was CMC, Color Melodies Combo. They were a rather atypical group because they worked together on commissioned projects but were from two entirely different worlds: Zero-T was a B-boy from Florence whose sneakers were always pristine, while Deemo was a talented punk who preferred to party with people from Isola and local writers like Rusty, Mined, Mirko, Marzia, Jurate, and Deda, who at the time tagged Shan R and played in a band called Rabid Duck. In Bologna Hip Hop and Punk shared the same spaces, and in those years they shattered the stereotype of writers/B-boys being into Breaking, Rap music, and oversized American styles.

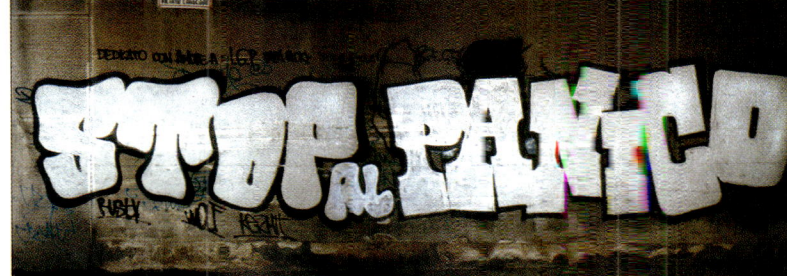

Stop al Panico by Rusty, Wolf, Kermit, an anthem of INK during in the very early 90s   — *Oida*

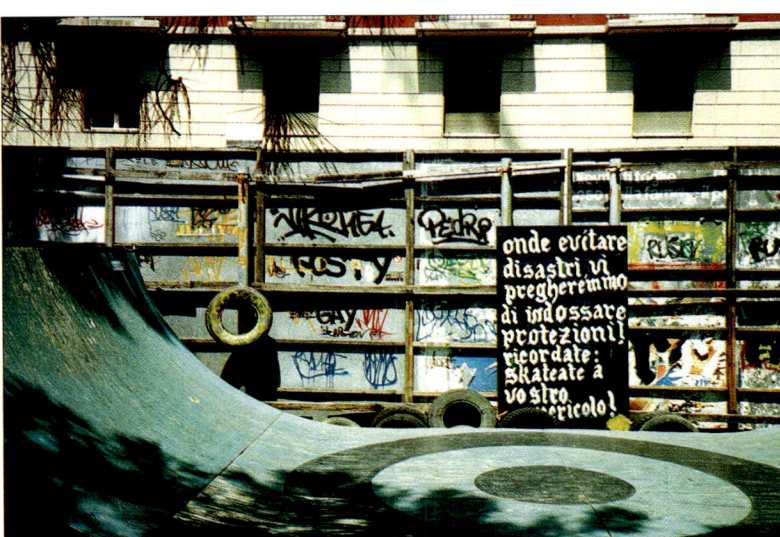

Half-pipe inside the spaces of Isola Nel Kantiere   — *Oida*

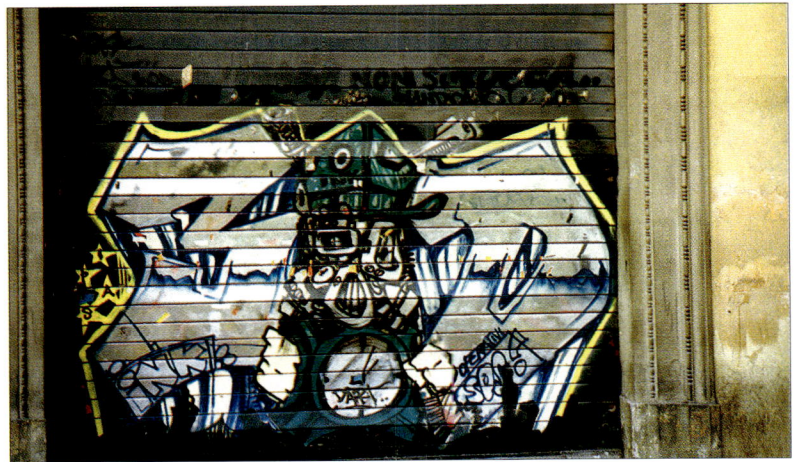

"3D" by Dayaky painted on the walls of INK in Via Indipendenza, Bologna. 1991   — *Oida*

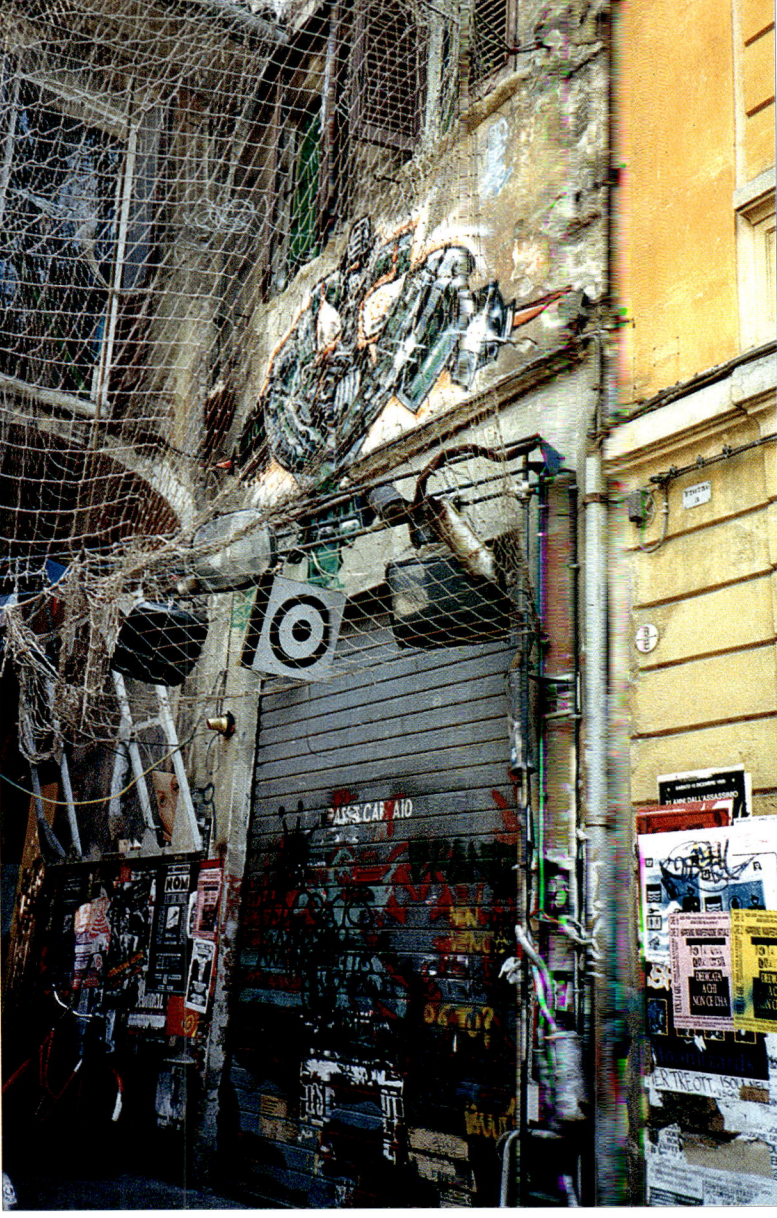

Installations, tags and flyers inside *Isola Nel Kantiere*   — *Rusty*

CENTRAL STATION

CIUFS

In front of Livello 57 there was a square of rail tracks that extended far beyond the eye could see and on which trains were parked, especially cars coupled in rather random ways. It was risky because directly attached to the central station and also close to the office of the railway police. In addition it was also a maintenance yard and therefore had workers around at

Trainspotting
>

A common faith

Oida
>

THE SOUND OF TRAINS

They say that European Writing evolved in the opposite direction with respect to New York, as it first appeared on walls and halls of fame and only later focused on trains and subway. If this is true, Bologna is a shining example. Apart from a couple of attempts by Dayaki in the first part of the 80's, whoever lived the first years of the scene could not have forgotten the walls of the railway track line or those surrounding the city's squats.

To be able to speak of a real train movement in Bologna, you had to wait until 1995, year in which the Italian scene exploded. It was Ciuffo that inaugurated the train cars of the Città Rossa, on which he would write…. "Treno"!

Inspired and motivated, Ciuffo, along with his faithful follower, Gino X, would search for the few adventure companions there were, gaining the trust of people like Smart and Ens in Florence, Done, foreigners like Honet, Pum from Paris and especially Rok from Piacenza.

With time the crews in Bologna started finding an identity that extended further than the city limits: Dirty Heroes was 50% Treno and 50% Rok from Piacenza. The PR's were less rooted to Bologna, seeing that

Done was from Cesena and others from Florence.

For this reason Chob Erik and I, pushed by an impetus of parochialism, decided to form WMN and then Ravone Burners with other kids: it was a dedication to the deposit inaugurated by Ciufs which would became our second home in the following years.

Rok
>

REVENGE

Piacenza, 1991, a year to remember, at least for me. I'm 14, my parents have separated so I live alone with my brother, which means everything you could possibly desire at that age: no curfew issues, going home whenever you want in whatever condition you may be in.

I register at the Technical-Industrial Institute. 1200 students of which 1190 males who mainly talked about football. As are the students, each Monday is the same: same shit, same topics, same ideas, same attitudes. There are some breaths of fresh air during the student strikes, one of the few activities I actively participate in (obviously not because I'm interested in politics), even attending those of other Institutes. It's clear my place is not in school and indeed I flunk the first year. I immediately understand that I don't belong there, I hate grades,

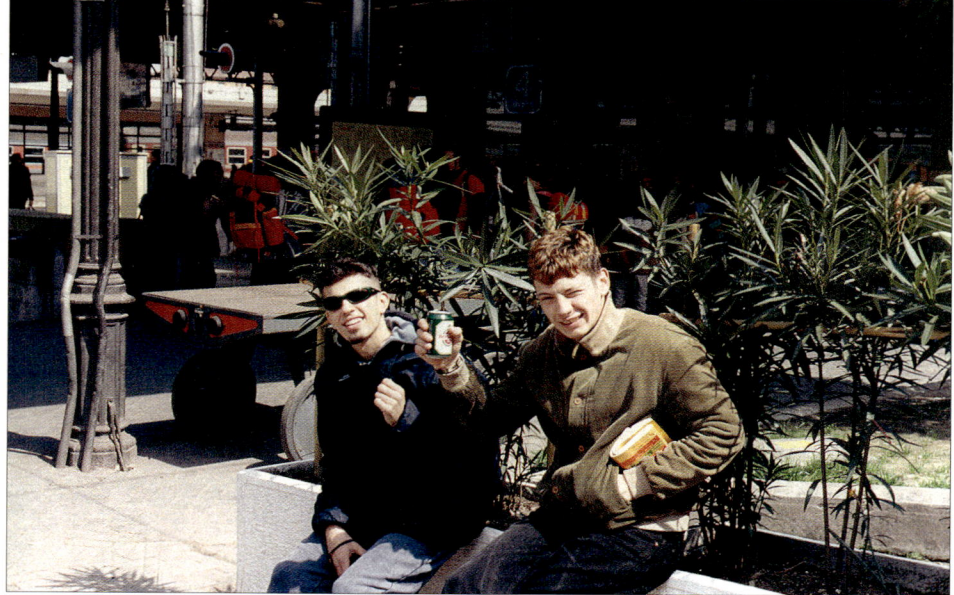

Ciuffo and Rok chillin' at Bologna central station, mid 90's   — Ciufs

classifications, report cards, and most of all I hate the Principal. Then one evening something changes. In appearance, nothing extraordinary. A movie on Rete 4, *Wild Style*: to me, pure spectacle. It was the first time I saw anything like it. I didn't even know what graffiti was, but seeing those kids bomb the New York subway gave me a sense of freedom, redemption. That same night, in the small and provincial town of Piacenza, other people crossed by the same thought started painting. I only found out six months later,

when I met Ryal and the Che. If in a small and ignorant city like Piacenza thanks to a fucking movie four or five kids started writing without even knowing each other, one can imagine the consequences in all of Italy… We were just waiting for someone to spark the fuse.

1992, summer. They invite us to paint some panels at the Festa dell'Unità of Piacenza, while people pass us by and watch. That's when we meet this kid from Rimini who was serving his military duty in Piacenza, Jessi (Eron), one of the first in

Italy to do passenger trains. With his advice it's a whole different story, he teaches us how to cut up the letters and sketch the trace, and along with Ryal we create TCS (*The Criminal System*). We immediately start bombing trains. I remember we would pick Jessi up at the barracks, he would crawl out the window while some comrades would cover for him. With Ryal we would crouch on the Po river bridge, where trains would arrive from Milan; whenever they stopped for a red light we had a couple of minutes to tag them all

The private lines
>

Suburbana

The suburban line of Bologna was the first out-of-town rail system to serve the heavy traffic of merchandise and passengers between the capital of Emilia and the other centres of the region, utilising limited-capacity trains. Though the Writing movement was gaining ground in the city, for over a decade the suburban line did not exert a strong attraction on writers, who preferred hitting the railway deposits of the national lines.

The dynamics changed when San Vitale station was closed and its railway traffic was diverted to Bologna's Central Station. Writers that were already there to take pictures of the FS trains started considering the opportunities offered to them by the suburban carriages, now in the same highly visible urban context.

On these trains the productions of crews born in the second half of the 90's was concentrated, BBS above all: hitting deposits repeatedly, they managed in the intent of regularly seeing trains with their pieces running.

The constancy with which the new generation of writers acted was decisive in breaking the existing balances in the context of Bologna's public transportation.

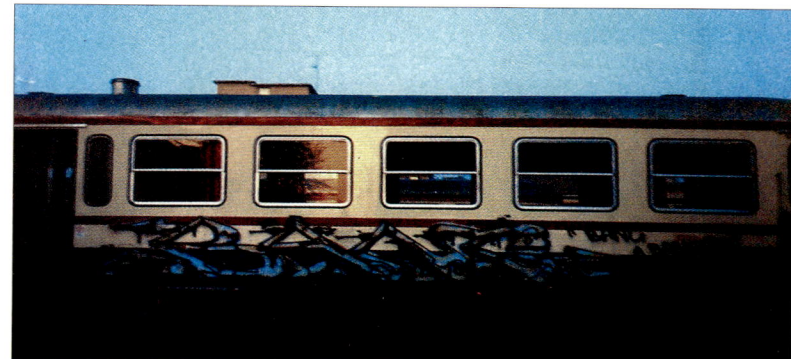

Bang by Clout – CKC from Treviso, together with Dayaki and Mace, first panel piece to be painted on the suburban train of Bologna, though it never ran   — Mace

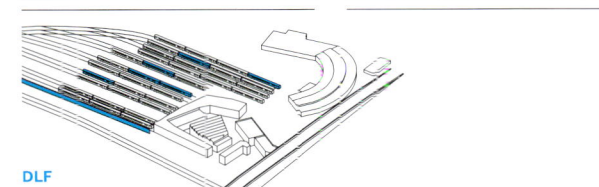

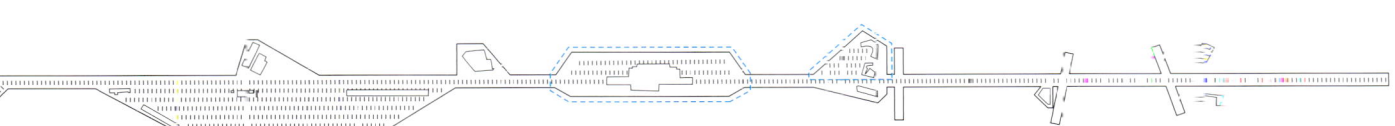

all hours, on one hand this allowed you to enter and move about freely, since it wasn't unusual for there to be people around at night, but on the other it exposed you to unexpected dangers.

over.....it was the shit, we would paint over the perplexed faces of the passengers staring from the windows. In that period with Ryal we were super active and also stubborn in bombing the yards we preferred, until obviously one night, the umpteenth night, while I was doing the *Inter-regionale* Milan-Ancona, two polfers (railway guards) pop up from the head of the train. Ryal runs incredibly fast and we manage to escape, slipping into a disgusting underpass that hid us amongst the bushes, between the rail tracks.

Four hours later I get up, go home, wash my hands and then get back to the station to take photos of the train. It's 1993, and it's pretty rare to see a bombed train in our stations, when I shoot the picture I'm real nervous and the flash goes off; an engine driver looks at me and leaves, two minutes later the polfer arrive, I'm fucked. Even though they have no evidence they withhold me until my mom arrives (I was a minor) and declares she recognises the bag full of spray cans that I had left earlier while running away. Fucked over by my mother, what a great feeling. The result: juvenile court in Bologna, without a lawyer. It took about thirty seconds.
"Did you paint the train?"
"No, not me, I only took some pictures".
Sentence: aggravated property damage, two months, a fine of one and a half million lire. My reaction can be summarised in the promise I made to myself as I watched the judge: "I swear I'ma start seriously writing. If they consider me a vandal, so be it". So a week later I was back to it, even more than before. Ryal and I discovered the yard in Codogno: calm, in the middle of a field, with two trains parked outside the station that regularly covered the route between Piacenza and Milan. I would often go alone also, hiding my car to then paint two or three pieces. One night after a fight with some friends I went to Codogno and did an end-to-end by myself....I didn't care for anything or anybody in that moment, I just wanted to write my name. ROK ROK ROK...
"The whole first carriage of the

regional train has been painted....with letters surrounded by yellow and black, a pretty well-done job from a graphics point of view, though obviously one cannot talk about art....": the article that appeared in a local newspaper the next day reminded me of my distraction in preparing the paint, and that yellow became the unusual and improbable outline.
In 1994 I went to one of the first jams in Rimini that put together writers from different parts of the country and I met some writers from Rome, of MT2 / ETC Of these, Sugo had a grandmother in Piacenza and would come through every once in a while. I remember this one time we went to BricoCenter hardware store, us incredibly skinny with these huge jackets, and we filled them with cans of Gioca-Colora-Lavora paint! Five minutes of fear until we left with eight silvers and two blacks each...that evening we drove to Parma, sweating buckets to cover the entire train car while a dog would not stop barking. We do the whole-car silver with coloured letters. That train was headed to Genoa, and I went all the way over there just to see how it looked, to take a photo: when I saw it arrive it still had the windows completely covered and I thought "This is so fucking hot!". I had hardly slept, ran away from school to go directly to Genoa, but the satisfaction of seeing it there in front of me, with style and arrogance among all those people, it repaid all our hard work....I think only someone who paints trains can understand what I mean. The energy it takes, the study, the endeavor, the effort, you do it for yourself, for your own fucking ego! There is no artist as free as us, disowning others means we can be ourselves. We don't need exhibitions, galleries and museums we take the spaces we want, and with that, fame and notoriety. In 1996 in Bologna, me, Treno and Ginox form the DH (Dirty Heroes) crew, and Gec joins in 1997. That period in Bologna was insane. With Ciuffo we do a whole car in the yard right in front of the social center Livello 57. From behind

> CONTINUES ON PAGE 252

Dopo lavoro yard

The passion for trains and for the railway as a blank canvas began in childhood, because my grandfather was also fascinated with the railway and would always take me to Central Station when I was little. He would talk to me about the various models, the cars, the locomotives, and with time it all came together in my imagination. I was living in the Bolognina district, to the North of the city, an area demarcated by the tracks of the railway; from Via Caracci you could enter the tunnel, an underground passage that distributes all the tracks leading to Central Station, to then emerge directly in it. Living in Bolognina, as a child my playground bordered the railway deposit and even before being involved with graffiti, my first Name had been written on a little FS cabin. Having come from that context, I was predestined. Initially only Deemo had a weakness for trains and especially yards, I think he had absorbed the emotion of climbing over a fence and into a new dimension through the pages of *Subway Art*. Apart from him, my first partners in bombing the F were Shorty and Wolf of FCE. I then continued alone, it made me feel good, especially at DLF, my yard. Things changed when I met Rok at Livello 57. I took him to every single deposit, and we then founded DH, a crew focused on the railway, and more specifically on life in the railway, because once we finished painting we would stick around the deposit; it was our dimension, a territory that as time went by we felt belonged more and more to us, we lived it with the enthusiasm of someone that discovers a virgin island and wants to keep it exclusively ours, unaware of any of the possible dangers it holds. — CIUFS

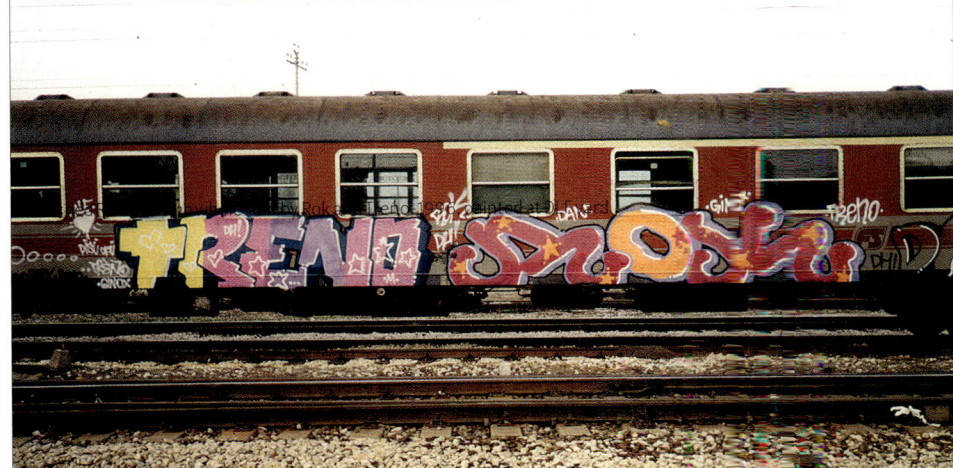

Treno and Rok, Dirty Heroes on Intercity train, 1996   — Ciufs

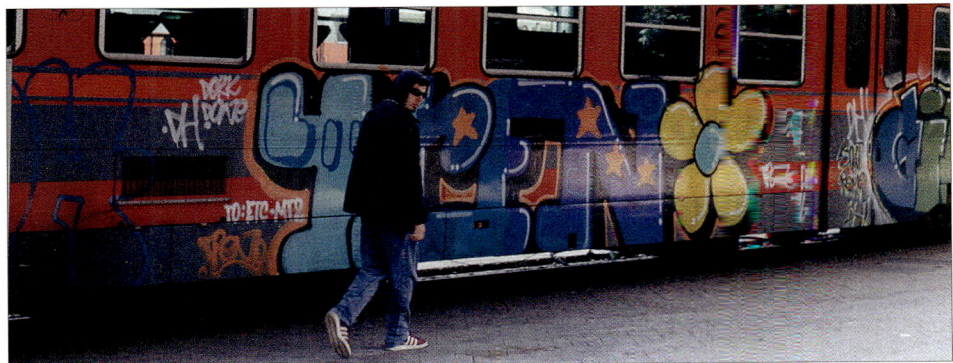

Treno – SPA, DH, taking a walk in front of his piece, parked at the central station, 1996   — Rok

MAIN YARD

Ravone by night

Chob
>

You'd wake up cold and dazed, you could feel the dust freeze the next day. Gec in your nose, your pants were moist and your shoes were still soaked from the night before because you had walked for kilometres in the deposit of Ravone in search of those bastard security guards who, in those years, would hide inside the trains to catch you.

I was so used to going to bed drunk that I didn't even have a headache the next day. Gec slept on the floor or even in the single bed with me, while Diego would plop himself down on his loft bed and usually forget to turn the lights off. Diego's stereo was covered in an inch of dust, during an acid trip it had been painted with yellow acrylic polka dots, almost every CD skipped except for a crappy compilation that had one good song by Weezer (Jamie), which we listened to ad nauseum every day and obviously every morning, together with Transformer by Lou Reed.

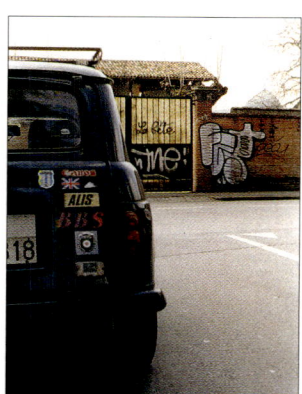

BBS mobile   – Diego Veronesi

From the bedroom window you could see the tracks on which the trains going to Rimini and the South travelled... Florence, Rome, every time we heard a train whistle we'd race to the window to see if our pieces were passing by, and they often were: we'd cheer, look at each other victoriously, and then start

preparing an explosive chiloom. There was something special about Bologna in the winter, that dense, heavy fog was more than just a fog, it enveloped the city, the brutal cold started at your toes and worked its way up to your fingertips, like a caress so cold you'd cry in delight as you drove your moped in Via Massarenti, towards a warm cappuccino in the city centre.

You'd sing stupid songs all day long, at times using the words from some jingle you heard on TV the day before, laughing like idiots the whole way: Gec should've done cabaret...not graffiti. BBS crew's strong point was Diego's vehicle: during the first years (more or less in high school), he had a fucking scooter (Forte MBK) that was painted with silver Capec spray paint, it was so ugly that he didn't even need to lock it up since we doubted anyone would ever steal it (though incredibly enough, I think a junkie dissappeared with it in Via Castiglione!); then he had a blue R4 car that tilted when curving, it represented us, with its trunk covered in BBS and Andrea Costa terrace stickers; I really think I loved that car and it still exists today, it was even professionally repainted.

When we were too stoned (we'd paint and do drugs "before, during, and after...") we usually stopped at Angelo's (Texas) in San Donato, who would open the door at 4 am with the usual remark: "Don't make noise... how much have you smoked?" Then we'd smoke another chiloom in the kitchen while Angelo showed us his latest purchase: a giant autographed photo of Jenna Jameson, just in from the States. In the afternoon we'd always take the Suburban train to Hobby&Legno in Villanova, a do-it-yourself store from which we'd steal Capec spray paint. At times we'd go there everyday, I still wonder how the blonde cashier could avoid noticing our bloated backpacks full of black and silver spray paint (those were the only colours we used), and the next day the shelves would be replenished once again.

Mind you, we were so fucked up I admit to having huge memory gaps regarding those years. But I'll never forget the times we

went to San Vitale to paint the Suburban trains: me, Diego, Gec, and Grom in his red Fiat Panda. We were so stoned and drunk, Grom felt so out of it that he decided to stay in the car while we went in and painted. Every now and then, Wanes would come too, he was the only member of BBS that didn't paint, he would just be our lookout. Once, we planned on driving Grom's red Panda (as always) all the way to Porretta to paint. While at a rest stop in Marzabotto, Wanes whips out a bag of ketamine and starts cutting lines under Grom's concerned eyes. The outcome: we were majorly fucked up, I was practically comatose in the front seat, the other three in the back were utterly wasted, and Grom was driving in total silence while leaning his head on the windshield. I'm surprised we actually made it to the train yard, we even painted and so did Wanes, he was incapable of

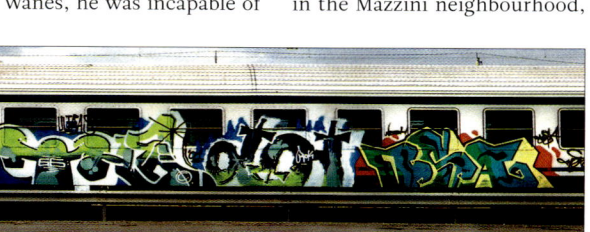

THE by Chob, DH by Gek, BSA by Repo, at Ravone Rialzo   – Diego Veronesi

holding a can of spray paint but nonetheless vandalised the front of a suburban car with one of his phrases. That crazy night was immortalised by a picture later published on *Il Treno* (The Train) magazine, sent by some trainspotter. The paragraph spoke about the new coating that would soon be applied to train exteriors to prevent graffiti. The caption beneath the photo read: "Explicit phrase written by a hoodlum on the local Bologna-Porretta line- I'd like to hoodlumise too, but I don't know how". And being the dickhead that I am, I think I actually lost the cutout of that article. It was the time of scratch-tags on city bus windows, pissing inside of public phone booths, breaking glass and scratching trains, dirty socks and paint-stained hands. On Sunday mornings we'd go to the stadium in search of more

gadgets to add to the R4 in support of the Bologna football team, led by the magic of Cruz and Signori. Every time foreign writers came to Bologna, we'd bring them to the stadium with us. Swedes, Germans, Danes, all on the sidelines with the team scarf around their necks, we would get them riled up by telling them to be ready to duke it out with rival hooligans... we had so much fucking fun. Then we'd get them drunk on Borghetti coffee liqueur and Cipster chips. I still remember Leroy and Stars (AOD) when Bologna scored the definitive 2 to 1 against Milan... Damn, they were screaming like madmen, they hugged us and wanted to toss homemade firecrackers onto the field. Football was always an important element for us, flipping through *Lo Stadio* sports newspaper at the bar, watching games on TV, playing football outside of Wanes' house in the Mazzini neighbourhood,

and away-games that we would always lose. We were captivated by the antagonism, by hooligans, fights, smoke bombs and banners, we identified with that stuff, and we practiced it in our own way in the world of graffiti: stadium slogans next to our pieces, BBS stickers that echoed coat of arms. And we attacked train buffers as if they were hooligans of rival teams.

Repo
>

It was a night towards the end of the 90's when the profound and silent difference between writer and common citizen presented itself to me in its totality: it certainly wasn't the first time,

but the combination of place and familiarity with what I was observing shed new light on my reflections. I had in front of me the roofs and lights of the city in which I was born and raised, an apparently normal view, common to the majority of my fellow citizens, but rendered unique by the position in which I found myself – a spot that suddenly gave me the consciousness that my perspective was shared by one per cent of the local population at most - I was looking at the night of Bologna from the roof of the assembling garage of the train deposit of Ravone.

That night Longe and I had entered the deposit without even a can, we had came to walk between the sheds and the rail tracks, to see the new ETR hangar with its entrance wall still missing, and to just wander around the train cars. I had already painted in Ravone several times and would continue to do so in the future, but that night was really something different. There was no real aim, no spot to check out or new entrance to try. A relaxing walk was transformed into an illuminating experience thanks to my companion's idea of showing me one of the garages.

We walked by huge shock-absorbing springs and crates full of batteries, between the muzzles of commuter trains and incomplete carriages, up and up, past the three floors that conduct to the terrace and there, from that roof, a view so familiar yet alien hits me like nothing before. On one side, behind me, the deposit, enormous and with a thousand different faces; on the other, small and provincial, Bologna. The difference between a writer and others is just here: to have something the rest of the world ignores - though they may have a vague idea due to that eternal incompleteness that is of those that do not practice - and to look at what is common to some from a position shared by few.

Of this immense deposit, one of the biggest and most important in Italy, beginning just outside the centre of Bologna, one could speak of for the length of an entire book, but I wouldn't be the most suited person to do so. One could narrate the incredible

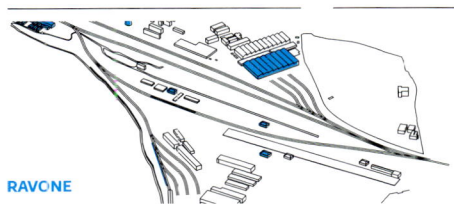

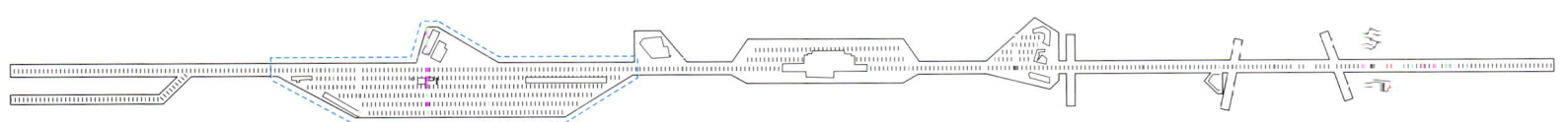

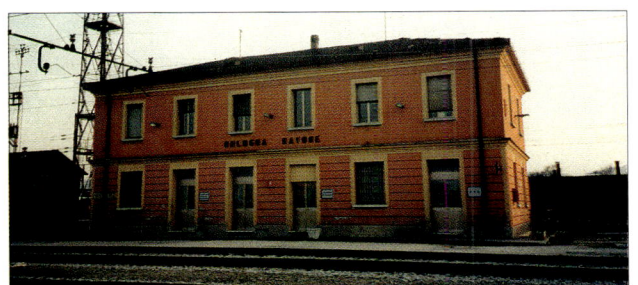

The railway building of Ravone   — Siso

and numerous prototypes that could be found here or the improbable encounters that many of us had, the hours passed on a single panel in the golden era or the close and not always successful escapes. One could talk about the historic spots like Casa di Ravone, Rialzo, or the Officina Meccanica, or describe the numerous entrances, the simple ones, the complex ones, the ones that still exist and the ones that have disappeared. It's a spot whose myth goes well beyond the city limits, especially thanks to the monumental and incessant activity of those that have made it great and brought it to everyone's attention: from the historic personalities of the Bolognese scene that first painted here, to the crews that immediately followed them and chose the name of the deposit as their own, creating a shock wave without precedents, so powerful as to make everybody talk about it. And then everyone that followed in the years, from Bologna, to the rest of Italy, France, Germany, Denmark, Sweden. Those that happened here by chance or those that came here so as to tell others: "I painted a panel in Ravone." And so as to tell themselves: "I also have my fragment of myth."
I believe that for those who lived it for real and not simply as meteors transiting the time it takes to paint a couple of panels, for those that explored the various zones and discovered new ways to access it, the mythological component of Ravone doesn't count a thing.
I believe that for many of us it was the ground for a personal growth and a profound change in our relationship with the city, a pair of glasses that you can't

take off even after your trips to the deposit become less frequent or stop altogether, a lens through which to see places everyone can see in a different, personal way, that gives you a sense of detachment yet at the same time belonging to the outside world. To be defined as particular types of citizens, to be defined as writers.

Longe
>

I began painting in 1993 after seeing pieces by Dayaki and SPA; the few fanzines that existed back then acted as further inspiration. I went through a second awakening in 1996 when I discovered trains, also thanks to the people I was hanging out with at the time. I was never a big fan of halls of fame, I preferred to bomb the city and the choice of trains meant even tighter time limits: I developed my throw-up at the time. Each time I tried to modify it a bit, adding a straight line instead of a curved line and vice versa; I added arrows, changed the filling, but I still felt the forms were outdated and my pieces barely covered two train windows. So I decided to start over from scratch. In order to do this I needed simple structures that could give space to this evolution, I found the solution and inspiration through a bomber I had recently met back then at a convention: Rok. Tubular letters of uniform volume, easy to learn and rather legible to all. My personal revolution occurred in the spring of '96 on Bologna's suburban train; I clearly and visibly

dedicated this piece to DH Crew (which Rok was a member of). It was the beginning of an intense train-bombing period, from then on I was painting practically every day, my life revolved around it. The same old five letters began to change with slightly more complex structures, the dimensions acquired more subtle extremities. My frenetic activity brought about rules, in fact I never allowed myself to make the same outlines on different pieces, I never used more than two similar colours to fill, and I always made sure not to reuse the outline colour on the same piece. I started using edges, the soft extremities of the letters became sharper and more elongated, to the point where they melted together. I only painted trains, all my pieces now started with a straight line at the bottom. My letters now stood up and expressed gravity, my style became more solid. At first I used regular geometric forms, circles and semi-circles, then I started using sharp edges, I started slicing through the softness of the forms. Pieces that barely covered two windows were a thing of the past, my pieces now often covered over four windows. The French influence, which Chob and I had already learned about through magazines, exploded after the first encounter with Honet and Pum in Italy; thus we began us-

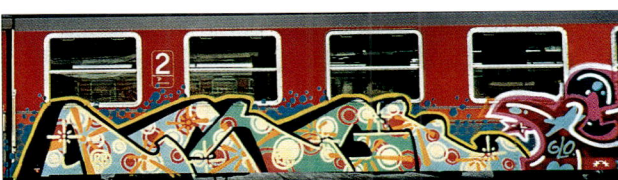

Longe - PR, RB, 1998   — Longe

ing pseudonyms and looking for inspiration from sources other than Writing. The fill-in colours increasingly resembled Expressionist paintings, the diagonal shading was inspired by comic books... We used more elastic lines, which eventually evolved in the opposite direction, with more solid volumes, angular icebergs sculpted into many letters. Northern European styles began to influence us, it was all part of a

linear evolution that did without delirious stylistic swings. Back then, Italian trains were rarely ever cleaned of graffiti, so you could see various stylistic periods on one train, five or six cars painted by us. In one year, 1997, we painted over 200 trains. Under layers of paint, the letters constantly changed, sources of inspiration were harder to interpret, my own contribution became increasingly true to an individual journey that was calibrated upon dynamism and the geometry of the train cars in the Bologna-Ravone yard.

Oida
>

While the bigs of SPA were painting serious stuff, I met the kid with the robotic arm, Longe. Excluded from the loop, we dedicated ourselves to freight trains for the whole winter of 1995: it was our training ground. One evening Longe told me he had an appointment with a young graffitist (writer was a bit much) and wanted me to meet him as well. "Well, no problem" I said. Along the way he explained that the kid painted in Imola and was looking for others with whom to form a group. I still remember how that immediately demora-

lised me, a) because Imola had no scene and so anyone coming from there was surely a Toy. And b) because it had been years that I was hoping to join the kings of the city, SPA, and certainly not a toy. The day of the meeting, the kid was sitting on the steps of the Arts Institute while waiting for us. He was young, but definitely the tallest among us. As we got closer he immediately recognised Longe. He got

up, and shit, he was really tall! With a big smile plastered on his face (I think he was much more excited than us) he introduced himself. I liked him straight off the bat, he conveyed something other writers often loose, the desire to create and share something with friends. Right then and there even though we had just met he decided we went fine by him. At that point it was a done deal. He lost some points only when he told me he tagged Chobin, but whoever is familiar with the scene can tell you how many points he recovered when he shortened it to Chob.
I remember the first time we went out we didn't feel we were ready to hit real trains, so we had decided to throw ourselves on buses, except there was something strange in the air, so we inevitably had to fall back on trains but maybe that's just the way it was supposed to go. Thanks to Longe we met the PR's from Florence, which we had often heard of in that period. We visited them various times, and vice versa, but in the end only Longe was included in the crew. Other friends joined us and in a brief amount of time we had created a new group, stronger and more active, that took on the name of Ravone Burners: Longe, Goe, Choe, Texas, Jed, Trota and Lego. Between '96 and '97 there were only two choices in Bologna: you were either painting with DH or with R.B, there was nothing else. Those were years of pure Writing, we met the kids from Ancona, Texas merged with Nerds from Florence, Choe and Goe joined THE from Rome and even Robin and Dumbo from Milan would come through. All this continued even when, (because of a not altogether successful Inter-Rail trip around Europe together), the relationship between Longe and an emerging Chob went sour, until it brought to the break-up of RB and the formation of BBS. In 1998 Bologna Bombers, captained by the same Chob and followed by the faithful Texas, found new strength in elements like Jack, Fish, Race and Oi, until including the extremely young kids of MPS, Leon, Aner, Star, Acme, Schoe, Prock and Babbo. But this is all recent history.

Enclave of the city

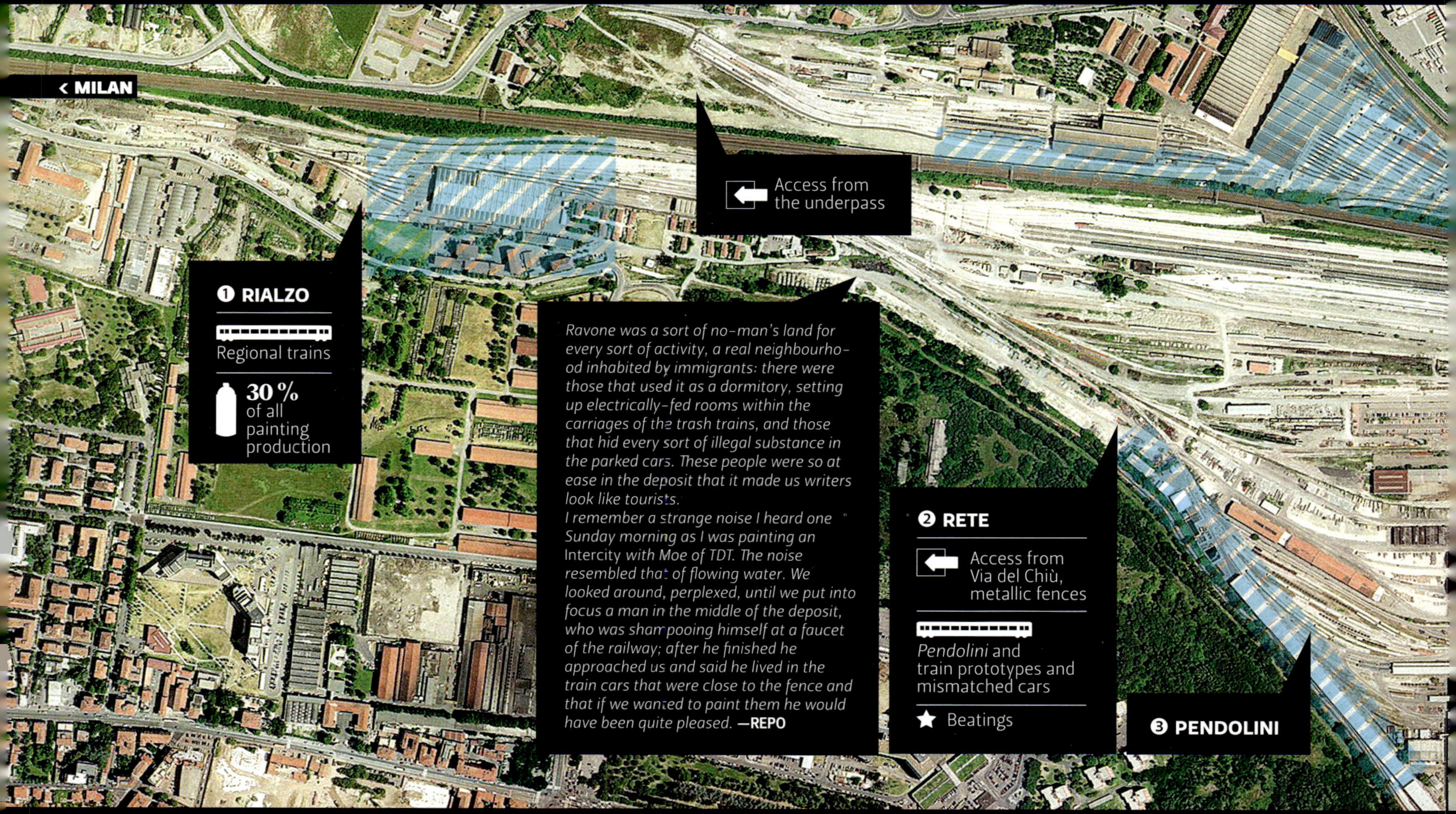

< MILAN

❶ RIALZO

Regional trains

30 % of all painting production

Access from
the underpass

Ravone was a sort of no-man's land for
every sort of activity, a real neighbourhood inhabited by immigrants: there were
those that used it as a dormitory, setting
up electrically-fed rooms within the
carriages of the trash trains, and those
that hid every sort of illegal substance in
the parked cars. These people were so at
ease in the deposit that it made us writers
look like tourists.
I remember a strange noise I heard one
Sunday morning as I was painting an
Intercity with Moe of TDT. The noise
resembled that of flowing water. We
looked around, perplexed, until we put into
focus a man in the middle of the deposit,
who was shampooing himself at a faucet
of the railway; after he finished he
approached us and said he lived in the
train cars that were close to the fence and
that if we wanted to paint them he would
have been quite pleased. —REPO

❷ RETE

Access from
Via del Chiù,
metallic fences

Pendolini and
train prototypes and
mismatched cars

★ Beatings

❸ PENDOLINI

At Rialzo

_onge

he trains that arrived to *Rialzo*
ame for a check-up, it was a
arge maintenance centre:
breaks were reviewed, wheels
were changed, the order of car-
iages was inverted. The nice
hing was that we painted an
ndividual car and didn't know
where they would then insert it,
nor on which line, nor even next
to which other carriage. We did
the panel and it was then attached wherever they wanted.
It was like playing Russian rou-
lette. We painted the pieces and
then the railway workers composed the puzzle. They might put
one on the line to Ferrara, and
attach another to the train for
Piacenza. Usually we worked on
the cars of the Bologna-Ravone,
which was abbreviated on the
base of the train as Bo Rav, because we were sure that those
would travel through much of
Emilia Romagna. But then again
it wasn't always the case.

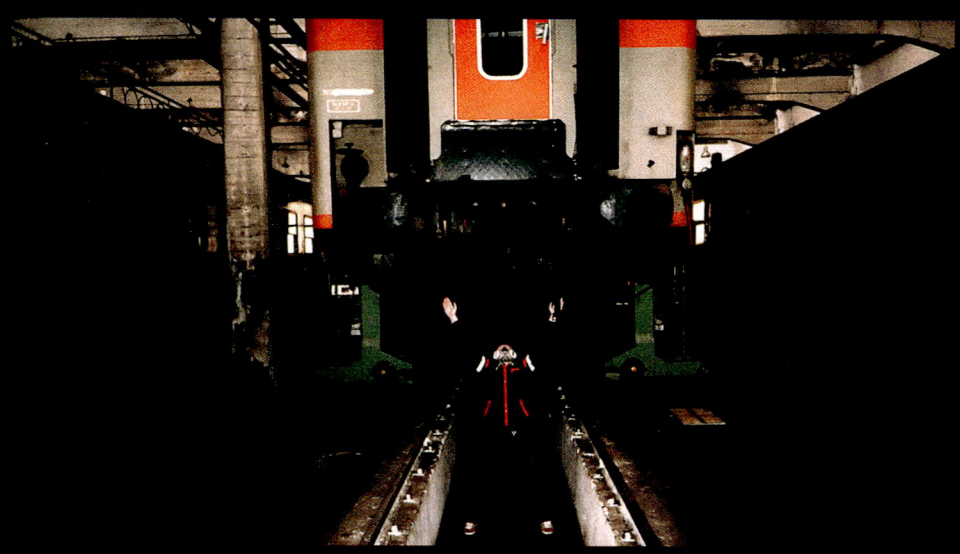

The *Rialzo* structure inside the railway deposit

— *Dafne*

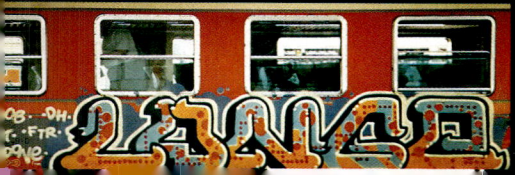
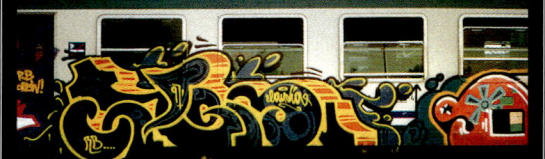
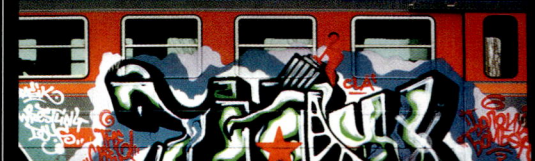

CHOB

Around Ravone there was always an incredible to-ing and fro-ing of trains, we lived that spot as if it was a neighbourhood. In the end Ravone had become a small meeting centre, as if it was a piazza of the city. People were really hanging out there, even on weekends.
We were always painting there, usually the *Inter-regionali* train, the long one, on the Milan –Ancona line, which was red, and had a multitude of windows. We would do end-to-ends on it because it had great proportions. The question was really not only about seeing your name travel, but also about cutting it and trying to create a powerful composition on an aesthetically valid convoy.

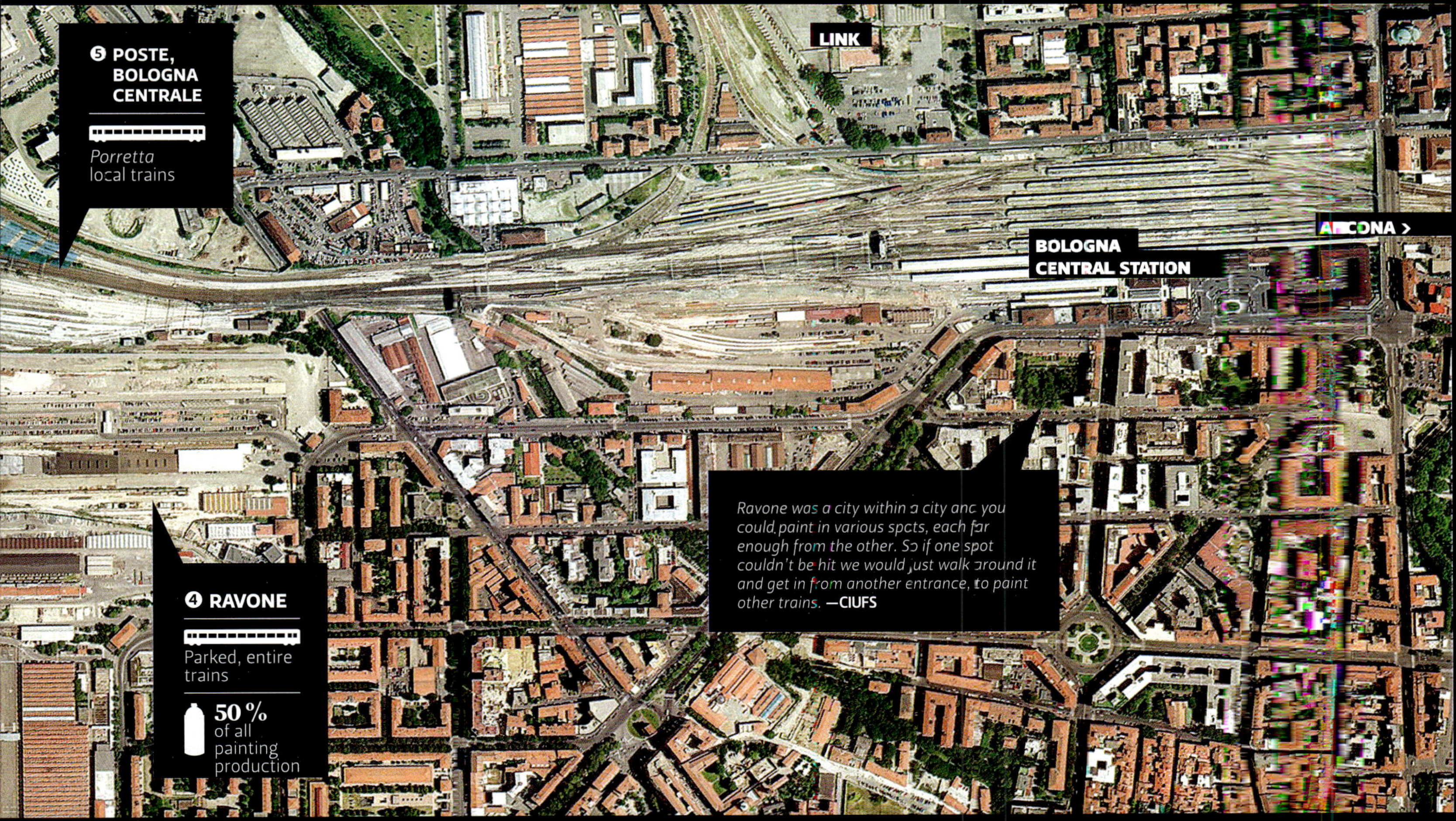

⑤ **POSTE, BOLOGNA CENTRALE**

Porretta local trains

LINK

BOLOGNA CENTRAL STATION

ANCONA >

④ **RAVONE**

Parked, entire trains

50% of all painting production

Ravone was a city within a city and you could paint in various spots, each far enough from the other. So if one spot couldn't be hit we would just walk around it and get in from another entrance, to paint other trains. —CIUFS

Contact sport

Chob
>

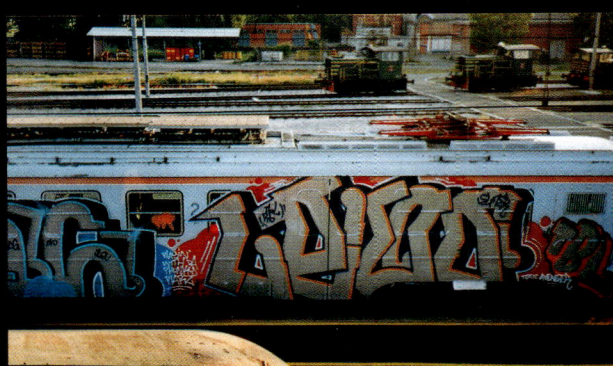

T2B by Lego at the *Poste*

— ACW archive

Towards the end of the 90's the FS started recruiting night guards to enforce security in the railway area. In the space of a month the entire population of immigrants that hung around the station disappeared, and us writers became their new target. The night they busted us we were a group of eight or nine people, among whom Pum, Oida, Jack, Fish and me. A dog, in full Rex-style, jumped out of the window of a train, followed by two guards. They caught Gec immediately, who was the unlucky one closest to the doors they came out of. They had been waiting for us in there. We started running like crazy with the other guard following us. After a few minutes everyone else had disappeared and only Oida and I remained. We were headed towards the wire fence, with the guy behind us still running and shooting in the air, and we were almost out of breath. I decided to throw myself in the bushes, conscious of the fact I would never have been able to climb over the fence; not seeing me anymore, the guard concentrated his efforts on Oida. Hidden behind those bushes, I saw the whole scene: Oida, as he was climbing over the fence, fell and lost his glasses. The guard took advantage of this and aimed his gun straight at him, shouting that he come back immediately. At first Oida refused, but then the guard started getting pissed and fired some shots in the air. When Oida decided to give in and turn back, that one started beating the crap out of him. I could hear him crying out and begging "please! please!", while his ribcage resounded with the kicks it was receiving but I didn't have the guts to come out. I have never felt as cowardly as that time. In the end, Oida was covered in blood. In the hospital they gave him fifteen stitches on the head and two weeks of observation! Gec had also gotten it pretty bad. When we went to the railway police to describe what had happened they told us to come back with a medical report so we could denounce the guards. Years later however, in court, the same police officers that had invited us to press charges were witnesses against us. We lost the case because we had 'resisted arrest'.

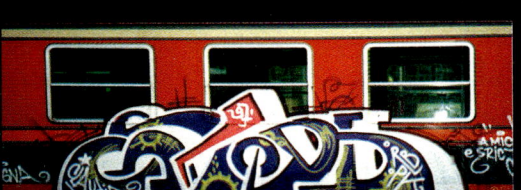

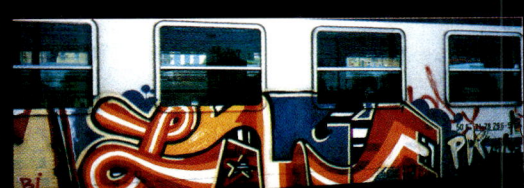

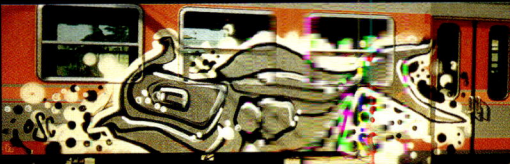

Love of indifference

> CONTINUES FROM PAGE 233

the open atmosphere of the 60's: the events that occur at the end of the 70's are more sombre, dramatic, and certainly less celebratory than the events of the past. Students reveal their dissatisfaction and concerns; Bologna (much like Milan, Turin, and Rome) opens itself to new linguistic solutions, which are already well known in the U.S. but are certainly new in our small peninsula.

Rage unites with personal and collective creativity, generating a new way of speaking, communicating, and embracing the 'no future' stance of other scenes.[3] There's no future, there's not much to be proud of, and part of the civilised community rallies together to stop the disintegration in progress. The 'game' begun by the Neo-avant-garde movements of the 60's is supplemented by the linguistic nonsense that begins to increasingly appear on the walls of various Italian cities: Bologna kindly yet unwittingly welcomes this renewed attitude made of sarcasm, repressed desperation, detachment between public and private, and distrust in society. A contagious irony develops on the red-coloured walls of Bologna, where the various painted slogans represent a vague hypothesis for hope.

«Writing on walls is a violation of a social arrangement that assigns structured moments and channels to public communication. The difficulties that legislations regarding the press interpose upon the constitution of a newspaper, such as the necessity to have a registered editor-in-chief, are emblematic elements of the repression of one of the cornerstones of the bourgeois revolutions: freedom of speech and press. Therefore, writing on walls presents itself not as a "most uncivilised national tradition", but as the retrieval of a pre-condition of democracy».[4]

This is not to be confused with those who claim that the 'murals' of '77 are the forerunners of early 80's Writing. The felt marker graffiti and large 'frescoes' that appeared on the walls of Bologna in those years characterise a tradition that is different from the subsequent birth of Writing in Italy. Certainly, one of the chosen tools in '77 (much like in the early 80's) is the felt-tip marker with which many writers begin their activity. Yet the long mural in Via Belle Arti, like many others along the University axis of Via Zamboni, isn't to be considered an anticipation of what was to come, but rather the conclusion of a period whose origins lie in the dawning of techné and which, during the tragic days of March 1977, is exhausted in the name of its own liberating celebration. What occurred in those weeks was a continuation of unrepeatable events that were intended as the exemplification of a national punishment.[5] An ideological and cultural retaliation that was difficult to control, and led to repression and strict surveillance by the city administration, which could not (and did not, today as back then) welcome within its walls such a large number of free, creative people

[3] Let's not forget that 1977 is the year in which the English punk band The Sex Pistols is born and consecrated.

[4] P.BALDELLI, *Comunicazioni di Massa*, Milan, Feltrinelli, 1974, p.370.

[5] AUTORI MOLTI COMPAGNI, *Bologna mcrzo 1977…fatti nostri*, Bologna, Bertani Publishing, 1977.

with a limitless mindset.

Here lies the first substantial difference between the primitive and somewhat tribal coloured drawings found on the streets of Bologna and the ensuing phenomenon of Writing.

Furthermore, the mandators of this 'vision' were, for the most part, students from out of town. The new "Metropolitan Indians" are residents of Bologna who don't live within the walls of the city centre, but rather in the working-class neighbourhoods that were assaulted by invasive urbanisation.

The Bologna of the early 80's was alive, open to the multi-disciplinary creativity of non-local students, but also restrained by the boundaries of an increasing decay similar to the homeland of the first writers. It's clear that the social situation in Bologna is different from the very metropolitan scene of New York[6], but here too we see the energetic infiltration of new cultural expressions like Andrea Pazienza's comic books, crazy rock music by Skiantos, electronic music by Gaz Nevada, art by Renato Barilli's Nuovi Nuovi and Francesca Alinovi's Enfatisti.

The new communicative fluidity establishes itself as signifier: all that changes is the physical support upon which the new mutations are executed. Abandoned walls in the city outskirts, inviting train cars, neglected ex-industrial areas, are transformed into blank canvases upon which to mark one's passage and "engrave your name".[7]

«The days of either or are over, the days of and… and have begun. Artists have become greedy, insatiable, omnivorous, devourers, manipulators of figures, patterns, archetypes, models, fragments deposited in the collective imaginary, reshaped through the filter of individual sensibility […] Feeling free to coexist with images, next to signs, immersing oneself in adventures of reciprocal exchanges; because it's already known that the game is now completely open, and freedom is admitting one's own constrictions within the moulds».[8]

[6] A It was the summer of 1971 when The New York Times, a famous American newspaper, printed an article about a young man of Greek origin, known as Taki 183, who had "bombed" the American subway, spraypainting his name on the walls and streets of New York City.

[7] M.CANEVACCI in *Writing. Storia, linguaggi, arte nei graffiti di strada*, by D.LUCCHETTI, Rome, Castelvecchi, 2001.

[8] F.ALINOVI, *Registrazione di frequenza*, Bologna, Grafis Edizioni d'Arte, 1981, p.8.

Revenge

> CONTINUES FROM PAGE 247

us out comes this engineer, so we start leaving, without running though. Ciuffo was screaming to him in Albanian, and I almost get my foot caught in the rail switch as it changes points: "Shit that was close!". We climb over the wall, go inside Livello 57, hide under some wooden boards and five minutes later the cops arrive. We realise there is no way they can find us, looking for two Albanians in the middle of the thousands of techno-dancing bodies not altogether happy with the presence of police. In those days we were practically living in the street, where everything got mixed together: graffiti, drugs, yards, paint, raves. We would sleep

wherever we could, on buses and trains in the winter, sometimes somebody would host us, sometimes not. My buddies in action were Gec, Enist, Chob. One time me and Gec did this whole-car with Chob and then went to sleep in a trash train in the yard (sleep intended as a euphemism since we were on speed). We took it all night until there was enough light to take photos and shoot some videos….the workers were already cleaning the windows, and it was freezing cold….

Bologna was very different in those years, if they caught you with ten grams of hash or a little speed they would insult you and maybe even beat you up but they'd always let you go, otherwise they would have had to arrest everybody! Sure we abused of it a lot… We would sleep in the street, take drugs non-stop, hardly ever eat, I would spend my days looking for a drug pharmacy that would fall for my fake Roipnol prescription….we would take whatever we could get our hands on. One time me and Enist had this impossible hunger and so we went to the junkie soup kitchen to get some food, but we didn't have the member card and ended up eating their leftovers. That's when I started thinking we had hit rock bottom. But when you're like that you don't give a fuck: the beauty of the trip is inversely proportionate to your ability of doing without. Sometimes I would spend the entire day in the station to see if any of the trains we had painted would pass by, panhandling to get whatever money I could to the first pusher I could find in the Montagnola market. In '97 I started and in '98 I finished.

At one point they had me hospitalised: examinations, transfusions and by the end of it one thing was very different, I had clean blood. I understood that was my chance to get out of it. Writing and drugs were two heavily mixed worlds for me at that time, so I had to get away from both. Now I'm back in this world with a different state of mind. Last night I took Giangi's bike. A friend joins me in front of the yard. We enter and there's only one train, completely painted on one side too. "Should we do the other side while the freight train hides us?" "Okay but keep an eye out for the usual workers…" I start sketching the trace, then I pass him the gold and I do the tar black outline, mmmh my favorite smell…

We're finishing up together and finally the boy starts moving fast. From far away we hear the freight train being hooked up, so we leave and go eat a sandwich at Zona Franca snackbar, drink three beers and go back to the spot to take pictures, since our pieces are visible now that they moved the fucking freight train.

I enter the yard, get on our train and then it starts moving! Shit this sucks! Having to get off a train while it's running is easier said than done. In the end I jump off, run towards the exit, and there's a guard waiting for us: "What are you doing? Come here!" Pretending not to hear we go behind a carriage, I put on a railway worker's waistcoat and take leave of my friend (obviously it didn't make sense for us to stay together). I walk by some workers, one of them looks at me and says "Have you already finished on track 8?" "No no, I'm going now…"

I pass between two trains, and already I can see the flashing lights of police on the other side. I take my marker and start tagging like crazy.

ROK ROK ROK ROK ROK…

Page 268
>

Desert highways

The *Juice* jam of Ancona

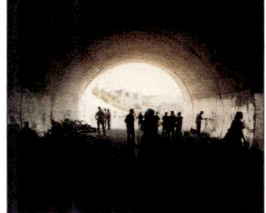

Page 271
>

Remembering New York

The elevated railway of Bari

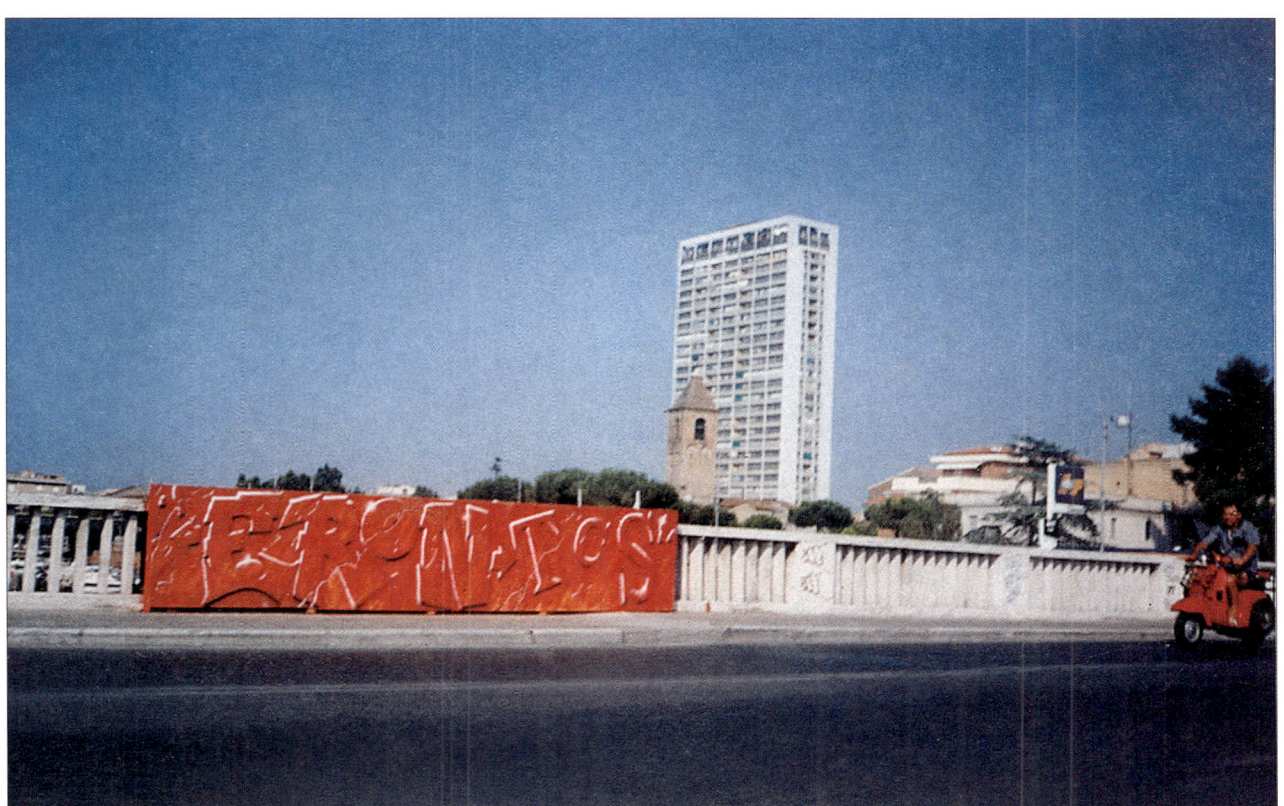

— Eron

Along the seaside

Rimini

Trait d'union

Along the railway line of the Adriatic Riviera, trains run parallel to the sea, directly serving the bathing areas of the beach underneath. In this case the railway and its immediate surroundings, usually forgotten by urban restyling programs, become an important window dressing opportunity to impress tourists, thus encouraging the local

> CONTINUES ON PAGE 258

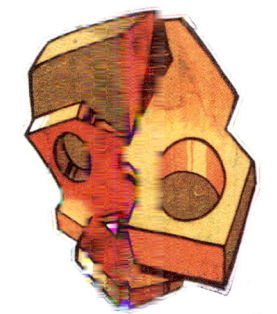

— Lego

Zelda

Open talk

The various sessions of Writing in Pesaro were marked by writers and crews that have the merit, for quality and quantity, of differentiating themselves from others and consequently entering the collective imagination of many toys, and of many people that were foreign to this world. These kids represented the

> CONTINUES ON PAGE 264

Damage

Direct experience

With it's crumbling neighbourhoods, it's lack of nightlife and the large amount of cement infrastructures that had been confiscated and abandoned, Ancona was the perfect scenario for a phenomenon like Writing, that is always looking for appropriate spaces. In the early 90's seeing a tag in the city was like sighting a rare animal in the forest, the scene was just starting and even though there were very

> CONTINUES ON PAGE 267

The Writing of the Adriatic coast developed in an anomalous scenario, an intermediate social and cultural context that maintains a provincial character though an almost metropolitan kind of infrastructural network. The Adriatic rail line, running along the entire Eastern coast of Italy, gives a sense of continuity in a maritime landscape that meets long stretches of compact buildings, where constructions appear without interruption for dozens of kilometres, like the Riviera in Romagna or in the Marche. The capillary transportation network shortens physical and mental distances between urban centres to such an extent that the Adriatic coast can read like a single large city of variable density. The provincial character of the single

areas, fragmented in various epicentres and distant from any strong social attractors, thus cohabits with a typically urban ease of mobility, that finds its apex in the summer time when seaside tourism allows people and especially ideas to circulate more freely with respect to a normal provincial situation, and tourists come from all the major region capitals of Italy. The Adriatic city becomes metropolis or provincial with seasonal tides, and the great receptive containers that empty during the winter months, or the structures of the now abandoned ex summer colonies of the fascist period, offer places under little control, ideal as spots to paint but also as potential buildings to occupy. Though less dynamic than an actual metropolis, the Adriatic city - with its pulsing

heart in the Riviera Romagnola - generated various groups tied to the different countercultures, local reactions to the great amusement and entertainment temples erected for tourists.

These groups here supported each other, for example allowing kids that belonged to other circumscribed local scenes, such as skaters or punks, to participate in the graffiti movement. The meeting ground for these realities were the first social centres, that formed around 1990 and immediately became places tied to counterculture movements, catalysers of energies that in a provincial setting synthesise the desire and necessity of being united and feeling part of a whole, which often represented the only diversion to the ordinary life of the province.

– TERRITORIAL BONDS

When the Hip Hop movement arrived to the Riviera, the impact of tags generated an immediate conflict with the city inhabitants and surroundings, all of which were completely unprepared for a metropolis phenomenon.

On a territorial scale this feeling of being distant from the norm and firmly dedicated to a particular belief became points in favour for a cohesion, a necessity to unite and form groups from isolated cases translated into a connection between small neighbouring centres along the coast. Rimini, Pesaro, Ancona, Bari, and Brindisi, though single, tangible realities since the earliest years, formed a bridge from city to city, made of phone contacts, visits to halls of fame,

> CONTINUES ON PAGE 254

ACW INTERNATIONAL / RIVIERA & SOUTH

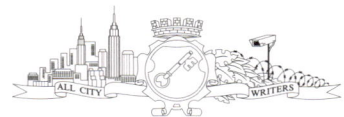

Main contributors:
Blast, Block20, Byr, Damage, Drugo, Eron,
Giose, Grim, Ikone, J-med, Just, Lego, Marco
/ Onè Sound, Move, Noem, Omaek, Ramon,
Reoh, Soap, Soevv, Vega, Wany, Word, Zart,
Zelda, Zest

In collaboration with:
ACT, ADR, BH, DCP, DSP, FDS, HV, JUICE crew,
KRUA, MG, NCE, PDB, RE Vandals, SMK, TCS,
TMA, TSK

Cover photo:
Eron, Rimini. 1996

Images page 255:
Ferruccio Farina - Balnea.net

K-RIMINI UNITED ARTISTS
—

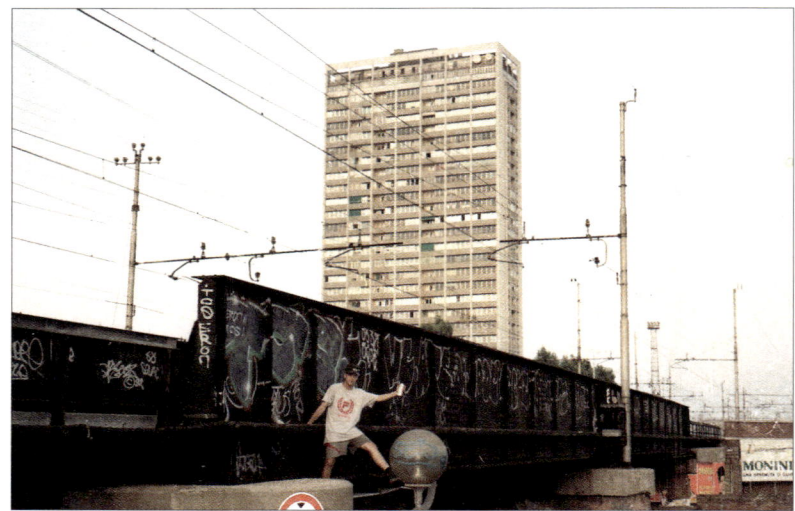

— Eron

Word
>

"S.O.S", three letters in silver, outlined by dark red, next to a black character, painted under the overpass of a peripheral area between '87 and '88. A 15 year old kid stares dreamy-eyed at this piece and is so impressed by it that once back home he starts elaborating his own ideas, hatched from the usual drawings of a school notebook.
Eron would then discover those letters and drawing were by Dayaki and Zero-T, two of the first Italian writers, later to become his mentors. In 1991 you could already see tags and throw-ups appearing around Rimini, and in his nocturnal rambles Eron was soon joined by Light7, a bomber renown for having entirely covered the iron bridge of the railway crossing on the harbour canal with the throw-up *"We are the motherfucker bombers"*: even though it's faded you can still distinguish it today. In that period many other characters that had until then observed the phenomenon in the shadows started emerging, the first crews formed and the B-boys of Rimini, along with the brothers from Bologna and Ancona that would come through, started meeting up in a gym in the city centre that was put at disposal of the breakers so they could train every Saturday afternoon, while on Sundays the regular hang-out was the club. Often at the end of the night writers would meet up, either to go hit a line, a train, or some spot in the city, and with time the various crews started identifying themselves through the first two digits of

their phone numbers. 38 Squad was immediately imitated first by 77 WestPower, who came from the Western fringes of the city, on the side farthest from the sea, and then by 74 Squad and 52NorthPower. In those years Rimini was experiencing a fall of its tourist industry due to the diffusion of mucilage[1], as well as the decline of the myth that had characterised the Riviera Romagnola in the 70's and 80's. The security of Rimini's seaside and beaches as tourist attractions was crushed in a single season, and while greedy businessmen started building colossal structures modelled around Las Vegas, the B-boys that represented the other face of the coast were searching for a new identity through street art. The reaction of the public towards the first tags was initially of skepticism and irritation, it was mostly the shopkeepers of the city centre and coastline that expressed their indignation, being the main representatives of power in a city dedicated primarily to tourism as is Rimini.
At the same time though, it was the same owners of seaside facilities that commissioned the first legal works from Eron, who through them was starting to express his full potential. In this context the Writing of Rimini reached its peak, sealed through the union of all the city's crews under the same initials: in 1993 K-RUA (*K-Rimini United Artists*) represented a group of teenagers that were separate and different from the cliché of Rimini techno clubs and beach life.

> ❶ Organic material that forms on the surface of highly polluted waters

> CONTINUE FROM PAGE 253
nocturnal actions and Zulu parties, immediately extending the local scenes into a wider representational idea distributed throughout the territory. Ancona in particular became a meeting point and a crucial centre in the wake of the connections initially created by the successive generations, who had established a strong bond first with Rimini, and then with Ascoli and Bari. All of whom had shared this same desire and practice of train bombing.

Initially this network could count only on the small scenes of primary urban centres, but with time more circumscribed realities belonging to all the towns of the Riviera and the hinterlands of the Marche and Abruzzo regions joined, fuelling this cohesion.
The kids of Cattolica were directly connected to the scenes of Pesaro, Foligno, Perugia and Ancona. In Bari an additional grouping of micro realities branched from the Puglia capital out to the rest of the region, while Brindisi, though more

RIMINI

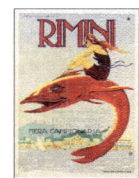

MARCELLO DUDOVICH
1922

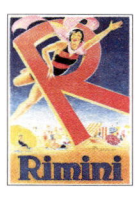

ADOLFO BUSI
1929

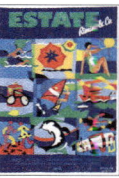

UGO NESPOLO
199

A new city icon
>

Eron: next on billboards

The relationship between the city of Rimini and mass tourism has its roots in the promotional iconography that the public administration launched at the beginning of the 20th century, firstly in order to communicate the idea of a unique bathing oasis, and secondly to convey the image of a territory consecrated to entertainment and recreational activities. The observation and comparison of the various posters commissioned to dozens of illustrators and artists, from Marcello Dudovich to Adolfo Busi, Ugo Nespolo and Milton Glaser, offer a panoramic view of how tourism and the manner of promoting the city's scenario both within national boundaries and abroad, has changed in the course of the century; a kind of continuous manifesto intended to evoke the attractiveness of a location that tries to always reinvent itself and encourage a vision of the Riviera as strongly connected to the summer season. It is indeed the seasons that are protagonists in this territory that sees itself transformed radically from one period of the year to the next: from the vitality of the summer, divulged through festive, colourful billboards, to the nostalgia of winter, where the absence of vacationers is synonymous with ordinary life. The Writing movement that appeared in the Riviera at the end of the 90's was strongly influenced by the promotional dynamics that have characterised the tourist policies of the coastal areas since the beginning of the century. It was in Rimini that the first Hip Hop parties were organised, with a recreational idea of event and meeting place in mind, indeed it was no accident that they were concentrated in clubs. The fact itself that Rimini offered an infinite amount of commission possibilities for writers during the summer season – from beach facilities, to restaurants, to hotels – is indicative of how this attention the territory had towards decoration and embellishment was steadily growing. The saltiness of the air, attacking plastered walls, ruined the aesthetic of these buildings: confiding in the decorative abilities of writers was the most immediate, efficient and economic solution. In an

analogous manner, the seasonal character of the tourist phenomenon, circumscribed to the four summer months, ended up influencing the actions of writers: that went from commissions to illegally painting the most visible spots of the city. This extensive presence of unauthorised and highly visible painting bothered the local administration, which instead pursued the idea of a clean and controlled city, tourist-friendly and solely tied to beach imagery. The metropolitan character of tags and throw-ups collided with the balance of certain compositions painted on commission. For over a decade the paradox of this condition was embodied by the figure of Eron, who more than anyone carried out commissions during the day to then hit trains, the walls of the track line and the city, by night.

This apparent incoherence was soon overcome by an intelligent stylistic evolution that in the course of a few years reconciled the idea of an invasive, all city bombing with the glossy, billboard aesthetic that was almost aimed at the general public more than to the writers themselves. The 'pop' bombing Eron did halfway through the 90's associated the promotion of the ego with the rules of advertisement marketing, in compositions that mixed the legible letters of the Riviera signage with aerosol aesthetics connected to graffiti; an iconography that allowed him to enter the collective imagery of every citizen and tourist, and at the same time ensuring himself the respect of writers in local and national scenes, generating a collective consensus around his persona. Eron's works could communicate a complete vision of his city, generating a style that was distant from the cliché of Rimini intended exclusively as a tourist destination: Eron expressed the more realistic image – sometimes even raw – of a location that is dressed also of the quotidian. The genius of this writer coincided with his ability to balance urban commissions – legal and conciliatory – with illegal actions in the historic centre. That is, to show the summer Rimini next to the winter one.

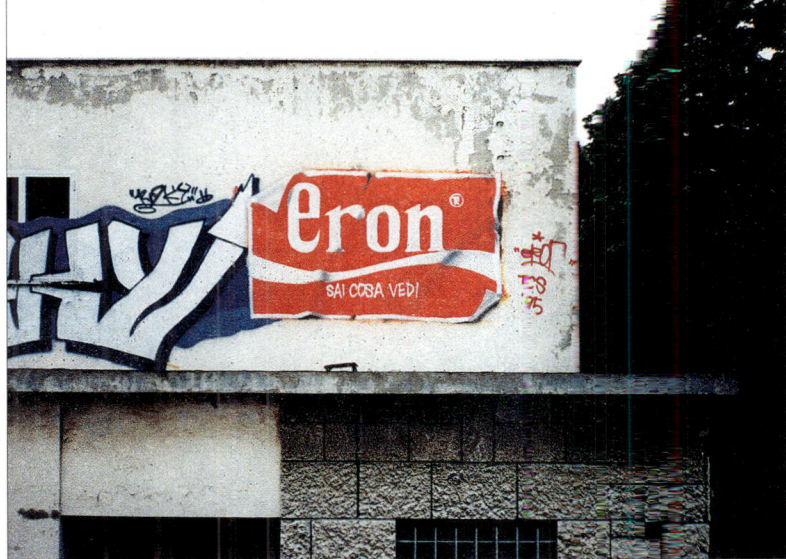

— Eron

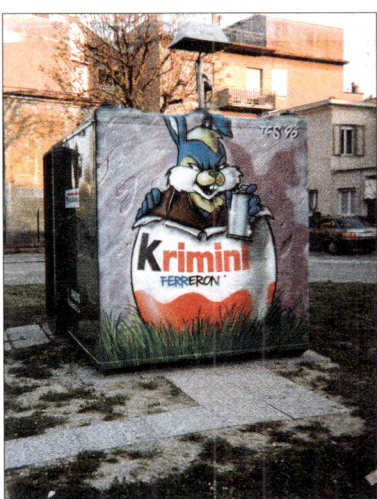

— Eron

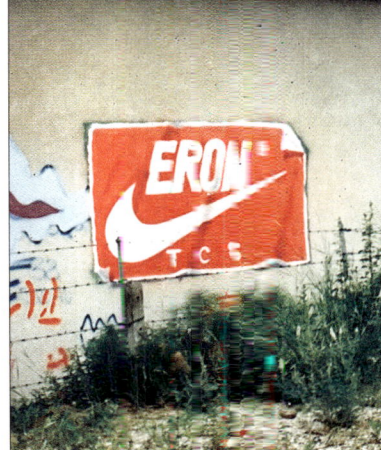

— Eron

isolated, constituted the first stronghold for the Hip Hop writing movement in Italy. Writing spread to Abruzzo: to Pescara with Dizney, who was also tied to the guys in Ancona, then to Aquila with Haero, who was more connected with the Roman scene.

When examining this issue in the broader context, it's important to first define and discuss the identity of some of the provincial centres that came to develop their own specificity within the movement. Rimini for example distinguished itself as

strongly linked to the Hip Hop scene in such groups as 38Squad, or high profile personalities such as Word.

The same bond with breaking is present in Ancona with 3Spirits and in Pesaro with DCace and some members of DSP; Bari on the other hand was rooted in a more independent reality, close to the skater circuit. Among all these cases Pesaro constitutes the most unusual because, though of limited dimensions, it immediately asserted itself as one of the most active and numerically important

centres of the Riviera. Influenced by the school of DSP, Pesaro came to count on a considerable number of writers that, with an almost New York-like mentality in painting any target – from the urban centre, to trains, to walls along the track lines – upset the identity of this provincial town, raised around the sea harbour, in less than a decade.

What then contributed to cementing the relationship between neighbouring centres were the jams, events on a national scale that found fertile ground in

the Riviera thanks to the amusement and entertainment culture typical of an area founded around the tourist industry.

In 1989 Rimini debuted in the organisation of the first parties in local clubs and in 1994 the same city proposed Indelebile, the first real event tied to Italian Writing. From 1995 onwards these opportunities to meet moved to Ancona, taking on the name of Juice and contributing in the further solidification of the ties between the cities of the Adriatic coast and the other national cities.

First connections
>

Rimini Indelebile 1994

Word
>

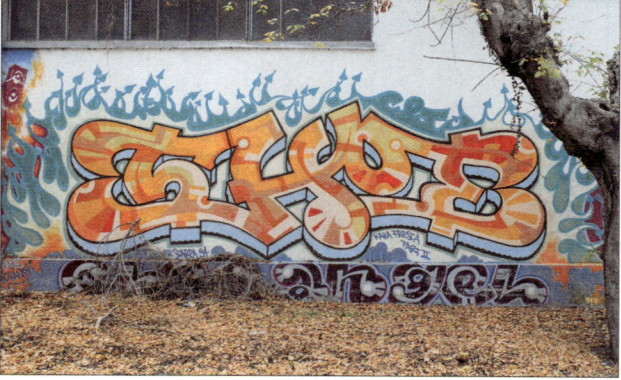

Shoe CTK from Amsterdam   — Zelda

Indelebile '94 was the first real International Hip Hop convention organised by the heads of the Italian scene, like Enrico "Crab" Arcangeli who, address book in one hand and phone in the other, put together all the connections accumulated throughout the years and contacted the main Italian representatives. An important contribution was also given by Deemo, thanks to whom we had the presence of Sangue Misto, a group that is still today considered one of the most influential in Italian Hip Hop. Word, Eron, Yurate and many other esteemed writers from Rimini also participated, before, during and after the three days of convention hosted in the biggest public park of Rimini, bordering the occupied social centre *Ex Anagrafe*, headquarters of the organisers. Indelebile marked an historical date for Italian Hip Hop, not only with respect to Writing but for all of the four elements, it included the main Italian MC's, breakers and DJ's of the time: from Deda, Neffa and DJ Gruff to Speaker Cenzou, Piotta, Lou X and Colle Der Fomento. The B-boys were not only coming from all of Italy, but also from Switzerland, France and Germany.

Among the many names that were hosted, the foreign ones stood out: Gasp, Shoe, Delta, Sender and Kraze from Amsterdam, Fume from Dusseldorf, Sharp from New York, and Mode2 from Paris. They painted the big wall in front of the social centre

entrance and those that were present will not have forgotten the crowd that gathered around Mode2; at the end of the piece Mode added a camera flash and a puppet in the shadows, next to the words "No photos", just to give an idea of the character.

Other than admiring these great masters at work and painting with them, *Indelebile* offered the opportunity for kids from all over Europe to get together: about 4000 people, full of enthusiasm and curiosity, participated in this event, which was organised by putting together the few political allies there were and trying to promote through magazines such as *AL*. The unexpected horde of writers caught both the organisers and the authorities off guard, a city so far dedicated to beach tourism became devastated by tags and throw-ups. In front of the freshly-painted wall and next to the park, kids would chill, bonding through their shared passions: the exchange of addresses and blackbooks, ghetto blasters playing the first demo tapes of Italian Rap that had just

come out of the 'posse' phase, breakers laying out linoleum on the grass and bare ground so as to practice at any hour of the day or night. Faces of people telling different stories and origins, but with something finally in common; *Indelebile* allowed us to no longer feel marginalised and alone, it shortened the geographical distance that divided us. For the first time, though we were different in ways and manners, we were united by a common intent and spirit.

Done
>

Rimini played a key role with regards to organising get-togethers tied to Italian Writing. The first parties of the 80's were held in the VIP room or secondary dance floor of clubs along the seafront, allowing the organisers of this new wave to host their events

in the "back" of the local discos, which were making most of their profits with house and commercial music on Sunday afternoons. In 1994 therefore, it couldn't be any place but Rimini to accommodate the biggest Italian convention of the time. News of the jam travelled primarily through *Aelle* and via phone, thanks to an invisible and disorderly network. Media attention was lacking, and information got around mostly thanks to word of mouth, but already from the station, that afternoon of June, the kids coming from all over the country understood that the wind was changing. People were incredulous to see dozens of teenagers descending from Inter-regional and Intercity trains, coming from anywhere between Puglia and Veneto. The cliché that for over a decade had seen the average Italian go around with Invicta backpacks in Rimini got confused by the baseball hats with peaked caps and the oversized pants. The troops that arrived to Marecchia park from the station caused a ruckus, but only due to the noisy backpacks full of spray cans: the

first to arrive kept silent, and didn't quite know what to expect. On the first day curiosity was at a peak and the tension could be felt in the air, it almost seemed as if all enthusiasm was missing. Then everyone got familiar with the environment and Indelebile exploded. On the grass it was a continuous battle between breakers and MC's, and every hour new clusters of people would form to watch those that were in the mood for improvising. In front of the foreign pieces Word from Rimini and Colle der Fomento would challenge each other with freestyles going from the Romagna dialect to the Roman one. The same battles would move onto the stage in the evening, where the Sangue Misto concert left a memorable mark on the event. The kids that had come from all over Italy to see them knew their lyrics by heart, perhaps because the SXM album was appreciated by Hip Hop heads as well as those that listened to Hardcore. Neffa came from a historic band of the Italian Hardcore scene called Negazione, Deda sang in

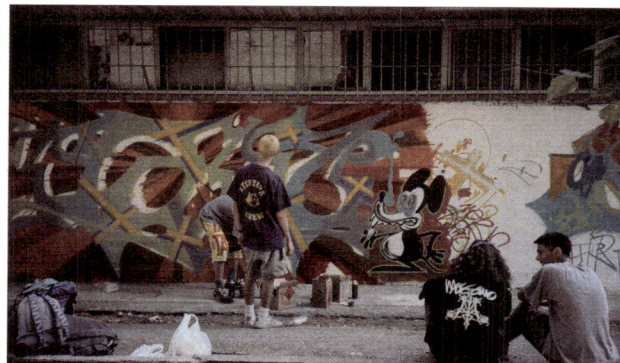

Dado SPA from Bologna   — Zelda

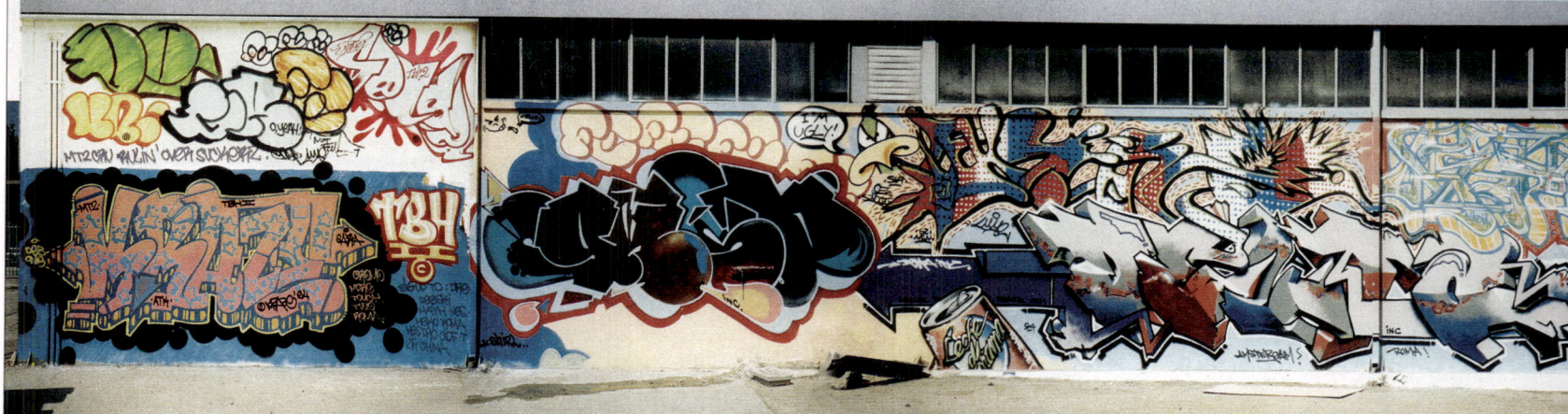

Kraze TBH   Gasp INC   Delta INC from Amsterdam (under), Fume MSN from Düsseldorf (above)   Sharp from New York City

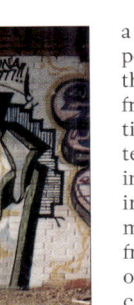

Omek DSP from Pesaro   — Zelda

the group Rabid Duck, while DJ Gruff had grown up in the Regio of Turin, a milestone for the Italian Hip Hop scene. Sangue Misto displayed remarkable firepower: the fact that Deda and Neffa belonged to distinct scenes was important in broadening the attention of the public of the time. It has to be taken into account that the middle of the 90's in Italy was a transitional period for skaters and writers, during which the line separating the two faded, and at times was even non-existent. The Sangue Misto concert left as much of a mark as the foreign murals did. In comparison the Italian walls mirrored the unripe state of the scene and when, months later, Gasp dared to openly declare so on *True Colorz*, a polemic ensued. In Milan everyone cried for revenge but a base of truth was there: the Italian Writing scene at Indelebile was still immature. Milan and Bologna had long traditions, Zero-T and Dayaki were experienced (actually they were stopping), Eron and DSF walked on their own two feet, but the Italian walls of Indelebile still could not measure up to the European

standards. For some reason during those days the entire platoon of Italian guests shot blanks: all Skah's potential came down to painting a single rose without a sole word. Sky4 and Flycat did pieces that were beneath their reputation on the same surface as Skah, a cement cylinder whose curved structure indeed did not help. Zero-T, in an act of high-handedness, took DSP's space and occupied it right in the centre with a nice character that however compromised the composition as a whole, so that in the span of a couple hours it had been filled with tags. On the walls of a social centre nearby SPA painted one of the best spaces, but unfortunately without being able to put in that much effort: the night before, the Sparvar cans Rusty had brought had been unexpectally stolen, and consequently their participation was only a mere act of courtesy. On the wall opposite that of the foreigners the groups MT2 and ETC, representing the Roman scene, were still painting pieces that were only two metres square each. Then, right at the entrance of the jam, Omek of DSP took possession of

a highly visible space and painted perhaps the best piece out of all the Italian ones. The fact he came from a town of limited proportions says a lot about the character of the Writing phenomenon in the early 90's: Indelebile was important because the Italian movement was not cohesive but fragmented, dispersed throughout the territory and hardly in contact. In that period, a first network was forming between city and city thanks to key figures like Sky4 and Rusty, bridges between Milan, Bologna, Treviso and Rome, that played cardinal roles within the Italian Writing scene for over two decades. The formation of the first "Intercity" crews, such as ADM or FTR, was anyway a sporadic case in a phenomenon that was still budding, and counted only a few dozen people in the province capitals. Other than this, connecting was difficult because the only magazine recognised on a national level was *Aelle* and jams were rare. Indelebile was therefore a pilot convention, in which for the first time realities that were distant and unimaginable could meet. If the beginning of the movement had witnessed a concentration of the national scenes in certain European metropolises (one can think of the role Paris played for France for example), in Italy, Writing was diluted in a subset of scenes that had difficulty connecting with each other and were thus weakened by this same dispersion. Perhaps for this reason during the first half of the 90's the Italian scene took longer than others to find its own stylistic and attitudinal direction; it was too eclectic, a victim of the more advanced European currents and the cumbersome presence of the New York masters.

EVENTS

Word

>

One of the earliest Hip Hop jams in Italy was organised by Deemo in 1989 at the Barcelona Disco, a well-known club on the Romagna coastline, and it became the very first meeting ground for the scenes of some Italian cities. That same year Crab and Wayne Brown, a DJ from New York that had recently moved to Riccione, organised a party at the Cellophane Disco, and in that occasion Toxic painted the whole outer face of a hotel wall, bringing the experience of the big apple to the Riviera. Following these two initial events numerous small parties started taking place in the private rooms of clubs in Rimini, to which many characters that would compose the core at the base of local Hip Hop would participate, among whom the MC and breaker Kallà, SpaceOne and Speed Roke, that would later become the best breaker of the local scene.

Mace

>

At Barcellona Disco the vibe was similar to the first Italian jams: people that had never gone out bombing showed up with blackbooks full of outlines, everyone was decked out; there were people from Florence, Bologna, Treviso, and Milan, as always I immediately hit it off with the troublemakers, the guys who wanted to have fun. Sher had just come back from Ibiza, Acid House was all the rage, and Fly was shouting "Estaiii i Locccaaaaa" while drinking Ceres beer. Most people ignored us. Imagine painting five or six cardboard panels with spray paint inside of

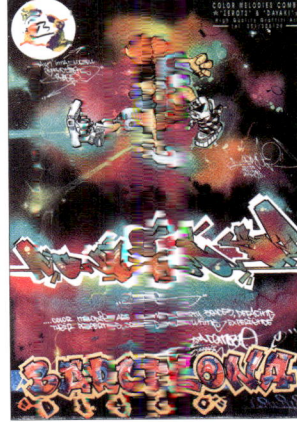

Flyer by Zero   — Zart

a club while people were dancing– it wasn't exactly healthy for us. I recall Deemo showed up with grey camouflage pants, like Professor Griff of Security of the first world, with Dayaki shaved into the back of his head. This was the last convention that would involve the members of the first generation, because then things changed: B-boys barely showed their faces at parties, except for Maurizio to on three occasions. I remember Doze, a breaker from Venice who was awesome at the time, he had learned the ropes at Beethoven (which then became Palladium) by challenging Americans, he even created a Breaking school in Treviso, he was awesome, both upright and on the floor. But these people didn't really understand what Writing was about. They considered it a backdrop for breaking, they had a 'disco' mentality, people who were used to performing on the dance floor with girls drooling over them since it was all the rage.

As writers, we were the losers, what else could we do? In any case, that first group at the Rimini gathering took things seriously and we can say that they created Italy's first real Writing scene.

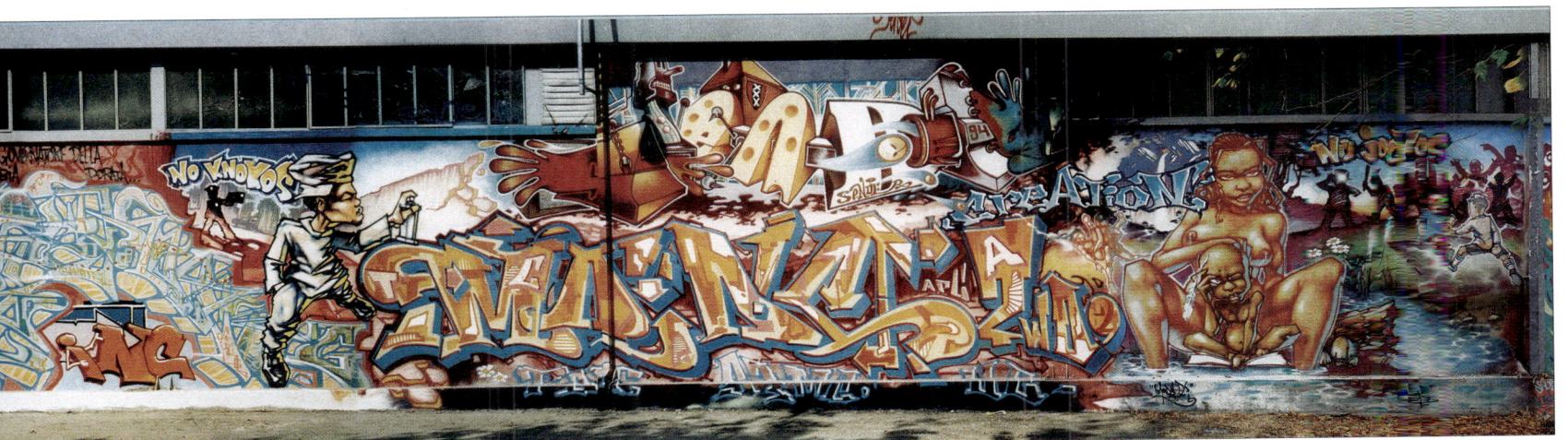

Mode 2 from Paris (under), Sender from Amsterdam (above)   — Zelda

Rimini and Pesaro line
>

Trait
d'union

> SEGUE DA PAGINA 253

administration to keep them in order and cared for, with particular efforts made at

making them attractive and hospitable during the summer period.

The fact these places are exposed to the sight of an elevated flux of people makes them also a primary target for writers, generating an open conflict with the local authorities. From the station of Rimini the track line proceeds bordered by a brick wall on one side, forming a stretch where Eron, Reoh, Lego and other writers of Rimini have concentrated the majority of their actions. One of the first radical

turning points occurred after an unexpected stance on the part of the local administration. Word, one of the principle protagonists of the Hip Hop scene in Rimini remembers:

In 1993, after years of bombing the track line of Rimini, an anti-graffiti team was assigned by the local municipality to clean our work. With their sand-blasting machines hundreds of square metres of paint were scraped off in a single day and the laterite-brick wall was returned to its natural state in less than 24 hours. That same night, every crew in Rimini planned a counter attack. The next day we painted one of the most imposing silvers in Italy. "Volete una città pulita fuori per non far vedere quanto siete sporchi dentro."[1] was the phrase composed by the letters Eron rapidly traced on the wall, that us other writers, about twenty-five in all, filled with silver spray paint. The news was in all the papers and from then on the track line was the property of us writers once again.

This same wall, erected in the vicinity of Rimini's central station, ends after a few hundred metres, whereas the railway line

continues towards the South, bordered by a prefabricated concrete fence that in fact erases any possibility of painting. Along this line you reach Pesaro, where the railway covers a suburban tract clenched between the mountains and the beach, coasting the highway to Fano.

In this stretch the wall is about two metres below the road level, thus completely hiding any writer's action, though the highway above dense traffick.

The part of landscape that writers appropriated for themselves was composed of a wall, two rails, and a mass of rocks sloping down directly to the longest stretch of free beach in the city, at points split by little portions of resort structures. So if greater parts of the wall faced the free beach, with little activity, in certain delimited points it winded past highly popular bathing facilities. The railway line is crossed here at various points by underpasses and overpasses giving access

❶ You want a city clean on the outside to hide how dirty you are inside

to the beach, and is regularly painted by writers. Except during the summer, it was very difficult for them to be caught in the act. At most they were seen by transiting engine drivers who just contented themselves to blowing the train whistle as they passed: those were the years of coloured pieces with backgrounds, painted during the day. The increasingly frequent incursions of the police however, changed the scenario: that type of graffiti moved to the so-called *fogne*, and their frequency on the railway line diminished.

When, in the second half of the 90's, Noem and Omaek began heavily painting the area again, they were doing pieces in silver and black and concentrating their activity in the dark hours of autumn and winter afternoons, to hide from the police. In the following years the free beach was considerably downsized, while the portions of seashore that required payment increased exponentially.

The bonfire parties DSP used to organise on the beach – that from word of mouth alone had gone from a meagre number

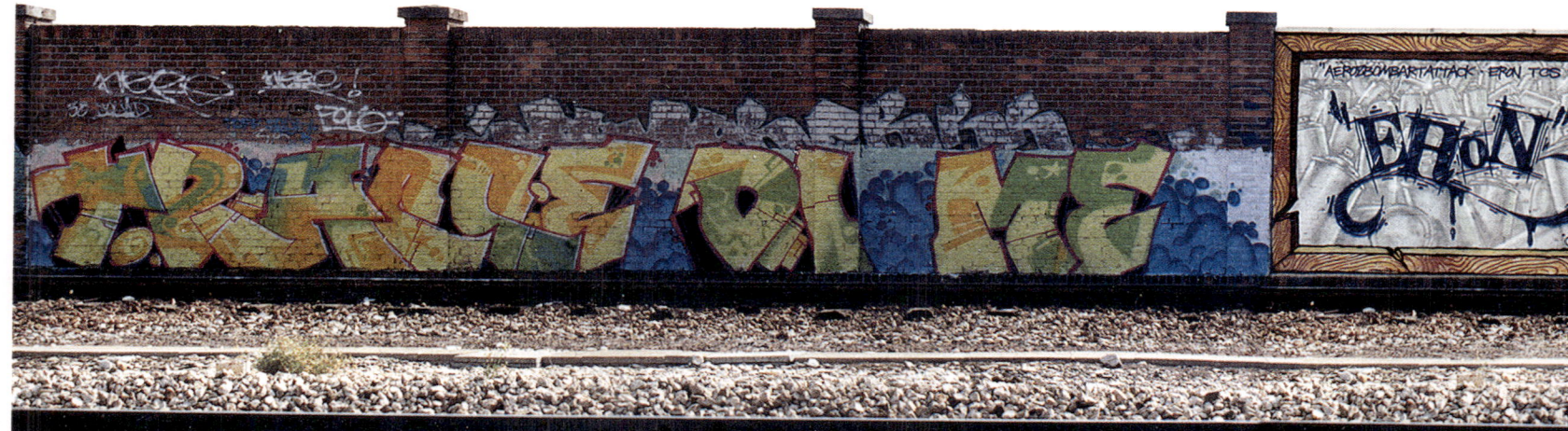

Tracce di me (Traces of me) by Eron-TCS, 1993

Eron-TCS

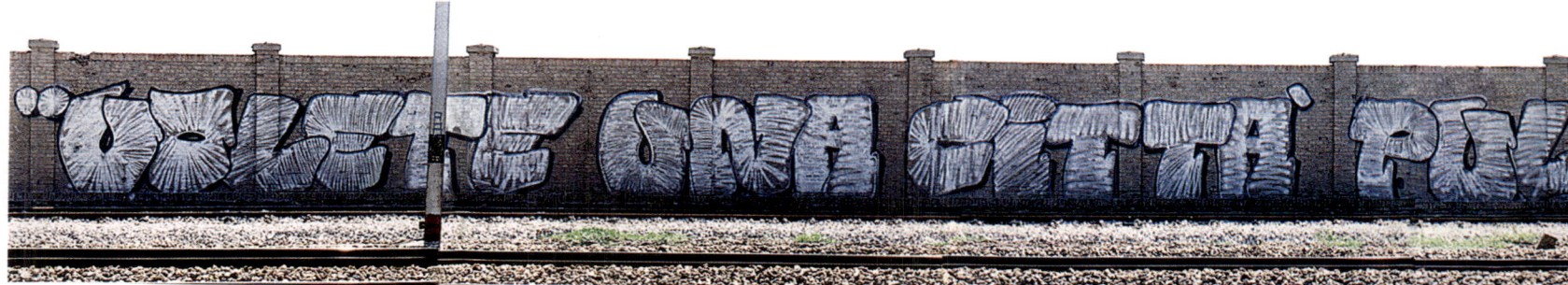

Volete una città pulita fuori per non far... (You want a city clean on the outside so as not to...)

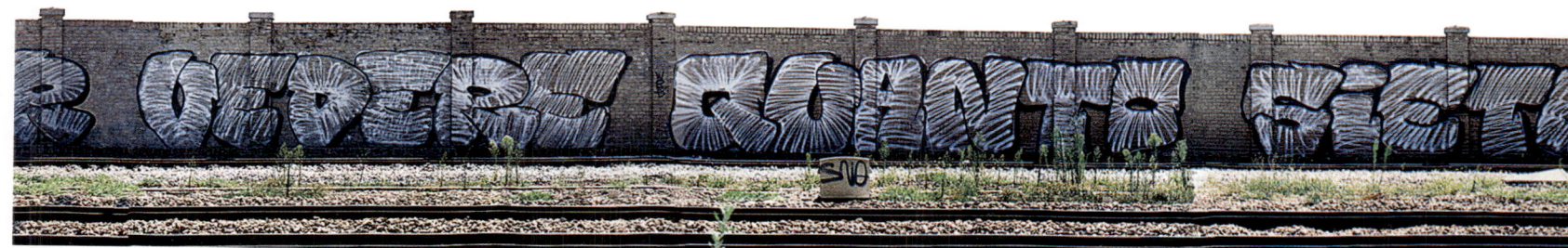

... vedere quanto siete sporki dentro (...show how dirty you are inside) by K–Rimini United Artists, 1993

of participants to hundreds of people
– had to give way to new bathing facilities, night clubs, and small bars along the
coast. The construction of a bicycle lane
connecting Pesaro to Fano now allows
you to reach the beach by bike or scooter, without having to pass through the
underpasses of the state road or walk for
over a kilometre in the sand, as you would
have in the 90's.

What was initially a place for freaks, lo-
ners, bums, swingers and homosexuals,
became one of the hippest authorised
summer spots of Pesaro, once a borderline environment and now a place for
cocktails at sunset. Today the bicycle
lane follows the rocky roadbed that lea-
des to the railway, fenced-in like a yard
and illuminated its entire length through
as if it were day light by an uninterrupted
row of street lamps, radically changing
the place's atmosphere. Despite this, the
transformation of the area and the bicycle
lane have given the track wall much visibility, making this railway stretch the
ultimate target now even more than in
the past, and constituting an even riskier
challenge for those that paint.

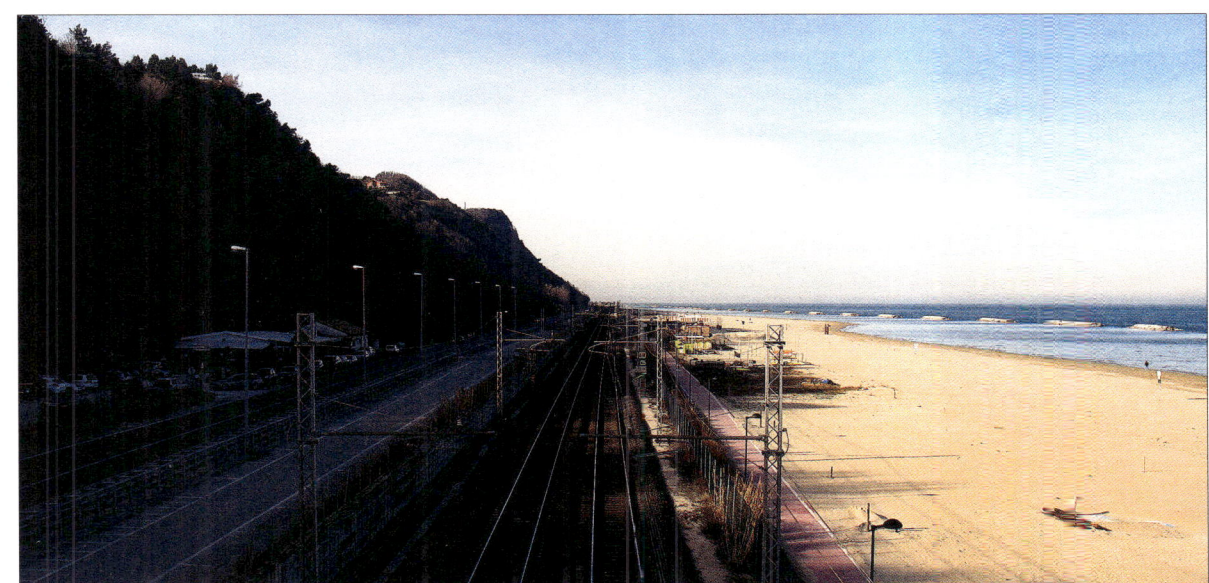

The railway line of Pesaro
— *Noem*

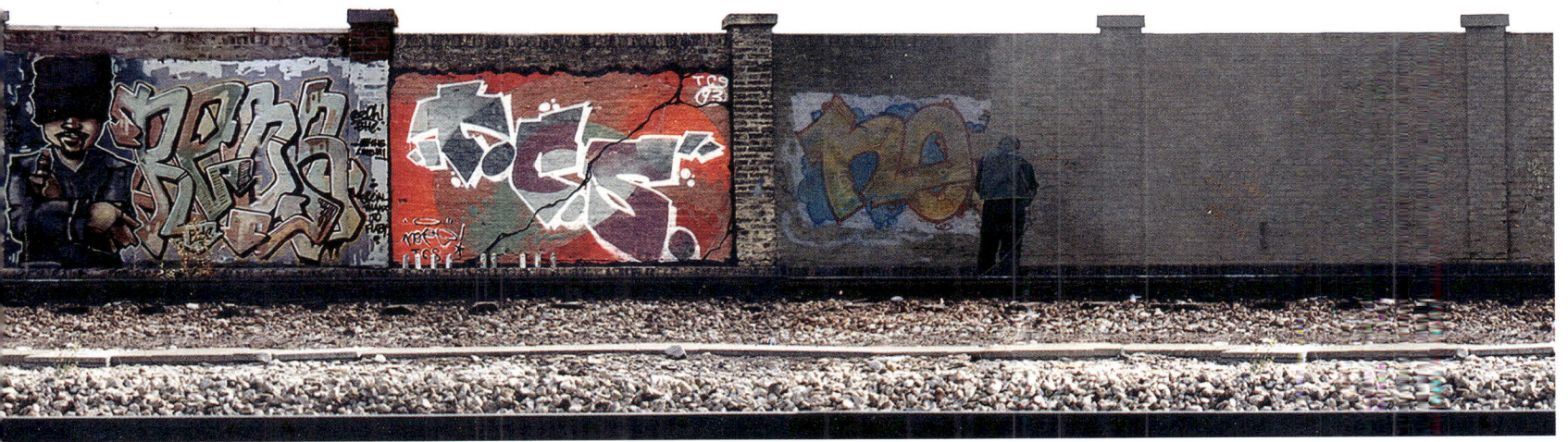

Reoh–BH   Eron–TCS
— *Eron*

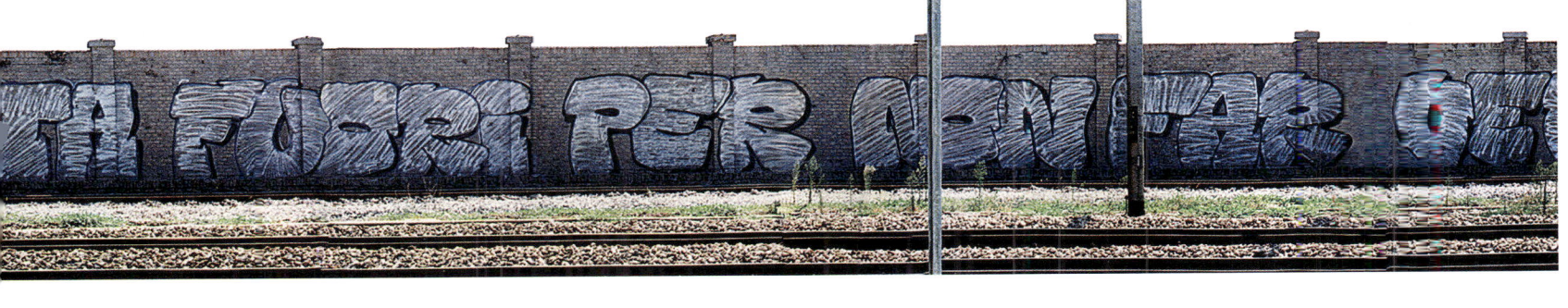

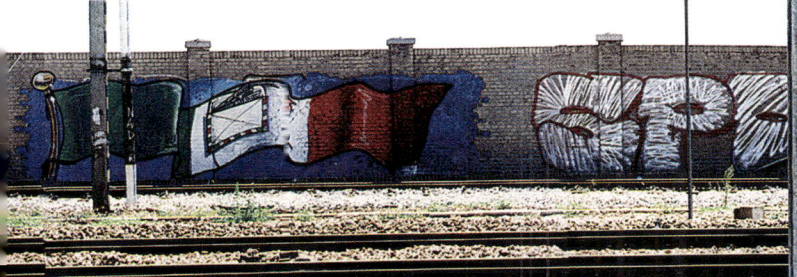
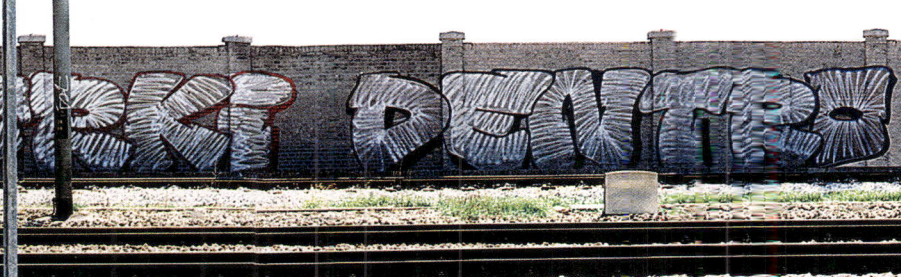

— *Eron*

PESARO

A small, rough town

The local scene's debut with DSP crew

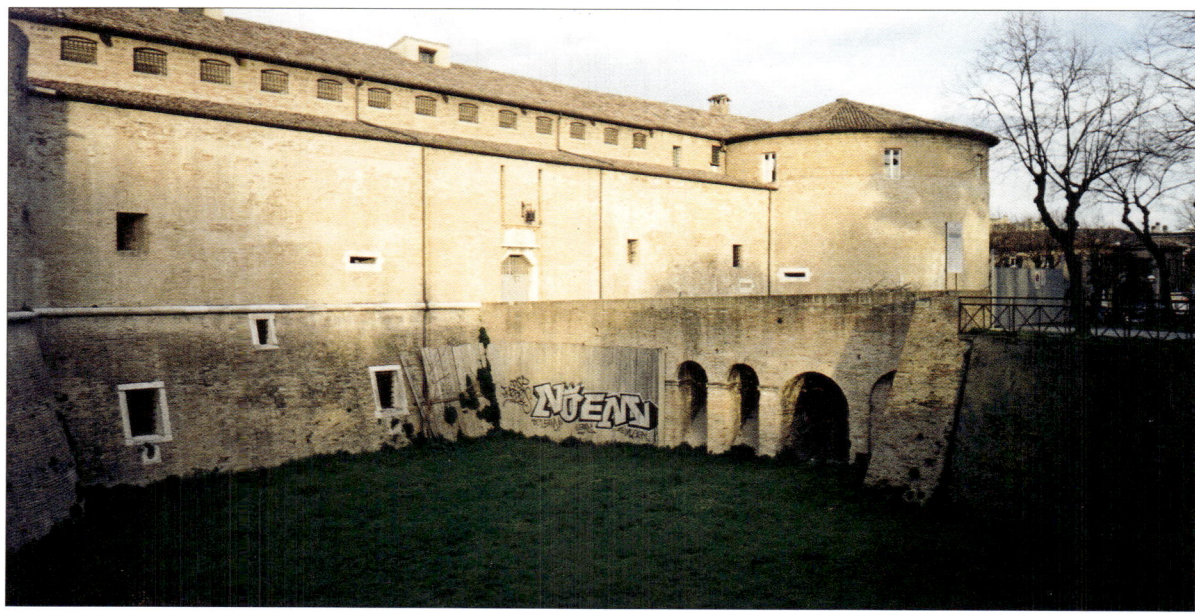

A Noem piece on the pailing of the Castle   — Noem

Tags started appearing in Pesaro in the late 1980's ('88–'89) thanks to two writers: Blaze and Noem507. Blaze was connected to the Italian Hip Hop scene through his friendship with DC Ace, one of the most important B-boys of the so-called 'old school'. Noem507 begins to tag the walls of his city after a trip to New York and he immediately establishes what will become Pesaro's first crew: DSP, *Da Skate Posse* (which then became *Dead Society Poets*). Blaze's career was high-quality but short-lived, unlike DSP crew's, despite the young age of its members and their non-involvement with the Hip Hop movement. A very important factor in the beginning was the connection with the vast, emerging local skate scene. Why? Because some of the writers from DSP came from Villa San Martino, a huge neighbourhood on the outskirts of the city, the place where the first skateshop was born and where most of the city's skaters flocked to. In this no-man's land, amongst tall buildings and underground garages, deserted streets and walls of semi-abandoned factories, DSP took action: underneath a bridge in Villa San Martino, they painted Pesaro's first hall of fame.

The encounter with Blaze, and through him, with Zart and Damage from Ancona, led to a thick exchange with this city of Le Marche, which already had its own steady scene. Zart and Damage are considered by the members of DSP (now with its definitive lineup: Noem507, Zinko, Sidermain, Ikone, Reeko, Omaek 193) to be true masters. But their encounters are few and far between and the crew remains very attached to the 'local' scene. 1990 and 1991 are turbulently informative years: the emergence of Hip Hop; the search for style through contacts with neighbouring cities; but above all, the relationship with Pesaro itself, in which in those years, behind the apparently idyllic façade, lurked a very chaotic existence for young people; the start of immigration; the young neighbourhood bar gangs (legacy of the 80s) associated with petty crime and fights who were also fascinated with graffiti due to its savage and adrenaline-charged nature. The amount of tags and graffiti increased and expanded from Villa San Martino into all neighbourhoods of the city, especially the historic centre and the vast beach front area. In 1991, DSP begins covering the state trains on the Ancona line with colourful pieces.

Up until the mid 90's, the wall running alongside the tracks was the most sought-after spot in the city, DSP defended it from toys and admitted very few others, only friends such as Dream. In 1991 FLY crew was born (J-Med, Neil, Sony7 and later, Move), the first true crew devoted exclusively to graffiti after DSP. 1992 is the year of the definitive consolidation of this phenomenon in the city, more and more crews are forming: RKS (Sony7, Nite1, Keim), SIP (Omaek193, Zinko, Dyno, Sezam), SMK (Vega, Sueno, Noem507, Sidermain, Keim), SPA (Ikone, Dream), NPS (Zest, Icekey, Dr. Stein); DSP's pieces generate converts while their style begins to break away from that of neighbouring cities, creating its own flavour that influences all of the city's writers. In Italy people begin to talk of a 'Pesarese style'; and in spring, the creation of "Epik" (Ikone and Noem507), a coloured piece in a key spot of Pesaro's historic centre, definitively reveals the existence of the largest local underground movement ever to residents, resulting in the development of a real urban legend. The summer ends with the first train (a freight train) ever painted

Bar Sport life

Pesaro neighbourhoods, due to the morphology of the territory or due to chance, are all different from each other: it's easy to spot the essential characteristics, to identify them and identify with them. Perhaps this is why, during the upsurge of petty crime in the 80's linked to heroin and drug dealing, kids in each neighbourhood created gangs with which to control their turf. Even though it was a small and isolated city, Pesaro had its share of gang-related crimes and occasional clashes between rival groups. Each gang guarded over their neighbourhood bar and spread their name by spray painting it all over the city.

Gangs would cross out other names to even the score, so clashes were inevitable. Piazza Redi belonged to ECLIPSE and COCIS. Eclipse wrote "spranga duro" (hard hitters) everywhere; Cocis, the more menancing group, wrote their gang's name

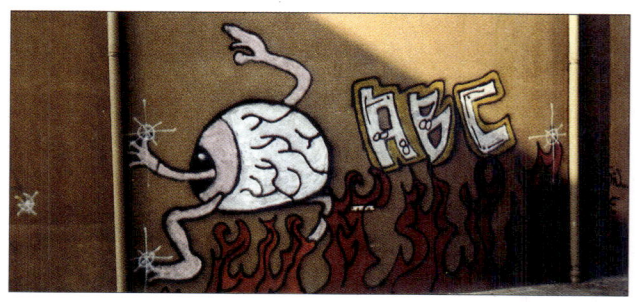

ABC bar division marking its territory   — Zelda

DIRTY EPIK
—

in Pesaro's history, thanks to Zinko and Sezam. This undertaking represents DSP's expansion onto metal.

In '93 NSA comes to life, amongst its members are two guys who will be the most important writers in the years to come: Byr and Zelda, who in '94 form ADR (*Apologia di Reato*), the first crew from Pesaro to have members from other cities (Lego from Rimini and Done from Cesena), apart from DSP that included Zart from Ancona. In 1994, thanks to Shiva, Ares, Depo, Soevv, and Emoy, ASG crew is formed, and with the contribution of Zelda, it then becomes TMA (*The Men Alive*), whose core members from Pesaro (Soevv, Depo, Ares, Zelda) represent one of the most prolific and long-lived crews in the city's history.

In its formative and affirmative years (1989-1994), the Writing phenomenon produces conflicting reactions among residents and the media, ranging from interest - during these years many newspapers write about the phenomenon, for example an entire page about DSP - to concern and criminalisation - some residents wonder if the North African immigrants are to blame for all these 'illegible' tags. In the early 90's, graffiti is very popular not only amongst real writers, but also amongst youths associated with petty crime. In fact, the DIGOS (Italian FBI) of Pesaro open an investigation on Writing, also due to the many complaints from residents. In those years the DIGOS become a sort of anti-graffiti squad. During this five year period, it's not rare for writers to be caught red-handed by Police or Carabinieri, and to be involved in shoot-outs in train yards or chases through the streets. Part of the local government tries to stress the illegal aspect of Writing, while the other part tries to stress its creative and artistic aspect by utilising this phenomenon in cultural events or by granting the writers spaces where they could legally paint. When DSP crew was formed they were completely removed from the Italian Writing movement. Its members' tags and throw-ups were based on Noem507's stories about his trip to New York. Soon enough, the discovery of neighbouring scenes in Rimini (38SQUAD) and Ancona (DCP), in addition to the study of books like *Subway Art* and *Spraycan Art*,

lead DSP crew towards a more conscious stylistic direction. In 1991, their style is a shy copy of European Bando-ism together with bubble-style throw-ups that had greatly influenced Noem507. The crew's trip to Paris in 1992 determines a progressive distancing from the styles of that time, towards a more Pesarese style, whose roots come from Paris (AEC, UK, NTM, VEP), from London's tube graffiti, from Holland's creativity, and from New York's various styles. One person who is influential in Pesaro's style evolution is Boogie from Padua, not for the shape of his letters, but for his wild yet refined approach towards graffiti.

Unlike other Italian crews that have a

> Part of the local government tries to stress the illegal aspect of writing, while the other part tries to stress its creative and artistic aspect by utilizing this phenomenon in cultural events or by granting the writers spaces where they could legally paint

specific group style, DSP does not, each writer develops a personal style and then blends it in with that of the others'. The DSP mentality becomes the city's mentality. Each writer tries to create his own style, and the aesthetics of Pesaro are based on this idea rather than on predetermined letter shapes: coloured pieces of large dimensions, complex murals with lengthy dedications, high-quality illegal pieces in silver, become a trademark of a city whose scene continues to make a name for itself in the Italian peninsula. From the mid 90's, the increasing accessibility to fanzines and the exponential development of train-bombing, influence the city's style without altering its core: even younger writers who are focused on trains (for example: Zelda and part of TMA), begin to integrate these new European influences with the matrix of

> CONTINUES ON PAGE 280

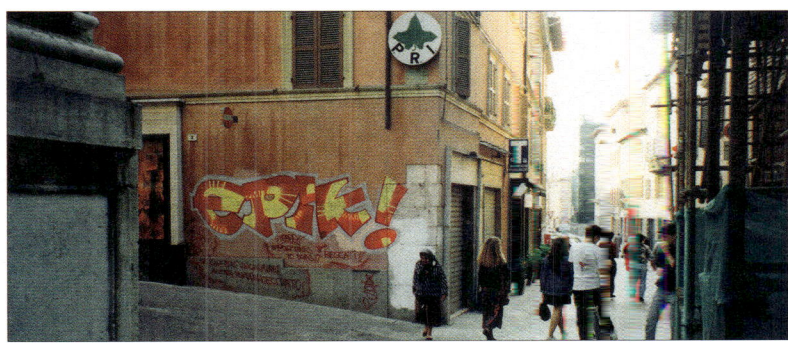

Epik by Ikone   — Noem

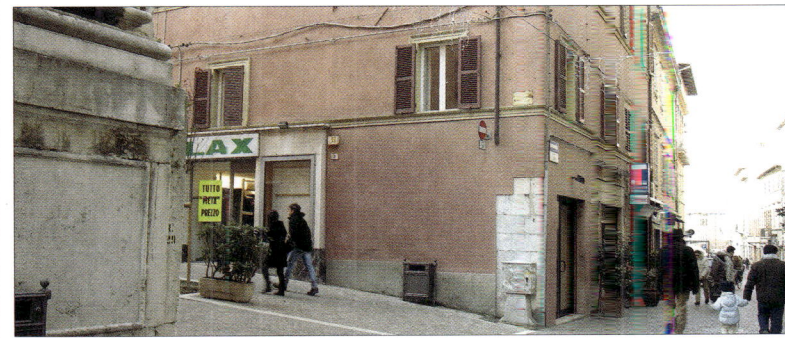

The spot after it was cleaned in 2008, 16 years later   — Zelda

I think "EPIK" was the most important piece in the history of graffiti in Pesaro. Considering the period and the place in which it was painted, it was also the most beautiful. Absolutely illegal, on an old building that was a political party's headquarters in the historic centre of Pesaro. And to boot, it was coloured.

That piece made it clear to everybody, even those who didn't want to know, that something new had risen and was growing in the city. Graffiti was no longer only hidden underground, in the outskirts, or on garbage bins. I was there, badge of honour. But from the start to the very end, Ikone did it, he was the most talented and inconsistent motherfucker in the crew. My duties were: making sure nobody interrupted our work and writing (upon Ikone's request) a phrase that was very 1992: "IF ART IS A CRIME, THEN FORGIVE US!". Rookies. The coolest thing was that night transcended the photograph immortalising it. First we painted the shutters of a newsstand black with a roller, then we were off to go paint "EPIK" but had two unpleasant encounters: one with a bored se-

curity guard and the other with a local crook who hung around for 20 minutes, fascinated by our nocturnal activity. Once we finished, we went back to the newsstand and I did my piece, a declaration of love for a girl I dumped a month later. The next morning, we were kings. I bet Zinko, the notorious vandal of the early 90's, still gets a stomachache when he thinks about it... ah ah! That's what DSP was like, we were against everyone but in competition amongst ourselves. To attract less attention, we usually worked in pairs instead of in a group, and in those days me and Ikone were 'the duo'. Since we couldn't be out too late due to our curfew, we became early birds: we'd get up at 4 am, a simple tactic. I'd go downstairs and Ikone would be waiting for me with a bicycle loaded with spraycans. It's now 2007 and "EPIK" is still there it has faced but it's still standing. Epic "EPIK"! I randomly caught sight of my newsstand many years later, it was being towed away. I followed it as far as I could, but I'll never know where the fuck it ended up.
— NOEM

---

with the profile of a guy smoking a joint. The Bowling guys reigned over Ledimar, and for ages, the Porto gang controlled the neighbourhood they named themselves after. Nearby was Baia Flaminia, a bad place to go looking for trouble since some of the locals were really good boxers. Obviously, there were gangs in Villa San Martino, especially around Il Sole mall, which wasn't very far from the 5Torri neighbourhood. There were lots

of hotheads who had experience with punches and spraycans in 5Torri. That neighbourhood led straight to Pantano, which was near the stadium. The largest number of gangs was found in this area, they often identified themselves through their neighbourhood bar: ABC gang, Graziella gang, Jamaica gang... not to mention GruppoBlando and Bar Coop, whose acronyms covered the more popular streets and parks in the neighbourhood.

The violence between these two groups was legendary amongst youngsters, their writings were untouchable, unless of course you were looking for trouble. "Greg" from GruppoBlando and "Dyno" from Bar Coop, were the most important writers from this microcosm. They painted lots of murals, but with a mentality and method different from traditional writers. We did our pieces furtively, fleeing from any risky situations, whereas they usually

painted in broad daylight, as if they owned the neighbourhood, with no fear of passersby or of the police. One year, the Cocis gang from Piazza Redi started crossing out all of Bar Coop's tags. The Bar Coop guys, high on amphetamines and armed with brass knuckles, flocked there to give their rival gang a good thrashing. That's how things were. In small towns, football is what usually fires up the local hotheads. This held true in Pesaro

too, but unlike other cities, once the football match was over, the bonds that were formed inside of the stadium quickly dissolved in favour of local gangs. Somewhat like in England when die-hard fans gather in support of the national team under St. George's cross: once they set their common flag down, they go back to championship games and group clashes to defend their own team's name. — DSP

Cityscape
›

The sewer, recepticle of local styles

Pesaro is traversed by a winding canal that runs below and above ground revealing the city's dark side. The sewers, or Fogne as we call them, provide no public service anymore even though they slice through many of the city's neighbourhoods like an endless intestine, surrounded by smooth walls that penetrate two-three meters below ground, running alongside abandoned homes, streets, and neighbourhoods. Although this territory is isolated from the rest of the city (normal residents don't set foot in it), it is still intimately tied to the city, making it an ideal free zone for writers due to the expanse of high-quality walls and the ease with which one can paint here, in fact it becomes a second home to many writers. The best parts of the sewer become hall of fames for each crew. In accordance with the unwritten urban rules, the best spots belong to the most respected crews in the city.

Those of us in DSP ended up painting in the sewers because the wall of the rail line that served as our hall of fame had become too limiting for the standards we wanted to achieve. We needed a space that was taller since we had more than enough length. Along the walls of the sewer there were small pieces, colour tests, crappy tags: basically stuff by aspiring writers with no talent and no balls to paint outside of that cement intestine. We system-

> ❝
> If crews got into fights,
> they would usually cross out
> pieces on the streets, not the
> ones in the Hall of Fame.
> What was the point of fucking
> up something that the other guy
> took no risk to create?!

atically covered everything. Zinko, Reeko, Omaek193, Ikone, Sider and I were the only ones who knew how to paint such difficult walls. Endless metres of walls. From beginning to end. It was summer of '93, soon enough, other crews started claiming sections of the wall in various neighbourhoods of the city. Some days you would paint in your own neighbourhood then hop on your bike and go paint your friend's wall. You'd jump down or take the maintenance stairs, look at new pieces, chat with people, drink or smoke something; then you'd disappear into the dark tunnel (keeping an eye out for rats) and reappear in another crew's hall of fame, hopefully not your enemies'. You could paint as much as you wanted in the sewers, but only street-writers were respected. And if crews got into fights, they would usually cross out pieces on the streets, not the ones in the hall of fame. What was the point of fucking up something that the other guy took no risk to create?! – NOEM

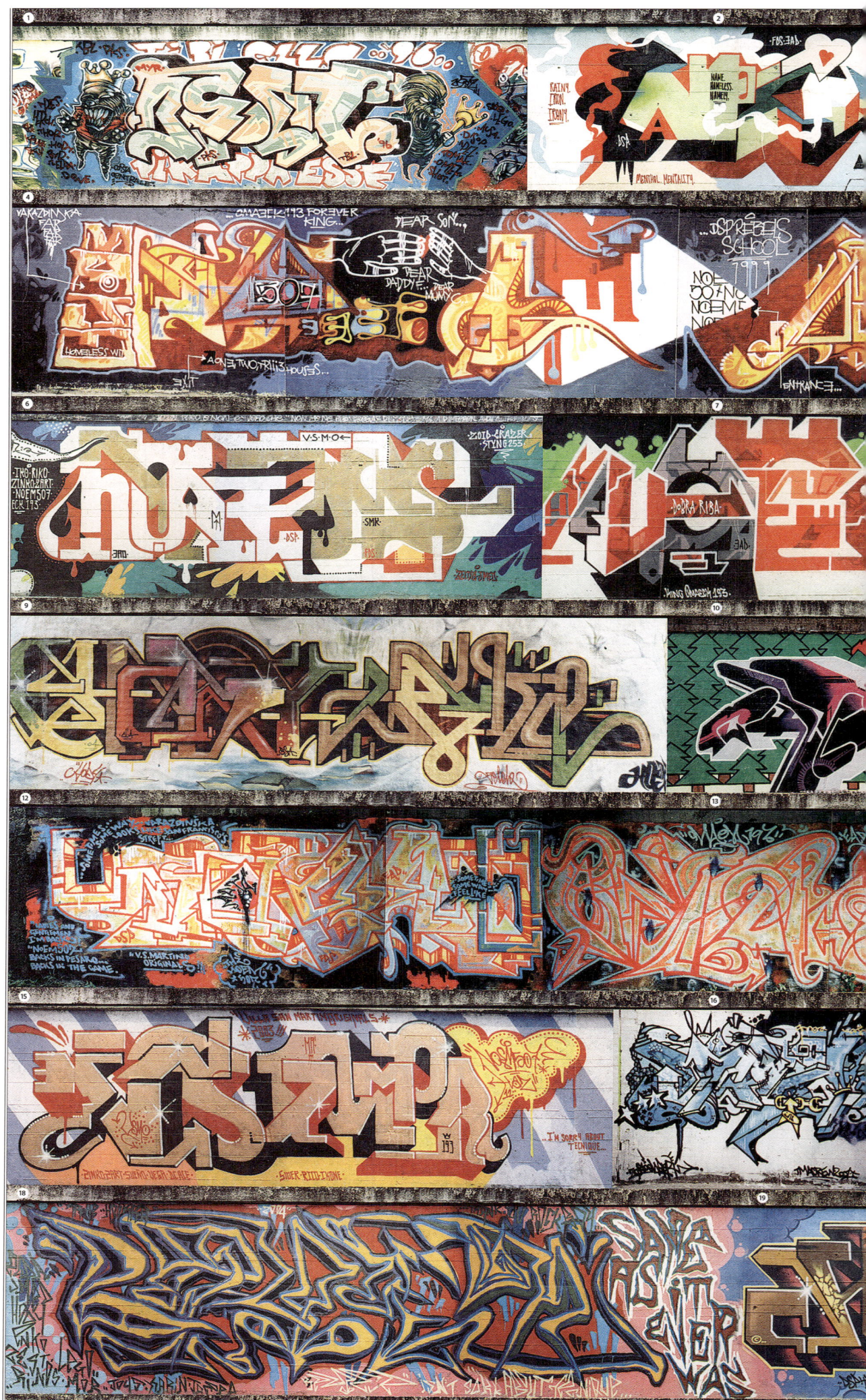

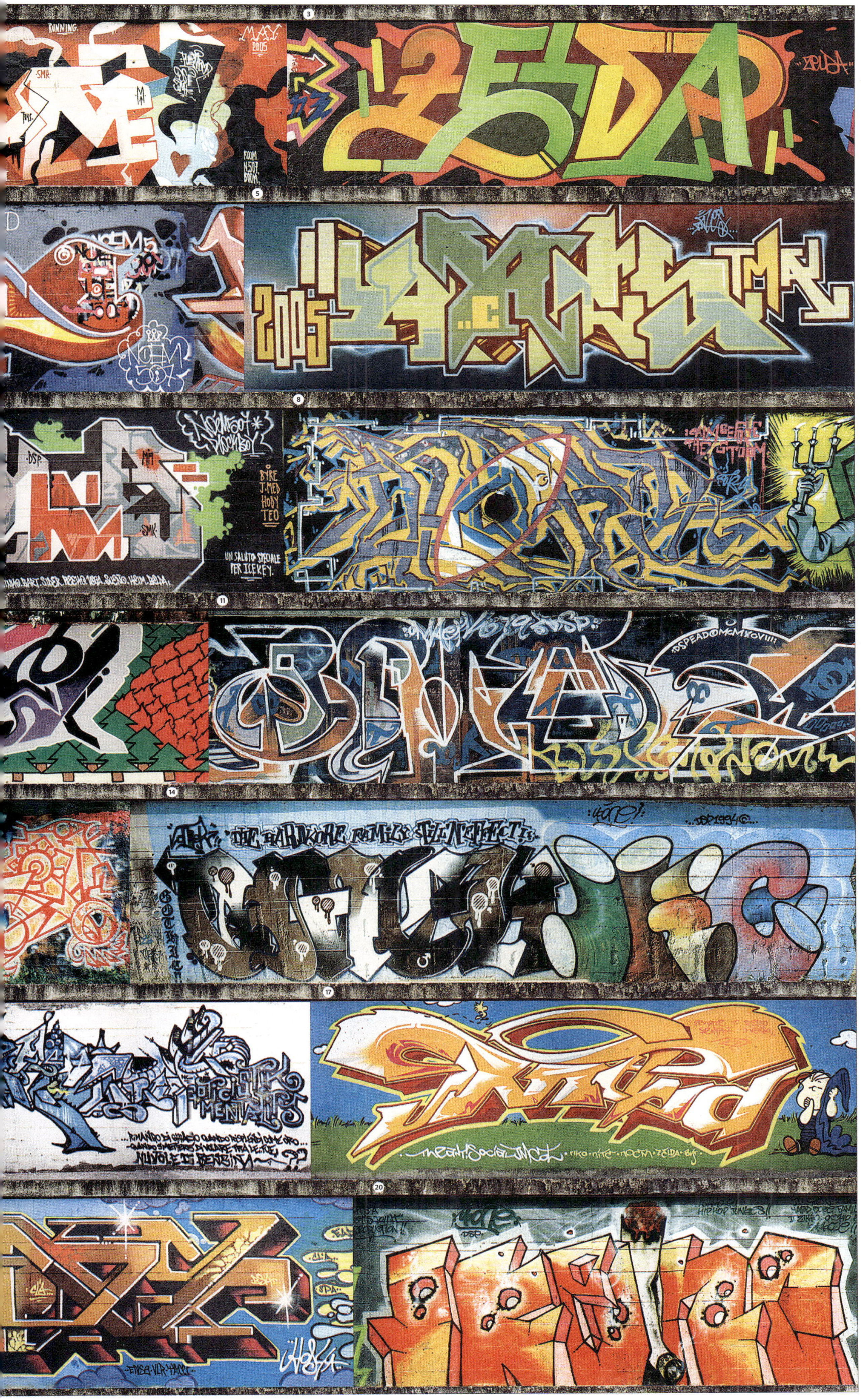

1 ZEST
2 NOEM 507
3 ZELDA
4 NOEM 507
5 ARES
6 NOEM 507
7 NOEM 507
8 BYR
9 HODY | ZELDA
10 C-UNO

11 DMAEK 193
12 NOEM 507
13 DMAEK
14 DMAEK | IKONE
15 NOEM 507
16 GOEVV
17 MED
18 BYR
19 HODY
20 IKONE

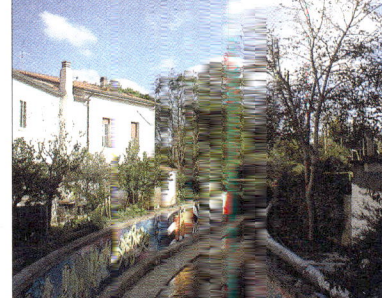

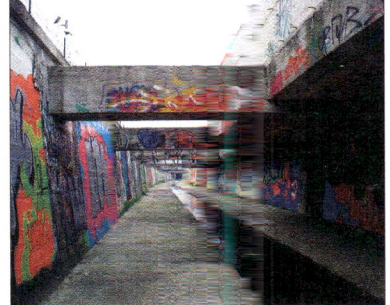

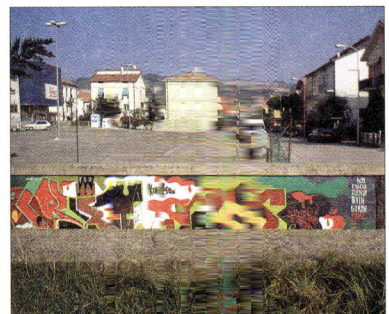

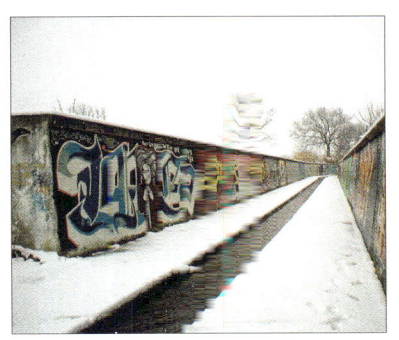

Storytellers
>

Open talk

Zelda
>

>CONTINUES FROM PAGE 253

quintessential writer or city crew, earning the respect and esteem of those who were just starting out. Given a certain period of incubation, in Pesaro the phenomenon literally exploded between 1991 and 1993 and a piece that is symbolic of that time for many of my generation was surely the puppet on a vespa scooter painted by Zinko, which was then re-baptised by everyone "la vespa di Zinko". When all the kids in the city started talking about this vespa I thought they meant Zinko had painted a real scooter and naively I would go around the city centre hoping to see it pass by! Then I found out it was a drawing painted in the old abandoned Colonie Marine buildings, an enormous structure from the Fascist era at the gates of the city, in the direction of Fano. This building represented a real forge for Writing in Pesaro, as well as a shelter for the many homeless that inhabited it. From that moment Zinko became a point of reference for me, he is a writer I remember with particular fondness and admiration. Apart from the historic pieces done in that hall of fame such as "Navicella spaziale" or "Scribbles" along the track line, his presence in Pesaro was felt through tags and bombings. His tags, even with different names such as Dynamo, Onesin or Lupen, were simple and easily legible, with clean lines given by the gold Bac cap that allowed you to distinguish and easily remember them: the right tags in the right places. In those years the desire to emulate him was so strong on the part of many toys that an enormous amount of tags beginning with the letter Z started proliferating throughout the city, like Zakoo, Zade, Zmeik. This was considered the sickest letter you could choose as an initial for your name, but it was also equally bitch-ass to draw, as I soon found out, after the initial euphoria. Yeah well the origin of my name also obviously wasn't tied to other reasons!

Ikone
>

WILD PIECES

When I was 16-17 years old, the most thrilling moment for me was discovering that the city was no longer a remote entity, dominated and controlled by unknown forces, something I traversed as an outsider, home- school- bar- home. We discovered that together, we could dominate it, we could take possession of every corner and mark it as our own, we could finally be protagonists and transform it into a giant work of art signed by us. What euphoria, an epic feeling. The

problem was, at times my omnipotence complex caused me to overlook the people who had dominated this city before me: the police, or worse - gangs. More than once, I risked being clobbered due to a naiveté worthy of Buster Keaton, to the point where people wondered if I was crazy for writing "What's that?! DSP kings!" next to a mural by Gregory from GruppoBlando: "But it sucked!"... It took me a while to realise the risks I ran, and the meaning and value (aesthetically speaking as well) of those wild pieces.

Omaek 193
>

BONES BRIGADE

Now that I think about it, growing up in the 80's with skateboarding and graffiti was no big deal, it was almost a cliché of troublemakers in the small city of Pesaro and Villa San Martino, a neighbourhood in the outskirts. The skate shop was the meeting spot for most of the first generation writers, all of them were considered outcasts, including me and Zinko, but we were privileged since we were already in our own territory. Zinko was an utterly reckless kid, completely incapable of understanding the repercussions of his actions, and I followed suit. He was the best big brother ever and I hope he feels the same about me. Our first real graffiti piece was *Bones*, an homage to Powell and Peralta's Bones Brigade, the first big illegal coloured piece with no compromises, a few metres of letters filled in with Max Meyer paint we had bought at the hardware store, strictly red, blue, and green. Technically it was all Zinko's, I just helped fill in with blue paint - it kept dripping -, but we were together, with our skateboards nearby ready to flee. Spots for painting and time to do it in were limited, underground garages in the afternoon, factory walls on Sunday morning, Saturdays spent painting our masterpiece on a soggy wall under the bridge, with our feet in the mud and the Carabinieri who would stop and chat when they passed by. Kids with spraycans under a bridge in the city's outskirts weren't a problem, the problems in those days were politics - the Brigate Rosse were out and about - and drugs - heroin during the AIDS epidemic -. Graffiti was still emerging, especially in the city outskirts, kids still tagged with Uni Posca markers, DSP had yet to become that uncontrollable phenomenon it was, and the city didn't know us yet, it didn't hate us yet. I don't know about other cities, but all that mattered to us was the beauty of the letter. Once you found a good letter, you'd work around it. My first good letters formed *Arth*, which meant nothing but I did it all the same, with six white spray cans on a cement wall that was like a sponge. Perhaps it's just an impression, but in Pesaro we didn't want one uniformed style like many other cities seemed to have, we all wanted to be

unique. We searched for a personal style that could distinguish us from others, that's the only way we were alike. My aesthetics were sacrificed to the symbols I attempted to integrate into letters or represent through them. Even though I eventually stopped focusing on the beauty of the letter itself, I still considered letters the foundation of a construction that may have been ugly, but had to be erected.

J-Med
>

THE RAIL LINE

Of all the post-DSP writers, I think Neil and I are the only ones who got started without having seen their pieces. It was the beginning of 1991, we were kids, the world we explored from the seats of our bikes didn't extend past the boundaries of our neighbourhood, Pantano.
In Pantano you could see graffiti by *Spray-Master* and *GruppoBlando*, but nothing by DSP. The walls of the park near the stadium that were painted by GruppoBlando, the dominating crew of that area, sparked our interest. On those same walls, in an empty corner, we did our first piece at lunchtime, after school, taking turns as lookout. We imitated the letters found in *Skate* magazine that Neil had bought since he was trying his hand at skating.
We had no idea what a tag was - so we never signed -, nor what Writing was, much less what Hip Hop was, we ignored the presence of other graffiti in the city and we couldn't care less about how the

We suddenly noticed the increase in marks around the city, and we realized that the ones we liked best seemed to be made by the same hand.

phenomenon had reached our neighbourhood; we were just thrilled by the fact that we could do it, that walls could become enormous blank canvases, that we could colour and modify the city; a notion that always stuck with me, which is why I preferred walls to trains or other surfaces. Our first encounter with DSP was visual: "Mamma" by Zmit (Ikone), an illegal white and red piece, we had no idea such high-quality work was possible as we'd never seen anything like it before.
We suddenly noticed an increase in the marks left in the city and realised that the ones we liked best seemed to be made by the same hand. We were more interested in the 'how' than the 'who', because after weeks of attempts - even with other classmates -, we weren't able to achieve significant improvement. Then we finally met the creators of those masterpieces in

person, and we learned about Bac, Talken, Dupli-Color, particular codes and dynamics, all about this awesome world.
We looked at the older, more experienced, and more talented guys with more than respect, it was almost a sense of fear, also due to their rather rigid behavior. DSP gave nothing away, even the disclosure of their 'secrets' was rationed. I recall we eagerly eavesdropped as they often spoke about "the rail line" without fully understanding what it meant, they merely told us it was a wall between Pesaro and Fano where they often went. That was more than enough to incite us to hop on our bikes and go out in search of it. After 5 kilometers - that felt like 500 - we were about to give up and go home when I saw some colour on the

What struck me most was that even though they had also just begun, they already had a well-defined style. At that point, I needed to be a part of it

upper part of a wall that ran alongside the tracks. I climbed down - it was slightly below street level - and started shouting for the others. We had found it! I recall the joy of that venture, of that discovery, of the beauty that appeared before my eyes, as if it were yesterday.
Nothing we'd seen before could measure up to the rail line. After the initial frenetic visual feast, we stopped to compare some of the pieces, viewing them from various distances to determine which were better, but it was no easy task. If a train had passed it would have run over these kids with astonished smiles and glistening eyes! That place immediately had a special meaning to me, and it still does. Nostalgic, it hurt me to see it handed off to other writers I deemed unworthy or to see it raped with impunity by the silver spray paint of the new generations. Even in 2002, when Zelda and I decided to create a roller piece that could be seen from the trains and the beach, I decided to do it on a wall that was far from the 10-year-old pieces, far from that historic spot that was 'magical' to me.

One day a classmate comes up to me and

Zest
>

LEGS SHAKING

says: "Want to do graffiti with me?", and I said yes. The problem was I didn't have the slightest idea what graffiti was.
My friend introduced me to a writer from Rimini: Spyke, my first mentor. In fact it was him that explained, with endless patience, the world of graffiti to me.

It was 1991, and on that day my life completely changed. From then on I began to look around and discover the city was different. I began to observe all vertical surfaces, I studied, analysed, and discarded various styles. Us writers of the post-DSP generation were lucky: we had been imprinted by the best. I'll never forget the turquoise tags by Desy (Ikone), the vermillion throw-ups by Noem, and the black faces by Zinko. What struck me most was that even though they had also just begun, they already had a well-defined style. At that point, I needed to be a part of it. Me and my friend founded N.P.S. (*New Power Street*) and we immediately started searching for alter egos. I picked Bad Taste and he picked Ycekey; which then became Icekey (R.I.P.). One more person joined us: Dr. Stein. Kick-ass name, if you ask me.

I stole it from him later on, but he never noticed. I'd go pick up Icekey at 6 am and we'd spend an hour tagging the city centre. Then we hit the bus to Urbino. My tags were horrible, his were better.

It was 1992 and we had no work under our belts, no murals, nothing. Icekey suggested we do a Bart Simpson character saying "Yo man" - they'd just started airing *The Simpsons* on TV. We argued. I told him that if we wanted to start right we needed to start with our own sketch. After that, I recall we spent entire afternoons drawing at my house. We came up with an idea and did it. Our first wall was on the rail line, a long wall that ran alongside the tracks and the sea. A truly amazing place, still to this day. Timidly, we asked the members of DSP for permission, since it was their territory. Much to our surprise, they agreed. We bought five Talken spray cans and stole two gold Bac caps. The night we painted our piece, everyone was there: DSP, FLY crew, Anthea, Mees, and all of our friends, plus a writer from Milan. It was a real rite of initiation. My legs were shaking, whereas Icekey was good and ready. Our finished piece was the most beautiful thing I had ever seen. I clearly remember that the ride back home on our bicycles was silent. I

The "new generation" was considered a threat. We had to earn their respect doing as much damage as possible elsewhere

kept staring at my hands, stained by that beautiful blue paint. Then Icekey broke the silence and said "I think it came out good..." He barely finished his sentence when I said "Damn, we just did graffiti!" He burst out laughing. My legs were still shaking. From then on things constantly evolved. I recall the afternoons spent at the beach camps doing graffiti and throw-ups. I dove head-first into painting, I was doing a piece a day.

I began hanging out with DSP crew. My ego was fulfilled. Omek (who became Omaek 193) was part of that crew, I painted my first legitimate piece with him. It was on a wall at the beach, and if I'm not mistaken it was done during the winter. He wrote Omek. Needless to say, he killed it. He used other tones with endless 3D effects that I'd never seen in my life.

Mine was a Zest piece with stone-like effect and 3D copied from Omek. From a distance, our two pieces made quite an impression - his did from up-close too -. Our lookouts were Vega and Sueno from SMK, the entire time they were spying on a couple that was fucking in a car. I became part of SIP together with Zinko, Omek, and Ice Dyno, I did my best to keep up with them. Ikone and I founded TVE (*The Vaginal Explorers*), the crew I'm proudest of. The crew's rule was to only paint surfaces with wheels: trains, trucks, vans, and excavators. Awesome. We had a blast. And then there were a series of crews that sprung up and died, to the point that having a crew made no sense anymore. Noem told me that first and foremost, a crew had to be a group of friends, and since my friends were all rebels, it seemed like the perfect setup: we could each do what we wanted with whomever we wanted.

My style never reached a peak in maturity, it was just a display of technique and an imitation of other styles. That's how I liked it. I carried on with small personal challenges and set objectives for myself like: "PCP crew uses dark colours as the base and then shades with lighter colours like with oil paints, let's see if I can do that too..." Or: "Can I apply complex, contrasting colours to my lettering?". Pure and utter fun.

In 1992, I became intrigued by those

Byr
>

BLOOD, SWEAT AND PAINT

---

strange letters I kept seeing appear on walls. They had nothing to do with the usual political or football-related slogans, they were symbols that indicated group affiliation, exclusive criminal organisations I wanted to belong to at any cost. I started imitating those strange letters on paper, then in March of '93, together with two friends from school, we formed NSA (*New School in Action*) and that summer, I did my first real coloured piece.

During that time, I also became part of Zelda's crew, he was the only person I hung out with in the outskirt neighbourhood I lived in. The dominant crew was clearly DSP, the mother of us all.

The age difference between me and them was rather slight, but the difference in quality and quantity was astronomical. We were rookies and they made it clear to us. Noem 507 once told me: "You are what you do. If you don't do shit, you are shit". He was right. But it wasn't easy back then to work your way up: we weren't allowed to paint in a lot of places because they were DSP's territory... The 'new generation' was considered a threat.

We had to earn their respect doing as much damage as possible elsewhere. Their opinion about our work was important to us. Back then, they were like a mini-regime that controlled everything with military force. Unfortunately, it was impossible to outdo them because they were too fucking talented, each one better than the next. In '94 NSA broke up, me and Zelda changed the crew's name to ADR (*Apologia di Reato/Another Deformed Reality*) and shortly later Lego from Rimini, and Done from Cesena joined our crew.

About two years later the crew broke up

due to a sort of inertia. I began writing more and more and in '96 I developed an entirely personal style I defined "tripnotic", based on the idea of not making aesthetically pleasing designs, but rather complicating the understanding of the piece with letters that were filamentous, almost organic, incredibly knotted up.

We weren't allowed to paint in a lot of places because they were D.S.P's territory...

A style that was blatantly enigmatic, symbolic, and hard to decipher.

Furthermore, it minimised the need for sketches - later on to be completely eliminated -, I only used them to finalise the intertwining of letters or to have a rough idea of the piece, but the majority of it was freestyle. ADR was my first 'real' crew, later I decided I didn't want to belong to any crew at all.

Being a 'free spirit' allowed me to paint with everyone without being tied to one group in particular. From 1996 to 2001 - the year I decided to quit -, I painted incessantly with Hody from Cattolica, Enko from Riccione, and JMed and Zest from Pesaro. I'd say I definitely closed the circle when, for a rather long period of time, I painted assiduously with Omaek and his 193 styles, and Noem 507: the guys who, more than anybody else, inspired me to start Writing back then. We spent lots of time doing huge coloured murals and throw-ups we were the first crew in our city to do entire walls of throw-ups with silver and black in inverted roles; meaning we used black to fill in and silver to outline. Even though we belonged to different worlds and had very different styles, the three of us were joined by the desire to not only do pieces with letters that were more or less stylish, but to give the world a piece of us that indelibly commemorated that period or a specific day. We gave it our all: blood, sweat, and paint!

It's odd that even though 15 years have

Vega
>

CONTENDING THE CITY

---

passed, I still view the people I painted with in Pesaro in the same light as when we were writers. I'm neither a romantic nor a freak who can't adapt to changes, but my experience as a vandal is the only thing I really contributed to society. That is why graffiti was so important. I'm not sure if you can understand me, with your photos organised into folders on your computer: New York, Paris, black pieces and silver pieces, trains, etc... I'm not criticising you for this because we are all the product of our own eras, and perhaps the emotions I felt back then while writing are what you feel now while doing other things - like bombing a police headquarters wall on Second Life. Nowadays there aren't many opportunities - and there weren't back then in 1992 either - to put a young man to the test: only people in poor countries usually go to war, and

adventure has been ch...own by GPS, distant spots have bec...oser through Ryanair. Our world ...ad', it's just profoundly inhuman ...grammed to handle communities ...e rather than single individuals: ci...en immigrants, Catholics, queers, int... the silent minorities, crowds... ...e overpopulated, poorly organise... on the verge of stupid. But with gr...in 30 minutes you knew who you were... here do you paint? What do you ...it? How do you paint? What risks are ... ...ning tonight? Illegality puts you to the... est. You start over from square one ...no acquired rights, with no mone...daddy, with no qualifications.

It's a completely new ...where your worth is based on wh...re and what you do. That's how i...for us writers. Our society has forgot...that we're animals: we're drown...Marxism, the myth of equality and ...ulturalism. We marked walls wit... paint like lions mark their terr... et it? That's not exactly what the A...ador of Integration and Global A...s would like to hear, but it's true. We...re real. As I said: I still feel the same... t the people I painted with in Pes... the guy who had talent but was w... the guy who was good and got luck... nobody, the guy who quit writing af... three weeks and bought himself a... guitar, the coward. I realise this i...thy, times have changed, and is ye...ter, many of us writers are happily int...ted in society as architects, lawye... ...e workers... So maybe I should sta... ...dering other aspects of these peopl... s, but I just can't. I still see these p...the friends they used to be. For ex... here's a guy I know who is now a...ful, intelligent business man that I r...into every now and then at soph...Left-wing artsy cinema events... ...fortunately for me, he'll always be...y who was never able to do more... three twirls of a windmill. There wa... ...er guy who clashed with the cops...beaten up but was still standing. We... touch for years, then one day I...o visit him at the hospital and we...d the same primitive smell as wh...vere kids. I shouldn't be saying t... ...ings because it's not healthy. It... make sense to respect someone j...cause they had the most tags in t... or despise someone because they...ainted illegal pieces under bridge... outskirts of

Illegality puts you t...est. You start over from...e one with no acquired rig...vith no money from dad...

the outskirts... But tha... it is! Thanks to graffiti, I saw the ...de of many people, I saw what wa...d the narcosis of the men in grey...beyond the conventions of this soc...ere nobody is denied anything

I was lucky, I got to pe...r the wall, and now I know the...know what really counts in life: tw...arms, loyalty to friends, and havi... in any and all situations.

ANCONA

Re–inventing the city
>

A private playground

Zart
>

The landslide of 1982 provides a golden opportunity for the writers of Ancona

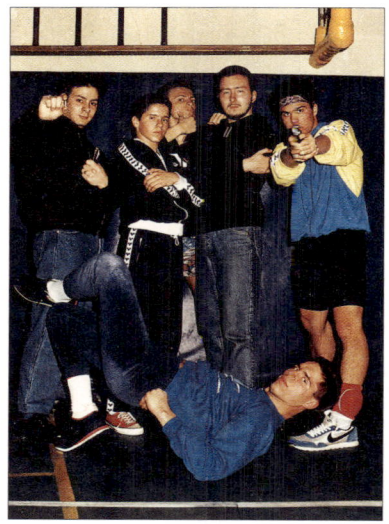

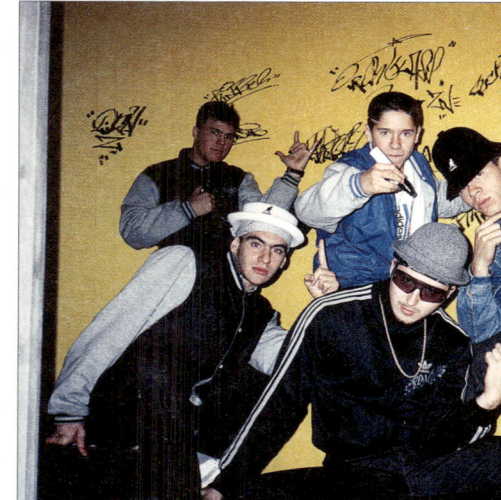

Local B–boys, 1985   – Zart

The first writers to be active in the city of Ancona were part of a B–boy group formed by Nasty, Nick and his brother Lil' Fly, who have been dancing since 1983 and were well known within the Italian Breaking scene. They would meet up at the Luna Ballerina gym located in the Del Piano area of Ancona.

In that period the first Zulu parties were being organised, and though at the time no more than fifty people would attend, it was in any case a way to meet others. It was at such parties that we got in touch with kids from outside, like Zero-T and Nicola JC from Florence. At an Afrika Bambaataa concert with Iron I met Massimo Colonna and Scacio. We also got in contact with the guys in Pesaro, thanks

> I started getting interested in graffiti thanks to a mythical local figure that fascinated every teenager, Tom Tattoo, a tattooist that had been in the U.S.A and wrote "Hip Hop"

to Carlo DC Ace. A few of his pupils would later form DSP and one day, at Arnold's sandwich stand, would ask me to go painting with them and join their crew. I often went to Pesaro's hall of fame, we did various pieces there, without ever managing to take pictures however cause I would return to Ancona the same night. Generally connections were made at the exit of Zulu parties, especially in the summer: many of these events were being organised in Rimini where people would come from all over Italy.

In Ancona I started getting interested in graffiti thanks to a mythical local figure that fascinated every teenager, Tom Tattoo, a tattooist that had been in the U.S.A and wrote "Hip Hop" on a little wall next to the Duomo of Ancona, done only with a black outline. It was the early 80's and to imitate him I also started writing phrases and naïve designs on walls. This was also done without even knowing about the

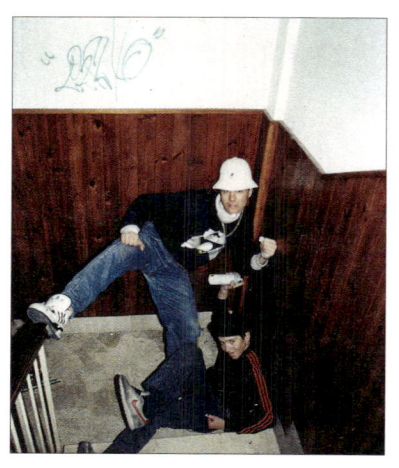

Zart and Lil' Fly   – Zart

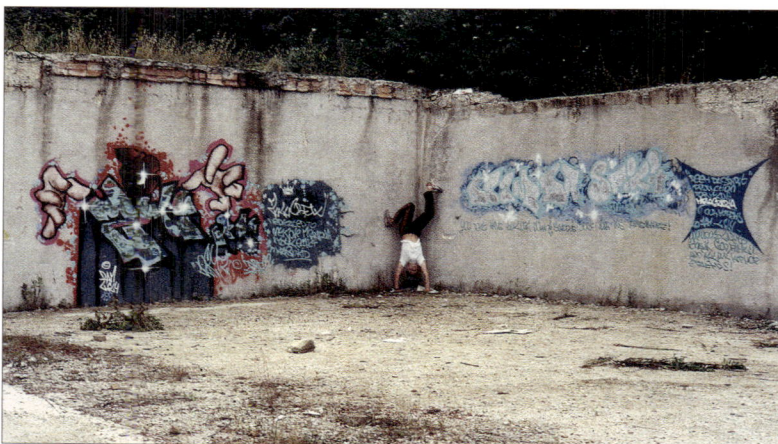

Posatora, the foundations of the geriatric hospital   – Zart

Hip Hop movement and with what I saw on skating fanzines as the only reference. I did a fluorescent yellow and green piece with the word "Pigs" and some arrows pointing outwards.

When I met Damage, who was also into graffiti, he became my first Writing partner and we formed a duo. My first serious piece in black and white was along a street in the Tavernelle neighbourhood, the night before its inauguration. In that period they were building all the connections between the industrial zones on the outskirts and the highway of Ancona. Our first hang-outs were inside the city, the Corso and the Galleria, a convenient place because when it rained you were sheltered. We would all meet up there: we'd

talk about Metal or Punk music, but you could also dance because there was a little bit of flooring in beautiful marble. Skaters used to go there as well.

In parallel to these sporadic episodes, distributed without a precise logic throughout the city, the first generation of writers in Ancona had their base in an abandoned area, Posatora.

At the time I was 12 or 13 years old and together with Damage I started hanging around that ghost quarter of the city, that had once risen on top of the hills but was completely destroyed in 1982 due to a landslide. Half of the neighbourhood slid towards the sea: the Hospital of Oncology and Geriatrics also disappeared, leaving only the foundations and some walls of

the garage at the ground floor, which became the perfect surface for our private hall of fame. The first time we entered Posatora was in the middle of winter and it was ice cold, we found shelter in some evacuated apartments and the first pieces we painted were indoor, on the walls of the abandoned landing.

Then when summer arrived we started painting the crumbling surfaces of the foundation: sure, it wasn't a very visible spot, but it could be easily reached, you just climbed over the gate and painted.

For us it was like a playground without rules, more dangerous but much more fun. In that dilapidated quarter of the city we created our teenage metropolitan fantasies.

DRUGO
Not a lot of time went by before
I started tagging Drugo '74, the
Name some friends to whom
I always spoke of *A Clockwork
Orange* had started calling me

BLAST
Between '93 and '94 we started
noticing that in certain cities
neighbouring the Adriatic coast,
other individual writers were doing
the same thing

DAMAGE
In the early 90's seeing a tag in
the city was like sighting a rare
animal in the forest, the scene
was just starting and even though
there were very strong stylistic

influences coming from Europe,
these experiences were living their
original, rugged and pure phase

Direct experience

Damage
>

> CONTINUES FROM PAGE 253

strong stylistic influences coming from Europe, these experiences were living their original, rugged and pure phase. This is when I started giving a meaning to what I was writing on the walls of the commercial neighbourhood Palombare, where I would spend entire nights in the streets, deserted once the warehouses closed. From Palombare I then moved to tagging and bombing other parts of the city, meeting other writers like Zart, and increasing my knowledge of the movement by observing the works of Dayaki and Zero-T, or the flyers of the Barcelona Disco in 1989. I remember the road trips to Rome with the newly formed MT2, Crash Kid (R.I.P.), the parties organised in Rimini and the first trains I hit with Cool5 in a deposit on the seafront, an area known for the presence of transexual prostitutes.

We didn't have a driver's license yet so at dawn we would wait for the bus along with them: we would sit down and observe each other, they were intrigued by our dirty clothes and our jangling backpacks. In those years the first Italian writers could be recognised by their Invicta backpack covered with tags; you could hear them arrive from a distance, with all that ruckus the spray cans make when you move!

Blast
>

One of the first traces of spray paint in Ancona was by Tom Tattoo at the beginning of the 80's, when he returned from a trip to New York and wrote "Hip Hop" on a fairly visible wall of the city. Those words will remain one of the few isolated cases until the end of the 80's, when Zart initiates the phenomenon of

Writing in the city. Even though I didn't know much about it in those years, I couldn't help but notice the tags and pieces on the walls of cities I would visit with my parents, like Berlin, Copenhagen, and Paris. I remember when we went to see the Berlin Wall, completely covered in Writing, it was the first time I say every single piece on that long coloured wall. Incited by this enthusiasm, as soon as I got home I started writing my Name on the streets of Ancona, together with Elel and Lilfly, one of the most authentic writers.

It was during this period, in the early 90's, that the first crews started forming in Ancona; first Zart and Damage's DCP and some time later 3Spirits, which also included Cool5, a breaker of German origin that brought with him the Munich style and attempted to communicate it to the whole crew.

Between '93 and '94 ACT and ICS were formed, that would later become 365. At the same time we started noticing that in certain cities neighbouring the Adriatic coast, other individual writers were doing the same thing: in Pesaro Zart joined DSP, while Dayone and I moved to Rimini where we had often painted with Eron, Reoh, Spike and Rose between '92 and '94. Almost all of us were concentrating on doing large coloured walls and only in 1992 did we start noticing train stations. Eron, Rok, Dayone, Reoh, Ryal, Tomak, and I entered the yard of Central Station for the first time, and it was full of immaculate trains. Ancona is unlike Rimini, Pesaro and Bologna, because it doesn't have a wall to paint along the rail line, but on the other hand that means you can enter the yard directly from the tracks without obstacles or barriers along the way. At this point the writers in Ancona divided into those that did trains and those dedicated to walls and halls of fame.

Because of Tangentopoli[1], the city was not lacking surfaces to paint, and the tolerant politics is why 90% of the writers preferred the large walls of the unfinished expressways to the risks of the yard; only a minority of us

chose trains and so until 2000 the scene remained pretty calm, no beef due to overcrowding in the yard. In this perfect situation, me, Pusher, Dash, Bois and Folse continued hitting one train after another, painting together with RE Vandals, one of the crews that was most present on this railway route during the middle of the 90's.

[1] or 'Bribesville', used to indicate the corruption-based system of politics in Italy during the 1980's and early 1990's.

Drugo
>

The pairing of two classes in the 11th grade of the Arts Institute I was attending was a real

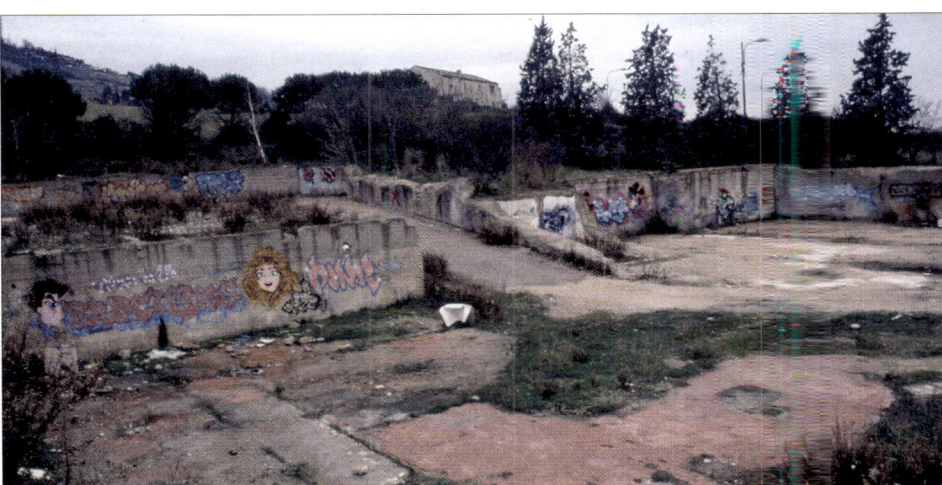

Posatora neighbourhood after the landslide of 1982 — *Blast*

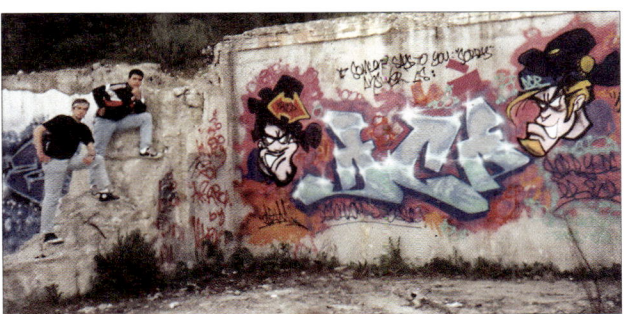

Zart and Damage next to the *DCP* piece — *Zart*

turning-point for me: I met Swift, with whom up until then I had at most only shared a smoke session at school. However being the kids we were, we became friends in a matter of minutes. He explained to me the meaning of the letters I would copy from the flyers of local parties and he spoke to me about this thing called Hip Hop, of the disciplines that it included.

He made me some tapes with the hottest shit of the moment and I played them on my broke-ass stereo in heavy rotation: N.W.A, 2 Live Crew, Run DMC, but also Isola Posse and Onda Rossa. Swift introduced me to his crew, 3 Spirit, which included Cool 5 and Rosky Race. From that moment we started skipping school, going to Rimini by train to jack rap records.

Not a lot of time went by before I started tagging Drugo '74, the Name some friends to whom I always spoke of *A Clockwork Orange*, had started calling me. Before choosing that tag, I had already written my Name on the walls of Ancona, but more than Writing those were the traces of my affiliation with a local hooligans football team.

The football hooligan movement and Hip Hop are so distant that it's difficult to find a motivation, I simply found myself sharing these two very separate passions, each with its own rules and code of conduct. Besides football, my 90's were shared with people from my city but mostly with the guys that came from the hinterlands of Marche or the cities close to the coastline; thanks to Elel in 1994 I met Oskie, and together with Estro, Korea and Crack became part of 3MW, the first crew to include kids from Ancona and also from Foligno. This same commixture of guys from different cities in a single crew happened again years later when I joined MG, a group that was formed in the second half of the 90's and was primarily focused on the trains running the line of the Eastern coast: from Ancona, Ascoli, and Bari. For years MG was the most active crew on the Riviera, with hundreds of train cars travelling up and down the Adriatic coast, embracing the mythology of the New York subway during the fabulous 70's.

Ancona Juice party

In the second half of the 80s, a large renovation project was programmed for the area between Via Flaminia and the East axis (in the Pinocchio, Tavernelle, and Colombara neighborhoods), which included new junctions connecting the city of Ancona with the A14 Ancona Sud highway. Unexpectedly, the works which began in the early 90s, were halted by the public prosecutor's office; investigations revealed irregularities in the bidding process during a period of wide-ranging judicial scrutiny against corruption in Italy, which was called "Tangentopoli".

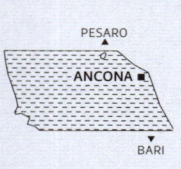

The area, where a viaduct was to be constructed leading to the highway entrance, was closed off for about 10 years, leaving the Tavernelle and Pinocchio neighborhoods unfinished.

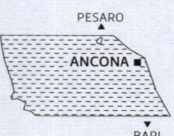

The first writers appropriated this court-seized area, making it their urban Hall of Fame, a linear continuum extending along the drivable infrastructures, all the way to the tunnels, which continued for hundreds of meters through the bowels of the hills. In order to paint the innermost sections, writers had to use flashlights. The route was about 600 meters long, with supporting walls and white surfaces that had been completely covered. It wasn't the first time infrastructures had been targeted: years before, beneath the bridge in the neighborhood that connected Tavernelle with Vallemiano, Lil'Fly and other local writers began occupying the foundations of these viaducts, painting the connecting pillars and beams. This action was a preview of what would happen years later when writers' expressive action was concentrated on surfaces, on the highways themselves.

In the mid 90s, the vector spanned by this highway was transformed into the fulcrum of all of Ancona's graffiti. Without delay, Buso, Drugo, and other local writers took advantage of the many "ghost neighbourhood" to organize one of Italy's most impressive jams: Juice. An unexpected and uncontrollable number of people, circa 3,000, showed up for the event.

An army of writers participated, covering the surrounding areas with tags, a direct and inevitable consequence of all of the first jams; the repercussions in the media were devastating. Not one single aspect of the event was highlighted or interpreted in a positive manner: Juice was one of the most prominent events ever; it managed to attract writers from all over Italy and Europe,

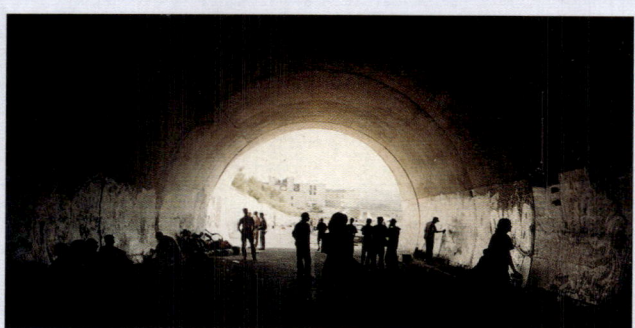

1 The Juice tunnel, 1995   — Blast

ready to display the esthetic value of their painted walls and also display the energy of an entire movement in full expansion. Yet, only a few newspapers focused on the open-minded nature of the city of Ancona, ready

to welcome such a large number of young people. Until then, the city council had shown signs of understanding; as a first concession, the city offered Galleria del Risorgimento - located in the center of Ancona – to anyone who wanted to paint, but it was never really used due to the heavy smog that hindered the paint from sticking to the walls. Subsequently, the situation further improved when the Q2 neighborhood council decided to allow street-level walls to be painted. Ancona is a city that begins at the port and extends toward the hills, where terraced land, sliced by drivable roads, characterize with their reinforced cement partitions, every residential neighborhood perched above the city.

For 10 years, these vertical containment surfaces, part of the infrastructure, were entirely painted, emphasizing how open-minded the city was.

Despite this, in the course of 10 years, territorial politics imposed a change of direction in regards to the previous concessions given to writers: graffiti slowly disappeared and the surrounding landscapes went back to looking out onto untouched reinforced cement walls.

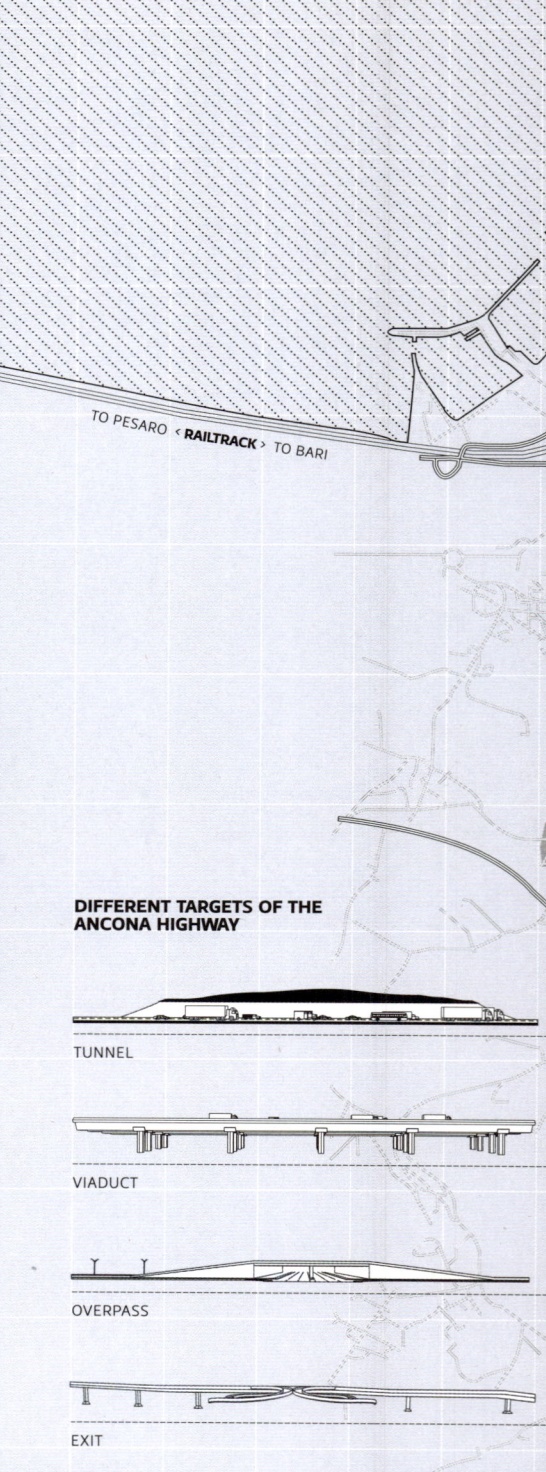

TO PESARO ‹ **RAILTRACK** › TO BARI

**DIFFERENT TARGETS OF THE
ANCONA HIGHWAY**

TUNNEL

VIADUCT

OVERPASS

EXIT

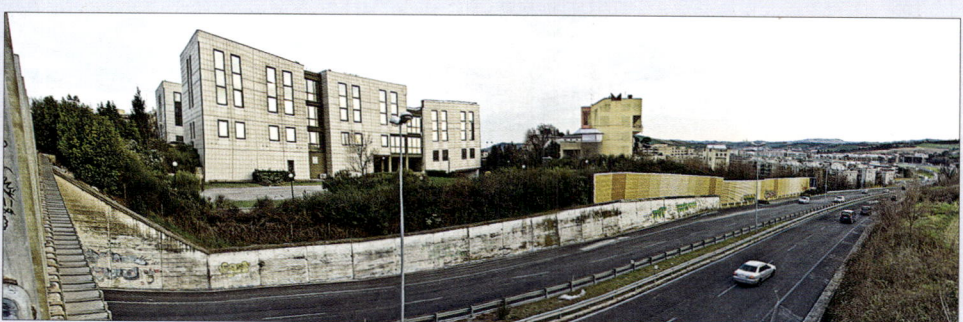

2 The Ancona highway in 2009   — Alessio Occhiodoro

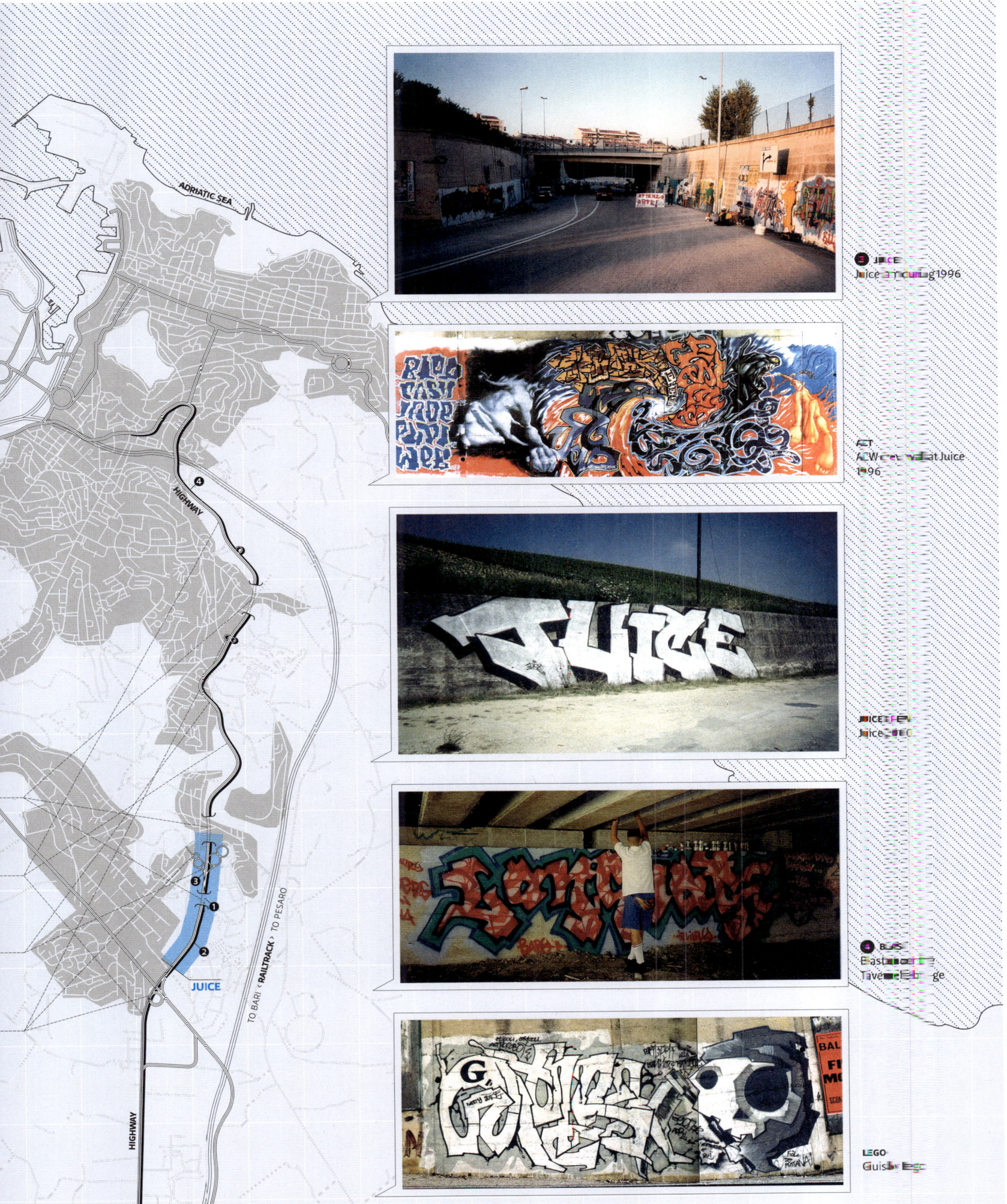

JUICE
Juice at crossing 1996

ACT
ACW crew wall at Juice
1996

JUICE FEV
Juice SEO

BLAS
Eastside ...
Tavernelle bridge

LEGO
Guislo Lego

BARI

If the kids are united

Giose
>

I n Bari the first kids to really get into
Writing came from the skating scene:
Move, Giose and Loco301, who can be
considered the first real writer of the city.
Everything started one afternoon skating
in the neighbourhood of Poggiofranco and
at the Santo Spirito Station, that would
later become the first two real spots of
the city. Between a trick and another we
would exchange sketches and draw pieces
with Uni-posca markers on the boards of
friends. The turning point was when Iave
arrived, a skater and writer from Vicenza
who explained the basic know-how of
Writing to everybody, and started talking
to us about mythological characters such
as Bando, Shoe, and a couple of national
legends such as Mace from Treviso.
At the eve of the 90's the little information that arrived came from the pages of
XXX Magazine, *Skate&Snowboard*, and *Uniform* notebooks, or the photos of *Subway
Art*. *XXX* and the other skate magazines
didn't consider the Hip Hop phenomenon
much, as it was still in a very early phase in
Italy, but a couple of pools and half-pipes
were painted and that 'scenography' was

> In the South of Italy any
> sub-culture was destined to be
> isolated from any information

enough to put our imagination to work.
Already the following year, in 1991, the
first crews of Bari gradually formed: Lo-
co301, Giose, Move and Iave became KNR
and soon later others followed; KMD, SRP,
FS and finally NCE, created through the
friendship between KNR and Creeda, and
Keba's rap group called Allarme Rosso.
NCE reunited the cream of the Bari crop of
the time, writers, breakers such as Electro
Smurfs, and Dj Argento.
The first convention of the city was organised at the social centre Fucine Meridionali, and it drew the likes of Sone
from Ostuni along with Wany and TSK
from Brindisi. Graffiti in Italy in that period was still closely tied to very politi-
cised contexts, like the radical Left, and
often colourful political messages would
be sprayed rather than personal tags;
when NCE and Kode started painting

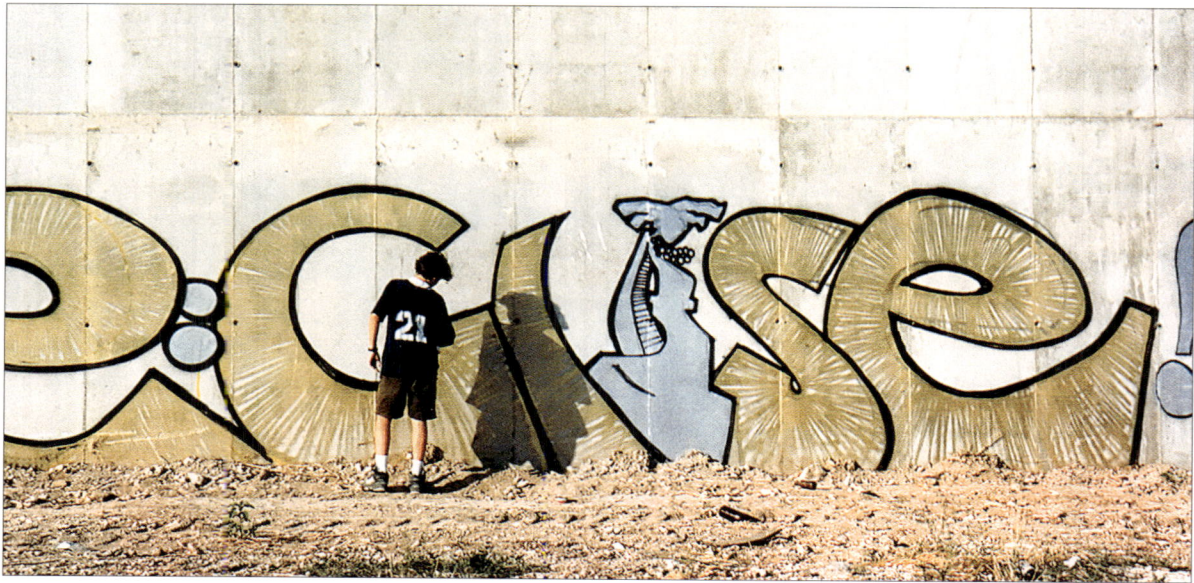

Giose – NCE, Bari, 1992

— Giose

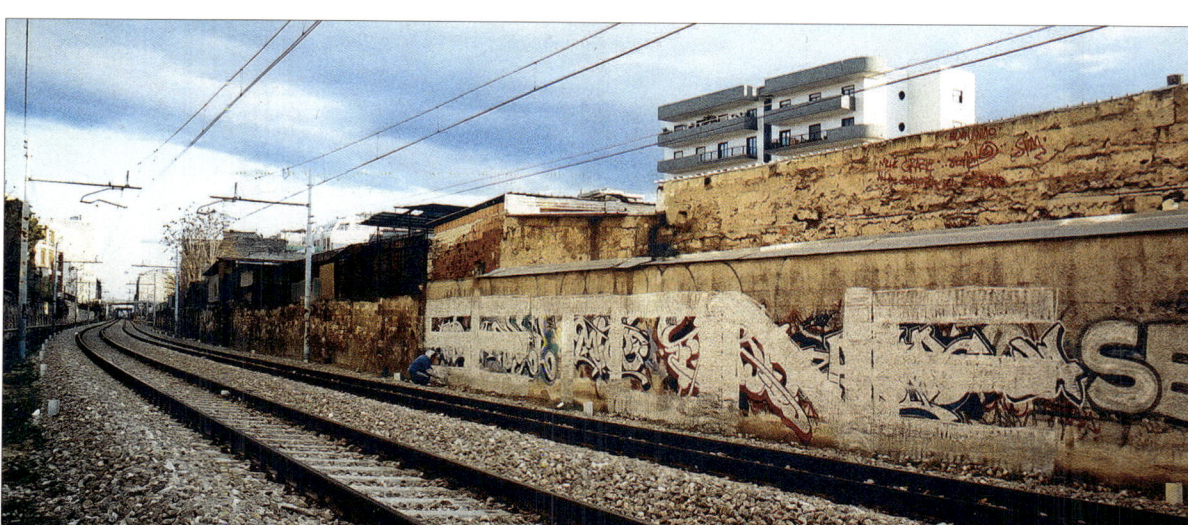

Setone, a blockbuster long the railway track line

— Giose

silver flops it turned into a controversy
with the social centre's organisation, who
were used to picturesque and coloured
backgrounds with strong political con-
notations. It was at the Fucine that the
contrast clearly emerged between those
that utilised Writing to communicate a
message and those that had adopted it as a
culture and were concentrating on style. I
remember hearing things like "This is not
Writing", "There has to be a message", or
some such bullshit. The context in which
Bari's Writing was developing was sterile

and lacking any reference points, in the
South of Italy any subculture was destined to be isolated from any information
and from the experiences of other people
belonging to it, but the one thing we had
understood from the zines and from *Subway Art* concerned the importance of a
Name, of choosing an alias and of slamming it in everyone's face, whether they
liked it or not.
Moreover, in the city of Bari Writing
wasn't a real concern for either police
or local authorities, there were so many

other forms of criminality to fight. This
allowed many pieces to stay up for a long
time, such as the enormous silver that
KNR did on the most important bank of
the main road of the city centre, which
remained intact for over a year, to our
surprise. The city's historical hall of fame
is in the railway station of Santo Spirito
and we would paint it in plain daylight,
nobody ever complained. From that moment on other kids started writing, such
as the guys in RNS: with Zoca, Mong,

> CONTINUES ON PAGE 280

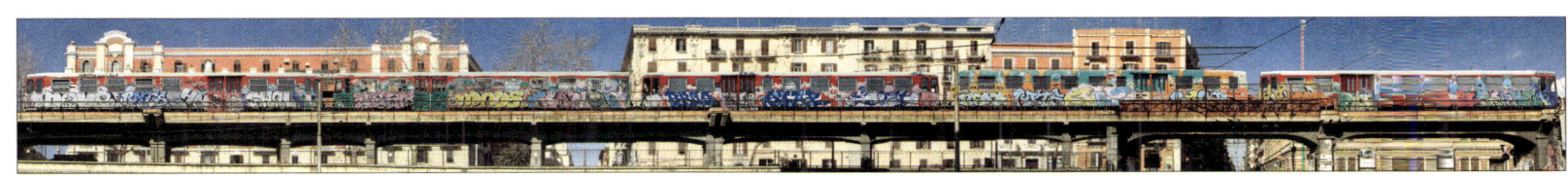

Remembering New York

Just
>

An anomalous railway line generating a distant photographic testimony, reminiscent of Martha Cooper's shots of New York

The Ferrovie Appulo-Lucane manage three railway lines that connect the region of Puglia with that of Basilicata, travelling through the Bari basin, the territory of Le Murge, and the Apennine valleys of Lucania. The old diesel trains working the line travel on tracks with a narrow rail gauge and carry a number of cars that is insufficient for the numerous passengers. The biggest inconveniences weigh on the commuters of the Bari tract that use, willy nilly, the F.A.L as a suburban line. In the last decades, the F.A.L, like other minor railways, have come to be considered by many as a dry branch of the line, to be substituted with more convenient buses. Only recently, with the reevaluation of local transport on iron and the plans for a subway line for Bari and its hinterlands, have the F.A.L gone back to thinking of their future on rail tracks. In the next few years they will probably become more efficient, comfortable, and less bankrupt, but with difficulty will they be able to maintain the atmosphere that several generations of kids from Lucania and Puglia experienced, the old rural stations that are now suppressed, the small red cars completely painted over by writers, the rudimental level crossings next to which plain brick walls bordered the fields. Although the Writing phenomenon was never the biggest problem of this railway line, starting in 2000 the first measures against graffiti were adopted, like the application of a white film on the old red cars so as to allow for a more immediate and efficient removal of spray paint. These heavily bombed old red trains had always represented a very sought-after target for the

> This portion of railway reminds of Martha Cooper's shots of the subway cars of New York

writers of the city and province of Bari, ever since '95-'96, when CDS and NZS - Code, Nudh and What- started to go to the Bari deposit. From there it only took a minute for NWC. Seto in particular, and HVS to start getting up on that line. Between '97 and '98 the East and Move were hitting it as well, followed by A'Left, TIE and 2AM, who have been systematically targeting F.A.L since 2002. In recent years white trains have increased in number, and painted trains have a very brief life span, in the best case they last a week. This is why many feel the need for an accurate photographic testimony, and if initially a few stolen night shots were sufficient, there was soon a switch to a more attentive study of the best angles. One of the favourite views from which to take photos is the elevated stretch that passes through the centre of the city, before ending at the station of Bari Centrale: even if for a brief distance this portion of railway reminds of Martha Cooper's shots of the subway cars of New York, as if all of a sudden a window on the past had been opened.

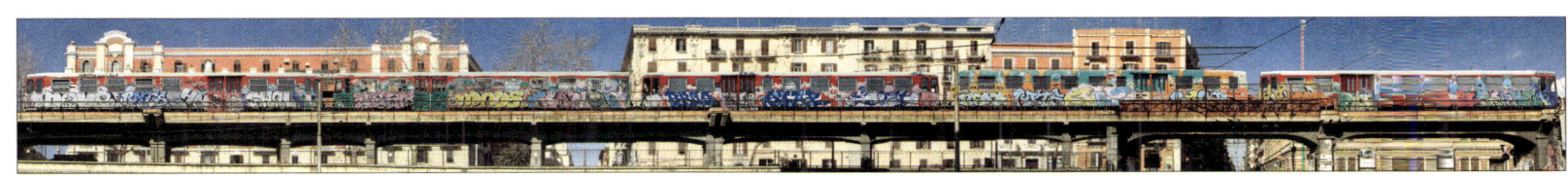

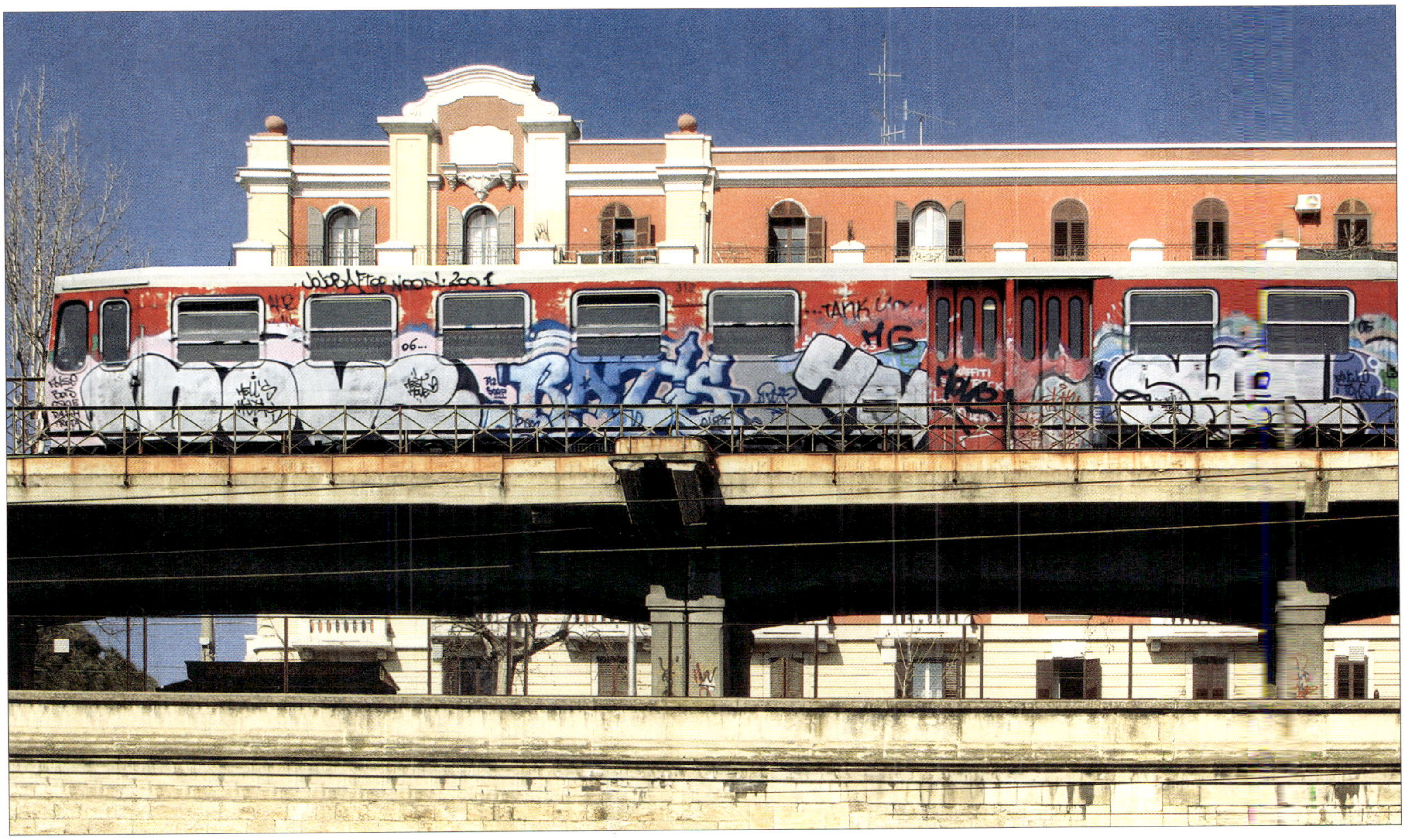

Move, Rats, Hv, Swal

— Just

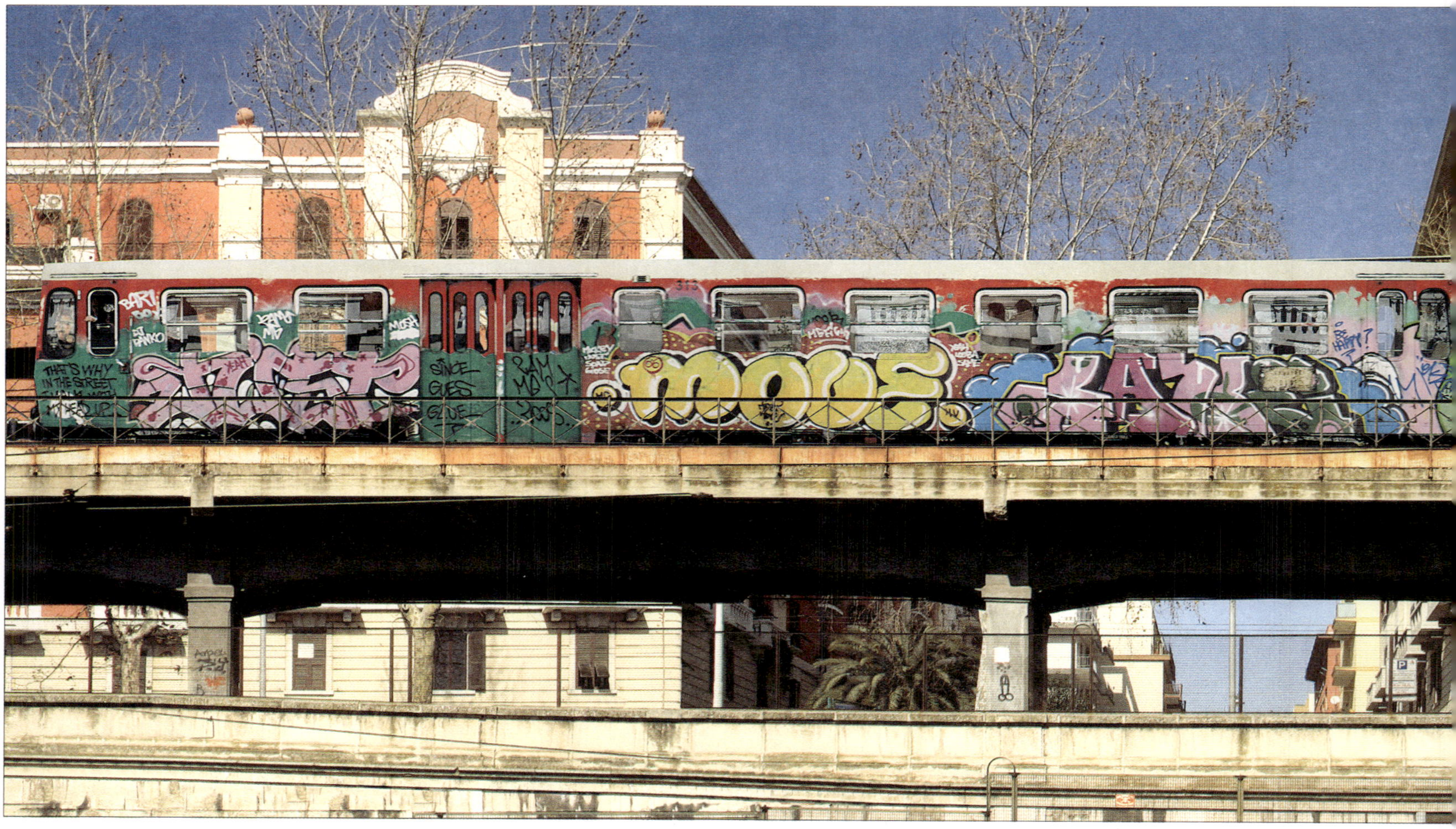

Just–MG   Move–HV   Jake AOD from Amsterdam

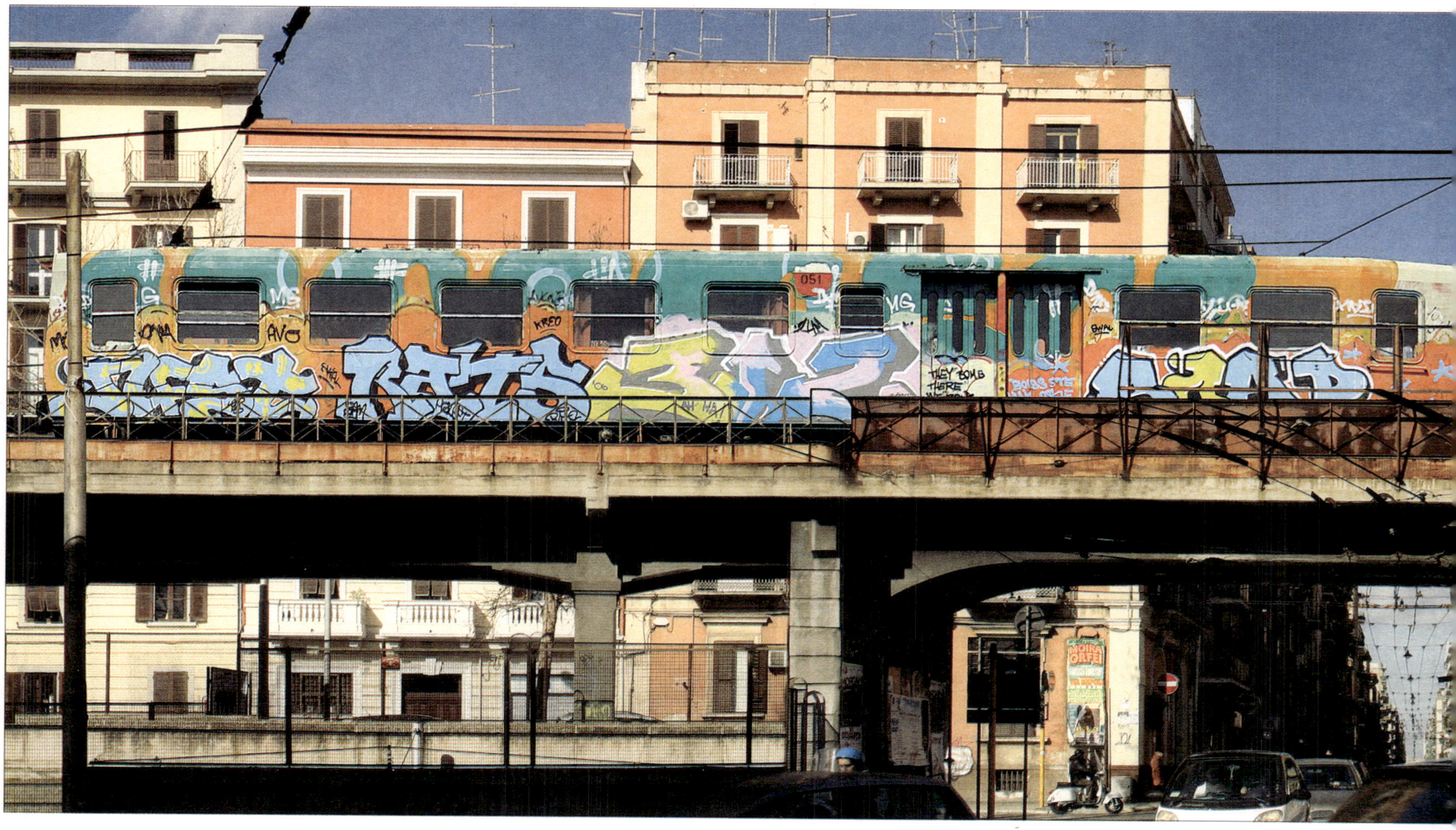

Just–MG   Rats   312 crew   Soap–MG

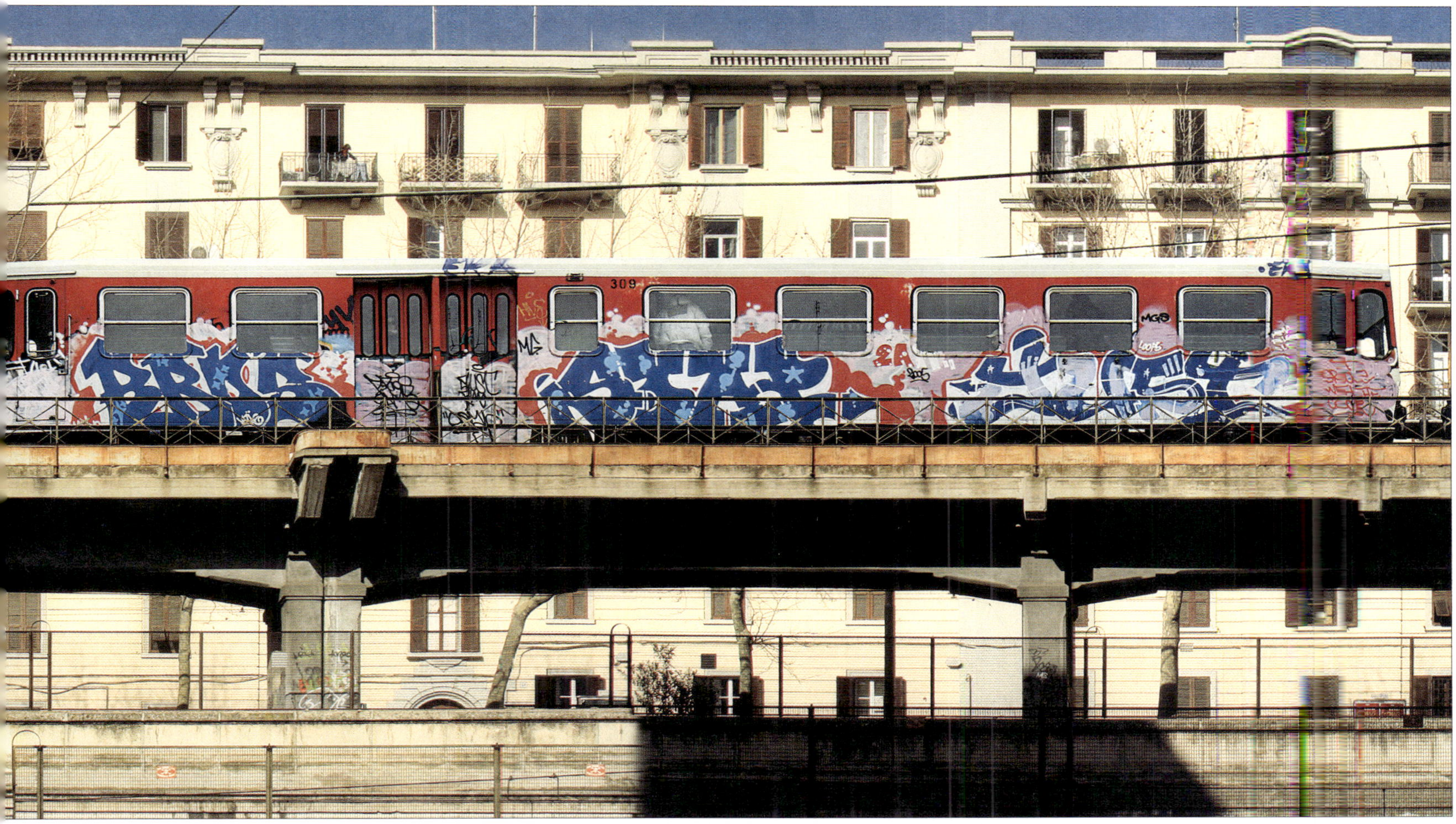

Bros–MG from Ancona   Soap–MG   Just–MG   —*Just*

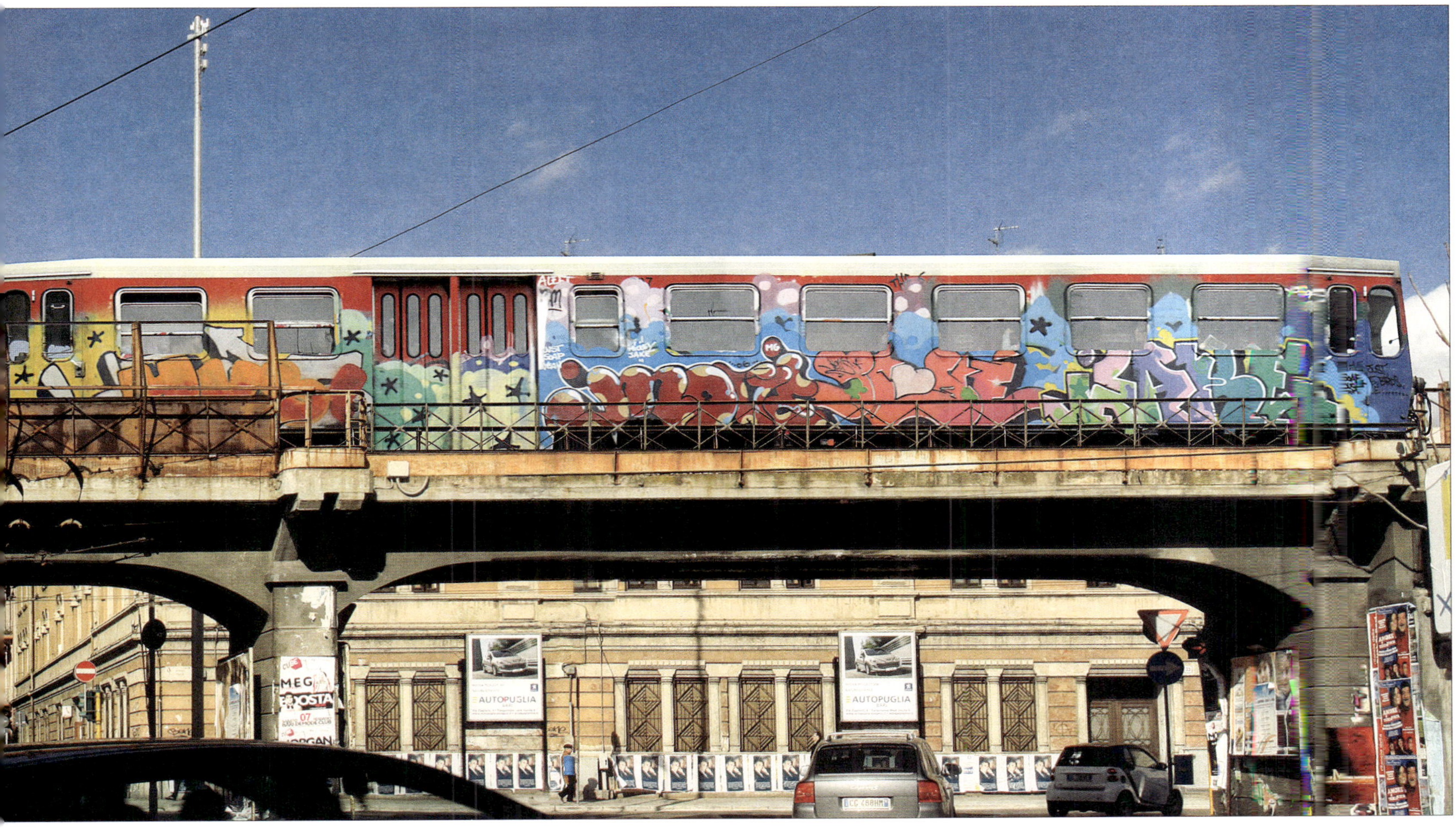

Move–HV   Giose–HV   .ake–AOD from Amsterdam   —*Just*

Puglia
>

Boundless Brindisi

Wany
>

The "Z's" of Zulu Nation started appearing all of a sudden all over Brindisi in the early 80's. Nobody knew what they meant or who the authors were. Teddy and Tony, the two brothers responsible for this aerosol raid, had recently moved to Brindisi from Paris, bringing with them the passion for a movement that was in full fervor in their hometown. Shortly after arriving to Brindisi they met Arturo, who had been studying and developing his Breakdance moves for a while. Teddy, later called King of the Family, his younger brother Tonasty and Arturo-Help, made Brindisi become one of the first Italian cities to be contaminated by the Hip Hop virus.

In the following years, until '89-'90, the city hosted numerous generations of B-boys, DJ's and writers; the tags and crews that left the strongest legacy are Positive Force, Fresh Kids, and TAA. Numerous were also the French writers and breakers to come to Brindisi, such as Frosty, Gaban, and JC, who, along with Teddy, did the first graffiti in the city. In those years life in Brindisi was still that of a harbour city of the South, in which half the population was dedicated to smuggling cigarettes, including each of the characters that have been cited above. The information regarding Hip Hop culture was close to none, based on word of mouth and not much else. Many writers didn't even have a tag, at most they used a nickname such as the ones that are often used in Southern Italy for certain types of families.

When they painted they didn't even take photos, it was just the Name of the crew or a message they wanted to leave for every passerby. At age 11 I started noticing that Bozzano, my neighbourhood, was one of the most heavily hit; I remember a graffiti with the word "Rane" written by Master Zombie and Bombi, whereas in the Sant'Angelo district, an unadvisable area to pass through both at night and during the day, Cioccolata aka Sud Star and others had occupied an abandoned nursery school close to the project houses/parking lots where I lived.

That nursery school became a gym in which breakers could practice and Sud Star had his own personal room in which to try his moves out alone, those moves charged with an instinctive ferocity, the same ferocity that would characterise not only his style of Breakdancing, which reached the highest levels of power moves, but also his style of life, that would see him get involved in crime, loose both his brothers and encounter numerous problems with the law. Fights and stolen scooters were daily events even in front of the church, which was a historic hang-out for writers who would meet up there and chill until it was dark enough to go out painting.

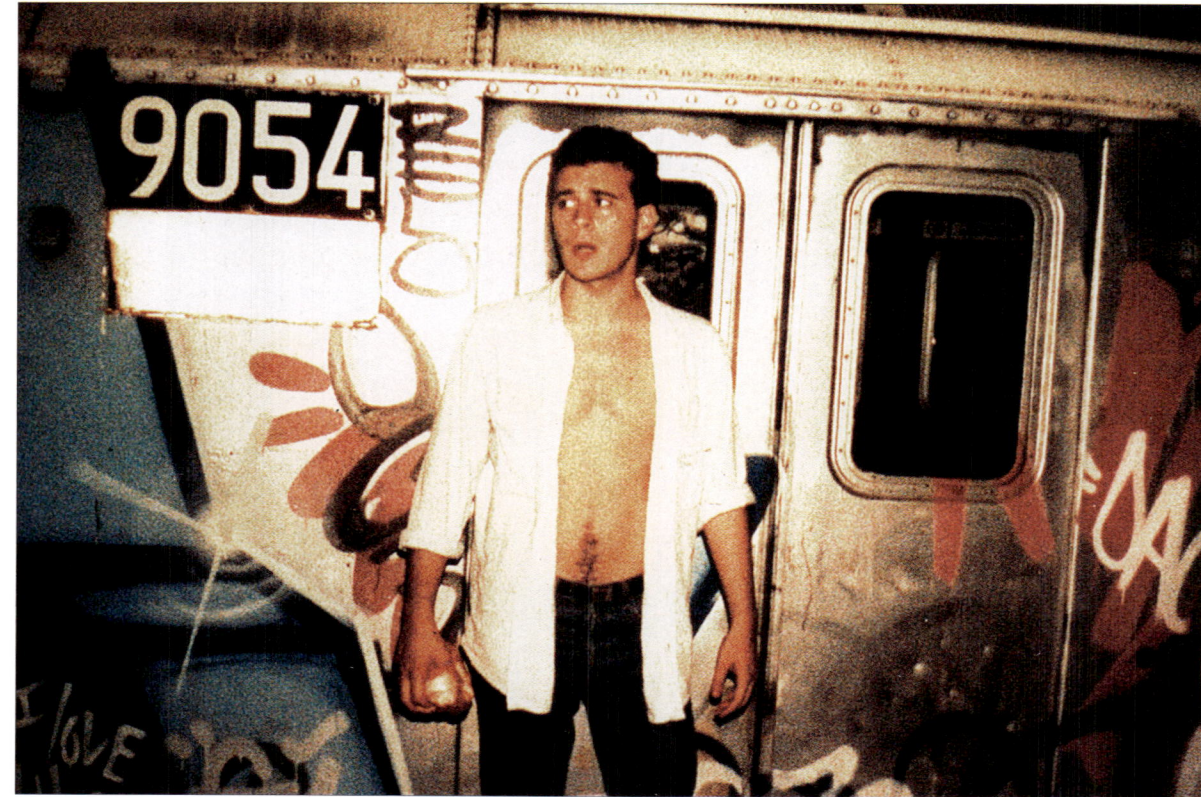

Teddy in the subway in New York, 1984

— Wany

This one time Checco, nicknamed Bambata because of his African somatic traits, and a kid he accidentally bumped into in one of the main streets of the Commenda district, right there at 4 in the afternoon challenged each other, dancing without music, to then end up fighting under the disbelieving eyes of all bystanders.

In the following years, after having witnessed various legendary battles between Cioccolata and Next One, the Fresh Kids started dropping out of the scene, conscious of the fact they had left a mark a bit everywhere.

In 1986 Teddy followed his dream and moved to New York, where in a brief amount of time he traded in his garbage collectors uniform and landed a job at the historic Hip Hop label Def Jam. And so photos from overseas started arriving to Brindisi in which Teddy was portrayed with various American pioneers: Lee, Kase2, Henry Chalfant. Between the end of the 80's and the beginning of the 90's

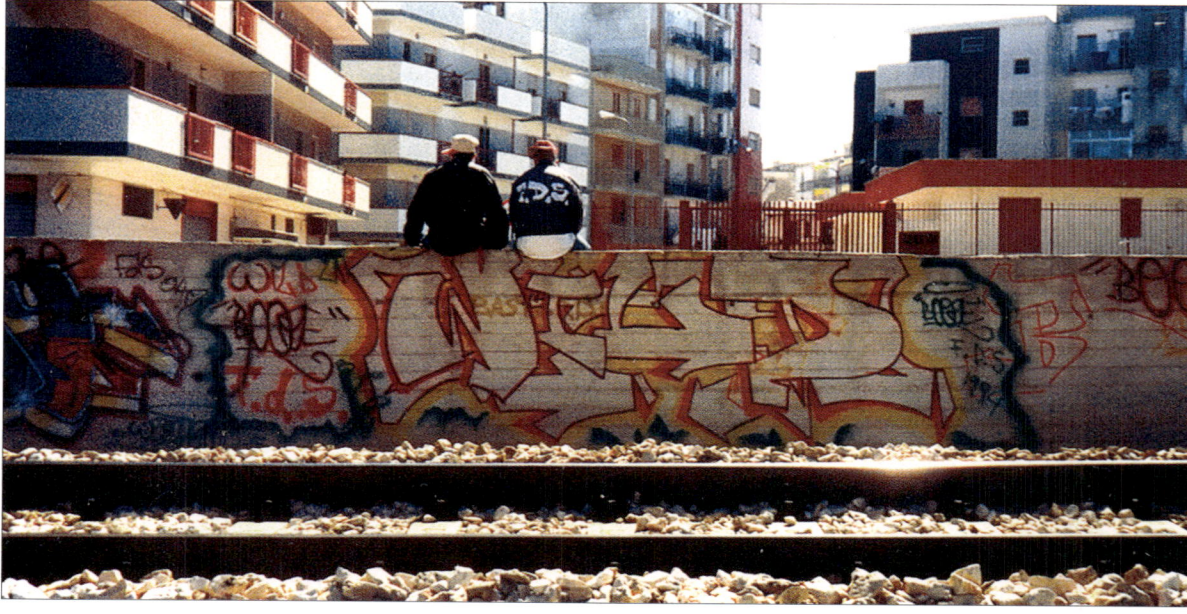

Wild by FDS crew, Brindisi, 1994

— Wany

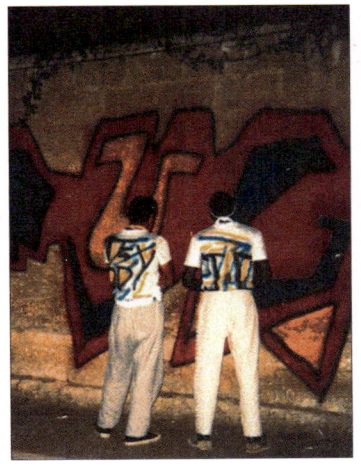

Teddy and Tony during 1985   — Wany

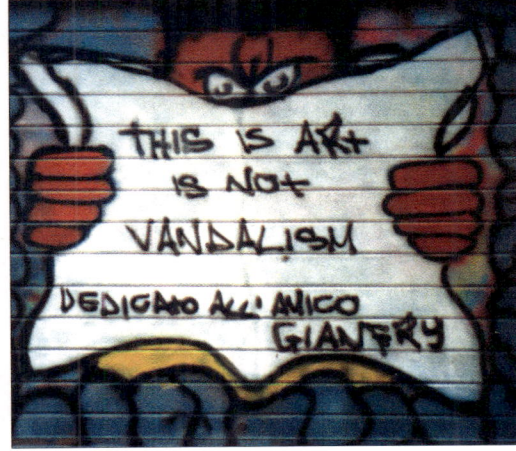

This is art, is not vandalism, 1990   — Wany

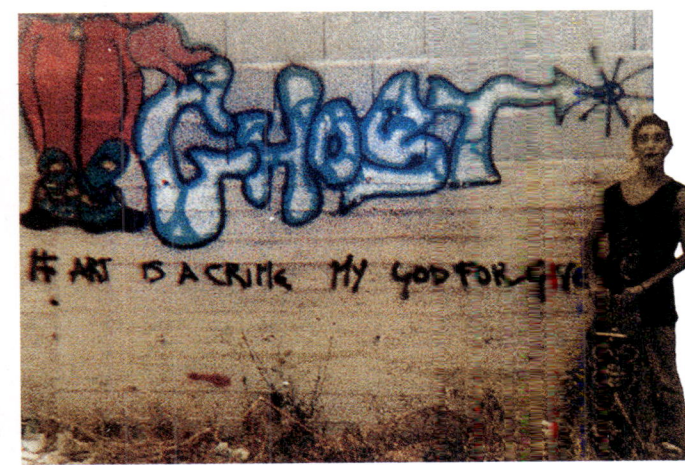

Ghost by Wany, Bozzano, 1991   — Wany

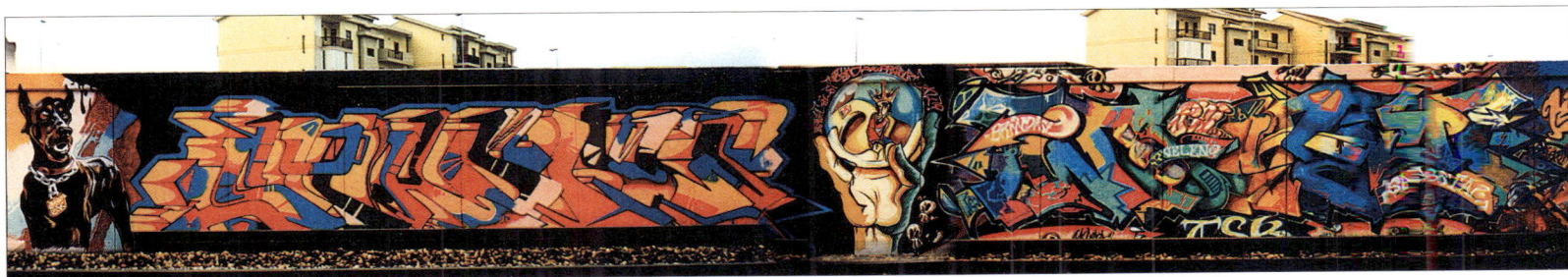

Shadow, Wany and Mac, TSK crew   — Wany

there was a distinct change, many of the old school veterans stopped writing and other Names denoting the passage of new writers and crews started appearing.
My first piece on a wall dates back to 1990, after having seen a tape of *Beat Street* that some friends I would skate with in that period brought over.

In those years the main spot us skaters would chill in was the Santa Chiara social centre and that's where I met Sone, a skater from Ostuni with whom I started painting on a factory in Bozzano; it wasn't legal, but nobody was minding us.
At the time everything was improvised: to defend Nicola Sad, a friend that around here is what is called a 'problem embracer', we decided to confront the two kids that were on his case. One of these was Vito Vinicolo, who would end up becoming a life-long travel companion, colleague, and brother for me. Him and Mac came from the previous generation and were already at an advanced stage of lettering, whereas I was already drawing characters, so we decided to form FDS crew (*Figli Della Strada* - Sons Of the Street). We anyways had to deal with TAA, who had been at the top for years and often verbally abused us.... I think it was their way of teaching us something. We all used this terrible quality spray paint, like Briolux or Happy Color for certain colours, and then we discovered Nitex and rather rarely got our hands on Fly, that had a larger variety of hues as opposed to the simple primary colours we were accustomed to.
There were no halls of fame in Brindisi, we would mostly paint on the walls of abandoned factories or of Bozzano's state buildings, with time we moved on to the adjacent neighbourhoods, from Commenda, the areas inside Brindisi City, Santa Chiara, Sant'Angelo, Casale, Minnuta, La Rosa, Sant'Elia, Paradiso, Perrino and San Paolo, all the way to the city centre. Each district obviously had its peculiar characteristics to consider, on the basis of the availability of accessible walls but mostly on the basis of the people living in it: you had to learn if the wall belonged to someone and who that someone was, to avoid problems. Like for example that time Marvel painted the balcony of an

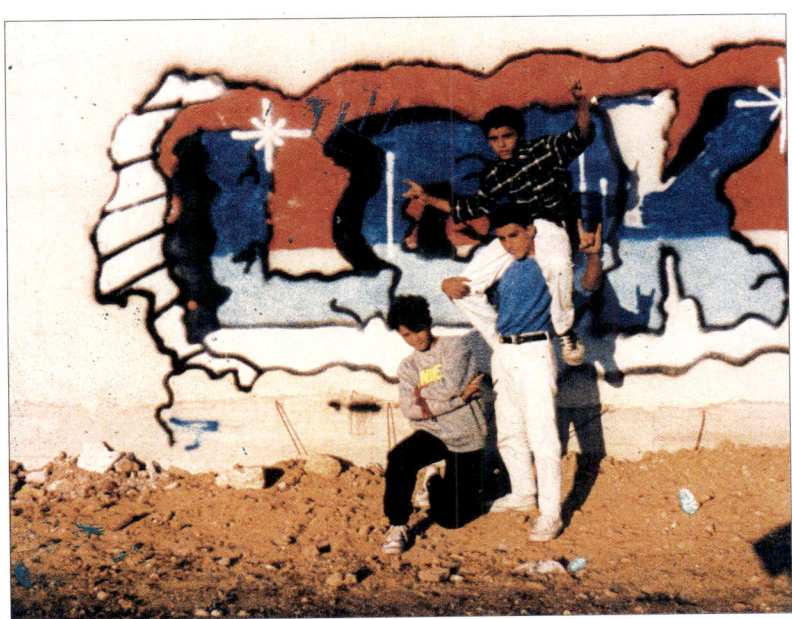

Brindisi B-boys, 1988   — Wany

apparently vacant apartment of Brindisi City, a conglomerate of houses that is half occupied and half abandoned; nobody could have known the owner was a dangerous person, who hunted Marvel down for months on end. We weren't too worried about the police, the problems were primarily tied to private citizens because if you touched the wall of a gangster you were in serious trouble.
In Sant'Elia we were lucky because we obtained some commissions from the car dealership of Zio Mimmi of the Cacafave family, owners of a gambling room he asked us to paint. In other neighbourhoods we had to know exactly what could be hit and what was better left untouched, Shadow and Ghost for example always researched which walls were off limits due to shady owners. Once I went to Perrino with Mauro Zac to paint a dragon on the boat of a family of notorious smugglers, who lived in a huge mansion with no end in sight. I was also asked to plan and design a ratchet mechanism for some not altogether....legal exploits. Independently from where we were painting, we would anyway try to write a positive message for the people that would see it the next day, using contrasting colours that would often result a little kitsch. This allowed our Names to become known throughout the city in a brief span of time, and the real competition between us and the old guard began. To use the words of Pablo, the Brindisi style was 'compact'. It was crew against crew to conquer the city.

First contacts with the italian scene and the exodus from the city

>

One way ticket

The first contact with other scenes in Italy dates back to 1992-'93, when Damage moved from Brindisi to Ancona, where he met Zart, with whom he started painting. When he got back home Damage painted a graffiti piece that would have a strong influence on the city's style, so much so as to be considered a real star, whom people would ask for autographs and sketches.

In those same years the first hall of fame in Brindisi appeared, "No alla guerra di colore" (No to the war of colours) signed by FDS, that thus asserted their technical and stylistic superiority with respect to other crews. That was the beginning of a new era for graffiti in Brindisi: new Names started appearing on the scene, and the city people started taking notice, often commissioning works. There was a strong demand to paint clubs, gambling rooms, bars, speedboats, or simply neighbourhood walls where members of the Sacra Corona Unita family lived, an organisation that is Puglia's mafia equivalent, comparable to the Camorra in Campania. One of them even commissioned us to paint a tiger on a leash, this was the crazy reality back home!

In spite of all the commissions however, the public continued to consider us martians, wondering why we would spend our money to challenge the law in a period and context of scarce economic resources, and in which problems with the law were already quite frequent. It got even worse in '93, after we decided to invest the money earned in a big commission on our first trip; with Buz and Marvel we hit the road in the direction of Wag's store, all the way in Milan, the only known Hip Hop-oriented clothes store, where we bought baggy pants and belt buckles with the letters FDS. It cost us many a brawl back home seeing we were stared at like circus clowns on the loose. On the way back to Brindisi we stopped at Ancona, where we met Damage and Zart, who gave us a ride on his white Mercedes to Pesaro to show us the pieces by DSP in the infamous sewers of the city. That night, while we wandered around Ancona waiting for the train, we met other kids that had our same passion, 3Spirit, with whom we started Breakdancing 'til our departure. In '94 there was a jam at the Fucine Meridionali centre which brought us to Bari for the first time and from that moment we started bombing other cities and towns of Puglia. That same night Sone had a terrible car accident that put him in a coma for months, so me and other friends would record tapes for him to listen to, reminding him of our nocturnal adventures and escapes, and he would half-smile. He eventually awoke from the coma, and a year and a half later I took him to the railway of Brindisi to paint a piece: it was like starting all over again and in a short amount of time he was back to great shape. Between the end of '94 and the beginning of '95 FDS broke up, even though people had started to accept and appreciate our tenacity and art in the streets, for me and Buz everything was

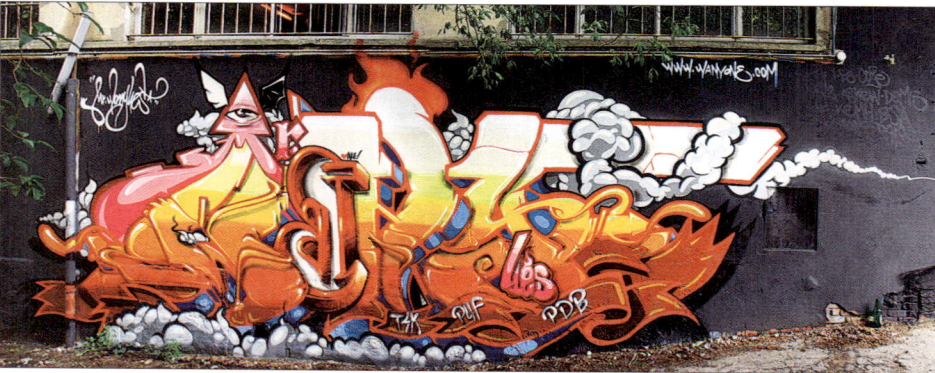
Wany in Bologna   — Wany

moving much too slowly. So in 1995 we attended the jams that would make history in Italian Hip Hop: Indelebile and Juice. I have never seen so many B-boys all together, it was mad crazy, fights and legendary battles like those between Body Gum and Crash Kid. I met Can2, Dare and Mode2, who was my hero, but also Sir2, Blef, Onuk and Dafne, who invited me to join PDB and I just had to accept.

In '95-'96 Buz and I founded TSK, a group that embraced all disciplines of Hip Hop, and soon Shadow, Body Gum, Dj Zorlak and Bisbinto joined. We were adopted by Dj War and Dj Gruff and started touring towns with our show based on Rap, Graffiti, Breaking and scratching. In '96 the Ferrovie dello Stato made us a huge present, building a wall that was two metres high and numerous kilometres along the Brindisi-Bari line, one of the biggest halls of fame on a train line in Italy. I remember the time me, Mac and Shadow left my house with a two metre-long ladder and travelled on foot through three neighbourhoods and over a kilometre of wall skirting the track line.

On the way back we reached the level crossing and I got in a fight with two guys on motorbikes that expected us to raise the bar for them, they received a lot of punches and I got jabbed with a knife. The fight ended with the older brother of one of the two, a well-known smuggler of Brindisi, apologising and kicking his brother around.

In '97 I left to study in Rome, there was a big concert and a lot of battles, it was crazy. I left behind a really strong imprint and many friends in my city, reminiscing all the situations we went through together, our big and small realities, the evenings spent talking in the street trying to put together enough cash for a bottle of wine, drinking it while

freestyling, two bars each and if you messed up you'd just smile. The fights ending in scars and bruises, the indelible experiences and situations now far away, the escapes, the nights spent scheming the most visible spots and the best routes to break out. The colours, the cops, the bitch-asses on our case, the gangsters, the untouchables, the abuse of power, the bad looks that would end up in beef, the defense of our identity and belonging, our neighbourhood, people just pas-

sing by and eternal friendships, from here it was back to point zero. Rome wasn't just a pivotal change in my life but the beginning of a broader vision of the concept of crew and bombing, tied to life in a metropolis. It was in Rome that PUF, one of the biggest crews of Southern Italy, adopted a group of local writers, generating a connection that would bring Brindisi new inputs from the capital. At a distance of years the scene in Brindisi continues to survive, though penalised by the heavy emigration that often challenges its sense of unity and makes it hard to keep up. We're all spread out between Milan, Venice, Bologna, Rome, or Pesaro, and others even outside Italy, like Barcelona, Pablo

who is in Ibiza and Hunto who is in Canada, others unfortunately are in jail, or have just come out thanks to an indult. Many from my generation have abandoned or just do other things, trapped between work and family.

Only during the summer holidays and Christmas vacation do we get to meet up and organise something. This is the story of Writing in Brindisi, whether for better or worse it has forged and accompanied us to where we are now. What we've been through

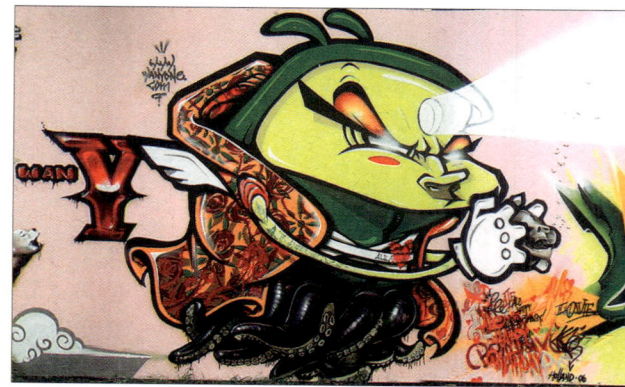
Wany in Amsterdam   — Wany

makes us neither gangsters nor better people, we're often just victims of a very deep-rooted system and of a treacherous historical period. When I see guys in Italy that front like they're bad boys, constructing this artificial ghetto and acting out their gangster soap opera, it almost makes me laugh, some people have no idea what organised crime is, they compare it to micro-delinquency, idealise it, without understanding that kind of life sucks. As far as I'm concerned, I thank God for letting me find an escape from this in Hip Hop and allowing me the possibility to change, because I understood that not everything I had done to that moment was right. — WANY

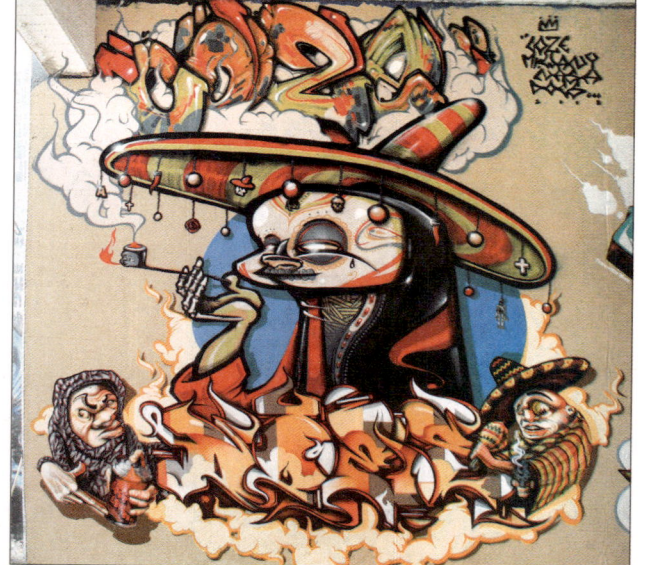
Wany in Germany   — Wany

The first italian magazine
>

AL, a bridge to South Italy

The importance of *Aelle* magazine in the national scene

The story of Italian Writing in the early 90's seems to be closely connected to the genesis of *Aelle* magazine – the acronym of Allenza Latina – founded in Genoa by Claudio "Sid" Brignole. Towards the end of the 80's Sid had collected an impressive quantity of material about writers who were beginning to paint in Italian cities, building a small network formed by about twenty people among whom were Skah and Onis from Vicenza, Flyat and TDK from Milan, Sha-1 and Polo from Naples, Eron from Rimini and Dayaki from Bologna. Each of them contributed to the project with material, texts and photos that were photocopied on A4 format paper in black and white. The deadline of each number, though not quite systematic, tended to be bimonthly. *Aelle*, like most European fanzines, was initially distributed thanks to word of mouth, and subsequently through a primitive subscription system that allowed it to grow in terms of quality as well as distribution throughout the territory. The first coloured pages appeared when the fanzine started networking in Footlocker stores throughout Italy.

When the Hip Hop movement tied to the Italian music scene exploded, *Aelle* tripled its subscribers, becoming for all effects and purposes a real magazine, sold in newsstands since the mid 90's. If before the diffusion of the magazine the connections between crews occurred mainly through jams, the capillary distribution of *Aelle* allowed local scenes to connect into a single network.

The sales of *Aelle* at the newsstands accelerated its diffusion throughout Italy, and represented an enormous step forward for the movement. It then had the opportunity to reach those urban centres of the peninsula that had been excluded from the interaction process.

Perhaps this magazine did not manage to

The distribution of *Aelle* at newsstands allowed the sudden amplification of the network

fully represent all the facets of the movement, but not only was it the only medium to gather the different Writing scenes of a fragmented territory like Italy, for years it also remained nonetheless a reference point for those who painted and a barometer of the phenomenon's status. Towards the end of the 90's *Aelle* received an essential contribution from Southern Italy. The Hip Hop scene in the

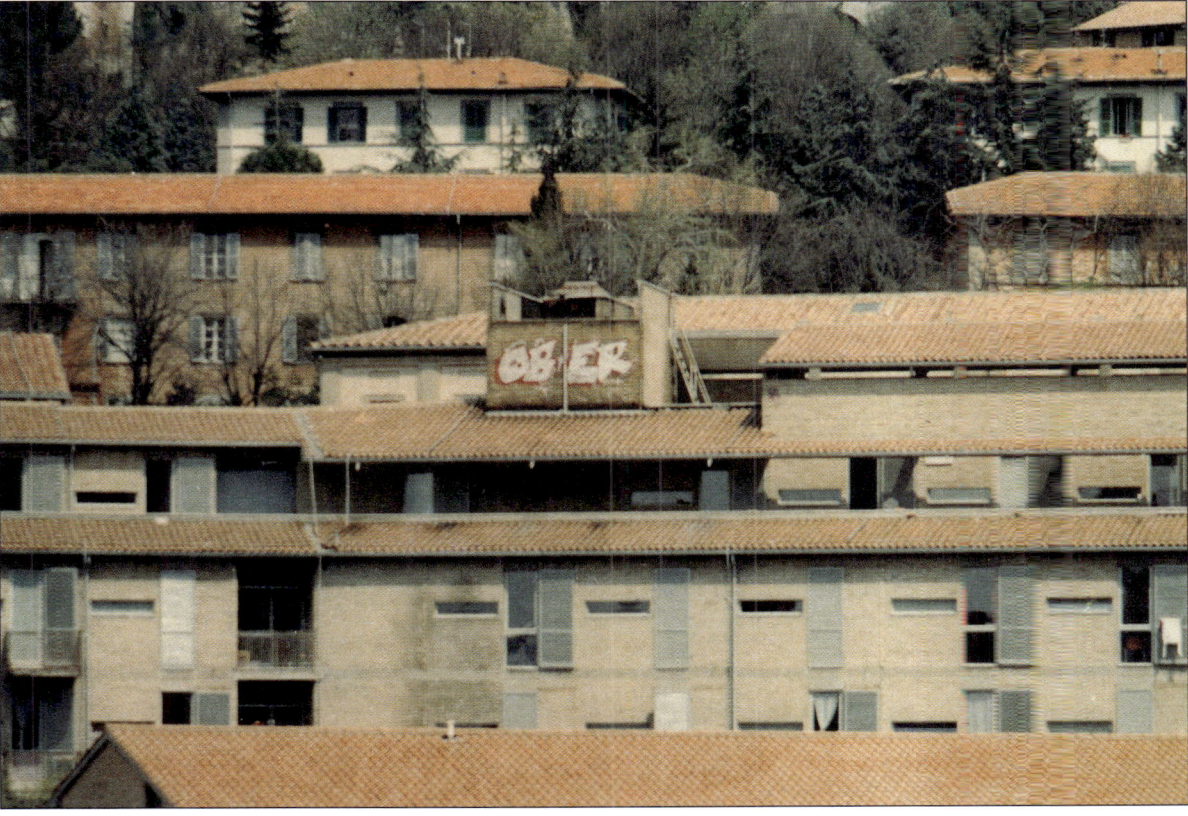

Ober on the laterite rooftops of Perugia

— *AL archive*

South suffered from the problem, typical of Southern cities, of having difficulty staying connected to the rest of Italy. The first signs of Writing arrived almost fortuitously through the sons of immigrants who had moved to the North to study, or the resident writers of the North who had Southern origins and, when returning to

their town, disseminated the little information there was.

The distribution of *Aelle* at newsstands allowed the sudden amplification of the network to these regions: writers in Southern Italy abandoned their isolation, sending thousands of photographs of their pieces to the magazine.

Despite the difficulties they endured in the South, writing established itself as an self-constructed and vernacious reality, deeply rooted to a territory that is usually quite separate. Various unceuses of kids kept the interest for Writing alive until the arrival of *Aelle* at the newsstand officially recognised its existence.

CONSEQUENCES

—

Aelle s photographic archives represent an interesting observatory on the status of Writing productions in Italy. The quantity of material – photos and cover letters – sent to the editorial office, gives a sense of the extent to which *Aelle* was a benchmark and an objective for writers throughout the Italian peninsula. Southern Italy's fundamental contribution was an important photographic corpus, a mirror reflecting a Writing scene that was less connected with and known in other Italian regions. The drive to emerge and witness their presence pushed many writers of the South to intensify their activity: the thousands of images sent from Campania, Calabria, Sicily and Sardinia portrayed the actions of local writers in an atypical context, rural and completely removed from the metropolitan condition in which Writing was born. The locals confronted surfaces that were entirely different: from megalithic edifices to stone walls, and painted

on any means of transportation: from cranes to tractors, bulldozers and containers. All this gave an idea of how New York imagery had been reinterpreted and applied to the local landscape, creating a new take on it, in a context that was very different from the urbanised European scenarios. Consequently, even the approach to photography was different. If the way of portraying works was usually focused on the aesthetic of the painted piece, on the stylistic level and the quality of design, the images that arrived to *Aelle* from Southern Italy were centred on the background against which the pieces were produced. This photographic choice was in part due to the recognition of a yet unripe stylistic evolution, but especially due to the desire to emphasise such characteristic surroundings. The push to have their voices heard and get in touch with the neighbouring scenes persuaded Southern writers to embark on an intense production

of fanzines, though generally they were low quality because they were completely self-produced and lacking once. In contrast, the contents of these fanzines revealed to be more thorough and analytical than many Northern magazines that, perhaps due to the possibility of being published in colour and including higher definition pictures, often relied on typical art catalogue cliches, presenting an infinite sequence of photos. On the contrary, the fanzines of the South concentrated especially on articles, on a series of information and news regarding the status of the Hip Hop scene in the South, focusing attention for example on a jam in a small town lost in the countryside of Calabria, and presenting a rich and complete report on it. Southern fanzines constituted real pul e irs of information that updated the readers on the recent happenings, the present realities and the future events of the Writing world.

Sardinia
>

The imaginary subway of

Grim
>

Between the end of the 80's and the beginning of the 90's, a second generation of writers in Nuoro came to life. During those years, there were already numerous pieces from the first writers of the past decade like Wave, Free D, Mr. Robot, Float, W2ORKart, and Kid Loose, and pieces made after the late 80's by Grim, Shade, Shark, Whiz, Eroe, Daze, Zone, and Stew. And subsequently Naves, Kino, and Nat51. I recall, more or less during the same period, other Sardinian writers: Dens and Skim from San Teodoro; Nero 91, Def One, Zisto, Drim, and Farfa, from Iglesias, Cagliari, and Quartu Yoghi; Palolo, Randa, Stile, Blaza, Joka, Noise, and Kiza from Sassari and Porto Torres. I met Whiz in '92 and we realised that for a few years we had both been painting separately in two distinct neighborhoods of our city- Monte Gurtei and Mughina - without ever knowing about each other. In those years, a strange energy pervaded those streets, and some of us kids began painting with the desire to make our own pieces and write our own Names in the neighborhood. In my neighborhood, there were already some pieces by guys who were older than me: a crew of breakers who danced at the start of the 80's and would challenge other crews from different areas of the city. I grew up looking

at their graffiti, going to see new pieces every time they painted, studying those letters. In the beginning, they didn't tag, they just painted pieces and characters that were associated with Hip Hop culture. The piece beneath the church of San Paolo- Fontanella neighborhood- "The Magnificent Sprayer" (TMS), was the first hall of fame from the mid 80's by the first crew of writers: Wave, Free D, Mr. Robot, and Float. At the time I was about 10 years old, but that wall is still stuck in my mind. Other pieces followed on that same wall: TMS painted a New York City subway train in almost 1:1 scale. For years, writers continued to paint that wall. We often skated on that street and witnessed the evolution of style and learned from it.

We were distant from everything, at least mentally, since we had no subways and no trains, so the distance between Nuoro and larger cities like Cagliari or the "mainland" (Italy) seemed immeasurable to us. But that subway train painted by TMS overstepped the frontiers. Seeing that graffiti from a young age inspired us to begin and to improve with time. Me, Shade, Whiz, and Shark (DCC) began going out around Nuoro in search of new walls to paint.

At times we'd end up in our own neighborhoods, the wall behind my house, facing the street, was our first hall of fame. There, we learned from each other. We used spray paint (Fly Color) that didn't cover well and I recall when we'd go see new pieces by the older writers, we'd scavenge for their forgotten or half-empty spray cans as if they were gold.

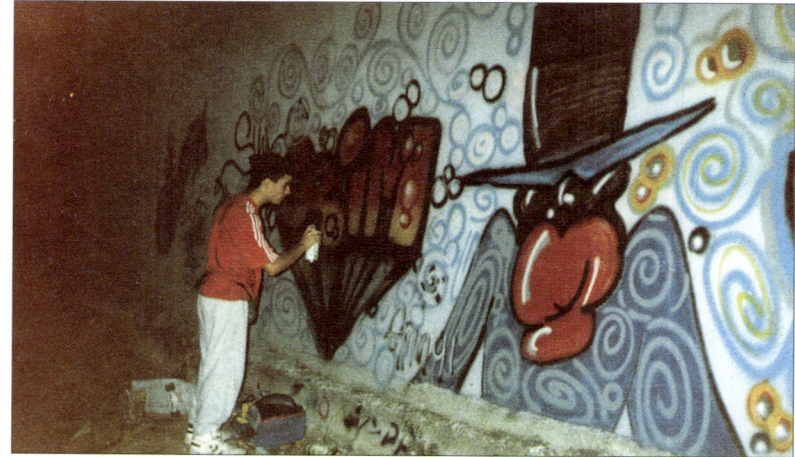

Grim in 1991
                                              — Grim

At times we'd find and use some SparVar spray paint leftover from Wave's trips, by now he'd moved to Florence for college. We'd modify the nozzles for a finer mist, we'd use caps from insect sprays and deodorants, or we'd use the spray cans upside-down. Apart from skateboarding and school, that's all we did, it was all spontaneous, we painted a lot and occasionally we'd steal spray cans and place them diagonally in our bags so the marbles wouldn't shake around and blow our cover. In the meantime, in other neighborhoods, writers like Zone, Eroe, and Stew got cracking. The confrontation and challenge with older writers impelled us

to quickly progress, to show determination and style, to discover something new every day, and to be creative and evolve. True and enduring bonds and friendships were formed, we learned from each other with great humility. Often, even those who weren't directly involved in this passion, took part in the nocturnal outings. In time, the first fanzines began to circulate and we were able to see the different styles of American or European writers, and extreme lettering we tried to compete with. There were no such things as jams in Sardinia so we learned about other writers strictly by word of mouth. At night we'd stay out late while sitting in front of a fire

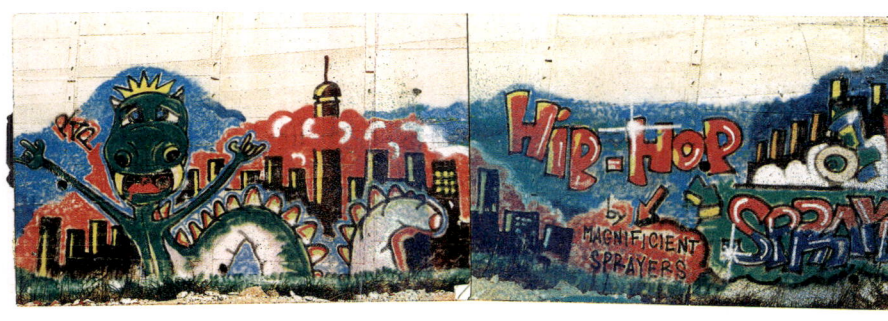
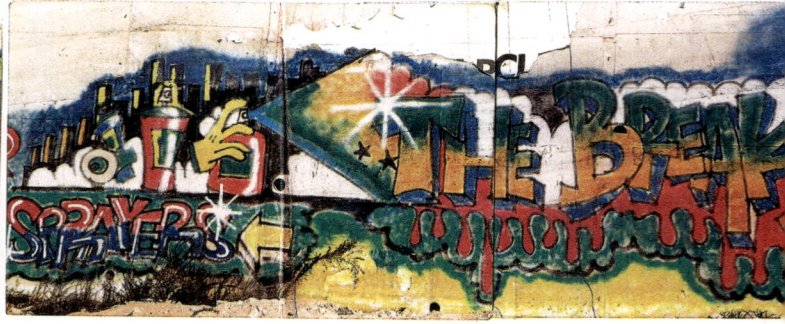

Hip Hop, The Break, Peace by The Magnificent Sprayers, Nuoro early 80's

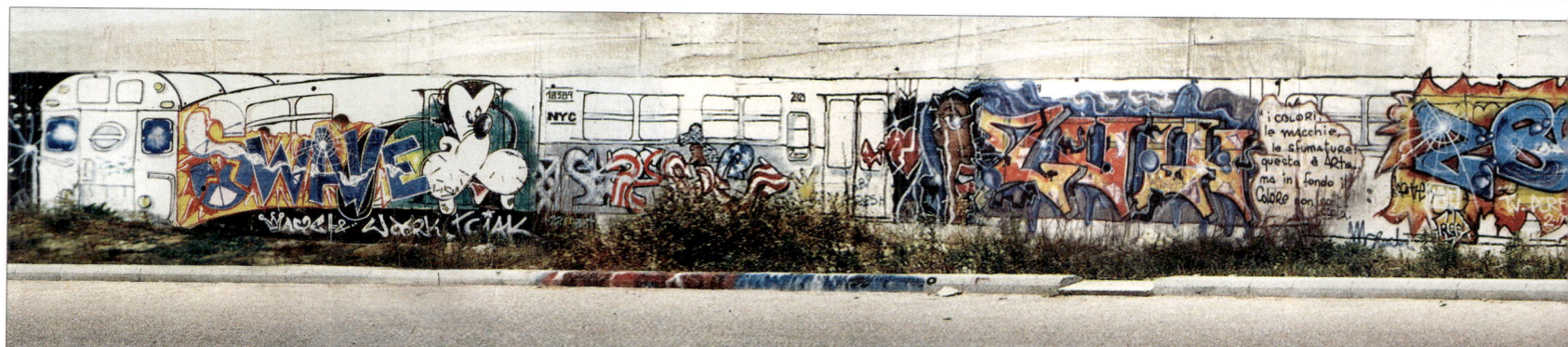

Wave, Zulu, Z Boys painted on a imaginary subway. Nuoro, 1989

Calabria
>

Nuoro | Ramon, Beat Street Cosenza

in an old rusty bin in Montagnetta- a park which was the meeting spot for many of the neighborhood's generations- in summer and winter. Apart from us there were those who danced or just watched them dance, but the mood that surrounded us was completely different than today's mood and obtaining the respect of the older writers was important but we spent more time focusing on having fun and painting. Things remained this way for quite some time, we never imagined there could be something else outside of our way of doing things. We knew what was going on in Italy thanks to articles and photos, but we were there, far away from everything and that was our dimension- a small city in the suburbs where we sought out visibility and risk nonetheless by painting the military barracks or the one train line we had that went from Nuoro to Macomer, we didn't even have those few trains that were parked in Cagliari, that were soon conquered by the area's writers (TNT). Subsequently, some of us went away for college and while living in new places, ended up painting with other writers and finally managed to conquer some yards (BCX).

Many years have gone by and many of us returned to Sardinia, creating a project which merges various crews: "All-capsproject", and even today, those who began all of this are still painting, like many of us from Nuoro and throughout Sardinia who began painting during that time. Nowadays I realise that the distance separating us from everything was, in reality, a blessing.

One Sound magazine

The movie *Flashdance*, the scene in which the main character stops in an alley to observe some street dancers. My whole story starts here; the power, the agility, the magic those dancers expressed, left me breathless, it was only a moment, but it lasts to this day.
I was 15 or 16 years old, I don't remember well, I was a very shy kid but when I left the movie theatre, kind of jokingly, in front of the incredulous eyes of my sister, I tried to imitate one of the dance steps I had seen in the movie. Strangely enough something came out right and I felt freer than I had ever felt before. Some time passed, not too much, and I went to see the movie *Breakdance*.
Once home I started trying (trying and trying again) those acrobatic moves I had seen at the movies, but unfortunately without a video player, without anyone to teach me the steps ... I was counting only on memory.

My name had started appearing everywhere and I became the worst nightmare of the citizens of Cosenza ("ia ara Madonna... ma chi ni ca... o è stu Ramon?")

I managed to do very little though when something did come out right, others looked at me dubiously and surprised. A while later I saw Electric Boogaloo (Breaking 2) and finally Beat Street at the movie theatre. The first two movies I had seen gave a somewhat distorted view of the Hip Hop world, but I only understood this later. Beat Street on the other hand opened my eyes: Rap, Breakdance and Writing, aka 100% Hip Hop. It was after that movie that I started sketching and planning the first mural pieces. My helper at the time was my classmate and my first tag was Spider Karate Man. All ideas were pretty confused, but the desire to emerge was plentiful. We bought three 350ml Unipol spray cans at the hardware store (one red, one white and one blue), metal caps, for a total of 3500 Lira. My first piece was taken from the newspaper clipping of *Beat Street*, with the words: "Se l'arte e' un peccato mio Dio perdonami" (If art is a crime may god forgive me). At 22:30 hours, on the wall of the bus station, with adrenaline at a peak. Me and my 'lookout' ended in about 30 minutes, the words were in block letters and the design was a simple outline, without fill, merely sketched, as if just begun. Other references came from articles on newspapers, sacred and difficult to find, a few rap songs and primarily movie soundtracks, but also Grandmaster Melle Mel that I got a hold of thanks to a DJ friend of mine. The year was '85 and me and my classmate Davide had enrolled in an Afro-American Breakdance school; we had bought a pair of low-top Nike shoes with pale

blue swoops and shirts also by Nike, we felt like two gods. It lasted a month, maybe two, and I didn't learn a thing. It only gave me the opportunity to practice in a larger environment than at home, and also to meet other weird kids like me that loved this dance. But of writers, not even a shadow
Then one day the funfair arrived to Cosenza, the travelling one, and I saw some kids there

We bought three 350ml Unipol spray cans at the hardware store (one red, one white and one blue), metal caps, for a total of 3500 Lira

that I had noticed Breaking under my house. I had spied on them in secret; I was dressed in my Nike shoes with the tongue out, jeans, Adidas sweatshirt and a Sheriff's pin with my name on it: Ramon. They noticed me immediately and one of them approached and invited

me to dance on the platform of the Tagadà ride: it was a challenge. One of them was black and was the best, DJ Lugi, at the time Luigino. We walked home together and he showed me where he lived. The next day I was already there, at his place, on the doorstep of his home, knocking on the door in an attempt to trade a Break move of his with a music tape I had brought. We practiced in his house, and that's where I met Daniele and Carmelo-Melo J. In the meantime me and Davide-Holmes had started doing pieces that got better and better, even in impossible places like Piazza Fera which is very busy. You have to keep in mind that at 11 pm (at the most), we had to be back home and so there were no nocturnal excursions. My Name had started appearing everywhere and I became the worst nightmare of the citizens of Cosenza: "ia ara Madonna... ma chi ni ca... o è stu Ramon?" (Lordy lordy....who the fuck is this Ramon?).
When Luigino, Adalberto, Carletto and I obtained permission to practice in a gym, we organised our first Breakdance show in June of 1986. By then graffiti and breaking had become a reason to live and survive in a city that offers little today, imagine in 1986.

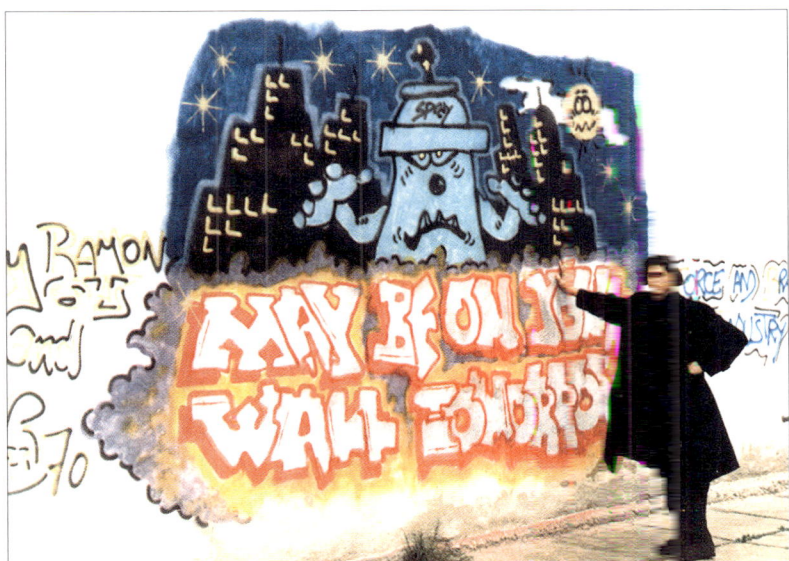

May be on your wall tomorrow by Ramon　　　— *One Sound archive*

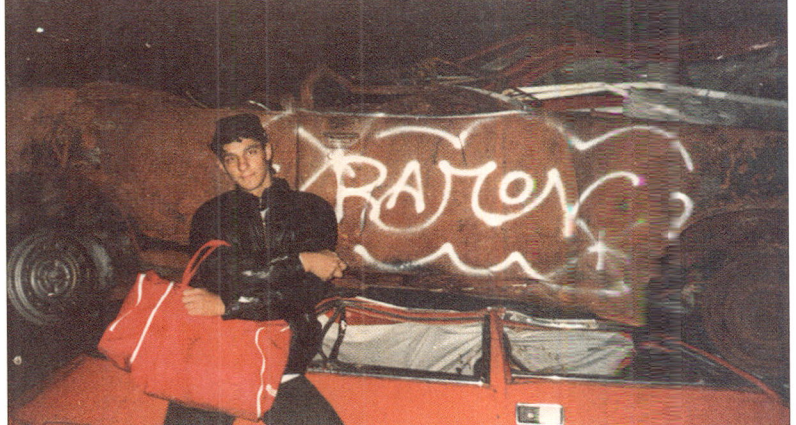

Ramon　　　　　　　　　　　　　　　　— *One Sound archive*

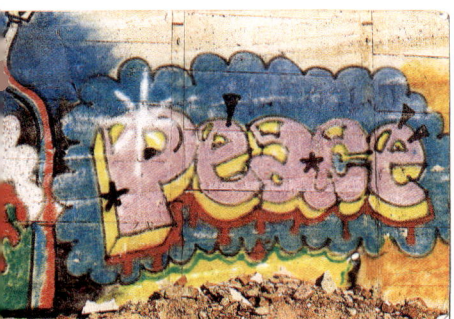

— *Grim*

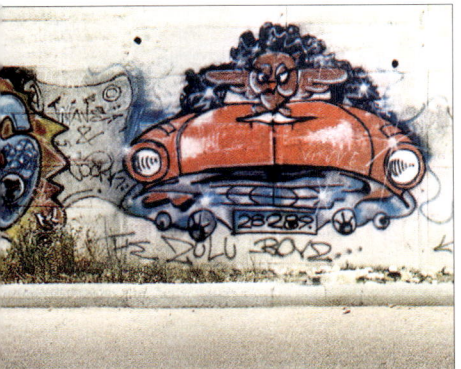

— *Grim*

A small rough town

> CONTINUES FROM PAGE 261

affiliation to Pesaro.

Writing in the hall of fame - not to mention the style of life intrinsic to it: spending lots of time alone outside of the normal city realm in places that are often dirty and smelly - and defending these places from other writers, become an inseparable entity for Pesaro's writers, part of the harsh "game" of graffiti, but none of this matters without a personal portfolio of bombing in all of the classic spots delegated by this discipline: walls, roofs, state train lines, trains. This mentality prevails throughout the 90's and still today, and this is one of the reasons why the upsurge of train-bombing - which skyrockets in the second half of the 90's - was never exclusive to the city of Pesaro, but instead spread homogeneously thanks to this system. The main goal in Pesaro is to give your name visibility, this is considered "the real thing", and even though painting trains commands pride and respect, the best way to gain fame is by painting in the city itself, with both quantity and quality.

—

If the kids are united

> CONTINUES FROM PAGE 270

Hulk, Soap. And like that, the scene of Bari took off.

Outside the city limits, Brindisi was the only other scene we encountered: that's where TSK came from, who had been active for much longer, but were subject to completely different influences, and would paint puppets, which here in Bari we never did, we were more attracted to throw-ups and big silvers. Move was a fan of the Swiss and Parisian scenes, like Bando, Steph, and Colt, whereas I was passionate about Mace, Rusty, Shad and Kray, whom I had seen on *Trap* magazine. Other influences were writers such as Odem and Amok from Berlin, or Delta, Gasp and Mellie from Holland, and naturally even before that, the pioneering work of Dondi. The isolation of the scenes in the region of Puglia, unavoidably limited by their geographical position, was interrupted thanks to trips to the Adriatic coast to attend various conventions, starting from the one in Rimini in 1994, *Indelebile*. This event left a mark on the writers of all Bari and all of Italy. That jam allowed us to establish friendships and collaborations that would last for years, in Rimini we met KTM from Naples, and Done, Rusty and Vince from Monaco.

And again during the various conventions we bonded with kids from Roma like Vela, Dale and Trota. As the years passed many of us moved, Creeda went to live next to Milan and met Shad, Rae and Kilos. Others spent some time in Holland, to then return the favour by hosting writers like Same, Jake and Mickey from TFP, who earned themselves the title of honorary citizens of Bari.

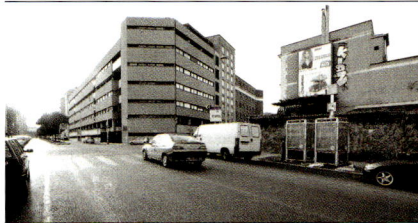

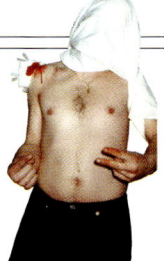

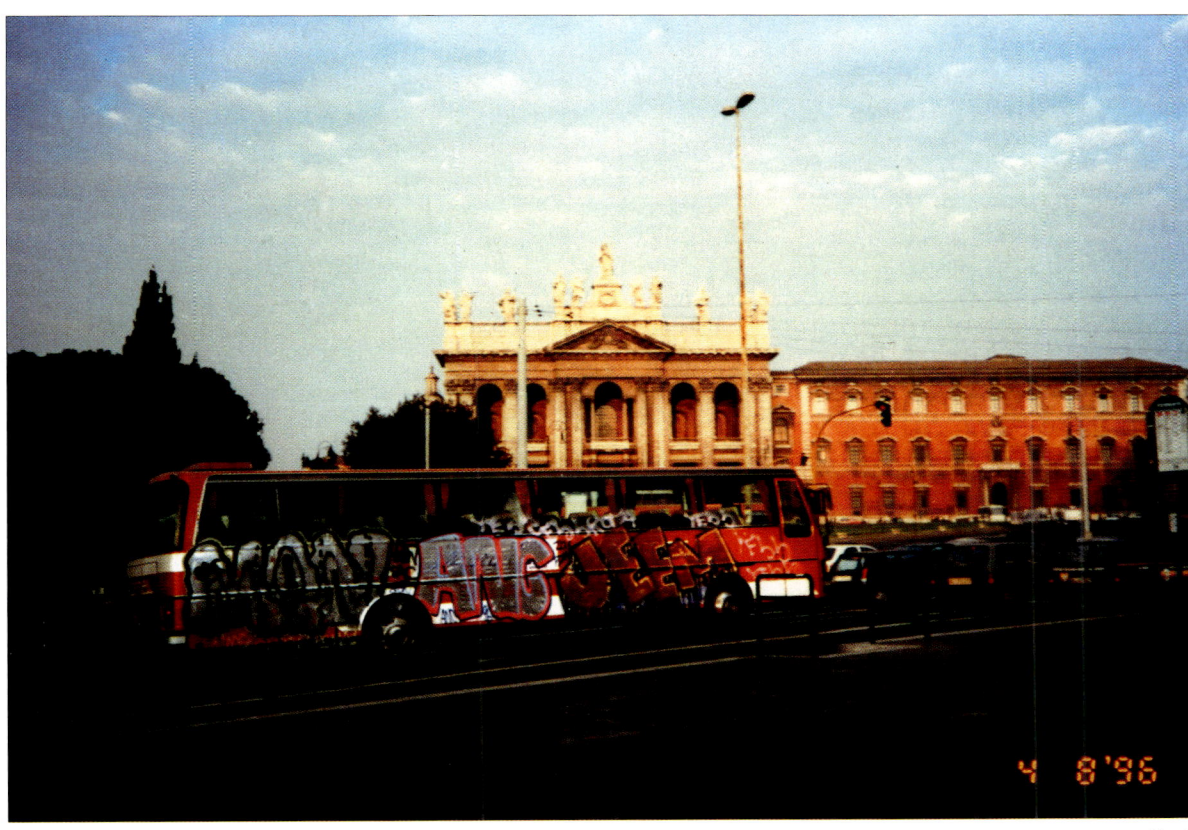

— Meneio

4 8'96

The infinite (sub) ways of Rome

I n the first years of 2009 Rome equalled a New York record. In the Italian capital, painted trains have circulated within urban traffic for 17 years, exactly as had happened in the Big Apple twenty years earlier. Though distant from the maze of the MTA subway, in Rome, as had previously occurred in New York, the train cars of the subway and of the urban and suburban railway lines represented the only possible target throughout the early 90's. The Roman scene thus took shape around the object of trains and their intrinsic nature, relegating walls to a secondary role. The communicative potential of this target was pushed to the extreme, determining the same character and practices of the local crews.

Their daily routine was spent in yards, and could be characterized by an attitude based on instinct, a voracious character personified by the local exponents, that reflected a spontaneous and unmistakable style.

The increase of security in yards and the congestion of the few available lines, in time generated a speedy approach, consciously animated by an aesthetic research similar to the so-called "unlearn how to paint" theorised by Picasso: an apparently raw style that chooses to forget virtuosity, control, and clean strokes in favour of immediacy.

What I liked about Rome was that many writers mantained the original feeling of Writing, about the action and still doing something spontaneous. The German writers are about planning, analysing, making a sketch and being perfect. Rome isn't about being perfect, it's about doing something. Rew, Berlin

The outlines were simple and purposely inaccurate because the piece was conceived as a moving vision, in conditions of disturbance with respect to the hall of fame contemplation. Approximation was preferred to precise strokes, just as had occurred with the New York styles of the 70's: the impact of train cars painted with the original spray and cap hit the mark exactly because of the dynamism of the fluctuating letters, where the finish of the outline was not taken into consideration. In the height of the first decade, the intensity of graffiti on subway carriages was proportionate to the succession of the most important groups, from the

> CONTINUES ON PAGE 282

A–LINE
The subway of Rome

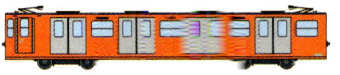

The A-line of the subway became operative in 1980. It runs from Battistini to Anagnina, cutting through the city from North-East to South-East. With 486 runs a day it transports more than 450,000 passengers.

> CONTINUES ON PAGE 288

B–LINE
The subway of Rome

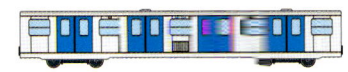

The subway of the B-line became operative in 1955, though planned and begun in the 30's during the Fascist era for the Universal Exposition of '42. It runs from Laurentina to Rebibbia.

> CONTINUES ON PAGE 296

LIDO LINE
The subway of Rome

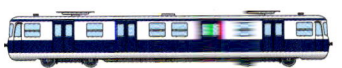

The Lido line was the first suburban railway to be built with the characteristics of a subway. The Lido line goes from the station of Roma Porta San Paolo up to the southern limit of the coastal neighbourhood of Ostia lido.

> CONTINUES ON PAGE 304

We'd filled our hearts with courage, like we'd filled all those cars with paint. The yard was now ours, we conquered it from top to bottom

— JON, ZTK

ACW INTERNATIONAL / ROME

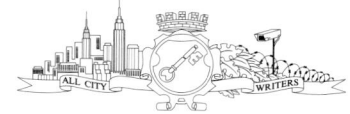

Main contributors:
Anek, Clown, Coma, Far, Fonzi, Fume, Gast, Gel, Joe,
Jon, Hiom, Manjar, Mencio, Monia Cappuccini, Napal,
Nico, One, Pane, Panda, Poison, Stand, Sugo, Syla,
Tekne, Trota, Tuff, Vela, Ver, Washe

In collaboration with:
00199, ETC, KIDZ, MDF, MT2, NSB, PAC, THE,
TRV, ZKM, ZTK

Cover photo:
Men, ANC, Geem in front of San Giovanni in
Laterano.

Through lay

Nico
>

In Rome, all lay-ups have nicknames, kind of like a tag that's instinctively given: "Spaghetti", "Il Ponte" (The Bridge), "Magliana con dentro l'Americano "(Magliana featuring the American), "Riparazioni" (Repairs), "Entuend" (End-to-End), "Le Prime e le Seconde Banchine" (The First and Second Platforms), "la Linea" (The Line), and then the stations of Laurentina, Ostia, Anagnina, Ottaviano and Rebibbia. All these lay-ups are exclusively for painting the A and B subway lines and the Ostia line, basically nothing but subway cars. Any line is good but some lines are better than others because they have their own individual characteristics.

The B line starts at the yard on Via Tiburtina, a consular road that's been around since the time of the ancient Romans. Along this road sits an industrial hinterland. The Eastern deposit is called Rebibbia, like the state prison located next to it. For the first stops, the train runs

aboveground. Santa Maria del Soccorso is the stop for people from Colli Aniene, a neighbourhood with buildings that hold 500,000 people. The train already runs underground at the Pietralata stop. Above it is a neighbourhood made of old blocks, bars, mechanic shops, and junkyards. This stretch ends at Monti Tiburtini, after passing through a sort of limbo known as the Quintiliani ghost station - for years it has yet to be opened. Then the train heads toward the upper neighbourhoods: first Termini Station and then the historic centre. The train sees the light of day again at Piramide station where the last of the tourists get off, making way for the Filipinos, a historic Roman community which goes to work in the EUR neighbourhood; when the train cars take off again, they run parallel to the Ostia line all the way to Magliana station. It's important to see things in the light of day, but this isn't possible on the A line.

The A line is a mistake: kilometres of escalators, tourists, nuns, commuters, too many people, too little space. The South-Eastern yard is situated in a neighbourhood that's in the open, where movies and good white wine are made, but both products have good years and bad years. Each day the A line runs along Via

> CONTINUES FROM PAGE 281

first formations of MT2 and ETC, who later merged with TRV, to the following groups: MDF, ZTK, ZKM - later THE - PAC and many others.

The maximum concentration on a single target of reference determined the same character of the local crews: writers coming from all over Rome would find themselves hitting the same places, forming groups of people coming from different neighbourhoods, intent on reaching the yards of the city together. Roman crews never boasted strong territorial possession, because their targets would move

> In the 90's Rome became the main tourist destination for crews from all over Europe

in space and the set meeting spots were so reduced as to transform them into real catalysers. Initially, strongholds within the territory of Rome were extremely rare, if you exclude the example of Nomentana station and the neighbourhood of San Lorenzo.

Writers coming from abroad also contributed to the evolution of subway dynamics. In the 90's Rome became the main tourist destination for crews from all over Europe: the possibility of admiring their painted trains circulate in a subway system attracted a unique wave of thematic tourists, previously equalled only by Amsterdam and later Warsaw. The fleeting

yet devastating presence of foreigners was witnessed by the variety of styles on the painted carriages.

The subway scenario began to change in the second half of the 90's. Security adopted control systems that were becoming more radical: in yards the habit of shooting on sight of anyone brought certain crews to fall back on secondary objectives. Among these, the local railway line to Velletri; the one in the direction of Pantano, which includes the small trains of the Casilina; the white and red trains of the Roma Nord; the greens to Fiumicino airport; and the network of national railway lines that go outside the city. Even trams were transformed into a relief valve. The juxtaposition of these painted landscapes constituted the setting of Roman Writing, in which the suburban stretches were gradually reconsidered as valid alternatives to a subway system that was becoming too dangerous and limited. The Roman transport system, maily composed of surface vehicles, forced the movement to confront the city and the infrastructures connected to railway transportation. In the 90's, this combination coincided with the axes of maximum concentration of local styles, where the phenomenon of graffiti on trains had formed and developed.

At the end of the decade, when the number of Roman writers grew excessively, crews decided to target the walls on the side of the track line and the consular roads on which trams and driving traffic circulated.

Once again, considering the local writers characteristics, a condition for contemplating their pieces was a moving gaze.

ups and gypsy camps

Tuscolana, underneath densely populated neighbourhoods that popped up next to the cinema industry's headquarters: Cinecittà. The A line links the three basilicas of St. John Lateran, St. Mary Major, and St. Peter, next to the military barracks and the Court in the Prati neighbourhood. All of the stops are underground, there's no way to look at the train.

The cars reveal themselves in the various stations, opening their doors on different sides each time. Pietro Nenni Bridge is the only stretch where you can see the train in broad daylight, filtered by glass barriers that become more and more yellow each day. But at least trains are clearly visible here since they pass over the bridge slowly. The Ostia train is completely exposed and naked. It's composed of various types of cars: the older ones are tapered with rounded edges while the new ones have sharper edges. From the new Piramide depot, the train takes a scenic route through many buildings, with the B line running parallel to it all the way to Magliana yard. Through gypsy camps, racetracks, illegal homes, and fenced-off fields with "For Sale" signs, the train makes its way to Ostia Antica where the smell of pine trees fills the air and the city appears once again.

Far
>

Writing comes seriously alive in a metropolis when the latter reaches its peak saturation, both social and communicative. People walk through the city without even seeing it, without looking at each other; TVs and radios are left on without any interest, advertisements are continuously less noticed and search for new stratagems to attract attention. All this makes everyone less sensitive to what happens around them: a kind of protective invisible wall is created that isolates people inside their inner I, in themselves, in their wandering through the city thinking only of their own needs and welfare. The necessity to reach down into the soul arises when a superficial perception of surrounding people and things is no longer enough: what is created is the need to show what we have inside, to show emotions and feelings through new, unconscious modalities through which to sensitise and directly communicate the most hidden part of us. To show

is quite different then to tell. That is why at this point the city lives a sort of artistic-therapeutic Renaissance that awakens sentiments through the traumatic impact of those that move in the underground. All this is reflected in the places that people flock to in the street, and long (or on top of) every metropolitan infrastructure, such as the subway.

There you have it that people are willing to shed their exterior image, kids are ready to connect and impose their Name before the eyes of everyone, to live in risk and illegality so as to communicate. A new world is formed on the multiple urban surfaces: friendships and conflict, messages and threats, judgements and doubts between individuals that perhaps never even met. The people that seriously practice Writing are able to notice the arrival of a stranger from the signs he leaves behind. They might even understand what type of person he is and what feelings or desires they have in common. Writing is a way of leaving a mark that says more than "I was here" because those that reach full maturity in this discipline are able to transmit their identity, with only a signature and a personal style. It is hardly ever understood to what extent Writing constituted the

bursting relief valve of generations and generations, obviously it was an invasive presence in the urban landscape but it also provided a containment and "alternative" in terms of criminality: how many of us were "saved" by concentrating our energies on a train car. Aside from this "therapeutic" effect, Writing is anyway considered one of the principle causes of urban decay, but in this case as well we are facing the usual clichés and rhetoric. For one reason or another, the attention of those of us that paint is towards the more visible spots of the city and often the areas that are most frequented, those that the city has forgotten. If these areas, already degraded, are improved or not is difficult to say but what counts is the symbiotic process that is writers established with the city; an intense absorption, a thorough knowledge of places, a consciousness of the metropolitan condition that most people are forgetting. This symbiotic role that Writing can assume in urban space is not only limited to walls but can work on public transportation as well, on the cars of subway trains and their tunnels, on any vertical surface, because Writing neither damages nor penalises the function of things, it only changes their external appearance.

FRAME BY FRAME
—

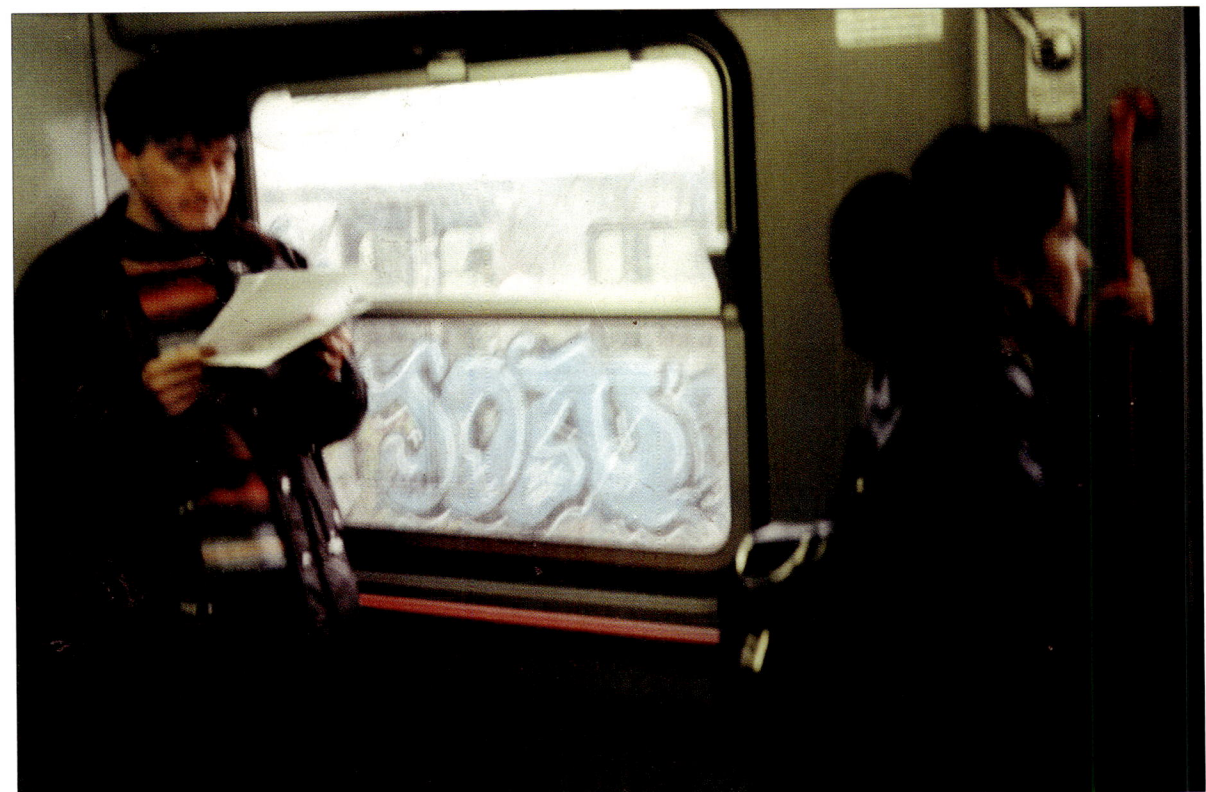

Jon
>

Painting subway trains during the day implies that my Name will be in motion most of the time. I can manage to see it only a few seconds at a time when it stops in stations. While people get on and off I only have a few seconds to take a photo. While I paint, I try to imagine my Name the next day as it moves and I try to give it that sensation I want to feel when I see it running. It's that impression that what you've just seen will pass you by and leave you within a few short minutes — which will not be like a fixed image, but more like a blurred memory. It's hard to notice all the details of a painted car as it races past you, looking dynamic slightly different every time when seen from different angles, under the sun or in the shadow of a station. The sun fades all kinds of spray paint, and the acid used to clean the windows usually finish the job. A painted piece changes over time, it moves, it gets older and eventually dies. When speaking of bombing and throwups, and of the effect I want to provoke in viewers, I imagine that the train moves frame by frame, like a movie reel. My Name has to be present on every frame, so that the horizontal motion of the train generates the repetition of my Name. A painted subway system becomes like an incredible live animation in which motion is the essence.

— Jon

A decade on the subway
>

Train car stratigraphies

Jon
>

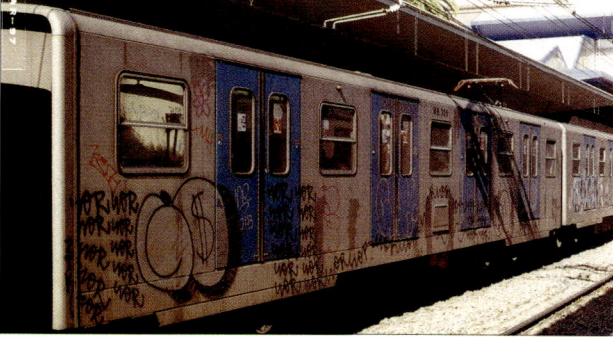
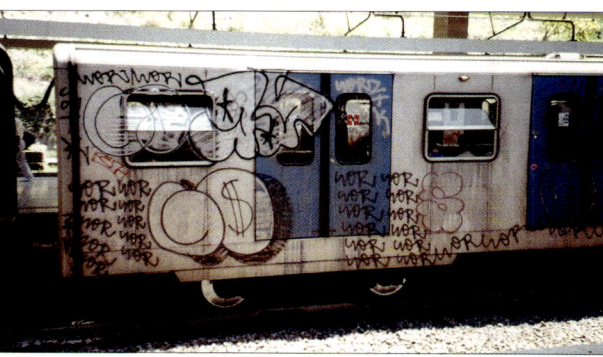
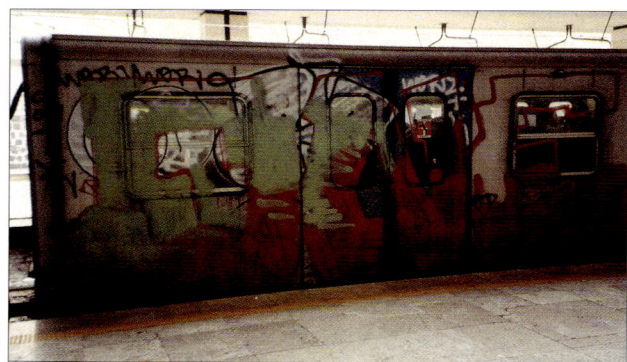
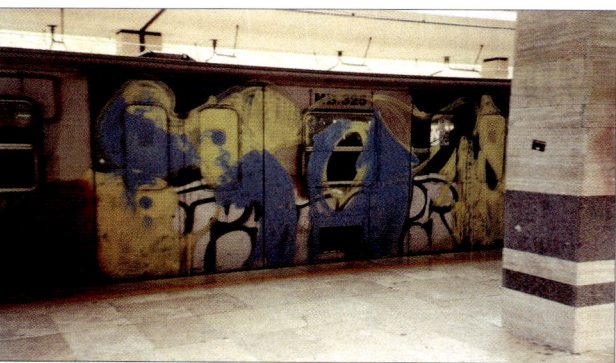
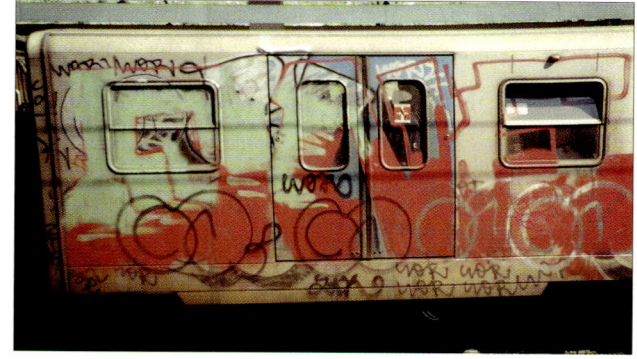
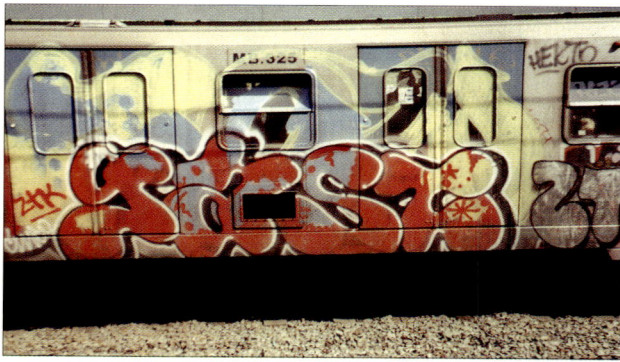

This was supposed to be a One, Jon and Gast whole-car on wagon MB 325, but we never got to finish it cause the guards managed to surprise us, and actually even started shooting. We hid the whole night in the bushes to the side of the rail tracks of the Ostia-Lido line, while the railway police were looking for us in and out of the deposit. That night Chico and Gor were with us and had also attempted a whole-car on the train in front of ours. In that period we painted so much that it wasn't hard to catch a previously unfinished piece and be able to paint it over. In this case Gor and Gast found *our* car parked in the 08 shed where broken trains were repaired, so they took advantage of the previous colouring of the top-to-bottom as filling for the new piece. Notice how under One's T2B there's a "GO-GA" throw-up from '97 on the glass windows, again by Gor and Gast, and another throw-up by Gor in '96 on the bottom and to the right a "CH" by Chico from '95! In those years we bombed and painted the same train cars so many times it wasn't difficult to see four, five or more layers of ZTK. I still wonder how in the hell it's possible for those trains to arrive at the platform without getting caught in the thickness of the accumulated paint.

—Jon

From the heart
>

I'm Joe, and I'm an infamous writer

Joe
>

My name is Joe and I'm an infamous writer. I was never very good at writing, nor at drawing or stealing high-quality spray paint: if you have no skills you have to have heart. When I first began to paint I tried to imitate things that didn't belong to me, stuff I saw in fanzines. I wasn't painting from the heart, I wasn't Joe, I was just some kid who did graffiti. But then things changed, I began to paint without thinking about Seen or Mode 2. I began to disregard technique and my style became more feral, I began doing outlines with regular caps and used highlights and shading wherever I wanted. I became Joe, an Infamous Writer. In Rome there were two generations of writers: the first generation saw graffiti for the first time in books, the second generation doesn't even remember that once upon a time Rome's subway trains were clean, they grew up seeing the trains we bombed. Me and my crew, The Riot Vandals, unlike the second generation, focused on theory too, with *Subway Art*, *SprayCan Art*, and Andrea Nelli's legendary *Graffiti in New York*, we even went on a pilgrimage to New York. After us, writers (I'm referring to good writers) no longer needed to look at fanzines and books because all of the subway trains had been bombed. Graffiti in Rome is in a natural state of grace with a past and an eternal present, making it seem as if bombing will never fade away. Seeing the trains in Rome is really striking because they're all painted and they all

Graffiti in Rome is
in a natural state of grace
with a past and
an eternal present

have a rather particular style. Roman pieces are ugly, dirty, and mean; writers leave threats for rival crews instead of leaving dedications. The style seems to have stopped at *Subway Art*, almost entirely ignoring any European style. It seems as if graffiti is and always has been a Roman thing. Writers paint with the right mindset because they're in the condition to be able to do so. There are no conventions in Rome and only toys paint in the Hall of Fame. We're the infamous writers: we like to paint with normal caps instead of skinny caps, we look at trains instead of fanzines, we're not into characters, we're more into throw-ups.

1994

One of the first end-to-ends
to be painted on the cars of
the Lido line: Fume - MSN from
Düsseldorf, *Win* by Stand - MT2 TRV,
Soa by Joe - ETC TRV, *Hes* by Sugo - ETC
TRV, *Wist* by Pane - TRV.

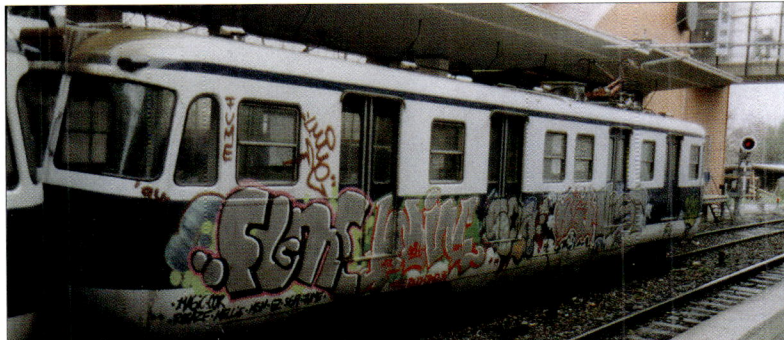

— Mark Todt

1995

The end-to-end UV crew from Paris
painted a year later, over the piece
by Fume and the other Roman writers.
This is a photo of the pane by Vanz-UV.

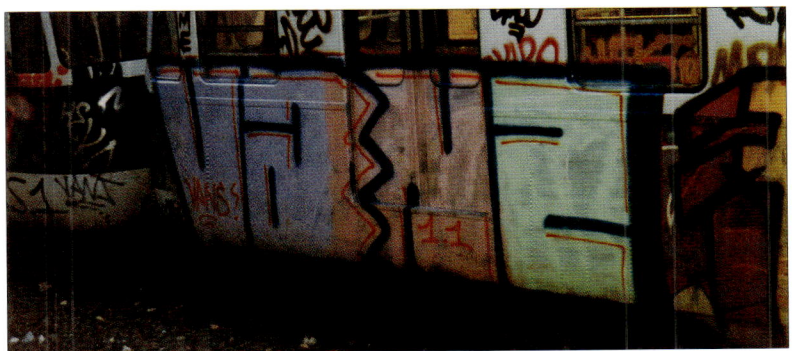

— Fuzi

1996

End-to-end by Milk and Nois
from Helsinky, *Tyson*
by Stand, painted over
the French pieces.

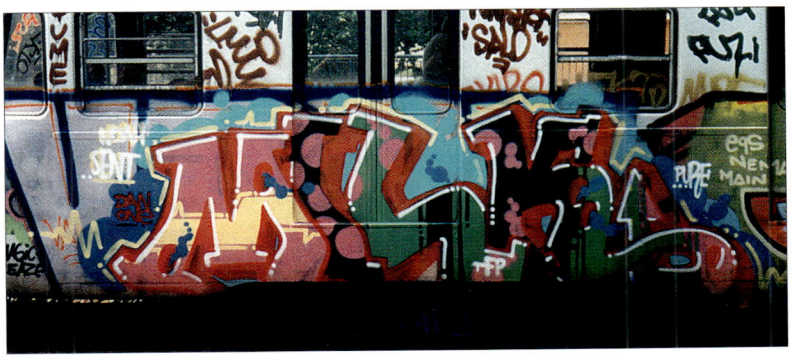

— Trota

1997

Throw-up by Gaz - UV CFK crew
from Paris.

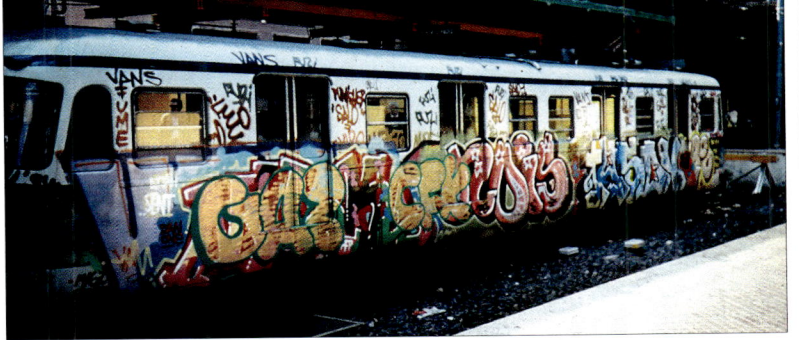

— Mencio

1998

Jon - ZTK, part of an end-to-end
that Castel and Nico -TRV, painted
years later on the same car.

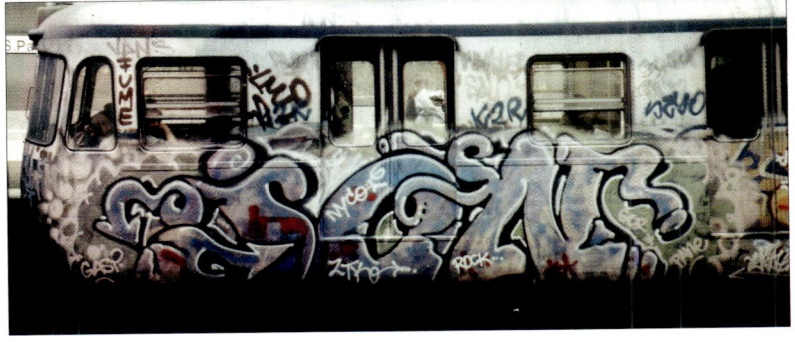

— Jon

FOREIGNERS
—

Trota
>

The crew that most changed the way of painting in Rome was RCB, who arrived from Berlin
in 1995. They came by van from Germany and
stayed in the city for more or less a month,
hitting any place at any time, in both quantity
and quality: A Line, B Line, Lido, trains from
the Ferrovie Nord, Pantano, Fl, they even
painted the 'gasolino' in Viterbo, cause we
found their tags in the deposit down there.
They came without knowing or contact-
ing anyone in Rome, but they anyway had a

> RCB couldn't care less about
> preserving spots and so entered
> by force

good hook up: Heat from SM had come here
to paint months earlier. Thanks to his tips
RCB debuted with a series of end-to-ends
and whole-cars that are still remembered
today. Super precise and enormous pieces,
silver with 10 cm black outline: well, Ger-
manic stuff that stood out in the general
scene of Rome. In Anagnina they made a huge
hole in the fence with wire cutters. We would
climb over it or leave very few traces but RCB
couldn't care less about preserving spots and
so entered by force. Many kids were looking
for them with baseball bats, cause they had
covered a shit load of people: it was inevitable.

Panda
>

Among the many foreigners that came to
Rome to paint, UV contributed in influencing the local Writing scene; probably because
they came rather early, in a period in which
any foreigner was taken as a reference point.
Fizz and company were raw, when we went
with them to the paint shop of Vertecchi,
it would turn into a raid: we entered, filled

> UV were bombing pretty heavily
> until they got caught in the end
> station of Rebibbia

our backpacks, emptied them outside and
went back in for another round. In '95 we did
some whole-cars together in Lido a couple of
times, and I took them to La Laurentina where
they did other whole-cars. They were bombing pretty heavily until they got caught in the
end station of Rebibbia, with a kitchen knife
and a hammer on them: during the preceding week they had clashed with some local
writers in Magliana and revenge was in the air.
After they got arrested in Rebibbia, they were
directly expatriated.

San Lorenzo Kidz

Napal
>

San Lorenzo suffered with my heart, its survivors and its dead have left an open road inside of me. This is how Elio Filippo, poet from San Lorenzo and pupil of Ungaretti, concluded his story about the American bombings of San Lorenzo on July 19th, 1943. San Lorenzo, a working-class neighbourhood located near Rome's central train station, has always been a place of interaction, cultural turmoil, delinquency; an inspiration for poets, writers, painters, and distinguished film directors like Pier Paolo Pasolini. Obviously, the neighbourhood has had its share of years of glory and years of misery:

"Respectable people only come to San Lorenzo once they're dead", Maria Montessori wrote back in 1907, and this reputation stuck with the area for many years... The actual urban layout of the neighbourhood- an elongated quadrilateral shape enclosed by ancient Roman walls, which contain a freight yard, a cemetery, and Via Tiburtina- demarcate it and isolate it from the rest of the urban fabric, rendering it a full-blown town within the city itself. During WWII, San Lorenzo became headquarters of the Nazi-Fascist Resistance, and this climate influenced and saturated the neighbourhood's mentality throughout the years: in the 70's during the proletarian struggle, in the 90's with student protests, and even in our days. Still today, despite the fact that property speculators and city councilmen would like to clean San Lorenzo up and make it more bourgeois, it is still a working-class

neighbourhood that embodies the real spirit of Rome. As soon as you set foot in San Lorenzo, it is clear that it's a hotspot for working-class politics, from aggressive Left-wing movements, to Roma football fan clubs, to Anarchist groups. D. Orano wrote: "The same people live and struggle in the hideous apartment blocks of San Lorenzo. This social context provides fertile terrain for the diffusion of Anarchist thought as a direct reaction to the widespread state of decay. Still today, it is common to find amidst bona fide San Lorenzo locals and those who often go there, a slight matrix of Anarchism". The phenomenon of spray painting San Lorenzo's walls began at the end of the 70's with the increasing presence of politically-charged writing associated with important squat structures like Via dei Volsci and Radio Onda Rossa (the historical radio station of the local movement), and with Roma soccer

fan clubs like C.U.C.S (Commando Ultrà Curva Sud) and THE BOYS. In addition to this, 10 years later, Roman writers began to mark San Lorenzo's walls making it one of the first neighbourhoods of the city to have numerous tags and bombings already by '87-'88, thanks to Kidz crew, who at the time were still called NFA (*New Fresh Artists*). In the years to come, it became a source of inspiration for other writers, even though access to its walls was prohibited for many years. Motivated by an uncommon gang spirit, the Kidz protected their turf by writing their name everywhere and covering other crew's tags. An atypical coexistence of various and peculiar underground groups that are poles apart in ideology but united by the spirit of the place: Roma football club hooligans (not Lazio hooligans), political activists (only Anarchists or radical Left-wing supporters), and writers too: but only the Kidz.

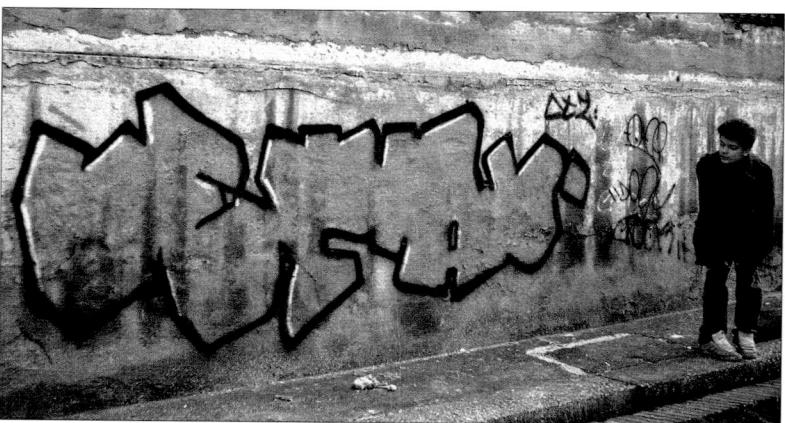

San Lorenzo, 1989   *— Napal*

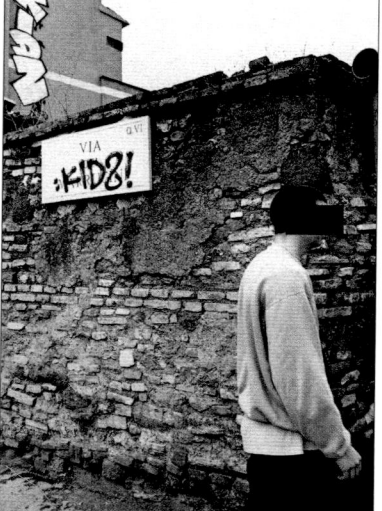

Patrizio, I wish everything could be like before   *— Napal*

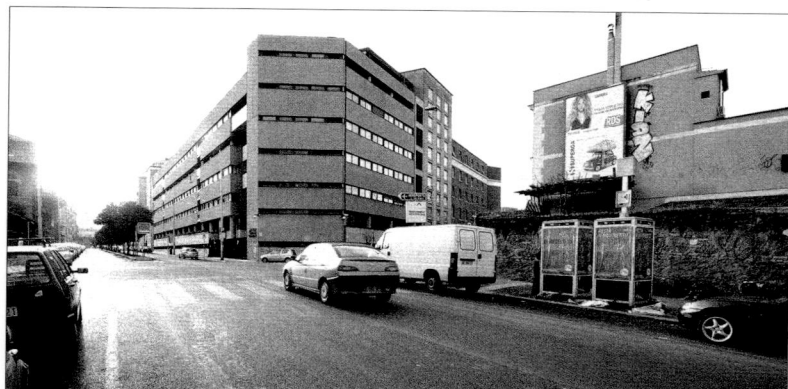

Via Cesare de Lollis   *— Napal*

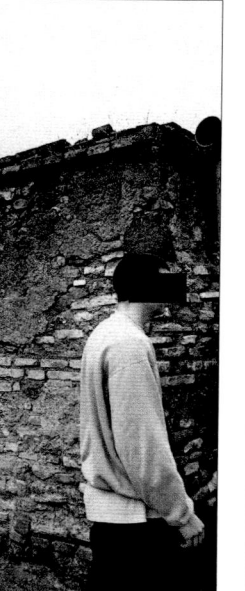

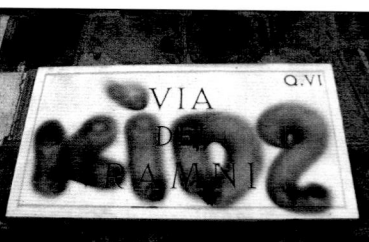

San Lorenzo skinheads   *— Napal*

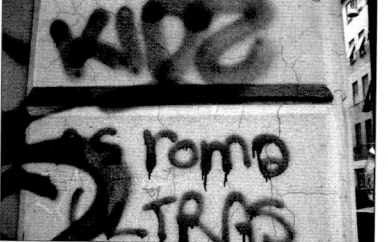

AS Roma ultras (football team fans)   *— Napal*

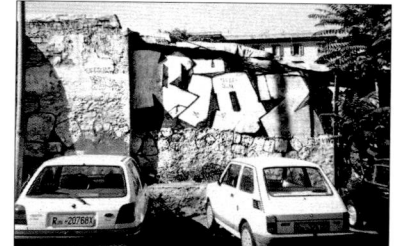

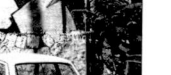

Via dei Varruggini   *— Napal*

Via dei Ramni   *— Napal*

The discovery of an abandoned area
>

Nomentana ghost station

Monia Cappuccini
>

Eastern beltway, Fonte delle Valli. It all happened by chance in the 'Africano' neighbourhood of Rome. Located between the Aniene River and Villa Ada, it was built in the 30's (and expanded after the war) in celebration of Italian colonialism. Breezy G and Cheecky P grew up in these streets and squares that bear the names of ill-omened victories (Viale Libia, Viale Eritrea, Viale Somalia, Piazza Gondar).

They were barely 21 when they decided to leave home and go to London, where they got acquainted with the black community and culture. Upon their return, they told lively tales of dancehalls, parties, crews of rappers, and naturally, graffiti.

They did more than just talk, they quickly organised an action with a "Graffiti is not a crime" piece on a wall near their house. New York writers added a number to their name to show what part of the city they were from... Well soon enough, the crew's name was: 00199, the zip code for the Africano neighborhood.

> And voilà, as if by magic you'd find yourself at the Rome–Nomentano station.
> The train schedule, the platform with red awnings and kilometres upon kilometres of asphalt instead of tracks: a ghost station, a world within a world.

The Ferrovie dello Stato began construction of the Rome Nomentano station in preparation for the 1990 World Cup games in Italy. Not only would it be a passageway for trains coming from the North, but Nomentano was also meant to be one of the first stops on the commuter train line that went from Fara Sabina (on Via Salaria, beyond the beltway) all the way to Leonardo da Vinci airport.

But the construction was soon halted, it wasn't completed in time for the World Cup and the site was left half finished. You could get there from Viale Etiopia, over the pedestrian crossing that linked the Africano and Monte Sacro neighbourhoods. The first exit led straight to the station, at first it was open but soon enough they put it under lock and key. So in order to get in you had to go to the Rome–Salario line), walk along the platform beyond the "Do not go beyond this point" sign, walk for a few more metres, then turn left into a passageway, cross the Rome–Milan tracks

(making sure no trains were coming), and voilà, as if by magic you'd find yourself at the Rome–Nomentano station.

The train schedule, the platform with red awnings, and kilometres upon kilometres of asphalt instead of tracks: a ghost station, a world within a world. It didn't take Breezy G and Cheecky P long to track it down: it was right across the street from them, by simply exchanging glances they knew what move to make next.

They were the first to defile it together with Drenni and Panama (other members of the crew, I joined them later) and their piece read "Buon compleanno Tansì", signed Onda Rossa Posse. It was November 1990. That piece marked the beginning of a history that was, for the most part written on these walls. From the heroic phase of *Due Pesi Due Misure, Tessere la Ragnatela, Fiume in Rotta, Senza Paure, Non è Mai l'Ultima Volta*, to life's sad moments and the many phrases and messages of love after the death of Cheecky P in April 1991.

We'd go there to paint, to test colours, to take pictures, to "check" if there were any new pieces, to ease our suffering by staring at Cheecky P's graffiti, to look for friends, to show the place to others, to smoke joints.

We felt at home in that abandoned place. With long strides, smiling as we walked, as if we were at the centre of the world. Cheecky P, Breezy G, Panama, Drenni, and Baby were our names. I never fully understood if being an all-girl crew worked to the advantage or disadvantage of our reputation. Undoubtedly, the fact that we 'discovered' Nomentano worked to our advantage, this plus the fact that we were girls certainly made our story unique.

The world of Writing is predominantly male (but non sexist), we knew we were an exception and the gender difference in never caused us to feel uncomfortable. Plus, in the beginning there were so few of us that things were mellow; as the level of competition grew, so did the level of machismo, but we were out of the game by then. It happened naturally, it wasn't premeditated: the fact that we were all girls created a more intense sense of complicity and granted us an image we liked. Some of us studied, some worked, some did both; we were all more or less on our own already. Even without Writing we were emancipated, and we were probably big enough for graffiti, but Writing opened up another chapter in the story of our independence, and nobody can say we didn't give it our all. Together we made the best of what we knew, we leafed through books ad nausea (we looked at Lady Pink in *Subway Art* and thought: We can do it!), we spent entire afternoons drawing and sketching. It became our obsession, our urban compass; although we weren't experts on technique, we certainly knew enough about 'behavioural codes'.

At first, there weren't many pieces at Nomentano, only about a dozen around the platform. Slowly but steadily though, the walls were being covered. The scene existed and was growing, totally unaware that

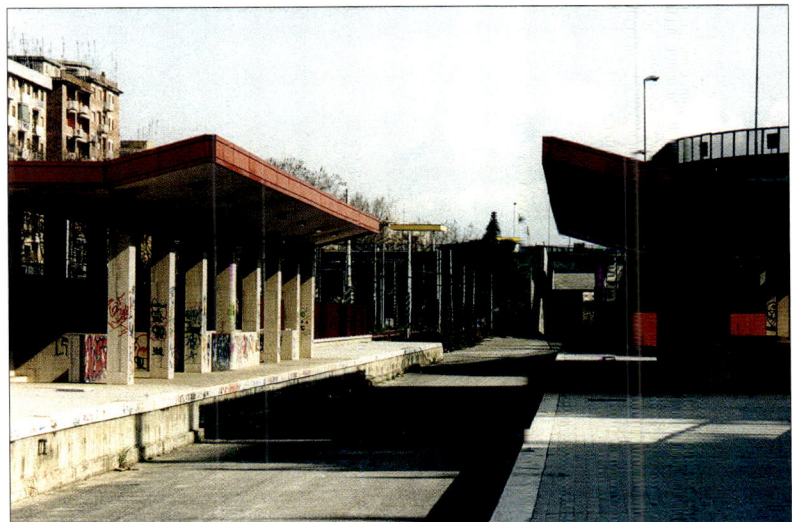

Nomentano Station before the opening of the railway line, 1990   — *Monia Cappuccini*

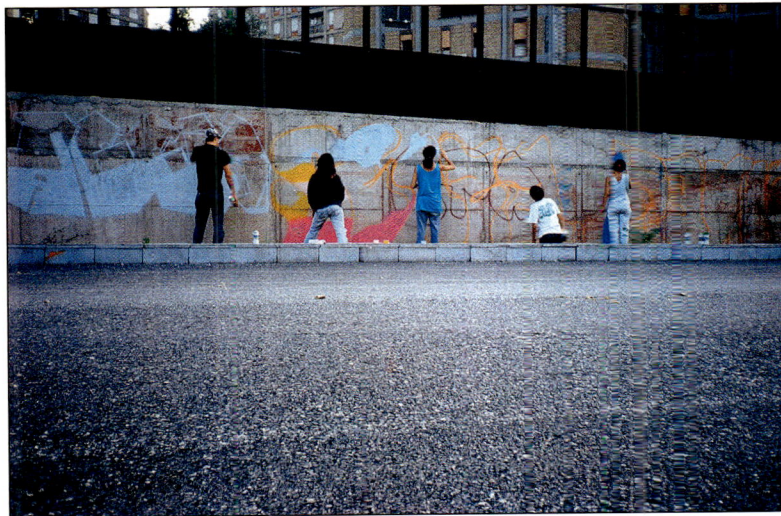

00199 crew in action on the railtrack wall of Nomentano   — *Monia Cappuccini*

it reached a point of no return. The entire Roman old school was there: Licensed to Art, Crash Kid and Napal (whose name at the time was Ioice, future king of San Lorenzo with The Kidz) with their manga faces and giant pieces executed with the nozzle technique to control the pressure; "Do it" by Fab137 (he called himself that because he lived near the 137 bus depot at Val Melaina) with a character like Radio Raheem (from *Do the Right Thing* by Spike Lee) with a spraycan in hand instead of a tape deck; "Messaggio" by Lion Horse Posse, special guests from Leonkavallo (historic social centre in Milan) and Kino, who was also from Milan, together with 00199 on "Mura da abbattere"; a blockbuster by Painters Squad 113 in white and silver. And Check, a writer from London who spent a few months in Rome, noticeably raising the technical and stylistic level and outshining local writers. He did two pieces together with Breezy G at Nomentano. One was: "Hell hath no fury like Heaven" – it truly seemed like heaven

and hell had collided on those 20 metres of wall — and "Angel" with a dolphin for Breezy.

– A POINT IN THE MIDDLE OF NOWHERE
At this point, starting from zero, the cultural sun was so low on the horizon that our energy was what warmed us, and even our nano traces at Nomentano station managed to cast long shadows.

For quite some time, that was the only noteworthy hall of fame in the city, and the later generations continued to go there as if on a pilgrimage to their homeland. In 1992, Assalti Frontali (ex-Onda Rossa Posse) released the album Terra di nessuno; on the cover was a night shot of Rome Nomentano with a solitary traveller walking away from the camera: "A point in the middle of nowhere" raps Militant A in the song "Terra di nessuno". An inspiring place, a resource. But the end of Nomentano's golden age was near. In 1997 it definitively returned to its original function.

A–LINE
The subway of Rome

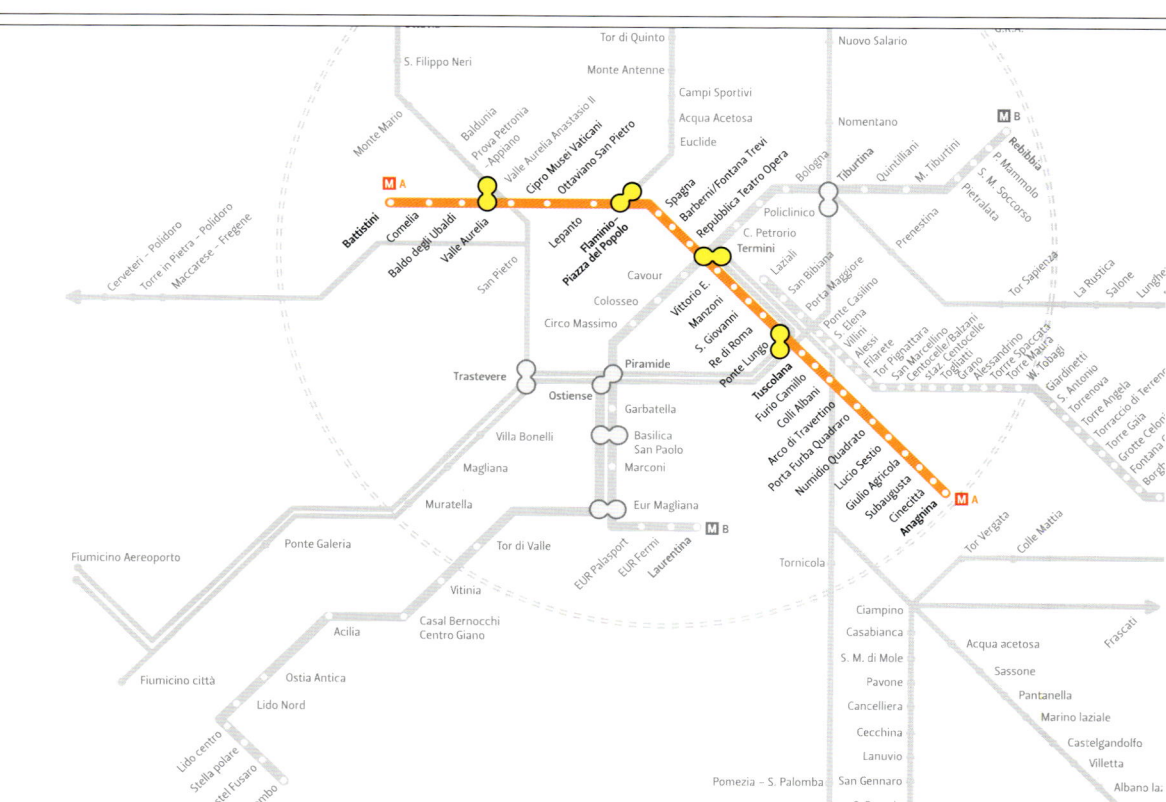

The A–line of the subway became operative in 1980. It runs from Battistini to Anagnina, cutting through the city from North–East to South–East. With 486 runs a day it transports more than 450,000 passengers. The excavation works were represented in the Fellini film *Roma*.

The A line yard
>

Inside Anagnina

Pane
>

Painting the yard of Anagnina during the day. Adventures, Sunday picnics, and missions among trains.

I'm sure of the date because it's written on the photo, it was a day in April 1994 and the yard was the one in Anagnina. I also remember that was the first time we painted during the day in that yard, I entered alone while the others were watching my back and checking the situation outside. It was a test to see if it was possible to paint during the day. It turned out positive and from that mo-

> 66
> Painting during the day greatly changed our perspective, we took mad photos in front of our pieces

ment on we often visited Anagnina. We'd go there on Sundays towards 1 o'clock, when activity in the yard was at a minimum and we could make sure we had the maximum amount of time possible among the train cars.
Painting during the day greatly changed our perspective, we took mad photos in front of our pieces, using flashes at night was not advisable and so pictures didn't

come out as well; other than that during the day we also brought our lunch with us, especially Joe, whom we called "scuccamella" because of his habit of bringing pasta in tupperware containers. Then, once we had finished painting, we would spend the rest of the day together, with the taste of the yard and the train pieces we had painted still fresh on our lips, the excitement accompanying us the whole day through. Sometimes we'd go to Stand's room, where he'd let us hear the latest Funk records he had bought at the flea market, and where we'd look at photos (when it came to archiving photos

he was the biggest nerd). Then he would always offer us some cognac in the appropriate glasses and some tea of the finest quality, he was a good cook and so we'd often stay for dinner. One time, after Anagnina, we went to the "Sagra del Vino" in Castelli, a place not too distant from the yard. In that occasion the wine spurts out from a fountain and you can drink it in all possible forms, and we started doing the 'caprone' on the street, a particularly advanced Breakdance step that comes out better if you've filled up on some wine; that step also helped us expel the excess alcohol in various corners of the town.

Going to Anagnina in the day time was a blast. Not much later we even started bringing some foreign friends, and we did so for quite a while, until we had an argument with the old man that had his home right next to the yard. It was useless trying to explain to him that we weren't causing any harm, he kept on threatening us with his dog, saying he would call the police. So we loosened the hold and started hitting other spots.
I've been told that area has now changed a lot, where once was a road they now expanded the yard that reaches the housing projects. I also saw some videos of

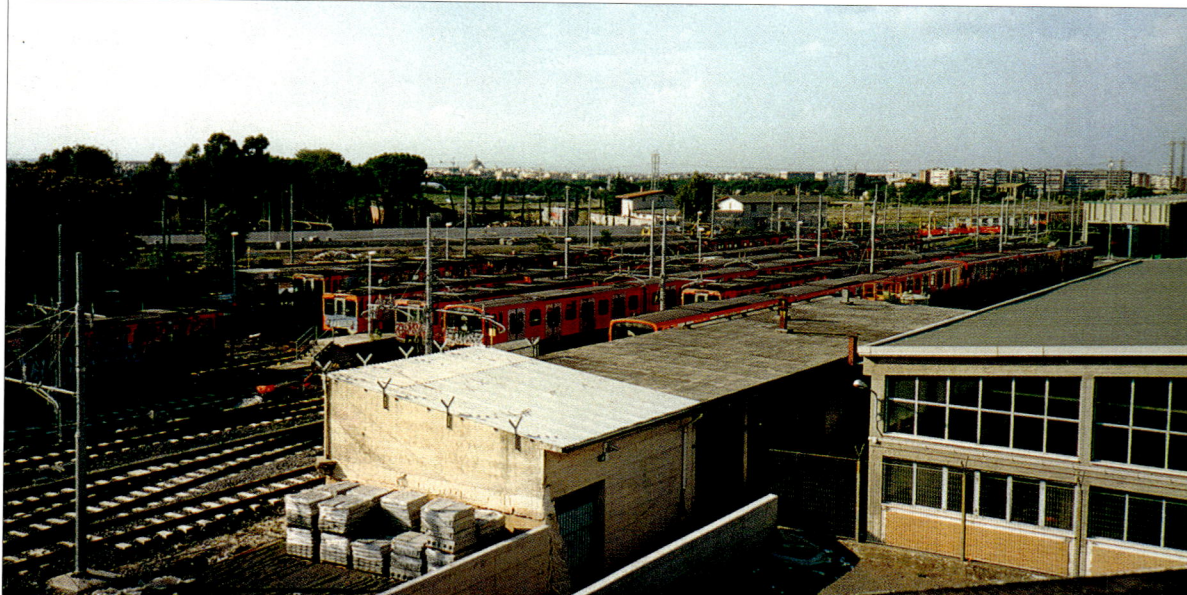

View from above of Anagnina deposit, before the graffiti boom

— *Mark Todt*

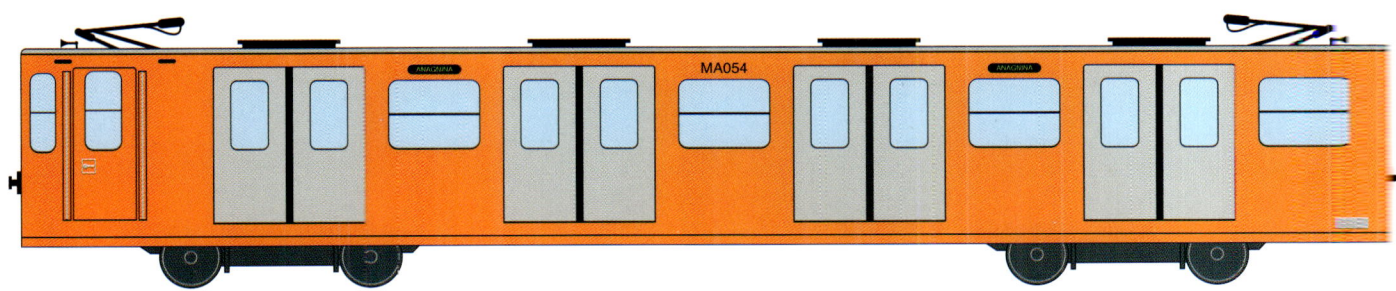

"Rome's subsoil is unpredictable. Every 100 metres there are important ancient ruins and any underground work naturally suffers from this. It's a very difficult job. We simply wanted to solve a problem related to urban traffic, build a circular subway such as in Munich or Dublin, but here the soil has eight layers and we have to turn into archeologists, speleologists. The first time there was talk sof a subway in Rome was in 1871, exactly 100 years ago. Burocracy is even more unpredicatble than the subsoil, the correspondence exchanged between us and the authorities of Rome could fill the entire subway route.".

From *Roma* by Federico Fellini, 1972

---

stone-throwing fights with the railway police... it's just not the place we used to picnic in on Sundays anymore.

– RIDERS OF THE STORM

Me and Giaime didn't do much together and we weren't even in the same crew, but that night no-one from my crew wanted to go on a mission, so for the first time we organised to paint a train together.

It was raining heavily, but I would never give up a night painting. I lived on the Northern outskirts of Rome, in the area where the city's ring road crosses Via Boccea, next to the Aurelia road, in a neighbourhood called Selva Candita. From there to Giaime's house, which was in Prati, at full speed on my Red Rose 50 motorcycle took about twenty minutes, and once at Giaime's it was another good half hour at least to the yard of Anagnina, where we had decided to go.

We were hoping it would stop raining, because long storms in Rome are rather rare, but this was going to be one of those. Wishing it would end, we arrived at the yard of Anagnina, as drenched as a dishwashing sponge, or a shower sponge abandoned at the bottom of the tub after a long bath. When we got there we were

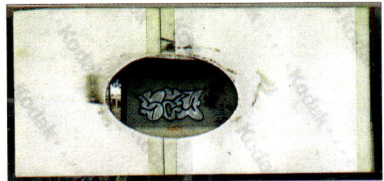

Say, throw-up by Giaime   – *Pane*

in a bad mood, wanting to be anywhere else, but we didn't tell each other this. We brushed it off like it was nothing and after parking the Red Rose we walked towards the fence of the yard by way of a little dirt road. There were project houses in that neighbourhood but the area around the yard was open countryside, and even included a farmhouse and corn fields. When we got to the wire fence Giaime tried climbing over it; in spite of my physical help and my moral encouragement in the form of "come on, hold on there, now pull up your foot, lift your leg...", he couldn't make it. So I got in the yard alone, with even less desire to be there. I did a couple of trains, some silver and black flops, and apart from my tag I also wrote Giaime's. The result being that, because of the rain, the colours didn't stick, and when I got back to the other side of the fence all that was left was a muddle of paint on the metal.

We approached the Red Rose, parked next to a small building which held the electricity metres that fed and served the entire project neighbourhood. Before leaving, Giaime did a flop in silver and black on a wall of this building, he wrote "Say", that was one of his names, and I did something else on another wall. Giaime, in things that did not involve getting over walls and fences, was really good, and you could tell by looking at his flop that he had

> 66
> You could tell by looking at his flop that he had put in a lot of time studying it

put in a lot of time studying it, but perhaps it wasn't just time, because I also spent it doing the same but never came out with a flop like this. We didn't say anything to the others regarding this meagre mission, much time has passed so I can talk about it now. What remains, other than the memories, is this photo of SAY by Giaime on that little building of electricity metres, which I took some time later, when I had gone there with some kids from my crew that knew how to climb over a fence.

DAYTIME ACTIONS
—

Towards the middle of the 90s we would go to Anagnina at any hour; morning, afternoon, evening. I remember for a period we had accepted a commission by AvantA , a clothing brand that asked us to paint the 5x3 metre advertising spaces spread through out Rome directly with spray cans. They gave us I don't even know how many Felts and naturally we used about half. One morning went real early to paint for AvantArt and I then decided to hit Anagnina: I went to check the situation at lunch but ZTK had just bombed , the paint was still fresh. So with Vela I went to take a look around Cinecittá, to then return around 6 in the evening: Vela was no expert of the deposit and followed my every step. When we got in we saw a train being maneuvered along the tracks, and so decided to station the trash train on lookout. We waited some time and then advanced towards the front of the car to check out the situation. Igot quite a shock when I arrived to the head of the locomotive and found a guard two metres away from me: he had kept an eye on us ever since we were outside the yard and had decided to walk towards us instead of waiting for us to come his way. I shouted for Vela to run along the dead track line but due to his inexperience he had no idea of which pylon to take advantage of in climbing over the fence.

We both started panicking because we could hear gun shots without actually seeing the guard that was shooting since he was running parallel to us but on the other side of the train. I guided our escape from the yard towards an antique Roman aqueduct that brought you into an enormous field full of ancient ruins: today it's an archeological park. Entering the park was always a risk as you could get caught by the guards on car, but luckily the end of the aqueduct we saw a bus. The driver was waiting for us, thinking we were running to catch it: we got on at once, completely covered in sweat, we looked at each other and started laughing, but I'll never forget how much we threw up once we got off – TRST2

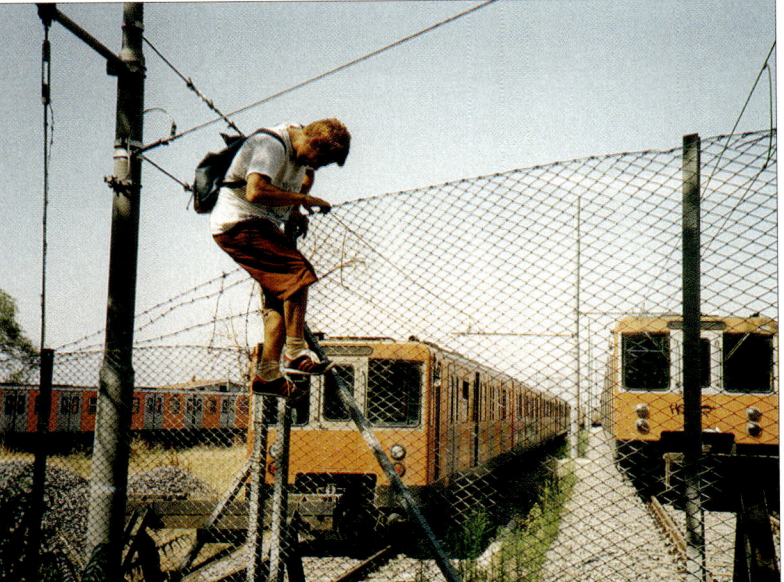

Pane as he climbs over the fence of Anagnina yard   – *Mark Todt*

Notes from the underground
>

Fragments of the A-line

Mencio
>

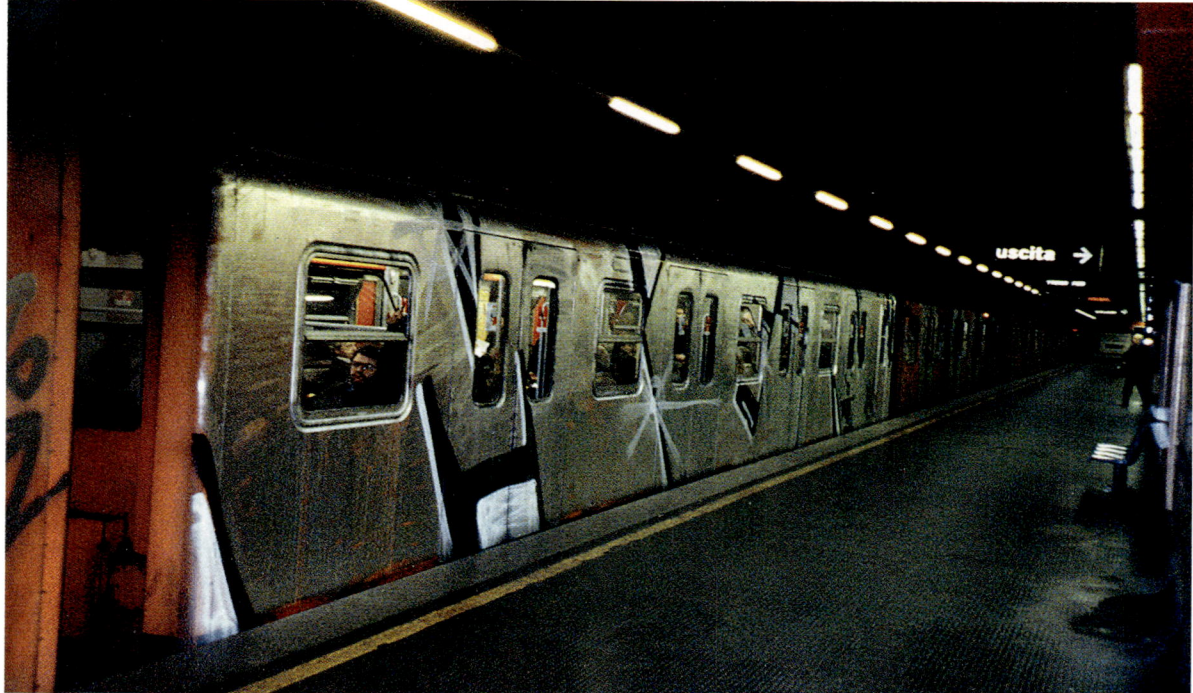

One man whole-car of Mencio-PAC, A-line

— *Mencio*

I think it was 1996. The A line, the one with reddish-orange cars, the most underground, hadn't been regularly bombed since ETC's regular raid period. A few pieces came out during the holidays or on rainy nights, but still, the line was mostly clean. Too much. And everybody knows the harder it gets, the more prestigious it is. When a line is regularly painted it means it's basically for practice. When it's hard, maybe only the bravest, most badass writers do it, but it's still possible. When a line is more or less virgin there are more uncertainties, so the crew or the writer opening the way gets the credit - recognised or not – in Writing's micro-history.

The beginning of the change coincided with a very precise episode, with a train parked in the tunnel before San Giovanni station, the one leading to the famous Basilica. This meant that if you wanted, you could reach the cars from the platform. What a spot! I was with Foe, a writer from Bordeaux, who was my guest at the time. I had gathered some 'free' Buntlack spray; even a tag would have been worth it with that paint, but to enter the tunnel right in front of the cameras and the people was risky. The adrenaline told us to "Go!" and then "Let go…" After some brisk reasoning, we decided to move when the passengers were getting out of the train, so that the crowd all over the platform would keep the camera screens busy. At the same time, everybody was turning their back to us because they were heading towards the exit, while the awaiting passengers were pushing to get on. There! We made it. We were in the tunnel and we were running along a tight sidewalk. Let's stop at the first car! No, at the second! At the third one then, so that the engine driver doesn't see us when he comes to take his train back. Everything's dark, every passing subway almost takes us away with its uproar. Along with my heart beating like mad in my chest, the scent of paint engulfed us. That I'll see the traces we left on the cars everyday, excites me. About fifteen minutes, no more, even though the temptation to stay is strong. We wait for the next train to stop at the

We feel relaxed, exalted and strong

station, we run after it like mad, we reach the platform. The luminosity blinds us, we feel light, everything surrounding us appears unfamiliar, distant. We feel relaxed, exalted and strong… it's the magical feeling you get post train-writing. It's the very search for this feeling that

always leads me to do trains. I feel full, satisfied, even though afterwards I'm already fired up for the next one. Finally, a spot at rush hour, out of the regular Roman standard. I don't remember if we waited at the station or if I saw the piece later on. Foe was a little disappointed by his silver and black, but I was in seventh heaven. The joy we felt seeing our pieces along the

Only Rome can offer such a considerable contrast: the genius of the ancient town close to a subway warehouse

A line pushed us to repeat our deeds. We had to find other solutions. So, like with the orange train line, we took advantage of the shorter days of winter and autumn. This had to be the timetable, not painting while the yard slept during the night, but while the yard was wide awake; it's ten times better. The A Line deposit, South-East of Rome, was a suggestive place. With the new district council and an interest in crumbling ruins and Roman aqueducts, the whole area contiguous to the warehouse was fenced off. Only Rome can offer such a considerable contrast: the genius of the ancient town close to a subway deposit. Fragments of an important era next to the culture diffusion of Writing, first from New York and then from Europe. For Romans, the ancient and modern have always coexisted. Every afternoon, me and PAC Crew go to the warehouse. Our gear is always the same, not really striking, not really Hip Hop. We pack a plastic bag with

a six-pack of spray cans and sport gloves and a wool hat to make us unrecognisable, keep us warm, and at the very least a little mask to keep us from inhaling too much aerosol. The wall we have to climb over is high on the way in and even higher on the way back, because you have to start from a lower level; but agility is a challenge as well. The contrast between artificial lights, underground shades and the coming of the night disguises you well on the one hand, but on the other deceives you about the presence of guards, workers, or train drivers. We always paint on the side closest to the wall, the first pieces are nickel silver, small and unsatisfactory. As we get acquainted with the yards and our reconnaissance improves, we move towards the central platforms.
Once our control of the place increases, we clearly understand that we can dare to

Only The contrast between artificial lights, underground shades and the coming of the night disguises you well on the one hand, but on the other deceives you about the presence of guards, workers, or train drivers.

paint at any moment of the day. This same reasoning is carried out on the rail routes that connect the city to the seaside. PAC crew bombed the A line.
We did the first whole-car pop up, the first

end-to-end. And on New Year's Eve, the first whole-train. The frequency of our tags and pieces increased. The line became ours, and the stories multiplied. I can't tell you how many times the cops have shot at us. In that moment, you have no fear. You just think of running and trying not to get screwed. You don't want to stop on the painted train, you don't want to stop. Besides the action, snapping pictures took

Finally, a spot at rush hour, out of the regular Roman standard

a lot of time and patience. Writing can be very ephemeral when you have no images to hand out, to swap, to publish. By day we used to go out of the yard to do our trainspotting in turns; hours of waiting for a car that never comes. Also the control tower noticed us, and we were chased several times. Trivial compared to our need to write our pieces. Wonderful years, I can't tell you the satisfaction of seeing a train roll by with your Name written on it; the signature, the signs of wanting more, more than others dared. Every story is just a little fragment. The moments, the days, the awaiting, the escapes, the feeling of omnipotence, overcoming your fears: you can't start all this over again. That's why those who bomb a lot of trains can't be associated with those who only paint walls. Trains travel with you, embodying your desire of ubiquity, a desire that runs through intensely populated territories; even if cleaned, the fragments of the A line will forever belong to us.

A spot discovered at the end of the 90's
>

Down the rabbit hole

Trota
>

The idea of a totalising crew stemmed from seeing the Scandinavian examples of VIM, MOAS, AOD, and so on. We knew some of them thanks to a series of trips to Stockholm and visits on their part to Rome. At the time we were ZKM, and Vela, Puer, Fox, Dale and I were thinking of joining PAC to form a mega group. With time Mencio, Syla and company got tight with Hiom and Fonzie and the whole thing faded, ZKM broke up and we five opted for THE. The beginning certainly wasn't of the best, on a visit to Naples we went through a tough night in the yard of Quarto, a lot of tension and panic. So when we got back to Rome

we immediately abandoned the whole idea.
After a period of indecision, one evening we talked about it and decided to take the thing seriously: drop our respective names to only write THE. That's how the whole deal began: by December we had already counted 120 pieces between whole-cars, panels, end-to-ends, and up to two one-man whole-trains on the A line. Other writers turned pale.
Perhaps the biggest blow was the discovery of the underground yard of Anagnina. Walking through a plowed field, in the middle of nothing, we finally found the two manholes that led to the underground tunnels. There had to be an emergency exit in the whereabouts of Anagnina because right next to the yard the subway goes beneath the surface of the ground and trains pass right under the cultivated field. On this level two

trapdoors existed, one with a ladder and the other without: both went down two floors, arriving first at a mezzanine and then directly into the tunnel with the cars.
In winter, when it rained, we would descend with plastic bags on our feet and take them off on the first level so as not to leave

> 66
>
> To preserve the secret I went around saying I knew the security guard on duty at the deposit of Anagnina

footprints in the yard; we were so obsessed by this place, we even avoided painting the new train models with rhombus-shaped doors and aimed only at

the old trains, already painted. To preserve the secret I went around saying I knew the security guard on duty at Anagnina, which is the deposit in the open where everybody painted, and that kept the other groups at bay, at least for a while.
When we went to paint and passed this plowed field we would bring bags full of spray cans and also empty bags because on the way back we'd stop to load up on vegetables: it was like going to the grocery. And in winter they would keep the cows there; initially it was pretty funny but then it became a problem because with the cold the cows would all heap on top of the trapdoor, as the warm air would come up from the underground. One time moving them was so hard that we had to give up, without knowing it the company managing the Roman subway had found the best guards they ever had.

Train authors
>

1. SNOY ZTK
2. JON ZTK
3. PANDA MDF THE
4. CROMO MT2-TPV
5. DEBS MT2-TRV
6. WAZ BY STAND TRV
7. STINK BY STAND TRV
8. COMA ETC-TRV
9. HESTRO ETC-TRV
10. ANEK MDF THE
11. THE CREW
12. YESS
13. DOME

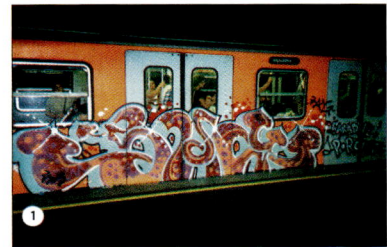

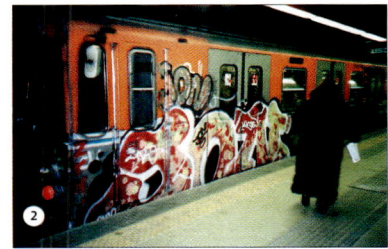

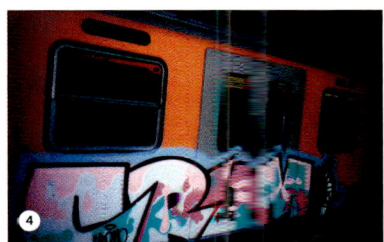

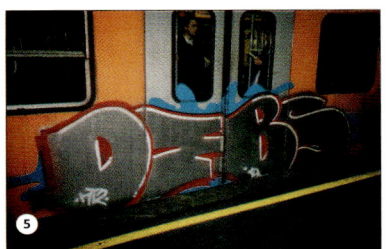

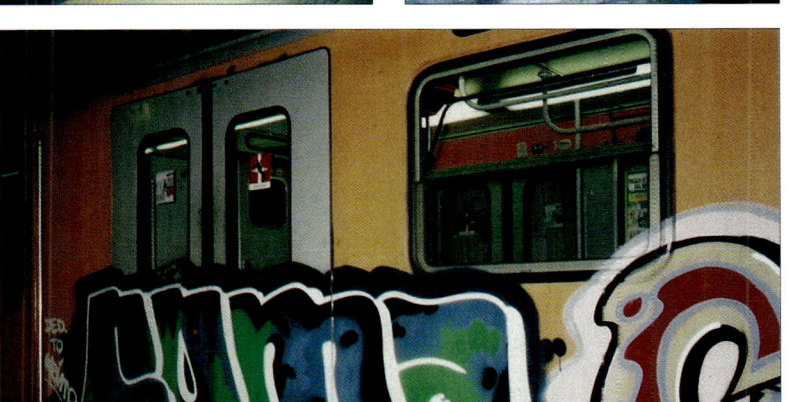

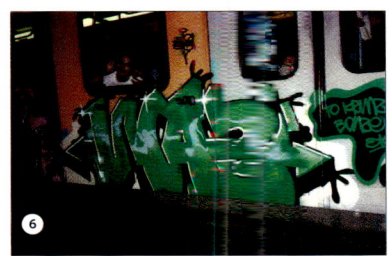

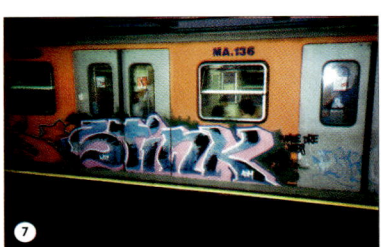

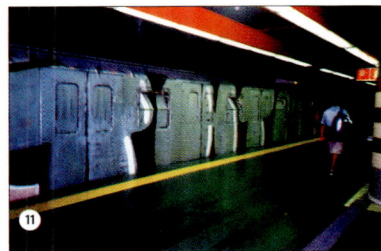

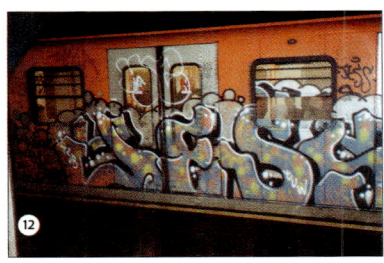

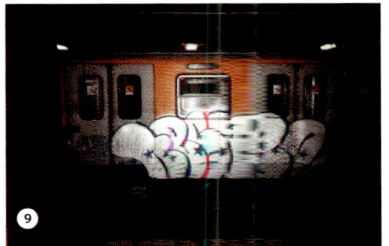

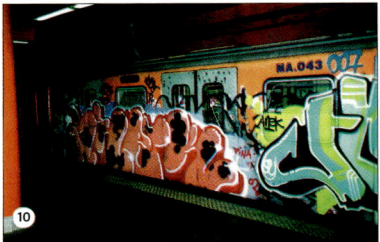

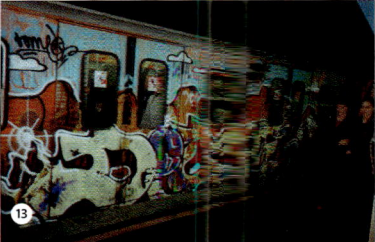

INVERSE RULES

—

One ZTK

>

The most representative yard of the A line might be Anagnina, though there are many smaller and more charming ones. Anagnina however has similar characteristics to Magliana: it's in the open and has various possible entries, it also has the same type of cement platforms in the same disposition; and here as well the guards were trigger–happy on a daily basis. It was one of the first yards that went from nocturnal graffiti to daytime actions, right under the sun.

When they defend something too much, having the power to do so, it's no use resisting but rather try to locate the 'constants' and change them so as to try to make the difference. During the day the guards were much more relaxed, their rounds were less frequent; before the first shot had been fired an incalculable quantity of cars had already been painted and all this was considered by us not as a victory but rather as an incentive to continue winning; our evolution required a constant transformation.

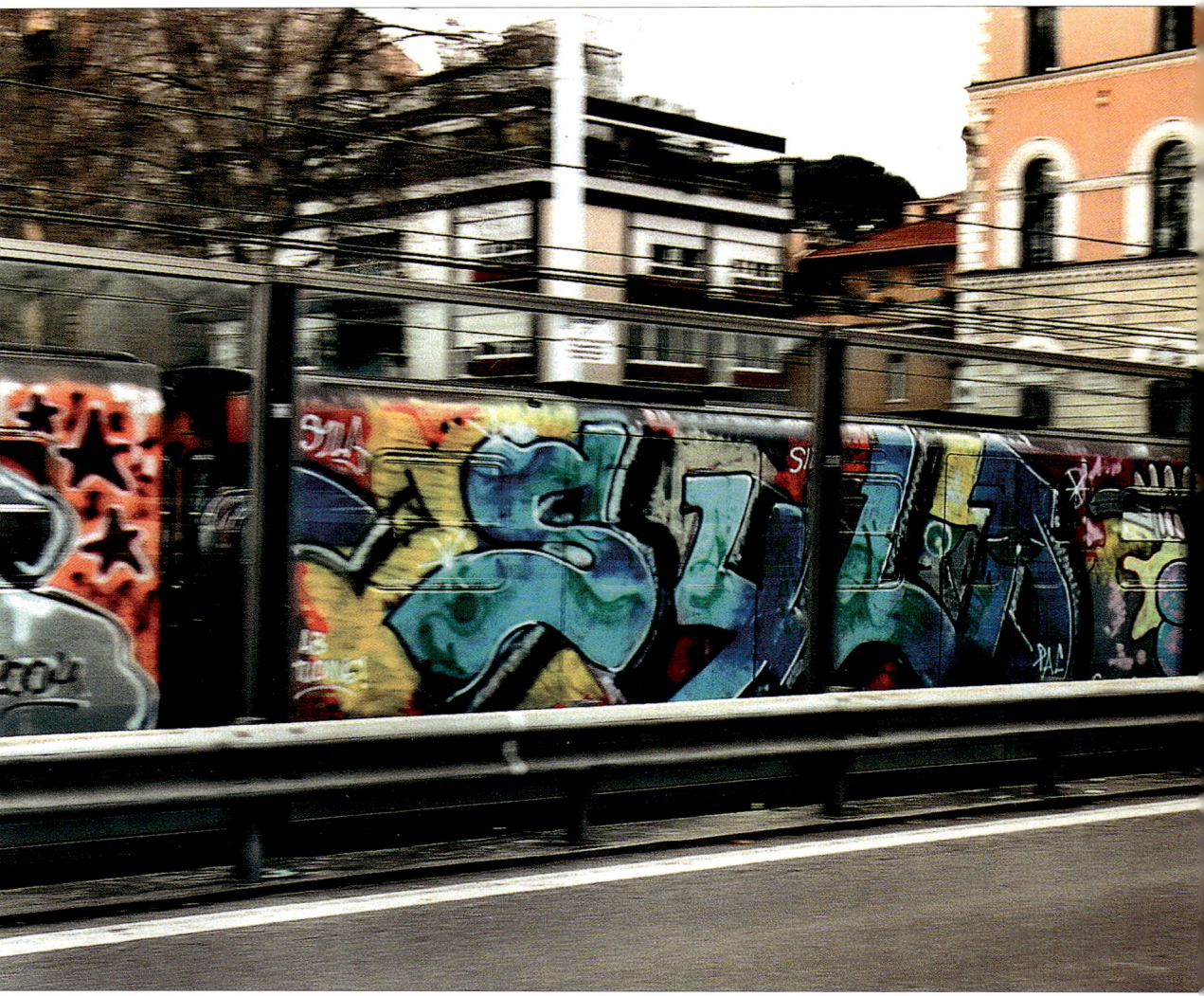

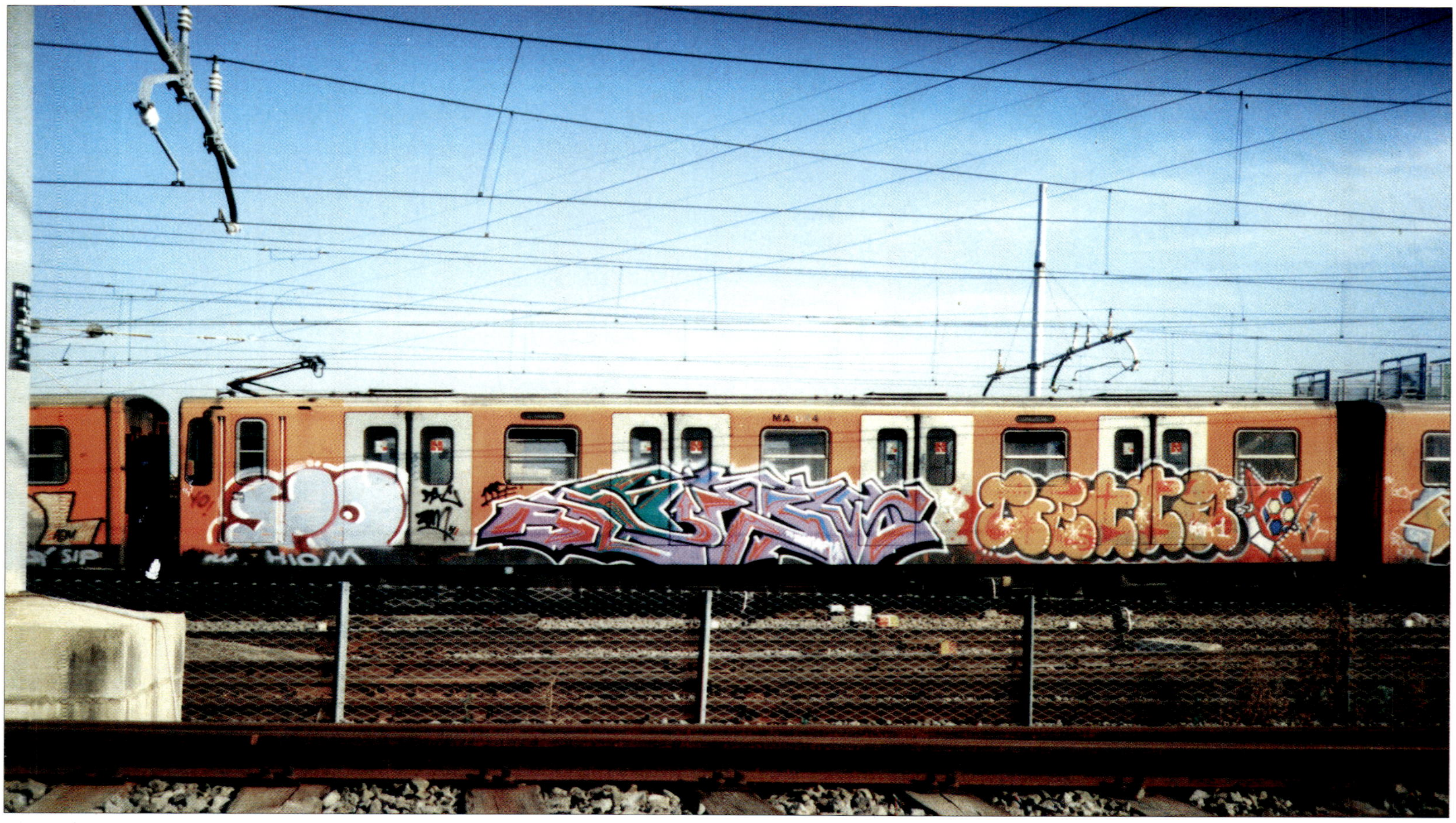

— Mencio

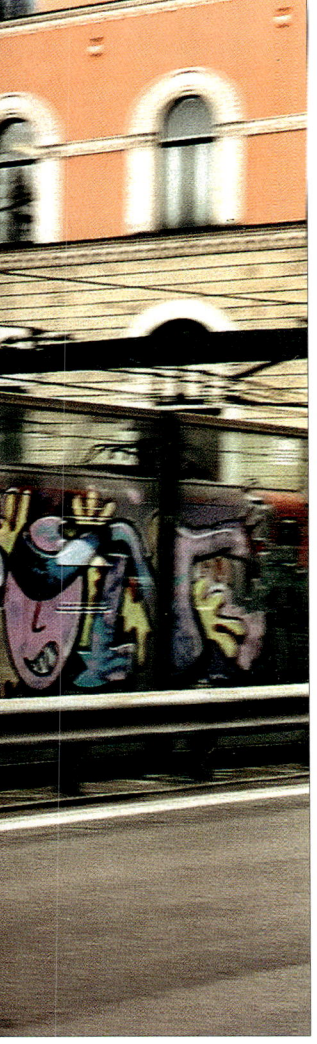

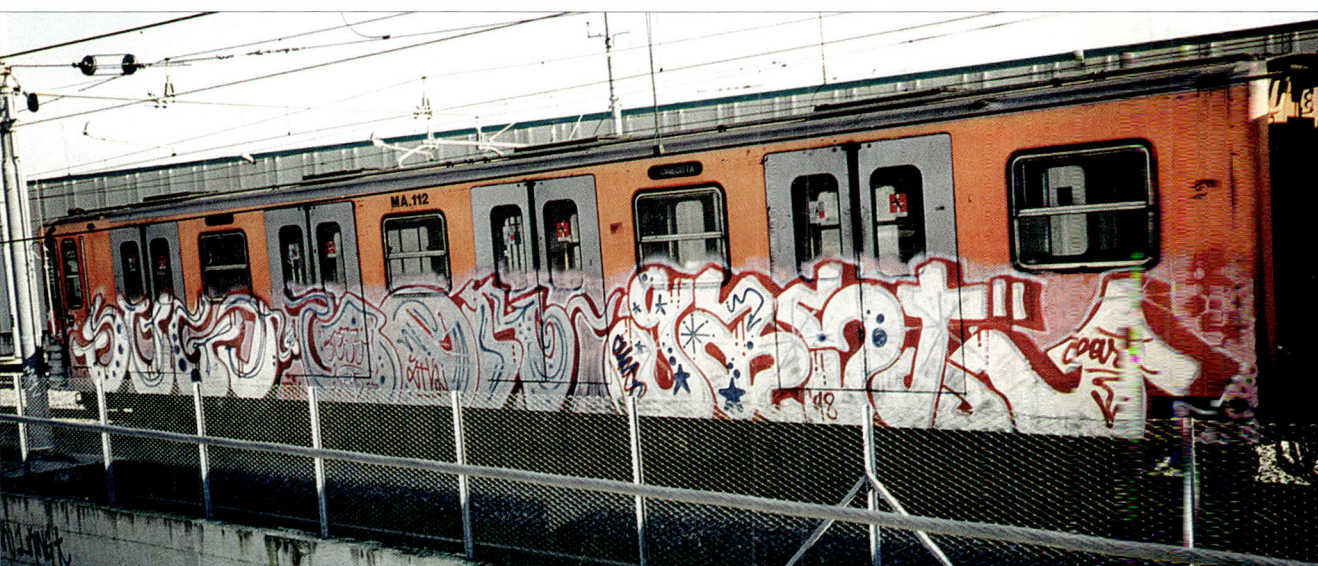

— Mencio

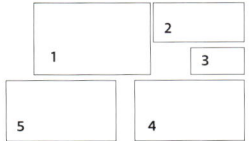

1. Syla PAC-ZTK, Jon-ZTK, whole-car transiting over Pietro Nenni bridge
2. Sugo-TRV, Gor-ZTK, Gast-ZTK, end-to-end, 1998
3. Dale ZKM crew, 1997
4. Zeir-PAC, Gor-ZTK
5. *Yo* by Hiom, Asme PAC and *Getty* di Fonzy, 1996

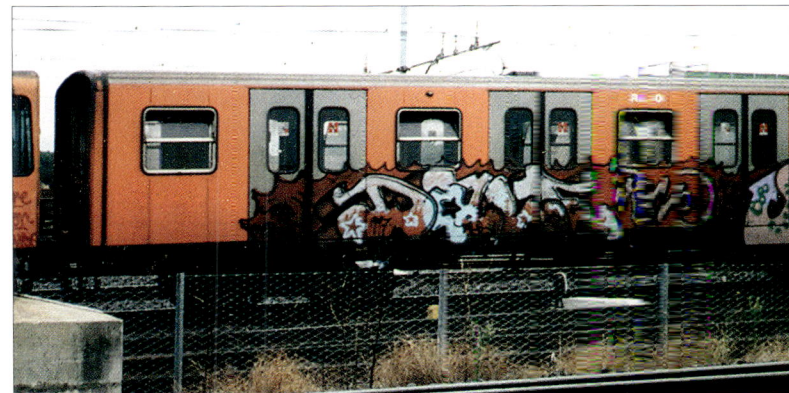

— Son

— Maccaroni archive

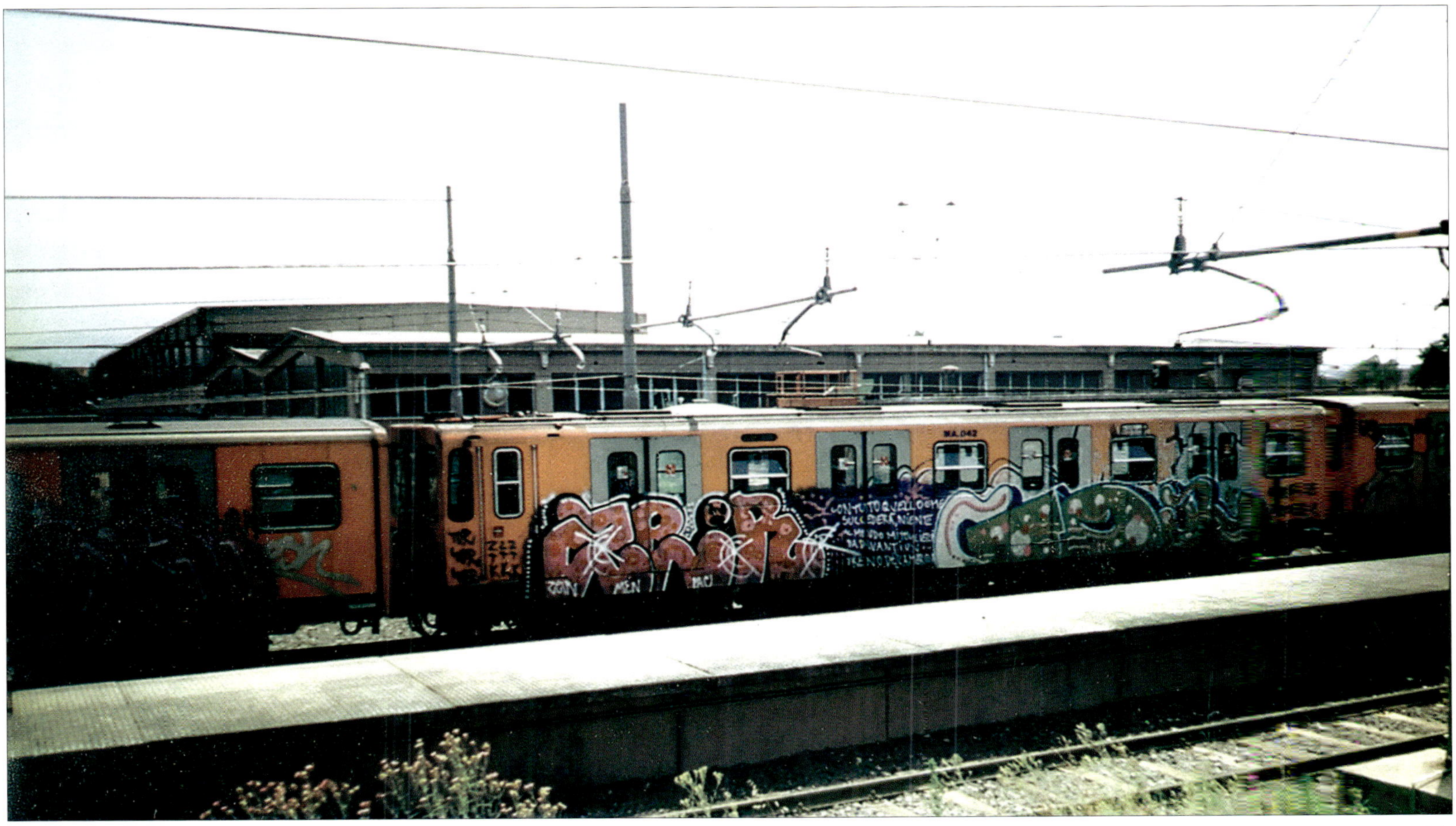

— Trota

MISCELLANEA
—

They called Cornelia 'seven floors' because to get to the rail tracks you had to descend seven storeys of stairs. Between each set of steps is a rickety landing, so we'd jump over each one like Tarzan in order to not make any noise.

The stairway had a metallic coating, like a tube, and these tubes are black so from the get go you have to wear gloves in order to keep your hands clean. Each staircase is more or less five metres distance from the next, you descend quite far down, maybe it's because of the ancient ruins that it goes down that deep. The only lights are the emergency ones. When you arrive in the tunnel it's full of giant rooms that we would go check. There was an enormous, futuristic—like room, real weird, full of large round things like motors or fans. The air is mad stuffy cause nobody went there, it was full of dust and some rooms hadn't been entered into for ages. Once you got to this floor with thousands of doors, you had to go through the one that was hardest to open, which took you to a small, dark room, then you had to walk until reaching a fence you had to climb over to get in, and if you were lucky, there was a train down there. It wasn't at the platform but in the tunnel, and to get out you had to go back the way you came, it wasn't easy because there was only one hole to get out from and if the guards came down that way you were fucked because there was no other exit in the other direction. — SYLA

I remember when we'd enter the trapdoor that was next to the Anagnina yard on the A line of the subway. There was a passage from that opening that took you to a fan room that produced a deafening noise, then a door, and "poof" a train in front of you. Mad adrenaline. I was literally shitting myself cause I didn't know if I would ever get safely out of that tomb. The steps were close, like a fire-escape ladder that descended down to the underworld. In the beginning the two trapdoors that took to that tunnel were used by the few writers that were in the know, then, as in all things, those passages got played out and our toy was broken: they put locks on both of them. I'll never forget the illumination down there, the neons blended with the darkness creating a surreal light.

This evocative scenario was joined by the noise of the sewers, if you closed your eyes they seemed underground rivers beneath the sleeping city. Once outside, we'd feel a chest pain, due to our lungs being full of spray paint. — GEL

We went painting after lunch, and were loaded with Marabus: Cinecittá had commissioned an enormous amount of work that had resulted in hundreds of spray cans, all Marubu, the best of the best. We entered Poggi store and in a single blow we compensated all the thefts of the previous months by buying (and paying for them this time) all the paint on the shelves. We often worked for Cinecittá because they were always in need of some backdrop or scenography for their movies, as soon as they understood the economic advantage in having them spray painted the gates of heaven were opened for certain writers. Anyway, that day we went to Anagnina loaded with quality spray paint but shortly after we had started, the usual sheriff straight out of the far west appeared: holster in one hand and steel in the other. So the typical guards and robbers chase ensued, with him shooting in the midst of the trains, and us in front running away: at the time all guards belonged to Roma Urbe, the first security company, with pretty aging guards that were out of shape, and to compensate the gap in age and physical fitness they could do nothing but shoot. Hekto, tall and skinny, got to the fence and was the first to climb over it; I had the opposite physical proportions and got there late. On that side of Anagnina there were three wire fences and the race turned into an obstacle course: once over the first and second fence I got to the last one, but as soon as I tried to throw my bag to the other side all the cans spilled out: I looked around and saw the Marabu white, the black, the yellowish, all those marvelous colours laying on the ground. With the rifle-range still shooting away behind me I picked them up one by one, to then throw the whole thing to the other side.

We fled together through the fields, and between the August sun at a peak and my full stomach, I started feeling dizzy, until I fell to the ground: I started vomiting my soul out and because I couldn't manage to speak Hekto started worrying I had been shot, searching me for the wound. — PANDA

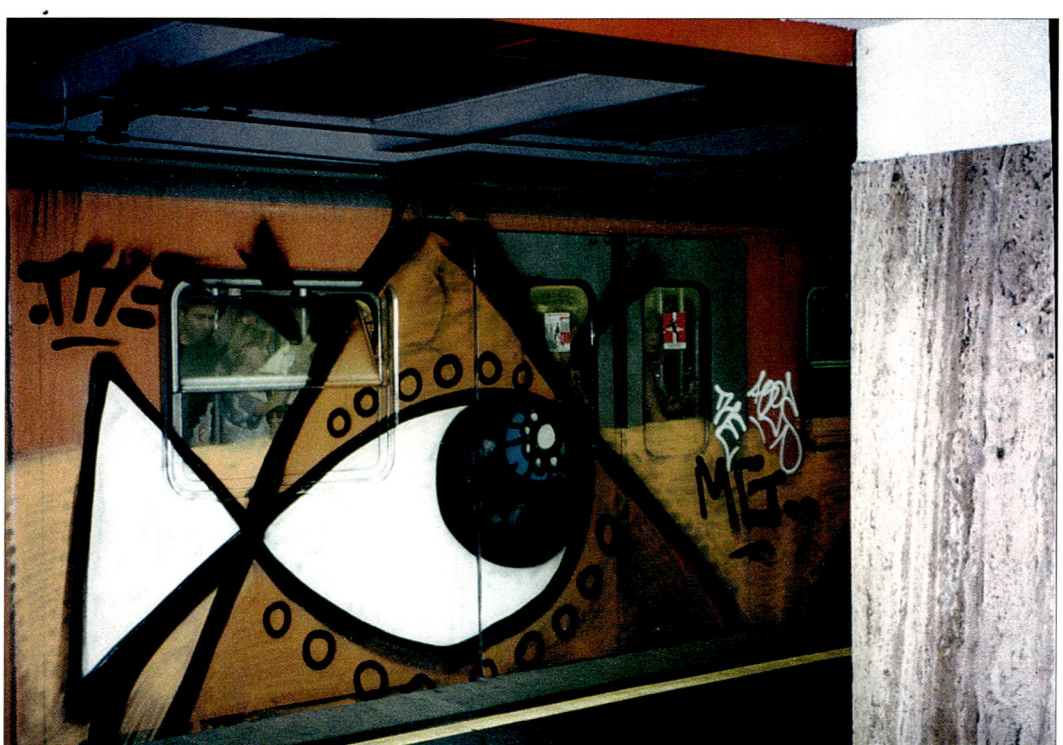

— Trota

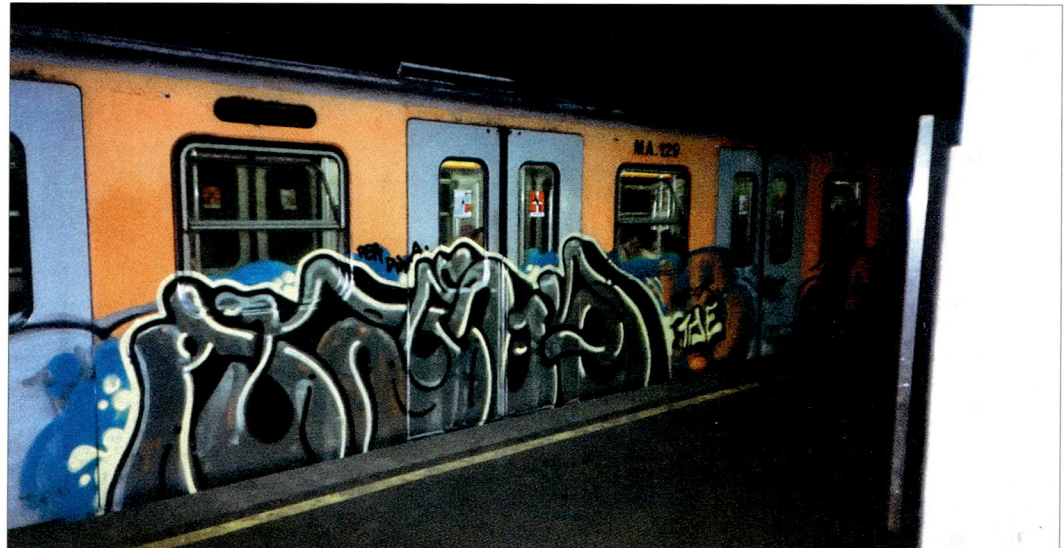

— Trota

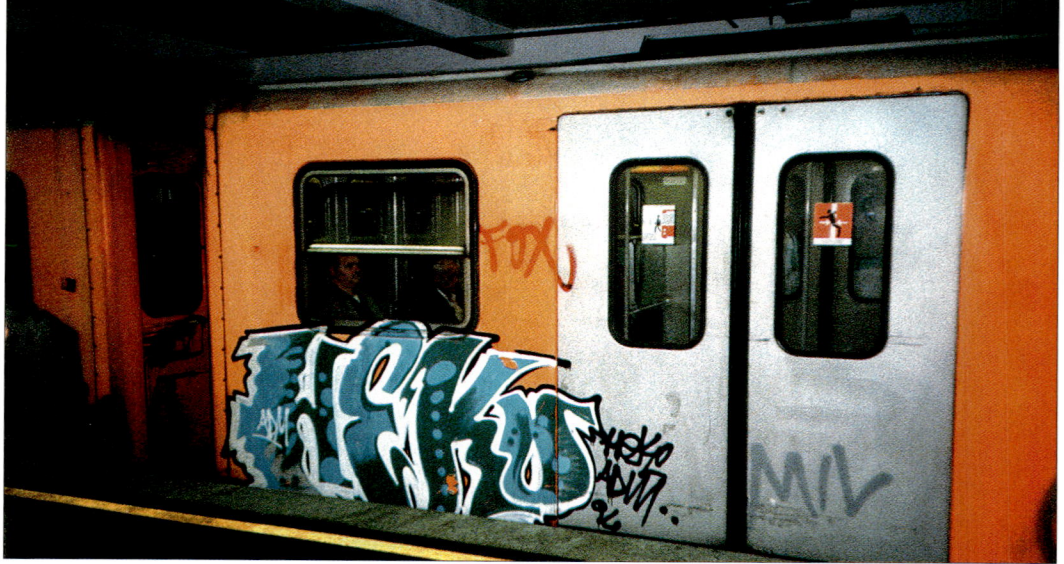

— ACW archive

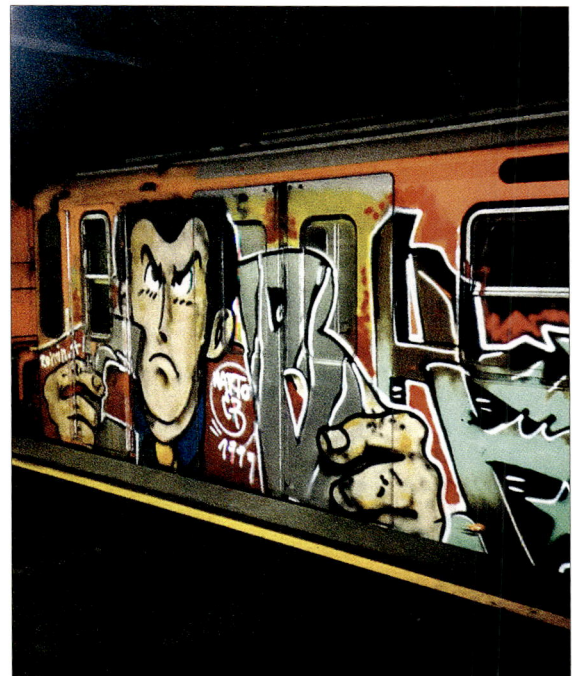

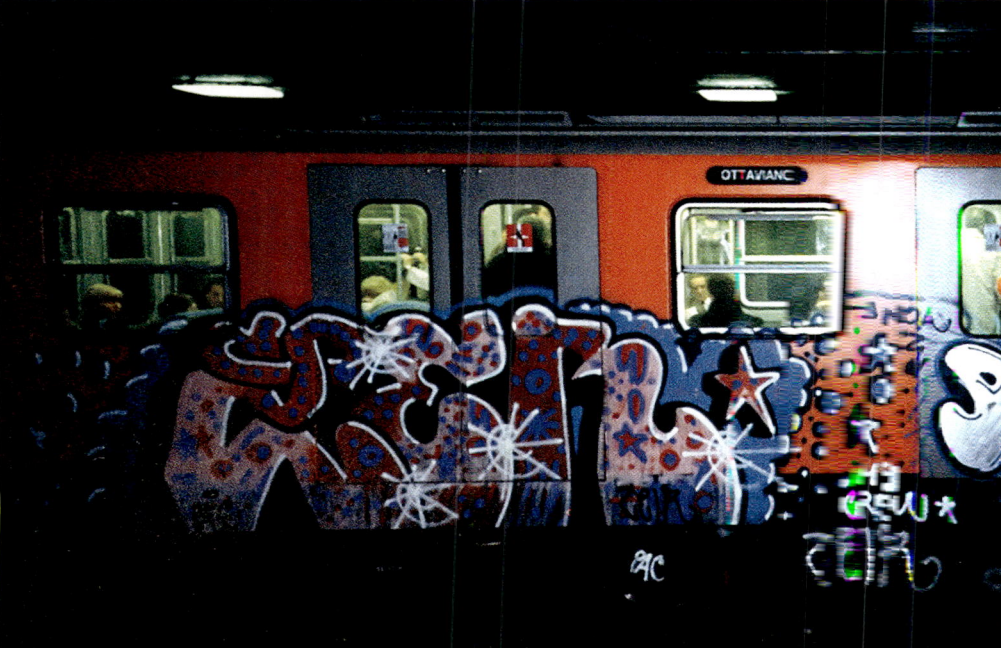

— *Trota*

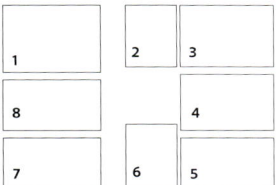

1		2	3
8			4
7		6	5

1 THE logo by Vela – THE crew

2 Arsenio Lupen character painted by CB crew, 1999

3 Zeir – PAC

4 THE crew

5 *My life is written on trains* by Jon–ZTK

6 Mencio inside the A line wagon

7 Heko – TRV, 1994

8 Anek – THE

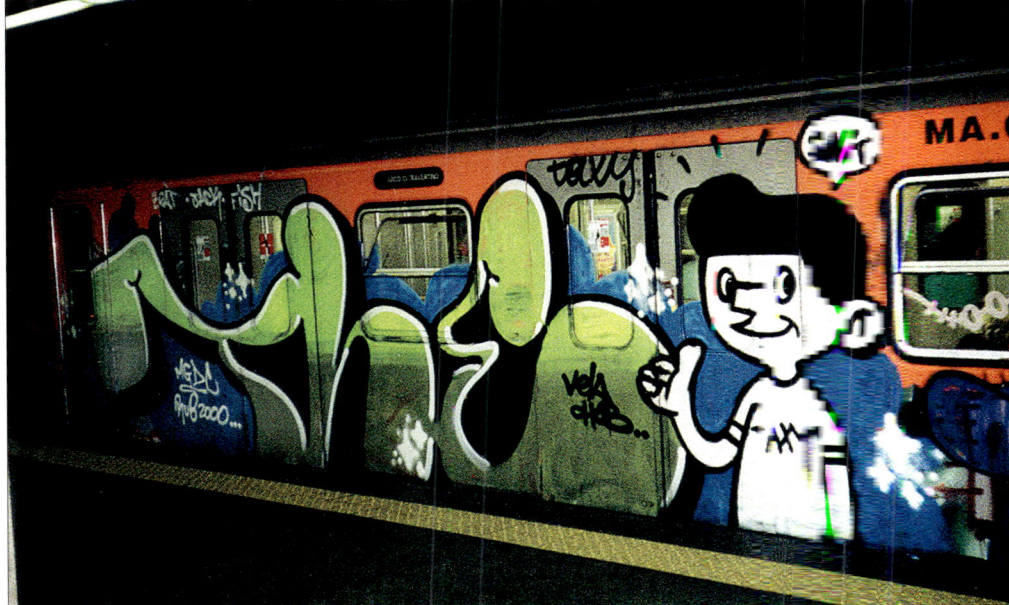

— *Trota*

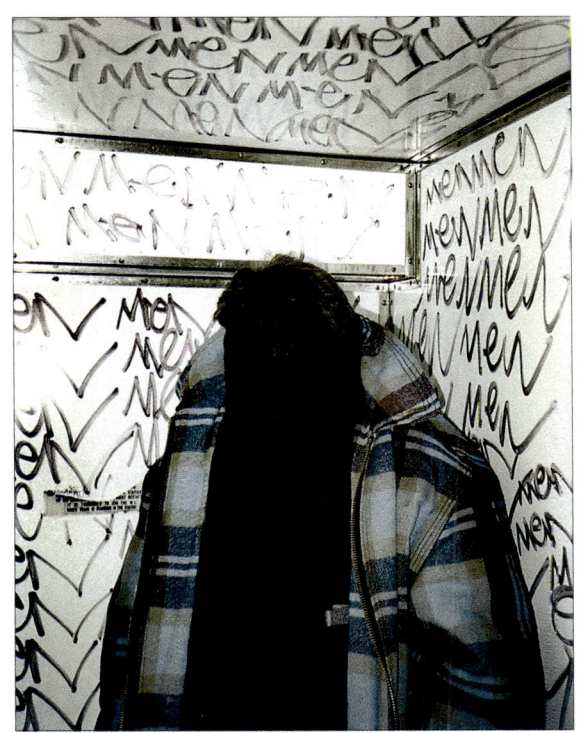

— *Mencio*

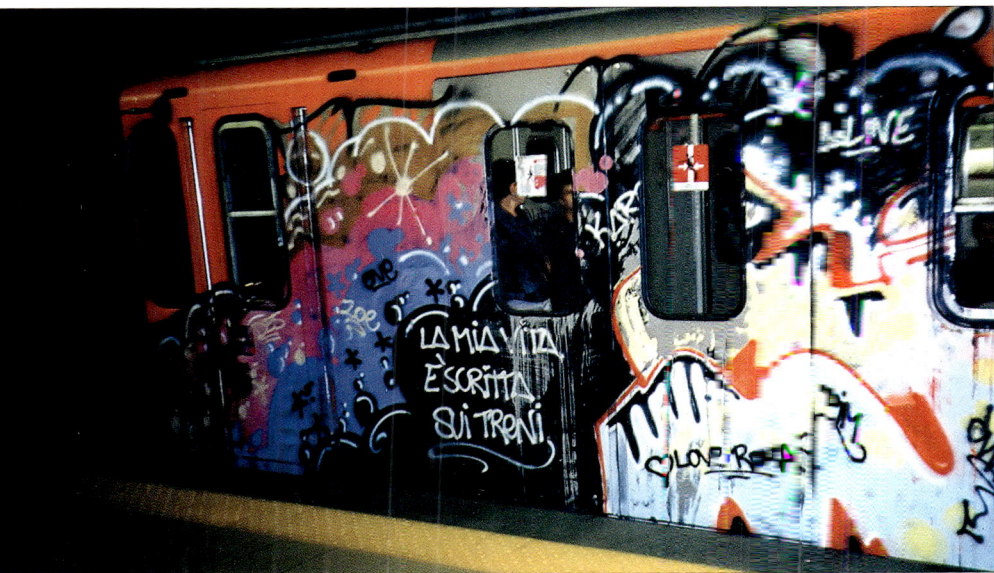

— *Trota*

B–LINE
The subway of Rome

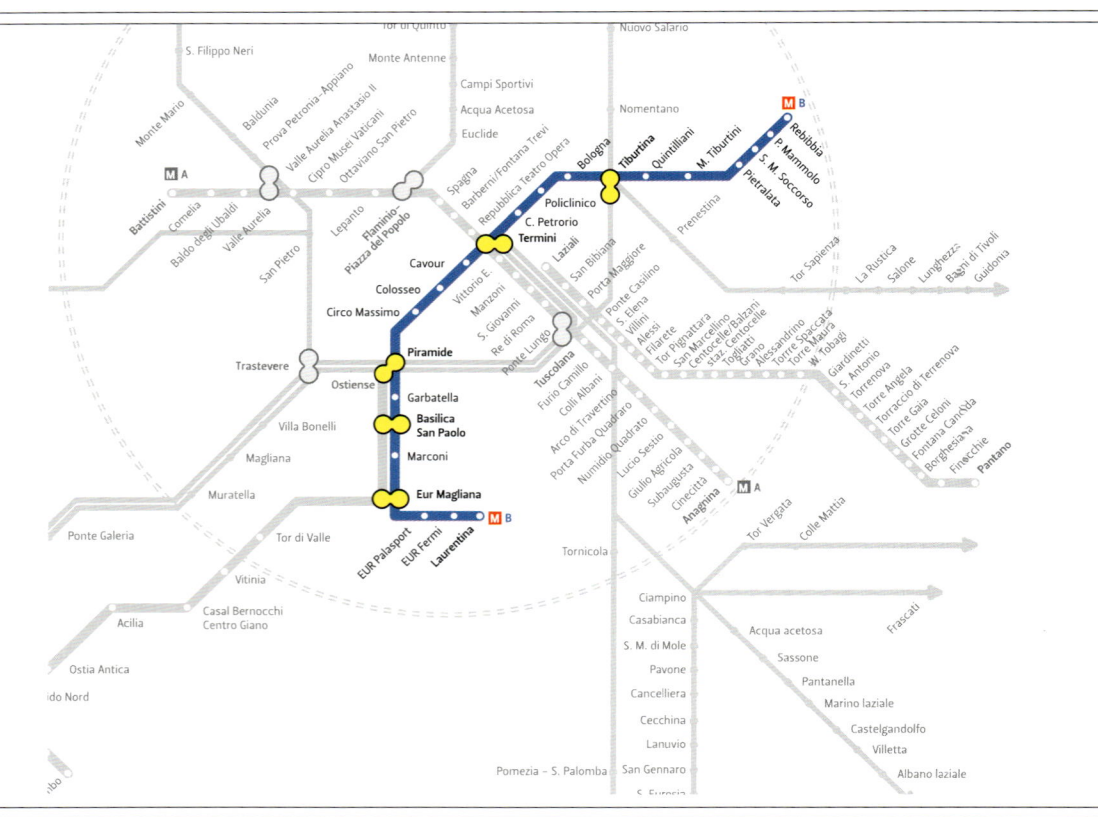

The subway of the B-line became operative in 1955, though planned and begun in the 30's during the Fascist era for the Universal Exposition of '42. It runs from Laurentina to Rebibbia, cutting through the city from North-East to South. With 377 runs a day it transports more than 300,000 passengers.

The battleground of the scene
>

Discovering Magliana

Jon
>

The first subway train I ever painted was on the Roman B line in Magliana yard, August 1995, together with One, Far, Pim, Chico, and Cartun. We were out there on the tracks of the Ostia Lido line checking out the yard. Back then, most of the B line's trains were clean. In fact, the sight of those clean trains kind of triggered a sense of anxiety and impotence: How could we ever cover them all? It seemed like an impossible mission. I'll never forget how the subway cars glistened, the shiny metal and the blue doors lit by the yellow lights of the platforms where the trains rested before heading out at dawn the next morning.
From that moment on, we made sure there were fewer and fewer clean trains, and more colours in motion.
I remember we would always use the lookout technique, it's pretty simple: one of us would lay down on the far end of the last platform and would keep watch over the security guard booth from under the trains. If one of them came out of the booth, the lookout could see his feet and would run to warn the others. Then everyone would abandon the platforms to go hide in different spots behind the trains while watching the guard's every movement. Right then and there, your heart is pounding and it seems as if time is standing still. You have an altered perception of reality. Tension is high and you feel like

you're doing something amazing. If the guard would get too close, we'd back up and hide in the bushes near the tracks or lie down along the tracks themselves, motionless, barely breathing.
We quickly realised that if we stood still in the dark, we were invisible even at close range. Once the guard finished doing his rounds, he'd go scour another area or go back to the booth. Then we'd each do our part: monitoring the areas where we could sneak back to the platform and complete the cars we were painting.
We'd sneak back one or two at a time, while the others made sure the coast was clear. Depending on where the guard had gone, we'd reposition the lookout by calculating from what direction danger might approach us again. At times, the situation was more difficult because the guards knew we were in the area due to the fresh spray paint on the trains, but they never saw us since we had three lookouts who knew the yard and its hiding places better than they did.
They'd come out every two minutes, every five minutes, so in order to finish a whole-car it would take us two to three hours because we constantly had to run and hide. At times we barely managed to make it back onto the platform and paint at all before the guard came out again, making us repeat the whole routine.
It was insane: we were kids at the time and we managed to outsmart the subway guards and change the colour of every car. Every day new, different, coloured pieces were in motion. The cars kept changing thanks to us. That's right, we changed them all!
Shortly later, this idea inspired "ZTK'95" and "BOOM", both were whole-car pieces

in black, which was totally unheard of. A car that was entirely black!!! In that moment it seemed like the most incredible idea, something everybody would have noticed. There's no colour more evil and more damaging than black.
I'd get home at 5:00 am and could never fall asleep because I was so excited, all I could think about was what I had just done and wanted to do again. I nearly shit my pants out of fear, but I managed to overcome it and I was loving it. We were living in a new dimension, it seemed like a game, a video game. We were really close-knit and overly confident, we kept moving on to the next piece, earning more points

We'd filled our hearts with courage, like we'd filled all those cars with paint. The yard was now ours, we conquered it from top to bottom

and fame. The riskier it was, the more fun we had concocting ways to paint night after night, day after day.
We ruled the Magliana yard with full-fledged military-style attack and defense strategies. We knew everything about the yard, train schedules, which trains would leave first the next day, etc… We'd always hit the train that was parked in "08", the repair depot for broken trains.
It was easier to paint there because the guards didn't expect it. I'm talking about

'95-'96, when there were lots of clean cars still and every night we'd paint to see our names in motion on all the subway trains of Rome's B line. There were two older crews who dominated that line and inspired us: TRV and MT2 who, apart from inspiring us when we were rookies, also motivated us to compete with them and the rest of the city. Each day we'd go to the station with the crew to see our new pieces pass by and to see those by Stand, Clint, Nico, Pane. This encouraged me to improve, I wanted to paint, I wanted to paint my own mega-piece.
Every night me and my friends would plan that night's mission. I can't begin to describe how it felt to stand in front of rows and rows of subway cars in the yard.
We were so small and the yard was so enormous. We were swallowed by its magnitude and were in another time dimension. The night seemed endless.
Once we left the yard, nothing counted anymore. No matter what happened inside, we were still happy and euphoric. We were on top of the world, as if we were looking at the yard from above, as if we were omnipotent beings who, each night, decided to change the destiny of the city and the perception its inhabitants have of it. When we had to back up, we'd hide in a huge ditch full of greenery, it was practically a crater, or we'd hide in the bushes along the tracks, from here we'd keep tabs on the comings and goings of trains, the guards, and the workers, then we'd decide how and where to strike. It depended on the night, on the period, on how long we had been painting clean cars, and above all if we had painted lots of windows. The guards would go crazy because despite their efforts, they'd notice

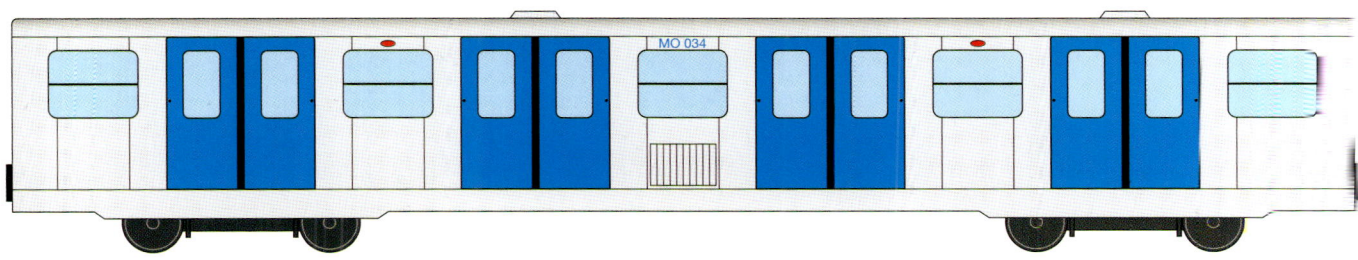

Back then, most cf the B line's trains were clean. In fact, the sight of those clean trains kind of triggered a sense of anxiety and impctence: How could we ever

cover them all? It seemed like an impossible mission. I'll never forget how the subway cars glistened, the shiny metal and the blue doors lit by the yellow lights of the

platforms where the trains rested before heading out at dawn the next morning.
From that moment on, we made sure there were fewer and fewer

clean trains, and more colours in motion. —JON

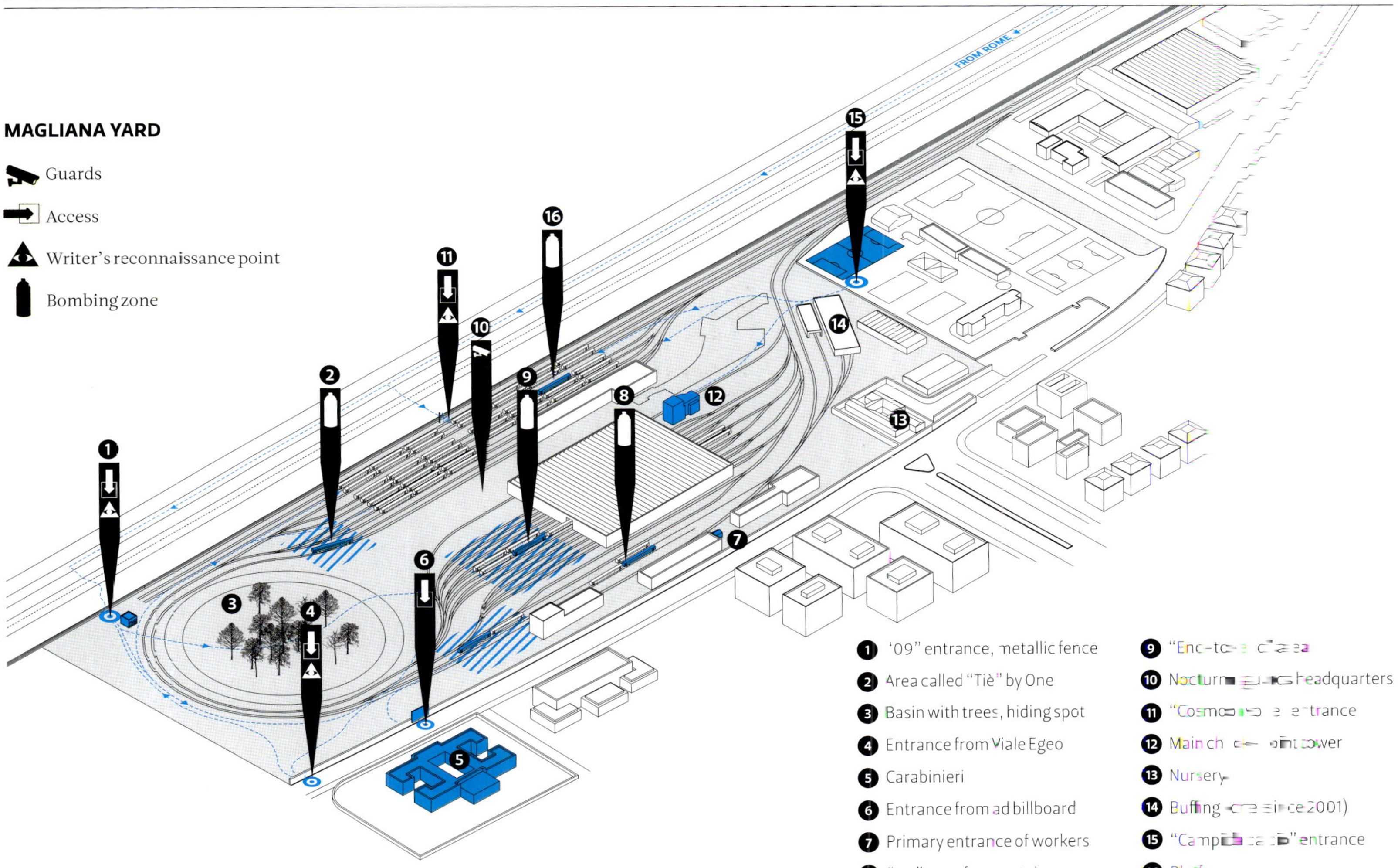

MAGLIANA YARD

📹 Guards

➡️ Access

🔺 Writer's reconnaissance point

🔋 Bombing zone

1 '09" entrance, metallic fence

2 Area called "Tiè" by One

3 Basin with trees, hiding spot

4 Entrance from Viale Egeo

5 Carabinieri

6 Entrance from ad billboard

7 Primary entrance of workers

8 "08" zone for mantainance

9 "Enc-tc-e c^a=a

10 Nocturn= ≡⌐⊏ Headquarters

11 "Cosmœ⊃⋅⊃ ≥ e⊓trance

12 Main ch c⊨ ⊃ínt cower

13 Nursery

14 Buffing ⊂≥ ≡⊩ce 2001)

15 "Campi≡=⊏ ⊏⊏" entrance

16 Platform⊑

newly-painted trains the next morning but had no idea how it was possible. This is also one of the reasons why they started to shoot at us more often, they even managed to wound a few of us! With time the guards became more clever and would sometimes surprise us, approaching from different directions. So we simply utilised new techniques to adapt to their new surveillance tactics. They were adapting to our activity and in return we altered our

method of moving through the yard. All those nights spent monitoring the guards' rounds, waiting for the right moment to strike, flashbacks of all those adventures under the influence of adrenaline, were slowly becoming experience.
By now, wherever we looked we'd see trains we had painted on every and any track. Seeing our trains all over the yard gave us confidence. We'd filled our hearts with courage, like we'd filled all those

cars with paint. The yard was now ours, we conquered it from top to bottom. Like ghosts, we evaded the guards hundreds of times so we could express our fantastic world on the metal surface of trains. Going in there was like being in a terrifying nightmare, but we, with our coloured letters and all our rage, faced the evil monsters and defeated them. We felt invincible, immortal, elusive. We increasingly felt it in the air, an unstoppable flow,

like electricity running through the wires above our heads. It was all around us, within us, everywhere it was spreading through the city and more people joined us, causing it to grow ever more. We were living intensely. We gave life to the letters ZTK, enhancing them with meaning and expanding our imagination and perception of what surrounded us by creating a new city for ourselves, in which we could feel at ease.

Strategies
>

A yard in three acts

One ZTK
>

In Rome there are three subway lines and these lines travel through the physical body of the city, in its insides, passing right next to the Coliseum and reaching as far as the coast.
line A, line B, and the Lido line. These are the three fundamental lines, relentlessly defended by the night guards. They represent Rome, and whoever paints them creates an image for it. Not everyone knows how to paint these carriages, or better, repeatedly target them, as it is a virtue that few have; but it's a known fact that this is the only way to experience them for real, not just going a couple of times in a lifetime but painting them so often that it's scary when you don't... for the simple fact you're no longer up to date with the situation there. The graffiti on these subway cars would bump up and down the city, while other carriages would be left resting, a pause that could sometimes last over a year. By regularly painting these lines you learn the times and the modalities of car circulation; you understand which run the most and especially which ones not to 'touch'; if you're there, and do what you do, there has to be a reason, and that reason is right in front

of you, it's that train. When you absorb a discipline by practicing it so much, inevitably it transforms you into another person, distant from whoever you used to be. By painting again and again on these lines – in which if you don't finish your piece it's because someone's shooting at you – we started developing a certain familiarity that transformed into experience, and then transformed us.

– PHASES
The three lines inspired us to describe and divide our daily experiences in three fundamental and distinct phases; the moment before climbing in, what happens after you've taken a piss, and that in which you climb back out, again with the necessary care so as not to be seen...to then go back the next day. When you arrive at the yard a long and accurate check of the situation takes place before actually climbing into it, sometimes even lasting various hours. This is when you merge with everything that surrounds you, noticing the slightest movement, sound or noise to understand whether it looks like there could be an ambush: sometimes it's a feeling, but more often it's a verified risk. You advance like ghosts to then meet up under the train, spray cans in hand, ready to be used.
The second moment starts with the first spray of paint and lasts, if it lasts, all the necessary time to do what you had in mind or what that situation allows you to do. Sometimes we would have to get back

out and return in, repeating the ceremony of the first moment. The third moment is the most extravagant, unimaginable and sometimes unreal, but mostly unexpected. It can be when you'd be putting the empty cans in a bag and, looking back towards the train, feel like you're invincible even if a guard were to arrive. When you've finished painting you have an extra energy, you're ready for anything. Otherwise it might be when you find yourself suddenly running away from stray bullets. Or even when you suddenly stop painting because you've noticed someone watching, maybe for some time even, and sense things around you are turning into a mounting ambush. The reaction, the speed, the intuition in choosing the next action to take, advised by experience, will decide the rest. Wounded, dead, beat up, arrested or....free!

– MAGLIANA
The security in the yards along these three lines allow for this last phase to proceed with neither coherence nor logic. Among them, my favourite has always been Magliana, on the B line: an enormous yard in the open in which one guard, no matter how driven, is not sufficient to catch you. Most of the time, it was him against you. One on one, in two distinct positions, with hardly anywhere to close you in. It took them years before they figured out that closing us in would have been the right move. We relied on our speed and

dexterity in spotting any security and in changing position at this sight. One or two guards would arrive, maybe from opposite directions, and would wander by the trains, armed and sometimes desperate, or better exhausted. We had developed our own technique to allow them to make their inspections: between one and the other, sometimes even during their rounds, we would crouch under the train right under their noses with an end-to-end and get back up with one or two whole-cars. With the passing of years, little did it matter if we were two or four, one of the most recurring questions in front of that fence was: "with or without a lookout?" With a lookout it was impossible to be caught but we were in for almost twice as long. Without a lookout it was much more hardcore and everyone would be on watch in turns, face to the ground, all five senses open and aware. And then standing again, painting. I can say I have painted on any day, during whatever sporting or world event, in any weather conditions, rain, hail, flood or wind so strong it wouldn't allow the paint to stick. When it was freezing cold and when the heat made the train cars burn... pun intended. Painting is great how it is, whatever you do and practice in a way that makes it yours so that you think of it differently to when you started. Because the game becomes a great game only if it continues. If it is continuous, it transforms into an expression of yourself, your way of being.

NINJA SECURITY
—

Panda
>
Around '97-'98 the main guard of Laurentina, though actually pretty old, was completely nuts. He was always on duty, and that in itself was weird; plus he always dressed in black: others were in uniform but he had shoes, jacket and hat all in black, with a flash-

LAURENTINA

The end stop of the B line was built in the 30's in the neighbourhood of Giuliano Dalmata. In the 80's the station was completely demolished and rebuilt. The current structure was inaugurated in 1990

light/billy stick about half a metre long. We would go in the day: Laurentina was an end-station that hosted as many as three trains of the B line even in the day, on three different rail tracks; the

guard would hide between the trains but he was pretty clumsy and sooner or later would easily be spotted: we threw rocks at him while shouting "Get out we see you!" but he would stay hidden, get out his radio and call the other guards. At the time certain subway security staff had a contractual clause that forced them to persecute writers: every newly painted train would be deducted from their salary. The costs of cleaning the wagons that had eluded their control were covered by the guards. Naturally whole-cars became their nightmare, both for the dimensions and for the fact that windows would be painted over, certifying it had been a recent hit. One day, after the zillionth whole-car by Hekto, we returned at sunrise and found the usual ninja dressed in black but this time he was also wearing a pair of fluorescent yellow latex gloves: he was cleaning all the windows of the subway train so as to pretend it had not been recently painted.

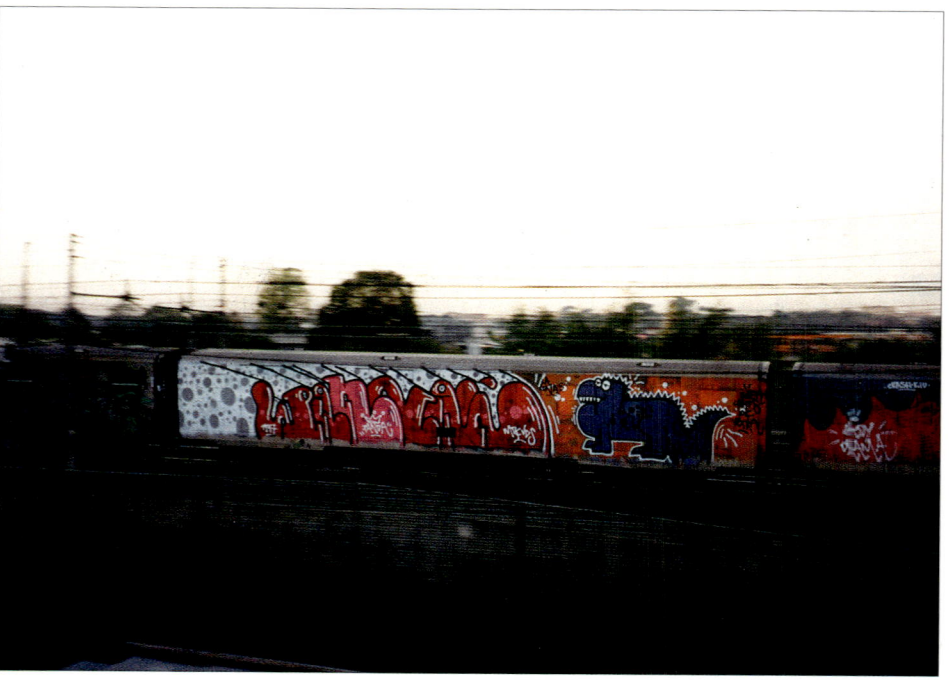

Panda MDF-THE: one man whole-car painted at Laurentina yard, 1997

– Panda

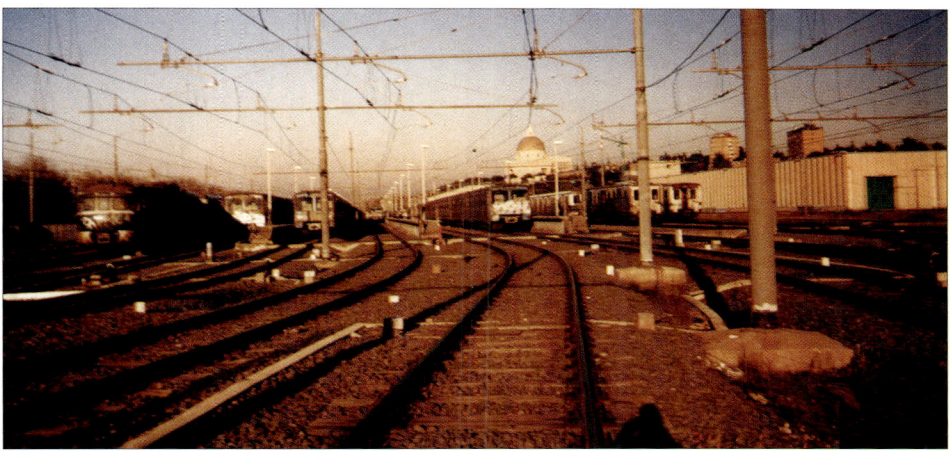

— Jon

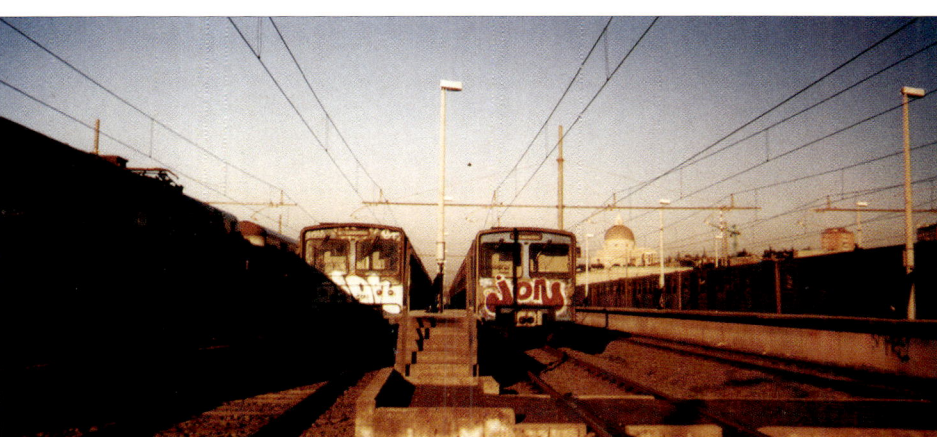

— Jon

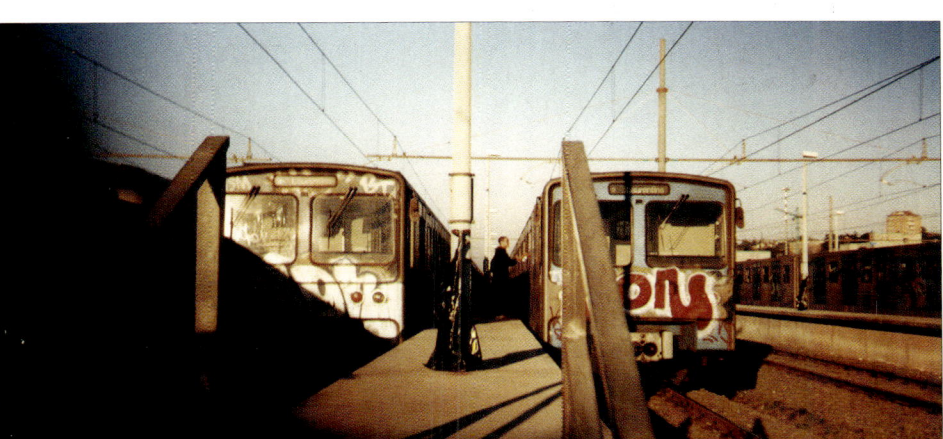

— Jon

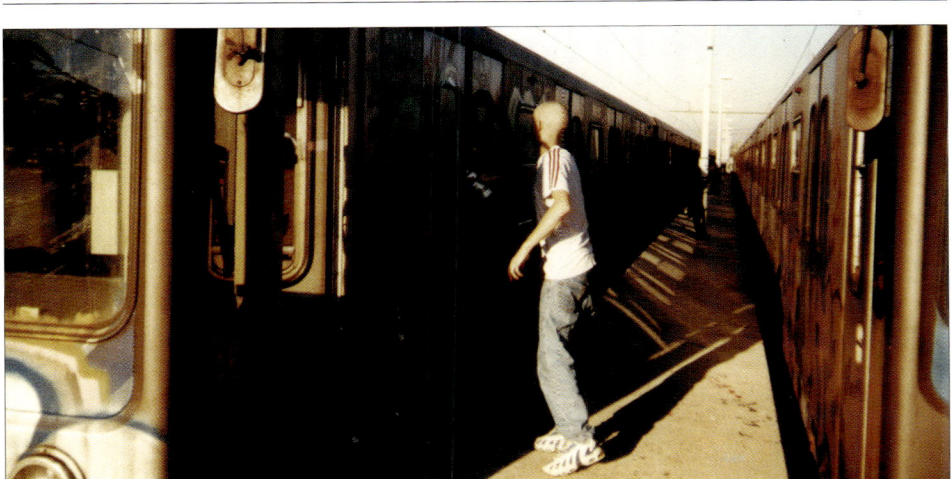

— Jon

THE SUBWAY SHOOTING
—

That morning I was at the beach of Ostia: on my way back to Rome I stopped at the deposit to check out the situation in Magliana: there was a strange atmosphere, anomalous, it was full of guards, investigating the area around the trains. I didn't get it, I thought maybe they were mounting sensors and video cameras. In those years ETC crew was hitting it down pretty hard in Magliana and everyday the same game would repeat: guards and robbers. Enter the yard, start painting, anticipate the arrival of the guards and their guns, run away and wait a while outside, then get back in and repeat the game to exhaustion, until the pieces are finished. The guards would end up worn out plus they would get heavily reprimanded from their superiors every time any new paint would be detected on a train. Considering that in Magliana everybody painted top-to-bottoms and whole-cars, the vigilantes quickly took control of the situation by shooting anybody that approached the train cars. Going back to the subway after Joe got hit was different because that was the tangible evidence they were shooting at bodies and not in the air. Not that this was unknown beforehand, (everyone had heard the grating of the bullets as they grazed the sides of the train cars), but that event generated even more tension in the deposits. — TROTA

The night they shot Joe I had been in the same deposit a few hours earlier. My mother knew everything, about the subway, the trains, and she was on my case so much in that period she demanded to know in which yard or station I was going to paint every time, because "if something happens, I know where to find you". She had worn me out and I ended up telling her I was going to Magliana. After painting I went to a friend's house to sleep. The next morning my mother almost fainted while reading the local papers: the articles talked about a kid that had been hit by a gunshot in the Magliana deposit that same night. Obviously she lost it and when I got back home she pinned me to the wall: I didn't know about the shooting and thought she had actually gone mad because of me. I think if the parents of writers had to imagine we were doing trains and deposits at the time there were no halls of fame

> "
> the vigilantes quickly took control of the situation by shooting anybody

in Rome. We had Nomentano but that was an isolated episode in both time and space. Since everyone in Rome was talking about the pieces on the subway, from writers to ordinary citizens a parent seeing his son grow up with a passion for spray cans certainly couldn't imagine anything else. Vela for example had to be home by 2.00 am: "my parents don't know anything" he would tell me, but that was his own conviction because one day at breakfast his dad said: "Mizio, drink this te (THE) and go full sail (VELA)". — LANDA

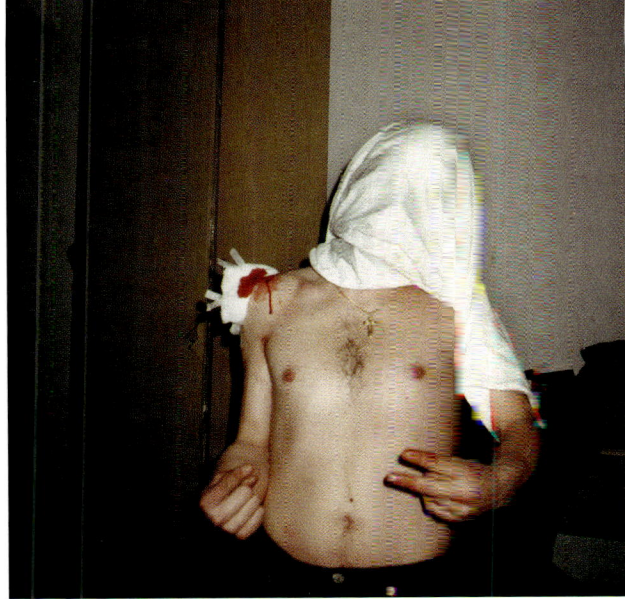

A photo of Joe, taken by Jon, after the shooting in the yard of Magliana   — Tuff

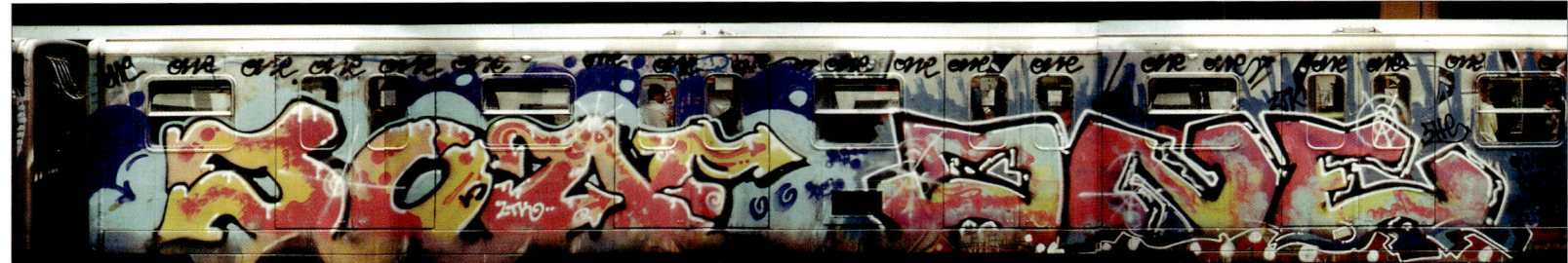

Jon, One – ZTK. "Quando la rabbia si sfoga e si trasforma" (When rage vents and is transformed)   *– Jon*

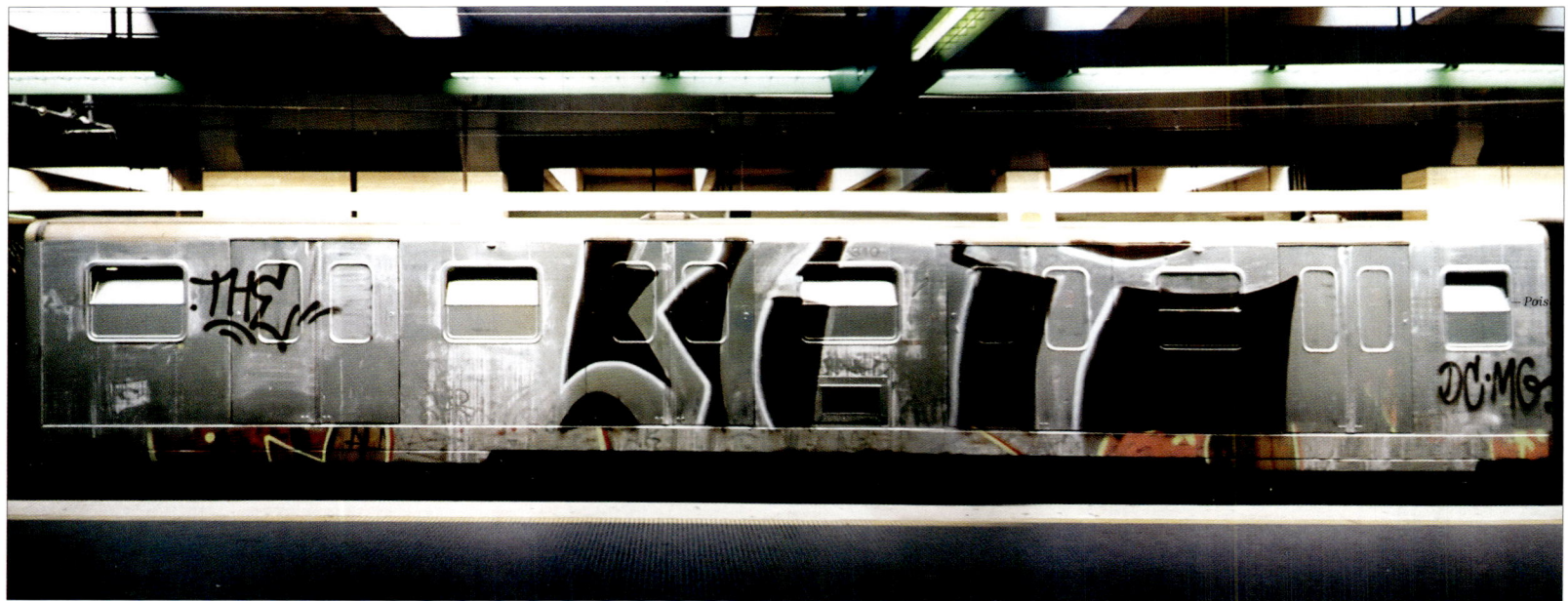

THE whole-car painted at Rebibbia   *– Trota*

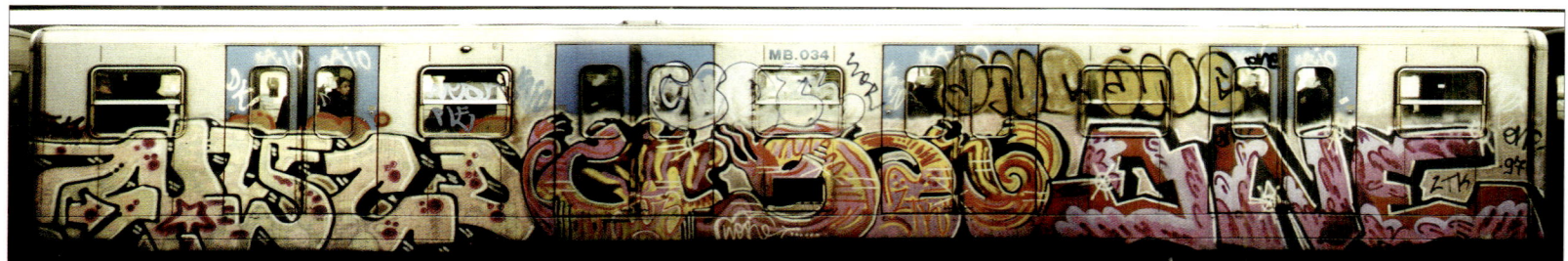

Nyco by Nico – ETC TRV, Gor e One – ZTK,1997   *– Jon*

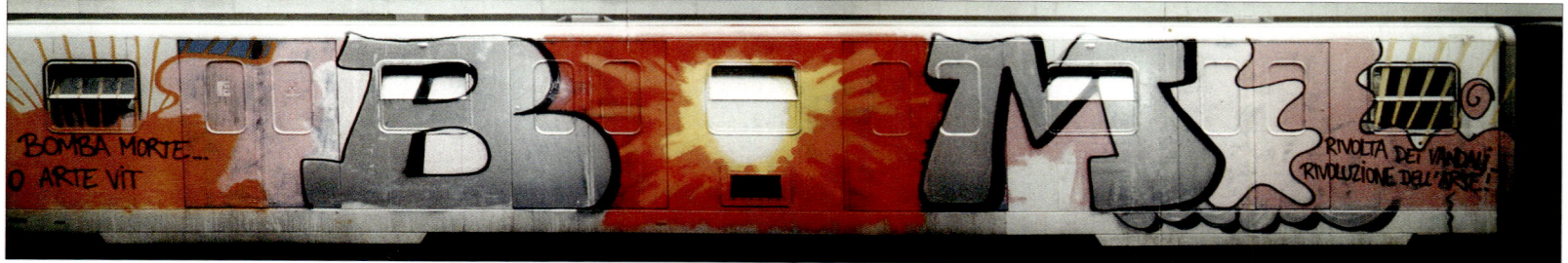

BM unfinished whole-car by Jon ZTK, "Bomba morte… o arte vit" (Bomb death…or art life), "Rivolta dei vandali, rivoluzione dell'arte!" (Revolt of the vandals, revolution of art!)   *– Jon*

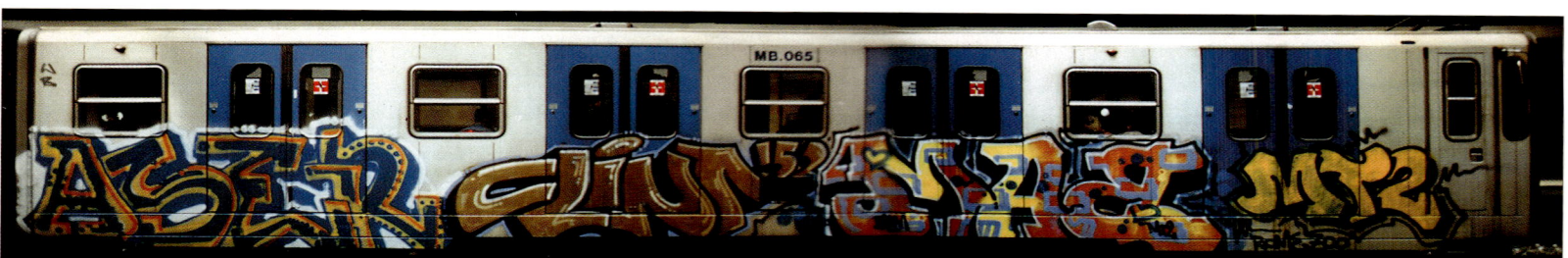

Aser by Nico – ETC TRV, *Clint 152* by DebOne – MT2 ADM, by Stand – MT2 ADM TRV   *– Mencio*

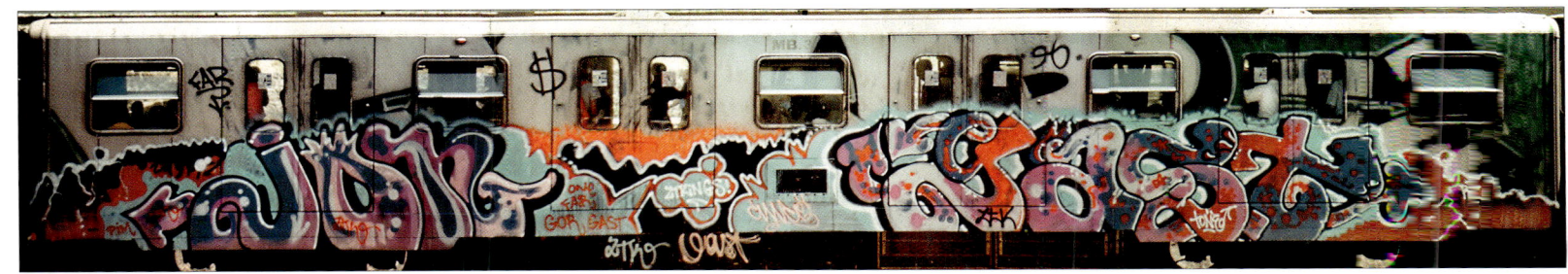

Jon and Gast – ZTK

— Jon

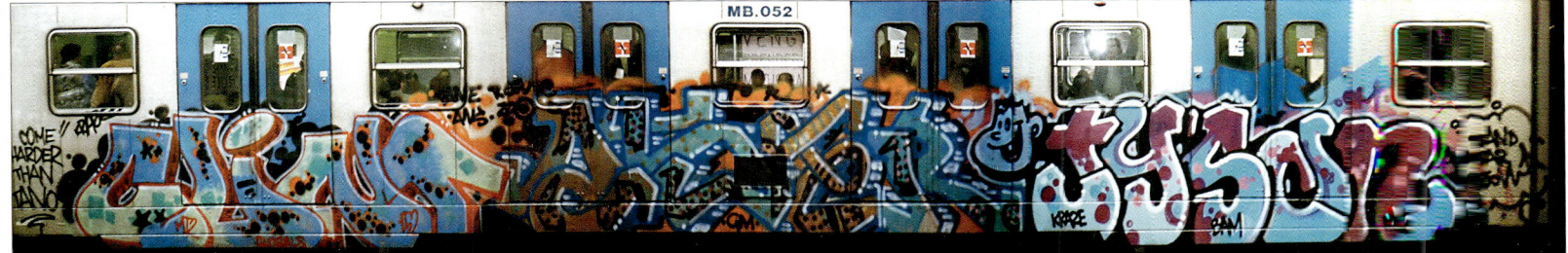

Clint 152 by DebOne – MT2, Aser by Nico – TRV, Tyson by Stand – TRV

— cccroni archive

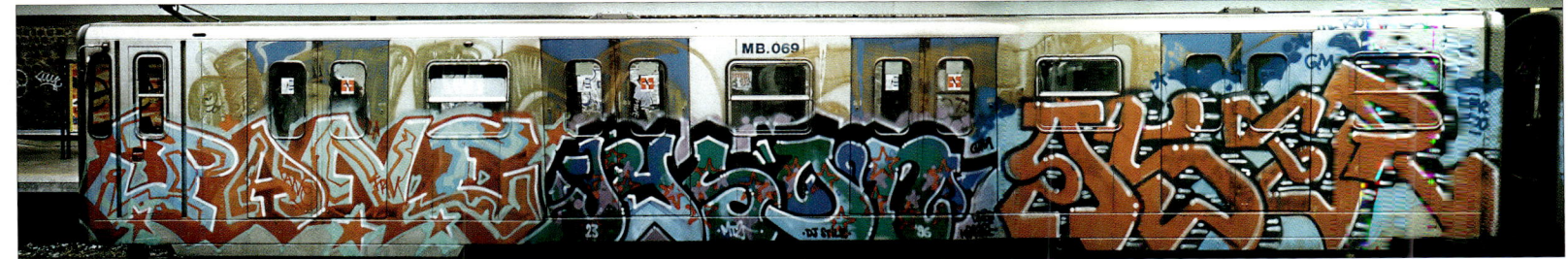

Pane, Tyson by Stand, Aser by Nico, TRV crew, 1996

— cccroni archive

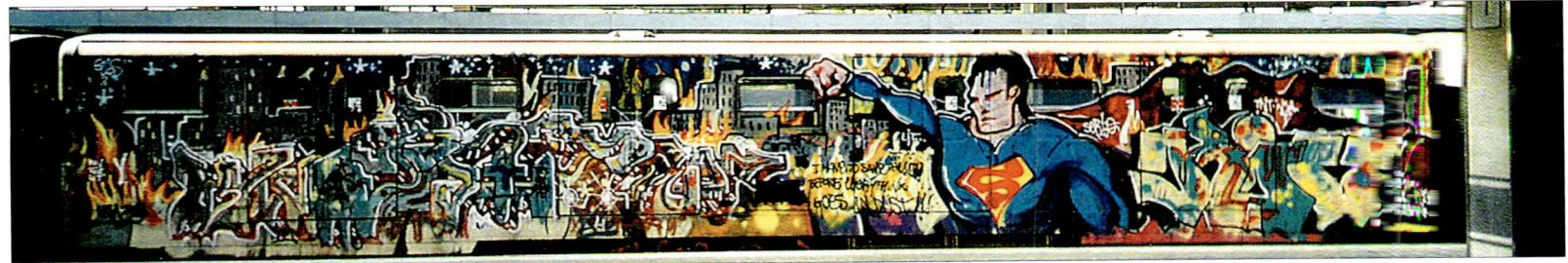

Full colour whole-car by CB crew

— Poison

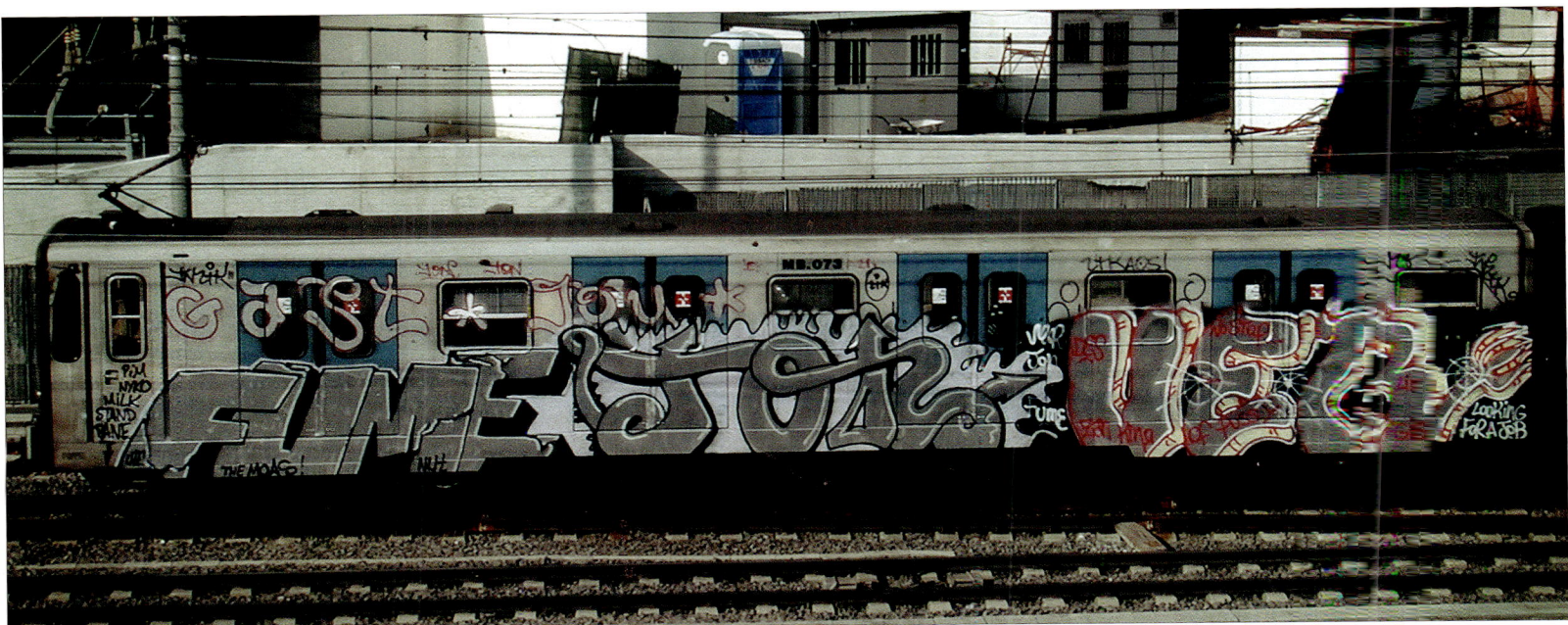

Fume MSN, Jon – ZTK, Ver – NSA, e2e painted at Magliana yard

— Jon

A MOTHER'S PERSPECTIVE
—

As a mother it's hard to speak impartially of one's son, especially if he spent his life painting the city without permission. I would however like to acknowledge all the years he passed on trains cars as if they were part of an anomalous artistic path, parallel to his growth, a constant that has accompanied us during his adolescence and the years to follow. A path brimming with infinite preoccupation, unsettling episodes that as a mother initially I could not accept. I remember a distant summer in the early 90's, Luca was in a subway deposit, one of the many he would visit. He was with a friend of his and towards 3 in the afternoon, as they were painting the train cars, a security guard saw them and started shooting in their direction; Luca and his friend started running away and after climbing the wire fences around the deposit my son fainted due to a sunstroke, immediately toppling to the ground. His friend, desperate, went back to get him, with the risk of getting caught, thinking Luca had been hit by a bullet the guard fired. Some years later more or less the same thing happened to some other kids, except this time it didn't go as smoothly and one of them got shot. The dramatic nature of these moments belongs to those memories that with the years one would prefer to forget, but they never go away. I recognise that at the time our relationship was based on this non-conventional passion of his, of course I couldn't be openly happy about this new world I discovered through him. In the beginning I couldn't even believe it, but as time progressed I followed his transformation and development, I learnt to understand and appreciate it. I've always wanted to know where he was going, I was scared; I demanded it, it was our deal. **– PANDA'S MOTHER**

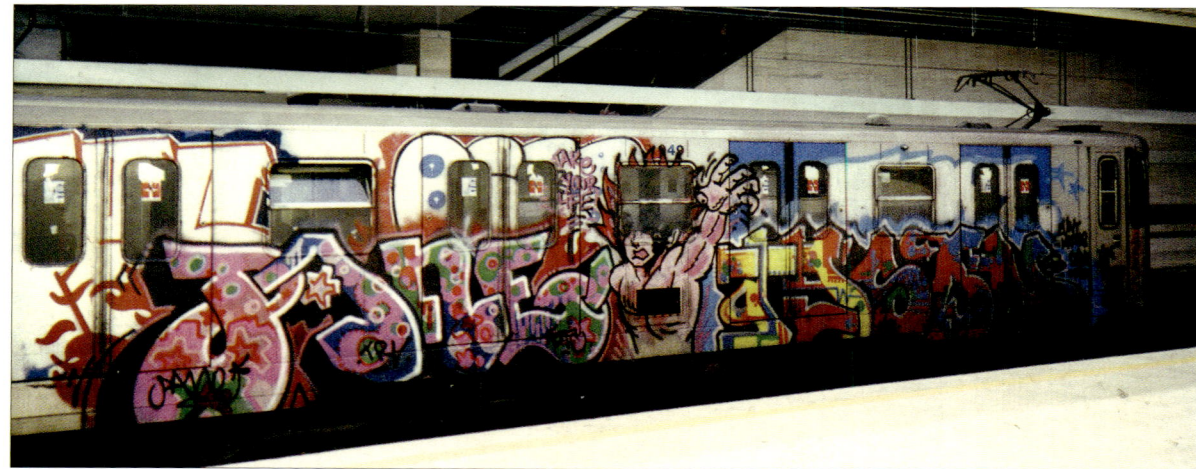

— Jon

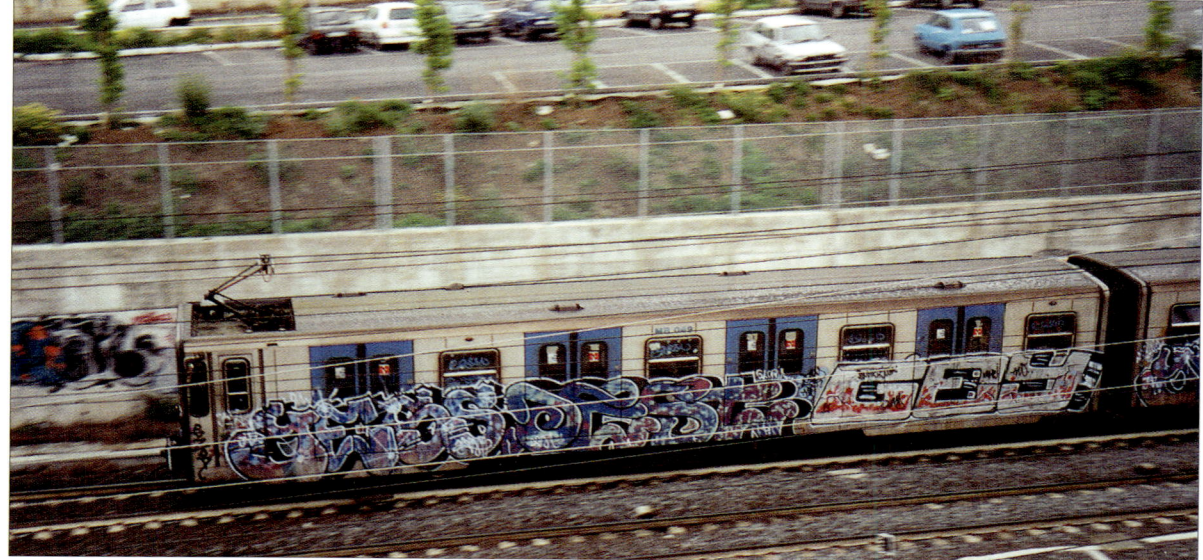

— Jon

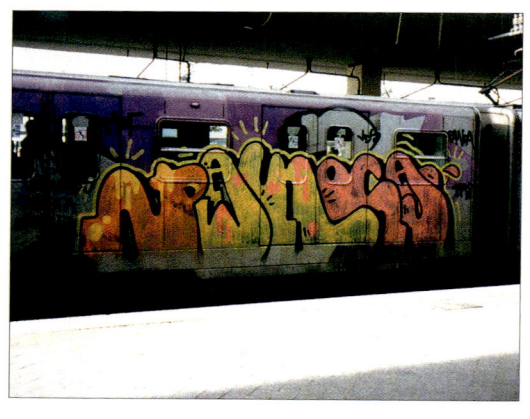

— Panda

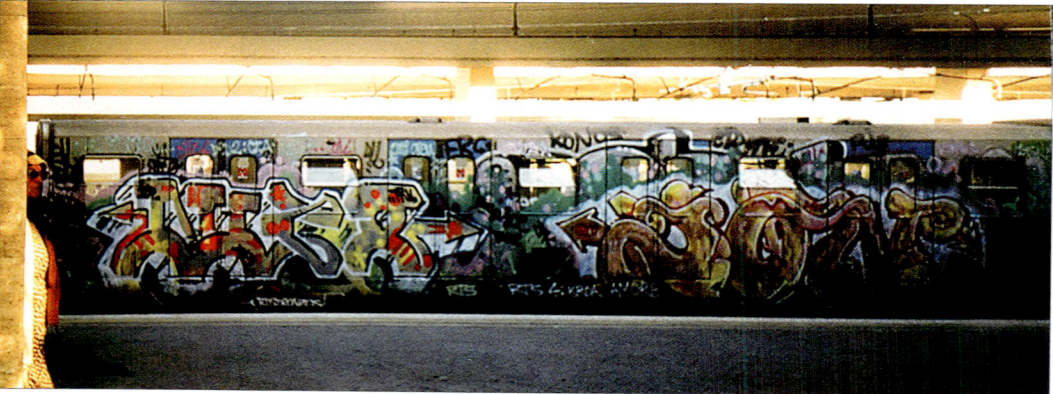

— Mascaroni archive

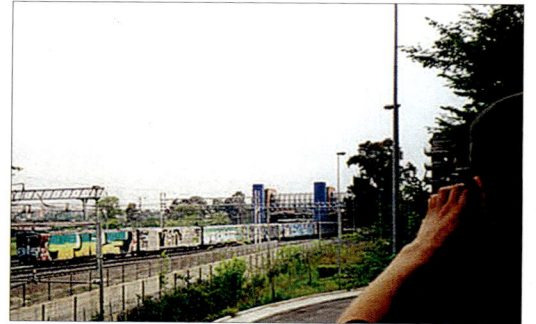

THE by Trota

— Trota

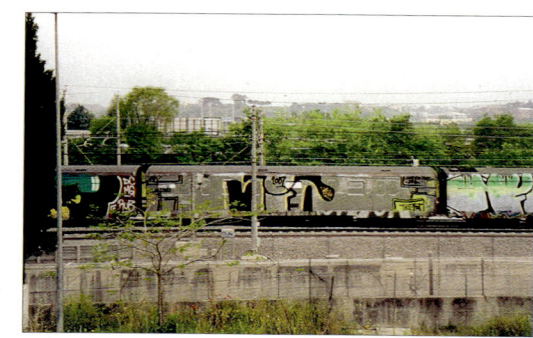

Min-THE

— Trota

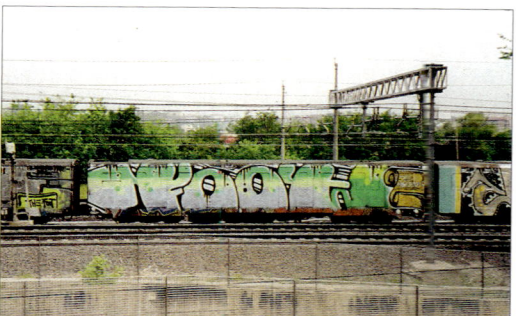

Foot

— Trota

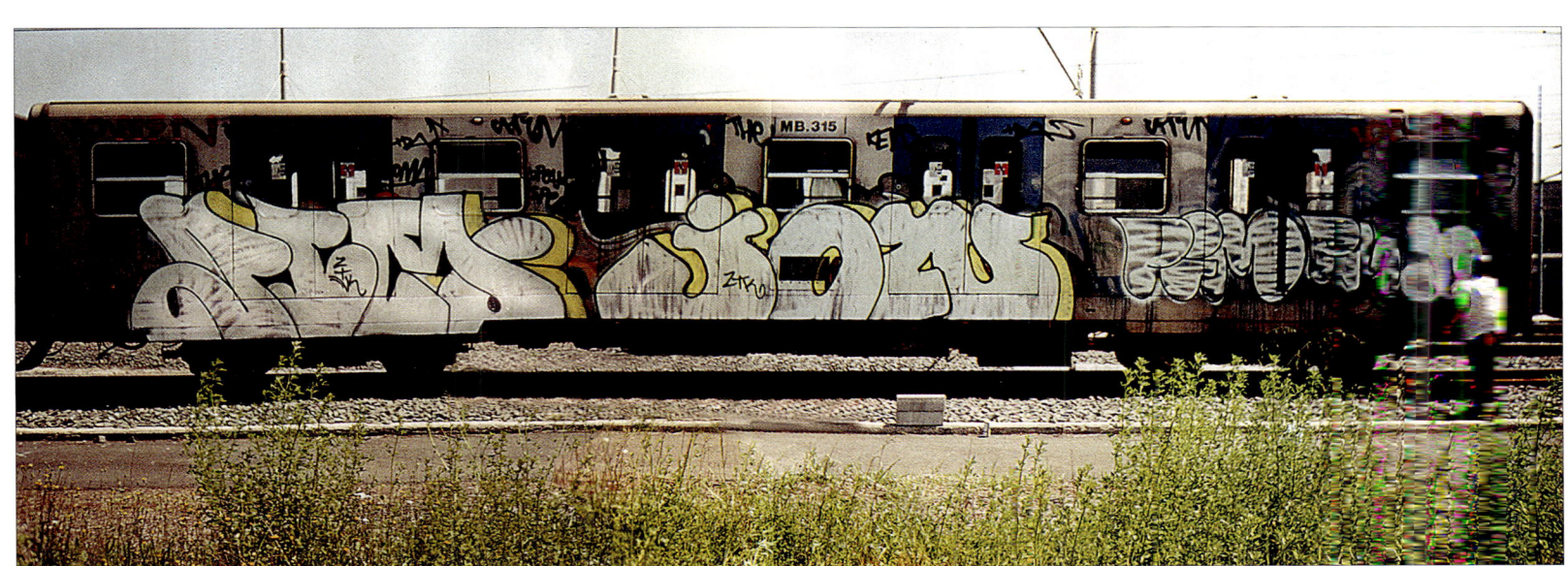

— Pim

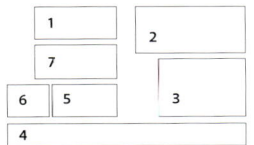

1. Pane, *Tyson* by Stand, 1996
2. Pim and Jon–ZTK
3. *Net* by Honet, *Tyson* by Stand
4. Whole-train painted on the B line subway cars, 1996
5. Nico TRV–Jon ZTK, 1999
6. Panda MDF–THE, 1998
7. Yess, Dest, Gey

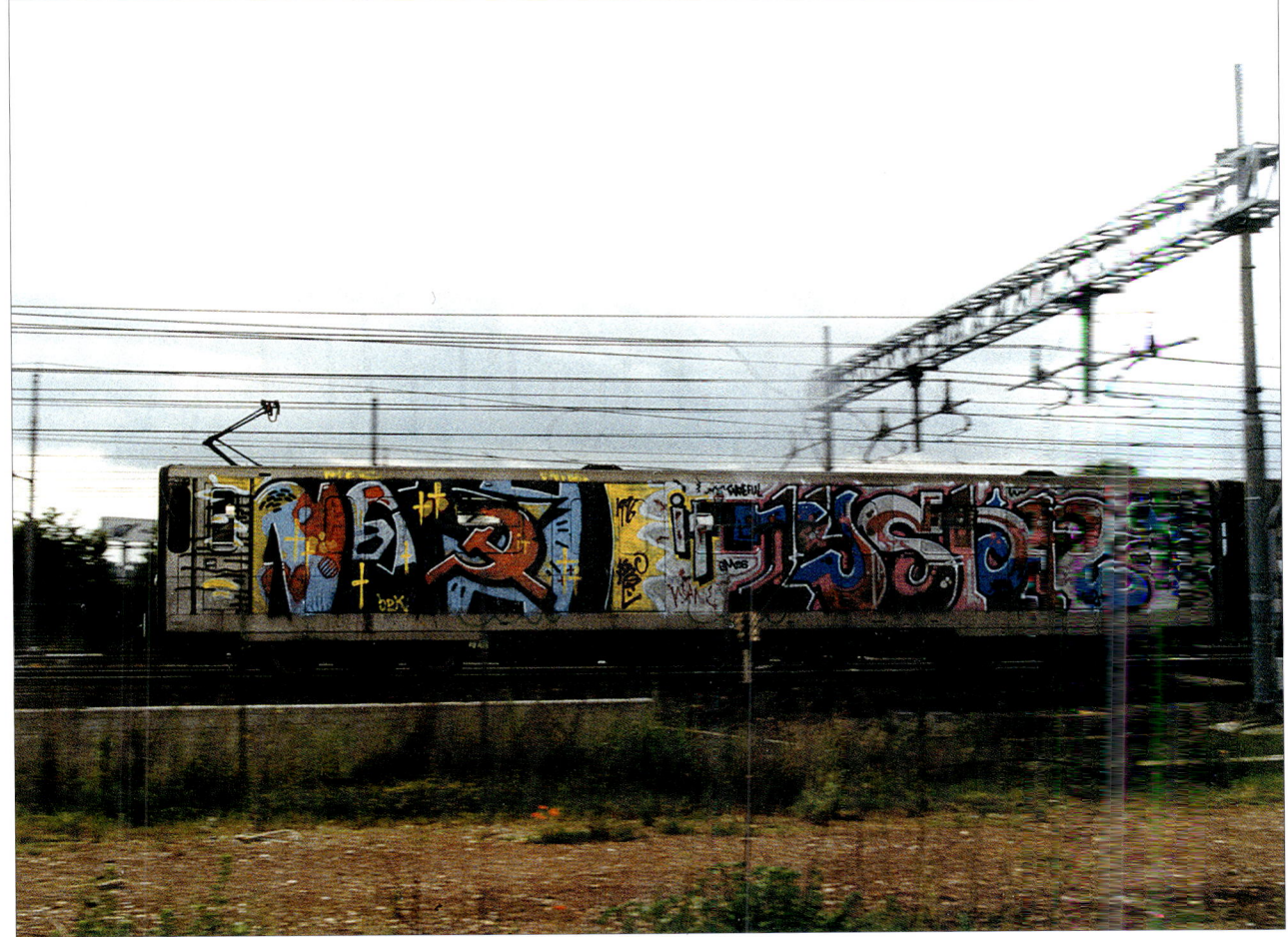

— Mark Todt

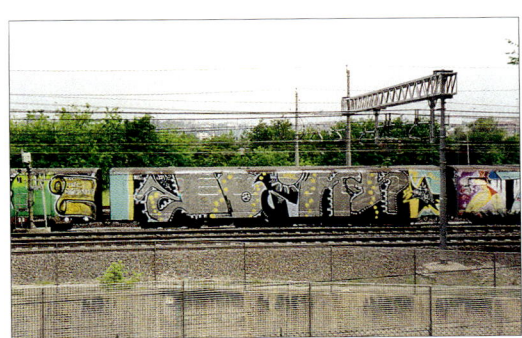

Moke

— Trota

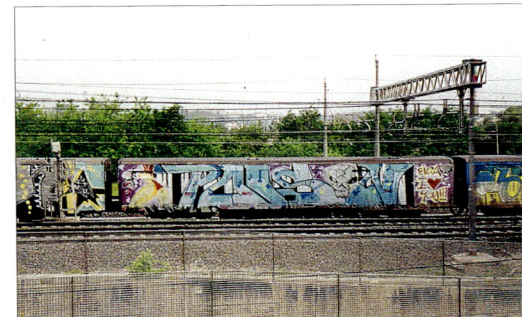

Posion

— Trota

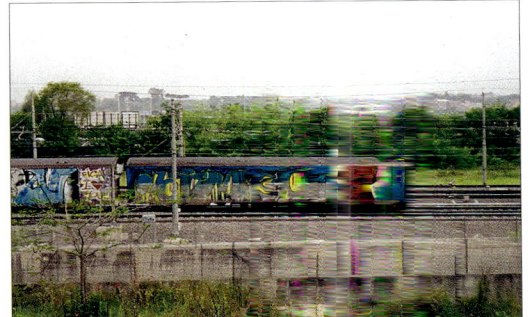

Bimko

— Trota

LIDO LINE
The subway of Rome

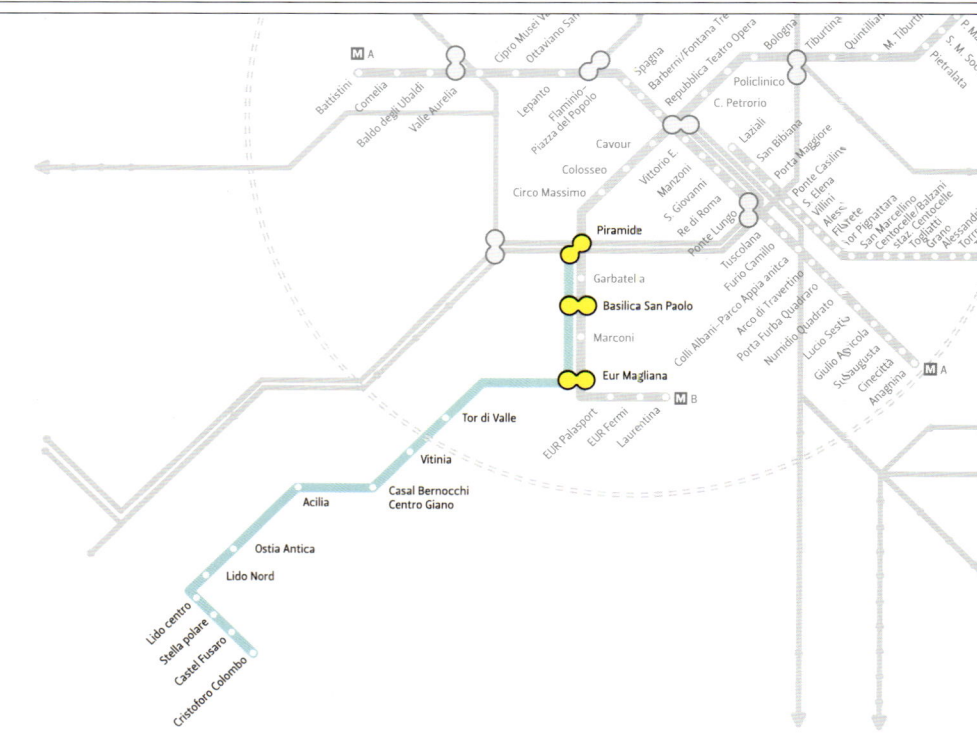

The Lido line was the first Italian railway to be built with the characteristics of a subway. The Lido line goes from the station of Roma Porta San Paolo up to the southern limit of the coastal neighbourhood of Ostia lido. Part of its internal route is shared with the B-line of the Roman subway, though they have independent rail tracks. It was inaugurated in 1924 by a Gr 910.045 steam locomotive with Mussolini on board.

The pine wood of Ostia
>

Into the wild

Anek
>

Colombo, end of the Rome-Lido line of Ostia. The station is between the coastal road and the pine woods of Castelfusano, an enormous forest that extends for many kilometres. If you wanted to get in that was your only way, up and down dunes of sand, bushes, trees and roots that come out of the ground all over the place: you had to take that narrow path that begins in the pine forest and then borders the whole yard, until you reached the little bridge over the rail tracks that takes you to via Cristoforo Colombo. You could find anything there: junkies, bums, various desperates that had built shacks in the woods, or even people fucking, since the roads around the yard had and still have today dozens of whores and transvestites...what a nice environment right? Which is why there were some kids that never wanted to be first (but neither last) in the line of people that took that path. Down there it was the darkest dark I've ever seen, only with a full moon could you discern anything. We often brought flash lights, though we didn't use them the whole way for fear of being seen by the station guards. The final stretch of

the walk is uphill and brings you on top a little rise that has an electricity pylon covered by tags, with cans and caps lying a bit everywhere. This was where you stopped and got ready, you could observe the yard from above, study the movements of the guards and check if somebody else was already painting. A cigarette, a piss, and then we'd go in.
From the pylon to the wire fence of the yard was the worst bit: a

steep descent through thorns and bushes, but it's the last effort. At night the station held four trains: three parked on the platforms and the fourth train, the one furthest from the station, 'unplatformed' and close to the yard fence. This was the train that, thanks to its position, guaranteed the swiftest and safest escape, and was thus the preferred target (if there was space on the cars). We would stay two-three hours, dozens of us: often

while we were painting other writers would come, their arrival anticipated by the noise they made coming through the forest vegetation, and if someone finished early he'd roll a joint and pass it to the others. Well, a paradise, also and mostly thanks to the carelessness of the guards, who preferred to sleep as opposed to spending the night 'defending' completely devastated trains. And anyway there was always someone on lookout. If a

guard came, all it took was a whistle and we were all in the forest where he would never be able to find us. In that case however we had to leave by another route, avoiding the path we had used to get in (as there was the possibility of finding the police waiting for us after a call from the yard guards). This alternative path takes you to the part of the forest that belongs to the estate of the President of the Republic, with military guards that

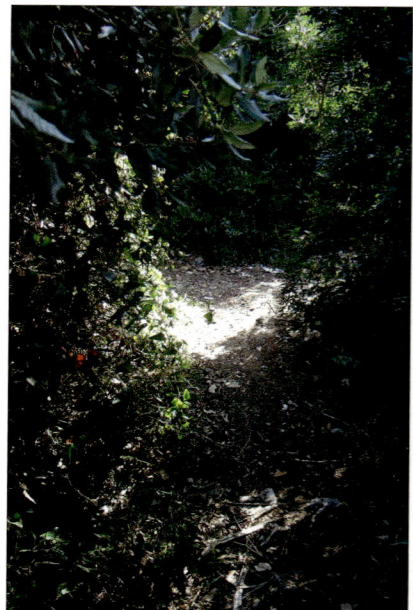

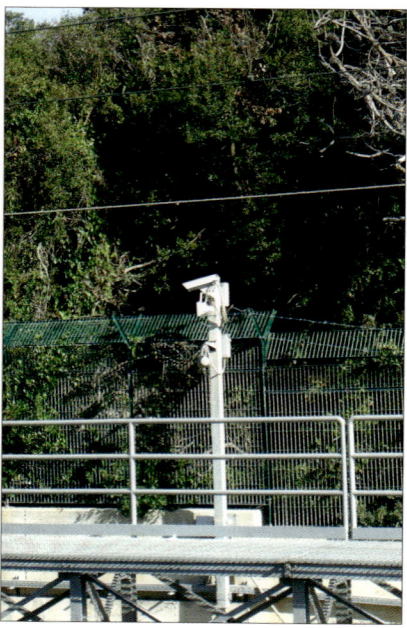

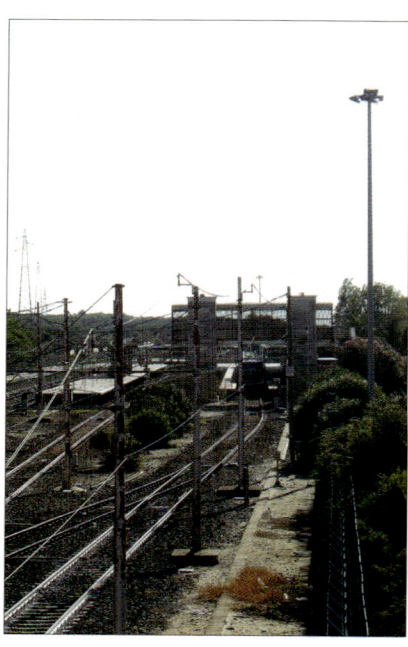

—Anek

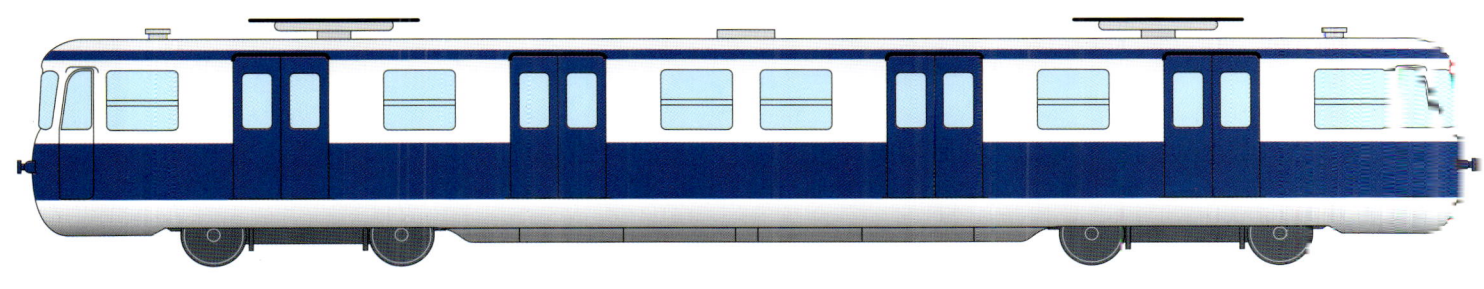

Ostia is one of the worst neighbourhoods of the Roman outskirts. Ostia's young inhabitants (including me) spent their teenage

afternoons doing jack shit, and when we did scrape up some cash we'd spend it on drugs. Our hang-out was the piazza in front of the

Lido Centro station amidst junkies, gypsies, and bums. It wasn't exactly the best spot but when you had nothing to do, you'd stop by

there and always run into someone so you would end up hanging out in the square, running into more people..—VER

---

patrol on horseback.It was in one of these escapes that we had a particular encounter: we had run away from the yard and had been walking for a while on this 'other' path. All of a sudden we hear noises, something getting closer to us.... it was the sound of horses (or so we thought). In total panic, sure it was the patrol, we hid in the bushes, laying on the ground almost without breathing, waiting to understand what was happening. I saw

I wasn't scared, more surprised, fascinated. I had in front of me a wild boar

the outline of what looked like a pig come towards me, except it was taller and stockier, it had an enormous snout and horns at the sides of its mouth. All at once it stopped, motionless just like us... as if it had sensed our presence. It stood still some seconds, but to me it seemed like minutes. I wasn't scared, more surprised, fascinated. I had in front of me a wild boar. It grunted, in a similar way to that of a pig, and then ran quickly away: sounding exactly like a galloping horse, I still remember it! We all got up and started running towards the exit (it wasn't far now), we hid the spray cans and got out on the coastal road. The Spanish kids that had come with us were incredulous, I hardly spoke until we got to the car, thinking back to that animal. It was the first

and last time in my life I ever saw a boar, in the pine wood of Ostia (where they say they are plentiful) or anywhere else. I never had this luck again, but that's part of the beauty of graffiti Writing: it often puts you in unthinkable situations, nocturnal adventures that you would never encounter during the day. Today the yard of Colombo looks like a fort: wire fences everywhere, sensors, cameras, two security guards 24 hours a day, and almost all the trains new and clean.... when I pass in front of it, perhaps to reach the beach, remembering everything that went down in that station, it sucks. It's been years now, I'm 'old' and I'll probably never venture that path again with a backpack full of cans... but what really gets me down is to think that nobody else takes that path to go into that yard either. Today that spot is dead; it lives only in the memories of the people that had a chance to enjoy it.

Ver
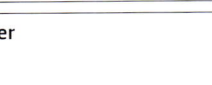
>

Ostia is one of the worst neighbourhoods of the Roman outskirts. Ostia's young inhabitants (including me) spent their teenage afternoons doing jack shit, and when we did scrape up some cash we'd spend it on drugs. Our hang-out was the piazza in front of the Lido Centro station amidst junkies, gypsies, and bums. It wasn't exactly the best spot but when you had nothing to do, you'd stop by there and always run into someone so you

would end up hanging out in the square, running into more people. I was the only member of the crew who painted in ZTK style, and everyone considered me a toy for this. K2R crew thought they were hot stuff just because they had painted a few pieces along the beach (except for Desma). They thought they could base their reputation on the dozen pieces they had each done and that that was sufficient to judge other people's styles. They would always warn me about ZTK by saying: "They're jerks, they steal spray paint from kids for no reason, they beat you up, they cross out everyone's tags!" etc... So I started to look down on them too because of these legends I kept hearing. A few years passed, it was 1998 and K2R crew had pretty much vanished. That year I began bombing the Lido line with Fone, giving rise to our crew: *No Stop Actin'*. One day we decided to go to Magliana to paint the B-line subway, all of a sudden this guy comes at us with a club... Fone says: "I think that's One, we're fucked!" I freaked out and started thinking all the rumours I'd heard about them were true. He walks toward us and asks who we are. We say "Ver and Fone", he asks if we're there to paint. We nod yes and he tells us he's looking for some losers who had crossed out his pieces and whatnot, then casually says: "Let's go in together and take turns acting as lookout". I couldn't believe it, I kept wondering: "When is he going to steal our spray paint and beat us up?" But instead he asked us to go in with him! We had never touched ZTK's pieces, that's why he was chill when he heard who we were. I realised

that all the stories about their violence and bullying were based on hostility towards them.
That afternoon changed my entire adolescence, all of my convictions crumbled and I realised how much I had been influenced by the stories I'd heard about them, even though in reality I didn't know jack shit. So for years our NSA crew was considered ZTK's ass-kissers; and before that ZTK crew was considered TRV's ass-kissers. Now, 10 years later, NSA, ZTK, and TRV are all united and we fight against the commercialisation of graffiti. As always, there are lots of nasty stories about us, but we don't give a shit- the facts speak for themselves! Unfortunately for them, they're not making history or changing it.

Gel

>

I remember the nights spent with Jon, Sila, Gor, One, Gast and P_m in the yard of Lido with beer bottles and bags full of spray cans, under the star-filled sky, the smell of summer piercing our nostrils. I've always seen Lido as somewhat of a playground. We would go there as if we were on a field trip, with our six-packs of Peroni and a party in our hearts. I remember we would have to take this pathway through the pine woods where you would sometimes meet wild boars. The pinewood of Ostia is an absurd place, with prostitutes at its entrance on the street of Colombo, and in a split second you could get lost. I was very passive and trusted

the people at the head of the line who acted as lookouts, also because I was hardly ever sober when I went painting. Once we had entered it, the wood seemed to never end it was a labyrinth of trees I would explore in a state of trance as if I was part of a video game a psychedelic trip towards the yard. Sometimes we'd meet rival writers from Rome or abroad, nearly every crew couldn't wait to get into a fight with these Lido boys. I don't give a damn, I was terrorised and at most was there ready to afteryard: a public space in which to spend the rest of the night. After crossing the pinewood we arrived in front of the train, it was all surreal and it was magic. Complete silence, just the noise of the spray cans.
Once we finished painting we'd do the whole journey backwards, apart from a couple of times we went to the platform of the station to hit the windows of the trains, still pretty clean at the

Once we had entered it, the wood seemed to never end, it was a labyrinth of trees I would explore in a state of trance as if was part of a video game

time. It was a true sensation, our names everywhere ready to travel. At the end of the field trip we would pass by the bar and then take the bus that would bring us safely and soundly back to Rome

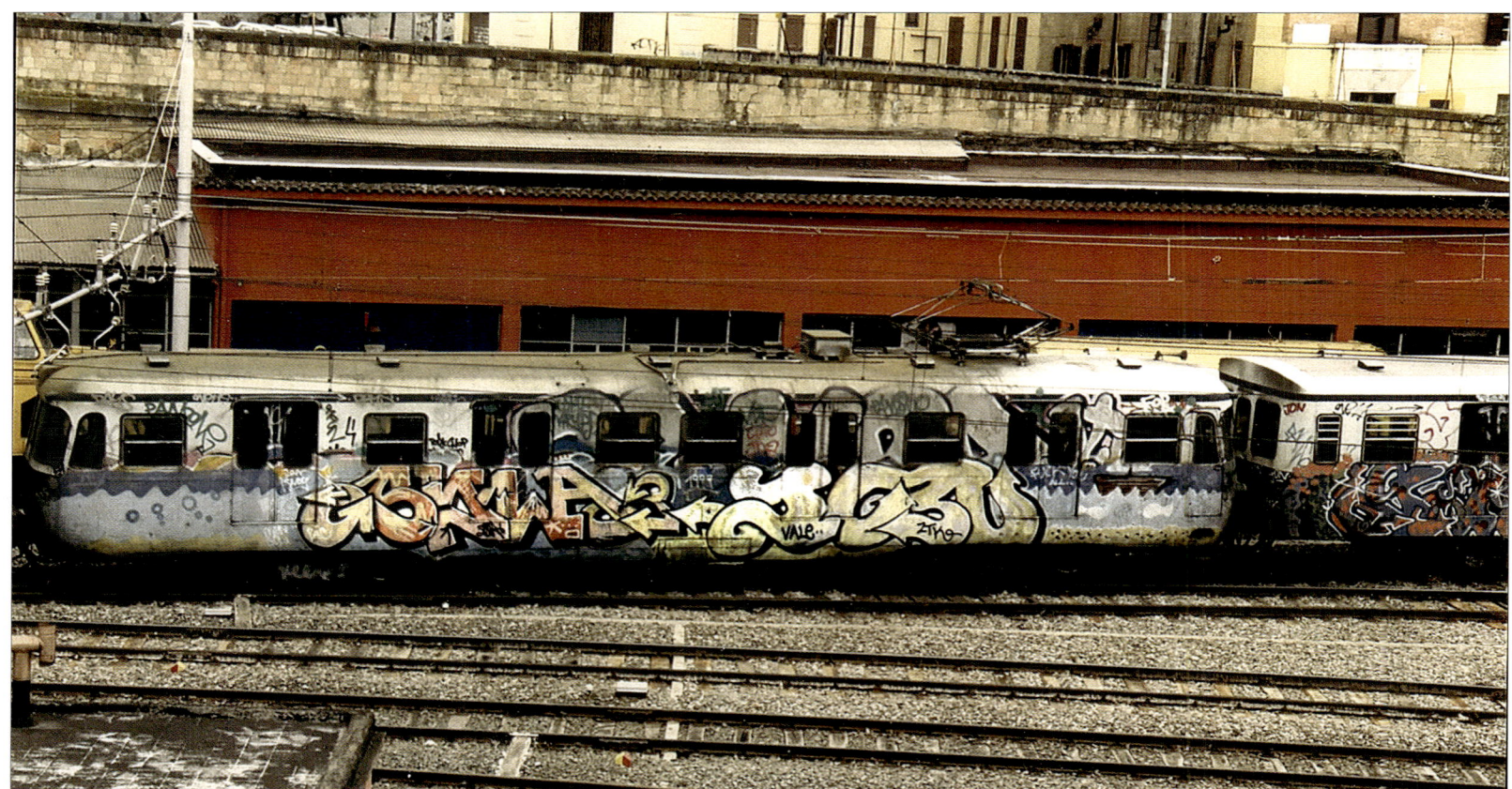

— Maccaroni Archive

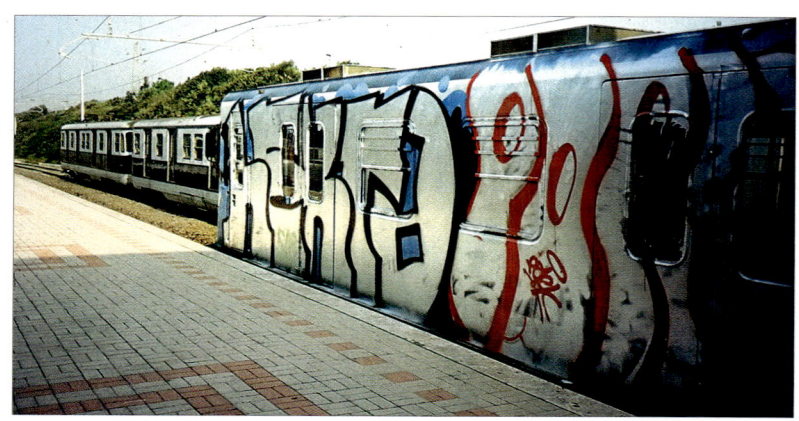

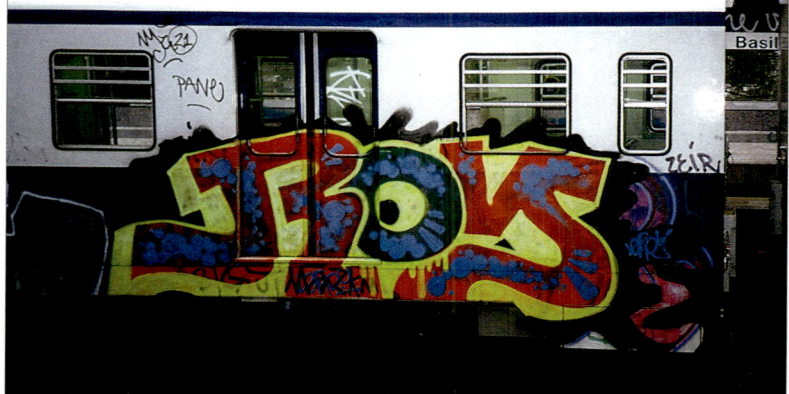

— Trota

— Trota

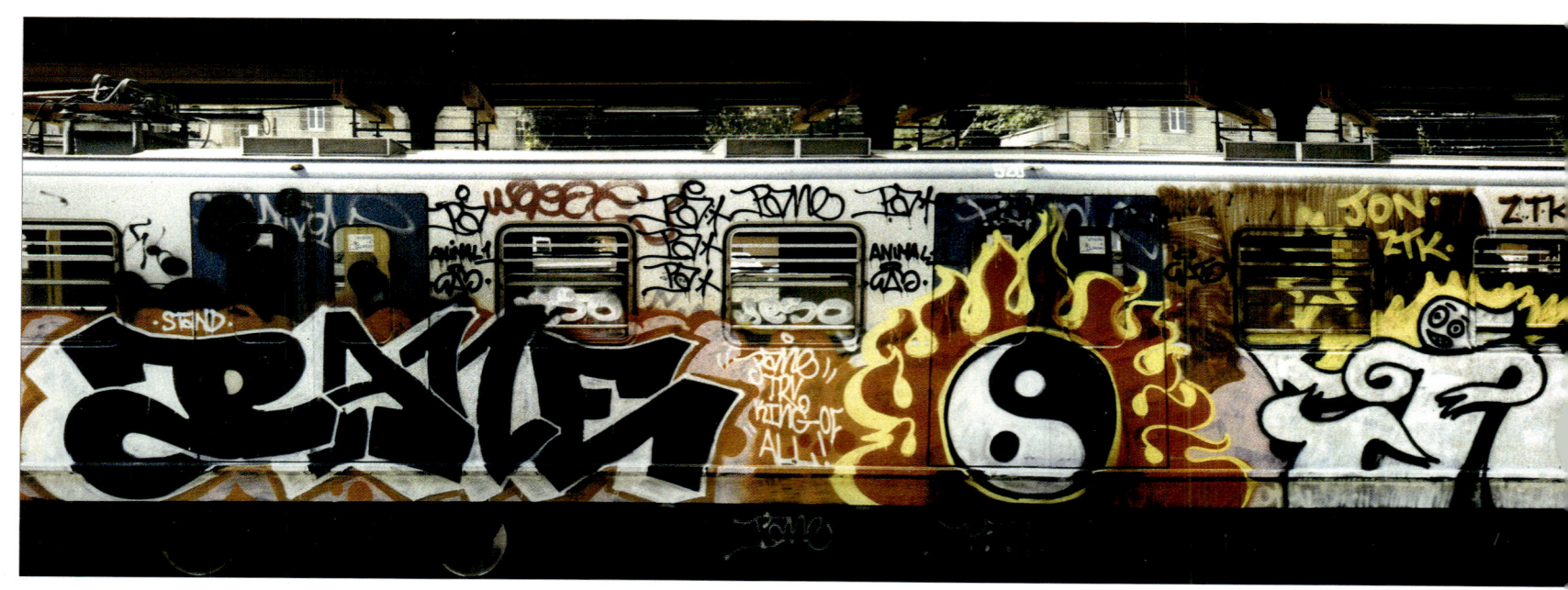

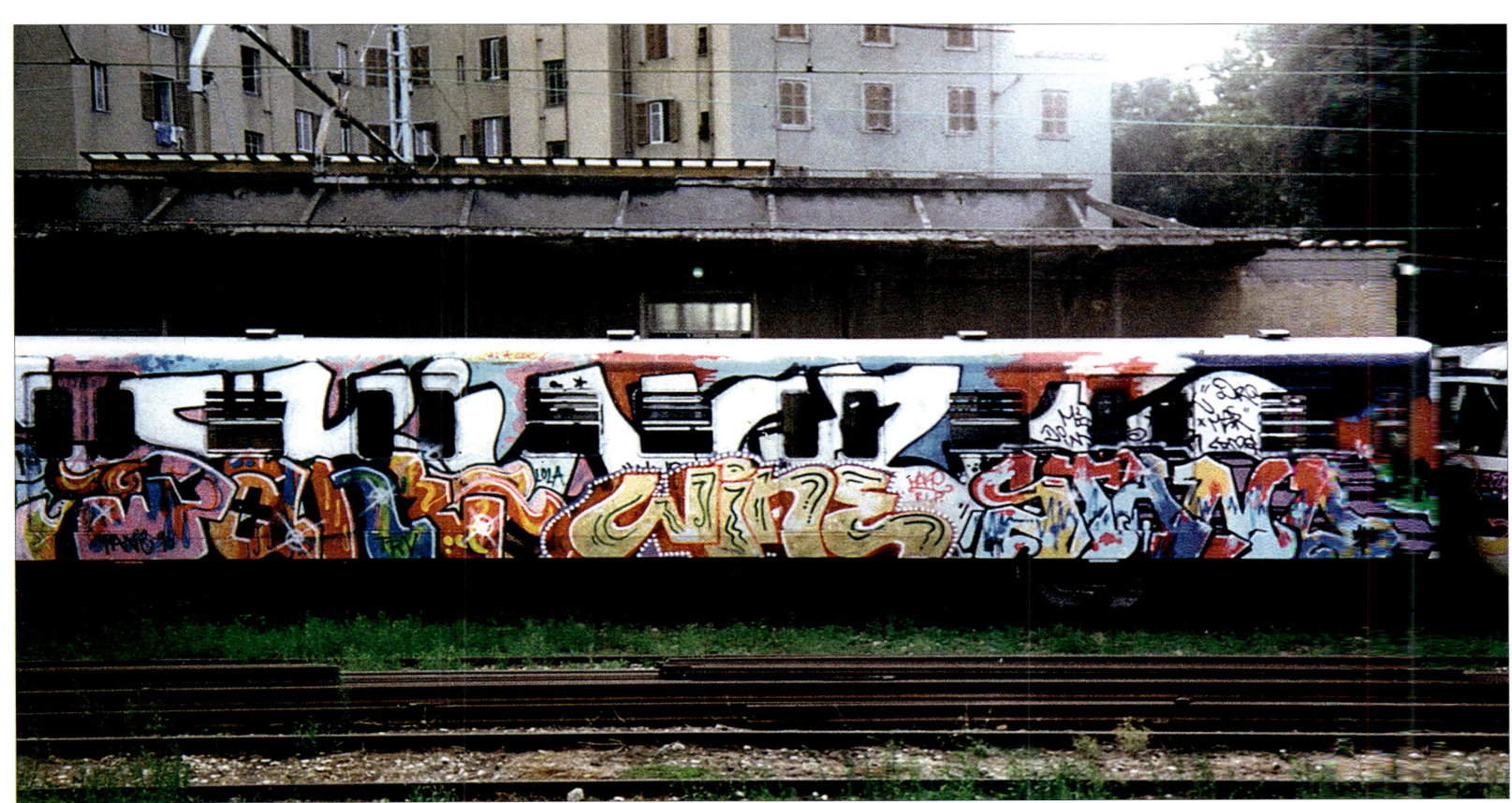

– Mencio

1		2
7	6	3
5		4

1 Unfinished end-to-end by Syla–PAC–ZTK, Jon–ZTK, 1998

2 Pane TRV, *Wine* by DebOne MT2, Stand–TRV

3 Joe

4 PAC crew in action

5 Pane–TRV, Jon–ZTK

6 Roy by DebOne–MT2 TRV

7 Hekto MDF

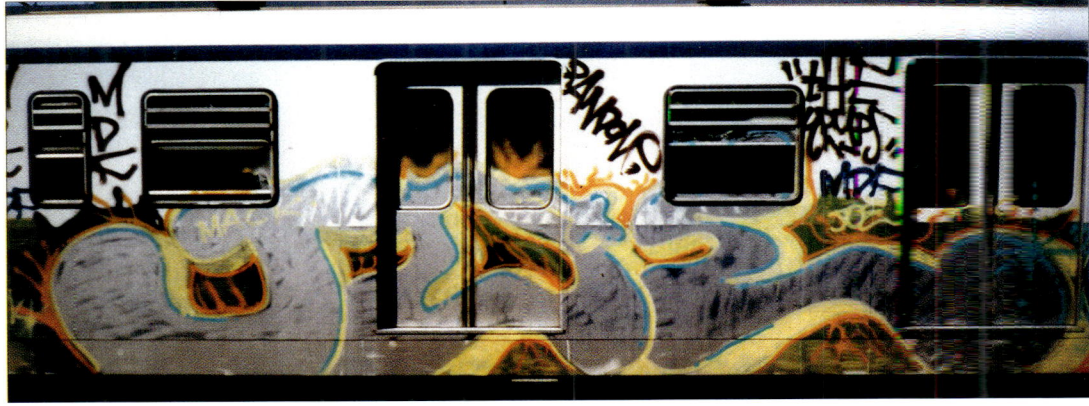

– Mencio

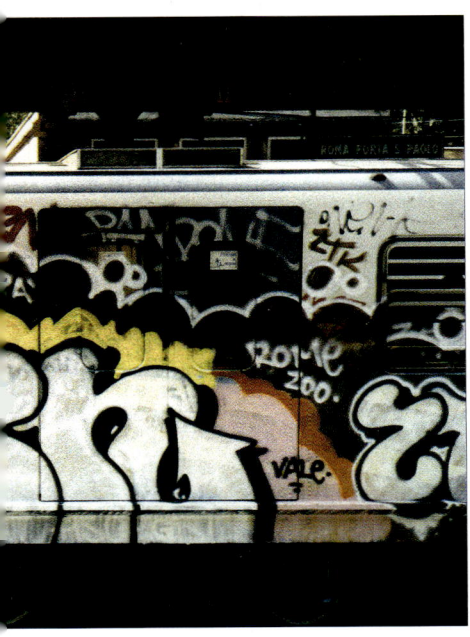

– Mencio

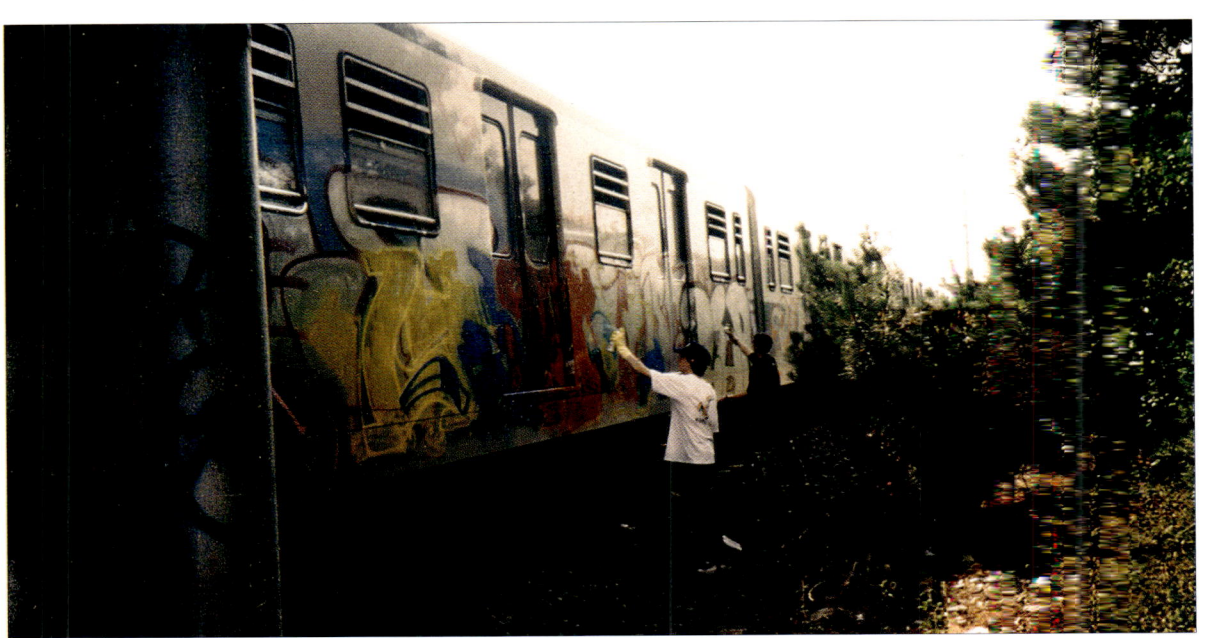

– Trota

END OF THE CITY
—

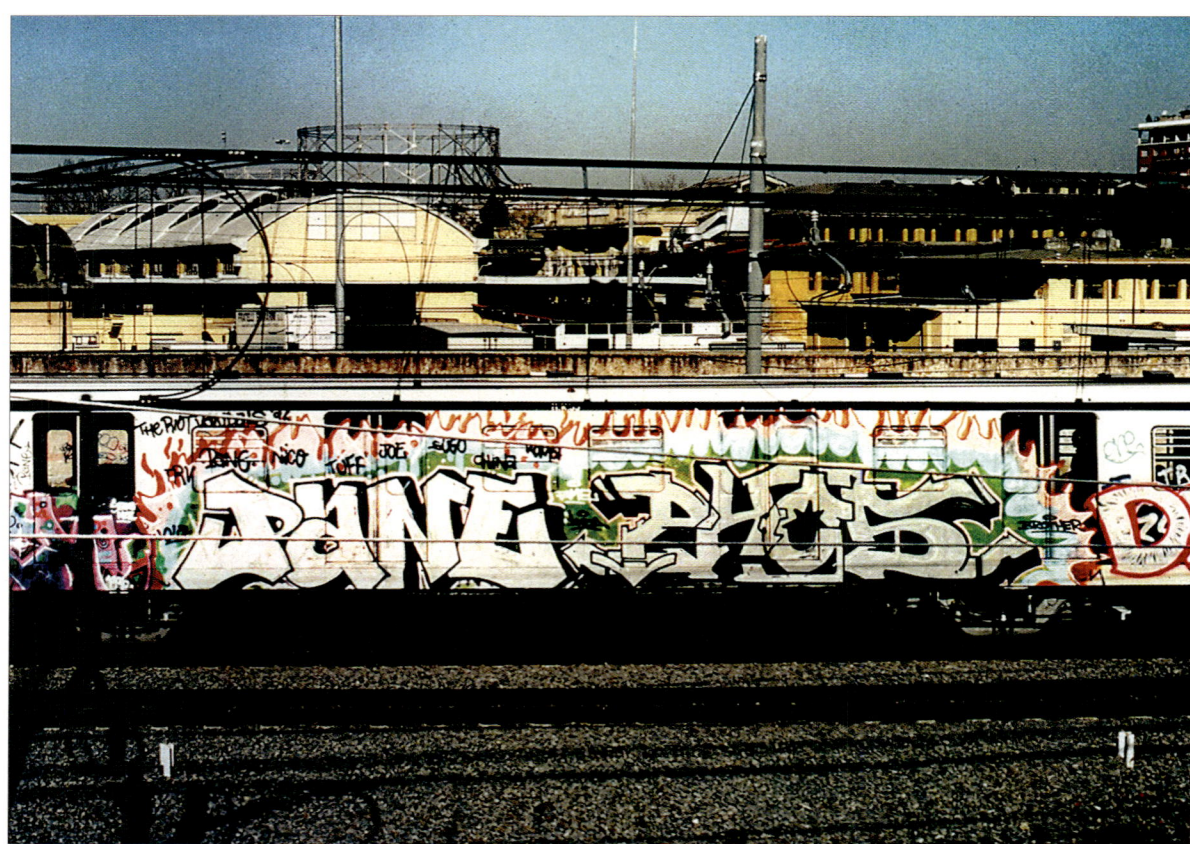

— *Maccaroni Archive*

One ZTK
>

To paint the Lido line, once the golden days of
the Roman mini-yards had ended, we were
forced to go as far as the end stop of Ostia. To
get to the train you had to take a 30 minute
walk through the pine forest and certain
nights it was so ghoulish we felt much safer in
the yard, a feeling that would then become a
constant in almost all deposits.
I remember certain ambushes that took place
between the yard and the woods, back when
instead of a fence delimiting the area of the
yard there were only bushes: it was riskier this
way, because fences have always been more
of a barrier for the guards than for us, we would
fly over them. Without the wire fence, in the
dark, seeing armed guys come out and start
shooting at you as you run away, was even
more dangerous. Getting to the train was in
fact similar to a war movie, where camouflag-
ing yourself isn't just a safety precaution but
more of a shrewd move: we wanted to paint
regardless and it would have been difficult to
see us go home with clean hands.

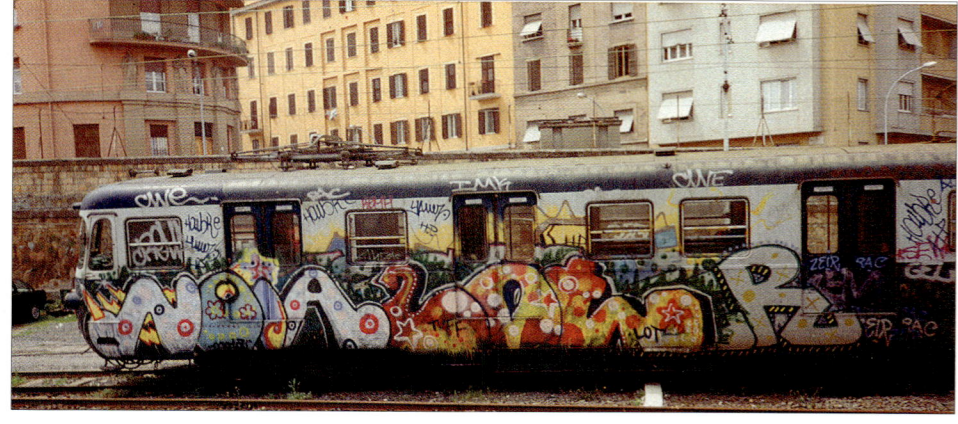

— *Tuff*

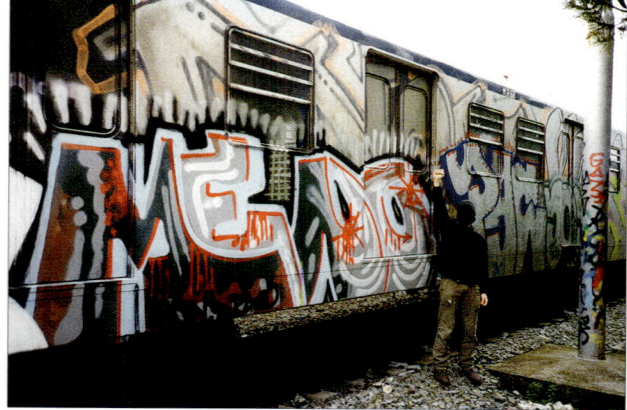

— *Trota*

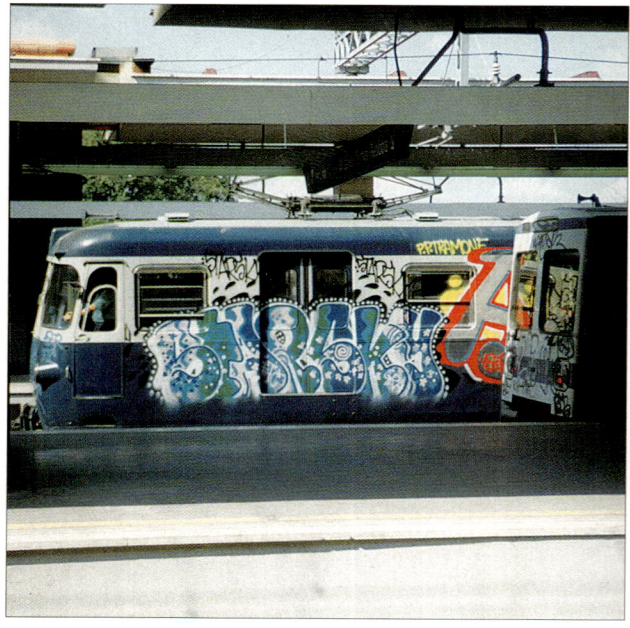

— *Mark Todt*

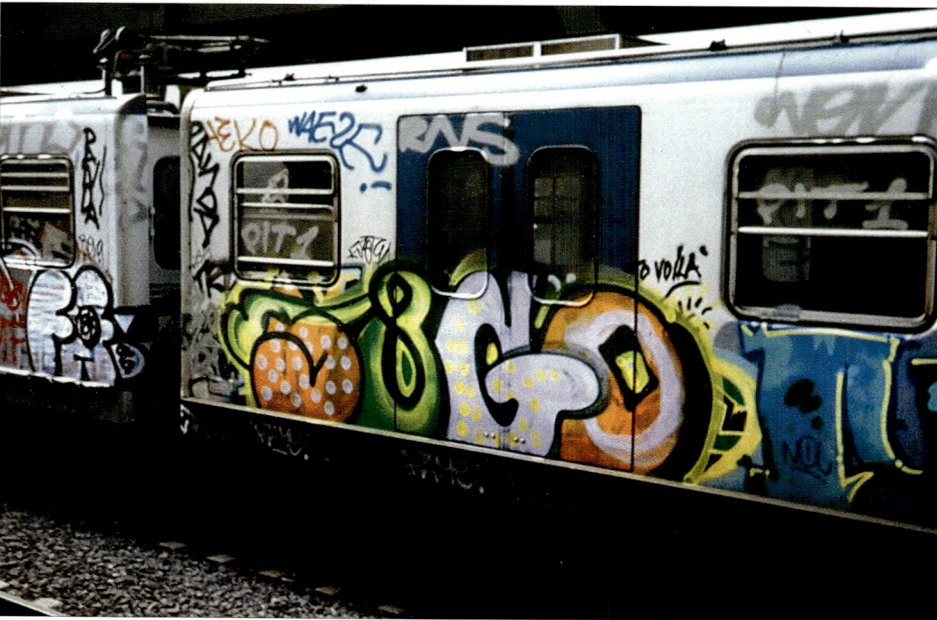

— *Trota*

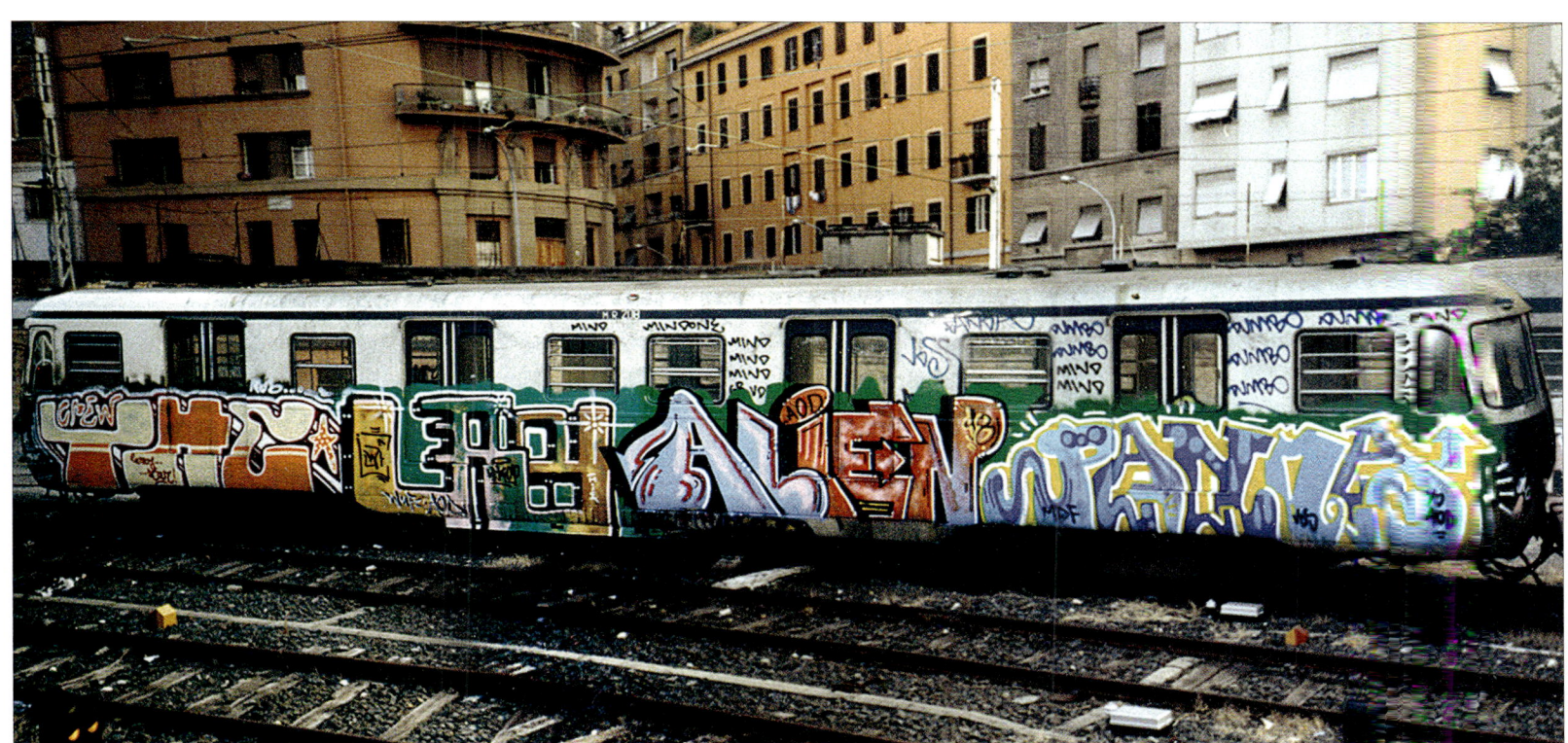

— Trota

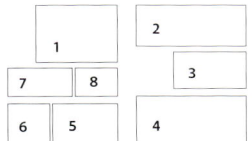

1. Pane TRV, Phos from Berlin
2. THE, Leroy and Alien AOD from Scandinavia,
   Panda THE–MDF
3. *More touch two* by Stand, Kraze and Clown,
   one of the first pieces to be painted on the Lido line
4. *Adam* by Stand–MT2 ETC TRV, Washe–NSB
5. Sugo TRV, 1996
6. *Starsky* by Pane TRV
7. Noia, Lot by Tuff
8. Mencio PAC photographed in the yard in front of the
   pinewood of Ostia

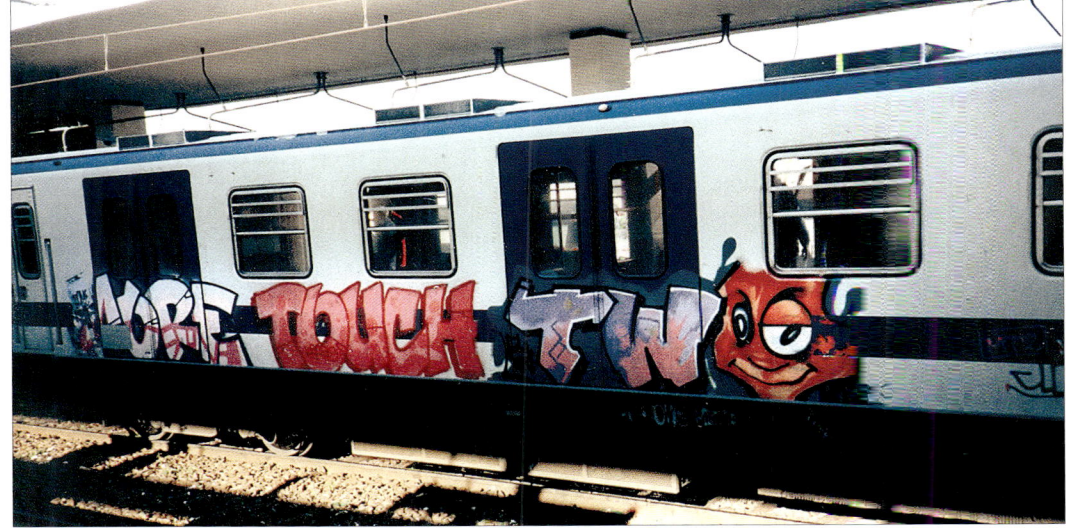

— Mencio

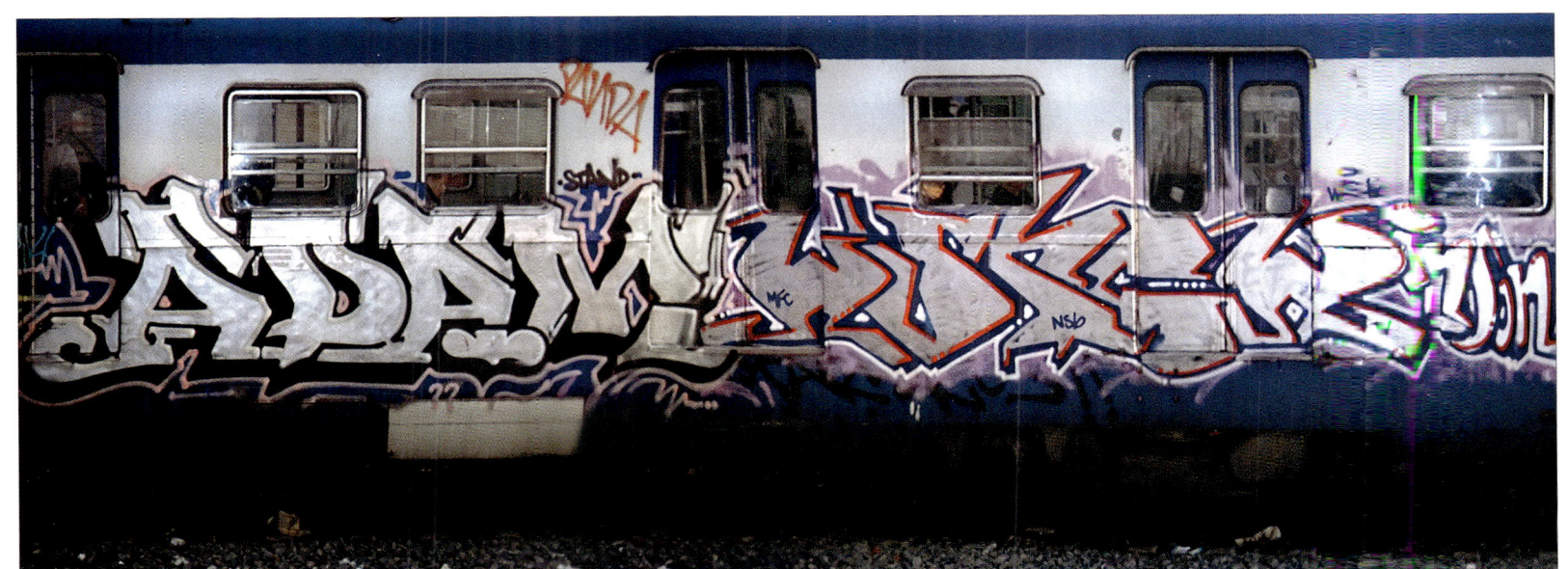

— ACW archive

Piramide station, 2009

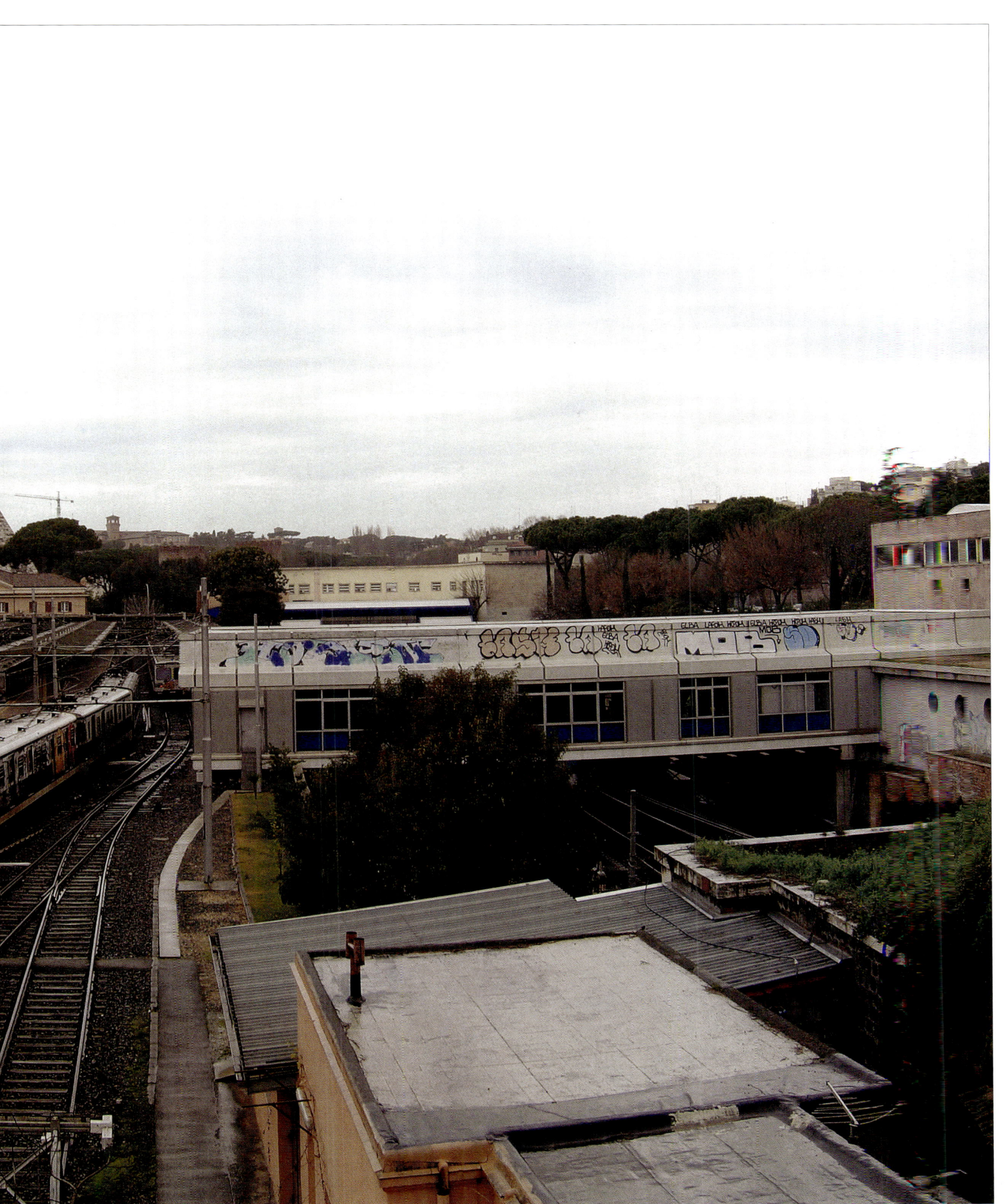

The attraction exerted by the Roman subway on European and American writers

>

Strangers in Rome

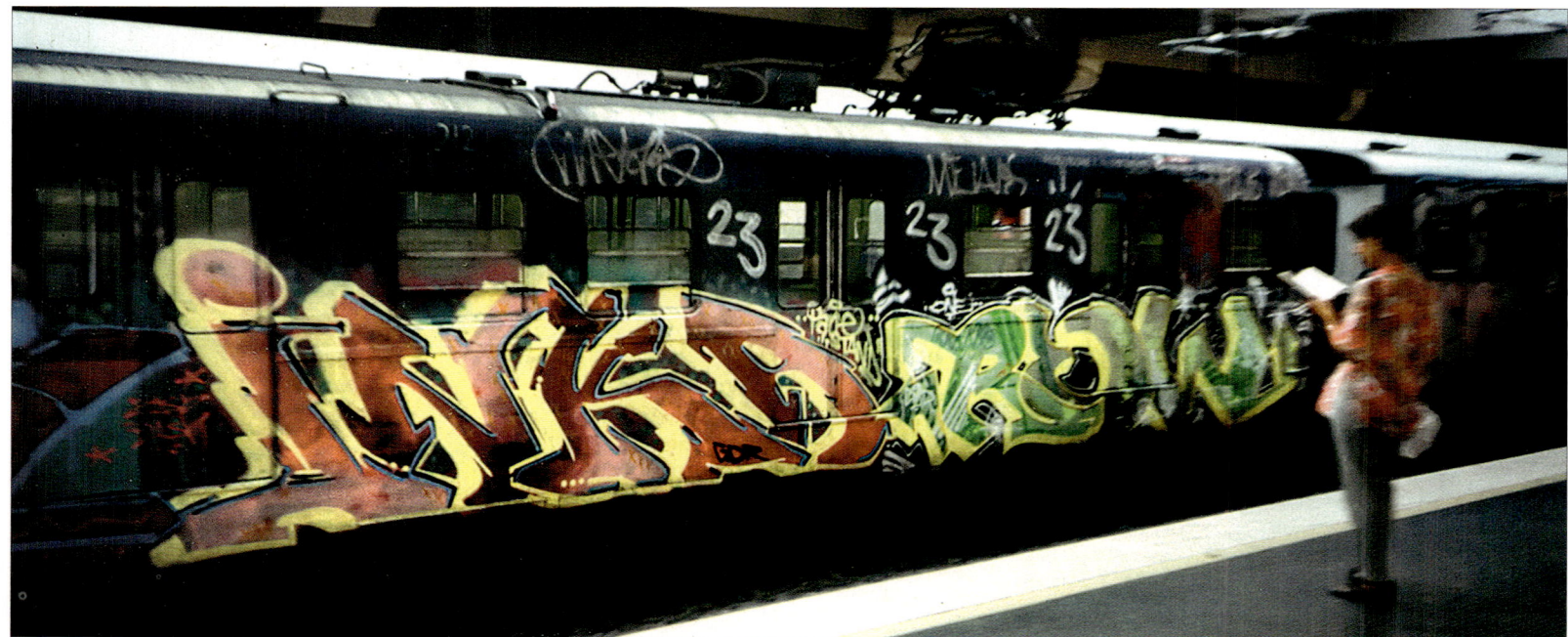

— Trota

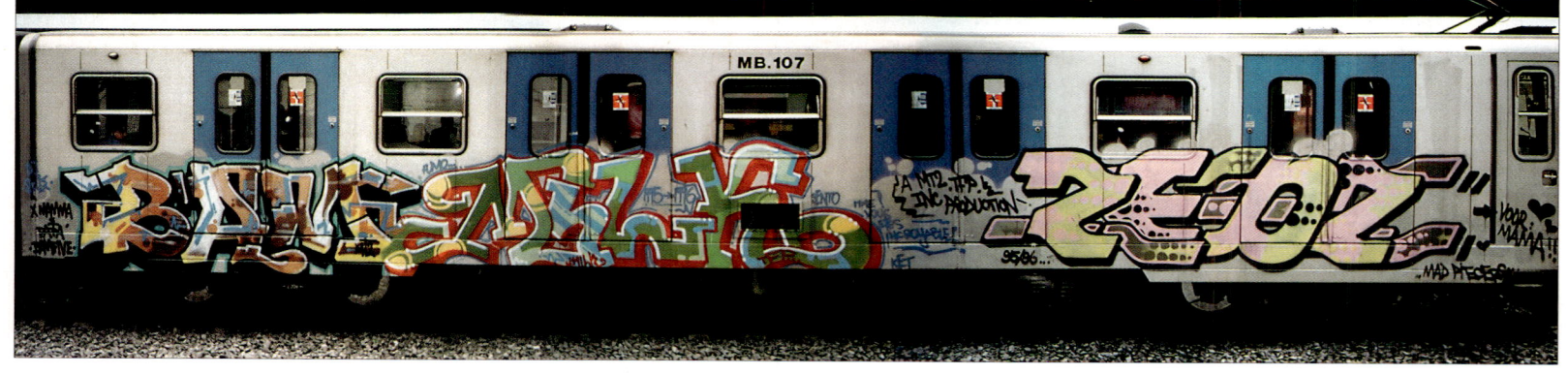

— Maccaroni archive

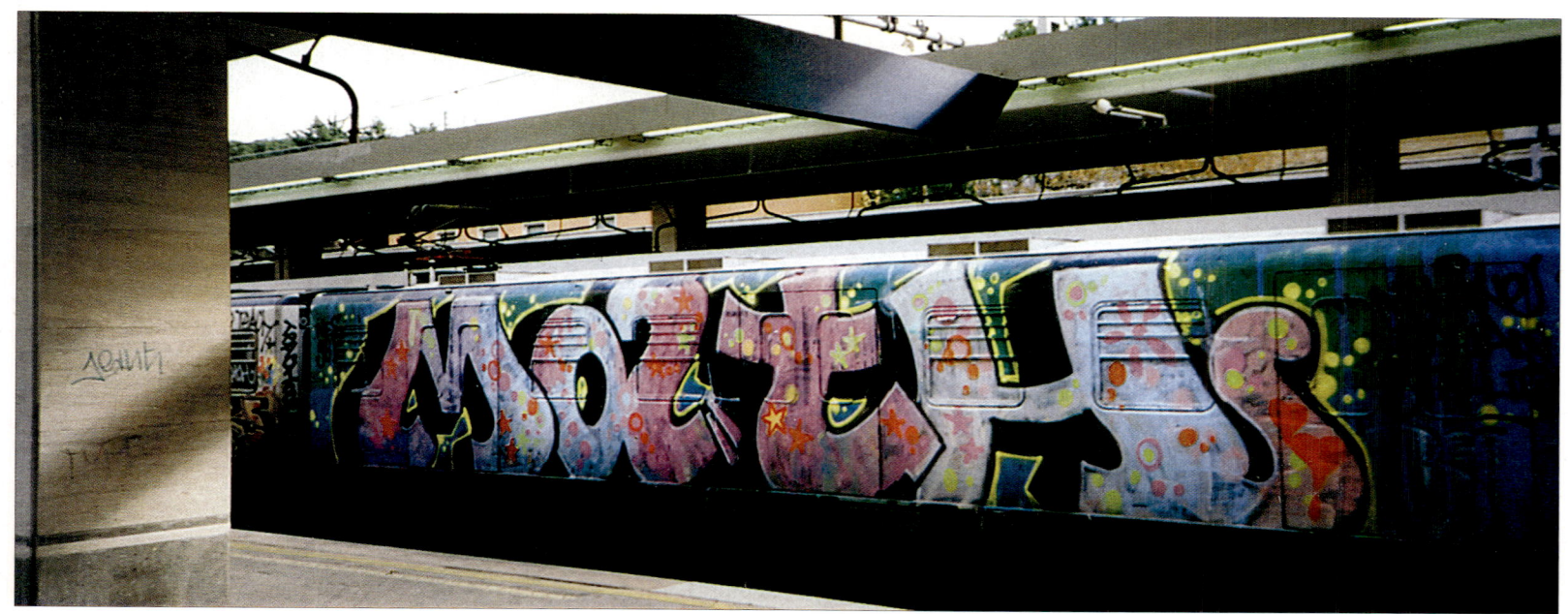

— Maccaroni archive

ALL CITY WRITERS   CITY CHRONICLES
ROME

SUBWAY

STRANGERS
IN ROME

313

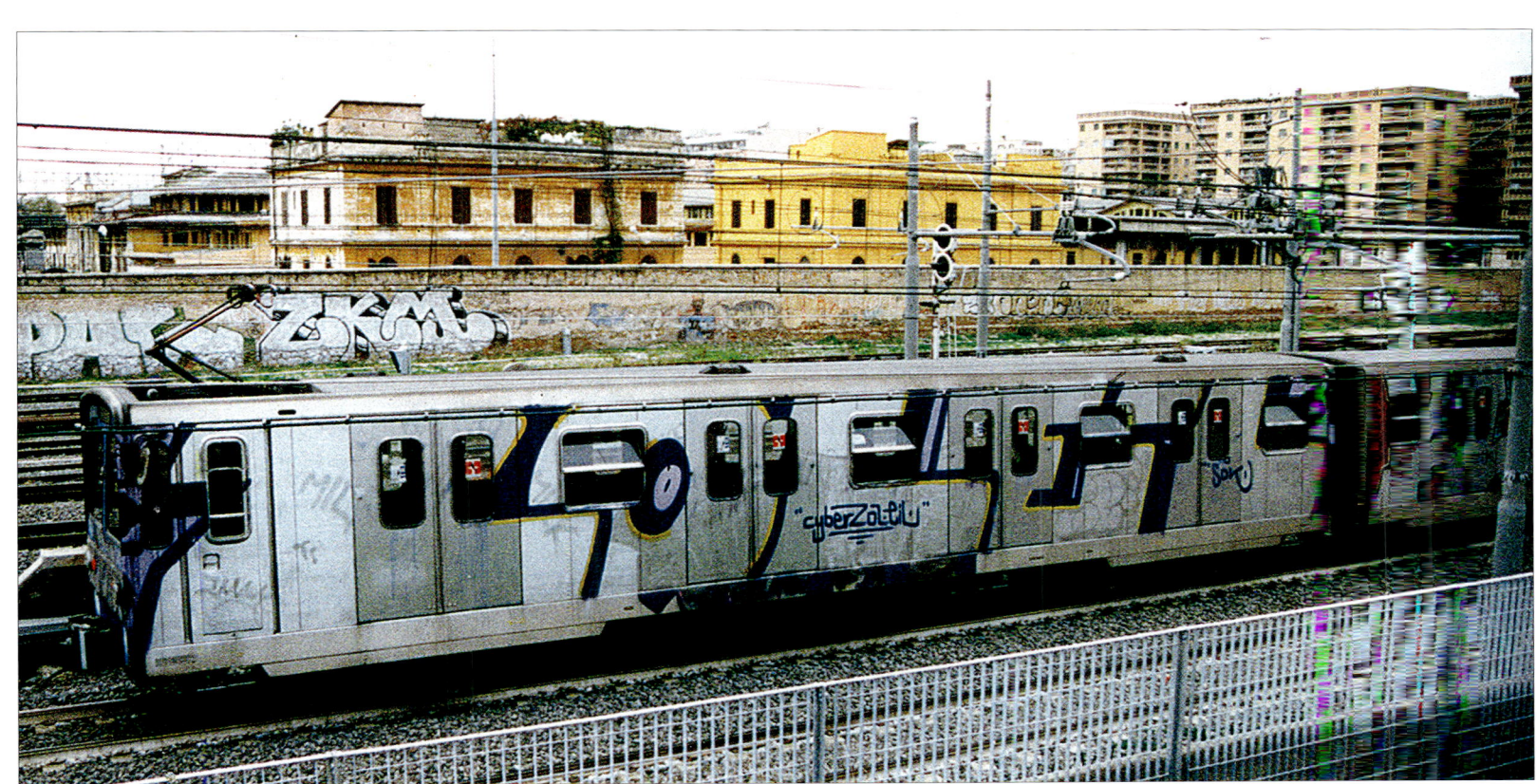

— Vencio

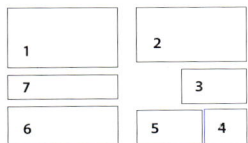

1	2
7	3
6	5	4

1 Inka, Rew from Berlin

2 One man whole-car by Soleil-SDK from Paris, in the background pieces by PAC and ZKM can be seen on the track wall

3 *All Pal* by All from Barcelona, 1995

4 Jase from Hamburg, 1996

5 Zimok from Germany, 1999

6 One man whole-car by Math from Amsterdam

7 End-to-end, *Bam* by Stand-TRV, Milk-TFP from Munich, Zedz from Amsterdam painted on New Year's Eve of 1996

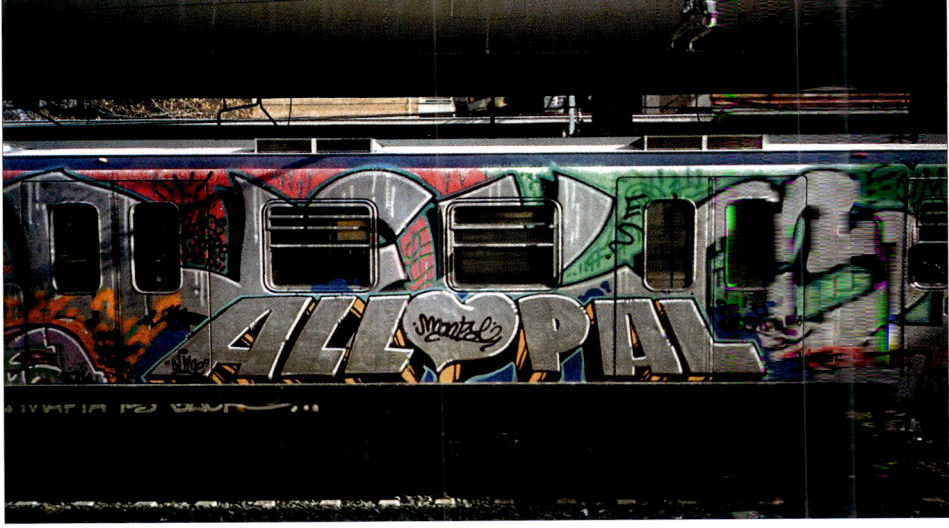

— Museum archive

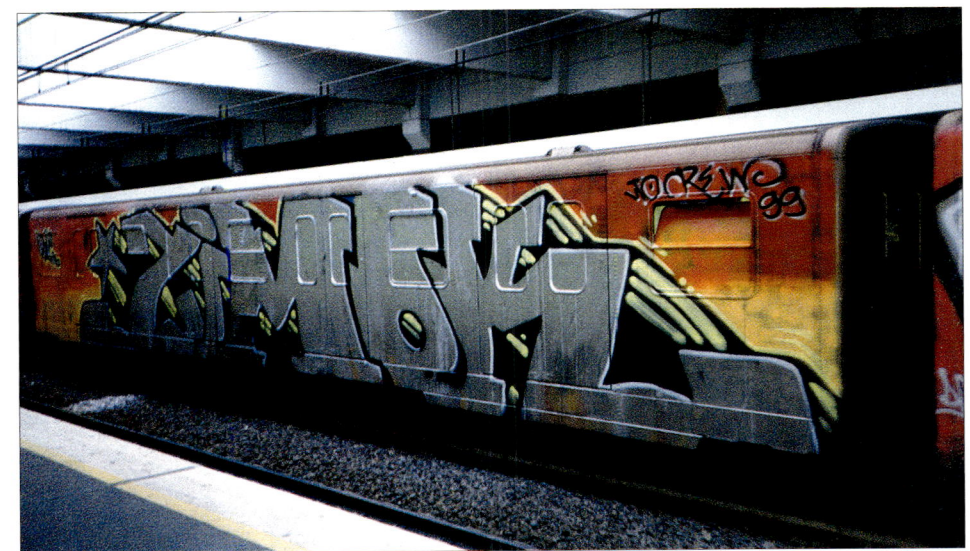

— Trota

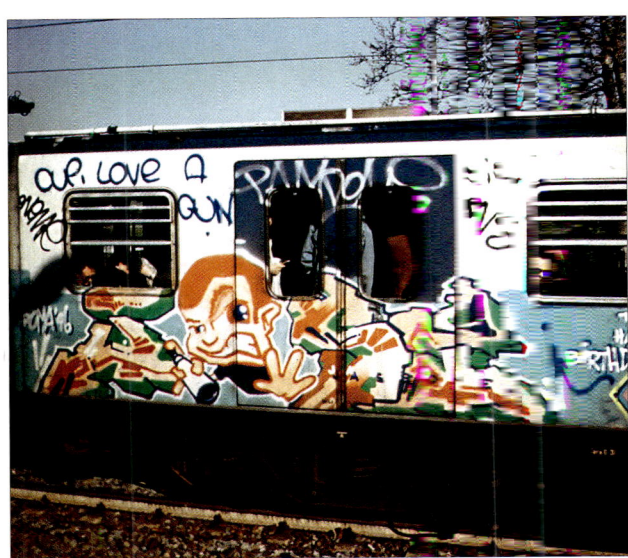

— Trota

INDELIBLE MARKS
—

When UV crew came to Rome they basically bombed every line, the A and B subway, the Lido and the trains of the Roma Nord. They were the first to bring glossy French inks, like the ones you can buy at FNAC department store, that are more permanent than Nero Inferno, you just can't remove them and they were used for tagging trains. Those tags lasted real long and dripped like crazy. I got my hands on two or three of those ink bottles and when I tagged it trickled way too much and you would do a couple of stations this way, Rome was completely black, that ink was fierce.

Not everyone in Rome understood the guys in UV, a couple of people had a similar mentality but they indisputably imported a new way of painting, even more instinctive than the Roman one. Zemar told me they had this weird method, they never put their cans down, it was a continuous movement, they did one piece and then another. We had three colours for the fill, the outline, and maybe more, they started painting I don't even know how many pieces, while in the meantime you would have maybe finished two.

They never quit and that way they managed to do more, while also crossing other people's stuff. They didn't look at jack, not even your piece right next to theirs. ZTK has this "let's do throw-ups" attitude, they pick up the silvers and start covering everything... but at least they also do pieces. UV was more wild, they had the French simplicity, with separated letters, elementary, but killing everything, without ever stopping. — **SYLA**

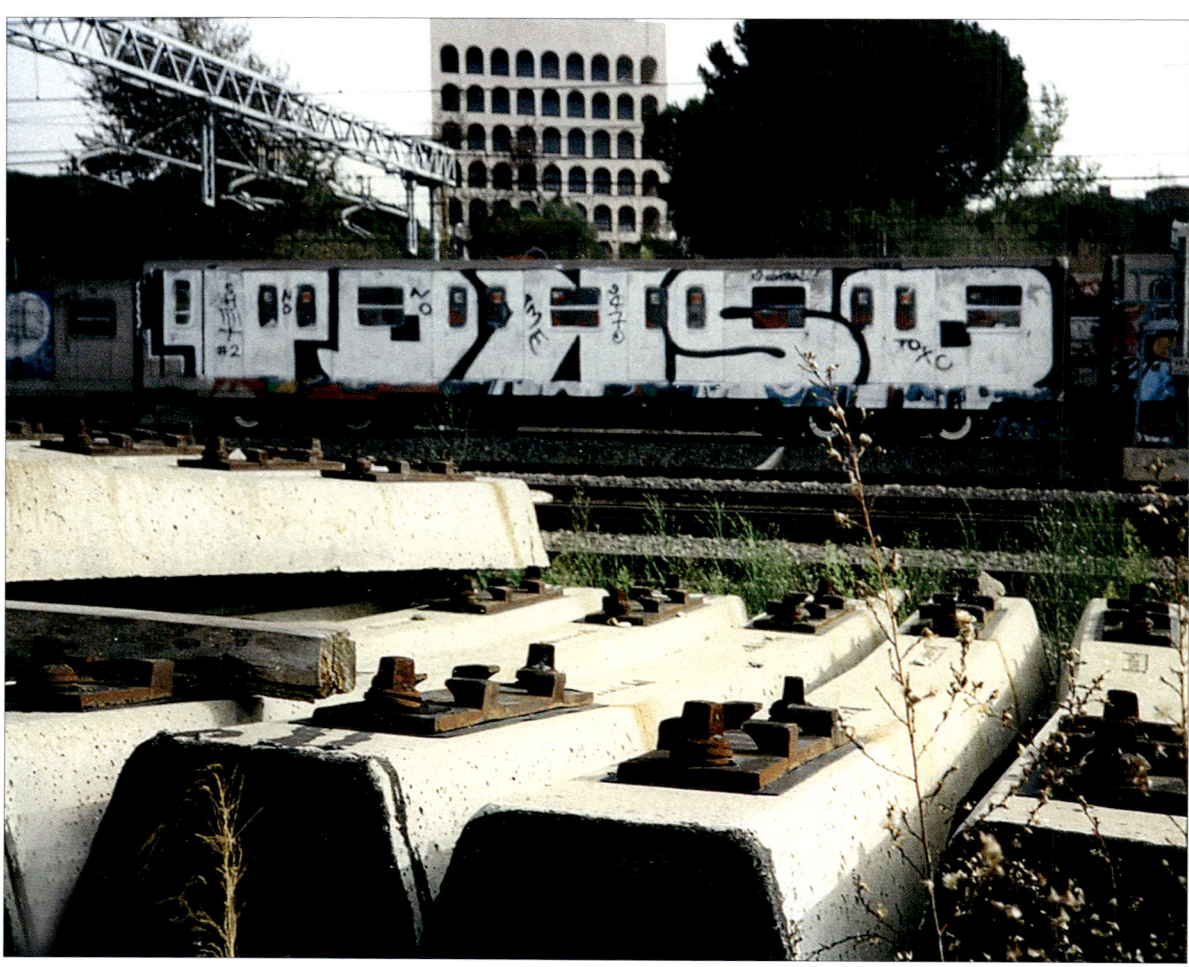

— Maccaroni Archive

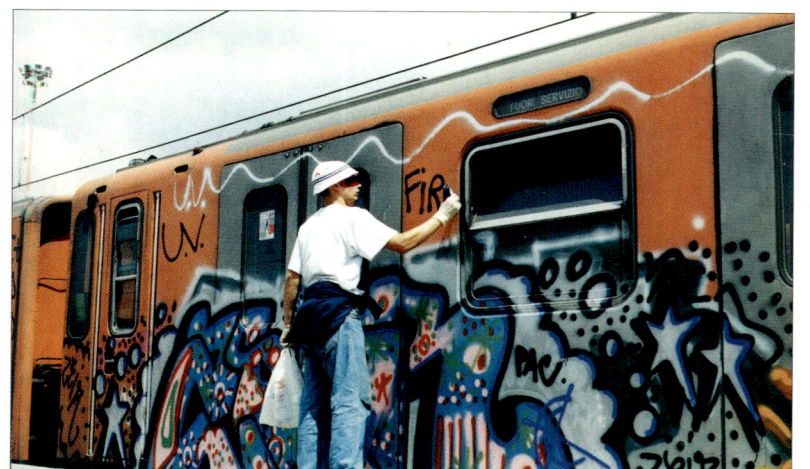

— Mencio

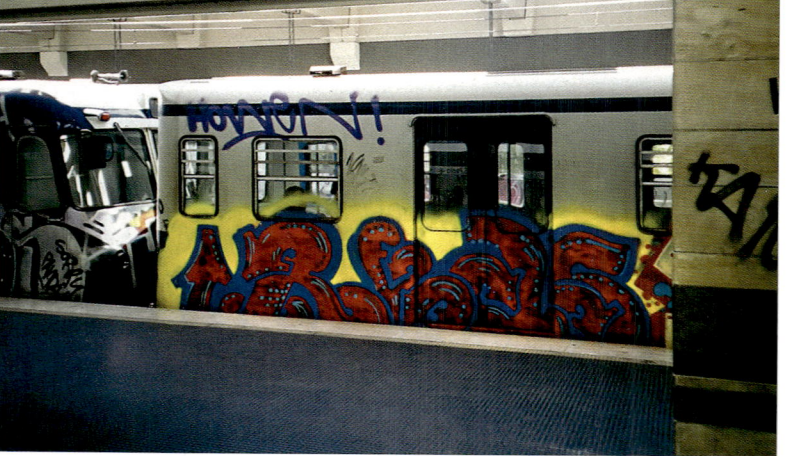

— Trota

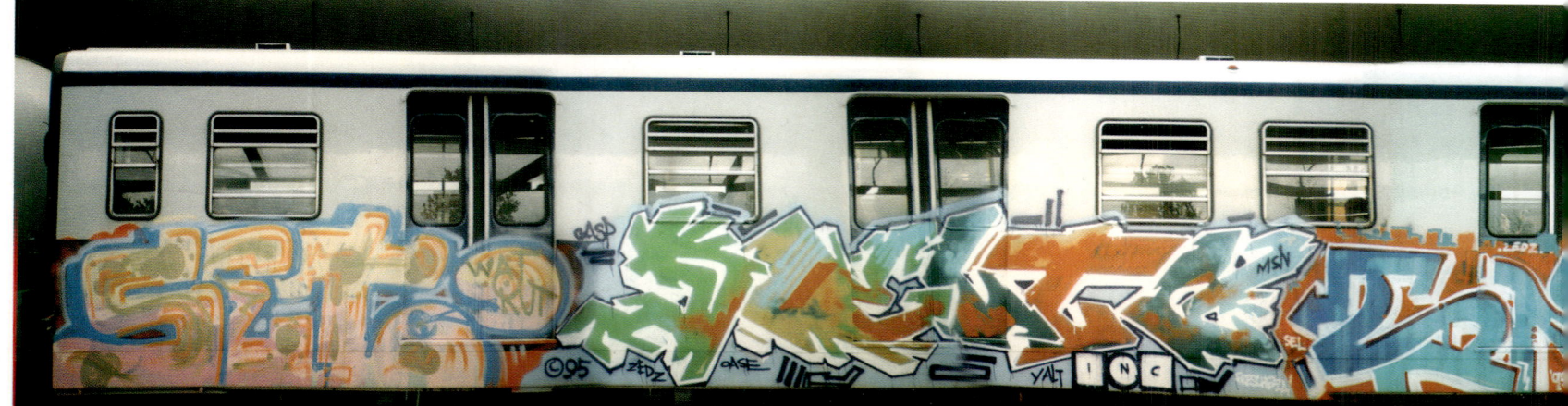

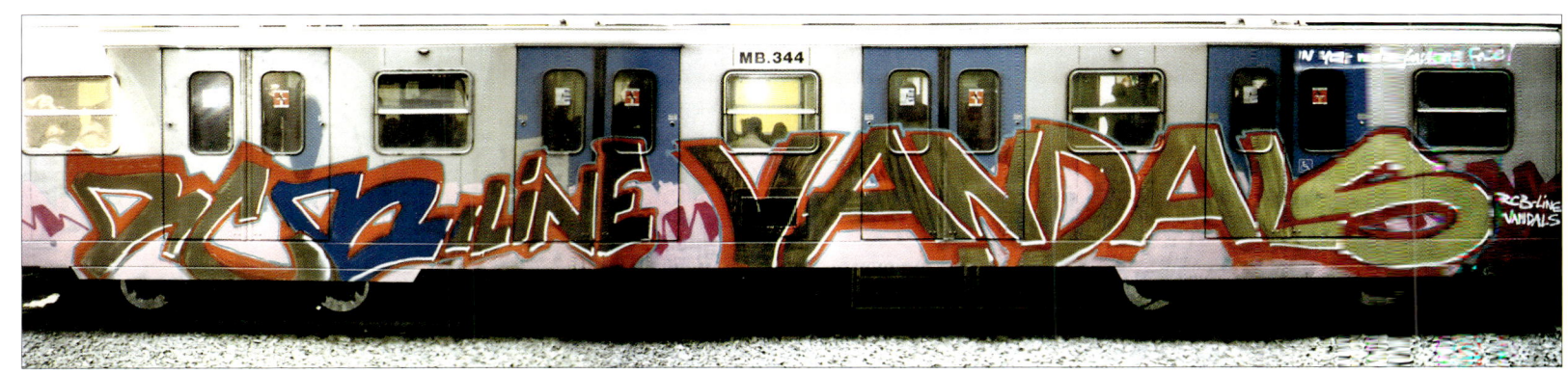

— Mazzarini Archive

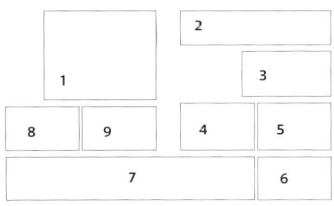

1 *Toxo* by Oame - PME from Bordeaux

2 *RCB line vandals* by RCB crew from Berlin

3 *Shas* by Sha from Madrid

4 Fume - MSN from Düsseldorf

5 Chintz from Dortmund. 'È pericoloso sporgersi''

6 Nois - CDC from Helsinki

7 Set, Delta, Sel from Holland and Bam

8 Firo - UV from Paris, tagging the A-line cars

9 Reas from New York, €2e painted with Smart from Firenze and Trota - THE

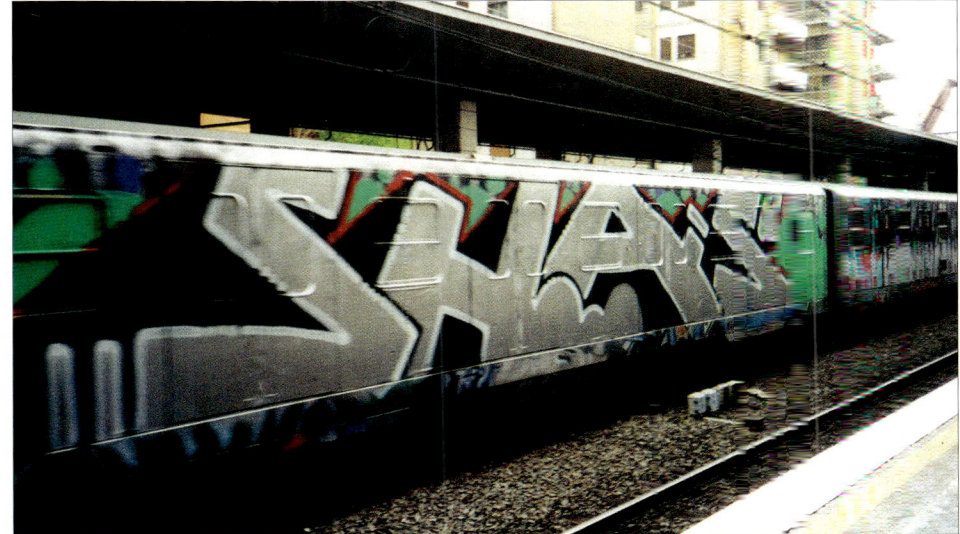

— Trota

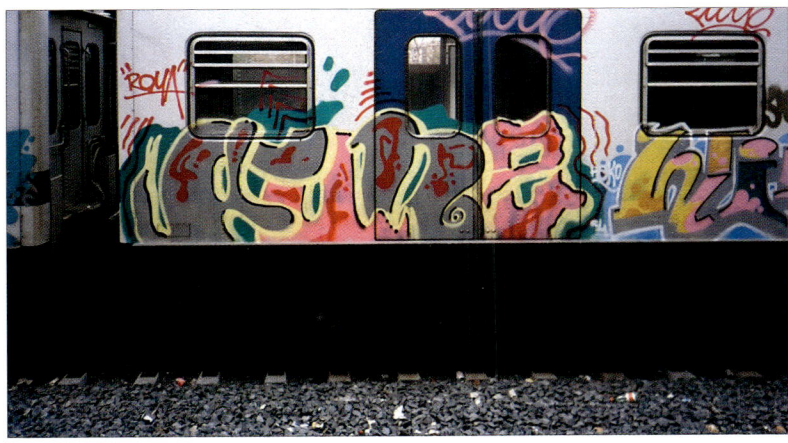
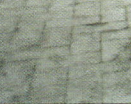

— Trota

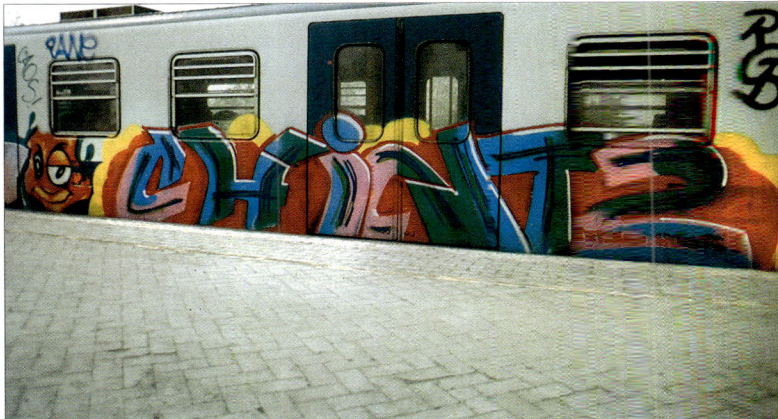

— Benzio

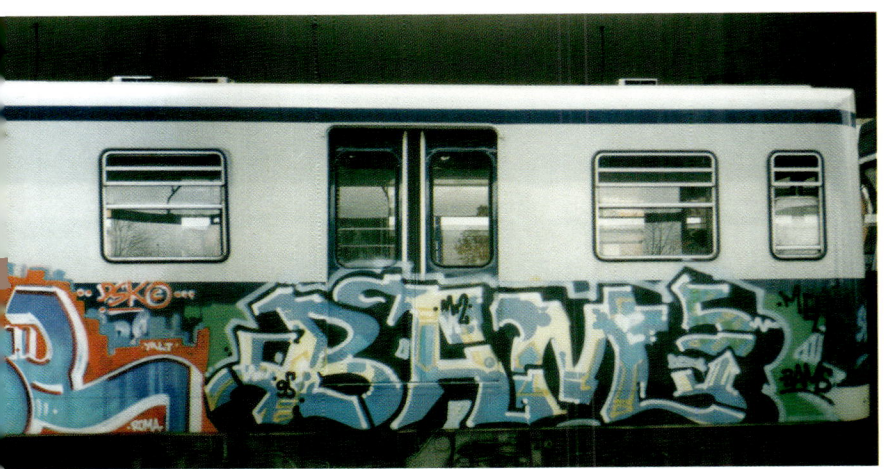

— Trota

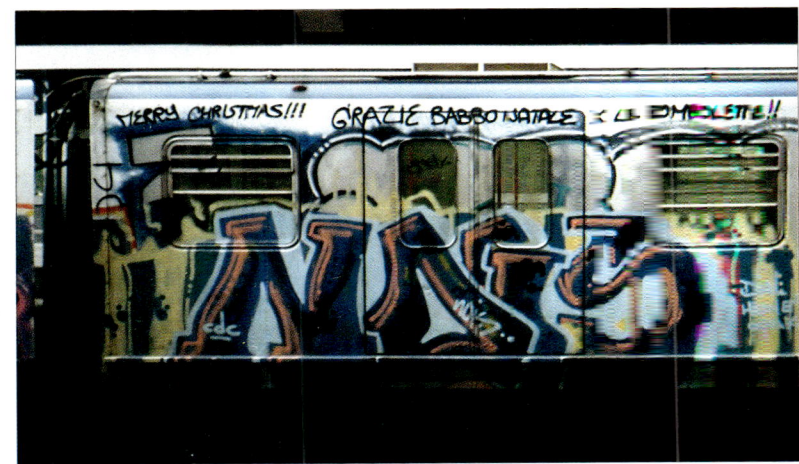

— Trota

316   ALL CITY WRITERS   CITY CHRONICLES
                                       ROME

OVERGROUND
RAILWAYS

ROMA
VELLETRI

ROMA VELLETRI
Overground Railways

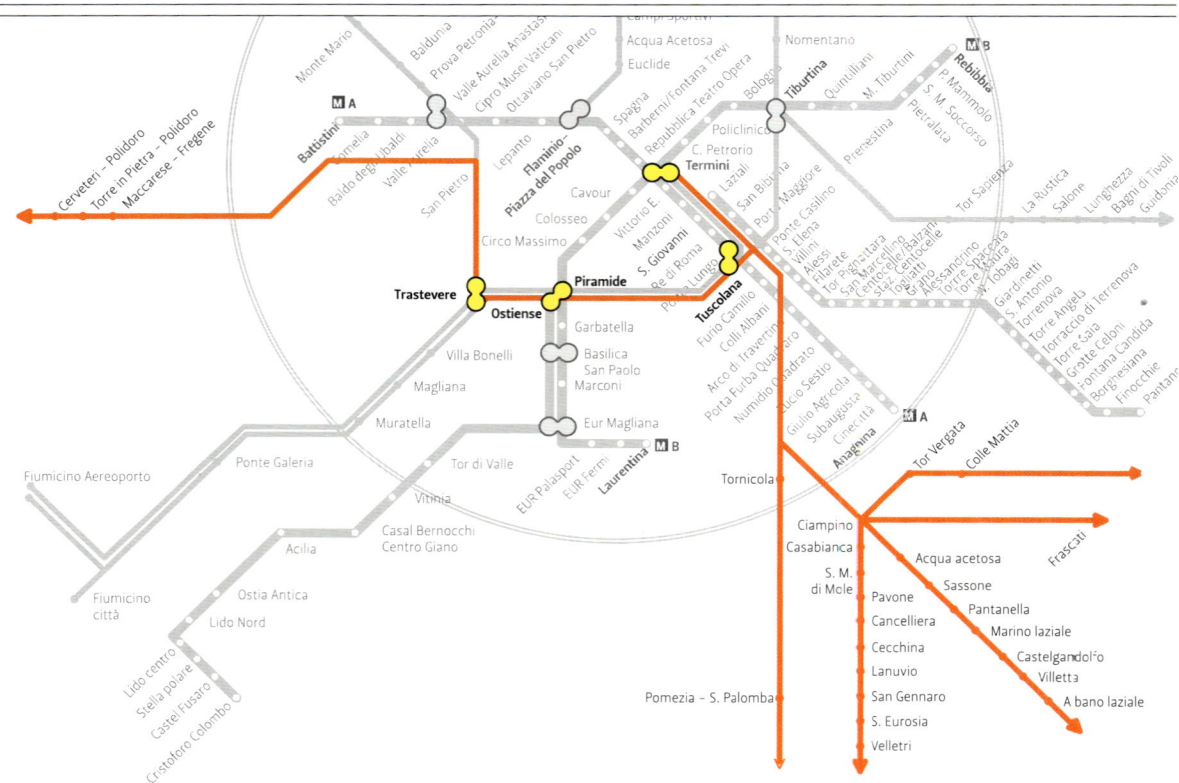

Run by Trenitalia, the FR4 is one of the regional railways that utilizes the three lines serving the basin of Roman Castles, to the South of the city, branching out towards Frascati (first opened in 1858), Albano Laziale and Velletri. The frequence is about a train every hour.

An alternative to the subway
>

The Orange trains: PAC's

Mencio
>

Every writer that paints trains knows there's nothing better than having a line you can bomb with your whole crew. Even better if the line has big, homogenous panels and runs the whole length and width of the city, the province and the principle stations where visibility is at a peak. All this happened on the metropolitan railway line of the *arancioni*. Before us no-one else, apart from a couple of sporadic hits, had painted it. There was a nice car by Legs, Octez from Paris and NSB running, because that train had also stopped in another deposit, but the systematic devastation of the line was ours. Living outside of Rome, that was the line I always took going to school and back. I noticed that on Saturdays, while most trains arrived and immediately left this end station, there was one train standing nice and still on the third track for a good hour, while its driver and staff were eating at the restaurant in front of the station, renown for its fresh fish. So I thought that while the fish was cooking I might as well attempt a flop and some tags. It worked.

The whole crew was informed. Rendez-vous at 1900 hours, with backpacks, gloves, spray cans and caps. To reach the train from behind you had to take a wide route, walking on a dark, narrow street with an abandoned house on the corner which was clearly a drug dealership seeing the traffic of not altogether clean cut

faces coming and going. At one point you left the road to your left and arrived at the foot of a hill that took to the rail tracks. Here, amidst the bramble, bushes, trees, rubble and the usual garbage, we'd get ready. Climbing upwards, hidden among the trees, you would find the usual shacks that sadly animate the surroundings of marginal territories, witnessing the social divarication. Which translated means "unwelcome foreign presences". For the purpose of convenience we established our headquarters for all future missions halfway up the hill. Having ter-

When the pieces have been completed everybody smiles, cause we understand it's the probable beginning of a growth for our crew

minated our quick preparation, looked at the time on our watches, and done a first reconnaissance, we all approached the train. Everything seemed silent and unreal. The train car named desire was within our reach. So move it, put the caps on the spray cans and hurry up because the cloud of paint quickly reaches the station. These were perhaps the first trains for us, around 1994, our hands were shaking, our hearts were beating fast, the excessive silence made us flinch at every little noise, only the hiss of the

spray paint can hypnotise you and calm you down. But there's no time left and you trace the outline not quite the way you had imagined it on your sketchbook. The important thing is to overcome your fears as a novice, if everything turns out well you can only get better. The first of us finishes and starts tagging instead of being on lookout. The usual writer self-ishness. At the same time seeing others think only for themselves pushes you to finish the piece and not get fossilised by the tension. So you also start tagging. And others follow suit. Everybody says "let's go, let's go" but then they all still want to write. Voraciousness. When the pieces have been completed everybody smiles, cause we understand it's the probable beginning of a growth for our crew. And that's exactly what happened, because from that moment our weekends were

tinged of silver and later of various hues. Sure, the limit of colours was still tied to the availability of cheap spray paint. I remember that in order to stock on a load of silvers and blacks we went to Naples, next to the harbour where a guy was selling his own production called "Magracca", at insignificant prices. In that period we never really posed ourselves the question of colours, just painting the train was enough of a satisfaction.

This is how Saturdays went down. Those who could, would take the train from Rome and reach the end station in this way. As for me, without a car, I would try to hitch a ride with my parents when possible, but with time, to avoid raising suspicion, I took to bicycling with my backpack on my shoulders, 8 km of ups and downs one way, a considerable effort, together with the angst of not knowing

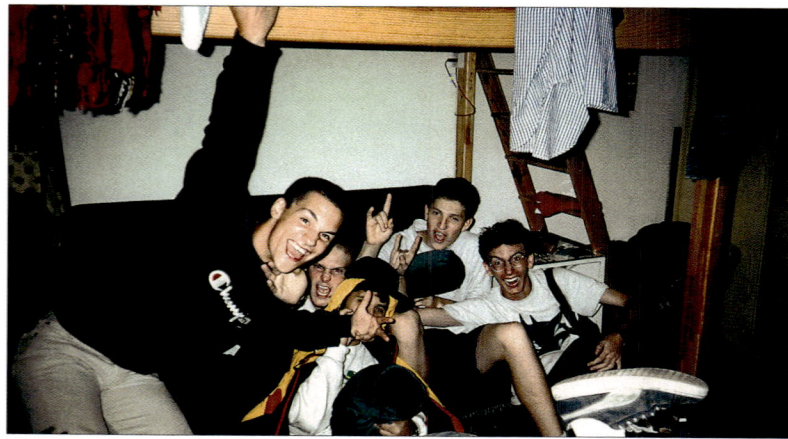

Young French writers and PAC crew.

— Mencio

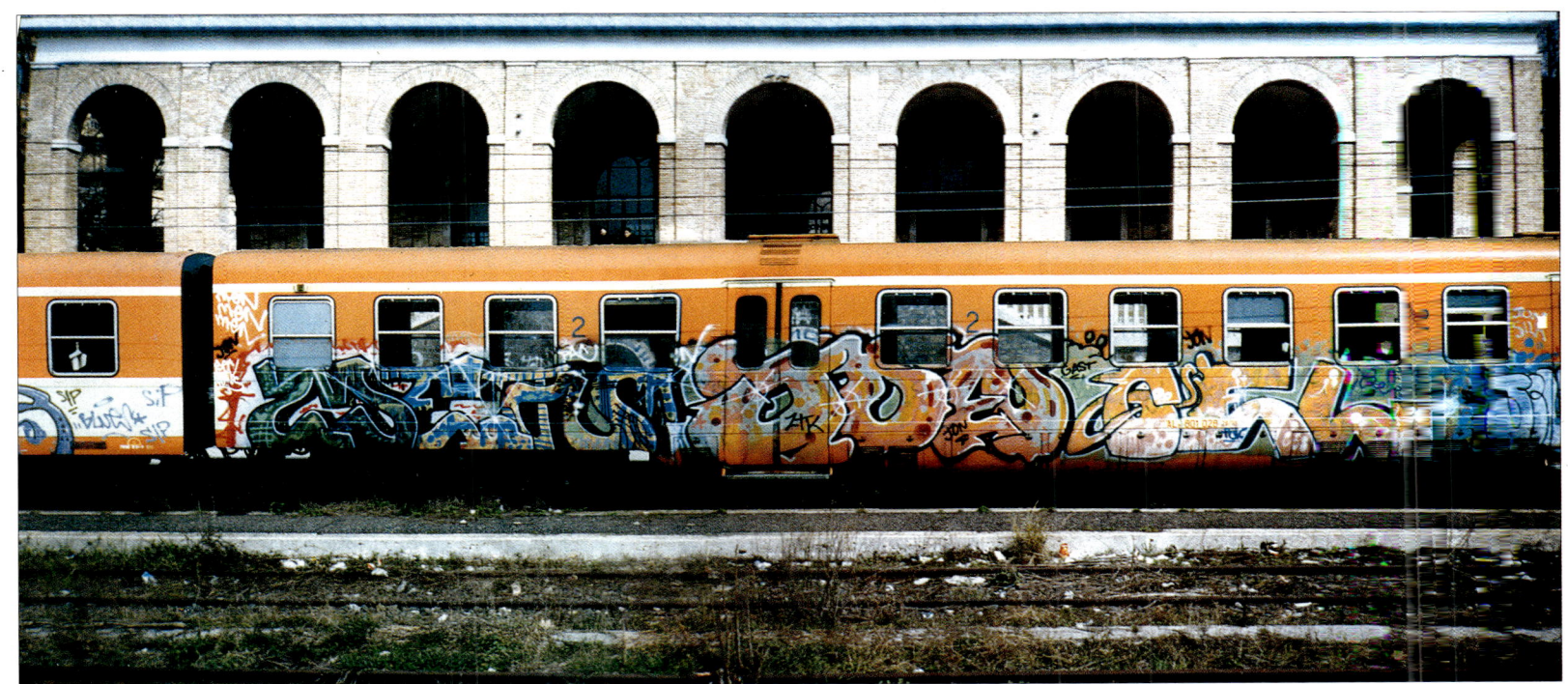

Mencio – PAC, Jon – ZTK, Gei – PAC   — Mencio

playground

whether I would arrive in time to paint. For weeks we would bomb even two times a night due to the switch in trains parked there. In the intermissions between this change, our hands still dirty with paint, our backpacks hidden in some thicket, we'd all go to the pizzeria: at first we would just eat single slices in the piazza, but with time they became whole round pans with beers, we were getting older! It was a blast. How do you give this up? It's hard to accept a fasting once you've mastered the art, you have more ideas but also more hunger. Your appetite grows the more you eat. You can't give it up. It takes you less time to paint, there's no more fooling around; even the twins (Snoy and Sila/Clone) had become more disciplined. If at first we made a racket, after a while only the noise of the cans could be heard, if before we vaguely kept track of time, now we were taking 15, 20 minutes, tops. You had to consider that it was a very small station with few tracks, people arrived at the platform and waited for their train, and they were always ready to notice any anomalies like coloured clouds of paint coming from the back of a train car. If the *arancioni* spot didn't get played out it was because we were so careful. If we had left empty spray cans lying around, tagged a bit everywhere, on pylons and on the ground, started acting overconfident, bombing like crazy, surely there would have been more adrenaline, but there would not have been any continuation. Nobody really knows how long you can keep writing your Name on panels. The result was that our discretion regarding the yard permitted us to monopolise the line. Everyone, from Zemar, Asme, Zeir, Sila and Snoy knew that any disclosure

PAC crew exiting Tuscolana station   — Mencio

would have been treason. I often insisted on this point. Any advantage must be cultivated. In a city like Rome, where pieces were running for years and the scene was still relatively young, (we belonged to the second generation along with ZTK), strengthening one's position is the least you can do amidst new crews sprouting and growing all over. The joy of knowing a spot belongs to you hypes you up. On one hand you can and others can't, and on the other you get close and personal with the

trains, you greet them, get fond of them, from objects to subjects. Modern souls. Other than the *arancioni* we also started bombing other subway lines. But when the time came to choose between a "Men" whole-car on the A line or a piece on the *arancioni*, there was really no question. Around 1999-2000 a new saga began for these trains. By now at least two new crews were taking advantage of a spot in another station. And so there's no holding back. All the front cars have to be ours,

as the best end-to-ends. This time I'd go painting with my friends Ien and Vico. One of my last *arancioni* is tied to a cranial trauma I suffered. That night we went alone, and about halfway through the other writers arrived, among them was Iota. Ascon

> Today the *arancioni* no longer exist, they're covered by a sticky film that makes them white

as I finished the piece I climbed onto the train car as always, to tag higher up. But as I got down I lost my balance and footed, and fell from a height of over two metres, hitting my head on the cement platform. I hear voices all around me, it's the other writers trying to help. "Come on we're taking you to the hospital". I start cursing, take some spray cans and paint the highlights (in a rather disturbed manner to say the least). When I think I'm done, I run off home by car with a strong pain in the head. I take a shower but without realising it at 6 in the morning my sister takes me to the hospital: a week's stay for cranial trauma.

Today the *arancioni* no longer exist, they're covered by a sticky film that makes them white. I always see them, every day in the station, it took me real long to get excited every time they pass me by. The same for all the other lines. But I'm still convinced that's a part of the city that belongs to me: whenever I'll feel like it there I'll be, still painting my trains.

ROMA PANTANO
Overground Railways

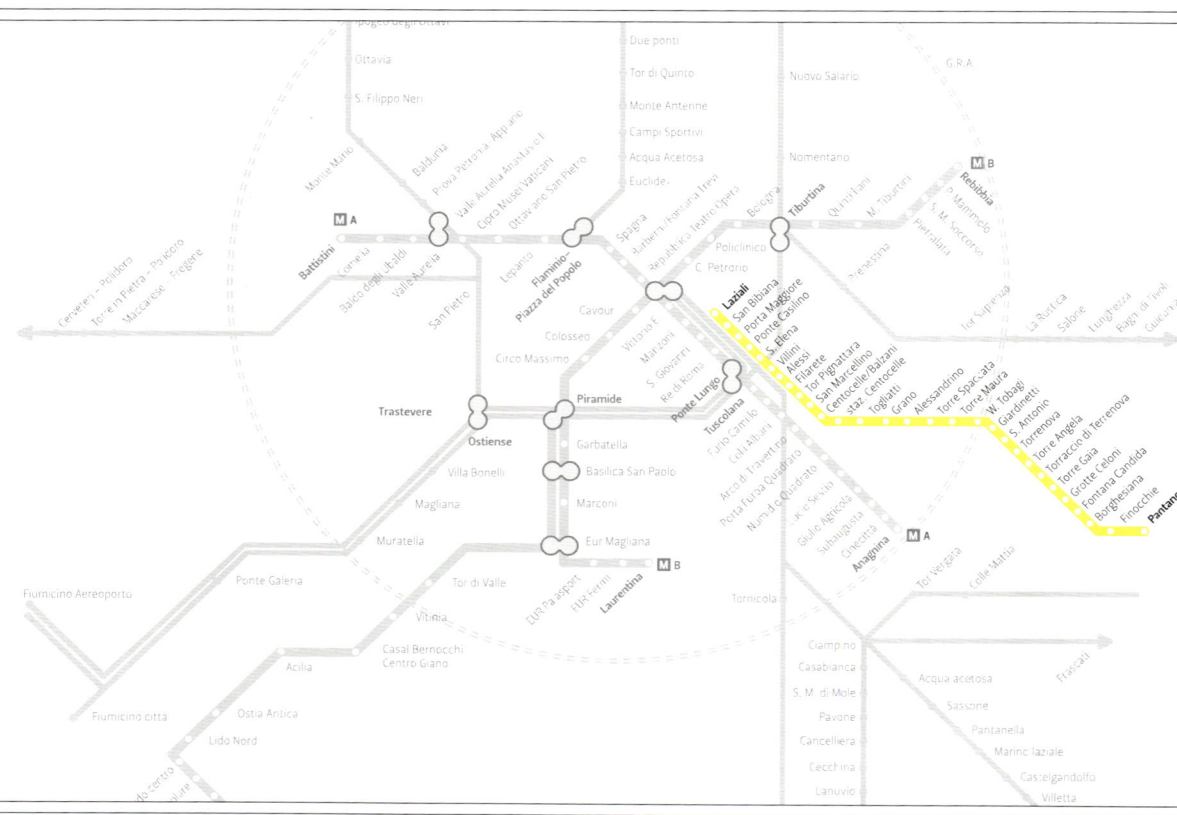

The Casilina line operates on a narrow gauge railroad whose characterstics are similar to that of a tram's. It serves the province of Rome between the end stops of Roma Laziali and Giardinetti. The Region of Lazio holds the the property of the line while it is managed by Met.Ro.company.

An evening along the Casilina

Monia Cappuccini
>

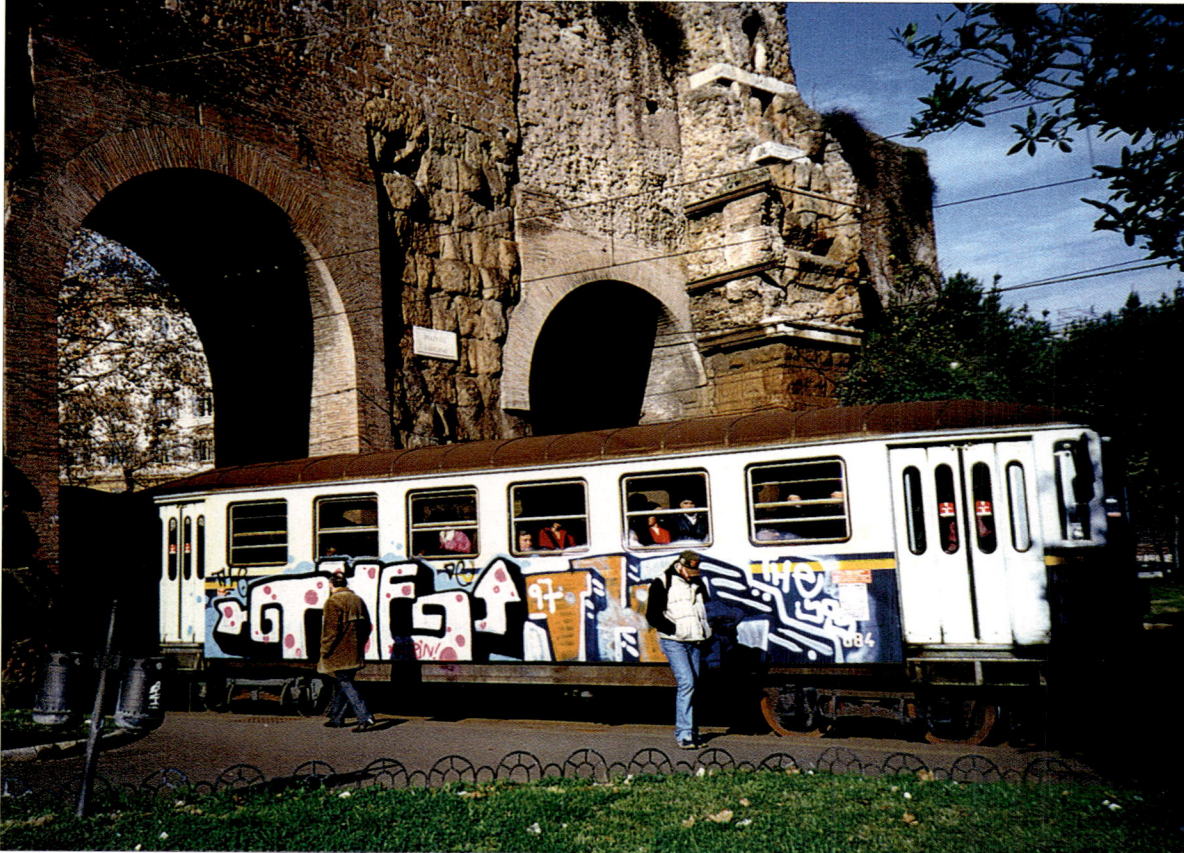

DoubleTHE by Trota and Vela, 1997, photographed under the arch of Porta Maggiore

— *Trota*

1992-1993, the "Corto Circuito" social centre in Cinecittà, a neighbourhood in the South-Eastern outskirts of Rome. Here, 00199 crew, Heko, Jam, Voice, Sharc, Hestro, Bingo, Puffo, Napoleone, and HP crew joined together to form a group with a resounding name: Bombolette Kalibro 38 (BK38). Objective: to create 100 anti-fascist and anti-racist graffiti pieces in the city. This campaign was part of the social centre's 'activities': they brought the group together, they clashed heads with City Hall to get permission to paint the walls, and they provided us with spray paint.

We met up once a week to decide where we'd paint and what we'd paint, each crew was in charge of a letter of the chosen phrase. The outcome: some nice murals and some sweet financial backing, but the project was destined to be short-lived. It was inevitable - Writing culture is allergic to sedentariness, and the fact that the crew was tied to a social centre acting as the promoter of our work made it all eventually seem lacking in spontaneity. Not to mention, we only completed a dozen of those 100 graffiti pieces we had planned to create due to bureaucratic snags with paradoxical implications.

A situation bordering on the absurd, too much even for those of us who greatly believed in this project, unlike many others who were part of BK38 just to get free spray paint and propel their illegal urges beyond the known boundaries,

throughout the city. Besides, it was high time for Writing to make its grand entrance into society.

Up to that point, what distinguished us from others was our gender, but with BK38, for the first time it was age, in fact that period felt like a sort of changeover for us. It was very clear, even for me - I was 20 and was the youngest member of 00199, hence the name Baby - one night we all went to the Casilino yard together: it was winter, it was cold, we showed up in a car, the others came by scooter, and

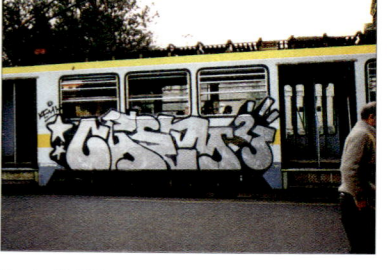

Kemh, 23 REC, 1997

— *Trota*

we realised we were the only legal adults on this expedition.

The end of BK38 allowed a new and more active generation of writers to make a name for themselves in the city. Especially ETC crew - eager, more so than others, with their minds elsewhere - they took it upon themselves to push Writing into a more metropolitan dimension. Together with MT2, they began systematically bombing the subway; with the name TRV they became the most active writers in Rome from 1992 to 1997.

ROMA NORD
Overground Railways

FIUMICINO LINE
Overground Railways

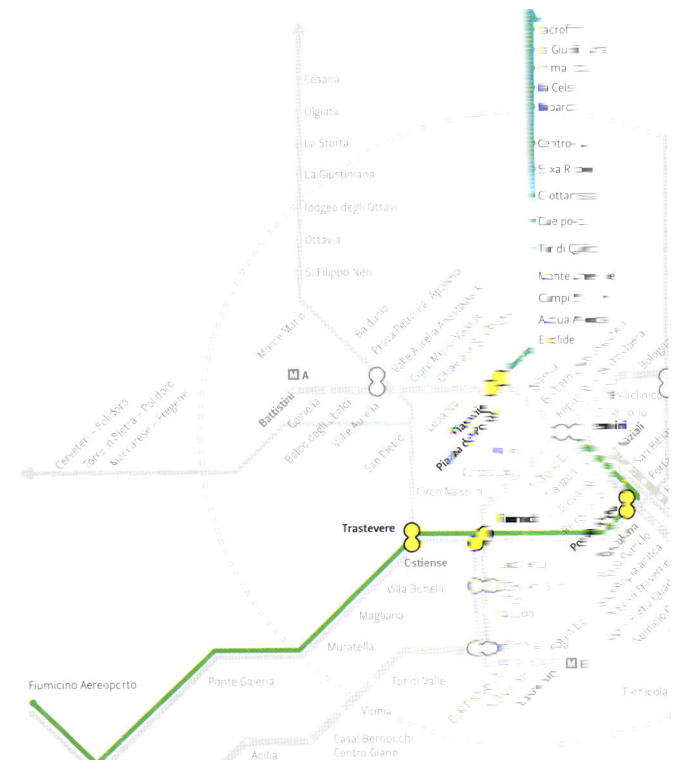

Inaugurated in 1913, the railway connects the Capital to Viterbo, long a route of 102 km. The line runs parallel to the Flaminia up to Civita Castellana, also serving as a means of transportation inside the city. "Roma Nord" originates from the name of the old company managing it.

From 1994 the regional railway FR1 connects the airport of Fiumicino to the province of Rieti every 15 minutes, crossing through Rome from North-East to South-West, where it serves as a subway.

The green airport trains

Vela
>

Of all the yards, there was one I preferred, it was the deposit of the *verdi*, or the greens, trains that took to the airport for those that remember them.

They were really beautiful, green and grey, well it was just a pleasure painting them. I also liked the spot and the sensations it gave me, at times it was almost more for the yard than the trains that I actually went there.

To enter we would pass under some road signs and wait for the right moment, then cross a series of heavily trafficked rail tracks, climb up a hill, often involving high grass covered in frost, then walk along the track line until we arrived at the illuminated hangar, in front of which were one or two trains that by now were practically ours.

The silence, interrupted sometimes by the noise of some passing train, the night and the light of the moon, the winter cold, the colour of a partly illuminated train, all this made the place magical and precious.

I remember I would go out to party, we'd drink without pause and halfway through the night I'd go there with Dale; one night, Trota, Kimo, Cole and I were all real drunk and before going in the deposit we started throwing up almost contagiously, I don't even remember who started but we couldn't stand too close to each other because the sound of one of us gagging would get the others started again.

Years later, after we had started writing THE, I was with Fox and Puer and we got involved in a brief stone-throwing fight in our deposit, because as we were getting in we saw Jon and Stand doing throw-ups over the pieces that we had painted a couple days earlier, and our first thought was to get them to stop. I've never understood these things, but anyway it's part of Writing. Rome is different from other cities, it has very few deposits so it's impossible to say this is my yard, or even to fairly distribute them among writers, but that place really felt like it belonged to me and its memory will never fade because it represents the most beautiful mental picture that a writer can bring home after a night out with friends.

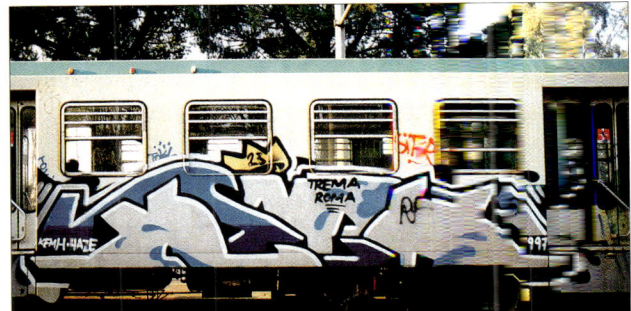

Kemh, 23 REC, on the trains of the Roma Nord, 1997   —Trota

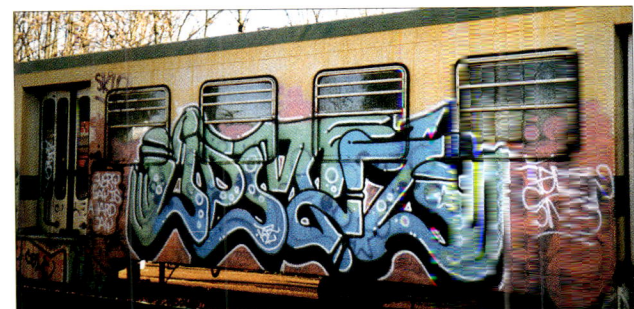

Iemz Rome Zoo, Roma Nord line, 1997   —Trota

MY 1990'S
—

Syla
>

For me, the 90's were characterised by the discovery of graffiti. We painted non-stop and spray paint was our source of adrenaline. Flames, water, devils, burning buildings, blood, and ice were our symbols. We had fire in our bellies, curiosity, competition, and above all, lots of positive energy; nothing could stop our tidal wave, we were one and the same. Rome like New York? It seemed like a dream, but in the end it was actually true; without realising it we were following in the steps of our predecessors from NYC. By reinterpreting what belonged to the kings we developed a Roman style mixed with the Mediterranean, and a genuine essence that belonged to us. Phrases like: "Kings will survive", "Still running on this way", "Back in the yard once again", became: "Adrenalina a palla" (Full-blown adrenaline), "Come, dove e quando vogliamo" (How, where, and when we want), "Contro lo stato attentato" (Against the state's attack), "Disagio urbano" (Urban unrest), "Mai abbastanza" (Never enough). In the mid 90's, Italy (and Rome in particular) began to develop its own identity, neighbourhoods in the outskirts were painted and whole-cars circulated intact: in our area, trains were the most artistic thing you'd see. During these early years writers were not under [...] the American phenomenon of graffiti [...] was not yet recognised [...] had [...] been experienced firsthand [...] was a person, a person who was unite with a handful of others in [...] ve rest that we expressed to the [...] y through train cars. Graffiti is social and [...] b cart [...] t at the same time it s extre [...] im [...] and private, something that [...] ys o y[...] i n and makes its way straight [...] ur heart

TRAMS & BUSES
Overground Railways

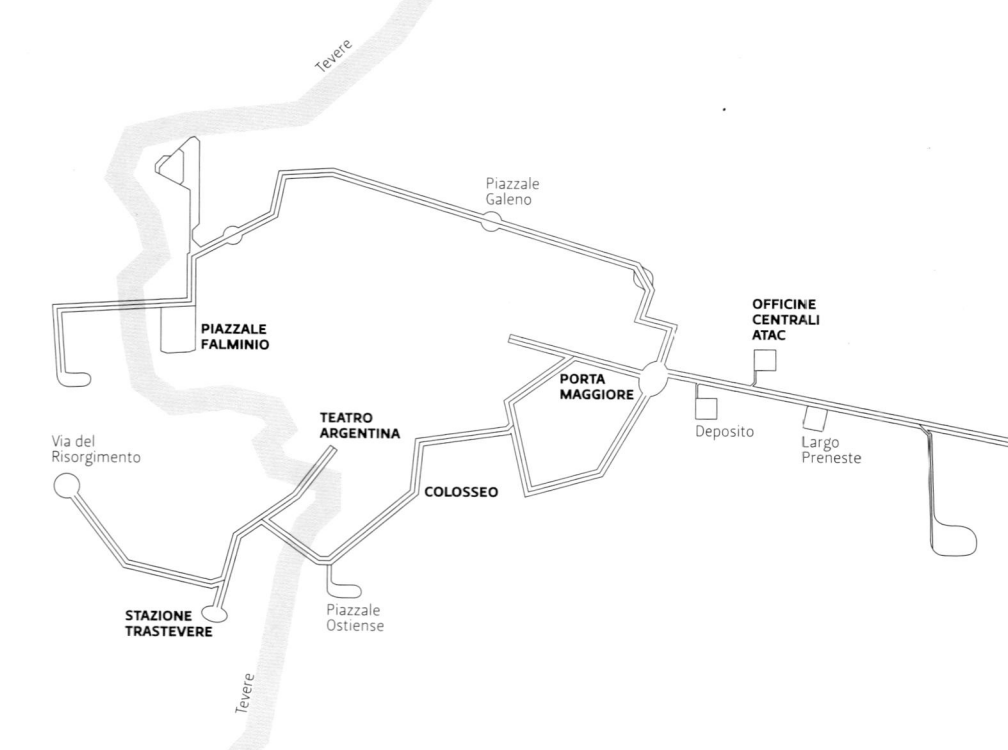

For the past 130 years the trams of Rome have supplied an indispensable support to the demographic and urbanistic growth of the Capital. Today they are just the residue of a network that used to be the most extended in Italy. Inaugurated in 1845, it was a line of horse-drawn omnibuses that left only once the carriage was full.

Memories of a bomber
>

A tuff experience

Tuff
>

An 'invisible' writer in the day, freeing his instinct at night. His tag, always different, spreads.

I was wearing a buttoned down shirt and Timberlands when I did my first tags... At the end of the 80's, Rome was a provincial city, people would look at you funny just for wearing a baseball hat. You see, Romans always tend to mock people, it's in their DNA. In any case, as a kid I covered the walls of my house by writing Luca Lazio Luca Lazio Luca Lazio... from the bathroom, to my closet doors, to the kitchen. The first timid excursions outside of my building were all part of my learning experience: I brought along a felt marker to extend my range of writing to the stairwell, the landings, the entrance hall. I had no idea what graffiti and tags were, I just wanted to write my name like a troublemaking teenager who causes ruckus with cousins, friends, etc. A pastime just like fireworks and homemade fire-crackers, gratuitous vandalism on the trams of Northern Rome. My debut in the city was

accompanied by my first nickname: "Duke", not because I was trying to be American, but because they called me Luca er Duca (Luke the Duke). It all took form quickly, as a consciousness-raising writer, I added the number one to Duke and completed the circle: Duke-One. The first person who told me about Hip Hop was Quickie, thanks to him I saw a series of movies like *Turk 182* and *Colors*... most of us had this same experience. Through Writing, I found an outlet that calmed me deep down inside: before I would break tram windows and write "LUCA", but with Duke and Tuff, it was a purely calligraphic and graffiti release, a sort of artistic vandalism.

– RE-INVENTING ROME
In Rome, it all developed in stages, in a rather instinctive way, nothing was planned. A few times we tried to organise ourselves: in Rome there were no sticker tags so when those of us in TRV crew started doing that, everyone else followed along, and the same holds true for tagging the ACOTRAL buses. That's why we set concrete objectives when it came to buses: the trams were clean (meaning, disgustingly dirty with trash and dust, but tag-free) and the subway was bombed, so we had to even things out and bring our Names into the spotlight. In '95, me and

Joe organised Rome's first bus contest: we had to hit any and all of the city's major bus lines. Largo Argentina, a key passageway for city buses, became the judges' stand; we counted how many tags from each writer and each crew we saw. The person with the most tags inside and outside was the winner.
During that time, students occupied most of the schools; high schools were paralysed by the student movement protests so me and Joe cruised around them looking for new recruits. I remember during the first or second contest, ZTK crew, composed of fiery teenagers, bombed everything. Soon enough, me and Joe were considered 'unwanted guests' even in the occupied high schools, the students wouldn't let us in because they didn't want us to bomb their classrooms or steal their textbooks.

– TARGET: BUSES
One of my favourite places to tag on was the black indentation near the bus taillights, I noticed that tags never got buffed from there. After that, I started to bomb the strip that was above the bus windows: they would buff tags on there but it was still fun because you had to do it from inside, leaning out of the window while the bus was in motion. Other favourite spots were obviously inside the bus near

the seats, right at eye level. The outside of the bus was good for throw-ups or bigger pieces done with spray paint. Some bus lines were immediately buffed, while others, oddly enough, weren't buffed for days. The bus depot in Trastevere neighbourhood was a historic spot that was bombed by me and others. Soon enough I noticed that amidst all this chaos, my tags were the only ones being buffed: Tuff had been deciphered, it was now read and recognised even by outsiders. The climax occurred in the mid 90's when ACOTRAL bus company gave me a real 'shout out' in the magazines they distributed for riders: there was a puzzle where you had to colour in the dotted pieces to see the final image – lo and behold, it was my tag, in black boldface, as aggressive as my mark: Tuff. I had conquered them!

– METHOD
With time I realised that in order to carry on with my nocturnal mission, I had to disappear - meaning become invisible by becoming part of the masses, by imitating all those people who walk by unnoticed. That meant no baseball caps and no baggy pants. Instead, I had to wear 'normal' clothes, take my dog out on a leash, and look like any ordinary person. During that time, I managed to steal whatever I needed: not just spray paint

and felt markers (shop owners would start to catch on after a while), but even new clean shoes and 'normal' clothes since mine were always stained with ink. I didn't have any money so I stole whatever I needed to in order to paint. I started going out during the day. Who would have suspected anything by day?! At night you have freedom, but during the day the adrenaline intensified, just like my self-taught invisibility classes. With some practice, I learned how to write without looking, with both my left and right hand, I could even write with my hand behind my back. If you look me in the eyes and I'm standing against a wall, I can still manage to tag Tuff, it might be slanted but it's still legible. Between football games and moped accidents, I spent months with a broken right arm, which forced me to use my left hand, but it ended up being useful for my cause. In Rome, there were kids who would meet up on Saturdays to go out tagging, but there weren't many people who always had a felt marker in their pocket who made tagging a normal daily practice, just like buying bread or reading the newspaper.

– SCRIBBLES IN THE CITY
When I first started tagging in Rome, it was random- I would occasionally take the surface, height, and nature of the chosen

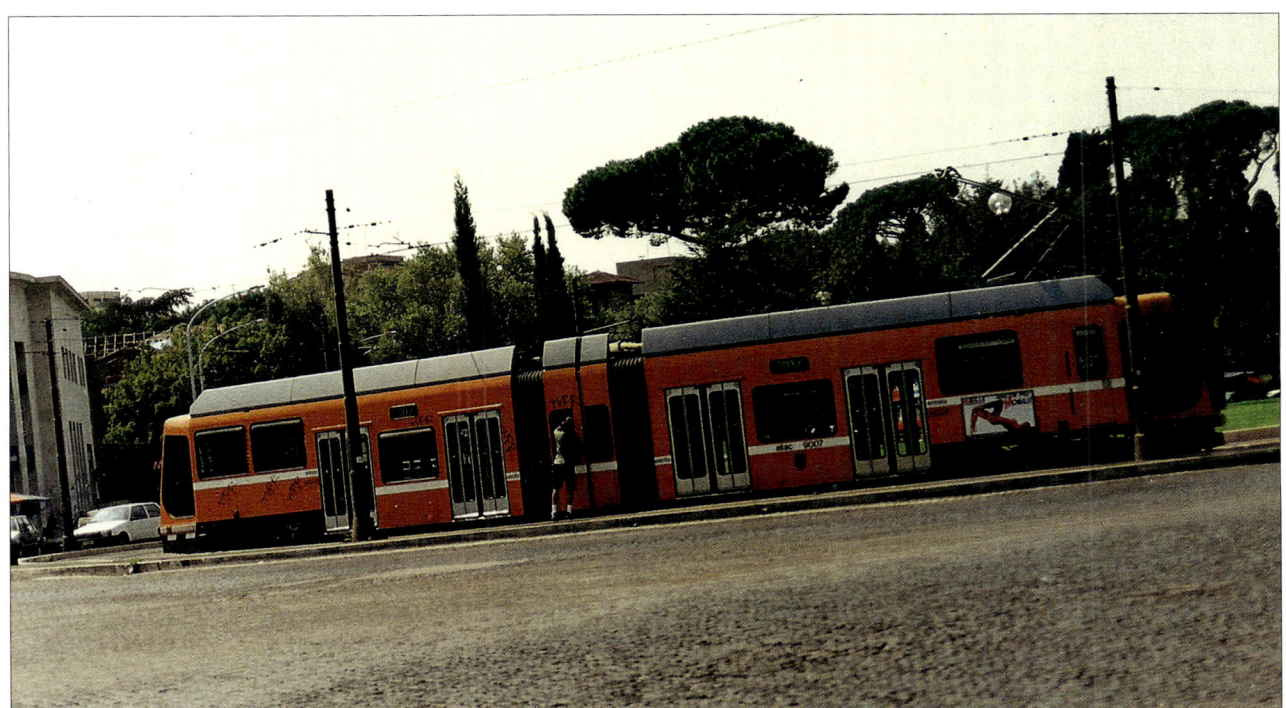

Tuff as he tags a Roman tram   – *Tuff*

spot into consideration. As time went on, I began to plan my activity and the chosen spots: I began in the heart of the city, the historic centre, and expanded outwards. I decided that my path should coincide with the historic axis roads that linked Rome to the rest of the world. These

> You'll never see
> a *Tuff* tag that looks like
> another, because each
> *Tuff* tag is created
> in distinct conditions

ancient roads were now major passageways for both private and public (trams and buses) vehicles. Writing on these Roman roads meant being hyperexposed to passersby, it's no coincidence that these same roads

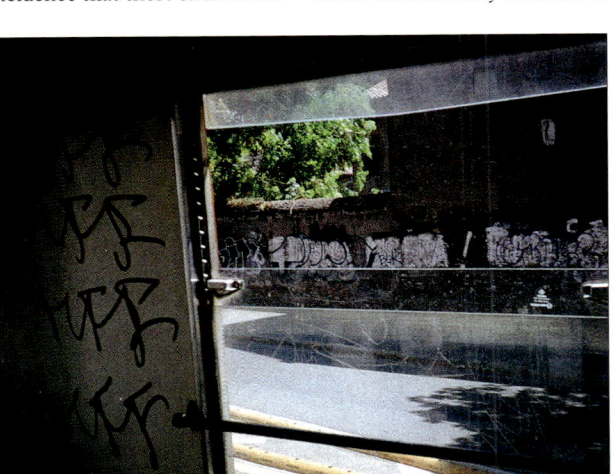

Tuff inside a bus and outside, along an ancient Roman road   – *Tuff*

are now a hot spot for advertising billboards. These roads link all of Rome's neighbourhoods through the centre: the Prenestina road leads to Centocelle, the Pontina road leads to EUR, and so on. In order to get home or to the centre of the city, you had to pass by here and you couldn't help but notice my Name written on the seat of a tram or on the column of a bridge. In the centre, there were two recurring targets for me: garbage bins and power boxes. Everybody targeted garbage bins and power boxes because PVC is the best surface for black felt markers. When it came to garbage bins, I had a specific spot I always bombed- the part between the two holes where you'd insert trash. Once, I saw a truck that was delivering and setting up garbage bins in the early morning; without thinking twice, I jumped onto the truck and started tagging my favourite spot on all the bins, one after the other. And then they took care of

spreading my name throughout the city...

– **ANIMAL INSTINCTS**

I never cared much for calligraphy, lettering, or style, unless the style was connected to the actual act of tagging: you'll never see a *Tuff* tag that looks like another, because each Tuff tag is created in distinct conditions: some people pass by, some look, some don't even notice you. Thus, the writing changes, the speed with which I write changes, where I direct my eyes changes, I hardly ever look at my hand while writing. "T", two orthogonal lines, "U", a wedge, and double "F", which closes my mark. When you get into a car you turn the key, start the car, and put it in first gear: you carry out this sequence of actions without thinking, it's instinctive and mechanical. I write my Name in the same way, without filtering the immediacy of the gesture. A tag reflects presence, an incision that's dictated by animal instincts; the idea of sketching and modifying a tag on paper couldn't be further from my mindset. I did write at home too, but only because I was a graff maniac and I had to write at all hours in order to speed up my process... the fridge, my closet doors, and my bedroom became my personal playground, in total privacy and for my eyes only.

– **GIAIME**

Me, Quick-E and Grandi Numeri had formed a crew called TMC, that is Too Mother Crew (which was literally italian for: ya mama crew) cause we had the habit of joking about everybody's mom. At first people would get mad but after a while they got used

to it. The crew grew bigger with Giaime, DJ Baro, Amir and Joe. Other than kidding around we were also quite active and when we painted our aim was maximum visibility; we had to be real quick, we'd pick a drawing and do it all together, needless to say when Giaime would come we'd always pick his. He'd do it in a flash, with a style that was really avant-garde for the time; he was the first real bomber in Rome, he continuously talked about flops, tags, if he was still with us today he would surely be the undisputed King of the city for style and quantity. In the brief period in which he painted he left an enormous inheritance to the scene in Rome and even if new writers don't know his name they owe him a lot.

Giaime was a special kid, real sensitive and meticulous, always

> We'd pick a drawing and
> do it all together, needless
> to say when Giaime
> would come we'd always
> pick his

innovative; he spent hours and hours studying letters until completing the whole alphabet with the same style. He also had a huge amount of records he knew by heart, in those days we didn't have access to many photos of pieces from the States, and he would point out the flops on the background of many album covers. I called him the alien cause he didn't live in our world but on planet Hip Hop.

ONE LOVE

Cel
>

Ever since I was a little kid I was fascinated by the writing on the walls, and ever since I was a little kid I've had problems with the law. I was 13 years old when the guards stopped me next to the railtracks. I was writing with spray paint along with some friends. They accused us of throwing rocks at the trains - it was the period in which some severe car accidents had been caused by kids tossing stones from the overpass of the highway - but we hadn't even touched one. The second time I was older and they found me in the station of C... in Mencio... PAC, after we had done some trains. The polfer caught us and the trials began, with lawyers and all that stuff. In recent years they arrested me because I was writing on the walls of the city. They wrote up the arrest report and charges but nonetheless, in spite of the inconveniences and trouble I have not lost the habit of writing. It's a reaffirmation of the soul, an extension of your thought. Meeting Gast was inevitable, I became part of ... and caught the 'vandal' bug. Before that group I was in a crew called SIP, along with Frappa, Trota, ... Flom, Kim and

> The common denominator
> between everyday life and
> the yards was tags

Gast. The weeks following a night in the yard were some of the evenings in Trastevere were savoured better with a little dose of love. I had "worked" played with spray-paint and rightly reserved the nights of alcohol and crap that were awaiting; for a while I felt satisfied, until the depression of common life, of routine, would set in which is when you go out painting again. The common denominator between everyday life and the yard-dimension was tags. I primarily tagged during the day, I would rarely ever scribble at night, or rather, I never intended to do so. It sometimes happened but was anyway never a routine practice, you did it in the light of day, in anticipation of the adrenaline of the yard. My adventures with graffiti are something that I will take with me my whole life, though, even now that I'm busy doing other things the virus sometimes comes back and I get that sickness of years after my first hits, still fall for the temptation and ever into that ... so, my last police report was caused by a throwup I dedicated to the women I love. The love that has always accompanied me. Love for women, for success, and for graffiti.

Rome, dynamic city

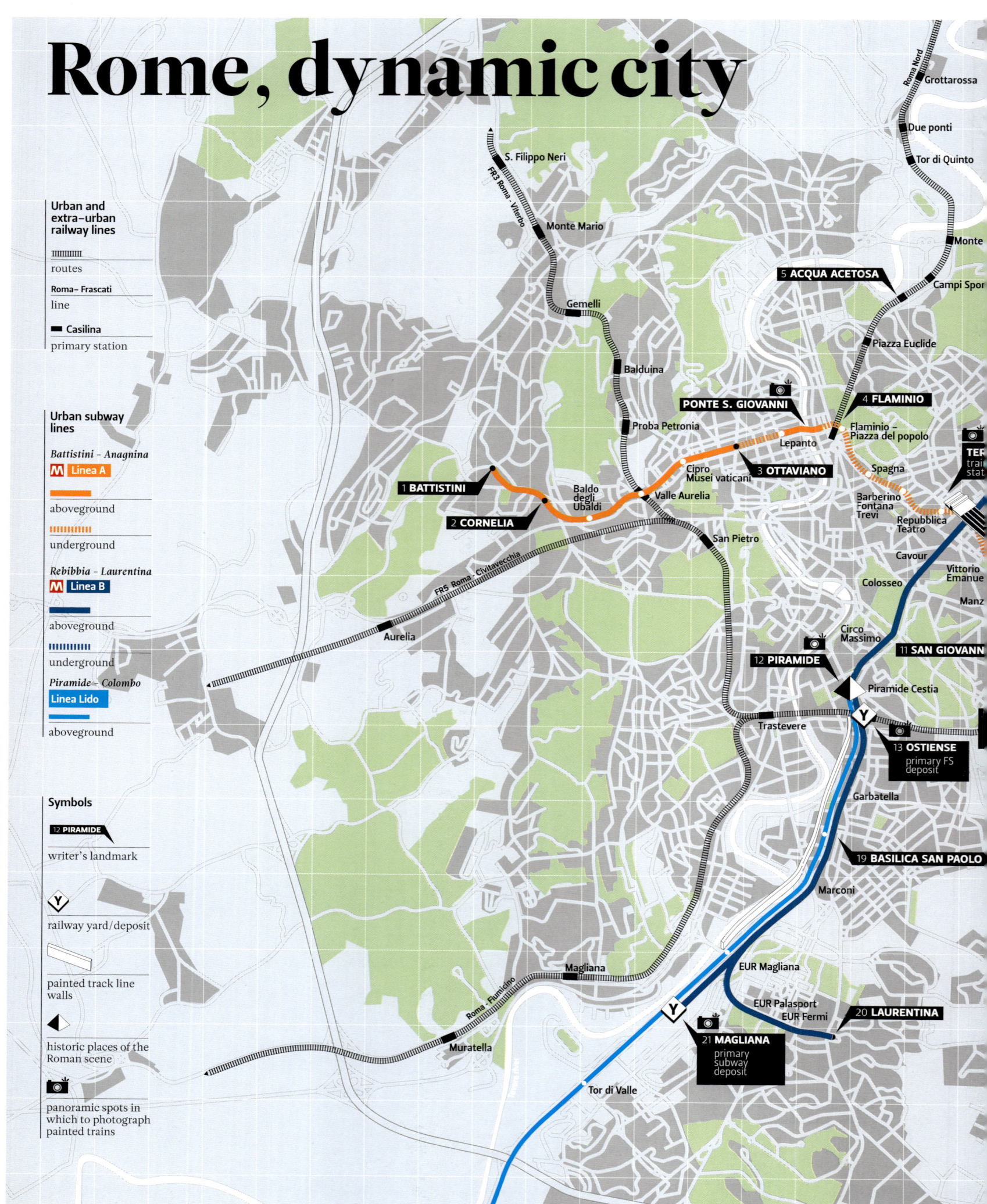

Urban and extra–urban railway lines

routes

Roma– Frascati line

Casilina

primary station

Urban subway lines

Battistini - Anagnina

Ⓜ Linea A

aboveground

underground

Rebibbia - Laurentina

Ⓜ Linea B

aboveground

underground

Piramide - Colombo

Linea Lido

aboveground

Symbols

12 PIRAMIDE

writer's landmark

Y

railway yard/deposit

painted track line walls

historic places of the Roman scene

panoramic spots in which to photograph painted trains

S. Filippo Neri

FR3 Roma – Viterbo

Monte Mario

Gemelli

Balduina

Proba Petronia

PONTE S. GIOVANNI

1 BATTISTINI

Baldo degli Ubaldi

2 CORNELIA

Cipro Musei vaticani

Valle Aurelia

3 OTTAVIANO

Lepanto

4 FLAMINIO

Flaminio – Piazza del popolo

Spagna

Barberino Fontana Trevi

Repubblica Teatro

5 ACQUA ACETOSA

Piazza Euclide

Roma Nord

Grottarossa

Due ponti

Tor di Quinto

Monte

Campi Spor

TER
trai
stat

San Pietro

FR5 Roma - Civitavecchia

Aurelia

Cavour

Vittorio Emanue

Manz

Colosseo

Circo Massimo

11 SAN GIOVANN

12 PIRAMIDE

Piramide Cestia

Y

Trastevere

13 OSTIENSE
primary FS deposit

Garbatella

19 BASILICA SAN PAOLO

Marconi

EUR Magliana

Magliana

Roma - Fiumicino

EUR Palasport
EUR Fermi

20 LAURENTINA

Y

21 MAGLIANA
primary subway deposit

Muratella

Tor di Valle

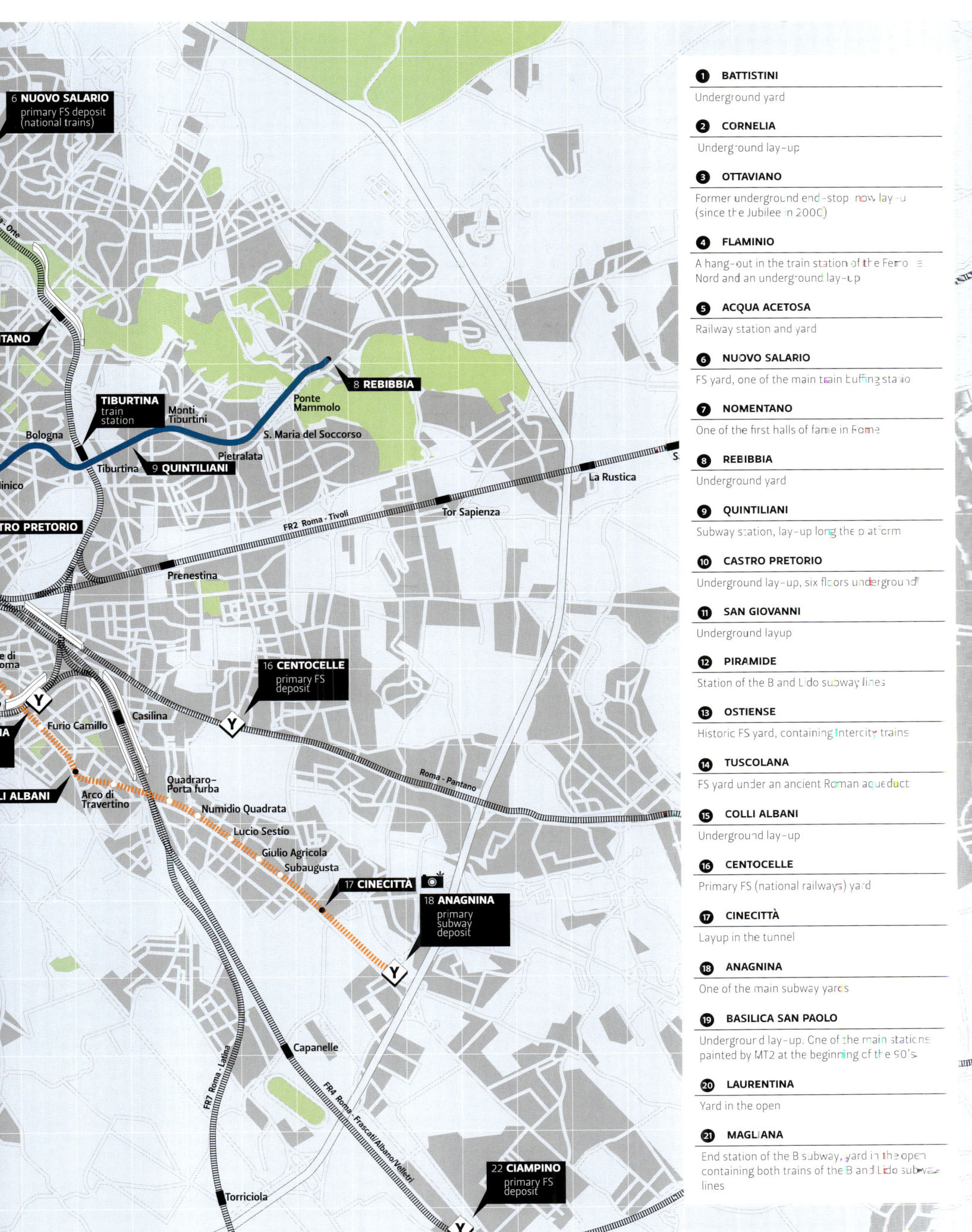

1 **BATTISTINI**
Underground yard

2 **CORNELIA**
Underground lay-up

3 **OTTAVIANO**
Former underground end-stop now lay-u
(since the Jubilee in 2000)

4 **FLAMINIO**
A hang-out in the train station of the Ferro e
Nord and an underground lay-up

5 **ACQUA ACETOSA**
Railway station and yard

6 **NUOVO SALARIO**
FS yard, one of the main train buffing statio

7 **NOMENTANO**
One of the first halls of fame in Rome

8 **REBIBBIA**
Underground yard

9 **QUINTILIANI**
Subway station, lay-up long the platform

10 **CASTRO PRETORIO**
Underground lay-up, six floors underground

11 **SAN GIOVANNI**
Underground layup

12 **PIRAMIDE**
Station of the B and Lido subway lines

13 **OSTIENSE**
Historic FS yard, containing Intercity trains

14 **TUSCOLANA**
FS yard under an ancient Roman aqueduct

15 **COLLI ALBANI**
Underground lay-up

16 **CENTOCELLE**
Primary FS (national railways) yard

17 **CINECITTÀ**
Layup in the tunnel

18 **ANAGNINA**
One of the main subway yards

19 **BASILICA SAN PAOLO**
Underground lay-up. One of the main stations
painted by MT2 at the beginning of the 90's

20 **LAURENTINA**
Yard in the open

21 **MAGLIANA**
End station of the B subway, yard in the open
containing both trains of the B and Lido subway
lines

Reference points
>

Colonna's gallery

Monia Cappuccini
>

The breakers from Galleria Colonna, the Special Breaking Crew, were masters. They had settled in under the arches of a central Roman piazza (along Via del Corso, facing the Parliament Building) amidst the palm readers selling luck. Smooth marble floor, maximum visibility: the perfect spot. They started to pop up in the mid 80's, at first on Saturday afternoons, then as the word spread, you could even find people there during the week. Many a time they were asked to leave, and many a time they came back: Galleria Colonna was the first meet-

A generous soul, Zulu Nation soldier, a reference point for both new and old schools

ing spot of the city. The key column was Crash Kid, a.k.a. Massimo Colonna (an unintentional play on words, "colonna" means column in Italian), a generous soul, Zulu Nation soldier, a reference point for both new and old schools. He didn't give a shit about factions, he acted as an intermediary between everyone, he never got tired of saying: "Breakers, writers, MCs, DJs must be united". In the fall of 1997, at a young age, he passed away leaving an immense void on the floor and in the community. Shortly after, the writers found their own version of Galleria Colonna at the Rome Nomentano station in the late 80's-early 90's. The relationship with the city was 0 to 0 and Writing finally abandoned the episodic nature it had possessed until then.

Washe
>

I met Massimo on an autumn evening in Rome. It was the first time I was painting the B line of the subway, we were in five, and happy to be there. Massimo already instilled strength and security, it was like looking at someone who knew exactly where to go and what to do. About him I only knew what had been told to me, I had not yet lived what he was a part of: Italian Hip Hop, Breakdancing, bombing, the subway.
To me Massimo was like a page of history: his photo of the first train in Rome, his stories of trips abroad, his Africa Bambaataa-style necklace, the Run DMC adidas. The night in which we met didn't turn out that well, we ended up running away from the

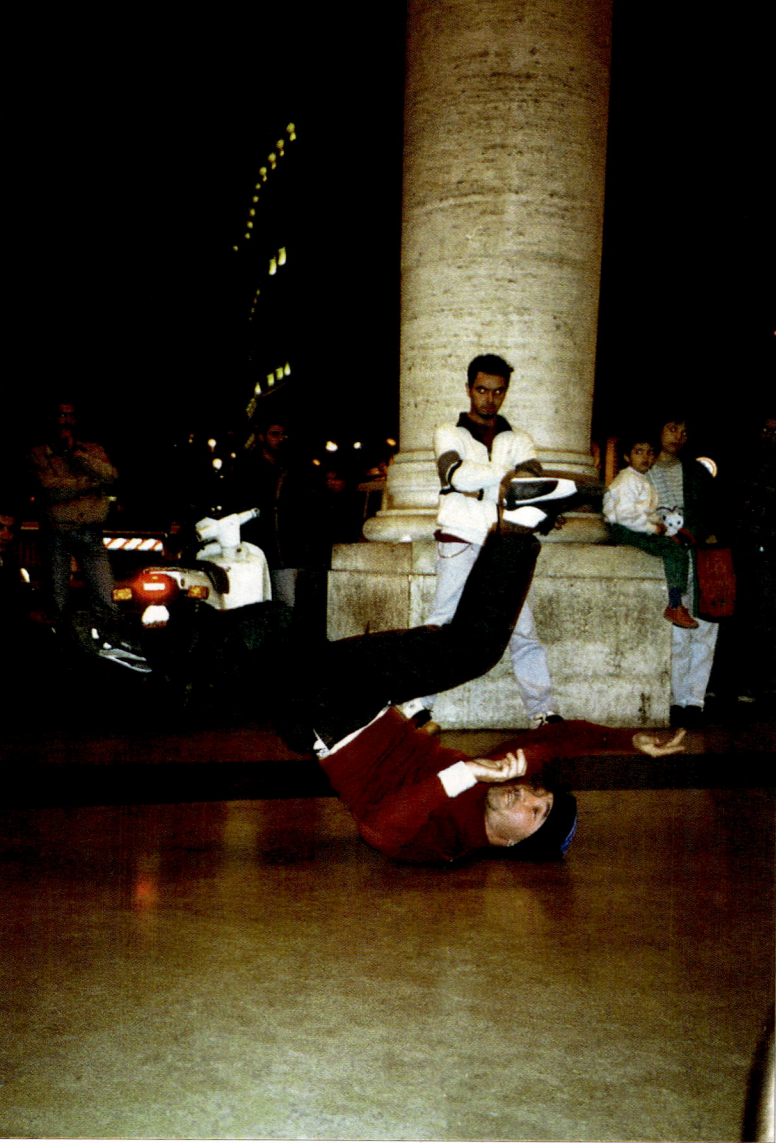

Crash Kid a.k.a. Massimo Colonna as he dances in 'his' gallery in Rome: Galleria Colonna   — *Washe*

security guards. Massimo and I hid under two cars during the getaway, waiting in silence for things to calm down. The next morning, with the adrenaline of the night before still running through my body, I went to his house to pick up the scooter that had spent the night there. It was the first time I saw his crib and his parents, who really didn't understand what he was up to and who he was, he had fat laces in every possible colour to be worn on his Pumas, and caps from New York that fit all paint cans. Massimo had a tough and direct way of talking to you, there was no joking about him and what he did.
I remember him this way, tough and pure. We spent more time hanging out than actually painting, but this was normal for us, for the way we approached Writing: more than a competition it was a unique form of expression we shared. Massimo admired what we did, I think we even managed to change his mind on a couple things; it was

no longer about painting to kill it and be better than everyone else, it had become a challenge with your own letters, and an excuse to get together just like a dinner among friends. His strengths were the consciousness with which he did things, the will to share what he was learning and especially the energy he conveyed: when Massino entered a B-boy circle he did so in a direct manner, no fuss, much substance. Everyone around him would stare as he turned on his head for hours, with his home-made beanie, doing his show, taking off his pants while spinning, until he was in his underwear.
Massimo had this urge inside to pass on to others what this life had given him, what he had earned with blood, sweat and tears, with a natural passion.
It was perhaps one of his best traits, being able to be close to him and know that every thought and breath was deliberately shared with us.

Clown
>

On one side we had the 'Clown' crew and Riccardo "Maelo", and on the other side we had Massimo "Crash Kid" and Marcello "I-O-Ice", AGR crew, and LTA crew. There was intense rivalry between us, practically a war, which is ridiculous considering that in all of Rome there were only five 'graffiti artists' back then, we could still call ourselves that). But it was a way to be part of a larger global scene which included Public Enemy, Zulu Nation, Chalfant's books, and white subway trains. LTA *License to Art* was a more talented crew, during one of their trips abroad, they learned something that those of us in AGR were oblivious to. Massimo and Marcello's pieces began to shine with a variety of colours that were unknown to us, with a definition and precision that seemed miraculous, how did they do it? Due to the rules of the game that we ourselves had established, Riccardo and I didn't have access to that secret so we were condemned to spending our afternoons searching for alchemic formulas to transform our pathetic Duplicolor spray paints into something that could remotely resemble theirs. The rivalry between Massimo and us was just a game, in reality we were bonded by a friendship for the fact that we began a journey together. He was

The rivalry between Massimo and us was just a game, in reality we were tied by a friendship that was born from the fact that we began a journey together. He was a Sherpa and we were his explorers, Massimo was our window on the world.

a Sherpa and we were his explorers, Massimo was our window on the world.
When I first met him at Termini train station in Rome, I was blown away, he was the image of Hip Hop with his Adidas-logo earring, his buckle and ring in the shape of his tag. He was 'fresh', Massimo was the Roman Afrika Bambaataa, through him I could grasp a world that up until then, had always been light years away.
We began a journey together, Crash revealed the secret of their colours, skinny and fat caps appeared, fanzines, the first crews, new friends joined in, we saw new countries, new styles, and above all, new ideas. I'm very grateful for that moment in my life when I had the opportunity to see Riccardo's painted backpack and I had the courage to approach Massimo for the first time.

NATIONAL RAILWAYS

CITY CHRONICLES

Pages 330–337
>

Central stations
Santa Maria Novella

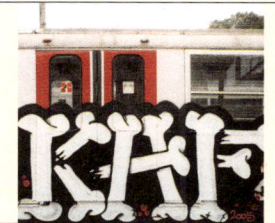

Pages 342–347
>

Alternative tentacles
The case of Naples

Styles and communication along the railways
>

A long–distance network

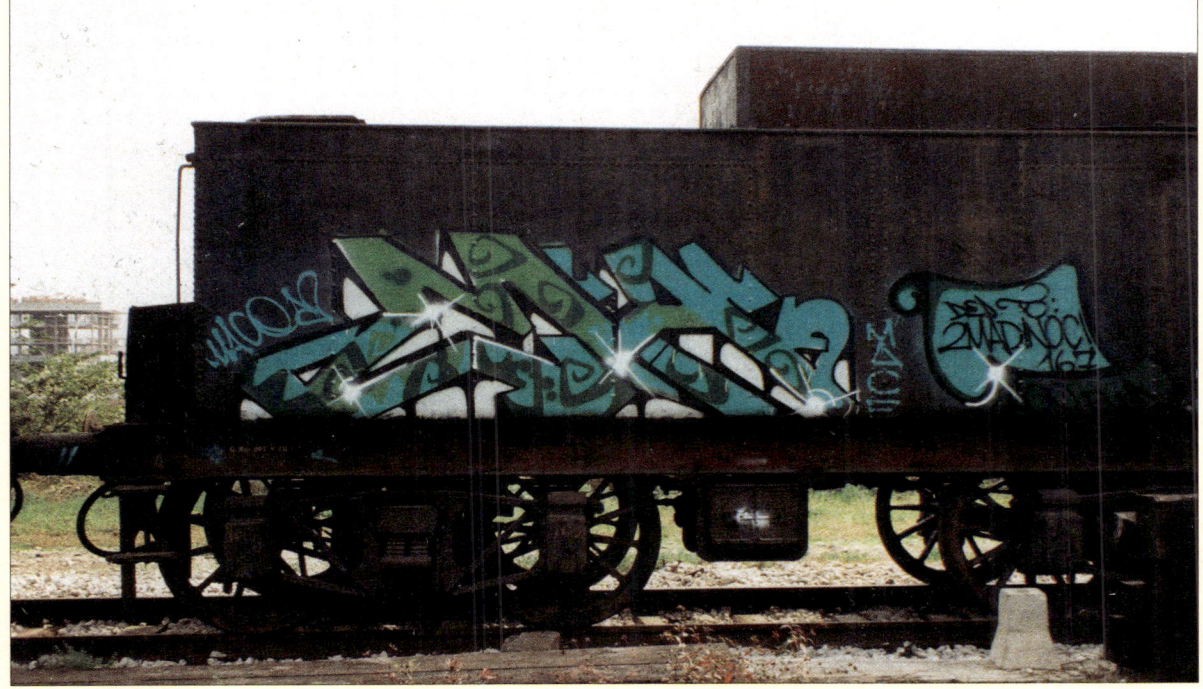

Halfway through the 90's, any Italian writer who did not paint trains risked anonymity, especially if he or she concentrated their activity in the province. The attention of many national exponents shifted in mass from walls and vertical surfaces in general, to local transportation systems. The switch to trains as the primary target radically reconfigured the identity of the Writing scene in Italy. As in the rest of Europe, the myth of the New York subway was absorbed and transformed in the larger urban centres: from the carriages of the Ferrovie Nord in Milan, to the Roman subway. In the province, on the other hand, the lack of a metropolitan rail system redirected local writers towards long-distance trains.

The first Italian scene was thus born with a DNA that owed much to 'intercity' crews, among whose ranks could be found predominantly residents of minor cities. PDB group for example, one of the first formations dedicated to train-bombing, was fuelled by a thick network that covered the entire 'boot' , from Brindisi (Wany), touching on Vercelli (Riso), Genoa (Blef), Bergamo (Verb), Turin (Muko), and other towns. Various other important writers found themselves operating in similar conditions, based in Piacenza (Rok), Rimini (Eron and Lego), Pisa (Fra 32), Ancona (Blast) and many more.

Moving along the primary railway axes of the country was the only way to become part of an extended scene that could give an identity of national scope. The "provincials" who did not follow this path were left out of the loop. It was a mandatory choice that conferred to the Italian context radically different characteristics and dynamics with respect to those typical of the New York subway.

In Italy, the national train yards were often delocated in scarcely populated areas: this allowed actions to take place undisturbed, without the risk of encountering private vigilantes. When the movement exploded towards the end of the 90's, the state railway struggled to contain it due to the expansive transportation network and the difficulty in controlling yards spread throughout the territory.

On the opposite front, writers had their own share of obstacles to conquer. The time frame in which to hit a train depended on its route: given the extension of the railway circuit, the probability of repeatedly seeing the same painted convoy was much slimmer. Photographs, essential medium through which to immortalise the accomplished work, became an important testimony that often coincided with a single, furtive, night shot.

Another difference between the reality in Italy and that of the New York subway was the dimension of the carriages, where the

> CONTINUES ON PAGE 326

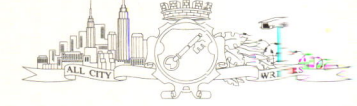

ACW INTERNATIONAL / NATIONAL RAILWAYS

Main contributors:
Bees, Blast, Egs, Ens, Fra32, Ghos, Hence, Hiom, Kaf, Kein, Mee, Manjar, Peggio, Polo, Reas, Ento, Sera, Smart, Riso, Tekne, Vashe

In collaboration with:
PR's, NSB, ZKM, CDC, AOK, KTH, KH, PDB, RE Vandals, FTR, NERDS, PWO

Cover photo:
Mace, freight train.Treviso 99

> CONTINUES FROM PAGE 325

former surpassed the latter by a great deal. Painting end-to-ends and whole-cars on certain Intercitys entailed a considerable effort.

Moreover, among the various long-distance lines in Europe, the Italian case was unique because it enjoyed a singular condition: Intercity, Inter-regional and Regional trains were allowed to circulate painted throughout the 90's, without any censorship or preventive measures. For the Italian railway company it had been a complicated decade: other than facing a phenomenon that was difficult to restrain they also had to address a serious corporate deficit. The state lines, already plagued by problems tied to security, the quality of service and maintenance inside trains, did not succeed in containing the work of writers, who managed to completely modify the aspect of national liveries for over a decade.

By the second half of the 90's, the presence of graffiti on trains was a constant. The stations of Milano Centrale, Roma Termini, Firenze Santa Maria Novella and Genova Porta Principe became a thermometer by which to measure the stylistic evolution of Writing scenes hundreds of kilometres distant from one another. As had occurred on the platforms of the New York subway, where writers lingered to comment on their works, the situation was reproduced in Italian railway stations, in an equally intense process, though more diluted in space and time.

———————   Main national routes
————————   Main local routes
■   Primary stations
•   Secondary stations

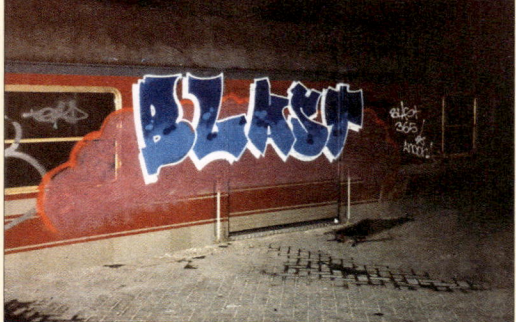

Blast, early window-up piece, 1992   —Blast

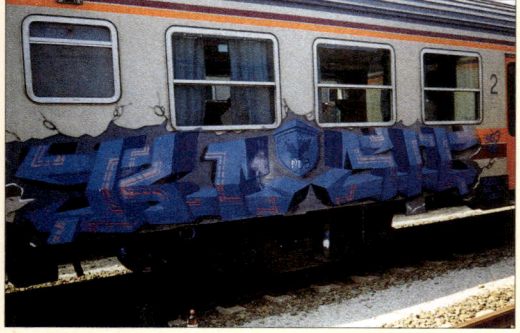

Riso – PDB   —Fra 32

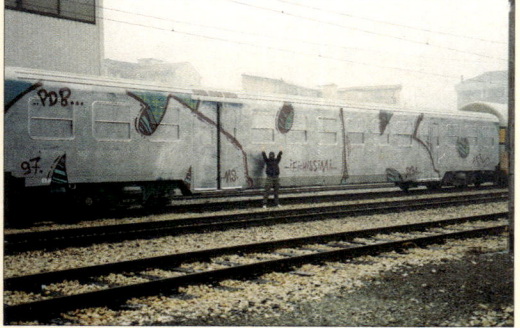

Muko – PDB   —ACW archive

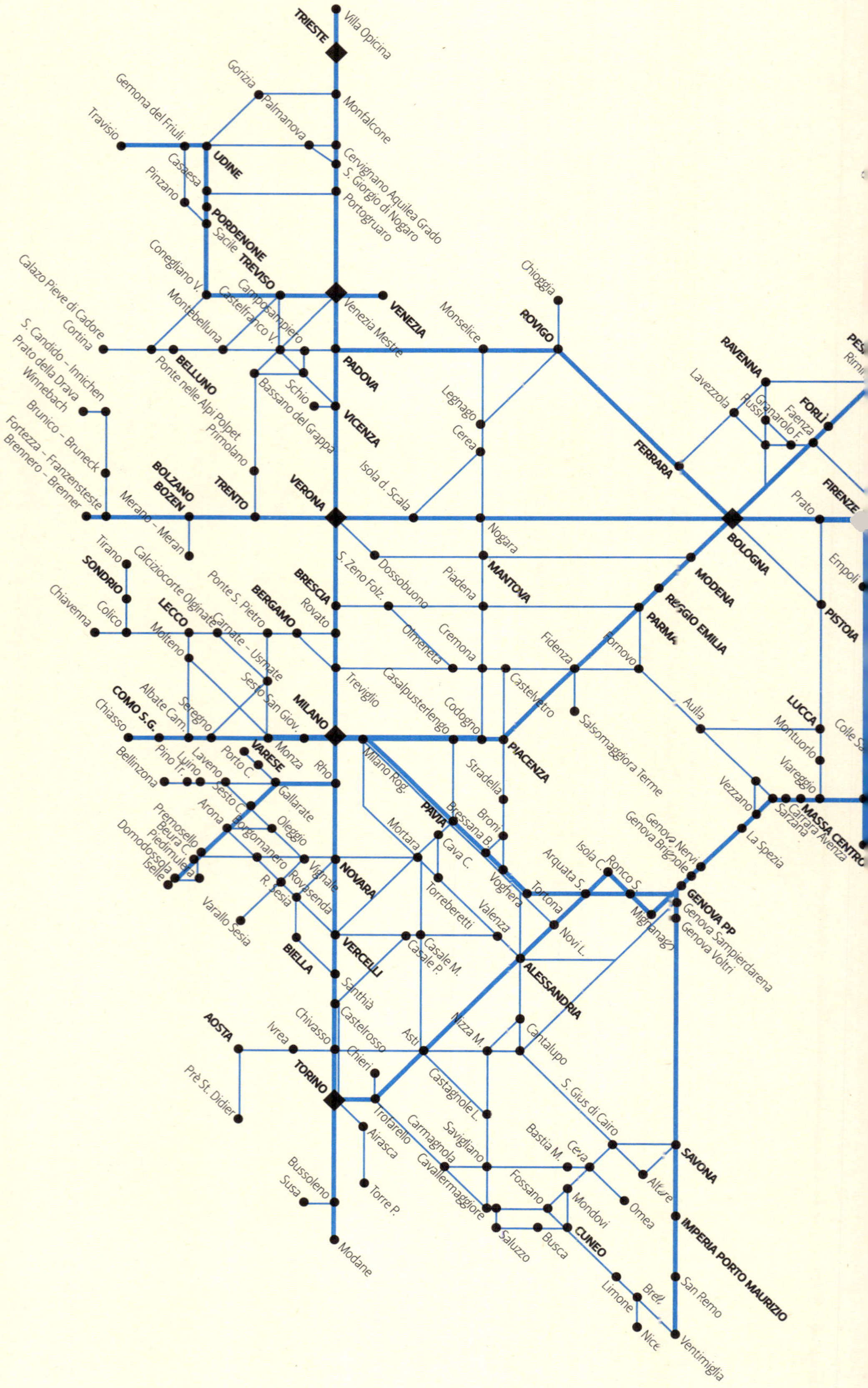

THE NATIONAL CIRCUIT DURING THE 90'S

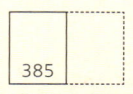

385

LOCAL NETWORK
TUSCANY

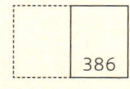

386

CENTRAL
STATIONS
SMN FLORENCE

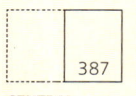

387

CENTRAL
STATIONS
ROMA TERMINI

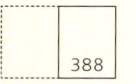

388

YARDS
ROMA OSTIENSE

389

MULTIPLE SYSTEMS
NAPLES

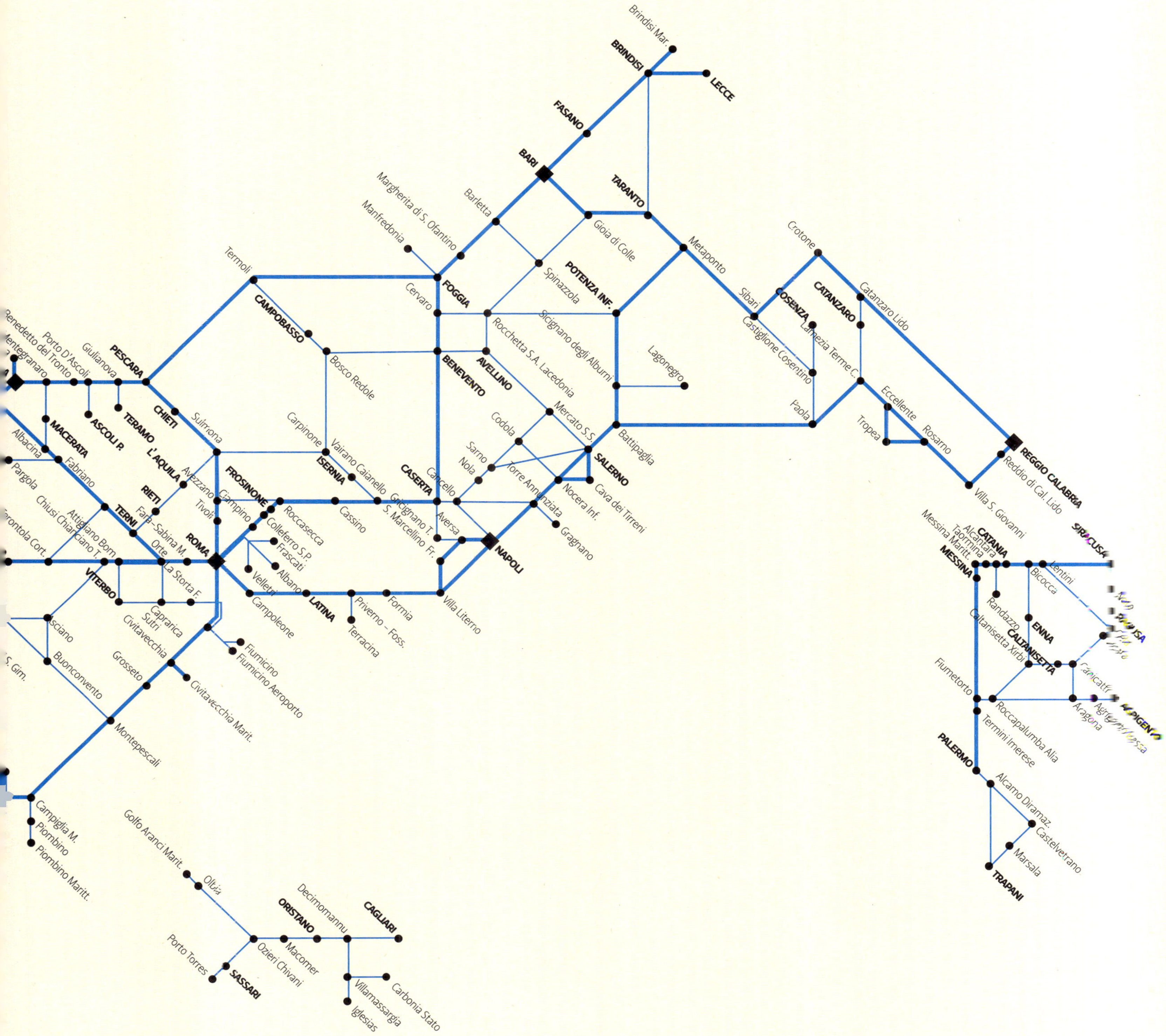

Brindisi Mar.

BRINDISI

LECCE

FASANO

BARI

TARANTO

Barletta

Gioia di Colle

Metaponto

Crotone

Margherita di S. Ofantino

CATANZARO

Catanzaro Lido

Manfredonia

Spinazzola

POTENZA INF.

Sibari

Termoli

Cervaro

FOGGIA

Rocchetta S.A. Lacedonia

Sicignano degli Alburni

Castiglione Cosentino

COSENZA

Lamezia Terme C.

CAMPOBASSO

AVELLINO

Lagonegro

BENEVENTO

Bosco Redole

Paola

Eccellente

Rosarno

Benedetto del Tronto

Porto D'Ascoli

PESCARA

Carpinone

Vairano Caianello

Codola

Mercato S.S.

Tropea

Giulianova

Sulmona

Mercato S.S.

Battipaglia

CHIETI

TERAMO

ASCOLI P.

Sarno

REGGIO CALABRIA

MACERATA

L'AQUILA

Avezzano

Campino

ISERNIA

Nola

Torre Annunziata

SALERNO

Reddio di Cal. Lido

Albacina

Fabriano

Tivoli

FROSINONE

CASERTA

Cancello

Nocera Inf.

Cava dei Tirreni

Villa S. Giovanni

Pargola

RIETI

Roccasecca

S. Marcellino Fr.

Gragnano

SIRACUSA

Chiusi Chianciano T.

TERNI

Fara - Sabina M.

Colleferro S.P.

Cassino

Aversa

CATANIA

Frontola Cort.

Attigliano Born

Orte

Frascati

Alcantara

MESSINA

ROMA

La Storta F.

NAPOLI

Taormina

Messina Maritt.

VITERBO

Sutri

Albano

Campoleone

LATINA

Villa Literno

Randazzo

Bicocca

Capranica

Velletri

Lentini

Isciano

Buonconvento

Civitavecchia

Priverno - Foss.

Formia

Caltanissetta Xirbi

ENNA

S. Gim.

Grosseto

Fiumicino

Terracina

Fiumetorto

CALTANISSETTA

Fiumicino Aeroporto

Roccapalumba Alia

Campiglia M.

Civitavecchia Maritt.

Termini Imerese

Aragona

Piombino

Montepescali

Agrigento

Piombino Maritt.

PALERMO

Alcamo Diramaz.

Golfo Aranci Marit.

Castelvetrano

Olbia

Marsala

Decimomannu

CAGLIARI

TRAPANI

ORISTANO

Macomer

Porto Torres

Ozieri Chivani

SASSARI

Villamassargia

Carbonia Stato

Iglesias

A suburban reality
>

Across Tuscany

The Tuscan railway network is structured into two primary long distance axes: the Genoa–Rome Tyrrhenian coastline and the internal axis of Florence–Bologna. The work of the first crews to be active on the Intercity train routes circulated long this double system in the first half of the 90's. Among these, FTR were one of the first groups to form with members coming from different cities: Dust and Chief from Milan, Dork, Duke-1 and Enist from Florence, Etnic from Empoli and finally Polo and Kaf from Naples.

At the same time writers from Rome and Liguria were also appearing long these stretches, by painting UIC-X models, Intercity trains commonly known as *Bordeaux* or *Marmotta*.

On a regional scale on the other hand, the railway network is a capillary web of lines distributed throughout the territory, trafficked by trains that are recognisable for the precise design of their exterior: the cream and light blue *Littorine* that connect Florence to Faenza, or the train models called *Metropolitani*, preferred by Florentine writers due to the height of the panel under the windows.

In the Province, already by the mid 90's the realities of Viareggio, Pisa, Empoli and Grosseto were further adding to the density of painted trains, to be summed with those of Florence. In this suburban dimension, Fra32 and KNM crew became the main reference points. Availing themselves of the better conditions of deposits scattered around the territory, this group transferred onto trains a stylistic approach that generally belongs to hall of fames: their compositions were based on complex letters and figures and since the second half of the 90's have contributed in identifying the aesthetic of these regional trains.

Fra 32
>

I seriously started painting the walls of Pisa in '95, my earlier works were marked by the political undertones that have always been present in Pisa, social centres and student collectives have been active since the 70's. Left-wing factions and groups would gather everywhere; I remember in '93 they incorporated into their cliché the new underground musical culture that was emerging directly from the United States: posses and the very first Italian Hip Hop groups were importing the political message of Public Enemy and company. In Pisa most of the Hip Hop movement was experienced in a confused way, the idea of a combination of DJs, MCs, writers and breakers wasn't clear either, music was radically removed from the American baggy aesthetics, we were just kids from the province that were actually rather anti-American, with an attraction to underground culture and

protest. Graffiti was intended in that sense, as an attempt to amplify this protest message in the context of our cities, with Writing that initially echoed the legendary phrases spray painted in Italy and Europe in the 70's, "potere operaio" (power to the working-class), and such slogans. In those days our group was called SVC, and more than a crew, it was a real collective that comprised skaters, DJs, writers and artists, we were somewhat the motor behind everything that was being organised in Pisa, contests, jams and rave parties.

I remember my first piece was "AK47", at the time I didn't even take pictures, the idea of tagging with your own Name didn't exist, we would just concentrate on the political and social message. Only in '94 did I pick a tag, Noiz, to then become Fra32 after dozens of other choices, and with time I met other guys like Ozmo, already connected to Florence via Etnic and Duke1, and to Milan via Dust of MNP. But the radical turning point for Pisa came through Dra from Milan, who in '95 opened all our eyes by breaking it down the way it was, from the choice of a Name, to what a crew was, to the discovery of the first yard.

He brought us the first decent spray paint from Milan, Sparvar, and caps, and the first issues of *Tribe* magazine. Obviously Milan was taken as a reference point. Other than Dra I remember other contacts with the kids from Viareggio on holiday: Dust, sometimes Chief, and one time even Drop from CKC, basically the Wildstyle of Milan was an essential reference that however fell short with us, since we still lacked the basics and the mentality. The influence of the Milanese scene lingered for years, it was a common ground for all the kids in Pisa, from me to Sera, Etnic, Ozmo and Aris, and then K3 from Viareggio who imported the B-boy aesthetics: baggy clothes, strictly Hip Hop music, and an 'Americanised' slang.

In comparison we were freaks, with our flared pants, long hair, we were the offspring of the 70's. Among all this confusion, underground culture and political ideals, it's a miracle that Writing got through to us, even though more than Writing in general, one might directly speak of a train-scene. Already in 1995 painted Intercity trains could be seen in Pisa and its province, especially end-to-ends by FTR in Florence. We couldn't wait to hit a train panel until one day the name Dra appeared on a couple trains that had been painted in the yard of Pisa. For Ozmo and me it was the beginning of everything, I remember Dra made sure we all kept the yard clean, no caps lying around, no cans left on the rail tracks, few tags on the nearby street lamps and no gratuitous damage, well he had years of experience under his belt. In that period I think in all of Italy the number of painted trains was still limited, like a panel a week, nothing compared to what was to come.

The yard was a sort-of sacred place, untouchable except for targeted actions.

> CONTINUES ON PAGE 348

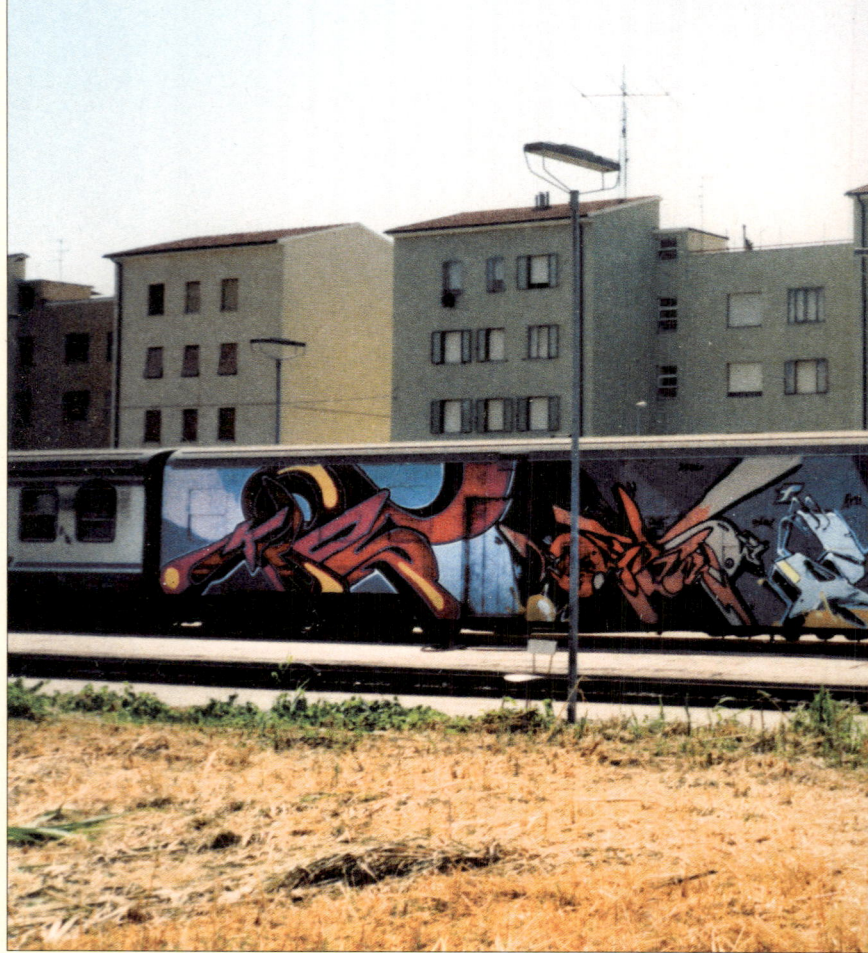
Full colour whole-car by KNM crew and *Kros* by Blef, from Genoa

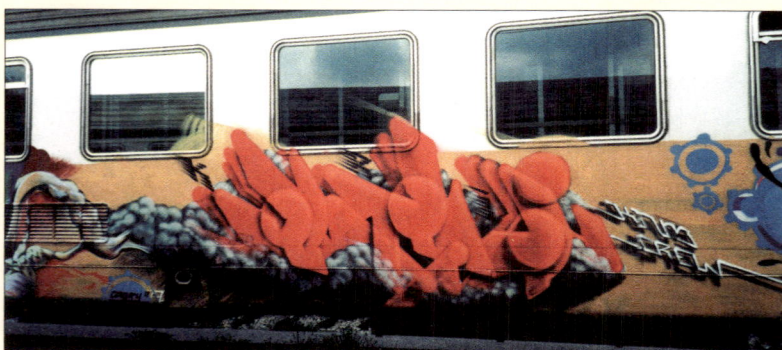
Krisa   — Sera

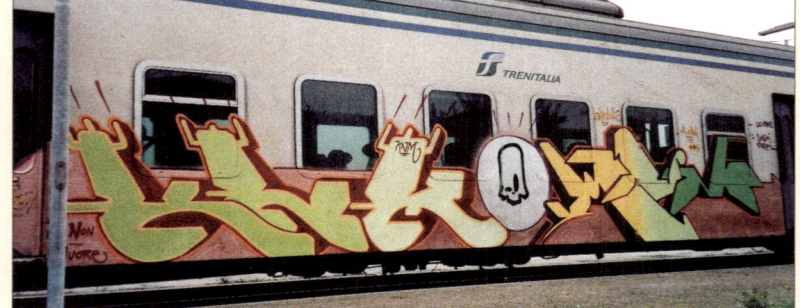
Karma   — Sera

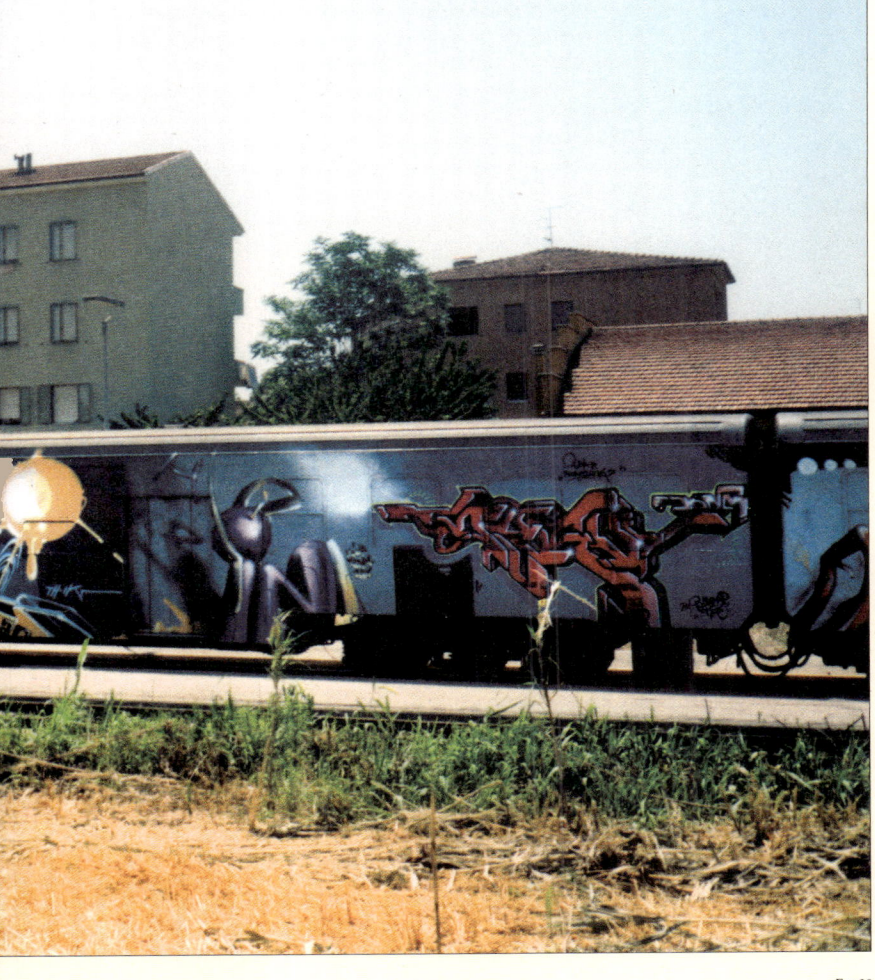

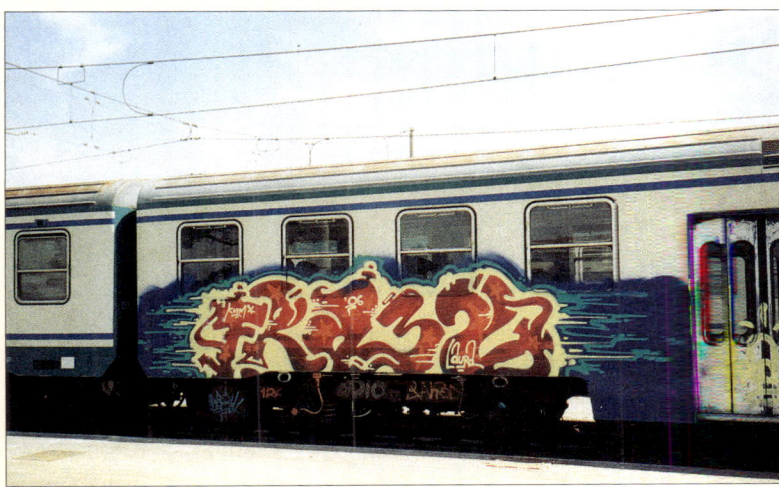

Fra 32

— Fra 32

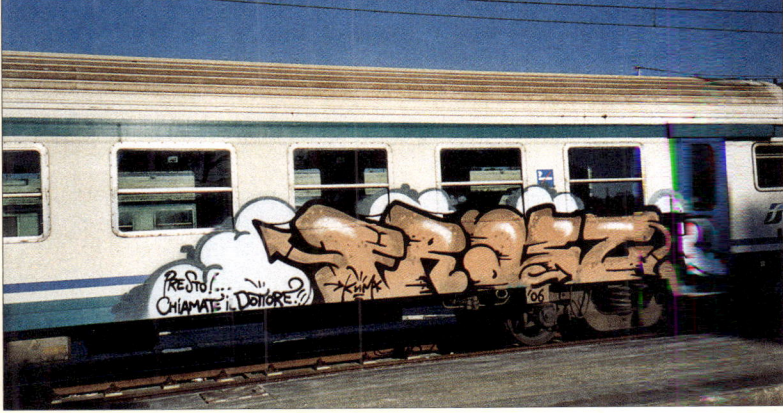

— Fra 32

— Fra 32

Fra 32

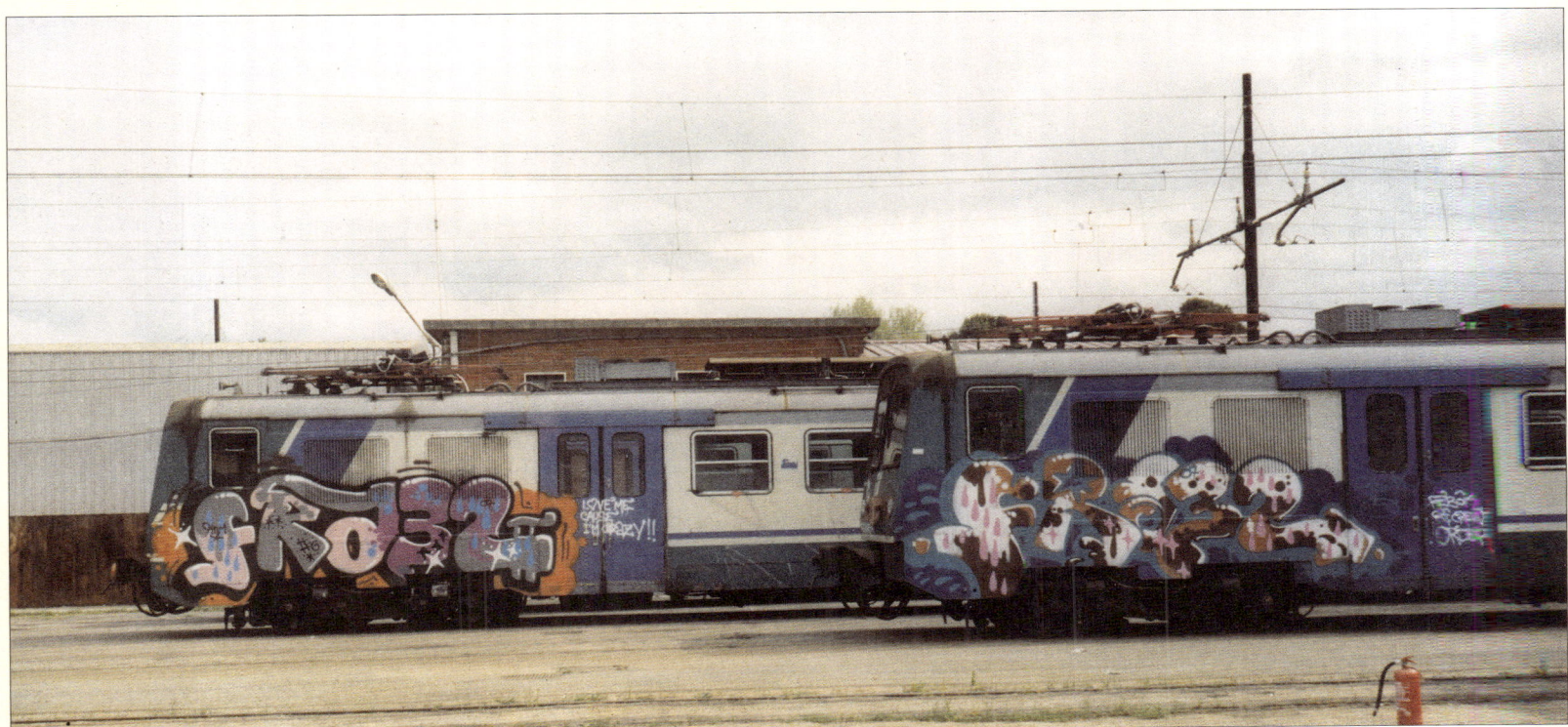

Fra 32 double hit on Tuscan regional trains

— Fra 32

CENTRAL STATIONS

Parallel tourism
>

Straight to the city centre

Some Italian train stations are terminuses rather than pass-through stations, forcing trains to pull in and reverse their direction in order to leave. For example: Florence's Santa Maria Novella, Milan's Central Station, and Rome's Termini. Positioned in the historic center of the city, Santa Maria Novella has always been a starting point for mass tourism: in fact, from the station one can walk to the Duomo, Uffizi, Ponte Vecchio, and every other tourist landmark. When the local Writing scene exploded in the 90's, the city was faced with an unusual situation: the first painted trains began pulling into Central Station, painted by key figures such as Smart, Enist, Kein, and other members of PR's and Nerds crew. The station, designed by Michelucci, began to resemble a large container: dozens of painted trains parked on coplanar and parallel tracks multiplied the visual impact of the station. Florence

offered unexpected scenes that catapulted it into a metropolitan dimension, totally shattering the expectations of newly arrived tourists. The allure of Santa Maria Novella, as well as some other factors, led to a high concentration of American writers for over a decade. An immensely charming city of art, home to many Universities for American students (namely Syracuse University), Florence was the epicentre for some rather permanent visitors from North America who came to find distant relatives and see friends who were temporarily in the city. The local scene benefitted from these conditions: thanks to this influx of people travelling from North America to Florence, and trips to California and New York by local writers like Chero and Smart, a constant exchange of visits occurred between the Tuscan capital and major American cities, inevitably influencing styles and habits.

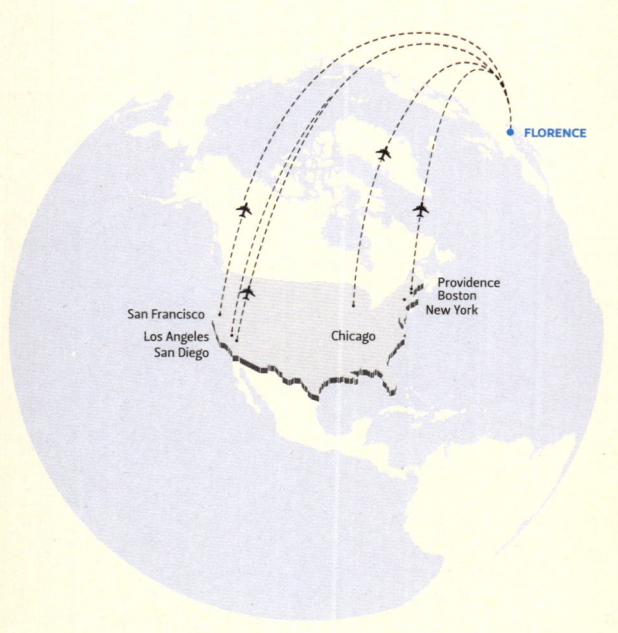

Open talk with PR'S crew and foreign writers
>

Meeting at Santa

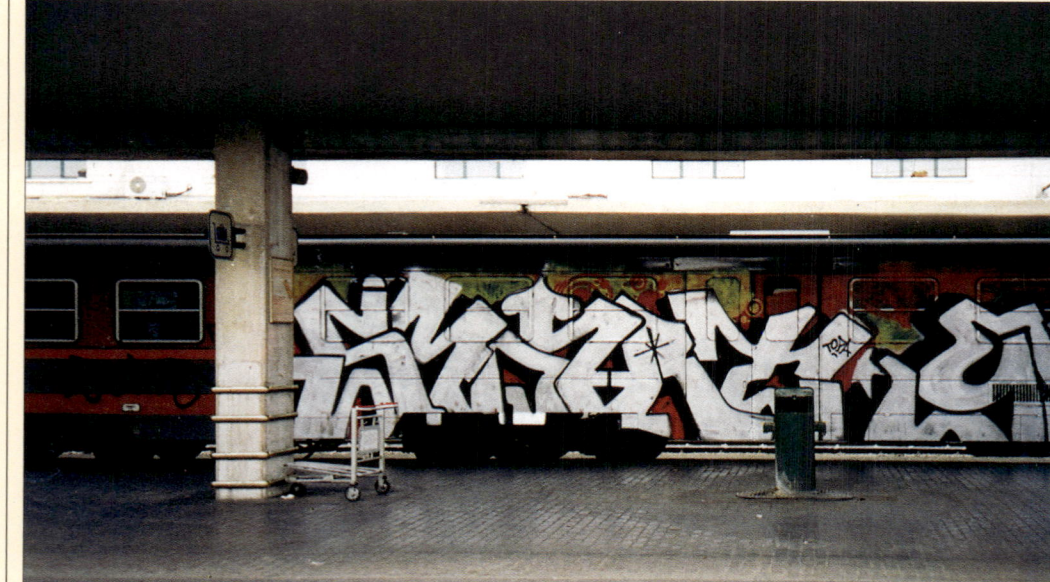

PR's whole-car by Smart, Guim, Ens parked in Santa Maria Novella

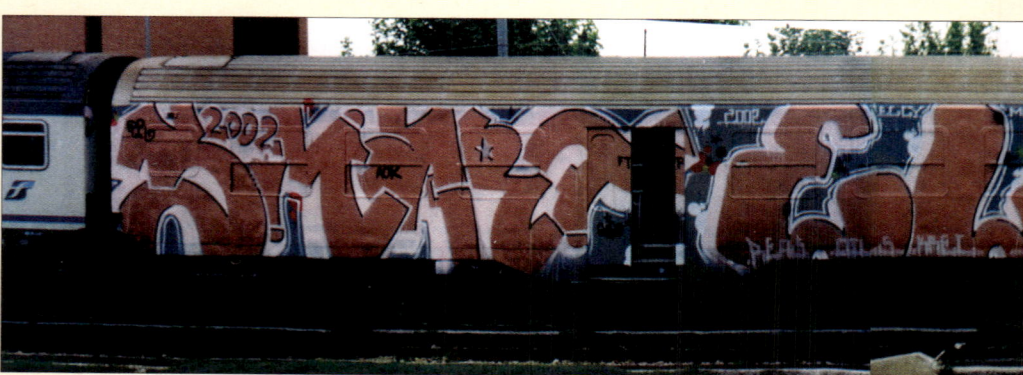

Smart, Elk from London, Ens

Starting around the middle of the 90's, and lasting for over a decade, a bond was created between the scene of Florence and many American writers. How did this exchange take place and what allowed it to flourish and last so long?

SMART- There is no exact date or precise episode that gave way to everything, but rather a mix of experiences tied to trips that allowed the writers of Florence to link up with crews from overseas. Florence is an exceptional tourist attraction for those coming from the U.S and this surely played in favour, but it wasn't the only reason for those travels. Often writers came to visit

family and friends that perhaps studied at the Italian site of Syracuse University, but most of the time the trips were individual, sometimes planned with the sole intent of painting trains and seeing the main station of Santa Maria Novella. Vice versa, we would take New York and California as reference points in America and the reciprocal visits cemented the connection.

What about the foreign writers that came to Florence, who were the first to arrive and how did the early encounters evolve into a solid network that lasted for over a decade?

SMART- Apart from Toxic of TDS

who had been living in Tuscany for years, the first foreign name we started noticing around was Teach of TN7; I never actually met him, not until a trip to New York many years later, but in '94 at the Cure, a wall along the track line that goes underneath an overpass, I started seeing pieces by him. To see a piece with such style was a shock because there were so few of us in Florence that we all knew each other. Then he did some throw-ups around, and wrote "New York" under a couple of them and this fuelled the legend even more, so we tried to find him. We'd make stickers with mini throw-ups and tags, leaving notes around what we thought was his area, in the

Maria Novella

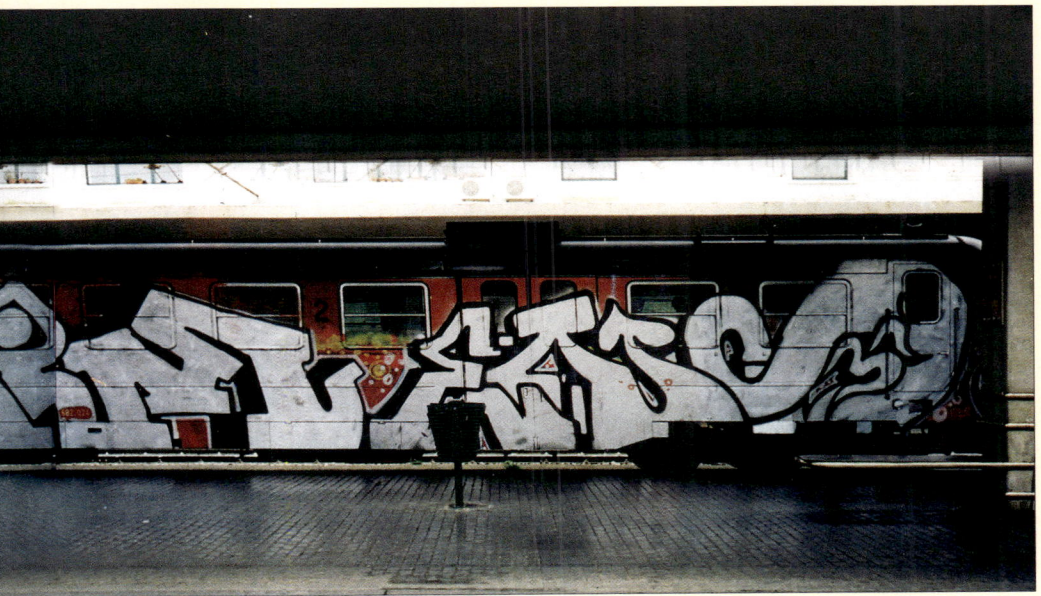

— Smart

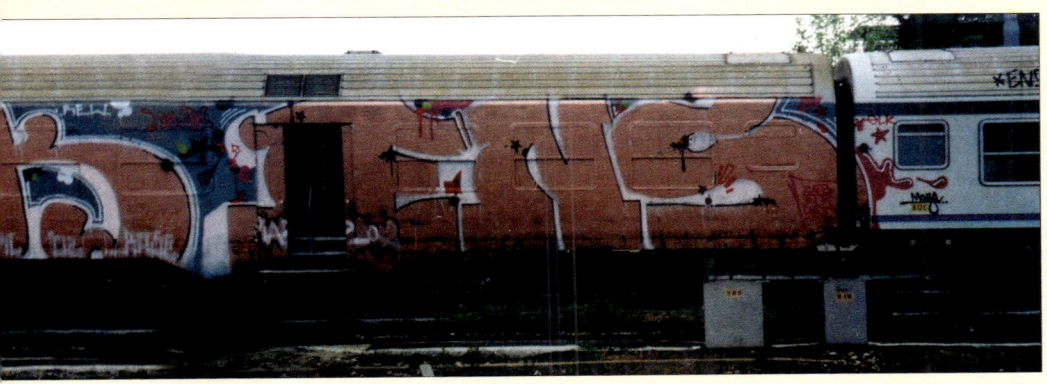

— Smart

Santo Spirito neighbourhood. We would write "Let's meet at Ultra", one of the first street stores in Florence. We thought he had come with Yes2 cause we saw some stuff by him as well. Years later Teach returned with Ivory and some other American guys.

ENS- Apart from seeing stuff by Toxic and Teach around, I think the first writer I met from America in Florence was Vender from San Francisco. He was the man that never felt pain, we'd play football and he had the American rugby approach, he'd throw himself on everyone, except we would be playing on the hard cement. People started fouling him and even with his knee all messed up and swollen, he kept on running, "I'm ok, everything's ok" he'd say. He was a hardcore bomber, in Florence he did mad trains, what a character. I remember one day we were benching at Central Station and taking pictures of the train we had painted the night before. At one point he goes "Wait, wait, I want a photo with me in the window above the piece". So he boards the train and sticks his head out the window, except all of a sudden the doors shut and the train starts moving, off to the deposit! He runs to the door but it doesn't open, so he returns to the window and tries to get out from there, only he's a pretty big guy so he gets totally cut up trying to squeeze through that hole, throwing himself off as the train is running.

SMART- As soon as Vender came we started doing panels, whole-cars, a shit load of stuff and when he went back to the States people there got mad hyped, not that many writers were doing passenger trains in San Francisco. Naturally once he had gotten home Vender had pulled out all these flicks... news got around of all the trains done in Santa Maria Novella and the whole thing blew up, many writers from Cali started organising trips to come out here.

BEES- Yeah, when I went to California and showed all the pictures of Florence, cats there were bugging. One time at breakfast I pulled out an envelope of train photos that Smart had sent from Florence and those guys were losing it, seeing all those painted trains circulate, they couldn't believe it and would protest "but they're trash trains", and I'd say "no no, look at the people behind the windows!".
And boom, total surprise: cause in '94 apart from freights not much was circulating painted in California, so they weren't expecting to see all those passengers from Italy.

ENS- At Cascine me, Bees, Smart, Dust. and il Magagna did a couple whole-cars with Vender. He was used to doing freight trains so he just went nuts; Cascine was like a playground, when a train was laid up there we could spend the whole night painting.

SMART- It has to be said that the night of the whole-cars at the Cascine with Vender was a stroke of luck cause that wasn't even a yard, it wasn't anything. Except once a year they organised a trip to Lourdes and the train left from the station of Leopolda, which was abandoned and used only for that single train; it was basically a work station, not a station from which trains transited much, but that one train left from there and they parked it at the back of Cascine, lost in the middle of nothing. By chance that night it was there, at the time I would loot 30-40 cans a day, so we went all out and painted all the carriages.

ENS- After Vender, his friend Jolts came and he didn't want to leave. He stayed at my place for like a month, then I don't even know how long at a friend's crib, he was also from San Francisco. Me and Jolts racked crazy spray paint, I would take him around to all the stores. I had always looted paint, but all the writers I met from America were on another level, so I always had a good time taking them 'shopping' in stores. Since then it was like a chain, a friend, a friend of a friend and so on...
I especially remember Elk from London. He had contracted Smart, saying he was coming with the necessary paint to do a golden whole-car with us! I guess I have this thing that I get along with anybody whose tag begins with an "E" and has three letters. Ditto for Egs, who came here various times and we painted non-stop together.

How did you get acquainted with the Italian scene and what were your connections in Florence?

EGS- The first foreign writer I met was Storm from Florence on a language course in England in the summer of 1988. He had fat laces and a name, so me and my friends went to talk to him. We exchanged addresses and later that year my Finnish friend received some letters and photos from him. Among the pictures there were some amazing Wildstyle sketches by Zero-T that really impressed us. Those photos were the first stuff I had seen from Italy and I immediately got interested in the Italian scene. Years later a friend of mine went to Rimini for a holiday and brought back some flyers done by Dayaki and Zero-T. They were dope.
In the early 90's I go to see a bit more Italian graffiti in some magazines. To my pleasure Italian styles varied a lot from Wildstyle burners by Flycat to crazy panels by Sherif and of course the amazing work done in the Roman subway by Starz and friends. In 1995 I got to meet Smart and Done in Helsinki and a year later Smart came back with Ens and my connection to Florence got stronger. In 2004 I visited Florence for the first time and hung out with Bees, Smart, Ens and the crew. We had fun painting, eating delicious food and drinking wine and grappa. I really enjoyed that city and definitely share a passion with the local writers for good food, great wine and dope graffiti styles.

How did the meeting with foreign writers take place? Were they deliberately planned and preceded by letters and

> CONTINUES ON NEXT PAGE

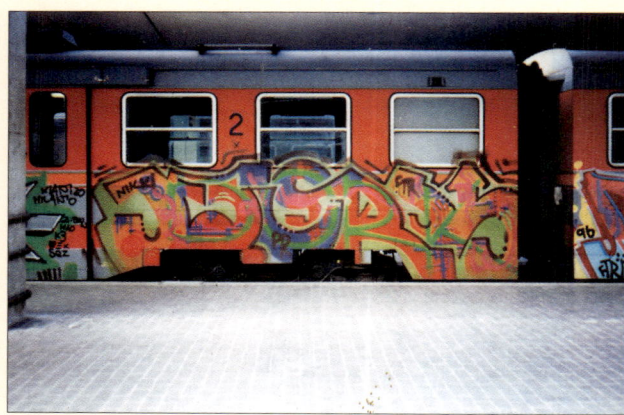

Dork, former Name of Smart — *Smart*

> CONTINUES FROM PAGE 331

phone calls or rather chance encounters?

BEES– We often met directly along the platforms of Santa Maria Novella. For instance that's how we got in touch with Prey, an old school writer from Boston; he was there looking at trains because many writers were obviously trainspotting. Duel RIS was also here briefly in '97, but he didn't get the chance to hook up with anybody really, so he ended up missing out on a great year!

In the mid 90's Central Station was full of bombed trains.

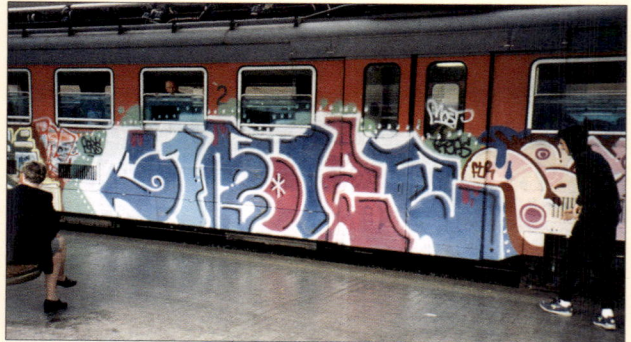

Amaze from San Francisco — *Smart*

We could check out trains from all over Italy but obviously our favorite were the *Metropolitani* on the Firenze-Viareggio line. It became almost automatic to chill there after a while, it turned into a kind of hang-out for us writers in Florence and for the Americans/foreigners that for one reason or another were passing through. The rate of painted trains rolling through Santa Maria Novella could be compared to a subway line, because the abundance of tracks meant they would arrive and leave with a high turnover of pieces. In any given day, you would see new pieces, either by your crew, or other writers from different cities. At the time I was working so I would also bench trains during my lunch break, or right after work. I benched them in the morning too. I would get my croissants and a cappuccino

to go and chill at a nearby, small train station for commuters. I was takin' pix, checkin' what was being done, and simply enjoin' it. Often co-workers would wonder why I would disappear at lunch, to then return an hour later with my camera strapped around my neck!

When did your first trip to New York take place and what do you remember most vividly about it?

SMART– In my case it was in '95, when I went there with my mom. I spent my days looking for tags and pieces in every neighbourhood. Not knowing where to go, I would take the subway and whenever I would see something, I'd get off to photograph it.

At one point on the elevated line I saw this building totally covered in graffiti, Five Points, earlier called Phun Factory. I got off the subway and started taking pictures, first from the street, then I saw some pieces higher up and started climbing up the gutter pipes; a guy came out looking pissed and said "what the fuck you doing here?!" and I didn't know much English but I tried to explain I was just taking photos. He asked me: "But do you know who Iz the Wiz is?" I did know who he was, but I had never seen him nor did I have any idea of what he looked like. This guy took me with him in his office and asked me if I wanted to meet him, then he passed me the phone. Iz was on the line and he

invited me to his place for dinner to look at his blackbook. I remember he was in Queens, next to JFK airport and he showed me *Faith of Graffiti* for the first time, I had never seen it... obviously I would talk to him about *Subway Art* but he insisted *Faith of Graffiti* was the real writer bible, of those that had started tags in New York. Then he pulled out his collection of photos... markers... sketches. I had been painting a couple of years already but that trip to New York marked a kind of new beginning. From then onwards the U.S became a set destination whenever possible. With the fact I was hosting all the American writers in Florence I could automatically guarantee myself a place to stay when it was me travelling.

Among all the American writers you encountered, was there someone that particularly influenced you?

ENS– Probably Reas, who came to Florence with Daze, invited by Enrico Coveri who already had some canvases by him and Crash. Actually it was Crash that was supposed to come, but he couldn't make it for some reason so Reas took his place, and him and Daze stayed at Coveri's apartment to sleep. I remember reading the news in the paper and Smart immediately got in touch with him since there had already been some communication between them in New York.

SMART– Yeah, through Drax. Drax had come to Florence from London in '96 and we had painted together, he was the one that linked me up with Reas since I was about to leave for New York. Except for a series of circumstances me and Reas ended up never hooking up in the States and met directly at Coveri's the next year. I remember he first stopped at Santa Maria Novella and was impressed by the intensity with which panels were circulating. He got to the station and it must have been somewhat of a nostalgic experience.

Seeing the total devastation of trains must have taken him back a decade because it was '97-'98, I had about a piece on every train, or at least on every train car. Naturally in a matter of days we organised a series of actions and he came back the following year cause he had had such a blast. He managed to get one trip sponsored by *Vibe* together with the editor of *Mass Appeal*, Sacha Jenkis.

When he got back I told him Rome was also totally bombed and that if he wanted we could go check it out, so we went to hit the subway. Reas was struck by the affinity between the styles in Rome and Ghost. "Cats love Ghost here!" he would say.

What were your impressions of the train station in Florence and the subway scene in Rome, and how would you compare them to New York?

REAS– In Florence it was overwhelming to see how many pieces were running, I mean on different train lines. You could read the dates under the pieces were two years old or more, so nothing was being cleaned. I even saw a silver Sharp piece, it was nice to catch it all the way out there. It seemed like most of Italy's trains were pieced, not just a subway system in one place, it was pretty massive. It

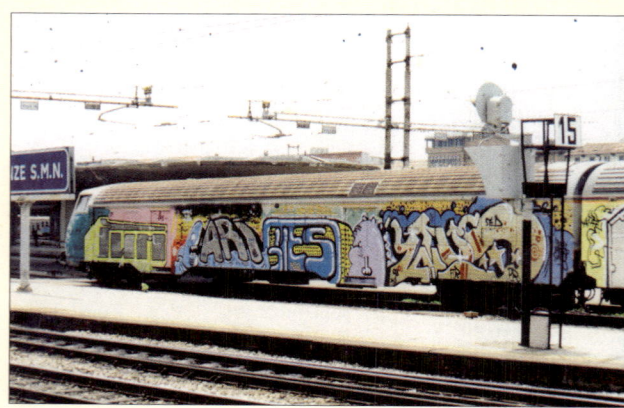

French writers and Ens at SMN — *Ens*

was as close to NYC as I have ever seen and I've been to Amsterdam which was also impressive, but different. Those two places are really my favourites outside NYC. Then with Smart I took the train to Rome and on the way I saw everything was covered. In Rome you had the sickest subway scene, all the styles were like from the mid 70's and you'd have different cats like Stand, Clint, Joe, Trota/THE doing it up and then a few guest appearances from the likes of Sento with stuff running. There were top-to-bottoms window-downs and then kids with markers bombing the insides.

GHOST– The cool thing with Florence was standing in a train station and seeing pieces on trains running, but it was nothing compared to the way trains were bombed when I was a kid

in New York. Our subway scene was really second to none. When I first arrived to Florence the train scene was different from that of NYC when I was growing up. The subway system in New York was devastated and there was more of a scene as far as writers on platforms waiting to watch trains, which I didn't really feel as much while I was there. Maybe I wasn't really there long enough to really experience it...but I did some bombing and then hung out on the platforms waiting to get flicks, which was something I hadn't experienced in a long time, I thought it was cool.

HENCE– When I got to Florence I saw an end-to-end by local writers with some decent pieces, which set a nice tone. Compared to NY it is more relaxed. There is a sense of space, light and air in the Florence train station. Arriving in the New York stations you're underground, the light is artificial and it's packed with people going into narrow corridors. There are less people around Florence's main station compared to NY and Rome. Rome has a similar vibe to NY because of all the people and action around you from the minute you get off the train, of course it's a matter of infrastructure but graffiti-wise the impact was different.

I imagine the dynamics involved in painting the yards in New York as opposed to those in

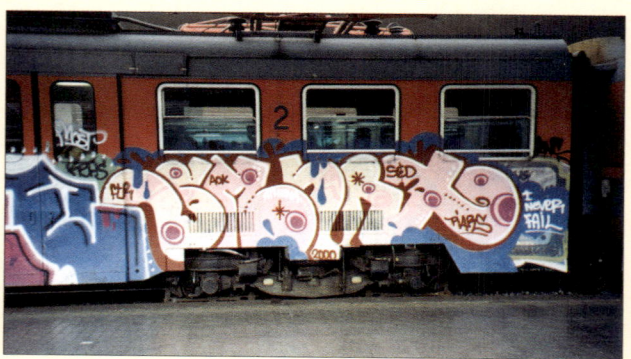

Smart, PR's — *Smart*

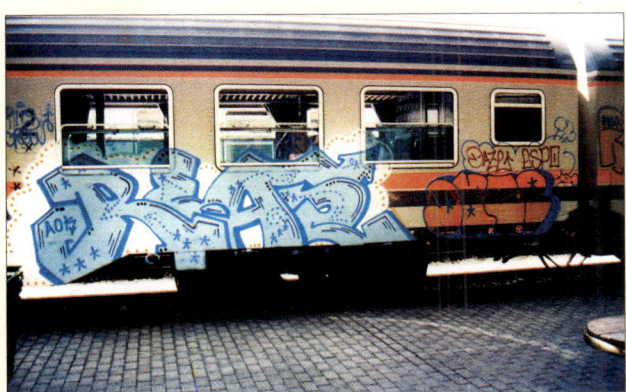

Reas – AOK from New York   — Chero

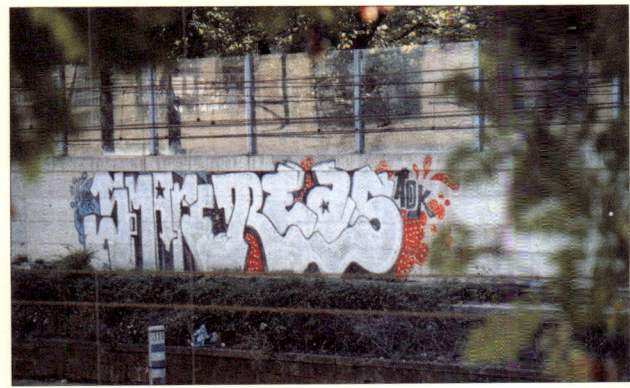

Smart and Reas along the Florence tracks   — Chero

Florence or the rest of Europe are radically different. What do you think the main differences are?

GHOST– Compared to New York it was totally different, back in the day you could paint in yards and lay-ups all day and night. When I first went to Europe I hooked up with Sabe from Copenhagen, we went to paint S-trains and when them cats were almost finished I was still putting the fat cap on the can… we did a simple piece and then I went to do throw-ups, cause that's how I would bomb in New York. I started to do a few throwies and they started to say "We have to leave!". I thought someone had come but that's just how they rolled, they only spent a few minutes doing a piece and then you had to break out cause of security… which I didn't really understand, I figured you should stay 'til you're finished. That was really the only difference I had experienced. It was like, as soon as we got there we had to leave, I made sure I would piece really fast just so I could go bomb throwies cause that's all I really wanted to do. Anyway the next day seeing it run was cool.

What was your impression of the styles you were seeing in Florence and Italy compared to those of New York and the rest of Europe?

REAS– Florence had a bunch of different styles and basically all the trains had been painted. It seemed like dudes were having fun. Guim was doing really crazy stuff, you had that kind of experimental work and Ens and Smart and the PR's crew were doing a mix of crazy and traditional styles. Rome really had a kind of 70's vibe with 80's classic NYC stuff and you'd get a mix of other Euro cats in there.

You, Ghost and the whole AOK /RIS have been to many Italian writers what T-Kid was for Berlin, meaning that a lot of people looked up to you and were inspired by what you were doing. How do you feel about this?

REAS– What better country than

Italy to have had some inspirational impact on, if that's the case. To be honest, I felt that there were a lot of guys influenced by 70's stuff or the spirit of breaking rules and not being afraid of just doing something crazy-looking. To me AOK RIS was very much about our approach to Writing, which was sort of fun and uninhibited and included an appreciation for older 70's stuff in a time when

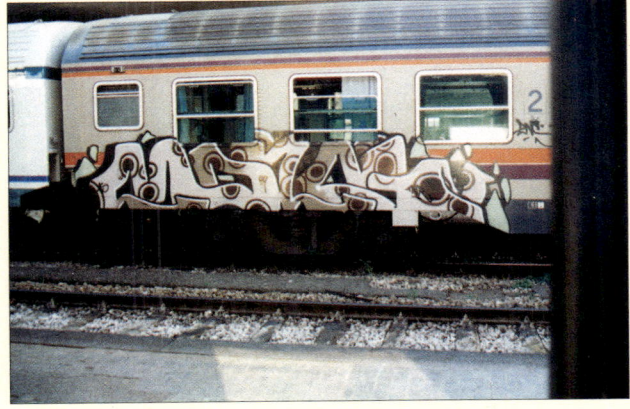

Mag by Magagna   — Ens

people were not doing that at all. The only other guy into that back then was Sane and he was a good friend of ours. The guys I met in Italy, Smart, Guim and Ens were doing this kind of thing when I met them. Smart picked up on some styles but more than that he added onto them and did some stuff I was inspired by. That's the difference between someone just copying and someone who can work with a style and build on it.

Were the inputs that were coming from Reas mainly stylistic or did they also concern the way of painting and planning letters?

ENS– Reas was sick cause he could do any style. He'd say he wanted to recreate a mid 80's New York vibe and he'd do it, he'd write his name with that style. He could do any graffiti genre from the 70's onwards, it was incredible cause he could choose and perfectly control the styles. No doubt he flipped my take on sketches; as a kid I

would spend hours doing them, I would sit there with a pencil and eraser and notice he would just get out his book, grab a pen and do a Wildstyle without the structure, he wouldn't erase and retrace, he had this way of putting it down right away, without the structures.
I on the other hand, never got it right the first time, and had to redo my letters over and over, erasing and redrawing so as to get the construction of the letters right. Maybe Reas also did that when he started, but he had assimilated the process so well that it all came automatic to him then.

Who came after Reas?

SMART– Grey I think. Naturally one contact led to another and it was Reas who told me about him, he said Grey was in Europe, that he was a chill guy and he recommended I meet him; so in 1997 he came and we were immediately on the same wavelength. I remember our discussions on tags, Grey would sit for

hours at the table filling pages with tags, with this incredible style. Pages and pages of small tags, one after another. He really drummed this thing about signing your name into me, because before meeting him I had done some throw-ups but not that many tags.

BEES– I remember Grey from when I was in San Francisco, even years earlier he had a style that was recognisable and dope. I had bumped into him there and when he came to Florence I didn't recognise him immediately because in the States I had a different recollection of him, he was dressed in a different way. Reas influenced all of us, he really opened some doors, he made us appreciate the older stuff, especially the 70's style, even some 80's. Stuff like Blade that until then had not been considered that much. Reas brought back styles and letters from previous writers and eras and made them legit and fresh to us, I remember there were some

painted styrofoam panels floating on the river, for an exhibition that was happening at that time, which him and Daze came down for. So we were checkin' those floatin' panels, and Reas pointed to some of them, made by some kids. Well, we agreed on the "so whack it's fresh" thing, as some of the swirls and connections of these letters were actually dope.

ENS– I definitely absorbed something from Grey's style. Being influenced was inevitable because during the 90's American writers were coming every month, it was non-stop if you consider the visits were reciprocated from Florence to New York or California.

SMART– The difficult thing was keeping up contacts long-distance but gradually we managed it, especially with those coming from New York and San Francisco because these were cities we were visiting every year. Perhaps these assiduous trips to the States are what sparked the link with AOK, with Ghost and Reas, because we were fascinated and attracted by New York, as many writers are, and vice versa the writers from NYC came back to Florence every year to find those acceptable train-writing conditions that allowed them to relive the emotions you get when you see a train running with your Name on it.
I remember one night we went to paint in Borgo with Reas, he did a throw-up writing "Daze", cause Daze couldn't come and

so it was his way of getting him up anyway, kinda like a tribute. Before painting we had gotten in the car with Guim, who was tripping balls, he drove like a madman, at an absurd speed, he knew the way real well but still he was going so fast and Reas was behind all tense. Then as soon as we arrived inside the yard its unique atmosphere greeted us: misty, calm. Basically the car trip to and from the yard with Guim was more dangerous than the actual action itself.

Did the constant contact with writers coming from abroad and namely the U.S, affect Florence's approach to Writing?

ENS– No doubt tagging was re-evaluated. Personally the thing that brought me to do graffiti is the tag tradition, I was especially impressed by the scribbles I saw in the centre of Florence by JC, Zero-T and Druid, a guy I never met. Then this attention to signing your name stopped and it seemed that in Florence and Italy nobody cared for it, everyone was focusing on finding caps for the best outlines and attempting impossible 3Ds, completely forgetting about tags.
The arrival of Reas in Florence was important because it dug up this thing about signing your name and also because it became a connection to a whole series of contacts like Grey or Amaze that came in the following years. In the States they've always had a tradition for hand

> CONTINUES ON PAGE 334

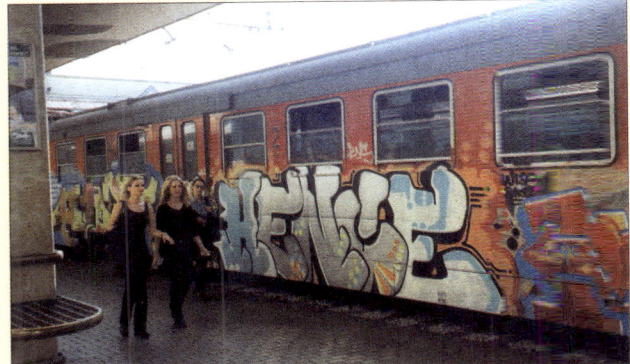

Hence from US   — Hence

> CONTINUES FROM PAGE 333

style, they already had it in the 70's and still in the middle of the 90's this pursuit continued. In the States you might catch someone that was a disaster at doing a piece but when it came to tagging he killed it more than all the hall of fame fanatics. I remember my first signature well before Grey came and it was something to be ashamed of. Not that they wanted to teach us anything, it was more of an induction process: we'd go out, tag together, and they might point something out, do a scribble in our book, and that slowly improved our tagging style. Bees picked up many things about

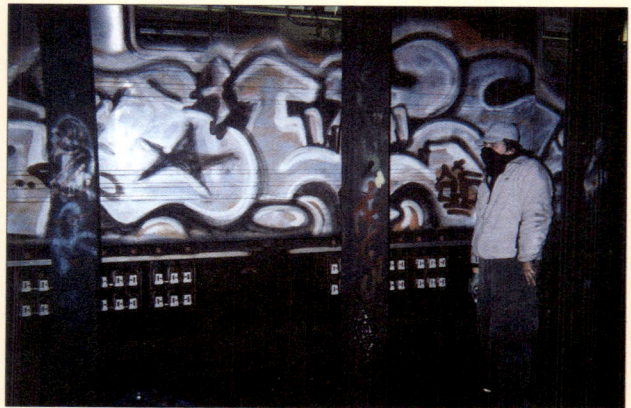

Bees by Chero on the New York City subway   *— Ens*

good tagging when he was staying in San Francisco.
BEES- Product placement! That's what I'm saying! Sometimes you see mad tags all over, but those don't work, or better still, don't really meet my tastes, even if I appreciate the bombing itself anyway. I prefer to have less and better placed tags instead. I remember a tag Grey did on a door knob in S.F. Well, that tag stuck in my memory more than all the other stuff done by kids out there, but hey, you know, it's probably just me.
I think that tagging next to a pole is something that Grey or Amaze must have mentioned, to place a tag next to objects that draw the eye, as that might increase the likelihood it will attract attention. For example we

often avoided billboards because they're already colourful. You should concentrate on objects that are present in the urban landscape but that are anonymous, that need personalisation, customisation.

The styles of tags present in the U.S varied in radical ways and that must have struck you coming from Italy.

BEES- Yeah but the style of some American Writing you would see in California had already been absorbed in Italy through other channels, Cholo Writing is an example, but my recollection of Cholo Writing goes way back, as I remember articles about LA gangs on some mags that I had read years ago. For example in 1990 Italy had already seen a boom of skaters and many of us came from there. Before becoming writers we were skaters. Me and Smart spent our days at the CPA with Fiore and others and naturally the references we had were from Americans, the whole skateboarding movement, all the bmx and skate mags I used to buy, not only for the skate flix, but also to check the sneakers, clothing and all that! The Powell-Peralta boards and all the imagery tied to Bones Brigade and their logo, which stylistically recalled the Cholo letters. The border between skater and writer wasn't that defined in the early 90's and so we drew

inspiration from everywhere. For sure more from the skater world than Hip Hop. Smart came from the punk scene and breakers weren't even considered.

After visiting Florence in distinct periods of time, from the 90's through to the next decade, have you noticed changes in the style of the local writers?

HENCE- I've noticed a difference in tags and throw-ups in the street. People are more into doing streets now compared to when I first visited Florence during the 90's. Many guys are going for a certain kind of bubbly throw-up style with a sense of the past that is influenced by the major Italian writers looking at older New York writers. The work is clean because of the paint that is now available.
It was cool to see some writers really getting up on the streets. It definitely motivates people to try it. On the streets I hope people can respect the old architecture because it would be a shame to deface the historical buildings and draw negative attention.
Where I live in New York there's new bombing in the street every night. I think there is much more starting to happen again in the U.S. I see people scheming on spots and I sometimes see them bombing. Years ago I used to yell at the kids when I would catch them doing their street art thing or the kids who have stupid names. I used to try to scare them away for fun but now its just as much fun to see them once in a while and just observe what they do. Often they don't notice that somebody is watching them and that's weird to me.

Where do you prefer painting? Streets, yards or halls of fame?

HENCE- I like to paint in different situations and not get stuck on one thing. I have been able to experience the streets, yards, halls of fame and other walls. Trains are always a favourite but it's nice to do different things.
Back in '99 I met Smart and he took me to do trains. I got to spend some time and do some quality pieces compared to other

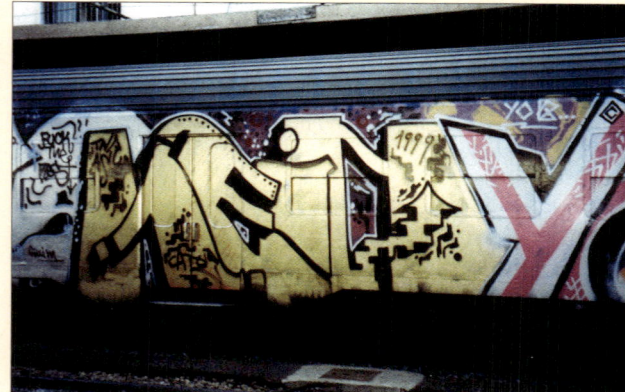

Kein, Nerds crew   *— Kein*

places where I had to rush to get something on a train. It was definitely more relaxed than NY, Holland, Stockholm and Rome. In these other places I've had more stressful situations.

In the States it was mostly long-distance freight trains that were being painted. How did it work in Florence? What type of trains came to Santa Maria Novella? And since all lines from Rome to Northern Italy pass through Florence, have you ever particularly concentrated on hitting long-distance trains?

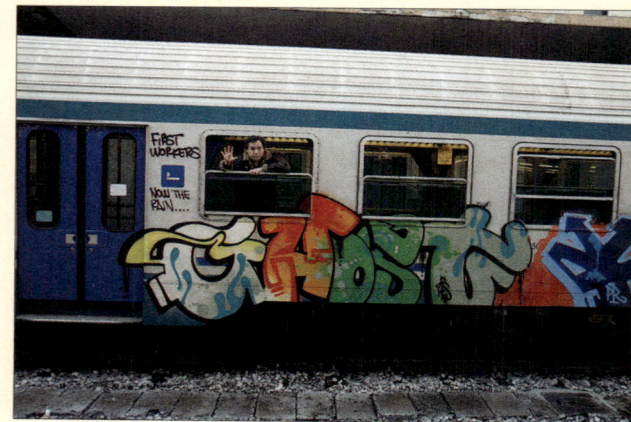

Ghost-AOK from New York City   *— Smart*

ENS- Obviously there were Intercity trains in the deposits of the city, but they were always my last resort because

they travelled farther away from Florence and I wasn't able to see them. I liked to have my pieces on regional trains so I could see them at the station every day and it felt good. The idea was to be able to catch your train pieces regularly, like you would in a subway. There were a lot of freight trains too but who was considering those?

BEES- I can agree with him on the fact that freight trains are worth jack... but at the same time I think they create a network. I mean, ok, you bomb, you want to be known and all

that but there's also the urge to create, to have an avalaible surface. In the U.S. writers actually benched them, as I remember writers talking about people they saw "up", so a writer from back East would be known all the way to the Midwest, thanx to a travelling car, painted miles away. I remember after we painted some freights back in California, we would write down the serial of the car, as we knew that there was a number you could call, and they would tell you where that very car was rolling in that moment.
Freights in the States, they're pretty important. I think that gave writers from smaller and graffiti-free areas the input to start a local scene and eventually become known in far away

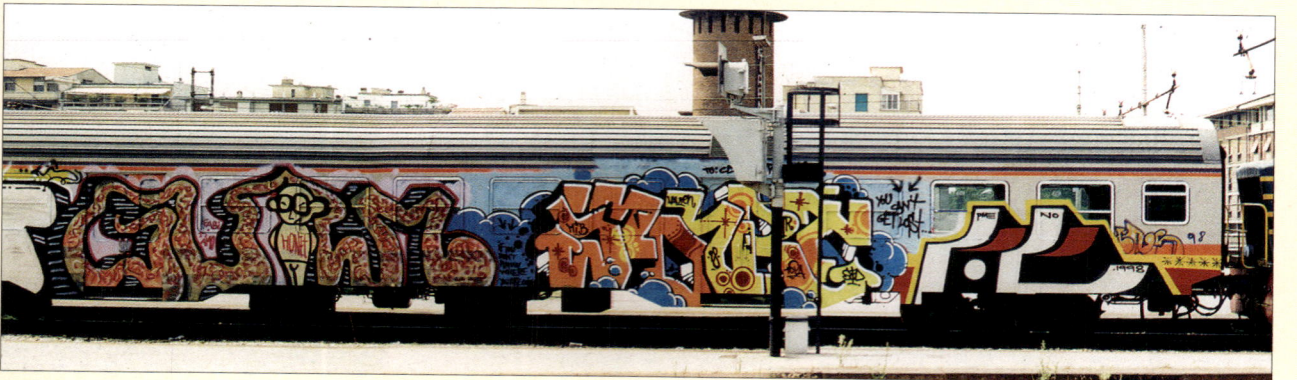

Guim, Smart and Foe from Bordeaux   *— Ens*

places. I guess that graff moves from the subway to a bigger, nationwide network. It depends on the context, you have to adapt to what surrounds you. We had local passenger lines plus we could move around by car, we'd go to Viareggio to paint the local lines. There was a train called the *Metropolitano* and it was our subway, it would go to Viareggio and within an hour it would be back in Florence, crossing through dozens of towns in Tuscany. And if an Intercity happened to be around, why not? We had pieces coming into Santa Maria Novella from Rome, Naples and other major cities. You spent a day at the station and saw all these styles from other cities, so every once in a while we'd also hit the long-distance lines.

SMART— If I had the possibility of hitting an Intercity I did.

wasn't a subway, had not even crossed my mind, I thought graffiti was for walls. We didn't have the subway, so what do you do? You paint walls, right? But I hadn't thought of all these local trains, maybe because I didn't take the train that often.

BEES— In Santa Maria Novella the tracks on the right are where the local styles painted on the *Metropolitani* are concentrated. To the left you have the national lines and I remember seeing end-to-ends from Padua, Rome. And a lot of stuff by Sherif. There were trains upon trains coming from Liguria with pieces by Sherif and the other writers of Genoa.

ENS— We mostly painted the local lines that were travelling between Florence, Viareggio, Livorno, Lucca, Montevarchi. Me and Smart were fixated on

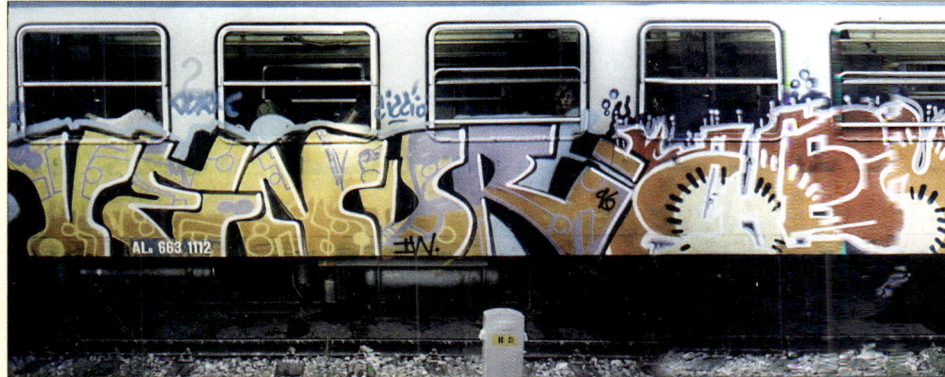

Vendr from San Francisco and *CHE* by Chero–PR's — *Chero*

which guards used dogs. Once when we were painting there two guards with dogs busted us, an anti-graffiti squad, and honestly we weren't expecting it, we weren't used to it.

a very important figure of the early 90's in Tuscany because he had a thing for trains and painting coloured hall-of-fame-type pieces on train cars. He stopped writing after a couple of years but he anyway laid the foundation for FTR which also included Chief from Milan, Polo from Naples and a bunch of other guys. We did end-to-ends, coloured, without a set theme, but each with his own piece, that all together had a powerful visual impact, at least for the time.
In Lamucchi we would paint on a dead track on which they would park trains. At the beginning they buffed everything, but from '94 to 2000 they stopped, abandoning the practice.

GHOST— Painting around Tuscan yards was pretty much a smooth ride except for one night, I think we had painted so much that it had gotten a little comfortable. Me and Sabe had done panels on one car, while Smart and Ens were doing another car with this other kid (sorry forgot what he wrote). As always I did the piece real fast so I could go do throw-ups, which is what I prefer. I started to bomb going towards the barn, when I heard talking. I didn't really pay it

front of the train. The security guard was just on the other side, they didn't even know we were there cause they were talking. Smart started to yell something and run. I followed him cause I didn't know my way around. The guard was on the opposite track and I ran past him as he started to chase Smart. I don't even think he noticed I was there! Man, I started running, I had a bag of my empties over my shoulder with my camera in the bag and with my video camera in the sleeve of my hoody. I heard him yelling in Italian and as I was running I lifted my bag over my head to throw it away 'cause it was weighing me down. Man it's nice to know I can still boogie at my age... I came across the tracks and when I turned around he had stopped cause I think a train was coming, I'm glad for that cause I couldn't run no more. I was out of breath. Sabe and Smart were gone. I had started walking, trying to catch my breath. Well, I lost my camera and I had broke the video camera but at least I didn't get caught.

ENS— It was chill to paint for the first couple of years, but when they moved the trains from the

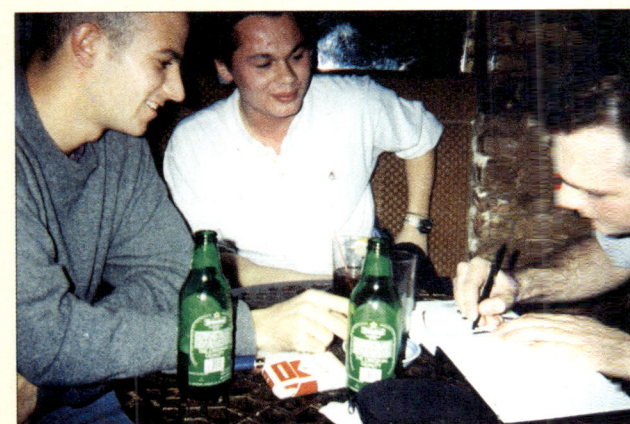

FTR was a temporary experience but in Campo di Marte, a yard in Florence, every once in a while we'd target long-distance trains. The thing was that since I spent a large quantity of my painting years without a camera I would never see the pieces again, which was a bummer, while the Regionals in one way or another would circulate and it would be easier to get my hands on someone else's picture. The few Inter-citys I did do I either didn't have the picture of or had a night flick with an over-exposed flash shot.

ENS— In any case if I have to do something I prefer it to be on Regionals, even for the shape of the trains that in my opinion are more suited, the metropolitano had a lower floor that left over a metre of clear surface under the windows to paint. In Santa Maria Novella the frequency with which these trains passed was real high, almost like a subway, and that's what got me doing them. In the beginning I didn't even consider trains, not until I met Smart, who in this sense had the intuition to get the importance of these lines right away. Before him the idea of doing a piece on a normal train, that

those trains, at a certain point we had about a piece each on every car. Instead of going to school, I would spend my day in Santa Maria Novella, trainspotting. Naturally when we painted in Campo di Marte, which didn't hold locals but Intercitys, there wasn't that much waiting to do because it was an implicit fact that the next day the train would be in who knows what city, perhaps transiting ithrough Central Station but any way for only a brief amount of time.

How was the yard in Campo di Marte? Were there also other yards in which you would paint?

BEES— Campo di Marte was a big yard, a transition yard. There were trains from all over Europe, Germany, Belgium, something coming from the local lines of Naples. A strange ensemble, especially the International trains like the *Tens*, blue trains with sleeping cabins cause they travelled by night. We painted several pieces there, but after a while, it was being patrolled with guards and dogs.

ENS— After a while we started avoiding Campo di Marte because it was the first place in

SMART— I think Campo di Marte is one of the first spots in Italy in which guards were seen patrolling with dogs, already in '96. When we bumped into them I decided to drop that yard for a while.

BEES— I remember a stairway we had to climb over diagonally.
ENS— Right on the side where we entered they had put a sticker that said "Area under Laser Surveillance", and the first time we saw it we asked ourselves what the fuck it meant, and then we understood it was just bullshit and so we continued going in from there. Anti-intrusion laser...something like that. Please. There wasn't shit there, we tested it once when we were drunk, and painted as usual.

SMART— Of the many yards, one of the most important was Lamucchi without a doubt, I painted there when I was still a kid. I was 14-15 years old, had no real means of transportation and that deposit was a 20 minute walk from my house. Dust from Milan would also go there, at the time he was going to University in Florence, he was about 18-20. Then there was Duke from Empoli. Duke is

Sketch session between local and American writers — *Chero*

much attention figuring it was from the street or it was one of us... Smart came over to tell me we should get out of there. I said "okay let me outline my shit", as Smart walked out past the

dead track the stakes got higher, we had to go at spitting distance of the deposit, where the guards were, to hit them. Everything got complicated when they

> CONTINUE ON PAGE 53

Ens–PR's crew — *Ens*

Outsiders
>

Reciprocal visit: America

Chero – PRs
>

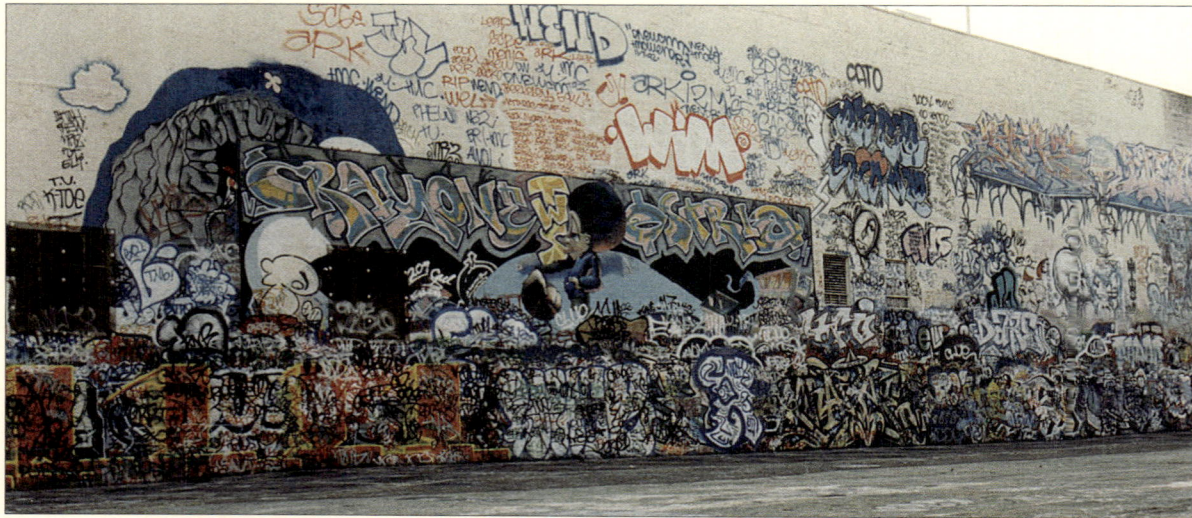

Psycho–city in San Francisco   — Chero

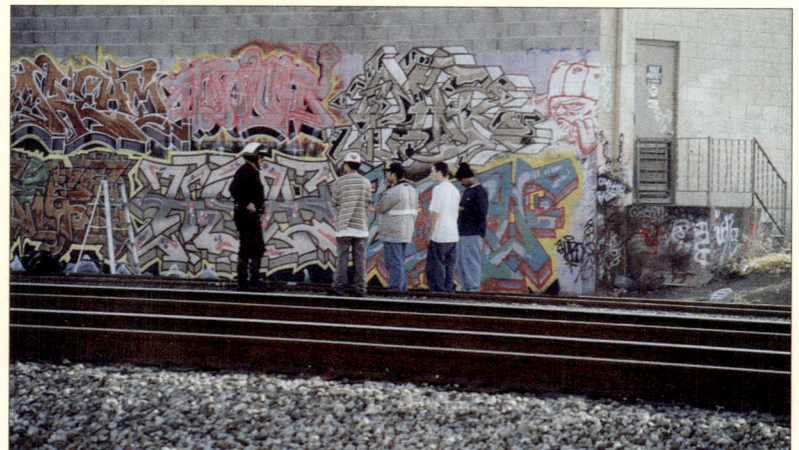

Dream and writers from San Francisco being stopped on the railway track line   — Chero

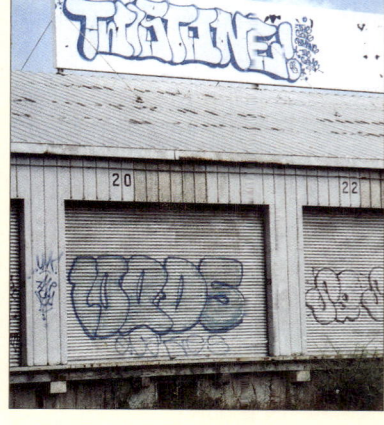

Lords crew flop and Twist, San Francisco   — Chero

In 1994 I moved to Chicago, as I had always wanted to try to live abroad and see what was happening on the other side of the pond. That time was mostly spent goin' to clubs and looking for graffiti. I was living in a sorta sketchy area, but I didn't care. I used to live somewhere near West Irving park and Broadway, close to the elevated and an old cemetery that was being used as a local hall of fame on either side. Many pieces were painted there, along with some gang graffiti. As I clearly remember on the street side of the wall, there was a huge "latin kings" with an eagle, but I would only understand more about it later in time. Since I had lots of free time I used to walk around, looking for graffiti or tryin' to hook up with people to go painting. I would get on the L train at the local station and travel all the different lines, looking for graff that I could eventually take a pic of. One day I was trying to get to a show at a local gallery, the show was on a local writer named Dzine, but as soon as I got on the bus I got off. I wanted to walk to the area hoping to catch pieces to photograph in the streets on my way there. Anyway, after walkin' for a long while, I realised how far away it was and walking there was definitely going to be a hike. So, I started to wander around, making my way to a nearby train track to take pix and check stuff out. To make a long story short, I ended up headin' West along Division Street and down towards downtown. Division is the street that would cross the Cabrini Green area of Chicago, and goin' through that area wasn't the safest thing to do, especially if you were white and didn't know your way around. Cabrini Green was considered one of the most, if not the most dangerous places in town (according to local sources). I'm still glad that I wasn't wearing my early Jordans that day! (been wearing those since day one, and yes, kids would stop me in the street for them!) So walkin' through the area, this little black girl who couldn't be older than 10, looked up at me and said "I'll kick your ass white boy" I was speechless, but I just kept on walkin', as I was worried more about my camera and film rolls than myself! After my wanderings and train rides, I would stop at a local Tower Records to check graff magazines for free, and hopefully, get to know people. Yes, I collected a good stack of mags over a period of four months, SP.ONE's Skills (love that mag to this very day), Graphic Violence, some euro mags that weren't available at that time in Italy, etc. On my way home, I would stop by my house, to check this sneaker spot called Tony Sports. I wasn't only checking the fresh kicks, but also looking at a piece on the side of the building by Reas, Wane and some other NY dudes. I was diggin' the

characters, they reminded me of some Hanna-Barbera cartoons I used to watch on TV when I was a kid. The colours, the style, and those details led me to believe that Reas was some sort of cartoonist, which I was able to confirm years later when I met him for the first time back in Italy. I got to Chicago in September, and it was now November. The city was getting cold as fuck, so, before goin' back home I decided to visit San Francisco as I had never been to California before. It was kind of a shock when I got there! I was expecting chicks on roller-skates and hot weather... NOT! It was chilly and grey, plus I was broke. Thanks to a friend that was living there, I had a place to stay for a short while, so I decided to work in a restaurant nearby the city's main intersection, which was Van Ness and Market Streets. One day after I got the job, I decided to check out the surroundings, you know, to see what the city had to offer. I stil clearly recall that day! I was flabbergasted! A combo of happiness and excitement, I could barely keep it all in! Walkin' around, I ended up being in SF's most famous graff spot, dubbed Psycho City. I recognised the place by some pieces that

were still up on it, and that I had previously seen in an Italian graff mag. There were pieces by Dream TDK (rip) Spie TMC, signs of past productions by TWS crew and characters done by Twist. Also, a piece by Loomit from Munich was still up on there. Meanwhile, on the other side of the street, there was the Franklin wall, with pieces by Giant AOT, Kept AWR, random bombings and an old production by Stockton's MPC crew. From that day, I was hooked! In between shifts I would stop there with a camera and rolls, and check the spot for new pieces and tags, mostly hoping to hook up with people. I eventually found out that hookin' up with people wasn't that easy. They had this thing goin' on, like they were ready for beef, simply frontin' on you, even if they didn't know who the fuck you were. I was there simply to paint and hang out, but again, the more I was running into people, the question was always the same... "whatchu write?" I was getting bored, so I stuck to myself for a while, checkin' Psycho City more randomly, and changin' the destination of my wanderings on a daily basis. Through a tattoo dude that was working in a local studio near my house, I was told

that there was this place called Coors building, and the guy explained to me what buses I needed to take to reach this destination. The next day, I was on my way there. Man, I took so many pix that day, but nobody was around It didn't matter though cause I knew the place, and I knew I was goin' to visit it again. After six months I was getting sick of simply working and checkin' graffiti, I wanted some action. I wanted to do something different. One night, on my way home from work, I saw these two dudes walkin' on the other side of the street, and I noticed that suddenly one of them pulled out a marker to catch a tag. I said to myself "Nah, I'm sick of trying to hook up with people" but then I thought "why not!" So I ran towards them, they saw me and they started to walk away faster. Then I kinda yelled at them "Hey, I'm not 5-o!" One of the dudes had a skateboard, and he was ready to hit me. So I went "Hey man, I'm not a cop! I write too!", keeping in mind that the whole thing was happening in one of the richest neighborhoods in SF, and the whole thing was getting more and more surreal! You know, the friendly approach, wasn't common at all. So,

on the road

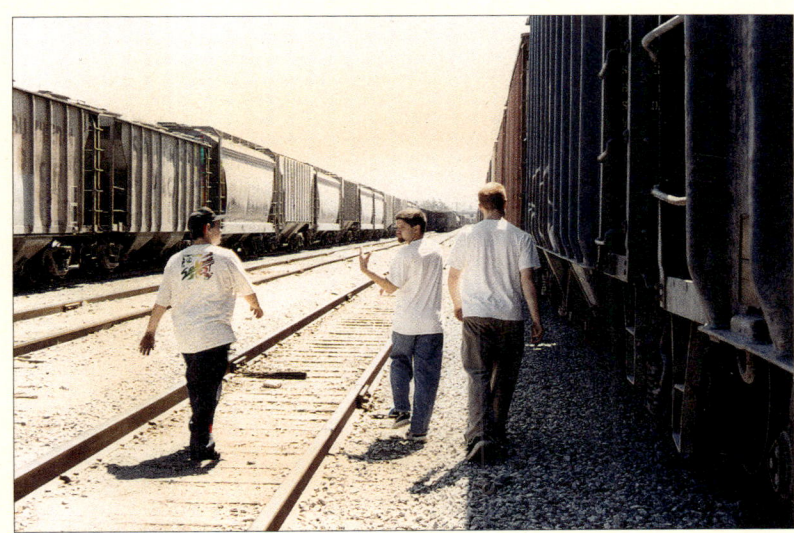

— Chero

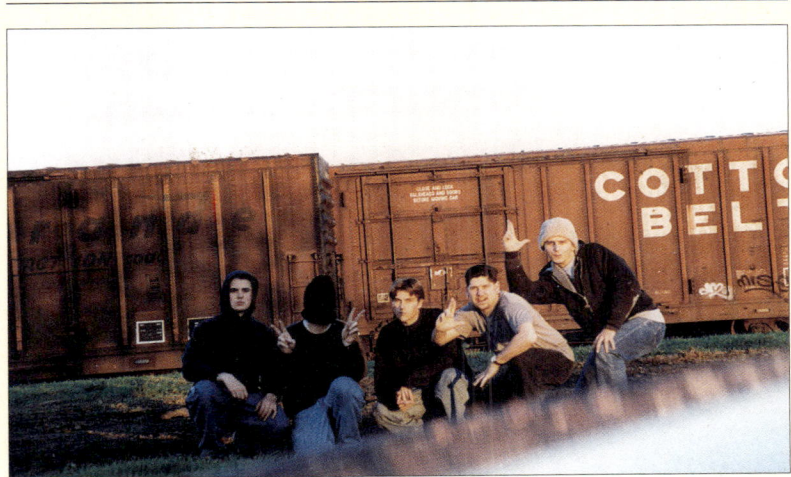

Chero and local writers among freight train yards

— Chero

I explained my situation to them, who I was and all that. They told me to call them the following week. From there I managed to paint a few freights somewhere between San Francisco and San José. Quake and Defie (these were their street aliases) also brought me to Emeryvile, Albany, Novato Spillway and the legendary Oakland tracks. Oakland tracks was a place that I used to visit almost once a week. I used to go there, check out what was being done in the East bay. I liked it a lot. One time as I was walking down the tracks, I ran into a group of little Mexican kids, and they simply said "Hey, I wouldn't walk any further if I were you, there is a dead body over there!" I was like "What!"; "Yes man, it's true." I stood there for a minute, then I thought "Fuck it! It's my day off!" So I kept walking, took some pix and came back. Rumours I heard afterwards did confirm that a body was actually found in between the tracks. I still remember when I was with Defie one day, we went to check out some other dudes that were painting along the line in Oakland. On the other side of the tracks, there was Dream TDK (RIP) finishing his piece on the famous "Tax Dollars Kills"

production. I was looking at him from far away, then suddenly the cops showed up and rolled on him. I have pix from that day. With time I met Dean of TME, he was half Italian and naturally we bonded because of that; years later he came to Florence on his honeymoon, a classic for Americans... except he was interested in bombing trains and we took him to do an end-to-end. I still have that photo hanging at home!

When I started getting to know people, on one of the last days at Psycho City I got arrested. Actually we all got arrested, someone even has a picture of it. A group of English guys photographed us sitting along the wall that was under the enormous piece by Giant, cops in front of us and all. I never painted much while I was there though, just a couple of walls and freight trains cause I was working two jobs. Smart would send me photos of the trains that in the meantime had been painted and were starting to circulate in Florence. For a while I lived in a sort-of guest house, half-starving cause I would only eat once a day. One time a guy from New York that was also staying there, another character, found a phone

card and explained to me the codes to me. I started calling everyone and their grandma, in the evening I would phone Smart, my folks, neighbourhood friends I had grown up with, at least I was taking advantage of the card and kept in contact with Florence.

I also remember Giant of AOT, the tattooist, who did the Bombing America pieces, he's from Alberquerque in Mexico and at the time was doing the graphics of *Think Skateboard*. Sick stuff ... he was on the rise. He had also lived in Chicago and I had stayed there before coming to California. In Chicago I had witnessed the strong presence of gangs, and was relieved when I got to San Francisco, safe and sound after such experiences. It was tense. If you crossed your arms a certain way it meant you were a member of a certain gang, either Folks or People, and you could wear your baseball hat backwards but in any other way it carried a whole other meaning. Hand gestures are part of a street code that is dead serious out there, no kidding around or imitating a pitch fork. You don't know these things when you get there, but in Chicago you learn real quick. I remember I spent my days at Tower Records because it imported a load of graff magazines like *Can Control*, one of the best mags of all time in my opinion. Definitely it was a 360° type thing, I wanted to check all the aspects of graffiti. After a while, my attention focused on stickers and mops. Stickers because a handful of kids were using random images, ripping them off magazines and gluing them on adhesive paper. They would later put their tags up on them and stick 'em up either around the city or in blackbooks. I liked the idea so much, that I brought it back to Florence, and for a while I did a series of porno ones. I remember I was makin' them after work and I would put them up around the city at night, while takin' a walk with Smart, Ens or other random friends. Back in SF I was also fascinated by mops, I have a soft spot for the so called "tools of the trade", the whole DIY approach of makin' your own markers, paint and whatever else you needed to get up. At that time I couldn't understand what type of marker writers were using to do tags with. It was such a cool, crisp, clean line, and I knew I wanted one too. The problem being, that I didn't know what they were using! What were they called? The answer came shortly thereafter. A dude from Oakland that I had met previously at Psycho City, schooled me about them. He explained that what I was after were the so-called Mops and those were nothing but shoe polish bottles, drained of the original content and filled with ink, mostly Marsh ink. There were some homemade colours too, such as silver. KR from New York was around at that time, so he was probably tagging around with his trademark Krink already, his homemade ink. He did have a lot of tags with silver pens and throw-ups, mostly on the Soma area of the city and along rail tracks. Twist was using them all over the place, rockin' characters too. I also remember Grey and

Geso using them. I bumped into Grey one day, as I was walking by the missior housing projects with Kocis, an acquaintance of mine that also knew him. At first I thought they were gonna fight but they were just fuckin' around. At the time, he looked like a squat type guy, you know, piercings and ragged clothes. I knew of him through his works that I had seen at a show called Completely Gore at a local gallery. He was doing graffiti but was also doing those paintings of cats, made with bucket paint, that were pretty cool in my book. There were a bunch of outta towners in SF at that time, and they were keeping themselves busy in the streets. Kids like Felon, with both letters and characters, Mr.Element, Grey, Geso, Twist, Kept and Bles AWR. Bles was doing a bunch of cool pieces, Jase, BA, the occasional Dug TMF and throw-ups by Gian. This dude, Orfn, was up even if he had quited for a while. I still remember the night that I got arrested inside the Duboce tunnel, he had the side of a rail track tagged for the whole length of the tunnel! I heard it took him three nights! When I got back to Florence I had suitcases full of markers, especially the fat, 2 inch-thick ones. Universes and all that good stuff! Markers that in America were used for posters but that in Italy weren't available. I got a deal through an Oakland writer, Poem TDK. He was doin' a magazine at that time, and was advertising those in the pages of it. So before my departure, I got a whole bunch as I knew that my friends were gonna like them back home. Once home, I started selling this stuff, word got around and they were calling me from Bologna and Rome. When, in 1996, I went to the In Linea jam in Bologna, Ciufs-SPA wanted one Mop, that he traded me six Beltons for one marker! A friend in Rome also wanted one and a few days later he received it, Rome heads started to call me on a daily basis.

While I was still living in San Francisco, one of the other things I was after were the so called "Meanstreaks". I looked for months but it was such a loosing battle. I would go to any art supplies store and they'd say "No, we don't carry them, it's a graffiti tool, nope ain't got 'em." Chance had it that when I got back to Florence, I would score an old, big, untouched stash of them, while rackin' paint with Smart. That day was somehow unreal. We entered the store, and like many times before we would use the same strategy. I would keep the lady busy and Smart would grab the cans. I kinda felt sorry for the woman cause she was actually ok, she had taken a liking to us. So while I'm talking to her, Smart nods at me from behind. That was the sign that he was loaded, so with a smile on my face, I asked Smart if he had found the color he was after. Walkin' out the messy little narrow corridor, he would say "NO!" So I turned me head in order to leave the shop. But halfway down the corridor and near the desk, a pile of dusty old boxes with the word Smart on it catches my attention. I was like "Wait a minute! I know that logo!" So I stopped,

> CONTINUES ON PAGE 348

Termini Station

Stazione Termini is a large hub, a node of the city in which the majority of inner and outer city transportation infrastructures meet. For this reason, in a European capital like Rome that has channelled the Writing phenomenon primarily onto dynamic targets such as trains and buses, Termini station in the 90's represented a synthesis of the local scene's productions. In that period the presence of writers was evident in the entire area of the station, which not only hosts the national trains of the Ferrovie dello Stato but also those of the local Casilina line as well as the A and B lines of the subway, which intersect exclusively at the stop of Termini. For the writers in Rome the station was therefore a densely trafficked urban niche that offered a panoramic view of the national train-bombing scene, or at least of that part of the movement that was particularly inclined to hitting long-distance trains. Pieces by Rok, Fra32, Blef, Dafne, Sherif and PDB arrived at the first platforms of Termini on a daily basis, painted on the sides of Intercity carriages. On the other hand the tracks that lead to the Roman hinterlands and those of the suburban lines – connecting the city to the neighbouring areas of the periphery – were targeted by local crews such as PAC, who used them as a training ground before painting the subway. The fact the two main subway lines of the city also happen to meet in Termini station made the quantity of pieces even

PIAZZALE
sorting area for
surface public
transportation

HALL
Termini Station
ticket counter
and shopping
area

TOWER
administrative
offices of the
FS Railway

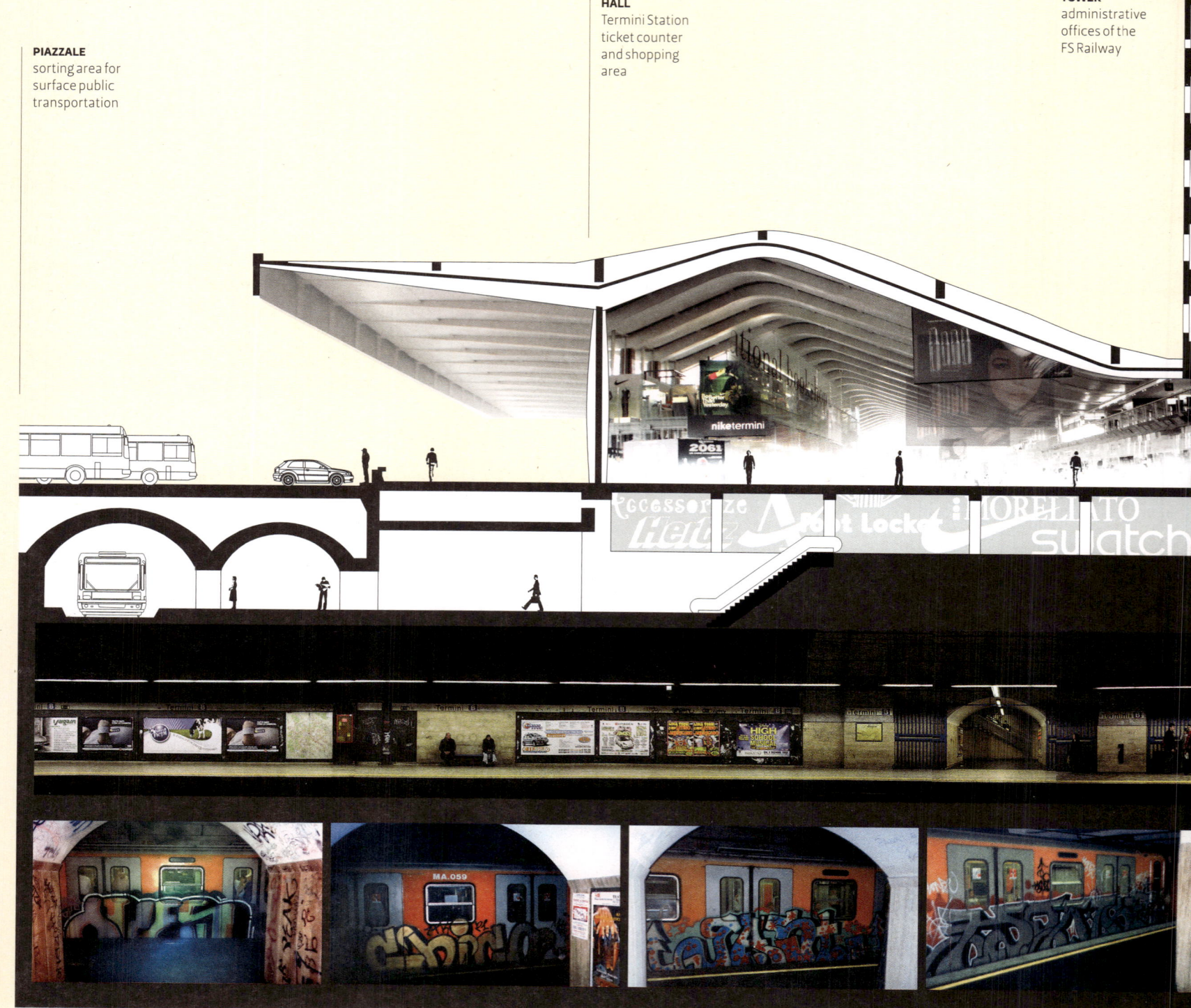

higher, between the trains on the surface and the cars of the A and B lines underneath. At this subway stop, the impact with the painted cars of the A line is particularly traumatic: once you descend the stairs you're in a congested, narrow section of the tunnel. To access the platform you cross a series of arches that channel passengers directly to the mouth of the trains, all saturated with tags and pieces. On the B line on the other hand, the bays of the tunnel roof present a more extended curve radius, and the grey and blue subway cars enter a more spacious and luminous environment, that becomes a frame for the moving pieces. The aesthetic of Termini during the 90's was dominated by two counter-phenomena of equally parasitic nature: one determined by the tradition of Writing on trains, the other tied to the dynamics of promotional advertisement. Termini station, with its evocative architecture, has always expressed strong communicative potential, to the extent that it became a privileged channel; every possible interstice has been turned into useful space for hosting advertising messages, whether it be on the slender pillars sustaining the primary facade, or the curvilinear beams of the roof, to the more recent flat screens along the rail platforms. Graffiti on trains is thus only one of the numerous, uncontrolled and undisciplined semantic layers that have stratified for over a decade on Termini station's hypertext

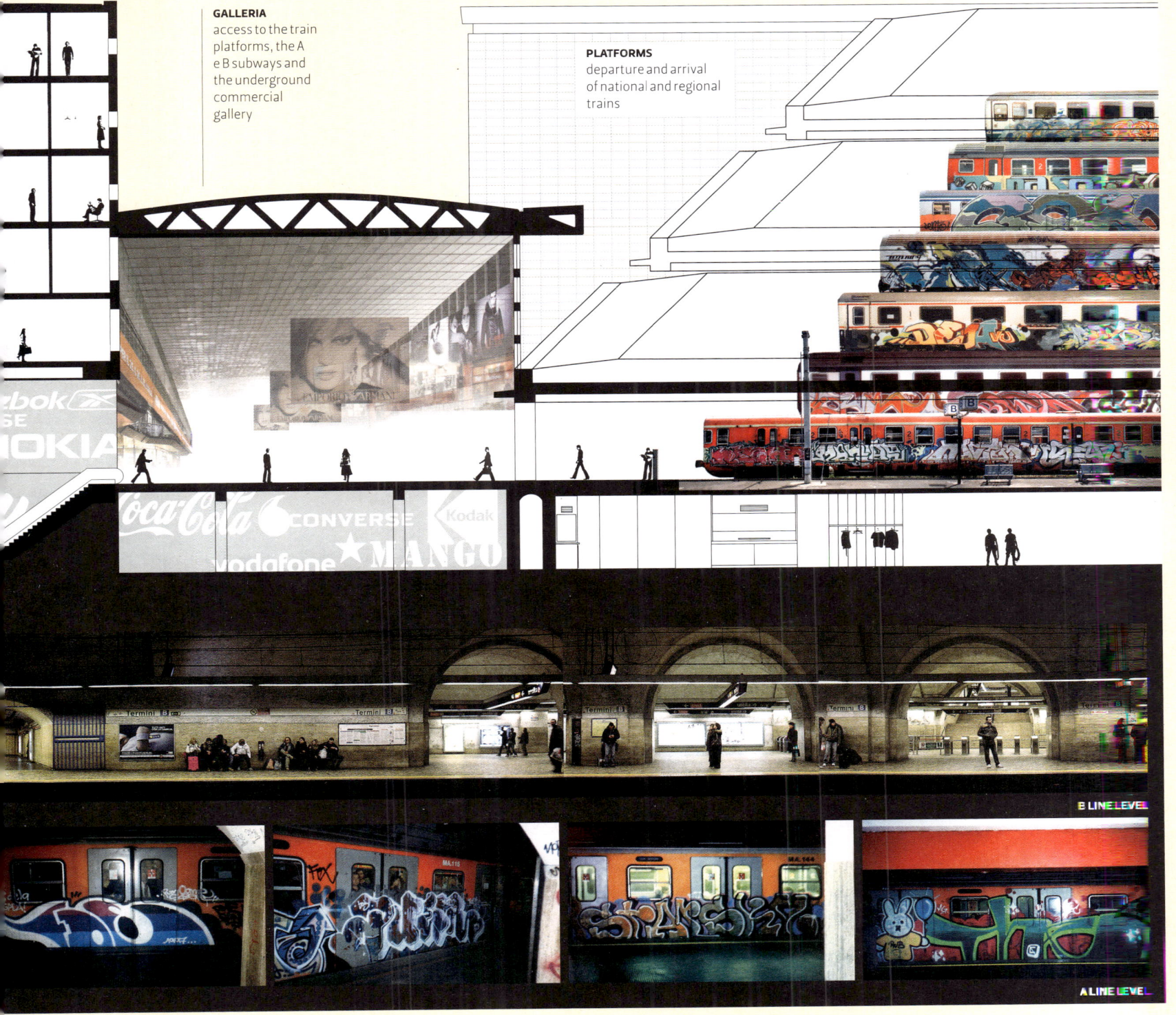

GALLERIA
access to the train platforms, the A e B subways and the underground commercial gallery

PLATFORMS
departure and arrival of national and regional trains

B LINE LEVEL

A LINE LEVEL

A Roman cadavre exquise

I met NSB crew thanks to Manjar in the summer of '94, after I had my own crew (TDM) for a few years and had been painting in Rome's Monteverde neighborhood. I saw tags by Manjar, Tekne, and Peggio (who later became Quero) and was captivated by them because I was sure they were from my neighborhood. I met Manjar for the first time at the "Festa dell'Unità" at Castel Sant'Angelo, he was painting a panel to liven up one of the stands. We hit it off immediately and the next day we went painting together: back then we mainly went into the train tunnels. We'd enter through Ponte Bianco, above Trastevere, and walk for an hour or two until we found the right spot and the

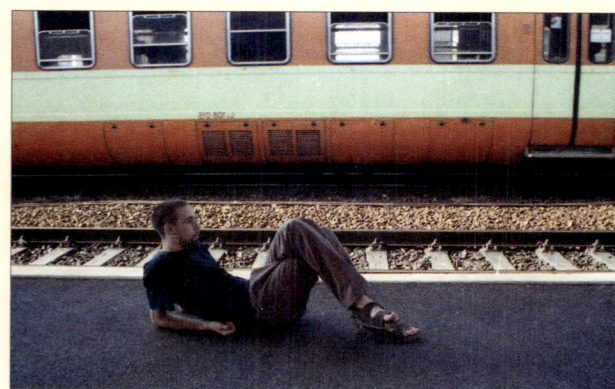
Manjar waiting for the train   — Washe

the entire afternoon, listening to Jazz, The Roots, US3, and Digable Planets. I make a point of mentioning this because it was all one and the same: Roman bread smeared with manjar, straight from Chile (Manjar's country of origin); pasta with tomato sauce, tuna, and cream; sketches; canvases; and a passion for projects. I recall those moments as the most creative in my life, at least in terms of graffiti.

We went to paint my first train at the Ostiense yard behind the Piramide subway station. I don't know why we were initially attracted to painting trains instead of subway cars. That first night we painted a Regional train with huge orange doors, I remember it took me quite a while, whereas Manjar, who had more experi-

it belonged to us. After painting we'd always go get a croissant in Testaccio and then go home. The next day, some of us went to high school, some of us would go to college and whatnot...

We painted at Ostiense with lots of friends, Italian and foreign; we rarely got chased because the yard was huge and open, so it was easy to keep in check. We mainly painted Intercity trains. From Via Marco Polo and the bridge over Via Cristoforo Colombo, we could check below if there were any trains and what the situation was like in order to size things up before going in.

MANJAR— Before we started painting trains, they were already a passion for some of us. Peggio was the most informed, the real train buff amongst us. In time, we accumulated a real knowledge on the subject. In fact, when we began painting trains later it was normal for us to call them by their proper names. We'd make mental notes: "Those model cars are found in this yard, that other model is found in that yard, and these other models... Damn, they never park them!" The Rome Ostiense yard was brimming with UIC-X cars: they were wine red with horizontal grey stripes that brought to mind an irresistible Adidas tracksuit. We'd peer over the bridge into the yard to get a panoramic view of the cars and check out the situation so we could surprise the trains in their sleep.

PEGGIO— Calling them "UIC-X" cars instead of "the red ones with stripes" made us feel like train aficionados... it may seem strange but apart from the obvious need to avoid the yard guards, we considered ourselves part of the family of trainmen, railroaders, and transit workers. Obviously, our job was very different from theirs. We even used to say "hi" to the trainmen back in the day when graffiti wasn't that widespread, when it was considered a marginal problem, when we were still considered rare.

MANJAR— The train yard is a world in itself, especially FS yards. Most of the time, they're inhabited by bums, vagabonds, whores, and writers. Occasionally, all at the same time! If you're not aware of this, as we weren't the first time, you end up scaring each other and running in opposite directions. But

at the Rome Tuscolana yard, we even ended up painting for an audience- the homeless, tramps and prostitutes were our nocturnal spectators.

PEGGIO— Jumping a fence to get into a yard or a station that's in disuse, allowed us to cross the line between our regular world of home, family, and school and the world living behind, under, or beyond a city. This gave us a profoundly different view of the urban landscape - on a physical and humane level - compared to other kids our age. Back then, these things weren't clear to me and maybe I wouldn't even have cared about them... all I cared about was painting!

WASHE— Wandering around the city with other kids wasn't the same thing: looking at a wall or a space, trying to find yours allows you to experience the world and your city as if it were a giant canvas. The mind, the colour, the sketches, the desire never quit, it didn't matter if it was a tunnel, a train, a wall, or a garbage truck!

TEKNE— We were young explorers in search of adventure. The

city became our nocturnal playground and yards were the most amazing roller coasters. After a night out, after a Pastaman flava feast, after smoking a joint in front of the wall, there was always something else, trains were like the icing on the cake.

MANJAR— Back in the day, we were really proud of the fact that once in a while we'd wait in the Ostiense yard for the pilgrim train heading to Lourdes the next day. The sight of a bombed train full of Red Cross nurses and infirm devotees filled us with excitement. The other trains went everywhere, mainly along the Rome-Pisa-Genoa line, some went all the way to France. All in all, that yard was a blast, even if it became a hot spot specifically for that reason. When trouble was brewing in the subway, it was best to let things settle down so FS yards were like a safety valve for everyone. But by 1994-1996 all of the yards in Rome were busy, both subway and FS yards. Writers from all over Europe came here to paint. Trains circulated for years without ever being buffed, it was heaven, the Eldorado of writers. I remember something BDB, a

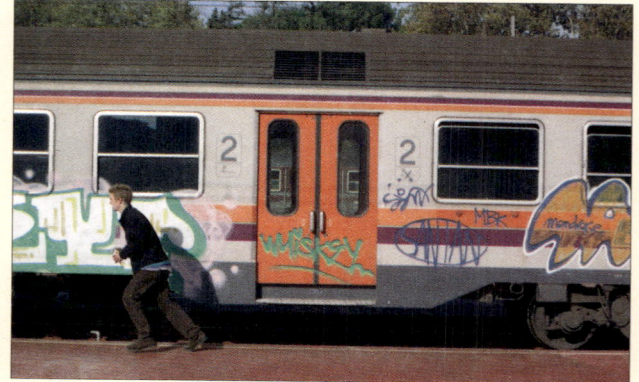
NSB stickers on the engine car   — Washe

right atmosphere, and we'd use our silver spray paint, the only colour that worked on those run-down walls, this allowed us to work on the outline from the start. Intercity and freight trains would pass by making deafening noises, and we'd be there, crouched down, watching them pass, almost in awe. We painted in the tunnels continuously for a few months, and in general we never stopped (it was like an obligatory gathering, like taking a break together), occasionally passing by "Villaggio Globale, Ex-Mattatoio", which at the time was home to some of the most colourful pieces and murals.

– SKETCHES AND OSTIENSE

At the time, Tekne was studying in Philadelphia, and since me and Manjar lived close to each other, unlike Quero, the two of us began to hang out constantly. And by constantly I mean that we'd hang out every day at my house or his and we would draw

ence, was faster. I filled in and added details to my piece very slowly with Marabu spray paint, which was a staple back then... The only way to access the yard was through a side street, before going in we sat in the grass and scoured the area, then we climbed over a low fence to get in. The fence would always be in the way when we tried to take pictures the next day, because by day we couldn't jump it so we had to take pictures from outside. From then on we painted a couple of times a week, in the same yard, trains became my passion, my favourite hobby, and Ostiense was like my training school. Tekne would come back in the summer and we'd all go out together with Quero who'd hang up his little posters on the trains, a predecessor of street art. After a while, Chaso joined us so we had a solid crew. Often, friends would come along to act as lookouts, or just for the fun of hanging out together. Ostiense was our kingdom, we felt

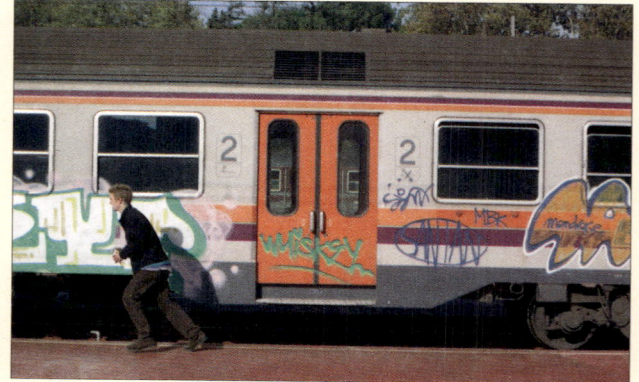
Washe during the mid-day show   — Washe

Dealing with foreigners

writer from Paris, said when he first went into the Roman subway yard in '96: "Merde! C'est New York!". Space was becoming scarce on subway cars, and in the city too.

PEGGIO— When we first started we were pretty spontaneous... we just liked doing graffiti, period. Crew rivalries, keeping spots secret, all this stuff came later. Maybe it's all part of the game.

MANJAR— NSB crew was in love with FS trains. Washe, Tekne, Peggio, Chaso, Santo, and Manjar, we were in our own fucking world: the city's isolated crew. We didn't care about Hip Hop and its rigid behavioral codes that others took too seriously. We didn't identify with it. All that mattered was our desire to paint on the streets, the rebel instinct that was part of it, and the new world that was revealed to us in doing this. We didn't paint pieces to photograph them and send them to fanzines. Years later I wrote a phrase on a wall in another city that more or less said: "Dreams are handmade without permission" That's the whole point. All we wanted was to paint, and we had no intention of asking anyone for permission. My real friends came from that period, as did some real enemies.

PEGGIO— Friendship was the base of everything. Many years after that era, we had a reunion: a simple gathering at night near a wall on the Rome-Fiumicino line. That night made it clear to me that what I had missed most was spending nights with those friends. Like mushroom hunting or fishing. That's it: something you simply do with people you like. Few words, hands soiled with grease and paint, going home at dawn, and having enjoyed the night. You might never tell anybody about it, for no reason, so it'll be a memory for you and those who were there.

WASHE— We all liked each other so much that it was a pleasure to allow new guests into our yard, and paint on our trains. It was an immense pleasure to share our passion with others, being open rather than closed, in anticipation of a single, swift motion.

TEKNE— Painting connected us not only as brothers but also as accomplices. Taking over unauthorised spaces was our mission and bringing them to life was

our lifeblood. We rarely went out to destroy because creating was much more gratifying. So we left an ephemeral mark that traveled to places we could not reach yet.

WASHE— First off, painting is a state of being. That doesn't mean nothing else existed back then, but trains and spray paint were all that mattered. We had long discussions, even with our families, drinking tea, trying to make them understand what it meant to us, but it was difficult, like it always is, to explain something that inexplicably comes from the heart. It went as far as the hand and the finger.

MANJAR— One night it was raining and the train was drenched. The spray paint wouldn't stick, it just dripped off with the rain. But we didn't want to leave empty-handed so we tore off the curtains in the train car and wiped down the whole side of the car. Now we could paint! Fuck yeah! I'm telling you, we were craving, hungry like wolves.

TEKNE— I recall the sleepy face of a gypsy who opened the train window while I was doing my outline on the car; in order to finish that piece I had to be immensely patient and diplomatic because that car was a temporary dormitory for them. We each experienced the train in a different way, but none of us bought tickets.

WASHE— The trains lived with us, they became a part of us and our colours. Manjar started doing pieces without filling them in, he'd leave the train's colour as the filling. Each part of the train belonged to us, from the moment we took possession of it in the dark yard. The signs indicating the destination, the small stairway leading up top, the sections of the train we'd hide in or in which we'd act like jackasses, a nocturnal journey while standing still.

MANJAR— When painting at night started to become predictable, we began painting at midday, during the railroaders' lunch break. We'd give ourselves 10 to 15 minutes at most. We called it the Midday Show. Insatiable! Unstoppable! This is the only way to paint, and other writers know it. This is real 'style'. "We are unstoppable! We are uncatchable!" like

> CONTINUES ON PAGE 348

Hiom

One of the first spots in which I painted was the deposit of Tuscolana station, a kind of right-angled triangle delimited by the tracks that begin there and take towards the stations of Tiburtina and Casilina. It must have had a dozen platforms, mostly in disuse or occupied by service convoys like the engine wagon, random machinery and various cars for the maintenance of the tracks and trash train. Only in the evening towards a certain hour would the regional train arrive, which we usually called 4-6-4, or if we were lucky, even a long distance train. To get in you had to take a small one-way street that zig-zagged between the railway and the Roman aqueduct. From there you took a small private street of the FS and you would easily enter the deposit from a gate whose lock was busted. We also befriended the Romanian community that lived in the trash train and the various abandoned buildings of the FS. Because we were so young we would primarily paint on the weekends, when they would get together to party and drink. Their parties were more or less their main socialising event: after a week spent working, on Saturdays they would each put in some cash, buy all the alcohol they could, and meet up; just like 'normal' people go to pubs, they were out in the open, on the platforms or in some train car dressed up as if it were a home, depending on the weather. These were pretty conspicuous and loud parties, one time they even lit a fire on the railway platform, but even if the service locomotive of the FS often passed, the railway police were never to be seen. Our first encounters with them did not go particularly well. Actually, a couple of times, scared by the shouting coming from the deposit, we even ran away cause there were way more of them than us. Then one time, I don't remember in what occasion, maybe it was the birthday party of one of them, the first close encounter took place. Some of them came out from the convoy they were in, and asked us what we were doing, so we answered we were writing our names on the train and I don't really know why, but it seemed like a good idea to them as well

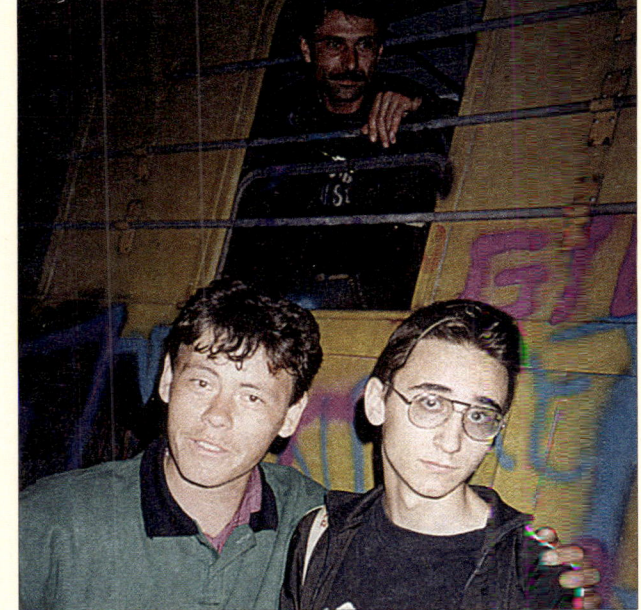

Gil, Giulian and Hiom feeling uneasy   —Hiom

and so they stopped to talk to us. Slowly the other components of the community also approached to come see what the fuck we were up to. They were all dressed in those clothes you only see at Mas convenience store, and every time you go in there you ask yourself who the hell would ever buy them. They were pretty young, between 19 and 40 years old, and some were actually kind of cool. And so, after having dedicated the piece to them, we left these guys our spray cans with the last drops of paint so they could also write their names. The next day, when we returned to the station to take photos, other than the pieces we had done, there was an entire car trashed with the wobbly names they had written with our cans. The only names I can still remember are Gil and Giulian Mindresti or something like that. Those two were kind of the 'bosses' there, or perhaps simply those that acted like it, and they had taken a liking to us. Gil in particular 'protected' us, he wanted to be called Giuliano Celentano and said he was the brother of Adriano Celentano; I remember him as enormous, and maybe the fact that in the middle of winter he would come out in sandals and a wife-beater made him even more fearsome in our eyes. Whenever somebody got too cocky or tried to grab the spray cans from our hands he would send them away. He always asked us to write his name next to our pieces and then bring him the photo the week

later, he would then send it to his relatives at home. Something about taking pictures together to then send them to family seemed to be particularly appreciated by the inhabitants of the deposit. Many group photos were published on the ending pages of *Maccaroni* fanzine, where they would make collages of screwed up photos, all distorted or modified. All the others, who knows, maybe they're in Romania now. This went on for various months, perhaps even over a year, until one day we read on the paper that there had been a series of arrests in the deposit of Tuscolana station following a shooting. When we went back to the deposit the gate had been closed with a chain, we looked from the outside for a bit, and then climbed over it. Nobody was there. We did the train and then left without having anyone to talk to before getting back home. Other people would later inhabit that deposit, mostly from Albania, hostile towards us because in their opinion our presence attracted the guards. They weren't totally wrong actually. Some time they ran after us with sticks, another time one guy shows up while we're painting, he gets all aggressive and takes out a blade, another time two of them held Fonzie and Trota hostage inside a train car with God knows what intentions (some say to rape them) until Fonzie took hold of the situation, and most importantly, bartered Trota's photo camera for their release.

Alternative tentacles

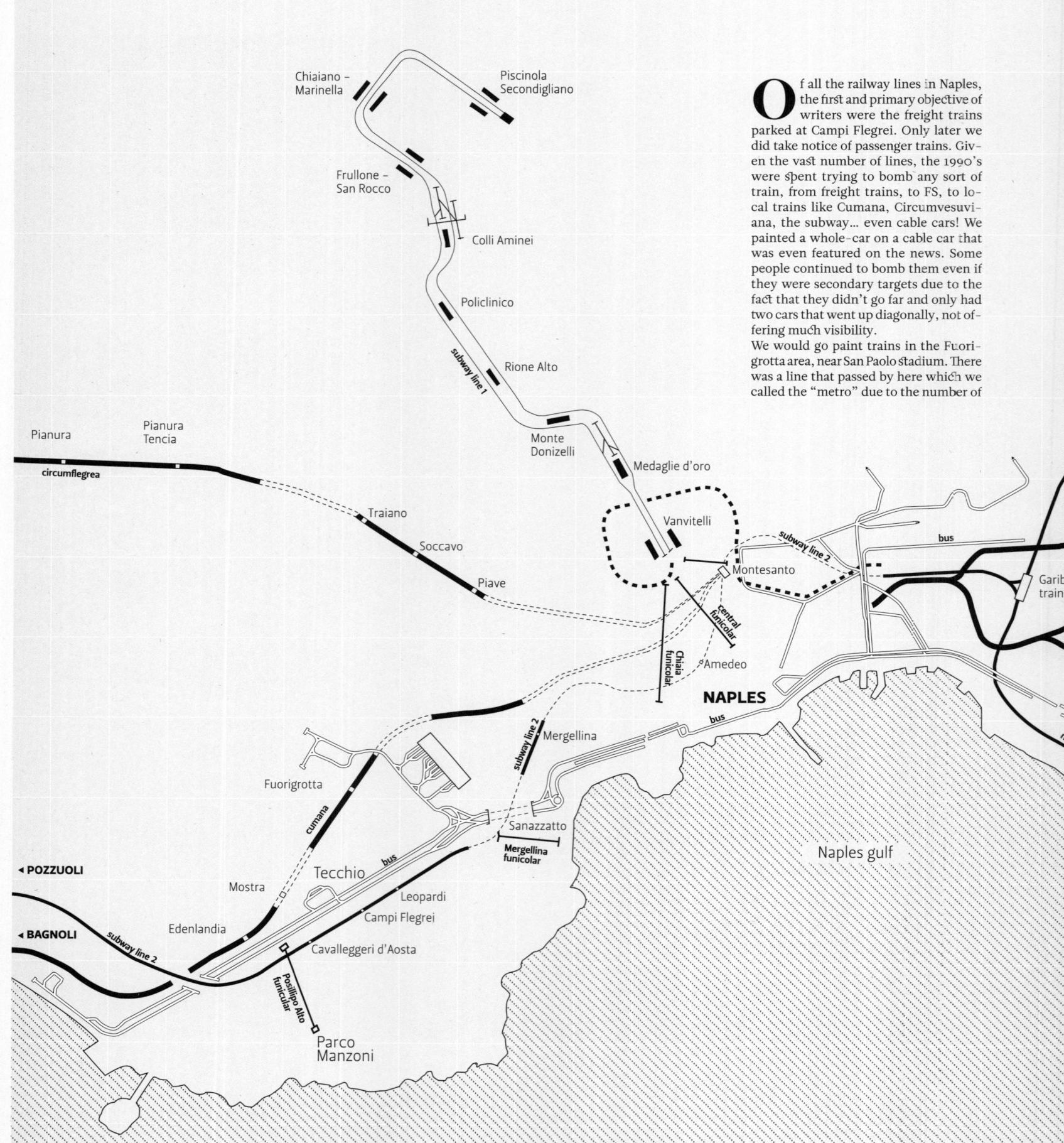

Of all the railway lines in Naples, the first and primary objective of writers were the freight trains parked at Campi Flegrei. Only later we did take notice of passenger trains. Given the vast number of lines, the 1990's were spent trying to bomb any sort of train, from freight trains, to FS, to local trains like Cumana, Circumvesuviana, the subway... even cable cars! We painted a whole-car on a cable car that was even featured on the news. Some people continued to bomb them even if they were secondary targets due to the fact that they didn't go far and only had two cars that went up diagonally, not offering much visibility.

We would go paint trains in the Fuorigrotta area, near San Paolo stadium. There was a line that passed by here which we called the "metro" due to the number of

Chiaiano –
Marinella

Piscinola
Secondigliano

Frullone –
San Rocco

Colli Aminei

Policlinico

subway line 1

Rione Alto

Monte
Donizelli

Medaglie d'oro

Vanvitelli

Montesanto

subway line 2

bus

Gariba
train s

Pianura

Pianura
Tencia

circumflegrea

Traiano

Soccavo

Piave

central
funicolar

Chiaia
funicolar

Amedeo

NAPLES

bus

◄ POZZUOLI

subway line 2

Mergellina

Fuorigrotta

Cumana

Sanazzatto

Mergellina
funicolar

Naples gulf

bus

Tecchio

Mostra

Leopardi

Campi Flegrei

◄ BAGNOLI

subway line 2

Edenlandia

Cavalleggeri d'Aosta

Posillipo Alto
funicolar

nat

Parco
Manzoni

stations it stopped at, but in reality it was like an FS train, the cars were the same as state trains. It was called the "metro" because it passed through the main areas. Later, a real subway was created from Piazza Dante all the way to Scampia, Secondigliano, and into more outlying areas. At times we would go paint on Sundays when the Naples football team played home games. Back then, the team was part of the A series, which meant the entire city was at the football field or glued to a radio, including security guards. So while the game was going on, amidst the chaos in the bleachers and people fixated on the game, Fuorigrotta became a sort of open-field for painting anything. The first pieces were painted on the Pozzuoli-Gianturco train line by Polo and Zemi. Most of the pieces were simple, monochromatic. The only colours available

were found in local paint shops. I recall Polo's top-to-bottom piece on four cars with blockbuster silver letters outlined in black. Those trains were published in AL and were quite a shock to many because Polo had painted the letters on separate cars, the "P" on the first car, the "O" on the second, and so on. It made quite an impression at the station. Contemporaneously, the Cumana lines, which went from Montesanto to Licola and Torregaveta, were also bombed. Cumana is one of the many urban lines with an undefined identity, a mix between a subway and a local train, but with the peculiarity of always running above ground toward the sea; in some ways it's like the Lido line in Rome, which always runs above ground, but the Cumana cars are red, grey, and blue. It's not the only aboveground train though: there's also

line 2, which goes above ground after Garibaldi and Montesanto, while crossing Campi Flegrei.
In time, attention was shifted mainly to the Cumana line. It was easy to paint, I often went with Paradiso and Dolce. Given the density of graffiti on this line, this is where the city made its first preventive attempts. They tried anti-graffiti coating and a series of other initiatives that were of no use. Before the coating came about, there were adhesive advertisements on trains, including the legendary Kimbo ad on line 2. With these adhesive ads, we noticed that our pieces were easier to clean so we began a series of crossings and reinterpretations of the Kimbo logo. Unlike the Cumana line, we had to be more careful painting line 2 because its yard was always guarded by the railway police. This surveillance was unusual in

a lawless place like Naples, but it was due to the fact that junkies would go there to steal copper. They would enter the yard, strip the rubber-coated cables, steal the copper wires, and resell them for money! When the railway company noticed, they stationed railway police in Cavallegeri, which was the biggest and most-targeted yard. The police were constantly on guard, mainly in search of thieves. In order to get in, we had made a hole in the metal fence with pincers, so they never even noticed. When they did see us it was trouble, every position in the yard was stressful for us and them. Naturally, if we were caught the first thing we did was pull out our spray cans so they could see we weren't stealing and were unarmed. This is how it works in Naples, when something happens, one always imagines the worst

POMIGLIANO
NOLA
BAIANO

circumvesuviana

S. ANASTASIA
POGGIOMATTINO
SARNO

circumvesuviana

SAN GIORGIO
A CREMANO

256
P. Vittorio
Emanuele II

bus

PORTICI

P. Sebastiano Poli

Palazzo Reale

P. San Ciro   P. Trieste

circumvesuviana

ERCOLANO

POMPEI
SORRENTO
POGGIOMARINO

bus

TORRE DEL
GRECO

national railways

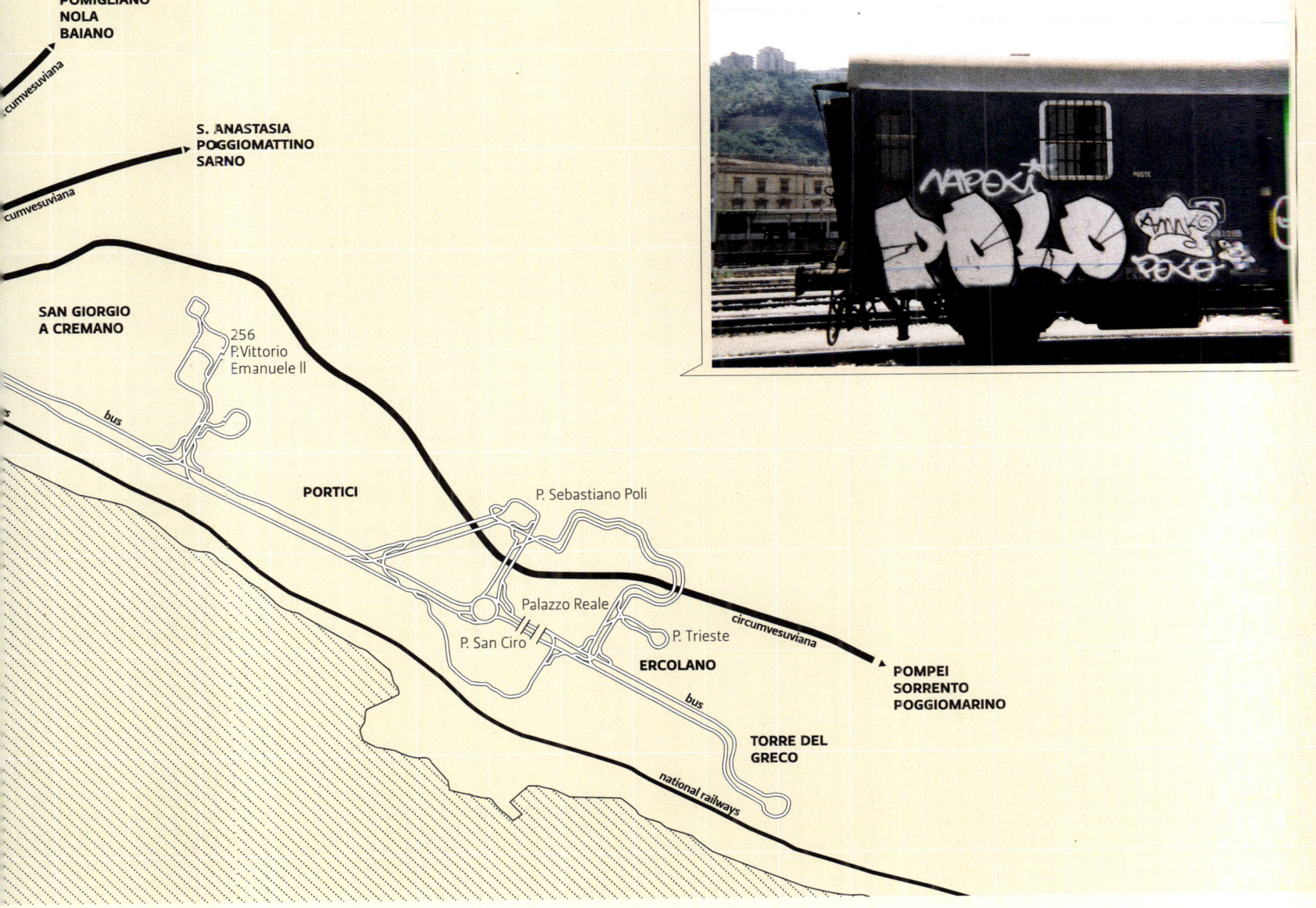

Circumvesuviana approach
>

Ultra

Kaf
>

One writer who radically changed the style of painting in Naples was Ultra, a Neapolitan guy who had immigrated to Dortmund years ago. Since he lived in one of the most devastated cities in Europe, he exported this obsession for bombing streets and trains. In Naples, we started noticing the tag "Ultra", and realised it was too stylish to belong to a football fan. Naples' Ultras (hooligans) wrote their name everywhere, but with a specific calligraphy and a precise style of their own.

There were also some anarchists and metropolitan poets who were active on the streets of the historic center, but we immediately recognised "Ultra" as a tag. We painted the Circumvesuviana for the first time with him since he'd already done it alone. It was then that we learned what bombing was. Circumvesuviana is a private line that starts at Central Station and stops in towns around the Vesuvius, all the way to Sorrento, in the opposite direction of Sarno. In many ways it's a completely different sort of line, even its cars are particular, they're ad hoc; their tracks are different from subway or FS trains and only allow certain cars to run on them. The cars have limited space upon which to paint because they are lower, but their colour scheme attracted many writers since they were completely white with red doors only. Upon going inside and watching Ultra, we quickly understood the Dortmund mentality: while we were still painting the first car, he had already done twelve! He repeatedly did tags and throw-ups everywhere... killing it, as we say here.

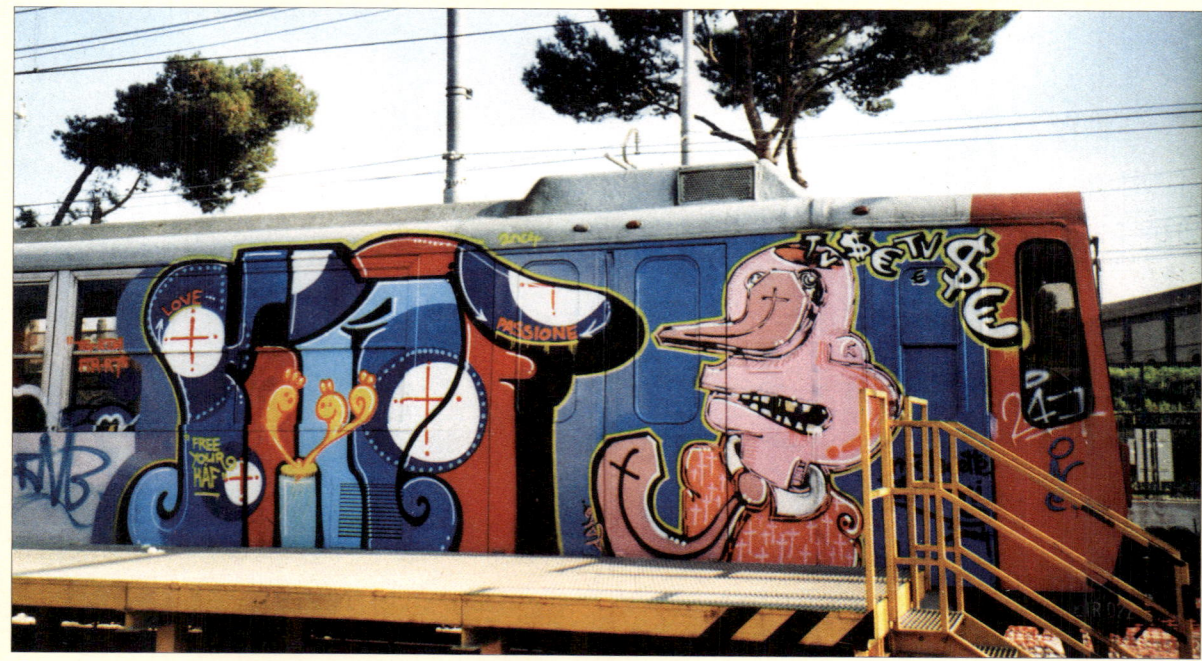

Cyop & Kaf – KTM

– Kaf

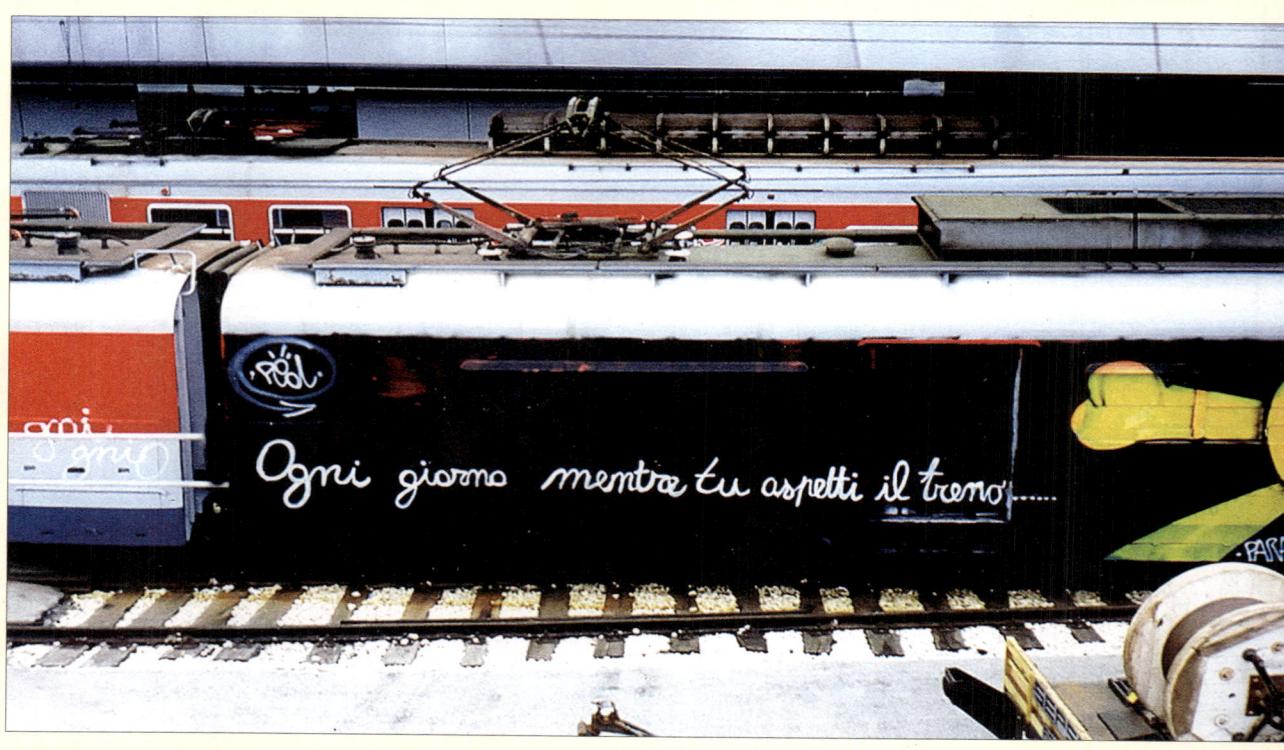

Whole-car by Paradiso and Dolce against capital punishment

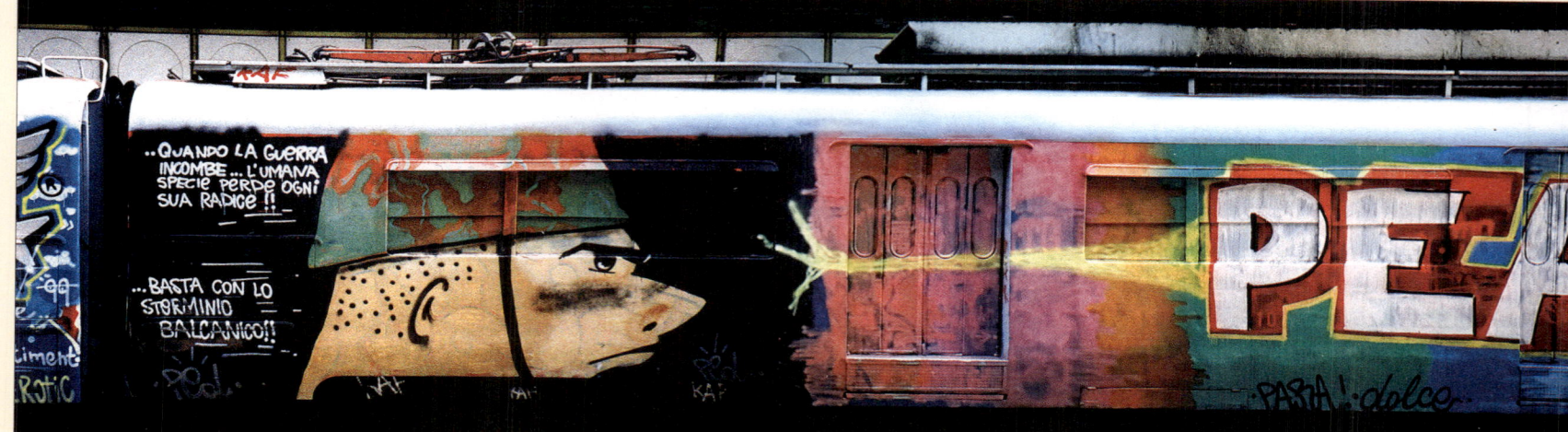

Peace, whole-car by Paradiso and Dolce against the Balkan Massacre

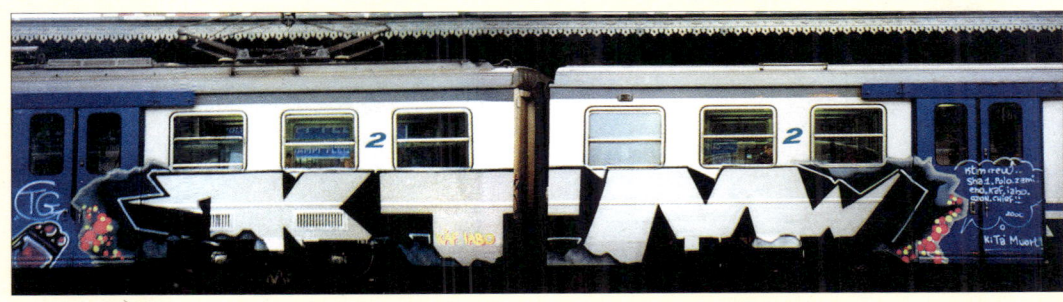

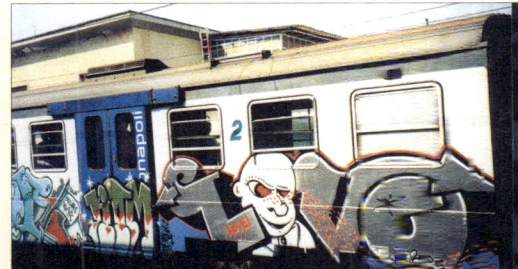

KTM by Kaf and Iabo — AL arcxive

Guen e Crisy – DCN — AL archive

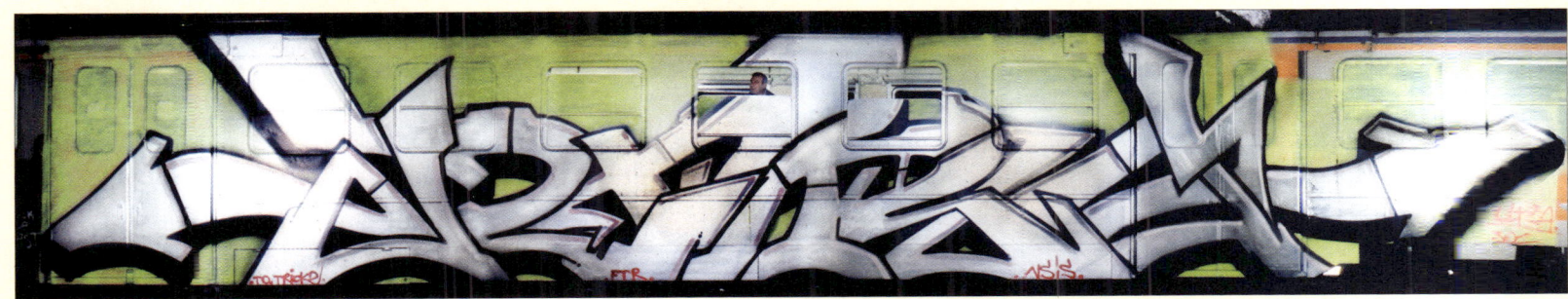

Ultra, Wildstyle whole-car — AL archive

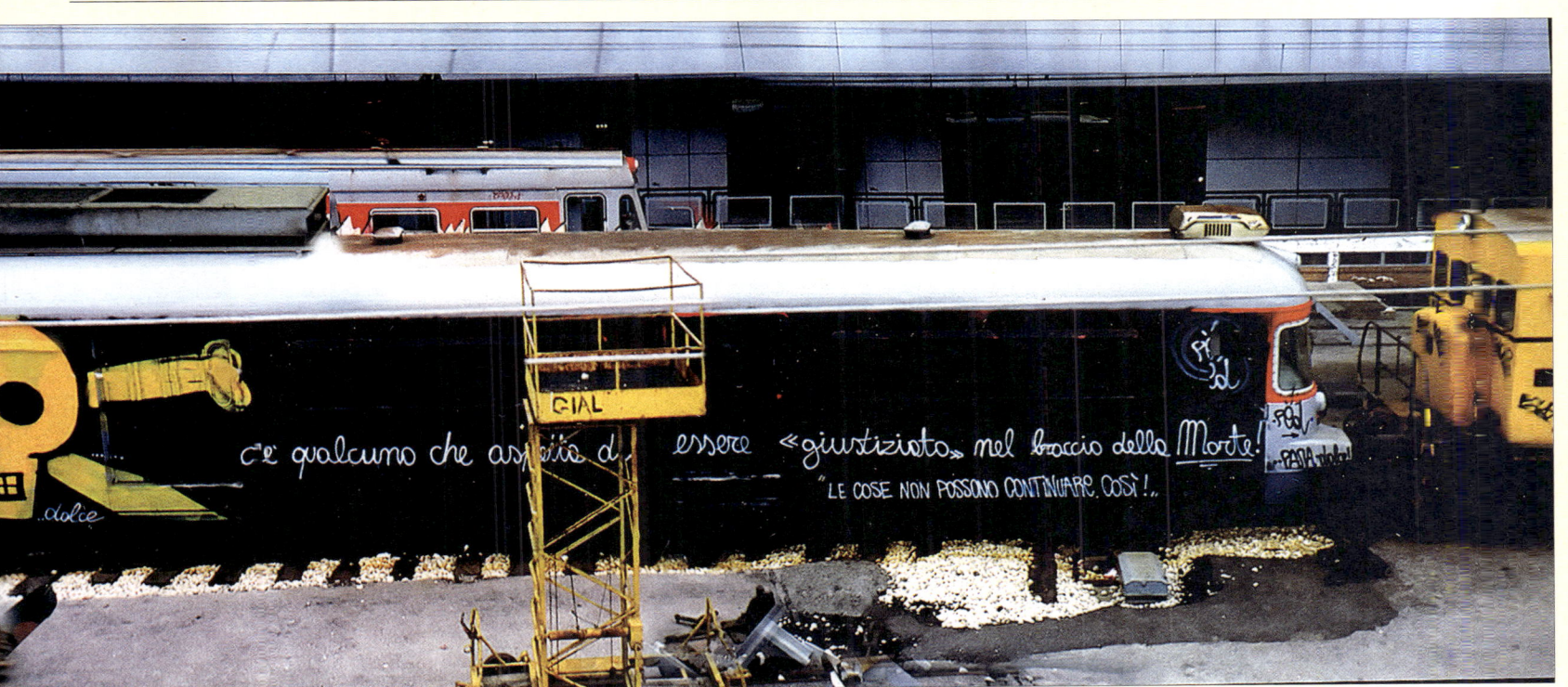

c'è qualcuno che aspetta d. essere «giustiziato» nel braccio della Morte! "LE COSE NON POSSONO CONTINUARE COSÌ !.."

— AL archive

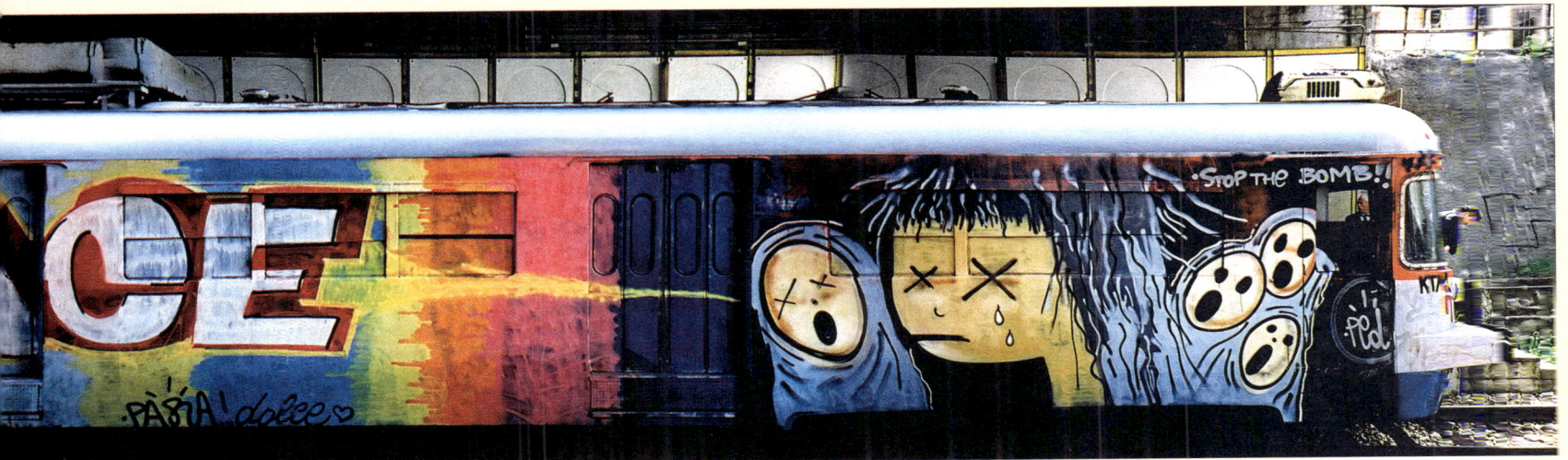

— AL archive

An anomalous context:

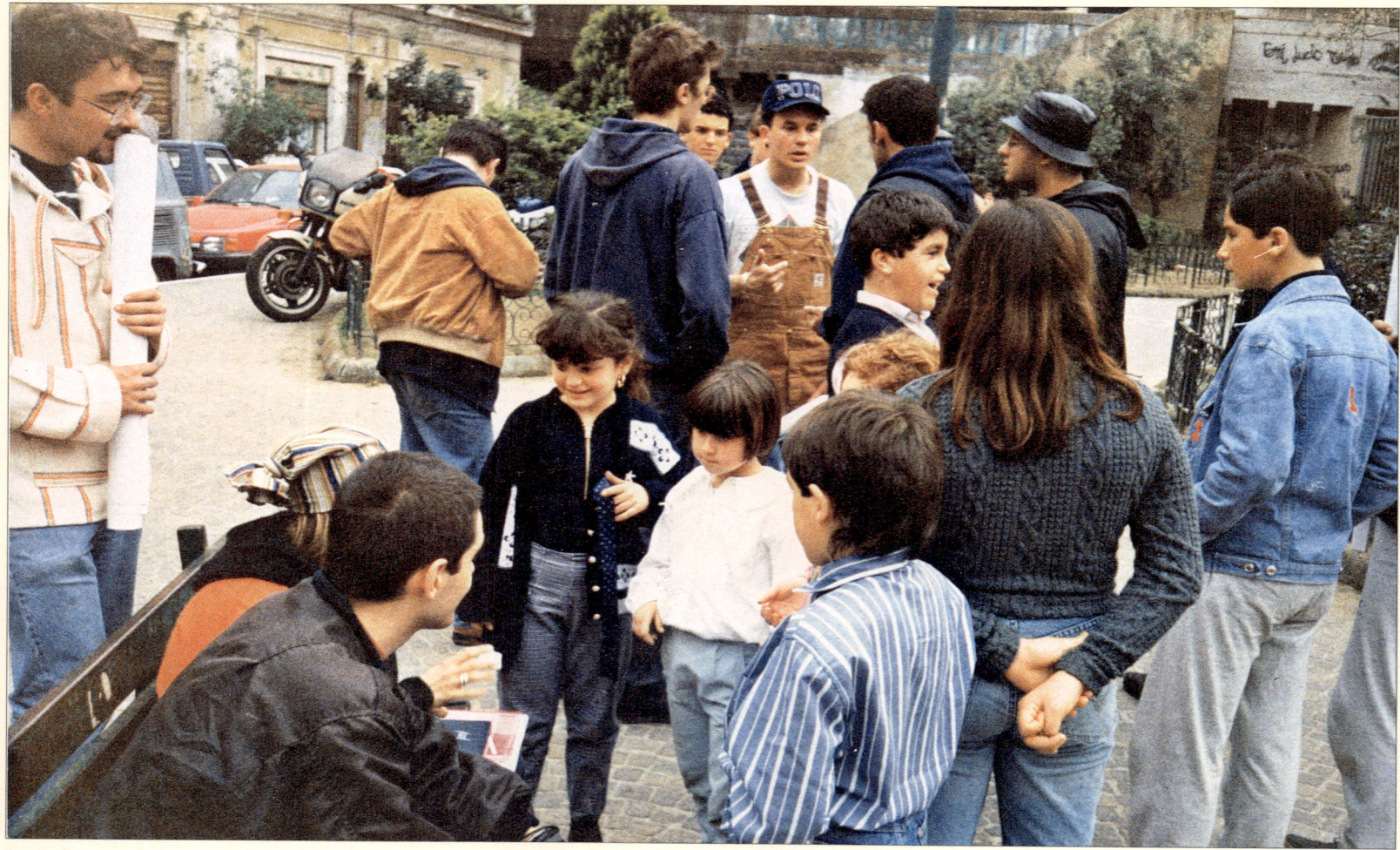

Polo and Neapolitan street kids during the early 90's

— Polo

Interview with KTM crew: Polo and Kaf

How did you handle the illegal aspects of this phenomenon in a city that is already rather problematic?

KAF – Being in a city that is difficult, often unlivable, causes you to live your daily life differently: a phenomenon like graffiti is considered the least of problems. More than anything, in the early 90's, people didn't understand why one would waste time doing something that wasn't considered a job or a hobby. Residents – and the police– didn't understand the point of painting with spray paint in the street. Many people would stop and ask who was paying us!
At times the problem went beyond the concept of painting in illegal spots. Once I was with Cyop painting the walls of the Cumana station on Corso Vittorio

Emanuele; in the distance I see some Carabinieri jumping a wall... instinctively I thought to run but then I said "I'd better not or they'll get scared and pull out their steel, shoot two shots in the air and who knows where the third will end up". We stayed there immobile. Three or four police cars pulled up, they seemed very pissed off. The first thing I showed them was the spray can. I shook the marble in the can and told them to stay calm... I recall one of them, a really young guy, was shaking like a leaf. In situations like these, an inexperienced cop- or even worse, one who isn't from the area – is dangerous because he's expecting the worse. They said they had seen us from afar and imagined we were thieves, but once they saw we were painting they calmed down, told us our drawings weren't bad, and left. We went back a few weeks later to finish our pieces.

POLO – When Zemi and I painted the first cars, lots of younger kids

followed in our footsteps. They saw us using spray paint and wanted to imitate the motion without understanding the rules of the game. In an instinctive manner, without criteria, without a specific mentality, they would devastate trains and break windows, etc... try explaining the difference between bombing and vandalism to them, there was such a fine line between the two that nobody understood it. Hence, the police intervened and began investigating. In a FS yard in Campi Flegrei they caught a guy who ratted out all the names of writers, Zemi and I being the first. The police called my house but I wasn't home- at the time I was living in Pescara – so I had to return to Naples with my lawyer. They interrogated me, but as it so often happens in Naples, it was completely informal: "When it was just you and Zemi, we had no problem because you did nice things, it was okay... but these new kids are a pain in our ass... see if you can fix the situation".

As soon as we left we convoked all of Naples' writers outside of the Campi Flegrei station. It was a Saturday afternoon, Zemi and I got there and there were about 50 kids from ages 10 to 15! We tried to explain to them how Writing worked, even if many of them had other ideas in mind. It was a historic episode, and those who were there, still remember it.

KAF – Slowly but surely, an important scene took shape from that small group of people, the idea of bombing and hitting trains became part of some people's DNA. For example, a crew like DIAS stood out because they painted- and still paint- local trains constantly, with no compromises. In Naples there was always a group of people whose pieces stood out on train cars, like Paradiso who, together with Dolce, left his mark in the mid 90's by painting numerous whole-cars. Those were exceptional pieces, at times they resembled the thematic subway

cars we saw in *Subway Art*, which were painted to spread a message rather than a Name.

How did people react to these painted trains?

POLO – Naples is such a chaotic and visually 'noisy' city, that a fully painted train could pass by and hardly be noticed. Our interaction with people usually occurred while we were painting, while in the act of spray painting trains. Most yards are surrounded by tall residential buildings, which face the yard. They're housing projects that are often in horrible shape. Many writers, like Paradiso, came from those projects and from his window he could see the painted trains circulating. From their balconies, people would watch us paint and often these individuals would mind their own business. They understood graffiti was illegal and against the State, and some of them appreciated it. So long as you didn't touch anyone's private property- in

Writing in Naples

which case you'd be screwed—but if you were just painting public property, most people would take your side. Obviously, there are 'fancy' areas like Chiaia, Vomero, Via dei Mille… as soon as those people saw something odd, they would call their local police friends. Vomero is like an entirely different city, people are different and cop cars are everywhere.

And in areas like Scampia, where Le Vele housing projects are located?

Polo- Painting there is riskier, you're dealing with ignorant people, as soon as you start you're surrounded by kids on scooters asking for spray cans, pressuring you to write "Mastiffs" or their girlfriend's name. So we avoided it, also because we were seen as outsiders, as aliens so we had to put ourselves at their level by talking and playing their game, we couldn't ignore them or they would get pissed off. In the alleyways there was total collaboration. Zemi did the first graffiti; drawings for football fans, he painted a huge lion in Piazza Carolina for an hooligan group called "Vecchi Lions". Then he began painting the logo for the Mastiffs in San Gaetano. We painted symbols for the hooligans from stadium section A, the most violent group, but also symbols for tough groups from section B, like Fedayn from San Giovanni. It was advantageous to paint for them because then you could rest assured in the streets, if you knew them you could roam freely. In Naples, each person lives day to day, and you need to find a way to make it to the end of the day without too many problems.

KAF – It's less convenient because in the street, if you see an hooligan stencil, you know not to touch that spot. In the beginning, the phenomenon was prevalently concentrated in the alleyways and around the stadium, but nowadays it's all over the city. There's no conflict between writers but at times they do contend for the same space. Writers still have the trains, which hooligan don't seem to care about. Whereas the railway walls themselves are often battle zones because section A groups have realised that they're highly visible spots. Competing for spots in the city is a game, which until now has been regulated by reciprocal respect.

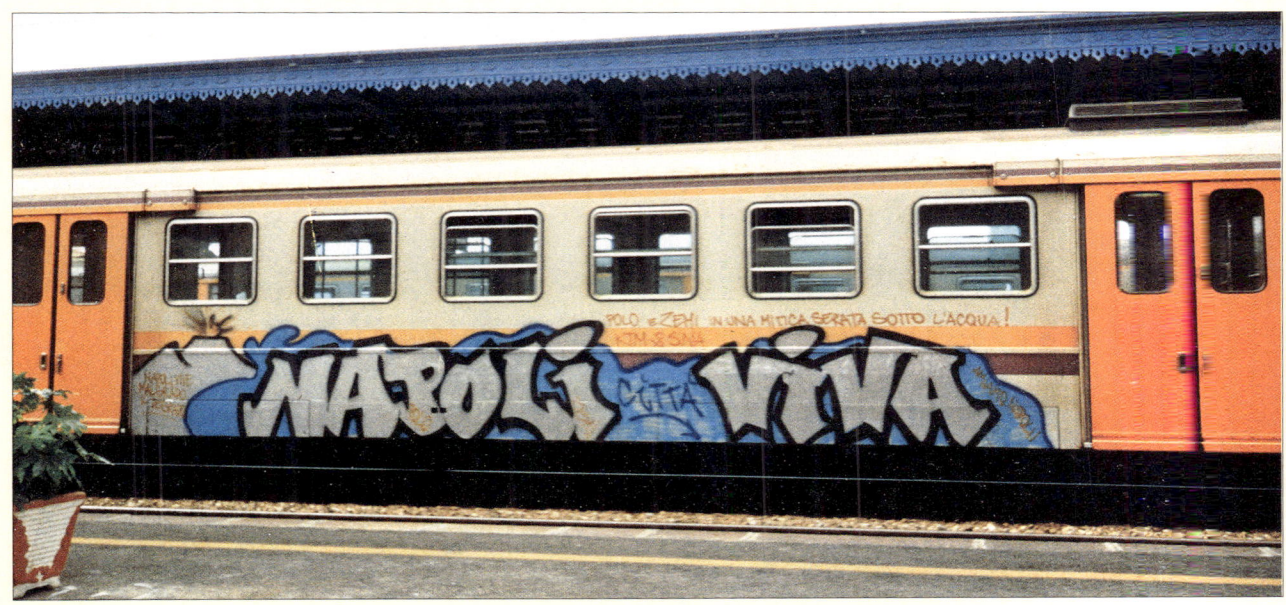

Napoli città viva by Polo and Zemi   – Polo

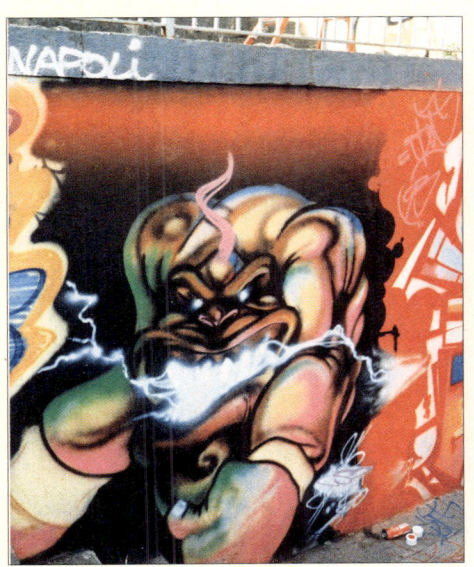

Zemi KTM   – Polo

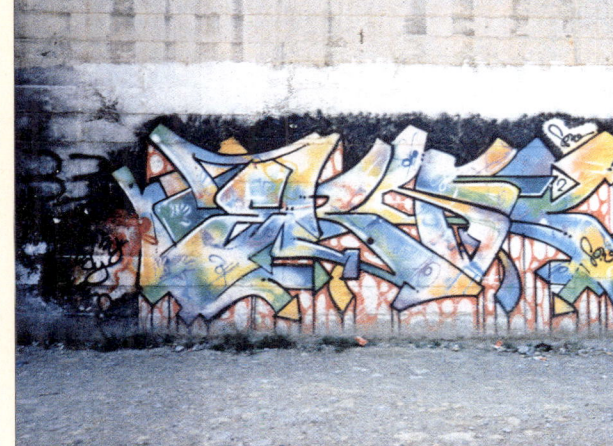

Early piece by Sha–1, first writer of Naples. Mid 80's   – Polo

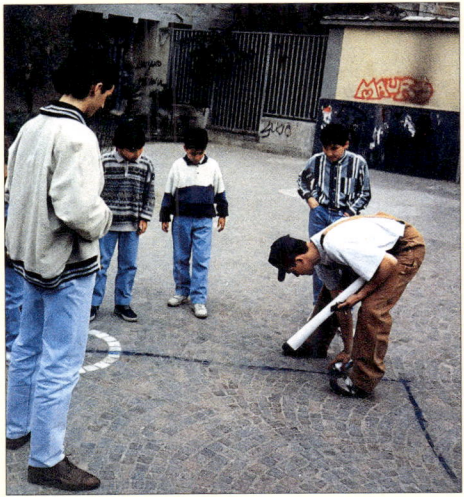

    – Polo

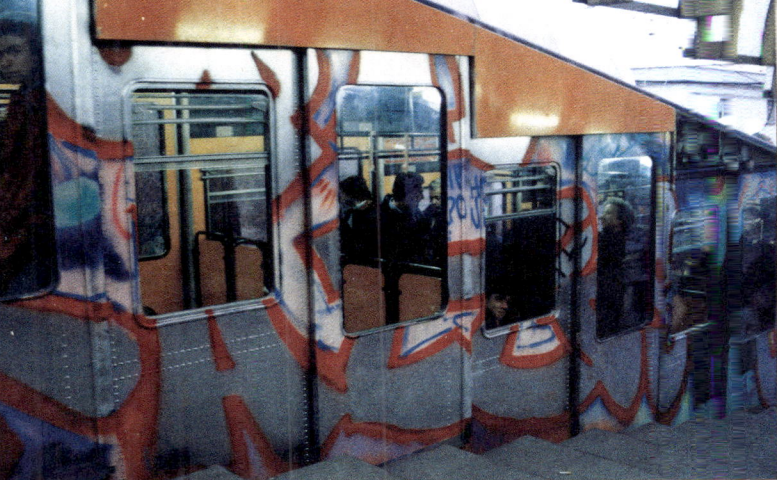

The funicular cars painted during the 90's   – Polo

Across Tuscany

> CONTINUES FROM PAGE 328

In all this I remember the pieces would travel for months, years, my first panel ran until 1999, four years up and down Italy, something unthinkable and yet it was a true reality for us then. Stylistically speaking things changed in '98, until then my provincial reality made of calm and accessible yards was rooted in a hall of fame-like style. We hardly cared about the impact of the whole in comparison to the single details. When you observe the pieces of that period you can recognise our fixations, the effects, the shading and the dozens of colours, we weren't that interested in dimensions either, top-to-bottom or whole-car, we preferred precise and intricate panels. All this ended abruptly when I went to Madrid on Erasmus for a year: I remember when I showed my pieces to the local writers they couldn't even read the name, and I realised I had lived a sheltered and weak reality when it came to impact and style. Madrid at the end of the 90's was already in the phase of backjumps, ten minutes per panel and out, I remember Sha would paint directly from the platform, during the day, with people on the train. It was him that had met up with Trota in Paris, word is the backjump-obsession was born on that Inter-Rail trip, but who knows? In Scandinavia it had probably been a standard practice for years. Madrid was anyway a turning point. It was 1998 and I met up with Sha a couple of times, but mostly with Wine and Buda, I remember dozens of adventures: one summer we went to Barcelona to paint the Cercanìas, the Spanish regional trains that were hard to hit in Madrid, but then we ended up attacking the subway instead, we arrived at 8 in the morning and had hit it twice by 11. All this determined a new concept of letters and pieces on trains, I was tired of the way I had painted, interweaving letters until they were unreadable.

Writing in Spain coincided with a forced choice, related with the context and the given modality, with 10 minutes per panel Wildstyle became ridiculous and I started painting different letters, softer and more legible. During my transfer in Madrid I met Artan from Rome, though he couldn't have been farther away from the stylistic standards of his city, obsessed as he was by German letters and by styles like Can2, which gave the final blow to everything I had always held into account as aesthetic reference points: the attention to detail, the intricate letters I had joined together without any apparent logic. Simplicity and compact letters became the foundation of our nocturnal discussions. When I returned to Pisa in 1999, nothing could be as it had before, I decided to change the pace and frequency of my actions, before we were all obsessed by the quality of pieces, by the specifics, by the idea of bringing the hall of fame style to the yard by painting the same panel for hours. In '99 we started bombing four-five times a week, finishing one, two, even three pieces the same night, until we were drained. The following years coincided also with a new target, at least an anomalous one, when associated to a crew who was basically dedicated to trains; concept walls done by the whole crew, in halls of fame, became as routine as panels. I remember Loomit came to Italy and fomented all this, he was himself

surprised at our murals around Tuscany, I think he didn't expect it. Actually it was a contradiction, trains and concept walls are poles apart in Writing. To be honest, I would often have periods of crises in this context and sometimes I would get lost when the themes were "prescribed", which colours to use, what measurements to keep, maybe the common denominators that tied everything together were the yard conditions that often allowed the aesthetics of concept walls to be transferred to trains. Some of these pieces were like canvases, hours were necessary to finish those end-to-ends or whole-cars, which were simply obsessive in their use of colours, letters and backgrounds.

In 2001 I decided do restart from scratch, I started experimenting everything, every style and letter, arriving at block capitals to then turn back again. I see many writers that after finding a more or less personal style then work on micro-variations on the theme, you have to confront dozens of panels in the arc of a year to perceive any evolution in the lettering. I wanted to give a radical cut every time, surprise people with pieces that were always different, I would advance by attempts, a kind-of continuous experimentation in line with what Phase II spoke of, to be always distinctive, and to get your panels running non-stop.

—

Meeting at SMN

> CONTINUES FROM PAGE 335

started moving trains, putting guards with dogs and especially when they added a film layer on the train cars which allowed faster and better buffing.

How did your way of painting change after the film layer?

BEES- It was traumatic for all train writers, especially because we were used to seeing our pieces run for months, sometimes years. It had become standard procedure to go to Santa Maria Novella and spend hours at a time, not even with the obsession of photos, but rather to experience a situation which is difficult to describe because all of a sudden the railway station of our city had become an exposition space that never closed and was updated daily. When they came out with the film layer we lost all that visual impact but I think that those that have been painting for years do it out of pure instinct, for the act itself of going to the yard. Maybe everyone is getting used to the fact pieces are no longer running like they used to years ago. For those that paint trains the approach is maybe similar to a skater towards a trick, it gets ephemeral, the actual action ...... how long does it last? An instant. But the emotion you feel at the moment you do it, though strictly individual, is eternal. I agree with what Skeme says in *Style Wars*: "I was there, I know I did it and so it's mine, then maybe we'll look back twenty years from now, we'll talk about it, look at the pictures, but I was there that day".

ENS- The film was a tough blow. Almost immediately all the stuff that had been running for years disappeared ... I liked being able to just go to the yard, paint and then just leave the station when I wanted

and eventually take a flick, there was no rush unless we did a whole-car where they would buff the windows. It was chill. Now you have to get well organised if you want a photo of your piece. It was while talking with Cesar from Helsinki that he made me notice the importance of pictures. The Scandinavian Writing culture is totally different: in Italy we were lucky to see our shit running, in Finland even if you do a wall they buff it after two days. He would say it can be a positive thing because if you take the picture you have your piece just to yourself, nobody else has that photo.

—

Reciprocal visits: on the road in America

> CONTINUES FROM PAGE 337

flipped the tab of the box and... BOOM! Smart was gawkin' over my shoulder, and I was speechless! Boxes, old boxes full of Meanstreaks! In every color you could think of! Cherry red, basil and sage green, blacks, whites, purples, yellows... I was dumbstruck. I immediately said "Listen m'am, how much do you want for these?" Her prices were off the top of her head, by instinct, "Dunno, like, a thousand lire each?" she then added, "... cause they're small". She based the cost of things on their size! She considered things that were small being of less value than things that were big, her shop was full of stuff and she didn't even know how much to charge for it! We bought a bunch, but we also racked a bunch on following missions. We showed them to Trota-THE, he was flippin' too. He also got a bunch, Roman kids still thanks us to this day! Let me tell you, that little lady was the greatest. I saw her open 'til 10 in the evening, city-that-never-sleeps-style... she was always open, even on Sundays sometimes. After a while, we bought them all, partly to feel less guilty about the spray paint we were racking.

—

A Roman cadavre exquise

> CONTINUES FROM PAGE 341

the kids from New York used to write 20 years before us.

SANTO— I remember every day after school, Washe would go get Chaso at school with his scooter and they would head to the Midday show. When possible, we would join them, I was in college and Manjar would come down from Venice occasionally. When he couldn't come down, he'd wait for the trains we had painted at midday to arrive in Venice, fantastic! Then we started getting too bold and got caught a few times. That, plus the fact that most of us left Rome, diminished the desire to go out and paint trains.

CHASO— Some time ago, Manjar and Peggio went out for a nighttime stroll through Rome, the next day we saw their tags all over, it was like a flashback of the days when we painted. I still remember Washe waiting for me outside of school...

and the nights spent at Santo's house sketching before going out in search of a wall or train. In those years, hanging out together, whether painting or not, was the most important thing. In those years I learned a lot and it remains with me to this day, even if there are no more traces of us on the walls.

MANJAR— If for any odd reason they were to perform an archeological analysis on some of the walls in Rome, they'd uncover the entire history of graffiti in the city, like layers of an onion.

TRAIN SYSTEMS

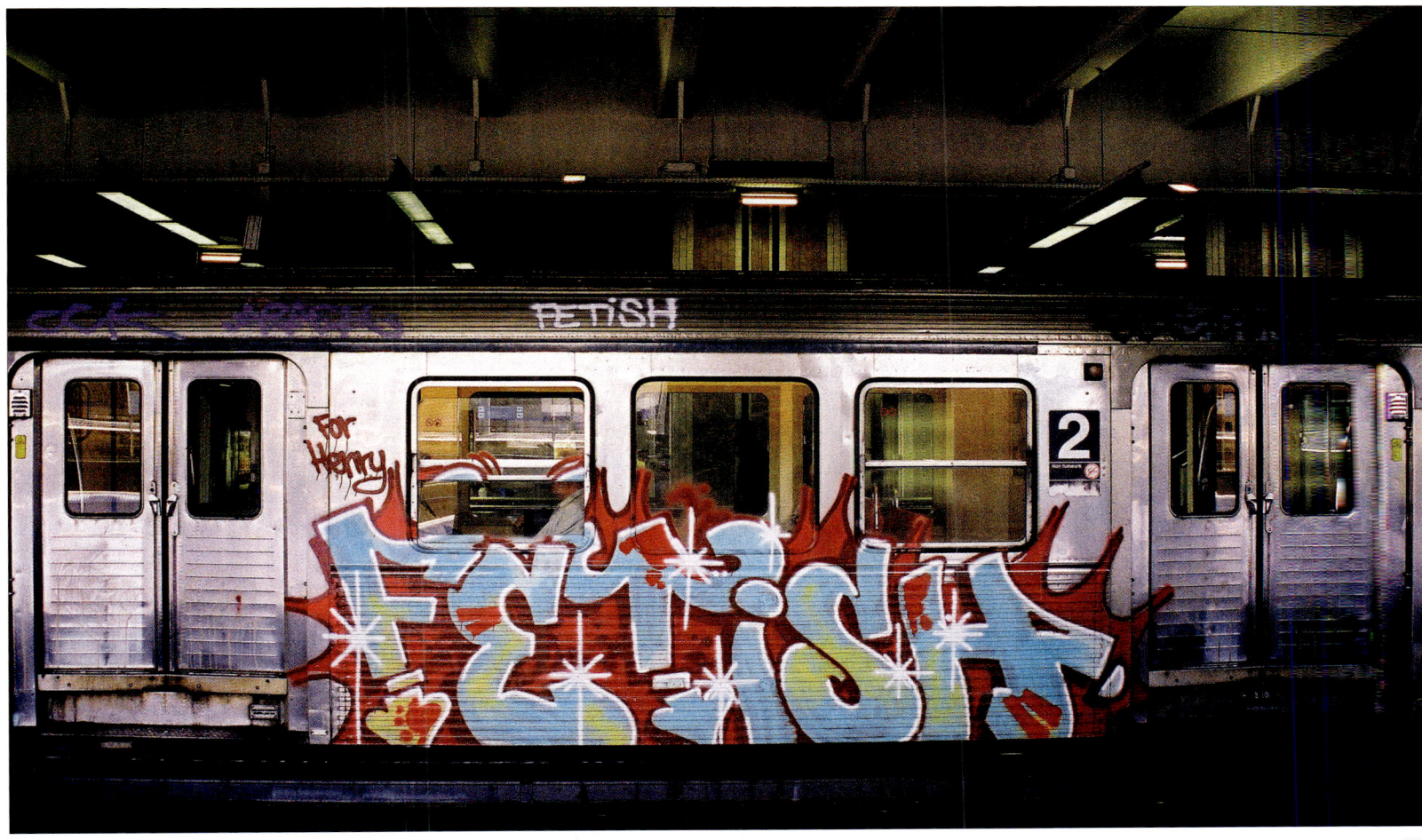

-RCF

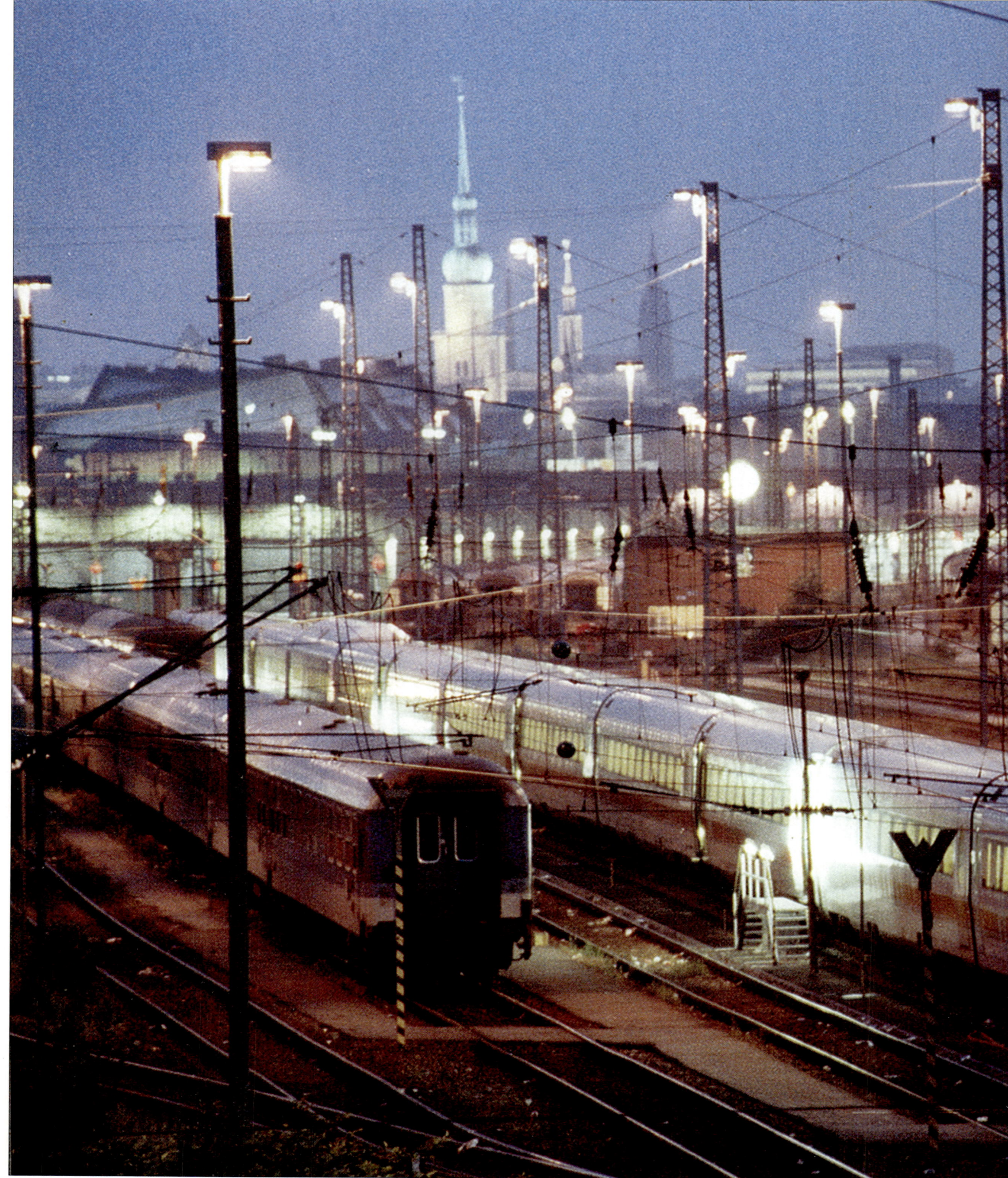

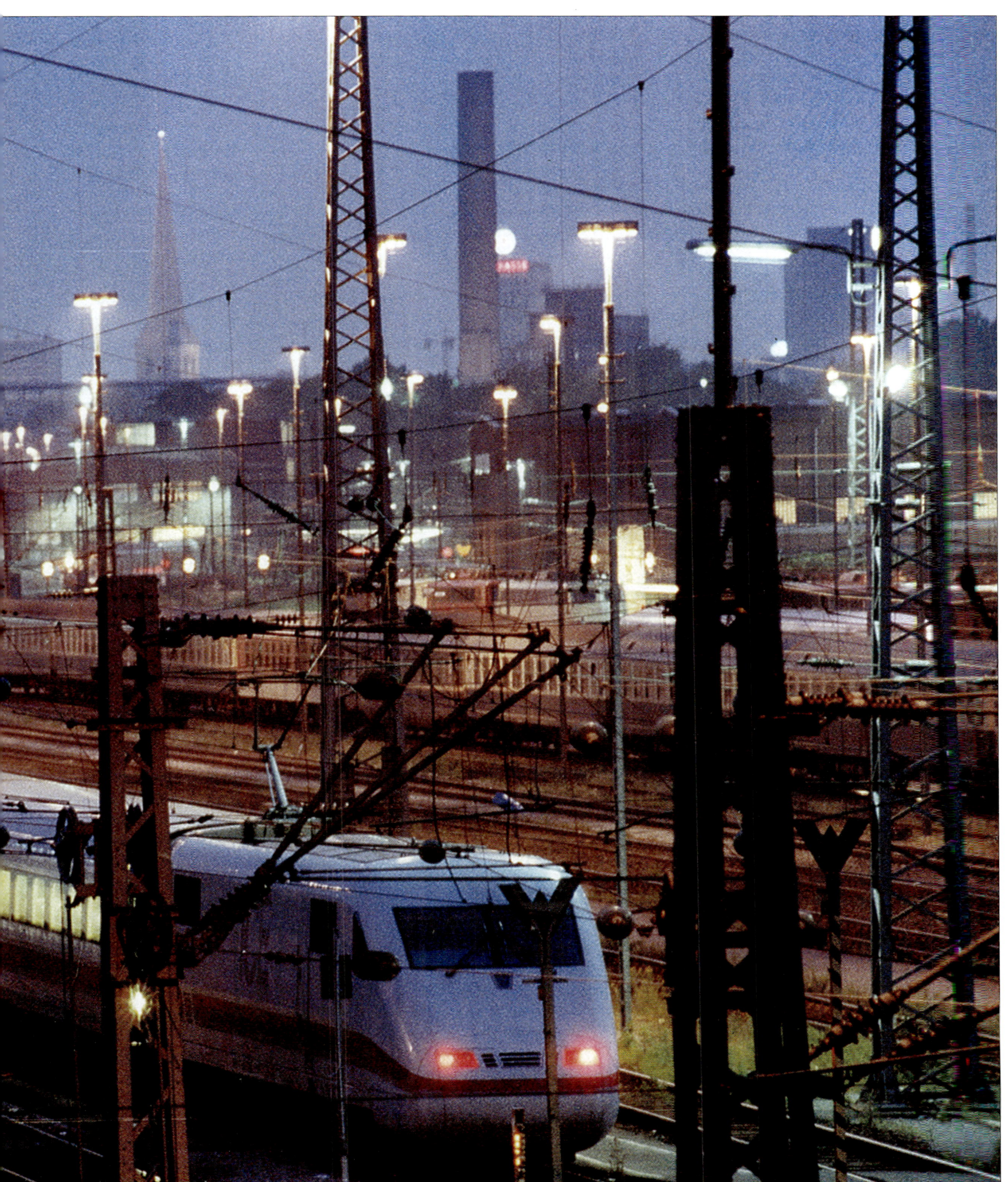

SUBWAYS

UNCONVENTIONAL STEPS

The tube: one of the most monitored public transportation systems of the world, described by someone who lived the adventure of its tunnels and deposits.

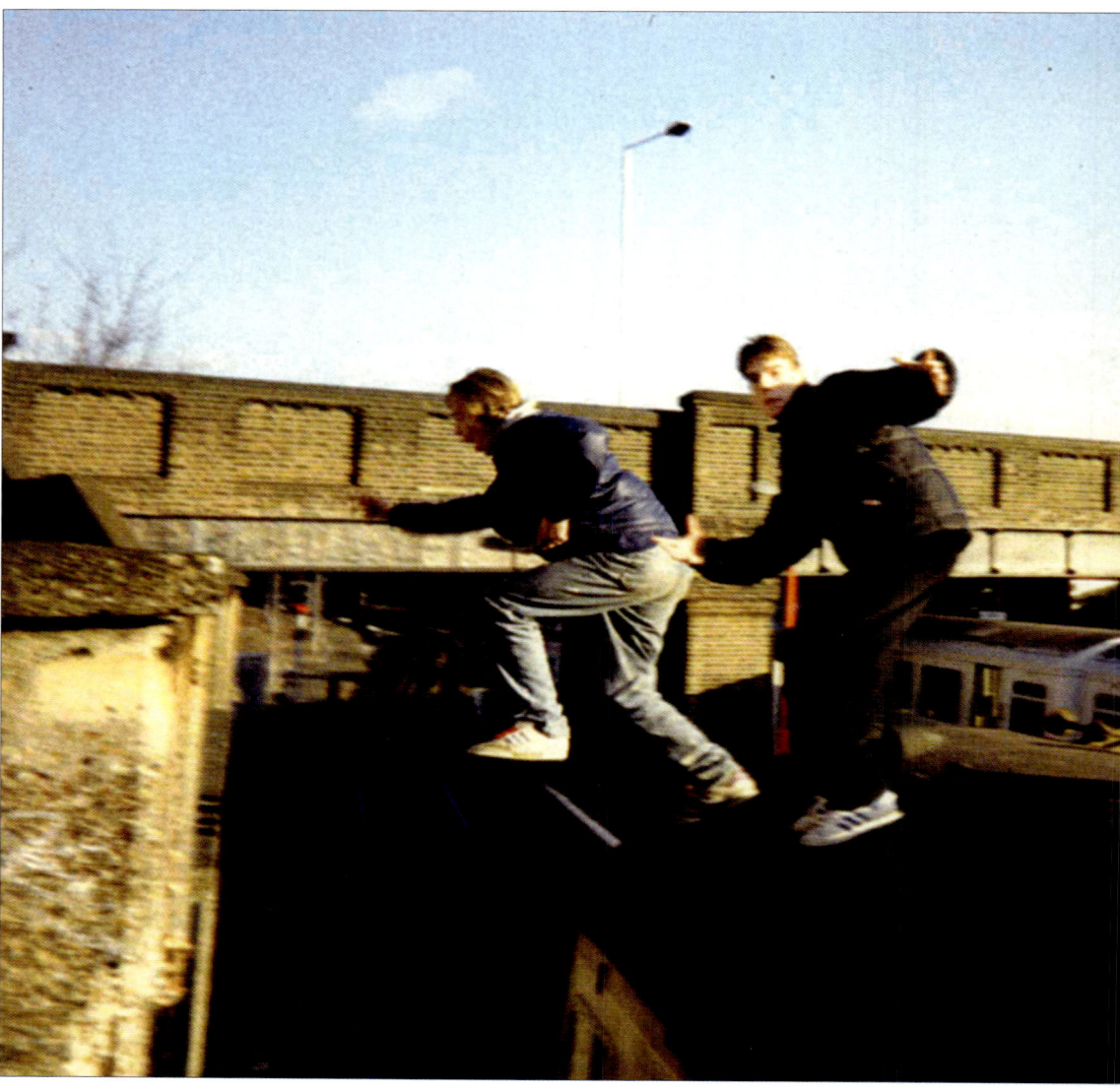

Don and Fued train hopping on the London tube

Coma / London
>

I was born Richard Sen in London in 1968 and spent my youth growing up in Wembley. Heavily influenced by the emerging Hip Hop culture of the mid 80's, my brother and I decided to visit relatives in New York in the summer of 1985. This trip changed my life! It was there that I witnessed the NYC subway graffiti movement at it's tail end and spent my holiday watching trains and burners as well as bombing the E and F lines where I was staying. Inspired by my NYC experiences, the films *Wildstyle* and *Style Wars* and the book *Subway Art*, I decided to start writing graffiti.

My first experience of painting a train was in autumn of 1985. I had been to a party along with some friends and we were all dressed in suits and had drunk quite a lot. A friend of mine, Reme, then said that he knew how to get into the Wembley Park sheds where they kept the Metropolitan line tube trains. We got some paint from Reme's house and then went to the yard, four of us still in our suits! It was easy to get into it in those days, with no se-

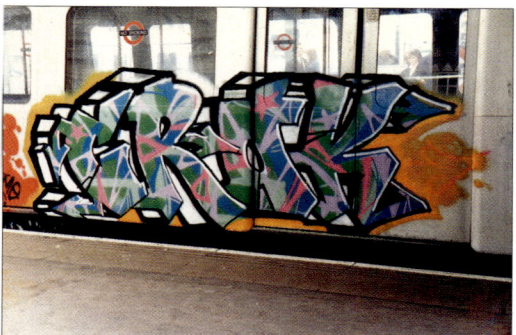

Crok by Coma   — Coma

curity. There was an open door at the back of the sheds, so after climbing over a small fence, we went in. I remember thinking how big the trains were because when you're on the platform, the wheels are below platform level. Myself and Reme started to paint while the other two (who weren't writers and just came for a laugh), kept a look out. I couldn't even reach the top of the panel and managed to do a really messy piece with bad car paint that soaked into the metal of the panel. The piece said "Rich" which was my tag at the time and was in purple I think. We finished and left quietly without any hassle and from then on, I was hooked...

After being arrested once, I changed my tag to Coma and quickly became one of the most prolific and famous writers on the London scene in the mid 80's. I concentrated most of my painting and bombing on the Harrow section of the Metropolitan Line (Big Met) and would regularly visit Rickmansworth and Wembley Park yards with fellow writers Tilt, Reme and Cast. Our days would be spent racking paint, and most evenings we would go out, usually meeting up in Harrow, have a few drinks and go bombing. This could include doing silver throw-ups or pieces along the trackside, bombing the insides with tags, or going to the yards to piece. We discovered that on Sundays there was no London Underground staff at Rickmansworth yard, so we would get the last train on Saturday night to Moor Park and walk down the tracks until we got to the yard. On the way there was a worker's hut where we would stay for a couple of hours before it was safe to go in. There we would drink more, get high and even listen to music, it was like we were having a party before going in! Then, we'd get in at around 2 or 3 am and spend the whole day there, we used to call these missions 'Rickmansworth all-dayers'. At one of these 'all dayers' about 10 to 15 of us painted a whole-train.

Among my many adventures, myself and Tilt were the first (to our knowledge) to paint a whole-car top-to-bottom, on the Jubilee line in 1986. We were also the first writers to be sent to prison for graffiti! This brought us instant fame and respect from writers all over London

ON THE LONDON TUBE

UNDERGROUND TALES

Drax – WD / London
>

Electro Magnetics Intercourse was painted at Farringdon with black Hammerite. In the late 80's/early 90's Britain was in the midst of 'Acid rave' culture.

This piece is a product of that time. Wobbly lines, heart blips, big eyeballs, lightning strikes, purple Om signs and basically a selection of images that related to the 'Acid house' scene. In essence 'tripping images'. I wasn't personally on acid at the time but I was spending enough

time in and around these clubs so knew what the vibe was. I also did quite a few banners for these clubs using white sheets and fluorescent spray paint. In essence here I've just transposed a little of the London club scene onto the tube network. Minus the f up paint of course.

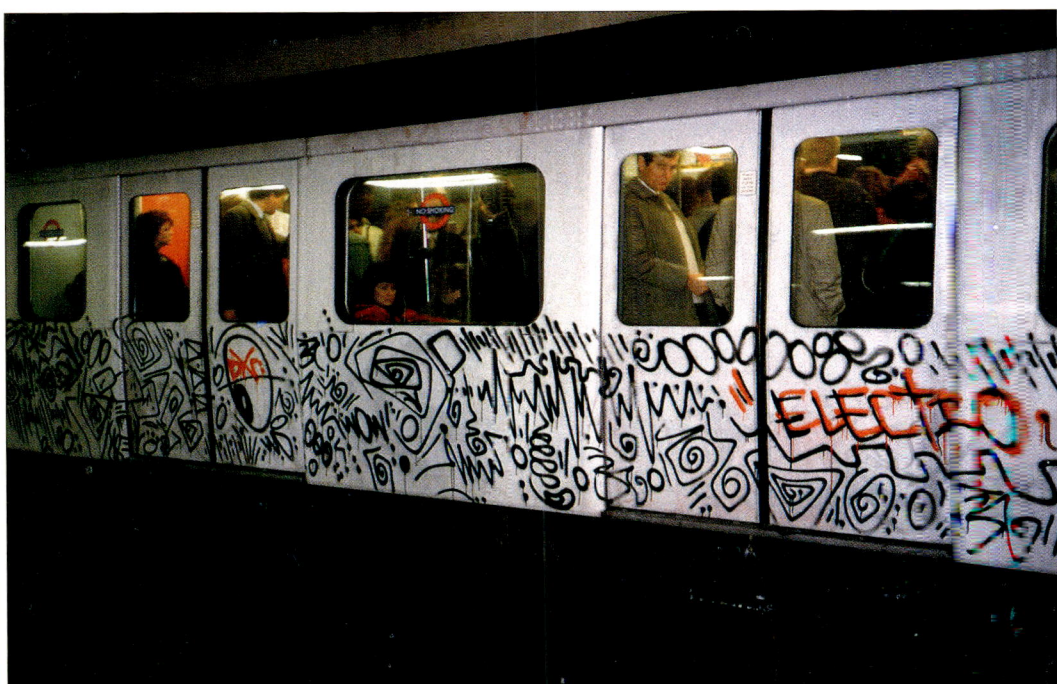

Electro Magnetics Intercourse by Drax, 1990

— PAC

Drax

and it definitely was no deterrent. Angrier and more determined, I continued bombing the Met and became accepted on the Hammersmith and City line (Little Met). Alongside Ladbroke Grove writers; Hate, Foam, Cazbee, Cade and Skam, I explored Gloucester Rd, Moorgate and New Cross yards also.

My last train piece was in 1988 with Hate at Gloucester Rd (Triangle sidings) where we both did semi-wild panel pieces. We used to call this yard "Big G" and it was special because it was the only yard that was underground. You could enter it by climbing a small wall on street level, then go down some stairs of a workman's entrance and arrive at the trains. It became one of the 'hottest' (unsafe) yards and was prone to raids by the British Transport Police regularly. Because there are so many lines on the London Underground, you had writers from different parts of London concentrating on one or two lines.

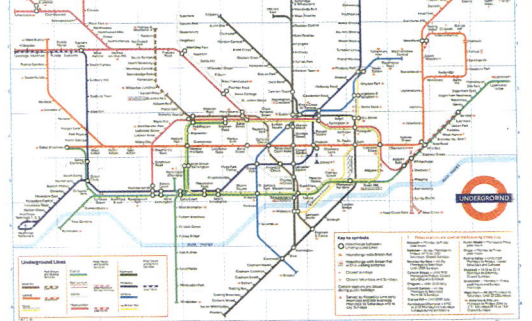

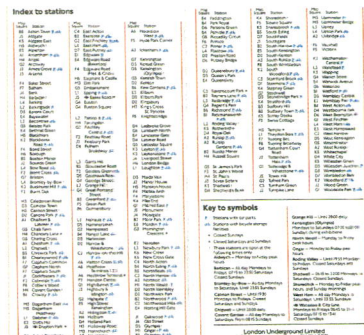

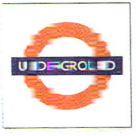

THE BIG AND LITTLE MET

Line after line, the London circuit as narrated by one of its most faithful followers. The cars and yards of the Tube compared to their European counterparts

Elk / London
>

The first things I ever saw produced with spray paint were the tags by punks and skinheads in Camden town, on the 31 bus. These were individual tags, these guys were taggers except they were punks and skinheads. The two main ones I remember were Rollo and Wilko. I don't know why but I just knew they were naughty, there obviously wasn't a grown-up behind them, it was something that just drew me in, and they were only ever in blue and red and black, there were no colours. This must have been in the late 70's, early 80's. What drew me initially to tagging was definitely pre-graffiti by punks and skinheads, and then of course it was TCA. In the beginning the scene was tiny, it was really, really small, and at this point I used to photograph every bit of graffiti in London, that's how small it was. By '89/'90 it had exploded, but before that it was basically focused in South London and West London, a bit in North London, but the main areas were South and West. I was essentially a West-Londoner, but I was aware of all the graffiti going on in South London, and all the tagging styles. Interestingly the area it came from had no subway, so we would all bomb the tube trains and they would bomb buses. I used to get a bus that came from South London to go to school, I could either take the bus or the subway, so one day I'd catch tags on buses. On the tubes you wouldn't see any of the South London writers but on the buses you'd get to see all their crazy styles, they had a really distinctive hand style. For me one of the most significant parts of London graffiti was their tagging style, it was so different, they were tagging on buses so they had different shapes to put their tags on.
I grew up on the Metropolitan line, which is the purple; the nearest yard that I could walk to was Queens Park, and then there was Wembley Park. The first lay-up I ever went to however was Rickmansworth, on the purple, which is miles away, out in the country; literally it's in the countryside, a long way out. So I grew up seeing the stuff on the big Met, that is the Metropolitan line, which is one of the two best lines to hit.
Basically in the London underground there are trains that look like New York trains, and then there are the classic London trains, which are the tube trains called 'bubble trains'. The lines that looked more like New York were the more respected lines, so the Metropolitan was a big line, the District line was a big line. Then the Circle line, along with the pink, which is Hammersmith & City, and the part of the District line that goes to Wimbledon, all have the same subway cars. Each line has different train models, the District line had one type of model and the Metropolitan had another model, but these three lines, the pink, the yellow and that part of the green from Wimbledon to Edgware Road, all had the same model of train. So if one day you painted at Wimbledon the train would run on that line but then tomorrow it could be on the pink line or the Circle.
At the time Hammersmith & City, the pink, was called the Metropolitan line as well as the purple, so there were two Metropolitans, for Japanese tourists it must have been a nightmare; we called one the big Met and the other

little Met, as an abbreviation of Metropolitan, cause one was slightly bigger than the other, and those two were the best lines to paint. Actually some people used to call this group of trains the inner Met, I would call it the little Met because I was on the big Met. I grew up there and all the first graffiti I saw was on that line, then in the early 90's I moved to the little Met. I also went to Holland Park School which is one down from Notting Hill and so I was on this line a lot. This is where I did most of my shit, when I started writing in 1990.
The competition was just to fucking get up and do shit, personally speaking I don't really think there's ever been an incredible amount of competition between writers. When I was a kid we used to joke as to who was better between the big Met and the little Met but really they were equal until the 1990's. Post 1990 I don't think the big Met ever had a big movement again. I see myself

When I was a kid we used to joke as to who was better between the big Met and the little Met but really there were equal until the 1990's

roughly as second generation in London, and then third generation is Teach and DDS and they always focused on the Circle line and on the Hammersmith & City. Every line got painted but those were the most desirable, again the District line, Hammersmith & City, Circle and Metropolitan; all look like New York trains, is that a coincidence?
I love painting the tubes cause they're so London. The reason why we have tube trains is that the earth is very soft, while Manhattan is rock, it's all solid and so makes for a good foundation. This is also why we don't have so many tall buildings in London. In New York they can just dig out and build in, in London you have to tunnel down and tunnel through which is why we have these small trains, and I love them because they're quite unique.
For the most part however the tube trains aren't the most desirable target. One reason why people didn't like them very much was that if you wanted to do top-to-bottoms there wasn't any top to the train, it just curves over. If you were doing panel pieces it didn't matter, but when we started doing top-to-bottoms you wouldn't want to do them on the bubble trains, I've done some and you're like "where the fuck do I end the piece?". Personally, if I paint a top-to-bottom I don't want tops to the letters, some people have tops, but I always want them to cut off, so the bubble trains were terrible for that.
Anyways, the situation in England with regards to train circumstances was a worst-case scenario. I once had one panel piece run for two weeks and that was like, legendary. I was completely used to never seeing my pieces

running, ever. I reckon I've photographed one third of my paintings, maybe one half at most. It was really depressing and not cool. I think London has always been one of the most difficult places to paint, we've had more money spent on security, more infra-red cameras, more hidden cameras, CCTV, touch pads in the ground, most of that came after the IRA bombings in the early 90's, but even before that it was difficult to paint. It's cold, it's wet, it's grey, there's no sun on your colours. If you got photographs you were lucky. It was really difficult, I feel like the photos I have are really special documents because it was such a privilege to get them and they were precious. We never swapped photos for example, which is something that happened in a lot of other countries If you were a London writer though, you never showed anyone your photographs except your best friend. I think one part of why we didn't show them off and give them to magazines is because you went to prison in this country. No country in the world has ever sent as many people to prison for graffiti as England, that's a fact. In Amsterdam for example, during the same time, getting caught for graffiti was like a civil offence, which is like getting a parking ticket, whereas here you would go to prison. If you think about the psyche, you also get your house raided. I remember the first time I went to Italy, and people had all their sketchbooks and everything in their room the Draconian nature of graffiti in London just had me in disbelief. I lived in Rome for a little bit and I couldn't believe I could have a sketchbook, leave it at my house, then I'd go and paint, and then I'd come home to sleep, I wouldn't stay up all night cause my piece is gonna run, then you get a photograph and you stick it on your wall. In London I never kept a sketchbook until the mid 90's. When we first used to paint trains when we came out of the stations we'd rack old tube tickets and do little outlines on the back and then chuck them away in the tunnel We'd sketch a little bit but we'd never take anything with us, you had no evidence, nothing in your house, nothing on your body. Because if you got caught and the photographs were the evidence. It wasn't until 2005 that for the first time in my life I took a photograph of a London tube train of mine with the sun shining on it, and I did my first train in '86, so that was nineteen years later. It was normal though, it didn't matter, if anything it makes me respect my movement, or our movement even more, because it shows we are 100% real, it was a true passion. For instance I got into Art school in this country, I applied to Glasgow School of Art which is a respected Art School, and I showed them my whole cars, and I was honest, I wanted to get in for me, for who I was. I was unsure but I got in and I met lots of people in there when I went to the interview, and I really felt they were the most un-genuine, non-passionate group of artists, it was sort of like a fashion statement, and it made me realize that the graffiti community, not only in London and England but International y, was honestly passionate and pure, and I felt this was special. There have always been 'fashion' writers, that did it as a trend, but they came and went quickly, and obviously the bigger the scene gets the more of those people they are.

The Farringdon lay-up

Drax – WD /London
>

Infected by the germs of life was done on my own in Farringdon lay-up. The fill is done with a selection of Beltons and the outline is Japlac. Farringdon was the sickest yard. I loved that place and painted it many times. A three train lay-up sunken deep into the bowels of Smithfield meat market, it stunk of stale blood and was appropriately a virtual tomb if you got raided by the British Transport Police (BTP). It felt like an underground yard, though it was actually open to the elements. Steep walls descended on all sides and access was only available through a labyrinth of British Rail tunnels, tube tunnels, underground car parks, doors that only 'the knowing few' knew about and old warehouses that were once part of the Smithfield meat market empire. A now crumbling empire, in fact the whole area was a relic of it's former glories. 'F' as we called it oozed mystique as only it and 'G' (Gloucester road a.k.a Triangle sidings) could. They were the two most legendary spots on the London Underground system and those that got to paint them were privileged. Trains that ran out of F usually ran on the Circle line or the little Met (now known as the Hammersmith and City line). This piece ran for most of a day on the Circle line before it disappeared into the buffers graveyard at Hammersmith depot, never to be seen again. The title "Infected by the Germs of life" basically means 'you are what this world makes you', which was poignant at the time as I was knee deep in court cases and trotting out the tired old excuse that I'm merely a product of society. Which to some extent was true. The Germs of life had indeed infected me but it's fair to say that I wasn't avoiding them so much as 'soaking them up'.

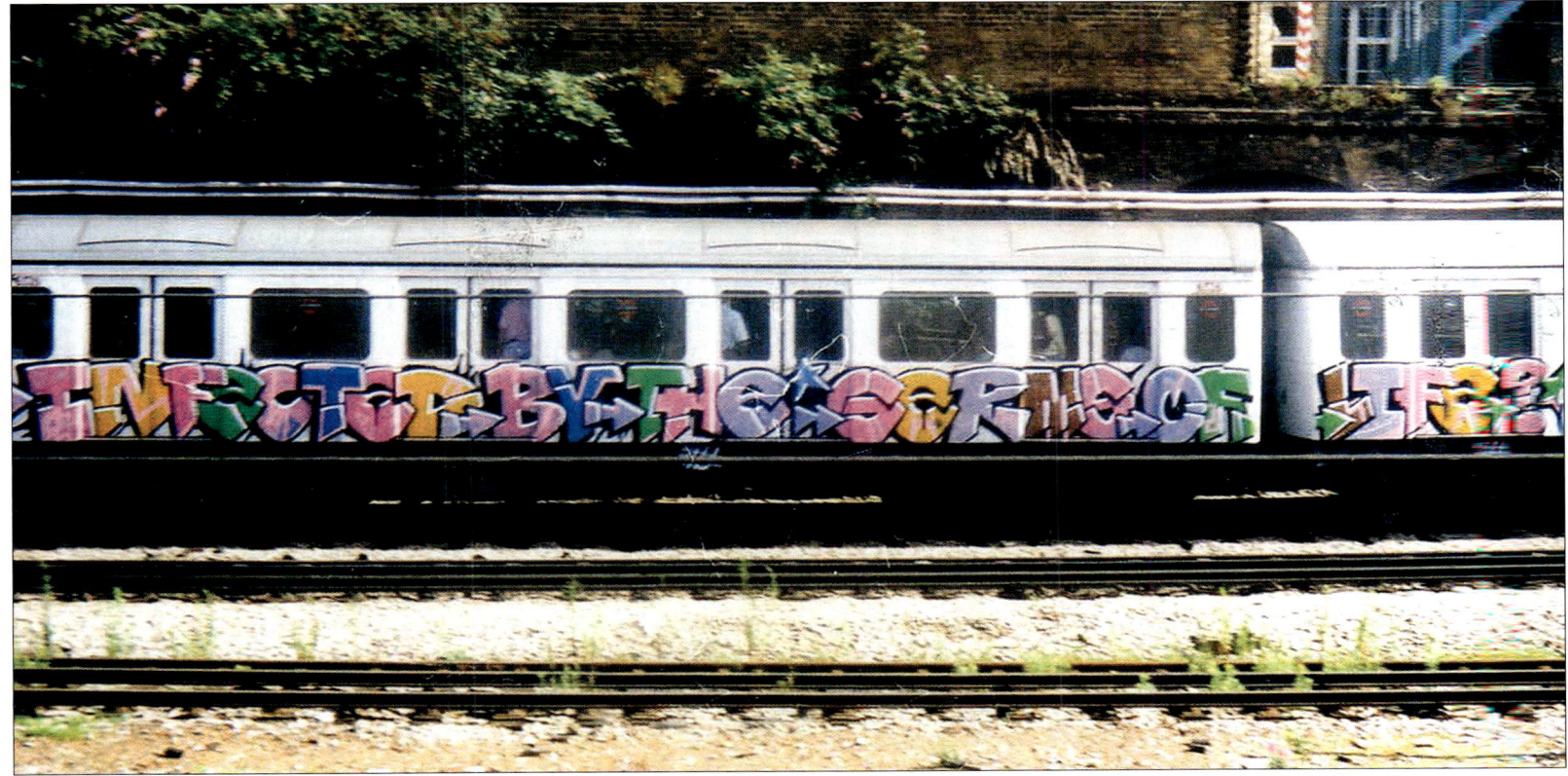

Infected by the germs of life by Drax, 1991

NO POLL TAX

—

"No poll tax" was done at Farringdon: this piece was next to an Elk piece which is on the next car. The fill-in s done in Red Cover-Plus, for the doodles I ponced a few spits off Elk (probably Homestyles) and the outline is in Hammerite. I think Prime painted as well that night but I'm not sure.

During the late 80's Britain was in the grip of what we now call Thatcherism. Margaret Thatcher (Maggie to some) was Prime Minister and she had become very unpopular, especially amongst the working classes. After riding a nationalistic wave, circa the Falklands war in the early 1980's, Thatcher was now being blamed for a government policy termed 'boom and bust'.

Tenants had been encouraged to buy their council houses, banks had been throwing out business loans and the British public had discovered the credit card. The early 80's had been a boom time but now it was 1989 and everyone was in debt. Thatcher had crushed the trade unions and many had been thrown on the unemployed scrapheap as the Industr-

ialised industries had gone into meltdown. The early 80's had seen riots in Brixton, Toxteth, Moss side, Chapel town and across the UK. In 1985 more riots erupted and a policeman was killed at the Broadwater farm in Tottenham, North London. The nation was simmering.

Then Thatcher unveiled the Poll Tax, a money making government scam that some termed 'a tax on life'. It was considered particularly unfair by the working classes who would have to pay exactly the same amount as Maggie's perceived chums, the big business 'fat cats' of the city. Protests were organised and it was no surprise when riots broke out in Central London. Throughout these times a common slogan on the cities walls was 'No poll tax'. I simply plagiarised it and brought a little political commentary to the London Underground. I think it ran for about a day. Maggie lasted a bit longer but she got kicked out at the next election. The poll tax was disbanded but soon re-appeared as the slightly fairer re-branded 'Council tax'. It's still a fucking rip off.

NO COUNCIL TAX!........ Now where's my cans.

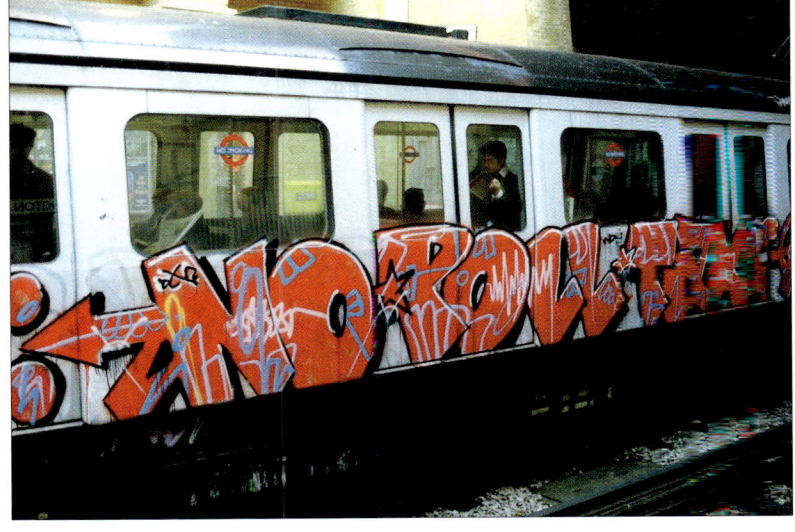

No poll tax by Drax, 1989

THE CHRISTMAS WHOLE

Drax – WD /London
>

This was done at Moorgate with the all time King of London train bombing, Robbo. It's painted in Chrome Spectra, a selection of Cover plus and black Hammerite. We didn't have any white with us but the next day I went back with a can and put the highlights and a few more dedications in. Christmas eve has always been the traditional night that writers do big productions. The whole tube network shuts down from late on that night until 7-8 am. Boxing day morning. 30 or so hours with the whole system to ourselves. An opportunity not to be missed. We usually obliged. It was 1988 and me and Robbo had made plans to meet up with Elk WD and Steam TU after they'd completed a mission that they were doing earlier that evening at 'Neasden' I think, or one of them other spots out in the badlands of North West London. Our target was Moorgate station, a major tube station and 'sometimes' a lay-up for two tube trains. Moorgate is in the City of London, the banking district. It's a part of town that's dead when the financial machine of London isn't in full swing. Walking the streets in this area late at night is hazardous, the police are suspicious of anyone that 'shouldn't be there'. With this in mind we planned to attend a local club that was nearby. If we got stopped en-route we'd explain the paint by saying we'd been asked to paint banners at the club. Once inside all we had to do was hang out for a few hours waiting for Steam and Elk, then slip out under cover of the departing crowd and make our way to the prize, Moorgate. A brilliant plan, or so we thought.

Something happened with Steam and Elk and they ended up spending half the night hiding in bushes as the police looked for them. This was a few years before the mobile phone onslaught so in those days if you didn't make a rendezvous there was no chance to re-arrange. We waited until 2-3-4 am but still they hadn't arrived. "Come on lets go" I said, but something had happened, the Rob seemed distracted. He looked at me confused, like he'd no idea what I was talking about. Oh shit! The Moorgate mission was in danger of not happening, Robbo was pissed. What a fool I'd been to think that I could take a party legend like him into a club for 3-4 hours and then get him to leave whilst the tunes were pumping and the beers were still flowing.

Elk and Steam's non-arrival had really fucked us, it was 5 am and the Rob was rocking. The Mission was off. In desperation I tried one last, corny attempt to get him to leave. I announced, 'probably untruthfully', that I'd leave without him, find my way into Moorgate (he knew the way) and paint a top-to-bottom whole-car without him. It worked, ten minutes later we were on the march with Robbo ranting "you'd never find your way in without me and if you did you'd kill yourself climbing down the walls". Brilliant! Now a pissed geezer was the only thing between me and a lonely death, crumpled and twisted at the foot of a tube station wall. We weaved through the backstreets of Moorgate, sticking our heads out to check for police cars, then eventually we reached 'the entrance'. A six foot wall led up to a roof of mesh wire. Rob jumped up and pulled me up after him. Amazingly he now seemed completely sober, a true professional. His crew ain't called We Rock Hard for nothing.

Through the mesh, about 30 feet below could be seen a room full of generators and other equipment. Robbo edged across the mesh roof feeling for a hole where bolt cutters had been previously used to cut it with. He found it and pulled the wire back so that we could ease our way in. Hanging off the wall, 30 feet up in the air, we dangled precariously trying to maneuver ourselves down on to the top of one of the generators. First he dropped down then slowly he helped me find my way down to safety. He was right, I would have killed myself without him. In

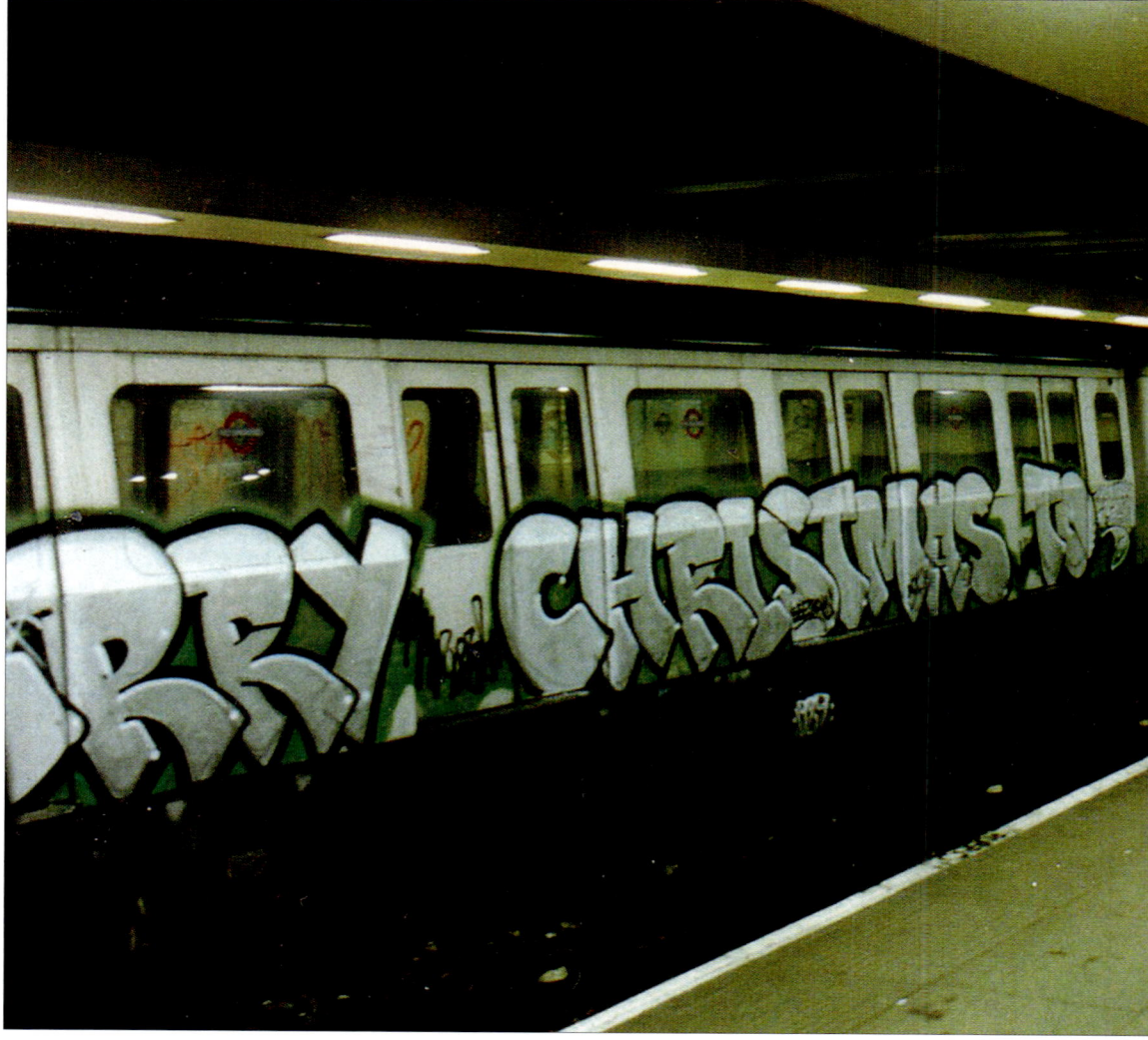

The X-mas window-down whole-train painted by Drax and Robbo in 1988

the generator room, which is behind the platforms for the Circle/Met line, we could hear the tell tale hum of a train's generator as it ticks over. Things sounded promising. Next we edged ourselves behind a dust covered platform wall, squashed up against years of soot and muck. We looked like coal miners by the time we emerged in the tunnel at the end of the main platforms. Our faces and clothes black with soot and grime. Vigilant eyes stared out from behind the dirt as we scanned the area for signs of life. The place looked dead. There was no sign of any staff, security or police. Everything was perfect. The vultures had circled for hours and were coming to feast.

Originally we hadn't planned to do a window-down at all. The paint we brought with us was meant to be enough for two top-to-bottom whole-cars. But there was a problem, there was only one train here tonight. Moorgate is a station where the Northern lines and the Little Met/Circle lines interchange. Upstairs, where the Met/Circle's pass through there are two extra dead-end platforms where two trains sometimes lay-up. We'd hoped that this would be the case or at least there'd be a train in the first lay-up with it's left side against that platform. Perfect for top-to-bottoms. But there was only one train and it was in the second slot. This meant that if we wanted to paint facing the tracks on which the trains would run past in just over 24 hours then we would have to paint standing on the tracks where the other train would have been. Devoid of ladders we would have to paint "window-down". I can't remember which one of

us suggested doing a "whole-train" but as soon as it was mentioned we were 'havin it'.

It took us four or five hours and we barely had enough paint, we barely finished before it ran out.

I remember something funny about the night, when we arrived and started painting we were quiet as mouses but after two hours it was so relaxed that we were shouting at each other from three cars away "got any black left" "how does this look" etc. The WRH yard bag had produced three-four bottles of beer and we were rocking. Robbo turned to me at one point and said "I wished we'd brought a box, we could have had some tunes". He wasn't joking. We were half dead from paint fumes, covered in all sorts of shit and making so much noise that any security-mindedness had gone right out the window.

This was real train bombing. It looked, felt and 'smelt' like everything I'd ever read about in all those famous New York Subway art books. Only this wasn't the South Bronx, the 1970's or the New York subway system. This was a London Underground station in the 'City of London', one of the richest square miles on the whole planet and we were just two lads from Islington/Hackney 'havin a go'. When it was done we'd painted London's first window-down whole-train. A little Met is six cars long. The first car said MERRY CHRISTMAS, the next four had the names of a selection of London writers and crews and the sixth car said FROM ROBBO AND DRAX. On Boxing day, when the system re-opened, it sat there all day as the public and Writing community checked it out (this photo

TRAIN

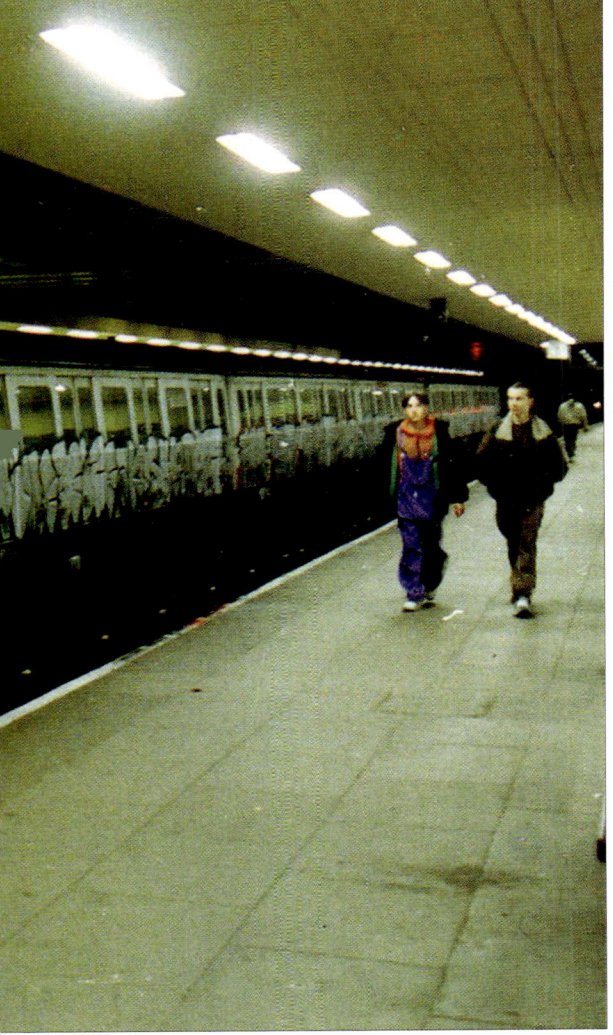

— Drax

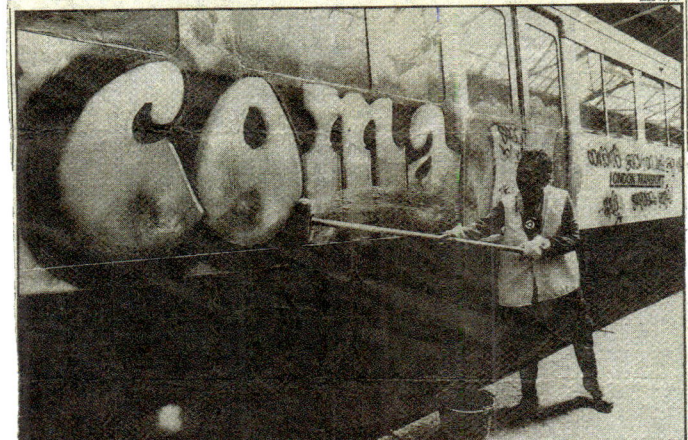

SUNDAY TELEGRAPH JUNE 14 1987

Liba Taylor

Cleaners scrub off graffiti from a tube train.

Graffiti art course angers train users

by John Kesby

A LEFT-WING plan to organise "graffiti art" courses for youngsters at a community centre yards from a London Underground depot plagued by paint-spraying vandals has sparked a dispute between passengers' representatives and the local council.

London Transport and British Rail have issued new figures which show that cleaning rail coaches and buses is costing more than £2 million each year.

The growing cost was disclosed as a transport watchdog group sent an angry protest at the latest proposals of Brent Council.

The London Regional Passengers' Committee said Brent was prepared to sponsor "graffiti classes" for 11 to 16 year olds at their St Raphael's Community Centre. The centre is just 100 yards away from Neasden London Transport Underground

Depot which, it is claimed, is the depot worst affected by paint-daubing hooligans.

Mr Rufus Barnes, secretary of the committee, has written to Brent complaining that children who have been taught the skills of designing and carrying out graffiti are likely to want to put their skills into practice "more destructively."

The watchdog group claimed that the St Raphael's Centre has advertised for someone to teach its junior youth club "the skills involved in designing and doing graffiti artwork."

In his letter to Brent, Mr Barnes said the majority of graffiti on trains was carried out when they were "stabled" overnight in London Underground depots, and Neasden was one of the worst affected.

The Passengers' Committee and London Transport fear that the capital's Underground system may follow the course of New York's, which is almost literally covered in "graffiti art."

Mr David Mitchell, the Transport Minister, has written to Mr Barnes confirming that the classes set up in Brent could be construed as "encouraging vandalism." Home Office officials also share fears of growing vandalism and the problems facing London Transport in keeping the Underground system safe and attractive.

In his complaint to Brent, Mr Barnes said that the very many people who wrote to his group, the perpetrators of graffiti regarded as vandals, not artists.

The moves for a tough line come as the cost of graffiti continues to grow. The latest figures show that London Transport spends £750,000 a year on cleaning paint off buses and £580,000 on cleaning Underground trains. It is estimated British Rail spends more than £1 million a year on cleaning.

The Government has taken note of the figures and the committee has been told that in future magistrates' courts will be urged to make greater use of

the powers they already have, including sending offenders to prison for up to two years.

The Home Office has told the London Regional Passenger committee that although the Home Secretary is not in a position to influence the court's sentencing policy, there was the possibility that the Lord Chancellor would underline the seriousness of the problem when speaking to magistrates in future.

Among the powers available, but seldom used, are under the 1973 Act to order the forfeiture of any property which an offender used, or intended to use, in the commission of an offence punishable with more than two years' imprisonment.

Under the Criminal Damage Act 1971, there could be penalties for vandalism of up to 10 years' imprisonment, or an unlimited fine on conviction on indictment, and up to six months' imprisonment and a fine of £2,000 or both, on summary convictions.

— Coma

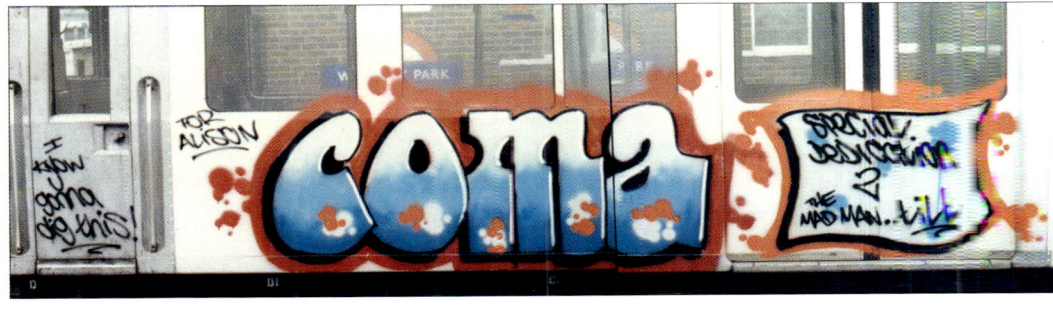

Coma piece

— Coma

Don / London
>

It was back in 1986, when I was at school, and just 15 years old; I was about to go into class when Gunja approached me on a stairwell and mentioned that Ice3 had started writing "Don"!
My heart dropped as I had been writing and bombing Don for a year... trains, streets, buses. So I thought about it for a bit and decided I wasn't going to back down, so I kept on writing it. Ice 3 was a king at the time, he still is, and in a short period of time had pulled off a couple

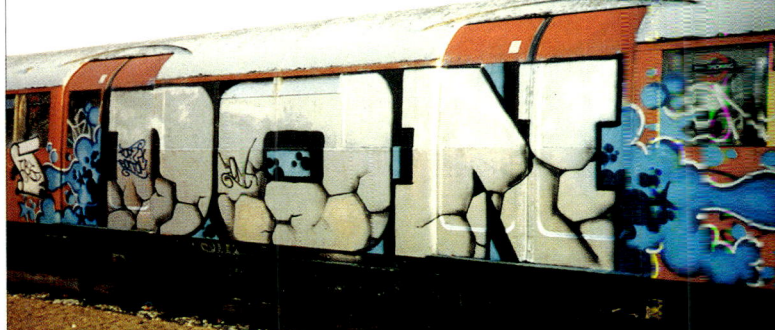

Don, blockbuster top-to-bottom

— Don

of classic trains, a panel piece on the Circle line and an end-to-end at Acton Town yard. He really nailed it, but all in

all, I was still the original Don! I have the utmost respect for Ice3, and still do even today, as for me he was a pionier.

Respect! But I'met there today doing my Don thing, and I look forward to doing a piece with him in the future...

was taken at that time). A professional photographer took pictures that made it on to TV via ITV news and into the press via the Independent newspaper. He later made postcards of the first car, the "MERRY CHRISTMAS" car and they sold them in shops all over the country. We'd never expected exposure like this.

It's mad to think back over 20 years ago and realise that a night which had started with fairly modest aims and that had decended first into drunken mayhem and then into near farce, found itself re-packaged as 'one of the most famous nights in UK graffiti history'. Across the capital trains were painted everywhere that Christmas. The train at Moorgate even got painted again on Christmas day as Shuto, Excel502, Sub and other members of the infamous Newave crew painted a top-to-bottom on it's other side and battered what was left of Moorgate station. I even popped back in there with Elk and a can of white Hammerite, adding highlights and a few dedications to mine and Robbo's work. After that we walked through the tunnels to Farringdon and bombed the three trains laid up there. A lot of stuff got done that year.

At the time we didn't know it but thinking about it now it was a crazy time. We were doing something that many writers never get to do: we were out there 'doing it', marching through tunnels, hanging off high walls, bombing trains, living the life of outlaws, existing in a vacuum consumed by a subculture we had embraced, creating what we now view as history. It was a special time. We lived the dream.

INSIDE THE AMSTERDAM

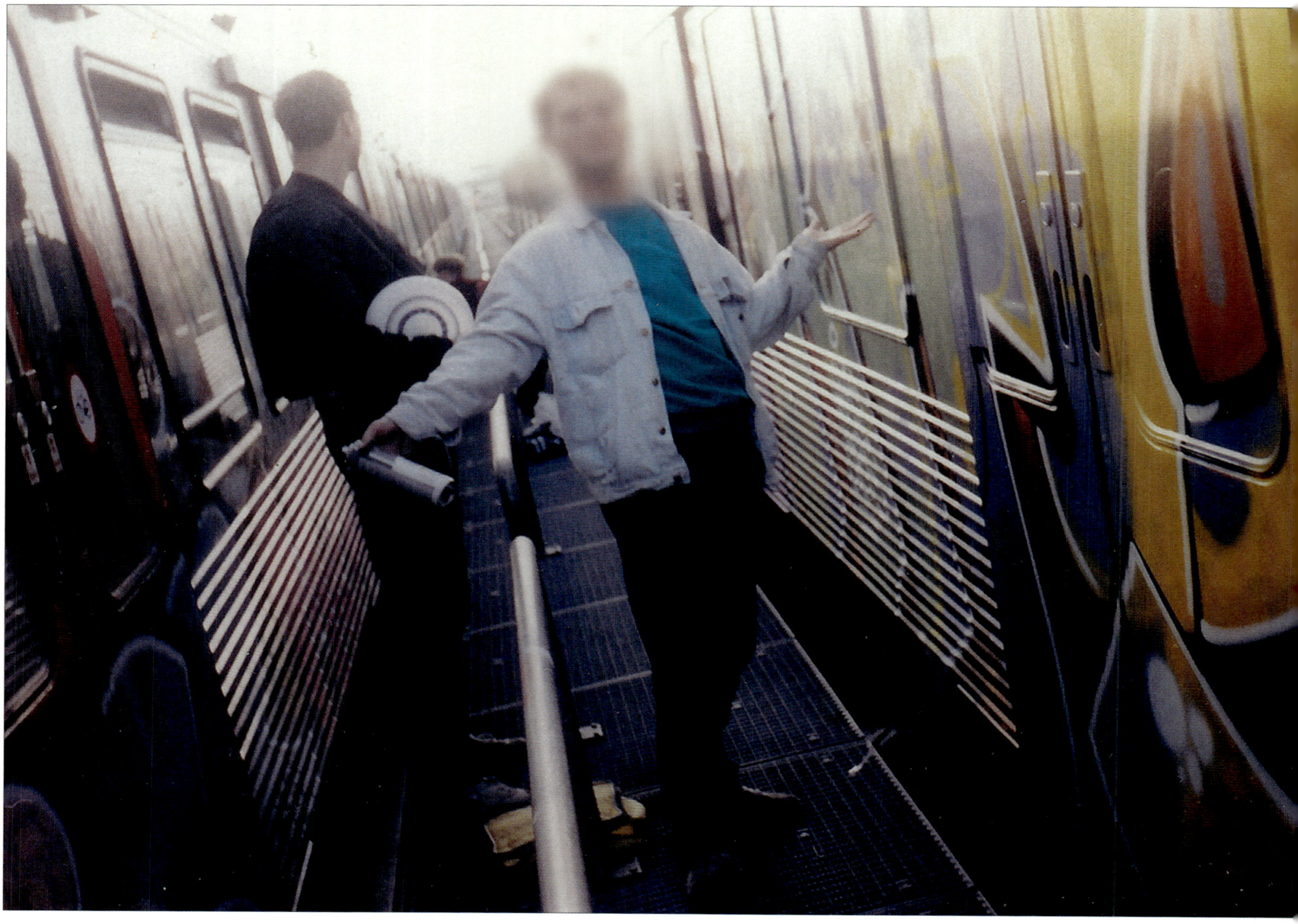

During the 80's the tram system became a main target in Amsterdam, especially for the boys who lived in the south of the city, even if High, CBS and others started to consider the subway network as a main attraction. In those days, the CBS crew and the posse around Sonic were the main forces in East Amsterdam, and they were fighting for the territory and for the subway end-stations. Those guys had already burned cars, but when I showed them beautiful stuff from New York, they were shocked by it. They were ashamed to show me photos of the subway cars they'd done.

Of course I was reacting tough, but in my mind I was wondering how the fuck had they done all that on the subway. I wanted to do that, too. Tek and Cula showed me photos of their blockbusters, and when I saw those cars, they blew my mind. I knew a guy from CBS who worked in a supermarket, so I told him I wanted to get in contact with Pengo, because I knew he was doing trains. A couple of days later he talked to Pengo, and Pengo said he had seen my stuff. We met at 11pm near the flat where Pengo lived, and we waited outside. All of a sudden the window of a flat four floors high opened and a wire came out. A guy climbed down, came up to me and said "I'm Pengo, CBS". I thought it was a great introduction. It couldn't have been better.

So he said "We're going to bomb trains?" "Yeah!" "One thing: if you get caught you don't know me and if I get caught I don't know you." "I can live with that." So we walked from his house to the tracks. The first station you meet on that route is Amstelstation, but it's an elevated station. While walking on the tracks we could see some people working there. I was thinking about leaving the tracks and walking on the street, but of course that's not how it worked with Pengo.

He said "Ok let's just keep walking on the tracks." "But we'll get arrested!" "No we won't." So we kept walking, and when we got to the station the workers asked us who we were and nothing happened. The next stop was

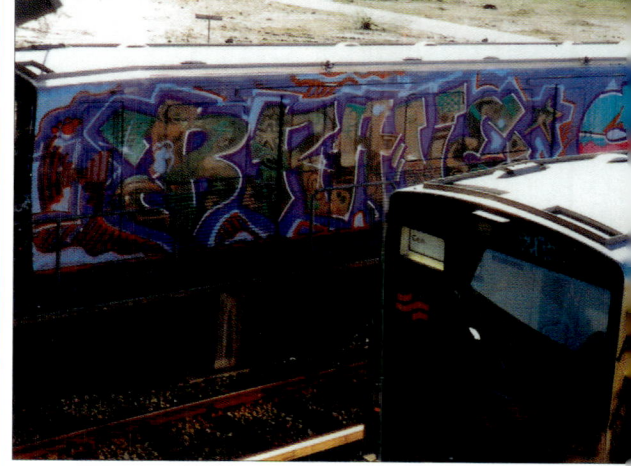

Brave by Rhyme and Chintz from Germany

SUBWAY

OCTOBER 4TH, 1992

RHYME

Painting and playing Frisbee in the yard with Reas and Pure. That day, 4 October 1992, a Boeing 747 of the Israeli airline El Al, crashed into the Bijlmermeer area of Amsterdam. Lots of people died just a few hundreds meters away from the yard.

Spaklerweg. That's where the trains stand. He wasn't worried about the guards so we started bombing. I did filled in throw-ups like I'd seen in New York, while they did their tags. I don't remember if we got chased but we killed those trains! The next day I called my partner in crime, Jaz, and told him to watch the trains because I had bombed them the night before. So we watched the tracks and the train was running. It was crazy! He wanted to go too, so the next week we did the same thing in Spaklerweg, but we got seriously chased. It scared me off because I wasn't familiar with the territory. So at that point, I stopped with the trains. That was in '85-'86.

The subway in Amsterdam exploded in the 90's, but a year or two earlier with Sprite we had already been doing window-down end-to-ends. It was beautiful. It had never been done before. We started doing them almost every weekend but never did one of those cars pull out. One pulled out straight to the buff, so that's the only picture I have. But of course we didn't give up. Not all the fame goes to us though; Shenk, Cobia and Shei deserve as much credit as we do. They lived next to the yards and so did Chase and Echo. Unfortunately almost none of the pieces were running and we were sick and tired of it so we decided to do whole-cars. First Ces 53 came from Rotterdam and we did a Pone, Milk and Ces wholecar but with different names. When it pulled out it went straight to the buff. At the time we were bombing strong but the situation was still under control.

Then when I came back from a holiday around '89-'90, all of a sudden I saw a Nug piece with some other guy from the Vandals in Motion crew. They'd done something on a train. Gasp called me and told me the train had been running for three weeks! I was so angry, I had done so many cars that were immediately buffed and that crew from Stockholm had a train running!

That's when the system literally exploded and our wholecar period started: the German guys came, the English guys came and I remember one weekend there were seven whole-cars standing in the yards ready to pull out. We had 44 cars. The guys playing this game were DSKings, Milkyboy, Fume, Ces 53, the French dudes, the French guys, some writers from Scandinavia, a few New Yorkers, and us. At one point I had three whole-cars ready to pull out. I was excited but a few days later I got a phone call "They took something from your car" "What do you mean?" "They scratched off some paint!"

Workers saw there was a lot of graffiti so they just cleaned it on the tracks. The problem was that the products they cleaned with were dripping into the ground causing an urgent sudden environmental alert.

They needed to build a complete structure to collect these chemicals which took months, and in that period they were not allowed to buff. I had one piece running for years and pieces on walls were being buffed before the trains! After that I stopped. My goal had been reached.

— Rhyme

— Rhyme

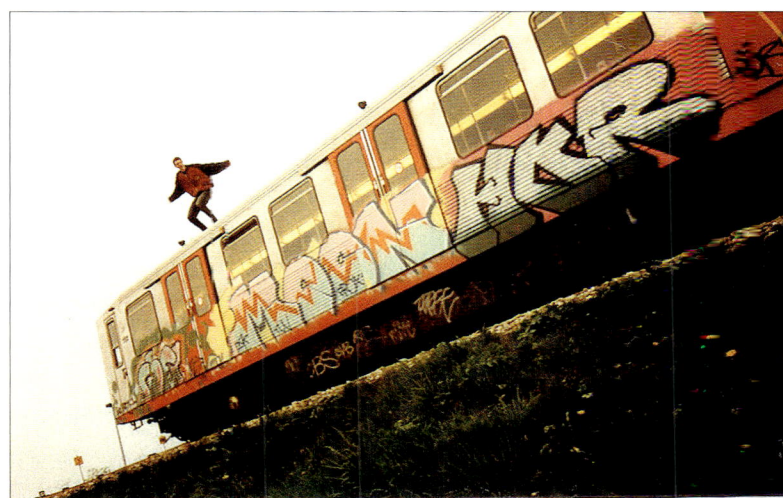

Moon surfin' on his panel piece   *— Moon*

Moonwalking

A government prohibition becomes a great opportunity for writers

Moon – DSK / Amsterdam
>

I think it all started after the first wholetrain on the 21st of April, 1990. A large team of workers cleaned the whole-train at the Spaklerweg yard and one of them passed out from the cleaning fumes of the solvent used to buff the painted trains; he wasn't wearing a gas mask. When the cleaner collapsed, an ambulance came to pick him up and take him to the hospital. The event made prime-time news and newspaper headlines, and even Greenpeace voiced their concern, making an inquiry into what kind of poisons were in the cleaning solution. It was soon discovered that by cleaning the painted trains, the subway company was essentially poisoning the earth, and so from that moment on the Government banned the cleaning of trains. It was then that writers like Dice, Bus, Moon, Shei, Days, Fat, Chaze of DSK, plus Shenk, Cad and later on Rhyme, Pone, Delta and Gasp started to hit the subways really hard. I can remember one night when crews like DSK, GVB, CBS and LHS hooked up at the Gaasperplas yard to kill the last clean car! It was so cool having over 25 guys running around the four track lay-up in the park, destroying all the cars with panels, throw-ups, top-to-bottoms and tags!

After that action a small group conceived a plan to go to the buff yard at Venn in Stuard Weg to do another whole-train. Eleven guys did the second whole-train and also a double end-to-end on the rail tram! It was a "GVEomb-Bus" whole-car, "Empee" from Days, "Djoez-Moon", Dice and at the end an LHC one; every whole-car was full colour and beautiful, but then when everybody started to bomb the other clean trains all of a sudden the cops arrived and there was a huge riot. Oh boy! Hell on earth!!

THE SITUATION IN 1990
—

Rhyme – GVB / Amsterdam
>

When the subway cars started getting frequently bombed it was a job done by Bus, Shei and Dice in 1990: at some point the subway company wasn't cleaning the trains anymore so we figured they weren't allowed to. We read in the newspapers that the poison found in the cleaning chemicals was going into the ground and because of pollution the company couldn't clean the cars anymore. That's when it became total madness. This was a dream come true for us, we started to do pieces like maniacs and every piece was running! Every car was hit with pieces, whole-cars, end-to-ends.

The news travelled fast and all of a sudden there were people from all over Europe coming to Amsterdam to start bombing. Graffiti writers were coming from Germany, England, France, Scandinavia. We ended up at some point with 20 guys in the yard, the security guys couldn't manage anymore... total chaos. Also Reas and Pure came from New York, we did a whole-car together. Sometimes you could go even in the daytime, which I think was better.

It wasn't controlled even though there were wholecars. Trains kept running for months, it was getting boring: I wasn't so motivated in the end, it was too easy. I saw pieces of mine running for a year! It was the dream of a life time, but when it came true it wasn't so interesting anymore.

Strangers around the corner

The Amsterdam boom of the early 90's, an International tourist attraction for every writer

Fume – MNS / Düsseldorf
>

During the middle of the 80's, Amsterdam was already a goal for every guy of the Ruhr-area: we only needed a couple of hours inside those gates of freedom, where apparently everything was legal, even bombing on the streets: the buildings were so full of tags that it became a quotidien behaviour, a daily routine for the group of locals. The first time I visited the city during 1985, I was just a naïve kid convinced that us writers of Dusseldorf were the only ones in Europe, apart for a couple of guys in Dortmund. But when my mother drove me there and I jumped out at Waterloo Plain, I was shocked: style-wise the locals here were even more ahead than us! Amazing letters, amazing colours! Since then I tried to go over there every month and have a look at the pieces, the hall of fame, checking how the whole style was improving and getting better and better.

The first person I ever met was this guy who writes Alien, who was into death metal. Me and my friends walked around Amsterdam tagging everywhere, we thought it was legal because everything was bombed. All of a sudden we bumped into a group of taggers that were renown for ripping off tourists and stealing cans from other writers. Oddly enough, when we told them we were from Düsseldorf they told us to come with them to see some halls of fame. I think one of the guys was Zar; I later heard that he was a very violent person but maybe he was just having a friendly day. We kept walking and tagging with them until we finally arrived at the spot: a large wall in the centre of the city where there was an Alien burner in the middle and two space commancers painted on either sides by Jesus and Jazz. Later on Cat 22 did a "Crime" piece on top of it.

Amsterdam back then was really an open-air museum for every writer coming from outside with street bombing everywhere and the best burners on walls. The whole perspective changed in 1990. During that year I went to a jam in Heidelberg where I painted my first panel piece. It was in service for more than three months, and I was on fire. Despite painting for years, trains had never been considered before. That achievement twisted the

Finally, in Europe somehow the New York myth of a bombed system got evoked and the local scene of Amsterdam became International

expectations and the lifestyle of a whole group of guys that gradually kept that target as their main mission in life. When I heard about subways, I started wondering if they had trains similar to the New York ones. Of course you always had this idea of New York in mind, so Amsterdam became the main focus: even if the system was incredibly small, the subway had steel trains running. With Sers, Rio from Dortmund and Shen from Koln, we went to Amsterdam and I remembered I still had Alien's phone number. He'd already stopped but he hosted all of us, and his flatmate, Forz, took us to the subway. It was a weird night. We went there, into the rows of trains, checking the guard from far away.

While we did pieces, Forz was just tagging every possible car until suddenly we saw him running like an animal. We had already finished our pieces, we were still watching the trains and rolling joints; in our stoned condition

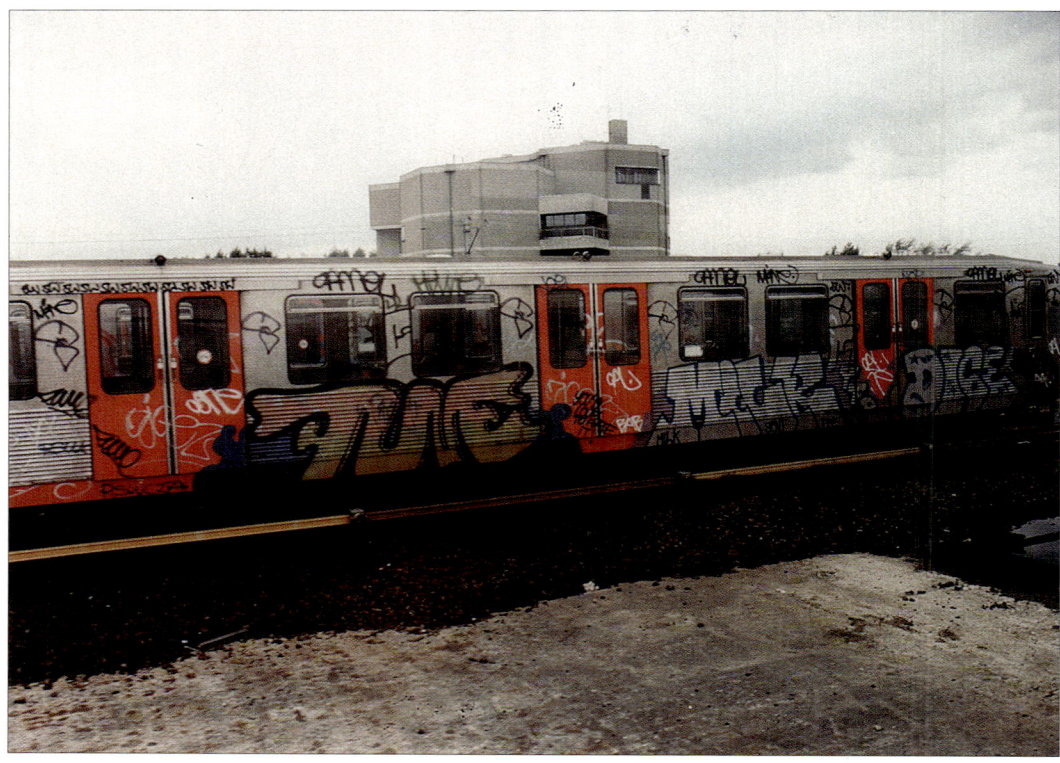

Pone – GVB, 1991   — *Mark Todt*

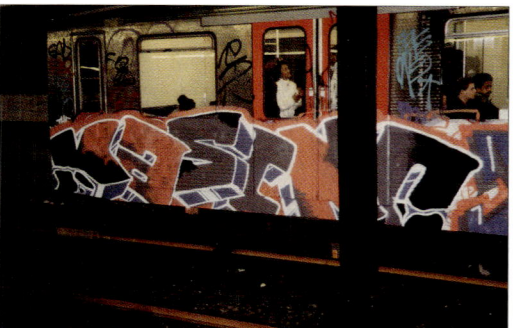

Kasino from Brisbane   — *Mark Todt*

Colorsz from Paris   — *Mark Todt*

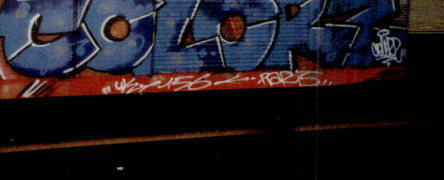

Nug, Aman from Stockholm, Sak from Germany, 1992 — *Mark Todt*

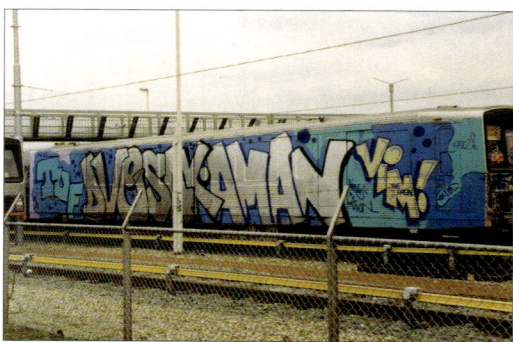

Swet from Danimark   — *Mark Todt*

it seemed like a joke, but a few minutes later the police came by car and it was only by chance that we got away safely. The next day the train ran straight to Amstel station, standing there in broad daylight! The excitement of seeing painted cars run was high and contagious back then, and that same year the whole of the Amsterdam subway system literally exploded.

Finally the New York myth of a bombed system was being evoked in Europe and the local scene of Amsterdam instantly became wider and more International. Writers from the Ruhr area began travelling to the Netherlands every week, like commuters of train bombing. Amstel

station became the spot in which to take pictures and meet the locals on the platforms. Even the most renown yards became hang-outs: one time I got in with some German writers and then suddenly a bunch of Dutch guys arrived... we almost had a panic-attack until we saw they were just writers too! Then five minutes later a whole squad of Londoners come in and all of a sudden we figured out there were 15 guys there, coming from all over Europe and with one goal in mind. This frequent co-operation built some of the most important crews and Amterdam's bombed subway became a symbol of unstoppable Writing in Europe.

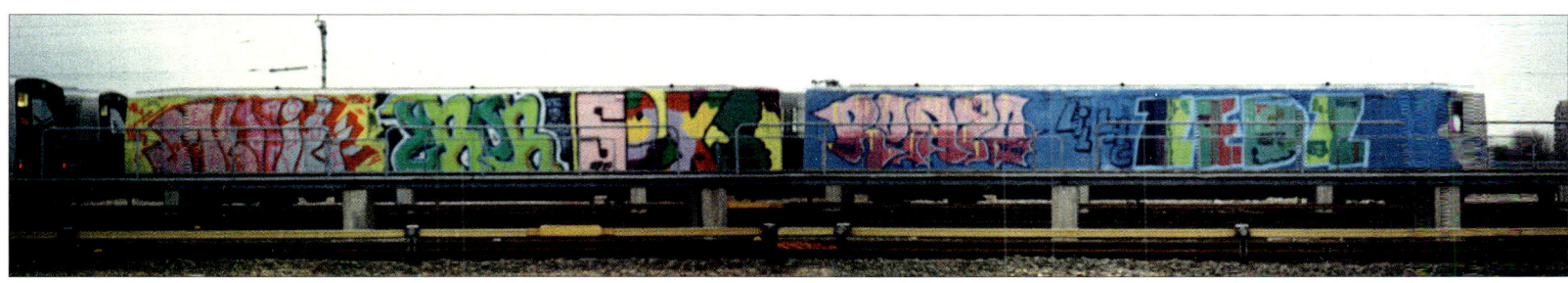

Mellie, Eror, Sek, Reaze, Zedz, 1993   — Reaze

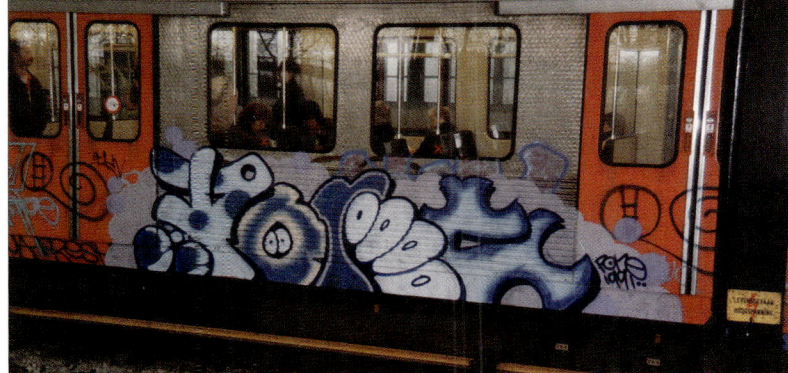

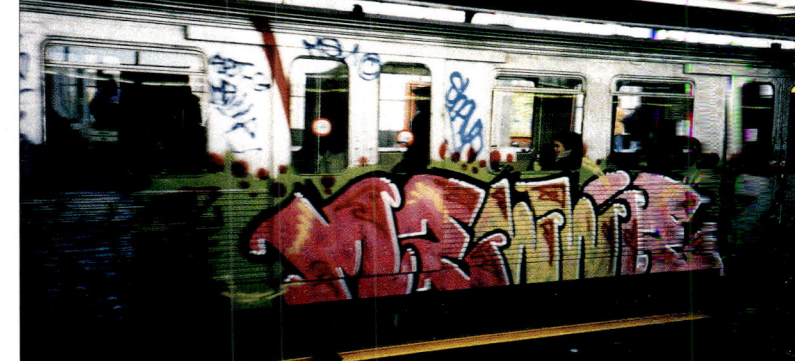

Pone-GVB, 1991   — Mark Todt   Mellie - MSN   — Actor Aive

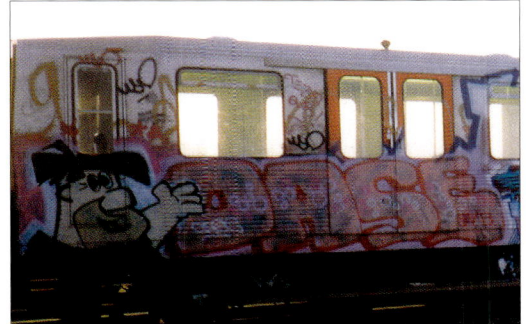

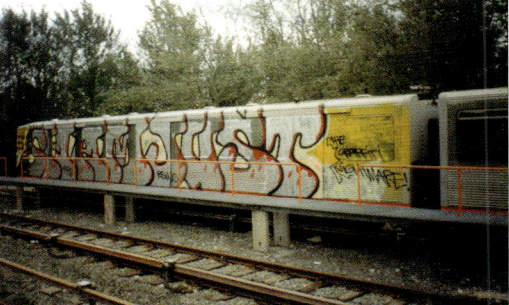

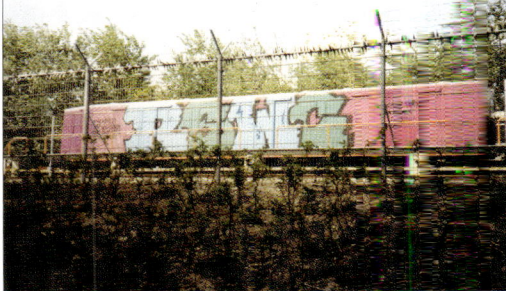

Oase - GVB   — Rhyme   Shame and Just, "The graffiti nightmare"   — Mark Todt   Ces53 and Shame, unfinished RSWC whole-car   — Mark Todt

A SUBWAY BULLETIN
—

From True Colorz magazine, issue 6 (1995)

>

Over five years of getting fucked up, painted by tons of writers from all over the world and it's still driving from Central station to Gein with its thick layers of paint. Done over and over again as if it were part of an everyday cycle.

At the moment there are three lines: one that goes from Central station to Gein (the bombed line), one that goes from Central station to Gaasperplas, which used to be bombed but got totally cleaned in 1993, year in which a new line was put in service. This line drives from Central station to Amstelveen Middenhoven and only includes new models of subway trains called sneltrams. These are not bombed. In 1997 a new line will be completed, going from the North to the South of Amsterdam. The GVB will buy new sneltrams for this line and will build new yards and lay-ups.

–THE SITUATION UNTIL MID FEBRUARY 1995

The GVB has 44 steel cars for the Gein and Gaasper lines, about 17 of these are still fucked up. It's easy to see if you look at the numbers of the cars. The numbers of the steel cars go from 1 to 44 and the sneltrams go from 45 to 69. Each numbers is in fact two cars that are always connected, also known as a DINGDONG, this counts for both steel cars and sneltrams. If you look at these figures it's obvious they have to connect clean cars to bombed cars or use totallly clean cars on the Geinline.

The 24 sneltrams are all clean. These sneltrams are property of the GVB which is very proud of them. As I said earlier these cars are not bombed while in service, but they do get bombed while in yards and lay-ups.

If a sneltram is hit while the GVB is sleeping they drive it to the buff immediately, as soon as they see it. Usually these whole-cars never see the light of day whereas whole-cars done on steel cars stand in the yards or lay-ups where everybody can see them for days. The last few months were good times in the history of Amsterdam subway bombing. A new crew came up, ASD (Amsterdam Subway Destroyers or All System Down) who surprised everybody with a hugh amount of panels and whole-cars within a short period of time. A married couple

whole-car by KL-crew (which had not happened since the one by Chintz, Atome, Sento, Milk). KL-crew, which is a train crew from its origin, took care of several end-to-ends and panels mostly by Down and Lench. Now, March 1995, we can say Joe from ASD has the most panels behind his name if we look back at the last few months. Some of them are just panels but mostly with a detailed character in fresh colours. Another new writer on the front is Lench, he came out with several fresh panels and took part in some whole-cars with Joe. Zedz of DSK crew went out on the warpath several times, sometimes alone and sometimes with Cece. Next to some panels on the steel Gein-cars he managed to put some panels on the sneltrams.

Whole-cars on sneltrams are done by Yalt, Cece and Zedz, a top-to-bottom by Math from the NES-crew also on a sneltram. Math put some new panels on both clean and bombed cars. Other new and very active crews are SMD-crew (Suck My Dick) and 2TS (2 Trash Subways) they both came out with several panels on the Gein cars and bombed the Gaasper cars. The same with VASR and homies,

they hit dozens of cars, though mostly clean ones. Foreigners, mostly from Germany, came out with a few end-to-ends and worried-couple whole-cars. Through a crazy amount of new panels and whole-cars some old INC pieces that had been burning for over three years were destroyed. Also a lot of Mellie pieces were destroyed. Mellie almost had a panel on each side of painted cars so he had to concede a lot of space to the heavy bombing. In the last few months only a few wholecars from his hand were spotted.

In issue 2 we reported about the new barbed wire fences around the yards of Gaasper and Gein. Well it ain't that new any more, the GVB had to spend thousands of guilders filling holes. Moon: Cleaners used to have an "I don't care" attitude. Sometimes cleaners even walked up to writers while they were painting panels and whole-cars in the daylight to have a talk like: "You're not allowed to do this.", and would just walk away while writers continued. Some writers and cleaners know each other pretty well back in the cars (90-91). Nowadays cleaners can earn a 100 gulders bonus if they catch a writer.

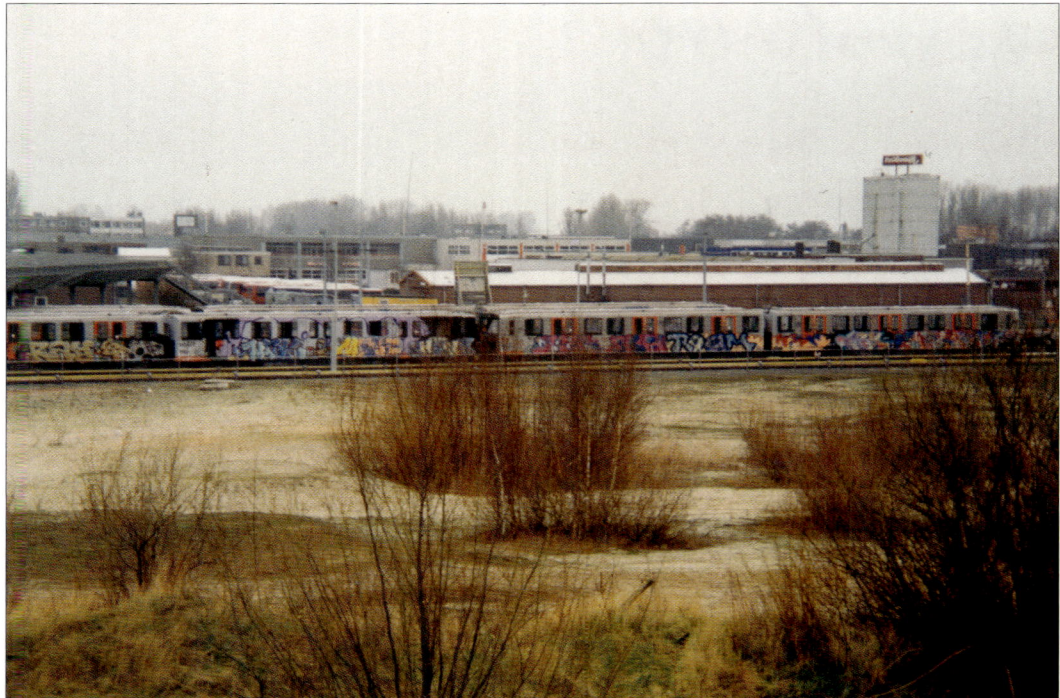

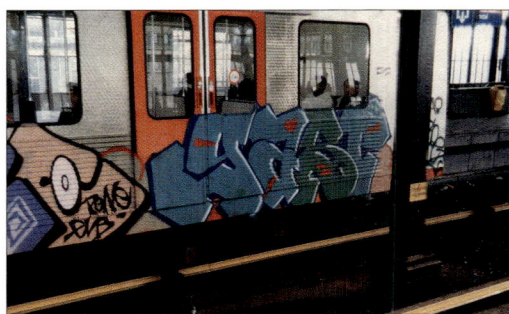

— Mark Todt

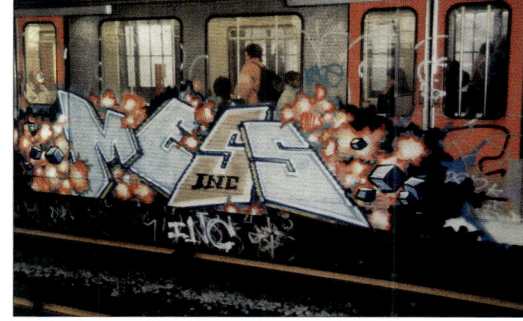

— Mark Todt

— Mark Todt

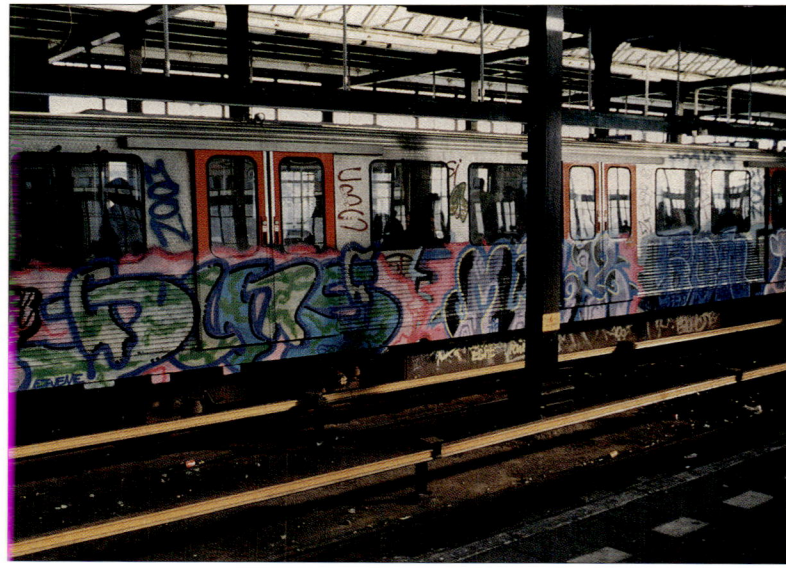

— Mark Todt

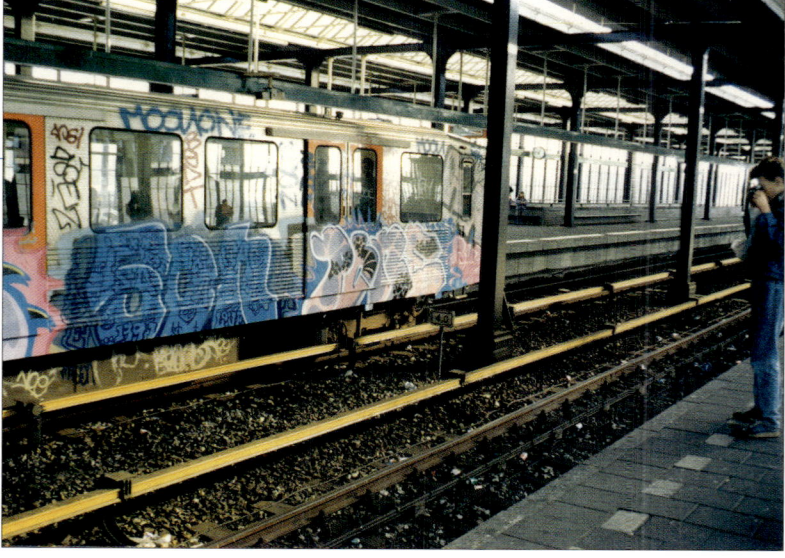

— Mark Todt

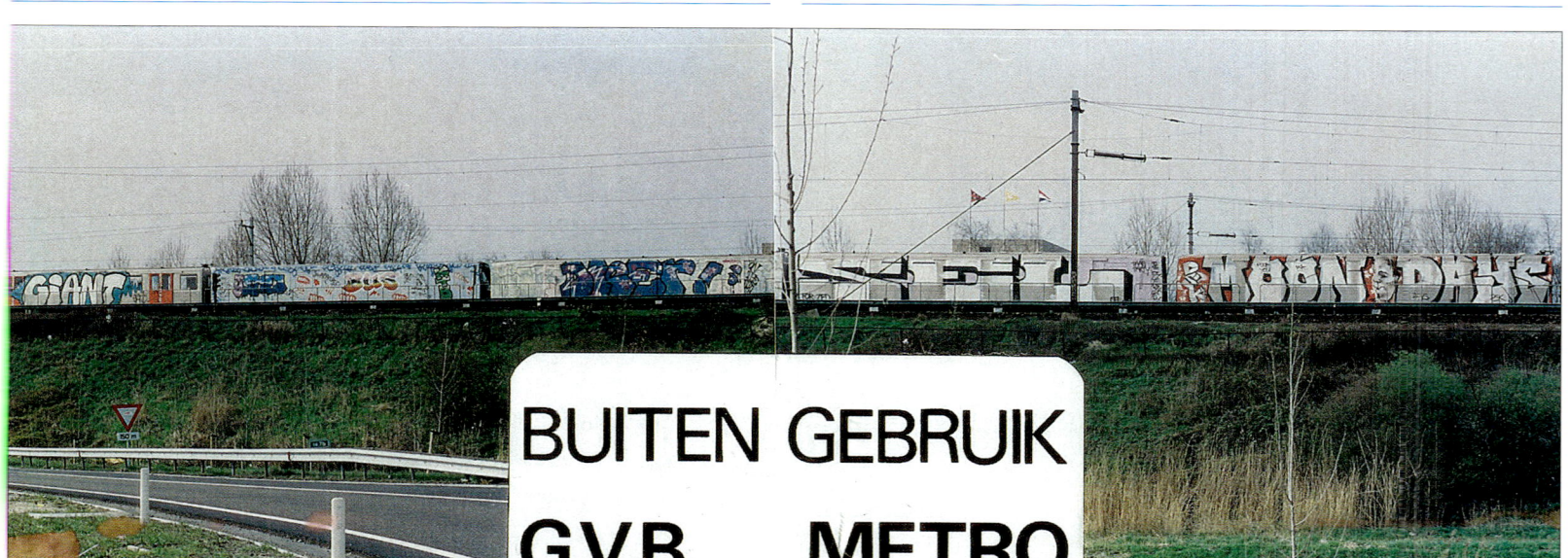

— Moon

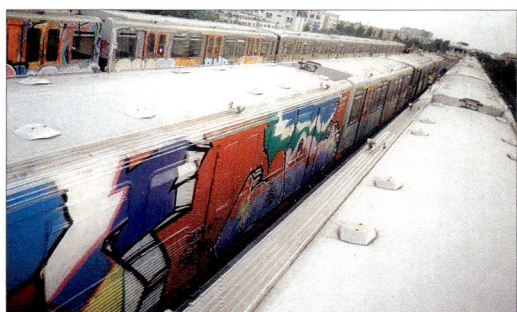

— Moon

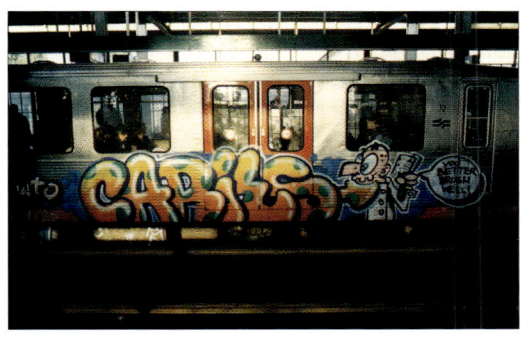

— ACW Archives

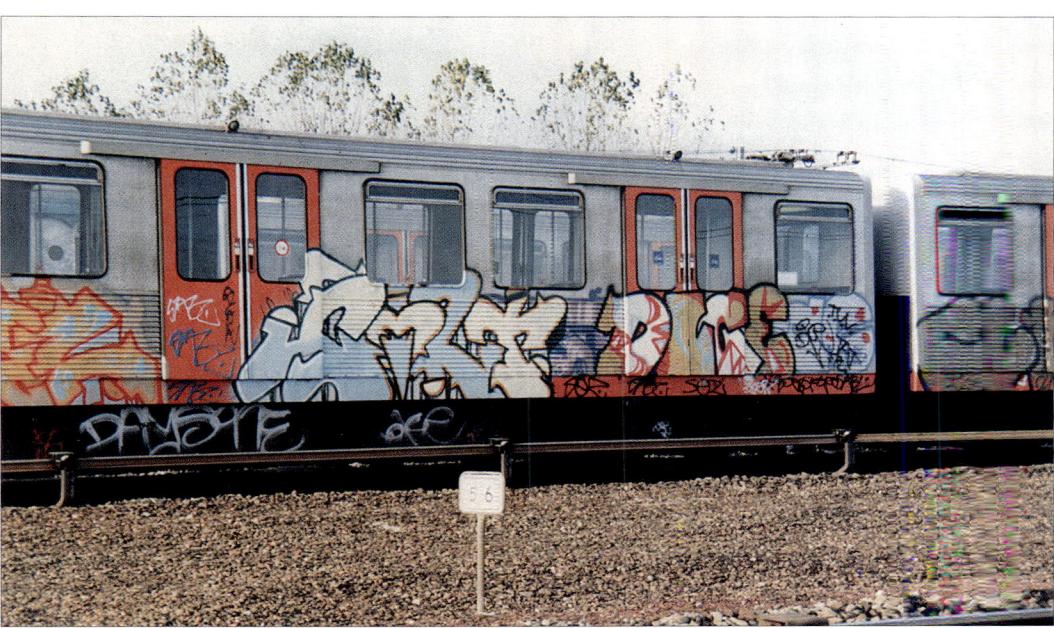

— Nick Todt

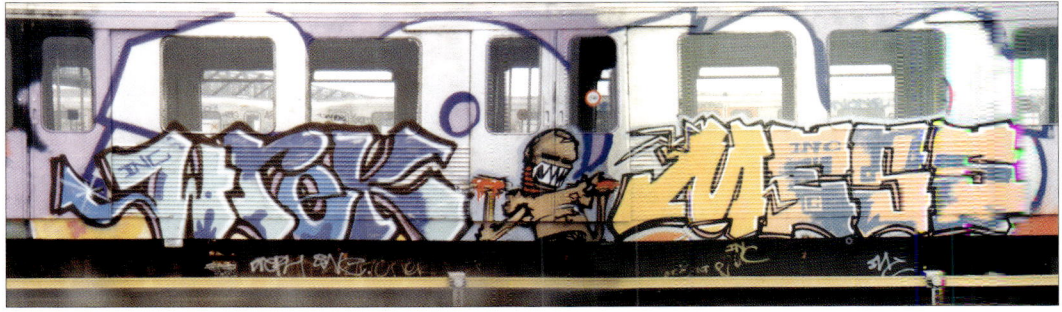

— Nick Todt

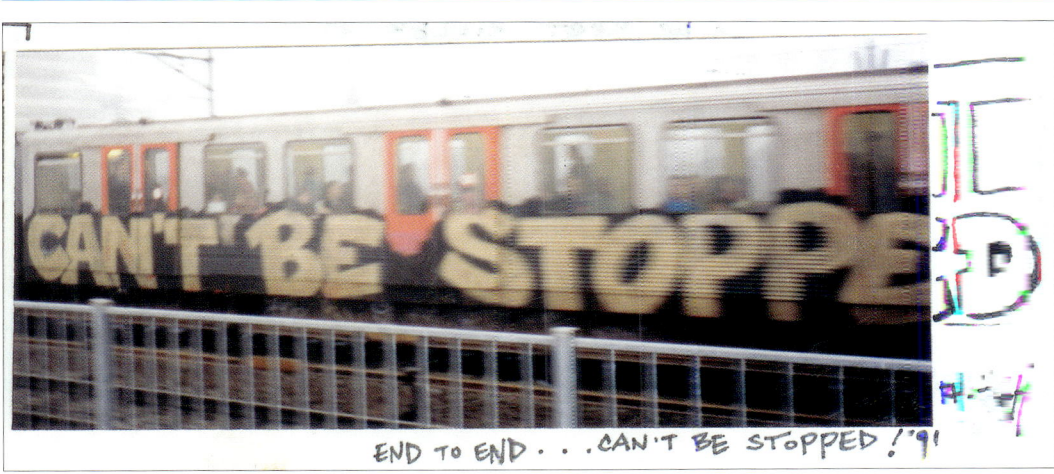

END TO END . . . CAN'T BE STOPPED! '91

— Home

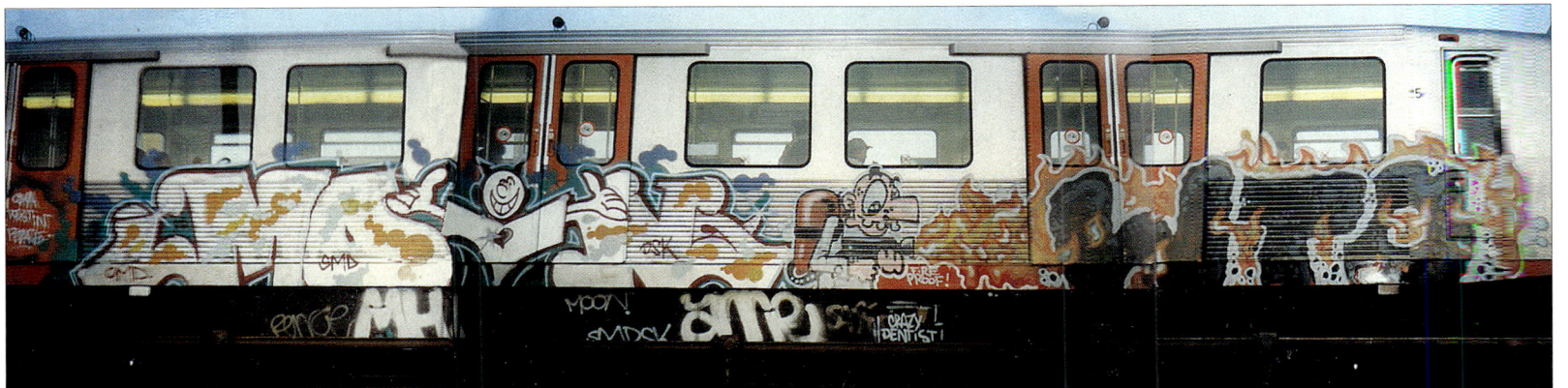

— Nick Todt

	2		4		
1			5	6
	3			7
11	12			8
10		9	

1. Ray, Wrek, Mess, Dice, Shei, Roam, DSK at the main Buff Yard called Verrijn Stuart

2. Gasp – INC, 1991

3. Mess explosion, 199

4. The subway scenaric of Amsterdam during 1990

5. *Caries* by the crazy dentist, WTO crew

6. Cot and Dice

7. Wrek by Gasp and Mess by Delta, INC crew

8. *Can't Be Stopped in traffic*, by Rhyme and High

9. Moon and WTO

10. DSK whole-train

11. *Duns* by Fume–MSN from Dusseldorf, Milk–TFP from Munich

12. *Son* by Mason from Dortmund and Pone–CTK

METRO MADRID

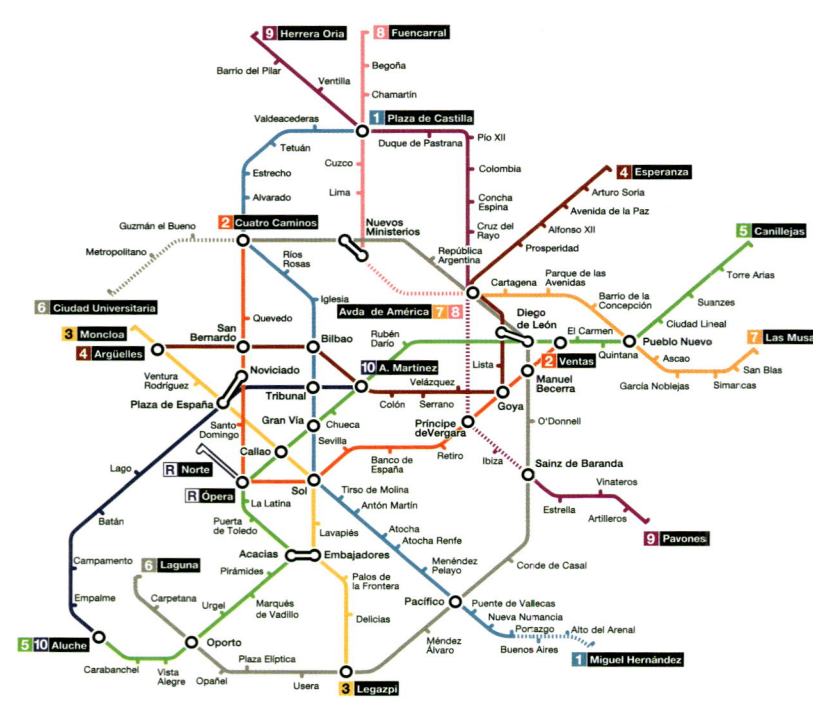

The primary subway lines of Madrid in the 80's, a golden age for local Writing

Fernando Figueroa
>

The first appearance of Writing in Madrid can be dated between 1984 and 1985, though the beginning of activity for the majority of old-school writers is concentrated between 1986 and 1988. First tags appeared and then, once technique and style were grasped, pieces developed. Just like New York in the early 70's. The factors that favour the development and stable presence of Writing are various, but the principle aspect that encouraged it here was the existence of a generation of local youths living in peripheral neighbourhoods or dormitory-cities, middle and lower class kids that were growing up in a democracy that had only recently been constituted from the ashes of the Francoist regime, and were therefore open to the cultural influences coming from the United States. These kids would be the motor behind a process of assimilation and definition of Writing and the Hip Hop movement in the national context.

Even though some groups between the 80's and 90's established ties with the scenes of New York and Miami, in the Madrilenian definition of Writing a clear European influence is manifested (from France, Germany, Netherlands, Scandinavia), as well as an interrelation with other Spanish cities outside the Province of Madrid, especially Alicante and Barcelona. In this sense travelling, exchanging photos, the publishing of fanzines and exhibitions in art galleries were fundamental.

The arrival of Writing to Madrid cannot be understood without taking into account the neighbouring urban centres because it is in some of these satellite-municipalities that the quantity and quality of production was concentrated in the early years. More specifically, to the East of

Madrid we have Torrejón de Ardoz, which includes an area that had an important influence; then the Hispanic-North American military base of Coslada, and to the South the cities of Móstoles and Alcorcón, which were authentic capitals in the territory of the Comunidad, or Province, of Madrid during the 80's and 90's. Evidently this co-existence of neighbouring and communicating fires (especially thanks to the Cercanías trains) increases the feelings of competition and facilitates the trips and exchanges between crews in different territories.

In a similar manner to the Province, the city of Madrid also had its 'nucleuses' of activity particularly distributed in peripheral neighbourhoods. It's in the South of the capital that the most important groups are concentrated (Latina-Carabanchel), followed by the Northern area (Tetúan-Chamartín) and the South-East (Vallecas-Moratalaz, Usera-Villaverde). Each of these areas would have a central place of reference, or hang-out, such as the pedestrian complex of piazzas and terraces of Nuevos Ministerios, that would become a meeting point for all the old-school B-boys of the 80's.

– THE SUBWAY OF MADRID

The first pieces to appear on the subway cars of Madrid started circulating in 1986, after the first carriage was hit in the station of Aluche. The autochthonous writers, the so-called Flecheros, were the first to write in the subway, though they limited themselves to marking other surfaces without actually touching the cars themselves: usually they deliberately chose to scribble over the rail signals that had a light blue background. With regards to the process that brings Madrilenian Writing to the cars

of the subway, a key role is played by the diffusion and knowledge of information regarding subway Art. Also of great importance was the T.V broadcast of *Style Wars* by Tony Silver and Henry Chalfant in 1986, and after that the publication in Spanish of *Getting Up* by Craig Castleman in 1987. The Spanish translation of Castleman was particularly important because it favoured a comprehension void of doubts regarding certain terms and aspects that were difficult to grasp in books and documentaries in English. Influenced by these media, the writers of the city started to emulate the practices and aesthetics of the original New York B-boys: though we never went as far as to reproduce the suburban landscape of 70's New York in all its magnitude, in a few years Madrid had an active scene that was widespread throughout the territory.

In its development an essential role was played by the formation of crews whose main activity was painting the cars of the subway, thus increasing the sense of competition regarding the quantity and quality of pieces done.

The most relevant actions of the 80's are almost always attempts at realising whole-cars, which had become the objective of every crew. In this sense an action to remember is the one on Christmas Eve of 1989 in the station of Aluche, in which the first whole-car was realised, and, curiously enough, even some Flecheros participated, though unfortunately it was never allowed to circulate. The most active lines between 1986 and 1992 were the 1 (Plaza Castilla-Portazgo), the 5 (Aluche-Canillejas), the 6 (Laguna-Ciudad Universitaria) and the 10 (Aluche-Alonso Martinez). The 5 and 10 lines had the added bonus of circulating outside the tunnels and creating an impact on the landscape that resembled the classic images from

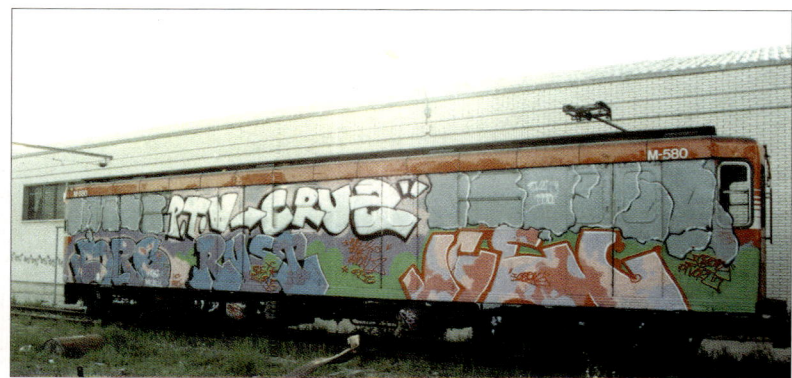

PTV Crue by More, Rust e Ice –PTV, whole-car painted along line 5th in 1990   *– Felipe Gálvez Archive*

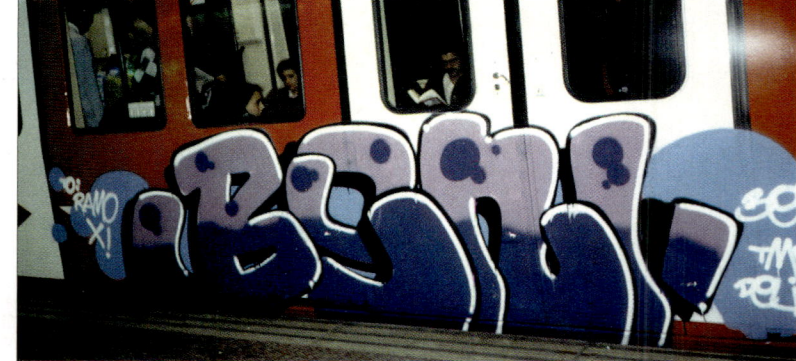

Beni –TMF on line 4th, 1992   *– Felipe Gálvez archive*

New York. Other lines were also running painted, like the 4 (Argüelles-Esperanza), the 8 (Fuencarral-Avenida de América) or the 9 (Herrera Oria-Pavones), but the autochthonous writers seemed to prefer the 10 and 3 lines. Any action wasn't limited to just the train cars but also naturally expanded to include the stations and their tunnels. The first whole-car to circulate painted could anyway not be seen until 1992, along the 6, during a period remembered for the great rivalry that existed between crews that had the sole objective of obtaining the most visibility throughout the metropolitan network. The peak of this rivalry, in both size and virulence, would arrive in the same 1992, through a series of wars for the control of the subway cars and lines. This incandescent atmosphere, thanks to which dozens of painted trains were circulating, provoked an intense and inevitable reaction from the authorities: the sanctions increased, preventive and dissuasive measures were taken (such as the strengthening of barriers and video surveillance), buffing technology was developed and civic education programs were created, as were campaigns against graffiti. Thus a crisis in the activity of the subway develops between 1993 and 1994. In the second half of the 90's a good opportunity for entering the stations and painting was provided by the works for the expansion of the subway network. In parallel to this, the possibility of working with the walls that follow the track line started being considered, thus turning them into the new, important target to hit in the name of visibility. Along these walls the future styles of Madrid were developed, and a consequent generational turnover took place. In a similar manner to other European cities the divulging of painted trains occurs through photographical testimonies of the actions, a nocturnal snapshot meant immortalising the work and allowing it to circulate in magazine and fanzine circuits. Following this, at the end of the 90's, some train cars started running painted again thanks to carefully programmed kamikaze-actions: risky solutions at the limit of possibilities, like the so-called 'palancazos'. During these actions writers entered the subway cars in service with their spray cans hidden under their clothes. Once the train exited the tunnel and reached the surface, they would pull the emergency brake and open the doors of the cars. The writers would then take advantage of the few minutes of time before the train would set off again to paint some pieces on the outer sides, with the guaranty of seeing them run for at least a couple of hours. That was a last resort that, though extreme, became the only alternative left for those that could not resign themselves to seeing the subway of their city clean.

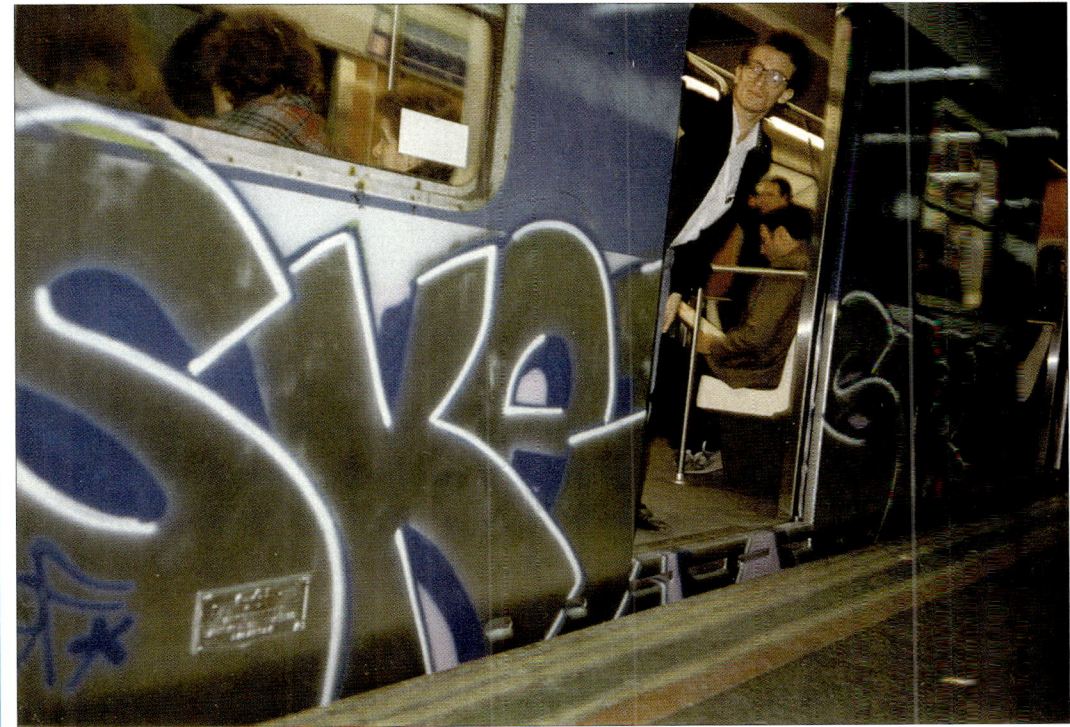

Sker and Stron by Speaker and Strone – SNF, CZB. Line 6

– Felipe Gálvez archive

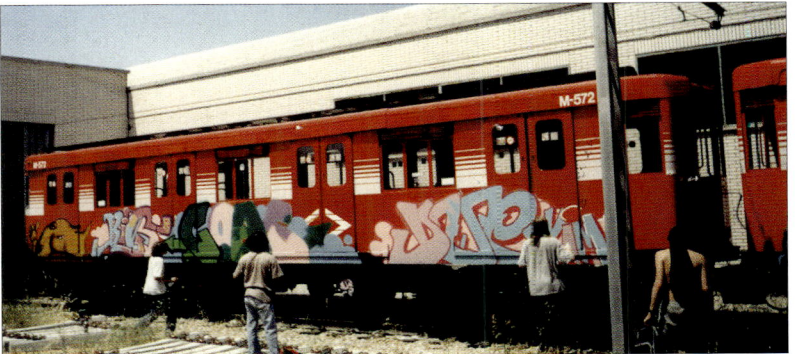

Rig, Coas, Due VIM by Rig, Koas and Nug from Stockholm.

– Felipe Gálvez archive

UNION

This car was painted by local writers and VIM crew from Stockholm at Canillejas subway station on July 21st, 1991.

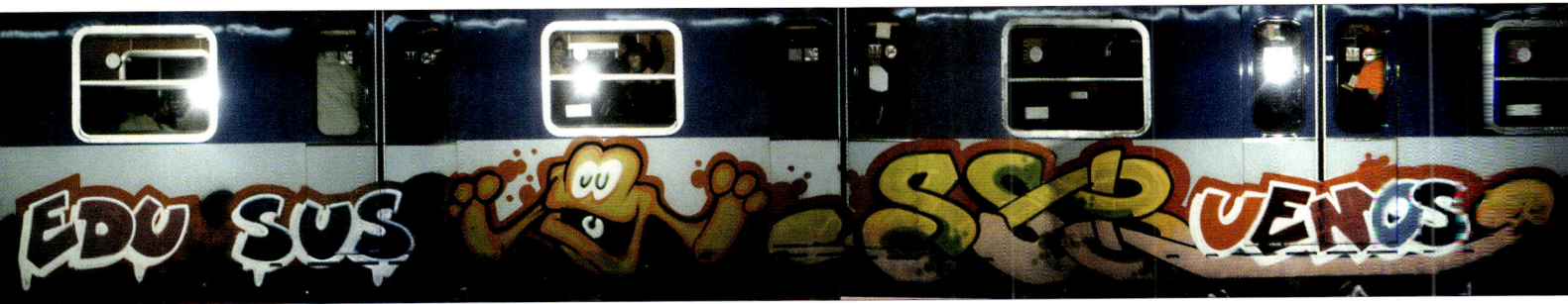

Edu, Sus, SSBuenos by Suso 33 and Edu – SSB. Line 9

– Felipe Gálvez archive

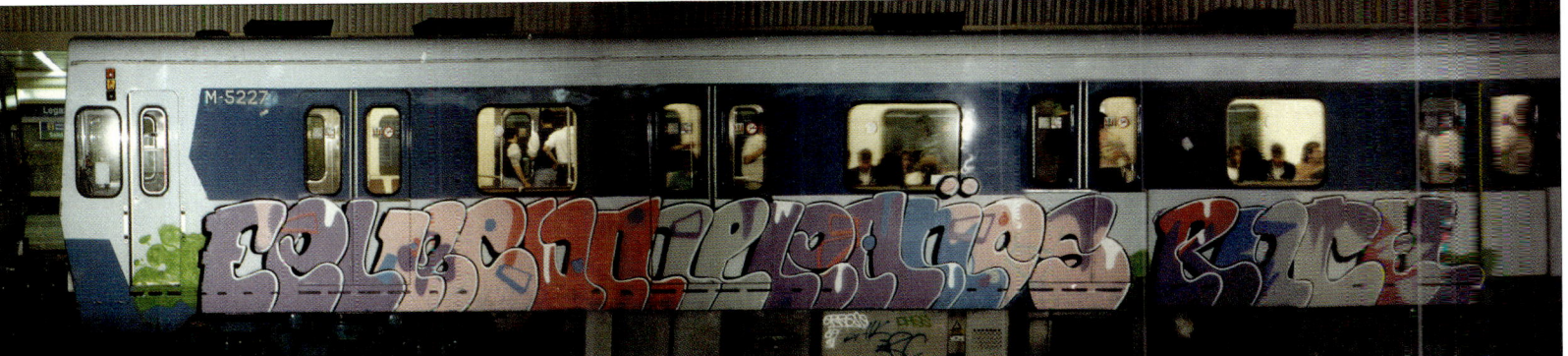

Feliz cumpleaños Ruth by Arrasa – SPC 69, TMF. Legazpi station, line 6th, 1992

– Felipe Gálvez archive

Suso draws up his battle lines

Suso 33 / Madrid
>

The words I am writing belong to my personal memories, experiences and accomplishments, though the history of the Madrilenian subway is inevitably also tied to many other people and stories. I seem to recall that the first thing I saw in the subway was basically scribbles, especially on empty ad billboards, seeing they had a large surface and their light blue background greatly emphasised tags, allowing them to last longer. In the second half of the 80's the first actual carriages started being painted, hit primarily by people from Southern Madrid, though in the early 90's the quantity of writers and crews active on this target increased noticeably.

The first subway trains I hit were done alone, but subsequently the people I started painting with most were Sec, Thor and Eduone; the lines I preferred – because they were the ones I used most and on which I could see painted cars run – were the 6 and the 9. On Line 6 there was maintenance work being done in the stations, which weren't operative, so we could enter in various ways, to then walk down the tunnel until reaching the carriages parked at the end of the line; it was here that we unleashed our creativity, between two trains in an underground tunnel from which we could see the station. We had to be very quiet and avoid creating a cloud of paint dust because otherwise the smell would have

We were learning to live and perhaps Writing was the perfect excuse

spread excessively. Many times there was hardly any light to see your pieces in and when you finally saw them circulating, the result was very different from what you had expected. The other end of the line was also a spot we tried to paint in but it was much more difficult, it was in a University area that was deserted during the night, so if they noticed you loitering nearby, you would most definitely be seen as suspect.

Line 9 was another of my favourites, it had a large deposit above ground and you could access and exit it from various places. We almost always entered from the locker rooms of the subway workers, taking advantage of their shift changes. There were big sheds with many rail tracks and various carriages; I liked going there on

weekend mornings because you could choose the better-positioned train, plus, being the weekend, train activity was much less frequent. The trains however stayed turned on, they could be moved at any moment, leaving your work half done – as has occurred on some occasions. In one of these deposits I remember painting one of my favourite pieces with Eduone, it was an end-to-end with many colours and it ran for weeks, often I got on that exact train to go to class.

The 8, though harder to do, was another of the better lines. I especially liked its deposit – similar to that of line 9, the only difference was that it had air-conditioners on the wall, through which, if you disassembled them, you could get in after having jumped over an obstacle. And if they saw you, there was always the possibility of exiting without the subway vigilantes knowing where you were getting out from.

The 1 line seemed impossible to us but it was a primary line that crossed through the city and playing on the ad slogan "La Linea 1 se pone guapa" (The 1 Line becomes beautiful), we did an end-to-end that read "La Linea 1 la ponemos guapa" (We make the 1 Line become beautiful). We painted it at an end station but they saw us before we had time to finish the outline so we had to get out in a hurry. We waited for them to open the next morning and before the train left we finished painting it in a heartbeat, we then had to run out of that tunnel in a rush as the moving train whistled behind us. Deposits, end stops, stations, lay-ups, these were the various locations in which you painted so as to avoid constantly hitting the same place and leaving traces. We managed to get our hands on the key that opened many of the doors and restricted access ways, so we decided to attempt painting all the lines in a single weekend, by taking advantage of the holidays. We were convinced we had everything planned and under control but we never made it, though it was a memorable attempt, with various frights and dangerous getaways. The paint we could get our hands on in that period wasn't great quality and the spray cans painted really slowly, so to produce bigger stuff we made our own caps. To have a wider variety of colours we then mixed the paint of one can with another, heating one to cool the other, pressing them together with a little tube blocked between the two caps.

In '93 and '94 the quantity of painted subway cars diminished notably and many writers stopped painting, because the anti-graffiti measures started getting real heavy. Other than putting guards and physical obstacles the carriages that got painted were no longer circulating – which discouraged many – and it was then that the long-distance Cercanias trains started being targeted,

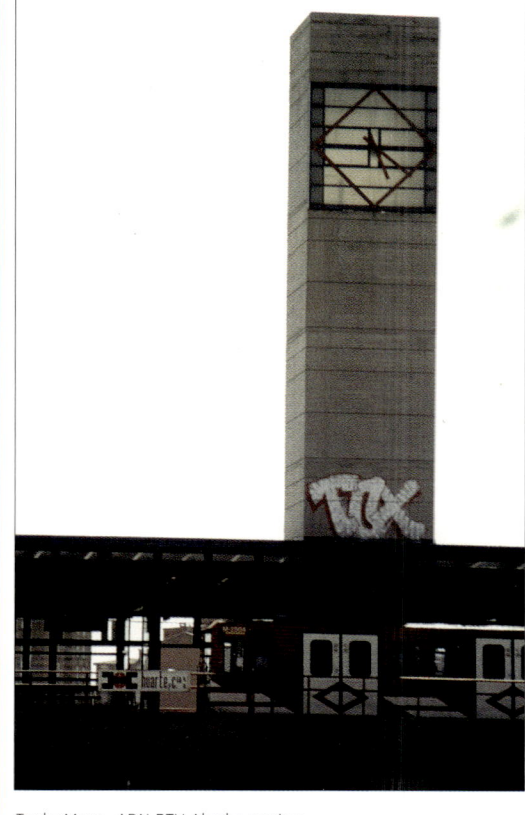

Tox by More – ADN,PTV. Aluche station   *– Felipe Gálvez archive*

though they were not considered as highly as the subway cars. It was also a time during which techno music and pills were causing a bloodshed. I have wonderful recollections of the feelings and sensations of that period. I was very young, I was discovering the world and at the same time feeling part of it when I was drawing. When I saw pinted trains running, the city that seemed so big would start becoming smaller. I feel especially tied to the people I lived the first experiences with, I felt free without thinking I was committing a crime. We were learning to live and perhaps Writing was the perfect excuse. Because the actual moment of painting wasn't the only relevant part, it was everything that surrounded the act itself that made it special: the fact of moving about the city and meeting so many people made me feel human.

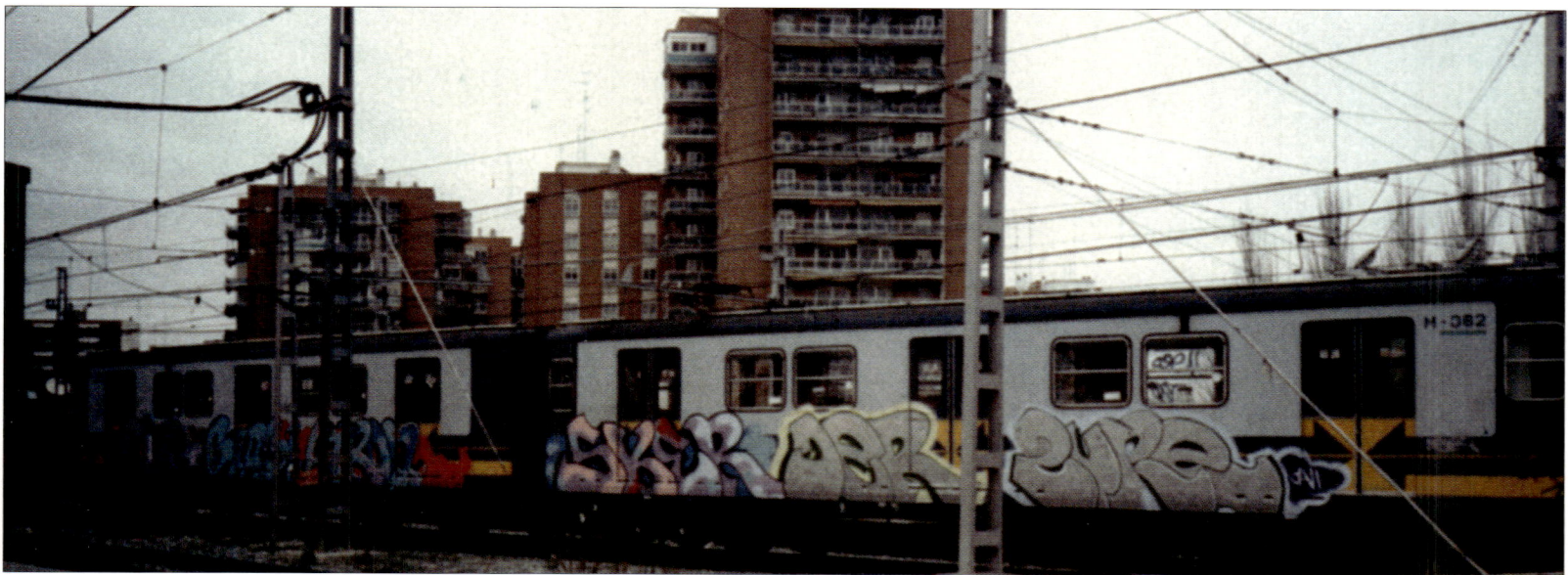

Sine, unknown, Stron, Sker, Jer, Zure by Trase, Poser, Strone, Speaker, Jer and Zure – CZB. Painted on the lay-up between Aluche and Empalme stations, line 10th   *– Felipe Gálvez archive*

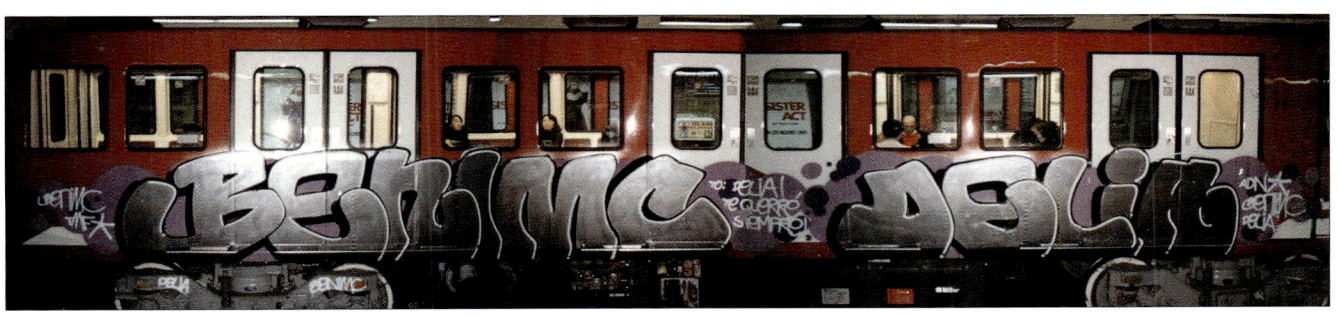

Benimc Delia by Beni – ADN, TMF. San Bernardo station, line 4th, 1992   *— Felipe Gálvez archive*

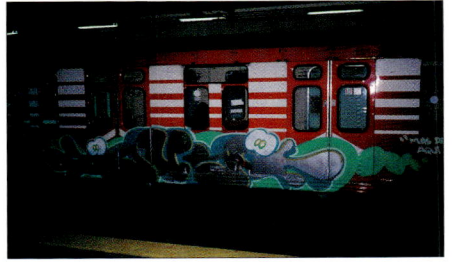

Suso 33 panel piece   *— Suso 33*

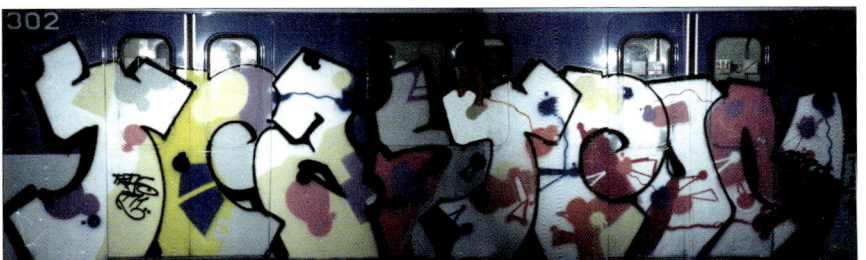

Trastron by Trase and Strone – CZB. Ciudad Universitaria station, line 6th, 1991   *— Felipe Gálvez archive*

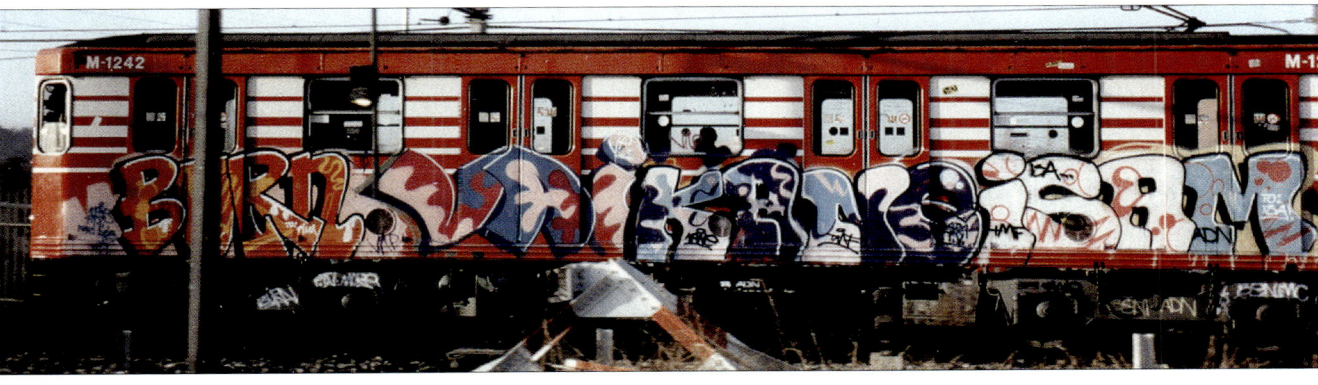

Burn, Vai, Kane, Isam by More, Vape, Kane and Eeni – ADN, TMF. Aluche lay–up   *— Felipe Gálvez archive*

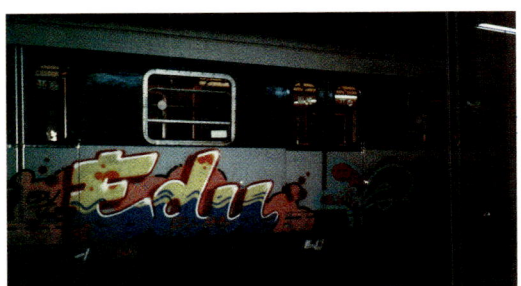

Edu – SSB, line 9   *— Felipe Gálvez archive*

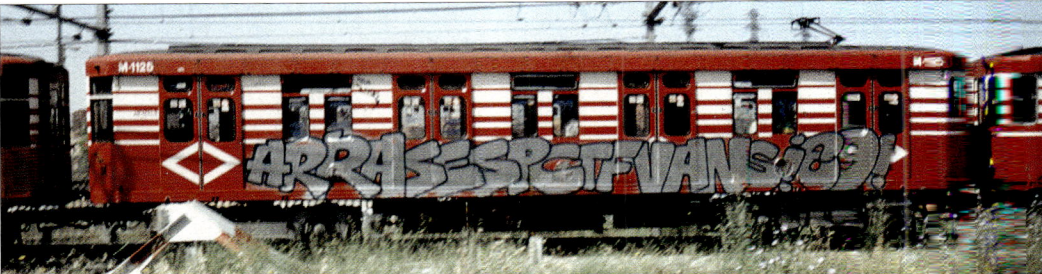

Arrasespctfvans.¡69! painted by Arrasa – SPC, TFV at Aluche lay–up, early 90's   *— Felipe Gálvez archive*

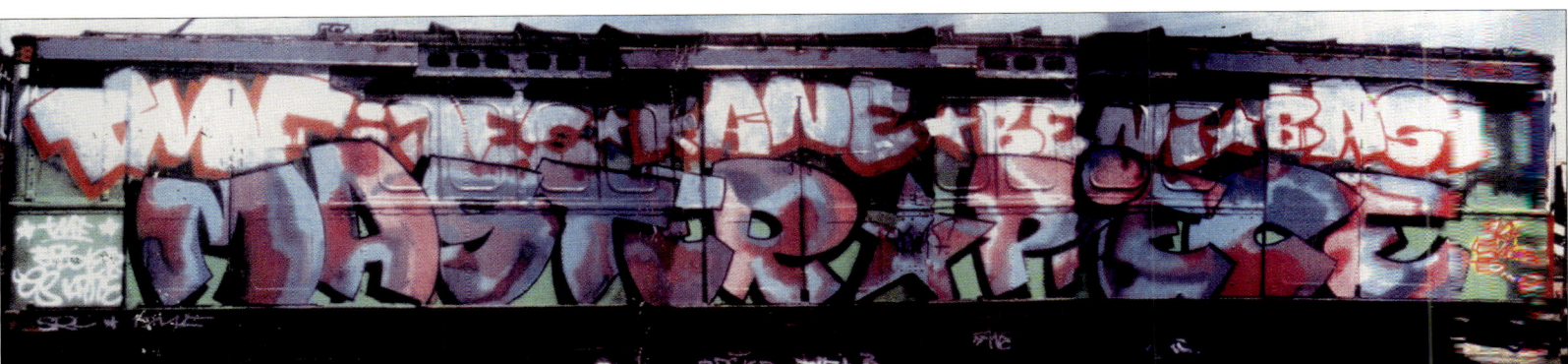

Master Piece by Jes, Kane, Beni y Basi – TMF. Line 3rd, 1991   *— Felipe Gálvez archive*

CLOUD 9

SUSO

Line 9 was one of my favourites, it had a large deposit above ground and you could access and exit it from various places. We almost always entered from the locker rooms of the subway-workers, taking advantage of their shift changes.

S-TRAIN SYSTEMS

COPENHAGEN RED CARPET

The red trains of the local lines in Copenhagen: a direct comparison of precursory styles and the main crews of the early 90's

Sabe FYS, COD / Copenhagen
>

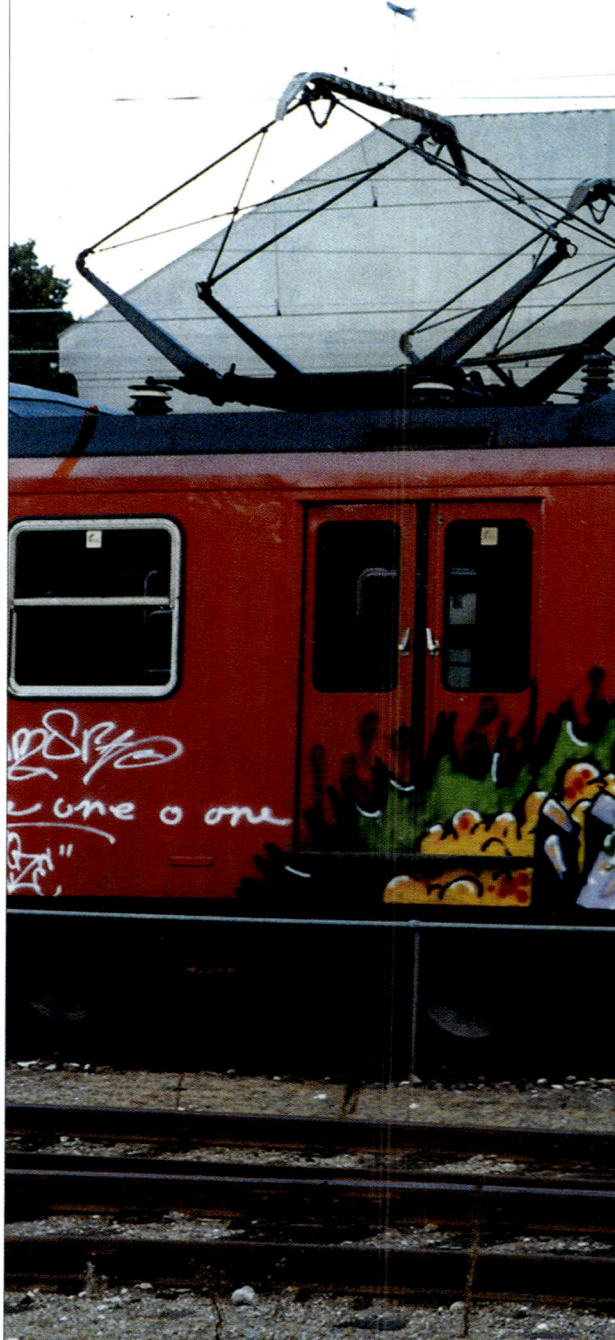

Rebel by Smurf, Date, Scale, fuse.1985

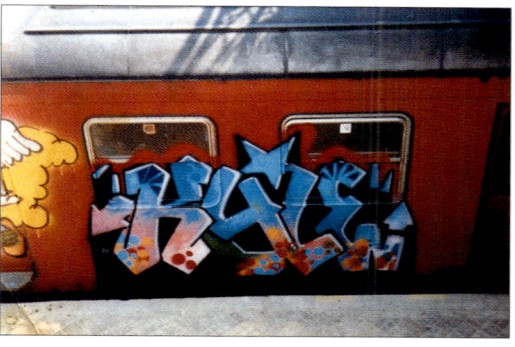

Kype piece in 1985   — Sketzh

As the Danish graffiti movement started pretty early on, the red S-trains have witnessed different generations of writers come and go since the early 80's. I think I belong to generation two. I started painting seriously in '85-'86 but there were already guys doing crazy whole-cars. The first train pieces in Copenhagen were painted in '84, I saw a photo of a piece Kyle had done that year. Then the scene kind of faded out in the middle of '87. The most beautiful whole-car in Denmark was done in '85; it was a full-colour, top-to-bottom whole-car. Nobody has ever beaten that, I think it was painted by a Danish guy called Freeze. When I started I knew I was way behind, some writers were already quite experienced and a Danish graffiti book had already been published. I had so much to catch up on, I started thinking maybe it was too late for me, but then again I had the 'right' feeling inside so I just kept on practicing. Trains have always been a target for me, I could see them go by my window every day on the elevated tracks. I'd be eating my cornflakes every morning before going to school and would watch the trains go by. The first time I really bombed by myself was in a yard in '86. I went alone and did some big tags with a fat cap, I was really shitting my pants, I was afraid. The yard was an hour away from Copenhagen. The second time I bombed was on New Years Eve of '86/'87, I did two main pieces in a yard and some little ones here and there. Between '87-'90 people weren't really painting, of course there were some pieces around but it had slowed down a lot. At the Public Enemy concert Rens showed me a whole-car he'd done in 1990. I thought he was fucking crazy, I hadn't seen pieces on the A line except his productions with Sek... they were TAV, The A-line Vandals! Me and Rens hooked up in '89 and did some stuff together. He was doing a lot of trains at the time while I was just doing them sporadically. Rens did really beautiful pieces because he took his time, he was really doing his thing. He was an inventive type of guy, figuring out how to paint a whole-car with a spray pump, doing it in just a few minutes! But above all, he was the one that came up with the idea of mixing paint. Rens kept his secret for a while. He had these crazy colours like baby blue while at the time there were only a few colours produced by a spray can brand called Quick, coming from Norway; they had 10-12 basic colours, in Copenhagen we were all limited to choosing from this colour spectrum and the tones of the pieces were basically the same. You could immediately recognise Danish panels by the red background of the S-trains and the primary colours of the pieces! They only had blue, yellow, green and a few other hues. After ten years of using the same colours, we were fed up with them and Rens found a solution. One night I was out painting and I saw a piece with a baby blue outline. It was Rens, even if at the time he was writing another name. I couldn't believe the colour I was seeing, I was shocked. A few weeks later he told me this lie about the factory. The story he told me was that his mother knew a girl working in a paint factory who would give him faulted spray cans produced by mistake with strange colours that were unsuited for the market. Writers went crazy and started giving him two ultra colour cans – which were luxury colours back then– in exchange for one of his fucked up spray colours. He was probably laughing his ass off because the reality was that he was just putting cans in the freezer and then mixing them by using a plastic straw! As we did a lot of stuff together he finally told me the truth. We laughed together about it for a long time and since then everybody else started using this method... of course the aesthetics of the pieces totally changed. By the early 90's the S-Train scene was quite strong. In Copenhagen there are different lines and different yards and considering that there were a lot of actors playing the same game, crews started to get more and more organised. Of course even the control systems got tougher: to paint whole-cars or even panels actions had to be organised so that a group of people would get together to do just one piece. One guy would be on watch, one would do the outline, one would do the fill and so on. That's how some writers started working, like a collective action. Crews were and still are really hardcore, painting a lot of stuff as they used to go to lay-ups and yards with seven-eight people doing whole-cars in 10-15 minutes. Everything was planned and they did crazy productions. Normally writers used to put up their own name on the S-Trains if they were working alone and the crew name if they were working as a crew. Personally I've always chosen to use my name but it's not that important what you write. It's important how you write it. In my opinion you have your tag or your crew name and you have to put it up in different styles, depending on the different moods or situations you're in. The personality in a name is really important to me. I love to see pieces by people who have been out painting together because you can see the different aspects of every individual person. You can see when someone is in a rush or is taking their time. Somehow, styles on trains mirror the writer's attitude.

Next pages
>

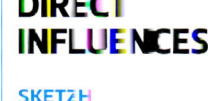

DIRECT INFLUENCES

SKETZH

Before Mode and Bando came to Copenhagen, the local styles were progressing by following New York, but with a local flavour, quite naïve. Then they came and did some pieces, even on trains. Back then CTK used to write small letters and spooky characters, with nice shapes and colours. These guys came along and blew everything away! It was really impressive to see how everything changed, style wise. Everybody started to do what they were doing, characters and letters. Of course they were experienced because they had met the New Yorkers in Amsterdam, they had a different vision with respect to us. I think it was good that they came but sometimes I wonder how our own style could have progressed without them.

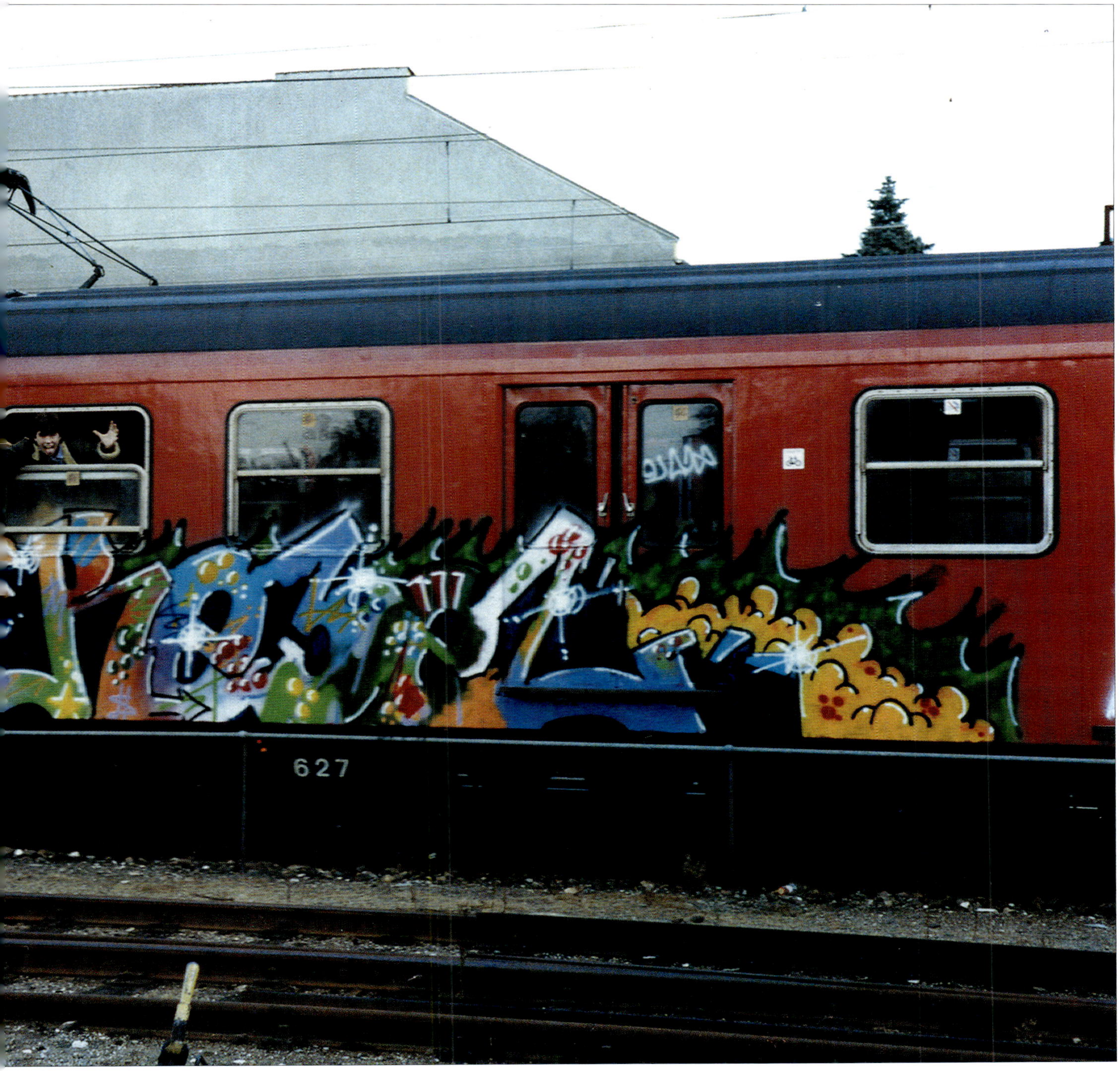

— *Sketzh*

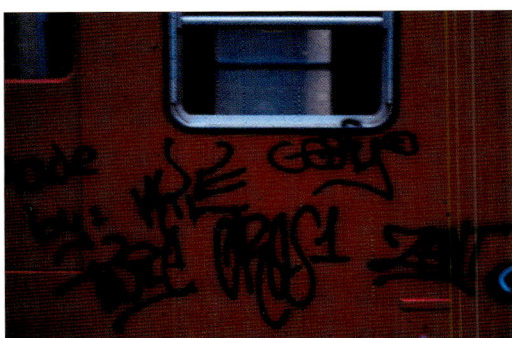

Cayle, Twice, Cros1, Goofy, Zent: Copenhagen early tags   — *Sketzh*

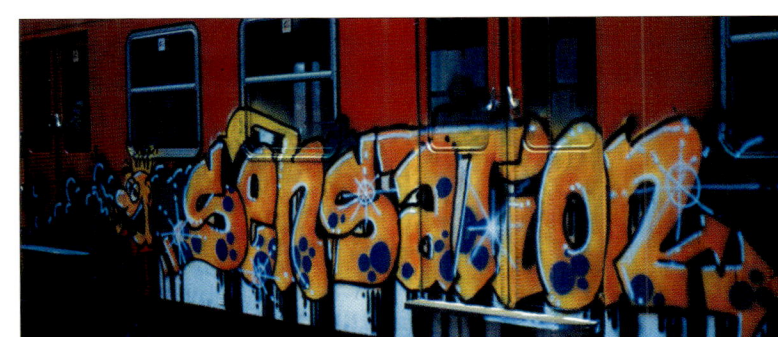

Sensation by Whap Gang, 1985   — *Sketzh*

A WAR OF MY OWN
—

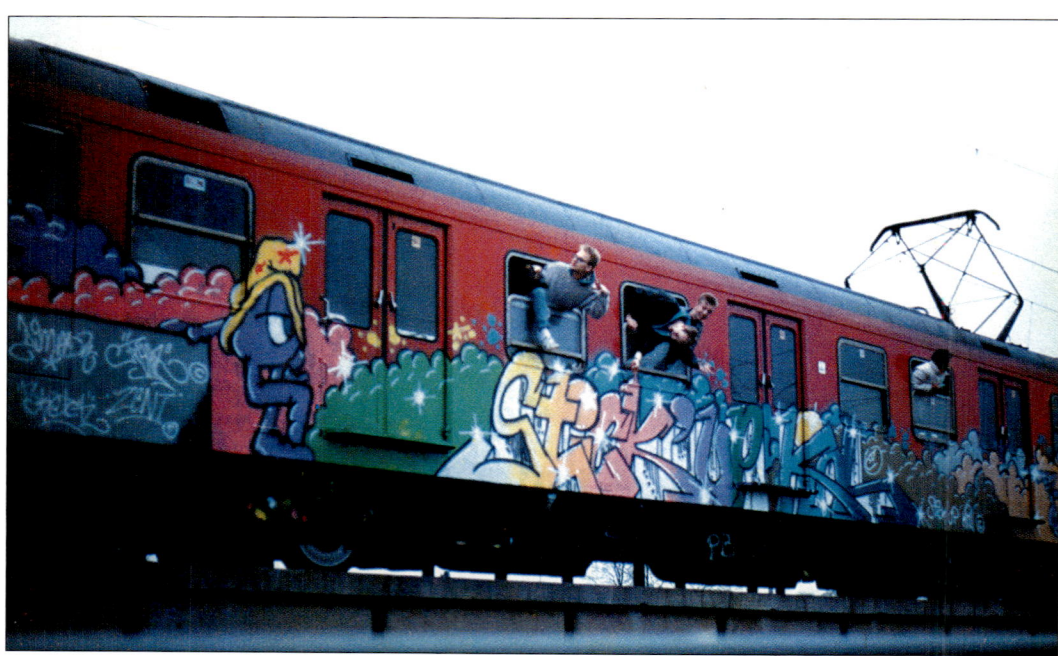

— Sketzh

Sek – TAV / Copenhagen

Back in 1985 there were no guards on the trains of Copenhagen, only workers. One of them would pick up extra train sets during rush hour; he was usually an old tipsy man on a mini bike. When we painted there it had to be before rush hour or you could be spotted from the track control centre, further down the tracks. I remember riding my BMX bike to the yard after school with my newly racked Poschas and Penols, hiding my schoolbag in the woods and sliding down the little hill, next to the trains.
And then climbing up and squeezing in between train doors to get in and tag on the brown and beige seats or the blue ones, which were simply the best! Sometimes I did panels with my crew at night but mostly we did them in the day, cause being 12 years old meant sneaking out at night was hard.
I remember one day in the yard we were painting a panel and the old man on the mini bike came to pick up a set of 'rush-hours'; when he saw us painting he was so shocked! He steered wrong and fell from the bike. It was the first time we got caught and we ran like crazy, cans were flying everywhere.
In 1985 the first whole-car was done as well as a lot of panels and window-downs. In 1986 the trains were guarded by a guy named Kledahl: this guy was very dedicated to his work and not only guarded the train yards but could also show up in the most active spots along the lines, and he was not shy about releasing the dog when he spotted writers. He had an old broken dog leash so when the police would come and he had caught writers, he'd simply tell the cops the leash had broken! He was a legend and a myth. I remember the first time I met him: I was in a lay-up with the legendary Freez who had gotten chased and caught by him several times. We were painting in the lay-up and suddenly a car parked in the back, Freez said: "Thats Kledahl!". We started running down the hill but since this lay-up was in the rich suburbs of the city, it was hard to get around: every property was surrounded by high fences. Right across from there was a lake surrounded by these big-ass houses; we ran non-stop, jumping fences, but after four fences we realised this could be a long trip! Just behind the lake I spotted a small rowing boat... Freez didn't know how to row so I had to do it. When we were in the centre of the lake we saw Kledahl with his dog and a flashlight looking in the bushes by the lake! When Freez came home after our sailing trip Kledahl was waiting on the ground floor of the 14-storey building we lived in. Freez went to the basement to take the elevator up and waved at him while passing by! Even though Kledahl was dedicated to his work in 1986 more trains than ever were painted. Later that year he got fired when it came out that he didn't have a clean record... moreover some guy that Freez knew checked

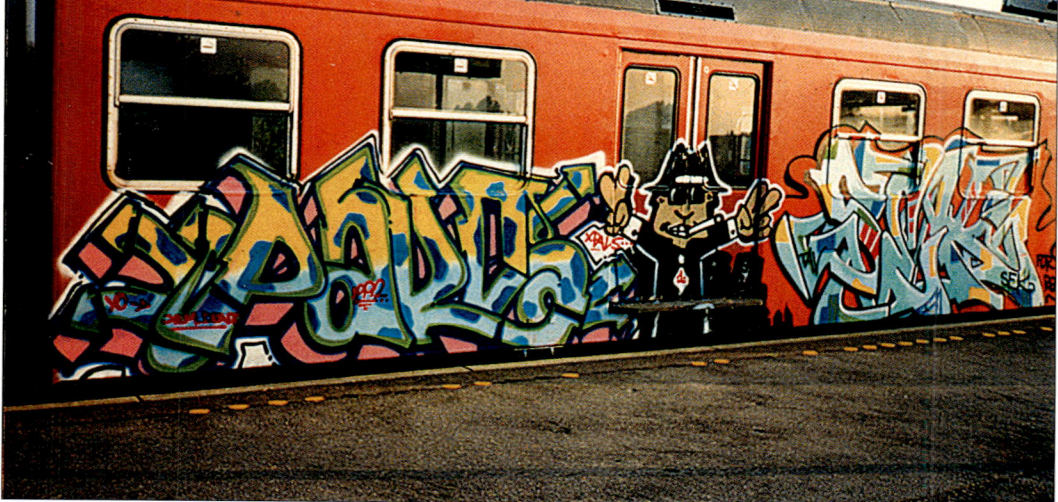

— Sek

> **Rens would check up on the yard near where he lived everyday and ended up figuring out the guards' routines**

his name in the ID centre system and it turns out he had killed his ex-wife's lover!
Around 1989 me and Rens got real busy on the trains after founding the A-Line Vandals. At this time there where a lot of guards in the yards. I remember we did the "TUFF" whole-car in 25 minutes even though those were tuff times for painting trains. In 1990 there were still guards, some stayed at the station all night checking the yards on the regular basis but we hid in the bushes and would wait for them to leave; sometimes someone came back by surprise and we had to run...it was a continuous game between them and us.
Rens would check up on the yard near where he lived everyday and ended up figuring out the guards' routines: on one special day of the week at a specific time the yard was completely empty; finally, we started hitting that yard regularly and indeed that was a golden era for TAV crew.

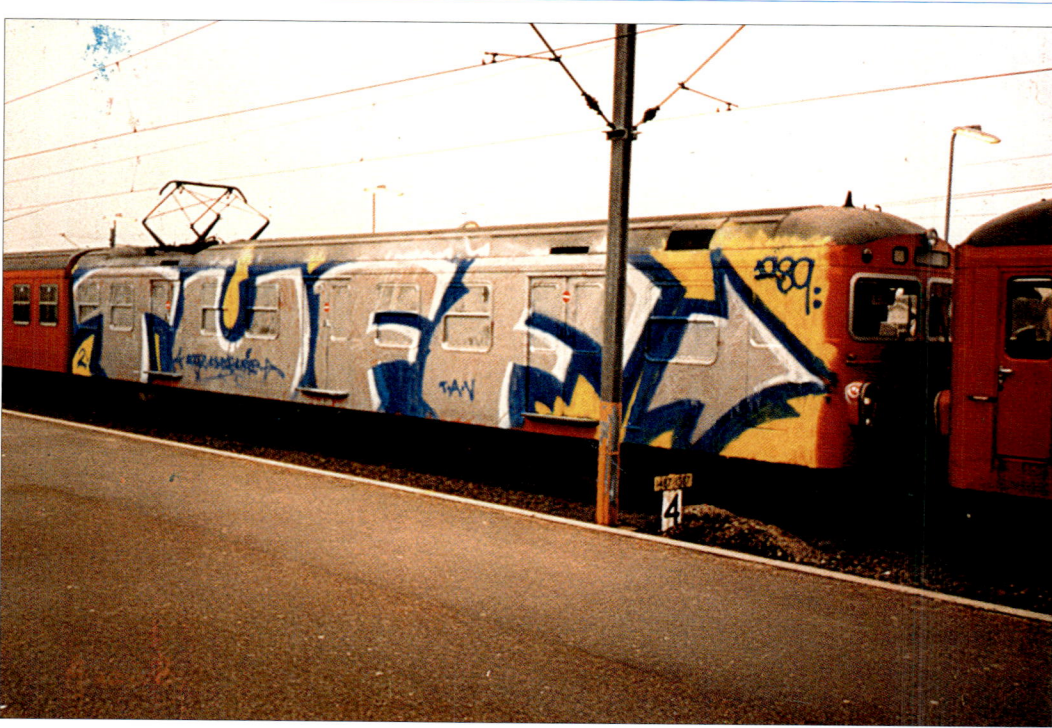

— Sek

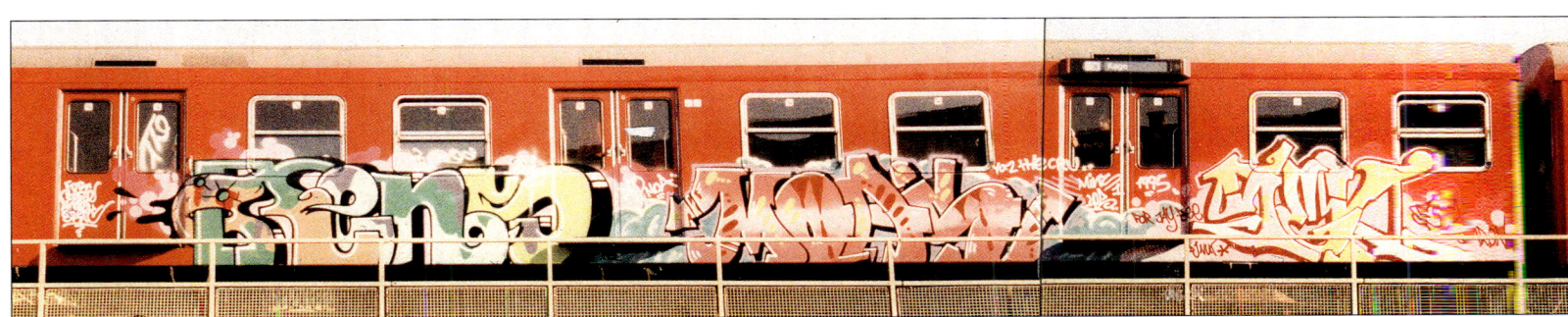

— Rens

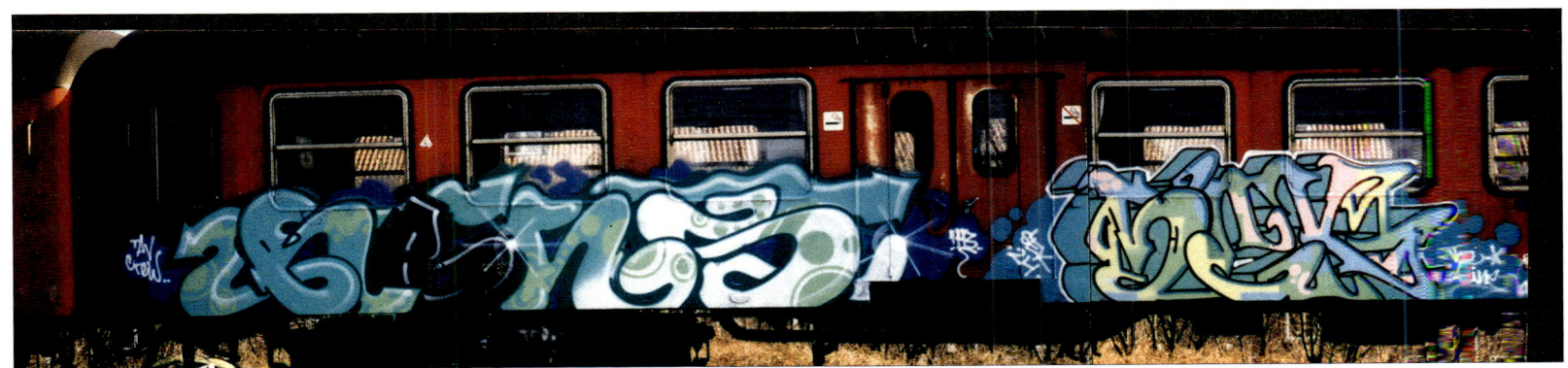

— Rens

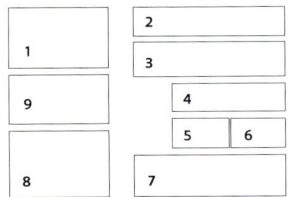

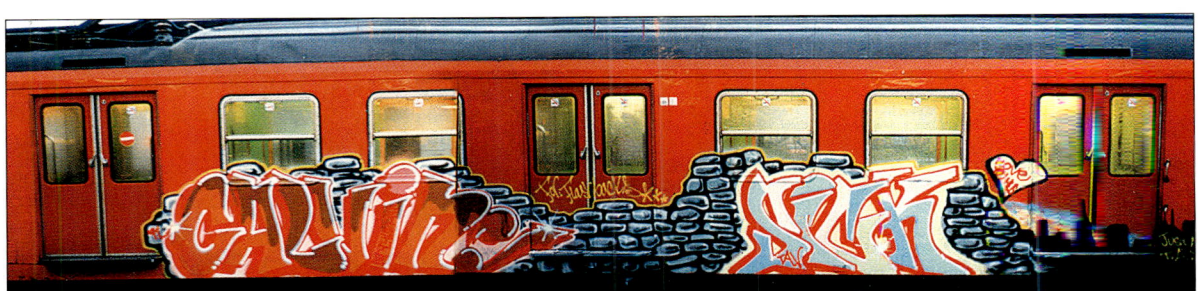

— Sek

1. *Stick up kids* by Freez, Sketzh, Dimmer, Zenith, 1985

2. End-to-end by Rens-TAV, the MOAS and Sek-TAV. 1995

3. Rens and Sek –TAV, 1993

4. Calvin by Rens and Sick by Sek, TAV

5. Rens celebrating his panel piece at Copenhagen central station, 1994

6. *Jassabe* by Jass and Sabe, 1995

7. The Copenhagen typical landscape: Les One, Mins and Sabe burners

8. *Tuff* whole car by Sek, 1989

9. Paks and Sek burners, 1992

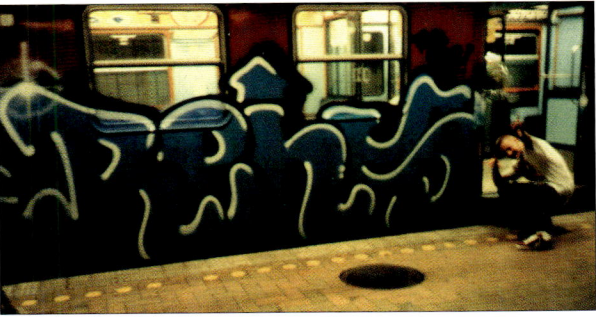

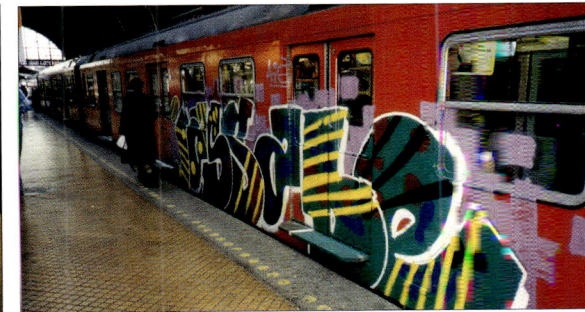

— Rens   *ACW archive*

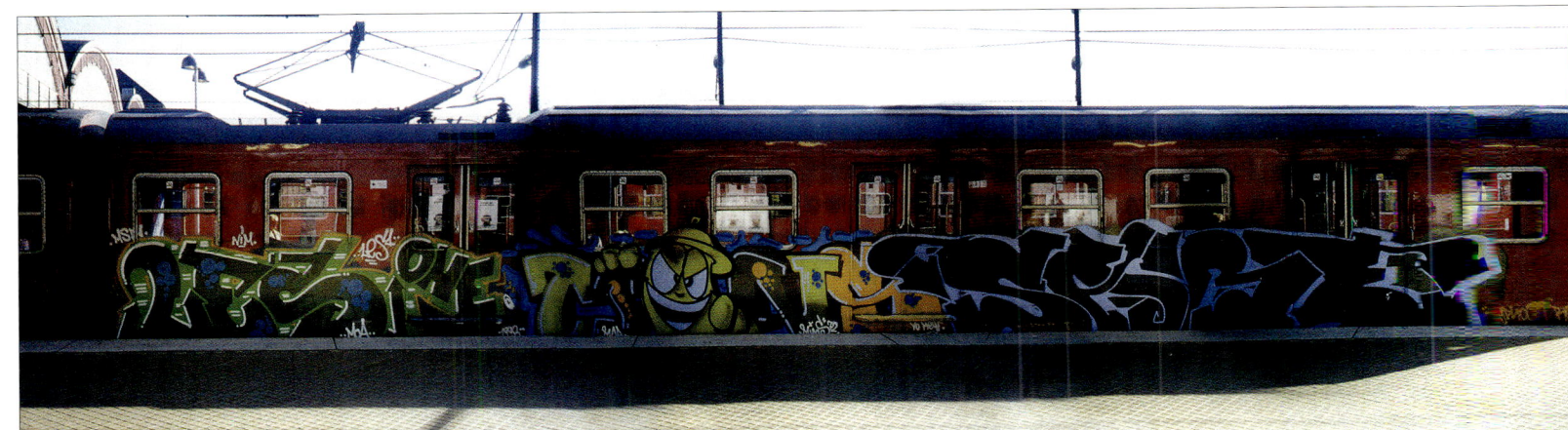

ACW archive

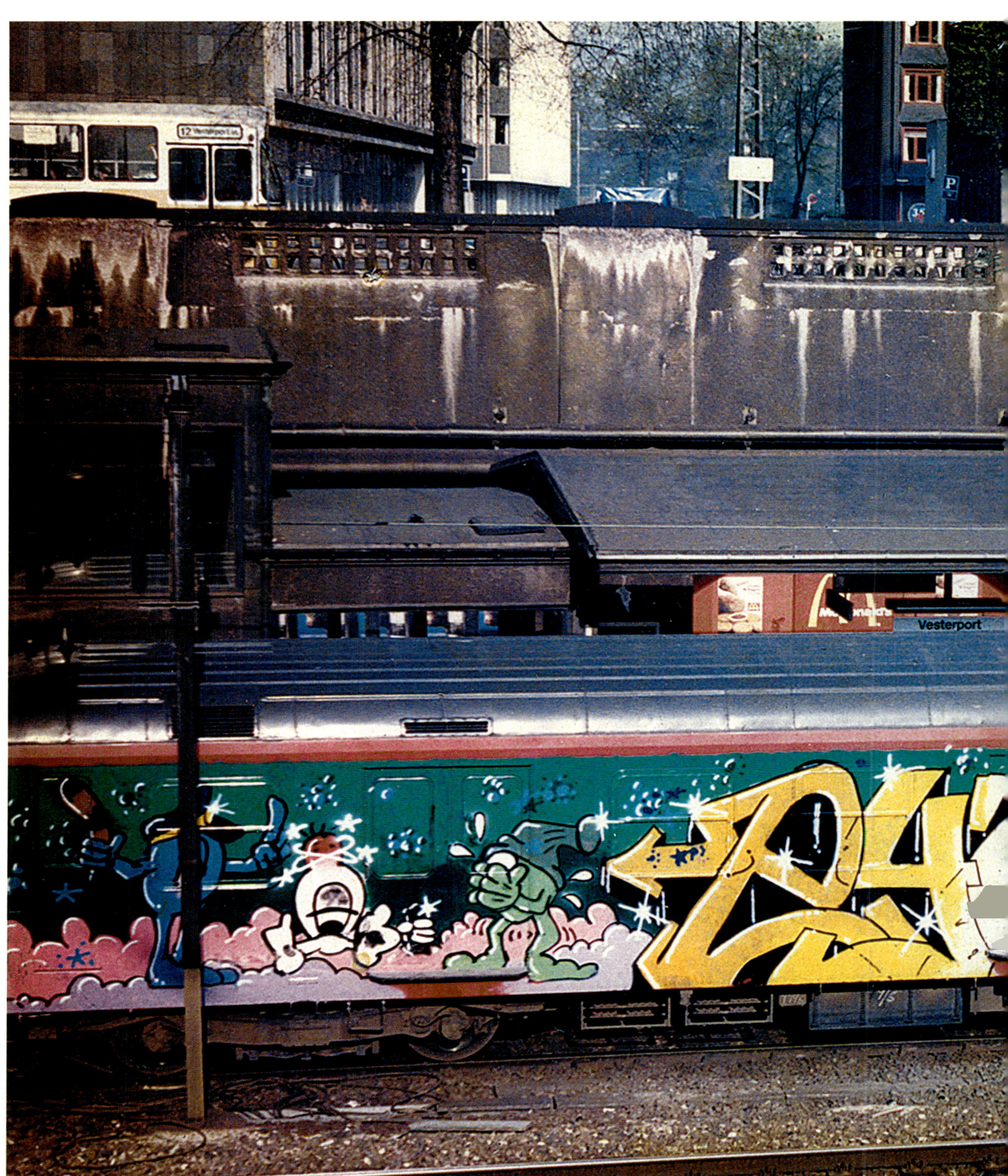

Eyes by Freez, Dinner and Zenith, 1985

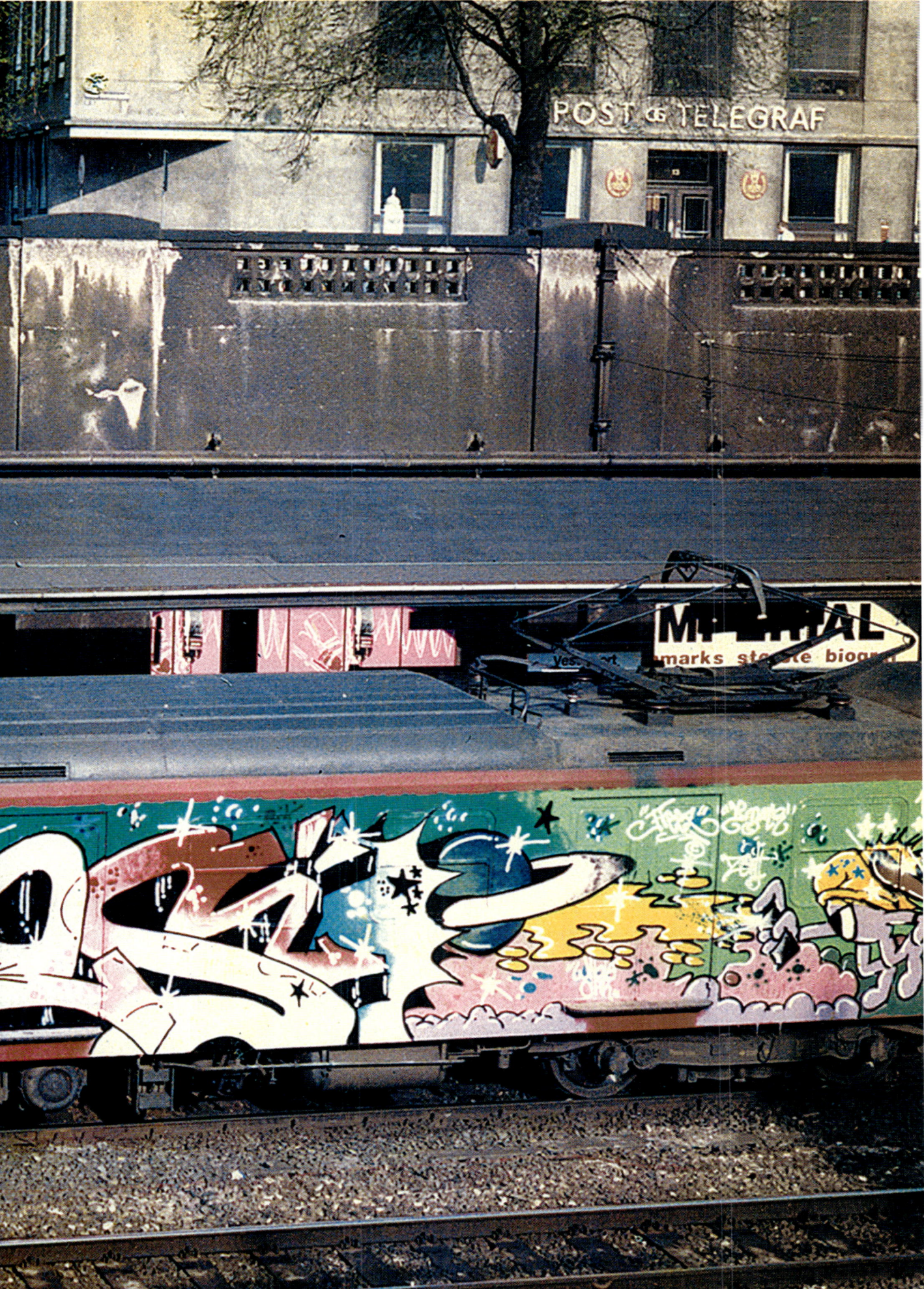

MEDIA COVERAGE

ALEX PISTOLA

Halfway through the 80's we went to Copenhagen, but without being able to see much. We had no money. So we went up there by car, and returned the same night. Only just before leaving to come back did we meet a guy who had a newspaper. He told him that spoke of a whole-car, with a picture of it as an incredible whole-car photo printed by a journalist and published in a daily newspaper. It was something so surprising that during the trip back it made us wonder what was going on in Copenhagen.

— Sketzh

MUNICH NIGHTS

The tight control of the police
on S–bahn trains in Munich, ground
for comparisons and challenges.
The personal experiences of Cemnoz
and Neon

Cemnoz – FBI / Munich
>

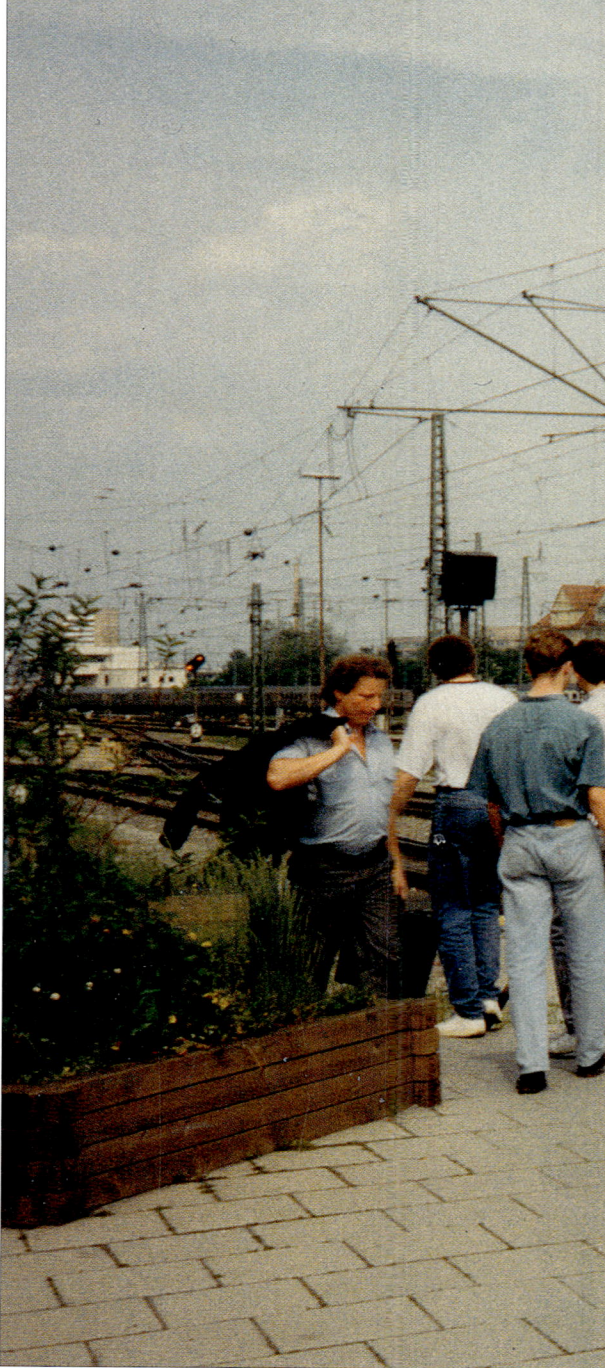

With regards to the first Writing scene, Hamburg-Dortmund-Mainz became the main network in Germany, besides Munich, which was a very open-minded city in the 80's. It had a left-wing mayor and the residents were very receptive to different things. If they saw something new come up they would promote it and that happened to graffiti as well. They gave us commercials to do and at the Flohmarkt we had the space in which to develop the scene quite rapidly. Munich also had a very tight S-bahn system and after CTK came we discovered how to really bomb it. At the time we'd go to a village that was 45 minutes away, where there was only one train. Somehow the S-trains then became the main target of a whole generation. Of course painting pieces during the 80's meant disturbing the media and society, it was pretty uncommon. The first train we did was all over the media, they were wondering whether it was a terrorist act! When they figured it out, the immediate reaction of the government was to create a special squad; the first Vandal Squad in Europe especially designed to arrest train writers. That decision really fucked everybody up... we were kids and no one could imagine this kind of repression. All of a sudden we had to be real careful, but we created something that they couldn't control anymore... year by year new kids took part in the S-train movement in Munich and the game got harder. Of course this incited a general sense of suspicion amongst us, no one was trusting anyone, police once arrested a writer that was forced to give up the names of other writers. We knew we had to have small groups and that we couldn't

talk to each other. This is probably the reason why writers chose the S-trains as their main target rather than a hyper-controlled system like the Munich subway. Furthermore, almost every subway line in the city was underground whereas we could take good photos of the S-bahn in the open-air stations. Those trains were running through the city and serving the suburbs as well, spreading the name all over. S-train yards were easier to hit, as some of the places were far from any congested and controlled urban scenarios, and you could even relax. Once I went with Cheech and Katmandoo to paint a train in the woods.

A journalist of a Munich paper was with us as she wanted to publish an article about train writing at its onset. I was doing some trains at that time, while Cheech probably did the first whole-car in Munich. Somehow, we thought we were pretty experienced and so we decided to take this person with us. It was all very toyish in the beginning, we felt the risk of course but at the same time we didn't feel like we were doing anything wrong. We covered ourselves since she was taking photos of us while we painted the trains but once the article was published in the newspapers, a whole investigation started. The photographer, who had a sick mother, was essentially threatened and forced to give up information, and consequently Katmandoo and Cheech were caught. They were the main contacts she had, while I was just taken along with them as the third guy, in the background. I was saved that time, but I learned that no place was safe in Munich, and S-train bombing gradually become hush-hush and a common practice only among a few followers.

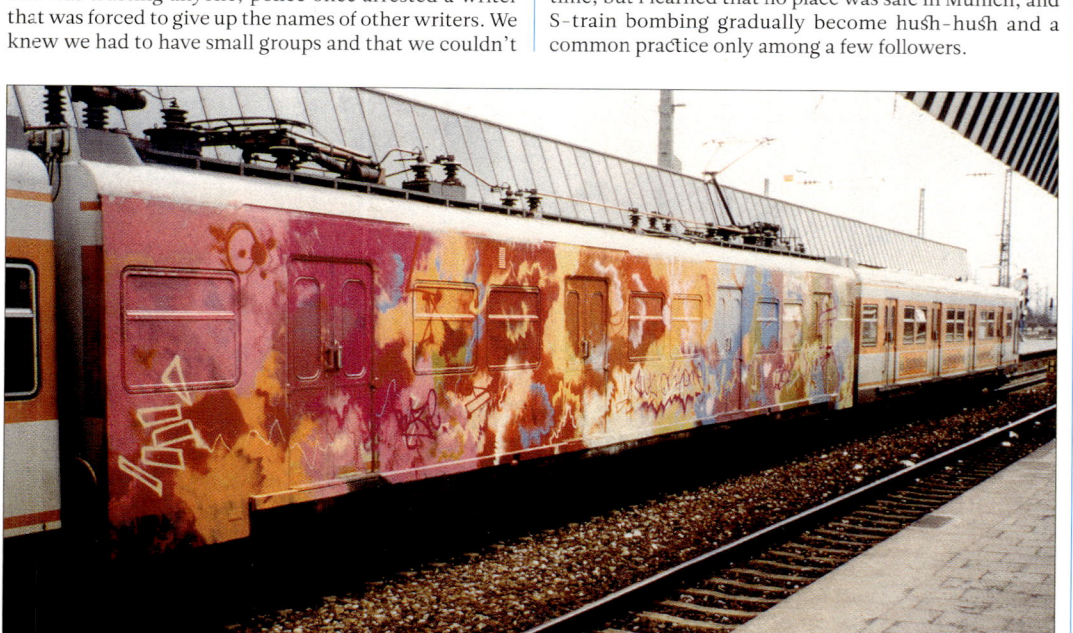

Raze and Sioux of Club of Rome crew, Munich 1988

– Stone

Neon –TFP / Munich
>

The boom for train Writing in Munich began in 1984 when almost all writers were targeting this objective, but as soon as they realised how stressful it was many of them went back to legal walls. Train bombing was and is a phenomenon that is directly related to a person's attitude, a balance based on risk and adrenaline that makes this scene almost a whole separate movement. Munich was a city that immediately put

you to the test under this aspect. Already in the early years police were on the back of the writers that chose the S-train as their primary target. The urban network was excluded immediately because it was even harder to paint. The company that managed it was private, with even more controls and a network of infrastructures that developed primarily in tunnels. The fact itself that the U-trains didn't rise above ground was a real deterrent with respect to the S-trains that travelled in the open and

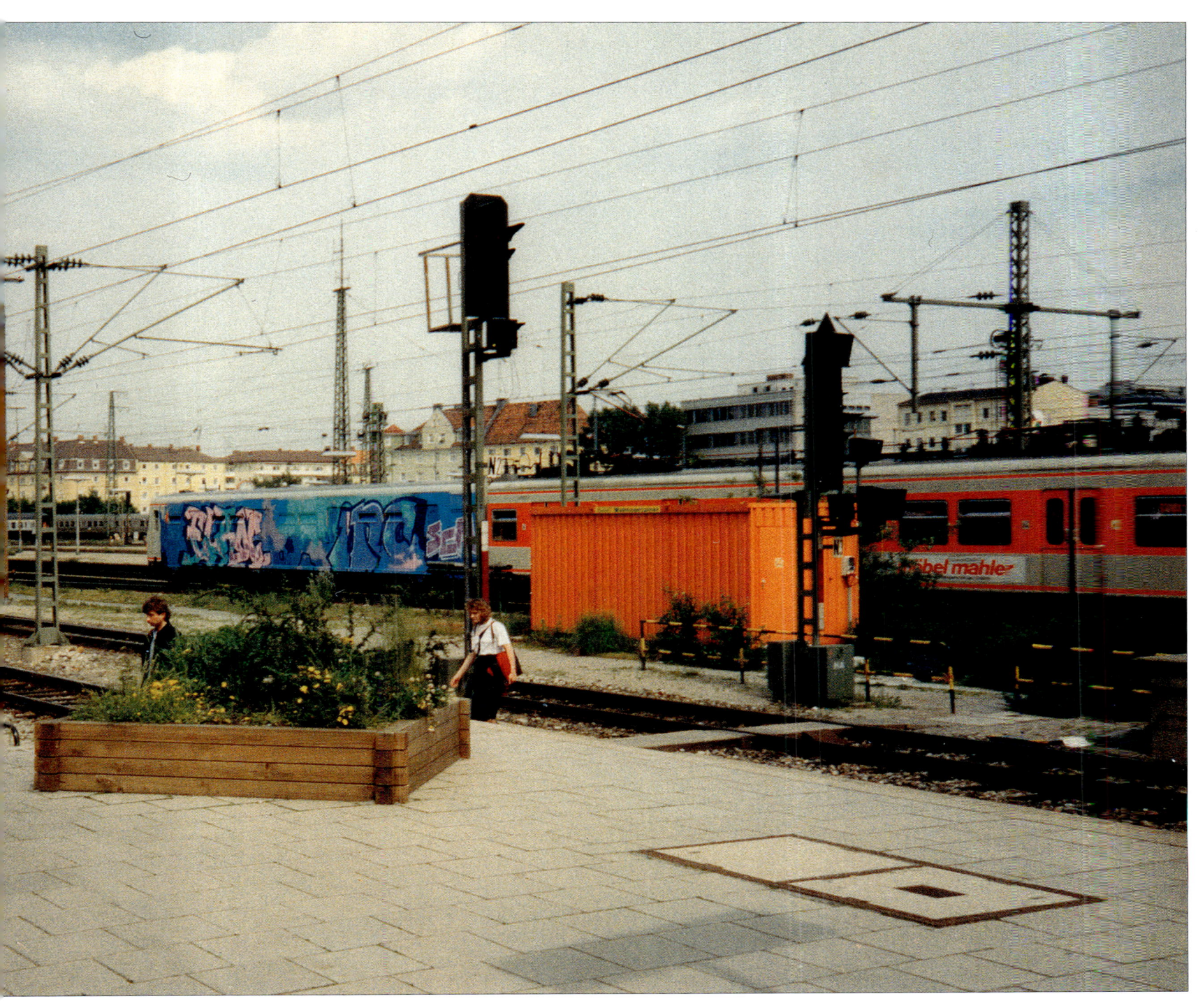

Mark Todt

HAVING A DOUBLE IDENTITY IS THE FIRST RULE
—

were property of Deutsche Bahn, the State company. The first contacts between writers occurred in an informal manner in the station, almost through intuition because the cliché tied to clothing didn't exist yet, kids didn't recognise each other thanks to fat laces or name belts. We were all involved in these crazy train dynamics, attracted to the world of the railway and to the carriages, and it wasn't important to dress and follow a trend because once on the platform it was easy to recognise the gaze of a kid that was infected by your same virus. If you really want to write your name and see it travel, if that's all you want to see, it

becomes automatic to meet in the station, notice the same recurring faces spying on each other. At the time I still sported my boots and the regular jeans of an Italian cousin, the whole clothing thing didn't exist! So we would board the same trains we were painting, to then arrive at Stachus station for our respective daily business, in the middle of all these kids looking you up and down, all just standing there waiting, wanting to meet each other but held back by the typical shyness of teenagers that can't find the guts to make the first move. When, month after month, kids started getting to know each other and to regularly hang out

in central station, the situation degenerated; even though trains from all the lines of the S-Bahn passed through Stachus the police were starting to increase their presence and the place became dangerous. The guys decided to move first to Isartor towards 1988-'90 and then towards Ost Bahnhof.

The Vandal Squad, or anti-graffiti police team, became standard in Bavaria already in the first years, so all of us created a double alias: the legal one, that we would use on walls like Flohmarkt, and a secret one used for painting trains. We were forced to keep a double tag because the Vandal Squad was extremely

organised and could work its way directly to your home address. Munich is not a metropolitan-minded city, it has a limited mentality and its inhabitants all have a very high sense of social awareness. It is mostly a very rich city that loves order and if this order is disturbed you get checked out on principle. Paradoxically in the 80's it was one of the cities with the highest rate of junkies in Germany, kids that were adrift yet didn't end up on the street but rather died at home, in their apartments. Munich is a city in which a lot goes on behind closed doors, in silence. This 'discretion' can also be found in the attitude of

certain train writers who avoided even discussing the topic among 'colleagues', some denying the authors of certain panel to avoid being double-crossed and strayed. When the first train was painted the police thought it was related to terrorism, to RAF, the German red brigade, and from that moment on they never cut any slack, even when soon enough they figured out that a group of teenagers was behind it, 16 year old kids that soon came up with every possible strategy like ski gloves so as not to leave fingerprints balaclavas, walkie-talkies and specially "keeping your mouth shut" cause you couldn't trust anyone.

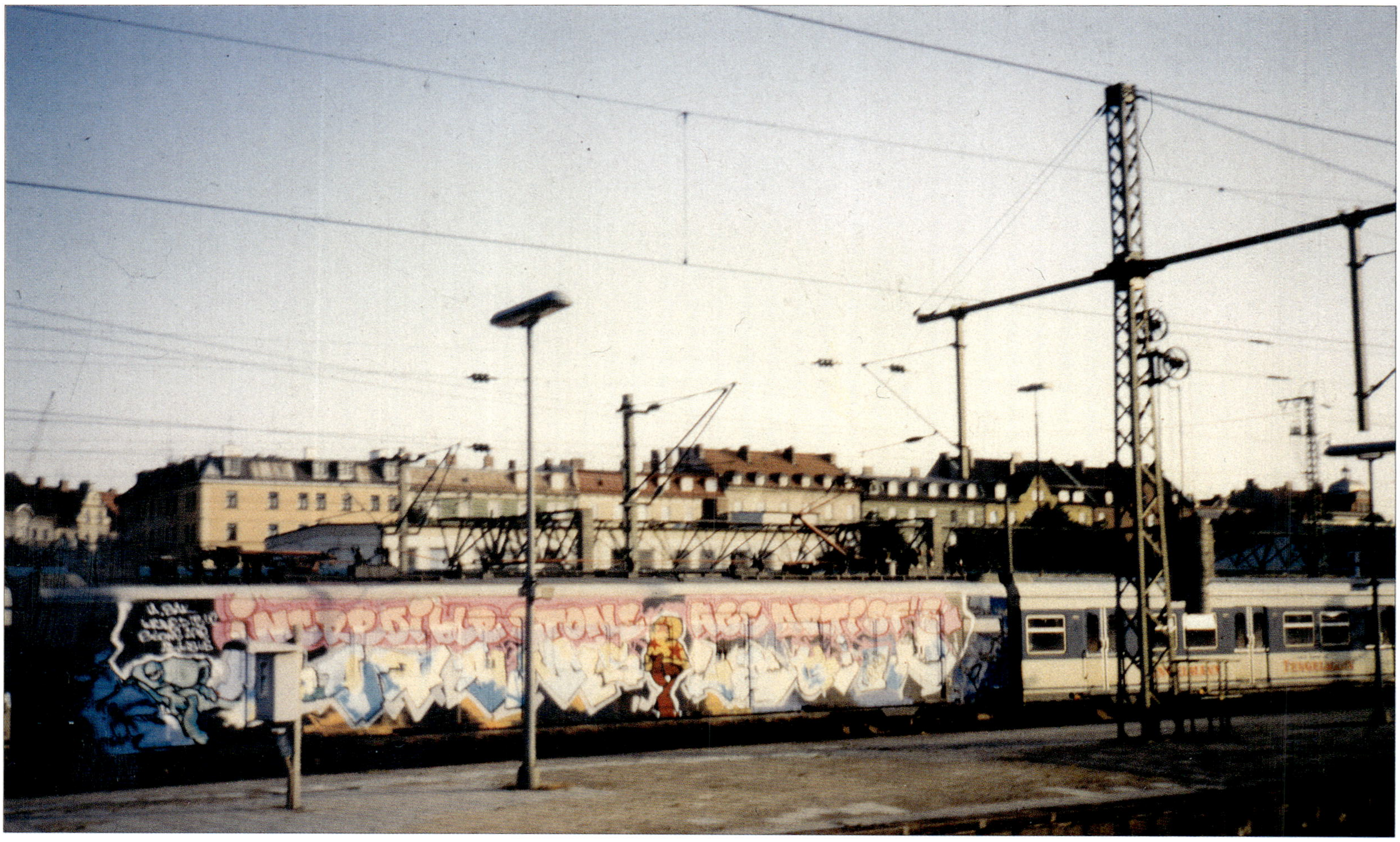

— *Mark Todt*

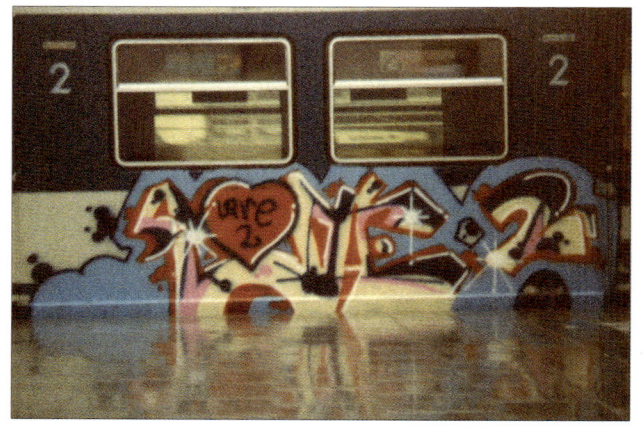

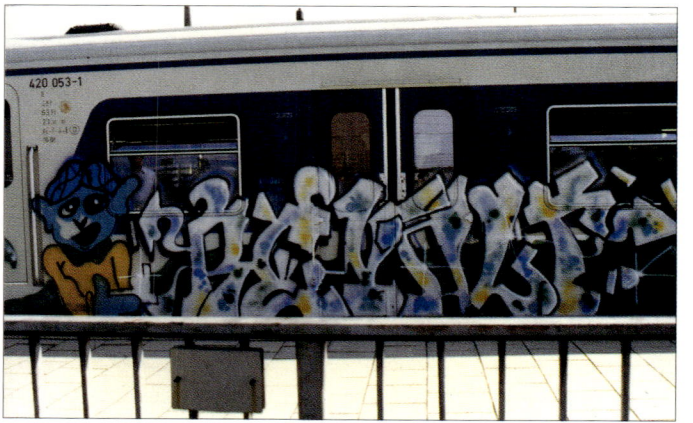

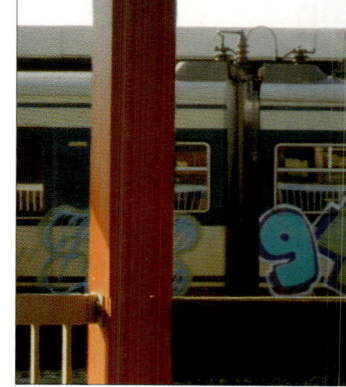

— *Stone*   — *Stone*

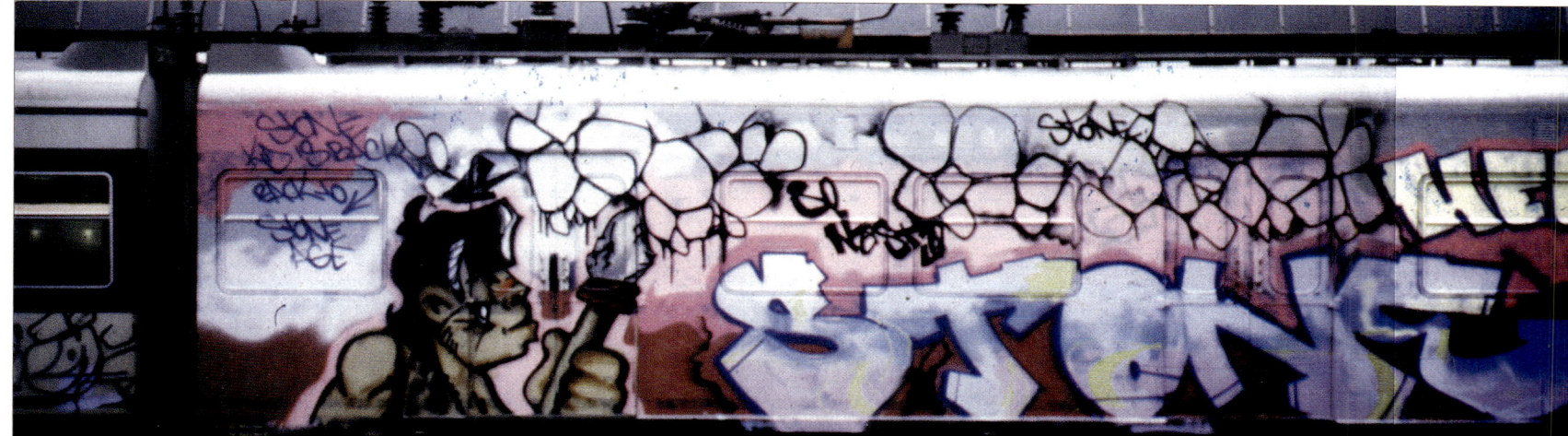

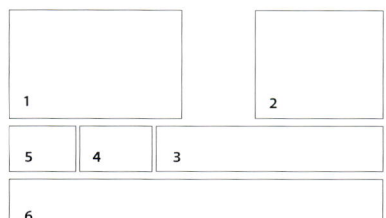

1. Satan's Legion: Incredible Stone Age Artists. Munich 1988
2. Raze, Sioux. First Club Of Rome wholecar. Munich 1987
3. Sento from New York and Stone, with Mein. TFP enc-to-end on Munich S-bahn. 1994
4. Sonic, 1987
5. Cowboy 69, ABC crew, 1986
6. Stone Age Kids, Munich 1987

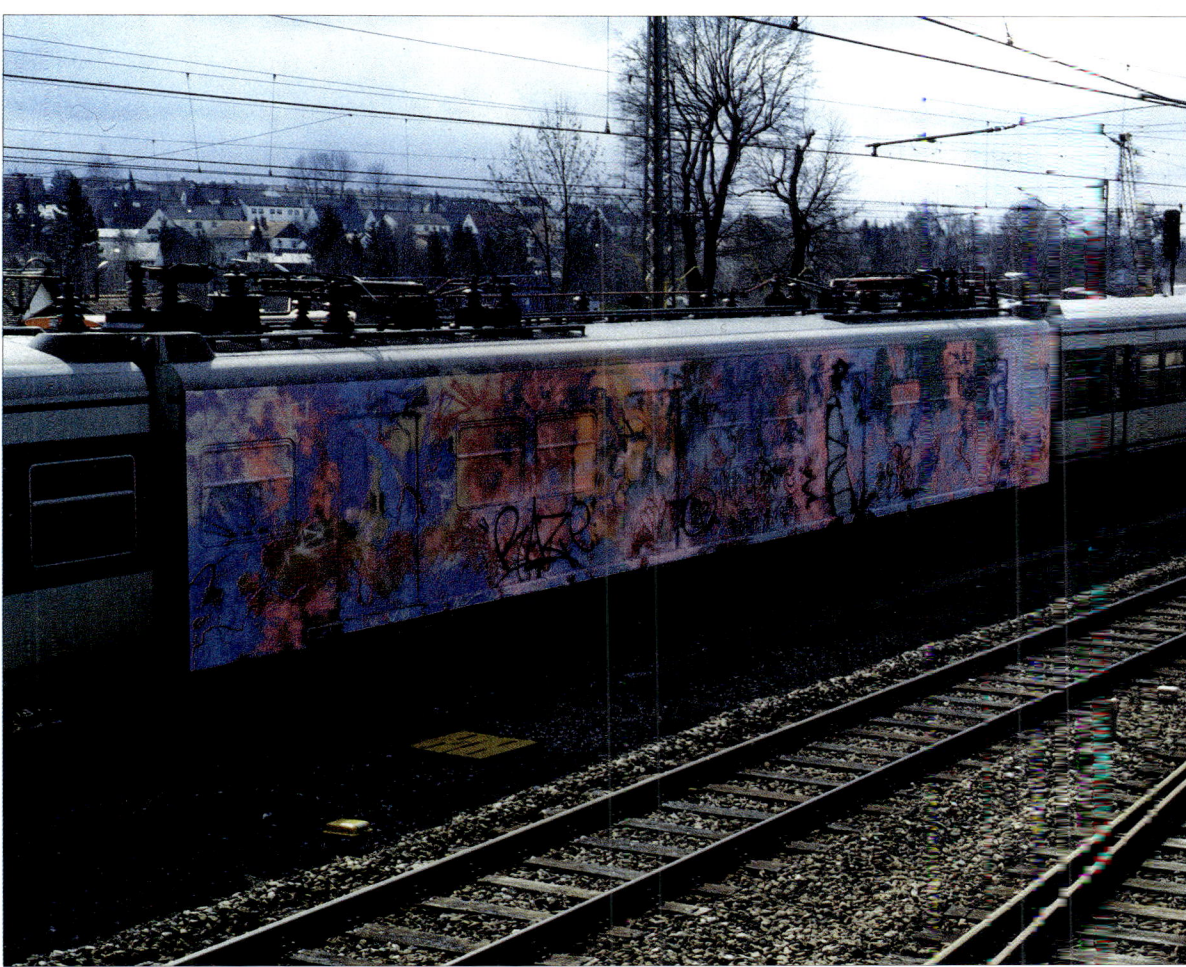

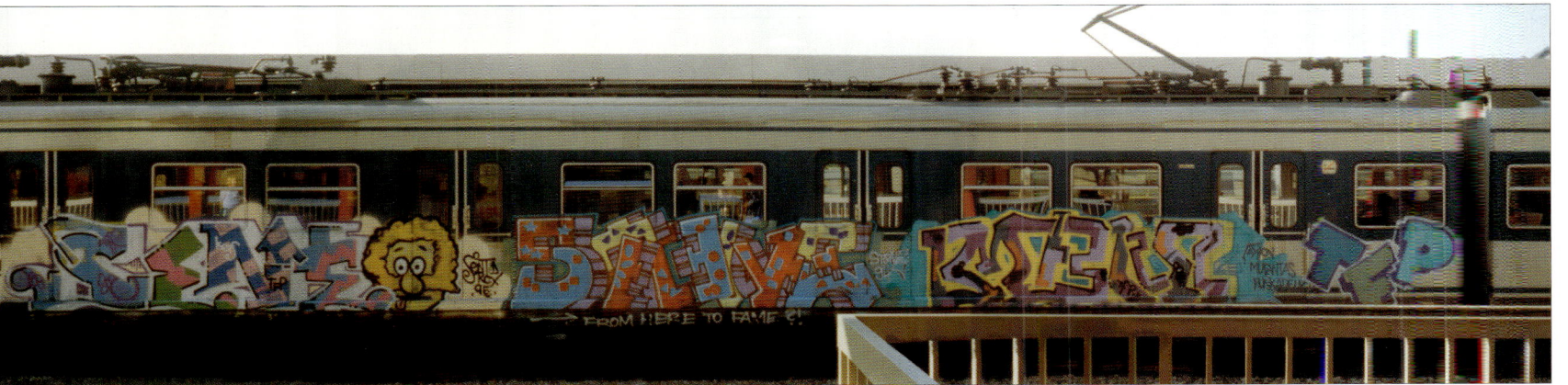

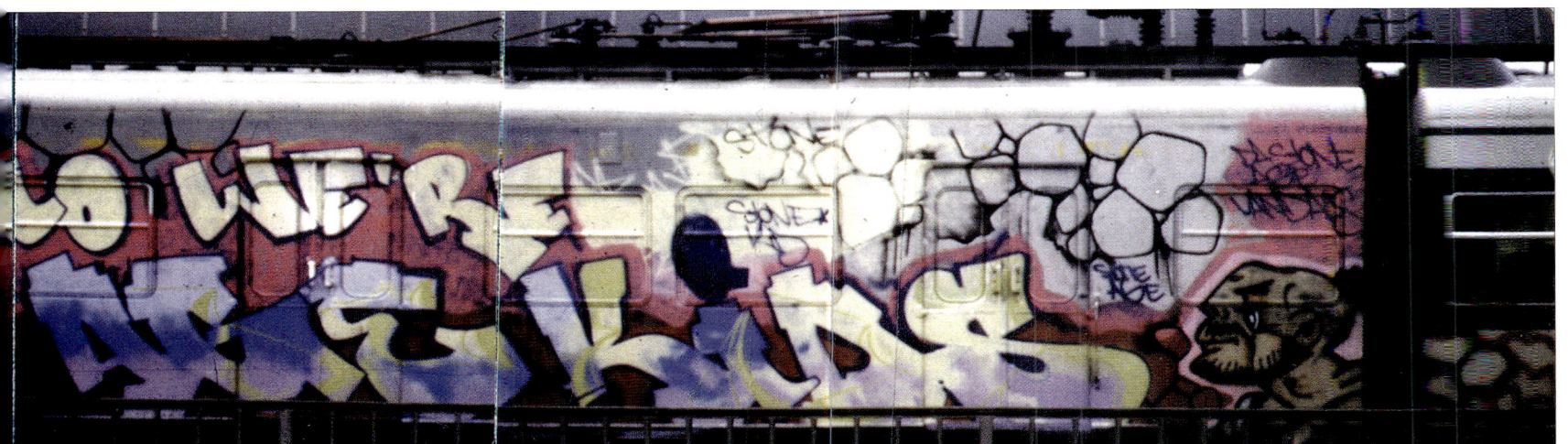

ECHOES FROM THE NORTH

The double system of subways
and commuter trains in Stockholm,
narrated by Malcolm Jacobson,
one of the most esteemed researchers
on the subject

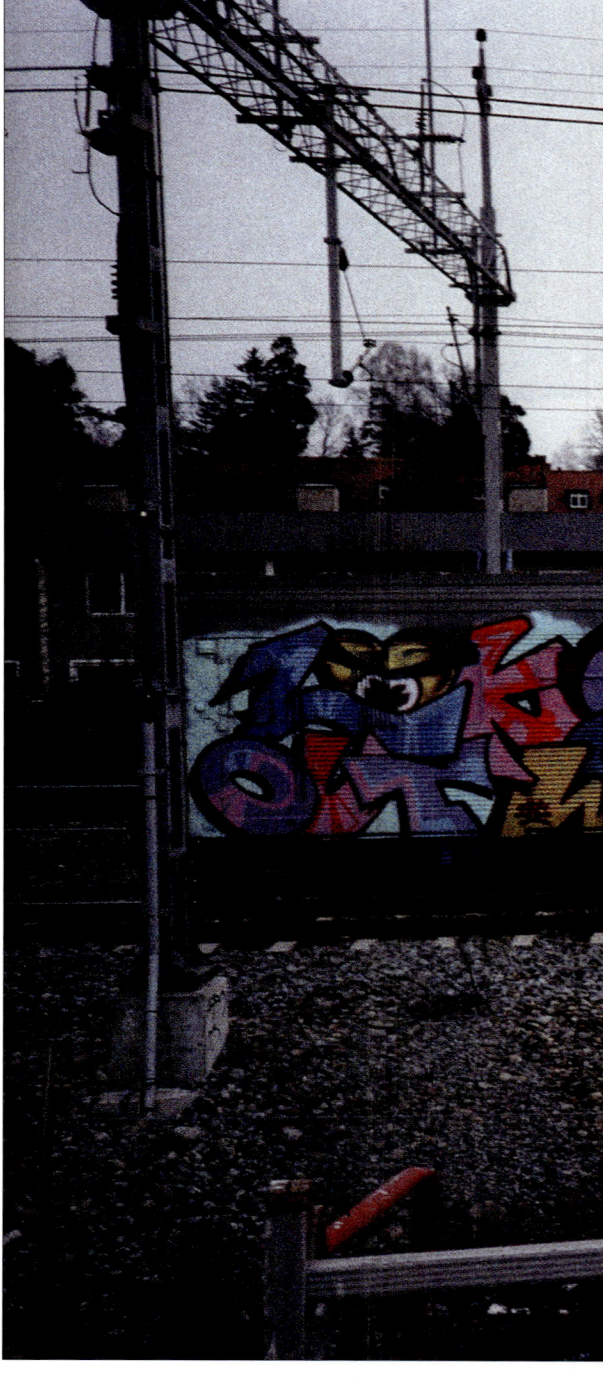

Look out crazy eraserz by Erse on Stockholm commuter train

Interview with Malcolm Jacobson
\>

As Stockholm has different public transportation systems, I would like to know whether there was a hierarchy with regards to the choice of targets. What was the first and most valued system for writers?

Most of the pieces during the late 80's were on the commuter-trains; the subway was very bombed but mainly on the inside, which was done while the trains were in traffic. I guess there were several reasons that gradually identified a different way of painting these two train systems in Stockholm. For instance if we look at the yards, while the subway ones are in the city, the commuter deposits are mostly outside, across the countryside, allowing you to paint in a more relaxed and quiet context. Originally commuters were painted in the lay-ups as there was only one yard in Älvsjö, whereas there were various lay-ups on every line, quite far out. Certain lay-ups or certain lines were preferred by certain writers, often depending on which part of town they lived in. Upplands Väsby for example was very painted, and also Kungsängen and Södertälje. On the other hand, you

hardly saw anything on the outside of the subway because it was more difficult to enter the subway yards. In the 80's backjumps weren't really common yet; painted trains were rarely allowed to circulate, so the attention of many crews immediately switched to commuter-trains. The situation changed during the 90's when people started doing backjumps on the subway, I think that the whole generation after Nug and VIM assumed backjumps were the natural way to let pieces run on the subways.

Do you think the lack of a metropolitan atmosphere, given the abundance of vast natural landscapes instead of crowded buildings and streets, might have played a role in the development of backjumps?

Some of the commuter trains go out into the wild and these conditions probably helped some of the big productions. During the 80's these lay-ups were almost unguarded, for instance along the Märsta line all that can be seen out of the train window is farms. The subway though is inside the city and even if the suburbs are still full of trees and nature, most of the backjumps were done around the stations where they would be visible, which is why they had to be completed quite fast. The

train was painted while people were climbing on board, so it was running painted for at least a few stations. Very often pieces were being finished right as the train was leaving and it was a matter of minutes. In the beginning I believe writers were worried about the people entering the train or the driver, but gradually they started to care less about their 'audience' and more about the painting; probably because writers noticed that most of the people riding the train didn't pay them much attention.
Maybe it's typically Swedish for people not to interfere much when they see certain criminal behaviors; they are afraid to raise their voice. Most of the backjumps were done at end-stations, such as Ropsten, but among the many backjump spots, Åkeshov was done quite a lot. Some trains stop in Åkeshov and just stand there, in the middle, between the two platforms on which the trains from Hässelby pass. The train station is flat and a couple of metres above ground, so when writers would paint there they were totally visible to the public walking outside of the station.

What was the Vandal Squad's reaction to the backjump behaviour?

In the 80's there wasn't really any specialised Vandal

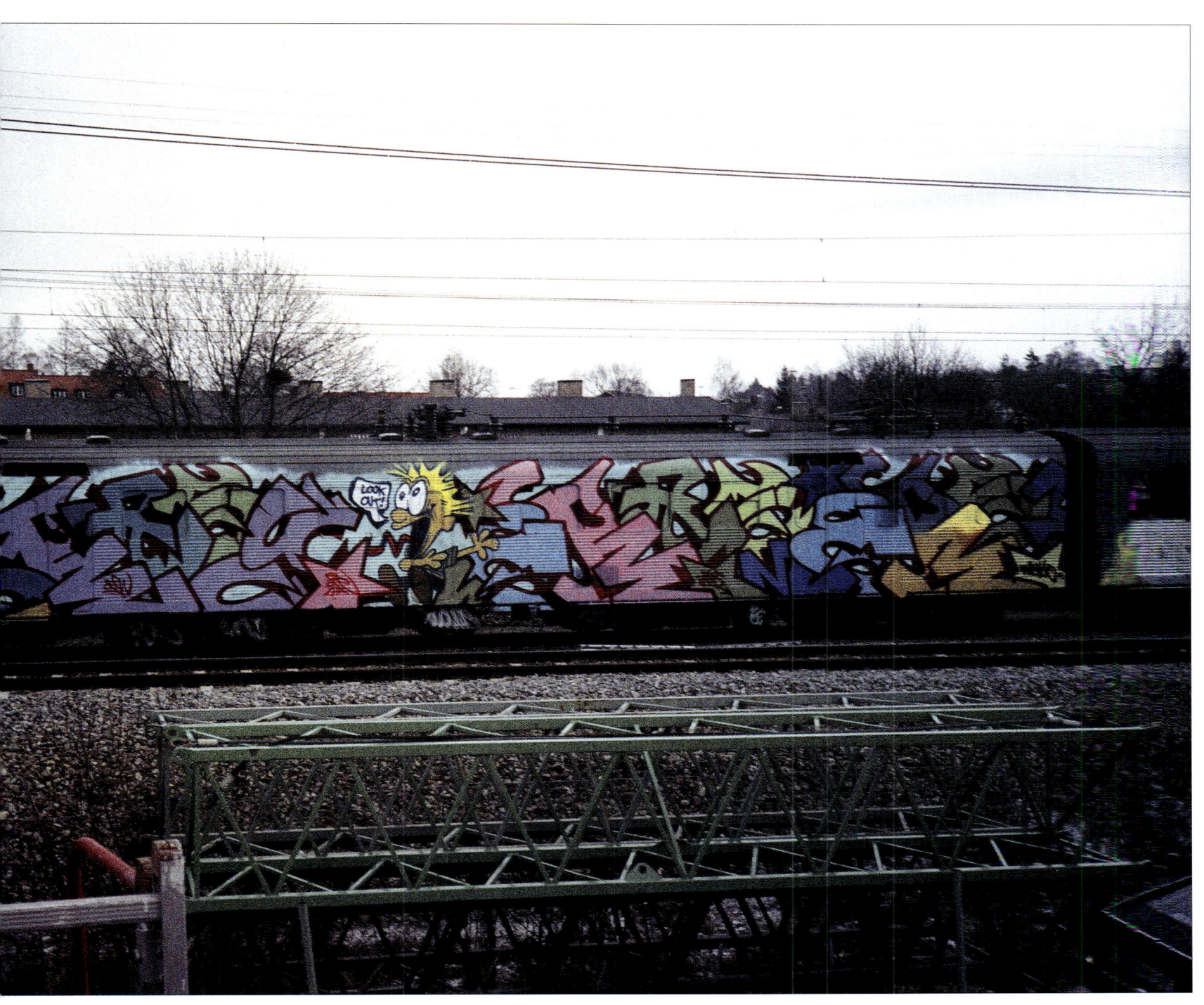

UP archives

Squad for trains, but somewhere around the late 80's or early 90's they had Kontrollgruppen (KG), a control group, which was actually just guys checking whether you had paid the fare or not. These guys, more or less

During the 80's these lay–ups were almost uncontrolled; along the Märsta line, if one looks outside the train window they'll see farms

on their own initiative, started going to lay-ups to see if writers were there. I think it was sanctioned by the transit authority, not by the police, it wasn't like they were trained guards. I think they were actually going beyond their ordinary job of checking tickets. Then word got out that they were supposedly beating up writers, so writers got organised to fight back in retaliation, add a bit of bad

press into the mix and you'll understand why soon the whole thing was shut down.

Before the KG it was possible to go to the lay-ups more or less undisturbed, there was the risk of someone seeing you and calling the police, but nobody was really concentrating on the writers. After the KG stopped there wasn't a Vandal Squad for a while, not until the Falck security started in the 90's. I think they were a bit concerned about the backjumps because it was a new phenomenon. The Falck worked very differently from the KG because they actually followed people and didn't just stay at lay-ups or end stations waiting for writers, they were almost harassing them, waiting outside their houses and stuff like that.

In magazines during the 90's it was mainly only end-to-ends and panel pieces on commuter trains that were being published, not that many top-to-bottoms or whole-cars. Were there any specific motivations for this behaviour?

There were no platforms in the lay-ups so it's a bit more difficult to do a top-to-bottom, but I also think the risks were a reason. Many of the lay-ups are situated in such

a manner as to be seen from the roads so if you move in front of the windows you can be easily spotted by either a guard or a person passing by, it compromises everything. In some lay-ups like Södertälje and Nynäshamn there are platforms, but they're pretty far off, and in the 80's and 90's most of the writers didn't have cars; these places are also not very connected by public transportation at night so perhaps that's the reason why not that many people went there. Nynäshamn also had a boat club on the other side, so writers had to pay attention to the guards watching over the boats as well.

Was there a particular place for taking pictures? I wonder whether these spots became corners where writers would habitually meet…

Karlberg Station was the best place for taking pictures of commuter trains because it was an outdoor station back then there were only three stations in which both commuter lines passed: Karlberg, Central Station and Älvsjö. In Karlberg there was a wide overlook and the least interference from the guards or staff of the transit company. For instance in Älvsjö there was a big yard in which

> CONTINUES ON PAGE 380

> CONTINUES FROM PAGE 379

many people worked on trains and taking photos didn't feel very comfortable. Besides that, Karlberg is a really beautiful station, and especially in summer it makes for a great backdrop for photos, with all the old buildings and a sunrise that hits the trains just at the right moment to make them sparkle. The main reason why writers would go to Älvsjö to take pictures would be if they had missed their train at Karlberg, Älvsjö is where they would buff the trains. At Karlberg people were gathering and hanging out and waiting for the trains in the morning, like a writer's corner. During the 80's the Stockholm writer spot was at Plattan, near Central Station, a place where people went to meet other writers. These meeting places changed during the years, before Plattan it was Sergelarkaden a.k.a. 'The writers nest' and later on Hötorget. Karlberg though was different cause kids didn't really go just to hang out and meet other people; meeting other writers was just a consequence and it happened mostly in the morning when they were taking photos and seeing their pieces.

When I was taking lots of photos in the middle and late 90's I used to take my bicycle to get there early, I planned to be there by 6:56 am because that was when the train from Upplands Väsby arrived and quite often there were pieces on that train. The tracks were curved so when I stood there I could actually see the other side of the train before it entered the station, you could then go over the tracks or up the stairs. Mostly you had to know which side was supposed to be painted at what time, as there were two trains standing in Upplands Väsby, so the writers usually painted in between them. So while waiting for the train from Upplands Väsby in the morning you would stand on one side and then after half an hour the other train came and you would stand on the other side. So we could see from both ways. When it left in the opposite direction from where it had come you could then see the back. Sometimes I just went to look but eventually when I starting taking more photos people would call me and so I knew when something new had been done.

Can you tell us about the blue paint buffing that took place? Crossing pieces with stripes was quite common, like in Germany, but in Stockholm the railway company decided to re-paint the train using the same background colour...

In the 80's and the beginning of the 90's commuter trains were running with pieces. The trains standing in the lay-ups were usually extra trains used during rush hour, put in service at the beginning of the day and late in the afternoon, when people stop working. The railway company would let these pieces run just cause they needed the trains, then the carriages would be put out of service after rush hour; sometimes they were put back in the lay-up and would run again in the afternoon, though this was quite rare.

It was a considerably smaller gap of time in which to paint, but this condition of having only a few minutes became a standard

When the blue painters started it was around 1994; most writers were painting in the middle of the night, and then the blue painters would come right before the trains went to service. So if the train would start running at 6:00 in the morning, the painter was there at 4 or 5. Since the painters had to travel to different spots, writers eventually learned their schedules and starting to paint trains after they had been made blue. It was a considerably smaller gap of time in which to paint, but year after year this typical condition of having only a few minutes became a standard for the Stockholm train scene and writers got used to it. It was often a game of watch and wait to see if the blue painters were there, followed by a rush before the driver came ... I guess you could say that people learnt to do everything in a hurry!

BLUE BUFF

MALCOLM JACOBSON

In the mid-nineties, Transit Authority staff started painting over graffiti on commuter trains in blue paint before putting them in traffic. Writers later learnt the blue-painters' timetables and now start painting the trains after the bluepainters have been to check the trains
From "They call us vandals", Dokument Forlag

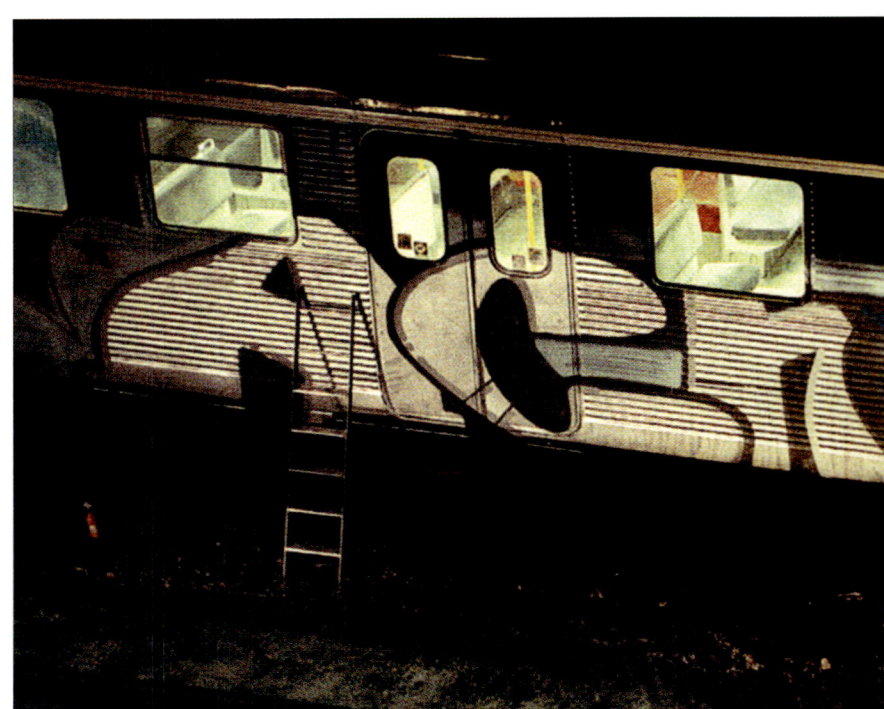

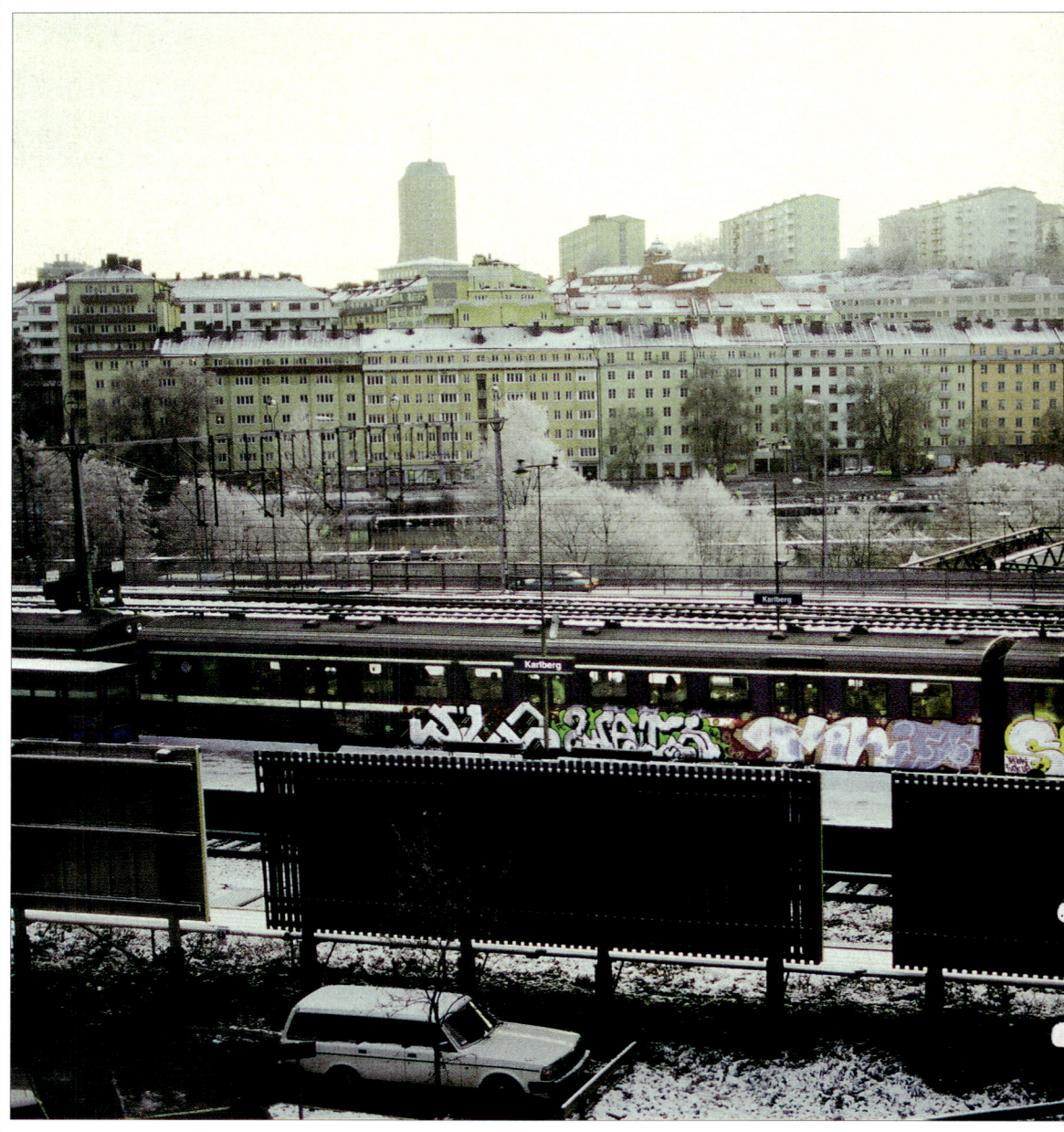

Karlsberg station overview, panel pieces by Slo and Wacs from Finland, Kliff, Silk, Kiff. 1997

Most attractive lines

The direct testimony of Jacob Kimvall during an open dialogue regarding the places and modalities of Writing in Stockholm: from hang-outs in stations to the great gatherings next to the Royal Gardens

Jacob Kimvall
>

In the 80's and at least up until the 90's there were two separate scenes: the commuter trains and the subway. For those of us living on the subway lines it was the subway, and only the subway, that counted. From 1986 to 1990 almost every car was hit inside, some of the older ones hardely got buffed at all for a couple of years so they were completely covered, and even when they were buffed only certain parts were concentrated on. The seats were fake leather and those couldn't be cleaned because the paint would soak in, so everyone was tagging on them. The metallic panels at the bottom of the car doors got bombed a lot too because they were never buffed either. Some cars were totally covered, it was really looking like New York in the early 80's. The markers we used were homemade, like the flowpens, 20 and 30mm Poscas that we filled with Meto, an ink made for advertising in shop windows; if you fill the Posca with it you get a real nice flowpen that covered anything.

Most of my friends and I were living on the red line but the most prestigious line was the green, I don't know why but the big bombers were all living on the green line and those were the guys that had the best style until Crüel came out in '87; he had a really nice handstyle and he was from the South side of the red line, making it a bit more prestigious. The green however remains the most respected, also because it's the biggest line, it reaches the farthest and goes to central Stockholm. The blue was the least considered, perhaps because it was so small, it was known that you could spend just a few days bombing it and you'd be the king of the line. To be seen on the green line on the other hand you had to tag it heavily since everyone was hitting it. Even though the insides were heavily bombed, there weren't that many pieces done on subway exteriors. It was easier to do pieces on the commuter trains cause we didn't have a lot of subway lay-ups. Almost all the subway cars were parked in the yards, which are naturally under tighter security. There were a couple of subway lay-ups, one next to Hötorget which is one stop from Central Station: in the winter of '86 there was a big strike amongst the subway drivers and quite a lot of writers hit the subways, but otherwise most people were doing pieces in the commuter train lay-ups at the end stations of pretty remote areas, usually in fields with high bushes, so it was much easier to hit them. Upplands Väsby was a beautiful spot with a hedge in front of the train so you could really sneak in, then there was Kungsängen, and also Nynäshamn. Nynäshamn was a dangerous commuter lay-up because it was too remote and there was a police station pretty close. They were quite anxious to catch people writing on trains cause they had nothing else to do, plus it was hard to escape cause you got lost! I know quite a lot of people that got busted there.

The fact suburban areas merge with wild nature is a strange condition that in my opinion somehow changed the behaviour of the local scene; another peculiarity involves subway stations as targets during the winter, as many writers preferred these spots to the trains during the harshest months of the year like December and January. In winter it's usually -10° Celsius, and when it gets that cold you can't paint outside, or at least it's very hard to because pressure drops. So people that normally paint trains nine months a year decided to hit the subway stations in the winter cause it's warm and nice and you would anyway be seen by a lot of people. From '88 to the mid or late 90's there was an enormous amount of

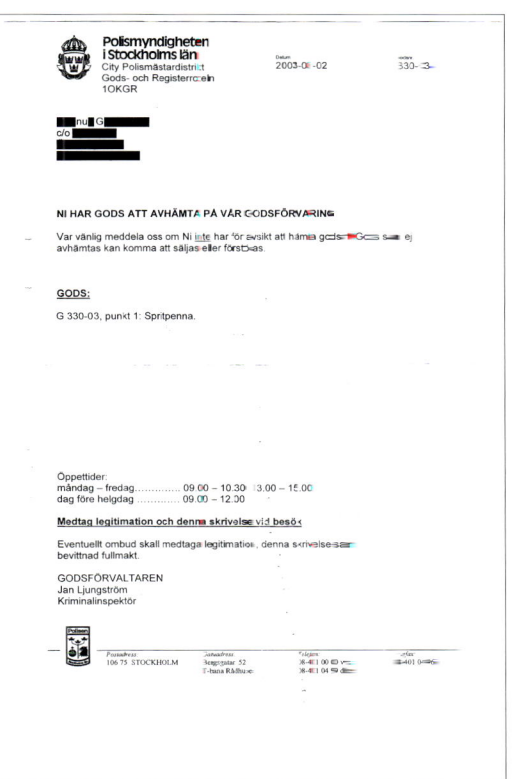

Stockholm police invite a local writer to pick up the tools they confiscated from him

subway stations that got painted. I even remember that a couple of writers got pissed off at people doing stations in the summer time when you were supposed to be painting trains! Our weather conditions also somehow shape the location of meeting places in Stockholm. For instance in the 80's, during the winter time, everybody used to meet at Plattan; it was like a writer's bench except it was much bigger. It was inside, just next to Central Station, and B-boys from all over Stockholm met, gathered and hung out there, checking their blackbooks and discussing styles. If you were hanging out at Plattan for sure everybody would immediately ask you what you did, and you had to prove yourself in a real social situation, face to face. There was respect between writers but there was also a pretty strict hierarchy, at least in the 80s. A few guys really counted, they were considered the best, from our point of view they were not only the best in Sweden but among the best in Europe and in the world.

Then, during the summer time, everybody met close in a place called Kungsan which is literally the Royal Gardens. There could be up to 2000 B-boys meeting there in the summer! There were a lot of people hanging out, though of course not all of them were writers but anyway part of the community more or less. It was a social spot, I remember very well that that's where you wanted to be seen and hang out with the right people. That disappeared in the early 90's, partly because it wasn't very smart to hang out there since you attracted the cops' attention and also because people got older and simply didn't have the same amount of free time in which to hang out. I know that the younger generation of writers meet at Hötorget every Saturday, they have like a writer's bench at the subway station.

From the early to mid 90's though the police started paying a lot more attention to graffiti, it became dangerous to have official meeting spots cause it was an easy way for them to gather information and take pictures of people. That affected the scene a lot, it got much more fragmented, you didn't know who people were, and then the internet came, where the chat forums have more or less taken up that role.

— Malcolm Jacobson

— Malcolm Jacobson

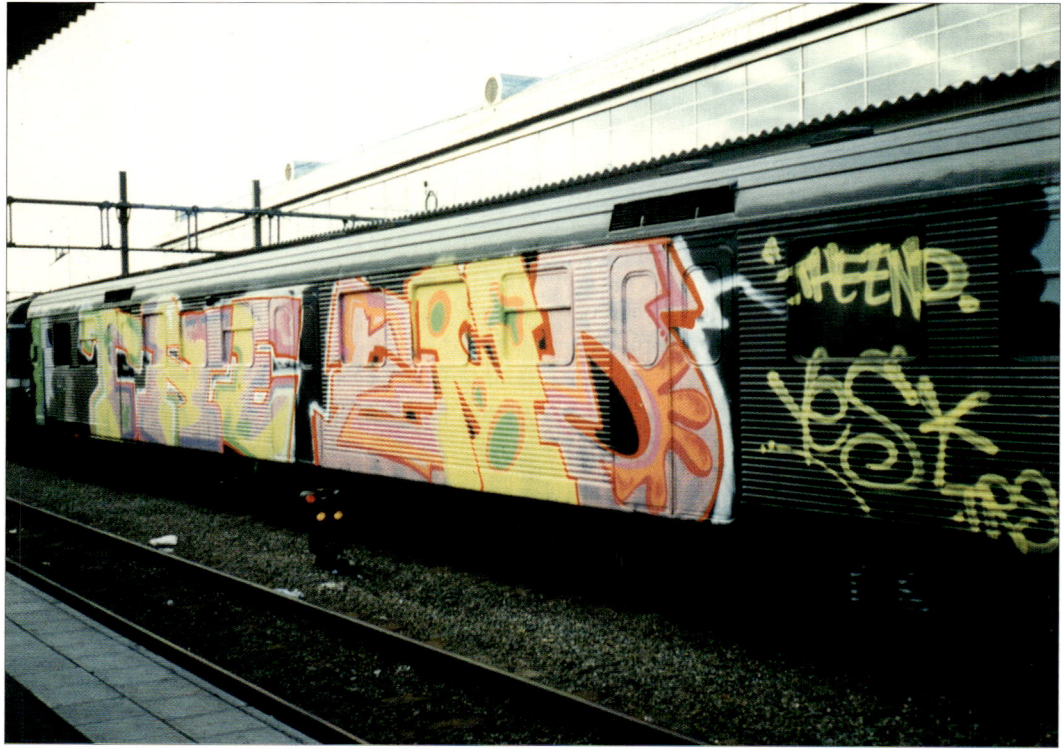

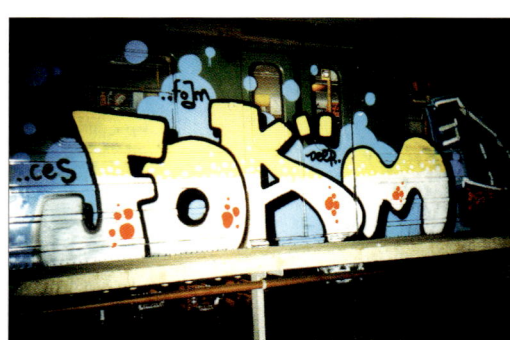

— ACW archive

— ACW archive

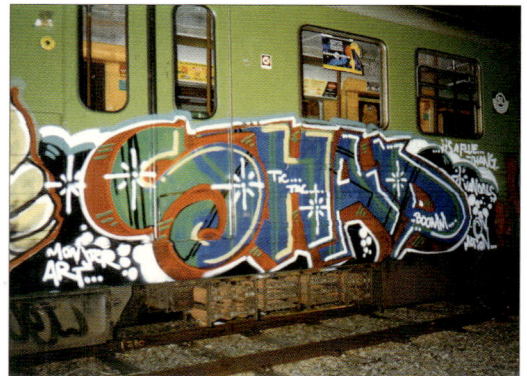

— ACW archive

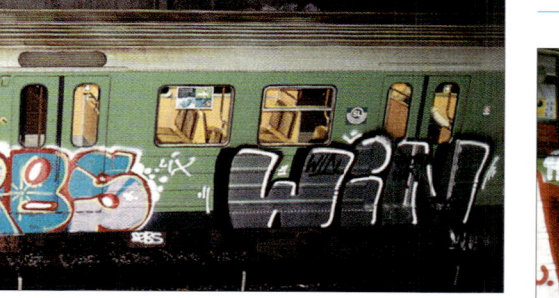

— Malcolm Jacobson

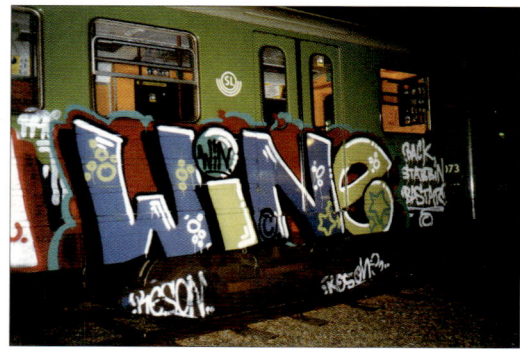

— ACW archive

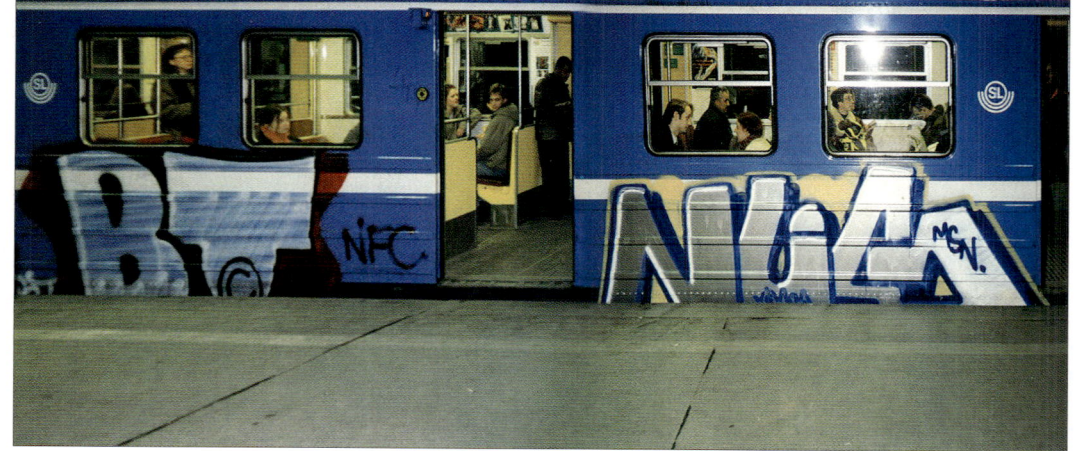

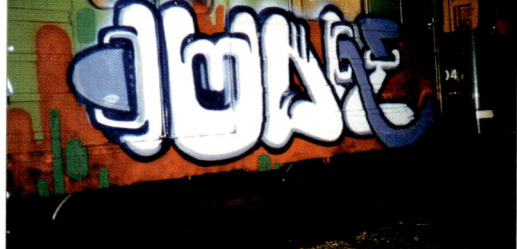

— Nug

— ACW archive

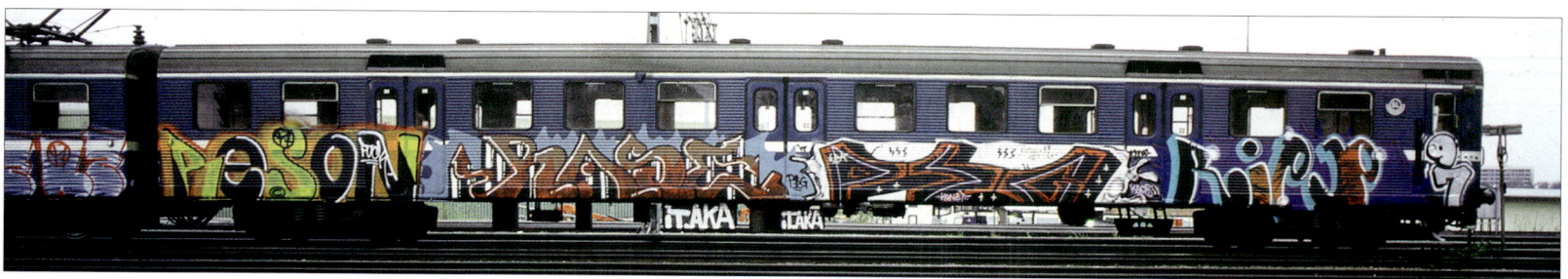

— Malcolm Jacobson

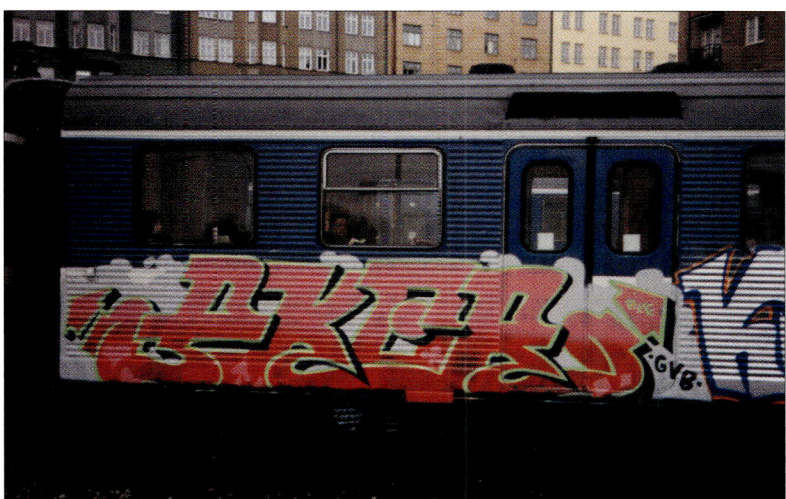

– Pike

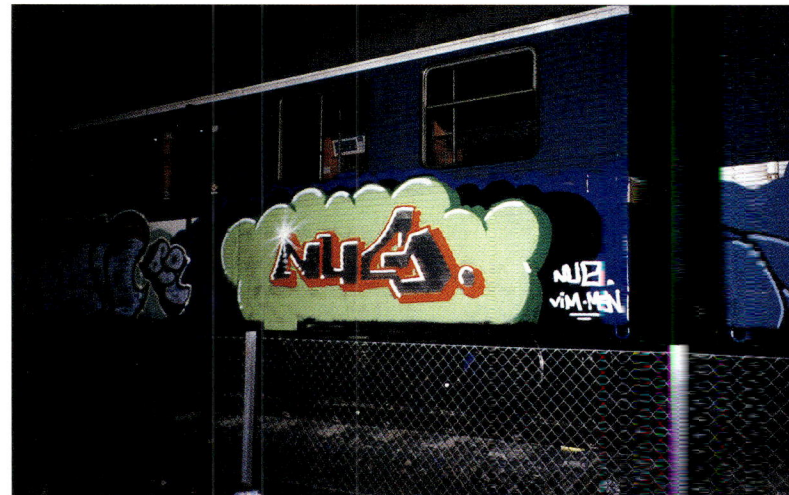

– Nug

9	10	1	2
	11		
8	12		3
7	13	4	
6		5	

1. Pike – VIM, 1992
2. Nug on a Stockholm S-train, early 90
3. Akay and The VIM on commuters, late 80's
4. Arse, Mask, Roes, Out, Älvsjö '96
5. Sos, Liroy, Obey, 1999
6. Reson, Rase, Psc, Ripp, Älvsjö, '97
7. Bt-bandit by Reson, Nug, on Stockholm subway
8. Ribe, Sebs, Win, Thorildspl, 1996
9. *The end* whole-car, 1991
10. 11. 12. 13. Foam, Shad, Wine, Duane on the subway

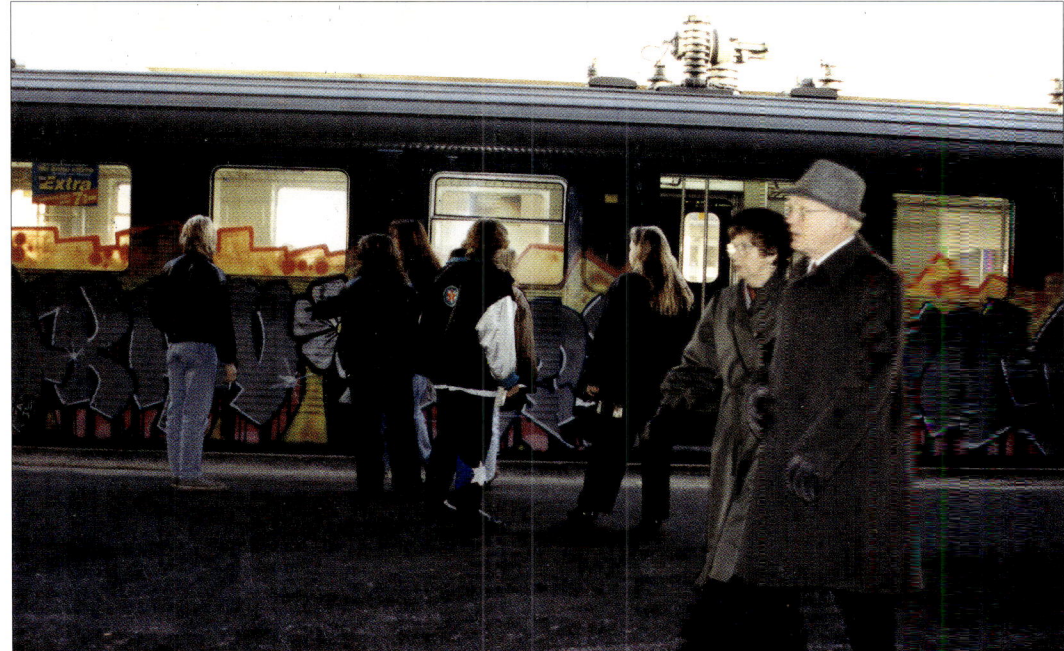

– Kaos

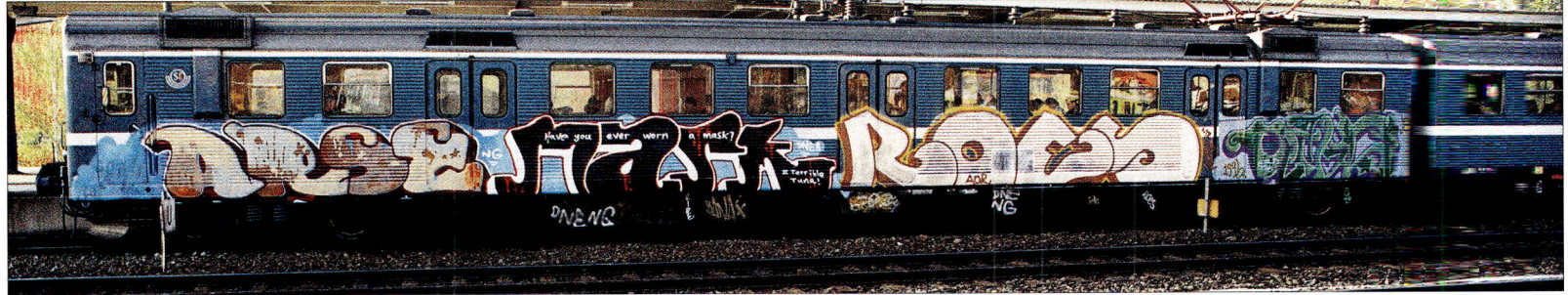

– corn Jacobson

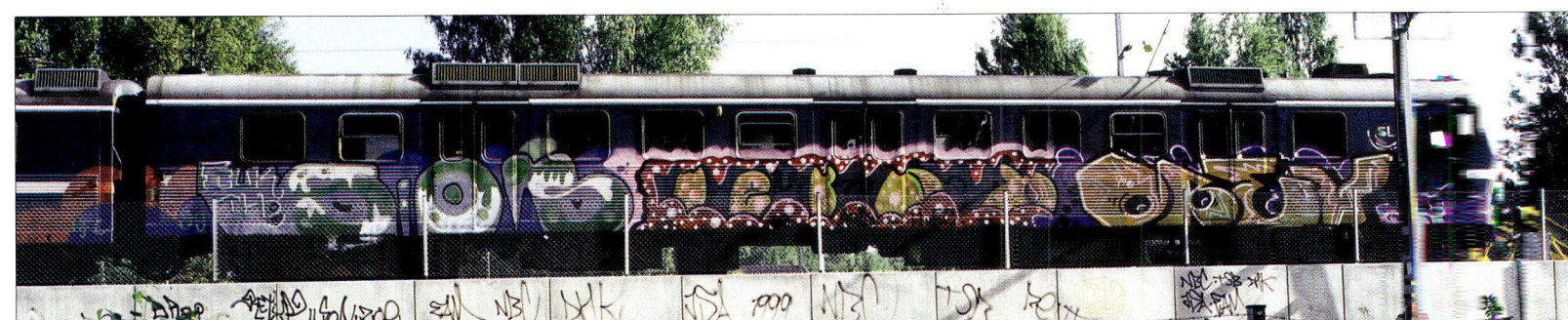

– corn Jacobson

DORTMUNDIANS

The experience of a protagonist in Dortmund's scene, capital of Writing on trains in the Ruhr during the 90's. The tenacity of an entire generation

Mason TFP, IFC / Dortmund
>

Dortmund used to be a working class town, back in the days the heavy industry forged the city's attitude in more than a way. Following a structural change, 60,000 people lost their jobs, it seems the profits weren't high enough for the steel or coal companies. Besides that, cultural choices were always low-brow. From a certain point of view I like the simple, straightforward life, but I also feel the constrictions resulting from all that.

Graffiti started in Dortmund like in most other European cities, around 1984, and almost immediately the first trains were painted as well. At the time it was a rare experience, but over the years it changed, and painting trains became the daily business. At that point almost every car was bombed and it was a great time. I remember how Fume and me did quick pieces at the central station yard. We would just cross over all the tracks, it was an open range, easily controlled by the main tower, but apart from us nobody paid trains much attention in those days. It was around this time that there was a "Dent" piece running and Sak had done a throw-up.

During the following weeks we realised that our stuff just kept on circulating. Before that, I did most trains in other cities; I just didn't see any opportunity to hit my own system, but now the area around Dortmund had become the main playground. I tried to find as many places as I could in which to paint the local trains, and so did a bunch of other guys. The first whole-cars we did around Dortmund were quite special, but even that became normal after some time. After a while it wasn't unusual to meet other writers or to enter a place and spot freshly done pieces.

– DAILY OPERATION

From 1991 'til 1993 I guess I was painting trains more or less five days a week. It also became customary to hit more than one place each night and paint more than one piece at once. It was a mixture of doing nice colourful pieces, taking one and a half hours to get them done, or just going to fuck the yard up with some chrome pieces. In that period there was a big transit breakdown, which wasn't so common in Germany, and trains were 'laid-up' for three or more days. I was living next to one of our local yards at the time and I remember I did seven pieces in one night, and in between we had to go to my house to pick up more paint. It was a damn gorgeous night.

I didn't have to seriously work much in those days, in a way I was totally free and I enjoyed that period as much as any writer would. During the day we would drive through the Ruhr area trying to steal as much paint as possible, while at night we would go painting, and in between we would try to catch flicks of the trains at central station. I could pay my bills from the money I made by selling paint, so it was all good.

A lot of friends from all over the world came to Dortmund during that period, because it was such a unique situation. It was a closed system of maybe 130 cars that were based in Dortmund, and there were about 40 possibilities to hit the trains, between backjumps on Sunday evenings, weekend lay-ups and regular yards.

We would play tic tac toe in the space between our panels, and just do whole-trains and a lot of general damage. We managed to bomb the small subway system so intensely that pieces were running for about three months. Because of the fact that the network is so small, there was no chance however of keeping up that rhythm and the local transit company took over after these few months.

We caused a big mess with the Dortmund trains, other writers from the Ruhr district started to do the same in Bochum, Essen and Düsseldorf, so after a while the local authorities decided to expand the resources against graf-

---

I think I realised the cops were following me from the beginning, and I don't know of any case in which they were successful with this

---

fiti, and a second generation Vandal Squad was instituted. The first had been founded around 1989, but they were not very successful. These new guys tried to be smarter. On the one hand they started crossing pieces, on the other they began a surveillance operation. I guess they wanted to fuck up pieces in the hopes of catching people fixing them, but that never worked out.

I think I realised the cops were following me from the beginning, and I don't know of any case in which they were successful with this. For about ten months the police were waiting next to my place, around the time when it would be getting dark. There were nights in which I did no painting, I would go from one club to the next, and the cops would follow me the whole time. There have been some close situations, where you might feel like beating them up or just making fun of them.

With the Squad on your heels, the usual route to a yard becomes more complicated. We would start by going in the opposite direction, making a lot of weird turns in the streets, until we were sure that nobody was on our ass. It was kind of sick, their only way of taking you to court was by inventing facts that never happened. Like that they saw someone, and of course it was almost daylight, and of course that guy didn't wear a mask, so they could fool the judge with that crap.

The Vandal Squad made some home searches in that period too, but it wasn't my first time with that, so like everybody else I was prepared for it. After a while they stopped trying to spy on people so much, they just checked the yards more often. The area in Dortmund in which we were painting trains was at a distance of like 150km from Dortmund, and the local transit police started supporting the Vandal Squad by checking their stations, so in that period it became routine for us to get regularly chased. I am quite happy that I never got caught painting a train. Shit used to happen while I was tagging in the streets or

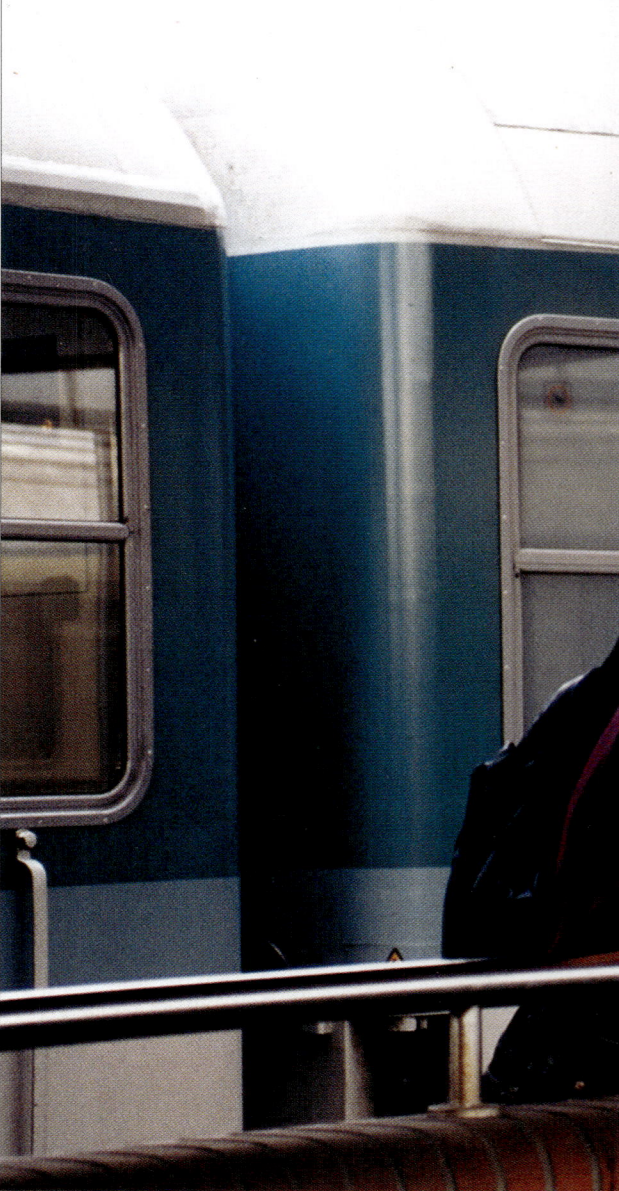

Dortmund local Vandal Squad, early 90s.

painting a wall in the centre, but never in a yard, though of course there have been some close calls. I remember one really bad night after doing an end-to-end and some panels; we were three guys all together, just on our way to leave the yard. While still walking along the tracks, at a distance of like 200 meters from the trains, I looked back and saw a bunch of guys coming around one of the trains. I just thought that the drivers or some work bums had arrived. Then I see more guys approaching us, about twenty, and I realise that they're all cops. And there were a lot of cops. I just shouted something and we tried to run. The area wasn't so good for hiding, it had some small houses on one side, and a factory on the other, and then there was the main street that led to central station. I managed to jump through some fucking bushes, but I got caught in them and scratched my eye, my whole face was dripping with blood. In the streets I could hear even more cops, so finally I ended up crouching to the ground, under a van that was parked behind a small house, and I had to wait there for like four hours without moving. It was winter and a really cold night, I guess between 5-10 below zero, so I was shivering for hours and just listening to the sounds of the police driving through the streets, accompanied by the barking of their dogs. I was sure that at least one of us had gotten caught. Once daylight came, the cops disappeared and I went to a gas station to wash up, I still remember the guy's expression when I came in with that bloody mess all over my face. At that time nobody had a mobile so it took a while 'til I got into

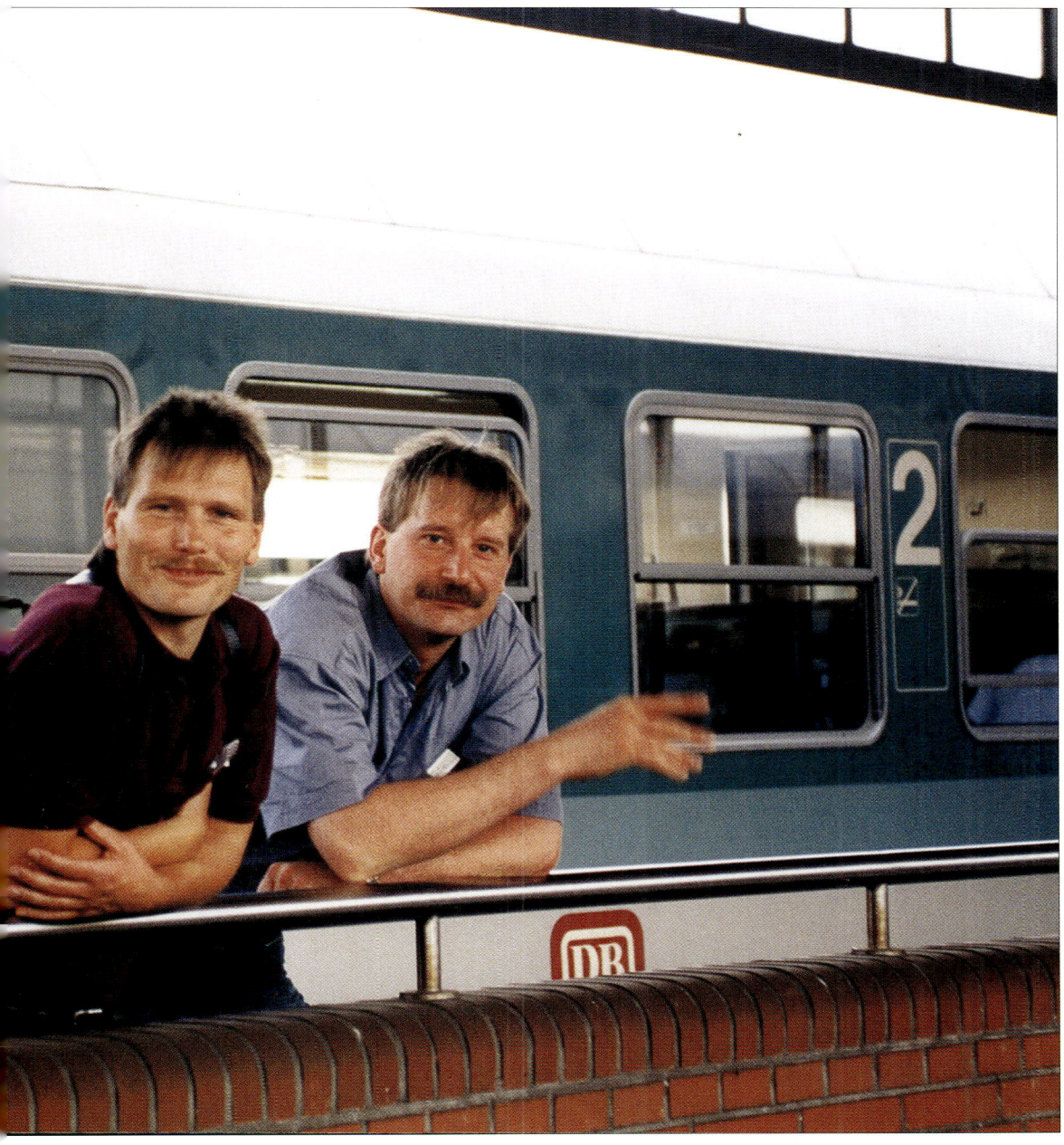

— *Mason*

contact with the others and the good news was that nobody had gotten caught. One guy was just hiding in the bushes next to the tracks and the flashlight of the cops even flittered across his body once. Of course there were a lot of funny situations as well. One night I was out to do a whole-car with Fume again. We found a corner, stashed our paint and went to check the inside of the train. On our way through the cars we ran into a girl sitting in a dark, empty car, alone. We both didn't expect her to be there, so at first we told her we were plainclothes over cops checking the train or some such nonsense, but after a while we decided to just tell her about our plan. We even ended up putting her name between our pieces and while we painted she would watch from time to time. Once we were done, we took her to the next train station and went home.

During the following years the local system started changing and trains were no longer based in town. Before this the 130 cars were running on totally different lines and had to be checked in Dortmund. So we ended up running in or next to the city. Now the last of these cars had been modified to some other cities. We could still paint them, but it was more difficult to see them run as often because the service range of these trains was much wider and in addition they were buffed much more often. The models in circulation also started to change and more and more spots where trains used to be parked just disappeared. Some lines just got closed and the newer train types were being checked all night by security.

I was still painting pretty frequently but around that time it started not to be as much fun anymore. There were weeks in which you'd try to hit a train maybe even three times, but only once would be successful. Going to a yard which is one hour away, parking your car in the middle of nowhere for safety, to then paint for maybe five minutes and have to wait for three hours the next day to take a photo just doesn't sound so interesting to me nowadays. There are still some opportunities here and there and I still love to see pieces running but in a way life has changed and I have work to do, responsibilities to take care of. Of course I still need a stress around now and then though.

– NEXT GENERATION

It's great to see that in a way so much has changed and I am quite curious as to what will come in the future. Younger kids do as many trains as they can, pieces don't run that long anymore, but you can still see stuff around. The style of letters and painting has also changed, but graffiti is still alive and kicking and it's good to see it around. Painting a train nowadays feels quite weird to me, I realise that my body isn't 20 years old no more - half of the police force is younger than me. But just going it makes you feel like sweet 16 or so.

Looking back at the very beginning, graffiti started as an outsider phenomenon. Newspapers wrote about these strange signs on the walls that nobody could read and there was a whole new world to be explored. Today graffiti just belongs to Dortmund like football or beer.

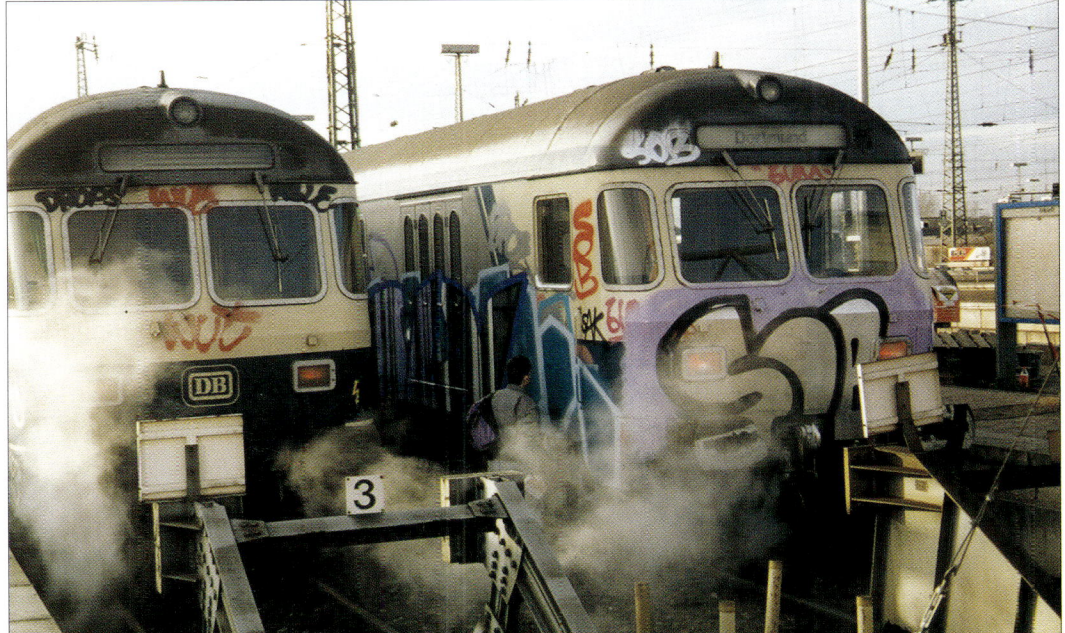

Sly, Sob on an old front car

— *Mason*

A CHANGE OF TUNE
—

Chana – TWS / Dortmund
>

The reason why Dortmund's scene became so strong and tough is due to the basic game of circumstance: competition. Graffiti-wise, similarly to what had happened in NYC, kids here initially competed with tags throughout the city, but once the first train was painted they soon switched to targeting the local lines of Dortmund. When the first panels were seen running word spread, and every writer soon started checking out the various yards of the territory, sometimes discovering city yards, sometimes just faraway lay-ups lost in suburbia. In all this yard-spotting Chintz was the one that had control of the whole situation from the beginning: yards, lay-ups, lines and the general system. Of course he never said a word about his secrets and discoveries. I once asked him about train spots and his answer was: "Hey, you know everything. Don't ask me".
So week by week the hunt for yards in Dortmund was having a traumatic effect on central station: the Bahnhof was totally full of bombed trains coming from every direction. As had occurred at Grand Concourse in NY, here too platforms started becoming writers' benches, the ideal spots from which to check out our results. The atmosphere however wasn't really that of the typical meltin' pot of young writers with blackbooks, sketches and ghetto blasters. At Dortmund bahnhof the heat has always been high and tangible. Over there kids weren't talking with each other, you could spend a whole afternoon on the platform spotting trains and watching the same people for hours: the same undercover cop, the same rail track guard, the same kid you already saw around the place 2000 times; he probably had recognised you as well, but he wouldn't come and comment. So a complacent game of 'peekaboo' would commence, a slight euphoria difficult to turn off considering that every ten minutes a new train with a new car was coming in with huge block letters. Those letters were the style paradigm of the city: straight, massive and with no mercy. Dortmund bahnhof was a silent place immersed in a conflictive atmosphere: fully coloured trains surrounded by the greyscale industrial city. An urban and social context impossible to avoid, in which the working class has no regard for anything that is not practical, useful or basic. Graffiti can be thought of as art or as mere vandalism, but here both cannot fit into a context based on white collar workers, beer, football and hooligans.
There's no plan B and obviously writers had to manage with what their surroundings were. Actually, they literally embraced the lifestyle and established a new form of graffiti in the European scene; undercover Writing took step here, also motivated by the tough methods the local police were adopting: house raids. Since the beginning there were very few kids giving names and facts to them, the Dortmundians became silent and suspicious, and "not speaking" became the first rule.

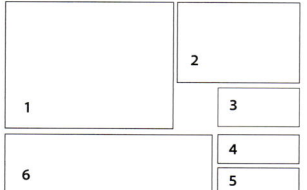

1   Iso, Massive Attack, Dance

2   Physo Senso, at Central Station

3   Abl getting buffed

4 5   Rad, before and after the cops messed it up trying to be funny

6   Dortmund central station during the early 90's: Rio, Sak, Sob, Vola whole-car plus bombed trains before and after

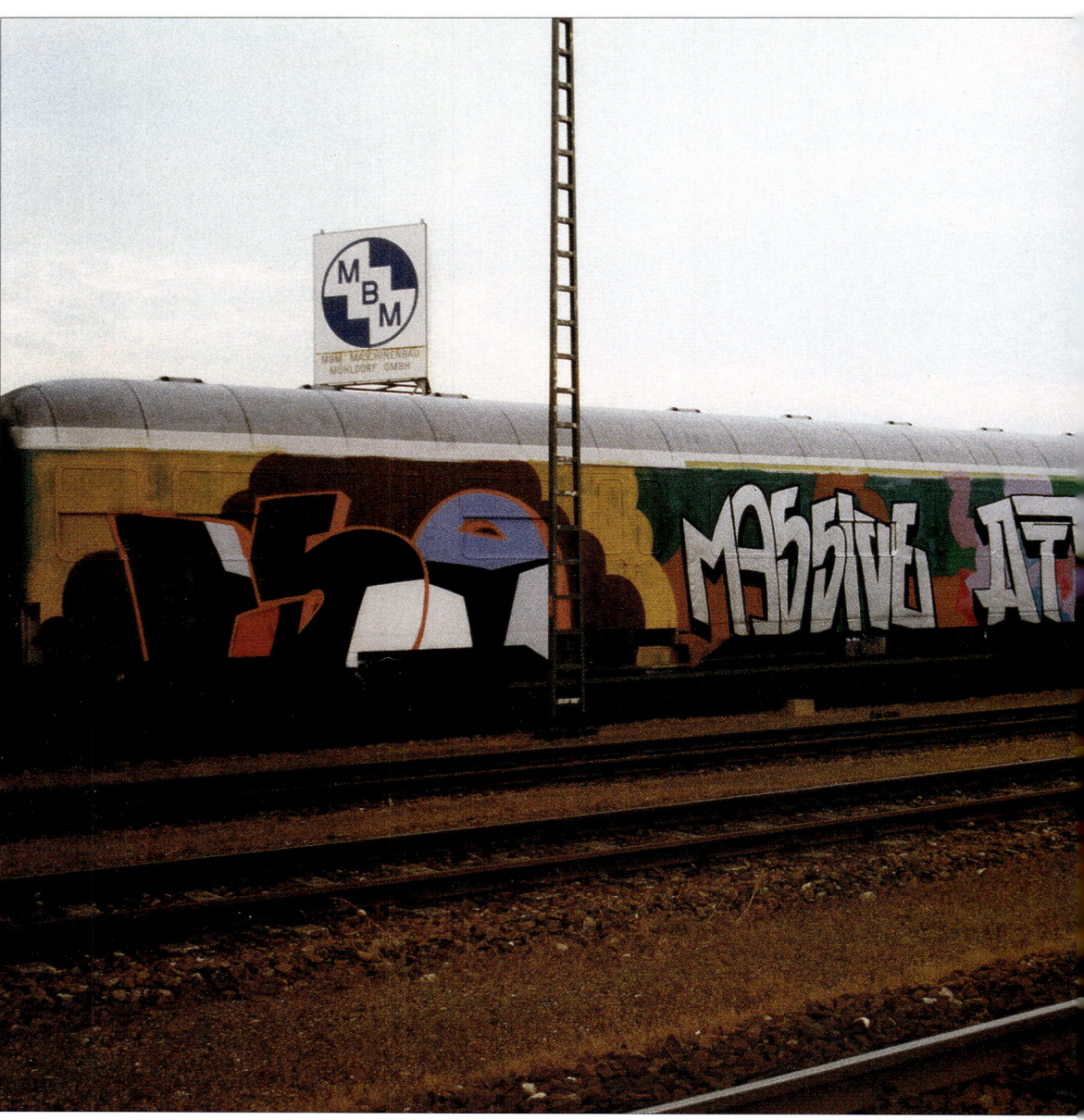

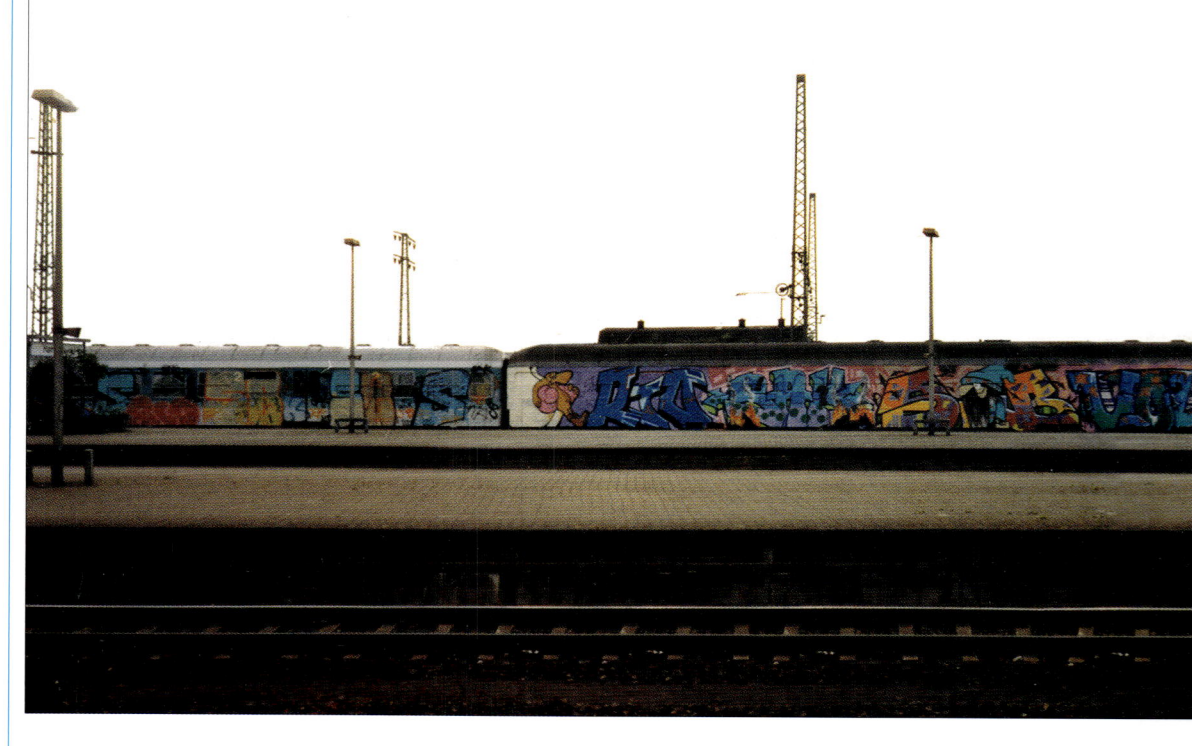

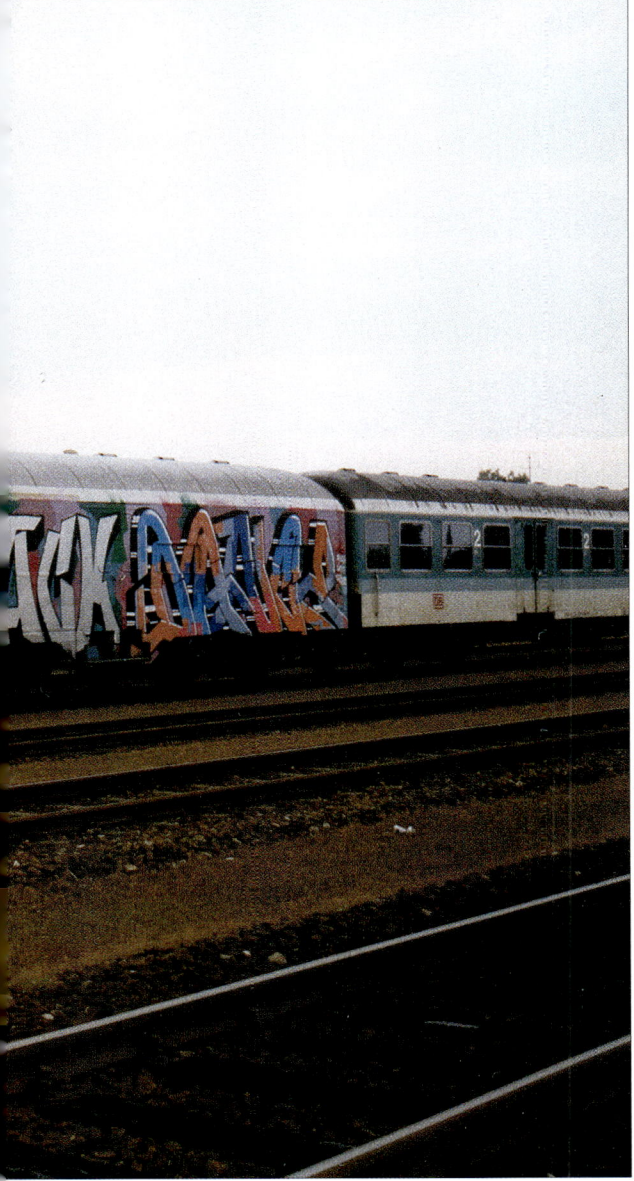

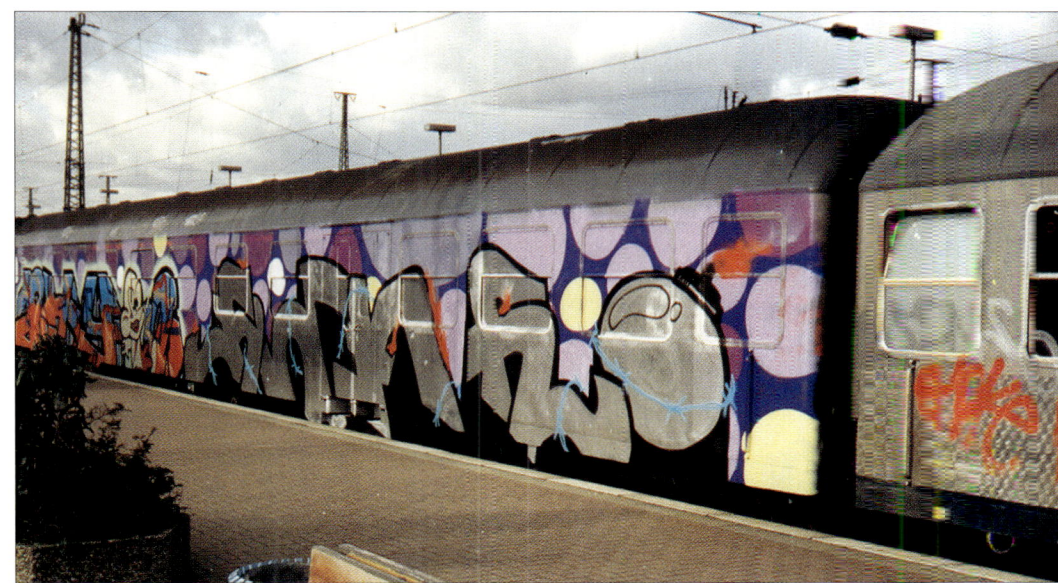

— Mason

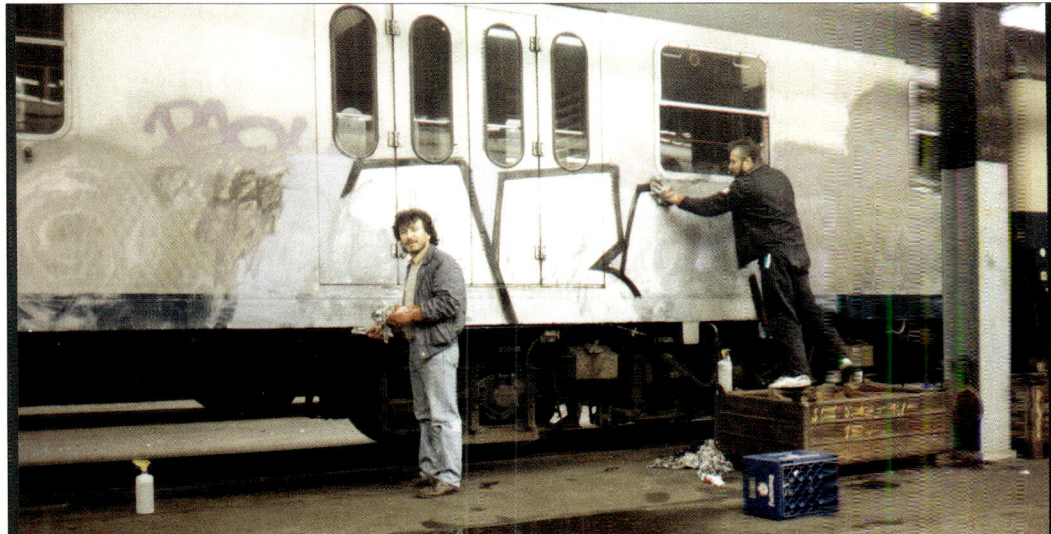

— Mason

— Mason

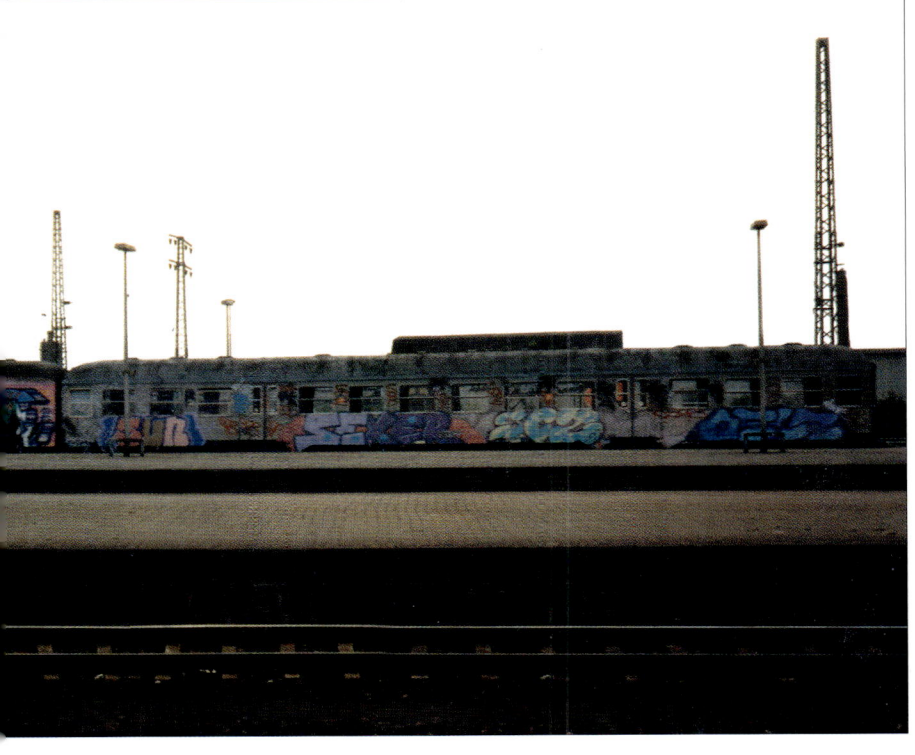

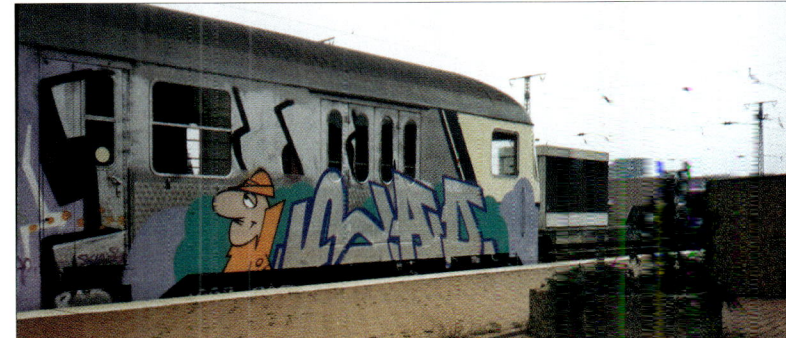

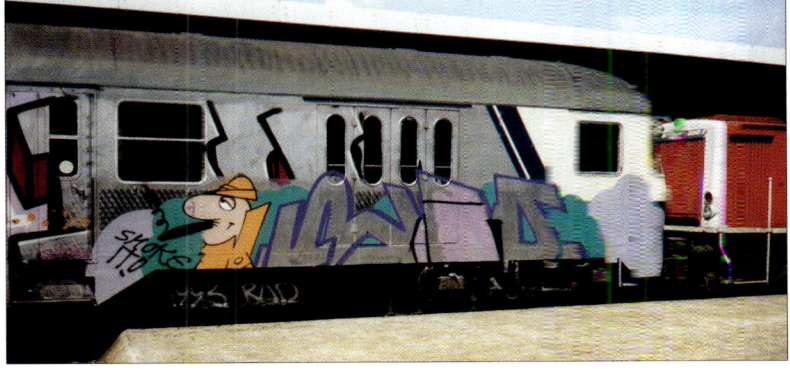

— ACW archive

— Mason

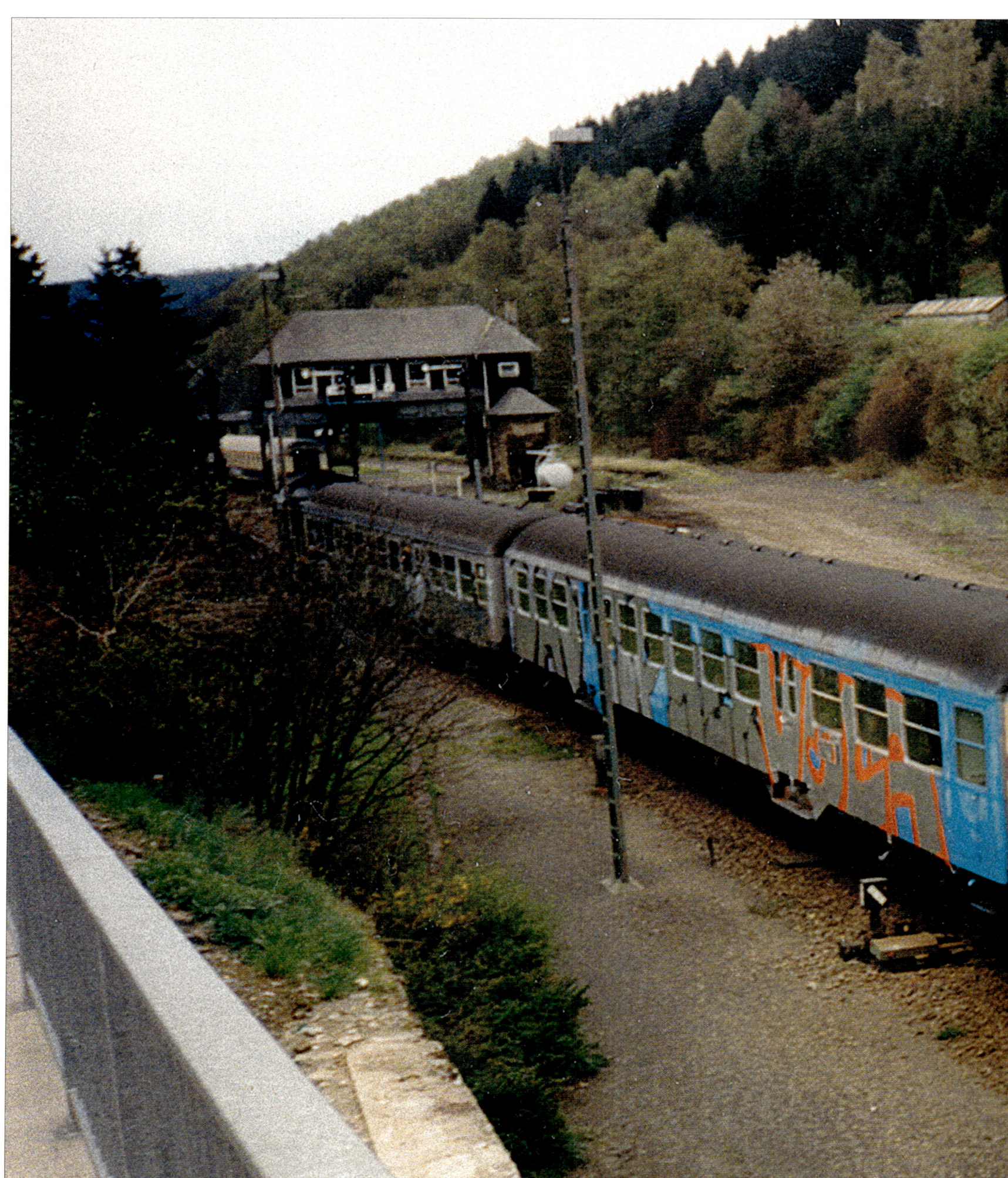

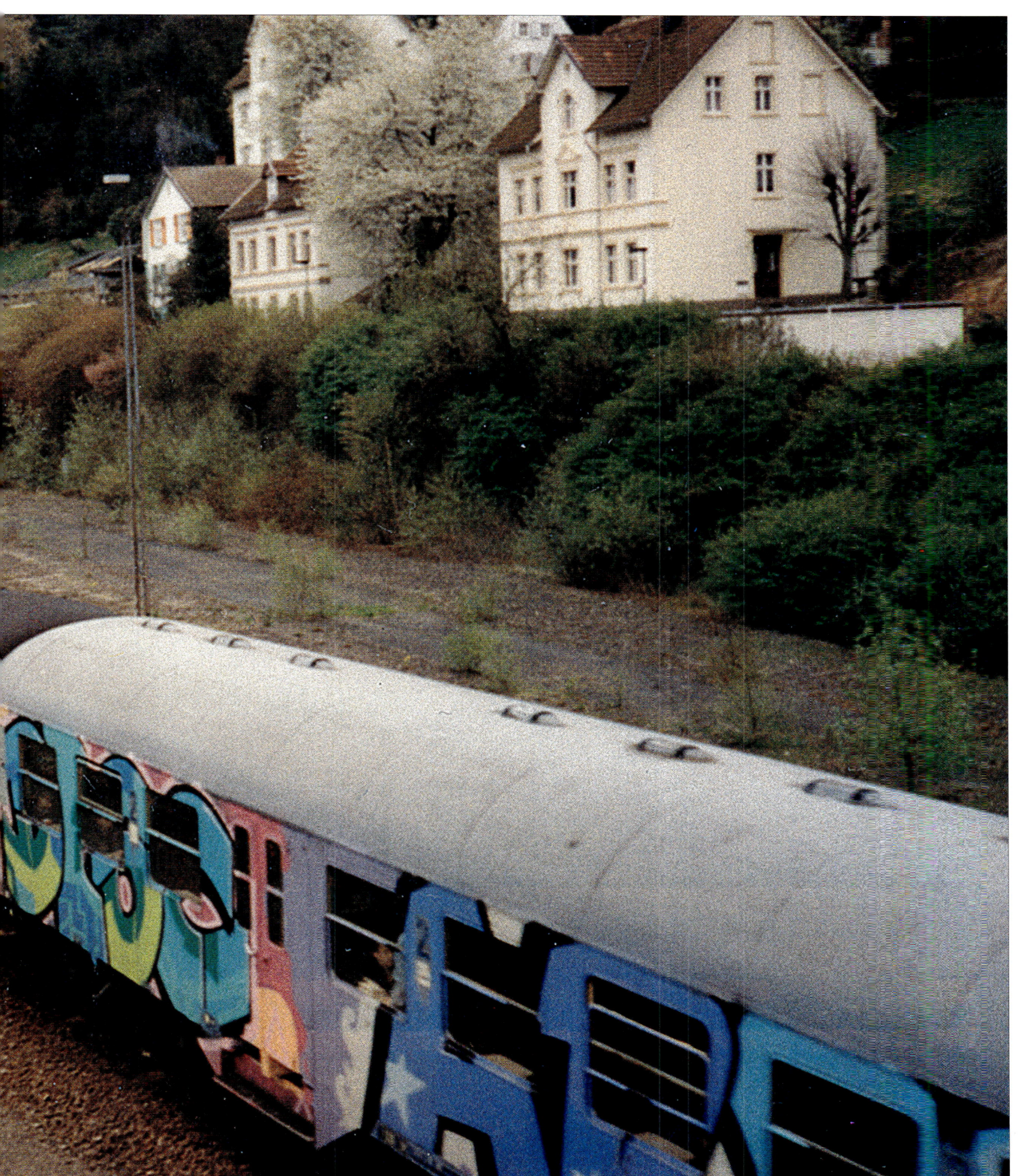

STRIKING CERCANIAS

The aesthetic reinterpretation of the local Cercanias trains, feather in the cap of the Spanish railway system

Kapi –BTP / Barcelona
>

During the 80's the Renfe was not seen as a valid ground for battles between writers; in certain stations, such as Sant Andreu, where trains were left on the platform for hours, hitting them was like painting the wall of your hall of fame. It would have been a party on the rail tracks. Then with the 90's this widespread opinion changed: on one side European fanzines were showing kids in Germany and Holland painting the Intercity and local lines, on the other, as soon as all interest for the Cercanias increased, they became much more risky to do and it was thus acceptable to paint them.

In 1992 two coinciding episodes occurred: the first number of *Game Over* came out, and the demand for the publication of train pictures increased, in an attempt to keep up with the pace of the European scene. At the same time Renfe changed the train cars of the Cercanias, substituting the old blue model with brand spanking new white ones, like those of the New York subway.

The cars were enormous, very long, with three doors. These lines served Barcelona and its province, you could see them at the station, waiting all day at Sant Andreu, until the Vandal Squad started taking photos of whoever was taking pictures of the trains.

Sant Andreu actually remained a place forgotten by the citizens and city of Barcelona, with its painted trains,

enormous halls of fame and abandoned factories. It was excluded from the program of urban renewal for the Olympics of 1992, and mostly stayed connected to the aesthetics of the 80's so that it became a second home for writers. During the first years the Renfe was painted by BTP, Bomb The Planet, formed by Kapi, Moockie, Musa, Zerok, Taran, and Tomak. In parallel to this, in the same period another group started painting it, Bandits (BTS), captained by Krash, who had already been painting the subway for some time and then switched to the Cercanias. On the platforms you could run into the members of a few other crews active on the Renfe, but when the company introduced cars with mirrors, the phenomenon exploded: the former Cercanias were too long and too high, almost impossible to fill.

On the other hand the new trains had a similar shape to that of certain European subways and the horizontal mirror added an incredible style to the pieces. The aesthetics of many local writers changed because of these new proportions and the mirror indirectly influenced you to plan letters and pieces that were long, thin and lower than before. Not that we wanted to respect the glass mirror, but on one hand it was a fascinating surface and on the other we thought that a car with clean windows had a higher probability of running as opposed to a whole-car. Also to consider is that we could see ourselves

reflected in the windows while we took photos, a double dose of narcissism that was even more satisfying to the typical writer ego. The first end-to-ends, whole-cars and whole-trains were painted by Moockie, Kapi and BTP. In particular, the first whole-car by BTP was seen as a real challenge towards those that were convinced that replicating the incredible 'worms' of the German writers was impossible in Spain. Silver "BTP", with rocks painted on the side and Moockie and Kapi's tags (Clyde and SPD). It never ran but at least we managed to photograph it, and that, before any whole-train, convinced everyone to raise the bar a notch.

With the Sant Andreu whole-train a chapter of Barcelona's history was written: every car had a leader that directed the work and traced the letters. Every leader had four people to fill the letters and the background. Kapi, Moockie and Krash did the names of all the people present and, as soon as the outline was traced, they started filling the space.

The whole-train was blocked in the station of Sant Andreu for an entire month, almost as if a temporary land-art exhibition had arrived: Renfe didn't know what to do with that enormous coloured snake, it was something unseen until then. Instead of moving or cleaning it, they left it in the station for weeks, during which Catalonian writers went to see it, as if on a pilgrimage.

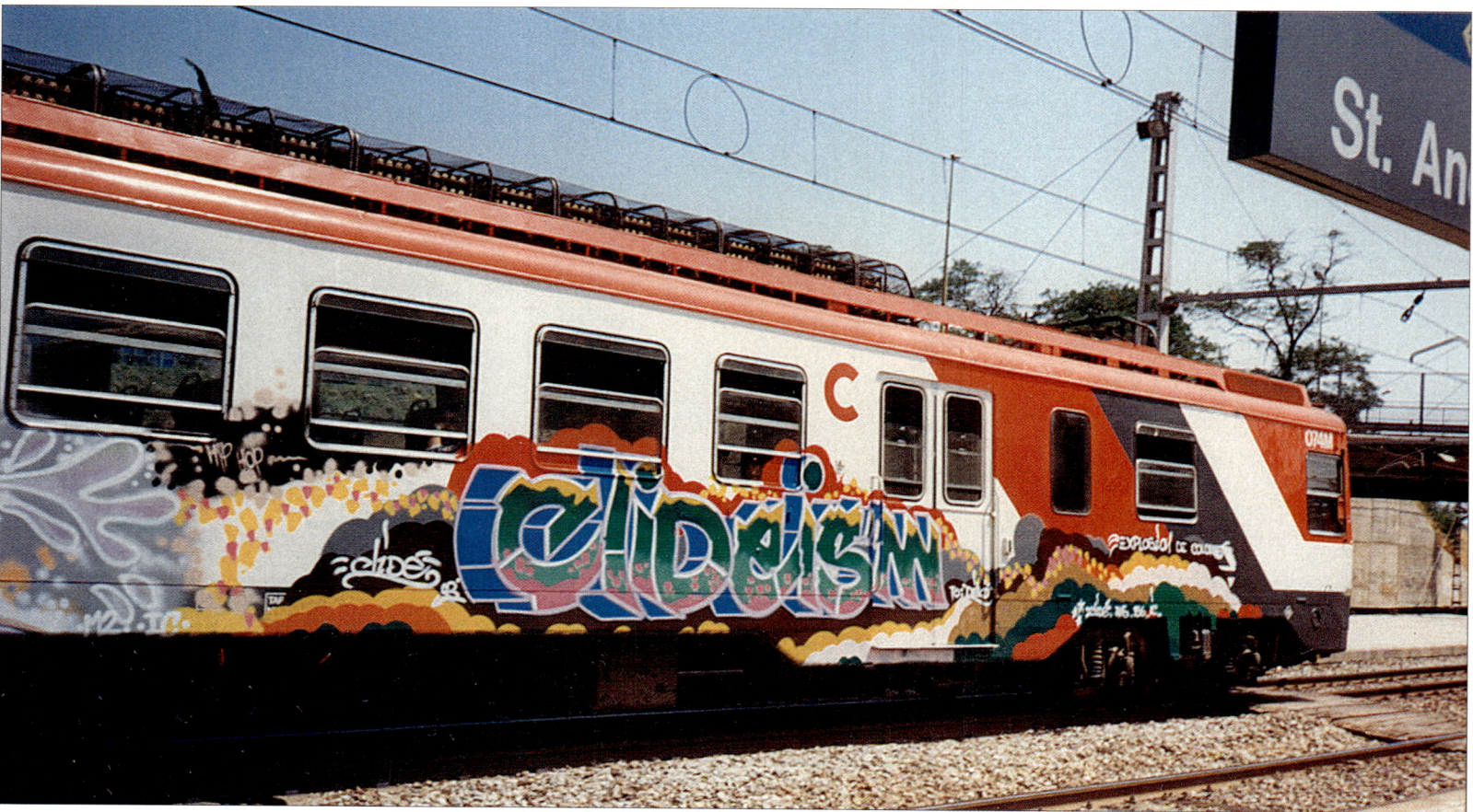

Clideism by Mockie – BTP

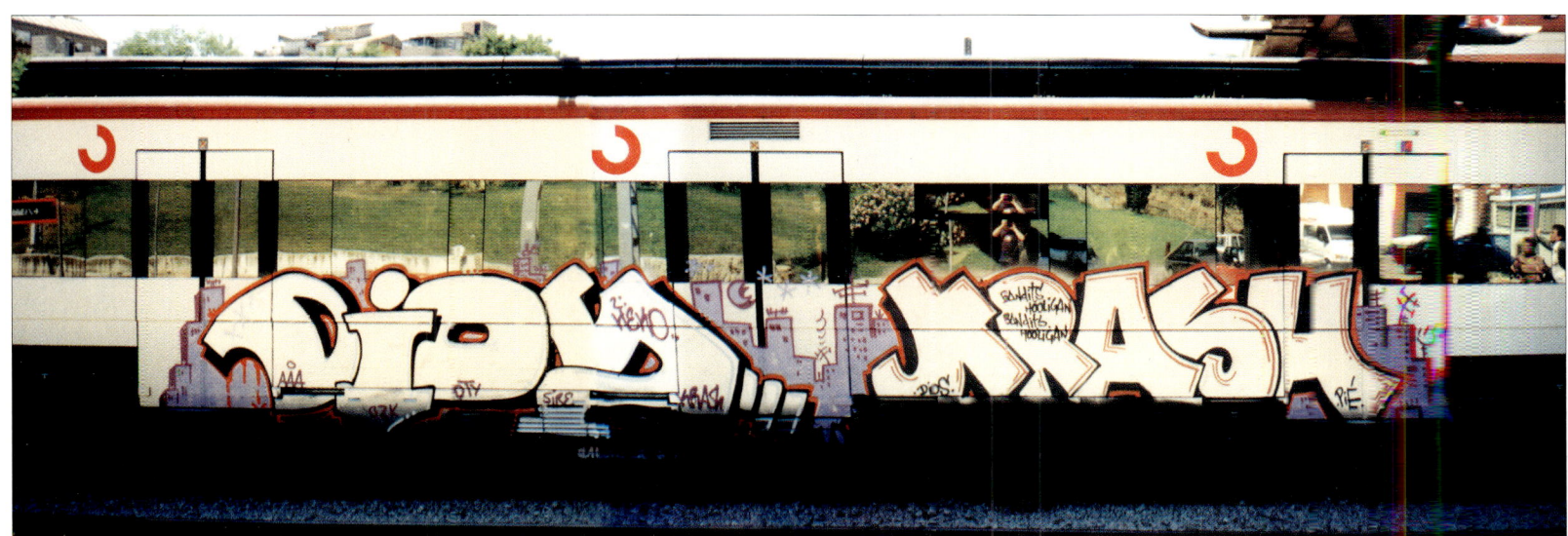

Dios and Krash, appearing above their pieces by the mirror-windows

– Krash

Mirror appeal

Vino – TSK / Barcelona
>

The Cercanías network of Barcelona is composed of seven lines, all crossing through the city centre and going from one side of the province to the other. Every station of the city is underground but once out of Barcelona the trains emerge into the open. The C1 line runs parallel to the Northern coast of the city, from Massanet to Martorell, and all its stops in the Northern area are on beaches. The same occurs with the C2 line that for its Southern stretch runs parallel to the sea. The C3 and C4 lines go towards the inlands, the prolongation of the C3 line now reaches as far as the Pyrenees.

Until 1992 the trains circulating on these lines were old, with a white and red coat, and before that they had been light blue and yellow. In 1992 the new trains arrived, with their mirror windows and for many years they were the most beautiful and modern trains in Europe – and they still are, for me. In 1994 the first double-deckers appeared, running solely on the C2 line. The old trains

> **In 1992 the new trains arrived, with their mirror windows, for years the most beautiful and modern trains in Europe**

were renewed with the same colours as the mirror trains, substituting the normal glass windows with mirror ones. In 2006 they changed the colours: now they are totally white with a red and a purple stripe. In 2007 the first CIVIA trains were then introduced, similar to the mirror trains, but with a more aerodynamic head, as if they were high-speed carriages.

Another peculiarity of the Cercanías is the yards, each very different from the others: some are completely isolated in the mountains, like Massanet. Others are in between the city and the mountains, like Manresa. Others are in the middle of the city, like Villanova or Sant Celoni. And others still are close to the sea, like Mataró, or Sant Vicente or Blanes. But they are all anyway very different

> CONTINUES ON PAGE 392

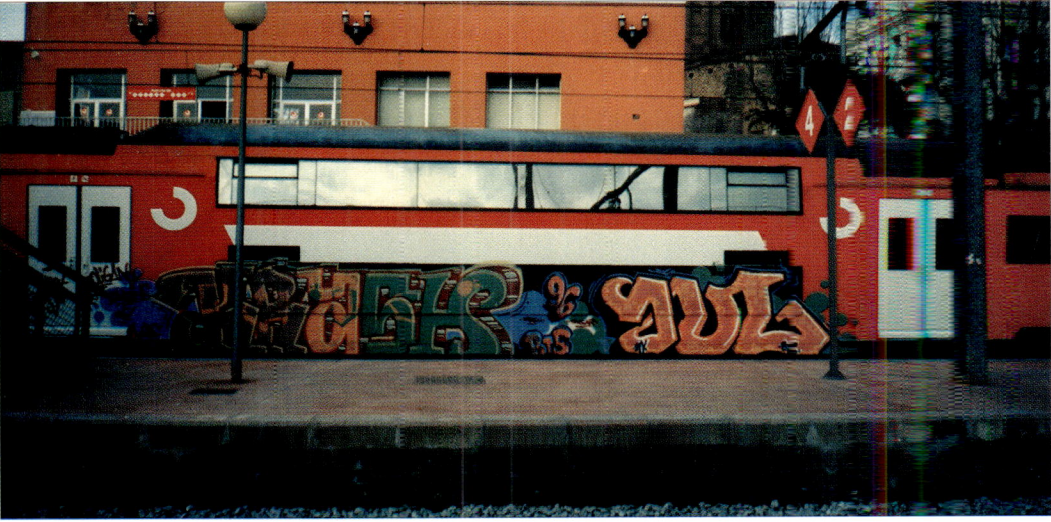

Krash and Sug –BTS on a double-decker Cercanias. 1996

– ACW archive

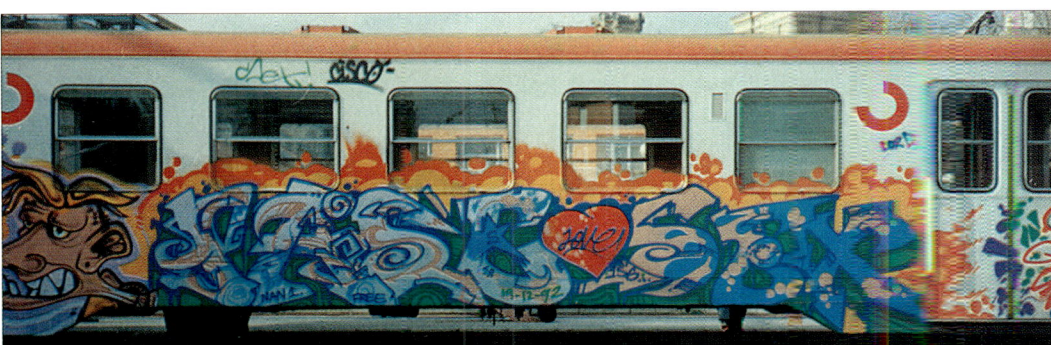

Fase loves sex by Fase, 1991

– Kapi

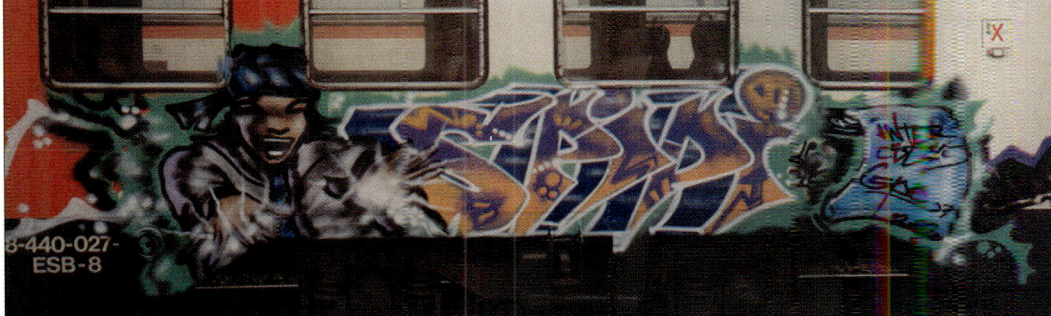

Panel piece and character by Spidi, Bomb the Planet crew. 1991

– Kapi

> CONTINUES FROM PAGE 391

from one another and the dynamics of painting always change. There are also various places for backjumps and end stations in which to paint.

In Barcelona, Writing on Cercanías started at the end of the 80's by the hands of Biz, Fase, Cad73, Sac and others, but the big boom occurred halfway through the 90's. I started painting trains in 1993 and in those days it was a whole new world to be discovered, there were still places where nobody had painted yet. Together with Blue, Snat, Busk, Sioc, Krash, Hove and groups like OTP, BTS or TRS, I painted in both known deposits and new spots we gradually discovered. In the beginning we painted sporadically, but with time we began doing so once a week and towards the end of the 90's even two or three times a week. We painted in every deposit and it was normal to bump into someone else doing the same thing or waiting to do so....in some cases we found ourselves being as many as twenty in the same deposit, doing

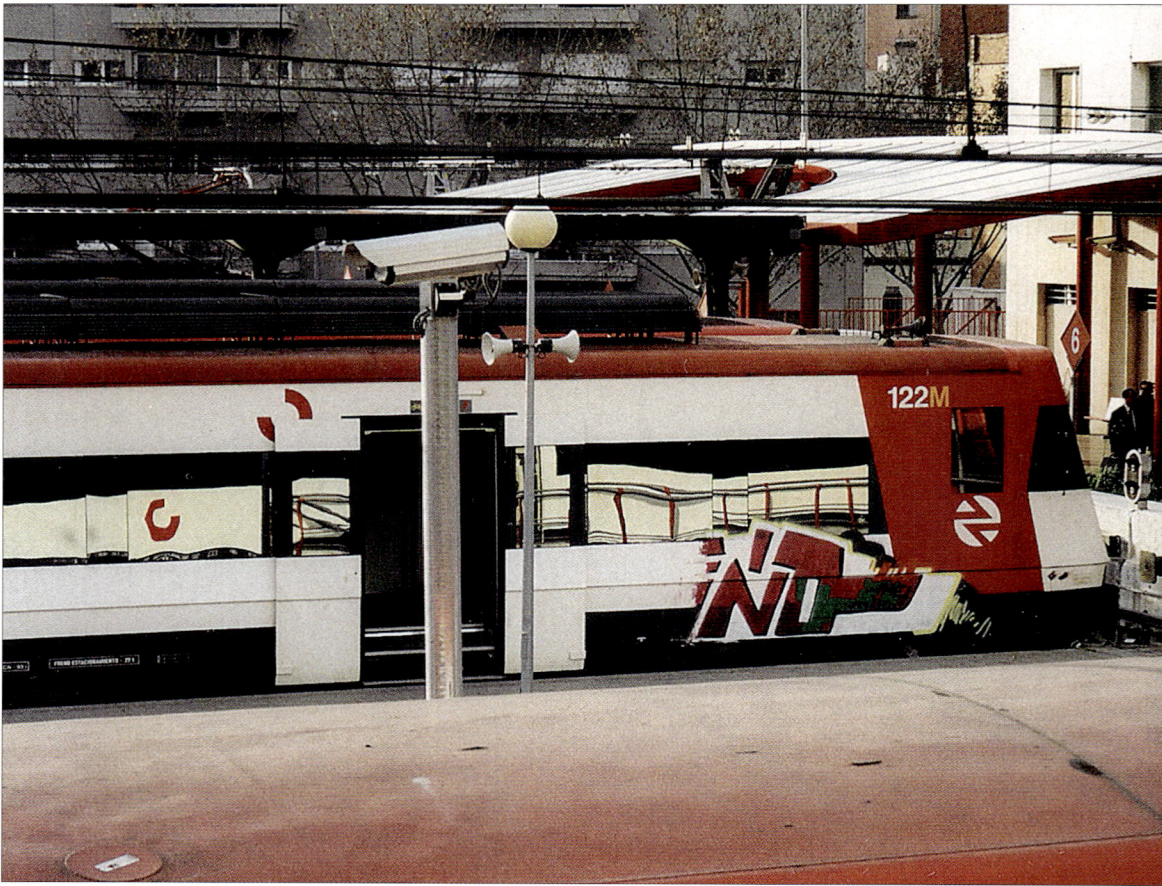

At the end of the 90's things changed. There was more security, you couldn't stay as long in the yard anymore

whole-cars and panels all night long! The panels then ran for weeks and it was incredible to hang out at the beach and see your train pass on the coastal line while you were sun tanning or taking a swim. Naturally sometimes you would find security guards hidden inside the train or the police would pass to check things out, but if the night was calm you could paint for over an hour. You got to the deposit, waited for the last train to arrive, and when they were finished cleaning inside it the party could begin. There were days in which you could see the cleaners go away by car and you would remain alone, or sometimes as you painted they would stop next to you and watch how you did your pieces. In some deposits writers had gotten to know the workers, who would let them write undisturbed. One time however while we were painting one cleaning guy gave some kind of signal and the police appeared from nothing....they caught ten writers in one go! Those were the good old days but people were too trusting and it's never a good idea to trust in people that much. At the end of the 90's things changed. There was more security, the police came more often and you couldn't stay in the yard as long anymore. We started doing backjumps, and so did many others. In the beginning it was easy, even though we had to be very fast, but with time that too became more difficult because they started increasing security, the police checked often and the train drivers looked into their mirrors! From 2002 the deposits were guarded 24 hours a day, only quick pieces could be painted while security was on lunch break, or else in areas of the deposit that were not under video surveillance, between rounds. There was security everywhere, even in deposits that were as much as 150km from Barcelona. While doing backjumps trains would arrive with guards on board and the police blocked the highways towards the deposits to catch anyone with painting equipment. Then, towards 2006, with the increase of regional police - Mossos d'Esquadra - it all just became almost too much.

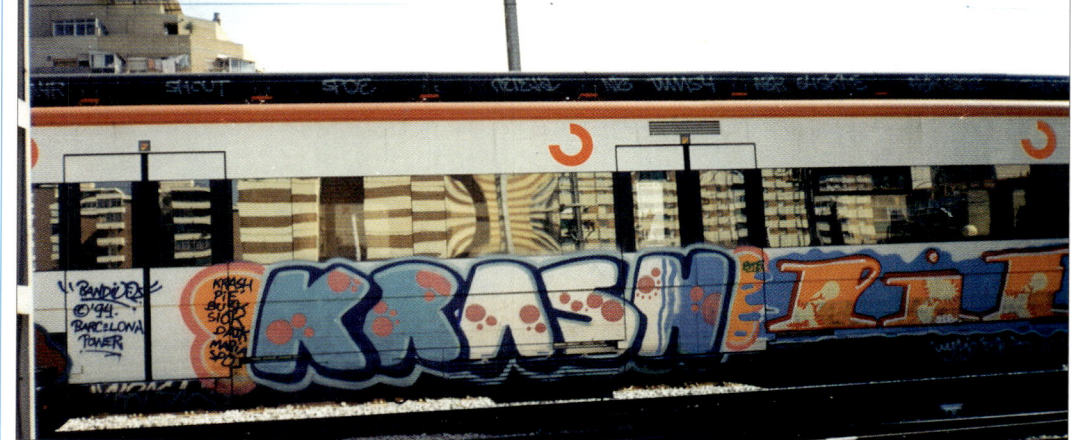

– ACW archive

There are currently very few places in which to paint and many people have been caught or have stopped. Groups like TSK, TMS, FGS, BFC, HCOM or people like Sorcek, Ogro, Peps continue doing panels, but they don't run for more than a couple of days, sometimes even only a few hours. In 2008 there was a period during which the buff squad couldn't use water due to the drought and so many panels circulated for weeks, even months. It was incredible. You might even go do a backjump and find you couldn't because someone had already painted there! Apart from these cases tied to a few exceptions though, things have changed.

For years we enjoyed a system that allowed us to paint trains with great ease, but if you want to continue doing so today the only possible strategy is to reinvent the rules of the game and adapt to the new dynamics.

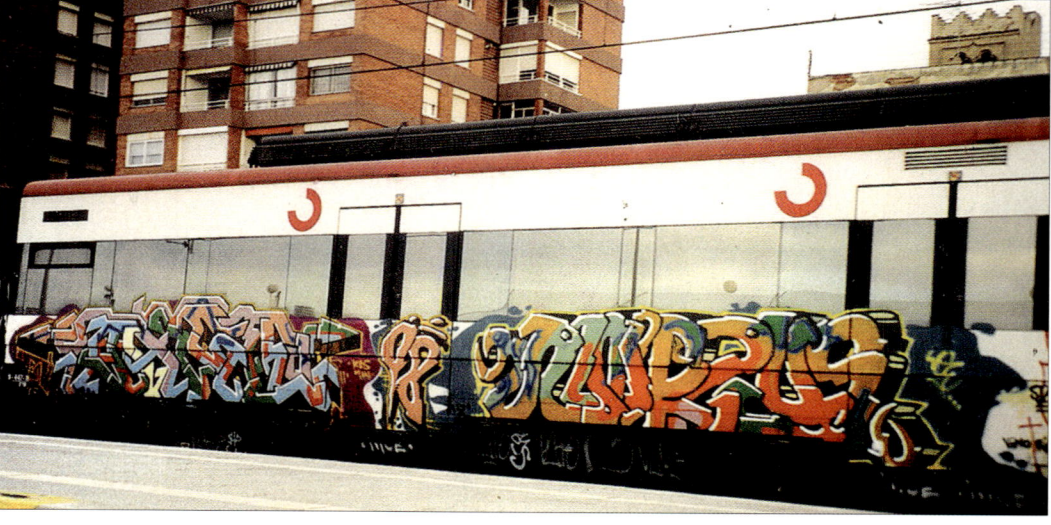

– Vino

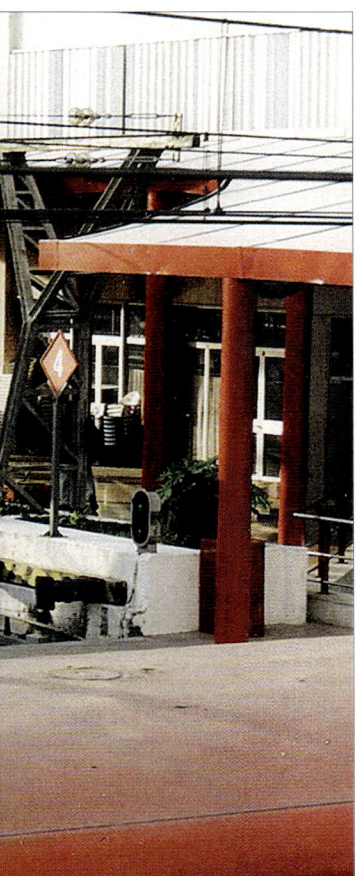

— Vino

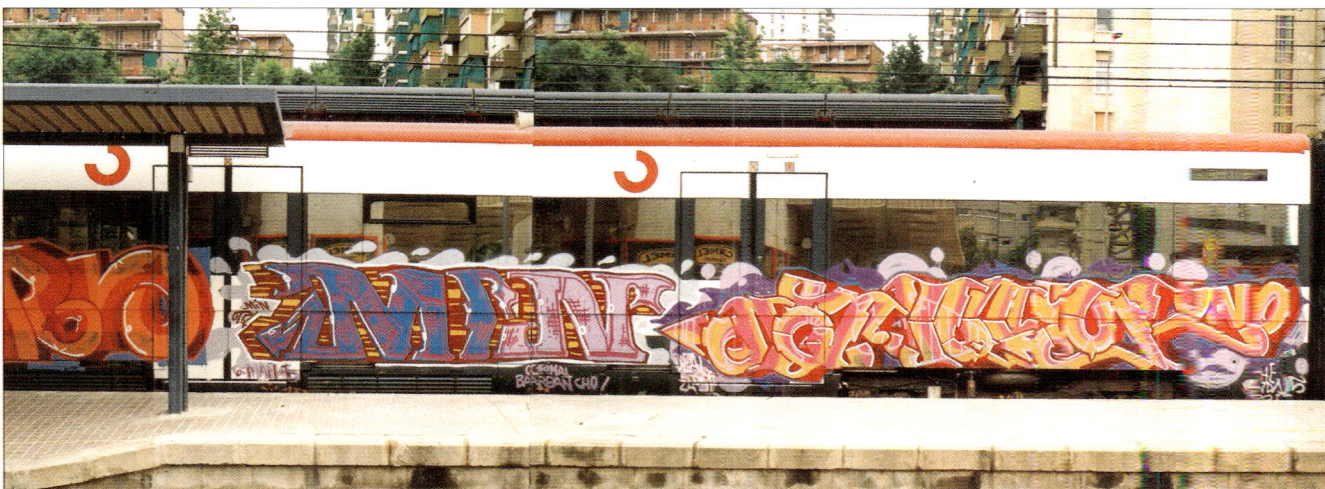

— Vino

1		2
8	9	3
7	6	4
		5

1 Hospitalet yard, 1998
2 Min, Ami, 1996
3 Bang, 1996
4 Blue, 1997
5 Bosh, 1995
6 Vino, 1998
7 Pako, Murzy, 1998
8 Krash
9 Dam, 1995

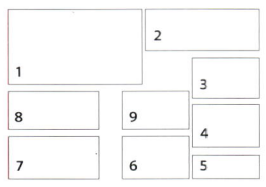

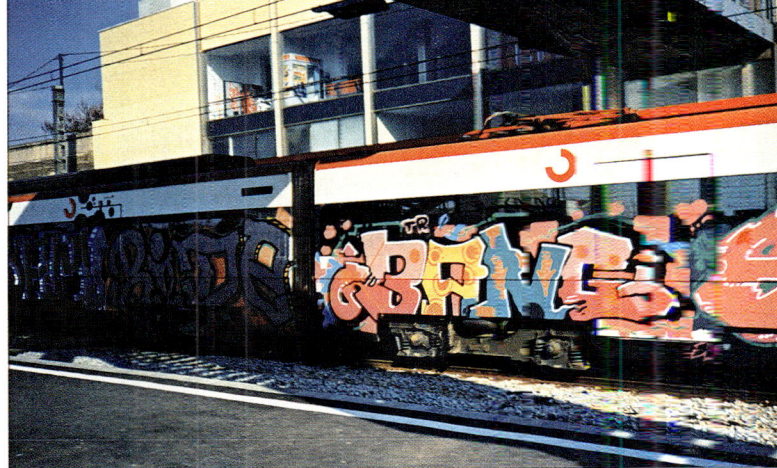

— ACW archive

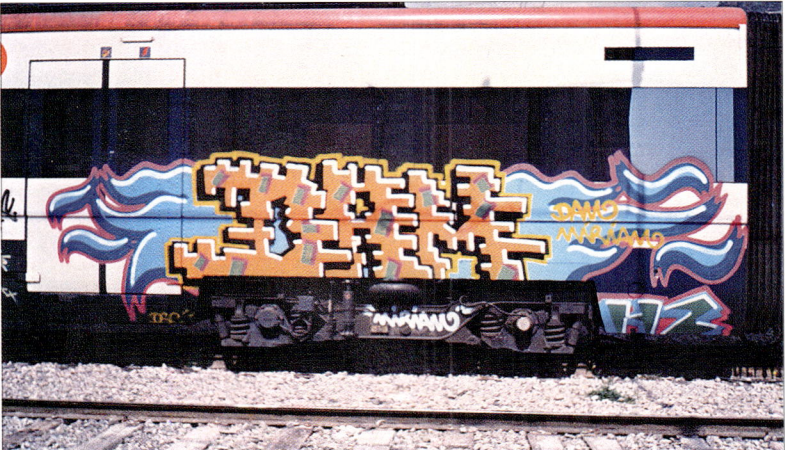

— ACW archive

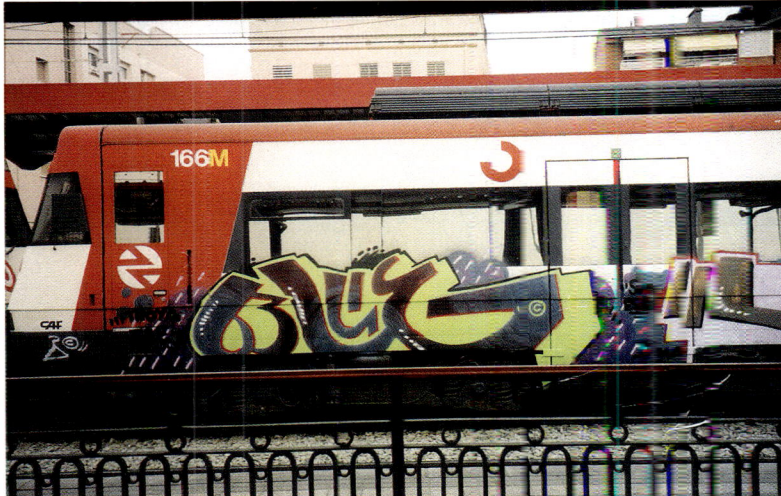

— Vino

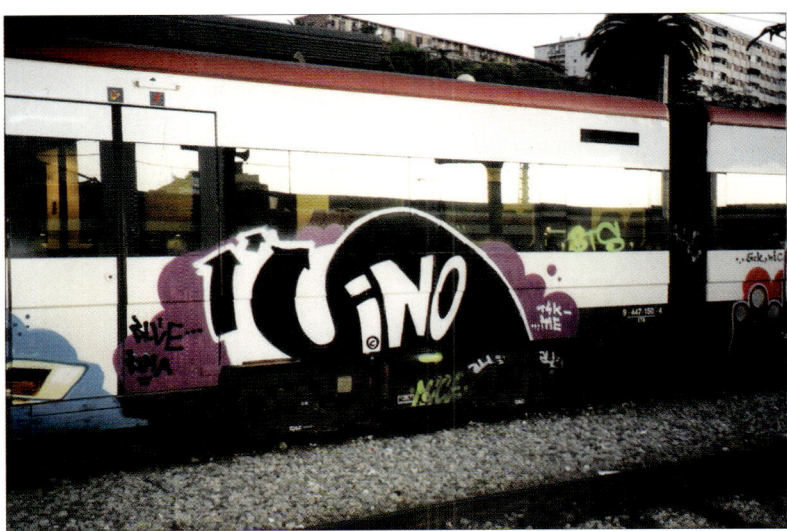

— Vino

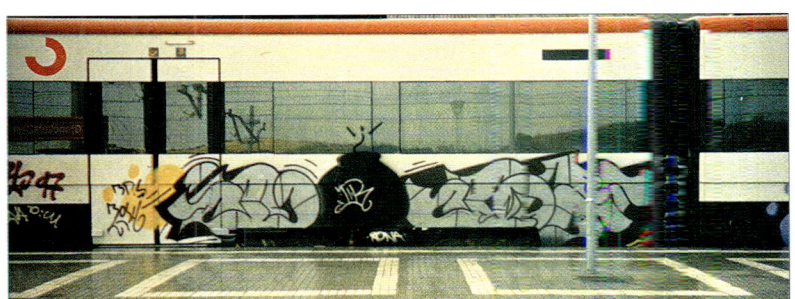

— ACW archive

BERLIN S–BAHN VISTA

From the archives of Rew,
a photographic abacus of Berlin's
S–bahn and U–bahn trains
that evokes the dawning of local
styles and portrays the writer
invasion of uncontrolled deposits
on the East side after the fall
of the Wall

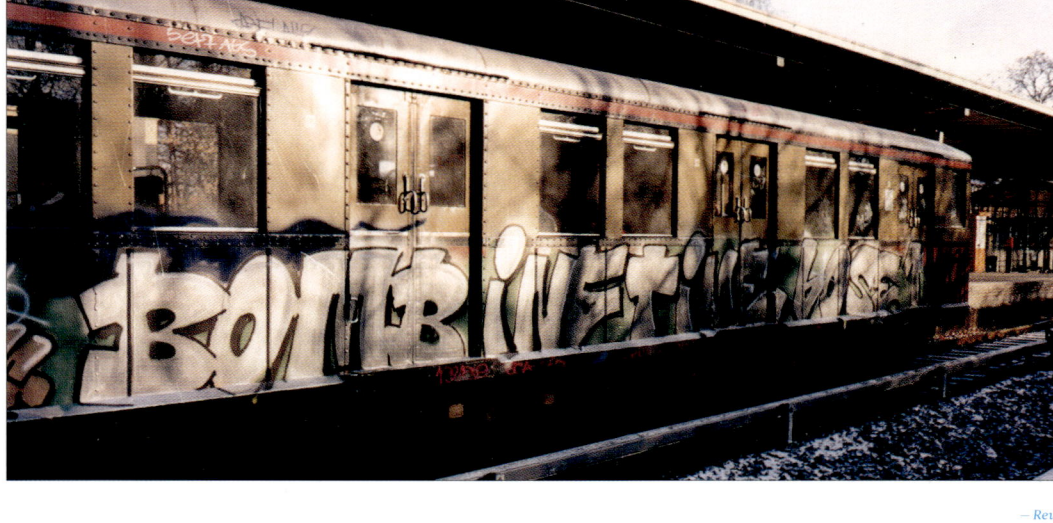

— Rew

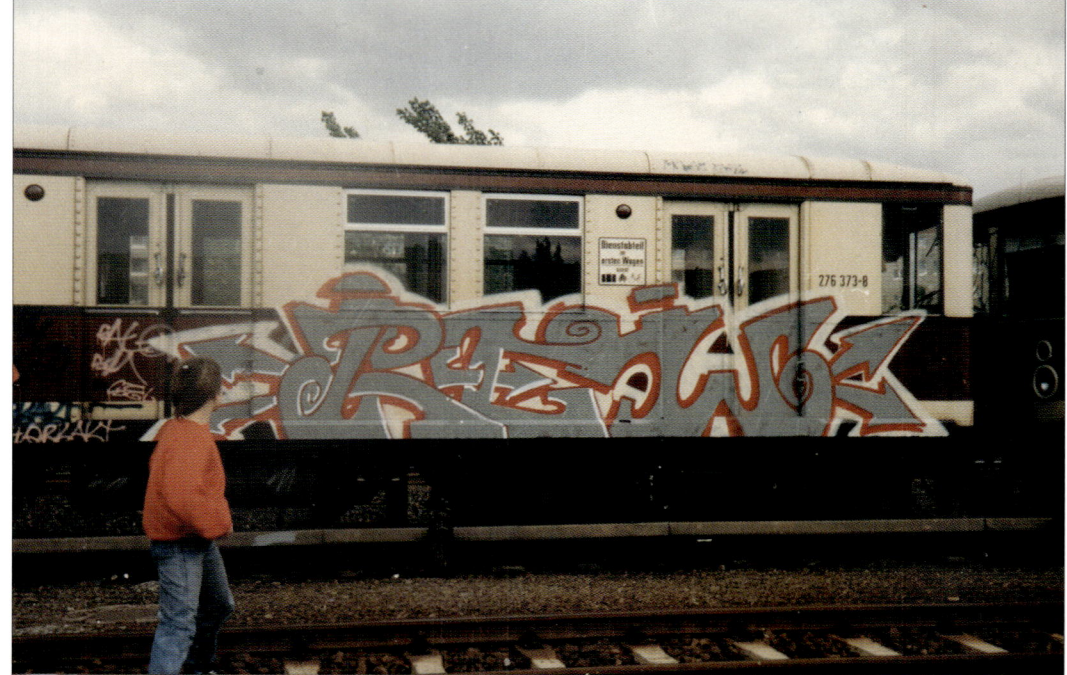

— Rew

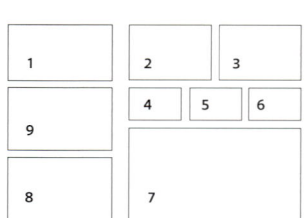

1		
	2	3
9	4 5 6	
8	7	

1. *Bombing time* by Bose
2. Rew, top–to–bottom, 1993
3. Rasta, 1992
4. Base, 1991
5. Bus, 1991
6. Kel, 1992
7. Wholecar by Shek, Some, Bisaz, 1991
8. Shek, 1991
9. Rew in front of Berlin S–train, 1991

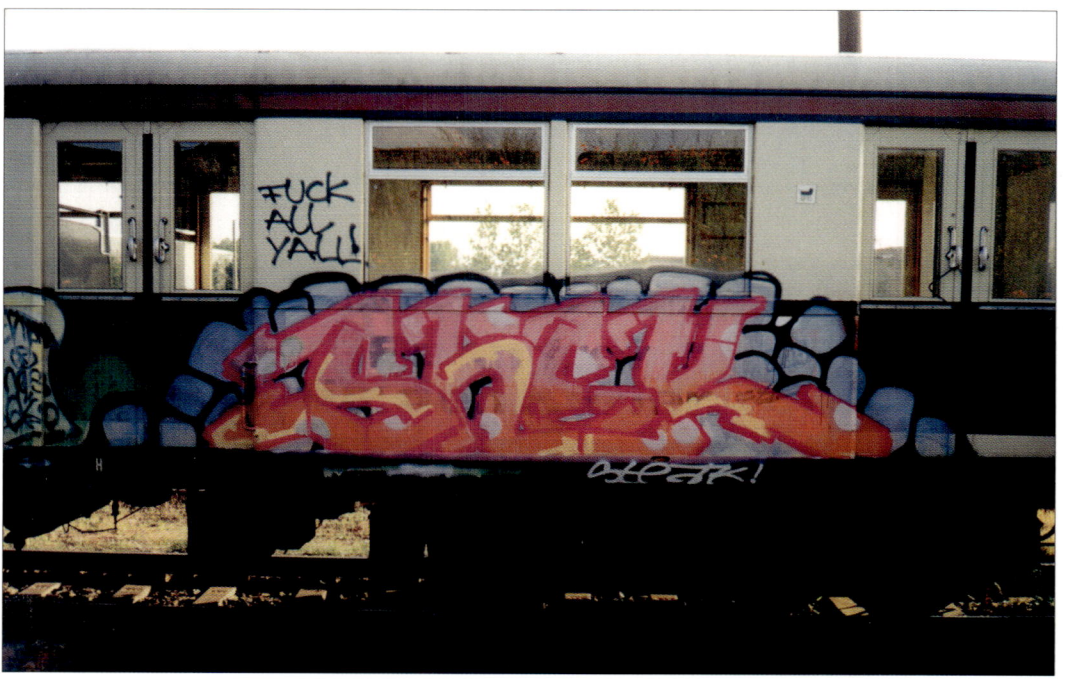
— Rew

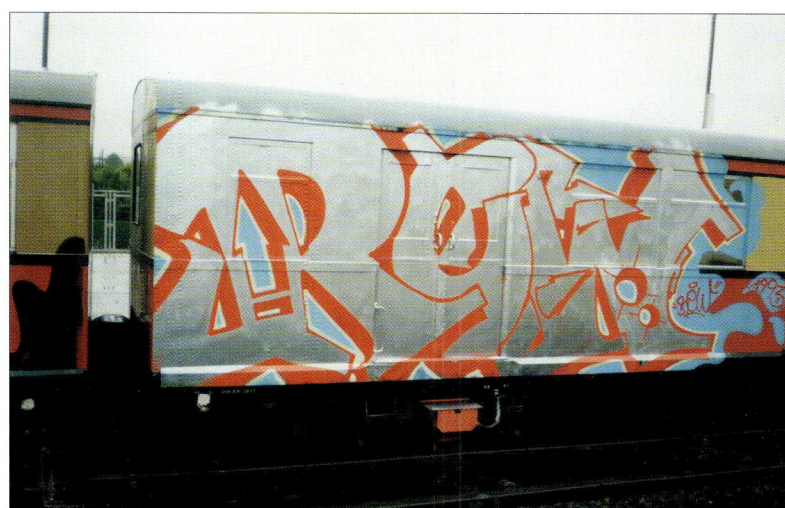

– Rew

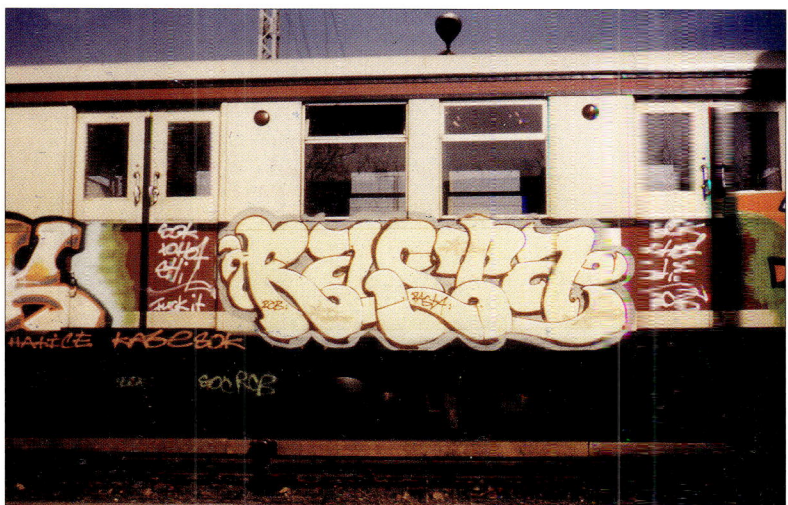

– Rew

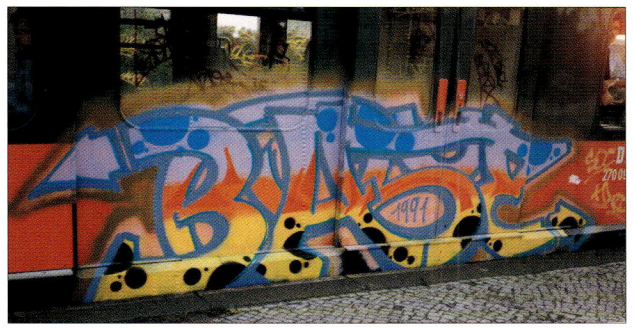

– Rew

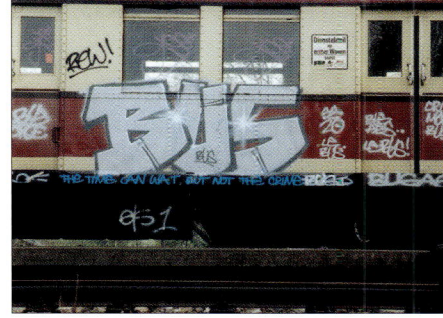

– Rew

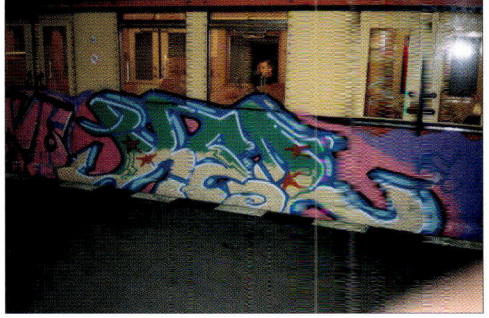

– Rew

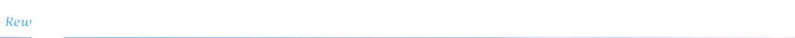

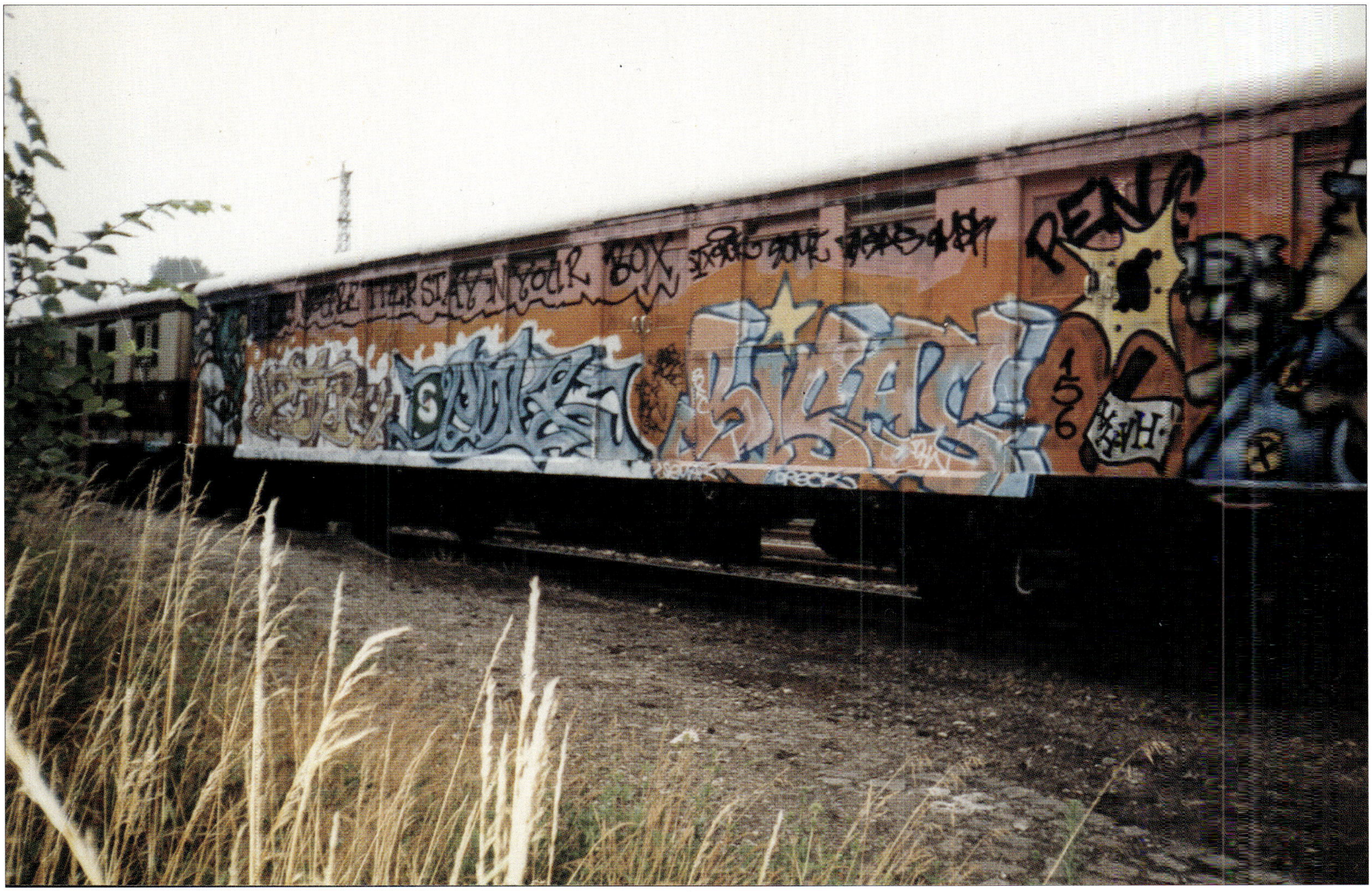

– Rew

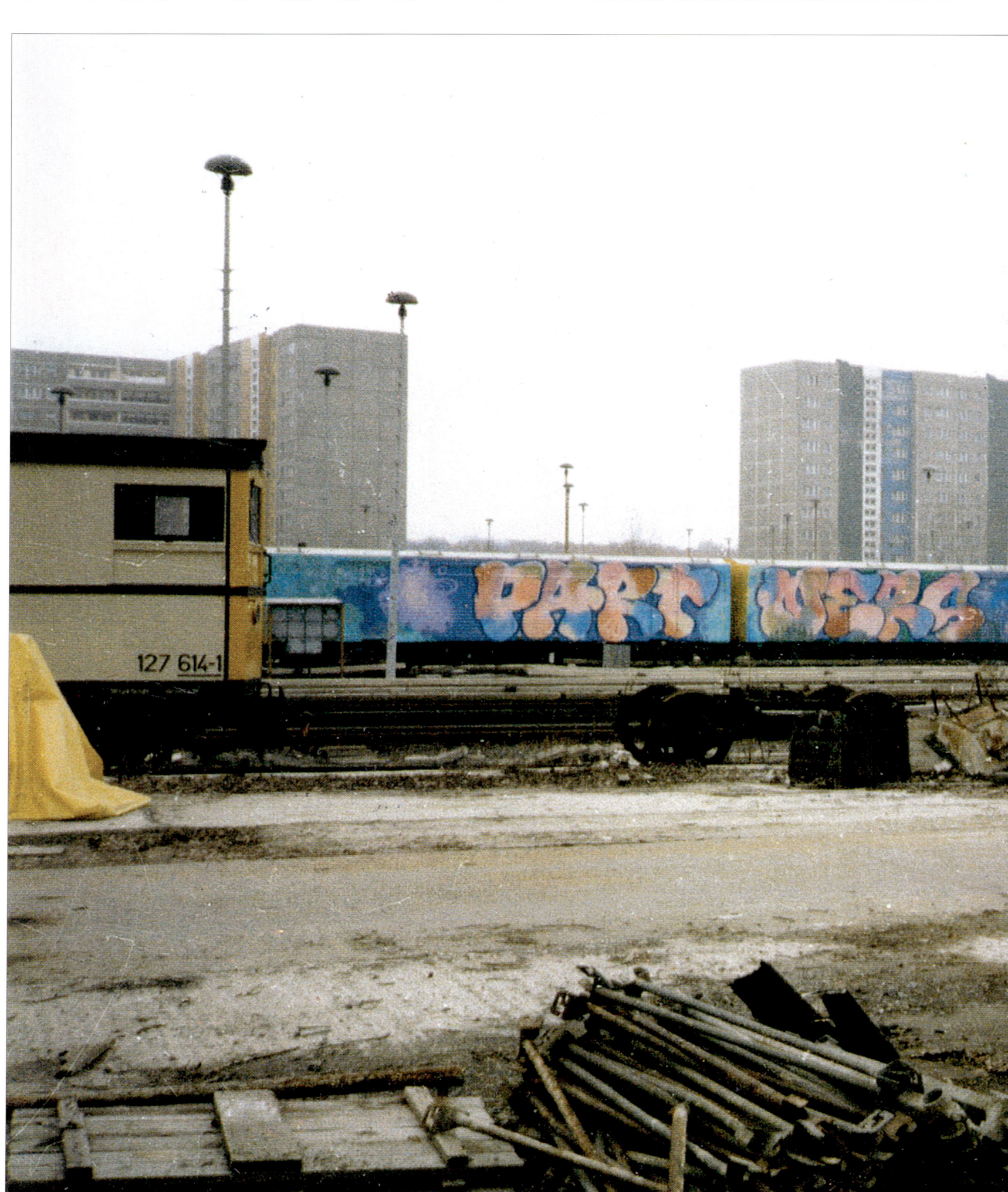

Partners of crime whole–train by POFC crew, Berlin subway, 1991

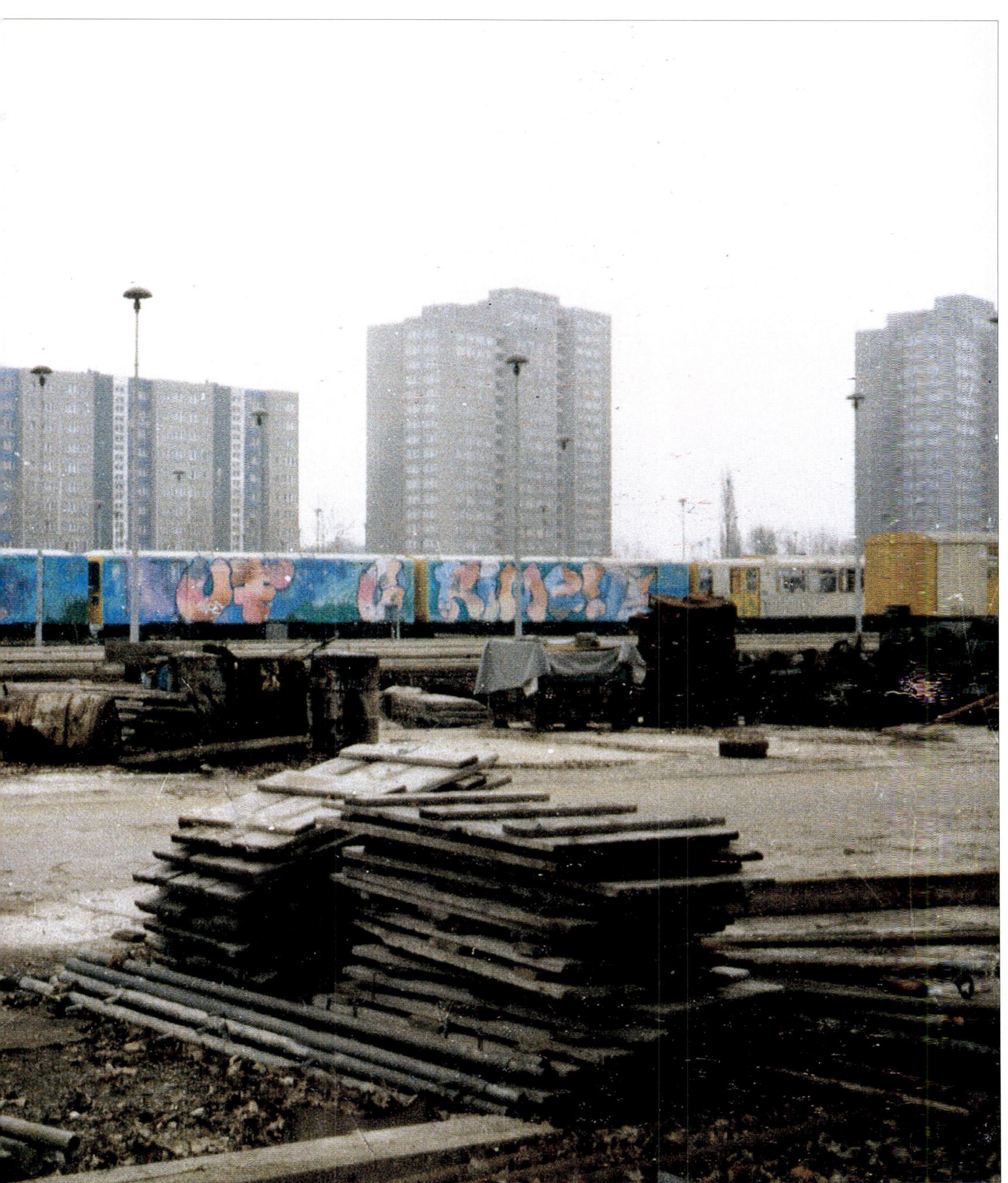

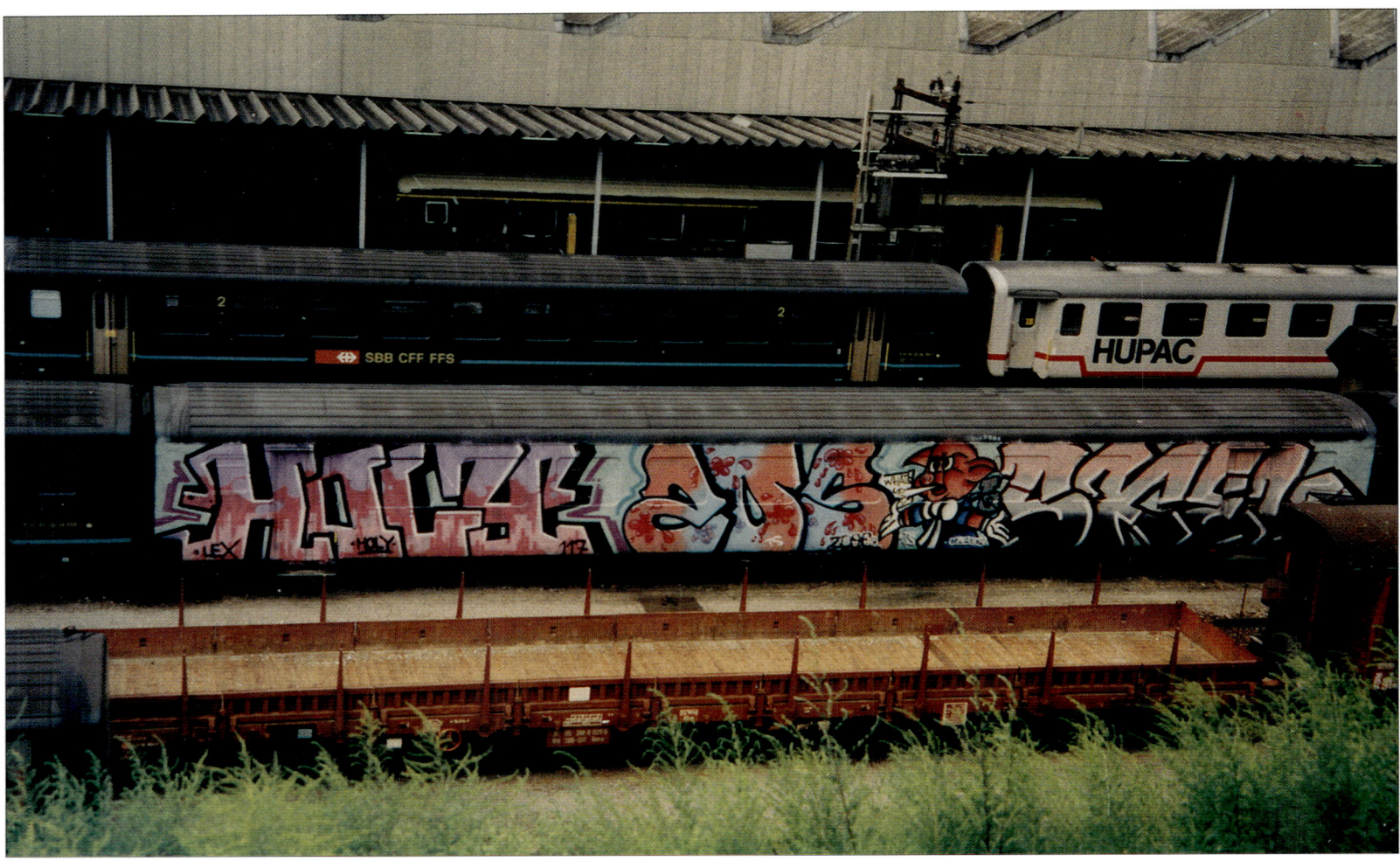

Whole-car by Holy, Zos, Skel

– Beka 70

ASSOCIATED WRITERS

"Red beans", "Greenpeace", "Colibri" are just a fraction of the infinite types of Swiss trains to be targeted. The guys of UC elaborate

Lord –UC / Zurich
Zimtic–UC / Zurich
>

The first writer scenario in Zurich took form in the early 80's and concentrated more on walls rather than trains. Between 1983 and 1986 an active battle proliferated long the walls of the track line, which saw the participation of between 20 and 25 writers. The 'Wild Writers' Gen and Bost, plus Lord and Ashes of URP crew were among the first to move onto the rail tracks.

Towards the end of the 80's a real push forward took place, involving new people; Takit, Pro, Pharao, Escof are some of the names that concentrated most on trains. In 1989 the phenomenon started causing a sensation, when the first International celebrities – among whom Loomit – left their traces on the Zurich railway network.

The phenomenon started to take a more serious turn starting in the summer of 1990. The forming of Upperclass Crew coincided with the activation of the Zurich S-bahn network, on May 27th 1990. A new combination of double-decker trains was inaugurated, which would travel through the whole canton and its neighbouring regions. Upperclass experimented in all the yards, lay-ups and end stops of out-of-town S-bahn stations. In the same year the first Swiss whole-car is painted in Zurich. The two-storey carriages were not particularly loved because they could be painted almost only over the windows but luckily older cars were also circulating on the lines of the S-bahn. During this period Upperclass systematically took advantage of the yards that were often concentrated in the end stations: because of this in the majority of cases trains would pass through Zurich. The SBB was initially overwhelmed and did not really manage to address the phenomenon. They were taken by surprise and thanks to this some whole-cars could travel painted more than once a day. The S5 line in Bulach and the S14 in Hinwil were surely the favourite deposits, you could paint for a couple of hours in total tranquillity; a convenient state that though definitely taken advantage of also had consequences: painting became difficult because the consistency with which it was being done slowly but surely caused each deposit to be put under tighter control. Upperclass thus decided to fall back on deposits localised in neighbouring cantons. In Brugge, Aarau, Schaffhausen, and Lucerna some yards were even bigger, perhaps less known but anyway useful because the majority of trains went to Zurich. In the first two years the members of UC were probably the only ones to pursue such a project, based on the study of railway lines and deposits. Meaning we knew when we had been there last

and when we could return. Then all of a sudden something changed. The whole-cars that were circulating started being noticed in the city and inspired new crews to start train bombing: thus began a real hunt for trains, fuelled by crews such as ZAT, UDO and Flash. Starting in 1993 crews from other cantons started to appear as well and the whole thing exploded! Let's rock!

At the time the Zurich S-bahn system was still divided into sections with different types of trains; there were the green trains nicknamed "Greenpeace" and the red express "Red Beans" that then became the legendary "S14", to this day one of the all time preferred targets for writers. Later entire fleets of trains would be modernised and many historic liveries would be replaced with the new white and blue double-decker models. There were then the "Colibri" and the two storey "Big Blues" commuter trains. All these models were regularly painted, and between 1993 and 1995 the phenomenon began to increase exponentially, until the SSB was no longer able to buff every train, there weren't enough substitutes to put them out of service.

Painted carriages would circulate for weeks and months, always during rush hour, a pretty unusual occurrence until then. This escalation clearly brought logistic problems: lay-ups that were usually easy to handle were fenced in or even closed. Some yards were put under tighter security or even barred off. Many writers were arrested and stories were circulating about writers having to pay 11.000 Swiss Francs for the costs of cleaning double-decker cars. This scared the newbies that interrupted their activity, only a group of them resisted. Thus began the second age! The active crews organised themselves into new formations and started opposing resistance. For tactical and security reasons the crews ended all activity for a brief amount of time, to then divide the yards into sectors. Each sector was painted only by a specific crew, UC, VTO, USO, TS and DC thus managed to keep in check the where, what and how of things being done. All in all this coalition worked pretty well seeing that the SBB police and security never managed to stop graffiti with their arrest strategies. Clearly the new crews that did not belong to this 'association' were not very enthusiastic about it: so the friction and rivalries in contending yards began, until these disagreements were resolved and things started working once more. In Zurich the train bombing scene picked up again without cessation: many foreign writers and tourists left their traces on the S-Bahn network. The presence of train pieces in the stations of Zurich was multiplying at all hours of the day, to such an extent that soon the situation was out of control. The SBB naturally noticed this and attempted to put these trains out of circulation or not allow them to leave at all. The company was primarily focused on cleaning the double-decker convoys, seeing all the large windows were painted and having them completely cleaned was very expensive. Every glass window had to be taken out and the gaskets had to be substituted. The entire train had to be scrubbed and then painted over with its official colours. In other countries train buffing took place through the use of a very strong chemical product, but in Switzerland this wasn't possible due to the environmental regulations. The SBB had had enough and was starting to defend its trains with an anti-graffiti protection; but these didn't last long either, after only two or three treatments the cars were again in terrible conditions and the trains of Zurich went back once again to their natural state: painted.

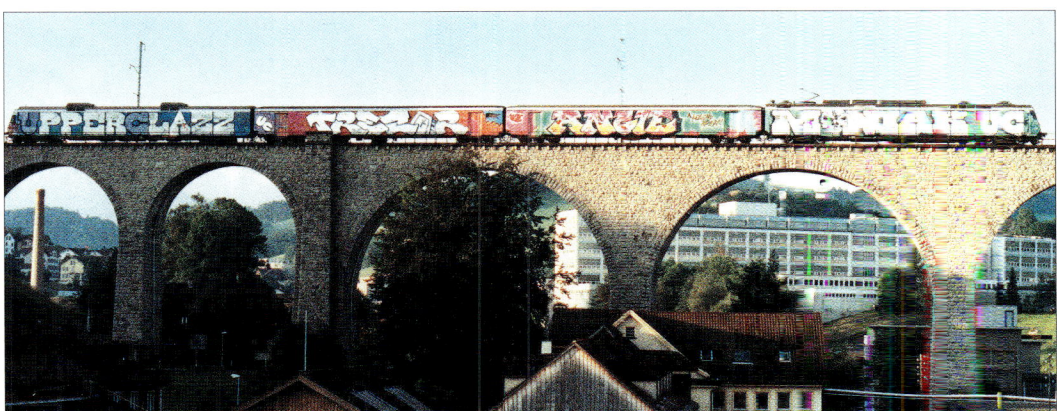

Upper clazz whole-train: Trezor, Angie, Maniak UC   — UC

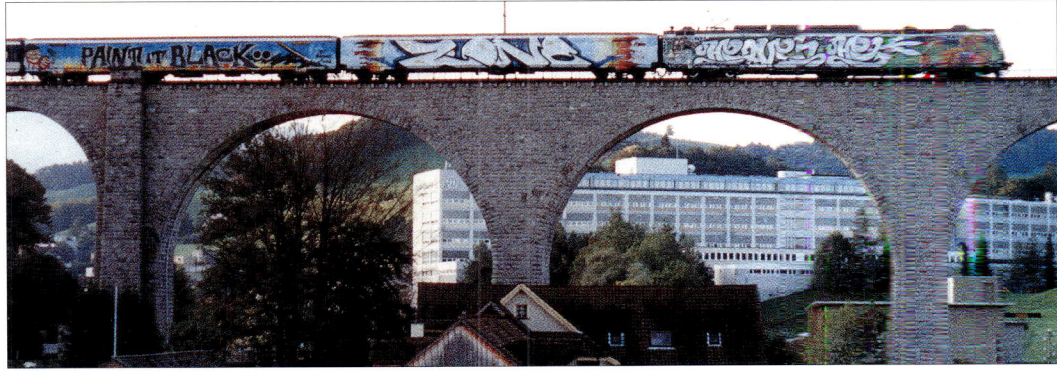

Triple whole-car: Painted it black, Zone, Heaven Hell   — UC

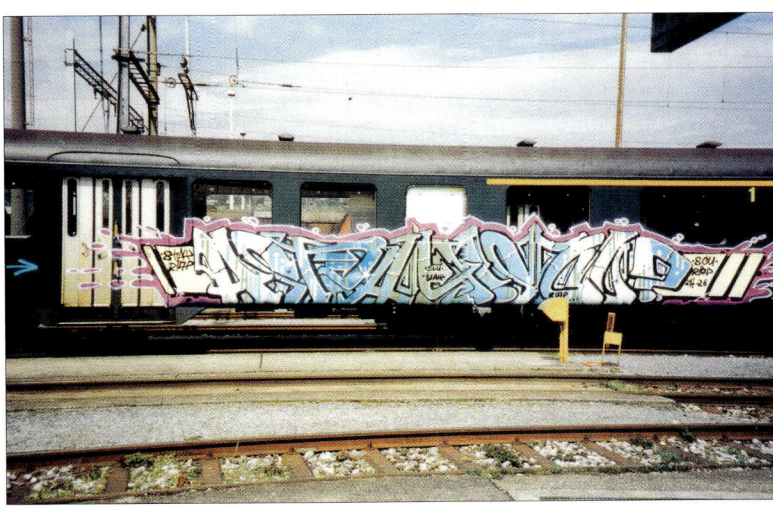

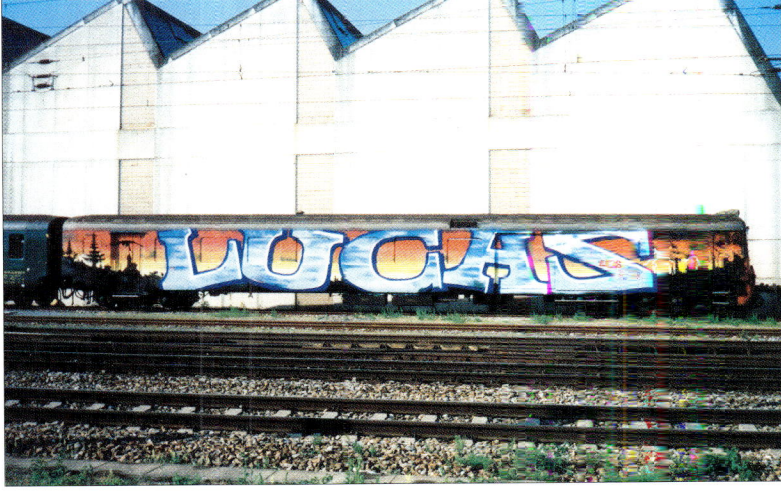

— UC   Lucas   — UC

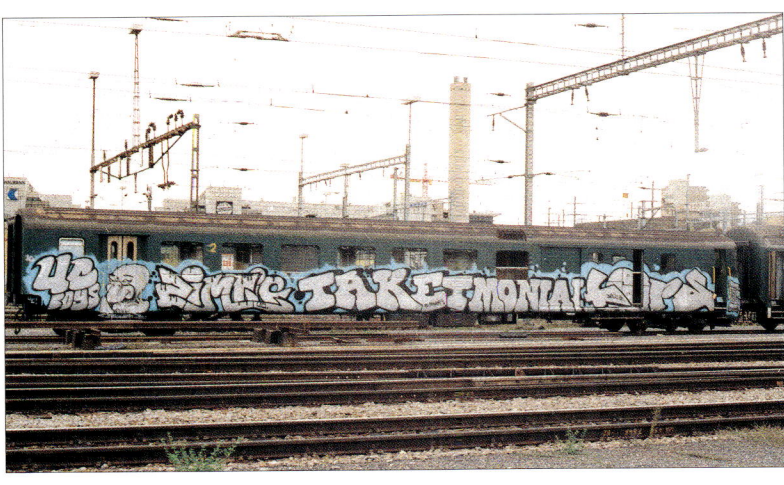

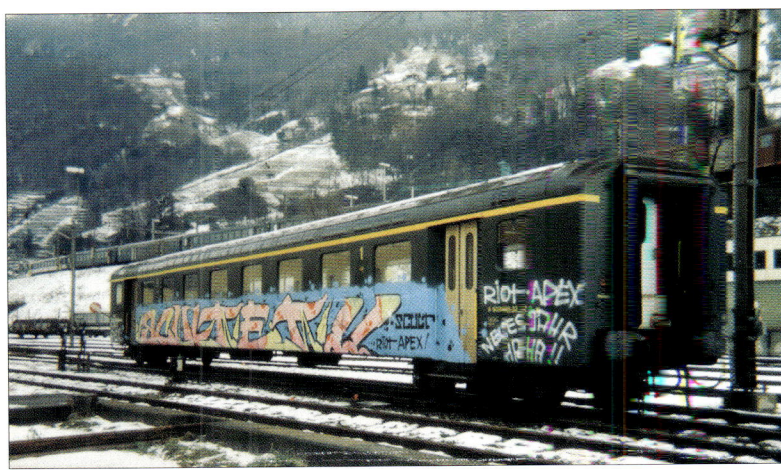

End-to-end Zimtic, Taket, Moniak, Lord   — UC   End-to-end by Scult   — UC

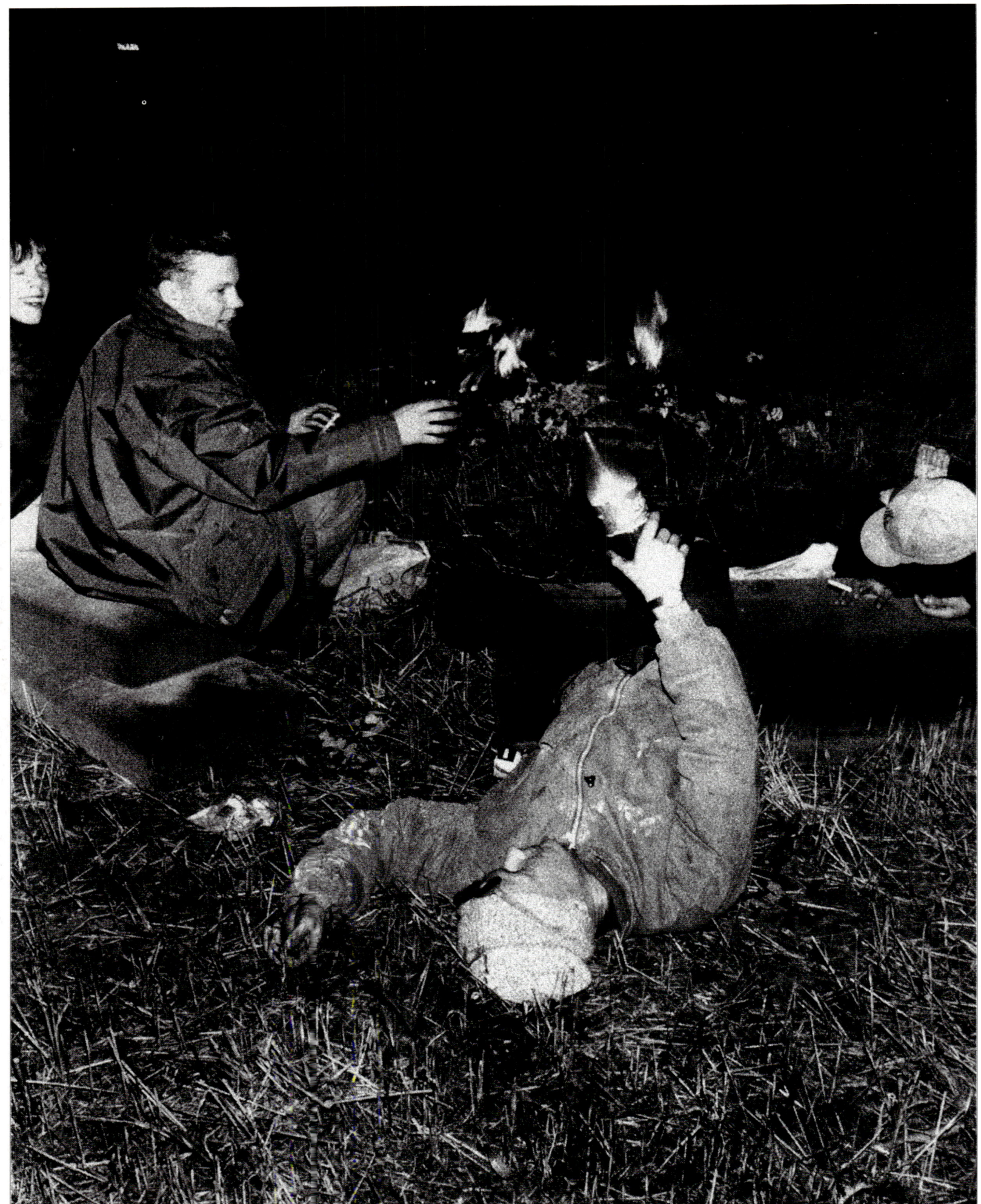

GLOSSARIES

TOOLS

Back-piece
A trapezoidal canvas decorated with letters and characters sewn onto the back of a jeans jacket. The materials used are fabric pencils, markers, acrylics, or paintbrushes. In the 70's in New York and the 80's in Europe, back-pieces were part of the dress code for writers.

Blackbook
A notebook containing photos of trains and walls painted by a writer, a reinterpretation of an artist's portfolio.

Canvas
Piece of canvas or Masonite upon which spray paint is used to create a work that is generally destined for art markets.

Cap
A mechanical device designed to control the flow of paint. More commonly, the nozzle of a spray can. Writers use caps from other cans in order to achieve specific results.

Fanzine
A fan magazine devoted to a specific interest. Often shortened to "zine".

Fat cap
Spray can nozzle that creates a wide jet.

Fat laces
Wide, coloured shoe laces used by B-boys to decorate sneakers.

Flick
A photo of graffiti.

Kangol Cap
A bell-shaped hat produced by the clothing brand Kangol, recognisable by its circular brim.

Krylon
A classic brand of American spray paint. Howard Kester invented the name by joining his surname with the word "Nylon".

Name-belt
Rectangular belt buckle used by writers, the buckle usually indicated the individual or crew's Name in chrome letters.

Skinny cap
Spray can nozzle used to create thin, precise lines.

Sketch
A rough pencil drawing made in a notebook before actually executing a piece.

Sketch book
In Europe, these notebooks often contained photos of completed pieces, thus becoming real personal "diaries" for writers.

Sparvar
A brand of German spray paint that was particularly common in Europe in the 90's, mainly used for details and for characters due to its slow jet.

Stickers
A form of leaving a tag in the city, usually drawn on adhesive labels which read "Hello, my name is", with space to include one's own tag.

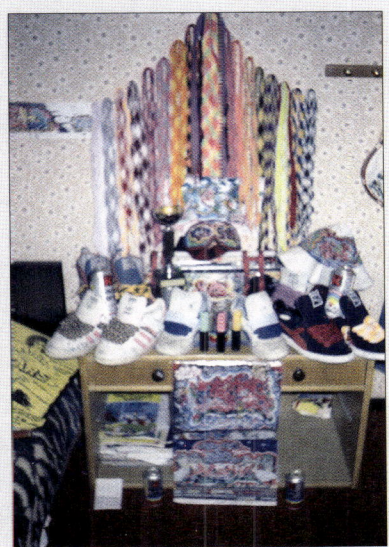

Fat laces — *Puppet*

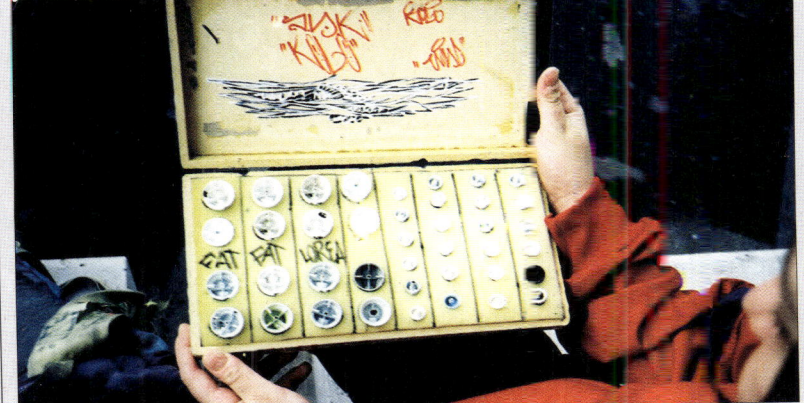

Caps — *Rusty*

BASIC GLOSSARY

Aerosol   A suspension of liquid particles dispensed from a pressurised container.

Aerosol Art   see "Writing"

All City   A writer who is particularly active on all urban surfaces with tags, throw-ups, pieces on trains, along track lines, and in every relevant spot.

Animation   see "Character"

Arrow   A key element in the composition of letters and complex styles such as Wildstyle. In Madrid in the 1980's, with the emergence of this symbol beneath tags, a peculiar movement of writers called "Flecheros" came to life.

B–Boy   A term which indicates a person who is involved in the Hip Hop movement, more specifically in the discipline of Breakdancing.

Background   Originally painted on train cars to emphasise a piece. On New York subway lines, considering the number of Names on trains, backgrounds were born out of necessity: they covered preexistent Names which rendered the piece hard to read. In halls of fame, they were considered a way to thematise compositions.

Backjump   A method used to paint train lines that are particularly well-guarded. In Europe in the 90's, it was one of the few methods to ensure one's name would circulate. Backjumps probably originated in Scandinavia with Nug and VIM crew. Trains are painted directly in the stations during the brief time they stop. It's a particularly risky and adrenalised action because it involves trains that are in service with passengers on board.

Battle   A competition whose scope is to resolve conflicts between individuals or crews. Battling can include different disciplines of Hip Hop such as Rapping, Breaking or Writing. Adversaries give their best while spectators judge. Afrika Bambaataa used battles to extinguish violence in the streets of the Bronx during the 70's.

Beef   Disagreement, argument, or eventual clash between individuals or crews.

Bench (*to bench*)   Waiting for painted trains at stations to photograph them. Writer benches were specific stations where writers would gather to comment on each other's styles in New York during the 70's.

Bite (*to bite*)   To copy the style of another writer. It's considered an intolerable act, although it is acceptable to borrow styles from other contexts, like comic books. Biting involves copying every element of a piece, from the structure and composition of the letters, to the colours, to the calligraphy of the tag. In some cases, there's a fine line between copying a style and being inspired by it.

Blockbuster   A piece with large block letters, often tilted to the right or left, and almost always filled with one colour, usually silver. This style was invented to cover other writers' pieces or cover an entire train in a short period of time.

Bodé, Vaughn (1941–1975)   An American comic book artist who was a reference for many New York writers. He created several famous characters like Dead Bone and Cheek Wizard, who were depicted on trains and walls worldwide.

Bomb/Bombing   When an individual or crew extensively covers a specific area with tags and throw-ups .

Breakdance   A technically complex, acrobatic street dance. It originated in the Bronx in the early 70's amongst Afro-American and Latino youth. It's a discipline of the Hip Hop movement, which expanded and reached its peak in the 80's.

Buff   A term used by writers when referring to the removal of graffiti from subway cars. Introduced by the New York MTA in March 1977, it used toxic chemical substances, causing health and environmental problems.

Burner   A piece with a recognisable style, usually carried out in Wildstyle. It was called this way because it seemed to "burn" off walls or trains. A burner is a piece that stands out from other pieces of the same aesthetic impact.

Character   A figure taken from comic books, cartoons, or popular culture in general, in order to add attraction to a piece and decorate the letters which make up the name.

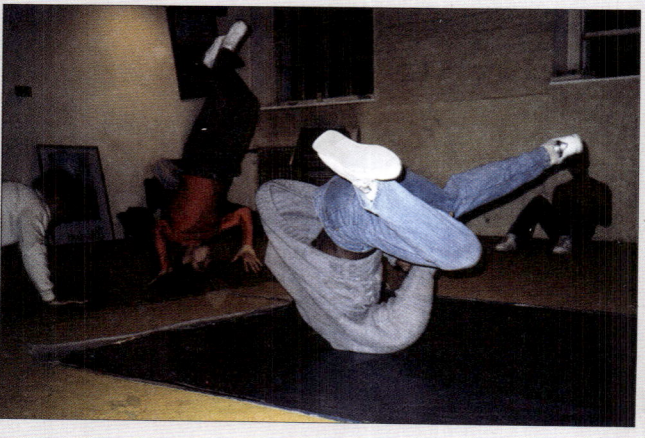

Breakdance
     - Mode 2

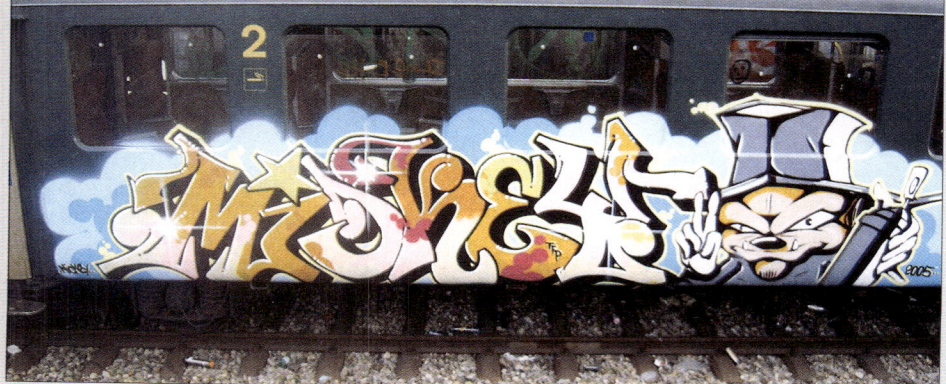

Burner
     - Mickey

Clique	A group of writers. See "Crew"	Adding light to letters to add a bright, sparkling effect to the piece. Highlights are usually white.	**Highlights**
Concept Wall	Pieces painted by various writers on a single, large legal wall. These productions are ascribable to New York crews like TAT, and European writers like Loomit, FBI, and ABC crew.	A cultural movement that originated in New York in the early 70's among Afro-American and Latino communities. It's commonly intended as a phenomenon that united the youth into cohesive groups who interacted by dancing, playing music, and singing to the rhythm of music. An essential social and cultural cornerstone for the Writing movement.	**Hip Hop**
Crew	A group of writers. A crew is indicated by an acronym. For example, TF5 stands for The Fabulous Five. Crew Names can be made up of two, three, or four letters, but are usually made up of three letters.	To tag any surface with one's Name.	**Hit**
Crossing out	Usually entails painting a line over another writer's tag or piece.	Commonly used to denote a person who is very close, almost a brother.	**Homeboy**
Design	Decorative element like stars, drips, bubbles, or dots painted on a piece.	Tags inside of subway trains.	**Insides**
Dress-code	Back-piece, name-belt, fat laces, and Kangol cap, were part of the dress code for many writers. They were fundamental elements in order to recognise each other during a time when the Hip Hop movement was not yet popular.	A gathering of groups of B-boys or writers, events which contributed to solidifying the connection between distinct European and national scenes.	**Jam**
		To excessively hit a city's wall or trains with one's Name.	**Kill**
End-to-end (E2E)	A piece painted along the entire length of a train car, below the windows. It's more precisely called: end-to-end window-down.	The best writer. This nickname is given to different writers, considering their skills, attitude and / or tenacity.	**King**
Fame	What a writer obtains when he paints constantly and persistently. One objective for writers is to obtain a certain level of fame among other writers.	Tracks where trains are parked overnight and on weekends.	**Lay-up**
Fill	The interior colour of letters on a piece or throw-up.	Two attached whole-cars painted at the same time. Originally in New York, it referred to two cars permanently attached, identified by their consecutive numbers.	**Married Couple**
Freight Train	One of the main targets of American writers. A secondary target for most European writers.	see "King"	**Master**
Getting up	When one's name is prevalent on a city's walls and trains. It means to hit up every surface in the city.	A high quality piece on a wall or train requiring time and elaboration.	**Masterpiece**
Going over	Covering another writer's Name with one's own Name. When the graffiti phenomenon first began in New York, Cap was the master of black and white throw-ups which covered other writers' Names.	*Metropolitan Transit Authority.* Corporation responsible for public transportation in New York City	**MTA**

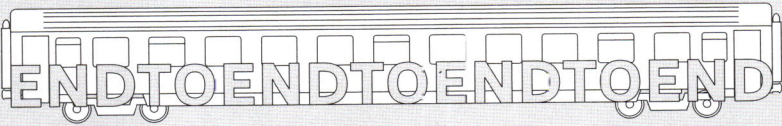

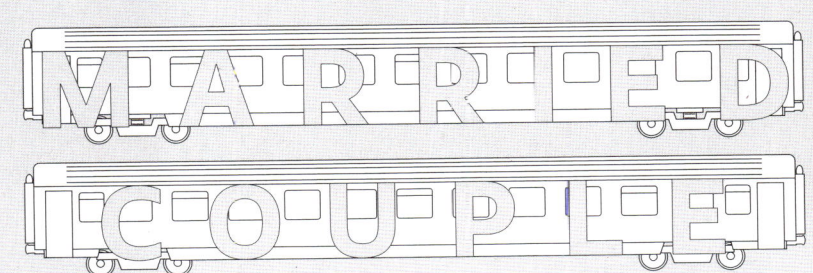

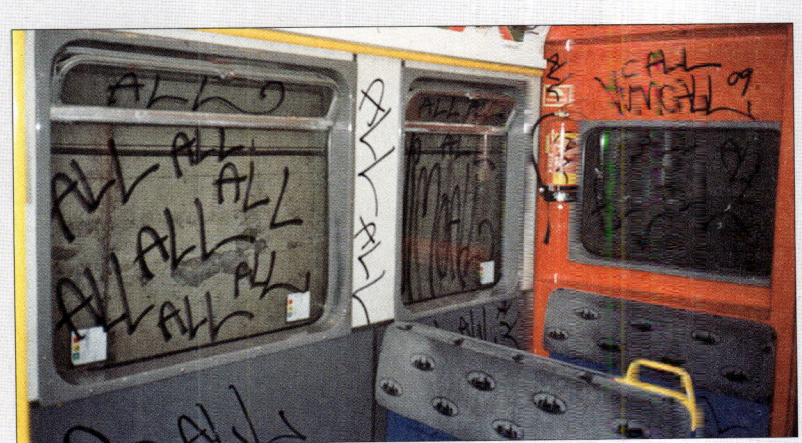

Insides

- ALL

Nickname Fictitious Name used by writers when signing pieces. The identity game is one of the main characteristics in the world of Writing. The chosen alias becomes the Name by which writers are known in this circle.

Old School Term denoting a writer who belongs to the first generation. Old school writers are respected for having been present when it all began. Old school New York writers are the most respected as true and tried pioneers of the movement.

Outline 1. See "Sketch" 2. A rough drawing of a piece or letters on a wall, which then gets filled in. 3. The final line drawn around the piece to finish it or define the shape of the letters.

Palanca A method similar to that of the backjump, most likely invented in Spain during the mid 90's. It consists in pulling the emergency brake, rushing out of the train, and painting the car in the brief time available before the train moves again.

Panel Piece Originally, a piece painted below the windows and between the doors of a New York subway car. Today, it's used for any piece on any type of train, still window-down, but it's no longer defined by the two doors but usually occupies two to four windows

Piece A painting by a writer, short for "masterpiece". Invented by Super Kool in 1972, it was later elaborated by every other writer.

Rack (to rack) To steal. Originally, New York writers would steal all materials for painting, this practice was later exported to Europe in the 80's and 90's.

Respect A sense of admiration for older, more experienced writers.

Scratchiti A tag which is engraved onto the windows of trains with a sharp tool. This phenomenon appeared in the late 90's as a response to the war waged on writers by the authorities.

Style, the concept of A writer who achieves a recognisable style and immediately earns the respect of the entire community.

Tag A writer's signature with a marker or spray paint, considered the most basic form of graffiti. Testimonial of the presence of a writer in a determined spot, usually executed quickly with connected letters. A tag is a writer's personal logo.

Tagger A writer who only does tags and throw-ups, not pieces.

Third rail On some subway lines, there is an extra rail that supplies power for trains. It's a lethal danger for writers when painting trains.

Throw-up A quickly-painted piece, usually composed of two colours and an outline, imperfectly filled in. It can consist of two single letters or an entire word.

Top-to-bottom Piece that extends from the top of the car to the bottom, covering it completely.

Toy Term for an inexperienced writer, usually assigned to writers who've just begun and have yet to earn recognition or respect.

Trainspotting See "Bench"

Whole-car A piece which covers an entire car from top to bottom (T2B) and from end to end (E2E).

Whole-train Covering an entire train with a series of whole-car pieces. Whole-Train Window-Down: a sequence of end-to-end pieces from window-down along the entire length of the train.

Wildstyle Construction of interlocking letters. A complicated style composed of arrows and connections. Complex pieces which are often undecipherable for non-writers.

Window-down A piece done below the windows of a subway car. See "Piece"

Writer A person who writes his Name on a city's walls or trains.

Writing Leaving a personal tag, throw-up or piece on mass transit or across the city.

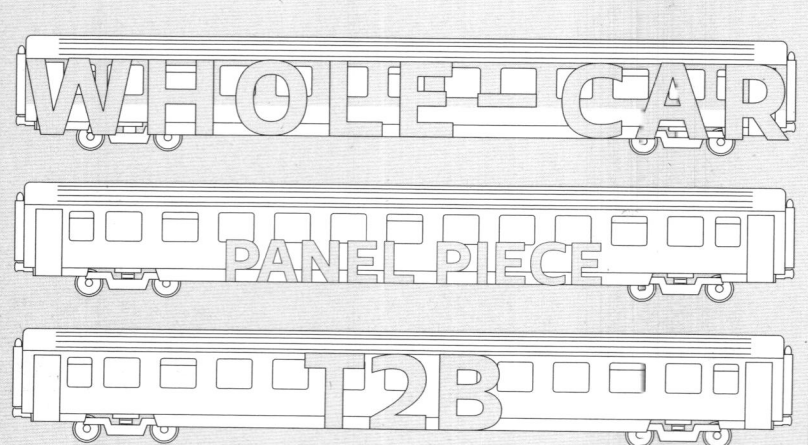

DYNAMIC TARGETS

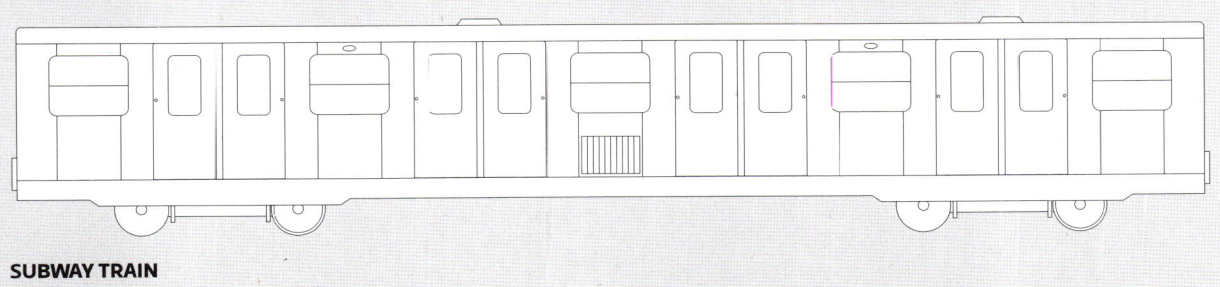

SUBWAY TRAIN

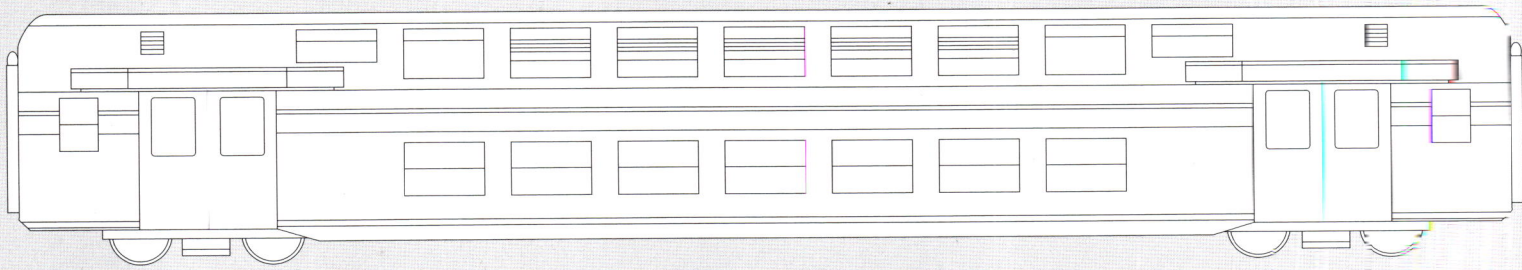

S-TRAIN

LONG-DISTANCE TRAIN

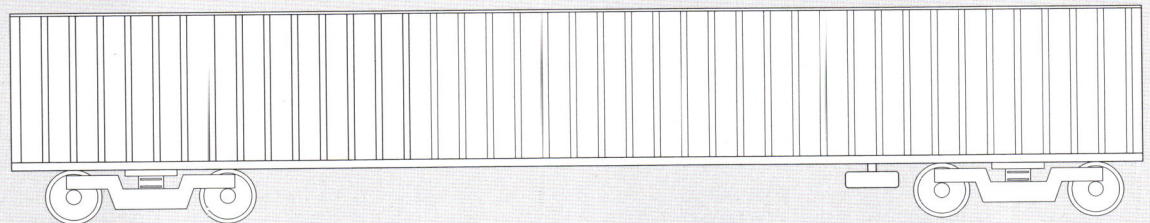

FREIGHT TRAIN

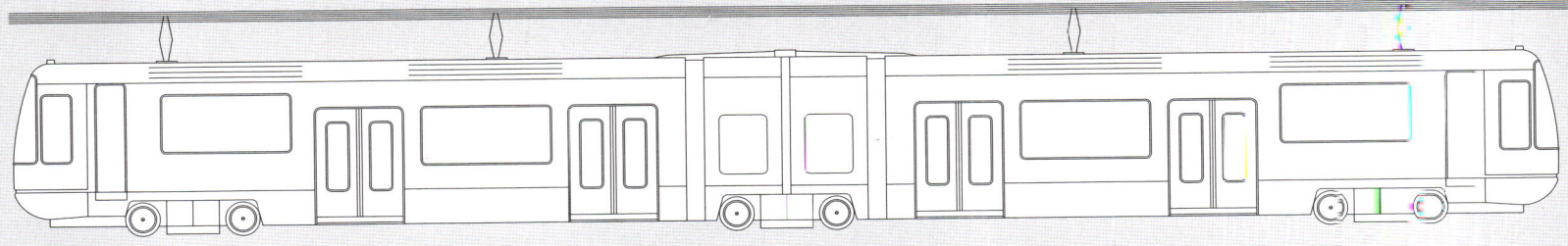

TRAM

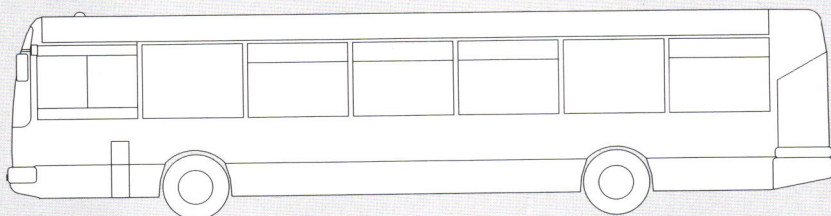

BUS

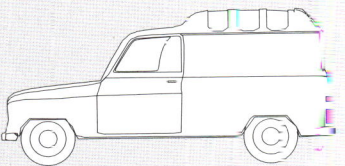

VAN

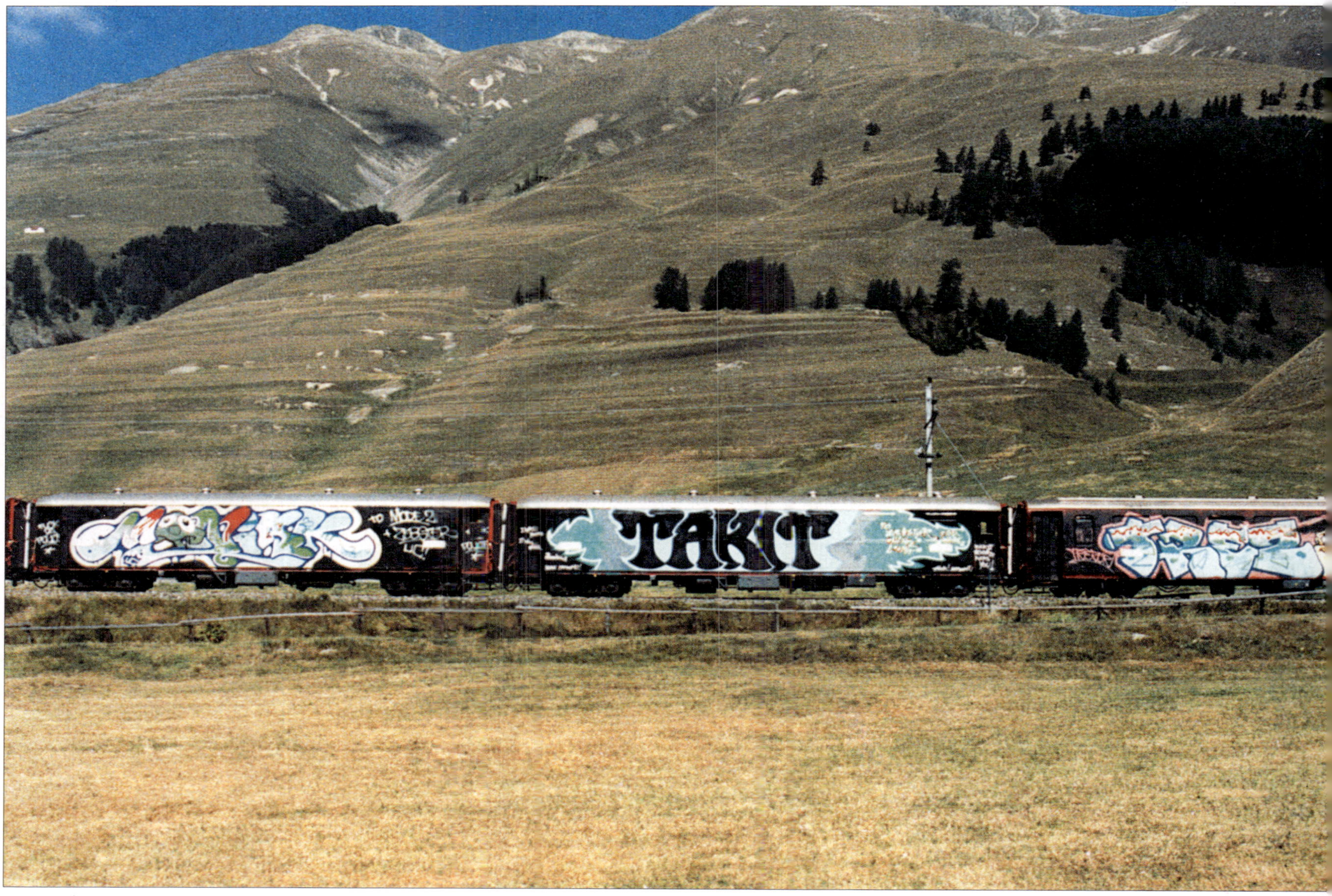

ment

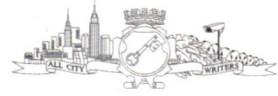

I would like to express my profound gratitude to those who contributed their memories and donated precious images. Without their support this work would not exist.

Charlie Ahearn, Airone, Alberto WAG, Aken, Amok, Anek, Ash, Atome, Atomo, Bando, Bang, Bates, Bean, Bees, Tobias Barenthin Lindblad, Dr. Massimo Bianchini/Met.Ro Roma, Cesare Bignotti, Blast, Blef, Block20, Boogie, Karim Brechbuehl, Claudio "Sid" Brignole, Byr, Cano, Capo, Monia Cappuccini, Cat22, Stefania Cavicchi, Cemnoz, Cento, Ces53, Chana, Chief, Chob, Ciufs, Clown, CMP, Cora, Crab, Craze, Cura, Dado, Dafne, Damage, Daze, Delta, Dizney, Don, Dosey, Dra, Draw, Drax, Drew at *All Ways New York*, Drugo, Dumbo, Dust, Echo, Egs, Elk, Emis, Emme, Enko, Ens, Ense, Eron, Esher, Alex Fakso, Far, Fernando Figueroa, Fish, Flycat, Fonzi, Fra32, Richard Galliano, Felipe Galvez, Gast, Xavier "Le Truc" Gauci, Gees, Gel, Gex, Ghost, Gio at *TOSHQ*, Giose, Goofy, Graffio, Grim, Hence, High, Hiom, Hody, Honet, Iave, J-mee, Just, Ikone, Lark, Lay-up, Lego, Lokiss, Loomit, Longe, Lord, Malcolm Jacobson, Joe, Bomber Johan, Jon, Joys, Kar, Kapi, Kaos, Kato, Kaso, Kein, Kid, Jacob Kimvall, Koa, Koma, Olivier Kosta-Thefaine, Krash, Johan Kugelberg, Mace, Magagna, Manjar, Sean Martin, Mastro K, Marco/Onè Sound, Math, Melie, Mencio, Mer, Mickey, Milk, Mind, Mins, Mode2, Moe, Moon, Renato Montecristi, Move, Fabio a Valdi, Napal, Natas, Andrea Nelli, Neon, Nico, Nico Cleyndert, Noem, Nug, Oida, Allegra Martin, Mason, Peter Michalski, Omaek, One, Opak, Pako, Pam, Pane, Panda, Enrico Pedrini, Peggio, Pengo, Ridder, PAC London, Rocco Pezzella, Phase II, Phobia, Pike, Alex Pistoja, Play, Poe, Poison, Polo, Pose, Pride, Pum, Pupi, Puppet, Pure, Ramon, Raptus, Steye Raviez, Rax-E, RCF1, Reas, Reaze, Rendo, Rens, Reoh, Repo, Rew, Rhyme, Riso, Robin, Rois, Rok, Rose, Jordi Rubio, Rusty, Sabe, Sand, Santo, Sat, Richard Sen, Sek, Sera, Shad, Shampo, David Schmidlapp, Shark, Sharp, Sherif, Shoe, Shot, Shorty, Sie, Sika, Siso, Sketzh, Skki, Slog, Torkel Sjostrand, Skah, Sky4, Smart, Soap, Paolo Soglia, Soevv, Soul Jazz Records London, Spino5, Spot, Stand, Stone a.k.a. Don M. Zaza, Stuko, Stying, Sugo, Suso33, Syla, Tabo, Tawa, Teatro, Tekne, Mark Todt, Trota, Tuff, Utero, Vega, Vons, Vela, Ver, Roberto Verona, Vime, Vino, Sigi Von Koeding, Wany, Washe, Wave, Wessels, Won, Word, Xeno, Zaki Dee, Zart, Zebster, Zedz, Bernard Zekri, Zelda, Zero-T, Zest, Zeta, Zimtic, Zuek.